POLITICS IN AMERICA

POLITICS IN AMERICA

Tenth Edition

2014 ELECTIONS AND UPDATES EDITION

Thomas R. DYE
Florida State University

Ronald Keith GADDIE
University of Oklahoma

PEARSON

Boston Columbus Indianapolis New York San Francisco Amsterdam
Cape Town Dubai London Madrid Milan Munich Paris Montréal Toronto
Delhi Mexico City São Paulo Sydney Hong Kong Seoul Singapore Taipei Tokyo

Editorial Director: Craig Campanella
Editor-in-Chief: Dickson Musslewhite
Acquisitions Editor: Jeff Marshall
Program Manager: Beverly Fong
Editorial Assistant: Kieran Fleming
Field Marketing Manager: Brittany Pogue-Mohammed
Product Marketing Manager: Tricia Murphy
Project Management, Team Lead: Melissa Feimer
Project Manager: Carol O'Rourke
Senior Procurement Superervisor: Mary Fischer
Procurement Specialist: Mary Ann Gloriande
Digital Studio Media: Tina Gagliostro
Art Director: Maria Lange
Cover Design: Pentagram
Composition and Full-Service Project Management: Saraswathi Muralidhar/Lumina Datamatics, Inc.
Printer and Binder: Manufactured in the United States by RR Donnelley
Cover Printer: Manufactured in the United States by RR Donnelley

Credits and acknowledgments borrowed from other sources and reproduced, with permission, in this textbook appear on appropriate page within text or on pages 719–720.

Library of Congress Cataloging-in-Publication Data

Dye, Thomas R.
Politics in America : 2014 election update / Thoma R. Dye, Florida State University, Ronald Keith Gaddie, University of Oklahoma. — 10th ed.
pages cm
Includes bibliographical references and index.
ISBN 978-0-13-401892-8 — ISBN 0-13-401892-3 1. United States—Politics and government—Textbooks. I. Gaddie, Ronald Keith. II. Title.
JK276.D926 2016
320.473—dc23

2014039885

Student Edition
ISBN-13: 978-0-13-401892-8
ISBN-10: 0-13-401892-3

A La carte
ISBN-13: 978-0-13-408155-7
ISBN-10: 0-13-408155-2

Instructor's Review Copy
ISBN-13: 978-0-13-408095-6
ISBN-10: 0-13-408095-5

3 4 5 6 7 8 9 10
V011

www.pearsonhighered.com

BRIEF CONTENTS

CONTENTS

7 Political Parties: Organizing Politics 212

13 Courts: Judicial Politics 478

PART V OUTCOMES

14 Politics and Personal Liberty 514

15 Politics and Civil Rights 560

TO THE STUDENT

To study politics is to be an American.

Ponder this question: Are you really politically empowered or do a few elites govern your decisions for you? Most Americans are growing increasingly cynical and think that politics only serves a narrow set of particular interests. Studying politics helps you understand what you are getting from government, and how (or whether) you can change what politics gives and takes from you. With this book, our goal is to educate you to be a critical consumer of political information so that you understand where you fit in American life.

As you read our book, you will see that we approach politics as an adversarial game—one that sparks acts of violence, leads some to create lasting works of philosophy and art, and prompts others to undertake tremendous acts of heroism. Any human activity that does these things *can't* be dull. Politics does these things because it *is* power; politics decides who will get what from government and when.

To understand this power, you have to understand the game: Who are the players and what are the rules? The game is played in multiple venues: elections, legislatures, executive mansions, courthouses, newsrooms. Different players act together or in opposition, battling to decide where the scarce resources of government go, whose values will prevail, and who will pay for everything.

So, why should *you* participate in politics, especially when it is made up of all these power players and elites and games? The answer is roughly equal parts philosophy, history, and self-interest. American politics assumes that the power of government originates in the individual. The people are the *sovereigns*, and the state and its government get authority from *your* consent. Our goal is for you to embody what Ronald Reagan called "*an informed patriotism.*" How our government defends our constitutional ideals and rights requires an informed vigilance on behalf of its citizens.

This is not a politically correct book. You will disagree with some (or much) of what you read, including, possibly, the central assumption that politics is about power and influence. It is our first goal that you can distinguish our empirical approach—we observe politics to be about power and costs and benefits—from whatever normative beliefs we have about how the world should be. To change the world towards a higher ideal, one has to first understand the world *as it is*. In this volume, we present a political world of institutions, players, and competitors who are trying to get what they want. But, we also want you to think about how other governments around the world do things; whether or not our government currently does the things it should do, and whether or not government needs to do things that it currently doesn't do. This creates a foundation for conversations about how political power is wielded—conversations we hope you have with your family, friends, and others long after you close the pages of this book.

Meet Your Authors

THOMAS R. DYE, Emeritus McKenzie Professor of Government at Florida State University, regularly taught large introductory classes in American politics and has served as president of the Southern Political Science Association, president of the Policy Studies Organization, and secretary of the American Political Science Association. He has taught at the University of Pennsylvania, the University of Wisconsin, and the University of Georgia, and served as a visiting scholar at Bar-Ilan University, Israel; the Brookings Institution in Washington, D.C.; and elsewhere.

RONALD KEITH GADDIE is Chairman of the Department of Political Science and Associate Director of the Center for Intelligence and National Security at the University of Oklahoma, where he regularly teaches the American Federal Government course. Author or coauthor of twenty books, he has been retained by corporations, trade associations, and state governments, and his work has been funded by the U.S. Department of Defense. Keith is also an award-winning radio broadcaster at NPR radio station KGOU (Norman, OK).

TO THE INSTRUCTOR

The struggle over who gets what in American politics

is as intense as ever. Battles over the size of government and how to pay for it define the struggle for power in Washington. The last presidential campaign between the Romney/Ryan and Obama/Biden tickets brought these contrasts and struggles to the fore. Conservatives say they seek to "starve the beast" of a fourth-generation welfare state while liberals say they try to preserve the gains to working and middle class Americans from the New Deal and the Great Society for posterity. The federal government sets about reorganizing health care, and in the process, sets off another round of struggles with state governments over how policy will reach citizens. But the choices offered by these parties and politicians confront a political process that requires either compromise and consensus, or overwhelming majorities for one party, to get things done. But with narrow, divided majorities in Congress and politics that are more polarized now than ever, the government has lurched from fiscal crisis to fiscal crisis as politicians played games with debt and spending deadlines. Electoral goals became more important than meeting the obligations to govern.

By using Harold Lasswell's classic definition of politics of "who gets what, when, and how" as its unifying framework, the tenth edition of *Politics in America* continues to present a stimulating introduction to what the American political system is and what is happening in it now. Politics consists of all the activities—reasonable discussion, impassioned oratory, campaigning, balloting, fund-raising, advertising, lobbying, demonstrating, rioting, street fighting, and waging war—by which conflict is carried on. Examining the power game of politics—the participants, the stakes, the processes, and the institutional arenas, *Politics in America* introduces your students to the political struggles that drive democracy. Throughout this text, students are not just presented with a study of politics; *they are asked what they think about those politics.* The successful study of politics requires one to stop and ask questions about events, institutions, systems, policies, and problems.

New to This Edition

The latest version of Politics in America is a significant update and revision of the text. After Barack Obama's dramatic reelection, new political drama unfolded in Washington D.C., mainly centered on the budget and efforts to defund the Affordable Care Act. Congress finally passed a budget, but relied on automatic spending cuts to bring the deficit down to just under a half-trillion dollars a year by 2015. In the Supreme Court, progressives were simultaneously elated and dismayed. The justices backed the expansion of marriage rights to same sex couples, but also overturned a key provision of the Voting Rights Act. As states passed restrictive voter identification laws, the lower courts proved a confounding mess of decisions either overturning or supporting the laws. And, record amounts of money flowed into congressional elections as the GOP continued to look for a new standard-bearer to oppose the presumptive Democratic Party nominee, Hillary Clinton.

To examine the recent political context and to continue to make this book the best possible teaching and learning tool, we made the following improvements in this new edition.

- Starting with the 10th edition of the text, every chapter now opens with a public policy or political story that provides contemporary context to the content of every chapter. About a third of these stories are updated, to identify emerging political leaders, explore issues such as citizens challenging state and national police power, and draw attention to the problem of confronting corruption and implementation failure in major bureaucracies such as the veterans' administration.
- Approximately 20% of the box programs have been changed to engage new issues, controversies, and puzzles in politics. Many others have been updated to account for changes in the law and politics.
- Over 20% of the photos in this edition are new. They capture major events from the last two years, of course, in order to illustrate politics' relevancy. They show political actors and processes as well as people affected by politics, creating a visual narrative that enhances rather than repeats the text. Also, all of the figures and tables reflect the latest available data.
- The graphics and tables are all updated to contain the very latest available information relevant to topics in the book
- Suggested readings and websites are updated for all chapters, so that the curious student can continue research and study beyond the pages of the text.
- Over 30% of the **photos** in this edition are new. They capture major events from the last few years, of course, but to illustrate politics' relevancy, they show political actors and processes as well as people affected by politics, creating a visual narrative that enhances rather than repeats the text. Also, all of the **figures and tables** reflect the latest available data.

BREAK THROUGH

To learning reimagined

REVEL™

Educational technology designed for the way today's students read, think, and learn

When students are engaged deeply, they learn more effectively and perform better in their courses. This simple fact inspired the creation of REVEL: an immersive learning experience designed for the way today's students read, think, and learn. Built in collaboration with educators and students nationwide, REVEL is the newest, fully digital way to deliver respected Pearson content.

REVEL enlivens course content with media interactives and assessments—integrated directly within the authors' narrative—that provide opportunities for students to read about and practice course material in tandem. This immersive educational technology boosts student engagement, which leads to better understanding of concepts and improved performance throughout the course.

Learn more about REVEL
<http://www.pearsonhighered.com/revel/>

Features

Politics is not a dull topic and textbooks should not make it so. We designed this book to challenge students to think and talk about controversial issues by integrating the basics of American government into our focus on conflict and controversy—the struggle for power.

Our framework is built on Harold Lasswell's classic definition of politics—"who gets what, when and how." The choice of Lasswell's approach is a tribute to its durability and its practicality as an approach to studying politics. "Who" are the voters, interest groups, politicians, and parties, all the potential beneficiaries of politics. "What" are the rewards gained from playing politics, whether it is a preferred law or policy, a tax break, a political position, or a position of power and influence. "When" is the timing of the payoff from politics. And "how" is the political means used to get what people get. With this as our central narrative, we examine the struggle for power: the participants, the stakes, the processes, and the institutions—in a way that provokes thinking and discussion. For the student as a potential participant, we pose one last question: Do individuals and groups drive the politics, or are they steered by elites who control the groups, the institutions, the parties, and the media?

Politics in America is organized somewhat differently from other American politics textbooks. In Part I, **Politics**, we start with an introduction to American politics from a Lasswellian perspective (who gets what?) and discuss the pluralist versus elitist approaches to politics. Then, in Chapter 2, we explore American political culture, including the sources of identity that reinforce political competition and political identity. In Part II, **Constitution**, Chapter 3 presents the founding and the framing of the Constitution, and Chapter 4 describes the development of the federal form of government. In Part III, **Participants**, the text turns to an examination of the individual and group players in mass politics and the mediating institutions that connect the people to their government. Chapter 5 explores Public Opinion, followed by a series of chapters about the connective tissue of politics – the Media (Chapter 6), Political Parties (Chapter 7), Campaigns and Elections (Chapter 8), and Interest Groups (Chapter 9).

Then, in Part IV, **Institutions**, we turn to the formal constitutional institutions of the national government and their legally constituted agencies–the Congress (Chapter 10), the Presidency (Chapter 11), the Bureaucracy (Chapter 12), and the Courts (Chapter 13). These chapters explore these institutions, and also their interactions with each other *and* also their connections to parties, voters, the media, and the Constitution. In Part V, **Outcomes**, we explore the outputs of government. Chapter 14 examines the role of government in defense (or violation) of personal liberties. Chapter 15 examines the increasingly complex development of law and policy related to Civil Rights, and explores the social movements that have expanded guarantees of rights.

Chapters 16 (the Economy), 17 (Social Welfare), and 18 (National Defense) examine major public policy areas to help students understand the relationship between the government, the economy it regulates, and two major sources of government spending in social and defense policy.

Politics in America presents balanced arguments on highly sensitive issues, including abortion, gun control, same-sex marriage, marijuana decriminalization affirmative action, race relations, and immigration reform. Each chapter contains a variety of special features designed to inspire discussion and controversy in the classroom:

- **Who's Getting What?** illustrates how political demands turn into government action, and examines how government picks beneficiaries (winners) and those excluded (losers) from public policy. This emphasis reflects the primary emphasis of Lasswell's pluralist approach to politics: Who benefits from the use of government power, and what do they get from the use of power.
- **A Conflicting View** challenges students to rethink conventional wisdom in American politics, by asking them to question what we take for granted, such as obeying the law or keeping our existing voting systems, and to then consider how changing assumptions might change political winners and losers or the balance of power.
- **What Do You Think?** asks students to take sides on controversial questions, and to consider some of the questions currently confronting American politics. In doing so, students are able to identify the players who will benefit or bear costs from government action, and also consider what government action is required, or whether government action is really appropriate.
- **Compared to What?** provides a comparative perspective on many key elements of the American political system. These features contrast the institutions, systems, and behaviors to explore how power is wielded in disparate political systems, and how they either resemble or are distinct from the American case.
- **A Constitutional Note** explains some constitutional dimensions of the topic of each chapter and examines the foundations and limits of constitutional grants of power to government.
- Every chapter includes a **marginal glossary** to support students' understanding of new and important concepts at first encounter. For easy reference, key terms from the marginal glossary are repeated at the end of each chapter and in the end-of-book glossary.

Taken together, these features build on the core material of the text to provide relevant illustrations of different aspects of politics. They expand on the student's understanding of the values, institutions, players, and products of politics. They help introduce the science and practice of politics through the use of both stories and data, and by offering examples of politics in practice. In the process they ask the student to return to the central theme: Who has power? How do they use power? Who is reaping the benefits or footing the bill for the benefits of government action? And, how can the student, citizen, and voter influence politics in an increasingly pessimistic and cynical political environment? In the process, it is our goal for the student to realize that politics is something that they can influence, rather than something that is done to them.

Supplements

Make more time for your students with instructor resources that offer effective learning assessments and classroom engagement. Pearson's partnership with educators does not end with the delivery of course materials; Pearson is there with you on the first day of class and beyond. A dedicated team of local Pearson representatives will work with you to not only choose course materials but also integrate them into your class and assess their effectiveness. Our goal is your goal—to improve instruction with each semester.

Pearson is pleased to offer the following resources to qualified adopters of *Government in America*. Several of these supplements are available to instantly download on the Instructor Resource Center (IRC); please visit the IRC at **www.pearsonhighered.com/irc** to register for access.

TEST BANK. Evaluate learning at every level. Reviewed for clarity and accuracy, the Test Bank measures this book's learning objectives with multiple choice, true/false, fill-in-the-blank, short answer, and essay questions. You can easily customize the assessment to work in any major learning management system and to match what is covered in your course. Word, BlackBoard, and WebCT versions available on the IRC and Respondus versions available upon request from **www.respondus.com**.

PEARSON MYTEST. This powerful assessment generation program includes all of the questions in the Test Bank. Quizzes and exams can be easily authored and saved online and then printed for classroom use, giving you ultimate flexibility to manage assessments anytime and anywhere. To learn more, visit **www.pearsonhighered.com/mytest**.

INSTRUCTOR'S MANUAL. Create a comprehensive roadmap for teaching classroom, online, or hybrid courses. Designed for new and experienced instructors, the Instructor's Manual includes a sample syllabus, lecture and discussion suggestions, activities for in or out of class, and essays on teaching American Government. Available on the IRC.

POWERPOINT PRESENTATION WITH CLASSROOM RESPONSE SYSTEM (CRS). Make lectures more enriching for students. The PowerPoint Presentation includes a full lecture script, discussion questions, photos and figures from the book, and links to MyPoliSciLab multimedia. With integrated clicker questions, get immediate feedback on what your students are learning during a lecture. Available on the IRC.

Acknowledgments

Every academic book is a collaboration, and the contributors extend beyond the names on the cover. This book draws on four generations of political science scholarship that was dedicated to seeking answers to a small set of important, pressing questions that confront people around the world: *What is politics and how does politics operate? Where does government come from? Why do representative democracies succeed or fail? Can the public control government? Who rules?* These are important questions. They are critical to understanding American politics. We would not know the answers to these questions without the efforts of the generations of great and obscure scholars—including our own teachers—who asked these questions, looked at the world, and provided answers. It is their body of accumulated knowledge that allows us to craft this text.

We are especially indebted to several friends and colleagues in the profession of political science. The feedback and guidance of those who have read and commented on drafts of the book over the years has proved invaluable in keeping the text accessible, topical, and relevant in a dynamic intellectual and political environment.

Our editors at Pearson have been tireless and enthusiastic in their support of our project and the development of the latest edition of this book. The evolution of the education marketplace makes a good team of editors and a supportive press invaluable sources of support and encouragement, and we are fortunate enough to work with a team of entrepreneurial, dedicated professionals who value our work and make it better.

1

Politics

Who Gets What, When, and How

So what are you getting from politics? Why?

Social insurance: Americans pay into a system of programs that was established four generations ago. For example, the typical retiree has worked roughly a half-century, paying into Social Security, for monthly payments of $1,230 a month. And among recently laid-off, unemployment benefits amount to about $300 a week, paid for by an insurance program, which is funded in part by payroll deduction.

Military security: The United States defense budget is $629 billion, unless you count all defense-related expenditures. Then it climbs to nearly $1 trillion. An Army lieutenant is paid about $43,000 a year with another $12,000 in additional benefits (housing). Three generarations ago, Congress created the Montgomery G.I. Bill, which provides for about $1,400 a month in additional education benefits for military personnel.

College loans: The average cost of going to college full-time and living on a public college campus is over $20,000 a year. The person sitting next to you in class will likely have $33,000 in student loan debt when they finish college—if they finish. The maximum Pell Grant is $5,730 a year—and 1.7 million students get them. They were created two generations ago.

Social welfare: There are 185 "means-tested" social welfare programs in the United States. They cost about $900 billion—and one third of social welfare recipients live in California. These programs were initially created four generations ago, expanded two generations ago, and reformed one generation ago.

Economic security: About $13 trillion was spent by the United States to save the collapsing banking industry starting in 2008. This happened because elites didn't want to repeat a depression from four generations ago.

So what are you getting from politics? Why? To understand politics, you have to understand who has political power, who gets to make choices for society, and who gets the benefits or bears the costs and risks.

1.1 Distinguish between politics and political science, p. 4

1.2 Compare and contrast governmental politics with politics in other societal organizations, p. 4

1.3 Identify the purposes for which government is established, p. 8

1.4 Outline the major principles of democracy, p. 9

1.5 Analyze the inherent conflict between majority rule and individual freedom, p. 15

1.6 Compare and contrast representational government and direct government, p. 18

1.7 Show how elitism and pluralism reach different conclusions about who governs in America, p. 20

1.8 Evaluate the implications of the elitist and pluralist views for the realization of American democratic ideals, p. 23

WHO GETS WHAT "Millennials" are a large, diverse generation. They are more community oriented and more inclined to organize than their parents' generation.

Politics and Political Science

1.1 Distinguish between politics and political science.

politics
Deciding who gets what, when, and how.

political science
The study of politics: who governs, for what ends, and by what means.

government
Organization extending to the whole society that can legitimately use force to carry out its decisions.

**olitics** is deciding "who gets what, when, and how."[1] It is an activity by which people try to get more of whatever there is to get—money, prestige, jobs, respect, sex, even power itself. Politics occurs in many different settings. We talk about office politics, student politics, union politics, church politics, and so forth. But political science usually limits its attention to *politics in government.*

Political science is the study of politics, or the study of who gets what, when, and how.[2] The *who* are the participants in politics—voters, special-interest groups, political parties, journalists, corporations and labor unions, lawyers and lobbyists, foundations and think tanks, and both elected and appointed government officials, including members of Congress, the president and vice president, judges, prosecutors, and bureaucrats. The *what* of politics are public policies—the decisions that governments make concerning taxation, social welfare, health care, education, national defense, law enforcement, the environment, "values," and thousands of other issues that come before governments. The *when* and *how* are the political process—campaigns and elections, political reporting in the news media, television debates, fund-raising, lobbying, decision making in the White House and executive agencies, and decision making in the courts.

Political science is the study of government and political processes, systems, and individual human political behavior. Political science is concerned with answering both the normative questions of politics (how things "should" be) and the empirical questions (how things are in the political world). Political scientists are generally concerned with three questions: *Who governs? For what ends? By what means?* Throughout this book, we are concerned with who participates in politics, how government decisions are made, who benefits most from those decisions, and who bears their greatest costs (see Figure 1.1).

Politics would be simple if everyone agreed on who should govern, who should get what, who should pay for it, and how and when it should be done. But conflict arises from disagreements over these questions, and sometimes the question of confidence in the government itself underlies the conflict (see *What Do You Think?* Can You Trust the Government?).

Politics and Government

1.2 Compare and contrast governmental politics with politics in other societal organizations.

hat distinguishes governmental politics from politics in other institutions in society? After all, parents, teachers, unions, banks, corporations, and many other organizations make decisions about who gets what in society. The answer is that only **government** decisions can *extend to the whole society*, and only government can *legitimately use force*. Other institutions encompass only a part of society: for example, students and faculty in a college, members of a church or union, employees or customers of a corporation. And individuals have a legal right to voluntarily withdraw from *non*governmental organizations. But governments make decisions affecting everyone, and no one can voluntarily withdraw from government's authority (without leaving the country, and thus becoming subject to some other government's authority). Some individuals and organizations—muggers, gangs, crime families, hate groups—occasionally use physical force to get what they want. But only governments can use coercive force and take a human

Who Governs: Participants

Governmental	*Nongovernmental*
President and White House staff Executive Office of the President, including Office of Management and Budget Cabinet officers and executive agency heads Bureaucrats Congress members Congressional staff Supreme Court justices Federal appellate and district judges	Voters Campaign contributors Interest-group leaders and members Party leaders and party identifiers in the electorate Corporate and union leaders Media leaders, including press and television anchors and reporters Lawyers and lobbyists Think tanks and foundation personnel

When and How: Institutions and Processes

Institutions	*Processes*
Constitution Separation of powers Checks and balances Federalism Judicial review Amendment procedures Electoral system	Socialization and learning Opinion formation Party identification Voting Contributing Joining organizations Talking politics
Presidency Congress Senate House of Representatives Courts Supreme Court Appellate courts District courts	Running for office Campaigning Polling Fund-raising Parading and demonstrating Nonviolent direct action Violence
Parties National committees Conventions State and local organizations	Lobbying Logrolling Deciding Budgeting Implementing and evaluating Adjudicating
Media Television Press Internet	Agenda setting News making Interpreting Persuading

What Outcomes: Public Policies

Civil liberties Civil rights Equality Criminal justice Welfare Social Security Health Education Energy	Environmental protection Economic development Economic stability Taxation Government spending and deficits National defense Foreign affairs Homeland Security Allocate morals and values

FIGURE 1.1 WHO GETS WHAT, WHEN, AND HOW

Political science is the study of politics. The distinguished political scientist Harold Lasswell entitled his most popular book *Politics: Who Gets What, When, and How*. The first topic of politics is "Who?" (That is, who are the participants in politics, both within and outside of government?) "When and how are political decisions made?" (That is, how do the institutions and processes of politics function?) "What outcomes are produced?" (That is, what public policies are adopted?) Shown here are some of the topics of concerns to political science.

CONFLICT ALL AROUND

Conflict exists in all activities as participants struggle over who gets what, when, and how. From the streets to Congress to the campaign trail, participants in the political process compete to further their goals and ambitions.

legitimacy
Widespread acceptance of something as necessary, rightful, and legally binding.

life legitimately—that is, people generally believe it is acceptable for the government to use force if necessary to uphold its laws, but they do not extend this right to other institutions or individuals. The government can rely on force only against relatively small numbers of offenders. Most of us, most of the time, obey laws out of habit—the habit of compliance. We have been taught to believe that law and order are necessary and that government is right to punish those who disobey its laws. Most people would say that they obey the law in order to avoid fines and stay out of prison. But if large numbers of people all decided to disobey the law at the same time, the government would not have enough police or jails to hold them all. Social order—and the widespread acceptance of social order—protects liberty, property, and conscience.

Government thus enjoys **legitimacy**, or rightfulness, in its use of force.[3] A democratic government has a special claim to legitimacy because it is based on the consent of its people, who participate in the selection of its leaders and the making of its laws. Those who disagree with a law have the option of working for its change by speaking out, petitioning, demonstrating, forming interest groups or parties, voting against unpopular leaders, or running for office themselves. Since people living in a democracy can effect change by "working within the system," they have a greater moral obligation to obey the law than people living under regimes in which they have no voice. However, there may be some occasions when "civil disobedience" even in a democracy may be morally justified (see *A Conflicting View*: Sometimes It's Right to Disobey the Law).

What Do You Think?

Can You Trust the Government?

Americans are suspicious of big government. Many do not trust the government in Washington to "do what is right." Trust in government has varied over the years, as measured by polls asking, "How much of the time do you think you can trust the government in Washington to do what is right? Just about always? Most of the time? Some of the time? None of the time?" Americans' trust in the national government used to be higher. Since the failure in the Vietnam War, the social unrest of the late 1960s, and the Watergate scandal that felled President Richard Nixon—the first resignation of a president in U.S. history—public confidence fell, and kept falling.[a] Americans have now expressed general distrust of their government for two generations.

Part of the decline is a function of public knowledge about government failure. Throughout this period of decline in trust, many negative images of government and government policy were televised for the first time. Television producers want news of scandal, violence, corruption, and incompetence; simple and sensational stories gain higher ratings, not good news or in-depth reporting of complicated issues. Media fragmentation through cable television and the Internet fed the growth of the "new media," where instant controversy drives viewership and readership. In turn, trust in the mass media has declined along with trust in government.

Economic recessions and policy failures also erode public confidence in government. People expect the president and Congress to lead them out of "hard times." Both President George H.W. Bush and President George W. Bush saw public confidence fall as economic issues overtook their military successes. And the skepticism over Middle Eastern wars and the national government response to Hurricane Katrina accompanied declining trust in 2005 and 2006. This continued to nearly historic lows during the Obama administration, despite aggressive spending and policy initiatives designed to alleviate the economic downturn.

But public confidence in government can be revived. In the 1980s, President Ronald Reagan's popularity restored the public's confidence in government.[b] The economic prosperity of the Clinton era revived Americans' trust in government. Trust doubled immediately after September 11, 2001, but then eroded as the war in Iraq dragged on. The election of Barack Obama inspired a modest upswing of trust corresponding to the "honeymoon" period that newly elected presidents enjoy. But as Obama's approval ratings declined, so did trust in government.

Many perceive that government is "captured" by a few special interests, and that government officials are basically corrupt. Most Americans believe that lobbyists (71 percent), corporations (67 percent), banks (67 percent), and the national government (58 percent) have too much power.[c] They also believe that leaders in Washington are "heavily influenced by special interests" (87 percent) and that politicians are "mainly concerned about getting reelected" (86 percent).[d]

The public trusts government more to handle foreign affairs than domestic problems. Among the national government institutions, people place the most trust in the courts, followed by the president, and then Congress. Local government enjoys greater trust than state government or the national government. And the people place the greatest trust in themselves: while only 19 percent trust the government to do the right thing, 69 percent place trust in the people to do the right thing.

QUESTIONS

1. Does distance from government institutions affect trust in government?
2. Why do you think people trust the courts more than Congress or the president?
3. Why do you think trust in media and trust in government both decline as the media reports more bad news about government?

[a]Marc J. Hetherington, *Why Trust Matters*. Princeton, N.J.: Princeton University Press, 2005.

[b]Arthur H. Miller, "Confidence in Government During the 1980s," *American Politics Quarterly* 19 (April 1991): 147–173.

[c]Gallup Poll, March 25–27, 2011, accessed at http://www.pollingreport.com/institut.htm.

[d]CNN/Opinion Research Corporation Poll, February 12–15, 2010, accessed at http://www.pollingreport.com/institut.htm

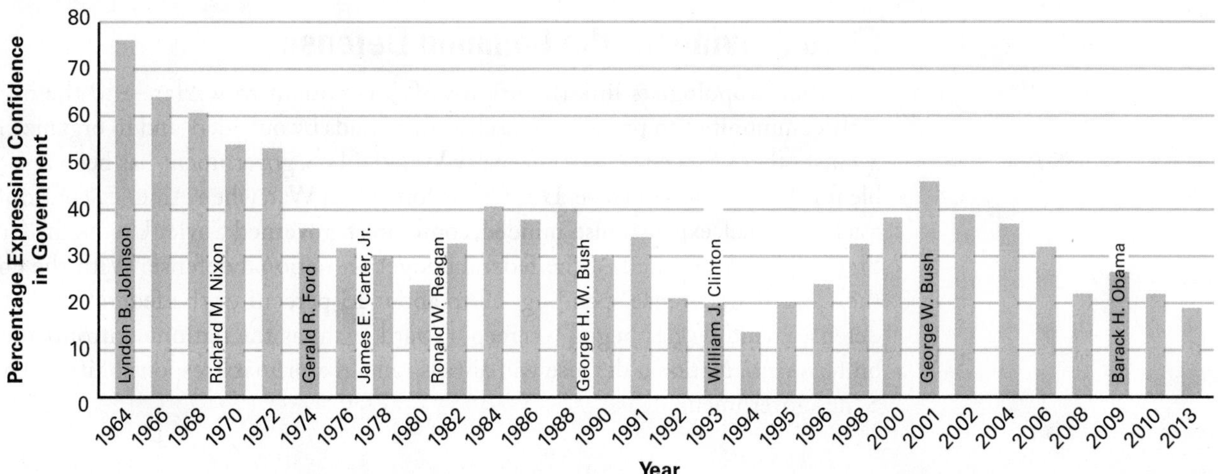

SOURCE: Data for 1964 through 2010 from Gallup Opinion Polls (http://www.gallup.com/poll/topics/trust_gov.asd). Data for 2013 from the Pew Research Center (www.people-press.org/2013/10/18/trust-in-government-interactive).

1.1
1.2
1.3
1.4
1.5
1.6
1.7
1.8

The Purposes of Government

1.3 Identify the purposes for which government is established.

social contract
Idea that government originates as an implied contract among individuals who agree to obey laws in exchange for protection of their rights.

public goods
Goods and services that cannot readily be provided by markets, either because they are too expensive for a single individual to buy or because if one person bought them, everyone else would use them without paying.

All governments tax, penalize, punish, restrict, and regulate their people. Governments in the United States—the federal government in Washington, the 50 state governments, and the more than 87,000 local governments—take nearly 40 cents out of every dollar Americans earn. Each year, the Congress enacts about 500 laws; federal bureaucracies publish about 20,000 rules and regulations, the state legislatures enact about 25,000 laws; and cities, counties, school districts, and other local governments enact countless local ordinances. Each of these laws restricts our freedom in some way.

Why do people put up with governments? An answer to this question can be found in the words of the Preamble to the Constitution of the United States:

> We the people of the United States, in Order to form a more perfect Union, establish Justice, insure domestic Tranquility, provide for the common defense, promote the general Welfare, and secure the Blessings of Liberty to ourselves and our Posterity, do ordain and establish this Constitution for the United States of America.

To Establish Justice and Insure Domestic Tranquility

Government manages conflict and maintains order. We might think of government as a **social contract** among people who agree to allow themselves to be regulated and taxed in exchange for protection of their lives and property. No society can allow individuals or groups to settle their conflicts by street fighting, murder, kidnapping, rioting, bombing, or terrorism. Whenever government fails to control such violence, we describe it as "a breakdown in law and order." Without the protection of government, human lives and property are endangered, and only those skilled with fists and weapons have much of a chance of survival. The seventeenth-century English political philosopher Thomas Hobbes described life without government as "a war where every man is enemy to every man," where people live in "continual fear and danger of violent death."[4] The American social contract is complicated by the agreement to limit the ability of government to interfere with the core liberties of human beings, including their beliefs and matters of personal conscience. This libertarian tradition is an enduring source of conflict in American politics, where the desire for order and safety confronts inalienable rights and freedoms.

To Provide for the Common Defense

Many anthropologists link the origins of government to warfare—to the need of early communities to protect themselves from raids by outsiders and to organize raids against others. Since the Revolutionary War, the U.S. government has been responsible for the country's defense. During the long Cold War, when America confronted a nuclear-armed, expansionist-minded, communist-governed Soviet Union, the United States spent nearly half of the federal budget on national defense. With the end of the Cold War, defense spending fell to about 15 percent of the federal budget, but defense spending has begun to creep upward again as the nation confronts the war on terrorism. National defense will always remain a primary responsibility of United States government.

To Promote the General Welfare

Government promotes the general welfare in a number of ways. It provides **public goods**—goods and services that private markets cannot readily furnish either because they are too expensive for individuals to buy for themselves (for example, a national park, a highway, or a sewage disposal plant) or because if one person bought them, everyone else would "free ride," or use them without paying (for example, clean air, police protection, or national defense).

Nevertheless, Americans acquire most of their goods and services on the **free market**, through voluntary exchange among individuals, firms, and corporations. The **gross domestic product (GDP)**—the dollar sum of all the goods and services produced in the United States in a year—amounts to more than $15 trillion. Government spending in the United States—federal, state, and local governments combined—now amounts to about $5 trillion, or an amount equivalent to one-third of the gross domestic product. (See *Who's Getting What?* Is Government Growing Too Big?)

Governments also regulate society. Free markets cannot function effectively if individuals and firms engage in fraud, deception, or unfair competition, or if contracts cannot be enforced. Moreover, many economic activities impose costs on persons who are not direct participants in these activities. Economists refer to such costs as **externalities**. A factory that produces air pollution or wastewater imposes external costs on community residents who would otherwise enjoy cleaner air or water. A junkyard that creates an eyesore makes life less pleasant for neighbors and passersby. Many government regulations are designed to reduce these external costs.

To promote general welfare, governments also use **income transfers** from taxpayers to people who are regarded as deserving. Government agencies and programs provide support and care for individuals who cannot supply these things for themselves through the private job market; this includes ill, elderly, and disabled people and dependent children who cannot usually be expected to find productive employment. The largest income transfer programs are Social Security and Medicare, which are paid to the elderly regardless of their personal wealth. Other large transfer payments go to farmers, veterans, and the unemployed as well as to a wide variety of businesses. As we shall see, the struggle of individuals and groups to obtain direct government payments is a major motivator of political activity.

free market
Free competition for voluntary exchange among individuals, firms, and corporations.

gross domestic product (GDP)
Measure of economic performance in terms of the nation's total production of goods and services for a single year, valued in terms of market prices.

externalities
Costs imposed on people who are not direct participants in an activity.

income transfers
Government transfers of income from taxpayers to persons regarded as deserving.

democracy
Governing system in which the people govern themselves; from the Greek term meaning "rule by the many."

To Secure the Blessings of Liberty

All governments must maintain order, protect national security, provide public goods, regulate society, and care for those unable to fend for themselves. But *democratic* governments have a special added responsibility—to protect individual liberty by ensuring that all people are treated equally before the law. No one is above the law. The president must obey the Constitution and laws of the United States, and so must members of Congress, governors, judges, and the police. A democratic government must protect people's freedom to speak and write what they please, to practice their religion, to petition, to form groups and parties, to enjoy personal privacy, and to exercise their rights if accused of a crime.

The Meaning of Democracy

1.4 Outline the major principles of democracy.

hroughout the centuries, thinkers in various cultures contributed to the development of democratic government. Early Greek philosophers contributed the word **democracy** ("rule by the many"). But there is no universal contemporary definition of *democracy*, nor any tightly organized system

Who's Getting What?

Is Government Growing Too Big?

President Barack Obama came into office with an extensive political agenda, including a bailout of the nation's financial institutions, a government stimulus package for the economy, a transformation of the nation's health care system, a new "cap and trade" initiative for dealing with climate change, and comprehensive immigration reform. Together, these policy initiatives envision a vast enlargement of the federal government, huge increases in federal spending, and the resulting skyrocketing of federal deficit levels. Republican congressional efforts to curtail the president's agenda are no more popular, and have done little to limit the growth of government. So, is government growing too big?

Over half of a national sample of adult Americans polled say that the government is trying to do too many things (57 percent), with others thinking that the government should do more (38 percent), and others expressing mixed feelings (4 percent). In another survey, when asked what the "biggest threat to the country in the future" is, respondents placed big government first (55 percent), ahead of big business (32 percent) and big labor (10 percent). Solid majorities of Americans believe that the national government "has too much power" and that the national government "is doing too much" to solve our country's problems. The number of Americans who view the national government as a "threat to rights and freedoms of ordinary citizens" has grown substantially since 2003.

In the depths of the 2008–2009 financial crisis, narrow majorities of Americans were willing to indulge short-term expansion of government (53 percent approved, 44 percent disapproved), and they did not see the expansion as being too great (40 percent said it was "too big an expansion," 46 percent said it was "the right amount," 10 percent said it was "too little"). The consequence was an expansion of the decade-long trend of deficit spending and a four-decade long expansion of federal spending. Confronted with massive deficits, the public has returned to its periodic preference for fiscal responsibility, and demands that government limit spending. When asked how to eliminate the deficit, the majority

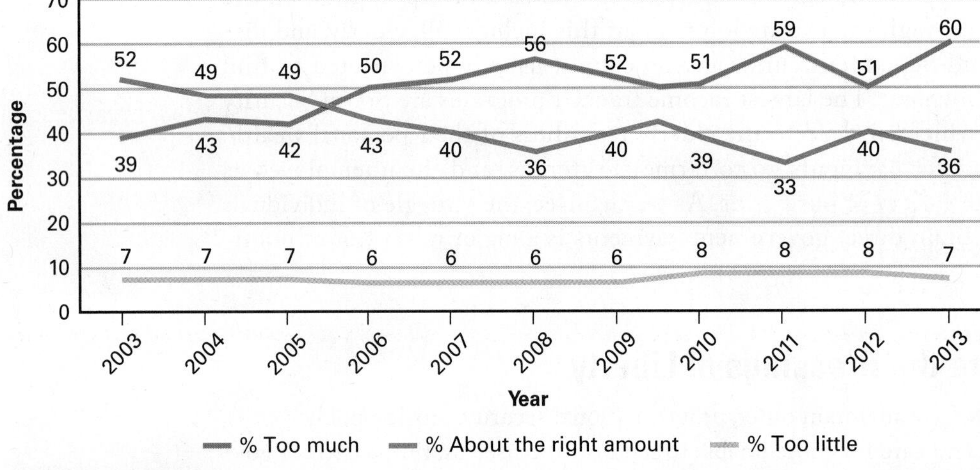

Do you think the federal government today has too much power, about the right amount of power, or too little power?

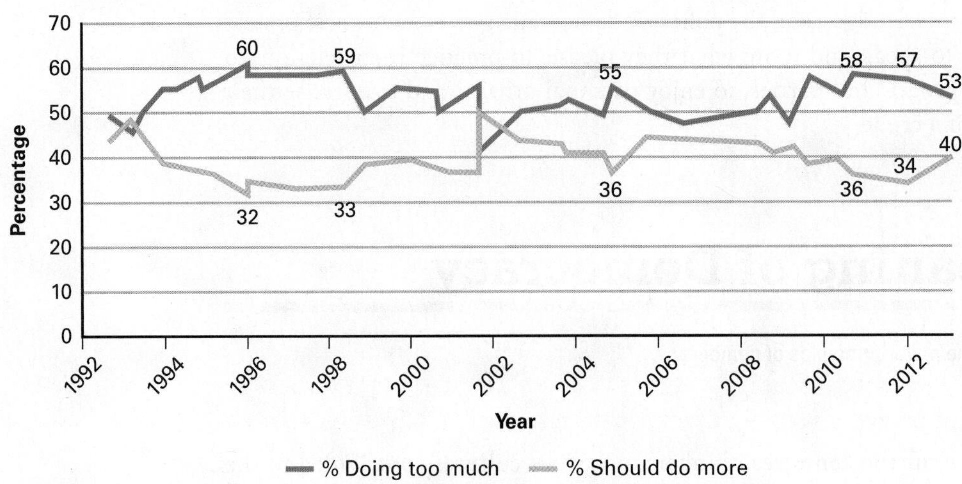

Is the government trying to do too many things to solve our country's problems?

(Continued)

(Continued)

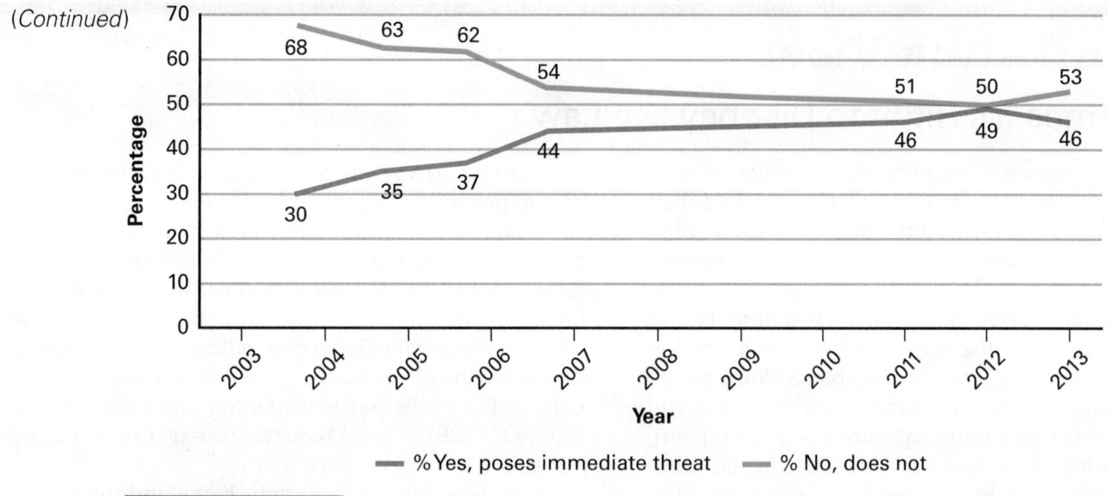

Is the federal government an immediate threat to the rights and freedoms of ordinary citizens?

preference—barely—is for spending cuts. Half of Americans (50 percent) want to balance the budget mostly or only with spending cuts, while just 11 percent want to do so mostly or only with tax increases. About a third of the public (32 percent) wants to use a balance of tax revenue enhancements with budget cuts.

For four generations, Americans turned to the government in Washington during hard economic times, such as during the New Deal expansion of government under President Franklin D. Roosevelt in the Great Depression of the 1930s. The "Great Recession" of 2009 gave the Obama administration and congressional Democrats an opportunity to offer a wide variety of new policy initiatives, a new "New Deal." But those initiatives did not generate the economic recovery promised, nor have they generated public confidence in government. The public is less trusting of government; see it as too powerful; and wish it would resolve its budget deficits by cutting spending.

QUESTIONS

1. So, do you think the federal government today has too much power, about the right amount of power, or too little power?
2. Is the government trying to do too many things to solve our country's problems?
3. Do you believe that the federal government is an immediate threat to the rights and freedoms of ordinary citizens? Why?[a]

[a]Time, June 15, 2009: 26.

SOURCES: Gallup opinion poll, 2010, reported at www.gallup.com.Gallup opinion poll, July 13, 2011, reported at www.gallup.com. Gallup Opinion Poll, 2009, as reported in *The Polling Report*, www.pollingreport.com.

of democratic thought. It is better, perhaps, to speak of democratic traditions than of a single democratic ideology.

The looseness of the term *democracy* allows it to be perverted by *anti*democratic governments. Governments that outlaw political opposition, suppress dissent, discourage religion, and deny fundamental freedoms of speech and press still claim to be "democracies," "democratic republics," or "people's republics" (for example, the Democratic People's Republic of Korea is the official name of communist North Korea). These governments defend their use of the term *democracy* by claiming that their policies reflect the true interests of their people. But they are unwilling to allow political freedoms or to hold free elections to test the people's agreement with their policies, and "democracy" becomes a political slogan rather than a true description of their government (see *Compared to What?* Political Freedom or Economic Freedom?).

A meaningful definition of democracy must include the following **democratic principles**: (1) recognition of the dignity of every individual; (2) equal protection under the law for every individual; (3) opportunity for everyone to participate in public decisions; and (4) decision making by majority rule, with one person having one vote.

democratic principles
Individual dignity, equality before the law, widespread participation in public decisions, and public decisions by majority rule, with one person having one vote.

A Conflicting View

Sometimes It's Right to Disobey the Law

Civil disobedience is the nonviolent violation of laws that people believe to be unjust. Civil disobedience denies the legitimacy, or rightfulness, of a law and implies that a higher moral authority takes precedence over unjust laws.

Why resort to civil disobedience in a democracy? Why not work within the democratic system to change unjust laws? In 1963, a group of Alabama clergy posed these questions to Martin Luther King, Jr., and asked him to call off mass demonstrations in Birmingham, Alabama. King, who had been arrested in the demonstrations, replied in his now-famous "Letter from Birmingham City Jail": "One has not only a legal but a moral responsibility to obey just laws. Conversely, one has a moral responsibility to disobey unjust laws."

King argued that nonviolent direct action was a vital aspect of democratic politics. The political purpose of civil disobedience is to call attention or "to bear witness" to the existence of injustices. Only laws regarded as unjust are broken, and they are broken openly, without hatred or violence. Punishment is actively sought rather than avoided, since punishment will further emphasize the injustice of the laws.

Dr. King took his inspiration for nonviolent civil disobedience from Mohandas Gandhi. A British subject born in India, Gandhi had worked as a young lawyer in South Africa where he repeatedly encountered de facto discrimination under what would later be the legally enforced apartheid regime. In response, he applied the principles of nonviolent civil resistance. Like King and other members of the subsequent American civil rights movement he was jailed and even beaten several times. He never responded violently or sued, but continued to resist the Jim Crow–style laws imposed by the white South Africans on black Africans and Indians. He later applied these same techniques in pursuit of Indian independence from the United Kingdom, achieved in 1947.

The objective of nonviolent civil disobedience is to stir the conscience of an apathetic majority and to win support to eliminate the injustices. By accepting punishment for the violation of an unjust law, persons practicing civil disobedience demonstrate their sincerity. They hope to shame the majority and to make it ask itself how far it is willing to go to protect the status quo. According to King, to break an unjust law while willfully accepting the penalty of breaking the law both showed respect for law and order while calling attention to injustice under the law.

Nonviolent protest took several forms during the American civil rights movement, and the use of nonviolent protest created several heroes of civil disobedience. The 1955 Montgomery bus boycott against the segregated public transportation in that city elevated Rosa Parks to iconic status for her refusal to surrender her bus seat to a white, and also propelled the recently arrived Reverend King to national status.

Lunchroom counter sit-in demonstrations by students in Durham, Wichita, Oklahoma City, and Greensboro popularized this form of disobedience between 1957 and 1960 and brought attention to the Student Nonviolent Coordinating Committee, which organized many of the protests. (Sit-ins had been used as early as the 1930s and 1940s by the Congress of Racial Equity [CORE] in New York to protest discriminatory restaurant hiring practices).

The Freedom Riders were black and white college students who challenged segregation in interstate by traveling together on buses across the South. Their journey in May 1961 was largely uneventful until they were met by an angry Ku Klux Klan-led mob in Anniston, Alabama. Their bus was attacked and burned, and the riders were assaulted and battered. A second bus, from Anniston to Birmingham, was similarly assaulted and several of the riders were beaten, including future Student Nonviolent Coordinating Committee chairman (later congressman) John Lewis.

Marches and other efforts at public display and protest were used in pursuit of the vote. The most famous of these took place in March 1965, in Selma (Dallas County), Alabama. John Lewis and another young activist, Hosea Williams, led a group of six hundred African Americans seeking to register to vote (Dallas County was solidly majority black but had almost no black voters registered). They were met at the Edmund Pettis Bridge by the state police. Lewis was beaten repeatedly about the head, one of several assaults he would endure while seeking civil rights. Lewis's dramatic televised appeal to President Johnson to intervene in the South was followed six months later by the passage of the Voting Rights Act.

Countless African Americans and whites worked in the civil rights movement, using nonviolent means to achieve social change. Many were arrested, or beaten, or even died in pursuit of equal rights. And, the change effected by their effort was so significant, it captured the eye of the media, and the attention of the world. In 1964 Martin Luther King, Jr., received the Nobel Peace Prize in recognition of his extraordinary contributions to the development of nonviolent methods of social change.

QUESTIONS

1. Does civil disobedience undermine the legitimacy of a protest movement?
2. As you move through the course, think about how the ability to communicate interacts with the ability to organize against perceived governmental or social injustice. Then return to these questions and ask yourself, "Is communication important to successful nonviolent protest?"

Individual Dignity

The underlying value of democracy is the dignity of the individual. Human beings are entitled to life and liberty, personal property, and equal protection under the law. These liberties are *not* granted by governments; they are inherent and belong to every person born into the world. The English political philosopher John Locke (1632–1704) argued that a higher "natural law" guaranteed liberty to every person and that this natural law was morally superior to all human laws and governments. Each individual possesses "certain inalienable Rights, among these are Life, Liberty, and Property."[5] When Thomas Jefferson wrote his eloquent defense of the American Revolution in the Declaration of Independence for the Continental Congress in Philadelphia in 1776, he borrowed heavily from Locke (perhaps even to the point of plagiarism):

> We hold these truths to be self-evident, that all Men are created equal, that they are endowed by their Creator with certain unalienable Rights, that among these are Life, Liberty and the Pursuit of Happiness.

Individual dignity requires personal freedom. People who are directed by governments in every aspect of their lives, people who are "collectivized" and made into workers for the state, people who are enslaved—all are denied the personal dignity to which all human beings are entitled. Democratic governments try to minimize the role of government in the lives of citizens.

Equality

True democracy requires equal protection of the law for every individual. Democratic governments cannot discriminate between races, or sexes, or rich and poor, or any groups of people in applying the law. Not only must a democratic government refrain from discrimination itself, but it must also work to prevent discrimination in society generally. Today our notion of equality extends to equality of opportunity—the obligation of government to ensure that all Americans have an equal opportunity to develop their full potential.

Participation in Decision Making

Democracy means individual participation in the decisions that affect individuals' lives. People should be free to choose for themselves how they want to live. Individual participation in government is necessary for individual dignity. People in a democracy should not have decisions made *for* them but *by* them. Even if they make mistakes, it is better that they be permitted to do so than to take away their rights to make their own decisions. The true democrat would reject even a wise and benevolent dictatorship because it would threaten the individual's character, self-reliance, and dignity. The argument for democracy is not that the people will always choose wise policies for themselves, but that people who cannot choose for themselves are not really free.

Majority Rule: One Person, One Vote

Collective decision making in democracies must be by majority rule, with each person having one vote. That is, each person's vote must be equal to every other person's, regardless of status, money, or fame. Whenever any individual is denied political equality because of race, sex, or wealth, then the government is not truly democratic. Majorities are not always right. But majority *rule* means that all persons have an equal say in decisions affecting them. If people are truly equal, their votes must count equally, and a majority vote must decide the issue, even if the majority decides foolishly. A democratic system must also be responsive and allow the electorate to change majorities with changing political preferences.

Compared to What?

Political Freedom or Economic Freedom?

How do you decide if a people are "free"? That depends on how you define and measure freedom. Freedom House, a New York–based think tank, regularly surveys political conditions around the world. It judges nations to be "free," "partly free," or "not free" based on the degree of democracy in their governmental system. Freedom House assesses political freedoms—enabling citizens to participate meaningfully in government—and individual liberties. Political freedoms include whether the chief executive and national legislature are elected; whether elections are generally fair, with open campaigning and honest tabulation of the votes; and whether multiple candidates and parties participate. Individual liberties include whether the press and broadcasting are free and independent of the government; whether people are free to assemble, protest, and form opposition parties; whether religious institutions, labor unions, business organizations, and other groups are free and independent of the government; and whether individuals are free to own property, travel, and move their residence. Currently Freedom House judges 89 of the world's 193 countries, with 46 percent of the world's population, to be "free." An additional 62 countries, with 20 percent of the world's population, are judged to be "partly free." Forty-two countries, representing 34 percent of the world's population, are judged to be "not free," including the world's largest country, China.

Another form of freedom is economic freedom. The conservative Heritage Foundation computes an Index of Economic Freedom (IEF) to determine how easily people can engage in business and trade, free from corruption or excessive interference by government. The freest economy in the world, according to the IEF, is Hong Kong, followed by Singapore, Australia, Switzerland, and New Zealand (The U.S. ranks twelfth). The five least free nations are Venezuela, Eritrea, Cuba, Zimbabwe, and North Korea. The United States is losing its ground to its economic competitors. In 2014 the United States fell from the ranks of the top ten freest economies. The nation experienced losses in property rights, freedom from corruption, and control of government spending.

Freedom House and Heritage have very different ways of defining freedom, but generally speaking, they identify the same countries as being more free. Countries with high Freedom House ratings also have high Index of Economic Freedom scores. Of 179 countries rated by both groups, there are 60 that score above average on both indices. All are considered "Free" by Freedom House (the top category). Of 30 countries that rank above for economic freedom but not for political freedom and civil liberties, 21 are "Partly Free" (including Mexico and Hong Kong) according to Freedom House, and nine are "Not Free" (including a variety of the Persian Gulf states). Fifteen countries are above average for political freedom and liberties but below average for economic freedom, including India, Brazil, Argentina, and Indonesia.

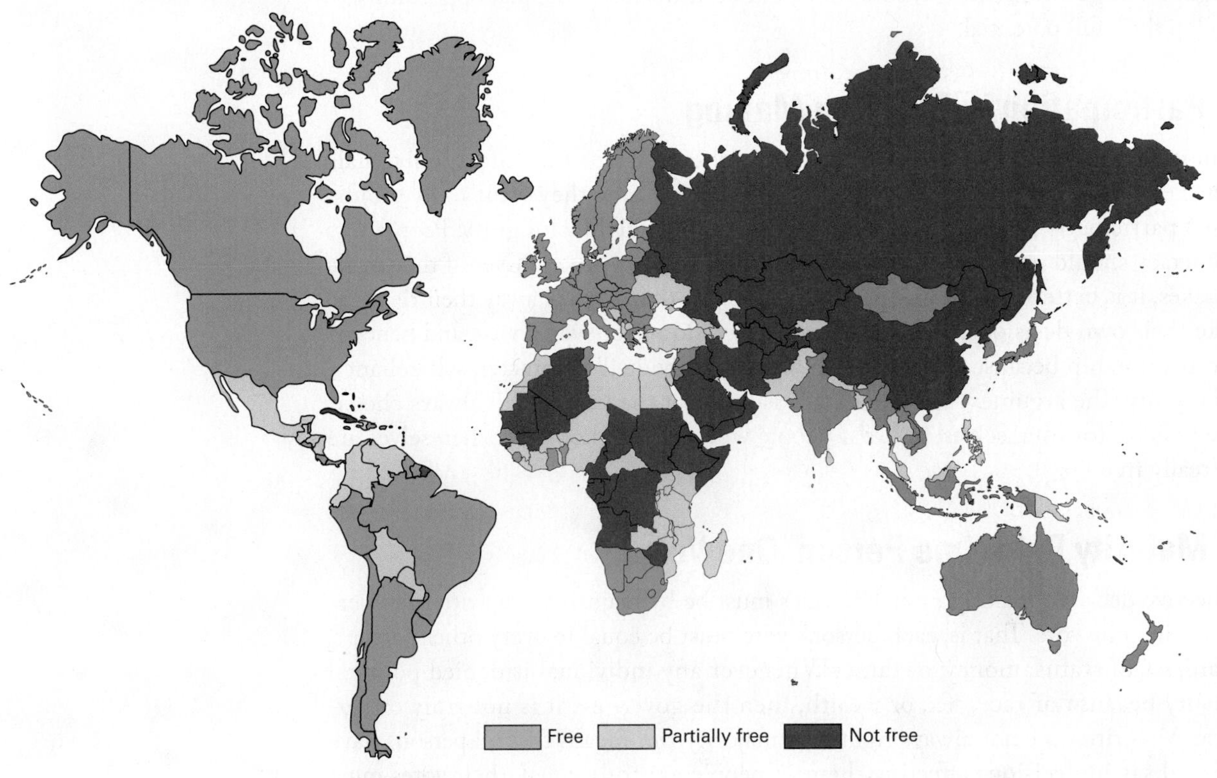

The most economically-free countries in the world are in western Europe, the Americas, and in south Asia and Oceania.

(Continued)

(Continued)

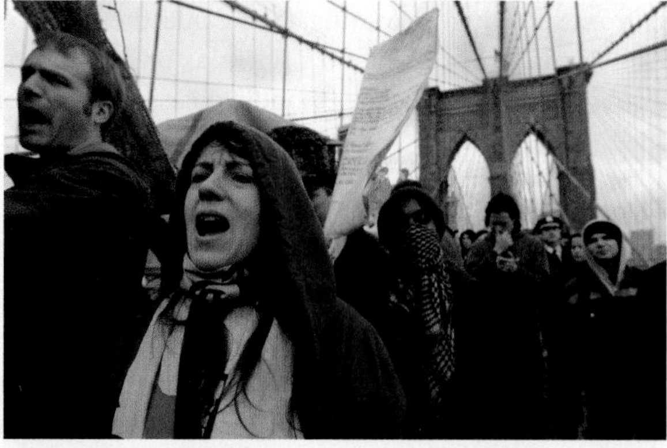

OCCUPY WALL STREET

The Occupy Movement brought attention to the economic and professional frustration of a generation of educated Americans who see their economic security and economic opportunities disappearing in a system that favors corporations. Here marchers cross the Brooklyn Bridge six months after the initial Occupy events.

Worldwide progress toward freedom and democracy made major strides after 1989 as a result of the collapse of communism in Eastern Europe and the demise of the Soviet Union. One assumption was that political freedom would bring market freedom, and that market freedom and economic growth would encourage demands for political freedom and civil liberties protections to defend economic gains. Economic freedom and political freedom generally grow together. But in recent years, Freedom House has detected a "gathering authoritarian push back," notably in Russia, China, Iran, and Venezuela, while revolutionary demands for greater political freedom are occurring in countries with limited economic and political freedom, such as Libya, Morocco, Tunisia, and Egypt.

QUESTIONS

1. Are economic freedom and political freedom separate concepts?
2. If market freedom leads to prosperity for some, but it is not accompanied by political freedom, what can motivate demands for political freedom?

SOURCES: Data on Freedom House Index obtained at www.freedomhouse.org. Index of Economic Freedom data from Heritage Foundation, *2014 Index of Economic Freedom*. Washington, DC: Heritage Foundation, 2014.

NOTE: Freedom House measures political freedom and civil liberties on a seven-point scale, where 1 is most free and 7 is least free. The two indices are strongly and positively correlated. The Freedom House index score in the accompanying figure is computed as follows: [(7 – PR) X (7 – CL)]/.36, where PR is the political rights score; CL is the civil liberties score; and the product is divided by .36 to normalize the score between 0 and 100.

The Paradox of Democracy

1.5 Analyze the inherent conflict between majority rule and individual freedom.

But what if a *majority* of the people decide to attack the rights of some unpopular individuals or minorities? What if hate, prejudice, or racism infects a majority of people and they vote for leaders who promise to "get rid of the Jews" or "put blacks in their place" or "bash a few gays"? What if a majority of people vote to take away the property of wealthy people and distribute it among themselves?[6] Do we abide by the principle of majority rule and allow the majority to do what it wants? Or do we defend the principle of individual liberty and limit the majority's power? If we enshrine the principle of majority rule, we are placing all our confidence in the wisdom and righteousness of the majority of the people. Yet we know that democracy means more than majority rule, that it also means freedom and dignity for the individual. How do we resolve this **paradox of democracy**—the potential for conflict between majority rule and individual freedom?

paradox of democracy
Potential for conflict between individual freedom and majority rule.

Limiting the Power of Majorities

The Founders of the American nation were not sure that freedom would be safe in the hands of the majority. In *The Federalist Papers* in 1787, James Madison warned against a direct democracy: "Pure democracy . . . can admit of no cure for the mischiefs of faction. . . . There is nothing to check the inducements to sacrifice the weaker party, or an obnoxious individual."[7] So the Founders wrote a Constitution and adopted a Bill of Rights that limited the power of government over the individual, by placing some personal liberties beyond the reach of majorities. They established the principle of

1.1 1.2 1.3 1.4 1.5 1.6 1.7 1.8

limited government
Principle that government power over the individual is limited, that there are some personal liberties that even a majority cannot regulate, and that government itself is restrained by law.

totalitarianism
Rule by an elite that exercises unlimited power over individuals in all aspects of life.

limited government—a government that is itself restrained by law. Under a limited government, even if a majority of voters wanted to, they could not prohibit communists or atheists or racists from speaking or writing. Nor could they ban certain religions, set aside the rights of criminal defendants to a fair trial, or prohibit people from moving or quitting their jobs. These rights belong to individuals, not to majorities or governments.

Totalitarianism: Unlimited Government Power

No government can be truly democratic if it directs every aspect of its citizens' lives. Individuals must be free to shape their own lives, free from the dictates of governments or even majorities of their fellow citizens. Indeed, we call a government with *un*limited power over its citizens totalitarian. Under **totalitarianism**, the individual possesses no personal liberty. Totalitarian governments decide what people can say or write; what unions, churches, or parties they can join, if any; where people must live; what work they must do; what goods they can find in stores and what they will be allowed to buy and sell; whether citizens will be allowed to travel outside of their country; and so on. Under a totalitarian government, the total life of the individual is subject to government control.

MORE THAN MAJORITY ROLE

The paradox of democracy balances the principles of majority rule against the principle of individual liberty. When the German people voted Adolf Hitler and the Nazi Party into power, did majority rule give the Nazis free rein to restrict the individual liberties of the people? Or did those who abhorred the trespasses of their government have the right to fight against the power?

SYMBOLS OF TOTALITARIANISM

Political sociologists have observed that the military in totalitarian societies has a distinct body language. Soldiers in communist North Korea use a "goose step" when on parade—a march in which the knee is unbent and the foot, encased in a heavy boot, is stamped on the ground, providing a powerful image of authority and force. In democratic societies, the goose step is not employed; indeed, it is regarded as somewhat ridiculous.

Totalitarian governments undertake to control all agencies of the government, including the military and the police, and virtually all other institutions of society including newspapers, television, schools, churches, businesses, banks, labor unions, and any other organization that might challenge their control. In contrast, democratic societies allow many other institutions to operate independently of the government (see *The Game, the Rules, the Players*: Confidence in American Institutions).

authoritarianism

Monopoly of political power by an individual or small group that otherwise allows people to go about their private lives as they wish.

AUTHORITARIANISM In many countries throughout the world, a single individual or ruling group monopolizes all *political* power, but allows people to otherwise lead their lives as they wish. **Authoritarianism** is mainly concerned with control of government. People can conduct business and trade, join churches, live where they wish, and otherwise conduct their *private* lives without government interference. But they have no role to play in politics, no control over their government, no competitive political parties, no elections, and are otherwise barred from political life. Authoritarianism appears somewhat less oppressive, at least in the everyday lives of the people, than totalitarianism.

Constitutional Government

Constitutions, written or unwritten, are the principal means by which governmental powers are limited. Constitutions set forth the liberties of individuals and restrain governments from interfering with these liberties. Consider, for example, the opening words of the First Amendment to the U.S. Constitution: "Congress shall make no law respecting an establishment of religion, or prohibiting the free exercise thereof." This amendment explicitly declares religious belief beyond the reach of the government.

1.1
1.2
1.3
1.4
1.5
1.6
1.7
1.8

constitutional government
A government limited by rule of law in its power over the liberties of individuals.

direct democracy
Governing system in which every person participates actively in every public decision, rather than delegating decision making to representatives.

representative democracy
Governing system in which public decision making is delegated to representatives of the people chosen by popular vote in free, open, and periodic elections.

The government itself is restrained by law. It cannot, even by majority vote, interfere with the personal liberty to worship as one chooses. In addition, armed with the power of judicial review, the courts can declare unconstitutional laws passed by majority vote of Congress or state legislatures.

Throughout this book, we examine how well limited **constitutional government** succeeds in preserving individual liberty in the United States. We examine free speech and press, the mass media, religious freedom, the freedom to protest and demonstrate, and the freedom to support political candidates and interest groups of all kinds. And we examine how well the U.S. Constitution protects individuals from discrimination and inequality.

Direct Versus Representative Democracy

1.6 Compare and contrast representational government and direct government.

In the Gettysburg Address, Abraham Lincoln spoke about "a government of the people, by the people, for the people," and his ringing phrase remains an American ideal. But can we take this phrase literally? More than 300 million Americans are spread over 4 million square miles. If we brought everyone together, standing shoulder to shoulder, they would occupy 70 square miles. One round of five-minute speeches by everyone would take over 3,000 years. "People could be born, grow old, and die while they waited for the assembly to make one decision."[8]

Direct democracy (also called pure or participatory democracy), where everyone actively participates in every decision, is rare. The closest approximation to direct democracy in American government may be the traditional New England town meeting, where all of the citizens come together face-to-face to decide about town affairs. But today, most New England towns vest authority in a board of officials elected by the townspeople to make policy decisions between town meetings, and professional administrators are appointed to supervise the day-to-day town services. The town meeting is vanishing because citizens cannot spend so much of their time and energy in community decision making.

Representative democracy recognizes that it is impossible to expect millions of people to come together and decide every issue. Instead, representatives of the people are elected by the people to decide issues on behalf of the people. Elections must be open to competition so that the people can choose representatives who reflect their own views. And elections must take place in an environment of free speech and press, so that both candidates and voters can freely express their views. Finally, elections must be held periodically so that representatives can be thrown out of office if they no longer reflect the views of the majority of the people.

No government can claim to be a representative democracy, then, unless:

1. Representatives are selected by vote of all the people.
2. Elections are open to competition.
3. Candidates and voters can freely express themselves.
4. Representatives are selected periodically.

So when we hear of "elections" in which only one party is permitted to run candidates, candidates are not free to express their views, or leaders are elected "for life," then we know that these governments are not really democracies, regardless of what they may call themselves.

The Game, the Rules, the Players

Confidence in American Institutions

Which institutions in society today enjoy the confidence of the American people? In somewhat of a paradox for a democratic society, the *military* enjoys the greatest confidence of Americans. The *police* also enjoy a great deal of confidence, although "the criminal justice system" (defined by most respondents as the courts) does not. Among branches of the national government, the president and the Supreme Court rate fairly high in confidence. But Congress is rated very low.

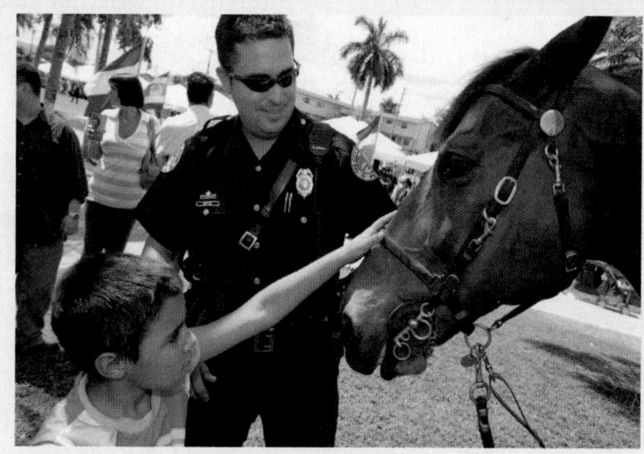

WHO DO YOU TRUST?

The police are, for most Americans, an institution that enjoys historic trust.

Q. I am going to read you a list of institutions in American society. Please tell me how much confidence you, yourself, have in each one: a great deal, quite a lot, some, or very little.

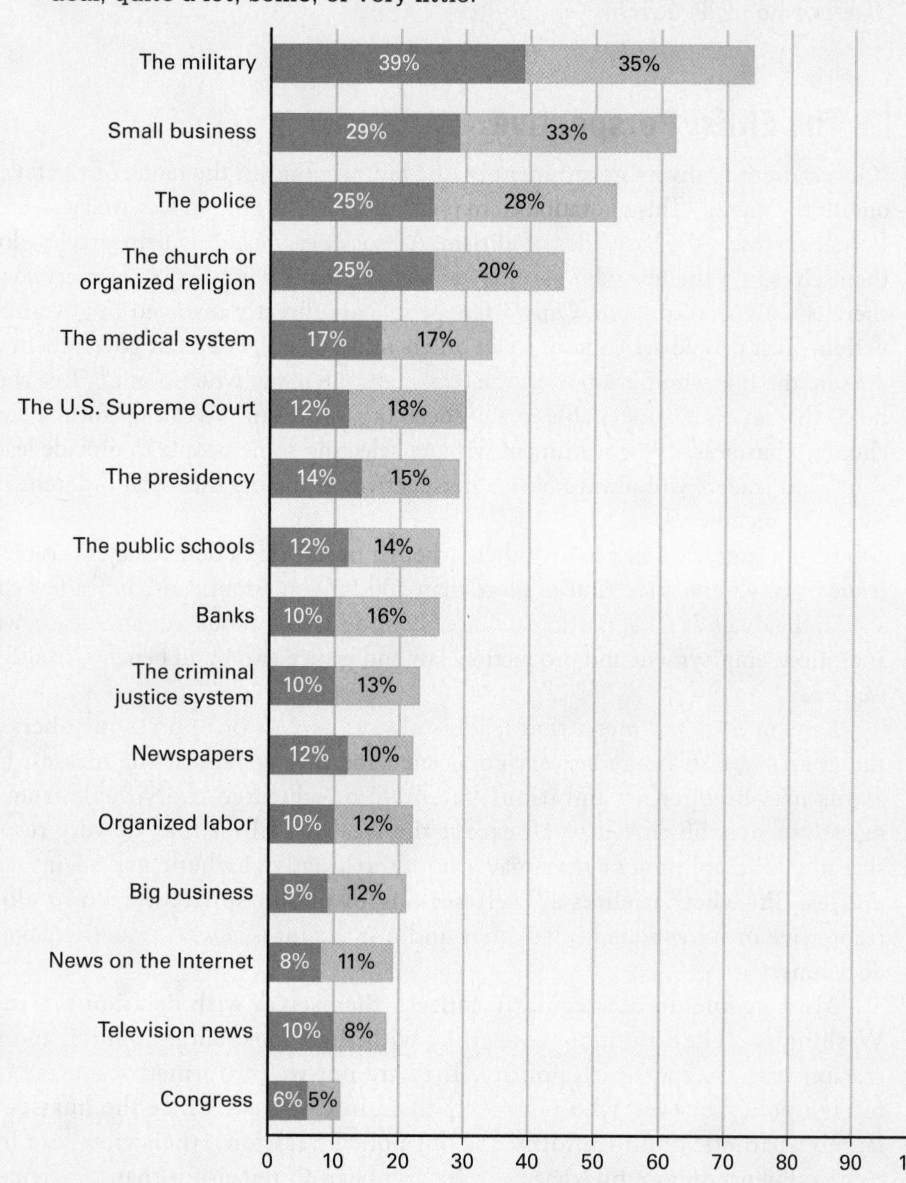

QUESTIONS

1. How much confidence do *you* have in these institutions?
2. What influences the level of confidence you have in these institutions? Is it based on your experience with them? Or, is it based on what you hear from the media, politicians, and other people?
3. How does your self-interest and goals relate to how you might evaluate an institution?

SOURCE: Copyright © 2011 The Gallup Organization.

1.1

1.2

1.3

1.4

1.5

1.6

1.7

1.8

elitism
Political system in which power is concentrated in the hands of a relatively small group of individuals or institutions.

Throughout this book, as we examine how well representative democracy works in the United States, we consider such issues as participation in elections—why some people vote and others do not—whether parties and candidates offer the voters real alternatives, whether modern political campaigning informs voters or only confuses them, and whether elected representatives are responsive to the wishes of voters. These are the kinds of issues that concern political science.

Who Really Governs?

1.7 Show how elitism and pluralism reach different conclusions about who governs in America.

Democracy is an inspiring ideal. But is democratic government really possible? Is it possible for millions of people to govern themselves, with every voice having equal influence? Or will a small number of people inevitably acquire more power than others? To what extent is democracy attainable in *any* society, and how democratic is the American political system? That is, who really governs?

The Elitist Perspective

"Government is always government by the few, whether in the name of the few, the one, or the many."[9] This quotation from political scientists Harold Lasswell and Daniel Lerner expresses the basic idea of **elitism**. All societies, including democracies, divide themselves into the few who have power and the many who do not. In every society, there is a division of labor. Only a few people are directly involved in governing a nation; most people are content to let others undertake the tasks of government. The *elite* are the few who have power; the *masses* are the many who do not.[10] This theory holds that an elite is inevitable in any social organization. We cannot form a club, a church, a business, or a government without selecting some people to provide leadership. And leaders will always have a perspective on the organization different from that of its members.[11]

In any large, complex society, then, whether or not it is a democracy, decisions are made by tiny minorities. Out of more than 300 million Americans, only a few thousand individuals at most participate directly in decisions about war and peace, wages and prices, employment and production, law and justice, taxes and benefits, health and welfare.

Elitism does *not* mean that leaders always exploit or oppress members. On the contrary, elites may be very concerned for the welfare of the masses. Elite status may be open to ambitious, talented, or educated individuals from the masses or may be closed to all except the wealthy. Elites may be very responsive to public opinion, or they may ignore the usually apathetic and ill-informed masses. But whether elites are self-seeking or public-spirited, open or closed, responsive or unresponsive, it is they and not the masses who actually make the decisions.

Most people do not regularly concern themselves with decision making in Washington. They are more concerned with their jobs, family, sports, and recreation than they are with politics. They are not well informed about tax laws, foreign policy, or even who represents them in Congress. Since the "masses" are largely apathetic and ill informed about policy questions, their views are likely to be influenced more by what they see and hear on television than by their own experience. Most communication flows downward from elites to masses. Elitism

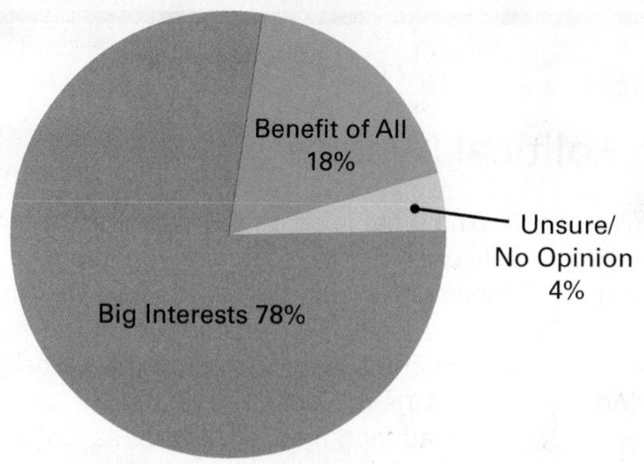

FIGURE 1.2 PUBLIC OPINION ABOUT WHO RUNS THE COUNTRY

Would you say that the government is pretty much run by a few big interests looking out for themselves or that it is being run for the benefit of all the people?

SOURCE: CBS/*New York Times* Poll, February 11, 2010, "The President, Congress, and Dissatisfaction with American Government."

argues that the masses have at best only an indirect influence on the decisions of elites.

Opinion polls indicate that many Americans agree with the elitist contention that government is run by "a few big interests" (see Figure 1.2).

pluralism
Theory that democracy can be achieved through competition among multiple organized groups and that individuals can participate in politics through group memberships and elections.

The Pluralist Perspective

No one seriously argues that all Americans participate in *all* of the decisions that shape their lives; that majority preferences *always* prevail; that the values of life, liberty, and property are *never* sacrificed; or that every American enjoys equality of opportunity. Nevertheless, most American political scientists argue that the American system of government, which they describe as "pluralist," is the best possible approximation of the democratic ideal in a large, complex society. Pluralism is designed to make the theory of democracy "more realistic."[12]

Pluralism is the belief that democracy can be achieved in a large, complex society by competition, bargaining, and compromise among organized groups and that individuals can participate in decision making through membership in these groups and by choosing among parties and candidates in elections.

Pluralists recognize that the individual acting alone is no match for giant government bureaucracies, big corporations and banks, the television networks, labor unions, or other powerful interest groups. Instead, pluralists rely on *competition* among these organizations to protect the interests of individuals. They hope that countervailing centers of power—big business, big labor, big government—will check one another and prevent any single group from abusing its power and oppressing individual Americans.

Individuals in a pluralist democracy may not participate directly in decision making, but they can join and support *interest groups* whose leaders bargain on their behalf in the political arena. People are more effective in organized groups—for example, the Sierra Club for environmentalists, the American Civil Liberties Union (ACLU) for civil rights advocates, the National Association for the Advancement of Colored People (NAACP) and the Urban League for African Americans, the American Legion and Veterans of Foreign Wars for veterans, and the National Rifle Association (NRA) for opponents of gun control.

Pluralists contend that there are multiple leadership groups in society (hence the term *pluralism*). They contend that power is widely dispersed among these groups; that no one group, not even the wealthy upper class, dominates decision making; and

The Games, the Rules, the Players

Complaints About the American Political System

Americans are highly patriotic, and most polls conducted in the United States and other democratic nations show Americans to be the most patriotic citizens in the free world. But American patriotism is not blind; it is skeptical and invested in knowledge and history, what Ronald Reagan called "an informed patriotism." Unfortunately for President Reagan's wish to reinforce patriotism through knowledge, traditional American skepticism instead evolved into a deep distrust of (and concern for) America's political system. Majorities of Americans think government is distant, incompetent, wasteful, and indifferent. The majority also thinks government is captured by individuals and groups who are not concerned about the public good.

The perception that the best people are not in government is widespread. In 2005, three-quarters of voters surveyed by the Pew Foundation said that elected officials are more concerned with reelection than "doing what is best for the country;" 7 in 10 say expensive campaigns discourage "good people" from seeking public office; and two-thirds said that campaign contributions have too much influence on elections. Voters also blame themselves, and the parties; nearly 7 in 10 Americans think citizens do not try hard enough to stay informed, and a solid majority says the parties are not "responsive enough to people's concerns."[X]

Over the past decade, a majority of American voters have generally lost confidence in the ability of government to deal with problems. More people think the government is wasteful, and cannot be trusted. The public increasingly thinks we cannot afford to do much to help the needy. Especially telling, they feel alienated from the political elite in Washington and also believe that corporations have too much power. And, as a consequence, the share of people feeling frustrated or angry with government has almost doubled in 10 years.[Y]

Key Issue	% Agree	
	2000	**2011**
Government is almost always wasteful and inefficient	52	55
The government today can't afford to do much more to help the needy	35	51
I prefer a large government providing more services	36	42
I trust government all or most of the time	40	29
Elected officials don't care about people like me	55	69
Too much power is placed in the hands of a few large companies	77	78
	Frustrated/Angry	
I am feeling frustrated/angry about the federal government	34/8	59/14

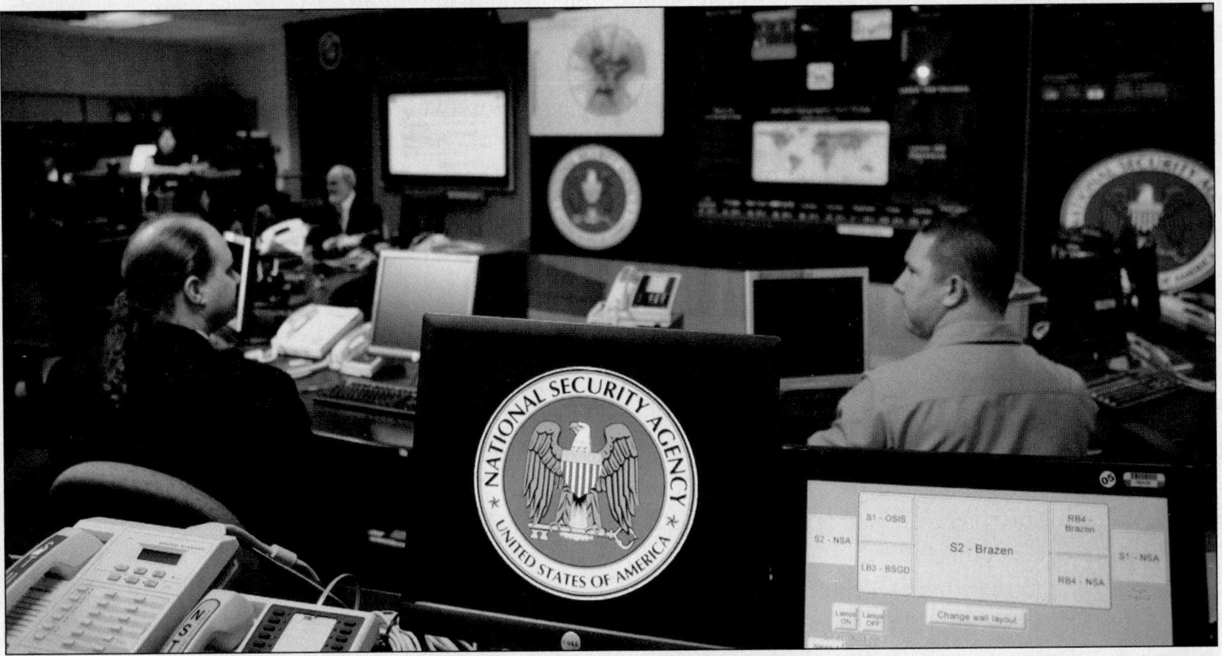

(*Continued*)

(*Continued*)

The consequence for government is that its image is at an all-time low, and the federal government is now the most-hated industry in America. Government is joined by other institutions of America's recent economic failure: the bankers, oil and gas, real estate, and health care. All of these industries have seen their positives collapse over the past decade, in no small part because they are all associated with increased lifestyle costs and a loss of economic security since 2007.[Z]

QUESTIONS

1. Do *you* think government officials care about *you* or what *you* want?
2. Government was not viewed nearly as negatively a few years ago as it is now. Why do you think things changed?
3. Do all of these institutions have anything in common that make them unpopular?

[X]From *Beyond Red and Blue*, Pew Research Center for the People & the Press, May 20, 2005.
[Y]From *Beyond Red and Blue: Political Typology*, Pew Research Center for the People & the Press, May 4, 2011. Copyright © 2011 by the Pew Research Center. Reprinted by permission.
[Z]Frank Newport, 2011. Americans Rate Computer Industry Best, Federal Gov't Worst: Image of Federal Government Is at An All-Time Low. Gallup Poll, August 29, accessed at http://www.gallup.com/poll/149216/Americans-Rate-Computer-Industry-Best-Federal-Gov-Worst.aspx.

1.1 1.2 1.3 1.4 1.5 1.6 1.7 1.8

that groups that are influential in one area of decision making are not necessarily the same groups that are influential in other areas of decision making. Different groups of leaders make decisions in different issue areas.

Pluralism recognizes that public policy does not always coincide with majority preferences. Instead, public policy is the "equilibrium" reached in the conflict among group interests. It is the balance of competing interest groups, and therefore, say the pluralists, it is a reasonable approximation of society's preferences.

Democracy in America

1.8 Evaluate the implications of the elitist and pluralist views for the realization of American democratic ideals.

Is democracy alive and well in America today? Elitism raises serious questions about the possibility of achieving true democracy in any large, complex society. Pluralism is more comforting; it offers a way of reaffirming democratic values and providing some practical solutions to the problem of individual participation in a modern society.

There is no doubt about the strength of democratic *ideals* in American society. These ideals—individual dignity, equality, popular participation in government, and majority rule—are the standards by which we judge the performance of the American political system. But we are still faced with the task of describing the *reality* of American politics.

This book explores who gets what, when, and how in the American political system; who participates in politics; what policies are decided upon; and when and how these decisions are made. In so doing, it raises many controversial questions about the realities of democracy, elitism, and pluralism in American life. But this book does not supply the answers; as a responsible citizen, you have to provide your own answers. At the completion of your studies, you will have to decide for yourself whether the American political system is truly democratic. Your studies will help inform your judgment, but, in the end, you yourself must make that judgment. That is the burden of freedom.

A Constitutional Note

Representative Government, Not Direct Democracy

Nowhere in the Constitution do we find a provision for national referenda voting on any topic, however important for the nation. Indeed, nowhere do we find the word *democracy* in the Constitution. Rather, the Founders believed in "republican" government, that is, decision making by representatives of the people, *not* by the people themselves. James Madison wrote, "the public voice, pronounced by representatives of the people, will be more consonant to the public good than if pronounced by the people themselves."

It was not until over a century later that "populism"—a strong political movement mainly in the Midwestern and Western states that appealed especially to farmers—succeeded in getting the initiative and referendum adopted, allowing *state* voters to vote directly on some issues. (The initiative allows citizens to place issues on the ballot by obtaining a certain number of signatures on a petition. The referendum is a popular vote that decides whether the issue becomes part of the state constitution or state law.) Today, about half of the states have the initiative and referendum. (The legislatures of all 50 states can place an issue on the ballot if they choose to do so, usually a change in the state constitution.) But Americans cannot vote directly on *national* issues.

National referenda on laws and constitutional amendments have usually been deemed impractical due to the expansive American geography and the large electorate. The problem of coordinating information and voting on national issues is deemed too complex. But communication technologies speed information and facilitate transactions in the economy, education, and even in government. Followers of reality entertainment programming such as *American Idol* commit to multiple weeks of electronic voting. Students take courses online, submit papers, take exams, engage in dialogue, and review sessions—and never leave home. And consumers make purchases ranging from groceries to cars through online retailers. Voting in referenda share aspects of all these activities. They involve using knowledge to make choices and then express preferences, based on the potential benefit of the result. The technologies exist to bring the mass public into decisions regarding policy and the Constitution.

QUESTIONS

1. Do we want to bring the public into these decisions?
2. Look again at the Constitution. Are the institutions designed to allow for easy popular control of government? Why not?
3. Do you think the Framers would support or oppose adopting a mechanism for unfiltered public decision making on constitutional issues or public policies? Why or why not?

Review the Chapter

Politics and Political Science

1.1 Distinguish between politics and political science, p. 4

Political science focuses on three central questions:

- Who governs?
- For what ends?
- By what means?

Politics and Government

1.2 Compare and contrast governmental politics with politics in other societal organizations, p. 4

Government is distinguished from other social organizations in that it:

- Extends to the whole society.
- Can legitimately use force.

The Purposes of Government

1.3 Identify the purposes for which government is established, p. 8

The purposes of government are to:

- Maintain order in society.
- Provide for national defense.
- Provide "public goods."
- Regulate society.
- Transfer income.
- Protect individual liberty.

The Meaning of Democracy

1.4 Outline the major principles of democracy, p. 9

The principles of democracy include:

- Recognition of individual dignity and personal freedom.
- Equality before the law.
- Widespread participation in decision making.
- Majority rule, with one person equaling one vote.

The Paradox of Democracy

1.5 Analyze the inherent conflict between majority rule and individual freedom, p. 15

The principles of democracy pose a paradox: How can we resolve conflicts between our belief in majority rule and our belief in individual freedom?

Limited government places individual liberty beyond the reach of majorities.

Constitutions are the principal means of limiting government power.

Direct Versus Representative Democracy

1.6 Compare and contrast representational government and direct government, p. 18

Direct democracy, in which everyone participates in every public decision, is very rare. Representative democracy means that public decisions are made by representatives elected by the people, in elections held periodically and open to competition, in which candidates and voters freely express themselves.

Who Really Governs?

1.7 Show how elitism and pluralism reach different conclusions about who governs in America, p. 20

Who really governs? The elitist perspective on American democracy focuses on the small number of leaders who actually decide national issues, compared to the mass of citizens who are apathetic and ill informed about politics. A pluralist perspective focuses on competition among organized groups in society, with individuals participating through group membership and voting for parties and candidates in elections.

Democracy in America

1.8 Evaluate the implications of the elitist and pluralist views for the realization of American democratic ideals, p. 23

How democratic is American government today? Democratic ideals are widely shared in our society. But you must make your own informed judgment about the realities of American politics.

Learn the Terms

politics, p. 4
political science, p. 4
government, p. 4
legitimacy, p. 6
social contract, p. 8
public goods, p. 8
free market, p. 9
gross domestic product (GDP), p. 9
externalities, p. 9
income transfers, p. 9
democracy, p. 9
democratic principles, p. 11
paradox of democracy, p. 15
limited government, p. 16
totalitarianism, p. 16
authoritarianism, p. 17
constitutional government, p. 18
direct democracy, p. 18
representative democracy, p. 18
elitism, p. 20
pluralism, p. 21

Test Yourself

1.1 Distinguish between politics and political science.

Politics is

a. the study of political science
b. the study of who gets what, when and how
c. the analysis of conflict
d. the "queen" of social sciences
e. the study of market transactions in the private sector

1.2 Compare and contrast governmental politics with politics in other societal organizations.

The widespread acceptance of something as necessary, rightful, and legally binding is

a. constitutionalism
b. democracy
c. legitimacy
d. equality
e. parsimony

1.3 Identify the purposes for which government is established.

The measurement which purports to show the total economic performance of the nation in terms of the production of goods and services is called the

a. prime development rate
b. gross development rate
c. domestic development rate
d. gross domestic product
e. gross national happiness

1.4 Outline the major principles of democracy.

Which of the following are considered "democratic ideals"?

a. one person, one vote
b. majority rule
c. widespread participation in public life
d. elites rule
e. limited access to government and politics among the lmasses

1.5 Analyze the inherent conflict between majority rule and individual freedom.

Unlimited government power over all aspects of life is a definition of

a. totalitarianism
b. authoritarianism
c. demagoguery
d. socialism
e. populism

1.6 Compare and contrast representational government and direct government.

The closest approximation we have to direct democracy in America is

a. the Native American Congress
b. the New England town meeting
c. Congressional elections
d. Presidential appointment
e. state legislative elections

1.7 Show how elitism and pluralism reach different conclusions about who governs in America.

The idea that democracy can be achieved in a large society by bargaining, compromise, and competition between interest groups would be consistent with

a. pluralism
b. classical liberalism
c. elitism
d. systems theory
e. egalitarianism

1.8 Evaluate the implications of the elitist and pluralist views for the realization of American democratic ideals.

Your text raises many questions about the realities of democracy

a. and finally comes down on the side of pluralism
b. and finally comes down on the side of elitists
c. and the authors say our society is some of both (i.e., elitist and pluralist)
d. but the authors say it is up to each of you to provide the answer to those questions
e. and concludes that democracy is a failed governing doctrine

Explore Further

SUGGESTED READINGS

Cronin, Thomas J. *Direct Democracy*. Cambridge, Mass.: Harvard University Press, 1989. A thoughtful discussion of direct versus representative democracy as well as a review of initiative, referendum, and recall devices.

Dahl, Robert A. *Democracy and Its Critics*. New Haven, Conn.: Yale University Press, 1989. A defense of modern democracy from the pluralist perspective.

Dye, Thomas R., and Harmon Zeigler. *The Irony of Democracy*. 14th ed. New York: Wadsworth, 2008. An interpretation of American politics from the elitist perspective.

Fukuyama, Francis. *Trust*. New York: Free Press, 1995. Argues that the breakdown of trust in America—not only in the government but at a person-to-person level—is burdening the nation with formal rules and regulations, lengthy contracts, bureaucracy, lawyers, and lawsuits.

Goidel, Kirby. *America's Failing Experiment*. Boulder, Colo.: Rowman and Littlefield Press. Advances the argument that expanded democracy impedes the governing of the U.S.

Lasswell, Harold. *Politics: Who Gets What, When, and How*. New York: McGraw-Hill, 1936. Classic description of the nature of politics and the study of political science by America's foremost political scientist of the twentieth century.

Mills, C. Wright. *The Power Elite*. New York: Oxford University Press, 1956. Classic Marxist critique of elitism in American society, setting forth the argument that "corporate chieftains," "military warlords," and a "political directorate" come together to form the nation's power elite.

Neiman, Max. *Defending Government: Why Big Government Works*. Upper Saddle River, N.J.: Prentice Hall, 2000. A spirited defense of how big government can improve the lives of people.

Putnam, Robert D. *Bowling Alone: The Collapse and Revival of the American Community*. New York: Simon & Schuster, 2001. An argument that Americans are increasingly disconnected from one another, harming the health of democracy.

Roskin, Michael G. *Political Science: An Introduction*. 11th ed. New York: Longman, 2010. A text introduction to the basic theories and concepts of political science.

Walton, Hanes, Jr., and Robert C. Smith. *American Politics and the African-American Quest for Universal Freedom*, 5th ed. New York: Longman, 2010. An introductory American government text that recognizes the influence that African Americans have had, and continue to have, on American politics.

SUGGESTED WEB SITES

American Enterprise Institute **http://www.aei.org**

A nonpartisan think tank dedicated to promoting libertarian and market solutions through public policy.

American Political Science Association **www.apsanet.org**

An association of college and university teachers advises students how to study political science.

Brookings Institute **www.brookings.edu**

A progressive centrist think tank that publishes studies and books on major issues confronting government.

Cato Institute **www.cato.org**

A conservative/libertarian think tank that publishes studies and books on major issues confronting government.

Council for Excellence in Government **www.excelgov.org**

A Washington-based think tank, relatively unbiased, that regularly publishes polls and studies on key issues facing the nation.

DefenseLink **http://www.defense.gov/**

Official site of the U.S. Department of Defense, with current news as well as links to the U.S. Army, Navy, Air Force, and Marines and other defense agencies.

Democracy Net **www.dnet.org**

The Democracy site of the League of Women Voters linking ZIP codes to your federal, state, and local representatives.

Freedom House **www.freedomhouse.org**

A think tank monitoring the ongoing evolution of global human rights and liberty; provides an annual world survey covering freedom's progress throughout the state system.

The Heritage Foundation **www.heritage.org**

A conservative think tank dedicated to promoting conservative public policies.

The King Center **www.thekingcenter.org**

This Atlanta-based center commemorates the life and teachings of Martin Luther King, Jr.

National Endowment for Democracy **www.ned.org**

This private advocacy group for worldwide democracy and human rights.

New Rules Project **www.newrules.org**

This organization advocates local government solutions and "direct democracy," including the New England town meeting.

U.S. Information Agency www.usinfo.state.gov/products/pubs/whatsdem

An official government site defining democracy, individual rights, and the culture of democracy.

The Zinn Education Project **ZinnEdProject.org**

A web site dedicated to alternate teaching approaches to American history and politics.

2

Political Culture

Ideas in Conflict

There is an ongoing debate in the United States about what constitutes being American. Ask any citizen, and that person will certainly say that an American is "someone like me." Yet according to the 2010 Census, the US population is growing more diverse in terms of race, ethnicity, religion, and philosophy such that America is becoming less white, less Protestant, and less conservative than one or two generations ago.

Half a century ago Americans confronted bigotry against Roman Catholics. In 2008, the radical social gospel of Barack Obama's minister, Jeremiah Wright, illuminated differences between white evangelical Protestants and parts of the black church. In 2012, Mitt Romney was the first major party candidate to come from the Mormon Church, America's first indigenous and modern religion.

Throughout his presidency, Barack Obama was dogged by accusations that he was not a true native-born American but a foreigner of Middle Eastern descent. That Mr. Obama is biracial illuminates the ongoing tensions in a country arising from racial tensions that are not merely topical, but deeply cultural.

The cultural shift in America continues to be captured in the immigration debate. Around the United States, many states pursue increasingly restrictive policies aimed at all illegal immigration, but most often driven by the general growth of Hispanic population. This demographic shift is not only changing the course of policy (since each demographic group brings their own interests to the ballot) but also what it means to be an American.

The majority of Americans are European whites, but the fastest growing segment of the population represent the newest wave of immigrants, Asian Americans and Hispanics.

Political Culture

2.1 Define the concept of political culture.

political culture
Widely shared views about who should govern, for what ends, and by what means.

values
Shared ideas about what is good and desirable.

beliefs
Shared ideas about what is true.

subcultures
Variations on the prevailing values and beliefs in a society.

Ideas have power. We are all influenced by ideas—beliefs, values, symbols—more than we realize. Political institutions are shaped by ideas, and political leaders are influenced by them.

The term **political culture** refers to widely shared ideas about who should govern, for what ends, and by what means. **Values** are shared ideas about what is good and desirable. Values provide standards for judging what is right or wrong. **Beliefs** are shared ideas about what is true. Values and beliefs are often related. For example, if we believe that human beings are endowed by God with rights to life, liberty, and property, then we will value the protection of these rights. Thus, beliefs can justify values.

Cultural descriptions are generalizations about the values and beliefs of many people in society, but these generalizations do not apply to everyone. Important variations in values and beliefs may exist within a society; these variations are frequently referred to as **subcultures** and may arise from such diverse bases as religion, racial or ethnic identity, or political group membership.

Contradictions Between Values and Conditions

Agreement over values in a political culture is no guarantee that there will not be contradictions between these values and actual conditions. No doubt the most grievous contradiction between professed national beliefs and actual conditions in America is found in the long history of slavery, segregation, and racial discrimination. The contradiction between the words of the Declaration of Independence that "all men are created equal" and the practices of slavery and segregation became the "American dilemma."[1] But this contradiction does not mean that professed values are worthless; the very existence of the gap between values and behavior becomes *a motivation for change*. The history of the civil rights movement might be viewed as an effort to "bear witness" to the contradiction between the belief in equality and the existence of segregation and discrimination.[2] Whatever the obstacles to racial equality in America, these obstacles would be even greater if the nation's political culture did *not* include a professed belief in equality.

Inconsistent Applications

And political culture does not mean that shared principles are always applied in every circumstance. For example, people may truly believe in the principle of "free speech for all, no matter what their views might be," and yet when asked whether racists should be allowed to speak on a college campus, many people will say no. Thus general agreement with abstract principles of freedom of speech, freedom of the press, and academic freedom does not always ensure their application to specific individuals or groups.[3]

Conflict

The idea of political culture does not mean an absence of conflict over values and beliefs. Indeed, much of politics involves conflict over very fundamental values. The American nation has experienced a bloody civil war, political assassinations, rioting and burning of cities, the forced resignation of a president, and other direct challenges to its political foundations. Indeed, much of this book deals with serious political conflict. Yet Americans do share many common ways of thinking about politics.

Individual Liberty

2.2 Outline the main principles of classic liberalism.

No political value has been more widely held in the United States than individual liberty. The very beginnings of our history as a nation were shaped by **classical liberalism**, which asserts the worth and dignity of the individual. This political philosophy emphasizes the rational ability of human beings to determine their own destinies, and it rejects ideas, practices, and institutions that submerge individuals into a larger whole and thus deprive them of their dignity. The only restriction on the individual is not to interfere with the liberties of others.

classical liberalism
Political philosophy asserting the worth and dignity of the individual and emphasizing the rational ability of human beings to determine their own destinies.

natural law
Rules governing human behavior that are morally superior to laws made by governments.

capitalism
Economic system asserting the individual's right to own private property and to buy, sell, rent, and trade that property in a free market.

Political Liberty

Classical liberalism grew out of the eighteenth-century Enlightenment, the Age of Reason in which great philosophers such as Voltaire, John Locke, Jean Jacques Rousseau, Adam Smith, and Thomas Jefferson affirmed their faith in reason, virtue, and common sense. Classical liberalism originated as an attack on the hereditary prerogatives and distinctions of a feudal society, the monarchy, the privileged aristocracy, and the state-established church.

Classical liberalism motivated America's Founders to declare their independence from England, to write the U.S. Constitution, and to establish the Republic. It rationalized their actions and provided ideological legitimacy for the new nation. The founders adopted the language of John Locke, who argued that a **natural law** guaranteed every person "certain inalienable Rights," among them "Life, Liberty, and Property," and that human beings form a social contract with one another to establish a government to help protect their rights. Implicit in the social contract and the liberal notion of freedom is the belief that governmental activity and restrictions on the individual should be kept to a minimum.

Economic Freedom

Classical liberalism as a political idea is closely related to capitalism as an *economic* idea. **Capitalism** asserts the individual's right to own private property and to buy, sell, rent, and trade that property in a free market. The economic version of freedom is the freedom to make contracts, to bargain for one's services, to move from job to job, to join labor unions, to start one's own business. In classical liberal *politics*, individuals are free to speak out, to form political parties, and to vote as they please—to pursue their political interests as they think best. In classical liberal *economics*, individuals are free to find work, to start businesses, and to spend their money as they please—to pursue their economic interests as they think best. The role of government is restricted to protecting private property, enforcing contracts, and performing only those functions and services that cannot be performed by the private market.

The value of liberty in these political and economic spheres has been paramount throughout our history. Only equality competes with liberty as the most honored value in the American political culture.

Dilemmas of Equality

2.3 Differentiate among the various kinds of equality.

Since the bold assertion of the Declaration of Independence that "all men are created equal," Americans have generally believed that no person has greater worth than any other person. The principle of equal worth and dignity was a radical idea in 1776, when much of the world

legal equality
Belief that the laws should apply equally to all persons.

political equality
Belief that every person's vote counts equally.

equality of opportunity
Elimination of artificial barriers to success in life and the opportunity for everyone to strive for success.

was dominated by hereditary monarchies, titled nobilities, and rigid caste and class systems.

As early as 1835, the French historian and visitor to America, Alexis de Tocqueville, wrote his classic analysis of American political culture, *Democracy in America*. He identified equality as a fundamental aspect of American society—the absence of a privileged nobility or notions of class that characterized European societies. Yet he also warned of the "tyranny of the majority"—the potential for the majority to trample the rights of minorities and individuals—and he believed that an independent judiciary formed a powerful barrier "against the tyranny of political assemblies."[4]

Belief in equality drove the expansion of voting rights in the early 1800s and ultimately destroyed the institution of slavery. Abraham Lincoln understood that equality was not so much a description of reality as an ideal to be aspired to: "a standard maxim for a free society which should be familiar to all, and revered by all; constantly looked to, constantly labored for, and even though never perfectly attained, constantly approximated and thereby augmenting the happiness and value of life to all people of all colors everywhere."[5] The millions who immigrated to the United States viewed this country as a land not only of opportunity but of *equal* opportunity, where everyone, regardless of birth, could rise in wealth and status based on hard work, natural talents, and perhaps good luck.

Today, most Americans agree that no one is intrinsically "better" than anyone else. This belief in equality, then, is fundamental to Americans, but a closer examination shows that throughout our history it has been tested, as beliefs and values so often are, by political realities.

☐ Political Equality

The nation's Founders shared the belief that the law should apply equally to all—that birth, status, or wealth do not justify differential application of the laws. But **legal equality** did not necessarily mean **political equality**, at least not in 1787, when the U.S. Constitution was written. The Constitution left the issue of voter qualifications to the states to decide for themselves. At that time, all states imposed either property or taxpayer qualifications for voting. Neither women nor slaves could vote anywhere—except, briefly, in New Jersey, where a property requirement on general suffrage (£50) enacted in 1776 (and repealed in 1807) explicitly allowed women to vote. The expansion of voting rights to universal suffrage required many bitter battles over the course of two centuries. The long history of the struggle over voting rights illustrates the contradictions between values and practices. Yet in the absence of the *value* of equality, voting rights might have remained restricted.

☐ Equality of Opportunity

The American ideal of equality extends to **equality of opportunity**—the elimination of artificial barriers to success in life. The term *equality of opportunity* refers to the ability to make of oneself what one can, to develop one's talents and abilities, and to be rewarded for one's work, initiative, and achievement. Equality of opportunity means that everyone comes to the same starting line in life, with the same chance of success, and that whatever differences develop over time do so as a result of abilities, talents, initiative, hard work, and perhaps good luck.

Americans do not generally resent the fact that physicians, engineers, airline pilots, and others who have spent time and energy acquiring particular skills make more money than those whose jobs require fewer skills and less training. Neither do most Americans resent the fact that people who risk their own time and money to build a business, bring new or better products to market, and create jobs for others make more money than their employees. Nor do Americans historically begrudge multimillion-dollar incomes to sports figures, rock stars, and movie stars whose talents entertain the public. And few Americans object when someone wins a million-dollar lottery, as long as everyone who entered the lottery had an equal chance at winning. Americans are generally willing to have government act to ensure equality of opportunity—to ensure that everyone has an equal chance at getting an education, landing a job, and buying a home, and that no barriers of race, sex, religion, or ethnicity bar individual advancement.

equality of results
Equal sharing of income and material goods.

Equality of Results

Equality of results refers to the equal sharing of income and material rewards. Equality of results means that everyone starts *and finishes* the race together, regardless of ability, talent, initiative, or work. Those who argue on behalf of this notion of equality say that if individuals are truly equal, then everyone should enjoy generally equal conditions in life. According to this belief, we should appreciate an individual's contributions to society without creating inequalities of wealth and income. Government should act to *transfer* wealth and income from the rich to the poor to increase the total happiness of all members of society.

Equality of results, or absolute equality, was referred to as "leveling" by Thomas Jefferson and was denounced by the nation's Founders:

> To take from one, because it is thought his own industry and that of his fathers has acquired too much, in order to spare to others who have not exercised equal industry and skill, is to violate arbitrarily…the guarantee to everyone the free exercise of his industry and the fruits acquired by it.[6]

The taking of private property from those who acquired it legitimately, for no other reason than to equalize wealth or income, was once widely viewed as morally wrong. Moreover, many people believed that society generally would suffer if incomes were equalized. Absolute equality, in this view, would remove incentives for people to work, save, or produce. Everyone would slack off, production would decline, goods would be in short supply, and everyone would end up poorer than ever.

But support for equality of results appears to be growing in recent years. For a century, Democratic presidents have proposed tax legislation that would increase income taxes on wealthy families and provide tax payments to middle- and lower-income families, while Republican presidents have largely promoted tax cuts or taxes that equalize the burden across all sources of income. Conservative critics claim that Democratic proposals to redistribute income is "socialism," and that it penalizes work, initiative, and talent. Americans generally believe in tax progressivity—higher income people can afford to be taxed at higher rates than lower-income people.[7]

Fairness

Americans value "fairness" even though they do not always agree on what is fair. Most Americans support a "floor" on income and material well-being—a level that no one, regardless of his or her condition, should be permitted to fall below—even though they differ over how high that floor should be. Indeed, the belief in a floor is consistent with the belief in equality of opportunity; extreme poverty would deny people, especially children, the opportunity to compete in life.[8] But few Americans want to place a "ceiling" on income or wealth. Generally, Americans want people who cannot provide for themselves to be well cared for, especially children, the elderly, the ill, and the disabled. They are often willing to "soak the rich" when searching for new tax sources, believing that the rich can easily afford to bear the burdens of government. But, unlike citizens in other Western democracies, Americans generally do *not* believe that government should equalize incomes.

The Tax Code Encourages Values

Even if Americans don't want government to equalize income, we readily use the tax code to encourage some values. Tax deductions for home mortgage interest encourage home ownership, for example, and dependent deductions advantage people with minor children. The federal tax code encourages businesses to purchase alternative-fuel vehicles, and to also produce alternative fuels, in order to reduce foreign oil dependence. It encourages investment in and production of renewable energy sources, such as wind and solar. Low-income individuals receive an earned income tax credit that is larger when they also have dependent children. And low-income individuals enjoy access to affordable housing in part because of a tax credit that encourages developers to build and maintain affordable, high-density housing. Employers can take advantage of a work opportunity tax credit that encourages employing persons who belong to groups with high unemployment rates, such as minority youth or veterans. Many credits and deductions are enjoyed by higher-income individuals and businesses. However, the targets of many policies arising from the credits are progressive, such as creating economic opportunity for the poor.

A Conflicting View

American Exceptionalism?

Is the United States different from other countries? For over six decades, the United States has consistently been the major economic engine of the world. American culture is infused with assumptions about the superiority of market capitalism and political egalitarianism, and that both manifest through republican democracy. Alexis de Tocqueville described the United States as "exceptional" due to the dominance of egalitarianism, liberty, and the protection of rights and liberties through rule of law in the post-Revolutionary America. The ability of American institutions to respond to the demands of protecting these components of the American Creed, it is assumed, renders the American nation immune to the disruptive and destructive historical forces that tore Europe apart in the nineteenth and twentieth century.

What separated the United States from Europe, and the European experiences with Marxist revolution, nationalist wars, and flirtations with fascism? One explanation is the deep investment of the American majority in protestant Christianity, especially protestant theologies that reinforced not only "millennialism"—the belief that a Christian golden age is imminent—but also values of individual responsibility and political populism. The metaphor of John Winthrop's "City on a Hill" sermon, taken from the Sermon on the Mount, has been repeatedly invoked as a symbol of American exceptionalism, most recently by Ronald Reagan.

Other explanations are developmental rather than cultural. North America, as virgin wilderness, offered ample resources and a frontier for relieving social stresses that plagued urban, developed Europe. Still another reason offered is that America's lack of a strict social system of rigid classes diffused the stressors that led to Marxist revolutions in Europe in the 1840s and later in twentieth-century Russia (other than the relic of slavery, which was dispensed in the Civil War, America had no feudal experience). Still others have argued that the dispersion of political power through federalism is a source, by keeping government power focused where it can be locally controlled. When combined with the broad-based consensus on the importance of protecting individualism, liberty, and property, federalism arguably emerges as a new political ideology in the late eighteenth century, which reinforces an ethos of capitalism and democracy in a developed United States.

Critics of the American exceptionalism argument find ample basis for their arguments:

- **Race and Caste:** The United States continued the feudal institution of slavery longer than any Western nation, and only resolved the issue through force of arms. The existence of the Jim Crow laws perpetuated a race-based caste system.
- **Closing the Frontier:** The demise of the frontier and the disappearance of the virgin resource base left Americans increasingly dependent on trade for critical resources.
- **The Social Welfare State:** The dramatic growth of the American social welfare state was a response to the market failures of the 1920s and 1930s. For nearly four generations, the United States has joined other developed nations in creating a social safety net that acts as a hedge against the imperfections of the market.

QUESTIONS

1. Do you think there is American exceptionalism? Why or why not?
2. Of the possible explanations for American exceptionalism, do any still stand unrefuted by historic events?

SOURCES: Dorothy Ross. 1991. *Origins of American Social Science.* New York: Cambridge University Press. Seymour Martin Lipset. 1997. *American Exceptionalism: A Double Edged Sword.* New York: W. W. Norton. Louis Hartz. 1955. *The Liberal Tradition in America.* New York: Harcourt, Brace, and World.

Income Inequality and Social Mobility

2.4 Characterize the trends affecting the current distribution of wealth and income and analyze the relationships among social mobility, inequality, and class conflict.

Politics in society is generated more often by inequalities among people than by hardship or deprivation. Material well-being and standards of living are usually expressed in aggregate measures for a whole society—for example, gross domestic product, average life expectancy, infant mortality rate. These measures of societal well-being are vitally important to a nation and its people, but *political* conflict is more likely to occur over the distribution of well-being *within a* society. Unequal distributions can generate conflict in a very affluent society with high levels of income and a high standard of living.

Inequality in America

Inequality in America is substantial, and it appears to be worsening over time. The percentage of the nation's total family income received by the poorest quintile of families (the bottom 20 percent) fell from 4.3 percent to 3.4 percent between 1975 and 2012 (Figure 2.1). The percentage of total family income of the highest quintile climbed from 43.6 percent to 50.3 percent. Put another way, the lowest earning families actually lost a fifth of their relative income while the top-earning families increased their relative income share by 15 percent.

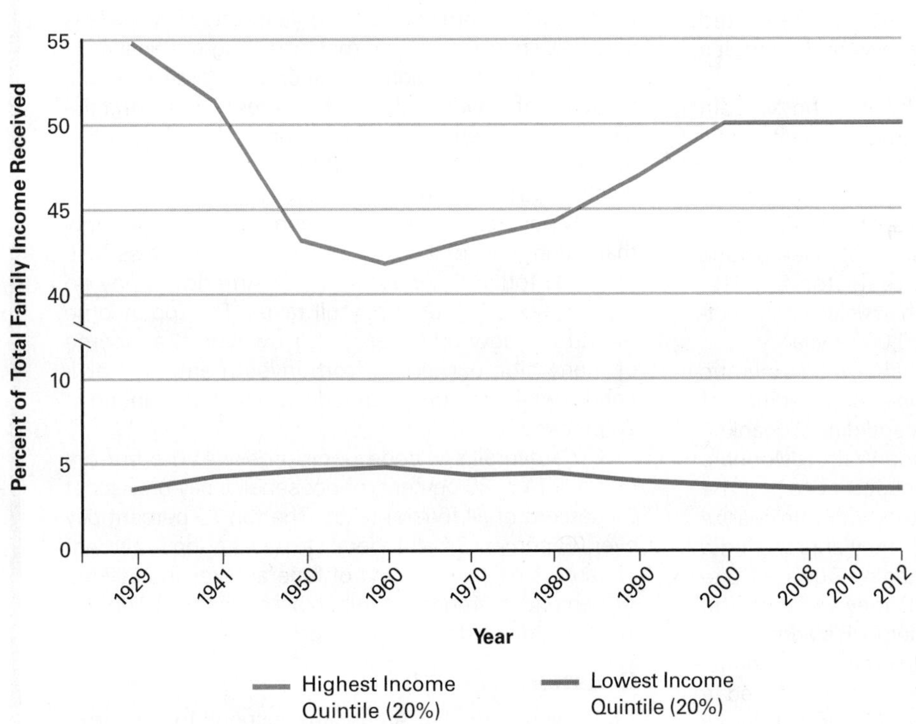

FIGURE 2.1 SHARES OF TOTAL HOUSEHOLD INCOME RECEIVED BY HIGHEST- AND LOWEST-INCOME GROUPS

Income inequality is growing. Roughly half of total household income in the nation goes to the top 20 percent of households. Less than 4 percent of total income goes to the bottom 20 percent of households.

social mobility
Extent to which people move upward or downward in income and status over a lifetime or over generations.

Why More Inequality?

There are several reasons why inequality has grown. The decline of the American manufacturing sector and the rise of an information and services economy produced many more low-paying jobs and fewer high-paying ones. Global competition has sent muscle jobs overseas, and, increasingly, also many communication and information jobs, thereby driving down wages. Demographic change produced an aging population with limited earnings potential, and also more female-headed households. Two-earner married households are doing well; households headed by single women are not.[9]

Social Mobility

Political conflict over inequality might be greater in the United States if it were not for the prospect of **social mobility**. All societies are stratified, or layered, but societies differ greatly in the extent to which people move upward or downward in income and

Who's Getting What?

Spreading the Wealth Around

In October 2008, presidential candidate Barack Obama encountered a guy named Joe Wurzelbacher. Joe was a plumber who complained that increasing taxes on "top earners" would get in the way of his plans to buy a small plumbing company. Joe complained that he would be "taxed more and more while fulfilling the American dream." Obama's long answer culminated with "I think when you spread the wealth around, it's good for everybody."

Republican presidential candidate John McCain seized on this statement as proof that the Democratic candidate was an advocate of redistribution politics—policies that take wealth from top earners and transfers it to the poor and working class. Other critics saw this statement as evidence of a "socialist" Democratic nominee. Obama won, and was reelected in 2012. A tax increase was approved after his reelection, affecting those persons making over $400,000 a year.

There was nothing new in charging Democratic candidates with socialism. There is a long tradition of "share the wealth" Democratic candidates. Franklin Roosevelt, George McGovern, and Walter Mondale all ran for president and were accused of taxing the rich. One class of wealthy investors were so fearful of a Roosevelt presidency in 1933, they approached a Marine Corps general named Smedley Butler to discuss a coup against Roosevelt (Butler exposed the "Business Plot" to Congress). Under FDR's administration in the 1930s, the top income tax rate hit a "confiscatory" rate of over 90 percent. This top rate stayed in place until the 1960s, when it fell to 75 percent during the Kennedy administration. During the Reagan administration, marginal tax rates were reduced further, and income tax credits were introduced to move tax burdens off the working poor.

Calling for tax increases is not popular. In 1992, President George H. W. Bush was defeated for reelection when he broke a campaign promise ("Read my lips – no new taxes") and agreed to one of the largest tax increases in U.S. history as part of a deficit reduction agreement in 1990. Tax rates went up under Bill Clinton, who promised to tax only the wealthy, and his party was punished in the midterm congressional elections in 1994. In the administration of George W. Bush, marginal rates were cut, albeit only temporarily, and the top rate was restored in 2012 as part of a deficit reduction agreement, after the outcome of the presidential election was decided.

Overall, top tax rates on income are far lower now than during the 1930s. The current top rate is less than half that today and nearly half of Americans pay no income tax other than payroll taxes. The top income tax rate is now 39.6 percent. However, the income of many high earners is from investments and dividends, which are taxed on a different scale, capped at 20 percent.

The overall tax code is progressive. The bottom four quintiles (80 percent) of households pay only about 31 percent of all federal taxes. The top 20 percent pay over 68 percent of all federal taxes. The top 1 percent of earners paid 28 percent of federal taxes in 2007. Yet 61 percent of Americans, when asked in the Gallup Poll in 2013, indicated that the rich pay "too little."

Questions

1. Do you think that Americans respond to economic appeals that involve higher taxes?
2. Can liberal politicians capture economic anger for redistribution, in the same fashion as conservative politicians do when demanding less taxation?

status over a lifetime or over generations. When there is social mobility, people have a good opportunity to get ahead if they study or work long and hard, save and invest wisely, or display initiative and enterprise in business affairs. Fairly steep inequalities may be tolerated politically if people have a reasonable expectation of moving up over time, or at least of seeing their children do so.

class conflict
Conflict between upper and lower social classes over wealth and power.

Income Mobility

America is the land of *opportunity*. While the nation is experiencing increased *inequality*, it continues to enjoy considerable income mobility, that is, people moving up and down the income ladder over time.

Measuring mobility requires following the ups and downs of individuals over time. The most reliable study of income mobility, conducted by the U.S. Treasury Department using tax records from 1996 to 2005, showed substantial mobility. Treasury analysts compared income of people inside five income quintiles (20 percent intervals) at the beginning of the study, then looked at where people in those quintiles ranked a decade later.

Of people who were in the lowest quintile in 1996, over half had moved up to a higher income bracket, while 42.4 percent remained in the lowest quintile. One in twenty had moved into the highest earning quintile. Of people who were in the highest quintile in 1996, nearly 70 percent remained in the highest quintile a decade later, and less than 6 percent had fallen into the bottom two earning quintiles. And, among people earning in the middle three quintiles, there was also substantial movement up and down the earnings ladder.

What does this tell us about mobility in America? Over half of the poorest Americans can expect to climb the earnings ladder, and to possibly climb very high in less than a decade. America is not a "caste" society. If it were, then everyone in the lowest earning quintile would likely remain there over time. The American nation experiences considerable income mobility will fall out of this top category (see *Who's Getting What?* Getting Ahead in America).

Mobility, Class Conflict, and Class Consciousness

Social mobility and the expectation of mobility, over a lifetime or over generations, may be the key to understanding why class conflict—conflict over wealth and power among social classes—is not as widespread or as intense in America as it is in many other nations. The belief in social mobility reduces the potential for class conflict

TWO AMERICAS

Income inequality in America has increased in recent decades. By 2012, record numbers of persons were receiving support from government social programs, including food assistance, in addition to the efforts of community and charitable organizations.

2.1 2.2 2.3 2.4 2.5 2.6 2.7 2.8

class consciousness
Awareness of one's class position and a feeling of political solidarity with others within the same class in opposition to other classes.

because it diminishes **class consciousness**, the awareness of one's class position and the feeling of political solidarity with others in the same class in opposition to other classes. If class lines were impermeable and no one had any reasonable expectation of moving up or seeing his or her children move up, then class consciousness would rise and political conflict among classes would intensify. Most Americans describe themselves as "middle class" rather than "rich" or "poor" or "lower class" or "upper class." There are no widely accepted income definitions of "middle class." The federal government officially defines a "poverty level" each year based on the annual cash income required to maintain a decent standard of living (approximately $22,000 in 2010). Roughly 12 to 13 percent of the U.S. population lives with annual cash incomes below this poverty line. This is the only income group in which a majority of people describe themselves as poor. Large majorities in every other income group identify themselves as middle class. So it is no surprise that presidents, politicians, and political parties regularly claim to be defenders of America's "middle class"!

Compared to What?

Income and Inequality

Capitalism has proven successful in creating wealth. The free market system has provided Americans with more purchasing power than any other people. ("Purchasing power parity" is a statistic used by international economists to adjust for the cost of living differences in measuring how much it costs to purchase a standard "basket" of goods and services.) However, relatively high incomes of average Americans exist side by side with relatively high inequality among Americans. The United States ranks well below many European countries in measures of income inequality. (The "Gini index" is a statistic used by economists to measure income equality/inequality.) However, poverty and inequality exist side by side in most of the world's less-developed countries (not ranked below).

Rank by Purchasing Power per Capita

1. Qatar
2. Luxembourg
3. Singapore
4. Norway
5. Brunei
6. UNITED STATES
7. Hong Kong
8. Switzerland
9. Canada
10. Australia
11. Austria
12. Netherlands
13. Ireland
14. Sweden
15. Iceland
16. Kuwait
17. Taiwan
18. Germany
19. Belgium
20. Denmark
21. United Kingdom
22. Japan
23. Finland
24. France
25. Israel
26. South Korea
27. The Bahamas
28. Saudi Arabia
29. Spain
30. New Zealand

30t. United Arab Emirates

Rank by Equality (Gini Index)

1. Sweden
2. Denmark
3. Slovenia
4. Iceland
5. Austria
6. Czech Republic
7. Finland
8. Luxembourg
9. Slovakia
10. Belgium
11. France
12. Germany
13. Hungary
14. Netherlands
15. South Korea
16. Bulgaria
17. Ireland
18. Spain
19. Canada
20. Greece
21. Italy
22. Switzerland
23. United Kingdom
24. Australia
25. Poland
26. Portugal
27. Japan
28. Israel
29. Russia
30. UNITED STATES

Question

1. Do you think there should be an obligation in public policy to reduce income inequality?

SOURCES: Rank by purchasing power, International Monetary Fund, *Word Economic Outlook Database*, 2013; rank by Gini index, Central Intelligence Agency, The World Factbook, 2005. Both sources rank many more nations.

Who's Getting What?

Getting Ahead in America

America is a land of opportunity. But how much of a chance do Americans *really* have of moving up the income ladder over time?

To measure mobility, we must observe the ups and downs of families *over time*. This calls for longitudinal studies—studies of the same families over a period of time to see how many move up or down the income ladder. The Pew Charitable Trust's Economic Mobility Project has examined the economic class changes of modern Americans, compared to their parents at the same age. Pew researchers have produced the following data about income mobility of American families.

Researchers began by ranking respondents' parents by income quintiles (20 percent intervals) from lowest to highest income, then ranking the respondents themselves by income quintiles. Then they compared where the parents and the kids were at the same stage of life. The table shows the percentage of each of the families from the parents' income quintiles that fell into current income quintiles in 2012.

The table is interpreted in the following way: The number 43 in the upper left-hand cell shows that 43 percent of two-parent families that started in the poorest quintile have kids who remained in the poorest quintile at the same stage of life. The remaining families in the lowest quintile moved up, most to the second and third quintiles. Very few, just 4 percent, made it all the way from the poorest to the richest quintile.

The table also shows that 40 percent of the respondents with parents that were in the richest quintile remained in the richest quintile in 2012. Many of them fell to the third and fourth quintile, but an unlucky few, 8 percent, fell all the way to the poorest quintile.

What does this table tell us about mobility? Children of over half of the poorest Americans moved up the income ladder in a generation. Over half of America's richest families can expect their progeny to fall out of the top category over the same period. America is certainly not a caste society; if it were, then 100 percent of the lowest quintile would remain there over time, and 100 percent of the highest income quintile would remain at the top, with no class penetration from top to bottom or vice versa. So America experiences considerable mobility. But it is not perfectly mobile either. While some families started poor and ended up rich and vice versa, poor families were more likely to stay poor and rich families were more likely to stay rich.

Questions

1. Is your family income-mobile?
2. Do you expect to do better, financially, than your parents or grandparents? Why or why not?

SOURCES: Robert S. Rycroft, *The Economics of Inequality, Discrimination, Poverty, and Mobility*. Armonk, N.Y.: M. E. Sharpe, 2009; Samuel Bowles, ed., *Unequal Chances: Family Background and Economic Success*, New York: Princeton University Press, 2005.

MOBILITY AMONG AMERICAN FAMILIES OVER TWO DECADES

Parents' Income Quintile at Same Age	Respondent's Income Quintile in 2012				
	Lowest	Second	Third	Fourth	Highest
Lowest	43	27	17	9	4
Second	25	24	18	20	14
Third	24	20	23	24	19
Fourth	9	20	23	24	24
Highest	8	10	19	23	40

SOURCE: Pew Charitable Trust, *Pursuing the American Dream*, accessed at http://www.pewstates.org/uploadedFiles/PCS_Assets/2012/Pursuing_American_Dream.pdf, July 2014.

Race, Ethnicity, and Immigration

2.5 Describe the current immigration trends and ethnic composition of the United States.

America has always been an ethnically and racially pluralist society. All groups were expected to adopt the American political culture—including individual liberty, economic freedom, political equality, and equality of opportunity—and to learn American history and the English language. The nation's motto "E Pluribus Unum" (from many, one) is inscribed on its coins. Yet each of America's racial and ethnic groups brings its own traditions and values to the American political culture.

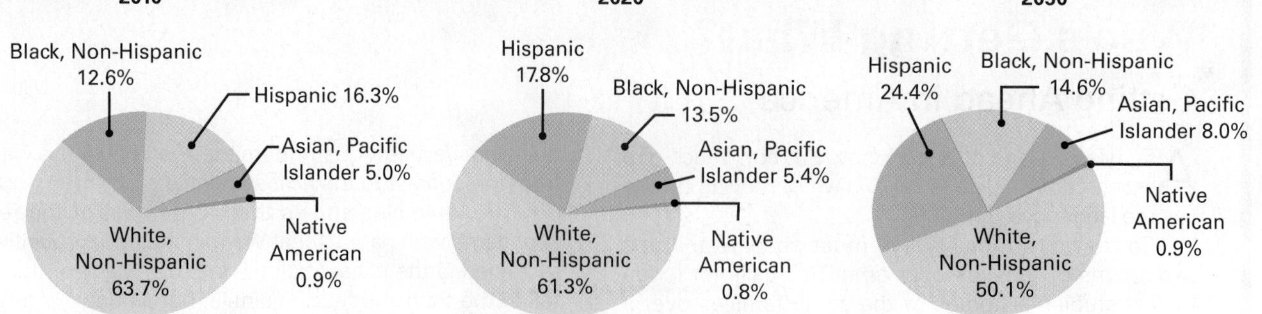

FIGURE 2.2 RACIAL AND ETHNIC COMPOSITION OF THE UNITED STATES IN 2010, 2020, 2050
Current trends in population growth and change suggest that America will become more ethnically and racially diverse over time.

SOURCE: U.S. Bureau of the Census (Middle Series). Two or more races not shown. www.census.gov.

☐ African Americans

Historically African Americans constituted the nation's largest minority. Blacks composed about 20 percent of the population at the time the U.S. Constitution was written in 1787 (although an enslaved African American was to be counted as only three-fifths of a person in the original Constitution). Heavy European immigration in the late nineteenth century diluted the black population to roughly 12 percent of the nation's total. As late as 1900, most African Americans (90 percent) were still concentrated in the southern states. But World Wars I and II provided job opportunities in large cities of the Northeast and Midwest. Blacks could not cast ballots in most southern counties, but they could "vote with their feet." The migration of African Americans from the rural South to the urban North was one of the largest internal migrations in our history. Today only about half of the nation's African Americans live in the South—still more than in any other region but less of a concentration than earlier in American history. Today, the nation's 40 million African Americans make up about 13 percent of the total population of the United States (see Figure 2.2). The African American political experience—the long struggle against slavery, segregation, and discrimination—has given African Americans a somewhat different perspective on American politics.

☐ Hispanic Americans

Hispanics are now the nation's largest minority. The term *Hispanic* generally refers to persons of Spanish-speaking ancestry and culture; it includes Mexican Americans, Cuban Americans, and Puerto Ricans. Today, there are an estimated 50 million Hispanics in the United States, or about 16 percent of the total population. The largest subgroup is Mexican Americans, some of whom are descendants of citizens living in Mexican territory that was annexed to the United States in 1848, but most of whom have come to the United States in accelerating numbers in recent years. The largest Mexican American populations are found in Texas, Arizona, New Mexico, and California (see Figure 2.3). The second-largest subgroup is Puerto Ricans, many of whom move back and forth from the island to the mainland, especially to New York City. The third-largest subgroup is Cubans, many of whom fled from Castro's Cuba. They live mainly in the Miami metropolitan area. The politics of each of these Hispanic groups differs somewhat.

☐ A Nation of Immigrants

The United States is a nation of immigrants, from the first "boat people" (Pilgrims) to the later Haitian refugees and Cuban *balseros* ("rafters"). Historically, most of the people who came to settle in this country did so because they believed their lives would be better here, and American political culture today has been greatly affected by the beliefs

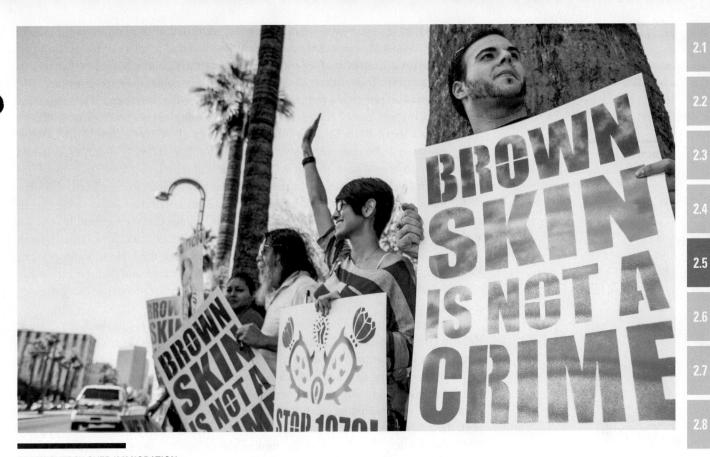

CONTROVERSY OVER IMMIGRATION

Many Hispanic Americans have protested against bills targeting illegal immigrants. The most aggressive efforts, by Arizona, prompted dramatic protests by Hispanics and also a series of challenges in the Federal courts. Immigration continues to be a source of tension in politics.

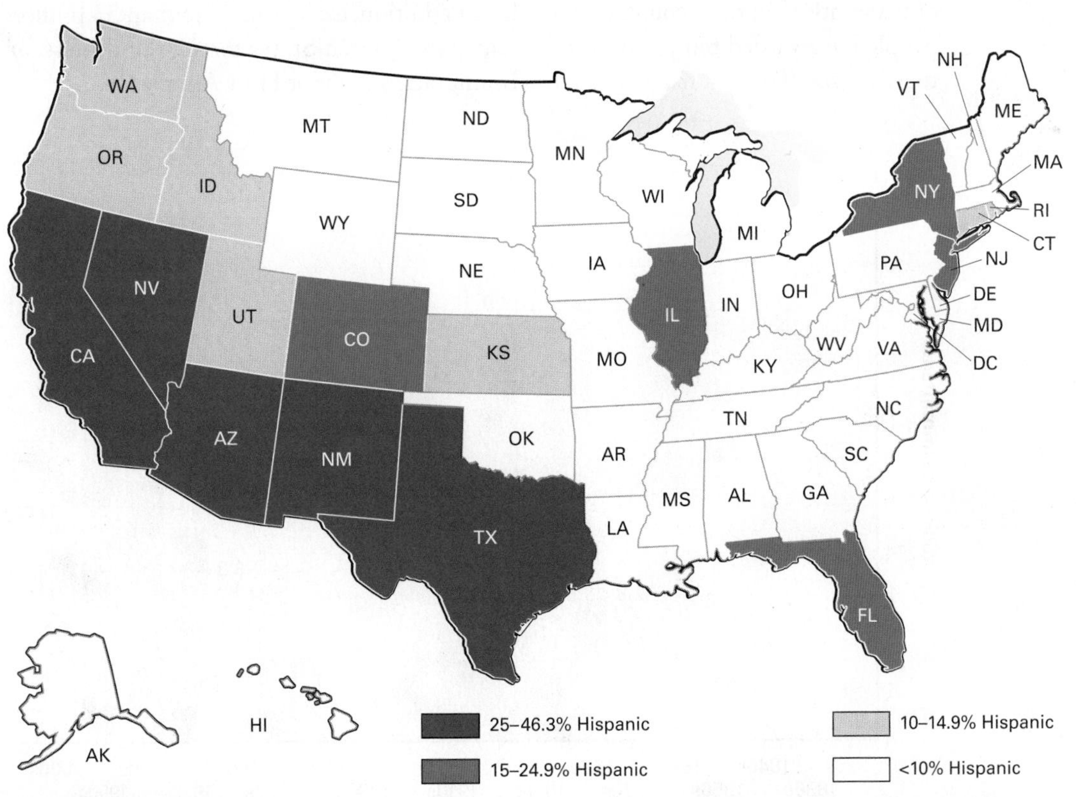

FIGURE 2.3 HISPANIC POPULATIONS

The Hispanic population in the United States is heavily concentrated in a few states—California, Colorado, Arizona, New Mexico, Texas, and Florida. Even within these states, Latinos are concentrated in particular counties, especially counties along the southern border as well as Miami-Dade County in Florida (Cubans) and New York City (Puerto Ricans). This concentration facilitates the continuing use of the Spanish language—in newspapers, television (Univision, TeleMundo), business, and commercial establishments. It often inspires bilingual education in public schools, colleges, and universities.

SOURCE: Map data from the 2010 U.S. Census; access at www.census.gov.

2.1 2.2 2.3 2.4 2.5 2.6 2.7 2.8

immigration policy
Regulating the entry of noncitizens into the country.

aliens
Persons residing in a nation who are not citizens.

amnesty
Government forgiveness of a crime, usually granted to a group of people.

and values they brought with them. Americans are proud of their immigrant heritage and the freedom and opportunity the nation has extended to generations of "huddled masses yearning to breathe free"—words emblazoned on the Statue of Liberty in New York's harbor. Today about 12 percent of the U.S. population is foreign-born.

Immigration policy is a responsibility of the national government. It was not until 1882 that Congress passed the first legislation restricting entry into the United States for persons alleged to be "undesirable" and virtually all Asians. After World War I, Congress passed the comprehensive Immigration Act of 1921, which established maximum numbers of new immigrants each year and set a quota for immigrants from each foreign country at 3 percent of the number of that nation's foreign-born who were living in the United States in 1910, later reduced to 2 percent of the number living here in 1890. These restrictions reflected anti-immigration feelings that were generally directed at the large wave of Southern and Eastern European Catholic and Jewish immigrants (from Poland, Russia, Hungary, Italy, and Greece) entering the United States prior to World War I (see Figure 2.4). It was not until the Immigration and Naturalization Act of 1965 that national origin quotas were abolished, replaced by preference categories for close relatives of U.S. citizens, professionals, and skilled workers.

Immigration "reform" was the announced goal of Congress in the Immigration Reform and Control Act of 1986, also known as the Simpson-Mazzoli Act. It sought to control immigration by placing principal responsibility on employers; it set fines for knowingly hiring illegal **aliens**. However, it allowed employers to accept many different forms of easily forged documentation and at the same time subjected them to penalties for discriminating against legal foreign-born residents. To win political support, the act granted **amnesty** to illegal aliens who had lived in the United States since 1982. But the act failed to reduce the flow of either legal or illegal immigrants.

Today, more than a million people per year are admitted *legally* to the United States as "lawful permanent residents" (persons who have needed job skills or who have relatives who are U.S. citizens) or as "political refugees" (persons with "a well-founded fear of persecution" in their country of origin). In addition, each year, more than 33 million people are awarded temporary visas to enter the United States for study, business, or tourism (see *What Do You Think?* Does Immigration Help or Hurt America?).

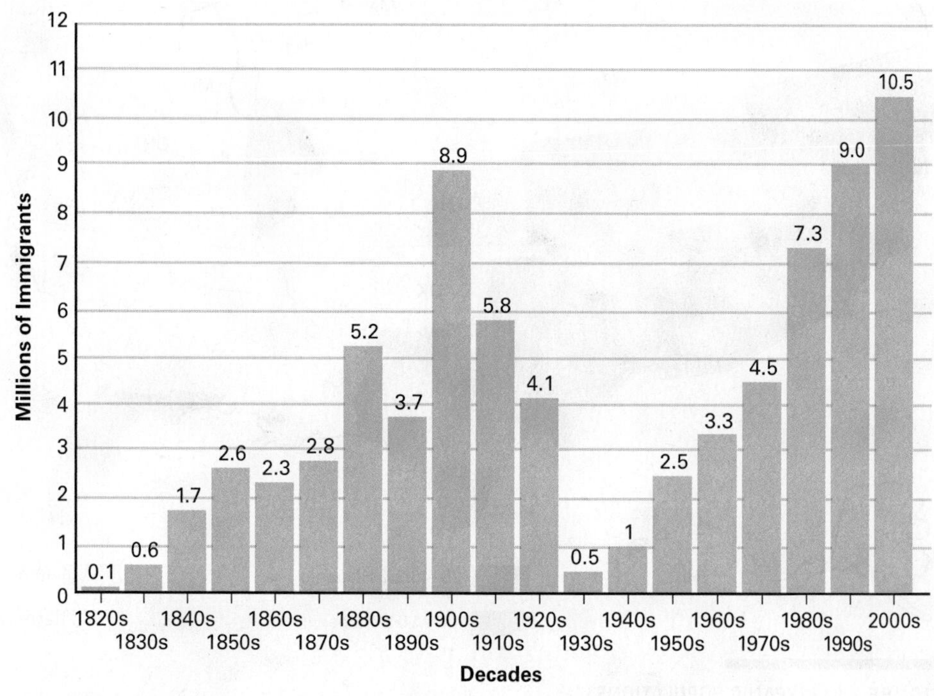

FIGURE 2.4 LEGAL IMMIGRATION TO THE UNITED STATES BY DECADES

Currently about 1 million legal immigrants are admitted into the United States each year. Today, the nation is experiencing its second great wave of immigration, following the great wave of the early 1900s.

SOURCE: *Statistical Abstract of the United States, 2012,* section 1, Table 44.

Illegal Immigration

The United States is a free and prosperous society with more than 5,000 miles of borders (2,000 with Mexico) and hundreds of international air- and seaports. In theory, a sovereign nation should be able to maintain secure borders, but in practice the United States has been unwilling and unable to do so. Estimates of illegal immigration vary widely, from the official U.S. Bureau of Immigration and Citizenship Services estimate of 400,000 per year (about 45 percent of the legal immigration) to unofficial estimates ranging up to 3 million per year. The government estimates that about 4 million illegal immigrants currently reside in the United States; unofficial estimates range up to 15 million or more. Many illegal immigrants slip across U.S. borders or enter ports with false documentation; many more overstay tourist, worker, or student visas. The responsibility for the enforcement of immigration laws rests with Immigration and Customs Enforcement, ICE (formerly the Immigration and Naturalization Service [INS]).

As a free society, the United States is not prepared to undertake massive roundups and summary deportations of millions of illegal residents. The Fifth and Fourteenth Amendments to the U.S. Constitution require that every *person* (not just citizen) be afforded "due process of law." The government may turn back persons at the border or even hold them in detention camps. The Coast Guard may intercept boats at sea and return persons to their country of origin.[10] Aliens have no constitutional right to come to the United States. However, once in the United States, whether legally or illegally, every person is entitled to due process of law and equal protection of the laws. People are thus entitled to a fair hearing prior to any government attempt to deport them. Aliens are entitled to apply for asylum and present evidence at a hearing of their "well-founded fear of prosecution" if returned to their country. Experience has shown that the only way to reduce the flow of **illegal immigration** is to control it at the border, an expensive and difficult, but not impossible, task. Localized experiments in border enforcement have indicated that, with significant increases in personnel and technology, illegal immigration can be reduced by half or more.

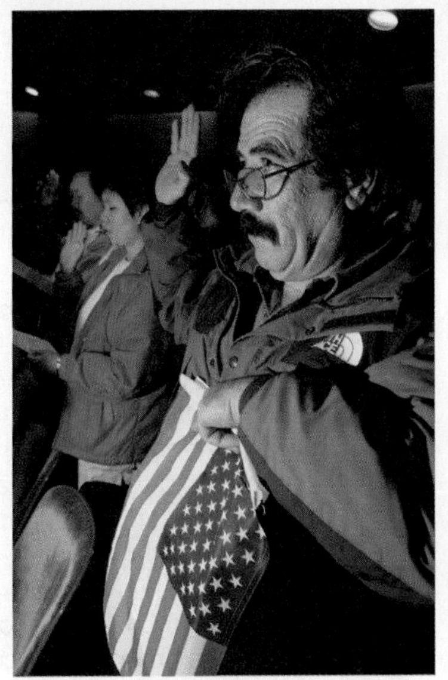

REFUGEES FROM TYRANNY

Many American immigrants sought political refuge in the 1970s, such as the Vietnamese who fled the fall of Saigon, or Iranians who fled the rise of theocratic rule. Here an Iranian immigrant takes the oath of citizenship in San Francisco.

illegal immigration
The unlawful entry of a person into a nation.

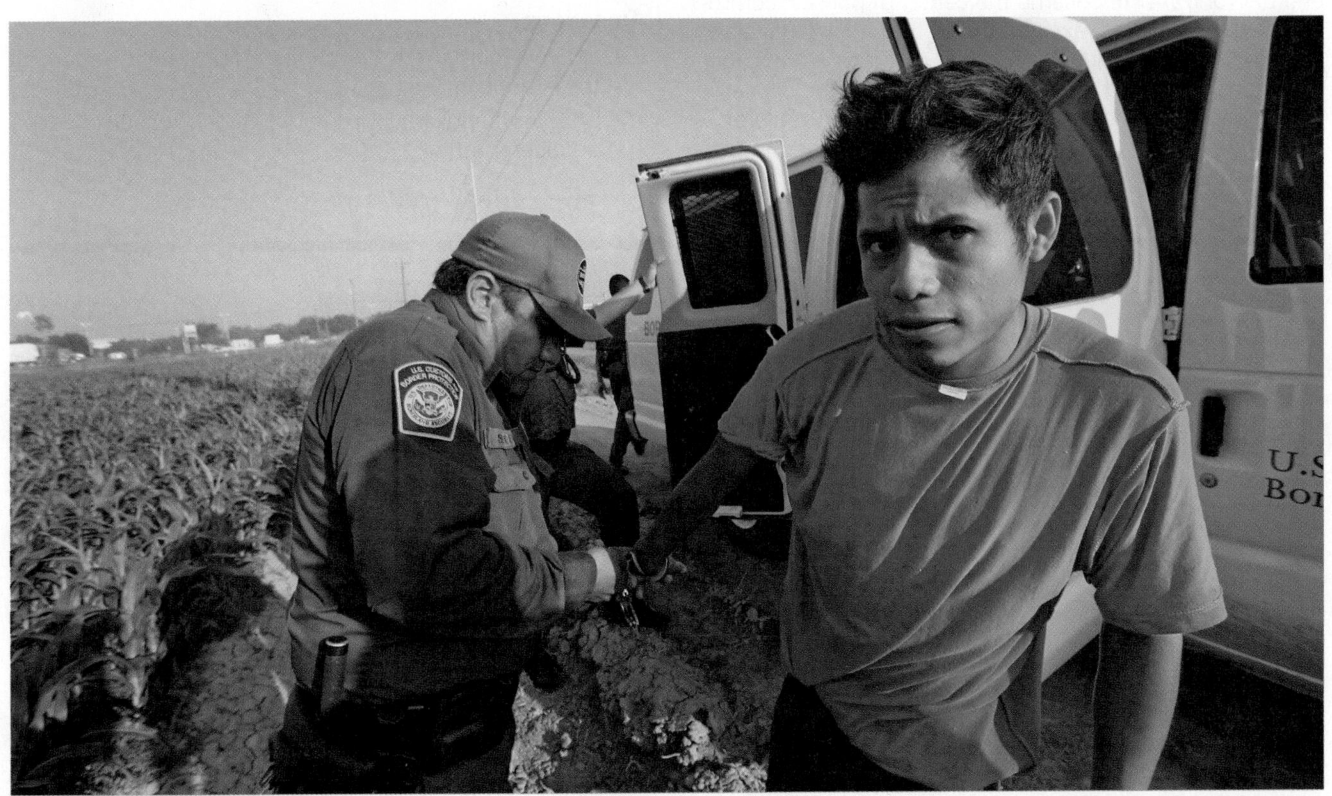

UNDOCUMENTED ENTRY

In addition to legal entry, illegal border crossing are a common means for immigrants to come to the United States, despite efforts of U.S. Border Patrol agents.

2.1 2.2 2.3 2.4 2.5 2.6 2.7 2.8

What Do You Think?

Should We Celebrate One Culture, or Cultural Diversity?

The Smithsonian Institute is one of the world's great repositories of knowledge and culture. It is known for its facilities in Washington, DC, dedicated to natural, cultural, and scientific history. The Smithsonian is also a source of controversy, as conflict grows over the treatment of culture and diversity in understanding American history.

Since the 1960s, the Smithsonian has increased its diverse cultural offerings—including the National Museum of African Art, the Anacostia Community Museum, the Arthur Sackler Gallery (Asian Art), the National Museum of the American Indian, a proposed National Latino Museum, and the National Museum of African American History and Culture—each representing the increased emphasis on American cultural diversity.

Critics see these new museums as dividing Americans. All of these institutions place an emphasis on culturally distinct ethnic, racial, and national minorities. Advocates argue that these institutions offer a perspective different from the dominant (white European) perspective. Critics contend that they impede conversations across diverse groups. U.S. Rep. Jim Moran (D-VA) observed, "I don't want a situation where whites go to the original museum, African Americans go to the African American museum, Indians go to the Indian museum, Hispanics go to the Latino American museum. That's not America."

The emphasis on diversity, and accompanying controversy, extends beyond these new museums. A proposed 1995 Smithsonian exhibit of the *Enola Gay*, the B-29 bomber that dropped the Hiroshima bomb that led to the end of World War II, became the center of political controversy when the initial exhibit emphasized the casualties arising from the bombing. American veterans groups and politicians protested the lack of emphasis on the cause of the war (Japan's attack on Pearl Harbor) or the role of the bomb in ending the war, as it averted the need for a costly invasion of the Japanese home islands. The exhibit was eventually canceled and the Air and Space Museum director, Martin Harwit, resigned his position.

About the Smithsonian

The Smithsonian Institute is the largest museum complex in the world. Founded in 1846 by Congress, the purpose of the Smithsonian is to facilitate the "increase and diffusion of knowledge." The original museums of the Smithsonian emphasized the natural science focus of its benefactor James Smithsonian. The oldest operating facilities—the National Museum of Natural History (1858) and the Smithsonian National Zoological Park (1889)—archived and displayed scientific knowledge at the height of the modern emergence of the natural sciences and the ascendancy of the scientific method.

The rise of the social sciences and a culturally and racially pluralist society accompanied the move of the Smithsonian toward diversity programming—and also the political land mines and criticisms that accompany a diverse examination of American politics, history, and culture.

The Smithsonian has grown to 19 museum facilities, many of which dominate the Mall between the Capitol and the Washington Monument. It also has nine research institutes and a zoo. It receives an annual appropriation from Congress of about $800 million, about $600 million of which is for salaries and operations. The Smithsonian is an independent trust governed by a 17-member board and run by a secretary who is appointed by the board.

Questions

1. Do you think there should be a National Museum of the American Latino?
2. Should tax dollars help fund cultural museums based on race or ethnicity?

SOURCES: www.si.edu (the Smithsonian Institution Web site). Kate Taylor. National Latino Museum Plan Faces Fight. *New York Times*, April 20, 2011, p. C1.

☐ Immigration Reform

Comprehensive immigration reform has been the subject of intense political conflict in Washington over the past two decades. Among the conflicting interests: employers seeking to keep immigration as open as possible in order to lower their labor costs; millions of currently illegal immigrants seeking a lawful path to citizenship; and residents seeking border security and opposing amnesty for illegal immigrants. "Comprehensive" reform implies compromise among these interests. In 2007, Congress considered a comprehensive bill co-sponsored by Senators Edward M. Kennedy and John McCain that included the following major provisions: strengthening border enforcement, including funding of 700 miles of fencing along the Mexican border; granting legal status to millions of undocumented immigrants currently living in the country; providing a path to citizenship that includes criminal background checks, payment of fees, and acquiring English proficiency; establishing a temporary (two-year) guest worker program; shifting the criteria for legal immigration from family-based preferences to a greater emphasis on skills and education. But opponents of one or another of these various provisions, both Democrats and Republicans, united to defeat the bill. Nonetheless, the major provisions of this effort at comprehensive reform are now a part of the Obama administration's own immigration reform efforts.

Citizenship

Persons born in the United States are U.S. citizens. People who have been lawfully admitted into the United States and granted permanent residence, and who have resided in the United States for at least five years and in their home state for the last six months, are eligible for naturalization as U.S. citizens. Federal district courts as well as offices of the Citizenship and Immigration Services (CIS) may grant applications for citizenship. By law, the applicant must be over age 18, be able to read, write, and speak English, possess good moral character, and understand and demonstrate an attachment to the history, principles, and form of government of the United States (see *The Game, The Rules, The Players*: Could You Pass the Citizenship Test?).

Citizens of the United States are entitled to a **passport**, issued by the U.S. State Department upon presentation of a photo plus evidence of citizenship—a birth

passport
Evidence of U.S. citizenship, allowing people to travel abroad and reenter the United States.

What Do You Think?

Does Immigration Help or Hurt America?

Most Americans think that immigration in general is a good thing.

Q. On the whole, do you think immigration is a good thing or a bad thing for this country today?

Good thing	61%
Bad thing	34%
Mixed or no opinion	5%

But Americans are divided as to the *effects* of immigration—whether immigrants make the United States a better or worse place. On the one hand, immigrants do work that others would not do. As the National Restaurant Association's legislative affairs director says, "Restaurants, hotels, nursing homes, agriculture—a very broad group of industries—are looking for a supply of workers to remain productive." He adds that in many parts of the country, workers are not available for such jobs at any price. On the other hand, the strong demand for cheap labor is just that: the demand by employers not to have to pay as much as they would to native-born Americans.

Q. Do you think immigrants mostly help the economy by providing low-cost labor or mostly hurt the economy by driving wages down for many Americans?

Mostly hurt	48%
Mostly help	42%
Neither	3%
Both	1%
Don't know	5%

Americans are more of one mind, though, when it comes to *illegal* immigration in particular—the 10 to 12 million persons in the United States who entered the country illegally.

A large majority of Americans agree that the U.S. government should take a tough stand on illegal immigration.

Q. When people are caught trying to enter the United States illegally, which do you think should be government policy?

Immediately send them back to their home country	61%
Allow them to appeal their case using legal representation and a court hearing	35%
Neither, don't know	4%

Q. Do you favor or oppose stricter penalties on illegal immigrants?

Favor	77%
Oppose	18%
Don't know	5%

Yet Americans are more tolerant of illegal immigrants if they meet various requirements, such as establishing how long they have lived in the United States, paying fees for residing in the U.S. illegally, and speaking the English language, among others.

Q. Which comes closer to your view about what government policy should be toward illegal immigrants currently living in the U.S.? Should the government deport all illegal immigrants back to their home country, allow illegal immigrants to remain in the U.S. in order to work but for only a limited amount of time, or allow illegal immigrants to remain in the U.S. and become U.S. citizens only if they meet certain requirements over a period of time?

Deport all	24%
Remain in the U.S. in order to work	15%
Remain in the U.S. and become citizens	59%

Question

1. Ask yourself these same questions. What did you answer?

SOURCE: Various recent national polls reported in Public Agenda, www.publicagenda.com, and in iPoll at the Roper Center.

The Game, the Rules, the Players

Could You Pass the Citizenship Test?

To ensure that new citizens "understand" the history, principles, and form of government of the United States, the CIS administers a citizenship test. Below is a sample of questions from the American government section of the test. Can you answer these questions?

1. What is the supreme law of the land?
2. The idea of self-government is in the first three words of the Constitution. What are these words?
3. What do we call the first 10 amendments to the Constitution?
4. How many amendments does the Constitution have?
5. Who is in charge of the executive branch?
6. Who makes federal laws?
7. What are the two parts of the U.S. Congress?
8. How many U.S. senators are there?
9. We elect a U.S. senator for how many years?
10. The House of Representatives has how many voting members?
11. We elect a U.S. Representative for how many years?
12. We elect a president for how many years?
13. In what month do we vote for president?
14. If the president can no longer serve, who becomes president?
15. If both the president and the vice president can no longer serve, who becomes president?
16. Who is the commander in chief of the military?
17. Who signs bills to become laws?
18. Who vetoes bills?
19. What is the highest court in the United States?
20. How many justices are on the Supreme Court?

SOURCE: Bureau of Citizenship and Immigration Services.

QUESTION

1. Take the test. How did you do?

Answers

1. The Constitution;
2. We the People;
3. The Bill of Rights;
4. 27;
5. The president;
6. Congress;
7. The Senate and the House of Representatives;
8. 100;
9. Six;
10. 435;
11. Two;
12. Four;
13. November;
14. The vice president;
15. The Speaker of the House;
16. The president;
17. The president;
18. The president;
19. The Supreme Court;
20. Nine.

visa
A document or stamp on a passport allowing a person to visit a foreign country.

certificate or naturalization papers. A passport enables U.S. citizens to reenter the country after travel abroad. When traveling abroad, your U.S. passport may be your most valuable possession. A **visa** is a document or stamp on a passport, issued by a foreign country, that allows a citizen of one nation to visit another.

Religion and Secularism in Politics

2.6 Assess the roles of religion and secularism in U.S. politics.

The United States is one of the most religious societies in the world. Over 90 percent of Americans report in polls that they believe in God. Over 80 percent say that prayer is part of their daily lives, and 60 percent say that they attend church at least once a month. Over 80 percent claim some religious affiliation. Evangelical Protestants are the largest single group and the fastest-growing (see Figure 2.5).

At the same time, however, most Americans are concerned about religious leaders exercising influence in political life. Most respondents say it is "not appropriate for religious leaders to talk about their political beliefs as part of their religious activities" (61 percent), "religious leaders should not try to influence how people vote in

2.1 2.2 2.3 2.4 2.5 2.6 2.7 2.8

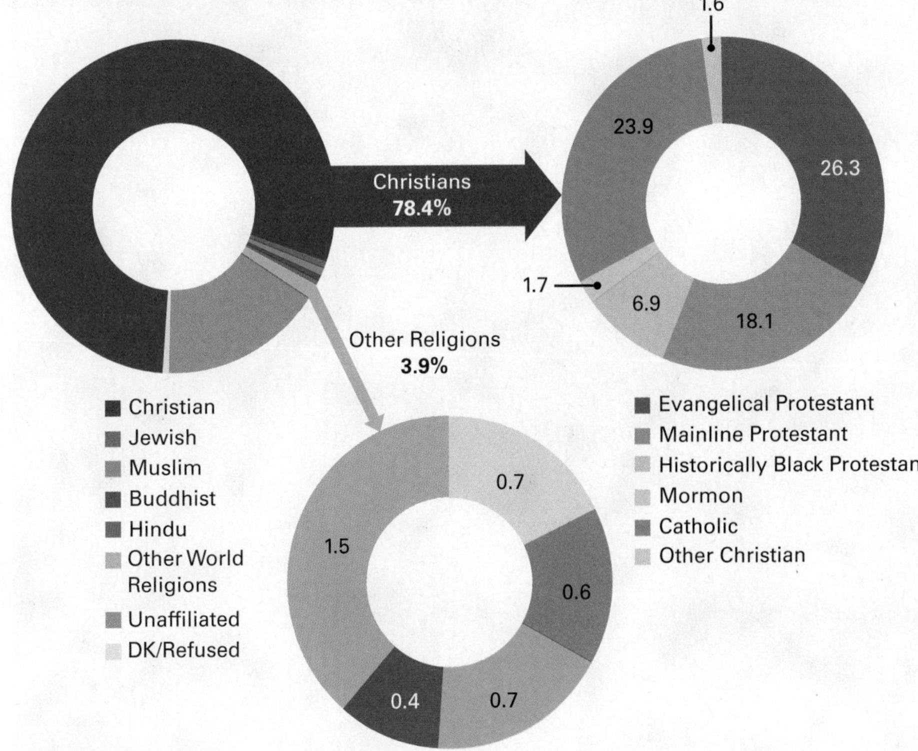

FIGURE 2.5 RELIGIOUS AFFILIATIONS OF AMERICANS

Americans are a religious people. Over 80 percent claim some religious affiliation. Evangelical Protestants are the largest and fastest-growing religious group in the country.

SOURCE: Data collected by Pew Forum on Religion & Public Life, *U.S. Religious Landscape Survey. Religious Affiliation: Diverse and Dynamic. February 2008.* Copyright © 2008 by The Pew Research Center. Reprinted by Permission.

elections" (64 percent), and "religious groups should not advance their beliefs by being involved in politics and working to affect policy" (54 percent).[11]

American's religious commitments and their belief in the separation of religion from politics sometimes clash.

secular
In politics, a reference to opposition to religious practices and symbols in public life.

☐ Challenging Religion in Public Life

There is a growing divide in America between religious faith and **secular** politics on a number of key public issues. The most religious among us, as determined by frequency of church attendance and belief in the literal interpretation of the Bible, generally support limitations on abortion, including parental notification when minors seek abortions, and would prohibit "partial-birth abortions" (intact dilation and extraction). They also support abstinence in sex education; oppose same-sex marriage, support the phrase "under God" in the Pledge of Allegiance; support the display of religious symbols in public places; and generally believe that religion should play an important role in addressing "all or most of today's problems."

In contrast, challenges to religion in public life are increasingly being raised in American politics, especially in the courts. Organizations such as the American Civil Liberties Union and Americans United for the Separation of Church and State are challenging many traditional religious practices and symbols in public life. Most of these challenges are based upon the First Amendment's "no establishment of religion" clause. Among these challenges: removing "under God" from the Pledge of Allegiance and eliminating the national motto "In God We Trust" from our coins; removing religious symbols—Christmas displays, the Ten Commandments, and so on—from public places; supporting the teaching of evolution and opposing the teaching of "creationism" in the schools; opposing the use of public school vouchers to pay for students attending religious schools; supporting gay rights, including same-sex marriages; and threatening to remove tax exemptions from churches whose religious leaders endorse candidates or involve themselves in politics.

2.1

2.2

2.3

2.4

2.5

2.6

2.7

2.8

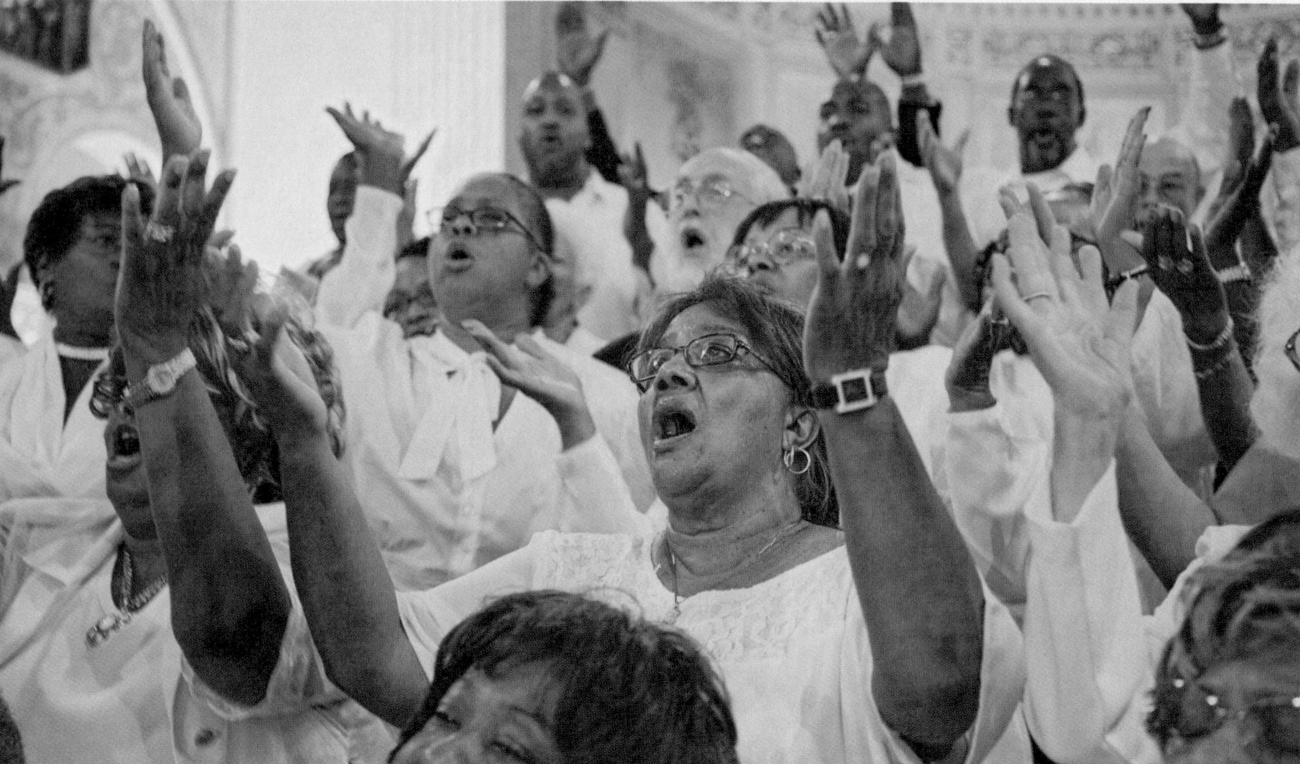

CHURCHES BUILD CIVIC ABILITY

Churches provided a critical basis for politically organizing African Americans during the civil rights era, and continue to be an important institution in not only the African American community, but in most of the United States.

ideology
Consistent and integrated system of ideas, values, and beliefs.

Religious/Political Alignments

Interestingly, the religious-versus-secular division on these issues does *not* depend upon *which* religion (for example, Protestants, Catholic, Jewish) that Americans identify themselves. Rather, this division appears to be more closely aligned with the *intensity* of people's religious commitments; in polls, for example, their self-identification as "born-again" or "evangelical"; their frequency of church attendance; and their agreement with statements such as "prayer is an important part of my daily life." An overwhelming majority of Americans (80 percent) say they have "old-fashioned values about family and marriage."

Increasingly, this division between religious and secular viewpoints is coming to correspond with the division between liberals and conservatives in American politics. Religious traditionalists are more likely to describe themselves as conservatives or moderates, while secularists are more likely to describe themselves as liberal in politics.[12]

Ideologies: Liberalism and Conservatism

2.7 Compare and contrast the main principles of conservatism and liberalism.

An **ideology** is a consistent and integrated system of ideas, values, and beliefs. A political ideology tells us who *should* get what, when, and how; that is, it tells us who *ought* to govern and what goals they *ought* to pursue. When we use ideological terms such as *conservatism* and *liberalism*, we imply reasonably integrated sets of values and beliefs. And when we pin ideological labels on people, we imply that those people are fairly consistent in the application of these values and beliefs in public affairs. In reality, neither political leaders nor citizens always display integrated or consistent opinions; many hold conservative views on some issues and liberal

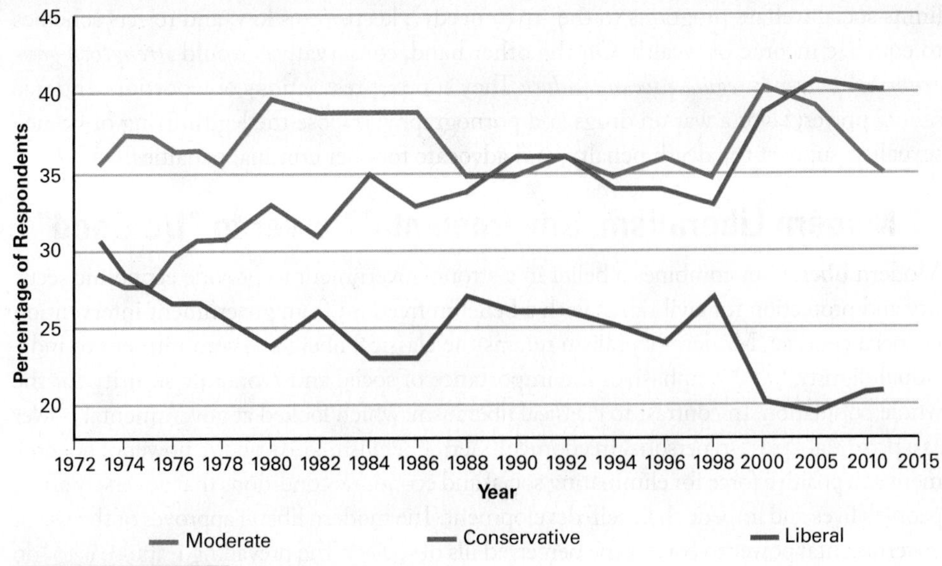

FIGURE 2.6 AMERICANS: LIBERAL, MODERATE, CONSERVATIVE

Americans are more likely to describe themselves as moderates or conservatives than as liberals.

SOURCE: General Social Surveys, National Opinion Research Center, University of Chicago; updated from Gallup polls to 2012.

views on others. Many Americans avoid ideological labeling, either by describing themselves as "moderate" or "middle-of-the-road" or by simply declining to place themselves on an ideological scale. But as Figure 2.6 shows, among those who choose an ideological label to describe their politics, conservatives consistently outnumber liberals.

Despite inconsistencies in opinion and avoidance of labeling, ideology plays an important role in American politics. Political *elites*—elected and appointed officeholders; journalists, editors, and commentators; party officials and interest-group leaders; and others active in politics—are generally more consistent in their political views than nonelites and are more likely to use ideological terms in describing politics.[13]

conservatism
Belief in the value of free markets, limited government, and individual self-reliance in economic affairs, combined with a belief in the value of tradition, law, and morality in social affairs.

Modern Conservatism: Individualism plus Traditional Values

Modern **conservatism** combines a belief in free markets, limited government, and individual self-reliance in economic affairs with a belief in the value of tradition, law, and morality in social affairs. Conservatives wish to retain our historical commitments to individual freedom from governmental controls; reliance on individual initiative and effort for self-development; a free-enterprise economy with a minimum of governmental intervention; and rewards for initiative, skill, risk, and hard work. These views are consistent with the early classical liberalism of Locke, Jefferson, and the nation's Founders, discussed at the beginning of this chapter. The result is a confusion of ideological labels: modern conservatives claim to be the true inheritors of the (classical) liberal tradition.

Conservatism is less optimistic about human nature. Traditionally, conservatives have recognized that human nature includes elements of irrationality, ignorance, hatred, and violence. Thus they have been more likely to place their faith in *law* and *traditional values* than in popular fads, trends, or emotions. To conservatives, the absence of law does not mean freedom but, rather, exposure to the tyranny of terrorism and violence. They believe that without the guidance of traditional values, people would soon come to grief through the unruliness of their passions, destroying both themselves and others. Conservatives argue that strong institutions—family, church, and community—are needed to control individuals' selfish and immoral impulses and to foster civilized ways of life.

It is important to note that conservatism in America incorporates different views of the role of government in economic versus social affairs. Conservatives generally prefer *limited noninterventionist government in economic affairs*—a government that relies on free markets to provide and distribute goods and services; minimizes its regulatory activity;

2.1

2.2

2.3

2.4

2.5

2.6

2.7

2.8

liberalism
Belief in the value of strong government to provide economic security and protection for civil rights, combined with a belief in personal freedom from government intervention in social conduct.

libertarian
Opposing government intervention in both economic and social affairs, and favoring minimal government in all sectors of society.

limits social welfare programs to the "truly needy"; keeps taxes low; and rejects schemes to equalize income or wealth. On the other hand, conservatives would *strengthen government's power to regulate social conduct.* They support restrictions on abortion; endorse school prayer; favor a war on drugs and pornography; oppose the legitimizing of homosexuality; support the death penalty; and advocate tougher criminal penalties.

☐ Modern Liberalism: Governmental Power to "Do Good"

Modern **liberalism** combines a belief in a strong government to provide economic security and protection for civil rights with a belief in freedom from government intervention in social conduct. Modern liberalism retains the classical liberalism commitment to individual dignity, but it emphasizes the importance of social and economic security for the whole population. In contrast to classical liberalism, which looked at governmental power as a potential threat to personal freedom, modern liberalism looks on the power of government as a positive force for eliminating social and economic conditions that adversely affect people's lives and impede their self-development. The modern liberal approves of the use of governmental power to correct the perceived ills of society. The prevailing impulse is to "do good," to perform public services, and to assist the least fortunate in society, particularly the poor and minorities. Modern liberalism is impatient with what it sees as the slow progress of individual initiative and private enterprise toward solving socioeconomic problems, so it seeks to use the power of the national government to find solutions to society's troubles.

Modern liberalism contends that individual dignity and equality of opportunity depend in some measure on *reduction of absolute inequality* in society. Modern liberals believe that true equality of opportunity cannot be achieved where significant numbers of people are suffering from hopelessness, hunger, treatable illness, or poverty. Thus modern liberalism supports government efforts to reduce inequalities in society.

Liberals also have different views of the role of government in economic versus social affairs. Liberals generally prefer an *active, powerful government in economic affairs*—a government that provides a broad range of public services; regulates business; protects civil rights; protects consumers and the environment; provides generous unemployment, welfare, and Social Security benefits; and reduces economic inequality. But many of these same liberals would *limit the government's power to regulate social conduct.* They oppose restrictions on abortion; oppose school prayer; favor decriminalizing marijuana use and victimless offenses like public intoxication and vagrancy; support gay rights and tolerance toward alternative lifestyles; oppose government restrictions on speech, press, and protest; oppose the death penalty; and strive to protect the rights of criminal defendants. Liberalism is the prevailing ideology among college professors (see Figure 2.7), though this liberalism is more pronounced among faculty at elite Ph.D.-granting universities and selective liberal arts colleges.

☐ The Ideological Battlefield

If Americans aligned themselves along a single liberal–conservative dimension, politics in the United States would be easier to describe, but far less interesting. We have already defined liberals as supporting a strong government in economic affairs and civil rights, but opposing government intervention in social affairs. And we have described conservatives as supporting a limited government in economic affairs and civil rights, but favoring government regulation of social conduct. Thus neither liberals nor conservatives are really consistent in their view of the role of government in society, each differentiating between economic and social affairs.

Yet some people consistently support strong government to regulate business and provide economic security, and also to closely regulate social conduct. While few people use the term *populist* to describe themselves, these people may actually make up a fairly large proportion of the electorate. Liberal politicians can appeal for their votes by stressing government intervention to provide economic security, while conservative politicians can appeal to them by stressing the maintenance of traditional social values.

And some people, often referred to as **libertarians**, oppose government intervention in *both* economic affairs and in the private lives of citizens. They are against most

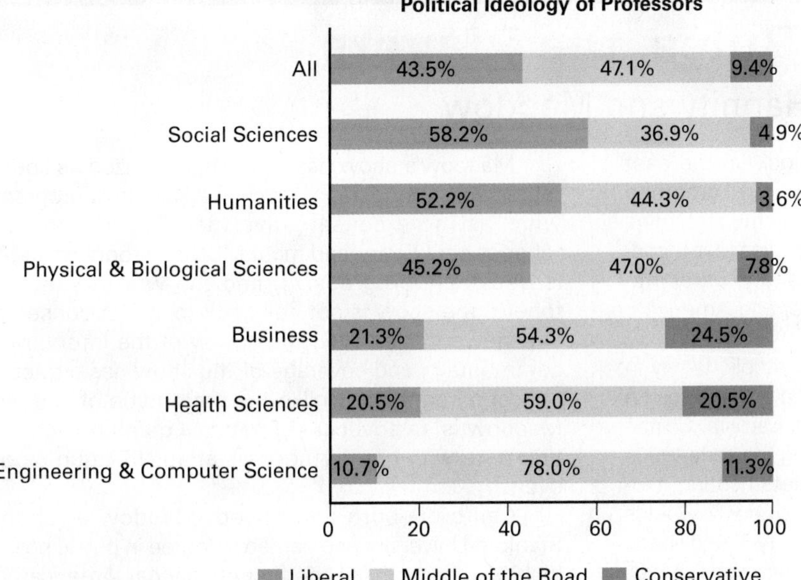

FIGURE 2.7 IDEOLOGY AMONG PROFESSORS

Most professors describe their politics as "liberal," especially professors in the humanities and social sciences.

SOURCE: Neil Gross and Solon Simmons. 2007. "The Social and Political Views of American Professors." http://www.wjh.harvard.edu/~ngross/lounsbery_9-25.pdf, accessed August 26, 2011.

environmental regulations, consumer protection laws, antidrug laws, defense spending, foreign aid, and government restrictions on abortion. In other words, they favor minimal government intervention in all sectors of society.

The result may be a two-dimensional ideological battlefield—identifying more or less government intervention and separating economic from social affairs—resulting in four separate groups—liberals, conservatives, populists, and libertarians (see Figure 2.8).

Youth and Ideology

Young people are more likely to hold liberal views than their elders. Especially on social issues, young people age 18–24 are more likely to describe themselves as liberals (see Table 2.1 on page 53). Older adults are more likely to describe themselves as conservatives on social as well as economic issues.

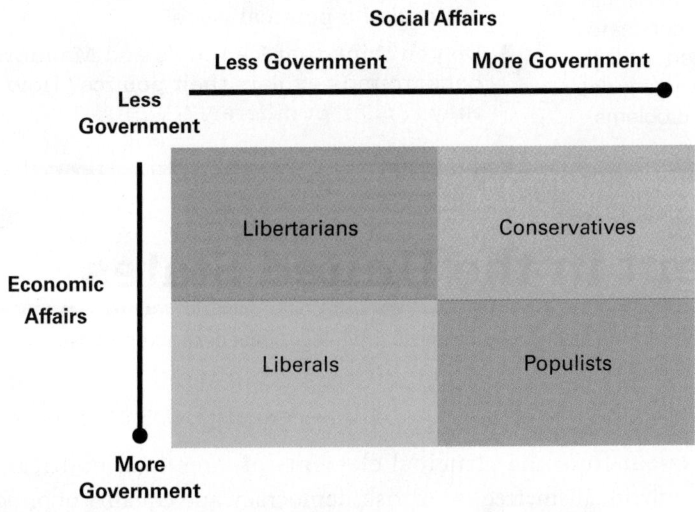

FIGURE 2.8 MAPPING THE IDEOLOGICAL BATTLEFIELD

We can classify people's views on whether they prefer more or less government intervention, first in economic affairs (the vertical axis), and, second, in social affairs (the horizontal axis). The result is a fourfold classification scheme distinguishing types (economic and social) of liberals and conservatives.

2.1
2.2
2.3
2.4
2.5
2.6
2.7
2.8

The Game, the Rules, the Players

Pundit Versus Pundit—Hannity and Maddow

Hannity: Every night at nine o'clock on the east coast, the voice of a square-jawed, well-groomed man roars in the name of Americanism on the Fox News Channel. Sean Hannity, a middle-aged, clear-eyed conservative, characterizes policy, politics, and party into two distinct camps: conservative, true, and American; and liberal, threatening, and alien.

Sean Hannity grew up in an Irish Catholic family in suburban Long Island. After dropping out of NYU, he broke into talk radio in the late 1980s in Santa Barbara, California, as a college radio host. After spending the early 1990s bouncing around southern media markets hosting mid-day political talk, Hannity was hired by the new Fox News Channel to host a show with New York City-based liberal talk host Alan Colmes. Though titled *Hannity and Colmes,* the stronger partner in Fox's interview–commentary program was the pugnacious Hannity. The product was a program that was popular among conservative viewers and that eventually rocketed past CNN's Larry King to be the top-rated nighttime news talk program on cable.

Hannity's products (he also hosts a popular syndicated talk radio program) are unabashedly Americanist in their worldview and presentation. His interviews and debates with liberal and moderate guests are often intense and ideologically charged—Cal Thomas, noted conservative columnist, identified Hannity as one of leading polarizers in American broadcasting.

Hannity's books clearly align conservative politics with American values, and characterize liberalism as an enemy of Americanism and the equivalent of terrorism. *Let Freedom Ring: Winning the War of Liberty over Liberalism; Deliver Us from Evil: Defeating Terrorism, Despotism, and Liberalism;* and *Conservative Victory: Defeating Obama's Radical Agenda* were all best sellers.

Maddow: Just up (or down) the cable dial from Sean Hannity, a similarly clean-cut, clear-eyed, Irish American commentator engages in witty, biting analysis of policy and politics that sides with progressive causes and casts a critical eye at conservative commentary. The commentator, Rachel Maddow, is not like Sean Hannity or Bill O'Reilly or Glenn Beck. In an industry dominated by middle-aged men with backgrounds in entertainment, Maddow is an intellectual, Generation X woman who advocates for progressive solutions to policy problems.

Maddow's show has been characterized as liberal rather than Democratic, much like Hannity's program, which is more conservative than Republican. The tenor of her show—and most MSNBC programming—is decidedly progressive, and the wry intellectual tone of the show is not designed to attract conservative viewers. However, the quality of the interviews, commentary, and coverage of the show has attracted critical recognition. Unlike the stereotype of liberals, Maddow is an advocate of national defense, and her first date with her partner was at an NRA gun range event.

California-born and raised, Maddow attended Stanford University and earned a degree in public policy. In 1995, she became the first openly gay American to win a Rhodes Scholarship. She did graduate research at Lincoln College, Oxford, and defended her doctoral dissertation, *HIV/AIDS and Health Care Reform in British and American Prisons,* in 2001.

Maddow moved into broadcasting in Massachusetts and was later an inaugural host of the effort at establishing a liberal talk radio network, "Air America." After building a substantial profile as a panelist and guest on numerous programs on MSNBC and CNN, and periodically guest-hosting for vitriolic former MSNBC host Keith Olbermann, Maddow moved into her own nightly show in 2008. The MSNBC audience in the time slot quickly expanded, though it still lagged Fox's numbers in the same time slot. Her first book, *Drift: The Unmooring of American Military Power,* is a best-selling examination of the emergence in the last half century of an America seemingly always at war.

QUESTIONS

1. **Watch a broadcast of Hannity's show and of Maddow's show on the same night. Do they seem to engage the same issues? Do they agree on basic facts when they do?**
2. **How does each commentator approach their critique of a political issue?**
3. **Do you think that Hannity's and Maddow's backgrounds explain their politics? How are they similar, or different?**

Dissent in the United States

2.8 Differentiate among various political ideologies that depart from conservatism and liberalism.

Dissent from the principal elements of American political culture—individualism, free enterprise, democracy, and equality of opportunity—has arisen over the years from both the *left* and the *right*. The **left** generally refers to socialists and communists, but it is sometimes used to brand liberals. The **right** generally refers to fascists and extreme nationalists, although it is sometimes used to stamp conservatives.

left
A reference to the liberal, progressive, and/or socialist side of the political spectrum.

right
A reference to the conservative, traditional, anticommunist side of the political spectrum.

Antidemocratic ideas have historical roots in movements that originated primarily outside America's borders. These movements have spanned the political spectrum from the far right to the far left.

Fascism

At the far-right end of this spectrum lies **fascism**, an ideology that asserts the supremacy of the state or race over individuals. The goal of fascism is unity of people, nation, and leadership—in the words of Adolf Hitler: "*Ein Volk, Ein Reich, Ein Führer*" ("One People, One Nation, One Leader"). Every individual, every interest, and every class are to be submerged for the good of the nation. Against the rights of liberty or equality, fascism asserts the duties of service, devotion, and discipline. Its goal is to develop a superior type of human being, with qualities of bravery, courage, genius, and strength. The World War II defeat of the two leading fascist regimes in history—Adolf Hitler's Nazi Germany and Benito Mussolini's fascist Italy—did not extinguish fascist ideas. Elements of fascist thought are found today in extremist movements in both the United States and Europe.

Marxism

Marxism arose out of the turmoil of the Industrial Revolution as a protest against social evils and economic inequalities. Karl Marx (1818–83), its founder, was not an impoverished worker but rather an upper-middle-class intellectual unable to find an academic position. Benefiting from the financial support of his wealthy colleague Friedrich Engels (1820–95), Marx spent years writing *Das Kapital* (1867), a lengthy work describing the evils of capitalism, especially the oppression of factory workers (the proletariat) and the inevitability of revolution. The two men collaborated on a popular pamphlet entitled *The Communist Manifesto* (1848), which called for a workers' revolution: "Workers of the world, unite. You have nothing to lose but your chains."

It fell to Vladimir Lenin (1870–1924) to implement Marx and Engels's revolutionary ideology in the Russian Revolution in 1917. According to **Leninism**, the key to a successful revolution is the organization of small, disciplined, hard-core groups of professional revolutionaries into a centralized totalitarian party. To explain why Marx's predictions about the ever-worsening conditions of the masses under capitalism proved untrue (workers' standards of living in Western democracies rose rapidly in the twentieth century), Lenin devised the theory of imperialism: advanced capitalist countries turned to war and colonialism, exploiting the Third World, in order to make their own workers relatively prosperous.

Communism

Communism is the outgrowth of Marxist–Leninist ideas about the necessity of class warfare, the inevitability of a worldwide proletarian revolution, and the concentration of all power in the "vanguard of the proletariat"—the Communist Party. Communism justifies violence as a means to attain power by arguing that the bourgeoisie (the capitalistic middle class) will never voluntarily give up its control over "the means of production" (the economy). Democracy is only "window dressing" to disguise capitalist exploitation.

TABLE 2.1 IDEOLOGY AND AGE

Younger people are more likely to describe their views as "liberal" than older people.

Age	Conservative	Moderate	Liberal
18–29	28%	40%	28%
30–49	40	36	21
50–64	44	33	20
65 and older	49	31	16

SOURCE: Gallup Poll, reported January 12, 2012. Copyright © 2012 by The Gallup Organization.

fascism
Political ideology in which the state and/or race is assumed to be supreme over individuals.

Marxism
The theories of Karl Marx, among them that capitalists oppress workers and that worldwide revolution and the emergence of a classless society are inevitable.

Leninism
The theories of Vladimir Lenin, among them being that advanced capitalist countries turned toward war and colonialism to make their own workers relatively prosperous.

communism
System of government in which a single totalitarian party controls all means of production and distribution of goods and services.

socialism
System of government involving collective or government ownership of economic enterprise, with the goal being equality of results, not merely equality of opportunity.

The Communist Party justifies authoritarian single-party rule as the "dictatorship of the proletariat." In theory, after a period of rule by the Communist Party, all property will be owned by the government, and a "classless" society of true communism will emerge.

Socialism

Socialism shares with communism a condemnation of capitalist profit making as exploitative of the working classes. Communists and socialists agree on the "evils" of industrial capitalism: the concentration of wealth, the insensitivity of the profit motive to human needs, the insecurities and suffering brought on by the business cycle, the conflict of class interests, and the tendency of capitalist nations to involve themselves in imperialist wars. However, socialists are committed to the democratic process as a means of replacing capitalism with collective ownership of economic enterprise. Socialists generally reject the notion of violent revolution as a way to replace capitalism and instead advocate peaceful, constitutional roads to bring about change. Moreover, many socialists are prepared to govern in a free society under democratic principles, including freedom of speech and press and the right to organize political parties and oppose government policy. Socialism is egalitarian, seeking to reduce or eliminate inequalities in the distribution of wealth. It attempts to achieve equality of results, rather than mere equality of opportunity.

The End of History?

Much of the history of the twentieth century was the struggle between democratic capitalism and totalitarian communism. Thus the collapse of communism

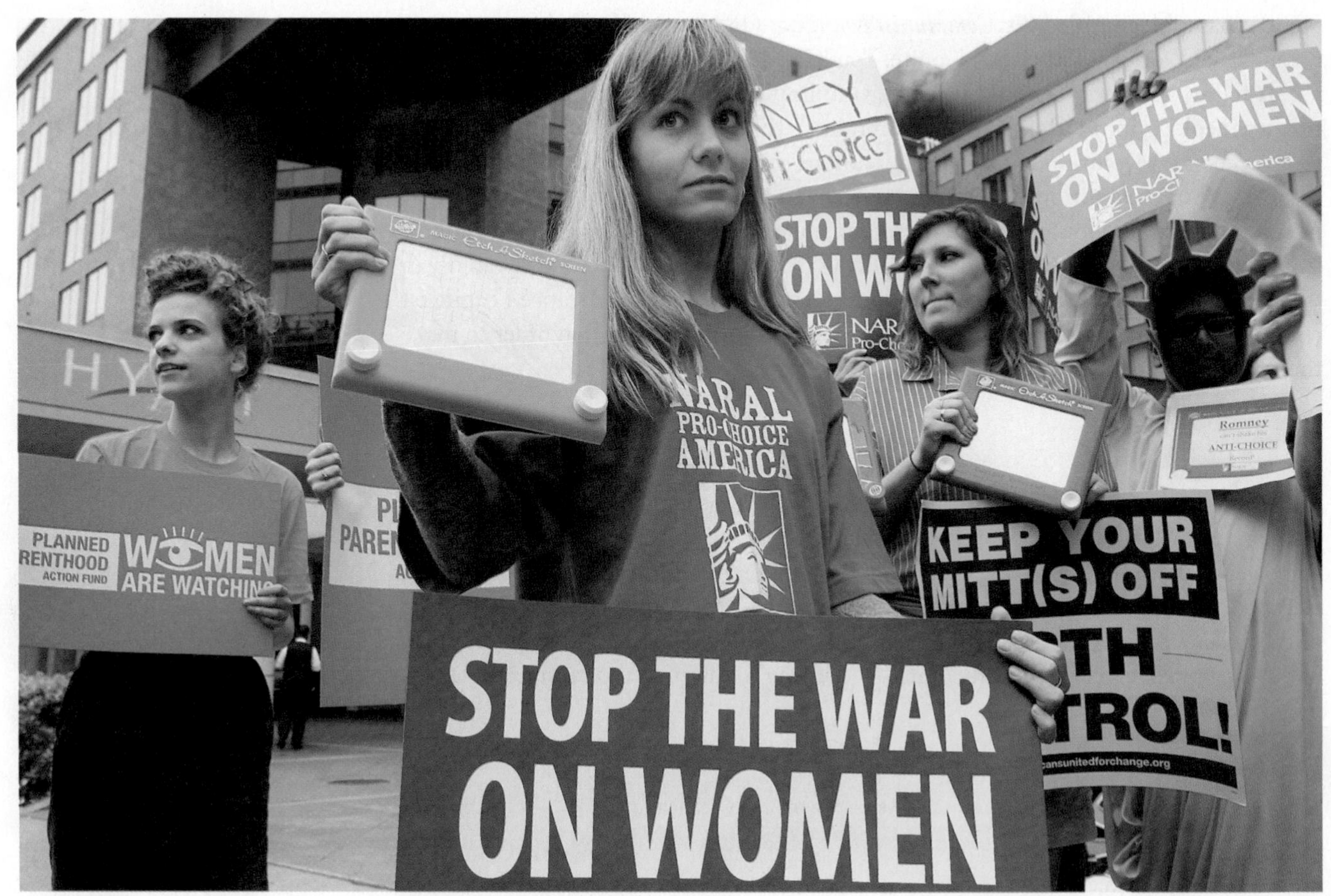

IDEOLOGIES IN ACTION

Liberals' concern about efforts to curtail social welfare programs reflects their support of strong government, while defending against encroachments on individual liberties. Here, an American woman protests in defense of reproductive freedom outside a Mitt Romney campaign event in 2012.

What Do You Think?

Got Grid? Conceiving of Culture

Sometimes, politics isn't as simple as left versus right, conservative versus liberal, or Democratic versus Republican. Can we think about politics in terms that describe their politics more precisely?

What if you are conservative on economics, but you also don't like war and you think the government is intruding on your privacy too much?

What if you think security and defense is important, but you also think that we need to spend even more money on national defense?

What if you want to see your social or religious values enforced by the government, but you also think government needs to shrink the welfare state?

What if you think that the government taxes too much, but you also think it has no business defining marriage?

All of these perspectives exist, but they don't fit easily into the left-right, Democratic-Republican boxes of American politics. People who study "political culture" say that instead of thinking about politics through party or ideology, you have to understand the worldviews of people. Then, you can understand their political choices.

According to the cultural theorists, there are two dimensions most people use to relate to the organization of society:

Group: Do you see yourself as part of a social unit (class, race, ethnicity, gender, cultural group)?

Grid: Are your activities more or less limited by rules and laws?

Based on how people score (high or low) on each of these dimensions, you can cluster them into four groups:

Hierarchs: Americans who score high on "grid" (rule-bound) and "group" (strong group identity) have a *hierarchical* worldview. They put the group ahead of the individual. They want a world with defined roles, procedures, and defined lines of authority. They want a strong state to reinforce those roles. A hierarch would probably agree with these statements:

> *The best way to get ahead in life is to do what you are told to do.*
>
> *Our society is in trouble, because we don't obey those in authority.*
>
> *Society would be much better off if we imposed strict and swift punishment on those that break the rules.*

Individualists: Americans with low "grid" (liberty over rules) and low "group" (strong individual identity) are individualists. They do not have much group identity. They are highly libertarian—and they are a growing segment among young Americans. An individualist would probably agree with these statements:

> *Even if some people are at a disadvantage, it is best for society to let people succeed or fail on their own.*
>
> *Even the disadvantaged should have to make their own way in the world.*
>
> *We are all better off when we compete as individuals.*

Egalitarians: These are people who are low-grid (they place liberty over rules), but they are also high-group. They have a strong cultural, class, or gender identity, but they do not like rules that set people apart by group. They also see some obligation of government to fix poverty associated with group identity. An egalitarian would probably agree with these statements:

> *What our society needs is a fairness revolution to make the distribution of goods more equal.*
>
> *Society works best if power is shared equally.*
>
> *It is our responsibility to reduce the differences in income between the rich and the poor.*

Fatalists: These high-grid, low-group people feel limited by social rules and norms. They also feel excluded from important social groups, and think that the "deck is stacked" against their opportunities. A fatalist would probably agree with these statements:

> *Most of the important things that take place in life happen by random chance.*
>
> *No matter how hard we try, the course of our lives is largely determined by forces outside our control.*
>
> *It would be pointless to make serious plans in such an uncertain world.*

This approach to understanding politics has deeply penetrated the political culture of the United States. An application of this approach to identifying people's politics is "The World's Smallest Political Quiz," an online application that draws heavily on Herb McClosky and John Zaller's classic book *The American Ethos*.

Questions

1. Consider the 10 statements above. Ask yourself how much you agree with them. What type are you?
2. Do you think a cultural approach is better than using ideology to describe a person's politics?

SOURCES: Herb McClosky and John Zaller. 1987. *The American Ethos*. Cambridge: Harvard University Press. Mary Douglas & Aaron Wildavsky. 1982. *Risk and Culture*. Berkeley: University of California Press.

2.1
2.2
2.3
2.4
2.5
2.6
2.7
2.8

end of history
The collapse of communism and the worldwide movement toward free markets and political democracy.

politically correct (PC)
Repression of attitudes, speech, and writings that are deemed racist, sexist, homophobic (antihomosexual), or otherwise "insensitive."

in Eastern Europe and the Soviet Union, symbolized by the tearing down of the Berlin Wall in 1989 as well as the worldwide movement toward free markets and democracy at the end of the twentieth century, has been labeled the **end of history**.[14] Democratic revolutions were largely inspired by the realization that free-market capitalism provided much higher standards of living than communism. The economies of Eastern Europe were falling further and further behind the economies of the capitalist nations of the West. Similar comparative observations of the successful economies of the Asian capitalist "Four Tigers"—South Korea, Taiwan, Singapore, and Hong Kong—even inspired China's communist leadership to undertake market reforms. Communism destroyed the individual's incentive to work, produce, innovate, save, and invest in the future. Under communism, production for government goals (principally a strong military) came first; production for individual needs came last. The result was long lines at stores, shoddy products, and frequent bribery of bureaucrats to obtain necessary consumer items. More important, the concentration of both economic and political power in the hands of a central bureaucracy proved to be incompatible with democracy. Communism relies on central direction, force, and repression. Communist systems curtail individual freedom and prohibit the development of separate parties and interest groups outside of government.

Capitalism does not *ensure* democracy; some capitalist nations are authoritarian. But economic freedom inspires demands for political freedom. Thus market reforms, initiated by communist leaders to increase productivity, led to democracy movements, and those movements eventually dismantled the communist system in Eastern Europe and the old Soviet Union.

The worldwide ideological battles of the twentieth century—notably the struggles between democracy, fascism, and communism—may no longer drive world politics. But this is not the end of history or the end of global political conflict. The principal sources of conflict in the twenty-first century are likely to be cultural and religious—a clash of civilizations.[15] Western civilization—modern, secular, and democratic—now faces challenge from the Muslim world—traditional, religious, and authoritarian. Nation states may increasingly find themselves aligned along Western versus non-Western civilizations.

☐ Academic Radicalism

Marxism survives on campuses today largely as an academic critique of the functioning of capitalism. Contemporary Marxists argue that the institutions of capitalism have conditioned people to be materialistic, competitive, and even violent. The individual has been transformed into a one-dimensional person in whom genuine humanistic values are repressed.[16] Profitability, rather than humanistic values, remains the primary criterion for decision making in the capitalist economy, and thus profitability is the reason for poverty and misery despite material abundance. Without capitalist institutions, life would be giving, cooperative, and compassionate. Only a *radical restructuring* of social and economic institutions will succeed in liberating people from these institutions to lead humanistic, cooperative lives.

To American radicals, the problem of social change is truly monumental, because capitalist values and institutions are deeply rooted in this country. Since most people are not aware that they are oppressed and victimized, the first step toward social change is consciousness raising—that is, making people aware of their misery.

The agenda of academic radicalism has been labeled **politically correct (PC)** thinking. Politically correct thinking views American society as racist, sexist, and homophobic. Overt bigotry is not the real issue, but rather Western institutions, language, and culture, which systematically oppress and victimize women, people of color, homosexuals, and others.

Academic radicalism "includes the assumption that Western values are inherently oppressive, that the chief purpose of education is political transformation, and that all standards are arbitrary.[17] In PC thinking, "everything is political." Therefore curriculum, courses, and lectures—even language and demeanor—are judged according to whether they are politically correct or not. Universities have always been centers for the critical examination of institutions, values, and culture, but PC thinking does not really tolerate open discussion or debate. Opposition is denounced as "insensitive," racist, sexist, or worse, and intimidation is not infrequent.

☐ A Clash of Cultures?

Is American cultural identity under attack? As Samuel Huntington asks, "Do we have any meaningful identity as a nation that transcends our subnational ethnic, religious, racial identities?"[18] Historically, Americans shared a common set of values and beliefs—"the essential dignity of the individual human being, the fundamental equality of all men, and certain inalienable rights to freedom, justice and fair opportunity." While other nations define themselves by a common ethnicity and ancestry, Americans came from all over the globe and united behind Jefferson's notion of "inalienable rights to life, liberty and the pursuit of happiness." For over two centuries, American culture emphasized the rights of the individual, the people as a source of political power, government limited by law, and the free enterprise economy. Political sociologist Seymour Martin Lipset defined the American "civic culture" as including at its core: individual liberty, egalitarianism (of opportunity and respect, not result or condition), individual achievement, popular control of government, and free enterprise economics.[19] Assimilation into American culture meant the personal acceptance of these values and beliefs.

☐ Moralism to Relativism?

For most of the nation's history, Americans were religious and patriotic. Patriotism peaked with President John F. Kennedy's 1961 inaugural address: "Ask not what your country can do for you—ask what you can do for your country." And the American

EXTREMISM, LEFT AND RIGHT

Political extremists on the left and right often have more in common than they would like to admit. Although decidedly different in their political philosophies, both members of radical left wing groups and members of white supremacist groups typically reject democratic politics and assert the supremacy of the "people" over laws, institutions, and individual rights. Militant environmentalist Alex Cornelissen (left) captains a vessel that actively confronts Japanese whaling fleets; the young men on the right are members of a U.S. neo-Nazi group that rejects principles of equality embodied in the Constitution.

culture included a strong moralism—work hard and play by the rules. Or, as a Cuban American advised his fellow immigrants: "Welcome to the capitalist system. Each of you is responsible for the amount of money you have in your pocket. The government is not responsible for whether you eat, or whether you are poor or rich. The government doesn't guarantee you a job or a house. You've come to a rich and powerful country, but it is up to you whether or not you continue living like you did in Cuba."[20]

☐ Culture Wars?

But in recent years, much of American politics is centered on "the cultural wars." American religious and patriotic traditions have come under challenge, particularly in the mass media. The notion of a unifying American culture is now being tested. The idea of America as a "melting pot" has given way to that of a "mosaic" or "salad" of diverse peoples. America has been "liberated" from the dominant Western European culture. American education has shifted from teaching children the English language and American history and culture to the teaching of the cultures of different races, ethnic groups, and social classes. The nation's motto, "E Pluribus Unum" ("from many, one"), has been redefined to mean "within one, many." "Diversity" and "multiculturalism" are widely praised. There is an increased tendency of immigrants to maintain dual identities, loyalties, languages, and even citizenships. America is being transformed into a multilingual, multicultural society, and religion is increasingly excluded from the public forum. Challenges to America's traditional cultural identity have inspired countermovements—support for English-only schooling, opposition to racial preferences, calls for teaching of American history and civics, efforts in universities to restore Western classics to the curriculum, and renewed support for Christian values and symbols in public life. The resulting "cultural wars" increasingly define American politics.[21]

A Constitutional Note

Natural Born Versus Naturalized Citizenship

The Fourteenth Amendment to the Constitution requires the states, and by implication the national government, to treat natural born and naturalized citizens the same: "all persons born or naturalized in the United States, and subject to the jurisdiction thereof, are citizens of the United States.... No State shall make or enforce any law which shall abridge the privileges or immunities of citizens of the United States....." But there is one key difference between natural born and naturalized citizens written into the original Constitution of 1787: "No Person except a natural born Citizen, or a Citizen of the United States, at the time of the Adoption of this Constitution, shall be eligible to the Office of President...."

In at least three elections, the potential eligibility of a presidential candidate or president has been called into question over the matter of native birth citizenship. In 1880, Chester A. Arthur, the GOP vice-presidential nominee (and later president) confronted repeated allegations that he was born in Ireland or Canada. In 1964, a California lawyer tried to get GOP presidential nominee Barry Goldwater knocked off the California ballot because Goldwater was born in Arizona territory before it became a state. In 1967, Michigan Governor George Romney faced some questions about his birth status because he was born at a Mormon colony in Mexico. And in 2008, both John McCain (born in the Panama Canal zone) and Barack Obama (born in Hawaii but hounded by conspiracy theories that he was born overseas) both confronted eligibility challenges.

Requiring that the president be born in the United States is the only constitutional difference between U.S.-born and naturalized citizens. Perhaps this difference made more sense in 1787, when many aspiring politicians had only recently moved into the country. Democrats and Republicans alike have had popular governors (Jennifer Grantholm, D-Mich., Arnold Schwarzenegger, R-Calif.) who looked like solid presidential contenders, except they were born overseas.

Questions

1. Is it relevant today to require the president to be a native-born American?
2. Does this requirement deny some very qualified people the opportunity to run for the nation's highest office?

Review the Chapter

Political Culture

2.1 Define the concept of political culture, p. 30

The American political culture is a set of widely shared values and beliefs about who should govern, for what ends, and by what means.

Americans share many common ways of thinking about politics. Nevertheless, there are often contradictions between professed values and actual conditions, problems in applying abstract beliefs to concrete situations, and even occasional conflict over fundamental values.

Individual Liberty

2.2 Outline the main principles of classic liberalism, p. 31

Individual liberty is a fundamental value in American life. The classic liberal tradition that inspired the nation's Founders included both political liberties and economic freedoms.

Dilemmas of Equality

2.3 Differentiate among the various kinds of equality, p. 31

Equality is another fundamental American value. The nation's Founders believed in equality before the law, yet political equality, in the form of universal voting rights, required nearly two centuries to bring about.

Income Inequality and Social Mobility

2.4 Characterize the trends affecting the current distribution of wealth and income and analyze the relationships among social mobility, inequality, and class conflict, p. 35

Equality of opportunity is a widely shared value; most Americans are opposed to artificial barriers of race, sex, religion, or ethnicity barring individual advancement. But equality of results is not a widely shared value; most Americans support a "floor" on income and well-being for their fellow citizens but oppose placing a "ceiling" on income or wealth. Income inequality has increased in recent years primarily as a result of economic and demographic changes. Most Americans believe that opportunities for individual advancement are still available, and this belief diminishes the potential for class conflict.

Race, Ethnicity, and Immigration

2.5 Describe the current immigration trends and ethnic composition of the United States, p. 39

The United States is a nation of immigrants. For many years, favoritism was granted to European immigrants, but in 1965, the national origins quota system was abolished. Today, preferences are granted to professionals, relatives of U.S. citizens, and skilled workers. About 1 million legal immigrants enter the country each year. Our immigration policies have resulted in a society where Latinos now outnumber African Americans and they have become the largest minority in the United States. Illegal immigration continues but it is affected by the state of the economy and the potential for finding employment.

Religion and Secularism in Politics

2.6 Assess the roles of religion and secularism in U.S. politics, p. 46

A great majority of Americans claim religious affiliation. But there is a growing divide between religious and secular viewpoints on the role of religion in public life. Secularists have challenged many traditional religious practices and symbols, such as the words *under God* in the Pledge of Allegiance.

Ideologies: Liberalism and Conservatism

2.7 Compare and contrast the main principles of conservatism and liberalism, p. 48

Conservative and liberal ideologies in American politics present somewhat different sets of values and beliefs, even though they share a common commitment to individual dignity and private property. Generally, conservatives favor minimal government intervention in economic affairs and civil rights but support many government restrictions on social conduct. Generally, liberals favor an active, powerful government to provide economic security and protection for civil rights but oppose government restrictions on social conduct.

Dissent in the United States

2.8 Differentiate various political ideologies that depart from conservatism and liberalism, p. 52

Many Americans who identify themselves as conservatives or liberals are not always consistent in applying their professed views. Populists are liberals on economic issues but conservative in their views on social issues. Libertarians are conservative on economic issues but liberal in their social views. This makes it difficult to cleanly define political belief systems in the United States.

The collapse of communism and the worldwide movement toward free markets and democracy undermined support for socialism throughout the world. Marxism survives in academic circles as a critique of the functioning of capitalism, while Fascism sustains itself among some white separatism and supremacist groups.

Learn the Terms

political culture, p. 30
values, p. 30
beliefs, p. 30
subcultures, p. 30
classical liberalism, p. 31
natural law, p. 31
capitalism, p. 31
legal equality, p. 32
political equality, p. 32
equality of opportunity, p. 32
equality of results, p. 33
social mobility, p. 36
class conflict, p. 37
class consciousness, p. 38
immigration policy, p. 42
aliens, p. 42
amnesty, p. 42
illegal immigration, p. 43
passport, p. 45
visa, p. 46
secular, p. 47
ideology, p. 48
conservatism, p. 49
liberalism, p. 50
libertarian, p. 50
left, p. 52
right, p. 52
fascism, p. 53
Marxism, p. 53
Leninism, p. 53
communism, p. 53
socialism, p. 54
end of history, p. 56
politically correct (PC), p. 56

Test Yourself

2.1 Define the concept of political culture.

Political culture refers to

a. the division of values and beliefs
b. shared ideas about what is good
c. the various subcultures in society
d. widely shared ideas as to who should govern for what ends, and by what means
e. a culture of politics that is vested only in religious values

2.2 Outline the main principles of classic liberalism.

Classical liberalism does not include a belief in which of the following?

a. natural law
b. limited government
c. the social contract
d. redistribution of wealth from the rich to the poor
e. individuals have free will

2.3 Differentiate among the various kinds of equality.

The famous French observer of the early American scene, Alexis de Tocqueville, thought that the distinguishing characteristic of American political values was the belief in

a. a mixed slave and free market economy
b. liberty
c. equality
d. the pursuit of individual happiness
e. a strong social welfare state

2.4 Characterize the trends affecting the current distribution of wealth and income and analyze the relationships among social mobility, inequality, and class conflict.

Recent rises in measurements of income inequality may be explained by which of the following elements?

I. the decline in the manufacturing sector
II. demographic trends
III. global competition
IV. failure of the social contract

a. Only I, II, and IV
b. Only I
c. Only I and II
d. Only I, II, and III
e. I, II, III, and IV

2.5 Describe the current immigration trends and ethnic composition of the United States.

With regard to immigration and ethnic change in the United States, the current political and social environment is characterized by which of the following?

I. A growing immigrant population that is heavily Hispanic and largely composed of legal immigrants
II. An Anglo white population that makes up a smaller and smaller proportion of the overall population
III. A conservative political backlash against immigrant populations in several states
IV. An increase in the relative size of the African-American population compared to the Hispanic population

a. only I, II, and III
b. I, II, III, and IV
c. only I and III
d. only II, III, and IV
e. I, II, III, and IV

2.6 Assess the roles of religion and secularism in U.S. politics.

In the modern American political climate, Protestant religious fundamentalists are most likely to be

a. conservative Democrats
b. conservative Republicans
c. liberal Democrats
d. liberal Republicans
e. apolitical

2.7 Compare and contrast the main principles of conservatism and liberalism.

The belief that the government should not intervene in economic or social affairs would be consistent with

a. liberalism
b. libertarianism
c. Marxism
d. "compassionate conservatism"
e. egalitarianism

2.8 Differentiate among various political ideologies that depart from conservatism and liberalism.

The *End of History* refers to which of the following?

I. the rejection of communism in favor of free markets
II. tearing down the Berlin Wall
III. a surge toward democratic values
IV. a rejection of the arbitrary division of church and state.

a. only I
b. only I and IV
c. only I and III
d. only I, II, and III
e. I, II, III, and IV

Explore Further

SUGGESTED REFERENCES

Ball, Terrance, and Richard Dagger. *Political Ideologies and the Democratic Ideal*. New York: Longman, 2009. An overview of the major political ideologies, their origins, and development.

Baradat, Leon P. *Political Ideologies: Their Origin and Impact*. 10th ed. New York: Longman, 2009. Text coverage of the evolution of political ideologies over the past three centuries.

Bishop, Bill, and Robert Cushing. *The Big Sort.* Boston: Houghton-Mifflin, 2008. Book argues that political polarization is caused by Americans self-segregating based on lifestyle and politics.

de Tocqueville, Alexis. *Democracy in America* (1835). Chicago: University of Chicago Press, 2000. Classic early assessment of American political culture by a French traveler.

Dolbeare, Kenneth M., and Michael S. Cummings. *American Political Thought*. 6th ed. Washington, D.C.: CQ Press, 2009. A compilation of key writings and speeches from Franklin, Madison, Adams, and Paine, to Bill Clinton, Ronald Reagan, Pat Buchanan, Al Gore and Barack Obama.

Garcia, Chris, F., and Gabriel Sanchez. *Hispanics and the U.S. Political System: Moving into the Mainstream*. New York: Longman, 2008. Historic, contemporary, and future role of Hispanics in American politics.

Huntington, Samuel P. *The Clash of Civilizations and the Remaking of World Order*. New York: Simon & Schuster, 1996. The nation's leading political scientist assesses the state of world politics after the fall of communism. He explains how conflict between "civilizations," for example, Western versus Islamic, have replaced nations and ideologies as the driving force in global politics today.

Huntington, Samuel P. *Who We Are? The Challenges to America's National Identity*. New York: Simon & Schuster, 2004. A controversial argument that our national identity, including the English language, individualism, and respect for law, is being eroded by the problems of assimilating massive numbers of immigrants. The author argues the need to reassert the core values that make us Americans.

Jacobs, Lawrence R., and Theda Skocpol, eds. *Inequality and American Democracy*. New York: Russell Sage Foundation, 2005. A series of essays on the political consequences of growing income inequality in America.

Love, Nancy S. *Understanding Dogmas and Dreams*. 2nd ed. Washington, D.C.: CQ Press, 2006. An introduction to liberalism, conservatism, socialism, anarchism, fascism, feminism, environmentalism, and globalism.

Rycroft, Robert. *The Economics of Inequality, Discrimination, Poverty, and Mobility*. Armonk, N.Y.: M. E. Sharpe, 2009. Text survey of the economics of growing inequality as well as mobility among income classes.

Wolff, Edward N. *Top Heavy*. 2nd ed. New York: News Press, 2002. A fact-filled report on the increasing inequality of wealth in America, together with a proposal to tax wealth as well as income.

SUGGESTED WEB SITES

Americans United for Separation of Church and State www.au.org
An interest group formed to keep religion out of public places, especially schools.

American Conservative Union www.conservative.org
Conservative news and views and rankings of Congress members on conservative index.

Americans for Democratic Action www.adaction.org
The ADA is the nation's oldest liberal political action organization.

Bureau of Citizenship and Immigration Services (CIS) www.uscis.gov/portal/site/uscis
Official site with information on immigration laws, citizenship requirements, etc.

Center for Equal Opportunity www.ceousa.org
Think tank advocating equality of opportunity over equality of results.

Center for Immigration Studies www.cis.org
Advocacy organization for strengthening enforcement of immigration law.

Family Religious Council www.frc.org
An interest group championing religion, family, and marriage, and government support of these values.

Global Policy Forum www.globalpolicy.org
Information on many global issues. Click to "social and economic policy" and then to "inequality of wealth and income" for cross national data.

The Heartland Institute http://www.heartland.org
Chicago-based think tank promoting public policy based on individual liberty, limited government, and free markets.

Heritage Foundation www.heritage.org
This think tank site includes a ranking of over 150 nations on an "Index of Economic Freedom." The U.S. ranks sixth; Hong Kong ranks first.

Immigration and Customs Enforcement (ICE) www.ice.gov
Agency responsible for enforcement of immigration and customs laws.

Monticello www.monticello.org
Biography, letters, and a "Day in the Life" of Thomas Jefferson.

National Association of Scholars www.nas.org
Association of college and university professors opposed to PC restrictions on campus.

People for the American Way www.pfaw.org
An influential interest group on the Left which, among other issues, strongly opposes religious symbols in public.

Pew Research Center http://www.pewresearch.org
Dedicated to researching American society to create and maintain a vibrant democracy.

Philosophy Pages www.philosophypages.com
History of Western philosophy and discussion of major democratic philosophers, including John Locke, Jean Jacques Rousseau, and Thomas Hobbes, among others.

Socialist Party USA http://sp-usa.org
News and views from America's Socialist party.

Young Americans for Freedom www.yaf.com
The "YAF" archives site contains background on the conservative organization and conservative views on key issues of the day.

3

The Constitution

Limiting Governmental Power

In 1789, Thomas Jefferson argued that a permanent and perpetual Constitution was impossible because "the earth belongs always to the living generation. They may manage it then, and what proceeds from it, as they please." Therefore, Jefferson argued that a new constitution be written roughly every nineteen years to reflect the will of the present.

James Madison's Constitution does not expire every nineteen years, but it does allow for amending. In 1978, Texas undergrad Gregory Watson discovered the text of a forgotten amendment that had been drafted as one of the original Bill of Rights, but only approved by eight states. Watson made it his goal to see the bill ratified, and in 1992, it was approved as the twenty-seventh amendment that states congressional pay raises do not take effect until after the Congress approving the raise completes its term. Speaker Tom Foley initially challenged the legality of the amendment because it was so old, but the Supreme Court ruled in 1939 that amendments without expiration dates were still eligible for ratification, and that amendments, as political questions, did not belong in the courts.

Four more proposed amendments await ratification: one from 1789 would change congressional apportionment to allow one member of the House for every 50,000 state residents; another from 1810 would revoke the citizenship of any American accepting a foreign title; a third known as the Corwin Amendment from 1861 would have made it unconstitutional to abolish slavery (made irrelevant by the 13th Amendment); and a 1924 Child Labor Amendment which would explicitly allow Congress to regulate child labor in the states.

All of these amendments are political, and represent efforts to alter a perpetual document to serve the needs of the political present.

3.1 Identify the major principles of constitutionalism and trace its evolution in the United States, p. 64

3.2 Assess the obstacles to nationhood, p. 66

3.3 Outline the principles on which the Founders were in agreement and characterize their areas of conflict, p. 69

3.4 Analyze the economic and security issues that the Founders faced and the solutions they reached, p. 73

3.5 Explain how the Constitution structured the new government, p. 77

3.6 Analyze the separation of powers and the checks and balances established by the Constitution, p. 81

3.7 Outline the arguments made for and against ratification of the Constitution, p. 83

3.8 Assess the protections provided by the Bill of Rights and determine the various means through which the Constitution may be changed, p. 86

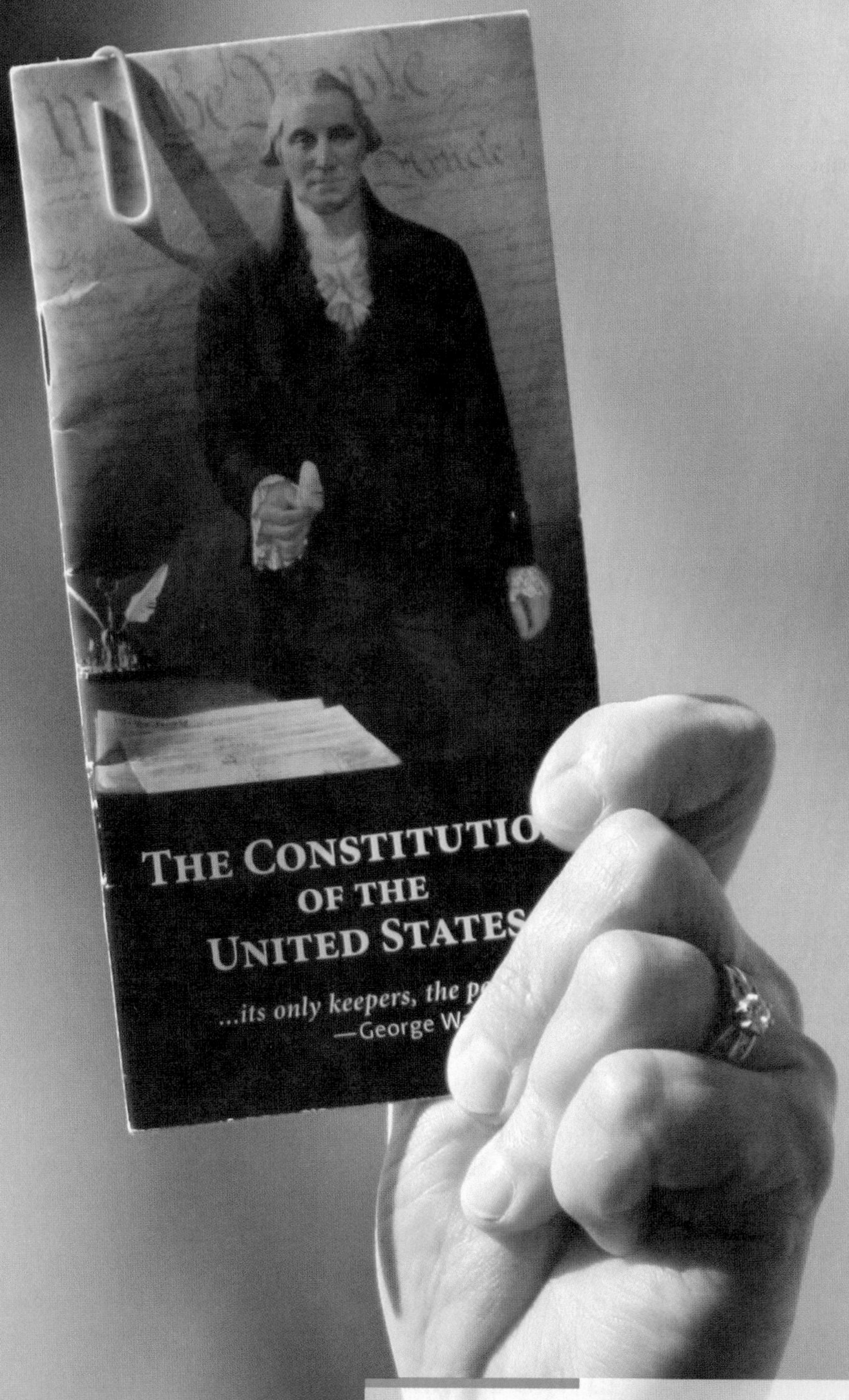

The American Constitution is the highest law of the land. It is also one of the dominant symbols of the American national identity.

Constitutional Government in America

3.1 Identify the major principles of constitutionalism and trace its evolution in the United States.

constitutionalism
A government of laws, not people, operating on the principle that governmental power must be limited and government officials should be restrained in their exercise of power over individuals.

constitution
The legal structure of a political system, establishing governmental bodies, granting their powers, determining how their members are selected, and prescribing the rules by which they make their decisions. Considered basic or fundamental, a constitution cannot be changed by ordinary acts of governmental bodies.

Mayflower Compact
Agreement among Pilgrim colonists to establish a government, setting the precedent of government by contract among the governed.

colonial charters
Documents granted by the English Monarch to individuals, companies, and groups of settlers in the new American colonies, authorizing a degree of self-government, setting the precedent of written contracts defining governmental power.

Constitutions govern government. **Constitutionalism**—a government of laws, not of people—means that those who exercise governmental power are restricted in their use of it by a higher law. If individual freedoms are to be placed beyond the reach of government and beyond the reach of majorities, then a constitution must truly limit the exercise of authority by government. It does so by setting forth individual liberties that the government—even with majority support—cannot violate.

A **constitution** legally establishes government authority. It sets up governmental bodies (such as the House of Representatives, the Senate, the presidency, and the Supreme Court in the United States). It grants them powers. It determines how their members are to be chosen. And it prescribes the rules by which they make decisions.

Constitutional decision making is deciding how to decide; that is, it is deciding on the rules for policy making. It is not policy making itself. Policies will be decided later, according to the rules set forth in the constitution.

A constitution cannot be changed by the ordinary acts of governmental bodies; change can come only through a process of general popular consent.[1] The U.S. Constitution, then, is superior to ordinary laws of Congress, orders of the president, decisions of the courts, acts of the state legislatures, and regulations of the bureaucracies. Indeed, the Constitution is "the supreme law of the land." Americans are strongly committed to the idea of a written constitution to establish government and limit its powers. In fact, the Constitutional Convention of 1787 had many important antecedents.

The Magna Carta, 1215

English lords, traditionally required to finance the king's wars, forced King John to sign the Magna Carta, a document guaranteeing their feudal rights and setting the precedent of a limited government and monarchy.

The Mayflower Compact, 1620

Pilgrim colonists, while still aboard the *Mayflower*, signed a compact, among themselves and other passengers, establishing a "civil body politic . . . to enact just and equal laws . . . for the general good of the colony, unto which we promise all due submission and obedience." After the Pilgrims landed at Plymouth, in what is today Massachusetts, they formed a colony based on the **Mayflower Compact**, thus setting a precedent of a government established by contract among the governed.

The Colonial Charters, 1624–1732

The **colonial charters** that authorized settlement of the colonies in America were granted by royal action. For some of the colonies, the British king granted official proprietary rights to an individual, as in Maryland (granted to Lord Baltimore), Pennsylvania (to William Penn), and Delaware (also to Penn). For other colonies, the king granted royal commissions to companies to establish governments, as in Virginia, Massachusetts, New Hampshire, New York, New Jersey, Georgia, and North and South Carolina. Royal charters were granted directly to the colonists themselves only in Connecticut and Rhode Island. These colonists drew up their charters and presented them to the king, setting a precedent in America for written contracts defining governmental power.

The "Charter Oak Affair" of 1685–88 began when King James II became displeased with his Connecticut subjects and issued an order for the repeal of the Connecticut

Charter. In 1687 Sir Edmund Andros went to Hartford, dissolved the colonial government, and demanded that the charter be returned. But Captain John Wadsworth hid it in an oak tree. After the so-called Glorious Revolution in England in 1688, the charter was taken out and used again as the fundamental law of the colony. Subsequent British monarchs silently acquiesced in this restoration of rights, and the affair strengthened the notion of loyalty to the constitution rather than to the king.

Declaration of Independence
The resolution adopted by the Second Continental Congress on July 4, 1776, that the American colonies are to be "free and Independent states." Drafted by Thomas Jefferson, it asserts natural law, inalienable rights, government by contract, and the right of revolution. John Hancock is said to have signed first in large letters so King George III could read it without his glasses.

The Declaration of Independence, 1776

The First Continental Congress, a convention of delegates from 12 of the 13 original colonies, came together in 1774 to protest British interference in American affairs. But the Revolutionary War did not begin until April 19, 1775. The evening before, British regular troops marched out from Boston to seize arms stored by citizens in Lexington and Concord, Massachusetts. At dawn the next morning, the Minutemen—armed citizens organized for the protection of their towns—engaged the British regulars in brief battles, then harassed them all the way back to Boston. In June of that year, the Second Continental Congress appointed George Washington commander in chief of American forces and sent him to Boston to take command of the American militia surrounding the city. Still, popular support for the Revolution remained limited, and even many members of the Continental Congress hoped only to force the king and his government to make changes—not to split off from Britain.

As this hope died, however, members of the Continental Congress came to view a formal **Declaration of Independence** as necessary to give legitimacy to their cause and establish the basis for a new nation. Accordingly, on July 2, 1776, the Continental Congress "Resolved, that these United Colonies are, and, of right, ought to be free and independent States." Thomas Jefferson had been commissioned to write a justification for the action, which he presented to the Congress on July 4, 1776. In writing the Declaration of Independence, Jefferson lifted several phrases directly from the English political philosopher John Locke asserting the rights of individuals, the contract theory of government, and the right of revolution. The declaration was signed first by the president of the Continental Congress, John Hancock.

The Revolutionary War effectively ended when British General Charles Cornwallis surrendered at Yorktown, Virginia, in October 1781. But even as the war was being waged, the new nation was creating the framework of its government.

Thomas Jefferson and the Declaration of Independence

Thomas Jefferson's opening words of the Declaration of Independence provide the most succinct summary of the role of government in a free society:

> We hold these truths to be self evident, that all men are created equal, that they are endowed by their Creator with certain unalienable Rights, that among these are Life, Liberty and the pursuit of Happiness. That to secure these rights Governments are instituted among Men, deriving their just powers from the consent of the governed. That whenever any Form of Government becomes destructive of these ends, it is the Right of the People to alter or abolish it, and to institute new Government. . . .

In this single paragraph, Jefferson asserts natural law and the natural rights derived from it, the social contract as the origin of government, government by the consent of the governed, and the right of revolution.

Jefferson was born into wealth and privilege in Virginia in 1743. He mastered Latin, Greek, and French and at age 14 inherited 5,000 acres of land and dozens of slaves on the plantation that eventually became known as Monticello. He graduated in two years from the College of William and Mary in Williamsburg with highest honors. He practiced law and served in the Virginia House of Burgesses and was sent by Virginia to the Continental Congress. There he was delegated the task of writing the Declaration of Independence, which was formally adopted July 4, 1776. He later served as governor of Virginia and as the American Minister to France, America's most important ally at the time. He did not attend the Constitutional Convention

3.1

3.2

3.3

3.4

3.5

3.6

3.7

3.8

Articles of Confederation
The original framework for the government of the United States, adopted in 1781 and superseded by the U.S. Constitution in 1789. It established a "firm league of friendship" among the states, rather than a government "of the people."

and gave only lukewarm support to the new Constitution, believing that it was flawed for lack of a Bill of Rights. After returning from France, he served as the nation's first secretary of state under President George Washington.

Jefferson can be credited with founding the American party system. In Washington's cabinet, he argued against the policies of Secretary of the Treasury Alexander Hamilton—policies that would strengthen the role of the federal government in business, banking, and commerce. He resigned from the cabinet and became the principal spokesperson for the emerging Anti-Federalists. He lost the presidency in 1796 to the Federalist candidate John Adams, but won enough electoral votes to become vice president. Prior to the election of 1800, Jefferson worked closely with Aaron Burr of New York to organize the Democratic-Republican party that would eventually become the Democratic Party. When all his party's electors cast their two votes for Jefferson and Burr, intending that Jefferson should be president and Burr vice president, the two men actually tied for the presidency. The Federalist-controlled House, after 36 ballots, and on the advice of Alexander Hamilton, finally elected Jefferson as president and Burr as vice president. Later Burr would kill Hamilton in a duel.

Jefferson's presidency was highlighted by the Louisiana Purchase, which doubled the size of the United States. He hoped that this purchase would provide the American people with farmland "to the hundredth and thousandth generation." When he spoke warmly of the wisdom of "the people," he was actually referring to those who owned and managed their own farms and estates. He believed that only those who owned land could make good citizens. He disliked aristocracy, but he also held the urban masses in contempt. He wanted to see the United States become a nation of free, educated, land-owning farmers. After leaving the presidency, Jefferson plunged into the planning and designing of the University of Virginia. His dream was realized with the opening of the university in 1825.

President John F. Kennedy welcomed 49 Nobel Prize winners to the White House in 1962, with his now famous tribute to Jefferson: "I think this is the most extraordinary collection of talent and of human knowledge that has ever been gathered together at the White House—with the possible exception of when Thomas Jefferson dined alone."

The Articles of Confederation, 1781–1789

Although Richard Henry Lee, a Virginia delegate to the Continental Congress, first proposed that the newly independent states form a confederation on July 6, 1776, the Continental Congress did not approve the **Articles of Confederation** until November 15, 1777, and the last state to sign them, Maryland, did not do so until March 1, 1781. Under the Articles, Congress was a single house in which each state had two to seven members but only one vote. Congress itself created and appointed executives, judges, and military officers. It also had the power to make war and peace, conduct foreign affairs, and borrow and print money. But Congress could *not* collect taxes or enforce laws directly; it had to rely on the states to provide money and enforce its laws. The United States under the Articles was really a confederation of nations. Within this "firm league of friendship" (Article III of the Articles of Confederation), the national government was thought of as an alliance of independent states, not as a government "of the people."

Troubles Confronting a New Nation

3.2 Assess the obstacles to nationhood.

Over two centuries ago, the United States was struggling to achieve nationhood. The new U.S. government achieved enormous successes under the Articles of Confederation: it won independence from Great Britain, the world's most powerful colonial nation at the time; it defeated vastly superior forces in a prolonged war for independence; it established a viable peace and won powerful allies (notably, France) in the international community; it created an effective army and navy, established a postal system, and laid the foundations for national unity. But despite these successes in war and diplomacy, the political arrangements under the Articles were unsatisfactory to many influential groups—notably, bankers and investors who held U.S. government bonds, plantation owners, real estate developers, and merchants and shippers.

☐ Financial Difficulties

Under the Articles of Confederation, Congress had no power to tax the people directly. Instead, Congress had to ask the states for money to pay its expenses, particularly the expenses of fighting the long and costly War of Independence with Great Britain. There was no way to force the states to make their payments to the national government. In fact, about 90 percent of the funds requisitioned by Congress from the states were never paid, so Congress had to borrow money from wealthy patriot investors to fight the war. Without the power to tax, however, Congress could not pay off these debts. Indeed, the value of U.S. governmental bonds fell to about 10 cents for every dollar's worth because few people believed the bonds would ever be paid off. Congress even stopped making interest payments on these bonds.

☐ Commercial Obstacles

Under the Articles of Confederation, states were free to tax the goods of other states. Without the power to regulate interstate commerce, the national government was unable to protect merchants from heavy tariffs imposed on shipments from state to state. Southern planters could not ship their agricultural products to northern cities without paying state-imposed tariffs, and northern merchants could not ship manufactured products from state to state without interference. Merchants, manufacturers, shippers, and planters all wanted to develop national markets and prevent the states from imposing tariffs or restrictions on interstate trade.

☐ Currency Problems

Under the Articles, the states themselves had the power to issue their own currency, regulate its value, and require that it be accepted in payment of debts. States had their own "legal tender" laws, which required creditors to accept state money if "tendered" in payment of debt. As a result, many forms of money were circulating: Virginia dollars, Rhode Island dollars, Pennsylvania dollars, and so on. Some states (Rhode Island, for example) printed a great deal of money, creating inflation in their currency and alienating banks and investors whose loans were being paid off in this cheap currency. If creditors refused payment in a particular state's currency, the debt could be abolished in that state. So finances throughout the states were very unstable, and banks and creditors were threatened by cheap paper money.

☐ Western Lands

Men of property in early America actively speculated in western land. But the Confederation's military weakness along its frontiers kept the value of western lands low. A strong central government with enough military power to oust the British from the Northwest and to protect western settlers against Indian attacks could open the way for the development of the American West. The protection and settlement of western land would cause land values to skyrocket and make land speculators rich. Moreover, under the Articles of Confederation each state lay claim to western lands. Indeed, Maryland's ratification of the Articles was withheld until the states with claims to lands west of the Appalachians were ceded to Congress in 1781 for "the good of the whole."

3.1

3.2

3.3

3.4

3.5

3.6

3.7

3.8

Shays's Rebellion
An armed revolt in 1786, led by a Revolutionary War Officer Daniel Shays, protesting the discontent of small farmers over debts and taxes, and raising concerns about the ability of the U.S. government under the Articles of Confederation to maintain internal order.

Annapolis Convention
A 1786 meeting at Annapolis, Maryland, to discuss interstate commerce, which recommended a larger convention—the Constitutional Convention of 1787.

Civil Disorder

In several states, debtors openly revolted against tax collectors and sheriffs attempting to repossess farms on behalf of creditors who held unpaid mortgages. The most serious rebellion broke out in the summer of 1786 in western Massachusetts, where a band of 2,000 insurgent farmers captured the courthouses in several counties and briefly held the city of Springfield. Led by Daniel Shays, a veteran of the Revolutionary War battle at Bunker Hill, the insurgent army posed a direct threat to investors, bankers, creditors, and tax collectors by burning deeds, mortgages, and tax records to wipe out proof of the farmers' debts. Shays's Rebellion, as it was called, was finally put down by a small mercenary army, paid for by well-to-do citizens of Boston.

Reports of **Shays's Rebellion** filled the newspapers of the large eastern cities. George Washington, Alexander Hamilton, James Madison, and many other prominent Americans wrote their friends about it. The event galvanized property owners to support the creation of a strong central government capable of dealing with "radicalism." Only a strong central government, they wrote one another, could "insure domestic tranquility," guarantee "a republican form of government," and protect property "against domestic violence." It is no accident that all of these phrases appear in the Constitution of 1787.

The Road to the Constitutional Convention

In the spring of 1785, some wealthy merchants from Virginia and Maryland met at Alexandria, Virginia, to try to resolve a conflict between the two states over commerce and navigation on the Potomac River and Chesapeake Bay. George Washington, the new nation's most prominent citizen, took a personal interest in the meeting. As a wealthy plantation owner and a land speculator who owned more than 30,000 acres of land upstream on the Potomac, Washington was keenly interested in commercial problems under the Articles of Confederation. He lent his great prestige to the Alexandria meeting by inviting the participants to his house at Mount Vernon. Out of this conference came the idea for a general economic conference for all of the states, to be held in Annapolis, Maryland, in September 1786.

The **Annapolis Convention** turned out to be a key stepping-stone to the Constitutional Convention of 1787. Instead of concentrating on commerce and navigation between the states, the delegates at Annapolis, including Alexander Hamilton and James Madison, called for a general constitutional convention to suggest remedies to what they saw as defects in the Articles of Confederation.

On February 21, 1787, the Congress called for a convention to meet in Philadelphia for the "sole and express purpose" of *revising* the Articles of Confederation and reporting to the Congress and the state legislatures "such alterations and provisions therein as shall, when agreed to in Congress and confirmed by the states, render the federal Constitution adequate to the exigencies of government and the preservation of the union." Notice that Congress did not authorize the convention to write a new constitution or to call constitutional conventions in the states to ratify a new constitution. State legislatures sent delegates to Philadelphia expecting that their task would be limited to revising the Articles and that revisions would be sent back to Congress and state legislatures for their approval. But that is not what happened.

The Nation's Founders

The 55 delegates to the Constitutional Convention, which met in Philadelphia in the summer of 1787, quickly discarded the congressional mandate to merely "revise" the Articles of Confederation. The Virginia delegation, led by James Madison, arrived before a quorum of seven states had assembled and used the time to draw up an entirely new constitutional document. After the first formal session opened on May 25 and George Washington was elected president of the convention, the Virginia Plan became the basis of discussion. Thus, at the very beginning of the convention, the decision was made to scrap the Articles of Confederation altogether, write a new constitution, and form a new national government.[2]

The Founders were very confident of their powers and abilities. They had been selected by their state legislatures (only Rhode Island, dominated by small farmers, refused to send a delegation). When Thomas Jefferson, then serving in the critical post of ambassador to France (the nation's military ally in the Revolutionary War), first saw the list of delegates, he exclaimed, "It is really an assembly of demigods." Indeed, among the nation's notables, only Jefferson and John Adams (then serving as ambassador to England) were absent. The eventual success of the convention, and the ratification of the new Constitution, resulted in part from the enormous prestige, experience, and achievements of the delegates themselves.

Above all, the delegates at Philadelphia were cosmopolitan. They approached political, economic, and military issues from a "continental" point of view. Unlike most Americans in 1787, their loyalties extended beyond their states. They were truly nationalists.[3]

the Enlightenment
Also known as the Age of Reason, a philosophical movement in eighteenth-century Western thought based on a belief in reason and the capacities of individuals, a faith in a scientific approach to knowledge, and a confidence in human progress.

natural law
The law that would govern humans in a state of nature before governments existed.

inalienable rights
The rights of all people derived from natural law and not bestowed by governments, including the rights to life, liberty, and property.

social contract
The idea the government originates from an implied contract among people who agree to obey laws in exchange for the protection of their natural rights.

republicanism
Government by representatives of the people rather than directly by the people themselves.

Consensus and Conflict in Philadelphia

3.3 Outline the principles on which the Founders were in agreement and characterize their areas of conflict.

The Founders shared many ideas about government, based on **the Enlightenment**. We often focus our attention on *conflict* in the Convention of 1787 and the compromises reached by the participants, but the really important story of the Constitution is the *consensus* that was shared by these men of influence.

Natural Rights to Liberty and Property

The Founders had read John Locke and absorbed his idea that the purpose of government is to protect individual liberty and property. They believed in a **natural law**, superior to any human-made laws, that endowed each person with certain **inalienable rights**—the rights to life, liberty, and property. They believed that all people were equally entitled to these rights. Most of them, including slave owners George Washington and Thomas Jefferson, understood that the belief in personal liberty conflicted with the practice of slavery and found the inconsistency troubling.

Social Contract

The Founders believed that government originated in an implied contract among people. People agreed to establish government, obey laws, and pay taxes in exchange for protection of their natural rights. This **social contract** gave government its legitimacy—a legitimacy that rested on the consent of the governed, not with gods or kings or force. If a government violated individual liberty, it broke the social contract and thus lost its legitimacy.

Representative Government

Although most of the world's governments in 1787 were hereditary monarchies, the Founders believed the people should have a voice in choosing their own representatives in government. They opposed hereditary aristocracy and titled nobility. Instead, they sought to forge a republic. **Republicanism** meant government by representatives of the people. The Founders expected the masses to consent to be governed by their leaders—men of principle and property with ability, education, and a stake in the preservation of liberty. The Founders believed the people should have only a limited role in directly selecting their representatives: they should vote for members of the House

3.1

3.2

3.3

3.4

3.5

3.6

3.7

3.8

nationalism
Belief that shared cultural, historical, linguistic, and social characteristics of a people justify the creation of a government encompassing all of them and that the resulting nation-state should be independent and legally equal to all other nation-states.

of Representatives, but senators, the president, and members of the Supreme Court should be selected by others more qualified to judge their ability.

☐ Limited Government

The Founders believed unlimited power was corrupting and a concentration of power was dangerous. They believed in a written constitution that limited the scope of governmental power. They also believed in dividing power within government by creating separate bodies able to check and balance one another's powers.

☐ Nationalism

Most important, the Founders shared a belief in **nationalism**—a strong and independent national (federal) government with power to govern directly, rather than through state governments. They sought to establish a government that would be recognized around the world as representing "We the people of the United States." Not everyone in America shared this enthusiasm for a strong federal government; indeed, opposition forces, calling themselves Anti-Federalists, almost succeeded in defeating the new Constitution. But the leaders meeting in Philadelphia in the summer of 1787 were convinced of the need for a strong central government that would share power with the states.

☐ Conflict

Consensus on basic principles of government was essential to the success of the Philadelphia convention. But conflict over the implementation of these principles not only tied up the convention for an entire summer but also later threatened to prevent the states from ratifying, or voting to approve, the document the convention produced.

The Game, the Rules, the Players

Locke, Guiding the Founders

The English political philosopher John Locke had a profound influence on America's founders. The Declaration of Independence is a restatement of Locke's basic ideas. Writing in 1690, Locke rejected the notion of the divine right of kings to rule and asserted the rights of human beings who are "by nature free, equal, and independent" to establish their own government by "social contract" to gain security from an unstable "state of nature."

Absent kings, organized governments, or societies, Locke assumed that there were laws governing men. These laws preceded government, and applied even in the presence of government. Several political philosophers, starting with Plato, had posited forms of natural law. Locke's natural law is often called "Liberal" natural law. The foundation of Locke's natural law was that men were born free, equal, and could only be ruled with their consent. Kings and theocrats could not presume to appeal to God for authority. Among the rights found in natural law were rights to life, to liberty, and also to the holding of property. If the government sought to deprive an individual of these rights, it would have to do so through procedures that recognized the individual's claims to sovereignty.

This agreement to procedures, laws, and rights was the foundation of an agreement, a social contract, between government and the people, in part to secure their rights. People consented to be governed to protect themselves and their property.

But if the government they create becomes arbitrary, enslaves its people, or takes away their property, then the people have the "right of revolution" against such a government. Locke had been read by most of the Founders, who accepted his ideas of a "social contract" as the origin of government, and even a "right of revolution" as a last resort to a despotic government. This liberal philosophy was the foundation of Jefferson's Declaration of Independence. In the statement crafted for the American people to the King, Jefferson delineated those natural rights held by free men. He then described how the King and his government had violated those rights. And, using this set of assumptions followed by evidence, he asserted the right of the people of the American colonies to declare their own sovereignty, freed from any previous obligation to the English monarch.

QUESTIONS

1. What are the main assumptions of Locke's approach to natural law?
2. Do you think government is necessary to defend one's rights and liberties?
3. As you proceed through this book, ask yourself: Is the changing relationship between the individual and the state and national governments protecting your liberty? Or impeding it? Do you need a new social contract?

Representation

Representation was the most controversial issue in Philadelphia. Following the election of George Washington as president of the convention, Governor Edmund Randolph of Virginia rose to present a draft of a new constitution. This Virginia Plan called for a legislature with two houses: a lower house chosen by the people of the states, with representation according to population; and an upper house to be chosen by the lower house (see Table 3.1). Congress was to have the broad power to "legislate in all cases to which the separate States are incompetent, or in which the harmony of the United States may be interrupted." Congress was to have the power to nullify state laws that it believed violated the Constitution, thus ensuring the national government's supremacy over the states. The Virginia Plan also proposed a form of **parliamentary government**, in which the legislature (Congress) chose the principal executive officers of the government as well as federal judges. Finally, the Virginia Plan included a curious "council of revision," with the power to veto acts of Congress.

parliamentary government
A government in which power is concentrated in the legislature, which chooses from among its members a prime minister and cabinet.

Connecticut Compromise
A constitutional plan that merged elements of a Virginia plan and a New Jersey plan into the present arrangement of the U.S. Congress: one house in which each state has an equal number of votes (the Senate) and one house in which states' votes are based on population (the House of Representatives).

Delegates from New Jersey and Delaware objected strongly to the great power given to the national government in the Virginia Plan, the larger representation it proposed for the more populous states, and the plan's failure to recognize the role of the states in the composition of the new government. After several weeks of debate, William Paterson of New Jersey submitted a counterproposal.[4] The New Jersey Plan called for a single-chamber Congress in which each state, regardless of its population, had one vote, just as under the Articles of Confederation. But unlike the Articles, the New Jersey Plan proposed separate executive and judicial branches of government and the expansion of the powers of Congress to include levying taxes and regulating commerce. Moreover, the New Jersey Plan included a National Supremacy Clause, declaring that the Constitution and federal laws would supersede state constitutions and laws.

Debate over representation in Congress raged into July 1787. At one point, the convention actually voted for the Virginia Plan, seven votes to three, but without New York, New Jersey, and Delaware, the new nation would not have been viable. Eventually, Roger Sherman of Connecticut came forward with a compromise. This **Connecticut Compromise**—sometimes called the Great Compromise—established two houses of Congress: in the upper house, the Senate, each state would have two members regardless of its size; in the lower body, the House of Representatives, each state would be represented according to population. Members of the House would be

TABLE 3.1 CONSTITUTIONAL COMPROMISE

A Senate with equal representation according to each state and a House with representation based on population, and a requirement that both bodies must approve legislation before it is enacted into law, was a political compromise between large and small states reached at the Constitutional Convention of 1787.

The Virginia Plan	The New Jersey Plan	The Connecticut Compromise The Constitution of 1787
Two-house legislature, with the lower house directly elected based on state population and the upper house elected by the lower.	One-house legislature, with equal state representation, regardless of population.	Two-house legislature, with the House directly elected based on state population and the Senate selected by the state legislatures; two senators per state, regardless of population.
Legislature with broad power, laws including veto power over passed by the state legislatures.	Legislature with the same power as under the Articles of Confederation, plus the power to levy some taxes and to regulate commerce.	Legislature with broad power, including the power to tax and to regulate commerce.
President and cabinet elected by the legislature.	Separate multiperson executive, elected by the legislature, removable by petition from a majority of the state governors.	President chosen by an Electoral College.
National judiciary elected by the legislature.	National judiciary appointed by the executive.	National judiciary appointed by the president and confirmed by the Senate.
"Council of Revision" with the power to veto laws of the legislature.	National Supremacy Clause similar to that found in Article VI of the 1787 Constitution.	National Supremacy Clause: the Constitution is "the supreme Law of the Land."

Three-Fifths Compromise
A compromise in the Constitutional Convention of 1787 between pre- and slave states in which slaves would be counted as three-fifths of a person for both taxation and representation.

directly elected by the people; members of the Senate would be selected by their state legislatures. Legislation would have to pass both houses to be enacted. This compromise was approved by the convention on July 16.

☐ Slavery

Another conflict absorbing the attention of the delegates was slavery. In 1787 slavery was legal everywhere except in Massachusetts. Nevertheless, the delegates were too embarrassed to use the word *slave* or *slavery* in their debates or in the Constitution itself. Instead, they referred to "other persons" and "persons held to service or labour."

Delegates from the southern states, where slaves were a large proportion of the population, believed slaves should be counted in representation afforded the states, but not counted if taxes were to be levied on a population basis. Delegates from the northern states, with small slave populations, believed that "the people" counted for representation purposes should include only free persons. The Connecticut Plan included the now-infamous **Three-Fifths Compromise**: three-fifths of the slaves of each state would be counted for purposes both of representation in the House of Representatives and for apportionment for direct taxes.

Slave owners also sought protection for their human "property" in the Constitution itself. They were particularly concerned about slaves running away to other states and claiming their freedom. So they succeeded in writing into the Constitution (Article IV, Section 2) a specific guarantee: "No person held to Service or Labour in one State . . . escaping into another, shall . . . be discharged from such Service or Labour, but shall be delivered up on Claim of the Party to whom such Service or Labour may be due."

Yet another compromise dealt with the slave trade. The capture, transportation, and "breaking in" of African slaves was considered a nasty business, even by southern planters. Many wealthy Maryland and Virginia plantations were already well supplied with slaves and thus could afford the luxury of conscience to call for an end to slave importation. But other planters from the less-developed southern states, particularly South Carolina and Georgia, wanted additional slave labor. The final compromise prohibited the slave trade—but not before the year 1808, thereby giving the planters twenty years to import all the slaves they needed before the slave trade ended.

☐ Voter Qualifications

Another important conflict centered on qualifications for voting and holding office in the new government. Most of the delegates believed that voters as well as officeholders should be men of property. (Only Benjamin Franklin went so far as to propose universal *male* suffrage.) But delegates argued over the specific wording of property qualifications, their views on the subject reflecting the source of their own wealth. Merchants, bankers, and manufacturers objected to making the ownership of a certain amount of land a qualification for officeholding. James Madison, a plantation owner himself, was forced to admit that "landed possessions were no certain evidence of real wealth. Many enjoyed them who were more in debt than they were worth."

After much debate, the convention approved a constitution without any expressed property qualifications for voting or holding office, except those that the states might impose themselves: "The Electors in each State shall have the Qualifications requisite for Electors of the most numerous Branch of the State Legislature." At the time, every state had property qualifications for voting, and women were not permitted to vote or hold office. (The New Jersey Constitution of 1776 enfranchised women as well as men who owned property, but in 1787 a new state law limited the vote to "free white male citizens.")

The Game, the Rules, the Players

George Washington, Founder of a Nation

From the time he took command of the American Revolutionary forces in 1775 until he gave his Farewell Address to the nation in 1796 and returned to his Mount Vernon plantation, George Washington (1732–99) was, indeed, "First in war, first in peace, first in the hearts of his countrymen." His military success, combined with his diplomacy and practical political acumen, gave him overwhelming moral authority, which he used to inspire the Constitutional Convention, to secure the ratification of the Constitution, and then to guide the new nation through its first years.

Washington was raised on a Virginia plantation and inherited substantial landholdings, including his Mount Vernon plantation on the Potomac River. He began his career as a surveyor. His work took him deep into the wilderness of America's frontier. This experience later served him well when, at age 21, he was appointed to be an officer in the Virginia militia. In 1754 he led a small force toward the French Fort Duquesne, but after a brief battle at makeshift "Fort Necessity" he was obliged to retreat. In 1755, British Major General Edward Braddock asked Washington to accompany his heavy regiments on a campaign to dislodge the French from Fort Duquesne. Braddock disregarded Washington's warnings about unconventional combat and parading redcoat forces were ambushed by the French and Indians near Pittsburgh, and the general was killed. Washington rallied what remained of the British forces and led them in a successful retreat back to Virginia.

Washington was subsequently appointed by the Virginia Assembly "Colonel of the Virginia Regiment and Commander in Chief of all Virginia Forces." When the British occupied Fort Duquesne (renamed Fort Pitt), Washington was given the task of garrisoning it. Washington left his military post in 1759 to return to plantation life. He married a wealthy widow, Martha Custis, expanded his plantation holdings, and prospered in western land speculation.

The Virginia legislature elected Washington to attend the First Continental Congress in September 1774. Washington was the most celebrated veteran of the French and Indian Wars who was still young enough (42) to lead military forces in a new struggle. John Adams of Massachusetts was anxious to unite the continent in the coming contest, and he persuaded the Second Continental Congress to give the Virginian command of the American Revolutionary forces surrounding the British Army in Boston in 1775.

Throughout the Revolutionary War, Washington persevered by employing many of the tactics later defined as the principles of guerrilla warfare. By retreating deep into Pennsylvania's Valley Forge, Washington avoided defeat and saved his army. His bold Christmas night attack against Hessian troops at Trenton, New Jersey, encouraged French intervention on America's behalf. Slowly, Washington was able to wear down the British resolve to fight. After a six-year campaign, he trapped the British at Yorktown, Virginia. Assisted by a French naval blockade, he accepted the surrender of Lord Cornwallis's 8,000 men on October 19, 1781.

Washington's greatest contribution to American democratic government occurred in 1783 in Newburgh, New York, near West Point, where the veterans of his Continental Army were encamped. These soldiers, unpaid and ignored by Congress, threatened to use military force if Congress continued to deny their benefits and invited Washington to lead them. Washington addressed the men and denounced the use of force to lead a coup against Congress. Washington chose to preserve representative government rather than assume military rule.

One of the few noncontroversial decisions of the Constitutional Convention in 1787 was the selection of George Washington to preside over the meetings. He took little part in the debates; however, his enormous prestige helped to hold the convention together and later to win support for the new Constitution.

QUESTIONS

1. What is Washington's most durable legacy?
2. Was he a "democrat"?

The Economy and National Security

3.4 Analyze the economic and security issues that the Founders faced and the solutions they reached.

The Founders were just as concerned with "who gets what, when, and how" as today's politicians are. Important economic interests were at stake in the Constitution. Historian Charles A. Beard pointed out that the delegates to the Constitutional Convention were men of wealth: planters, slaveholders, merchants, manufacturers, shippers, bankers and investors, and land speculators. Moreover, most of the delegates owned Revolutionary War bonds that were now worthless and would remain so unless the national government could obtain the tax

3.1

taxes
Compulsory payments to the government.

3.2

tariff
Tax imposed on imported products (also called a customs duty).

3.3

common market
Unified trade area in which all goods and services can be sold or exchanged free from customs or tariffs.

3.4

3.5

3.6

3.7

3.8

revenues to pay them off.[5] But it is certainly not true that the Founders acted only out of personal interest. Wealthy delegates were found on both sides of constitutional debates, arguing principles as well as economic interests.[6]

☐ Levying Taxes

A central purpose of the Constitution was to enable the national government to levy its own **taxes**, so that it could end its dependence on state contributions and achieve financial credibility. The very first power given to Congress in Article I, Section 8, is the power to tax: "The Congress shall have Power to lay and collect Taxes, Duties, Imposts and Excises, to pay the Debts and provide for the common Defence and general Welfare."

The financial credit of the United States and the interests of Revolutionary War bondholders were guaranteed by Article VI in the Constitution, which specifically declared that the new government would be obligated to pay the debts of the old government. Indeed, the nation's first secretary of the treasury, Alexander Hamilton, made repayment of the national debt the first priority of the Washington administration.

The original Constitution placed most of the tax burden on consumers in the form of **tariffs** on goods imported into the United States. For more than a century, these tariffs provided the national government with its principal source of revenue. Tariffs were generally favored by American manufacturers, who wished to raise the price paid for foreign goods to make their home-produced goods more competitive. No taxes were permitted on *exports*, a protection for southern planters, who exported most of their tobacco and, later, cotton. Direct taxes on individuals were prohibited (Article I, Section 2) except in proportion to *population*. This provision prevented the national government from levying direct taxes in proportion to income until the 16th Amendment (income tax) was ratified in 1913.

The power to tax and spend was given to Congress, not to the president or executive agencies. Instead, the Constitution was very specific: "No Money shall be drawn from the Treasury, but in Consequence of Appropriations made by Law." This is the constitutional basis of Congress's "power of the purse."

☐ Regulating Commerce

The new Constitution gave Congress the power to "regulate Commerce with foreign Nations, and among the several States" (Article I, Section 8), and it prohibited the states from imposing tariffs on goods shipped across state lines (Article I, Section 10). This power created what we call today a **common market**: it protected merchants against state-imposed tariffs and stimulated trade among the states. States were also prohibited from "impairing the Obligation of Contracts"—that is, passing any laws that would allow debtors to avoid their obligations to banks and other lenders.

☐ Protecting Money

The Constitution also ensured that the new national government would control the money supply. Congress was given the power to coin money and regulate its value. More important, the states were prohibited from issuing their own paper money, thus protecting bankers and creditors from the repayment of debts in cheap state currencies. (No one wanted to be paid for goods or labor in Rhode Island's inflated dollars.) If only the national government could issue money, the Founders hoped, inflation could be minimized.

☐ Protecting National Security

At the start of the Revolutionary War, the Continental Congress had given George Washington command of a small regular army—"Continentals"—paid for by Congress, and also had authorized him to take command of state militia units. During the entire war, most of Washington's troops had been state militia. (The "militia" in those days was composed of every free adult male; each was expected to bring his own gun.) Washington himself had frequently decried the militia units as undisciplined,

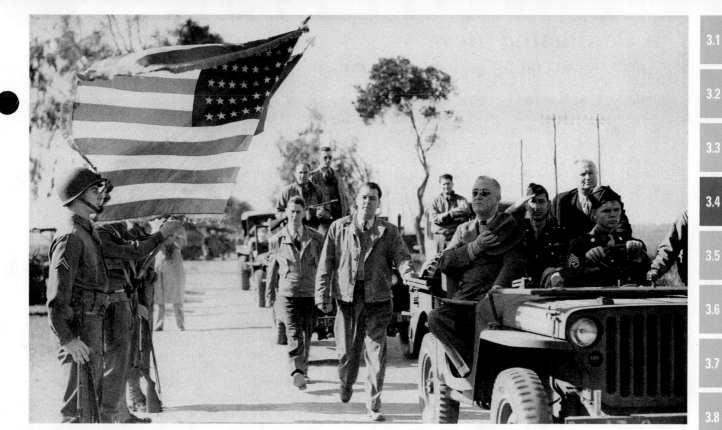

WARTIME CAN DEFINE A PRESIDENCY

One of America's most successful wartime presidents, Franklin Delano Roosevelt, led a comprehensive mobilization during World War II that fundamentally changed America into the world's leading power.

untrained, and unwilling to follow his orders. He wanted the new United States to have a *regular* army and navy, paid for by the Congress with its new taxing power, to back up the state militia units.

War and the Military Forces

Congress was authorized to "declare War," to raise and support a regular army and navy, and to make rules regulating these forces. It was also authorized to call up the militia, as it had done in the Revolution, in order to "execute the Laws of the Union, suppress Insurrections and repel Invasions." When the militia are called into national service, they come under the rule of Congress and the command of the president.

The United States relied primarily on militia—citizen-soldiers organized in state units—until World War I. The regular U.S. Army, stationed in coastal and frontier forts, directed most of its actions against Native Americans. The major actions in America's nineteenth-century wars—the War of 1812 against the British, the Mexican War of 1846–48, the Civil War in 1861–65, and the Spanish-American War in 1898—were fought largely by citizen-soldiers from these state units.

Commander in Chief

Following the precedent set in the Revolutionary War, the new president, whom everyone expected to be George Washington, was made "Commander in Chief of the Army and Navy of the United States, and of the Militia of the several States, when called into the actual Service of the United States." Clearly, there is some overlap in responsibility for national defense: Congress has the power to declare war, but the president is Commander in Chief. During the next two centuries, the president would order U.S. forces into 200 or more military actions, but Congress would pass an official Declaration of War only five times. Conflict between the president and Congress over war-making powers continues to this day.

A Conflicting View

An Economic Interpretation of the Constitution

Charles Beard, historian and political scientist, provided the most controversial historical interpretation of the origin of American national government in his landmark book, *An Economic Interpretation of the Constitution of the United States* (1913). Not all historians agree with Beard's economic interpretation, but all concede that it is a milestone in understanding the U.S. Constitution. Beard closely studied unpublished financial records of the U.S. Treasury Department and the personal letters and financial accounts of the 55 delegates to the Philadelphia convention. He concluded that they represented the following five economic interest groups, each of which benefited from specific provisions of the Constitution:

- ***Public security interests*** (persons holding U.S. bonds from the Revolutionary War; 37 of the 55 delegates). The taxing power was of great benefit to the holders of public securities, particularly when it was combined with the provision in Article VI that "all Debts contracted and Engagements entered into, before the Adoption of this Constitution, shall be as valid against the United States under this Constitution, as under the Confederation." That is, the national government would be obliged to pay off all those investors who held U.S. bonds, and the taxing power would give the national government the ability to do so on its own.
- ***Merchants and manufacturers*** (persons engaged in shipping and trade; 11 of the 55 delegates). The Interstate Commerce Clause, which eliminated state control over commerce, and the provision in Article I, Section 9, which prohibited the states from taxing exports, created a free-trade area, or "common market," among the thirteen states.
- ***Bankers and investors*** (24 of 55 delegates). Congress was given the power to make bankruptcy laws, to coin money and regulate its value, to fix standards of weights and measures, to punish counterfeiting, to establish post offices and post roads, to pass copyright and patent laws to protect authors and inventors, and to punish piracies and felonies committed on the high seas. Each of these powers is a specific asset to bankers and investors as well as merchants, authors, inventors, and shippers.
- ***Western land speculators*** (persons who purchased large tracts of land west of the Appalachian Mountains; 14 of the 55 delegates). If western settlers were to be protected from the Indians, and if the British were to be persuaded to give up their forts in Ohio and open the way to American westward expansion, the national government could not rely on state militias but must have an army of its own. Western land speculators welcomed the creation of a national army that would be employed primarily as an Indian-fighting force over the next century.
- ***Slave owners*** (15 of the 55 delegates). Protection against domestic insurrection also appealed to the Southern slaveholders' deep-seated fear of a slave revolt. The Constitution permitted Congress to outlaw the *import of slaves* after the year 1808. But most Southern planters were more interested in protecting their existing property and slaves than they were in extending the slave trade, and the Constitution provided an explicit advantage to slaveholders in Article IV, Section 2 (later revoked by the 13th Amendment, which abolished slavery), by specifically requiring the forced return of slaves who might escape to free states.

Beard argued that the members of the Philadelphia convention who drafted the Constitution were, with a few exceptions, immediately, directly, and personally interested in, and derived economic advantages from, the establishment of the new system. But many historians disagree with Beard's emphasis on the economic motives of the Founders. The Constitution, they point out, was adopted in a society that was fundamentally democratic, and it was adopted by people who were primarily middle-class property owners, especially farmers, rather than owners of businesses. The Constitution was not just an economic document, although economic factors were certainly important.

QUESTIONS

1. How are property rights incorporated into the Constitution? Why?
2. Why are private property and contracts important in Beard's analysis of the Constitution?
3. Do you think that framing the Constitution as an economic document reduces its democratic appeal?
4. Do you have to choose between property rights and political equality?

☐ Foreign Affairs

The national government also assumed full power over foreign affairs and prohibited the states from entering into any "Treaty, Alliance, or Confederation." The Constitution gave the president, not Congress, the power to "make Treaties" and "appoint Ambassadors." However, the Constitution stipulated that the president could do these things only "by and with the Advice and Consent of the Senate," indicating an unwillingness to allow the president to act autonomously in these matters. The Senate's power to "advise and consent" to treaties and appointments, together with the congressional power over appropriations, gives the Congress important influence in foreign affairs. Nevertheless, the president remains the dominant figure in this arena.

National Supremacy Clause
The clause in Article VI of the U.S. Constitution declaring the Constitution and federal laws "the supreme Law of the Land" superior to state laws and constitutions and requiring state judges to be bound thereby.

The Structure of the Government

3.5 Explain how the Constitution structured the new government.

The Constitution that emerged from the Philadelphia convention on September 17, 1787, founded a new government with a unique structure. That structure was designed to implement the Founders' beliefs in nationalism, limited government, republicanism, the social contract, and the protection of liberty and property. The Founders were realists; they did not have any romantic notions about the wisdom and virtue of "the people." James Madison wrote, "A dependence on the people is, no doubt, the primary control on the government, but experience has taught mankind the necessity of auxiliary precautions." The key structural arrangements in the Constitution—national supremacy, federalism, republicanism, separation of powers, checks and balances, and judicial review—all reflect the Founders' desire to create a strong national government while at the same time ensuring that it would not become a threat to liberty or property.

National Supremacy

The heart of the Constitution is the **National Supremacy Clause** of Article VI:

> This Constitution, and the Laws of the United States which shall be made in Pursuance thereof, and all Treaties made, or which shall be made, under the Authority of the United States, shall be the supreme Law of the Land, and the Judges in every State shall be bound thereby, any Thing in the Constitution or Laws of any State to the Contrary notwithstanding.

This sentence ensures that the Constitution itself is the supreme law of the land and that laws passed by Congress supersede state laws. This National Supremacy Clause establishes the authority of the Constitution and the U.S. government.

Federalism

The Constitution *divides power* between the nation and the states. It recognizes that both the national government and the state governments have independent legal authority over their own citizens: both can pass their own laws, levy their own taxes, and maintain their own courts. The states have an important role in the selection of national officeholders—in the apportionment of congressional seats and in the allocation of electoral votes for president. Most important, perhaps, both the Congress and three-quarters of the states must consent to changes in the Constitution itself.

Republicanism

To the Founders, a *republican* government meant the delegation of powers by the people to a small number of gifted individuals "whose wisdom may best discern the true interest of their country, and whose patriotism and love of justice, will be least likely to sacrifice it to temporary or partial considerations."[7] The Founders believed that enlightened leaders of principle and property with ability, education, and a stake in the preservation of liberty could govern the people better than the people

A Conflicting View

The Supremacy Clause at Work in the Curious Case of Cannabis

The legal status of marijuana is a source of ongoing political debate in the United States. This debate centers on three issues: (1) medical use, (2) production for controlled (medical) distribution, and (3) decriminalization of possession and production.

Many doctors, patients, and organizations contend that marijuana, medically known as cannabis, is valuable in the treatment of glaucoma, HIV-AIDS, nausea, and pain relief, especially in cancer patients. As of 2012, 15 states have enacted medical marijuana laws reversing state-level penalties for possession and cultivation when patients possess written documentation from physicians stating that they benefit from its medical use (eight additional states have decriminalized marijuana possession but do not allow for medical prescription).[a] Colorado and Washington State have gone even further, legalizing both medical and recreational use of marijuana. National polls regularly report that 75 percent of the American public support making marijuana legally available to seriously ill patients.

The Controlled Substances Act classifies marijuana as a Schedule I controlled substance, which means that it "has a high potential for abuse . . . no currently accepted medical use in treatment in the United States . . . [and] a lack of accepted safety for use of the drug or other substance under medical supervision." Schedule I substances cannot be prescribed. According to the DEA, a drug need not have the abuse potential of "proven" Schedule I narcotics like heroin or cocaine to be placed in Schedule I. Petitions to the federal Drug Enforcement Agency to declassify marijuana as a controlled substance and allow physicians to legally prescribe its use have been rejected. (There is no documented death from an overdose of tetrahydrocannabinol, the psychoactive substance in cannabis.)

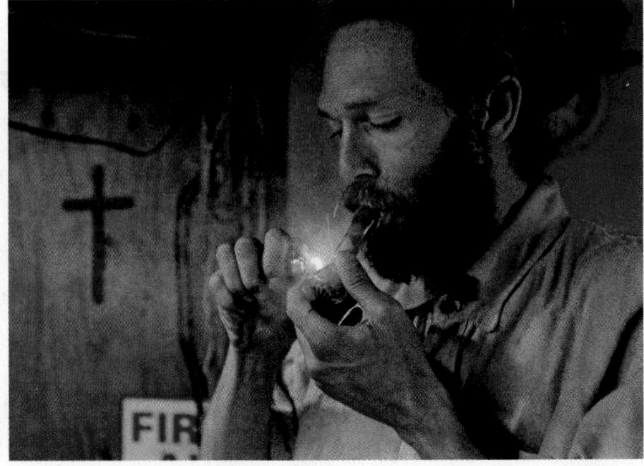

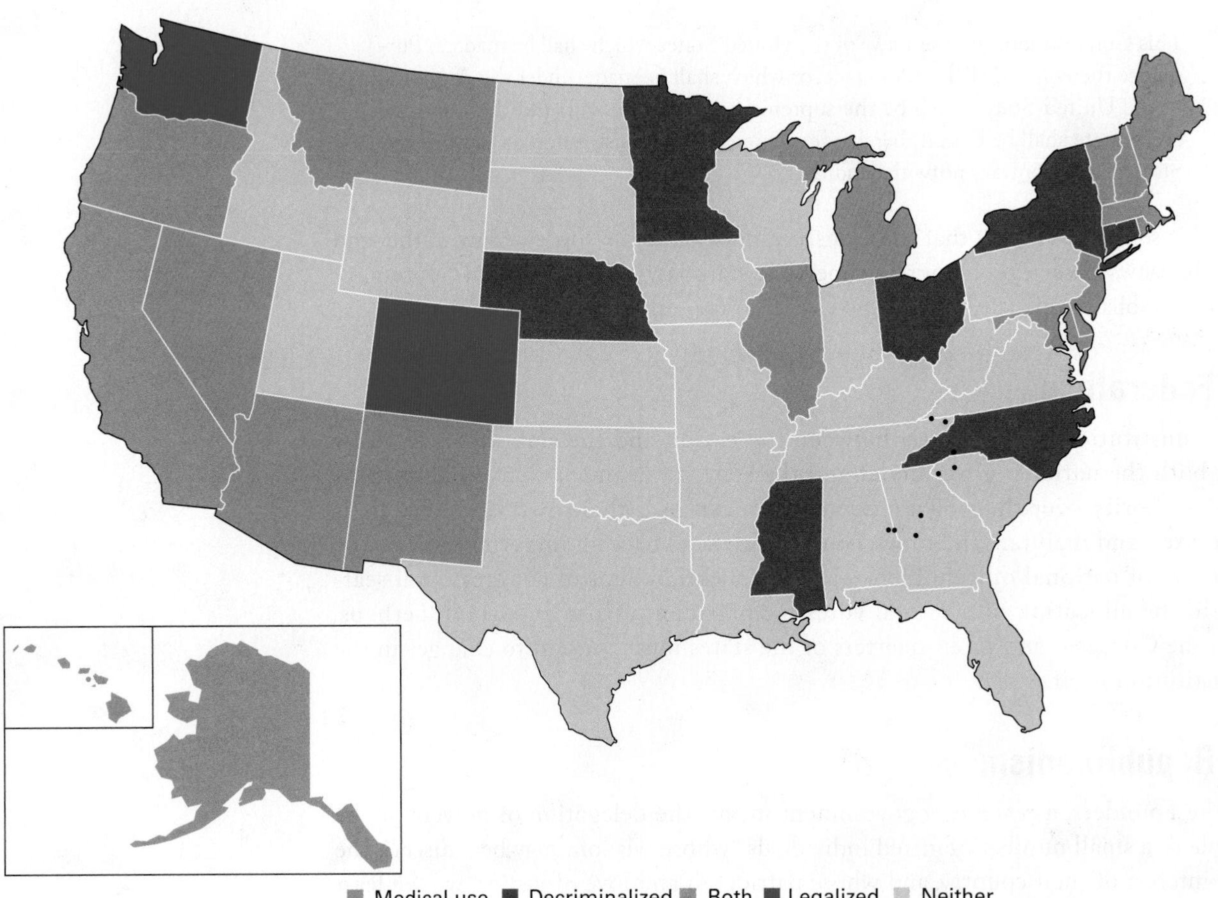

[a]National Association for the Reform of Marijuana Laws. www.norml.org.

(*Continued*)

Federal law is in direct conflict with the laws of many states on this issue. But the Supremacy Clause of the Constitution clearly requires that federal law prevail over state law in cases of conflict. When the issue reached the U.S. Supreme Court in 2001, the Court recognized that whether or not the activities of individuals or organizations regarding marijuana were legal under California law, they nonetheless violated federal law. The Court further held that "medical necessity" does not allow anyone to violate the Controlled Substance Act—Congress made no exemption in this act for medical necessity. "Under the Supremacy Clause, any state law, however clearly within a state's acknowledged power, which interferes with or is contrary to federal laws must yield."[b]

Prosecuting seriously ill patients or their doctors for using marijuana medically is not politically popular. Under President Obama, the U.S. Department of Justice announced that it would not "focus federal resources" on marijuana users who were in compliance with state laws. Nonetheless, there are limits to the cannabis revolution. Voters in some states where medical marijuana is legal appear to have reservations about further efforts to legalize marijuana. But voters in Washington and Colorado voters approved recreational use of marijuana in 2012. Both states have realized increased tax revenue from legalized cannabis use.

QUESTIONS

1. What are the circumstances that favor legalizing marijuana by state voters?
2. What are the main arguments in favor of decriminalizing pot? Against?

[b]*United States v. Oakland Cannabis Buyers Cooperatives* 523 U.S. 483 (2001).

could govern themselves. So they gave the voters only a limited voice in the selection of government leaders.

The Constitution of 1787 created *four* decision-making bodies, each with separate numbers of members, terms of office, and selection processes (see Table 3.2). Note that in the *original* Constitution only one of these four bodies—the House of Representatives—was to be directly elected by the people. The other three were removed from direct popular control: state legislatures selected U.S. senators; "Electors" (chosen at the discretion of the state legislatures) selected the president; the president appointed Supreme Court and other federal judges.

referenda
Proposed laws or constitutional amendments submitted to the voters for their direct approval or rejection, found in state constitutions, but not in the U.S. Constitution.

☐ Democracy?

The Founders believed that government rests ultimately on "the consent of the governed." But their notion of republicanism envisioned decision making by *representatives* of the people, not the people themselves. The U.S. Constitution does not provide for *direct* voting by the people on national questions; that is, unlike many state constitutions today, it does *not* provide for national **referenda**. Moreover, as noted earlier, only the House of Representatives (sometimes referred to even today as "the people's house") was to be elected directly by voters in the states.

TABLE 3.2 DECISION-MAKING BODIES IN THE CONSTITUTION OF 1787

The Constitution of 1787 established four decision-making bodies, only one of which—the House of Representatives—was to be directly elected by the people.

House of Representatives	Senate	President	Supreme Court
Members alloted to each state "according to their respective numbers," but each state guaranteed at least one member.	"Two senators from each state" (regardless of the size of the state).	Single executive.	No size specified in the Constitution, but by tradition, nine.
Two-year term. No limits on number of terms that can be served.	Six-year term. No limits on number of terms that can be served.	Four-year term (later limited to two terms by the 22nd Amendment in 1951).	Life term or until retirement
Directly elected by "the People of the several States."	Selected by the state legislatures (later changed to direct election by the 17th Amendment in 1913).	Selected by "Electors," appointed in each state "In such Manner as the Legislature thereof may direct" and equal to the total number of U.S. senators and House members to which the state is entitled in Congress.	Appointed by the president, "by and with the Advice and Consent of the Senate."

3.1

3.2

3.3

3.4

3.5

3.6

3.7

3.8

Who's Getting What?

Should We Call a New Constitutional Convention?

Does the United States need a new, more democratic, more perfect constitution? The U.S. Constitution was drafted more than 220 years ago for a small newly independent federation with about 3 million persons in 13 member states. Does it work today for the world's most powerful nation with over 300 million persons, 50 states, five territories, and global interests? Should we call a new Constitutional Convention?

What are the problems that exist with the present-day U.S. Constitution? Prominent political scientists have pondered this question and voiced the following concerns:

- The current Constitution gives small population states the same influence in the U.S. Senate as it gives large states. The current constitution severely dilutes the voice of citizens in large population states, such as California, Texas, and New York, and greatly amplifies the voice of citizens in small states, such as Wyoming, Alaska, and Vermont.
- Not only is the Senate a seriously undemocratic body, but the Electoral College (with the number of each state delegation equal to the number of its congressional delegation of members of the House and Senate) also distorts the voice of the American people in presidential elections. George W. Bush was elected president in 2000 despite losing the national popular vote.
- Members of the U.S. House face very few competitive elections, depriving voters of effective choices for their congressional representatives, largely because members of Congress work with state parties in redistricting to design electoral districts to maximize "safe" seats.
- Presidents can go to war and send U.S. troops into combat around the world, contrary to the wishes of Congress and the American people.

What should be done? Among the recommendations:

- Grant states up to four senators based on population size.
- Mandate nonpartisan redistricting for House elections.
- Establish term limits for representatives and senators, thus restoring the founders' principle of frequent rotation in office.
- Add a Balanced Budget Amendment, with appropriate escape clauses, in order to encourage fiscal fairness to future generations.
- Limit presidential war-making powers and expand Congress's oversight of war making by incorporating into the Constitution a requirement for congressional assent to ongoing wars at regular intervals.

But would a Constitutional Convention create more heat than light, more conflict than consensus, more threats than guarantees to individual liberty? Conflicts over the current hot-button social and cultural issues—immigration, abortion, prayer in schools, gay rights, the death penalty, the rights of criminal defendants, gun control, and the like—may poison debate and make compromise on these topics unlikely. "Any attempt to place constitutional provisions on either side of these cultural grenades would probably explode the process." Efforts to reform the structure of American government and politics would most likely give way to attempts to "strengthen" or "weaken" the Bill of Rights.

QUESTIONS

1. It has been argued that the purpose of the amending and convention process was to allow for periodic debate and revision of our framing document. Do you think that such a conversation is needed in the United States? What topics would you want to see addressed?
2. As you progress through this seminar, ask yourself, 'what changes would I propose in a new constitution?'
3. What do you think are the potential benefits of a new constitutional convention? The dangers?
4. Do you think the public would accept a new convention's proposed constitution as legitimate?

SOURCES: Sanford Levinson, *Our Undemocratic Constitution: Where the Constitution Goes Wrong (and How the People Can Correct It)*. New York: Oxford University Press, 2006. Larry J. Sabato, *A More Perfect Constitution: 25 Proposals, to Revitalize Our Constitution and Make America a Fairer Country*. New York: Walker & Company, 2007.

These republican arrangements may appear "undemocratic" from our perspective today, but in 1787, the U.S. Constitution was more democratic than any other governing system in the world. Although other nations were governed by monarchs, emperors, chieftains, and hereditary aristocracies, the Founders recognized that government depended on the *consent of the governed.* Later democratic impulses in America greatly altered the original Constitution (see "Constitutional Change" later in this chapter) and reshaped it into a much more democratic document. (See also *What Do You Think?* Should We Call a New Constitutional Convention?)

Separation of Powers and Checks and Balances

3.6 Analyze the separation of powers and the checks and balances established by the Constitution.

The Founders believed that unlimited power was corrupting and that the concentration of power was dangerous. James Madison wrote, "Ambition must be made to counteract ambition." The **separation of powers** within the national government—the creation of separate legislative, executive, and judicial branches in Articles I, II, and III of the Constitution—was designed to place internal controls on governmental power. Power is not only apportioned among three branches of government, but, perhaps more important, each branch is given important **checks and balances** over the actions of the others (see Figure 3.1).

separation of powers
Constitutional division of powers among the three branches of the national government—legislative, executive, and judicial.

checks and balances
Constitutional provisions giving each branch of the national government certain checks over the actions of other branches.

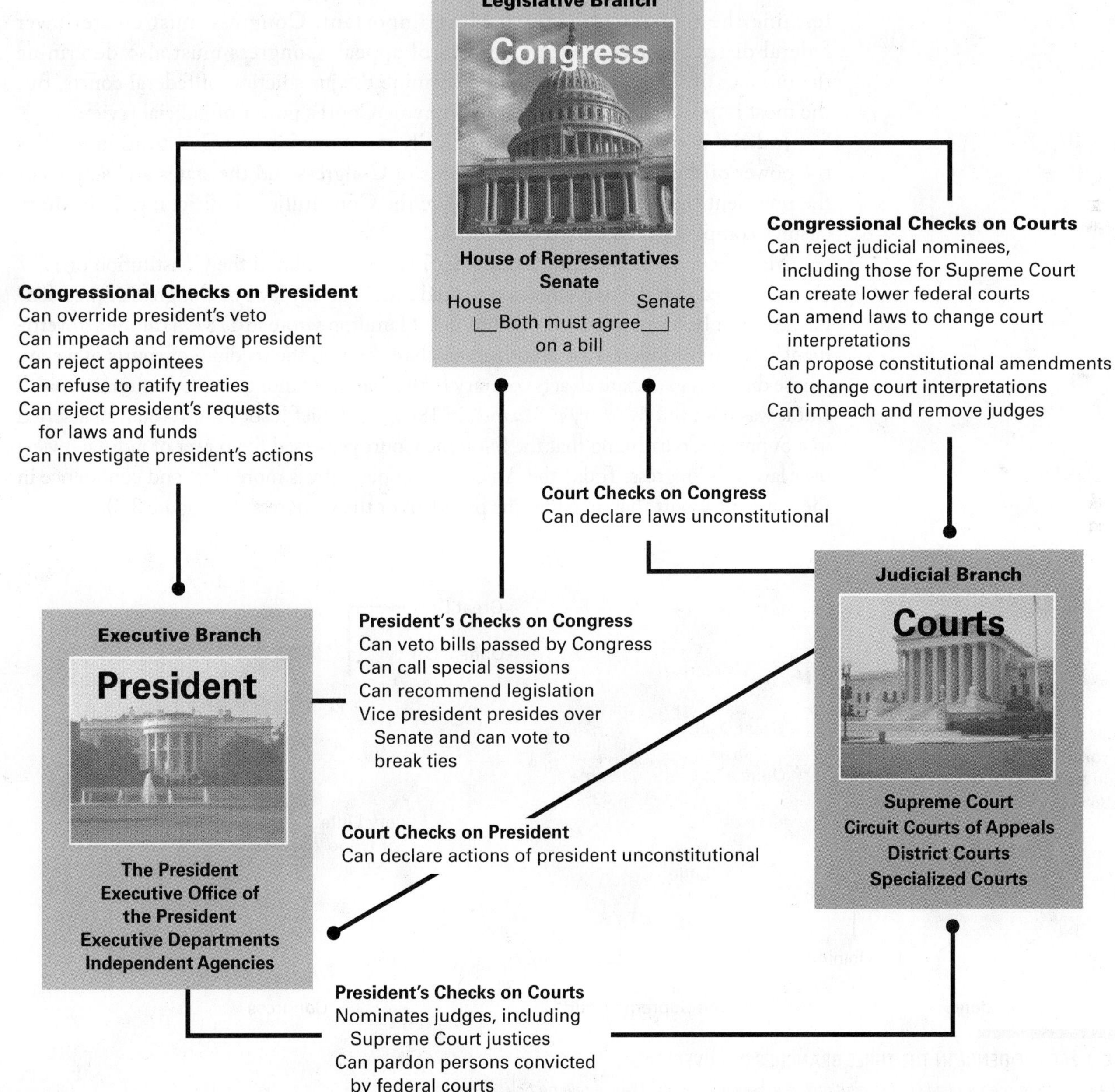

FIGURE 3.1 CHECKS AND BALANCES

3.1
3.2
3.3
3.4
3.5
3.6
3.7
3.8

judicial review
Power of the U.S. Supreme Court and federal judiciary to declare laws of Congress and the states and actions of the president unconstitutional and therefore legally invalid.

According to Madison, "The constant aim is to divide and arrange the several offices in such a manner as that each may be a check on the other."[8] No bill can become a law without the approval of both the House and the Senate. The president shares legislative power through the power to sign or to veto laws of Congress, although Congress may override a presidential veto with a two-thirds vote in each house. The president may also suggest legislation, "give to the Congress Information of the State of the Union, and recommend to their Consideration such Measures as he shall judge necessary and expedient." The president may also convene special sessions of Congress.

However, the president's power of appointment is shared by the Senate, which confirms cabinet and ambassadorial appointments. The president must also secure the advice and consent of the Senate for any treaty. The president must execute the laws, but it is Congress that provides the money to do so. The president and the rest of the executive branch may not spend money that has not been appropriated by Congress. Congress must also authorize the creation of executive departments and agencies. Finally, Congress may impeach and remove the president from office for "Treason, Bribery, or other High Crimes and Misdemeanors."

Members of the Supreme Court are appointed by the president and confirmed by the Senate. Traditionally, this court has nine members, but Congress may determine the number of justices. More important, Congress must create lower federal district courts as well as courts of appeal. Congress must also determine the number of these judgeships and determine the jurisdiction of federal courts. But the most important check of all is the Supreme Court's power of judicial review.

Judicial review, which is not specifically mentioned in the Constitution itself, is the power of the judiciary to overturn laws of Congress and the states and actions of the president that the courts believe violate the Constitution. Judicial review, in short, ensures compliance with the Constitution.

Many Federalists, including Alexander Hamilton, believed the Constitution of 1787 clearly implied that the Supreme Court could invalidate any laws of Congress or presidential actions it believed to be unconstitutional. Hamilton wrote in 1787, "[Limited government] . . . can be preserved in no other way than through the medium of courts of justice, whose duty it is to declare all acts contrary to the manifest tenor of the Constitution void."[9] But it was not until *Marbury v. Madison* in 1803 that Chief Justice John Marshall asserted in a Supreme Court ruling that the Supreme Court possessed the power of judicial review over laws of Congress. Today the American people express more trust and confidence in the Supreme Court than in either the president or the Congress (see Figure 3.2).

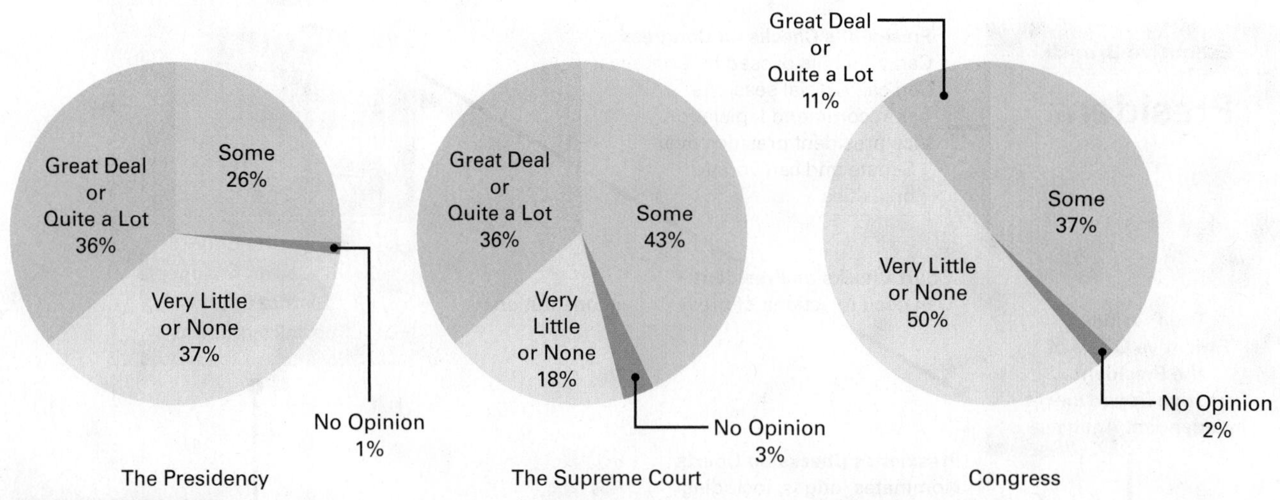

FIGURE 3.2 CONFIDENCE IN THE THREE BRANCHES OF GOVERNMENT

"Now I am going to read you a list of institutions in American society. Please tell me how much confidence you, yourself, have in each one—a great deal or quite a lot, some, or very little or none?"

SOURCE: Derived from Gallup, June 2009.

Conflict over Ratification

3.7 Outline the arguments made for and against ratification of the Constitution.

Today the U.S. Constitution is a revered document, but in the winter of 1787–88, the Founders had real doubts about whether they could get it accepted as "the supreme Law of the Land." Indeed, the Constitution was ratified by only the narrowest of margins in the key states of Massachusetts, Virginia, and New York.

The Founders adopted a **ratification** procedure that was designed to enhance the Constitution's chances for acceptance. The ratification procedure written into the new Constitution was a complete departure from what was then supposed to be the law of the land, the Articles of Confederation, in two major ways. First, the Articles of Confederation required that amendments be approved by *all* of the states. But since Rhode Island was firmly in the hands of small farmers, the Founders knew that unanimous approval was unlikely. So they simply wrote into their new Constitution that approval required only nine of the states. Second, the Founders called for special ratifying conventions in the states rather than risk submitting the Constitution to the state legislatures. Because the Constitution placed many prohibitions on the powers of states, the Founders believed that special constitutional ratifying conventions would be more likely to approve the document than would state legislatures.

Supporters of the new constitution, who become known as **Federalists**, enjoyed some important tactical advantages over the opposition. First, the Constitutional Convention was held in secret; potential opponents did not know what was coming out of it. Second, the Federalists called for ratifying conventions to be held as quickly as possible so that the opposition could not get itself organized. Many state conventions met during the winter months, so it was difficult for some rural opponents of the Constitution to get to their county seats in order to vote (see Figure 3.3 below).

ratification
Power of a legislature to approve or reject decisions made by other bodies. State legislators or state conventions must have the power to ratify constitutional amendments submitted by Congress. The U.S. Senate has the power to ratify treaties made by the president.

Federalists
Supporters of the ratification of the Constitution, who later coalesced into a political party supporting John Adams for president in 1800.

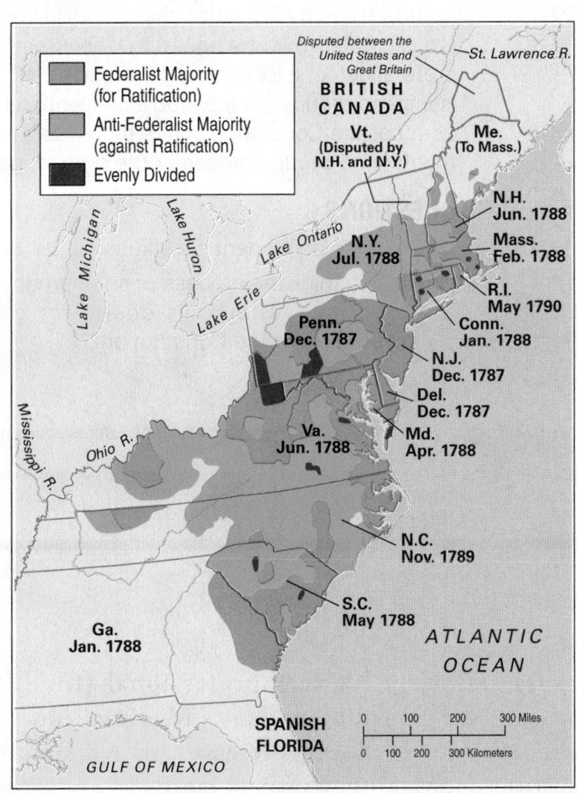

FIGURE 3.3 THE FIGHT OVER RATIFICATION

The vote for ratification of the Constitution of 1787 reflects divisions in the country, with support linked to a commercial economy and disapproval to more agricultural sectors.

3.1

3.2

3.3

3.4

3.5

3.6

3.7

3.8

Who's Getting What?

"The Earth Belongs to the Living": Generational Sovereignty and Constitutions

On September 6, 1789, Thomas Jefferson, author of the Declaration of Independence, was serving in Paris as U.S. ambassador. He penned a letter to James Madison, author of the proposed Constitution of the United States. Jefferson expressed a particular concern that the government and Constitution might prevent future generations from exercising their free will:

The question Whether one generation of men has a right to bind another . . . is a question of such consequences as not only to merit decision, but place also, among the fundamental principles of every government . . . I set out on this ground, which I suppose to be self evident, "that the earth belongs in usufruct[1] to the living": that the dead have neither powers nor rights over it.

. . . let us suppose a whole generation of men to be born on the same day, to attain mature age on the same day, and to die on the same day, leaving a succeeding generation in the moment of attaining their mature age all together . . . Each successive generation would . . . come on, and go off the stage at a fixed moment, as individuals do now. Then I say the earth belongs to each of these generations, during it's course, fully, and in their own right.

. . . it may be proved that no society can make a perpetual constitution, or even a perpetual law. The earth belongs always to the living generation. They may manage it then, and what proceeds from it, as they please, during their usufruct. They are masters too of their own persons, and consequently may govern them as they please. But persons and property make the sum of the objects of government. The constitution and the laws of their predecessors extinguished then in their natural course with those who gave them being. This could preserve that being till it ceased to be itself, and no longer. Every constitution then, and every law, naturally expires at the end of 19 years. If it be enforced longer, it is an act of force, and not of right . . .

. . . the power of repeal is not an equivalent. It might be indeed if every form of government were so perfectly contrived that the will of the majority could always be obtained fairly and without impediment. But this is true of no form. The people cannot assemble themselves. Their representation is unequal and vicious. Various checks are opposed to every legislative proposition. Factions get possession of the public councils. Bribery corrupts them. Personal interests lead them astray from the general interests of their constituents: and other impediments arise so as to prove to every practical man that a law of limited duration is much more manageable than one which needs a repeal.

This principle that the earth belongs to the living, and not to the dead, is of very extensive application and consequences, in every country . . .

Is a permanent Constitution unfair to rising or unborn generations? If we accept Jefferson's argument that no generation can bind the future, then the answer is "no." Then, the question that follows is whether we can defer to (or be bound by) the intentions and preferences of a long dead generation. Perhaps what is instead required is a periodic convention to consider whether the Constitution suits the values, requirements, and circumstances of the present generation.

QUESTIONS

1. How is a permanent constitution unfair to the future?
2. Do you think the process of amendment is sufficient to satisfy Jefferson's desire for generational sovereignty in the Constitution?

SOURCE: *The Founders' Constitution,* Volume 1, Chapter 2, Document 23, The University of Chicago Press. Located at http://press-pubs.uchicago.edu/founders/documents/v1ch2s23.html.

Notes: 1. *Usufruct* is an old Roman legal term that means the right to enjoy the use and advantages of another's property short of the destruction or waste of its substance.

The Federalists also waged a very professional (for 1787–88) media campaign in support of the Constitution. James Madison, Alexander Hamilton, and John Jay issued a series of 85 press releases, signed simply "Publius," on behalf of the Constitution. Major newspapers ran these essays, which were later collected and published as *The Federalist Papers*. The essays provide an excellent description and explanation of the Constitution by three of its writers and even today serve as a principal reference for political scientists and judges faced with constitutional ambiguities.

Nevertheless, opponents of the Constitution—the **Anti-Federalists**—almost succeeded in defeating the document in New York and Virginia. They charged that the new Constitution would create an "aristocratic tyranny" and pose a threat to the "spirit of republicanism." They argued that the new Senate would be an aristocratic upper house and the new president a ruling monarch. They complained that neither the Senate nor the president was directly elected by the people. They also argued that the new national government would trample state governments and deny the people of the states the opportunity to handle their own political and economic affairs. Virginia patriot Patrick Henry urged the defeat of the Constitution "to preserve the poor Commonwealth of Virginia." Finally, their most effective argument was that the new Constitution lacked a bill of rights to protect individual liberty from government abuse (see *What Do You Think?* Federalists and Anti-Federalists?.

Anti-Federalists
Opponents of the ratification of the Constitution, who later coalesced into a political party supporting Thomas Jefferson for president in 1800.

The Game, the Rules, the Players

James Madison and the Control of "Faction"

The most important contributions to American democracy by James Madison (1751–1836) were his work in helping write the Constitution and his insightful and scholarly defense of it during the ratification struggle. Indeed, Madison is more highly regarded by political scientists and historians as a *political theorist* than as the fourth president of the United States. His contemporaries at the convention, according to delegate William Pierce, saw Madison as exceptional: "What is very remarkable every person seems to acknowledge his greatness."

Madison's family owned a large plantation in Virginia. He graduated from the College of New Jersey (now Princeton University) at 18 and assumed a number of elected and appointed positions in Virginia's colonial government. In 1776, Madison drafted a new Virginia Constitution. While serving in Virginia's Revolutionary assembly, he met Thomas Jefferson; the two became lifetime political allies and friends. In 1787, Madison represented Virginia at the Constitutional Convention and took a leading role in its debates over the form of a new federal government.

Madison's political insights are revealed in *The Federalist Papers*, a series of 85 essays published in major newspapers in 1787–88, all signed simply "Publius." Alexander Hamilton and John Jay contributed some of them, but Madison wrote the two most important essays: Number 10, which explains the nature of political conflict (faction) and how it can be "controlled," and Number 51, which explains the system of separation of powers and checks and balances (both reprinted and annotated in the Appendix to this textbook). According to Madison, "controlling faction" was the principal task of government.

What creates faction? Madison believed that conflict is part of human nature. In all societies, we find "a zeal for different opinions concerning religion, concerning government, and many other points," as well as "an attachment to different leaders ambitiously contending for preeminence and power." Even when there are no serious differences among people, these "frivolous and fanciful distinctions" will inspire "unfriendly passions" and "violent conflicts."

Clearly, Madison believed conflict could arise over just about any matter. Yet "the most common and durable source of factions, has been the various and unequal distribution of property." That is, economic conflicts between rich and poor and between people with different kinds of wealth and sources of income are the most serious conflicts confronting society.

Madison argued that factions could best be controlled in a republican government extending over a large society with a "variety of parties and interests." He defended republicanism (representative democracy) over "pure democracy," which he believed "incompatible with personal security, or the rights of property." And he argued that protection against "factious combinations" can be achieved by including a great variety of competing interests in the political system so that no one interest will be able to "outnumber and oppress the rest." Modern pluralist political theory claims Madison as a forerunner.

QUESTIONS

1. What do you think Madison meant by "faction"?
2. Did Madison's constitution, and the effort to control factions, promote pluralism?

Amending the Constitution

3.8 Assess the protections provided by the Bill of Rights and determine the various means through which the Constitution may be changed.

Bill of Rights
Written guarantees of basic individual liberties; the first 10 amendments to the U.S. Constitution.

enumerated powers
Powers specifically mentioned in the Constitution as belonging to the national government.

amendments
Formal changes in a bill, law, or constitution.

t may be hard to imagine today, but the original Constitution had no **Bill of Rights**. This was a particularly glaring deficiency because many of the new state constitutions proudly displayed these written guarantees of individual liberty.

The Founders certainly believed in limited government and individual liberty, and they did write a few liberties into the body of the Constitution, including protection against ex post facto laws, a limited definition of treason, a guarantee of the writ of habeas corpus, and a guarantee of trial by jury.

The Federalists argued that there was really no need for a bill of rights because (1) the national government was one of **enumerated powers** only, meaning it could not exercise any power not expressly enumerated, or granted, in the Constitution; (2) the power to limit free speech or press, establish a religion, or otherwise restrain individual liberty was not among the enumerated powers; and (3) therefore it was not necessary to specifically deny these powers to the new government. But the Anti-Federalists were unwilling to rest fundamental freedoms on a thin thread of logical inference from the notion of enumerated powers. They wanted specific written guarantees that the new national government would not interfere with the rights of individuals or the powers of the states. So Federalists at the New York, Massachusetts, and Virginia ratifying conventions promised to support the addition of a bill of rights to the Constitution in the very first Congress.

A young member of the new House of Representatives, James Madison, rose in 1789 and presented a bill of rights that he had drawn up after reviewing more than 200 recommendations sent from the states. Interestingly, the new Congress was so busy debating new tax laws that Madison had a difficult time attracting attention to his bill. Eventually, in September 1789, Congress approved a Bill of Rights as 10 **amendments**, or formal changes, to the Constitution and sent them to the states. (Congress actually passed 12 amendments. One was never ratified; another, dealing with pay raises for Congress, was not ratified by the necessary three-quarters of the states until 1992.) The states promptly ratified the first 10 amendments to the Constitution (see Table 3.3), and these changes took effect in 1791.

The Bill of Rights was originally designed to limit the powers of the new *national* government. The Bill of Rights begins with the command "Congress shall make no law. . . ." It was not until after the Civil War that the Constitution was amended to also prohibit states from violating individual liberties. The 14th Amendment, ratified in 1868, includes the command "No State shall. . . ." It prohibits the states from depriving any person of "life, liberty or property, without due process of law," or abridging "the privileges or immunities of citizens of the United States," or denying any person "equal protection of the laws." Today virtually all of the liberties guaranteed in the Constitution protect individuals not only from the national government but also from state governments and their subdivisions, including cities, counties, and school districts.

Constitutional Change

The purpose of a constitution is to govern government—to place limits on governmental power. Thus government itself must not be able to alter or amend a constitution easily. Yet the U.S. Constitution has changed over time, sometimes by formal amendment and other times by judicial interpretation, presidential and congressional action, and general custom and practice.

TABLE 3.3 THE BILL OF RIGHTS

Thomas Jefferson, in a letter to James Madison in 1787, wrote: "A bill of rights is what the people are entitled to against every government on earth. . . ." This table summarizes and groups rights by their major purpose.

Guaranteeing Freedom of Expression
First Amendment prohibits the government from abridging freedoms of speech, press, assembly, and petition.
Guaranteeing Religious Freedom
First Amendment prohibits the government from establishing a religion or interfering with the free exercise of religion.
Affirming the Right to Bear Arms and Protecting Citizens from Quartering Troops
Second Amendment guarantees the right to bear arms.
Third Amendment prohibits troops from occupying citizens' homes in peacetime.
Protecting the Rights of Accused Persons
Fourth Amendment protects against unreasonable searches and seizures.
Fifth Amendment requires an indictment by a grand jury for serious crimes; prohibits the government from trying a person twice for the same crime; prohibits the government from taking life, liberty, or property without due process of law; and prohibits the government from taking private property for public use without fair compensation to the owner.
Sixth Amendment guarantees a speedy and public jury trial, the right to confront witnesses in court, and the right to legal counsel for defense.
Seventh Amendment guarantees the right to a jury trial in civil cases.
Eighth Amendment prohibits the government from setting excessive bail or fines or inflicting cruel and unusual punishment.
Protecting the Rights of People and States
Ninth Amendment protects all other unspecified rights of the people.
Tenth Amendment reserves to the states or to the people those powers neither granted to the federal government nor prohibited to the states in the Constitution.

☐ Amendments

A constitutional amendment must first be proposed, and then it must be ratified. The Constitution allows two methods of *proposing* a constitutional amendment: (1) by passage in the House and the Senate with a two-thirds vote, or (2) by passage in a national convention called by Congress in response to petitions by two-thirds of the state legislatures. Congress then chooses the method of *ratification*, which can be either (1) by vote in the legislatures of three-fourths of the states, or (2) by vote in conventions called for that purpose in three-fourths of the states (see Figure 3.4).

Of the four possible combinations of proposal and ratification, the method involving proposal by a two-thirds vote of Congress and ratification by three-quarters of the legislatures has been used for all the amendments except one. Only for the 21st Amendment's repeal of Prohibition did Congress call for state ratifying conventions (principally because Congress feared that southern Bible Belt state legislatures would vote against repeal). The method of proposal by national convention has never been used.

In addition to the Bill of Rights, most of the constitutional amendments ratified over the nation's 200 years have expanded our notion of democracy. Today, the Constitution includes 27 amendments, which means that only 17 (out of more than 10,000) proposed amendments have been ratified since the passage of the Bill of Rights. It is possible to classify the amendments that have been ratified into the broad categories of constitutional processes, Prohibition, income tax, individual liberty, and voting rights (see Table 3.4).

Amending the U.S. Constitution requires not only a two-thirds vote in both houses of Congress, reflecting *national* support, but also ratification by three-fourths of the states, reflecting widespread support within the states. The fate of the **Equal Rights Amendment**, popularly known as the ERA, illustrates the need for nationwide consensus in order to amend the Constitution. The Equal Rights Amendment is a simple statement to which the vast majority of Americans agree,

Equal Rights Amendment (ERA)

Proposed amendment to the Constitution guaranteeing that equal rights under the law shall not be denied or abridged on account of sex. Passed by Congress in 1972, the amendment failed to win ratification by three of the necessary three-fourths of the states.

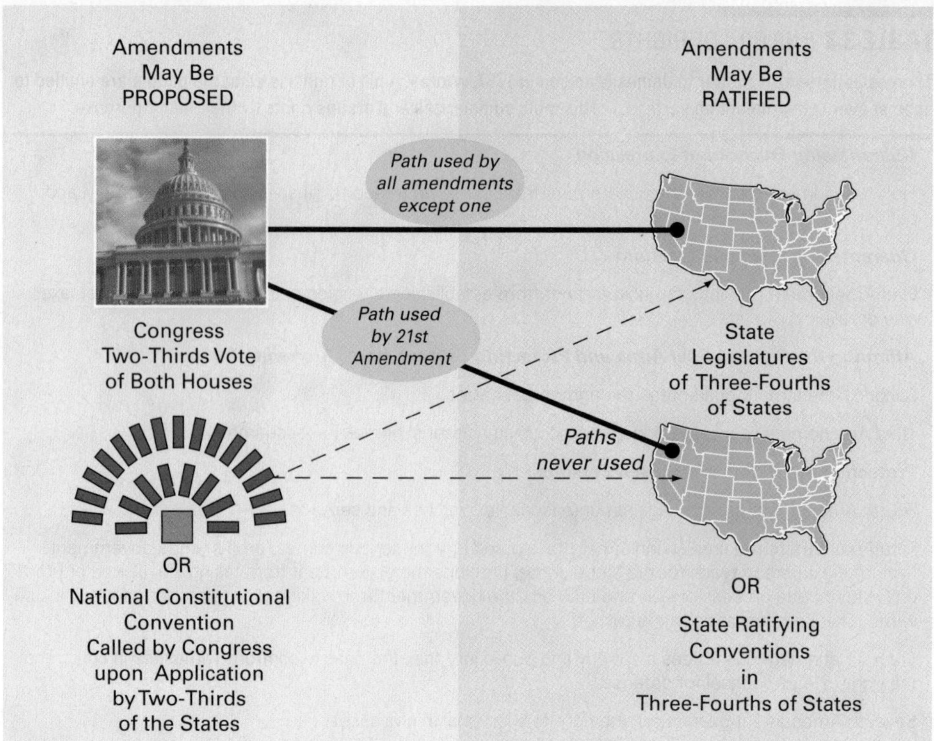

FIGURE 3.4 CONSTITUTIONAL AMENDMENT PROCESS

The Constitution set up two alternative routes for proposing amendments and two for ratifying them. One of the four possible combinations has actually been used for all except one (the 21st) amendment. However, in our time there have been persistent calls for a constitutional convention to propose new amendments permitting school prayer, making abortion illegal, and requiring a balanced national budget.

according to public opinion polls: "Equality of rights under the law shall not be denied or abridged by the United States or any state on account of sex." Congress passed the ERA in 1972 with far more than the necessary two-thirds vote; both Republicans and Democrats supported the ERA, and it was endorsed by Presidents Nixon, Ford, and Carter as well as most other national political leaders and organizations. By 1978, 35 state legislatures had ratified the amendment—three states short of the necessary 38 (three-quarters). (Five states subsequently voted to rescind, or cancel, their earlier ratification. However, because there is no language in the Constitution regarding rescission, there is some disagreement about the constitutionality of this action.) Promising that the "ERA won't go away," proponents of the amendment have continued to press their case. But to date Congress has not acted to resubmit the ERA to the states.

□ Judicial Interpretations

Some of the greatest changes in the Constitution have come about not by formal amendment but by interpretations of the document by federal courts, notably the U.S. Supreme Court.

Indeed, through judicial review, the U.S. Supreme Court has come to play the central role in giving meaning to the Constitution. Judicial review is the power of federal courts, and ultimately the Supreme Court, to declare laws of Congress and actions of the president unconstitutional and therefore invalid. This power was first asserted by Chief Justice John Marshall in the case of *Marbury v. Madison* in 1803. It is now an important part of the system of checks and balances (see Figure 3.1). This power is itself an interpretation of the Constitution, because it is not specifically mentioned in the document.

TABLE 3.4 AMENDMENTS TO THE CONSTITUTION SINCE THE BILL OF RIGHTS

The Constitution has been amended a total of 27 times, including the first 10 amendments of the Bill of Rights. This table summarizes and groups subsequent amendments by their major purpose.

Perfecting Constitutional Processes
Eleventh Amendment (1798) forbids federal lawsuits against a state by citizens of another state or nation.
Twelfth Amendment (1804) provides separate ballots for president and vice president in the Electoral College to prevent confusion.
Twentieth Amendment (1933) determines the dates for the beginning of the terms of Congress (January 3) and the president (January 20).
Twenty-second Amendment (1951) limits the president to two terms.
Twenty-fifth Amendment (1967) provides for presidential disability.
Twenty-seventh Amendment (1992) prevents Congress from raising its own pay in a single session.
The Experiment with Prohibition
Eighteenth Amendment (1919) prohibits the manufacture, sale, or transportation of intoxicating liquors.
Twenty-first Amendment (1933) repeals the Eighteenth Amendment.
The Income Tax
Sixteenth Amendment (1913) allows Congress to tax incomes.
Expanding Liberty
Thirteenth Amendment (1865) abolishes slavery.
Fourteenth Amendment (1868) protects life, liberty, and property and the privileges and immunities of citizenship and provides equal protection of the law.
Expanding Voting Rights
Fifteenth Amendment (1870) guarantees that the right to vote shall not be denied because of race.
Seventeenth Amendment (1913) provides for the election of senators by the people of each state.
Nineteenth Amendment (1920) guarantees that the right to vote shall not be denied because of sex.
Twenty-third Amendment (1961) gives the District of Columbia electoral votes for presidential elections.
Twenty-fourth Amendment (1964) guarantees that the right to vote shall not be denied because of failure to pay a poll tax or other tax.
Twenty-sixth Amendment (1971) guarantees that the right to vote shall not be denied to persons 18 years of age or older.

Supreme Court interpretations of the Constitution have given specific meaning to many of our most important constitutional phrases. Among the most important examples of constitutional change through judicial interpretation are the meanings given to the 14th Amendment, particularly its provisions that "No State shall . . . deprive any person of life, liberty, or property, without due process of law; nor deny to any person within its jurisdiction the equal protection of the laws":

- Deciding that "equal protection of the laws" requires an end to segregation of the races (*Brown v. Board of Education of Topeka*, 1954, and subsequent decisions).
- Deciding that "liberty" includes a woman's right to choose an abortion, and that the term *person* does not include the unborn fetus (*Roe v. Wade*, 1973, and subsequent decisions).
- Deciding that "equal protection of the laws" requires that every person's vote should be weighed equally in apportionment and districting plans for the House of Representatives, state legislatures, city councils, and so on (*Baker v. Carr*, 1964, and subsequent decisions).

□ Presidential and Congressional Action

Congress and the president have also undertaken to interpret the Constitution. Nearly every president, for example, has argued that the phrase "executive Power" in Article II includes more than the specific powers mentioned afterward. Thomas Jefferson

3.1

3.2

3.3

3.4

3.5

3.6

3.7

3.8

What Do You Think?

Federalists and Anti-Federalists?

Virginia's George Mason was a delegate to the Constitutional Convention of 1787. He refused to sign the final document and became a leading opponent of ratifying the new Constitution.

In 1776, Mason authored Virginia's Declaration of Rights, which was widely copied in other state constitutions and later became the basis for the Bill of Rights. An ardent supporter of states' rights, he attended the Constitutional Convention of 1787 and, according to James Madison's notes on the proceedings, was an influential force in shaping the new national government. Nonetheless, he refused to sign the Constitution and took leadership of the opposition to its ratification.

Mason and the Anti-Federalists' first objection to the Constitution was the lack of a Bill of Rights. He also objected to the powers given to the Senate, which was not directly elected by the people; to the federal courts; and to the independent executive. Mason and the Anti-Federalists were also wary of the Necessary and Proper Clause, which granted Congress the power to "make all laws which shall be necessary and proper" for carrying out the enumerated powers—those specifically mentioned in the Constitution—and he correctly predicted that this clause would be used to diminish the powers of the states.

Mason saw the lack of limitations on Congress as a danger to state sovereignty. He observed of the new Constitution that "under their own construction of the general clause at the end of the enumerated powers, the Congress may . . . extend their power as far as they shall think proper; so that the State Legislatures have no security for the powers now presumed to remain to them; or the people for their rights."

The Constitution was ratified, despite Anti-Federalist objections. And, a condition of ratification was the introduction of the Bill of Rights Mason demanded. But the Anti-Federalists did not go away. Instead, they entered the new political system and formed part of a political coalition that was the basis for the original Democratic-Republican Party (today's Democratic Party).

Within the Democratic Party, and especially in the southern states, Anti-Federalists continued to advance theories of federalism that limited the powers of the national government. They did so by using a "literal" interpretation of the Constitution—if it was not explicitly and literally said that the national government might do something, it could not do that thing.

The Tea Party and Anti-Federalists are examples of popular constitutionalist movements (PCMs). PCMs throughout American political history share a limited national government philosophy. They are characterized by a belief that the national government has exceeded its constitutional limits, and they often emerge during a real or perceived economic crisis, or because of major policy changes from an antagonistic national political majority. In this respect, the Tea Party resembles the Free Soil Movement (1848–52), the American Liberty League (1933–36), the states' rights massive resistance of the mid-twentieth century in the character of their Anti-Federalism.

History has not gone well for Anti-Federalist movements. Events consistently established that the national and state governments are not coequal. The courts have consistently reinforced national sovereignty. But Anti-Federalist movements persist, in part because political parties choose their philosophy of state–national relations based on where they hold power.

QUESTIONS

1. What were the major concerns with the proposed Constitution of the anti-Federalists?
2. The current Tea Party movement claims to be the successors to the Framers. Do you think they are Constitutionalists? Or are they anti-Federalists?
3. What threats to freedom or democracy arise from a United States with a smaller, weaker central government?

SOURCES: David Sehat. "Would Today's Tea Party Have Opposed the US Constitution?" *Christian Science Monitor*, February 10, 2011. Louise W. Knight. "The Tea Party Movement Has Deep American Roots." History News Network, March 15, 2010. Ilya Somin. "The Tea Party Movement and Popular Conservatism." *Northwestern University Law Review*, 105: 300-314, 2011.

purchased the Louisiana Territory from France in 1803 even though there is no constitutional authorization for the president, or even the national government, to acquire new territory. Presidents from George Washington to Richard Nixon have argued that Congress cannot force the executive branch to turn over documents it does not wish to disclose.

Congress by law has tried to restrict the president's power as Commander in Chief of the Armed Forces by requiring the president to notify Congress when U.S. troops are sent to "situations where imminent involvement in hostilities is clearly indicated" and limiting their stay to 60 days unless Congress authorizes an extension. This War Powers Resolution (1973), passed by Congress over President Richard Nixon's veto in the immediate aftermath of the Vietnam War, has been ignored by every president to date. Yet it indicates that Congress has its own ideas about interpreting the Constitution.

A Constitutional Note

How Democratic Was the Constitution of 1787?

The Constitution established *four* decision-making bodies—the House and the Senate in the legislative branch (Article I); the president in the executive branch (Article II); and the Supreme Court and "such inferior Courts as the Congress may from time to time ordain and establish" in the judicial branch (Article III). But in 1787, only one of these bodies was to be elected by the people—the House of Representatives. The other three bodies were removed from direct popular control: State legislatures selected U.S. senators; "electors," chosen in a fashion decided by state legislatures, chose the president; and the president appointed the Supreme Court and other federal judges "with the Advice and Consent of the [then unelected] Senate." Of course, over time, state legislatures provided for the direct election of presidential electors, and the 17th Amendment provided for the direct election of U.S. senators.

The Constitution of 1787 also recognized slavery—"persons held to Service or Labor" (Article IV, Section 2)—and even protected it, by requiring states that capture runaway slaves to "deliver up," that is, to return them to their owners. In terms of representation, the Constitution of 1787 distinguishes between "free persons" and three-fifths of "all other Persons" (Article I, Section 2), that is, slaves. And Congress could not prohibit the importation of slaves until after 1808 (Article I, Section 9).

QUESTIONS

As you move through the course (and this book), ask:

1. How do changes to the Constitution expand the concept of who gets to fully participate in public life?
2. Do we have too much democracy? Or too little? Why?

□ Custom and Practice

Finally, the Constitution changes over time as a result of generally accepted customs and practice. It is interesting to note, for example, that the Constitution never mentions political parties. (Many of the Founders disapproved of parties because they caused "faction" among the people.) But soon after Thomas Jefferson resigned as President Washington's first secretary of state (in part because he resented the influence of Secretary of the Treasury Alexander Hamilton), the Virginian attracted the support of Anti-Federalists, who believed the national government was too strong. When Washington retired from office, most Federalists supported John Adams as his successor. But many Anti-Federalists ran for posts as presidential electors, promising to be "Jefferson's men." Adams won the presidential election of 1796, but the Anti-Federalists organized themselves into a political party, the Democratic-Republicans, to oppose Adams in the election of 1800. The party secured pledges from candidates for presidential elector to cast their electoral vote for Jefferson if they won their post, and then the party helped win support for its slate of electors. In this way, the Electoral College was transformed from a deliberative body where leading citizens from each state came together to decide for themselves who should be president into a ceremonial body where pledged electors simply cast their presidential vote for the candidate who had carried their state in the presidential election.

Review the Chapter

Constitutional Government in America

3.1 Identify the major principles of constitutionalism and trace its evolution in the United States, p. 64

Constitutionalism includes the principles of a government of law, which is limited in power and where liberties may not be infringed upon even by the majority. Constitutions govern government and establish the legal authority for government. The American tradition of written constitutions extends back through the Articles of Confederation, the colonial charters, and the Mayflower Compact to the thirteenth-century English Magna Carta. The Second Continental Congress in 1776 adopted a written Declaration of Independence to justify the colonies' separation from Great Britain. All of these documents strengthened the idea of a written contract defining governmental power.

Troubles Confronting a New Nation

3.2 Assess the obstacles to nationhood, p. 66

The movement for a Constitutional Convention in 1787 was inspired by the new government's inability to levy taxes under the Articles of Confederation, its inability to fund the Revolutionary War debt, obstacles to interstate commerce, monetary problems, and civil disorders, including Shays's Rebellion.

Consensus and Conflict in Philadelphia

3.3 Outline the principles on which the Founders were in agreement and characterize their areas of conflict, p. 69

The nation's Founders—55 delegates to the Constitutional Convention in Philadelphia in 1787—shared a broad consensus on liberty and property, the social contract, republicanism, limited government, and the need for a national government. The Founders compromised their differences over representation by creating two co-equal houses in the Congress: the House of Representatives, with members apportioned to the states on the basis of population and directly elected by the people for two-year terms, and the Senate, with two members allotted for each state regardless of its population, and originally selected by state legislatures for six-year terms.

The Economy and National Security

3.4 Analyze the economic and security issues that the Founders faced and the solutions they reached, p. 73

The Founders were confronted with many economic problems, including conflicts over levying taxes, regulating commerce, tariffs, establishing a uniform currency and a common market, and resolving the questions over the national debt. The national government assumed power over the new country's foreign and military affairs, at first relying on state militias made up of citizen soldiers and later developing a professional army. The new Constitution gave the federal government authority to negotiate treaties with foreign nations and established the president as the Commander in Chief.

The Structure of the Government

3.5 Explain how the Constitution structured the new government, p. 77

The structure of the national government reflects the Founders' beliefs in national supremacy, federalism, republicanism, separation of powers, checks and balances, and judicial review. Some latitude for state action and initiative exists, but it is highly constrained by this structure.

Separation of Powers and Checks and Balances

3.6 Analyze the separation of powers and the checks and balances established by the Constitution, p. 81

The separation of powers and checks and balances written into the Constitution were designed, in Madison's words, "to divide and arrange the several offices in such a manner as that each may be a check on the other." Judicial review was not specifically described in the original Constitution, but the Supreme Court soon asserted its power to overturn laws of Congress and the states, as well as presidential actions, that the Court determined to be in conflict with the Constitution.

Conflict over Ratification

3.7 Outline the arguments made for and against ratification of the Constitution, p. 83

Opposition to the new Constitution was strong. Anti-Federalists argued that it created a national government that was aristocratic, undemocratic, and a threat to the rights of the states and the people. Their concerns resulted in the Bill of Rights: 10 amendments added to the original Constitution, all designed to limit the power of the national government, and protect the rights of individuals and states.

Amending the Constitution

3.8 Assess the protections provided by the Bill of Rights and determine the various means through which the Constitution may be changed, p. 86

The Bill of Rights provides for the protection of many liberties, including freedom of speech, press, religion, privacy, and the rights of criminal defendants. It intended to limit the power of the national government and protect the people's individual freedoms. Over time, constitutional changes have come about as a result of formal amendments, judicial interpretations, presidential and congressional actions, and changes in custom and practice. The most common method of constitutional amendment has been proposal by two-thirds vote of both houses of Congress followed by ratification by three-fourths of the state legislatures.

Learn the Terms

constitutionalism, p. 64
constitution, p. 64
Mayflower Compact, p. 64
colonial charters, p. 64
Declaration of Independence, p. 65
Articles of Confederation, p. 66
Shays's Rebellion, p. 68
Annapolis Convention, p. 68
the Enlightenment, p. 69
natural law, p. 69
inalienable rights, p. 69
social contract, p. 69
republicanism, p. 69
nationalism, p. 70
parliamentary government, p. 71
Connecticut Compromise, p. 71
Three-Fifths Compromise, p. 72
taxes, p. 74
tariff, p. 74
common market, p. 74
National Supremacy Clause, p. 77
referenda, p. 79
separation of powers, p. 81
checks and balances, p. 81
judicial review, p. 82
ratification, p. 83
Federalists, p. 83
Anti-Federalists, p. 85
Bill of Rights, p. 86
enumerated powers, p. 86
amendments, p. 86
Equal Rights Amendment (ERA), p. 87

Test Yourself

3.1 Identify the major principles of constitutionalism.

The Constitution established a government

a. of limited power
b. based on law
c. with three branches at the federal level
d. by executive fiat
e. based on religious principles

3.2 Assess the obstacles to nationhood.

Congress under the Articles of Confederation relied on ________ as a major source of funding.

a. the new income tax
b. loans from wealthy patriots
c. the sales tax
d. taxes on interstate commerce
e. foreign loans

3.3 Outline the principles on which the Founders were in agreement.

Which of the following was a principle that Founders had trouble reconciling?

a. the social contract
b. natural right to property
c. representation in Congress
d. natural right to liberty
e. the state church principles

3.4 Analyze the economic issues that the Founders faced and the solutions they reached.

Which of the following economic groups played little role in the development of the Constitution?

a. slave owners
b. land speculators
c. the government bureaucracy
d. bankers and investors
e. merchants and traders

3.5 Explain how the Constitution structured the new government.

The provision in the Constitution that makes state law inferior to federal law is

a. the full faith and credit clause
b. the interstate commerce clause
c. state inferiority clause
d. the national supremacy clause
e. the intrastate clause

3.6 Analyze the separation of powers and the checks and balances established by the Constitution.

It would be accurate to say that the power of judicial review provides that

a. Congress may review the financial affairs of the federal courts
b. the Supreme Court may declare an act of Congress unconstitutional
c. the executive has the authority to review the judiciary for impropriety
d. each state supreme court may review the constitutionality of federal statutes
e. Congress with the ability to overturn judicial decisions

3.7 Outline the arguments made for and against ratification of the Constitution.

How did the Framers deal with the issue of division between the various states over ratification?

a. The required unanimity, that all thirteen states ratify the Constitution for it to take force.
b. There was no minimum requirement to approve; any state ratifying the constitutions became subject to it.
c. They required nine of thirteen states to ratify in order to enact the Constitution.
d. They required a simple majority of the thirteen states (seven) to ratify in order to enact the Constitution.
e. They allowed the convention to impose the Constitution without ratification.

3.8 Assess the protections provided by the Bill of Rights and determine the various means through which the Constitution may be changed

The Bill of Rights were included into the new Constitution in order to

a. provide protection from ex post facto laws
b. outline the basic structure of the judiciary
c. provide safeguards and protections for individual liberties
d. provide for writs of habeus corpus
e. establish a church

Explore Further

SUGGESTED READINGS

Alexander, John K. *The Selling of the Constitutional Convention.* Boulder, Colo.: Rowman and Littlefield Press, 1990. How did the media of the late eighteenth century sell Americans on a new government? Here's the story of American politics' first effort at media management.

Beard, Charles. *An Economic Interpretation of the Constitution.* New York: Macmillan, 1913. A classic work setting forth the argument that economic self-interest inspired the Founders in writing the Constitution.

Dahl, Robert A. *How Democratic Is the American Constitution?* 2nd ed. New Haven, Conn.: Yale University Press, 2003. A discussion of the undemocratic features of the Constitution.

Epstein, Lee, and Thomas G. Walker. *Constitutional Law for a Changing America: Institutional Powers and Constraints.* 6th ed. Washington, D.C.: CQ Press, 2007. Supreme Court cases and explanatory narrative regarding the separation of power, federalism, national and state powers, national security, and so on.

Finkelman, Paul. *Slavery and the Founders.* 2nd ed. Armonk, N.Y.: M. E. Sharpe, 2000. A critical account of the Founders' attitudes toward slavery and the resulting three-fifths compromise.

Frohren, Bruce, ed. *The American Republic: Primary Sources.* Indianapolis: Liberty Fund Inc., 2002. Excellent collection of earliest American documents, from the Mayflower Compact to the Declaration of Independence.

Levin, Mark. *Liberty and Tyranny.* New York: Simon & Schuster, 2009. An argument that modern conservatism embodies the principles of the Founders—principles that can preserve liberty and defeat liberal tyranny.

Madison, James, Alexander Hamilton, and John Jay. *The Federalist Papers.* New York: Modern Library, 1937. These 85 collected essays, written in 1787–88 in support of ratification of the Constitution, remain the most important commentary on that document. Numbers 10 and 51 (reprinted in the Appendix) ought to be required reading for all students of American government.

Madison, James. *The Constitutional Convention: A Narrative History from the Notes of James Madison.* Edited by Edward J. Larson and Michael P. Winship. New York: Modern Library, 2005. An annotated firsthand account of the creation of the Constitution by its primary architect.

Mason, Alpheus Thomas, and Donald Grier Stephenson, Jr. *American Constitutional Law.* 14th ed. Upper Saddle River, N.J.: Prentice Hall, 2005. The now classic introduction to the Constitution and the Supreme Court through essays and case excerpts.

McDonald, Forrest B. *Novus Ordo Seculorum.* Lawrence: University Press of Kansas, 1986. A description of the intellectual origins of the Constitution and the "new secular order" that it represented.

Peltason, J. W., and Sue Davis. *Understanding the Constitution.* 16th ed. New York: Harcourt Brace, 2004. Of the many books that explain the Constitution, this is one of the best. It contains explanations of the Declaration of Independence, the Articles of Confederation, and the Constitution. The book is written clearly and is well suited for undergraduates.

Rossiter, Clinton L. 1787, *The Grand Convention.* New York: Macmillan, 1960. A very readable account of the people and events surrounding the Constitutional Convention in 1787, with many insights into the conflicts and compromises that took place there.

Sabato, Larry J. *A More Perfect Constitution.* New York: Walker, 2007. Proposals for a new Constitutional Convention to consider.

Storing, Herbert J. *What the Anti-Federalists Were For.* Chicago: University of Chicago Press, 1981. An examination of the arguments of the Anti-Federalists in opposition to the ratification of the Constitution.

Waldman, Steven. *Founding Faith: How Our Founding Fathers Forged A Radical New Approach to Religious Liberty.* New York, Random House, 2008. Explores the middle ground of the history of religion in America's founding as more than a stark choice between the concept of strict separation of church and state versus the view America as a Christian nation.

SUGGESTED WEB SITES

The Anti-Federalist Papers
www.thisnation.com/library/antifederalist
Essays by Anti-Federalists opposed to the ratification of the Constitution.

Constitution Society www.constitution.org
Web site includes comprehensive list of founding documents, essays, and commentaries on the Constitution.

Constitutional Law www.law.cornell.edu/topics/constitutional
Cornell University Law School's overview of the Constitution.

The Electoral College Official FEC site www.fec.gov/pages/ecmenu
Provides brief history of the Electoral College and a description of how it works.

George Washington Papers http://gwpapers.virginia.edu
The life of George Washington with images, maps, documents, and papers.

The Great Compromise www.jmu.edu/madison
James Madison University's Web site on Madison with information on constitutional compromises, including the slavery compromise.

James Madison www.jmu.edu/madison
The legacy of Madison organized by topic.

National Constitution, Center www.constitutioncenter.org
Located in Philadelphia's Independence Mall, this museum is devoted to explaining the U.S. Constitution.

Our Documents www.ourdocuments.gov
National Archives Web site with access to 100 "milestone documents" in American history.

U.S. History www.ushistory.org
The Independence Hall Association Web site with "Documents of Freedom" including Mayflower Compact, Declaration of Independence, Articles of Confederation, etc.

4

Federalism

Dividing Governmental Power

ho owns the public lands? Who gets to use them?

In most countries, there is land owned by the public and administered by government. In the United States, these lands can include national parks, defense installations, and other land acquired by the United States then organized into territories, which eventually became states.

Who gets to use the land depends on what part of government has jurisdiction. Substantial amounts of land in western states such as Nevada, Utah, Arizona, and New Mexico are owned by the United States and managed by the Bureau of Land Management (BLM). For decades, BLM has allowed western ranchers to graze herds on public land in exchange for paying "grazing fees." Many ranchers grumble about paying these fees, and, along with mining and fossil fuel exploration firms, they have sought freer access to public land for economic purposes.

For two decades, south Nevada rancher Cliven Bundy has had an ongoing dispute about grazing his herds on public land. This dispute erupted into open conflict in early 2014. Bundy refused to remove his herds or pay his fees. Supportive states-rights and gun activists came to help Bundy defend his land against a potential government removal of his cattle. Part of their claim? The public lands in Nevada shouldn't belong to the United States, but to Nevada, or, even more specifically, to Clark County.

So who should own the public lands? The people of the states? Or the people of the United States?

4.1 Distinguish the federal form of government from confederal and unitary forms and evaluate the arguments in favor of federalism, p. 98

4.2 Distinguish the delegated, reserved, concurrent, and denied powers granted to the state and federal governments, p. 104

4.3 Trace the evolution of American federalism, p. 108

4.4 Describe how the use of federalism leads to theories of political behavior, p. 112

4.5 Assess how court decisions in recent decades have impacted federalism, p. 117

4.6 Explain how federal grants impact the distribution of power between the federal and state governments, p. 118

4.7 Assess the impact of coercive federalism on state–national relations, p. 121

4.8 Describe coercive federalism and explain how it has altered state–national relations, p. 126

THE STATE OF THE STATE Nevada rancher Cliven Bundy set off a media storm with his resistance to paying grazing fees to use public lands.

4.1

4.2

4.3

4.4

4.5

4.6

4.7

4.8

Why Federalism? The Argument for a "Compound Republic"

4.1 Distinguish the federal form of government from confederal and unitary forms and evaluate the arguments in favor of federalism.

federalism
A constitutional arrangement whereby power is divided between national and subnational governments, each of which enforces its own laws directly on its citizens and neither of which can alter the arrangement without the consent of the other.

unitary system
Constitutional arrangement whereby authority rests with the national government; subnational governments have only those powers given to them by the national government.

confederation
Constitutional arrangement whereby the national government is created by and relies on subnational governments for its authority.

Dillon's Rule
Named for a legal decision by Judge John Forrest Dillon in 1868, this rule holds that local governments, as municipal corporations, exist and get their powers from the state legislature. Cities and counties have lesser standing than individuals or states, and only possess the powers delegated to them.

home rule
Power of local government to pass laws affecting local affairs, so long as those laws do not conflict with state or federal laws.

In December 1860, South Carolina seceded from the Union, and in April 1861 authorized its state militia to expel U.S. troops from Fort Sumter in Charleston harbor. Although there is no provision in the Constitution for states leaving the Union, 11 Southern states—South Carolina, Mississippi, Florida, Alabama, Georgia, Louisiana, Texas, Virginia, Arkansas, Tennessee, and North Carolina, in that order—argued that the Union was a voluntary association and they were entitled to withdraw.[1] President Abraham Lincoln declared these states to be in armed rebellion and sent federal troops to crush the "rebels." The result was the nation's bloodiest war: more than 250,000 battle deaths and another 250,000 deaths from disease and privation, out of a total population of less than 30 million.

Following the Civil War, Chief Justice Salmon P. Chase confirmed what had been decided on the battlefield: "The Constitution in all its provisions looks to an indestructible union, composed of indestructible states."[2]

Federalism divides power between two separate authorities—the nation and the states—each of which enforces its own laws directly on its citizens. Both the nation and the states pass laws, impose taxes, spend money, and maintain their own courts. Neither the nation nor the states can dissolve the Union or amend the Constitution without the consent of the other. The Constitution itself is the only legal source of authority for both the states and the nation, the states do not get their power from the national government, and the national government does not get its power from the states. Both national and state governments derive their power directly from the people.

American federalism differs from a **unitary system** of government, in which formal authority rests with the national government, and whatever powers are exercised by states, provinces, or subdivisions are given to those governments by the national government. Most of the world's governments—including France and Great Britain—are unitary. Federalism also differs from a **confederation** of states, in which the national government relies on the states for its authority, not the people (see Figure 4.1). Under the Articles of Confederation of 1781, the United States was a confederation. The national government could not even levy taxes; it had to ask the states for revenue. Like the United States, a number of other countries were confederations before establishing federal systems, and today new types of confederations with limited functions are being formed (see *Compared to What?* The European Union).

People in the United States often think of the *federal government* when the word *government* comes up. In fact, today there are more than 90,000 American governments. These state and local governments are important in American life, for they provide such essential day-to-day services as schools, water, and police and fire departments (see Table 4.1). However, the U.S. Constitution, the supreme law of the land, recognizes the existence of only the national government and the states. Local governments have no guarantees of power—or even existence—under the U.S. Constitution. States can create or abolish local governments, grant or withhold their powers, or change their boundaries without their consent. They are, according to "**Dillon's Rule**," creatures of the state. Some local governments have powers guaranteed in *state* constitutions, and some are even given **home rule**—the power to pass laws affecting local affairs, so long as those laws do not conflict with state or federal laws. About 60,000 of these 90,000 governments have the power to levy taxes to support activities authorized by state law.

In short, the American federal system is large and complex, with three levels of government—national, state, and local—sharing power. Indeed, the numbers and

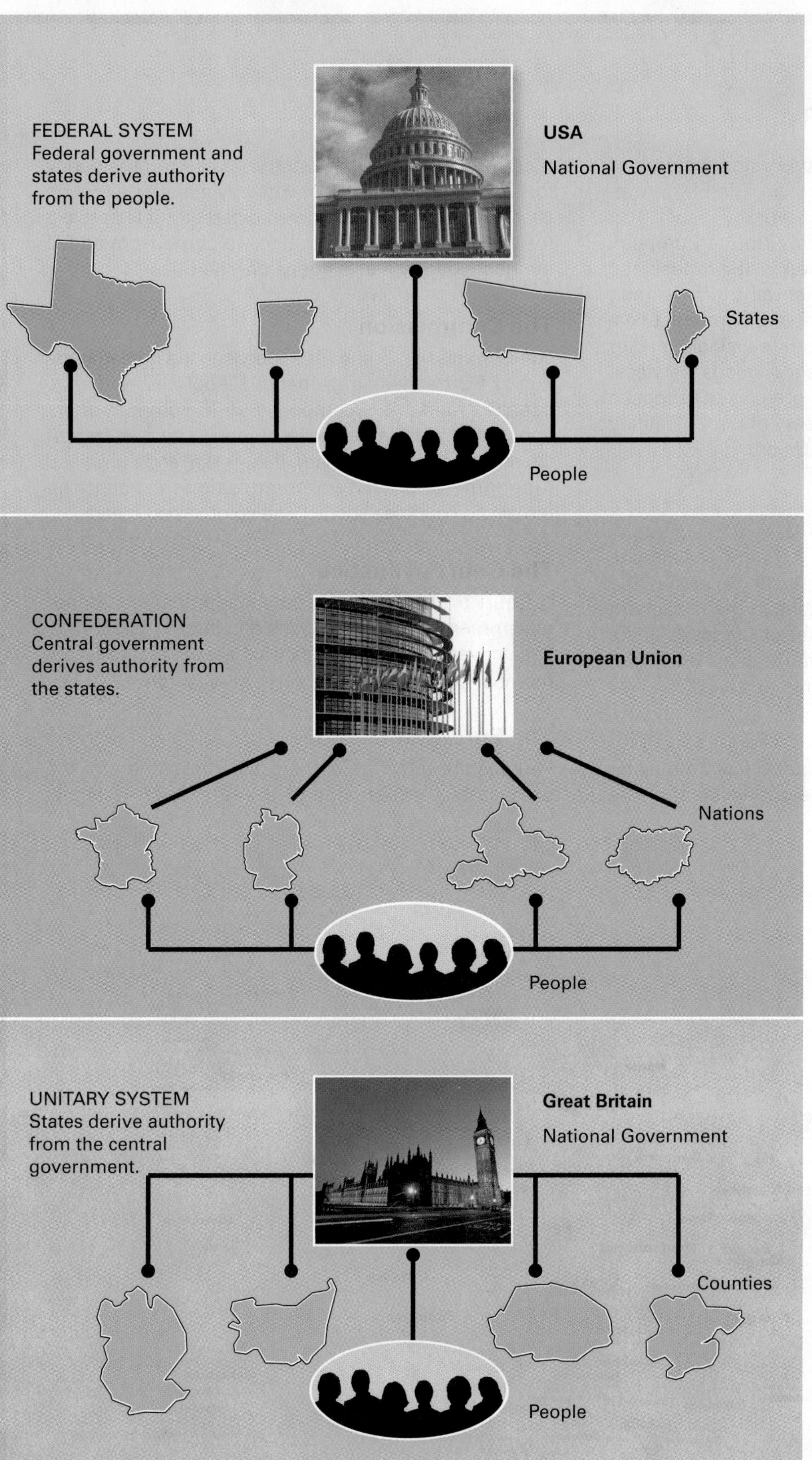

FIGURE 4.1 FEDERAL, CONFEDERATION, AND UNITARY SYSTEMS OF GOVERNMENT

In theory, power in a federal system is divided between a national government and the states; power in a confederation remains with the member states; power in a unitary system is concentrated in the national government. The United States, the European Union, and Great Britain resemble federal, confederation, and unitary systems; but no government completely conforms to these designs.

Compared to What?

The European Union

The European Union (EU) incorporates features of both federalism and confederation. The EU now includes 27 member nations and embraces more than 455 million people. It grew slowly from a European Economic Community established in 1957 (designed to reduce and eventually abolish all tariffs among member nations), through a European Community established in 1965 (designed to create a single market free of all barriers to the movement of goods, services, capital, and labor), to its much more unified European Union established in 1991. The Treaty of Lisbon, ratified in 2009, further strengthens the Union.

European Parliament

Deputies of the European Parliament are directly elected every five years by the EU's 455 million citizens. The major political parties operating in each of the member nations nominate candidates. The Parliament oversees the EU budget and passes on proposals to the Council of Ministers and the Commission. The Parliament also passes on new applicants to the EU.

Council of the EU

The Council is the EU's principal decision-making body. It is composed of the foreign ministers of the member nations. Each country takes the presidency for six months; the Council votes by majority, although each country's vote is weighted differently. It is possible for the president of the Council to come from an EU member country that is not part of the Council.

The Commission

The Commission of the EU supervises the implementation of EU treaties, implements EU policies, and manages EU funds. It is composed of 20 commissioners appointed by member governments. The five largest countries—France, Germany, Italy, Spain, and the United Kingdom—appoint two commissioners each; the remaining countries appoint one commissioner each.

The Court of Justice

A Court of Justice hears complaints about member governments' treaty violations and interprets EU treaties and legislation. Its 15 justices are appointed by the member governments and serve six-year terms.

The Euro

Perhaps the most far-reaching accomplishment of the EU was the introduction of the "euro" (€)—a single

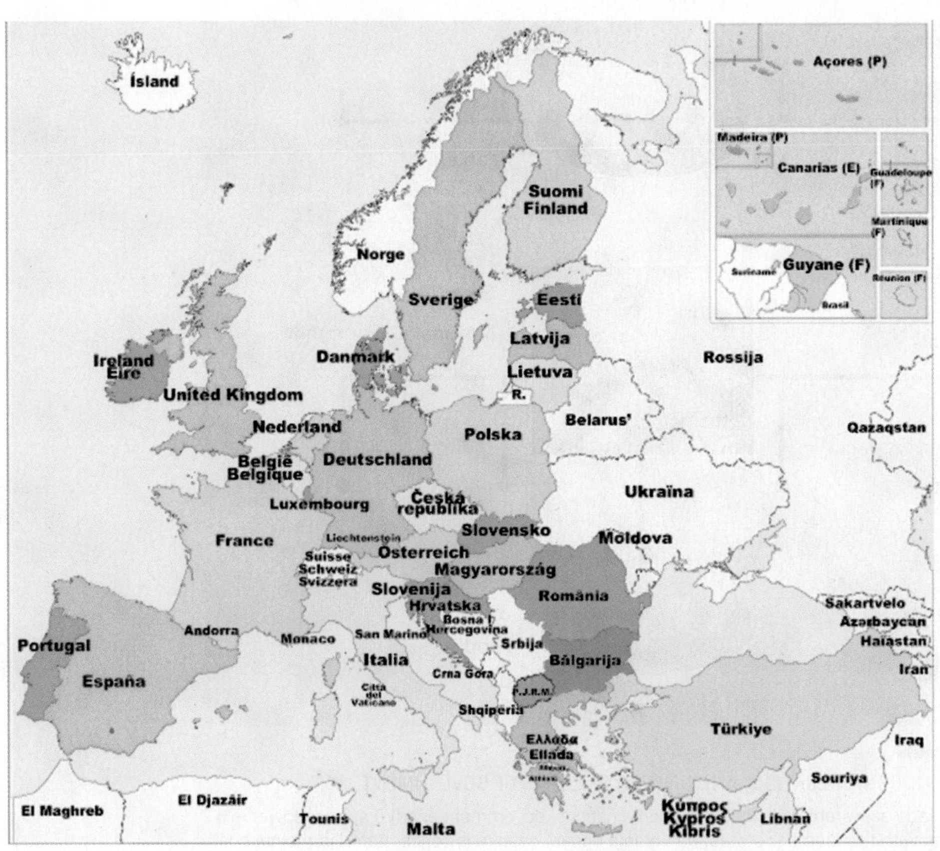

This map, produced by the EU, uses the languages of the nations portrayed. Test yourself by translating these names into English, for example Osterreich = Austria.

(*Continued*)

European currency for use in all member states. The euro was first introduced January 1, 1999, and officially replaced old national currencies—such as francs, marks, pesetas, and lira—on January 1, 2002. However, the United Kingdom, Sweden, and Denmark have refused to substitute the euro for their own currency, and the ongoing fiscal crisis in several EU countries threatens the long-term viability of the currency.

Unlike in American federalism, where there are limits on the ability of states to assume unbonded debt and the national government enjoys strong fiscal tools, the creation of the single-currency union left many member states with the ability to assume unsecured sovereign debt, but without the ability to manipulate currency. The euro crisis hit hard poorer European states that now lack a historic fiscal tool previously available to them—the ability to inflate their way out of a fiscal crisis.

The Treaty of Lisbon

The Treaty of Lisbon, ratified by all 27 member nations, moves the European Union closer to a federal union. It establishes an elected president and adds to the powers of the directly elected European Parliament. (Ireland and the Czech Republic were the last to ratify the Treaty, in 2009.) During the ratification process, many of the questions addressed by Europeans were the same as those discussed in the American Constitutional Convention of 1787.

Nationalist Backlash?

The 2014 European Parliament elections featured an increase in populist and anti-EU sentiment in several member countries such as Denmark, France, and Great Britain. In states hit hard by EU-supported austerity measures during the Great Recession, approval of EU leadership collapsed.

Questions

1. How does European federalism differ from that of the United States?
2. German federalism has a clearer delineation of state and national government authority than U.S. federalism. Do you think the American states need more control in their areas of traditional authority, as does Germany? Why?

TABLE 4.1 HOW MANY AMERICAN GOVERNMENTS?

Over 90,000 governments function in the United States. The U.S. Constitution recognizes only the national government and the states. Local governments are created and empowered by state laws and constitutions.

U.S. government	1
States	50
Counties	3,031
Municipalities	19,519
Townships	16,360
Special districts	38,266
School districts	12,880
All governments	90,106

SOURCE: *Census of Governments*, 2013.

intergovernmental relations
Network of political, financial, and administrative relationships between units of the federal government and those of state and local governments.

complexity of governments in the United States make **intergovernmental relations**—all of the interactions among these governments and their officials—a major concern of political scientists and policy makers.

The nation's Founders believed that "republican principles" would help make government responsible to the people, but they also argued that "auxiliary precautions" were necessary to protect the liberties of minorities and individuals. They believed that majority rule in a democratic government made it particularly important to devise ways to protect minorities and individuals from "unjust" and "interested" *majorities*. They believed that federalism would better protect liberty, disperse power, and manage "faction" (conflict).

Protecting Liberty

Constitutional guarantees of individual liberty do not enforce themselves. The Founders argued that to guarantee liberty, government should be structured to encourage "opposite and rival" centers of power *within* and *among* governments. So they settled

4.1

4.2

4.3

4.4

4.5

4.6

4.7

4.8

on both *federalism*—dividing powers between the national and state governments—and *separation of powers*—the dispersal of power among branches within the national government.

In the compound republic of America, the power surrendered by the people is first divided between two distinct governments, and then the portion allotted to each is subdivided among distinct and separate departments. Hence, a double security arises to the rights of the people. The different governments will control each other while each will control itself.[3] Thus, the Founders deliberately tried to create competition within and among governmental units as a means of protecting liberty. Rather than rely on the "better motives" of leaders, the Founders sought to construct a system in which governments and government officials would be constrained by competition with other governments and other government officials: "Ambition must be made to counteract ambition."[4] But the ability to use a competitive model to protect individual rights and liberties requires applying political will to ensure that the tyranny of local (or national) majorities does not abuse the rights and liberties of the political minority.

Dispersing Power

Federalism distributes power widely among different sets of leaders, including national as well as state and local officeholders. The Founders believed that multiple leadership groups offered more protection against tyranny than a single set of all-powerful leaders. State and local government offices also provide a political base for the opposition party when it has lost a national election. In this way, state and local governments contribute to party competition in the United States by helping to tide over the losing party after electoral defeat at the national level so that it can remain strong enough to challenge incumbents at the next election. And finally, state and local governments often provide a training ground for national political leaders. National leaders can be drawn from a pool of leaders experienced in state and local government.

Increasing Participation

Federalism allows more people to participate in the political system. With more than 90,000 governments in the United States—state, county, municipality, township, special district, and school district—nearly a million people hold some kind of public office.

Improving Efficiency

Federalism also makes government more manageable and efficient. Imagine the bureaucracy, red tape, and confusion if every governmental activity—police, schools, roads, fire fighting, garbage collection, sewage disposal, and so forth—in every local community in the nation were controlled by a centralized administration in Washington. Government can become arbitrary when a bureaucracy far from the scene directs local officials. Thus decentralization often softens the rigidity of law.

Ensuring Policy Responsiveness

Federalism encourages policy responsiveness. The existence of multiple governments offering different packages of benefits and costs allows a better match between citizen preferences and public policy. Americans are very mobile. People and businesses can "vote with their feet" by relocating to those states and communities that most closely conform to their own policy preferences. This mobility not only facilitates a better match between citizen preferences and public policy but also encourages competition between states and communities to offer improved services at lower costs.[5]

A Conflicting View

The Dark Side of Federalism

Segregationists once regularly used the argument of "states' rights" to deny equal protection of the law to African Americans. Indeed, *states' rights* became a code word for opposition to federal civil rights laws. In 1963, Governor George Wallace invoked the states' rights argument when he stood in a doorway at the University of Alabama to prevent the execution of a federal court order that the university admit two African American students and thus integrate. Federal marshals were on hand to enforce the order, and Wallace only temporarily delayed them. Shortly after his dramatic stand in front of the television cameras, he retreated to his office. Later in his career, Wallace sought African American votes, declaring, "I was wrong. Those days are over." (He got the votes.)

Federalism in America remains tainted by its historical association with slavery, segregation, and discrimination. John C. Calhoun of South Carolina argued forcefully in the years before the Civil War that slavery was an issue for the states to decide and that the Constitution gave Congress no power to interfere with slavery in the southern states or in the new western territories.

In the years immediately following the Civil War, the issues of slavery, racial inequality, and African American voting rights were *nationalized*. Nationalizing these issues meant removing them from the jurisdiction of the states and placing them in the hands of the national government. The 13th, 14th, and 15th Amendments to the Constitution were enforced by federal troops in the southern states during the post–Civil War Reconstruction era. But after the Compromise of 1876 led to the withdrawal of federal troops from the southern states, legal and social segregation of African Americans became a "way of life" in the region. Segregation was *denationalized*, which reduced national conflict over race but exacted a high price from the nation's African American population.

Not until the 1950s and 1960s were questions of segregation and equality again made into national issues. The civil rights movement asserted the supremacy of national law and in 1954 won a landmark decision in the case of *Brown v. Board of Education of Topeka*, when the U.S. Supreme Court ruled that segregation enforced by state (or local) officials violated the 14th Amendment's guarantee that no state could deny any person the equal protection of the law. Later, the *national* Civil Rights Act of 1964 outlawed discrimination in private employment and businesses serving the public.

Only after national constitutional and legal guarantees of equal protection of the law were in place was it possible to reassess the true worth of federalism.

Upending States' Rights: The Voting Rights Act of 1965

The Constitution places the conduct of elections in the hands of the states. And, in the Civil Rights Act of 1964, Congress acted within its powers under the Commerce clause. However, when states engaged in systematic discrimination designed to deprive African Americans of the right to vote, Congress took extraordinary action under the 15th Amendment to regulate the states and intercede to ensure the right to vote. It only took eight decades for Congress to act.

DALLAS COUNTY, ALABAMA, MARCH 7, 1965

On "Bloody Sunday," black residents of the majority-black county demonstrate to register to vote. Met with violence by local authorities in the county seat of Selma at the Edmund Pettus Bridge, the protesters will return twice more and prompt President Johnson to call on Congress to pass the Voting Rights Act of 1965.

Since 1883, Congress had taken almost no action to end racial discrimination in public accommodations or voting. Nearly all black voters in Mississippi and Alabama were disfranchised, and across much of the South, blacks confronted laws and practices that discouraged voting. The 1964 Civil Rights Act addressed segregation of public accommodations and also contained provisions to encourage black voter registration, but progress was not easy in the South. In March 1965, a group of black and white protesters in Dallas County, Alabama, sought to register black citizens to vote. Violence by local authorities was used to turn back marchers at the Edmund Pettis Bridge in Selma; President Lyndon Johnson demanded congressional authority to intercede in the conduct of election in select jurisdictions, and asked his attorney general Nicholas Katzenbach to "write me the goddamn best, toughest voting rights act that you can devise."

The product was the Voting Rights Act of 1965. The Act contained several ways for the national government to regulate state conduct of elections, when egregious acts of discrimination were taking place. The Justice Department could deploy registrars to register people to vote and monitor elections. In states where there was a history of low voter participation and the use of a literacy test to qualify to vote, any change in election law would have to be approved by the federal district court in Washington D.C. or by the U.S. Department of Justice. The states were presumed to be acting in bad faith and

(*Continued*)

(Continued)

had to demonstrate that any change in voting law doesn't make minority voters worse off. This provision, called Section 5, was an "emergency" provision originally enacted for three years, then extended several times by Congress, the last time in 2006 for a period of 25 more years.

The U.S. Supreme Court upheld the use of Congress's power in *South Carolina v. Katzenbach* (383 US 301 (1966)), deciding that Congress could exercise such extraordinary power under the 15th Amendment. The Act then stood, for nearly 50 more years. Then, in 2013, the Supreme Court determined in an Alabama case, *Shelby County v. Holder,* that the formula of electoral data and use of a device to qualify to vote was outdated and did not reflect the modern conditions in the South. The Court struck down the coverage formula that allowed the national government to review state election law changes, arguing that it violated the "equal sovereignty" of the states.

QUESTIONS

1. In the case of voting rights, Congress implemented a temporary, emergency law to subordinate state authority in order to address an "insidious and pervasive evil." Are there other areas of civil rights or liberties where you think the national government should subordinate the states' authority on behalf of citizens?
2. Where can Congress find authority in the Constitution without violating 'equal sovereignty' of the states?

SOURCE: Charles S. Bullock III and Ronald Keith Gaddie. 2009. *The Triumph of Voting Rights in The South.* Norman: University of Oklahoma Press.

laboratories of democracy
A reference to the ability of states to experiment and innovate in public policy.

Encouraging Policy Innovation

The Founders hoped that federalism would encourage policy experimentation and innovation. Federalism may seem "conservative," but it was the instrument of liberal reformers, and it is a novel and experimental form of government throughout the world. Federal programs as diverse as the income tax, unemployment compensation, Social Security, wage and hour legislation, bank deposit insurance, and food stamps were all state programs before becoming national undertakings. Today much of the current "liberal" policy agenda—mandatory health insurance for workers, child-care programs, notification of plant closings, and government support of industrial research and development—has been embraced by various states. The phrase **laboratories of democracy** attributed to the great progressive jurist Supreme Court Justice Louis D. Brandeis, accurately describes state experimentation with new solutions to social and economic problems.[6] Both conservative and liberal state governments engage in experimentation in state and local government.

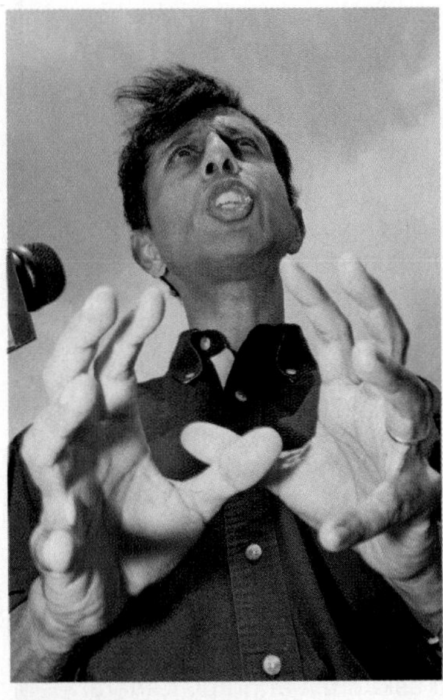

Louisiana Governor Bobby Jindal has confronted substantial criticism for dramatically reducing the size of Louisiana state government.

Some Important Reservations

Despite the strengths of federalism, it has its problems. First of all, federalism can obstruct action on national issues. Although decentralization may reduce conflict at the national level, it may do so at the price of "sweeping under the rug" very serious national injustices (see *A Conflicting View*: The Dark Side of Federalism). Federalism also permits local leaders and citizens to frustrate national policy, to sacrifice national interest to local interests. Decentralized government provides an opportunity for local NIMBYs (people who subscribe to the motto "Not in My Backyard") to obstruct the development of airports, highways, waste disposal plants, public housing, drug rehabilitation centers, and many other projects that would be in the national interest.

The Original Design of Federalism

4.2 Distinguish the delegated, reserved, concurrent, and denied powers granted to the state and federal governments.

The U.S. Constitution *originally* defined American federalism in terms of (1) the powers expressly delegated to the national government plus the powers implied by those that are specifically granted, (2) the concurrent powers exercised by both states and the national government, (3) the powers

The Game, the Rules, the Players

Do We Need New States?

Do we need more states? The history of the United States is one of expansion. From 1787 to 1912, a new state came into the union about every 3.5 years. The most recent states admitted to the Union, Alaska and Hawaii, entered after 47 years without state creation. Since their admission over a half-century ago, the U.S. has embarked on its longest period of stability in the number of states. But there is discussion across the country about the need to create new states.

Do we need new states? In the past, states were created from existing territories (such as the Northwest Territory or the territories from the Louisiana Purchase), the admission or annexation of "independent" republics (Texas, Vermont, California), or the partition of existing states (Maine used to be part of Massachusetts, and Kentucky and West Virginia were carved out of Virginia). States were created because the economic and political interest dictated that it was time for their creation.

So, what are the arguments for creating new states? Several reasons are advanced by new-state proponents:

Some states are just too big. California, Texas, Florida, and New York all have populations in excess of 19,000,000; one in three Americans lives in one of these states. These states have massive state budgets and diverse populations. They are also the physically largest states in their regions and have multiple urban population centers. Yet they elect just eight U.S. senators.

States have increasingly divergent interests and geographic minorities feel politically powerless. Multiple proposals to break up California, including one that passed the state Senate in 1965, focus on the divergent interests of southern California from northern California, or of coastal California from inland California. In 2013, a group of rural counties in Colorado held a failed referendum to create a separate Northern Colorado that would be freed from domination by Denver.

New centers of commerce, politics, and culture transcend old state lines. Many states were laid out in the eighteenth and nineteenth centuries, when patterns of settlement and commerce were different. Major economic and population centers have sprung up that cross state boundaries, often necessitating the use of interstate compacts and special administrative districts to manage public policy problems. A prominent example is a proposed state of Delmarva on the peninsula divided among Delaware, the eastern shore of Maryland, and peninsular Virginia.

Territories of the U.S. deserve statehood. Puerto Rico has often been touted as a potential candidate for statehood. Puerto Ricans are American citizens, and were it to become a state, it would have a population on par with Oklahoma or Connecticut. DC statehood has also been discussed. Guam, the U.S. Virgin Islands, American Samoa, and the Northern Marianas Islands all have populations sufficiently large to qualify for statehood.

QUESTIONS

1. Do we need new states?
2. If we admitted new states, what are the political considerations that could enter into the decision?
3. There are more people in California today than there were in the entire United States at the beginning of the American Civil War, and 10 times more Californians than there were Americans in 1790. Are there benefits for American citizens to create new states from the existing states? Should we make more states?

reserved to the states, (4) the powers denied by the Constitution to both the national government and the states, and (5) the constitutional provisions giving the states a role in the composition of the national government (see Figure 4.2).

Delegated Powers

The U.S. Constitution lists 17 specific grants of power to Congress, in Article I, Section 8. These are usually referred to as the **delegated, or enumerated, powers**. They include authority over war and foreign affairs, authority over the economy ("interstate commerce"), control over the money supply, and the power to tax and spend "to pay the Debts and provide for the common Defence and general Welfare." After these specific grants of power comes the power "to make all laws which shall be necessary and proper for carrying into execution the foregoing powers, and all other powers vested by this Constitution in the government of the United States or in any department or officer thereof." This statement is generally known as the **Necessary and Proper Clause**, and it is the principal source of the national government's **implied powers**—powers not specifically listed in the Constitution but inferred from those that are.

delegated, or enumerated, powers
Powers specifically mentioned in the Constitution as belonging to the national government.

Necessary and Proper Clause
Clause in Article I, Section 8, of the U.S. Constitution granting Congress the power to enact all laws that are "necessary and proper" for carrying out those responsibilities specifically delegated to it. Also referred to as the Implied Powers Clause.

implied powers
Powers not mentioned specifically in the Constitution as belonging to Congress but inferred as necessary and proper for carrying out the enumerated powers.

POWERS GRANTED BY THE CONSTITUTION

NATIONAL GOVERNMENT
Delegated Powers

Military Affairs and Defense
- Provide for the common defense (I-8).
- Declare war (I-8).
- Raise and support armies (I-8).
- Provide and maintain a navy (I-8).
- Define and punish piracies (I-8).
- Define and punish offenses against the law of nations (I-8).
- Provide for calling forth the militia to execute laws, suppress insurrections, and repel invasions (I-8).
- Provide for organizing, arming, and disciplining the militia (I-8).
- Declare the punishment of treason (III-3).

Economic Affairs
- Regulate commerce with foreign nations, among the several states, and with Indian tribes (I-8).
- Establish uniform laws on bankruptcy (I-8).
- Coin money and regulate its value (I-8).
- Fix standards of weights and measures (I-8).
- Provide for patents and copyrights (I-8).
- Establish post offices and post roads (I-8).

Governmental Organization
- Constitute tribunals inferior to the Supreme Court (I-8, III-1).
- Exercise exclusive legislative power over the seat of government and over certain military installations (I-8).
- Admit new states (IV-3).
- Dispose of and regulate territory or property of the United States (IV-3).

"Implied" Powers
- Make laws necessary and proper for carrying the expressed powers into execution (I-8).

NATIONAL AND STATE GOVERNMENTS
Concurrent Powers
- Levy taxes (I-8).
- Borrow money (I-8).
- Contract and pay debts (I-8).
- Charter banks and corporations (I-8).
- Make and enforce laws (I-8).
- Establish courts (I-8).
- Provide for the general welfare (I-8).

STATE GOVERNMENTS
Reserved to the States
- Regulate intrastate commerce.
- Conduct elections.
- Provide for public health, safety, and morals.
- Establish local government.
- Maintain the militia (National Guard).
- Ratify amendments to the federal Constitution (V).
- Determine voter qualifications (I-2).

"Reserved" Powers
- Powers not delegated to national government nor denied to the States by the Constitution (X).

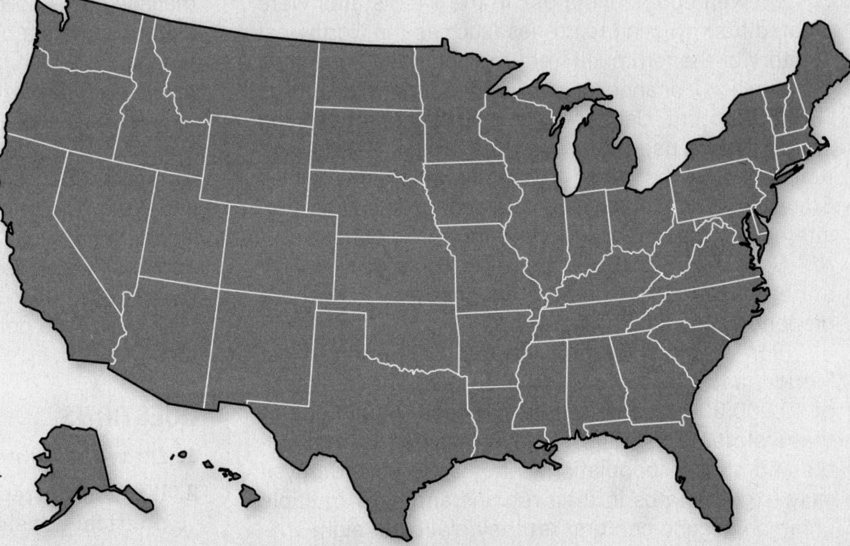

POWERS DENIED BY THE CONSTITUTION

NATIONAL GOVERNMENT
- Give preference to the ports of any state (I-9).
- Impose a tax or duty on articles exported from any state (I-9).
- Directly tax except by apportionment among the states on a population basis (I-9), now superseded as to income tax (Amendment XVI).
- Draw money from the Treasury except by appropriation (I-9).

NATIONAL AND STATE GOVERNMENTS
- Grant titles of nobility (I-9).
- Limit the suspension of habeas corpus (I-9).
- Issue bills of attainder (I-10).
- Make ex post facto laws (I-10).
- Establish a religion or prohibit the free exercise of religion (Amendment I).
- Abridge freedom of speech, press, assembly, or right of petition (Amendment I).
- Deny the right to bear arms (Amendment II).
- Quarter soldiers in private homes (Amendment III).
- Conduct unreasonable searches or seizures. (Amendment IV).
- Deny guarantees of fair trials (Amendment V, Amendment VI, and Amendment VII).
- Impose excessive bail or unusual punishments (Amendment VII).
- Take life, liberty, or property without due process (Amendment V).
- Permit slavery (Amendment XIII).
- Deny life, liberty, or property without due process of law (Amendment XIV).
- Deny voting because of race, color, previous servitude (Amendment XV), sex (Amendment XIX), or age if 18 or over (Amendment XXVI).
- Deny voting because of nonpayment of any tax (Amendment XXIV).

STATE GOVERNMENTS
Economic Affairs
- Use legal tender other than gold or silver coin (I-10).
- Issue separate state coinage (I-10).
- Impair the obligation of contracts (I-10).
- Emit bills of credit (I-10).
- Levy import or export duties, except reasonable inspection fees, without the consent of Congress (I-10).
- Abridge the privileges and immunities of national citizenship (Amendment XIV)
- Make any law that violates federal law (Amendment VI).
- Pay for rebellion against the United States or for emancipated slaves (Amendment XIV).

Foreign Affairs
- Enter into treaties, alliances, or confederations (I-10).
- Make compact with a foreign state, except by congressional consent (I-10).

Military Affairs
- Issue letters of marque and reprisal (I-10).
- Maintain standing military forces in peace without congressional consent (I-10).
- Engage in war, without congressional consent, except in imminent danger or when invaded (I-10).

FIGURE 4.2 WHO GETS WHAT?: THE ORIGINAL CONSTITUTIONAL DISTRIBUTION OF POWERS

Under the Constitution of 1787, certain powers were delegated to the national government, other powers were shared by the national and state governments, and still other powers were denied by the Constitution to the national government, other powers were denied to both the national and state governments, and still other powers were denied only to state governments. Later amendments especially protected individual liberties.

☐ National Supremacy

The delegated and implied powers, when coupled with the assertion of "national supremacy" (in Article VI), ensure a powerful national government. The **National Supremacy Clause** is very specific in asserting the supremacy of federal laws over state and local laws:

> This Constitution, and the laws of the United States which shall be made in pursuance thereof, and all treaties made, or which shall be made, under the authority of the United States, shall be the supreme law of the land, and the Judges in every state shall be bound thereby, any thing in the constitution or laws of any state to the contrary notwithstanding.

National Supremacy Clause
Clause in Article VI of the U.S. Constitution declaring the constitution and laws of the national government "the supreme law of the land" superior to the constitutions and laws of the states.

concurrent powers
Powers exercised by both the national government and state governments in the American federal system.

reserved powers
Powers not granted to the national government or specifically denied to the states in the Constitution that are recognized by the 10th Amendment as belonging to the state governments. This guarantee, known as the Reserved Powers Clause, embodies the principle of American federalism.

☐ Concurrent and Reserved Powers

Despite broad grants of power to the national government, the states retain considerable governing power. **Concurrent powers** are those recognized in the Constitution as belonging to *both* the national and state governments, including the power to tax and spend, make and enforce laws, and establish courts of justice. The 10th Amendment reassured the states that "the powers not delegated to the United States . . . are reserved to the States respectively, or to the people." Through these **reserved powers**, the states generally retain control over property and contract law, criminal law, marriage and divorce, and the provision of education, highways, and social welfare activities. The states control the organization and powers of their own local governments. Finally, the states, like the federal government, retain the power to tax and spend for the general welfare.

☐ Powers Denied to the States

The Constitution denies the states some powers in order to safeguard national unity. States are specifically denied the power to coin money, enter into treaties with foreign nations, interfere with the "obligation of contracts," levy taxes on imports or exports, or engage in war.

☐ Powers Denied to the Nation and the States

The Constitution denies some powers to both national and state government—namely, the powers to abridge individual rights. The Bill of Rights originally applied only to the national government, but the 14th Amendment, passed by Congress in 1866 and ratified by 1868, provided that the states must also adhere to fundamental guarantees of individual liberty.

☐ State Role in National Government

The states are basic units in the organizational scheme of the national government. The House of Representatives apportions members to the states by population, and state legislatures draw up the districts that elect representatives. Every state has at least one member in the House of Representatives, regardless of its population. Each state elects two U.S. senators, regardless of its population. The president is chosen by the electoral votes of the states, with each state having as many electoral votes as it has senators and representatives combined. Finally, three-fourths of the states must ratify amendments to the U.S. Constitution.

☐ State Obligations to Each Other

To promote national unity, the Constitution requires the states to recognize actions and decisions taken by other states. Article IV requires the states to give "Full Faith and Credit ... to the public Acts, Records, and judiciary Proceedings of every other State." This provision ensures that contracts, property ownership, insurance, civil judgments, marriages and divorces, among other things, made in one state are recognized in all states.

4.1

4.2

4.3

4.4

4.5

4.6

4.7

4.8

The Evolution of American Federalism

4.3 Trace the evolution of American federalism.

dual federalism
Early concept of federalism in which national and state powers were clearly distinguished and functionally separate.

merican federalism has evolved over 200 years from a state-centered division of power to a national-centered system of government. Although the original constitutional wordings have remained in place, *power has flowed toward the national government since the earliest days of the Republic.* American federalism has been forged in the fires of political conflicts between states and nation, conflicts that have usually been resolved in favor of the national government. Generalizing about the evolution of American federalism is no easy task. But let us try to describe broadly some major periods in the evolution of federalism and then look at five specific historical developments that had far-reaching impact on that evolution.

State-Centered Federalism, 1787–1868

From the adoption of the Constitution of 1787 to the end of the Civil War, the states were the most important units in the American federal system. It is true that during this period the legal foundation for the expansion of national power was being laid, but people looked to the states for resolving most policy questions and providing most public services. Even the issue of slavery was decided by state governments. The supremacy of the national government was frequently questioned, first by the Anti-Federalists (including Thomas Jefferson) and later by John C. Calhoun and other defenders of slavery.

Dual Federalism, 1868–1913

The supremacy of the national government was decided on the battlefields of the Civil War. Yet for nearly a half-century after that conflict, the national government narrowly interpreted its delegated powers, and the states continued to decide most domestic policy issues. The resulting pattern has been described as **dual federalism**. Under this pattern, the states and the nation divided most governmental functions. The national government concentrated its attention on the "delegated" powers—national defense, foreign affairs, tariffs, interstate commerce, the coinage of money, standard weights and measures, post office and post roads, and the admission of new states. State governments decided the important domestic policy issues—education, welfare, health, and criminal justice. The separation of policy responsibilities was once compared to a layer cake, with local governments at the base, state governments in the middle, and the national government at the top.[7]

Cooperative Federalism, 1913–64

The distinction between national and state responsibilities gradually eroded in the first half of the twentieth century. American federalism was transformed by the Industrial Revolution and the development of a national economy; by the federal income tax in 1913, which shifted financial resources to the national government; and by the challenges of two world wars and the Great Depression. In response to the Great Depression of the 1930s, state governors welcomed massive federal public works projects under President Franklin D. Roosevelt's New Deal program. In addition, the federal government intervened directly in economic affairs, labor relations, business practices, and agriculture. Through its grants of money, the national government cooperated with the states in public assistance, employment services, child welfare, public housing, urban renewal, highway building, and vocational education. The national government also used the control of grants to compel states to reshape or reform state agencies.

4.1

4.2

4.3

4.4

4.5

4.6

4.7

4.8

The Game, the Rules, the Players

Failed States' Rights Doctrines

The concept of states' rights has staying power in the American political conversation. Its history is colored by the race issue. Most contemporary states' rights movements are tied to racial issues—the resistance to the 'Second Reconstruction' in the 1950s and 1960s had strong states' rights rhetoric. But the most recent incarnation of states' rights rhetoric is not aimed at racial issues or policies, but instead at the scope of the national government in general. Intellectual concepts previously invoked in defense of slavery and segregation are coming back into the political debate. Legal and political scholars often term these "discredited" or "failed" states' rights doctrines. What are they?

Compact Theory of Union

This theory of the Constitution holds that the national Constitution was created by the states entering into a compact. As such, the national constitution and government become either subservient to, or just an equal partner to, state governments. The United States Supreme Court has consistently rejected this theory of the Constitution since 1793, in *Chisholm v. Georgia* 2 U.S. (2 Dall.) 419 (1793). The Court consistently holds that the Constitution finds its authority in the people, rather than in the states.

Nullification

Holds that a state legislature can determine whether a national law violates the Constitution. This doctrine was originally advanced by Thomas Jefferson in the "Virginia and Kentucky Resolutions" of 1798 as a mechanism to protest the civil liberties violations enshrined in the Alien and Sedition Acts. Nullification would later return in the early nineteenth century with regard to issues of slavery and tariffs on manufacturers coming to Southern ports.

Interposition

The other half of the nullification doctrine is Interposition. If a state determines that a federal law is unconstitutional, it can impede the implementation of that law in its borders. The assumption behind the doctrine is that because citizens are simultaneously citizens of states and of the United States, the states can protect their citizens from unconstitutional laws.

Secession

When a state withdraws from a political union or confederation, this is termed secession. Secession is a frequent occurrence in modern politics, as the dissolution of the Soviet Union, Yugoslavia, and Czechoslovakia readily demonstrate. In the United States, advocates of states' rights espoused (through the compact theory) a right to withdraw a state from the union. The effort to take theory and make it into action led to secession in 1860 and 1861 by 11 states and the creation of the Confederate States of America (which was explicitly framed as being a compact of states). The Civil War practically settled the issue, and four years after the end of hostilities, the Supreme Court reiterated its previous position, that secession was unconstitutional. Still, politicians—most recently Rick Perry of Texas—periodically wave the flag of secession, not being fully cognizant of its illegality under the Constitution.

These doctrines persist and return in our politics because the strong appeal of history; the desire for local popular control; and the existence of a politically, socially, and economically diverse country confront a Constitution that allows national majorities, through Congress, to regulate the states in order to guarantee equal protection under the laws for all persons. They also persist because American politicians pick theories of federalism based on political necessity. The antebellum states that were most dogmatic about states' rights in defense of slavery were also the most insistent that the sovereignty of other states be violated on behalf of slavery. That many of these states—mainly in the South—had far fewer democratic institutions only intensified the differences in political culture and the interpretation of the rights of persons, versus states.

QUESTIONS

1. **Are there any issues where your preferred position is advantaged by expanding states' rights?**
2. **How is the states' rights issue settled?**
3. **Does the experience of slavery and segregation permanently stain the legitimacy of states' rights rhetoric in the United States?**

This new pattern of federal–state relations was labeled **cooperative federalism.** Both the nation and the states exercised responsibilities for welfare, health, highways, education, and criminal justice. This merging of policy responsibilities was compared to a marble cake: "As the colors are mixed in a marble cake, so functions are mixed in the American federal system."[8] Yet even in this period of shared national–state responsibility, the national government emphasized cooperation in achieving common national and state goals. Congress generally acknowledged that it had no direct constitutional authority to regulate public health, safety, or welfare. Instead, it relied primarily on its powers to tax and spend for the general welfare, providing financial assistance to state and local governments to achieve shared goals. Congress did not usually legislate directly on local matters.

cooperative federalism
Model of federalism in which national, state, and local governments work together exercising common policy responsibilities.

4.1
4.2
4.3
4.4
4.5
4.6
4.7
4.8

centralized federalism
Model of federalism in which the national government assumes primary responsibility for determining national goals in all major policy areas and directs state and local government activity through conditions attached to money grants.

new federalism
Attempts to return power and responsibility to the states and reduce the role of the national government in domestic affairs.

Centralized Federalism, 1964–80

Over the years, it became increasingly difficult to maintain the fiction that the national government was merely assisting the states to perform their domestic responsibilities. By the time President Lyndon B. Johnson launched the Great Society program in 1964, the federal government clearly had its own *national* goals. Virtually all problems confronting American society—from solid-waste disposal and water and air pollution to consumer safety, home insulation, noise abatement, and even "highway beautification"—were declared to be national problems. Congress legislated directly on any matter it chose, without regard to its *enumerated powers* and without pretending to render only financial assistance. The Supreme Court no longer concerned itself with the reserved powers of the states, and the 10th Amendment lost most of its meaning. The pattern of national–state relations became **centralized federalism**. As for the cake analogies, one commentator observed, "The frosting had moved to the top, something like a pineapple upside-down cake."[9]

DEFINING MARRIAGE
Same-sex marriage is increasingly recognized across the United States. Some states have proactively recognized same-sex marriage, while others have had same-sex bans struck down in federal court on equal protection grounds.

New Federalism, 1980–85

New federalism was a phrase frequently applied to efforts to reverse the flow of power to Washington and to return responsibilities to states and communities. (The phrase originated in the administration of Richard M. Nixon, 1969–74, who used it to describe general revenue sharing—making federal grants to state and local governments with few strings attached.) New Federalism was popular early in the administration of President Ronald Reagan, who tried to reduce federal involvement in domestic programs and encourage states and cities to undertake greater policy responsibilities themselves. The result was that state and local governments were forced to rely more on their own sources of revenue and less on federal money. Still, centralizing tendencies in the American federal system continued. While the general public usually gave better marks to state and local governments than to the federal government, paradoxically that same public also favored greater federal involvement in policy areas traditionally thought to be state or local responsibilities. (See *What Do You Think?* Which Level of Government Does the Best Job?)

What Do You Think?

Which Level of Government Does the Best Job?

Americans appear to be ambivalent about federalism. On the one hand, most surveys show that Americans have greater confidence in their state and local governments than in the federal government. In general, they would prefer that power be concentrated at the state rather than the federal level.

TRUST AND CONFIDENCE

Generally speaking, which of the following cares more about the important problems that affect you personally?	
The governor, my state legislature	52
The president and Congress	36
Neither	10
Don't know/refused	2

Yet at the same time, most Americans want the federal government, rather than state or local governments, to run programs in many specific policy areas, like health care, the environment, and the economy.

For each issue, tell me whether the state government or the federal government should take the lead:

Issue	Federal	State	DK/Ref.
Education	24	75	1
Highways and roads	27	73	0
Health care	72	27	1
Crime	27	72	1
Environment	72	28	1
Jobs and the economy	56	43	1

SOURCE: "Immigration, Federalism." Andres McKenna Research. January 15–25, 2004.

Questions

1. Why do you think people have more faith in either state or national government, respectively?
2. Why do you think people generally choose state or local government to address different policy concerns?

☐ Representational Federalism, 1985–95

Despite centralizing tendencies, it was still widely assumed prior to 1985 that Congress could not directly legislate how state and local governments should go about performing their traditional functions. However, in its 1985 *Garcia v. San Antonio Metropolitan Transit Authority* decision, the U.S. Supreme Court appeared to remove all barriers to direct congressional legislation in matters traditionally reserved to the states. The case arose after Congress directly ordered state and local governments to pay minimum wages to their employees. The Court dismissed arguments that the nature of American federalism and the Reserved Powers Clause of the 10th Amendment prevented Congress from directly legislating in state affairs. It said that the only protection for state powers was to be found in the states' role in electing U.S. senators, members of the U.S. House of Representatives, and the president. The Court's ruling asserts a concept known as **representational federalism**: federalism is defined by the role of the states in electing members of Congress and the president, not by any constitutional division of powers. The United States is said to retain a federal system because its national officials are selected from subunits of government—the president through the allocation of Electoral College votes to the states and Congress through the allocation of two Senate seats per state and the apportionment of representatives based on state population. Whatever protection exists for state power and independence must be found in the national political process, in the influence of state and district voters on their senators and representatives. In a strongly worded dissenting opinion in *Garcia*, Justice Lewis Powell argued that if federalism is to be retained, the Constitution—not Congress—should divide powers. "The states' role in our system of government is a matter of constitutional law, not legislative grace.... [This decision] today rejects almost 200 years of the understanding of the constitutional status of federalism."[10]

representational federalism
Assertion that no constitutional division of powers exists between the nation and the states but the states retain their constitutional role merely by selecting the president and members of Congress.

HAND IN HAND

During the Great Depression of the 1930s, President Franklin D. Roosevelt and the Democratic-controlled U.S. Congress sponsored extended public works within the states. This image of WPA workers bagging a street in anticipation of spring flood is an example of cooperative federalism.

Other Political Science Theories of Federalism

4.4 Describe how the use of federalism leads to theories of political behavior.

fiscal federalism
The practice of different levels of government taxing different sources of revenue, based on the mobility of wealth and income.

environmental federalism
National laws that regulate environmental threats that cross state lines, and how the national government interacts with states on environmental policy.

competitive federalism
A theory that state and local governments compete for residents and industry by offering 'market baskets' of incentives, services, zoning, and taxes.

Fiscal federalism is the practice of deciding which fiscal (tax and spend) tools should be exercised by different levels of government. In the United States, different levels of government historically relied on different sources of tax revenue, based on the mobility of wealth and income. Local governments and state governments taxed property, because property is typically immobile—you can't move a section of land to another state. Most states rely on sales and transaction taxes, because such transactions were historically local. States and the national government tax income, because income is harder to move out of states (or out of the United States) than it is out of a locality. There are new issues arising in fiscal federalism. The traditional immobility of transactions and income are being altered by new technologies—Internet transactions are not subject to state and local sales taxes, for example, and in the densely populated areas that straddle multiple states, it is possible to move from state to state to seek relief from income taxes. Recent tax reform proposals by presidential candidates (such as Herman Cain) would have the national government start to tax sources of revenue usually taxed only by the states, such as sales transactions (see *The Game, the Rules, the Players:* Federalism Is the Enemy of Uniformity).

Environmental federalism refers to national laws and agencies that regulate "transboundary" environmental threats—threats that cross state lines. From the end of the 18th century until the 1960s, national government regulation of the environment focused largely on conservation and preservation of the public lands of the United States, ensuring the navigability of the waters of the United States under the Commerce Clause, or addressing specific public health threats, such as mosquito eradication in the Swamp Act of 1842. In the 1950s and 1960s, urban air quality issues and drinking water concerns became more widespread, and some states moved to address pollution challenges. The United States government under President Nixon recognized that these environmental threats required coordinated regulatory action, and in July 1970 Nixon sent (by executive order) Reorganization Plan #3, which created the Environmental Protection Agency as a coordinating agency to work with other national and state agencies to implement comprehensive environmental policy. Subsequent legislation—such as the Clean Air Act (1970), the Clean Water Act (1972), the Coastal Zone Management Act (1972), and the Endangered Species Act (1973) as well as successor laws—requires coordination of local, state, and national government to implement.

Competitive federalism is a modern empirical theory of federalism that treats state and local governments like firms in a competitive marketplace. Under competitive federalism, local governments or states compete with other governments for residents, businesses, and tax revenue. They do so by offering "market baskets" of taxes, land use zoning, and public policies designed to attract residents and businesses. A city might offer expansive public services, place a premium on good schools, build a hospital, or create public goods like parks and bike paths to attract residents. Or, a municipality might limit the construction of low-income housing through zoning and lot-size requirements. Most often, however, competitive federalism focuses on winning businesses. So, for example, a city government might create a special tax-increment financing district to encourage development of businesses in a part of its community. Or, the government might offer a property tax waiver to attract a "big box" store that will attract taxable sales revenues from surrounding communities, or to attract a manufacturer that will bring jobs and residents.

The two problems with competitive federalism are the "race to the bottom" and the "moat and gate" problems. In the race to the bottom, local governments are so aggressive in attracting potential businesses that the costs to government and the community outweigh the benefits of the new firm. Competing governments forced each

Who's Getting What?

Federalism Is the Enemy of Uniformity

Should taxes and services be uniform throughout the United States? Or should federalism allow variations among the states in tax burdens as well as the services provided?

Federalism allows citizens in each state to decide levels of public services (schools, transportation, police and fire protection, and other state and local functions) as well as how much they pay in state and local taxes. If some state voters want more public services and are willing to pay higher taxes for them, and voters in other states want fewer public services and enjoy lower taxes, then federalism allows for a better match between citizen preferences and public policy. Of course, the result is a lack of uniformity across the states.

Consider, for example, differences in per capita state taxes paid by residents of different states in 2010.

Rank	State	Per Capita	Rank	State	Per Capita
1	Alaska	6,361	26	Kentucky	2,197
2	Vermont	4,013	27	Montana	2,166
3	North Dakota	3,934	28	Nevada	2,161
4	Wyoming	3,756	29	New Mexico	2,144
5	Hawaii	3,556	30	Indiana	2,128
6	Connecticut	3,438	31	Mississippi	2,113
7	New York	3,278	32	Nebraska	2,086
8	Minnesota	3,245	33	Virginia	2,051
9	Delaware	3,085	34	Ohio	2,044
10	Massachusetts	3,062	35	Oregon	1,951
11	New Jersey	2,949	36	Louisiana	1,932
12	California	2,814	37	Oklahoma	1,887
13	Maryland	2,637	38	Idaho	1,883
14	Maine	2,627	39	Utah	1,842
15	Wisconsin	2,527	40	Alabama	1,712
16	West Virginia	2,512	41	Colorado	1,707
17	Arkansas	2,496	42	Florida	1,675
18	Rhode Island	2,441	43	Tennessee	1,657
19	Washington	2,395	44	Missouri	1,620
20	Pennsylvania	2,375	45	New Hampshire	1,614
21	Illinois	2,320	46	South Dakota	1,602
22	Michigan	2,289	47	Arizona	1,596
23	Kansas	2,276	48	Texas	1,567
24	North Carolina	2,256	49	Georgia	1,526
25	Iowa	2,235	50	South Carolina	1,471
	United States = 2,286				

SOURCE: U.S. Bureau of the Census and Bureau of Economic Analysis.

States Without Income Taxes		
Alaska	New Hampshire[a]	Texas
Florida	South Dakota	Washington
Nevada	Tennessee[a]	Wyoming

States Taxing Individual Income (rate ranges in parentheses)		
Alabama (2.0–5.0)	Kentucky (2.0–6.0)	North Carolina (6.0–7.7)
Arizona (2.6–4.5)	Louisiana (2.0–6.0)	North Dakota (1.5–4.0)
Arkansas (1.0–7.0)	Maine (2.0–8.0)	Ohio (0.6–5.9)
California (1.0–12.3)	Maryland (2.0–5.7)	Oklahoma (0.5–5.2)
Colorado (4.6)	Massachusetts (5.3)	Oregon (5.0–9.9)
Connecticut (3.0–6.7)	Michigan (4.2)	Pennsylvania (3.0)
Delaware (2.2–6.7)	Minnesota (5.3–7.8)	Rhode Island (3.8–6.0)
Georgia (1.0–6.0)	Mississippi (3.0–5.0)	South Carolina (2.5–7.0)
Hawaii (1.4–11.0)	Missouri (1.5–6.0)	Utah (5.0)
Idaho (1.6–7.4)	Montana (1.0–6.9)	Vermont (3.6–9.0)
Illinois (5.0)	Nebraska (2.5–6.8)	Virginia (2.0–5.75)
Indiana (3.4)	New Jersey (1.4–9.0)	West Virginia (3.0–6.5)
Iowa (0.4–9.0)	New Mexico (1.7–4.9)	Wisconsin (4.6–7.7)
Kansas (3.0-4.9)	New York (4.0–9.0)	

[a]State income tax is limited to dividends and interest only, and excludes wage income.

SOURCE: Council of State Governments, *Book of the States 2013* (Lexington, Ky.: 2013).

Questions

1. What state has the highest state tax burden? The lowest?
2. Pick one state with a high burden and one with a low burden. How did those states fare in the recent recession?
3. Why would a state not tax income?

WETLANDS AND ENVIRONMENTAL FEDERALISM

Transboundary pollution issues are regulated by Congress through the Commerce Clause, which grants the national government authority over "navigable waters." Wetlands are not in the waters, but they affect the water quality of navigable waters, thereby allowing the national government to regulate activities in wetlands through the Clean Water Act.

other to lower the tax obligations to the firm while increasing the cost of attracting and keeping the firm. The "moat and gate" problem arises from using zoning and public services to make a city or county unattractive or cost-prohibitive to many potential residents. By requiring large lots for homes, prohibiting multifamily dwellings, and not offering mass transit or social services, municipalities can limit population density and make their community unattractive to the poor and the working class. Segregation was another means by which competitive federalism was used to create zones of exclusion through state and local policy, and it is the history of segregation that is often used to criticize exclusive uses of local zoning authority.

Historic Landmarks in the Development of American Federalism

The American federal system is a product of more than its formal constitutional provisions. It has also been shaped by interpretations by the courts of constitutional principles as well as the history of disputes that have occurred over state and national authority.

MARBURY v. MADISON **(1803): EXPANDING FEDERAL COURT AUTHORITY** Chief Justice John Marshall, who presided over the Supreme Court from 1801 to 1835, became a major architect of American federalism. Under John Marshall, the Supreme Court assumed the role of arbiter in disputes between state and national authority. It was under John Marshall that the Supreme Court in *Marbury v. Madison* assumed the power to interpret the U.S. Constitution authoritatively.[11] The fact that the referee of disputes between state and national authority has been the national Supreme Court has had a profound influence on the development of American federalism. Since the Supreme Court is a national institution, one might say that in disputes between nation and states, one of the members of the two contending teams is also serving as umpire. Constitutionally speaking, then, there is really no limitation on national authority as there is against state authority if all three branches of the national government—Congress, the president, and the Supreme Court—act together to override state authority.

***McCULLOCH v. MARYLAND* (1819): EXPANDING IMPLIED POWERS OF THE NATIONAL GOVERNMENT** In the case of McCulloch v. Maryland, Chief Justice John Marshall provided a broad interpretation of the Necessary and Proper Clause:

> Let the end be legitimate, let it be within the scope of the Constitution, and all means which are appropriate, which are plainly adopted to the end, which are not prohibited but consistent with the letter and the spirit of the Constitution, are constitutional.[12]

The *McCulloch* case firmly established the principle that the Necessary and Proper Clause gives Congress the right to choose its means for carrying out the enumerated powers of the national government. Today, Congress can devise programs, create agencies, and establish national laws on the basis of long chains of reasoning from the most meager phrases of the constitutional text because of the broad interpretation of the Necessary and Proper Clause.

***SECESSION AND THE CIVIL WAR* (1861–65): MAINTAINING THE "INDESTRUCTIBLE UNION"** The Civil War was, of course, the greatest crisis of the American federal system. Did a state have the right to oppose national law to the point of secession? Regional tensions promoted discussion of New England secession in the early part of the nineteenth century, though no act was forthcoming. In the years between the War of 1812 and the Civil War, John C. Calhoun revitalized and refined secession doctrine, and argued that the Constitution was a compact made by the *states* in a sovereign capacity rather than by the *people* in their national capacity. Calhoun contended that the federal government was an agent of the states, that the states retained their sovereignty in this compact, and that the federal government must not violate the compact, under the penalty of state nullification or even secession from the Union.

The issue was decided in the nation's bloodiest war. What was decided on the battlefield between 1861 and 1865 was confirmed by the Supreme Court in 1869: "Ours is an indestructible union, composed of indestructible states."[13] Yet the states' rights doctrines, and political disputes over the character of American federalism, did not disappear with Lee's surrender at Appomattox. The 13th, 14th, and 15th Amendments, passed by the Reconstruction Congress, were clearly aimed at limiting state power in the interests of individual freedom. The 13th Amendment eliminated slavery in the states; the 15th Amendment prevented states from discriminating against blacks in the right to vote; and the 14th Amendment declared that "No State shall make or enforce any law which shall abridge the privileges or immunities of citizens of the United States; nor shall any state deprive any person of life, liberty, or property without due process of law; nor deny to any person within its jurisdiction the equal protection of the laws." These amendments delegated to Congress the power to secure their enforcement. Yet for several generations these amendments were narrowly construed and added little, if anything, to national power.

The issue of secession was not legally decided until 1869. In *Texas v. White* (74 U.S. 700 [1869]), suit was brought by the postwar Texas state government to recover $10 million in bonds sold by the wartime Confederate state government to New York City speculators George White and John Chiles. The U.S. Supreme Court had original jurisdiction over the case, and ruled that while certain civil acts of the rebel state governments were recognized as legal—marriages, divorces—activities designed to advance rebellion were "treasonous." The court took the opportunity to reject the notion that states could unilaterally leave the union, asserting that the Articles of Confederation had bound the states perpetually and that the Constitution strengthened the "indissoluble . . . perpetual Union." Despite Texas's assertions of having been an independent republic before joining the United States (Vermont, California, and Hawaii also enjoyed brief, independent sovereignty), the U.S. Supreme Court disagreed. A condition of readmission by states reconstructed after the Civil War was a provision in their state constitution acknowledging the final sovereignty of the national constitution and perpetual union.

THE INCOME TAX AND FEDERAL GRANTS (1913) With the money provided to Washington by the passage of the 16th Amendment (income tax) in 1913, Congress embarked on cash grants to the states. Among the earliest cash grant programs were the Federal Highway Act of 1916 and the Smith-Hughes Act of 1917 (vocational education). With federal money came federal direction. For example, states that wanted federal money for highways after 1916 had to accept uniform standards of construction and even a uniform road-numbering system (U.S. 1, U.S. 30, and so on). Shortly after these programs began, the U.S. Supreme Court considered the claim that these federal grants were unconstitutional intrusions into areas "reserved" for the states. But the Court upheld grants as a legitimate exercise of Congress's power to tax and spend for the general welfare.[14]

***NATIONAL LABOR RELATIONS BOARD v. JONES AND LAUGHLIN STEEL CORP.* (1937): EXPANDING INTERSTATE COMMERCE** The Industrial Revolution in America created a national economy with a nationwide network of transportation and communication and the potential for national economic depressions. Yet for a time, the Supreme Court placed obstacles in the way of national authority over the economy, and by so doing the Court created a "crisis" in American federalism. For many years, the Court narrowly construed interstate commerce to mean only the movement of goods and services across state lines, insisting that agriculture, mining, manufacturing, and labor relations were outside the reach of the delegated powers of the national government. However, when confronted with the Great Depression of the 1930s and President Franklin D. Roosevelt's threat to "pack" the Court with additional members to secure approval of his New Deal measures, the Court yielded. In *National Labor Relations Board v. Jones and Laughlin Steel Corp.* in 1937, the Court recognized the principle that production and distribution of goods and services for a national market could be regulated by Congress under the Interstate Commerce Clause.[15] The effect was to give the national government effective control over the national economy.

***BROWN v. BOARD OF EDUCATION* (1954): GUARANTEEING CIVIL RIGHTS** After World War I, the Supreme Court began to build a national system of civil rights that was based on the 14th Amendment. In early cases, the Court held that the 14th Amendment prevented states from interfering with free speech, free press, or religious practices. Not until 1954, in the Supreme Court's landmark desegregation decision in *Brown v. Board of Education* in Topeka, Kansas, did the Court begin to call for the full assertion of national authority on behalf of civil rights.[16] The Supreme Court's use of the 14th Amendment to ensure a national system of civil rights supported by the power of the federal government was an important step in the evolution of the American federal system.

VOTING RIGHTS ACT (1965) AND *BUSH v. GORE* (2000): FEDERAL OVERSIGHT OF ELECTIONS The Voting Rights Act of 1965 plunged the federal government into direct oversight of state and local as well as federal elections in an effort to end discriminatory practices. The act the Justice Department to approve any election law changes in states and communities covered by the act, to ensure no adverse discriminatory impact on minorities. This powerful tool was blunted by the Supreme Court in 2013 in the case *Shelby County v. Holder.*

In the contested presidential election of 2000, the U.S. Supreme Court confirmed national oversight of Electoral College voting and vote counting in *Bush v. Gore.*[17]

In this landmark case, the Court reversed a Florida Supreme Court interpretation of that state's election laws and ruled that voting and vote counting are entitled to Equal Protection and Due Process under the 14th Amendment.

Federalism Revived?

4.5 Assess how Court decisions in recent decades have impacted federalism.

The U.S. Supreme Court today appears to be somewhat more respectful of the powers of states and somewhat less willing to see these powers trampled upon by the national government.[18]

In 1995, the U.S. Supreme Court issued its first opinion in more than 60 years that recognized a limit on Congress's power over interstate commerce and reaffirmed the Founders' notion of a national government with only the powers enumerated in the Constitution.[19] The Court found that the federal Gun-Free School Zones Act was unconstitutional because it exceeded Congress's powers under the Interstate Commerce Clause. When a student, Alfonso Lopez, was apprehended at his Texas high school carrying a .38 caliber handgun, federal agents charged him with violating the *federal* Gun-Free School Zones Act of 1990.

The U.S. government argued that the act was a constitutional exercise of its interstate commerce power, because "violent crime reduces the willingness of individuals to travel to areas within the country that are perceived to be unsafe." But after reviewing virtually all of the key Commerce Clause cases in its history, the Court determined that an activity must *substantially affect* interstate commerce in order to be regulated by Congress. Chief Justice William H. Rehnquist, writing for the majority in a 5–4 decision in *U.S. v. Lopez*, even cited James Madison with approval: "The powers delegated by the proposed Constitution to the federal government are few and defined. Those which are to remain in the state governments are numerous and indefinite" (*Federalist*, No. 45).

In another victory for federalism, the U.S. Supreme Court ruled in 1996 in *Seminole Tribe v. Florida* that the 11th Amendment shields states from lawsuits by private parties that seek to force states to comply with federal laws enacted under the commerce power.[20] And in 1999, in *Alden v. Maine*, the Supreme Court held that states were also shielded in their own courts from lawsuits in which private parties seek to enforce federal mandates. In an opinion that surveyed the history of American federalism, Justice Kennedy wrote: "Congress has vast power but not all power. . . . When Congress legislates in matters affecting the states it may not treat these sovereign entities as mere prefectures or corporations."[21]

In defense of federalism, the Supreme Court invalidated a provision of a very popular law of Congress—the Brady Handgun Violence Protection Act. The Court decided in 1997 that the law's command to local law enforcement officers to conduct background checks on gun purchasers violated "the very principle of separate state sovereignty." The Court affirmed that the federal government "may neither issue directives requiring the states to address particular problems, nor command the states' officers, or those of their political subdivisions, to administer or enforce the federal regulatory program."[22] In addition, the Court held that in the Violence Against Women Act, Congress also invaded the reserved police power of the states.[23]

Will the Supreme Court continue its revival of federalism? Historically, the Court has interpreted the Constitution's Interstate Commerce Clause in a broad fashion, giving Congress extensive powers not originally envisioned by the Founders. The recent cases described above represent a modest change in the direction of recognizing the reserved powers of the states. No doubt the Supreme Court will continue to be called upon to consider the constitutionality of expanding federal powers.

Federalism and Direct Democracy

4.6 Explain how federal grants impact the distribution of power between the federal and state governments.

direct democracy
Decisions are made directly by the people, usually by popular initiative and referenda voting, as opposed to decisions made by elected representatives.

initiative
Allows a specified number or percentage of voters by use of a petition to place a state constitutional amendment or a state law on the ballot for adoption or rejection by the state electorate.

referenda
Proposed laws or constitutional amendments submitted to the voters for their direct approval or rejection; found in some state constitutions but not in the U.S. Constitution.

recall
An election to allow voters to decide whether or not to remove an elected official before his or her term expires.

Direct democracy means that the people themselves can initiate and decide policy questions by popular vote. The nation's Founders were profoundly skeptical of this form of democracy; they believed that the "follies" of direct democracy far outweighed any virtues it might possess. The U.S. Constitution has no provision for direct voting by the people on national policy questions. It was not until over 100 years after the Constitution was written that widespread support developed in the American states for direct voter participation in policy making. Direct democracy developed in states and communities and can be found today only in state and local governments.

Origins of Direct Democracy in the States

At the beginning of the twentieth century, a strong populist movement in the Midwestern and Western states attacked railroads, banks, corporations, and the politicians that were said to be under their control. The populists were later joined by progressive reformers who attacked "bosses," "machines," and parties as corrupt. The populists believed that their elected representatives were ignoring the needs of farmers, debtors, and laborers. They wanted to bypass governors and legislatures and directly enact popular legislation.

The populists and progressives were responsible for the widespread adoption of three forms of direct democracy: the initiative, referendum, and recall.

Initiative

The **initiative** is a device whereby a specific number or percent of voters, through the use of a petition, may have a proposed state constitutional amendment or a state law placed on the ballot for adoption or rejection by the electorate of a state. This process bypasses the legislature and allows citizens to both propose and adopt laws and constitutional amendments. Table 4.2 lists the states that allow popular initiatives for constitutional amendments.

Referendum

The referendum is a device by which the electorate must approve decisions of the legislature before these become law or become part of the state constitution. As we noted earlier, most states require a favorable referendum vote for a state constitutional amendment. **Referenda** on state laws may be submitted by the legislature (when legislators want to shift decision-making responsibility to the people), or referenda may be demanded by popular petition (when the people wish to change laws passed by the legislature).

Recall

Recall elections allow voters to remove an elected official before his or her term expires. Usually a recall election is initiated by a petition. The number of signatures required is usually expressed as a percentage of votes cast in the last election for the official being recalled (frequently 25 percent). Currently, 16 states provide for recall election for some or all of their elected officials (see Table 4.2). Although officials are often publicly threatened with recall, rarely is anyone ever removed from office through this device. A recall of a state elected official requires an expensive petition drive as well as a campaign against the incumbent. The recall has been actively used since 2010 as a tool of politics. In 2011, an effort by minority Democrats was made to recall 9 of 33 members of the Wisconsin senate, to flip party control away from Republicans after the passage of strict limitations on collective bargaining by

Who's Getting What?

Federalism and Obamacare

The Patient Protection and Affordable Care Act (PPACA, also known as "Obamacare") challenged traditional notions of American federalism. The centerpiece of the Act is the individual mandate, a requirement that all individuals either get health insurance or pay a penalty tax for noncompliance. Passed after lengthy legislative wrangling, the legislation provided a focal point for opposition to the new president and the Democratic majority in Congress.

The new law reinvigorated the use of federalism as a political strategy, in part because it relied on federalism to succeed. Therefore, opponents would have to use federalism to try and defeat it.

To advance the PPACA reform, states were expected to create health insurance exchanges (HIX) to help individuals locate affordable health insurance plans. The response varied tremendously. California, Vermont, and Massachusetts, where substantial health care reforms were already enacted, greeted the national reform and moved forward with the creation of exchanges. Many states, especially heavily Republican southern and western states, opposed the PPACA, and offered opposition at the grass roots, through state government, and in the courts.

Gov. Mary Fallin (R-Okla.) was one of the most durable opponents of the PPACA

The Legal Strategy

The National Federation of Independent Businesses sued the federal government to block the law. Twenty-eight states also filed suit or joined lawsuits challenging the PPACA. Opponents claimed that, by instituting a mandate to buy insurance, Congress created commerce in order to regulate it. In a controversial Supreme Court decision in 2012, Chief Justice John Roberts wrote the majority (5–4) opinion holding that the individual mandate cannot be upheld through Congress's power to regulate commerce. While Article I allowed Congress to *regulate* commerce, it did not give Congress the power to *compel* commerce by making people buy something. Ignoring the distinction undermines the principle that the national government has only limited and enumerated powers.

Later, in a nod toward federalism, Roberts held that Congress could not compel the states to expand their Medicaid programs by threatening to withdraw *all* existing Medicaid funds from states that refused to participate in the Act's expansion of the program. Roberts held that this provision of the Act "runs counter to this nations system of federalism." The threatened loss of all Medicaid funds leaves the states with no real option but to acquiesce in Medicaid expansion. To be constitutional under the spending clause of the Constitution, states must *voluntarily* accept the terms of the program. They cannot be compelled to participate.

The Return of Nullification and Interposition

In addition to the strategy of challenging the mandate, another strategy for was pursued, first in Virginia. In 2010 the legislature passed a law designed to "nullify" the individual mandate in the state of Virginia (a "nullification act" purports to render a national law invalid within a state on constitutional grounds). A lawsuit was then brought against the national government. An appeals court ultimately decided that a state, Virginia, had no authority to supersede or nullify a federal law under the Supremacy clause (Article VI, sec. 2).

Seventeen Republican-controlled states subsequently passed laws making it illegal to assist someone trying to find insurance on the PPACA website. These laws were aimed at impeding the efforts of "navigators"—persons placed in the field by the U.S. Department of Health and Human Services—in assisting the uninsured in finding insurance under the "Obamacare" mandate. This is a version in *interposition*, where a state tries to stop the national government from implementing national law.

The State Legislative Strategy

A critical component of PPACA was the creation of health insurance exchanges (HIXs) to allow individuals and businesses to shop for insurance plans. Many Republican-controlled legislatures were pursuing a strategy of nonpreparation or resistance to creating HIXs and also opting out of the proposed Medicaid expansions in the PPACA. Some states pursued this course anticipating a defeat of "Obamacare" in the Supreme Court. Many conservative governors and state legislatures refused to create HIXs or accept federal money to develop HIX. As a consequence, those states became part of the federal health exchange (FIX).

Other states passed Health Care Freedom Amendments (HCFAs). HCFAs were state constitutional amendments to set up a confrontation between state and federal authority, by creating a state "right" to not be made to participate in a health care plan subject to

(*Continued*)

(*Continued*)

a financial penalty. Advocates of these provisions knew they would be mooted in federal court as "nullification" and not valid under the supremacy clause.

The National Electoral Strategy

The national electoral strategy required Republicans to win control of all of national government—the U.S. House, the U.S. Senate, and the presidency. Then, the president and GOP majority would need sufficient will and a strong enough majority to push through an outright repeal of the law. Republican presidential nominee Mitt Romney promised such a repeal if he were elected. He did not succeed.

Obamacare and Federalism

The full effects of the Supreme Court's decision on Obamacare are difficult to predict. On the one hand, Justice Roberts' opinion seems to restrict the use of the interstate commerce clause as a vehicle to assert national government power over the states. On the other hand, the expansive interpretation of Congress's power to tax may give the national government new and unprecedented powers in areas previously reserved to the states.

Finally, the courts have shown no indulgence for old federal theories of state resistance. Despite applying an expanded theory of state equality in interpreting some acts of Congress such as the Voting Rights Act, the courts have not been receptive to interposition, nullification, or other states' rights strategies that attempt to defy the Supremacy Clause.

Questions

1. Is it in the interests of the public for states to symbolically resist federal authority when courts consistently reject states' rights theories of the Constitution?
2. If a state has no interest in helping implement federal law, should it be compelled to do so?

public workers. The effort failed. Recall efforts in Arizona in 2011 were more successful, removing the Republican president pro tempore of the state senate. He had sponsored significant state immigration reform laws. The "granddaddy of all recalls" removed California Governor Gray Davis from office in 2003. The *Terminator* movie star Arnold Schwarzenegger was voted in as his replacement.

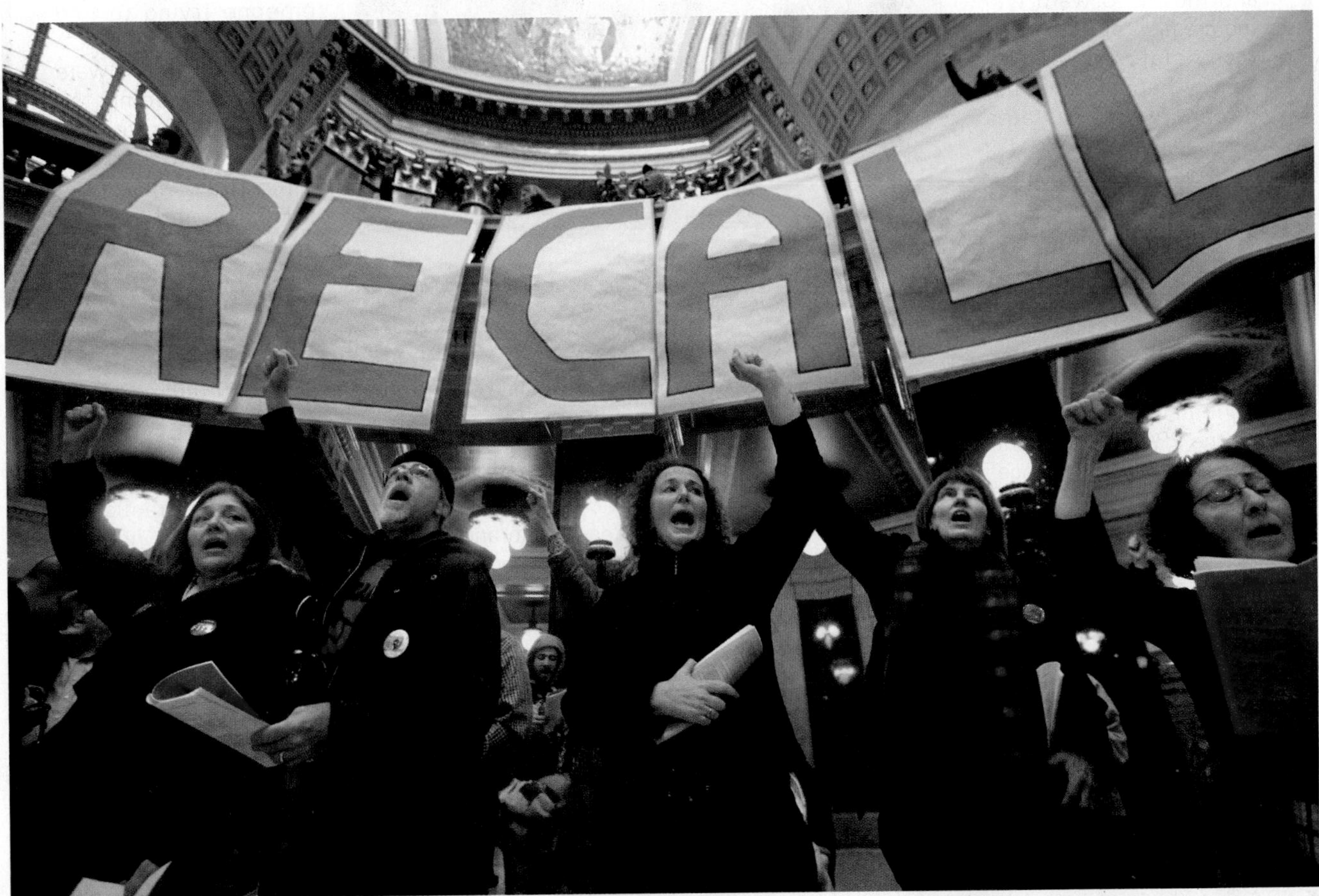

RECALL ELECTIONS

In 2011 the effort to recall Wisconsin's Republican governor, Scott Walker, set off recall efforts across the nation. Walker survived the recall, though some state lawmakers we recalled in Wisconsin, Colorado, and elsewhere.

TABLE 4.2 INITIATIVE AND RECALL IN THE STATES

Currently, 18 states allow voters by petition to place state constitutional amendments on the ballot. And 18 states allow voters' petitions to force a recall vote.

Initiative for Constitutional Amendments (Signatures Required to Get on Ballot)[a]	Recall (Signatures Required to Force a Recall Election)[b]
Arizona (15%)	Alaska (25%)
Arkansas (10%)	Arizona (25%)
California (8%)	California (12%)
Colorado (5%)	Colorado (25%)
Florida (8%)	Georgia (15%)
Illinois (8%)	Idaho (20%)
Massachusetts (3%)	Kansas (40%)
Michigan (10%)	Louisiana (33%)
Mississippi (12%)	Michigan (25%)
Missouri (8%)	Minnesota (25%)
Montana (10%)	Montana (10%)
Nebraska (10%)	Nevada (25%)
Nevada (10%)	New Jersey (25%)
North Dakota (4% of state population)	North Dakota (25%)
Ohio (10%)	Oregon (15%)
Oklahoma (15%)	Rhode Island (15%)
Oregon (8%)	Washington (25%)
South Dakota (10%)	Wisconsin (25%)

[a]Figures expressed as percentage of vote in last governor's election unless otherwise specified; some states also require distribution of votes across counties and districts.

[b]Figures are percentages of voters in last general elections of the official sought to be recalled.

SOURCE: Derived from Council of State Governments, *The Book of the States*, 2009 Edition.

☐ Politics of State Initiatives

State initiatives often reflect popular attitudes rather than the opinions of leaders in business and government. More popular initiatives in recent years include limiting terms for public officials, limiting taxes of various kinds, making English the official language, prohibiting same-sex marriages, allowing gambling, allowing marijuana for medical purposes, and allowing physician-assisted suicide. Of course, citizen initiatives are often backed by "special interests"—specific businesses or industries (such as the gambling industry), religious organizations, and so on. Often a great deal of money is spent for paid workers to gather the necessary signatures and then later to promote the initiative in the public.

Money and Power Flow to Washington

4.7 Assess the impact of coercive federalism on state–national relations.

Over the years, power in the federal system has flowed to Washington because tax money has flowed to Washington. With its financial resources, the federal government has been able to offer assistance to state and local governments and thereby involve itself in just about every governmental function performed by these governments. Today the federal government is no longer one of *enumerated* or *delegated* powers. No activities are really *reserved* to the states.

4.1

4.2

4.3

4.4

4.5

4.6

4.7

4.8

grant-in-aid
Payment of funds from the national government to state or local governments or from a state government to local governments for a specified purpose.

categorical grants
Federal grants to a state or local government for specific purposes or projects; may be allocated by formulas or by projects.

Through its power to tax and spend for the *general welfare*, the national government is now deeply involved in welfare, education, transportation, police protection, housing, hospitals, urban development, and other activities that were once the exclusive domain of state and local government.

☐ Grants-in-Aid

Today, grant-in-aid programs are the single most important source of federal influence over state and local activity. A **grant-in-aid** is defined as "payment of funds by one level of government (national or state) to be expended by another level (state or local) for a specified purpose, usually on a matching-funds basis (the federal government puts up only as much as the state or locality) and in accordance with prescribed standards of requirements."[24] No state or local government is *required* to accept grants-in-aid. Participation in grant-in-aid programs is voluntary. So in theory, if conditions attached to the grant money are too oppressive, state and local governments can simply decline to participate and pass up these funds.

About one-quarter of all state and local government revenues currently come from federal grants. Federal grants are available in nearly every major category of state and local government activity. Over 500 separate grant programs are administered by various federal agencies. So numerous and diverse are these grants that state and local officials often lack information about their availability, purpose, and requirements. "Grantsmanship"—knowing where and how to obtain federal grants—is highly valued in state and local governments. Federal grants can be obtained to preserve historic buildings, develop minority-owned businesses, aid foreign refugees, drain abandoned mines, subsidize school milk programs, and so on. However, welfare (including cash benefits and food stamps) and health (including Medicaid for the poor) account for two-thirds of federal aid money (see Figure 4.3).

Thus, many of the special projects and ongoing programs carried out today by state and local governments are funded by grants from the federal government. These funds have generally been dispersed as either categorical grants or block grants.

- **Categorical Grant.** A grant for a specific purpose or project. The project must be approved by a federal administrative agency. Most federal aid money is distributed in the form of categorical grants. **Categorical grants** can be distributed on a project basis or a formula basis. Grants made on a project basis are distributed by federal administrative agencies to state or local governments that compete for

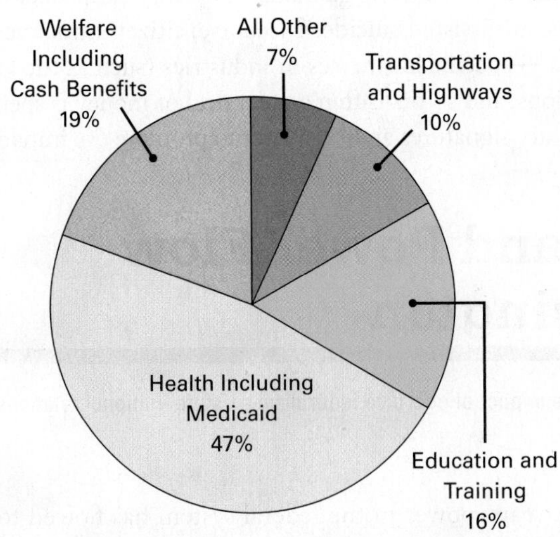

FIGURE 4.3 WHERE DOES GRANT MONEY GO?: PURPOSES OF FEDERAL GRANTS TO STATE AND LOCAL GOVERNMENTS

About one-quarter of all state and local government revenues are derived from federal grants. Federal grants-in-aid to state and local governments are especially vital in the areas of health and welfare.

SOURCE: Budget of the United States Government, 2015.

project funds in their applications. Federal agencies have a great deal of discretion in selecting specific projects for support, and they can exercise direct control over the projects. Most categorical grants are distributed to state or local governments according to a fixed formula set by Congress. Medicaid and SNAP (food stamps) are the largest categorical grant programs.

- **Block Grant.** A grant for a general governmental function, such as health, social services, law enforcement, education, or community development. State and local governments have fairly wide discretion in deciding how to spend federal block grant money within a functional area. For example, cities receiving "community development" block grants can decide for themselves about specific neighborhood development projects, housing projects, community facilities, and so on. All **block grants** are distributed on a formula basis set by Congress. Federal administrative agencies may require reports and adherence to rules and guidelines, but they do not choose which specific projects to fund.

block grants
Federal grants to state or local governments for general government functions allowing greater flexibility in the use of money.

State–Local Dependency on Federal Grants

Prior to 1980, state and local governments throughout the United States were becoming increasingly dependent upon federal grant money. From 1960 to 1980 federal grants as a percent of state–local spending rose from 14.8 percent to 27.4 percent. President Ronald Reagan made significant cutbacks in the flow of federal funds to state and local governments, and by 1990 federal grants constituted only 18.9 percent of state–local spending (see Figure 4.4). Reagan achieved most of this reduction by transforming categorical grants into block grants and then reducing the size of the block grants below the sum of the categorical grants. But following Reagan's efforts, federal grants again began to creep up under Presidents Bill Clinton and George W. Bush, and today federal grants again account for about one-quarter of all state and local government spending.

"Devolution"

Controversy over federalism—what level of government should do what and who should pay for it—is as old as the nation itself (see *A Conflicting View*: Liberals, Conservatives, and Federalism). Beginning in 1995, with a Republican majority in

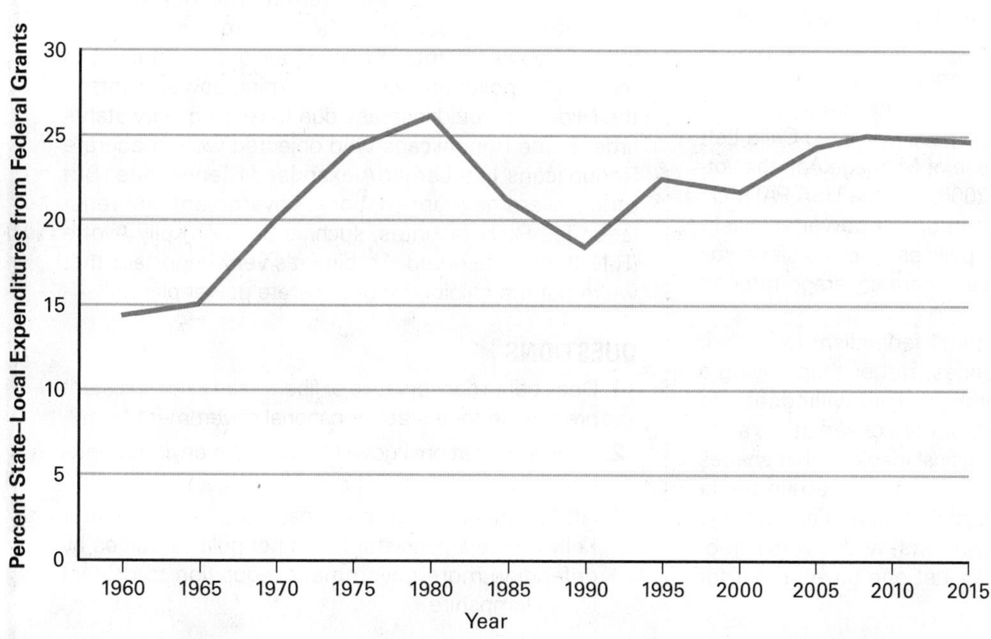

FIGURE 4.4 STATE AND LOCAL GOVERNMENT DEPENDENCY ON FEDERAL GRANTS

State and local governments depend on federal grants for about one-quarter of their revenues. This dependency declined somewhat during the Reagan administration in the 1980s but has since returned to previous levels.

A Conflicting View

Liberals, Conservatives, and Federalism

From the earliest days of the Republic, politicians and legal thinkers argued over federalism. When a political group was in the national majority and controlled the national government, they usually extolled the virtue of national supremacy. Political interests out of the control of the national government, but that had control of a region or some states, sang the praises of preserving the powers of the states.

For most of the twentieth century, battles over federalism followed traditional "liberal" and "conservative" political cleavages. Liberals come mainly from the North and Pacific Coast, and are part of the majority Democratic Party coalition. They sought to enhance the power of the national government. They believe people's lives can be changed—and bettered—by the exercise of *national governmental* power. The government in Washington has more power and resources than do state and local governments, which many liberals regard as too slow, cumbersome, weak, and unresponsive. Liberalism and concentrating power in the national government became closely related in American politics, especially from 1932 until 1968, when the national government made its greatest gains of power during the New Deal and the Great Society.

Conservatives historically want to return power to *state* and *local* governments. Conservatives are skeptical about the "good" that government can do and believe that adding to the power of the national government is not an effective way of resolving society's problems. The elections of Richard Nixon (1968), Ronald Reagan (1980), and George W. Bush (2000) were accompanied by calls from conservatives to limit the power and size of the national government.

But the reality of politics strains the relationship between ideology and theories of federalism. How one feels about federalism is as much about power as ideology. When conservative Republicans controlled the national government, they expanded government in size and reach as much or more so than the liberal, progressive Democrats, including the passage of No Child Left Behind legislation, the Defense of Marriage Act, the Voting Rights Act extension of 2006, and the USA PATRIOT Act. Liberal Democrats, when out of power in Washington, pursued progressive policies, such as same-sex civil rights and expanded health care coverage through state government.

Thus, Americans will "trim" federalism to fit their policy and political preferences, rather than having a consistent theory of federalism. This willingness to shape federalism to fit liberalism or conservatism actually turns federalism into a political ideology that shapes goals around the places where one can attain those goals based on having political power. It is an ideology that assumes many governments, and diverse geographic interests, rather than just one government for all geographic interests.

The Environmental Protection Agency is a frequent source of conservative criticism of the national government.

Yet another example of how federalism is trimmed to fit political values is in the ongoing challenge of environmental protection. Conservatives attack the federal government's Environmental Protection Agency (EPA). EPA exists to protect and manage our environmental resources, especially the quality of air and water. These activities have a major impact on business. One-seventh of all industries in the United States are directly affected by EPA air quality efforts alone. The Republican Party is the historic party of business, and therefore the party most commonly opposed to EPA. With the GOP takeover of the U.S. House of Representatives in 2011, conservatives set out to curtail EPA's power. Limitations on EPA passed a Republican-controlled House. In the Democratic Senate, all the anti-EPA bills stalled due to Democratic filibusters.

The exception was Kentucky Senator Rand Paul's proposal roll back some air pollution standards set in 2005. Democrats from the South and Midwest crossed party lines to support the bill, which still failed. And, some Senate Republicans voted with liberal Democrats against the bill. Why?

The reason was self-interest. The Republicans were from states downwind from the midwestern coal-burning power plants. Relaxing air quality standards meant that pollution from coal-burning power plants in the Midwest would increase due to lax air quality standards. Some Republicans who objected were moderate Republicans like Lamar Alexander of Tennessee. But others were new anti–national government, antiregulation Tea Party favorites, such as Senator Kelly Ayotte (R-NH) who observed, "I think it's very important that we're not the tailpipe for out-of-state power plants."

QUESTIONS

1. Does being conservative or liberal lead to a consistent preference for a state or national government?
2. Why is the national government in the environmental protection business?
3. NIMBY means "not in my backyard." Was Senator Kelly Ayotte inconsistent with her political values by defending more government regulation to protect New Hampshire?

SOURCES: Alison Croix. 2010. *The Ideological Origins of American Federalism*. Cambridge, Mass.: Harvard University Press.
David C. Nice and George H. Frederickson. 1987. *The Politics of Intergovernmental Relations*. New York: St. Martin's Press.
http://www.issues2000.org/2004/Al_Sharpton_Civil_Rights.htm

Who's Getting What?

Can Congress Regulate Marriage?

Same-sex marriage brings a variety of federalism issues into sharper focus. In September 1996, Congress passed the Defense of Marriage Act (DOMA), which defined marriage as one man and one woman and denied marriage benefits to same-sex partners under 1,100 federal programs. When the issue first came up in 1996, over two-thirds of Americans opposed same-sex marriage; 15 years later, a solid majority of Americans favor legalizing same-sex marriage, with the greatest support among younger voters, moderates, liberals, and more affluent Americans (see the figure). However, both state and local government have taken actions that set up potential federalism questions that might only be resolved by the federal courts:

Why Do States Worry About Same-Sex Marriage in Other States?

Under the Full Faith and Credit clause (Article IV, Sec. 1), "Full faith and credit shall be given in each state to the public acts, records, and judicial proceedings of every other state." A contract interpretation, record of deed or title, or judicial judgment in one state will be recognized in other states—including divorce decrees. Because a divorce in Nevada must be recognized in New York, the assumption of the public is that marriages have to be recognized too. So, a same-sex marriage in Hawaii, Vermont, or Massachusetts would be legal in other states, if Full Faith and Credit applied.

Does a State Have to Recognize a Same-Sex Marriage from Another State?

The original assumption of both advocates and opponents of same-sex marriage was "yes." But in fact, no state has yet been compelled to recognize a marriage that was not legal in the state. For example, states with interracial marriage bans were never compelled to recognize interracial marriages—*Loving v. Virginia* overturned such bans as unconstitutional under the Equal Protection clause. And a state need not recognize the legal marriage from another state of a person who does not meet the age of marital consent.

What Can States Do to Define Marriage?

In order to buttress heterosexual, monogamous marriage, 39 states passed laws or state constitutional amendments (mini-DOMAs) defining marriage as one man and one woman, creating a state constitutional barrier. However, states have been compelled to recognize adoptions by same-sex couples, indicating that Full Faith and Credit apply to a variety of other areas of family law involving same-sex couples. The challenge for the states is demonstrating that such definitions of marriage do not violate equal protection under the 14th Amendment.

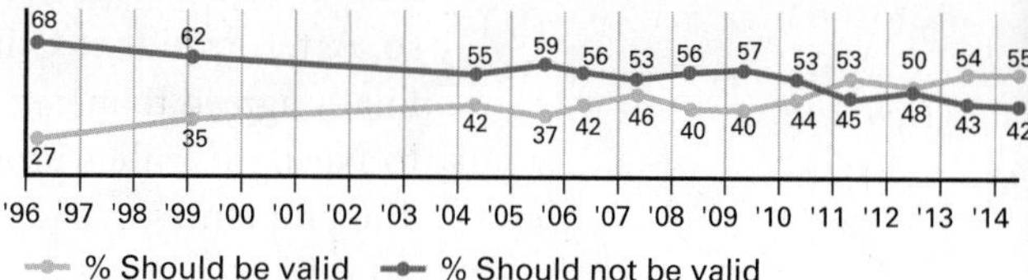

Death of DOMAs

The Defense of Marriage Act presented a federalism challenge. Article I of the Constitution does not give Congress the authority to regulate or define marriage. But under Full Faith and Credit, "the Congress may by general laws prescribe the manner in which such acts, records, and proceedings shall be proved, and the effect thereof." Supporters argued that, by defining the types of marriages that might be recognized under Full Faith and Credit, Congress acted within its scope of authority under Article IV. The Supreme Court disagreed.

In *United States v. Windsor* (570 U.S. ______ 2013), the survivor of a same-sex couple from New York, married in Canada, sought a surviving spouse exemption under U.S. estate law. The IRS refused the exemption, citing section 3 of DOMA. After three years of litigation, the U.S. Supreme Court held, in a 5-4 decision written by Justice Antony Kennedy, that DOMA constituted a "deprivation of the liberty of the person protected by the Fifth Amendment."

Meanwhile, down in the states, multiple federal district court judges struck down state constitutional or legal requirements that marriage be defined as one man and one woman. Within a seven-month period between December 2013 and June 2014, judges in Arkansas, Idaho, Kentucky, Michigan, Ohio, Oklahoma, Oregon, Pennsylvania, Texas, Utah, Virginia, and Wisconsin struck down state definition of marriage acts or amendments as violations of equal protection, due process, or both for same sex individuals.

The aggressive and consistent action by state and federal district courts in the mini-DOMA cases combined with the precedent at the national level from *Windsor* indicate that the full faith and credit concerns that compelled Congress and the states to defend marriage may well become moot.

Questions

1. Why do you think public opinion shifted regarding same-sex marriage?
2. Most states, including most of the most populous states, have definition of marriage amendments that were approved by the voters. If same-sex marriage is so popular, why is it banned by the voters in so many states?
3. Does your state have legal same-sex marriage? If you wanted to change the state law, how could you do so?

4.1
4.2
4.3
4.4
4.5
4.6
4.7
4.8

devolution
Passing down of responsibilities from the national government to the states.

both houses of Congress and Republicans holding a majority of state governorships, debates over federalism were renewed. The new phrase was **devolution**—the passing down of responsibilities from the national government to the states.

Welfare reform turned out to be the key to devolution. Bill Clinton once promised "to end welfare as we know it," but it was a Republican Congress in 1996 that did so. After President Clinton had twice vetoed welfare reform bills, he and Congress finally agreed to merge welfare reform with devolution. A new Temporary Assistance to Needy Families program replaced direct federal cash aid welfare "entitlements." The program:

- establishes block grants with lump-sum allocations to the states for cash welfare payments.
- grants the states broad flexibility in determining eligibility and benefit levels for persons receiving such aid.
- Limits the use of federally aided cash grants for most recipients to two continuing years and five years over their lifetime.
- allows states to deny additional cash payments for children born to women already receiving welfare assistance and allows states to deny cash payments to parents under 18 who do not live with an adult and attend school.

Since Franklin D. Roosevelt's New Deal, with its federal guarantee of cash Aid to Families with Dependent Children (AFDC), low-income mothers and children had enjoyed a federal "entitlement" to welfare payments. But welfare reform, with its devolution of responsibility to the states, ended this 60-year-old federal entitlement. Note, however, that Congress continues to place "strings" on the use of federal welfare funds, including a two-year limit on continuing payments to beneficiaries and a five-year lifetime limit.

Political Obstacles to Devolution and Federalism

Politicians in Washington are fond of the rhetoric of federalism. They know that Americans generally prefer governments closer to home. Yet at the same time they confront strong political pressures to "DO SOMETHING!" about virtually every problem that confronts individuals, families, or communities, whether or not doing so may overstep the enumerated powers of the national government. Politicians gain very little by telling their constituents that a particular problem—violence in the schools, domestic abuse, physician-assisted suicide, and so on—is not a federal responsibility and should be dealt with at the state or local level of government. So both federal and state politicians compete to address well-publicized problems.[25]

Moreover, neither presidents nor members of Congress are inclined to restrain their own power. Both liberals and conservatives in Washington are motivated to tie their own strings to federal grant-in-aid money, issue their own federal mandates, and otherwise "correct" what they perceive to be errors or inadequacies of state policies.

Coercive Federalism: Preemptions and Mandates

4.8 Describe coercive federalism and explain how it has altered state–national relations.

raditionally, Congress avoided issuing direct orders to state and local governments. Instead, it sought to influence them by offering grants of money with federal rules, regulations, or "guidelines" attached. In theory at least, states and communities were free to forgo the money and

ignore the strings attached to it. But increasingly Congress has been guilty of **coercive federalism**, undertaking direct regulation of areas traditionally reserved to the states and restricting state authority to regulate these areas. And it has issued direct orders to state and local governments to perform various services and comply with federal law in the performance of these services.

coercive federalism
A term referring to direct federal orders (mandates) to state and local governments to perform a service or conform to federal law in the performance of a function.

Federal Preemptions

The supremacy of federal laws over those of the states, spelled out in the National Supremacy Clause of the Constitution, permits Congress to decide whether there is **preemption** of state laws in a particular field by federal law. In **total preemption**, the federal government assumes all regulatory powers in a particular field—for example, copyrights, bankruptcy, railroads, and airlines. No state regulations in a totally preempted field are permitted. **Partial preemption** stipulates that a state law on the same subject is valid as long as it does not conflict with the federal law in the same area. For example, the Occupational Safety and Health Act of 1970 specifically permits state regulation of any occupational safety or health issue on which the federal Occupational Safety and Health Administration (OSHA) has *not* developed a standard; but, once OSHA enacts a standard, all state standards are nullified. A specific form of partial preemption called **standard partial preemption** permits states to regulate activities in a field already regulated by the federal government, as long as state regulatory standards are at least as stringent as those of the federal government. Usually states must submit their regulations to the responsible federal agency for approval; the federal agency may revoke a state's regulating power if that state fails to enforce the approved standards. For example, the federal Environmental Protection Agency (EPA) permits state environmental regulations that meet or exceed EPA standards. (See *What Do You Think?* Can a State Pass Its Own Immigration Law?)

preemption
Total or partial federal assumption of power in a particular field, restricting the authority of the states.

total preemption
Federal government's assumption of all regulatory powers in a particular field.

partial preemption
Federal government's assumption of some regulatory powers in a particular field, with the stipulation that a state law on the same subject as a federal law is valid if it does not conflict with the federal law in the same area.

standard partial preemption
Form of partial preemption in which the states are permitted to regulate activities already regulated by the federal government if the state regulatory standards are at least as stringent as the federal government's.

Federal Mandates

Federal **mandates** are direct orders to state and local governments to perform a particular activity or service or to comply with federal laws in the performance of their functions. Federal mandates occur in a wide variety of areas, from civil rights to minimum-wage regulations. Their range is reflected in some recent examples of federal mandates to state and local governments:

mandates
Perceptions of popular support for a program or policy based on the margin of electoral victory won by a candidate who proposed it during a campaign; direct federal orders to state and local governments requiring them to perform a service or to obey federal laws in the performance of their functions.

- **Age Discrimination Act, 1986.** Outlaws mandatory retirement ages for public as well as private employees, including police, firefighters, and state college and university faculty.
- **Asbestos Hazard Emergency Act, 1986.** Orders school districts to inspect for asbestos hazards and remove asbestos from school buildings when necessary.
- **Safe Drinking Water Act, 1986.** Establishes national requirements for municipal water supplies; regulates municipal waste treatment plants.
- **Clean Air Act, 1990.** Bans municipal incinerators and requires auto emission inspections in certain urban areas.
- **Americans with Disabilities Act, 1990.** Requires all state and local government buildings to promote handicapped access.
- **National Voter Registration Act, 1993.** Requires states to register voters at driver's license, welfare, and unemployment compensation offices.
- **No Child Left Behind Act, 2001.** Requires states and their school districts to test public school pupils.
- **Help America Vote Act, 2003.** Requires states to modernize registration and voting procedures and technologies.

4.1

4.2

4.3

4.4

4.5

4.6

4.7

4.8

What Do You Think?

Can a State Pass Its Own Immigration Laws?

Frustrated by the failure of the federal government to enforce existing federal immigration laws, several states, starting with Oklahoma, passed state illegal-immigration laws between 2007 and 2012. The most notable law passed to date, in Arizona, continued the legal fight over the ability of states to deal with what they deem a failure of the national government to meet its obligations to control immigration.

Confronting a serious immigration problem (there are an estimated 460,000 illegal immigrants in Arizona) and a lengthy border with Mexico, Arizona moved aggressively to deal with immigration. The 2010 Arizona law, SB 1070, mirrored the federal law dealing with aliens, requiring them to carry valid immigration documents, and made it a state crime to be in the country illegally. Police were given broad powers to detain anyone suspected of being an illegal alien.

The key provision of the Arizona law stated that: "For any lawful contact made by a law enforcement officer ... where reasonable suspicion exists that a person is an alien who is unlawfully present in the United States, a reasonable attempt shall be made when practicable to determine the immigration status of the person...." A "lawful contact" presumably means that a police officer has stopped an individual for violating another law, most likely a traffic stop. "Reasonable suspicion" may involve a combination of circumstances, but the law specifically prohibits officers from using race or ethnicity as factors in determining reasonable suspicion. The law also states that if a person produces a state driver's license or other state-issued identification, he or she is presumed to be in the United States legally. Once identified as illegal immigrants, persons can be taken into custody, prosecuted for violating Arizona law, or turned over to federal Immigration and Customs Enforcement (ICE) for deportation.

Citizens of Arizona, local governments, and the U.S. Justice Department all filed suit against the Arizona law arguing that it violates the Supremacy Clause of the Constitution: "A state may not establish its own immigration policy or enforce state laws in a manner that interferes with federal immigration laws. The Constitution and federal immigration laws do not permit the development of a patchwork of state and local immigration policy throughout the country." Although the Arizona law was written to ensure it was not in conflict with federal laws, federal courts must answer a related question, "Do federal laws preempt state laws on immigration?" Another constitutional question is whether the Arizona law poses a threat to the 14th Amendment's Equal Protection Clause by encouraging racial profiling in its enforcement. Federal courts may find that the Arizona law is an invitation to harassment and discrimination against Hispanics.

The federal district court for Arizona agreed with plaintiffs on these most controversial parts of the law. The court struck down the most controversial provisions of the law, including the "stop and check" provisions and providing for the ability of citizens to bring civil suits against the government for failing to implement the law. However, other portions of the law that had been challenged by Arizona residents and municipalities, including provisions preventing the creation of "sanctuary cities," were not overturned by the federal court. An appeal to the U.S. Ninth Circuit in San Francisco upheld the district court decision, in which the three-judge federal panel concluded that the state had intruded on federal government prerogatives. The political consequences weighed heavily in the mind of the majority, which wrote, "The Arizona statute before us has become a symbol. For those sympathetic to immigrants to the United States, it is a challenge and a chilling foretaste of what other states might attempt."

Arizona immediately appealed the case to the U.S. Supreme Court. The high court granted *certiorari* to the case and heard argument the following April. On June 25, 2012, the U.S. Supreme Court handed down its decision in *Arizona v. United States* (567 U.S. ________). Applying Article I of the Constitution and the Supremacy Clause (Article VI), the Court struck down three of four parts of 1070: section 3 (the 'carry your papers' provision), section 5 (the work application provision), and section 6 (the warrantless arrest provision) of the law while leaving intact the authority to determine immigration status during a legal stop. The majority argued that federal law preempted state action in these areas.

The decision invalidated similar provisions of state law in Alabama, Georgia, Indiana, South Carolina, and Utah, which had enacted SB 1070-style immigration laws in 2011. The political consequence includes a significant decline of state efforts to pass state immigration legislation. Where fifty immigration bills were introduced in thirty states in 2011, the next year bills were introduced in just five states, and none passed new immigration legislation.

Questions

1. Who bears the burden of implementing the law?
2. Is it possible to implement these laws without profiling people based on their color or ethnicity?

A Constitutional Note

How Is National and State Power Divided?

The Constitution gives to Congress—that is, to the national government—17 specific grants of power, the so-called "enumerated powers." These are followed by an eighteenth "necessary and proper" power—"to make all laws which shall be necessary and proper for carrying into Execution the foregoing powers, and all other Powers vested by this Constitution in the Government of the United States ... " (Article I, Section 8). It is this last "implied powers" or "elastic" clause that has been used extensively by the national government to greatly expand its power.

But what of the states? The Founders believed that the Constitution left all other governmental powers to the states. The 10th Amendment solidified that idea: "The powers not delegated to the United States by the Constitution, nor prohibited by it to the States, are reserved to the States respectively, or to the people." The "reserved powers" of the states are limited only by a few paragraphs in the text of the Constitution, notably Article I, Section 10, which, among other things, prohibits the states from entering into treaties with other nations, or coining money, or passing laws impairing the obligation of contracts, or granting any title of nobility, or placing taxes or duties on imports or exports, or engaging in war with a foreign power "unless actually invaded."

In brief, the original Constitution envisioned the states as having the principal responsibility for the health, safety, education, welfare, law enforcement, and protection of their people. This constitutional "division of power" remains in the Constitution, despite great shifts in power to the national government. Subsequent amendments prohibited slavery in the states (13th Amendment); prohibited states from abridging the privileges or immunities of citizens of the United States, or depriving any person of life, liberty, or property without due process of law, or denying any person within this jurisdiction equal protection of the laws (14th Amendment); or prohibiting citizens the right to vote because of race, color, or previous condition of servitude (15th Amendment); or denying the right to vote for failure to pay any poll tax or other tax (24th Amendment); or denying anyone 18 years of age or older the right to vote on account of age (26th Amendment).

So anyone reading the Constitution, without knowledge of the history of constitutional change in the United States, would not really understand the nature of American federalism.

Questions

1. How do the 13th, 14th, and 15th Amendments change how the 10th Amendment is read?
2. Do you think states need more latitude to make policy than they currently enjoy?

- **Homeland Security Act, 2002.** Requires states and communities as "first responders" to train, equip, and prepare for terrorist attacks.
- **Real ID Act, 2005.** Requires states to issue secure driver's licenses as defined by the Department of Homeland Security.

unfunded mandates
Mandates that impose costs on state and local governments (and private industry) without reimbursement from the federal government.

"Unfunded" Mandates

Federal mandates often impose heavy costs on states and communities. When no federal monies are provided to cover these costs, the mandates are said to be **unfunded mandates**. Governors, mayors, and other state and local officials have often urged Congress to stop imposing unfunded mandates on states and communities. Private industries have long voiced the same complaint. Regulations and mandates allow Congress to address problems while pushing the costs of doing so onto others.

Review the Chapter

Why Federalism? The Argument for a "Compound Republic"

4.1 Distinguish the federal form of government from confederal and unitary forms and evaluate the arguments in favor of federalism, p. 98

Federalism is the division of power between two separate authorities, the nation and the state, each of which enforces its own laws directly on its citizens and neither of which can change the division of power without the consent of the other. Federalism has also been defended as a means of increasing opportunities to hold public office, improving governmental efficiency, ensuring policy responsiveness, encouraging policy innovation, and managing conflict.

The Original Design of Federalism

4.2 Distinguish the delegated, reserved, concurrent, and denied powers granted to the state and federal governments, p. 104

The U.S. Constitution originally defined American federalism in terms of the powers (delegated, implied, reserved, and shared) that belong—or are denied—to the national and state governments. The Founders placed a larger emphasis on the powers of state and local governments to make public policy than is placed on them today.

The Evolution of American Federalism

4.3 Trace the evolution of American federalism, p. 108

Power has flowed to the national government over time, as the original state-centered division of power has evolved into a national-centered system of government. Among the most important historical influences on this shift in power toward Washington have been the Supreme Court's broad interpretation of national power, the national government's victory over the secessionist states in the Civil War, the establishment of a national system of civil rights based on the 14th Amendment, the growth of a national economy governed by Congress under its interstate commerce power, and the national government's accumulation of power through its greater financial resources.

Other Political Science Theories of Federalism

4.4 Describe how the use of federalism leads to theories of political behavior, p. 112

The expansion of national government authority in the 1960s and the growth of new areas of government involvement led to theories of politics rooted in federalism. These theories—fiscal federalism, environmental federalism, and competitive federalism—use intergovernmental relationships and the existence of problems that affect multiple and different levels of government to explain how public policies are made and implemented.

Federalism Revived?

4.5 Assess how court decisions in recent decades have impacted federalism, p. 117

The Supreme Court in its *Garcia* decision in 1985 removed all constitutional barriers to direct congressional legislation in matters traditionally reserved to the states. Establishing the principle of representational federalism, the Court said that states could defend their own interests through their representation in the national government. Some states are symbolically resisting national government power for political purposes.

Federalism and Direct Democracy?

4.6 Explain how federal grants impact the distribution of power between the federal and state governments, p. 118

Direct democracy means that people can initiate and decide policy questions without the intervention of elected officials. It was started by the Progressives and Populists and has been used in California most notably. Variations of direct democracy include initiatives, recall elections, and referenda.

Money and Power Flow to Washington

4.7 Assess the impact of coercive federalism on state–national relations, p. 121

Federal grants to state and local governments have greatly expanded the national government's powers in areas previously regarded as *reserved* to the states.

Coercive Federalism: Preemptions and Mandates

4.8 Describe coercive federalism and explain how it has altered state–national relations, p. 126

Although Congress has generally refrained from directly legislating in areas traditionally *reserved* to the states, federal power in local affairs has grown as a result of federal rules, regulations, and guidelines established as conditions for the receipt of federal funds.

Learn the Terms

federalism, p. 98
unitary system, p. 98
confederation, p. 98
Dillon's Rule, p. 98
home rule, p. 98
intergovernmental relations, p. 101
laboratories of democracy, p. 104
delegated, or enumerated, powers, p. 105
Necessary and Proper Clause, p. 105
implied powers, p. 105
National Supremacy Clause, p. 107
concurrent powers, p. 107
reserved powers, p. 107
dual federalism, p. 108
cooperative federalism, p. 109
centralized federalism, p. 110
new federalism, p. 110
representational federalism, p. 111
fiscal federalism, p. 112
environmental federalism, p. 112
competitive federalism, p. 112
direct democracy, p. 118
initiative, p. 118
referenda, p. 118
recall, p. 118
grant-in-aid, p. 122
categorical grants, p. 122
block grants, p. 123
devolution, p. 126
coercive federalism, p. 127
preemption, p. 127
total preemption, p. 127
partial preemption, p. 127
standard partial preemption, p. 127
mandates, p. 127
unfunded mandates, p. 129

Test Yourself

4.1 Distinguish the federal form of government from the confederal and unitary forms and evaluate the arguments in favor of federalism

The principle advantages of federalism include that it

a. centralizes power
b. leads to less governmental efficiency
c. prohibits local leaders from frustrating national policy
d. encourages policy innovation
e. encourages direct democracy

4.2 Distinguish the delegated, reserved, concurrent, and denied powers granted to the state and federal governments

The National Supremacy Clause provides for

a. a constitutional justification for a "my country right or wrong" mindset
b. a constitutional justification for judicial review of state laws
c. those powers not delegated to the states to be reserved to the national government
d. the constitution and national law to be the supreme law of the country
e. a Supreme Court to determine resolution to institutional conflict

4.3 Trace the evolution of American federalism

The case that did more than any other to expand national judicial power by giving the Supreme Court the power to interpret the Constitution was

a. *Marbury v. Madison*
b. *McCulloch v. Maryland*
c. *National Labor Relations Board v. Jones and Laughlin Steel Corporation*
d. *Brown v. Board of Education*
e. *Buffett v. Longboat Key*

4.4 Describe how the use of federalism leads to theories of political behavior

Two inequities that can arise from competitive federalism are ________ and ________

a. 'market baskets' and 'big boxes'
b. fait and transport
c. referenda and initiative
d. 'race to the bottom' and 'moat and gate'
e. dual inequities and parsed inequities

4.5 Assess how court decisions in recent decades have impacted federalism.

Recent decisions of the Supreme Court to take a more restrictive look at what type of federal regulations will be allowed under the interstate commerce clause involved policies on

a. gun control and crimes against women
b. marijuana legalization and taxation
c. gun control and taxation
d. crimes against women and legalization of marijuana
e. fait and transport of particulate pollutants

4.6 Explain how federal grants impact the distribution of power between the federal and state governments

Federal categorical grants differ from block grants in that they make specific provisions for how money allocated to state government-implemented programs will be spent. As a consequence, these grants result in:

a. increase state control over how money is spent on projects
b. increase local control over how money is spent on projects
c. increase national government control over how money is spent
d. nothing, because these grants are no longer used by the federal government
e. a result the same as earmarks

4.7 Assess the impact of coercive federalism on state–national relations

The federal government is now deeply involved in many activities that previously were the domain of the state and local governments because of

a. the 10th amendment, which gives manypowers to the national government
b. the federal power to ensure domestic tranquility
c. the power to tax and spend for the general welfare
d. the nationalist interpretation of the Full Faith and Credit Clause
e. the return to a Lochner-era court

4.8 Describe coercive federalism and explain how it has altered state–national relations

A component of the debate over federal government power concerns the use of congressional mandates to compel states to pursue policy goals. Sometimes these requirements come without any funding from the federal government. The use of "mandates" has allowed the federal government to

a. achieve more policy diversity at more economical costs
b. address public problems at more economical costs
c. achieve more policy experimentation and push the costs onto others
d. address public problems and the push the costs onto other governments
e. policy diversity that pushes the costs of policy onto other governments

Explore Further

SUGGESTED READINGS

Dye, Thomas R. *American Federalism: Competition Among Governments.* Lexington, Mass.: Lexington Books, 1990. A theory of "competitive federalism" arguing that rivalries among governments improve public services while lowering taxes, restrain the growth of government, promote innovation and experimentation in public policies, inspire greater responsiveness to the preferences of citizen-taxpayers, and encourage economic growth.

Dye, Thomas R., and Susan A. MacManus. *Politics in States and Communities.* 14th ed. Upper Saddle River, N.J.: Pearson, 2011. A general introduction to state and local government and politics, with an extended discussion of the politics of federalism.

Elazar, Daniel J. *The American Partnership.* Chicago: University of Chicago Press, 1962. Classic study of the historical evolution of federalism, stressing the nation-state sharing of policy concerns and financing, from the early days of the Republic, and the politics behind the gradual growth of national power.

Gaddie, Ronald Keith, and James L. Regens. *Regulating Wetland Protection: Environmental Federalism and the States.* Albany: SUNY Press, 2000. Explores the problem of state–national coordination on environmental problems through the example of the regulation of wetlands.

Gerston, Larry M. *American Federalism.* New York: M. E. Sharpe, 2007. A brief introduction to federalism, including "change events" that have shaped American federal principles over time.

LaCroix, Alison L. *The Ideological Origins of American Federalism.* Cambridge, Harvard University Press 2011. Examine show early ideologies in the United States affected the shaping of American federalism.

Nagel, Robert F. *The Implosion of Federalism.* New York: Oxford University Press, 2001. America's political institutions are collapsing into the center, reducing the opportunity for competition and participation.

Ostrum, Vincent. *The Meaning of American Federalism.* San Francisco: ICS Press, 1991. A theoretical examination of federalism, setting forth the conditions for a self-governing society and arguing that multiple, overlapping units of government, with various checks on one another's power, provide a viable democratic system of conflict resolution.

O'Toole, Laurence J., ed. *American Intergovernmental Relations.* 4th ed. Washington, D.C.: CQ Press, 2006. A collection of readings, both classic and contemporary, describing the theory, history, and current problems of intergovernmental relations in America.

Peterson, Paul E. *The Price of Federalism.* Washington, D.C.: Brookings Institution, 1995. Historical, theoretical, and empirical perspectives merged into a model of federalism that would allocate social welfare functions to the national government and education and economic development to states and communities.

Riker, William H. *Federalism: Origin, Operation, Significance.* Boston: Little, Brown and Co. 1964. A classic account of federalism that considers the history of federalism, compares federalism as applied in different countries, and describes and analyses its operational principles.

Van Horn, Carl E. *The State of the States.* 4th ed. Washington, D.C.: CQ Press, 2005. An assessment of the challenges facing state governments as a result of the devolution revolution.

SUGGESTED WEB SITES

The Close Up Foundation **www.closeup.org**

A nonprofit, nonpartisan citizenship education organization with excellent historical materials about federalism's evolution and information about federalism issues. A related link on the Close Up site contains the complete text of the pro-states' rights 1798 Kentucky and Virginia Resolutions (authored by Jefferson and Madison).

Council of State Governments **www.csg.org**

Official organization of U.S. states, providing information on their governmental structures, officials, and current issues.

European Union Online Official Site **http://europa.eu/**

Describes the structure of the organization, its membership, current issues, and so forth.

National Conference of State Legislatures **www.ncsl.org**

This conference site provides information on 50 state legislatures and the issues they confront.

Urban Institute **www.urban.org**

This Washington think tank offers viewpoints on federalism and issues confronting state and local government.

5

Opinion and Participation

Thinking and Acting in Politics

In the United States, people vote in local polling places that are located in courthouses, government buildings, schools, public meeting halls, neighbors' garages—and churches. And, where you vote might affect how you vote.

Do you vote at a school? You are more likely to support a school-funding initiative. This relationship is found among liberals and conservatives, young and old, and regardless of race or ethnicity.

Do you vote at a church? Regardless of your religiosity or your affiliation, you are more likely to vote for a conservative candidate or to ban same-sex marriage. The effect is more pronounced if "ecclesiastical images" like a crucifix are visible to the voter. And, the effect was more pronounced among Christian believers than other voters. This same effect was observed when people were asked to assign a jury verdict where the claimed injury (birth control pill litigation) might have offended their moral beliefs.

Political psychologists uncovered this relationship by running experiments and conducting surveys of voters in polling places in the U.S. These are called *priming effects.* When people grow up with or are socialized to symbols and values and word associations, exposure to symbols in a *context* can modify their subconscious behavior.

So does it matter where you vote? Yes. Does it matter where local government decides where you vote? Possibly, because a place has the ability to trigger latent attitudes or preferences when you go to express an opinion.

5.1 Analyze the relationships between politics, public opinion, and policy changes, p. 136

5.2 Explain how the agents of socialization influence the development of political opinions, p. 140

5.3 Determine the role of ideology in shaping opinion and describe the relationship between gender, race, and opinion, p. 144

5.4 Assess how and to what extent public opinion influences public policy making, p. 148

5.5 Identify the various ways in which a citizen may participate in politics, p. 152

5.6 Trace the expansion of the right to vote, p. 152

5.7 Analyze the political and demographic factors that influence voter turnout, and assess the consequences of nonvoting, p. 156

5.8 Characterize protest as a form of political participation, p. 165

POLLING PLACES Americans vote in government buildings, public halls, churches, and even the garages of their neighbors.

Politics and Public Opinion

5.1 Analyze the relationships between politics, public opinion, and policy changes.

public opinion
Aggregate of preferences and opinions of individuals on significant issues.

survey research
Gathering of information about public opinion by questioning a representative sample of the population.

halo effect
Tendency of survey respondents to provide socially acceptable answers to questions.

Bradley effect
Tendency of white voters to not express opposition to a black candidate to pollsters, in order to not appear racist.

For most Americans, politics is not as interesting as football or basketball, the sex lives of celebrities, or prime-time television entertainment. Although politicians, pollsters, and commentators frequently assume that Americans have formed opinions on major public issues, in fact, most have not given them very much thought. Nevertheless, **public opinion** commands the attention of politicians, the news media, and political scientists.

Public opinion is considered important in democracies because democratic governments rest on the consent of the governed. Major shifts in public opinion in the United States generally translate into policy change. Both the president and Congress appear to respond over time to *general* public preferences for "more" or "less" government regulation, "more" or "less" government spending, "getting tough on crime," "reforming welfare," and so on.[1] But public opinion is often weak, unstable, ill informed, or nonexistent on *specific* policy issues. Consequently, elected officials have greater flexibility in dealing with these issues—and, at the same time, there is an increase in the influence of lobbyists, interest groups, reporters, commentators, and others who have direct access to policy makers. Moreover, the absence of well-formed public opinion on an issue provides interest groups and the media with the opportunity to influence policy indirectly by shaping popular opinion.

Politicians read the opinion polls. And even though many elected representatives claim that they exercise independent judgment about what is best for the nation in their decision making, we can be reasonably sure that their "independent judgment" is influenced at least in part by what they think their constituents want. The cynical stereotype of the politician who reads the opinion polls before taking stands on the issues is often embarrassingly accurate—leading to the perception of "government by focus group."

All this attention to public opinion has created a thriving industry in public opinion polling and **survey research**. Polls have become a fixture of American political life (see *The Game, the Rules, the Players:* Can We Believe the Polls?). But how much do Americans really think about politics? How informed, stable, and consistent is public opinion?

Knowledge Levels

Most Americans do *not* follow politics closely enough to develop well-informed opinions on many public issues (see Figure 5.1). Low levels of knowledge about government and public affairs make it difficult for people to form opinions on specific issues or policy proposals. Many opinion surveys ask questions about topics that people had not considered before being interviewed. Few respondents are willing to admit that they know nothing about the topic or have "no opinion." Respondents believe they should provide some sort of answer, even if their opinion was nonexistent before the question was asked. The result is that the polls themselves "create" opinions.[2]

The "Halo Effect"

Many respondents give "good citizen" or socially respectable answers, whether they are truthful or not, even to an anonymous interviewer. This **halo effect** leads to an *underestimation* of the true extent of prejudice, hatred, and bigotry. A variant on halo effects, called the **Bradley effect**, occurs when white voters understate their opposition to a minority candidate. Such understatements by California voters in 1982 led to

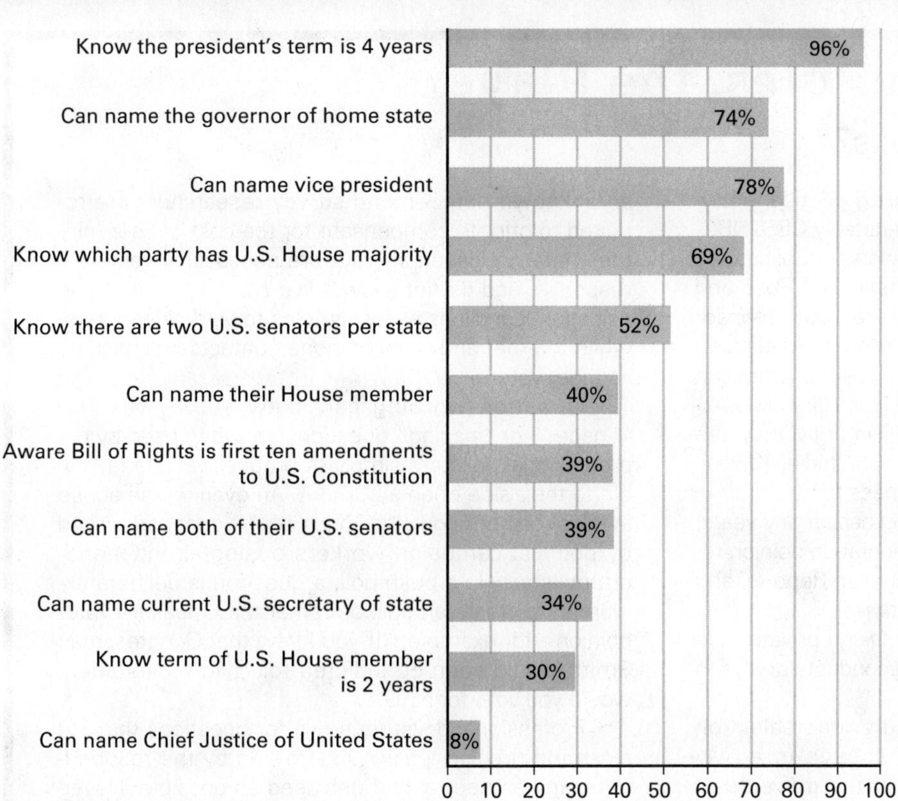

FIGURE 5.1 CAUSE FOR CONCERN?: WHAT AMERICANS [DON'T] KNOW ABOUT POLITICS

Politics is not the major interest of most Americans, and as a result, knowledge about the political system is limited. Less than one-third of the general public knows the names of their representatives in Congress or their U.S. senators, and knowledge of specific foreign and domestic matters is even more limited.

SOURCE: Data from Robert S. Erikson and Kent L. Tedin, *American Public Opinion,* 7th ed. (New York: Pearson Longman, 2007), p. 62, citing various polls.

an overestimation of support for African American Democrat Tom Bradley, who lost to Republican George Deukmejian. There were expectations of Bradley effects in the 2008 election of Barack Obama, but such effects were not detected.

Another common example of the halo effect is the fact that people do not like to admit that they do not vote. Surveys regularly report higher percentages of people *saying* they voted in an election than the actual number of ballots cast (for decades, political scientists have validated the statements that people voted with state election board records).[3] Moreover, postelection surveys almost always produce higher percentages of people who say they voted for the winner than the actual vote tally for the winner. So, for example, even though Jack Kennedy defeated Richard Nixon by less than a percentage point in 1960, in 1964 surveys, over 64 percent of voters recalled voting for Kennedy. Apparently poll respondents do not like to admit that they backed the loser.

□ Inconsistencies

Because so many people hold no real opinion on political issues, the wording of a question frequently determines their response. People respond positively to positive phrases (for example, "helping poor people," "improving education," "cleaning up the environment") and negatively to negative phrases (for example, "raising taxes," "expanding governmental power," "restricting choice").

The wording of questions, combined with weak or nonexistent opinion, often produces inconsistent responses. For example, when asked whether they agreed or disagreed with the statement that "people should have the right to purchase a sexually explicit book, magazine, or movie, if that's what they want to do," an overwhelming

5.1

5.2

5.3

5.4

5.5

5.6

5.7

5.8

The Game, the Rules, the Players

Can We Believe the Polls?

Survey research is a flourishing political enterprise. The national news media—notably CBS, NBC, ABC, FOX, and CNN television networks, publications like the *New York Times* and the *Washington Post*, and online content providers like YouGov—regularly sponsor independent national surveys, especially during election campaigns. Major survey organizations—the American Institute of Public Opinion (Gallup), Louis Harris and Associates, National Opinion Research Center (NORC), the Roper Organization, and National Election Studies (University of Michigan)—have been in business for a long time and have files of survey results going back many years, and there is a proliferation of next-generation opinion research firms like Survey USA, Rasmussen Reports, and Polimetrix providing survey content to media and industry. Political candidates also contract with private marketing and opinion research firms to conduct surveys in conjunction with their campaigns.

Public opinion surveys depend on the selection of a *random sample* of persons chosen in a way which ensures that every person in the *universe* of people about whom information is desired has an equal chance of being selected for interviewing. National samples, representative of all adults, all voters, or "likely" voters usually include only about 1,000 persons. In state and local surveys, samples often are as small as 384 persons. First, geographical areas (for example, counties or telephone area codes) that are representative of all such areas in the nation are chosen. Then residential telephone numbers are randomly selected within these areas. Once the numbers have been selected at random, the poll taker does not make substitutions but calls back several times if necessary to make contact so as not to bias the sample toward people who stay at home.

There are several potential sources of bias that arise, even when using random-selection procedures, and these can lead to samples that don't represent that population (or universe) represented in the survey. Some are random, and are a by-product of sampling error. Survey researchers estimate the *sampling error* through the mathematics of probability. The sampling error is usually expressed as a percentage range—for example, plus or minus 3 percent—above and below the sample response within which there is a 95 percent likelihood that the same response would be found if the entire universe were questioned. For example, if 65 percent of the survey respondents favor the death penalty and the sampling error is calculated at plus or minus 3 percent, then we can say there is a 95 percent probability that a survey of the whole population (the universe) would produce a response of between 62 and 68 percent in favor of the death penalty.

Another source of potential sampling error relates to survey mode. Americans are less likely to keep landlines in their home, which makes it harder for survey firms to get representative samples from calling homes. Cell phone users may be less likely to answer an unknown number, and survey researchers are required to offer to compensate for the cost of user minutes. Internet-based surveys are necessarily voluntary response, and do not allow a live caller to prompt participation. Landlines skew samples toward older voters, while Internet and mobile phone contacts help pick up younger voters.

Question wording can skew survey results. "Loaded" or "leading" questions are often used by unprofessional pollsters simply to produce results favorable to their side of an argument. An even worse abuse in telephone polling is the "push poll"—questions asked by political campaign workers posing as independent pollsters. In a push poll, a question is deliberately worded to create an opinion rather than measure voter opinion—for example, "If you knew that Congressman Smith would soon be indicted for child molestation, would you vote for him?"

Professional pollsters strive for questions that are clear and precise, easily understood by the respondents, and as neutral and unbiased as possible. Nevertheless, because all questions have a potential bias, it is often better to examine *changes over time* in response to identically worded questions. Perhaps the best-known continuing question in public opinion polling is the presidential approval rating: "Do you approve or disapprove of the way____ is handling his job as president?" Changes over time in public response to this question alert scholars, commentators, and presidents themselves to their public standing.

A survey can only measure opinions *at the time* it is taken. A few days later, public opinion may change, especially if major events that receive heavy television coverage intervene. Some political pollsters conduct continuous "tracking" surveys until election night in order to catch last-minute opinion changes.

An altogether different type of poll is the *exit poll*, during which Election Day voters are personally interviewed as they leave the voting booth. Exit polls are used by the media to "call" winners early on election night even before all votes are counted. Television networks now jointly contract with an independent company, VNS, to select voting precincts at random, interview voters, and fast-forward the results to the networks. The networks analyze the results and make their own "calls." In response to criticism that early calls reduce voter turnout, the networks have agreed not to call a state result until the polls close in that state.

QUESTIONS

1. **When you look at a poll, what kind of information should you look at to decide how much confidence to place in the results?**
2. **How are polls used in the political process? Do you think media polls are different from politician, party, or interest group polls?**

80 percent endorsed the statement. However, when the same respondents were also asked whether they agreed with the opposite statement that "community authorities should be able to prohibit the selling of magazines or movies they consider to be pornographic," 65 percent approved of this view.[4]

salient issues
Issues about which most people have an opinion.

Salience

People are likely to think more about issues that receive a great deal of attention in the mass media—television, newspapers, magazines. **Salient issues** are those that people think about most—issues on which they hold stronger and more consistent opinions. These are issues that people feel relate directly to their own lives, such as abortion. Salient issues are, therefore, more important in politics.

Salient issues change over time. In general, during recessions, the most salient issue is "Jobs, Jobs, Jobs!"—that is, unemployment and the economy. During inflationary periods, the issue is "the high cost of living." During wartime, the war itself becomes the public's principal concern. A gasoline shortage can turn public concern toward energy issues. These salient issues drive the political debate of the times.

Opinion Research

Politics in a representative democracy is fueled by feedback. And one of the main sources of feedback is opinion research: the polls and focus groups that lend numbers, balance, and comment to issues of the day. But there is more to opinion research than surveying the public. Opinion researchers also help their clients—politicians, interest groups, corporations, and media outlets—create messages to help shape public sentiment.

Public opinion researchers have to be adept at several aspects of social science, including sampling, question wording, instrument design, and the use and interpretation of statistics. Put simply, they need to have a professional ability to study small groups of people who are representative of a population their client wants to study; ask meaningful, fair questions using surveys or focus group scripts; and then organize and analyze those results so the client can understand them, even if the client is ignorant of numbers and statistics.

Most opinion researchers have backgrounds in quantitative social sciences like political science and sociology or in a discipline with related research tools: marketing. Many have advanced degrees and are often adept with statistical software designed to analyze data. Many are actually quite young. Pollsters such as Frank Luntz at Fox News were in their late 20s when they started their own opinion research operations. Often, opinion researchers started out in political campaigns, organizing voter targeting operations or phone banks for candidates or for party polling operations.

It does not necessarily take a lot of capital to start an opinion research firm. A full-service opinion research firm will have a calling center staffed with callers operating from computerized calling stations. The firm will likely also have a focus group facility, and possibly the capacity to automate calling and surveying (in robocall-based surveys where respondents interact with a taped survey, like SurveyUSA). Most of the costs of a given survey are completely absorbed by the client contract (personnel costs, the costs of compiling samples). Sometimes, the calling and programming of surveys can be outsourced to professional calling houses. The downside of outsourcing opinion research is that the firm loses some degree of quality control over its product.

The long-term prospects for most opinion research firms is dependent on two factors: developing a reputation for accuracy that creates a stable book of business, and expanding the clientele beyond campaign work by branching out to capture private-sector clients to maintain profits between election cycles.

Socialization: The Origins of Political Opinions

5.2 Explain how the agents of socialization influence the development of political opinions.

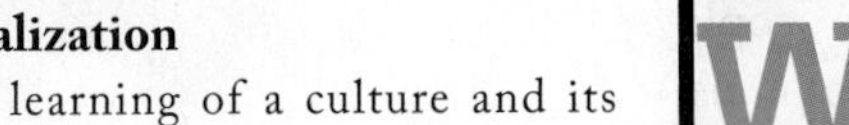

socialization
The learning of a culture and its values.

diffuse support (for the political system)
Goodwill toward governmental authority learned early in life.

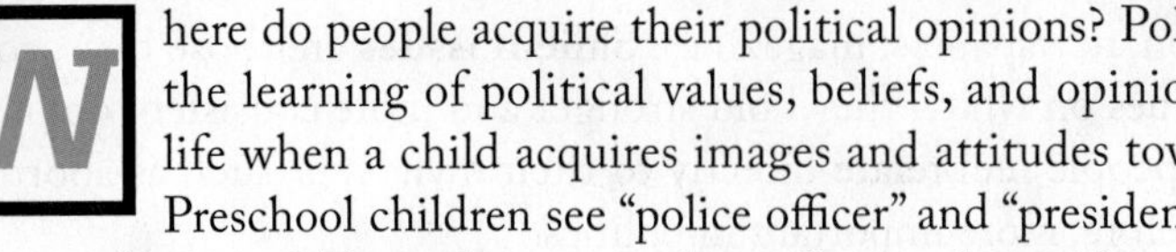

Where do people acquire their political opinions? Political **socialization** is the learning of political values, beliefs, and opinions. It begins early in life when a child acquires images and attitudes toward public authority. Preschool children see "police officer" and "president" as powerful yet benevolent "helpers." These figures—police officer and president—are usually the first recognized sources of authority above the parents who must be obeyed. They are usually positive images of authority at these early ages:

> Q: What does the policeman do?
> A: He catches bad people.[5]

Even the American flag is recognized by most U.S. preschoolers, who pick it out when asked, "Which flag is your favorite?" These early positive perceptions about political figures and symbols may later provide **diffuse support** for the political system—a reservoir of goodwill toward governmental authority that lends legitimacy to the political order.

Family

The family is the first agent of socialization. Children in the early school grades (three to five) begin to identify themselves as Republicans or Democrats. These childhood party identifications are almost always the same as those of the parents. Indeed, parent–child correspondence in party identification may last a lifetime. The children who abandon the party of their parents tend to become independents rather than identify with the opposition party. However, party identification appears to be more easily passed on from parent to child than specific opinions on policy questions. Perhaps the reason is that parental party identifications are known to children, but few families conduct specific discussions of policy questions.[6]

Recent research linking genetics to political behavior suggests that family may influence political behavior and attitudes through genetic inheritance as well as through environmental socialization. Identical twins are more likely to hold similar political attitudes than nonidentical twins. (Both types of twins share the same home environment, but identical twins also share the same genetic makeup.) The genetic influence appears to extend to the likelihood of voting, contributing to campaigns, running for office, and joining political organizations as well as to specific political opinions, including the death penalty, abortion, gay rights, and school prayer.[7]

"ALL GREAT CHANGE IN AMERICA BEGINS AT THE DINNER TABLE."
Ronald Reagan made this observation in his 1989 farewell address as president. Research shows that the kitchen table is one of the main places where people learn about politics and values.

School

Political revolutionaries once believed that the school was the key to molding political values and beliefs. After the communist revolutions in Russia in 1917 and China in 1949, the schools became the focus of political indoctrination of the population. Today political battles rage in America over textbooks, teaching methods, prayer in schools, and other manifestations of politics in the classroom. But no strong evidence indicates a causal relationship between what is taught in the schools and the political attitudes of students.

Certainly the schools provide the factual basis for understanding government—how the president is chosen, the three branches of government, how a law is passed.

TABLE 5.1 EDUCATION AND TOLERANCE: A STRONG CORRELATION

Tolerance generally increases with educational level.

Percentage Responding "Yes" (by highest degree completed)

	Less than High School	High School	Junior College	Bachelor	Graduate	Total
If such a person wanted to make a speech in your community, should he be allowed to speak? (Yes)						
Atheist	49%	69%	80%	87%	91%	71%
Racist	47%	58%	66%	74%	78%	61%
Homosexual	55%	74%	85%	90%	94%	76%
Should such a person be allowed to teach in a college or university? (Yes)						
Atheist	32%	46%	62%	72%	80%	52%
Racist	36%	40%	49%	57%	63%	46%
Homosexual	44%	64%	78%	85%	90%	68%

SOURCE: *General Social Survey, Cumulative Index*, 1972–2012 (Chicago: National Opinion Research Center).

But even this elemental knowledge is likely to fade if not reinforced by additional education or exposure to the news media or discussion with family or peers.

The schools *try* to inculcate "good citizenship" values, including support for democratic rules, tolerance toward others, the importance of voting, and the legitimacy (rightfulness) of government authority. Patriotic symbols and rituals abound in the classroom—the flag, the Pledge of Allegiance—and students are taught to respect the institutions of government. Generally the younger the student, the more positive the attitudes expressed toward political authority.[8] Yet despite the efforts of the schools to inspire support for the political system, distrust and cynicism creep in during the high school years. Although American youth retain a generally positive view of the political system, they share with adults increasing skepticism toward specific institutions and practices. During high school, students acquire some ability to think along liberal–conservative dimensions. The college experience appears to produce a "liberalizing" effect: college seniors tend to be more liberal than entering freshmen (see also *A Conflicting View*: College Students' Opinions). But over the years following graduation, liberal views tend to moderate.

Although no direct evidence indicates that the schools can inculcate democratic values, people with more education tend to be more tolerant than those with less education and to be generally more supportive of the political system (see Table 5.1). Higher education is also associated with greater political participation, including voting. But it is not clear whether education itself is a cause of political participation, or whether people who choose a college experience are predisposed to participate in civic affairs.[9]

□ Church

Religious beliefs and values may also shape political opinion. *Which* religion an individual identifies with (for example, Protestant, Catholic, Jewish) affects public opinion. So does *how important* religion is in the individual's life. It is difficult to explain exactly how religion affects political values, but we can observe differences in the opinions expressed by Protestants, Catholics, and Jews; by people who say their religious beliefs are strong versus those who say they are not; and between fundamentalists (those who believe in a literal interpretation of the Bible) and nonfundamentalists. Religion shapes political attitudes on a variety of issues, including

A Conflicting View

College Students' Opinions

College students' opinions today appear to be somewhat more conservative than they were a generation ago, in the 1970s. While most students identify themselves politically as "middle-of-the-road," there are somewhat more "conservative" self-identifiers and fewer "liberal" self-identifiers than 35 years ago. On policy issues, students today are more likely to support the death penalty, believe the courts are too lenient with criminals, and oppose legalization of marijuana. (However, students are somewhat more liberal on these issues today than in the 1980s and 1990s.) Students in the 1970s confronted an unpopular war in Vietnam, faced a military draft, and were more likely to experiment with drugs and alternative lifestyles. Today's students confront greater economic competition and increased educational requirements for employment. They are more concerned with their financial future than students were a generation ago.

College student ideology is largely unchanged over time. In 1972, about a third were liberal and a sixth were conservative. Liberalism declined among college students in the 1990s, but then went back up to about a third of all students by 2012. A fifth of college students have consistently been conservatives since the 1990s. With regard to party, about half of college students lean Democratic and about one in three lean Republican.

However, college students remain somewhat more liberal than the general population. Moreover, college seniors and graduate students are more liberal than first-year students; students at prestigious Ivy League universities are more liberal than students at state universities and community colleges; and students in humanities and social sciences are more liberal than students in engineering, physical sciences, and business. Over the years following graduation, many of these liberal predispositions tend to moderate.

QUESTIONS

1. On what issues are college freshman more liberal? More conservative?
2. How do your opinions on these issues differ from other college students in the UCLA survey?

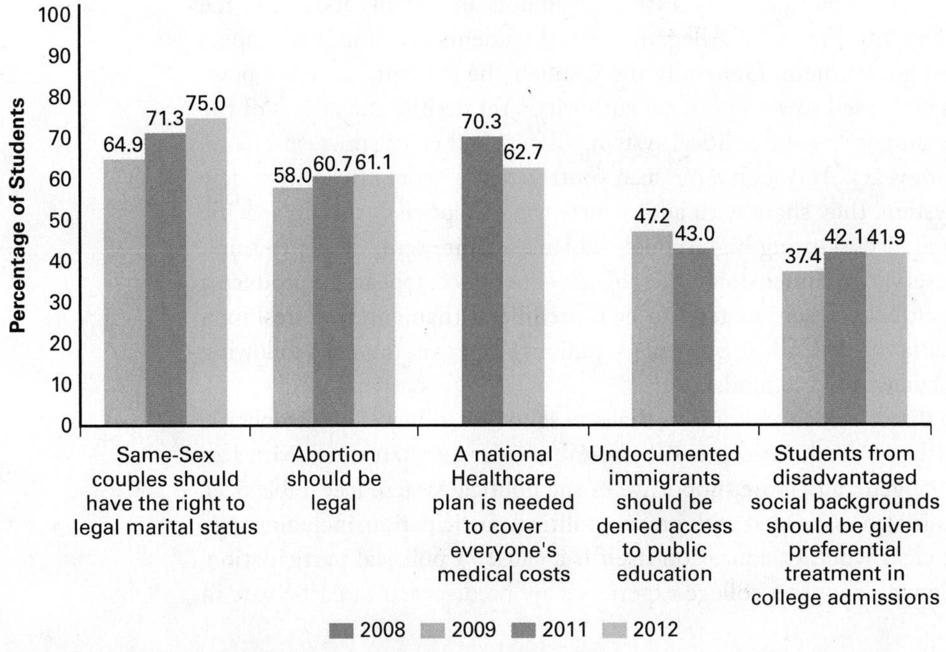

abortion, drugs, the death penalty, homosexuality, and prayer in public schools (see Table 5.2). Religion also plays a measurable role in political ideology. Fundamentalists are more likely to describe themselves as conservatives than as moderates, and very few accept the liberal label.[10]

At the same time, however, most Americans are concerned about religious leaders exercising influence in political life. Most respondents say it is "not appropriate for religious leaders to talk about their political beliefs as part of their religious activities" (61 percent), "religious leaders should not try to influence how people vote in elections" (64 percent), and "religious groups should *not* advance their beliefs by being involved in politics and working to affect policy" (54 percent).[11]

TABLE 5.2 RELIGION AND PUBLIC OPINION: IT'S STRENGTH OF CONVICTION, NOT CHURCH AFFILIATION, THAT MATTERS MOST

This strength of religious conviction is more important in shaping public opinion than church affiliation.

	Affiliation			Faith in God		Belief That the Bible is ...		
Opinion	Protestant	Catholic	Jew	The most Important	Not at all important	Literal word of God	Inspired by God	Book of fables
Abortion for any reason should be legal	36%	36%	78%	29%	83%	22%	45%	69%
Legalize marijuana	22	26	47	16	64	19	31	55
Support death penalty	73	73	70	77	74	71	75	67
Remove book that favored homosexuality from library	40	28	14	37	11	48	21	14
Support prayer in public school	68	60	18	71	11	79	55	32

SOURCE: *General Social Survey, Cumulative Index*, 1972–2012 (Chicago: National Opinion Research Center). Tabulations by Professor Terri Towner, Oakland University.

☐ Age and Opinion

Age group differences in politics and public opinion are sometimes referred to as the **generation gap**. On most of the issues shown in Table 5.3, older people appear to be more conservative than younger people. Older people are less likely than younger people to favor the legalization of marijuana, to allow abortion for any reason, or to allow homosexuals to teach in college; older people are more likely to identify themselves as "conservative."[12] Younger Americans in general appear to be less interested and involved in politics than older Americans; they are less likely to keep up with political news and, perhaps most importantly, are less likely to vote (see Table 5.3 and the discussion later in this chapter).

generation gap
Differences in politics and public opinion among age groups.

☐ Media Influence

Television is the major source of political information for Americans. More than two-thirds report that they receive "all or most" of their news from television, making newspapers, magazines, books, the Internet, and radio secondary to television as a source of political information. But for Americans under 40, television is declining

TABLE 5.3 AGE AND PUBLIC OPINION: OPINION AND PARTICIPATION CHANGE WITH THE YEARS

Younger people express somewhat more liberal opinion than the elderly, but younger people vote less often and have less interest in politics.

	Under 30	55 and over
Marijuana should be made legal	37%	18%
Allow homosexuals to teach in college	77	53
Allow abortion for any reason	42	34
Describe oneself as:		
Liberal	34	22
Moderate	39	40
Conservative	27	38
Read news about presidential campaign	60	80
Pay attention to national network news	44	59
Vote in 2008 presidential election	65	85

SOURCE: *General Social Survey, Cumulative Index*, 1972–2012 (Chicago: National Opinion Research Center) and *2008 National Election Studies* (University of Michigan).

5.1

5.2

5.3

5.4

5.5

5.6

5.7

5.8

as a primary news source, with internet-based sources emerging as the new, dominant channel.

But the effect of television on opinion is not really in persuading people to take one side of an issue or another. Instead, the principal effect is in *setting the agenda* for thinking and talking about politics. Television does not tell people *what* to think, but it does tell them what to think *about*. Television coverage determines matters of general public concern. Without coverage, the general public would not know about, think about, or discuss most events, personalities, and issues. Media attention creates issues, and the amount of attention given an issue determines its importance.

Ideology, Gender, Race, and Opinion

5.3 Determine the role of ideology in shaping opinion and describe the relationship between gender, race, and opinion.

Ideology helps shape opinion. Many people, especially politically interested and active people, approach policy questions with a fairly consistent and integrated set of principles—that is, an *ideology*. Liberal and conservative ideas about the proper role of government in the economy, about the regulation of social conduct, about equality and the distribution of income, and about civil rights influence people's views on specific policy questions.

To what extent do self-described liberals and conservatives differ over specific issues? Can we predict people's stances on particular issues by knowing whether they call themselves liberal or conservative? Generally speaking, self-described liberals and conservatives do differ in their responses to specific policy questions, although some take policy positions inconsistent with their proclaimed ideology (see Table 5.4). People who describe themselves as liberal generally favor governmental efforts to

TABLE 5.4 DECIDING WHO GETS WHAT: HOW IDEOLOGY INFLUENCES OPINION

Self-described "liberals" and "conservatives" differ over many specific policy questions.

	Percent Agreeing		
Opinion	**Liberal**	**Moderates**	**Conservatives**
The government should provide "more services even if it means an increase in spending."	53%	30%	15%
The government "should make it more difficult to buy a gun."	66%	51%	33%
The government should guarantee "that every person has a job and a good standard of living."	48%	32%	16%
Favor "government insurance plan which would cover all medical and hospital expenses."	61%	36%	16%
Favor laws to "protect homosexuals against job discrimination."	46%	38%	32%
Permit abortion "always" or "if needed."	81%	63%	45%
Favor "death penalty for persons convicted of murder."	55%	72%	80%
Favor "preferential hiring and promotion of blacks" to address historic discrimination.	31%	20%	11%
The United States "should spend less on defense."	49%	26%	21%

SOURCE: Data from the *2012 National Election Study* (University of Michigan).

reduce income inequalities and to improve the positions of African Americans, other minorities, and women. Overall, it appears that ideology and opinion are fairly well linked—that the liberal–conservative dimension is related to opinions on specific policy questions.

Gender Gap
A difference of opinion on issues or vote preference between men and women detected by opinion polling.

☐ Gender and Opinion

A **gender gap** in public opinion—a difference of opinion between men and women—occurs on only a few issues. Interestingly, a gender gap does *not* appear on women's issues: abortion, the role of women in business and politics, whether one would vote for a qualified woman for president, or whether men are better suited for political office. On these issues, men and women do not differ significantly (see Figure 5.2).

However, gender gap differences are apparent on a variety of contemporary issues (see Figure 5.2). Many polls report that women are more likely than men:

- To favor an activist role for government
- To oppose U.S. military intervention
- To support restrictions on firearms
- To support spending on social programs
- To support affirmative action

Politically, the most important gender gap is in party identification. Women are more likely to identify themselves as Democrats. This difference emerged in the 1980s, when men were more likely than women to support Republican president Ronald Reagan.[13]

☐ Race and Opinion

Opinion over the extent of discrimination in the United States and over the causes of and remedies for racial inequality differ sharply across racial lines. Most whites believe there is very little discrimination toward African Americans in jobs, housing, or education, and that differences between whites and blacks in society occur as a result of a lack of motivation among black people. Most African Americans strongly disagree with these views and believe that discrimination continues in employment, housing, and education and that differences between whites and blacks in standards of living are "mainly due to discrimination" (see Figure 5.3).

African Americans generally support a more positive role for government in reducing inequality in society. Approximately two out of every three believe that government should do more to reduce income differences between rich and poor. Blacks favor busing to achieve racial balance in public schools, a view not shared by many whites. Given these preferences for a strong role for government, it is not surprising that more blacks than whites identify themselves as liberals. However, about one-quarter of African Americans identify themselves as conservative. And indeed, on certain social issues—crime, drugs, school prayers—majorities of African Americans take conservative positions.

African American perceptions of the criminal justice system are especially negative. Police encounters with black civilians have inspired many of the most destructive riots and demonstrations. Most whites believe the criminal justice system is fundamentally fair; most blacks do not. Whites attribute police brutality to individual malfeasance by officers; blacks see it as racism when the victim is black. Blacks see the disproportionate percentages of blacks in prison as discrimination; whites see it as a product of greater criminality among African Americans.[14]

African Americans are more likely than whites to support governmental actions and programs to improve the position of black people and other minorities. Levels of support for affirmative action depend on the wording of the question, but

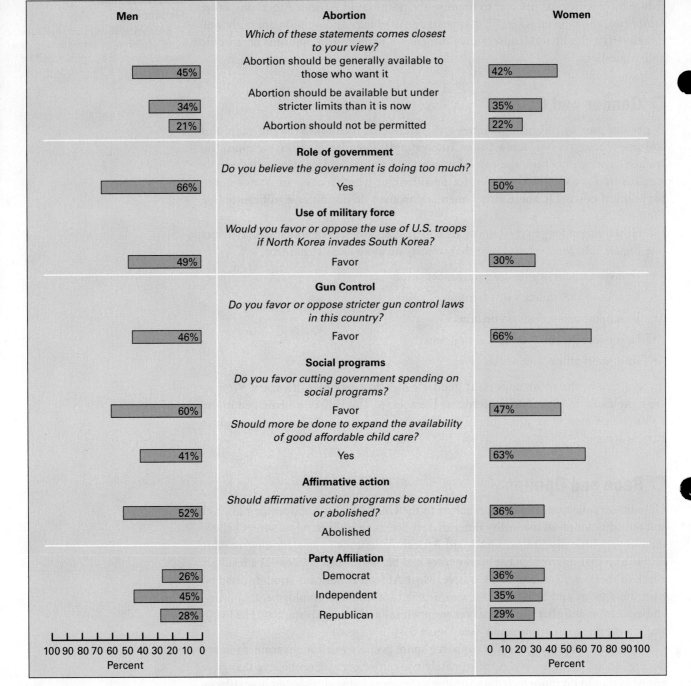

Men	Issue	Women
	Abortion *Which of these statements comes closest to your view?*	
45%	Abortion should be generally available to those who want it	42%
34%	Abortion should be available but under stricter limits than it is now	35%
21%	Abortion should not be permitted	22%
	Role of government *Do you believe the government is doing too much?*	
66%	Yes	50%
	Use of military force *Would you favor or oppose the use of U.S. troops if North Korea invades South Korea?*	
49%	Favor	30%
	Gun Control *Do you favor or oppose stricter gun control laws in this country?*	
46%	Favor	66%
	Social programs *Do you favor cutting government spending on social programs?*	
60%	Favor	47%
	Should more be done to expand the availability of good affordable child care?	
41%	Yes	63%
	Affirmative action *Should affirmative action programs be continued or abolished?*	
52%	Abolished	36%
	Party Affiliation	
26%	Democrat	36%
45%	Independent	35%
28%	Republican	29%

100 90 80 70 60 50 40 30 20 10 0 Percent — 0 10 20 30 40 50 60 70 80 90 100 Percent

FIGURE 5.2 THE GENDER GAP: DIFFERENCES IN POLICY OPINIONS

A gender gap exists in a variety of issues, but not on abortion. Also, women are more likely to identify themselves as Democrats than are men.

SOURCE: Reprinted by permission of Center for American Women and Politics, Eagleton Institute of Politics, Rutgers, The State University of New Jersey. *Note*: The data in this figure was compiled by authors drawing from information collected by the Center for American Women and Politics from a number of surveys conducted by various groups in the mid-1990s. For complete information, go to www.cawp.rutgers.edu.

regardless of wording, blacks are more likely to support racial and minority preferences than whites.

☐ Hispanic Opinion

Hispanic voters are the fastest-growing force in American politics.[15] While Hispanic voter turnout has been low (Hispanics made up only about 7 percent of the voters in the 2008 presidential election, despite accounting for about 15 percent of the U.S.

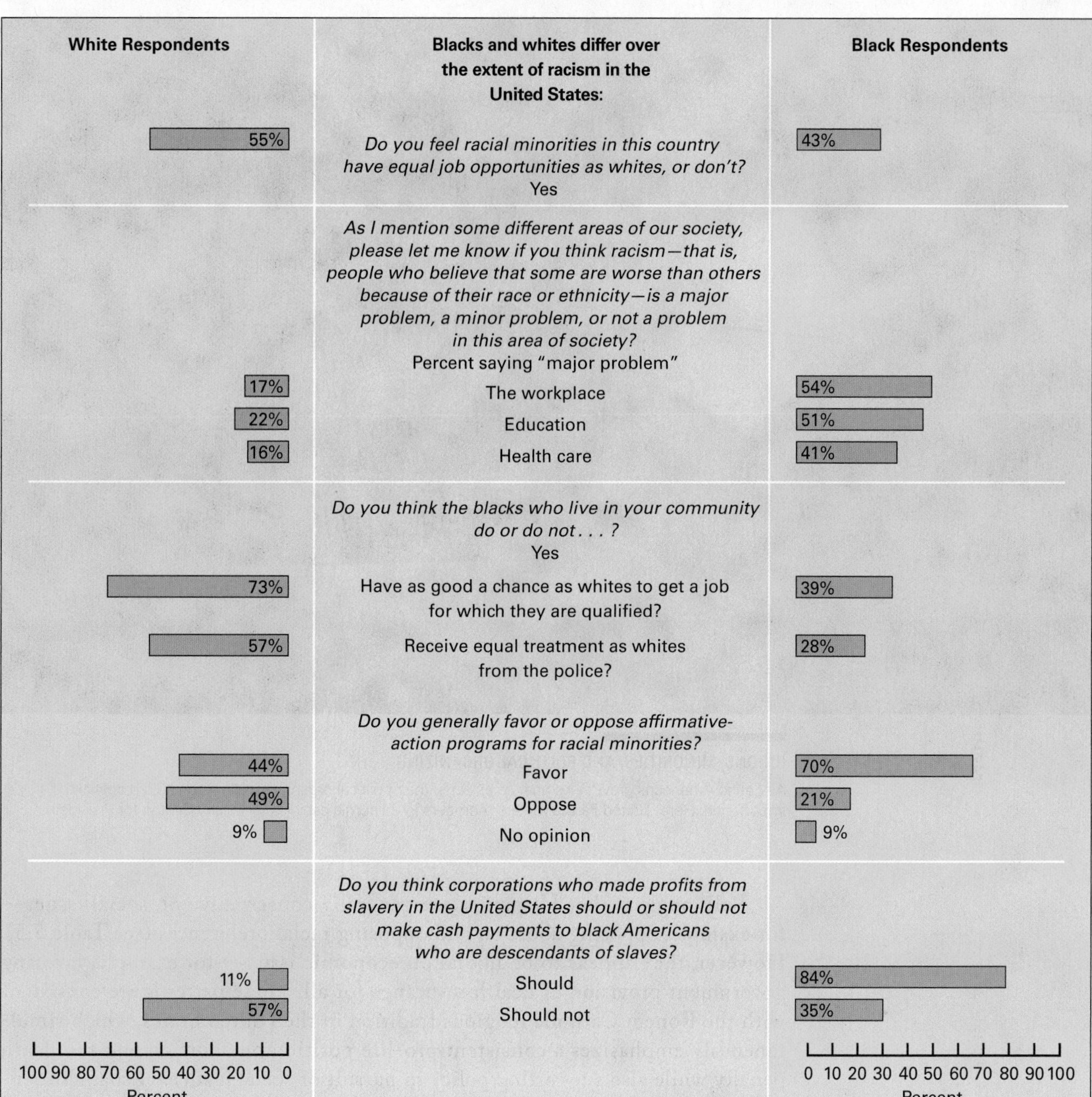
White Respondents
Blacks and whites differ over the extent of racism in the United States:
Black Respondents
55%
Do you feel racial minorities in this country have equal job opportunities as whites, or don't?
Yes
43%
As I mention some different areas of our society, please let me know if you think racism—that is, people who believe that some are worse than others because of their race or ethnicity—is a major problem, a minor problem, or not a problem in this area of society?
Percent saying "major problem"
17%
The workplace
54%
22%
Education
51%
16%
Health care
41%
Do you think the blacks who live in your community do or do not . . . ?
Yes
73%
Have as good a chance as whites to get a job for which they are qualified?
39%
57%
Receive equal treatment as whites from the police?
28%
Do you generally favor or oppose affirmative-action programs for racial minorities?
44%
Favor
70%
49%
Oppose
21%
9%
No opinion
9%
Do you think corporations who made profits from slavery in the United States should or should not make cash payments to black Americans who are descendants of slaves?
11%
Should
84%
57%
Should not
35%
100 90 80 70 60 50 40 30 20 10 0
Percent
0 10 20 30 40 50 60 70 80 90 100
Percent

FIGURE 5.3 THE RACIAL GAP: DIFFERENCES IN POLICY OPINIONS

Blacks are more likely than whites to perceive racism in the workplace, education, and health care as a "major problem," and blacks are more likely than whites to support affirmative action programs.

SOURCE: Various national opinion surveys reported on www.publicagenda.org (2007).

population), population projections forecast an ever-growing role for Hispanics in national politics.

The term "Hispanic" is a linguistic-group identifier and is used by the U.S. Census to formally identify persons with heritage in the Spanish-speaking countries of the Americas. Most Hispanics have no preference regarding the use of Hispanic or Latino(a) to describe their ethnicity. There is substantial cultural and political diversity among Hispanic Americans; in addition to the dominant Mexican, Puerto Rican, and Cuban populations, many Hispanic Americans come from Central and South America.

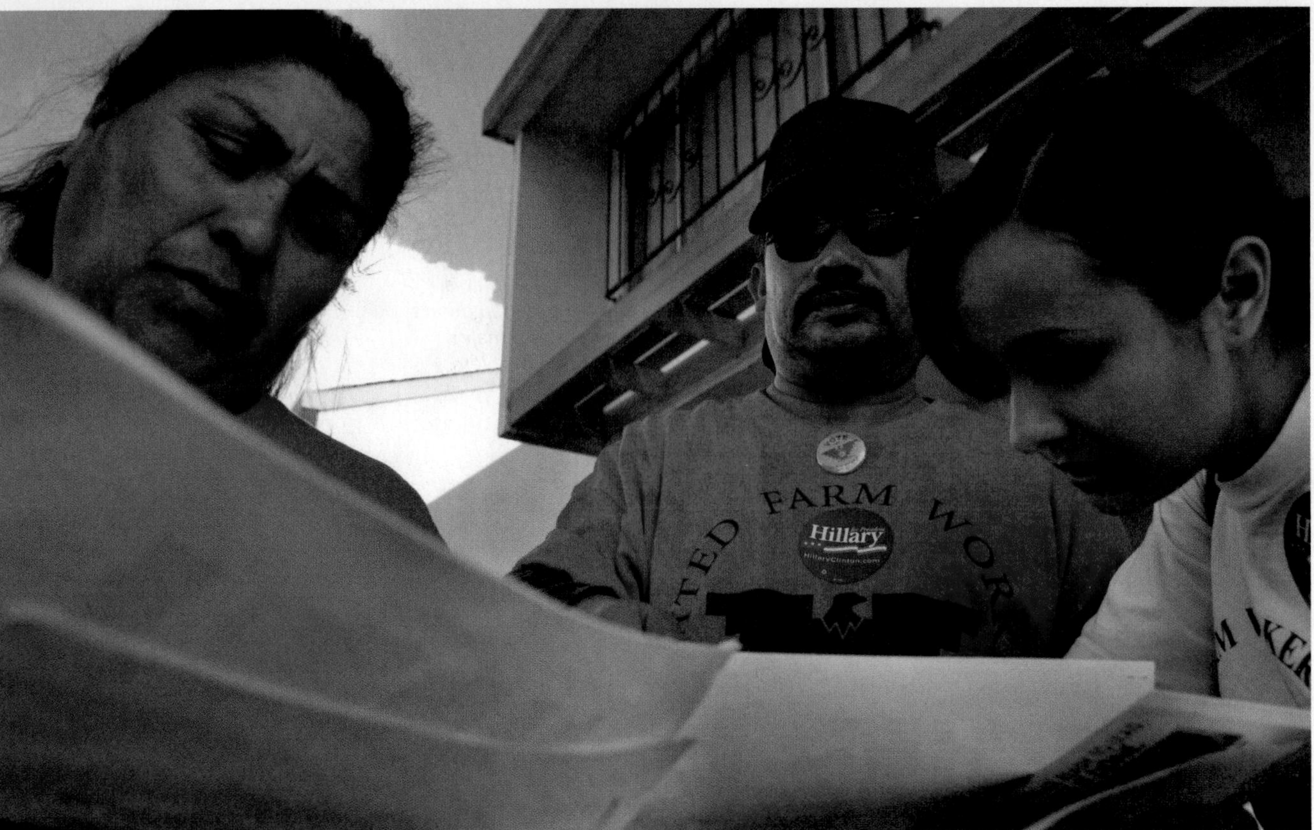

UNIONS, MINORITIES, AND POLITICAL ORGANIZING

As Latino Americans grow in number as citizens, their political organization takes on added political importance. Here, United Farm Workers members in California canvass for Hillary Clinton for President.

Polls suggest that Hispanics are generally conservative on social issues—for example, opposing abortion and opposing racial preferences (see Table 5.5). However, they appear to be liberal on economic issues—for example, favoring government provision of health insurance for all. These patterns are consistent with the Roman Catholic religious tradition in the United States, which simultaneously emphasizes a consistent pro-life position on abortion and the death penalty while also supporting policy in pursuit of social justice. Hispanics identify jobs and the economy as the most important problems confronting the country, followed by immigration. They generally believe that immigration helps the economy, and they oppose reducing the number of Latinos who come to work in this country legally.

Policy and Opinion

5.4 Assess how and to what extent public opinion influences public policy making.

Does public opinion determine government policy? It is widely assumed that in a democracy, government policy will be heavily influenced by public opinion. Yet, as noted earlier, public opinion is weak or nonexistent on many policy questions; it is frequently inconsistent and unstable; and it is poorly informed about many policy issues. Under these circumstances, political leaders—presidents and members of Congress, bureaucrats, judges, and other

TABLE 5.5 HISPANIC OPINION: POLICY PREFERENCES OF A GROWING DEMOGRAPHIC

Hispanic opinion tends toward conservatism on social issues and liberalism or economic issues. Hispanic opinion generally favors immigration and believes it helps the economy.

The terms *Hispanic* and *Latino* are both used to describe people who are of Hispanic or Latin origin or descent. Do you happen to prefer Hispanic or Latino? (2012)	
Hispanic	33%
Latino	15%
No preference	50%
Do you think abortion should be legal in all cases, illegal in most cases, or illegal in all cases? (2007)	
Legal in all cases	43%
Illegal in most or all cases	51%
Do you think the government should provide health insurance for Americans without insurance, or is this something the government should not do? (2007)	
Should	83%
Should not	14%
Should colleges sometimes take a student's racial and ethnic background into consideration when deciding which student to admit, or should they select students without considering their racial or ethnic backgrounds? (2007)	
Consider	40%
Don't consider	18%
Some people think the United States should allow more Latin Americans into this country to work legally; some people think the United States should allow the same number as it does now; and some others think it should reduce the number who come and work in this country legally. Which is closer to your opinion? (2006)	
Allow more	48%
Allow the same number	32%
Reduce the number	18%
Don't know	8%
Some people say undocumented or illegal immigrants help the economy by providing low-cost labor. Others say they hurt the economy by driving wages down. Which is closer to your view? (2007)	
Help the economy	72%
Hurt the economy	21%
Don't know	7%

SOURCE: Pew Hispanic Center, Latino Immigration Study, 2007, 2011, 2012. www.pewhispanic.org

public officials—are relatively unconstrained by mass opinion in policy decisions (see *What Do You Think?* Should Government Leaders Pay More Attention to Public Opinion?). Moreover, in the absence of well-formed public opinion on an issue, other political actors—lobbyists and lawyers, interest-group spokespersons, journalists and commentators, television reporters and executives—can influence public policy by communicating directly with government officials, claiming to represent the public. They can also influence public policy indirectly by molding and shaping public opinion.

The weakness of public opinion on many policy issues increases the influence of elites, that small group of people who are interested and active in public affairs; who call or write their elected representatives; who join organizations and contribute money to causes and candidates; who attend meetings, rallies, and demonstrations; and who hold strong opinions on a wide variety of public issues. According to political scientist V. O. Key, the linkage between ordinary citizens and democratic government depends heavily on "that thin stratum of persons referred to variously as the political elite, the political activists, the leadership echelons, or the influentials."[16] Thus political *participation* appears to be the essential link between opinion and policy.

5.1

5.2

5.3

5.4

5.5

5.6

5.7

5.8

Compared to What?

World Opinion About the USA

The image of the United States improved markedly in most parts of the world with the election of Barack Obama as president. U.S. standing in the world is lower today than during the Cold War years of 1950–90. The decline was especially pronounced during the administration of President George W. Bush. After initial world support following the September 11, 2001, terrorist attacks on New York and Washington, D.C., worldwide support diminished as the United States grew mired in Iraq, and Osama Bin Laden remained at large in Afghanistan and Pakistan. Over the past four years, positive assessments of the U.S. started to decline again. Overall, however, global public opinion believes that the United States is a positive influence on world affairs. The 2014 BBC World Service Country Rating poll of 24 countries found sharp increases in negative evaluations of the U.S., especially in Spain, Germany, and Brazil. The BBC concluded, "It is probably not a coincidence that the nations that showed the sharpest increases in negative views of the United States . . . are ones where extensive US surveillance activity has been discovered and widely criticized." The three most negatively viewed countries? Iran (60 percent negative), North Korea (58 percent negative), and Pakistan (58 percent negative).

Country	Positive Influence	Negative Influence	Net Positive
Germany	60	18	42
Canada	57	15	42
United Kingdom	56	21	35
France	50	22	28
European Union	47	28	20
Japan	49	30	19
Brazil	45	26	19
South Africa	39	31	8
United States	42	39	3
South Korea	38	34	4
India	38	36	2
China	42	42	0
Russia	31	45	–14
Israel	24	50	–26
North Korea	19	58	–39
Pakistan	16	58	–42
Iran	16	60	–44

Source: British Broadcasting Corporation World Service Poll: "Negative views of Russia on the Rise: Global Poll," June 3, 2014, accessed at http://downloads.bbc.co.uk/mediacentre/country-rating-poll.pdf. n = 24,542 in 24 countries, margin of error per country ranges from +/– 2.5 to 6.1 percent, with 95 percent confidence.

Questions

1. What is your perception of the countries named and evaluated in the BBC survey?
2. Why do you think global opinion of the United States has declined since the start of the Obama administration?

What Do You Think?

Should Government Leaders Pay More Attention to Public Opinion?

In 1774, the British parliamentarian Edmund Burke told his Bristol constituents: "Your representative owes you, not his industry only, but his judgment; and he betrays, instead of serving you, if he sacrifices it to your opinion." Since then, "Burkean representation" has come to refer to political delegates using their own judgment in decision making, without paying much or any attention to public opinion polls. Indeed, many politicians boast of their own courage and independence and of their willingness to ignore public opinion polls on major issues. And political experts in higher education and the media repeatedly point out that the American public is woefully ill informed about political facts—whether about American government or the world at large—that the public is unstable and vacillating in its opinions and priorities, and that Americans are often highly emotional in their responses to difficult and complex issues. Shaping policy to public opinion would be irresponsible and possibly downright dangerous.

But other experts believe that the country would be much better off if politicians paid more attention to public opinion. A number of political scientists point out that public opinion is much more stable and much more reasonable than policy makers and the media would have us believe. There is evidence in polling data over a 30-year period that shows the wisdom and steadfastness of the American public with respect to important issues in U.S. foreign policy—one of the chief areas in which policy makers are wary of the public's judgment.[a] Despite the fact that Americans have limited political knowledge and pay only scant and often fleeting attention to politics, they take reasonable positions: they seek international justice and domestic prosperity and not just security from attack, and they seek to pursue such goals in cooperation with other countries—multilaterally, that is—rather than on their own.

Polls show that the American public certainly believes that the country would be much better off if politicians paid more attention to public opinion.

Q. If the leaders of the nation followed the views of the public more closely, do you think that the nation would be better off or worse off than it is today?

Better	81%
Worse	10%

Indeed, most Americans believe that members of Congress should "read up on the polls" in order to "get a sense of the public's views."

Q. Please tell me which statement you agree with most: (A) When members of Congress are thinking about how to vote on an issue, they should read up on the polls, because this can help them get a sense of the public's views on the issue. (B) When members of Congress are thinking about how to vote on an issue, they should not read the polls, because this will distract them from thinking about what is right.

Should read polls	67%
Should not read polls	26%

But other evidence shows that most members of Congress do not put much stake in public opinion. When members of Congress were asked, "*Do you think the American public knows enough about the issues you face to form wise opinions about what should be done about these issues, or not?*," fewer than one-third (31 percent) said "Yes," whereas almost half (47 percent) said "No" (17 percent answered "Maybe").

Political scientists Lawrence R. Jacobs and Robert Y. Shapiro found that members of Congress did not so much use information on public opinion to guide their decisions, but rather used it for their own tactical reasons; they ignored public opinion polls when public opinion conflicted with their decisions, and they publicized their agreement with public opinion when poll results meshed with their own judgments.[b]

Questions

1. Do you think it is more important to elect leaders who follow public opinion? Or leaders who use their judgment?
2. Is the public sufficiently knowledgeable to have its opinion seriously considered in the decisions of government?
3. Do you think public opinion is sufficiently stable to be seriously considered in the decisions of government?

[a] Benjamin I. Page with Marshall M. Bouton, *The Foreign Policy Disconnect: What Americans Want from Our Leaders but Don't Get.* Chicago: University of Chicago Press, 2006.

[b] Lawrence R. Jacobs and Robert Y. Shapiro, *Politicians Don't Pander: Political Manipulation and the Loss of Democratic Responsiveness.* Chicago: University of Chicago Press, 2000.

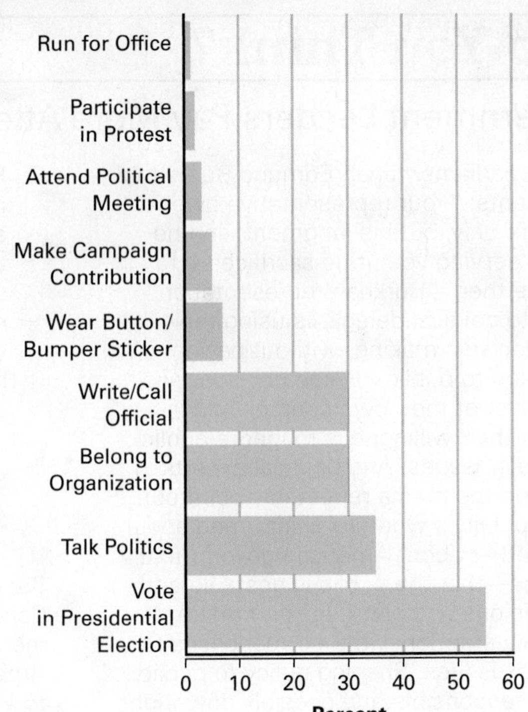

FIGURE 5.4 POLITICAL PARTICIPATION: HOW—AND HOW MANY—PEOPLE GET INVOLVED

Only a small percentage of the American people are actively engaged in the political process, yet they receive most of the media attention. Less than 1 percent of the population runs for office at any level of government, and only about half of all voting-age Americans bother to go to the polls even in a presidential election.

SOURCE: National Election Studies Cumulative File.

Individual Participation in Politics

5.5 Identify the various ways in which a citizen may participate in politics.

suffrage
Legal right to vote.

Democracies provide a variety of ways for individuals to participate in politics. People may run for, and win, public office; take part in marches, demonstrations, and protests; make financial contributions to political candidates or causes; attend political meetings, speeches, and rallies; write letters to public officials or to newspapers; wear a political button or place a bumper sticker on their car; belong to organizations that support or oppose particular candidates or take stands on public issues; attempt to influence friends while discussing candidates or issues; and vote in elections. Individuals may also participate in politics passively, by simply following political issues and campaigns in the media, acquiring knowledge, forming opinions about public affairs, and expressing their views to others. These forms of political participation can be ranked according to their order of frequency (see Figure 5.4). Only a little more than half of the voting-age population vote in presidential elections, and far fewer vote in congressional and state and local elections.

Securing the Right to Vote

5.6 Trace the expansion of the right to vote.

Popular participation in government is part of the very definition of democracy. The long history of struggle to secure the right to vote—**suffrage**—reflects the democratizing of the American political system.

☐ The Elimination of Property Qualifications, 1800–40

The Constitution of 1787 left it to the states to determine voter qualifications. The Founders generally believed that only men of property had a sufficient "stake in society" to exercise their vote in a "responsible" fashion. However, the Founders could not agree on the wording of **property qualifications** for insertion into the Constitution, so they left the issue to the states, feeling safe in the knowledge that at the time every state had property qualifications for voting. Yet over time, Jeffersonian and Jacksonian principles of democracy, including confidence in the judgment of ordinary citizens, spread rapidly in the new Republic. The states themselves eliminated most property qualifications by 1840. Thus before the Civil War (1861–65), the vote had been extended to virtually all *white males* over 21 years of age.

property qualifications
Early American state requirement of property ownership in order to vote.

☐ The 15th Amendment, 1870

The first important limitation on state powers over voting came with the ratification of the 15th Amendment: "The right of citizens of the United States to vote shall not be denied or abridged by the United States or by any state on account of race, color, or previous condition of servitude." The object of this amendment, passed by the Reconstruction Congress after the Civil War and ratified in 1870, was to extend the vote to former African American slaves and prohibit voter discrimination on the basis of race. The 15th Amendment also gave Congress the power to enforce African American voting rights "by appropriate legislation." The states retain their right to determine voter qualifications, *as long as they do not practice racial discrimination*, and Congress has the power to pass legislation ensuring African American voting rights. (The federal courts have also used the 14th Amendment to enforce equal access to the ballot.)

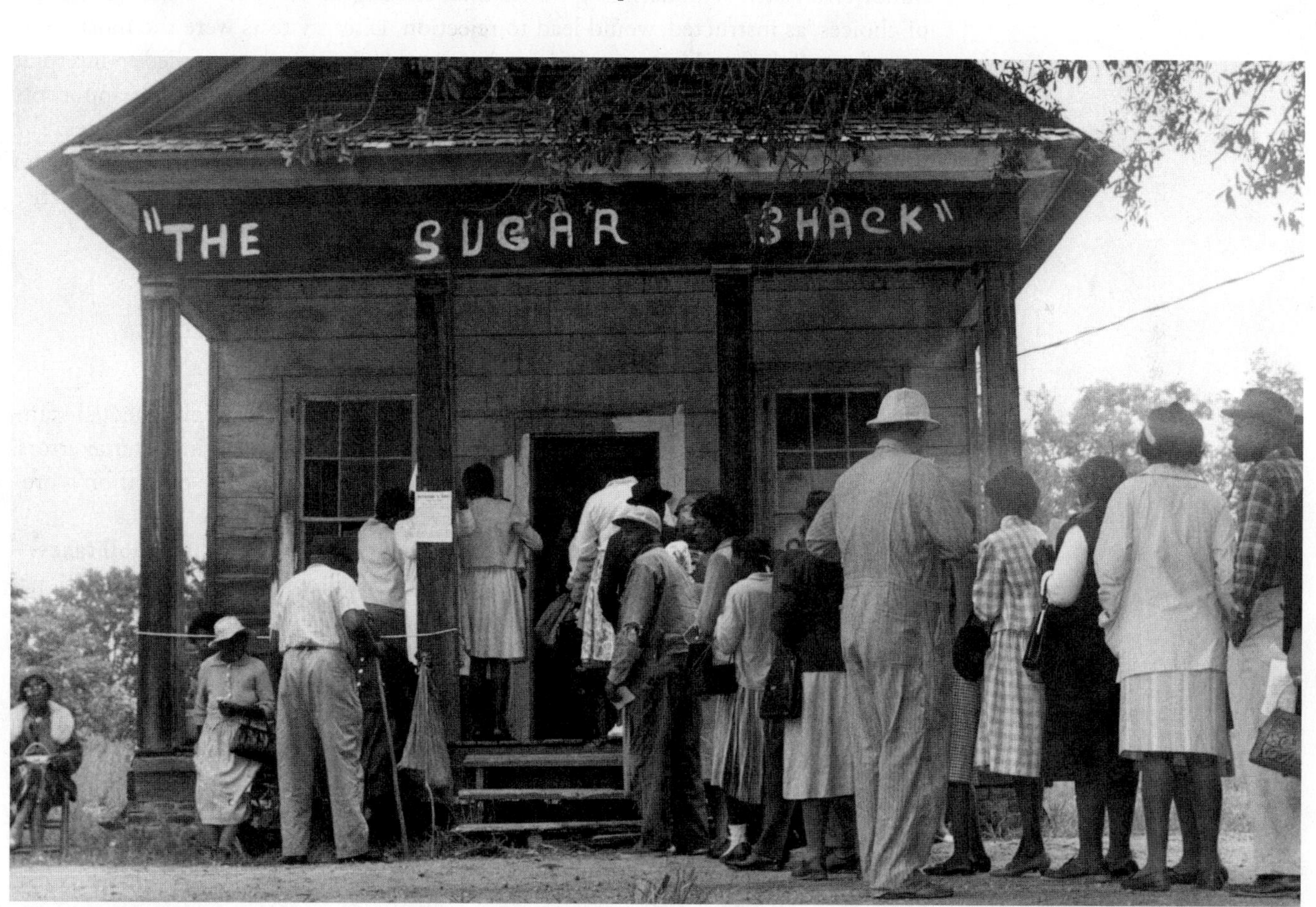

OPENING THE VOTING BOOTH

Passage of the Voting Rights Act of 1965 opened the voting booth to millions of African American voters formerly kept from the polls by a variety of discriminatory regulations in the south. Here, African Americans in rural Alabama in 1966 line up at a local store to cast their votes in a primary that focused on an issue central to their existence—segregation.

5.1

5.2

5.3

5.4

5.5

5.6

5.7

5.8

white primary
Democratic Party primary elections in many southern counties in the early part of the twentieth century that excluded black people from voting.

literacy test
Examination of a person's ability to read and write as a prerequisite to voter registration, outlawed by Voting Rights Act (1965) as discriminatory.

poll taxes
Taxes imposed as a prerequisite to voting; prohibited by the 24th Amendment.

Continued Denial of Voting Rights, 1870–1964

For almost 100 years after the adoption of the 15th Amendment, white politicians in the southern states were able to defeat its purposes. Social and economic pressures and threats of violence were used to intimidate many thousands of would-be African American voters.

There were many "legal" methods of disfranchisement, including a technique known as the **white primary**. So strong was the Democratic Party throughout the south that the Democratic nomination for public office was tantamount to election. Thus, *primary elections* to choose the Democratic nominee were the only elections in which real choices were made. If African Americans were prevented from voting in Democratic primaries, they could be effectively disfranchised. Federal courts threw out the white primary as early as 1927, in a challenge to the Texas white primary law called *Nixon v. Herndon*. Texas and other southern state legislatures resorted to declaring the Democratic Party in their states a private club and ruling that only white people could participate in its primary elections. Blacks were free to vote in "official" general elections, but all whites tacitly agreed to support the Democratic, or "white man's," Party in general elections, regardless of their differences in the primary. Not until 1944, in *Smith v. Allwright*, did the Supreme Court declare the white primary unconstitutional and bring primary elections under the purview of the 15th Amendment—finding that, because the states had delegated the effective function of running elections to a "private club" (the Democratic party), the party took on the equal protection obligations of the state.[17]

Despite the 15th Amendment, many local registrars in the south succeeded in barring African American registration by an endless variety of obstacles, delays, and frustrations. Application forms for registration were lengthy and complicated; even a minor error, such as underlining rather than circling in the "Mr.—Mrs.—Miss" set of choices, as instructed, would lead to rejection. Literacy tests were the most common form of disfranchisement. African American college graduates failed to interpret "properly" the complex legal documents that were part of the test. White applicants for voter registration were seldom asked to go through these lengthy procedures. The use of subjective and arbitrary power by county voting registrars (local officials who ran elections) resulted in widespread disfranchisement of African Americans and Hispanics. In many western states, Indians were disfranchised by law.

The Civil Rights Act, the 24th Amendment, and the Voting Rights Act, 1964–65

The Civil Rights Act of 1964 made it unlawful for registrars to apply unequal standards in registration procedures or to reject applications because of immaterial errors. It required that **literacy tests** be in writing and made a sixth-grade education a presumption of literacy. In 1970, Congress outlawed literacy tests altogether.

The 24th Amendment to the Constitution, ratified in 1964, made **poll taxes**—taxes required of all voters—unconstitutional as a requirement for voting in national elections. In 1966, the Supreme Court declared poll taxes unconstitutional in state and local elections as well.[18] (Many southern jurisdictions had voluntarily eliminated poll taxes in the 1930s and 1940s).

In early 1965, civil rights organizations led by Martin Luther King, Jr., demonstrated against local registrars in Selma, Alabama, who were still keeping African Americans off the voting rolls. Registrars there closed their offices for all but a few hours every month, and used other methods to keep African Americans disfranchised. In response to the Selma march, Congress enacted the strong Voting Rights Act in 1965. The U.S. attorney general, upon evidence of voter discrimination, could replace local registrars with federal registrars, suspend literacy tests, and register voters under simplified federal procedures. Southern counties that had previously discriminated in voting registration hurried to sign up African American voters just to avoid the imposition of federal registrars. The Voting Rights Act of 1965 proved to be very effective, and Congress repeatedly voted to extend it over the years.

The Act worked for almost 50 years. However, a key enforcement mechanism in the VRA was overturned by the Supreme Court in 2013, limiting the future impact of the law. The case, *Shelby County v. Holder*, held that the formula of events and fact used to place a state or county under VRA coverage was outdated and violated the equal sovereignty of states as applied.

19th Amendment
The 1920 constitutional amendment guaranteeing women the right to vote.

26th Amendment
The 1971 constitutional amendment guaranteeing 18-year-olds the right to vote.

The 19th Amendment, 1920

Following the Civil War, many of the women who had been active in the abolitionist movement to end slavery turned their attention to the condition of women in the United States. As abolitionists, they had learned to organize, conduct petition campaigns, and parade and demonstrate. Now they sought to improve the legal and political rights of women. In 1869, the Wyoming territory adopted women's suffrage; later, several other western states followed suit. But it was not until the **19th Amendment** was added to the U.S. Constitution in 1920 that women's right to vote in all elections was constitutionally guaranteed.

The 26th Amendment, 1971

The movement for 18-year-old voting received its original impetus during World War II. It was argued successfully in Georgia in 1944 that because 18-year-olds were being called upon to fight and die for their country, they deserved to have a voice in the conduct of government. However, this argument failed to convince adult voters in other states; qualifications for military service were not regarded as the same as qualifications for rational decision making in elections. In state after state, voters rejected state constitutional amendments designed to extend the vote to 18-year-olds.

Congress intervened on behalf of the 18-year-old vote with the passage of the **26th Amendment** to the Constitution. The states quickly ratified this amendment in

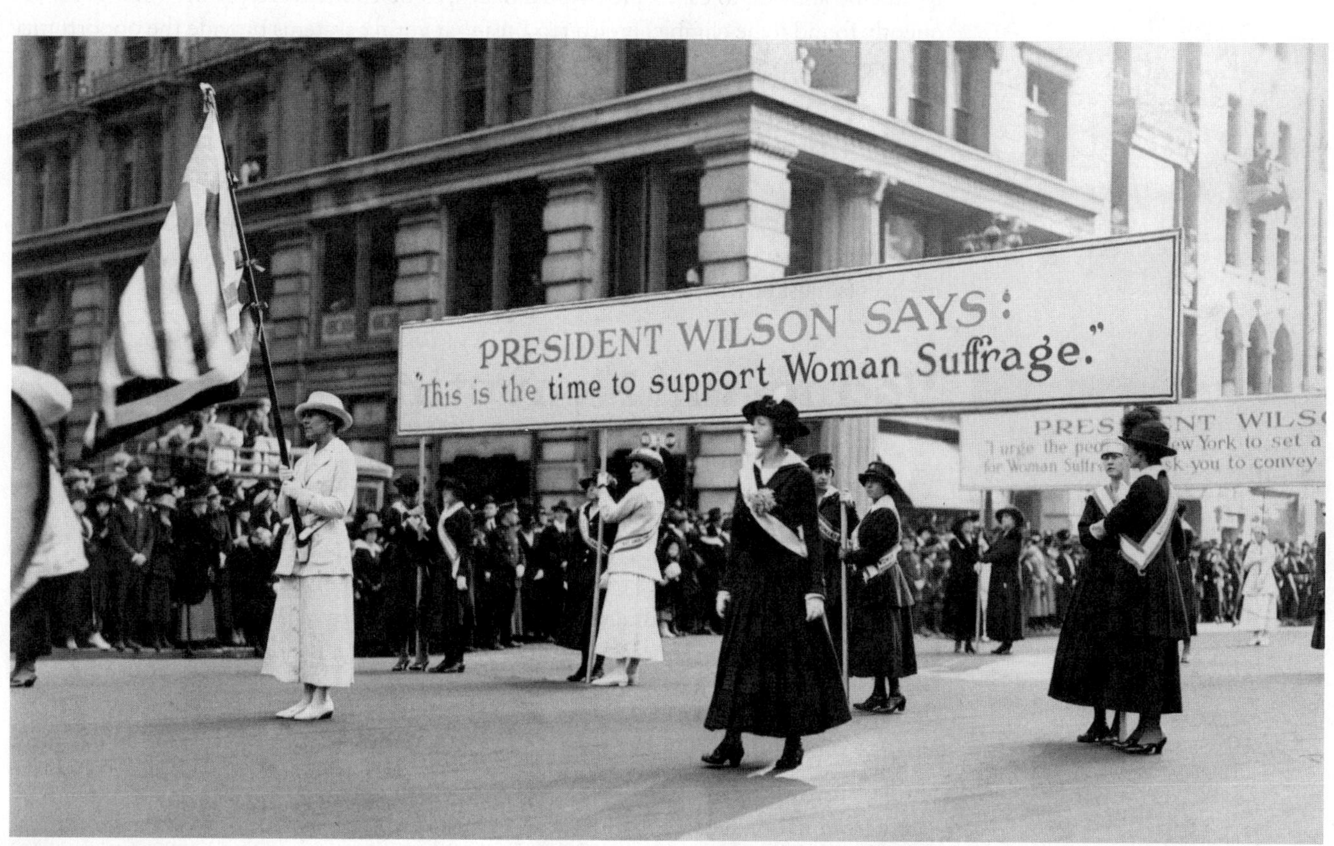

SUFFRAGETTE CITY

The turn of the century saw the acceleration of the women's suffrage movement. Although Woodrow Wilson expressed support for granting the vote to women even before he took office in 1912, it took the activities of women "manning the home front" during World War I to persuade the male electorate to pass the 19th Amendment and give women access to the ballot box throughout the nation.

"Motor Voter Act"
Federal mandate that states offer voter registration at driver's licensing and welfare offices.

turnout
Number of voters who actually cast ballots in an election, as a percentage of people eligible to register and vote.

1971 during a period of national turbulence over the Vietnam War. Many supporters of the amendment believed that protests on campuses and the streets would be reduced if youthful protesters were given the vote.

The National Voter Registration Act, 1993

The National Voter Registration Act of 1993, popularly known as the "Motor Voter Act," mandates that the states offer people the opportunity to register to vote when they apply for driver's licenses or apply for welfare services. States must offer registration by mail and also accept a simplified registration form prepared by the Federal Election Commission. Finally, it bars states from removing the names of people from registration lists for failure to vote. Has the **"Motor Voter Act"** worked? Careful research indicates that it has succeeded in increasing voter registration, but its effects on actual turnout at the polls have been very limited.[19] Apparently, easy registration does not automatically increase voter turnout.

HAVA, 2002

The failure of Florida voting technology led to the controversial 2000 presidential election recount. Congress passed the Helping America Vote Act (HAVA) to replace antiquated voting technologies, such as punch cards and level machines, with modern electronic systems. HAVA also created the Election Assistance Commission as a repository of information about election administration and a way to certify voting technology. States devise their own plans for upgrading voting practices, so considerable variations remain among the states. The act also mandates that each polling place have at least one voting system for individuals with disabilities, including the blind and visually impaired. It requires states to develop and maintain statewide voter registration lists. It requires that individuals who are determined at a polling place to be ineligible to vote be allowed to cast a provisional ballot, to be counted later if the voter is subsequently found to be eligible. It also requires that voting systems provide the opportunity for voters to change or correct any errors in their ballot before it is cast and counted.

The MOVE Act, 2009

The Military and Overseas Voter Act (MOVE) of 2010 was an amendment to the National Defense Appropriation Act. The law makes it easier for overseas citizens and military personnel to use absentee voting in federal elections. The act provides that absentee ballots must be transmitted to overseas voters at least 45 days in advance of an election.

Voting and Nonvoting

5.7 Analyze the political and demographic factors that influence voter turnout, and assess the consequences of nonvoting.

Deciding whether to cast a vote in an election is just as important as deciding which candidate to vote for. *About 40 percent of the voting-age population in the United States typically fails to vote, even in presidential elections.* Voter **turnout**—the number of actual voters in relation to the number of people eligible to register and vote—is even lower in off-year congressional and state elections, when presidential elections are not held. Turnout in local elections (for example, city, county, school board) is even lower when these elections are held separately from national elections. Voter turnout in presidential elections steadily declined for several decades (see Figure 5.5). The three-way presidential race in 1992 temporarily reversed the downward trend.

In 2004 and 2008 voter turnout surged to levels not seen since the 1960s. Various explanations have been offered: the expected closeness of these elections in key states, the experience of 2000 when only a few votes in Florida decided the outcome, the war

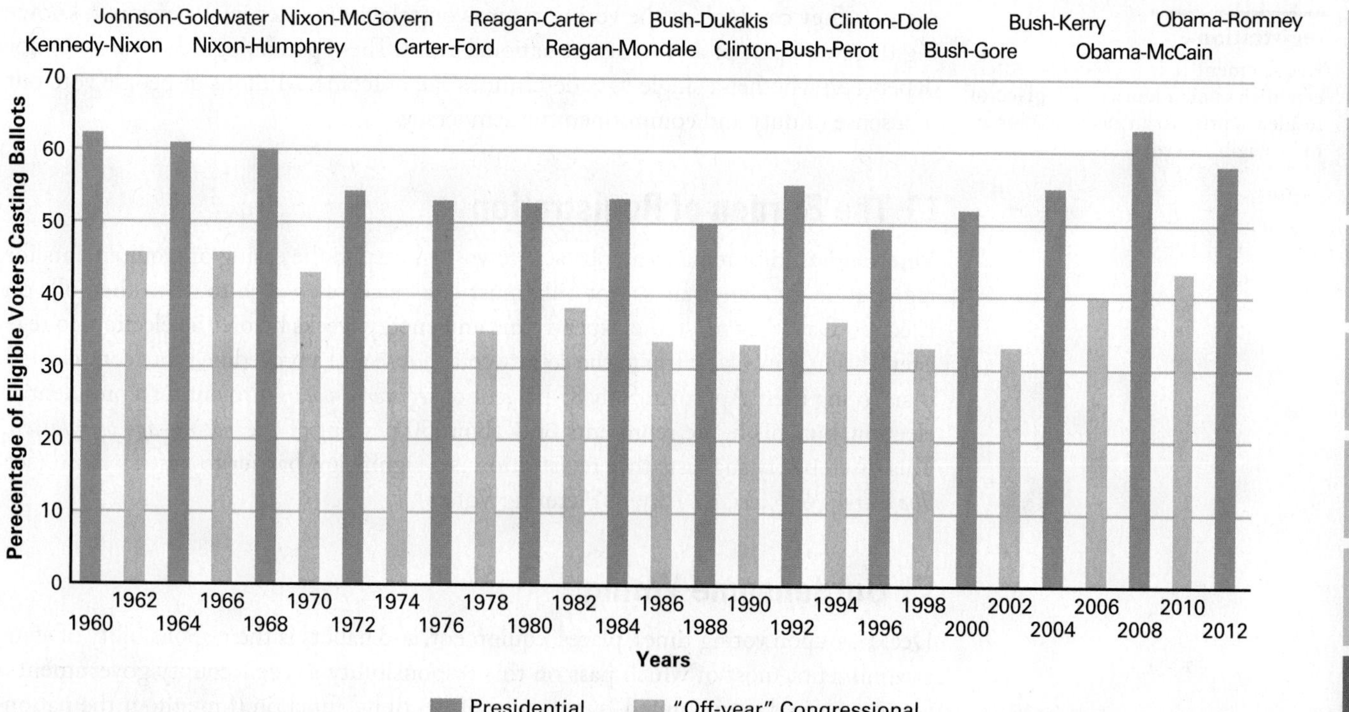

FIGURE 5.5 TRENDING UPWARD: VOTER TURNOUT IN PRESIDENTIAL AND CONGRESSIONAL ELECTIONS

Voter turnout is always higher in years with a presidential election. However, voter turnout has generally declined since 1960, even in presidential election years. The exception came in 1992, when intense interest in the contest between George H. W. Bush and Bill Clinton—spiced by the entry of independent Ross Perot—led to a higher-than-normal turnout. In 1996 fewer than half of voting-age Americans bothered to cast ballots. However, in 2004 and 2008 voter turnout rose to levels not seen since the 1960s.

SOURCE: Center for the Study of the American Electorate, 2012, report accessible at http://bipartisanpolicy.org/library/report/2012-voter-turnout

in Iraq, the financial crises in 2008, and the historic opportunity in that year to elect an African American president. Voter turnout in 2012 was estimated to have declined by about 5 million votes from the record 131 million who voted in 2008. The composition of turnout was a bit younger (19% of voters were under 30), less white (28% of the vote was cast by African Americans, Latinos, and Asians). The components of Obama's 2008 voting coalition were sufficiently represented to propel him to reelection.

Why vote? Usually, this question is asked in the negative: Why do so many people fail to register and vote? But greater insight into the question of voter participation can be obtained if we try to understand what motivates the people who do go to the polls.

☐ The Rational Voter

From a purely "rational" perspective, an individual should vote only if the costs of voting (time spent in registering, informing oneself about the candidates, and going to the polls) are *less* than the expected value of having the preferred candidate win (the personal benefits gained from having one's candidate win), multiplied by the probability that one's own vote will be the deciding vote. Why vote when registering, following the political news, and getting to the polls take away time from work, family, or leisure activity? Why vote when the winner will not really change one's life for the better, or even do things much differently from what the loser would have done? Most important, why vote when the chance that one individual vote will determine who wins is very small? Thought of in this fashion, the wonder is that millions of Americans continue to vote.

The "rational" model can explain voter turnout only by adding "the intrinsic rewards of voting" to the equation. These rewards include the ethic of voting, patriotism, a sense of duty, and allegiance to democracy. People exercise their right to vote out of respect for that right rather than for any personal tangible benefit they expect to receive. They can look at the voting returns on television later in the evening, knowing they were part of an important national event. These psychological rewards do not depend on whether a single vote determines the outcome. Millions of people vote out of a sense of duty and commitment to democracy.

registration
Requirement that prospective voters establish their identity and place of residence prior to an election in order to be eligible to vote.

The Burden of Registration

Voter **registration** remains an obstacle to voting, despite the easing of requirements for registration by many states. Not only must citizens care enough to go to the polls on Election Day; they must also expend time and energy, weeks before the election, to register. This may involve a trip to the county courthouse and a procedure more complicated than voting itself. Approximately 85 percent of *registered voters* turn out for a presidential election, but this figure represents only about 50 percent of the *voting-age population*. This discrepancy suggests that registration is a significant barrier to participation (see *The Game, the Rules, the Players*: Picturing Voters).

Burdensome Voting

Deciding upon voting times, places, equipment, and ballots is the responsibility of state governments, most of which pass on this responsibility to their county governments. County elected or appointed "supervisors of elections" function throughout the nation preparing ballots and handling the streams of voters on Election Day. Nationwide, over 1 million "poll workers," usually volunteers from the local Democratic and Republican party organizations, assist in the voting process and later the counting of votes.

The contested 2000 presidential election spotlighted many of the flaws of ballots and vote counting throughout the nation. That election revealed the variety of voting methods used among the states and even within the same state.[20] Some states and counties use traditional paper or mark-sense ballots, others older lever machines and punch-card ballots, while still others are progressing toward touch screen and other electronic voting equipment. Paper and punch-card ballots regularly produce "overvotes" (where voters mark or punch votes for more than one candidate for the same office) or "undervotes" (where voters fail to make a selection for a particular office), or otherwise spoil their ballot. These ballots are "uncounted"; nationwide, they usually amount to about 2 percent of all ballots cast. Many state laws are fuzzy regarding when and how to conduct "recounts"—requiring election officials to undertake a second or third counting of the ballots. Reformers generally recommend touch-screen voting machines; carefully designed ballot layouts; better training of poll workers; uniform rules for recounts; and better voter education programs, including sample ballots distributed well before Election Day. However, even electronic voting is subject to error. Opponents of "black box" voting argue that every vote on a single machine may be lost to computer error or malfunction. They urged the use of ballots that leave a "paper trail."[21]

States increasingly require photo identification at the polling place in order to ensure that voters are who they say they are. Opponents of photo ID argue that it has a disparate impact on poor and minority voters. The U.S. Supreme Court upheld the photo ID requirement in 2008, but the U.S. Department of Justice has used the Voting Rights Act to object to some photo ID requirements as diminishing the ability of minority voters to participate in elections.[22]

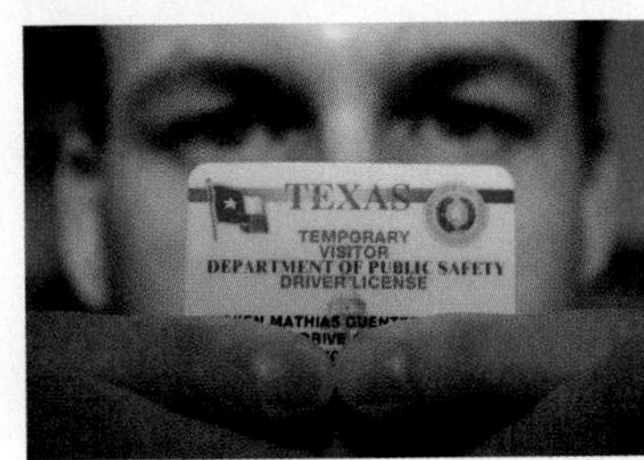

WHO ARE YOU?
Several states have tightened their voter identification requirements to be able to cast a vote, including narrowing the sort of photo identification that can be presented to vote. Advocates say it is a hedge against voter fraud, while critics contend it is an illegal effort to suppress the vote of the poor, elderly, and minorities.

The Politics of Voter Turnout

Politics drives the debate over easing voter registration requirements. Democrats generally favor minimal requirements—for example, same-day registration, registration by mail, and registration at welfare and motor vehicle licensing offices. They also support early voting. They know that nonvoters are heavily drawn from groups that typically support the Democratic Party, including the less-educated, lower-income, and minority groups. Republicans are often less enthusiastic about easing voting requirements, but it is politically embarrassing to appear to oppose increased participation.

The Game, the Rules, the Players

Picturing Voters

Who are you? Should you have to prove who you are to vote?

The voter identification battle has waged in the United States since 2004, when push-back against voter caging and ballot security, mainly by Republican and conservative organizations, prompted increased calls for voter identification. Starting in 2007, efforts have been advanced in several states to make voting more difficult, in response to alleged voter fraud. Advocates for a broader, freer franchised pushed back, challenging photo identification requirements as discriminatory and potentially a violation of the 24th amendment.

The Voter Fraud Argument

There are nearly 200,000 voting precincts in the United States. Usually representatives of both the Democratic and Republican parties are present at each precinct to ensure the honesty of the vote. Voters who have previously registered show their voter cards or present other identification and then sign their names on the voter registration lists. This ensures that the voters are who they say they are, and that they do not vote more than once. But registration by mail and absentee voting are rising over time.

Voter registration cards are widely distributed, filled out by persons eligible to vote, and then collected and sent to the county election office. As the election nears, registered voters may request an absentee ballot, to be filled out and mailed to the county election office. Party operatives and independent "get-out-the-vote" organizations go to nursing homes, assisted-living facilities, and other institutions housing the elderly, as well as large condominium projects, filling out registration forms for the residents as well as absentee ballot requests and then "helping out" in marking the ballots, collecting them, and mailing them en masse to voting offices. It has been alleged that some groups collecting registration forms and absentee ballots conveniently discard those that do not match the group's preferences.

Conservative commentators and some Republican state lawmakers contend that fraudulent nonvoters are voting and presumably doing so in large enough numbers to threaten election integrity. They allege that community organizing groups like the defunct ACORN exploited the voter registration system. Claims of fraud by in-person voters have not succeeded in turning up widespread or systemic fraud.

Efforts to require new voters to prove their citizenship or prove identity with photo identification were decried by liberal politicians as efforts to suppress the minority, poor, and elderly vote. These voters are less likely to have a driver's license. Litigation in Indiana and Georgia to challenge photo identification requirements did not succeed.

Strict identification states require a voter to produce photo identification at the polling place to vote. Voters can also cast a provisional ballot and then return with photo identification later to have their ballot officially counted. Eight states use a strict identification law—five of these are in the South, including Texas, which is the largest state to have a photo identification requirement.

SHOW YOURSELF

Some state voter identification laws have grown increasingly restrictive. This veteran was unable to use his federal VA identification to vote in Ohio in 2012.

Identification or affidavit states allow the voter to either produce a photo identification to vote, or sign an affidavit (statement) attesting to their identification. Seven states require photo identification or affidavit, three in the South. This includes Florida, which is the second-largest state to require identification.

Nonphoto identification states allow voters to show other forms of identification that lack a photograph, such as a Social Security card, voter registration card, or even a utility bill. Fifteen states have a nonphoto identification law.

The remaining 20 states have no identification requirement to vote. Of these, New Hampshire, Minnesota, and North Carolina have photo identification bills pass their legislature, only to see the proposal vetoed by the governor.

States with Some Voter Identification Requirement

Strict identification: Georgia, Indiana, Kansas, Mississippi, South Carolina, Tennessee, Texas, Wisconsin

Identification or affidavit: Alabama, Florida, Hawaii, Idaho, Louisiana, Michigan, South Dakota

Nonphoto identification: Arizona, Arkansas, Alaska, Colorado, Connecticut, Delaware, Kentucky, Missouri, Montana, North Dakota, Ohio, Oklahoma, Utah, Virginia, Washington

QUESTIONS

1. Do you think it is unreasonable for a voter to produce identification to receive a ballot?
2. Do you trust that your vote will be fairly and accurately counted when you go to vote? If not, why not?

5.1 5.2 5.3 5.4 5.5 5.6 5.7 5.8

political alienation
Belief that politics is irrelevant to one's life and that one cannot personally affect public affairs.

The Stimulus of Competition

The more lively the competition between parties or between candidates, the greater the interest of citizens and the larger the voter turnout. When parties and candidates compete vigorously, they make news and are given large play by the mass media. Consequently, a setting of competitive politics generates more political stimuli than does a setting with weak competition. People are also more likely to perceive that their votes count in a close contest, and thus they are more likely to cast them. Moreover, when parties or candidates are fighting in a close contest, their supporters tend to spend more time and energy campaigning and getting out the vote.

Political Alienation

People who feel politics is irrelevant to their lives—or who feel they cannot personally affect public affairs—are less likely to vote than people who feel they themselves can affect political outcomes and that these outcomes affect their lives. Given the level of **political alienation** (two-thirds of respondents agree with the statement, "Most public officials are not really interested in the problems of people like me"),[23] it is surprising that so many people vote. Alienation is high among voters, and it is even higher among nonvoters. Despite studies that show that increased voter turnout would not substantially change election outcomes, the nonvoters appear to be a potential Democratic constituency.

Intensity

Finally, as we might expect, people who feel strongly about politics and who hold strong opinions about political issues are more likely to vote than people who do not. For example, people who describe themselves as *extreme* liberals or *extreme* conservatives are more likely to vote than people who describe themselves as moderates.

Age and Turnout

Young people do not vote in the same proportions as older people (see Figure 5.6). After the electorate was expanded by the 26th Amendment to include persons 18 years of age and over, voter turnout actually dropped, from 60.9 percent in the 1968 presidential election to 55.2 percent in the 1972 presidential election, the largest turnout decline in successive presidential elections.

Who's Getting What?

The Voting Rights Act And Participating

The 1965 Voting Rights Act led to one of the most dramatic increase in voter participation in U.S. history. Forty-seven years after the enactment of the law, black voter participation outpaced white voting rates in many southern states and also nationwide.

The most effective part of the law, the "preclearance provision," allowed the national government to freeze local voting laws. Then, the attorney general would review changes in those laws to ensure that minority voters were not discriminated against by the change. States or counties with voter turnout or registration under 50 percent of those eligible in 1972, and a history of using a test or device to qualify to vote were subject to the law.

The US Supreme Court heard a challenge to this part of the law from Shelby County, Alabama in 2013 (*Shelby County v. Holder*). The Court threw out preclearance as outdated, citing dramatic gains in minority participation. They also determined that the law violated the "equal sovereignty" of the states. Critics contend that removing this protection will harm minority voting and lead to a return of "Jim Crow" politics.

Question

1. Do you think the national government should review all state voting practices? Why?

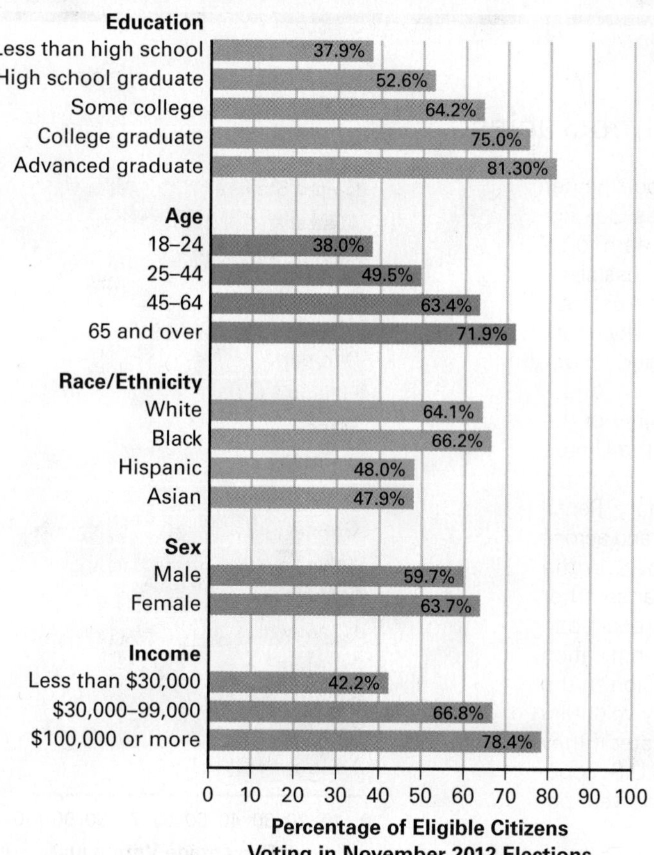

FIGURE 5.6 WHO VOTES

Voter participation increases with age and educational level. White and black participation levels are almost equal, but Hispanic participation lags. Women are somewhat more likely to vote than men.

SOURCE: Bureau of the Census, Data for 2012 presidential election, accessed at http://www.census.gov/hhes/www/socdemo/voting/publications/p20/2012/tables.html.

□ Party Organization

Strong party organizations can help increase turnout. But strong party organizations, or machines, that canvassed neighborhoods, took citizens to the courthouse to register them, contacted them personally during campaigns, and saw to it that they got to the polls on Election Day have largely disappeared. Organization of voters increasingly occurs through community and social groups with strong ideological ties to one party or the other.

Regardless of the explanations offered, it is interesting to note that most European democracies report higher voter turnout rates than the United States (see *Compared to What?* Voter Turnout in Western Democracies).

□ Voters and Nonvoters

Who votes? Who doesn't? Why? The perceived benefits and costs of voting apparently do not fall evenly across all social groups. Nonvoting would generate less concern if voters were a representative cross section of nonvoters. But voters differ from nonvoters in politically important ways.

Voters are better educated than nonvoters. Education appears to be the most important determinant of voter turnout (see Figure 5.5). It may be that schooling promotes an interest in politics, instills the ethic of citizen participation, or gives people a better awareness of public affairs and an understanding of the role of elections in a democracy. Education is associated with a sense of confidence and political *efficacy*, the feeling that one can indeed have a personal impact on public affairs.

Age is another factor affecting voter participation. Perhaps because young people have more distractions, more demands on their time in school, work, or new family responsibilities, nonvoting is greatest among 18- to 24-year-olds. In contrast, older

Compared to What?

Voter Turnout in Western Democracies

Other Western democracies regularly report higher voter turnout rates than the United States (see figure). Yet in an apparent paradox, Americans seem to be more supportive of their political institutions, less alienated from their political system, and even more patriotic than citizens of Western European nations. Why, then, are voter turnouts in the United States so much lower than in these other democracies?

The answer to this question lies primarily in the legal and institutional differences between the United States and the other democracies. First of all, in Austria, Australia, Belgium, and Italy, voting is *mandatory*. Penalties and the level of enforcement vary within and across these countries. Moreover, registration laws in the United States make voting more difficult than in other countries. In Western Europe, all citizens are required to register with the government and obtain identification cards. These cards are then used for admission to the polls. In contrast, voter registration is entirely voluntary in the United States, and voters must reregister if they change residences. Nearly 50 percent of the U.S. population changes residence at least once in a five-year period, thus necessitating reregistration.

Parties in the United States are more loosely organized, less disciplined, and less able to mobilize voters than are European parties. Moreover, many elections in the United States, notably elections for Congress, are not very competitive. The United States organizes congressional elections by district with winner-take-all rules, whereas many European parliaments are selected by proportional representation, with seats allocated to parties based on national vote totals. Proportional representation means every vote counts toward seats in the legislative body. Thus greater competition and proportional representation may encourage higher voter turnout in European democracies.

But cultural differences may also contribute to differences in turnout. The American political culture, with its tradition of individualism and self-reliance and its reluctance to empower government, encourages Americans to resolve their problems through their own efforts rather than looking to government for solutions. Government is not as central to Americans as it is to Europeans, and therefore getting to the polls on Election Day is not seen as so important.

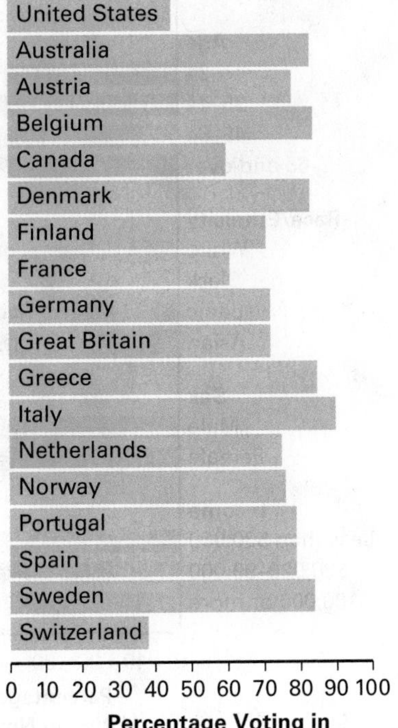

* Percent of voting age population casting ballots, average, in elections, 1991–2000.

Question

1. Do you think we should have mandatory voting?

Americans are politically influential in part because candidates know they turn out at the polls.

High-income people are more likely to vote than are low-income people. Most of this difference stems from the fact that high-income people are more likely to be well educated and older. But poor people may also feel alienated from the political system—they may lack a sense of political efficacy; they may feel they have little control over their own lives, let alone over public affairs. Or poor people may simply be so absorbed in the problems of life that they have little time or energy to spend on registering and voting.

Income and education differences between participants and nonparticipants are even greater when other forms of political participation are considered. Higher-income, better-educated people are much more likely to be among those who make campaign contributions, who write or call their elected representatives, and who join and work in active political organizations.[24]

Historically, race was a major determinant of nonvoting. Black voter turnout, especially in the South, was markedly lower than white voter turnout. African

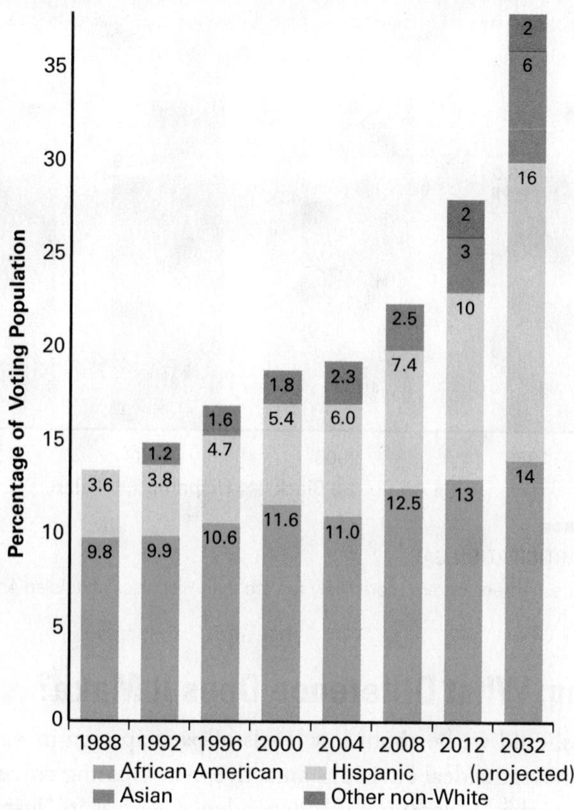

FIGURE 5.7 THE CHANGING AMERICAN VOTER

Since 1988, the American electorate has become more diverse, with far more Hispanic, Asian, and African American voters. See Paul Taylor, et. al., "An Awaked Giant: The Hispanic Electorate is Likely to Double by 2030." Washington, DC: Pew Hispanic Trends Research Project, Nov. 14, 2012.

Americans continue today to have a slightly lower overall voter turnout than whites, but most of the remaining difference is attributable to differences between blacks and whites in educational and income levels. Among blacks and whites at the same educational and income levels, blacks actually register and vote with slightly *greater* frequency than comparable whites. By the beginning of the 21st century, black voter participation is highest in the parts of the South that historically impeded minority voting the most.

The greatest disparity in voter turnout is between Hispanics and others. Low voter participation by Hispanics may be a product of language differences, lack of cultural assimilation, or noncitizenship status. Regardless of source, very low voter participation stands as the primary impediment to the full political empowerment of Hispanic citizens.

The Changing American Voter

The nation's voters in the 2012 presidential election were the most racially and ethnically diverse in American history. Over one in four votes was cast by nonwhites. The nation's three largest minority groups—African Americans, Hispanics, and Asians—each accounted for unprecedented shares of the presidential vote. Of the record 131 million people who voted in 2008, blacks made up 13 percent, Hispanics 10 percent, and Asians 3 percent. The white share of the electorate is the lowest ever, just under the 65 percent white share of the total U.S. population. The increasing diversity of the electorate was driven by increases both in number and in the turnout rates of minority voters. Levels of participation by Hispanics and Asians had decreased slightly in 2012. Record turnout by African Americans reduced the voter participation gap between minorities and white eligible voters. Hispanic and Asian participation levels also increased but they remain lower than blacks or whites. Voting projections do not indicate that the gap between Hispanics and Asians versus Anglo whites and African Americans will diminish in the next decade.

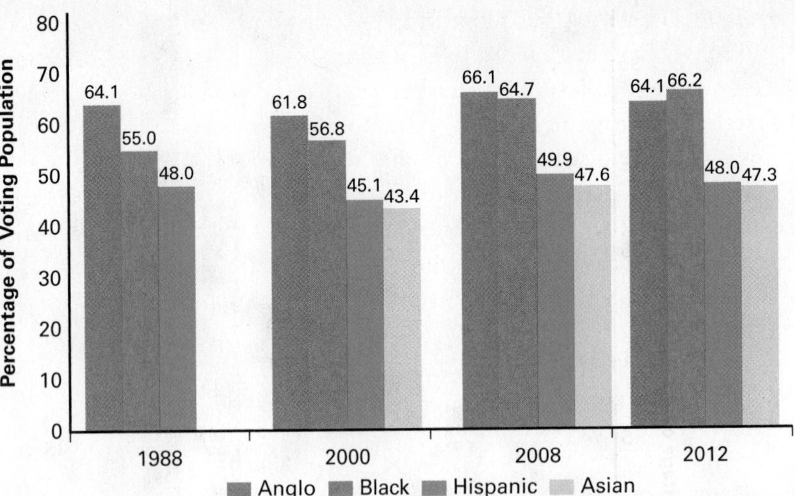

FIGURE 5.8 THE PARTICIPATION GAP

Anglo Whites and African Americans are more likely to vote than Hispanics and Asian Americans.

Nonvoting: What Difference Does It Make?

How concerned should we be about low levels of participation in American politics? Certainly the democratic ideal envisions an active, participating citizenry. Democratic government, asserts the Declaration of Independence, derives its "just powers from the consent of the governed." The legitimacy of democratic government can be more easily questioned when half of the people fail to vote. That is, it is easier to question whether the government truly represents "the people" when only half of the people vote even in a presidential election. Voting is an expression of good citizenship, and it reinforces attachment to the nation and to democratic government. Nonvoting suggests alienation from the political system.

However, the *right* to vote is more important to democratic government than voter turnout. The nineteenth-century English political philosopher John Stuart Mill wrote, "Men, as well as women, do not need political rights in order that they may govern, but in order that they may not be misgoverned."[25] As long as all adult Americans possess the right to vote, politicians must consider their interests. "Rulers and ruling classes are under a necessity of considering the interests of those who have the suffrage."[26] Democratic governments cannot really ignore the interests of anyone who can vote. People who have the right to vote, but who have voluntarily chosen not to exercise it in the past, can always change their minds, go to the polls, and "throw the rascals out."

Voluntary nonvoting is not the same as being denied the suffrage. Politicians can indeed ignore the interests of people denied the vote by restrictive laws or practices or by intimidation or force. But when people choose not to exercise their right to vote, they may be saying that they do not believe their interests are really affected by government. The late Senator Sam Ervin is widely quoted on the topic of nonvoters:

> I'm not going to shed any crocodile tears if people don't care enough to vote. I don't believe in making it easy for apathetic, lazy people. I'd be extremely happy if nobody in the United States voted except for the people who thought about the issues and made up their own minds and wanted to vote.[27]

Felon Disfranchisement

One of the major sources of nonvoting is felon disfranchisement. Section 2 of the 14th Amendment acknowledges the ability to disfranchise persons taking part in rebellion or other crimes, and the Supreme Court affirmed felon disfranchisement laws in 1974, in a California case, *Ramirez v. Richardson*. Felon voter eligibility is determined by the states, and they vary tremendously in restoring voting rights. Kentucky, Virginia, Florida, and Iowa have permanent felon disfranchisement (all but Virginia provide a mechanism for eventual restoration). Maine and Vermont do not disfranchise felons. All other states restore voting rights after completion of sentence.

There is a racially disparate impact of felon disfranchisement. There are over 1.5 million incarcerated felons in the United States, and nearly 5.3 million felons or former felons who are disfranchised. These numbers include over 1.4 million disfranchised African American men. It is estimated that one in seven black men is ineligible to vote due to felon status, and Hispanic men are also disproportionately disfranchised.

protests
Public marches or demonstrations designed to call attention to an issue and motivate others to apply pressure on public officials.

Protest as Political Participation

5.8 Characterize protest as a form of political participation.

Protests, marches, and demonstrations are important forms of political participation. Indeed, the 1st Amendment guarantees the right "peaceably to assemble, and to petition the government for a redress of grievances." A march to the steps of Congress, a mass assembly of people on the Washington Mall with speakers, sign waving, and songs, and the presentation of petitions to government officials are all forms of participation protected by the 1st Amendment.

Protests

Protests are generally designed to call attention to an issue and to motivate others to apply pressure on public officials. In fact, protests are usually directed at the news media rather than at public officials themselves. If protesters could persuade public officials directly in the fashion of lobbyists and interest groups, they would not need to protest. Protests are intended to generate attention and support among previously uncommitted people—enough so the ultimate targets of the protest, public officials, will be pressured to act to redress grievances.

Coverage by the news media, especially television, is vital to the success of protest activity. The media not only carry the protesters' message to the mass public but also inform public officials about what is taking place. Protests provide the media with "good visuals"—pictorial dramatizations of political issues. The media welcome opportunities to present political issues in a confrontational fashion because confrontation helps capture larger audiences. Thus protesters and the media use each other to advance their separate goals—though the growth of an increasingly corporate media may have initially impeded coverage of some protests.

Protests are most commonly employed by groups that have little influence in electoral politics. They were a key device of the civil rights movement at a time when many African Americans were barred from voting. In the absence of protest, the majority white population—and the public officials they elected—were at best unconcerned with the plight of black people in a segregated society. Protests, including a dramatic march on Washington in 1963 at which Martin Luther King, Jr., delivered his inspirational "I Have a Dream" speech, called attention to the injustices of segregation and placed civil rights on the agenda of decision makers.

Protests can be effectively employed by groups that are relatively small in number but whose members feel very intensely about the issue. Often the protest is a means by which these groups can obtain bargaining power with decision makers. Protests may threaten to tarnish the reputations of government officials or private corporations, or may threaten to disrupt their daily activities or reduce their business through boycotts or pressure on customers. If the protest is successful, protest leaders can then offer to end the protest in exchange for concessions from their targets.

The Game, the Rules, the Players

The Candidate: Are You Born to Run?

There are over a half million elected offices in the United States. They are all held by ordinary citizens who invested themselves in doing the public's business. There are rewards that come with elected office—the opportunity to help shape public policy; public attention and name recognition; and many business, professional, and social contacts. But there are many costs as well—the absence of privacy; a microscopic review of one's past; constant calls, meetings, interviews, and handshaking; and, perhaps most onerous of all, the continual need to solicit campaign funds. From local office to the White House, pursuing public office demands that individuals immerse themselves in the task of getting elected. And this task starts long before the first time someone puts their name on the ballot.

The Pre-Career: Getting Involved

Before someone has an elective career, there's usually a pre-career. Many people who seek public office start off by giving their time and effort over to religious, community, and business groups. This involvement teaches valuable organization, bargaining, and problem-solving skills. It also allows someone to create a circle of advisors, contacts, and supporters who are critical to any future elective career. Ways to get involved include:

- Neighborhood associations
- Chambers of commerce, business associations
- Churches and synagogues (become an usher, if possible, for visibility)
- Political groups (Democratic or Republican clubs, League of Women Voters, and so on)
- Parent–Teacher Associations (PTAs)
- Service clubs (Rotary, Kiwanis, Civitan, Toastmasters)
- Recreation organizations (Little League, flag football, soccer leagues, running and walking clubs, for example, as participant, coach, or umpire)

Deciding to Run: Know What You're Doing

In deciding to run, and choosing the office for which you wish to run, you should become thoroughly familiar with the issues, duties, and responsibilities. The political campaign is the most exciting and easiest part of the political career—as candidate, you are the center of attention. But in elective office, politicians have to share power and attention with other lawmakers or other officeholders. Getting elected will depend on understanding and explaining the job you are seeking to the voters who will entrust you to do the job. How do you get to know the job?

- Attend council or commission meetings, state legislative sessions, and/or committee hearings.
- Become familiar with current issues and officeholders, and obtain a copy of and read the budget.
- Learn the demographics of your district (racial, ethnic, and age composition; occupational mix; average income; neighborhood differences). If you do not fit the prevailing racial, ethnic, or age composition, think about moving to another district.
- Many officeholders started their career working in government, often for an elected official. Interning or taking a position with an elected official teaches the job of governing firsthand.

And, most important, have a brief (preferably less than seven seconds) answer to the question, "Why are you running?" If you can't give people three sound, brief reasons why they should vote for you, you'll probably lose their attention and not get their vote.

Getting in the Race

For most public offices, a phone call or visit to the Web site of your county or township election board should provide most of the information you need as a new candidate. Among the information and materials you will need are:

- Qualifying forms and information
- Campaign financing forms and regulations
- District and street maps for your district
- Recent election results in your district
- Election-law book or pamphlet
- Voter registration lists (usually sold as lists, or labels, or computer files)

If you are seeking a partisan office, contact your party's county chairperson for advice; convince the party's leaders that you can win. Ask for a list of their regular campaign contributors, but also recognize that donor information is often available through the state ethics board charged with regulating campaign finance.

Start Dialing for Dollars: OPM

The easiest way to finance a campaign is to be rich enough to provide your own funds. Failing that, you must go out and get other people's money (OPM). But, before you start taking in checks or accepting credit card contributions via the Internet, make sure you do the following:

- Establish a campaign fund and committee, according to the laws of your state.
- Find a treasurer/campaign-finance chairperson; if they know many wealthy, politically involved people, so much the better.
- Consider contracting a professional fund-raiser. Most fund-raisers work on a commission basis and will often defer part of their commission in exchange for a "win bonus" if you actually succeed in winning the election.

(*Continued*)

(*Continued*)

- Invite wealthy, politically involved people to small coffees, cocktail parties, dinners; give a brief campaign speech and then have your finance chairperson solicit contributions.
- Follow up fund-raising events and meetings with personal phone calls, e-mails, or personalized video messages.
- Be prepared to continue fund-raising activities throughout your campaign; file accurate financial disclosure statements as required by state law.

If you are unable to ask people for money, you will not win an election.

Getting Organized

Professional campaign managers and management firms almost always outperform volunteers. If you cannot afford professional management, you must rely on yourself or trusted friends to perform the following:

- Draw up a budget based on reasonable expectations of campaign funding.
- Interview and select a professional campaign-management firm, or appoint a trusted campaign manager. Like fund-raisers, some professional firms will defer part of their compensation in the form of a win bonus.
- Ask trusted friends from various clubs, activities, neighborhoods, churches, and so on to meet and serve as a campaign committee. If your district is racially or ethnically diverse, make sure all groups are represented on your committee.
- Decide on a campaign theme; research issues important to your community; develop brief, well-articulated positions on these issues.
- Open a campaign headquarters and make sure you have the appropriate communications apparatus and technology to run a contact-driven campaign. Much of the work of phone-banking, Internet contacting, and assembling and shipping mailings can be contracted out to professional consultants—the costs are less than you might expect.
- Arrange to meet with newspaper editors, editorial boards, TV station executives, influential online writers, and political reporters. Be prepared for tough questions.
- Hire a media consultant or advertising agency or appoint a volunteer media director who knows television, radio, Internet, and newspaper advertising.
- Arrange a press release and press conference to announce your candidacy. Notify all media well in advance. Arrange for overflow crowd of supporters to cheer and applaud. This is less important for local office—but make sure there is a press release of your candidacy that will be available for the news at the time of filing.
- Produce eye-catching, inspirational 15- or 30-second television and radio ads that present a favorable image of you and stress your campaign theme.
- Prepare attractive online and print media—but don't get too distracted by the task. A candidate who spends all day designing a logo for the campaign brochure just lost a day of voter contacting and fund-raising.
- Hire a local survey-research firm to conduct telephone surveys of voters in your district, asking what they think are the most important issues, how they stand on them, whether they recognize your name and your theme, and how they plan to vote. This firm should also be able to direct you to a phone-banking operation that will do phone-based advocacy for your campaign. Be prepared to change your theme and your position on issues if surveys show strong opposition to your views.

On the Campaign Trail

Campaigns themselves may be primarily media centered or primarily *door-to-door* ("retail") or some combination of both.

- Buy media time as early as possible from television and radio stations; insist on prime-time slots before, during, and after popular shows. You will pay more, but it will be worth it.
- Buy newspaper inserts. They are more colorful and attractive than ads placed in the print itself, and they cost less. Newspapers are dying as a political medium, so be aware that there is a cost-benefit tradeoff between papers and direct mail. However, if you spend enough money advertising with some papers, they will reciprocate with an editorial endorsement.
- Attend every community gathering possible, just to be seen, even if you do not give a speech. Keep all speeches short. Focus on one or two issues that your polls show are important to voters. As FDR said, there are three Bs in politics: "Be sincere; be brief; be seated."
- Personally canvass door-to-door with a brief (seven-second) self-introduction and statement of your reasons for running. Use registration lists to identify members of your own party, and try to address them by name. Also canvass offices, factories, coffee shops, shopping malls—anywhere you find a crowd.
- Recruit paid or unpaid volunteers to hand out literature door-to-door (door-knocking and door-dropping). New apps allow you to load voter data into a database for your PDA or hand-held device; to knock the door; record information from voters at home about their concerns; and, if they are not home, deploy a robocall to their phone.
- Organize a phone bank, either professional or volunteer. Prepare *brief* introduction and phone statements. Record names of people who say they support you. Phone banking can be supplemented with targeted automated phone calls and targeted e-mail.
- If you live in an early voting state, know the absentee and early voting rules and the locations of early voting stations for voters. Lock up voters before they can change their minds.

(*Continued*)

5.1
5.2
5.3
5.4
5.5
5.6
5.7
5.8

(Continued)

- Know your opponent: research his or her past affiliations, indiscretions if any, previous voting record, and public positions on issues.
- Have someone research you, too. The worst enemy of most politicians is the person they see in the mirror every morning.
- Be prepared to "define" your opponent in negative terms. Negative advertising works. But be fair: base your comments on your opponent's public record. Emphasize his or her positions that clearly deviate from your district voters' known preferences.

On Election Day: GOTV

Getting out the voters for your candidacy is the key to success. Election Day is the busiest day of the campaign for you and your staff. And remember that yours is likely one of several races on the ballot that day—so you will have lots of candidates from lots of campaigns trying to turn out the vote.

- Use your phone bank to place as many calls as possible to supportive voters in your district (especially those who have indicated in previous calls and visits that they support you). Remind them to vote; make sure your phone workers can tell each voter where to go to cast his or her vote. This is easier in general elections, where party identification efforts have located the most likely party voter.
- Solicit volunteers to drive people to the polls.
- Assign workers to as many polling places as possible. Most state laws require that they stay a specified distance from the voting booths. But they should be in evidence with your signs and literature to buttonhole voters before they go into the booths.
- Show up at city or county election office on election night with a prepared victory statement thanking supporters and pledging your service to the district. (Also draft a courteous concession statement pledging your support to the winner, in case you lose.)
- Attend victory party with your supporters; meet many "new" friends. But remember who got you there.

QUESTIONS

1. **If someone came to you and offered you a position in Congress at no cost (no campaign, no effort), would you take it?**
2. **Consider the aspects of candidacies. What are the personal, political, and financial resources you need to run? Could you go find them if you needed to? How?**
3. **Consider the commitment to a campaign described above. Can someone run for office as a part-time commitment?**

civil disobedience
Form of public protest involving the breaking of laws believed to be unjust.

Civil Disobedience

Civil disobedience is a form of protest that involves breaking what are perceived as "unjust" laws. The purpose is to call attention to the existence of injustice. In the words of Martin Luther King, Jr., civil disobedience "seeks so to dramatize the issue that it can no longer be ignored."[28] Those truly engaging in civil disobedience do not attempt to evade punishment for breaking the law but instead willingly accept the penalty. By doing so, they demonstrate not only their sincerity and commitment but also the injustice of the law. Cruelty or violence directed at the protesters by police or others contributes further to the drama of injustice. Like other protest activity, the success of civil disobedience depends on the willingness of the mass media to carry the message to both the general public and the political leadership.

Violence

Violence can also be a form of political participation. Indeed, political violence—for example, assassinations, rioting, burning, looting—has been uncomfortably frequent in American politics over the years. It is important to distinguish violence from protest. Peaceful protest is constitutionally protected. Often, organized protest activity harnesses frustrations and hostilities, directs them into constitutionally acceptable activities, and thus avoids violence. Likewise, civil disobedience should be distinguished from violence. Civil disobedience breaks only "unjust" laws, without violence, and willingly accepts punishment without trying to escape.

Effectiveness

How effective are protests? Protests can be effective in achieving some goals under some conditions. But protests are useless or even counterproductive in pursuit of other

PROTEST MEETS VIOLENT PROTEST

Efforts of civil rights protesters to bring political and social change to the South often met violence. Black and white Americans from outside the South traveled to the South to help organize non-violent protest and to challenge segregation laws governing transit and public accommodations. Here, one of the "Freedom Rider" buses burns at the Montgomery, Alabama, Greyhound Bus station in May 1961.

goals under other conditions. Here are some generalizations about the effectiveness of protests:

- Protests are more likely to be effective when directed at specific problems or laws rather than at general conditions that cannot readily be remedied by governmental action.
- Protests are more likely to be effective when targeted toward public officials who are capable of granting the desired concession or resolving the specific problem. Protests with no specific targets and protests directed at officials who have no power to change things are generally unproductive.
- Protests are more likely to succeed when the goal is limited to gaining access or representation in decision making or to placing an issue on the agenda of decision makers.
- Protests are not always effective in actually getting laws changed and are even less effective in ensuring that the impact of the changes will really improve the conditions that led to the protest.

Public officials can defuse protest activity in a variety of ways. They may greet protesters with smiles and reassurances that they agree with their goals. They may dispense symbolic satisfaction without any tangible results. They may grant token concessions with great publicity, perhaps remedying a specific case of injustice while doing little to affect general conditions. Or public officials may claim to be constrained either legally or financially from doing anything—the "I-would-like-to-help-you-but-I-can't" strategy. Or public officials can directly confront the protesters by charging that they are unrepresentative of the groups they are trying to help.

Perhaps the most challenging and sometimes most effective kind of "protest" is to run for public office. Whether at the local level, such as the school board, or at the state or national level, the participation of one individual as a candidate—even when not elected—can make a difference in public affairs.

5.1
5.2
5.3
5.4
5.5
5.6
5.7
5.8

A Constitutional Note

Who Can Vote?

The Founders generally believed that only property-owning free white males, 21 or older, should be entitled to vote. But they failed to include these qualifications in the original Constitution of 1787. Instead, they left it up to the states to decide who should vote: ". . . the Electors in each State shall have the Qualifications requisite for Electors of the most numerous Branch of the State Legislature" (Article I, Section 2). Why leave it up to the states to decide the voter qualifications for national elections? In committee and in floor discussions the delegates could not agree on what kind of property should qualify a person to vote. Plantation owners argued for qualifications to be expressed in land acreage; bankers wanted them expressed in the size of one's bank account; shippers and businessmen, in the value of their inventories or ships; and so on. In frustration, the delegates dropped the issue into the laps of the states, secure in the knowledge that in 1787, all the states had some form of property qualifications and no state permitted women, slaves, or persons under 21 to vote. But this opening in the Constitution began a long journey toward full voting rights in the United States. Jacksonian democracy swept the nation in the 1840s and property qualifications were dropped by the states themselves. Not until after the Civil War was the Constitution amended to prevent the states from denying the right to vote on account of race (15th Amendment, 1870). The long fight for women's suffrage finally resulted in a constitutional guarantee of women's right to vote (19th Amendment, 1920); poll taxes were constitutionally banned (24th Amendment, 1964); and 18-year-olds secured the constitutional right to vote (26th Amendment, 1971).

CARRIE CHAPMAN CATT

The women's suffrage movement took nearly eight decades to realize votes for women in the United States. Catt was a close friend of Susan B. Anthony and founder of the prominent League of Women Voters.

Questions

1. Should we amend the Constitution to include a national right to vote?
2. Should people under 18 be allowed to vote?

Review the Chapter

Politics and Public Opinion

5.1 Analyze the relationships between politics, public opinion, and policy changes, p. 136

Public opinion is the combined preferences and opinions of individuals on significant issues. Major shifts in public opinion usually translate into policy changes, although there is little agreement on whether public opinion should or should not direct government policy.

Socialization: The Origins of Political Opinions

5.2 Explain how the agents of socialization influence the development of political opinions, p. 140

Political socialization—the learning of political values, beliefs, and opinions—starts at an early age. It is influenced by family, school, church, peer group, and the media.

Ideology, Gender, Race, and Opinion

5.3 Determine the role of ideology in shaping opinion and describe the relationship between gender, race, and opinion, p. 144

Ideology also shapes opinion, especially among politically interested and active people who employ fairly consistent liberal or conservative ideas in forming their opinions on specific issues. On "women's issues" (e.g., abortion or the role of women in business and politics) there is no big difference between men's and women's opinions. The most important political difference between men and women is that more women identify with the Democratic Party than do men and that women tend to vote slightly more than men do. Political opinion continues to show a divide between whites and African Americans over the extent of discrimination that exists in the United States. African Americans tend to have a more positive view of the need for a more active government but are less sanguine about the American criminal justice system. Hispanics are the fastest-growing minority group in the United States and now the largest minority group, surpassing African Americans in total numbers. Hispanics are generally in favor of an activist government and strong welfare programs but at the same time have strong family values and are conservative on many foreign policy, social, and religious issues.

Policy and Opinion

5.4 Assess how and to what extent public opinion influences public policy making, p. 148

Political leaders, elites, and other decision makers are relatively unconstrained by mass opinion because it is unstable, ill informed, and inconsistent. The essential link between opinion and policy is political participation.

Individual Participation in Politics

5.5 Identify the various ways in which a citizen may participate in politics, p. 152

Individuals can exercise power in a democratic political system in a variety of ways. They can run for public office, take part in demonstrations and protests, make financial contributions to candidates, attend political events, write letters to newspapers or public officials, belong to political organizations, vote in elections, or simply hold and express opinions on public issues.

Securing the Right to Vote

5.6 Trace the expansion of the right to vote, p. 152

Securing the right to vote for all Americans required nearly 200 years of political struggle. Key victories included the elimination of property qualifications by 1840, the 15th Amendment in 1870 (eliminating restrictions based on race), the 19th Amendment in 1920 (eliminating restrictions based on gender), the Civil Rights Act of 1964 and Voting Rights Act of 1965 (eliminating racial obstacles), the 24th Amendment in 1964 (eliminating poll taxes), and the 26th Amendment in 1971 (extending the right to vote to 18-year-olds).

Voting and Nonvoting

5.7 Analyze the political and demographic factors that influence voter turnout and assess the consequences of nonvoting, p. 156

Many people do not vote due to feelings of political alienation and distrust of government. About half of the voting-age population fails to vote even in presidential elections. Voter turnout has steadily declined in recent decades. Voter registration is a major obstacle to voting. Young people have the poorest record of voter turnout of any age group. Some of the primary factors that influence whether or not someone is a voter include education level, age, and income. Historically, race has also been a factor. Currently, the greatest disparity in voters is between Hispanics and others. This lack of voters may be due to language differences, lack of cultural assimilation, or noncitizenship status. Voluntary nonvoting is not as serious a threat to democracy as denial of the right to vote. Nevertheless, the class bias in voting may tilt the political system toward the interests of higher income, better-educated, older whites at the expense of lower-income, less-educated, younger minorities.

Protest as Political Participation

5.8 Characterize protest as a form of political participation, p. 165

Protest is an important form of participation in politics. Protests are more commonly employed by groups with little direct influence over public officials. The object is to generate attention and support from previously uncommitted people in order to bring new pressure on public officials to redress grievances. Media coverage is vital to the success of protests.

Learn the Terms

public opinion, p. 136
survey research, p. 136
halo effect, p. 136
Bradley effect, p. 136
salient issues, p. 139
socialization, p. 140
diffuse support, p. 140
generation gap, p. 143
gender gap, p. 145
suffrage, p. 152
property qualifications, p. 153
white primary, p. 154
poll taxes, p. 154
literacy test, p. 154
19th Amendment, p. 155
26th Amendment, p. 155
"Motor Voter Act", p. 156
turnout, p. 156
registration, p. 158
political alienation, p. 160
protests, p. 165
civil disobedience, p. 168

Test Yourself

5.1 Analyze the relationships between politics, public opinion, and policy changes

Of the following possible characteristics of public opinion, it would be accurate to say that public opinion on specific policy issues is often characterized by which of the following?

I. specific policy issue opinion is ill-informed
II. specific policy issue opinion unstable
III. specific policy issue opinion is poorly organized
IV. specific policy issue opinion is consistent with individual political ideology

a. I, II, III, and IV
b. Only III
c. I and IV
d. only I, II, and III
e. Only IV

5.2 Explain how the agents of socialization influence the development of political opinions

Which of the following has the most influential impact on the development of political values and opinions?

a. the Church
b. the elementary and secondary schools
c. peer group values
d. the family
e. college faculty

5.3 Determine the role of ideology in shaping opinion and describe the relationship between gender, race, and opinion

In general, Hispanics believe that _________ the U.S. economy.

a. immigration helps
b. immigration hurts
c. immigration has little or no impact on
d. unemployment is high enough and it is time to curtail immigration before it hurts
e. We cannot tap Hispanic opinion on this issue due to halo effects

5.4 Assess how and to what extent public opinion influences public policy making

The lack of political knowledge and opinions among the masses increases the influence of

a. only the press
b. the press and labor leaders
c. only political leaders
d. both the press and political leaders
e. only labor leaders

5.5 Identify the various ways in which a citizen may participate in politics

Political participation in democracies occurs most frequently by citizens via

a. violent protest, like the Arab Spring uprisings
b. joining political organizations, like a party or a labor union
c. writing or calling public officials
d. wearing buttons, placing signs and bumper stickers
e. voting

5.6 Trace the expansion of the right to vote

In the effort to expand the right to vote, the first voter qualification barrier to fall were those regarding

a. race
b. gender
c. citizenship
d. literacy
e. property

5.7 Analyze the political and demographic factors that influence voter turnout, and asses the consequences of nonvoting

One of the great paradoxes of political science is the paradox of nonvoting. Nonvoting is often associated with

a. getting on in years
b. political socialization
c. political alienation
d. being middle class
e. Dying, except in Chicago

5.8 Characterize protest as a form of political participation

The right to peacefully protest an action of government is guaranteed in

a. the Declaration of Independence
b. the Articles of Confederation
c. the Bill of Rights
d. the Emancipation Proclamation
e. The Magna Carta

Explore Further

SUGGESTED READINGS

Asher, Herbert. *Polling and the Public: What Every Citizen Should Know*. 7th ed. Washington, D.C.: CQ Press, 2007. Explains methods of polling and how results can be influenced by wording, sampling, and interviewing techniques; also covers how polls are used by the media and in campaigns.

Burton, Michael John and Daniel Shea. 2008. *Campaign Craft: The Strategies, Tactics, and Art of Political Campaign Management*. Westport, Conn.: Praeger.

Conway, M. Margaret, Gertrude A. Stevernagel, and David Ahern. *Women and Political Participation*. 2nd ed. Washington, D.C.: CQ Press, 2004. An examination of cultural change and women's participation in politics, including treatment of the gender gap in political attitudes and the impact of women's membership in the political elite.

Drexler, Kateri M., and Gwen Garcelon. *Strategies for Active Citizenship*. Upper Saddle River, N.J.: Prentice Hall, 2005. A handbook for becoming active in politics.

Erikson, Robert S., and Kent L. Tedin. *American Public Opinion*, 8th ed. New York: Longman, 2010. A comprehensive review of the forces influencing public opinion and an assessment of the influence of public opinion in American politics.

Gaddie, Ronald Keith. 2004. *Born to Run: Origins of the Political Career*. Lanham, Md.: Rowman & Littlefield.

Graham, Bob. *America, The Owner's Manual: Making Government Work for You*. Washington, D.C.: CQ press, 2009. Student-oriented instructions by a former U.S. senator on how to advance a political issue.

Greenstein, Fred I. *Children and Politics*. New Haven, Conn.: Yale University Press, 1985. Early research on what children know about politics and how they learned it.

Jacobs, Lawrence R., and Robert Y. Shapiro. *Politicians Don't Pander: Political Manipulation and the Loss of Democratic Responsiveness*. Chicago: University of Chicago Press, 2000. A study of how politicians use public opinion to suit their own purposes.

Johnson, Dennis. 2010. *Campaigning in the 21st Century*. New York: Routledge.

Johnson, Jason. 2011. *Political Consultants and Campaigns: One Day to Sell*. Boulder, Colo.: Westview.

Stimson, James A. *Tides of Consent: How Public Opinion Shapes American Politics*. New York: Cambridge University Press, 2004. The movement of public opinion over time moves public policy.

Walton, Hanes, and Robert C. Smith. *American Politics and the African American Quest for Universal Freedom*. New York: Pearson Longman, 2010. A comprehensive American government textbook emphasizing the diversity of African American opinions and behavior.

Zaller, John R. *The Nature and Origins of Mass Opinion*. New York: Cambridge University Press, 1992. An effort to develop and test a conceptual model of how people form political preferences, how political views and arguments diffuse through the population, and how people evaluate this information and convert their reactions into public opinion.

SUGGESTED WEB SITES

Americans United for Separation of Church and State www.au.org
Advocacy organization opposed to religious influence in government.

ElectionStudies.Org
Data from over a half-century of polling by the American National Election Studies.

FiveThirtyEight.com
Nate Silver's website dedicated to election forecasting.

FairVote, The Center for Voting and Democracy www.fairvote.org
Reform organization devoted to expanding voter participation; Web site includes data on voter turnout nationally and by state.

Center for Women in Politics http://www.cawp.rutgers.edu/
Extensive information on women officeholders as well as gender gap data on voting and attitudes on public policy.

Christian Coalition of America www.cc.org
Organization advocating greater Christian involvement in politics and government.

Gallup www.gallup.com
Oldest public opinion organization, with latest polls and large archive.

National Urban League www.nul.org
Organization devoted to advancing the economic well-being of African Americans, often reflecting opinions of the growing black middle class. Publishes annual *State of Black America*.

Polling Report www.pollingreport.com
Recent public opinion polls on policy issues, political actors, government institutions, and so on.

Elections. Huffingtonpost.com/Pollster
Web site summarizing recent polls with links to blogs about polls and polling results.

Protest Net www.protest.net
Radical organization provides calendar of protests against military actions, world trade, animal experiments, and so forth.

Public Agenda Online www.publicagenda.org
Recent opinion polls on a variety of policy issues.

State of the Vote www.nass.org
Official Web site of the National Association of Secretaries of State (state voting officials), urging young people to register and vote.

6

Mass Media

Setting the Political Agenda?

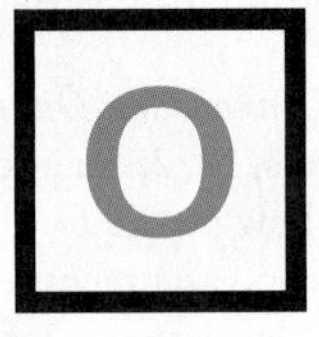

ne of the truths of American politics is that the camera is always on. It never blinks. And, when it comes to the media, nothing is ever really off the record. Many politicians carefully cultivate their images, only to find the facades come crashing down around them in so many shards. So, instead, they make their way into the media and create a brand that extends beyond the safe cookie-cutter image that needs protection.

These politicians often play against type, pitching themselves as the genuine article, impervious to the camera. Montana governor Brian Schweitzer is one such politician. A Democrat twice elected in conservative, western Montana, Schweitzer does not conform to the sophisticated, urbane politically correct image that plays so well with liberal cable media and core Democratic voters.

He deliberately plays against the type. And cable news loves it. When reporters come to interview him at his Montana ranch, if the news truck won't fit through the gate, he just cuts it down with a chainsaw. In characterizing southern Republicans who resist President Obama's initiatives, Schweitzer said that 60 or 79 percent of southern Republicans "set off his gaydar." Such pronouncements make Schweitzer, a potential presidential candidate, the stuff of which viral tweets and Internet posts are made. He stands in contrast to the Democratic intellectuals who populate party primaries and populate MSNBC.

But Schweitzer doesn't stop at making news—he participates. Like politicians such as Ed Rendell, Chris Christie, and Sarah Palin, he crafted a regular gig commenting on politics for MSNBC. This guarantees him access to an audience of core Democratic voters where he can not only comment on the news, but, sometimes, actually make the news depending on how pithy or snarky he feels that day.

MEET THE PRESS Brian Schweitzer (D-Mont.) is one of several former governors who have their face on cable news and their eye on a bigger career.

The Power of the Media

6.1 Identify functions and components of the media.

mass media
All means of communication with the general public, including television, newspapers, magazines, radio, books, recordings, motion pictures, and the Internet.

Politics—the struggle over who gets what, when, and how—is largely carried out in the **mass media**. The arenas of political conflict are the various media of mass communication—television, newspapers, magazines, radio, books, recordings, motion pictures, and the Internet. What we know about politics comes to us largely through these media. Unless we ourselves are admitted to the White House Oval Office or the committee rooms of Congress or dinner parties at foreign embassies, or unless we ourselves attend political rallies and demonstrations or travel to distant battlefields, we must rely on the mass media to tell us about politics. Furthermore, few of us ever have the opportunity to personally evaluate the character of presidential candidates or cabinet members or members of Congress or to learn their views on public issues by talking with them face to face. Instead, we must learn about people as well as events from the mass media.

Great power derives from the control of information. *Who knows what* helps determine *who gets what*. The media not only provide an arena for politics, they are also themselves players in that arena. The media not only report on the struggles for power in society, they are also themselves participants in those struggles. The media have long been referred to as America's "fourth branch" of government—and for good reason.[1] But technological innovations and changes in the journalism business model are challenging traditional approaches to the role of the media.

FACING THE MEDIA

Mitt Romney, Republican presidential candidate, campaigns in New Hampshire with a few friends from the media. Politicians on the campaign trail often confront a flurry of cameras and reporters, especially when controversy erupts on the campaign trail.

☐ The Power of Television

Television is still the most powerful medium of communication, though it is increasingly being challenged by new media. TV is a true *mass* communication medium. Virtually every home in the United States has a television set, and the average home has the set turned on for about seven hours a day. Television is regularly chosen over other news media by Americans as the most common news source, though this is becoming less the case as a new generation of media consumers comes of age.

For political news, Americans turn to television first. Local television is still the most popular source of information for local and state news. And, when it comes to national politics, Americans most often turn to television as their first source of news (66 percent of the public; see Figure 6.1). The Internet is now the second-most used source for political information (41 percent); followed by the rapidly declining newspapers at 31 percent; and radio, which attracts about one-in-seven news-seekers. Among television viewers, the main destination for national news is now the cable television networks—over a third of adults indicated that they primarily go to outlets such as CNN, Fox, or MSNBC to get national political news (Figure 6.2). The national network evening news shows (*NBC Nightly News, ABC World News Tonight, CBS Evening News*) have lost viewership in recent years but still attract about 22 percent of national news seekers, while 16 percent of the public said they go to their local news stations for national political news.

Television weekly news magazines, notably CBS's *60 Minutes*, have also become major sources of news for many Americans, though a growing number of Americans, especially young people, are turning to online news sources (see *Who's Getting What?*: The Generation Media Gap). During a national crisis—for example, the terrorist attacks of 9/11—Americans still turn to television for their news. When asked where they would go first for information during a crisis, 66 percent of Americans said they would turn on their TV sets. CNN was mentioned most often.[2]

☐ Accuracy and Fairness

Americans continue to lose confidence in the accuracy and fairness of the media. Just 29 percent say that news organizations generally "get their facts straight," the lowest

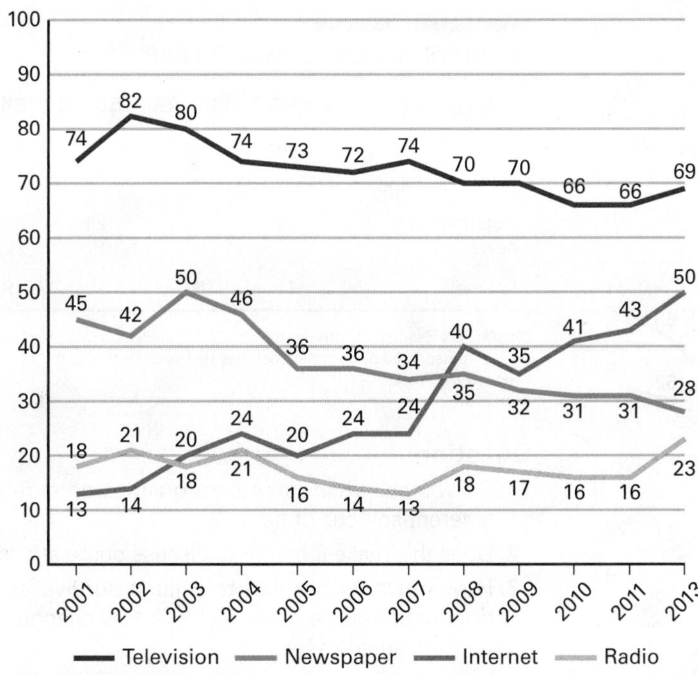

FIGURE 6.1 AMERICANS INCREASINGLY RELY ON THE INTERNET FOR NEWS

The Pew Research Center has tracked Americans' use of different news sources for over a decade. Since 2001, the Internet has had a surge in use as a news source, while television and newspapers have declined. (Question: "Where do you get most of your news about national and international issues?")

SOURCE: Pew Research Center. Survey taken July 11–13 2013. www.people-press.org.

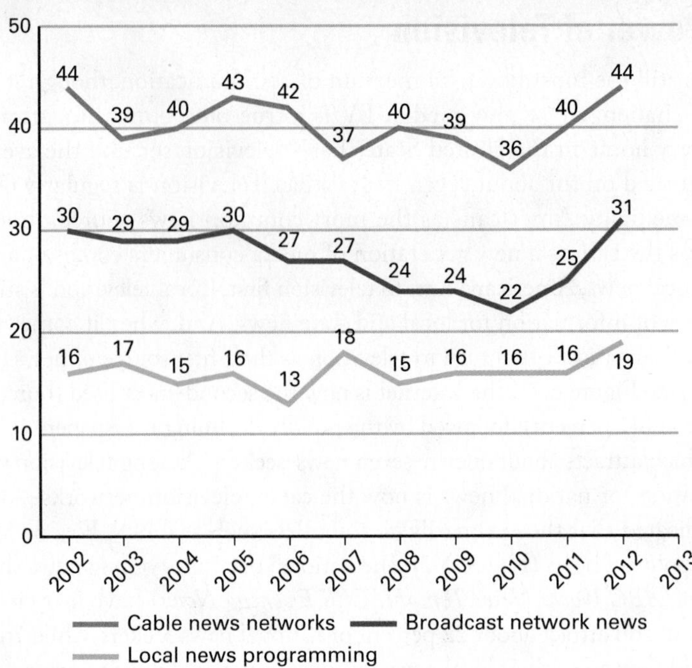

FIGURE 6.2 CABLE NEWS NETWORKS REMAIN THE MOST USED SOURCE FOR NATIONAL AND INTERNATIONAL NEWS

The Pew Research Center tracked Americans' preference for different television news sources. Since 2001, the Internet has had a surge in use as a news source, while television and newspapers have declined. (Question: "On television, do you get most of your news about national and international issues from . . . ?")

SOURCE: Pew Research Center. Survey taken July 20–24 2011, July 17–21 2013. www.people-press.org.

Who's Getting What?

The Generation Media Gap

Young people are less likely to spend time watching or seeking news than older people. And when old and young people seek news, they seek it from different resources. Older people are more than twice as likely to read a newspaper, while people under 50 are more likely consumers of online news and people under 30 predominantly use online resources.

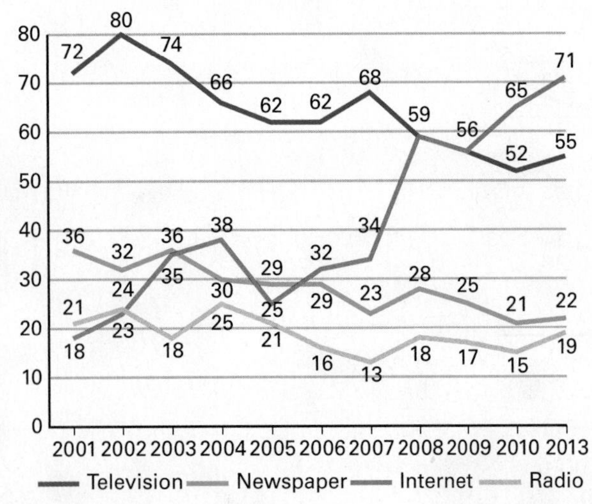

THE NEWS SOURCE GENERATION GAP

	18–29	30–49	50–64	65+
Television	55%	63%	77%	84%
Read newspaper	22	28	29	54
Listen to radio news	19	27	25	15
Internet	71	63	38	18

SOURCE: Pew Research Center for the People & the Press. www.people-press.org. Reprinted by permission of Pew Research Center for the People & the Press.

Questions

1. Do you and your parents (or grandparents) rely on different sources of news?
2. Does this make it harder to discuss public affairs?
3. How much longer can television survive as the dominant source of news? Will this change how people use news?

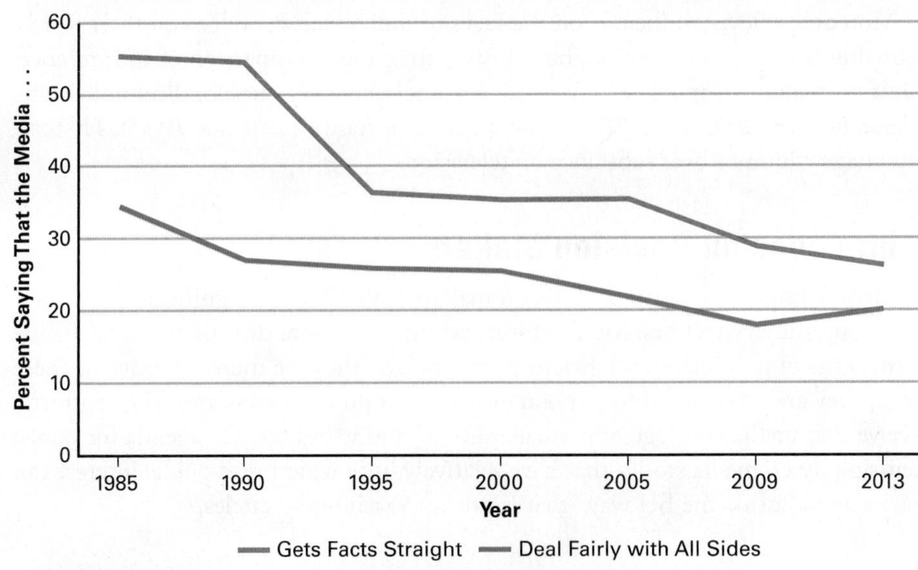

FIGURE 6.3 ACCURACY AND FAIRNESS IN THE MEDIA

Americans are losing confidence in the accuracy and fairness of the media.

SOURCE: Adapted from the Pew Research Center for the People and the Press, 2013. www.people-press.org.

level in more than two decades (see Figure 6.3). And fewer Americans believe that the media "deal fairly with all sides" in news reporting. Republicans and conservatives are more critical of the historic print and broadcast media, such as the national newspapers and traditional broadcast networks, while Democratic and liberal criticisms are largely directed at conservative cable news and talk radio outlets.

□ Newspapers and Magazines

Less than one-half of the adult population reads one of the nation's 1,400 daily newspapers. But the nation's prestige newspapers—the *New York Times, Washington Post*, and *Wall Street Journal*—are regularly read by government officials, corporate chiefs, interest-group leaders, and other media people. Stories appearing in these newspapers are generally picked up by daily papers around the country, and these stories almost always appear on national network television. The leading weekly newsmagazines—*Time, Newsweek*, and *U.S. News & World Report*—reach a smaller but more politically attentive audience than do newspapers. Magazines of political commentary—for example, the *Nation* (liberal), *New Republic* (liberal), *National Review* (conservative), *American Spectator* (conservative), *Weekly Standard* (conservative), *Public Interest* (neoconservative), and *Washington Monthly* (neoliberal)—reach very small but politically active audiences. All of these outlets are increasingly moving to Internet platforms and, as a consequence, revising their strategies for delivering content. There has been an increase in the number of Internet magazines providing sophisticated content (salon.com, Daily Beast, Politico, National Review Online) in competition with conventional news magazine outlets.

□ Television's Emotional Communication

The power of television derives not only from its large audiences, but also from its ability to communicate emotions as well as information. Television's power is found in its visuals—angry faces in a rioting mob, police beating an African American motorist, wounded soldiers being unloaded from a helicopter—scenes that convey an emotional message. Gripping pictures can inflame public opinion, inspire a clamor for action, and even pressure the government into hasty action—the "CNN effect."

6.1

6.2

6.3

6.4

6.5

6.6

6.7

6.8

narrowcasting
The emergence of news outlets on cable television and the Internet that offer specialty content for small, niche audiences.

fourth estate
The free news press and the people and institutions of the free press.

Moreover, television focuses on the faces of individuals as well as on their words, portraying honesty or deception, humility or arrogance, compassion or indifference, humor or meanness, and a host of other personal characteristics. Skillful politicians understand that *what* one says may not be as important as *how* one says it. Historically, image triumphs over substance on television.[3]

Influence on Decision Makers

The media's impact on political decision makers is vastly more significant than their impact on ordinary viewers. Media stories often relate more directly to the immediate concerns of politicians and government officials. They are more attentive to these stories; they are often asked to respond or comment upon news stories. They correctly perceive that media coverage of particular events and issues sets the agenda for public discussion. Even media stories that have relatively little widespread public interest can create a buzz "inside the Beltway," that is, within Washington circles.

The Myth of the Mirror

Media people themselves often deny that they exercise great power. They sometimes claim that they only "mirror" reality. They like to think of themselves as unbiased reporters who simply narrate happenings and transmit videotaped portrayals of people and events as they really are. But whether or not the editors, reporters, producers, or anchors acknowledge their own power, it is clear that they do more than passively mirror reality.

TV's New Media Conundrum

Television can no longer be considered in isolation. Internet resources quickly evolved to allow the **narrowcasting** of visual content—advertisements, fact-checks, commercials, and independently-created original content—through Web-based channels such as YouTube. In cable television's glory days, which ran through about 2006, network producers and advertisers could decide what visuals the public would be exposed to. The decline in the cost and expertise required to generate independent visual content, together with the lowering of barriers to make content publicly available, has made it possible for any event captured on video to potentially become a global story.

Sources of Media Power

6.2 Explain the sources of the media's power.

Government and the media are natural adversaries. Edmund Burke called the press the "**fourth estate**" of the realm (the others being nobility, the clergy, and the masses). The press is therefore deemed a social force; it's independent of the other estates yet exerts pressure on government, just like the others. (Thomas Jefferson once wrote that he would prefer newspapers without government to a government without newspapers. But after serving as president, he wrote that people who never read newspapers are better informed than those who do, because ignorance is closer to the truth than the falsehoods spread by newspapers.) Public officials have long been frustrated by the media. But the U.S. Constitution's 1st Amendment guarantee of a free press anticipates this conflict between government and the media. It prohibits government from resolving this conflict by silencing its critics—despite the best efforts of some administrations.

Media professionals—television and newspaper reporters, editors, anchors, and producers—are not neutral observers of American politics but rather active participants. They not only report events but also discover events to report, assign them political meaning, and predict their consequences. They seek to challenge government officials, debate political candidates, and define the problems of society. They see their profession as a "sacred trust" and themselves as the true voice of the people in public affairs; however, this degree of professionalism is increasingly called into question as confidence in media impartiality declines and new media sources challenge the conventional outlets.

newsmaking
Deciding what events, topics, presentations, and issues will be given coverage in the news.

agenda setting
Deciding what will be decided, defining the problems and issues to be addressed by decision makers.

☐ Newsmaking

Deciding what is "news" and who is "newsworthy"—**newsmaking**—is the most important source of media power. It is only through the media that the general public comes to know about events, personalities, and issues. Media attention makes topics public, creates issues, and elevates personalities from obscurity to celebrity. Each day, editors, producers, and reporters must select from millions of events, topics, and people those that will be videotaped, written about, and talked about—meaning that the media decides what is and is not "news."

Politicians have a love–hate relationship with the media. They need media attention to promote themselves, their message, and their programs. They crave the exposure, the name recognition, and the celebrity status that the media can confer. At the same time, politicians fear attack by the media. They know the media are active players in the political game, and that they seek sensational stories of sin, sexuality, corruption, and scandal in government to attract viewers and readers. Thus, the media pose a constant danger to politicians, and politicians understand the power of the media to make or break their careers.

☐ Agenda Setting

Agenda setting is the power to decide what will be decided. It is the power to define society's "problems," to create political issues, and to set forth alternative solutions. Deciding which issues will be addressed by government may be even more important than deciding how the issues will be resolved. The distinguished political scientist E. E. Schattschneider once wrote, "He who determines what politics is about runs the country."[4]

The real power of the media lies in their ability to set the political agenda for the nation, to decide what is news. Media coverage determines what both citizens and public officials regard as "crises" or "problems" or "issues" to be resolved. Conditions ignored by the media seldom get on the agenda of political leaders. Media attention forces public officials to speak on the topic, take positions, and respond to questions. Media inattention allows problems to be ignored by government. But, when TV acts, other actors respond. The long-time Time Magazine culture critic, William A. Henry III, observed over three decades ago that "TV is the Great Legitimator. TV confers reality. Nothing happens in America, practically everyone seems to agree, until it happens on television."[5]

Political issues do not just "happen." The media are crucial to their development. Organized interest groups, professional public relations firms, government bureaucracies, political candidates, and elected officials all try to solicit the assistance of the media in shaping the political agenda. Creating an issue, publicizing it, dramatizing it, turning it into a "crisis," getting people to talk about it, and ultimately forcing government to do something about it are the tactics of agenda setting. The participation of the mass media is vital to their success.[6]

☐ Interpreting

The media not only decide what will be news; they also interpret the news for us. Editors, reporters, and anchors provide each story with an *angle*, an interpretation that places the story in a context and speculates about its meaning and consequences. The interpretation tells us what to think about the news.

socialization
The learning of a culture and its values.

News is presented in "stories." Reporters do not report facts; they tell stories. The story structure gives meaning to various pieces of information. Some common angles or themes of news stories include:

- *Good guys versus bad guys*: for example, corrupt officials, foreign dictators, corporate polluters, and other assorted villains versus honest citizens, exploited workers, endangered children, or other innocents.
- *Little guys versus big guys*: for example, big corporations, the military, or insensitive bureaucracies versus consumers, taxpayers, poor people, or the elderly.
- *Appearance versus reality*: for example, the public statements of government officials or corporate executives versus whatever contradicting facts hardworking investigative reporters can find.

News is also "pictures." A story without visuals is not likely to be selected as television news in the first place. The use of visuals reinforces the angle. A close-up shot can reveal hostility, insincerity, or anxiety on the face of villains or fear, concern, sincerity, or compassion on the face of innocents. To emphasize elements of a story, an editor can stop the action, use slow motion, zoom the lens, add graphics, cut back and forth between antagonists, cut away for audience reaction, and so on. Videotaped interviews can be spliced to make the interviewees appear knowledgeable, informed, and sincere or, alternatively, ignorant, insensitive, and mean-spirited. The media jealously guard the right to edit interviews themselves, rejecting virtually all attempts by interviewees to review and edit their own interviews.

Socializing

The media have power to socialize audiences to the political culture. News, entertainment, and advertising all contribute to **socialization**—to the learning of political values. Socialization through television and motion pictures begins in early childhood and continues throughout life. Most of the political information people learn comes to them through television—specific facts as well as general values. Election coverage, for example, shows "how democracy works," encourages political participation, and legitimizes the winner's control of government. Advertising shows Americans desirable, middle-class standards of living even while it encourages people to buy automobiles, detergent, and beer, and entertainment programming socializes them to "acceptable" ways of life. Political values such as racial tolerance, sexual equality, and support for law enforcement are reinforced in movies, situation comedies, and police shows.

MADE FOR TV

Janice Dickinson and the Dickinson Models march on Hollywood Boulevard for the People for the Ethical Treatment of Animal's (PETA's) "We'd Rather Go Naked Than Wear Fur" campaign on August 20, 2007, in Hollywood, California. Stunts that challenge social mores or draw attention through humor or absurdity are a staple of modern protest in the United States.

Persuading

The media, in both paid advertising and news and entertainment programming, engage in direct efforts to change our attitudes, opinions, and behavior. Newspaper editorials have traditionally been employed for direct persuasion. A great deal of the political commentary on television news and interview programs is aimed at persuading people to adopt the views of the commentators. Even many entertainment programs and movies are intended to promote specific political viewpoints. But most direct persuasion efforts come to us through paid advertising.

Political campaigning is now largely a media battle, with paid political advertisements as the weapons. Candidates rely on professional campaign-management firms, with their pollsters, public relations specialists, advertising-production people, and media consultants, to carry on the fight.

Governments and political leaders must rely on persuasion through the mass media to carry out their programs. Presidents can take their message directly to people in televised speeches, news conferences, and the yearly State of the Union message.

Presidents by custom are accorded television time whenever they request it. In this way, they can go over the heads of Congress and even the media executives and reporters themselves to communicate directly with the people.

In short, persuasion is central to politics, and the media are the key to persuasion.

Agenda Control and the New Media

Television used to have a preeminent position in determining content, in illuminating or ignoring stories. In the Internet era, television efforts to impose agendas and pick stories have been challenged. In 1998, the major media attempted to ignore allegations of sexual misconduct by President Bill Clinton, only to have a little-known Internet news service called the Drudge Report break the story. In 2004, efforts by CBS news to promote a story about favoritism in the National Guard service of President George Bush was shown to be based on fabricated evidence by bloggers. And in 2011, arguably the greatest failure of television news agenda control came in the Occupy Wall Street protests. The major media outlets ignored the story for up to two weeks. Twitter and Facebook postings, together with Internet feeds, gave the movement visibility from the first day (September 17) and helped it spread to places beyond New York. The ability to use new media created a legitimate source of unfiltered information for many consumers, and mitigated against a single media framework being placed around the story when the television outlets and major print news outlets did cover it.

The Business of the Media

6.3 Describe the business of the media.

The business of the media is to gather mass audiences to sell to advertisers. Economic interest drives all media to try to attract and hold the largest numbers of readers and viewers in order to sell time and space to advertisers. Over one-quarter of all prime-time television (8–11 P.M.) is devoted to commercial advertising. Americans get more than one minute of commercials for every three minutes of news and entertainment. Television networks and commercial stations charge advertisers on the basis of audience estimates made by rating services. One rating service, A. C. Nielsen, places electronic boxes in a national sample of television homes and calculates the proportion of these homes that watch a program (the rating), as well as the proportion of homes with their television sets turned on that watch a particular program (the share). Newspapers' and magazines' advertising revenue is based primarily on circulation figures, while Internet media advertising is still working out proxy mechanisms for measuring eyes on content to determine rates.

Soft Fluff Versus Hard Programming

Lightweight entertainment—"soft fluff"—prevails over serious programming in virtually all media, but particularly on television. Critics of the "boob tube" abound in intellectual circles, but the mass public clearly prefers fluffy entertainment programming. Political scientist Doris Graber writes:

> Although "lightweight" programming draws the wrath of many people, particularly intellectual elites, one can argue that their disdain constitutes intellectual snobbery. Who is to say that the mass public's tastes are inferior to those of elites? . . . Proof is plentiful that the mass public does indeed prefer light entertainment to more serious programs.[7]

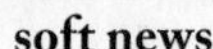

soft news
News featured in talk shows, late-night comedy, and TV news magazines—reaches more people than regular news broadcasts.

And it is the mass public that advertisers want to reach. Channels devoted to highbrow culture, including public television stations, languish with low ratings.

Public Television and Radio

The Corporation for Public Broadcasting (CPB) was created by Congress in 1967 to provide "noncommercial high quality programs … to inform, enlighten and enrich the public." As a nonprofit government corporation, CPB relies on taxpayer funding in annual appropriations from Congress. In turn, it provides the funding for Public Broadcasting Service (PBS) and National Educational Television (NET). PBS had some early successes in programming—*Masterpiece Theatre, Sesame Street*—but in more recent years commercial broadcasting has exceeded PBS in both quality and viewership. Commercial channels—History Channel, Discovery Channel, National Geographic Channel, and others—regularly broadcast high-quality programs to much larger audiences and do not rely on taxpayer funding. Opponents of continued government funding of PBS complain of left-leaning bias in its news and commentary (see *Who's Getting What?* Do We Still Need to Fund Public Broadcasting?).

News as TV Entertainment

Increasingly, news is being presented as television entertainment. In recent years, there has been a dramatic increase in the number of entertainment-oriented, quasi-news programming, sometimes referred to as the "soft news media."[8] **Soft news** comes in various formats: talk shows, both daytime and nighttime; and tabloid news programs (such as *60 Minutes, 20/20, Dateline NBC, 48 Hours*). Late-night entertainment hosts and programs—David Letterman, *The Colbert Report, The Daily Show with Jon Stewart*—include comedy monologues that often refer to political events or issues. Soft news is a major source of information for people who are not interested in politics or public affairs. It is true, of course, that most soft news programming favors celebrity gossip, murder trials, sex scandals, disasters, and other human interest stories. But on some high-profile news issues, these programs provide an otherwise inattentive public with what little information it absorbs.

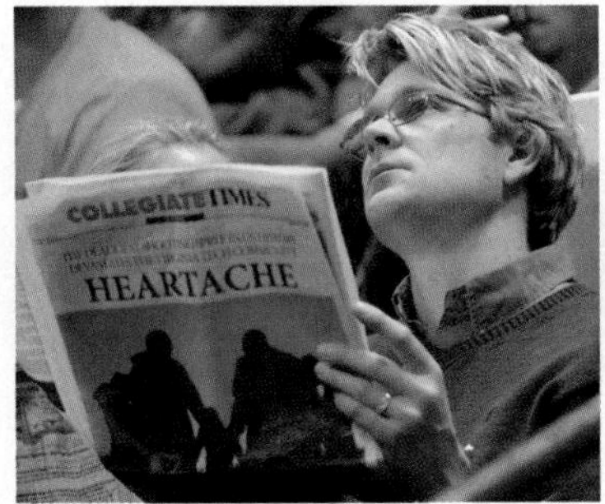

BAD-NEWS BIAS
The media favor bad news over good news. Wars, fires and natural disasters, and crime are all well reported. But good news about things going well, such as improved health, higher standards of living, or new construction going as planned, gets far less attention.

Politicians themselves have come to understand the importance of soft news programming in reaching segments of the public that seldom watch news programs, speeches or debates, or campaign advertising. Presidential candidates welcome invitations to appear with Jon Stewart, Jay Leno, or David Letterman, and try to reformulate their messages in a light, comedic style that fits the program. A variety of presidential aspirants and also former presidents have appeared on talk programs, but Barack Obama is the first sitting president to appear on late-night television, appearing on *The Tonight Show* (Leno), *The Late Show* (Letterman), and *The Daily Show* (Stewart) during his first term.

The Politics of the Media

6.4 Assess how the politics of the media are shaped by their economic interests, professional environment, and ideological leanings.

The politics of the news media are shaped by their (1) *economic interests*, (2) *professional environment*, and (3) *ideological leanings*.

The Game, the Rules, the Players

Jon Stewart

The twentieth-century cowboy humorist Will Rogers observed, "I don't make jokes. *I just watch the government and report the facts*." Four nights a week, a significant segment of the politically attentive public tunes in to Comedy Central and watches the self-described "neurotic" comedian from New Jersey, Jon Stewart, use politics and the corporate news industry as a source of unfiltered humor. In the process, Stewart and business partner Stephen Colbert have emerged as two of the most powerful critical voices of the American political media industrial complex with their shows *The Daily Show* and *The Colbert Report*. (Stewart owns Busboy productions, and Colbert owns Spartina Productions. They are in partnership to provide content for Comedy Central.)

Stewart's cutting comedy takes no prisoners. *The Daily Show* (TDS) is sometimes profane, usually topical, and always informative. The writers focus their humor on two primary sources of material: inconsistencies and bias in the broadcast media, especially the major cable news channels; and the activities of the political elite, especially presidents, presidential candidates, and congressional leaders. The show is also a highly sought interview slot for politicians, actors, and writers seeking to promote themselves and their projects.

The show has an unabashed progressive/libertarian slant, taking strong editorial positions on the use of forces overseas, terrorist detention, the preservation of individual rights and liberties, gay rights, and women's issues. However, in presentation, the show also challenges politically correct frailties of a contemporary media when dealing with issues of race, ethnicity, sex, and sexuality. TDS is a welcoming venue for libertarian-oriented conservatives such as Ron Paul and Buddy Roemer, and both conservative and liberal political icons such as John McCain, Condoleezza Rice, Donald Rumsfeld, Bill Clinton, and Barack Obama have been guests on the show. In 2012, Stewart joined Colbert in a satirical assault on the loopholes in the campaign finance industry that illuminated the hollow nature of the regulations that governed large-money, low-accountability Super PAC organizations. The quality content and Stewart's interviews won the show two Peabody Awards for distinguished and meritorious public service in broadcasting and 16 Emmy Awards.

Jon Stewart

The production of the show closely resembles the assembly of a regular network news broadcast. The writers for the show—including popular on-air players Wyatt Cenac and John Oliver, head writer Tim Carvell (who also writes for *Mad Magazine*), and veteran writers for NPR, Salon.com, and GQ—gather every morning to review headlines and stories in the mainstream media and from major online sources. The draft of the show is reviewed by Stewart, as the managing editor. A late-afternoon rehearsal is followed by a 6 P.M. Eastern time taping—four days a week, 40 weeks a year.

The impact of the show is substantial: it reaches nearly as many people as "serious" news programs on CNN and Fox, and research at the University of Indiana finds TDS content to be as—or more—substantial than that of the network and cable newscasts.

QUESTIONS

1. **Do you consume content from satirical news programs like The Daily Show? Why or why not?**
2. **Why do you think comedic content about news is popular?**

SOURCES: TheDailyShow.com. Julia R. Fox, Glory Koloen, and Volkan Sahin, No Joke: A Comparison of Substance in *The Daily Show with Jon Stewart* and Broadcast Network Television Coverage of the 2004 Presidential Election Campaign. *Journal of Broadcasting & Electronic Media* 51 (2007): 213–27.

☐ Sensationalism

The economic interests of the media—the need to capture and hold audience attention—create a bias toward "hype" in the selection of news, its presentation, and its interpretation. To attract viewers and readers, the media bias the news toward violence, conflict, scandal, corruption, sex, scares of various sorts, and the personal lives of politicians and celebrities. News is selected primarily for its emotional impact on audiences; its social, economic, or political significance is secondary to the need to capture attention.

6.1
6.2
6.3
6.4
6.5
6.6
6.7
6.8

Who's Getting What?

Do We Still Need to Fund Public Broadcasting?

The Corporation for Public Broadcasting (CPB) was created in 1967 to help fund public radio and television stations across the United States. Two generations of Americans have consumed PBS products, usually starting with children's education programming like *Sesame Street and Thomas the Tank Engine*.

CPB was originally created to foster intellectual and cultural enlightenment in the United States. Before the advent of cable television, PBS and NPR stations often brought the only in-depth news, educational programming, arts and entertainment to remote communities in the United States. The iconic *Sesame Street* was inspired by the Great Society program Head Start and sought to bring the benefits of Montessori-style early childhood education to all children. Public radio programs such as *Car Talk* have also become staples of popular culture on the most apolitical and inherently American topic of car repair.

Some conservative politicians complain that NPR and PBS have a "liberal" bias, and object to using taxpayer dollars to continue to subsidize the delivery of its content. Critics such as conservative blogger and law professor Hugh Hewitt contend that NPR has a double editorial standard for opinion—liberal opinions are fine, conservative opinions are not. So, for example, when NPR discharged correspondent Juan Williams in 2011 for comments he made on Fox News (that Muslims "make me nervous"), the cry was heightened to defund NPR. Then Public Broadcasting defenders responded that conservatives want to silence Elmo and Big Bird. And so it goes.

The conservative solutions to NPR and PBS bias are two: program content "balancing" or defunding. Content balancing would require that NPR and PBS balance the ideological content of their news, culture, arts, and music programming.

The defunding option is less draconian than it sounds. The federal appropriation for CPB is less than a half-billion dollars—just over one-one-hundredth of 1 percent of the total federal budget. The balance of the operating and content production costs of public broadcasting comes from state government appropriations, foundations, and endowments of state public broadcasting authorities, grants from private foundations, and charitable gifts from individuals and companies. Ninety percent of the funding for public radio, for example, comes from nongovernment sources.

What cannot be disputed is that public broadcasting is, by any measure, a broadcasting success. The market success and durability of Children's Television Workshop products like *Sesame Street* demonstrate that the content has brand appeal. The long-format television and radio news programs are also wildly successful—National Public Radio shows *Morning Edition* and *All Things Considered* reach broader audiences than any individual network newscast or cable news program. But the broader marketplace has changed. Cable networks have sprung up with dozens of outlets that provide news, history, arts, movies, and music—akin to what was once only available on PBS. Viewers purchase PBS program content for private use. And the Internet has opened a new medium for CPB to disseminate content without the need for transmitters. Given the size and commercial viability of the market for CPB programming—with listeners and viewers who are better educated and more affluent than most Americans, on average—has the time come to let public broadcasting compete more fully in the marketplace?

Questions

1. What are some reasons for continuing the funding of public broadcasting? Reasons against?
2. Do you listen to public radio or watch public television? When?

News must "touch" audiences personally, arouse emotions, and hold the interest of people with short attention spans. Scare stories—street crime, drug use, AIDS, nuclear power plant accidents, global warming, and a host of health alarms—make "good" news, for they cause viewers to fear for their personal safety. The sex lives of politicians, once by custom off-limits to the press, are now public "affairs." Scandal and corruption among politicians, as well as selfishness and greed among business executives, are regular media themes.[9]

☐ Negativism

The media are biased toward bad news. Bad news attracts larger audiences than good news. Television news displays a pervasive bias toward the negative in American life—in government, business, the military, politics, education, and everywhere else. Bad-news stories on television vastly outnumber good-news stories.

Good news gets little attention. For example, television news watchers are not likely to know that illegal drug use is declining in the United States, that both the air and water are measurably cleaner today than in past decades, that the nuclear power industry has the best safety record of any major industry in the United States, that the aged in America are wealthier and enjoy higher incomes than the nonaged, that the violent crime rate is down 50 percent since 1990, and that teenage pregnancies and abortion rates are both down significantly. Television has generally failed to report these stories or, even worse, has implied that the opposite is true. Good news—stories about improved health statistics, longer life spans, better safety records, higher educational levels, for example—seldom provides the dramatic element needed to capture audience attention. The result is an overwhelming bad-news bias, especially on television.[10]

muckraking
Journalistic exposés of corruption, wrongdoing, or mismanagement in government, business, and other institutions of society.

"feeding frenzy"
Intense media coverage of a scandal or event that blocks out most other news.

☐ Muckraking and Feeding Frenzies

The professional environment of reporters and editors predisposes them toward an activist style of journalism once dubbed **muckraking**. Reporters today view themselves as "watchdogs" of the public trust. They see themselves in noble terms—enemies of corruption, crusaders for justice, defenders of the disadvantaged. "The watchdog function, once considered remedial and subsidiary . . . [is now] paramount: the primary duty of the journalists is to focus attention on problems and deficits, failures and threats."[11] Their professional models are the crusading "investigative reporters" who expose wrongdoing in government, business, the military, and every other institution in society—except the media. The rise of new media has intensified this function.

Occasionally, muckraking episodes grow into "**feeding frenzies**"—intense coverage of a scandal or event that blocks out most other news. Two circumstances combine to create the frenzy. First, the increasing emphasis by cable news outlets in particular on immediacy pushes the sensational, breaking news story forward to dominate coverage. Second, a lack of solid and certain information about the scandal leads to a race for information and speculation that grows to fill the available broadcast space. Increasingly stiff competition among the media for attention and the need for round-the-clock cable news to fill long hours contribute to feeding frenzies—and then to analyzing the frenzy itself!

☐ Liberalism in the Newsroom

The activist role that the media have taken upon themselves means that the personal values of reporters, editors, producers, and anchors are a very important element of American politics. The political values of the media are decidedly liberal and reformist. Political scientist Doris Graber writes about the politics of the media: "Economic and social liberalism prevails, especially in the most prominent media organizations. So does a preference for an internationalist foreign policy, caution about military intervention, and some suspicion about the ethics of established large institutions, particularly big business and big government."[12] Most Americans agree that media news coverage is biased in a liberal direction (see *What Do You Think?* The Media Are Biased!).

☐ Liberalism in Hollywood

With a few exceptions, Hollywood producers, directors, writers, studio executives, and actors are decidedly liberal in their political views, especially when compared with the general public. Of the Hollywood elite, more than 60 percent describe themselves as liberal and only 14 percent as conservative,[13] whereas in the general public, self-described conservatives outnumber liberals by a significant margin. Hollywood leaders are five times more likely to be Democrats than Republicans, and Hollywood is a major source of Democratic Party campaign funds. On both economic and social issues, the Hollywood elite is significantly more liberal than the nation's general public or college-educated public.[14] (However, see *What Do You Think?* "Fair and Balanced" . . . Versus "Lean Forward").

What Do You Think?

The Media Are Biased!

Are the media biased, and if so, in what direction—liberal or conservative? Arguments over media bias have grown in intensity as the media have come to play a central role in American politics.

The American public is more likely to say that the news media are "too liberal" rather than "too conservative" or "about right." Political partisanship helps shape Americans' feelings toward bias in the news. Republicans and conservatives are much more likely to say that the media are "too liberal" than Democrats and liberals, who are more inclined to say that the media is "just about right."

Most journalists are personally liberal and vote Democratic, and the media's coverage of issues such as gun control, affirmative action, abortion, gay rights, and religion in America reveals a leftward slant.[b] Fox News, and the *Wall Street Journal* (now owned by the same News Corp.) are exceptions to the rest of the mainstream media. The elite newspapers (the *New York Times* and the *Washington Post*), the television networks (ABC, CBS, NBC, CNN), and the newsweeklies (*Time* and *Newsweek*) are liberal in tone and content. However, more than one in five Americans say that they get their news from talk radio—the programming of which is reported to be 90 percent conservative.[c]

Yet at the same time, Americans have high expectations of the role of the media in society: they expect the media to protect them from "abuse of power" by government, to hold public officials accountable, and to identify and help solve the problems of society.

Questions

1. How does someone's ideology influence their perceptions of bias in the media?
2. Do you think that news outlets need to be "objective," or can news consumers balance their news by using different sources?

Q. In general, do you think the news media are too liberal, just about right, or too conservative?[a]

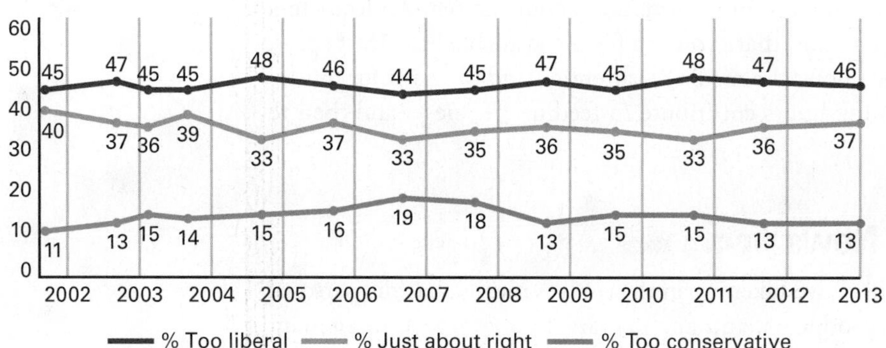

	Too Liberal	Just About Right	Too Conservative
All	44%	33%	19%
Democrats	20	53	23
Independents	40	37	19
Republicans	77	17	5
Liberals	16	45	37
Moderates	39	42	15
Conservatives	68	24	6

[a]Gallup News Service, September 5–8, 2013.
[b]Bernard Goldberg, *Arrogance: Rescuing America from the Media Elite.* New York: Warner Books, 2003.
[c]Robert F. Kennedy, Jr., *Crimes Against Nature.* New York: Harper Collins, 2005.

Conservatism on Talk Radio

Talk radio is the one medium where conservatism prevails. The top talk radio shows are the *Rush Limbaugh Show*—whose host regularly bashes "limousine liberals," "femi-Nazis," "environmental wackos," and "croissant people"—and *The Sean Hannity Show*.[15] Talk radio might be portrayed as "call-in democracy." Callers respond almost immediately to reported news events. Call-in shows are the first to sense the public mood. Callers are not necessarily representative of the general public. Rather, they are usually the most intense and outraged of citizens. But their complaints are early warning signs for wary politicians. However, it is worth noting that the average audience size for Limbaugh and Hannity are about the same as for NPR's "Morning Edition" and "All Things Considered." So the talking news is not all conservative, though the audiences are quite ideologically divergent and seek different types of news.

pundits
An individual who offers expert opinion to the mass media.

Professional Opinion Givers

The media do not just report stories and events. They also seek out "expert" commentary on events. The growth of the talk radio and cable news industry has resulted in increased use of professional expert opinion-givers, called **pundits**. The punditry is not new, but it has never been more vast. Once upon a time, it was confined to Sunday morning news shows, amidst a group of people that columnist Calvin Trillin calls "the Sabbath Gasbags." Now, every hour, on the radio and television, public intellectuals, former politicians, reporters, college professors, writers, consultants, and other self-designated experts utter commentary and opinion to show hosts, wrapped in the authority of their experiences. Much of this opinion is speculative—what will happen next rather than explanatory—putting what just happened into context. Political scientist Phil Tetlock and law professor Richard Posner have independently explored the extent to which political expert opinion is accurate and find the prognostications of experts to be lacking—public intellectuals are not especially good at predicting the future.[16]

Televised Incivility and Political Trust

Does watching political shows on television, in which hosts, guests, pundits, and others hurl insults at each other, interrupt and shout over each other, and use especially contentious and uncivil language, reduce levels of trust in politicians and government? One experiment, with some viewers watching friendly, polite, and simple political discussions, and other viewers watching rude, emotional, quarrelsome political confrontations, concluded that incivility has a detrimental effect on trust in government and attitudes toward political leaders.[17] Yet it is not likely that televised politics will ever become more civil. Politics for most people cannot compete with entertainment shows for TV audiences, so political shows are increasingly creating dramatic tension and uncivil conflict to gain viewers.

News Versus Entertainment

Cable television and the Internet have produced dramatic increases in available political information. Yet overall, political knowledge and turnout have not changed noticeably. The key to understanding this apparent paradox is the vast expansion in choices now available to viewers.[18] People can now choose from numerous cable channels and Web sites. Increasingly, there is a division between people who prefer entertainment programming and those who prefer news shows. There is some evidence that people who prefer news shows acquire greater political knowledge and go to the polls more often than those who mainly watch entertainment shows. Greater media choice, then, appears to widen the "knowledge gap." Because people who like news and take advantage of additional information in the media gain political knowledge, while people

6.1

6.2

6.3

6.4

6.5

6.6

6.7

6.8

What Do You Think?

"Fair and Balanced"...

For many years, conservatives complained about the liberal tilt of television news. But despite their ample financial resources, conservative investors failed to create their own network or purchase an existing one. Then Australian billionaire Rupert Murdoch came to the rescue of American conservatives.

Murdoch's global media empire, News Corp, includes Fox Network, Fox News Cable, 20th Century Fox, Fox Movie Channel, MySpace, the *New York Post*, the *Times* and the *Sun* of London, and 35 local TV stations. He began his career by injecting glitz and vulgarity into the previously dull Australian newspapers he inherited. The formula worked worldwide: The *New York Post* became a noisy tabloid after Murdoch took over (most memorable headline: "HEADLESS BODY FOUND IN TOPLESS BAR"), and Fox TV entertainment airs even more vulgar shows than the mainstream networks.

Murdoch himself is not particularly conservative, but he recognized an unfilled market for conservative views on American television. In 1996, he founded Fox News and hired Roger Ailes (former TV ad producer for Ronald Reagan) to head up the new network. Ailes signed Bill O'Reilly for an hour-long nightly conservative talk show. Brit Hume, one of the few prominent TV reporters considered to be a conservative, was made managing editor.

Fox proclaims "fair and balanced" news—"We report, you decide." The implication is that mainstream media has a liberal bias, and that Fox is rectifying it with its own fair and balanced reporting. According to Fox, if its reporting appears conservative, it is only because the country has become so accustomed to left-leaning media that a truly balanced network just seems conservative.

Regular news reporting on Fox is not much different than other networks, though there is strong editorial control to offer positive subtext to conservative issues and positions. Media watchdog groups Media Matters contends that Fox has a conservative skew, while the Project on Excellence in Journalism determined that 68 percent of news programming at Fox had an editorial subtext, compared to about 25 percent of stories at MSNBC and less than 5 percent of CNN stories.

It is the talk and commentary shows that outrage liberals and warm the hearts of conservatives. Former Democratic National Committee chairman Howard Dean referred to Fox as a "right-wing propaganda machine." Liberals bold enough to appear on Fox are badgered mercilessly, while conservative guests are tossed softball questions. The bottom line, financially as well as politically, is that Fox News is now the most watched cable news network, even surpassing CNN, and whatever its flaws, Fox has added diversity of views to American television.

... Versus "Lean Forward"

The long-standing criticism of the mainstream media was that it had a liberal bias, and there is some empirical evidence of a progressive tilt to the story selection and coverage of news stories in most major media outlets. According to political scientist Tim Groseclose, major media outlets, such as the broadcast network news programs and CNN, usually tilted against this criticism, which was often leveled by Fox News Channel, conservative talk radio, and conservative Internet sources. But in the past half decade, MSNBC has resituated itself as a news outlet delivering an openly progressive body of editorial content (the "lean forward" campaign), in contrast to Fox's conservative programming.

MSNBC started in 1996 as a partnership between Microsoft and the General Electric-owned National Broadcasting Company (NBC) in an Internet news unit, msnbc.com. Like Fox News, which premiered three months later, MSNBC was created to compete in the emerging 24-hour cable news market that was dominated by CNN and that had taken on prominence with CNN's coverage of the 1991 Gulf War. MSNBC took over the satellite transponder of another NBC project, "America's Talking" (created by current Fox News president Roger Ailes). NBC bought out the cable channel from Microsoft in 2005; since then, the network has systematically evolved to more talk-based content with an openly progressive agenda.

MSNBC moved to make politics a staple of its programming, with financial programming moving over to CNBC. The emergence of politically charged hosts such as Don Imus, Joe Scarborough, and former ESPN anchor Keith Olbermann brought a snarky, critical tone. Olbermann engaged in open conflict with Fox News, extensive criticism of the incumbent Bush administration, and regularly awarded Republican politicians his "Worst Person in the World" award. Unlike its ideological counterpart Fox, MSNBC has been more inclined to remove talent in the face of controversy. Imus and Olbermann both departed under controversy—but with their departure, the content has become openly progressive and in some ways more serious (morning host Joe Scarborough is the lone conservative voice at MSNBC). The anchoring evening program in the place of Olbermann features Rachel Maddow, who has a doctorate in philosophy from Oxford and was the first openly gay Rhodes Scholar to attend Oxford.

The networks have variable reach into the potential viewing public. About three-quarters of U.S. households receive MSNBC, compared to over 90 percent that receive Fox News and CNN. Daily viewership for the network is about 300,000 people—less than a third of the typical viewership for CNN or Fox. During the 2008 election, the network had a surge in attention from younger viewers, indicating that there may be a profitable future for the openly progressive network.

Questions

1. Given the numerous sources of information available for people to get news, is it important that news networks be "balanced"?
2. Do you find this entry to be "fair and balanced"? Why or why not?

SOURCE: Timothy Grosecloe, *Left Turn: How Liberal Media Bias Distorts the American Mind*. New York: St. Martin's Press. 2011.

who prefer entertainment programming learn less about politics, the mean levels of political knowledge in the population have essentially remained constant.

POPULAR VOICES?

Talk radio personalities like Rush Limbaugh once dominated political debates. An aging listenership that is not coveted by advertisers might spell economic (and political) trouble for right wing talk radio.

☐ The Shrinking Newsroom

The other challenge to the conventional media is the shrinking of its manpower. The primary source of news used to be content generated by print journalists with local and national newspapers. In broadcast, there are also fewer journalists, and many of those who remain are assigned to soft news or breaking news. The vacuum of content left by the shrinking corps of traditional journalists is filled by public relations firms, colleges, think tanks, and news-content packaging services. This content is often informative, but it is often designed to promote a client agenda.

☐ Polarization of the Media

Increasingly, media audiences are becoming politically polarized, with Republicans and conservatives, and Democrats and liberals, choosing to listen to and view separate media outlets. Listeners and viewers are choosing sides in their sources of news (see Table 6.1).

News audiences in the aggregate are somewhat more conservative than the general public. The Pew Research Center reports that of those who regularly watch, read, or listen to the news, conservatives account for 36 percent, moderates 38 percent, and

TABLE 6.1 WHERE DO PARTISANS GET THEIR NEWS?

Liberals and conservatives differ in their sources of news and commentary.

Regularly watch/ read/ listen to	Total	Rep.	Dem.	Ind.	Conservative Rep's	Liberal Dem's
Local TV news	50%	51	54	48	50	40
Daily paper	40	45	41	38	47	40
Community paper	30	35	30	30	37	26
Network evening news	28	27	30	27	23	24
Fox News	23	40	15	20	48	7
Morning shows	20	18	26	17	15	21
CNN	18	12	25	17	10	26
Sunday shows	11	11	13	11	11	13
NPR	11	6	14	14	6	23
MSNBC	11	6	16	10	5	18
O'Reilly (Fox)	10	21	3	9	27	1
News blogs	9	10	10	9	12	13
News magazines	8	7	10	8	7	16
CNBC	8	6	11	6	6	11
The Daily Show (CC)	7	4	9	8	3	14
Glenn Beck (Fox, now cancelled)	7	14	2	7	19	–
Sean Hannity (Fox)	6	15	1	5	20	–
The Colbert Report (CC)	6	3	7	7	2	11
New York Times	5	2	8	6	1	13
Rush Limbaugh	5	13	2	4	17	1
USA Today	4	6	4	4	7	3
Wall Street Journal	4	6	3	5	7	3
Hardball (MSNBC)	4	2	6	3	1	7
C-SPAN	4	3	5	3	2	3
Rachel Maddow (MSNBC)	3	1	4	3	1	7
Countdown (MSNBC, now canceled)	3	–	5	2	–	7

SOURCE: Pew Research Center, June 8–28, 2010.

6.1

6.2

6.3

6.4

6.5

6.6

6.7

6.8

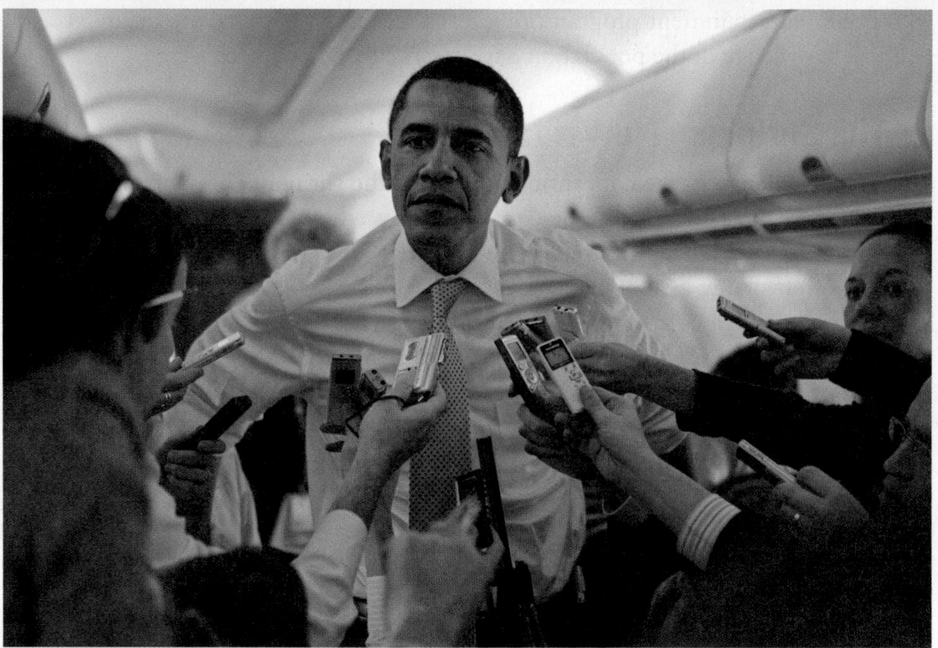

PRESIDENTIAL PRESS

Barack Obama enjoyed positive media coverage throughout the primary and general presidential elections in 2008 and 2012. Candidates do not always enjoy similarly balanced coverage from the media—and good relations with the press influences the coverage candidates receive.

liberals 18 percent. The favorites of conservatives are the *Rush Limbaugh Show* on radio and the *O'Reilly Factor* on Fox television, followed by religious radio, Fox News, business magazines, and call-in radio shows. Moderates and liberals turn to *Piers Morgan, Rachel Maddow*, the nightly ABC, CBS, and NBC news, National Public Radio, and literary magazines (which often deal with tangential aspects of public affairs).[19]

Mediated Elections

6.5 Analyze the role of the media in shaping campaigns and elections.

olitical campaigning is largely a media activity, and the media, especially television, shape the nation's electoral politics.

The Media and Candidate–Voter Linkage

The media are the principal link between candidates and the voters. At one time, political party organizations performed this function, with city, ward, and precinct workers knocking on doors, distributing campaign literature, organizing rallies and candidate appearances, and getting out the vote on Election Day. But television has largely replaced party organizations and personal contact as the means by which candidates communicate with voters. Candidates come directly into the living room via television—on the nightly news, in broadcast debates and interviews, and in paid advertising (see Table 6.2).

Media campaigning requires candidates to possess great skill in communications. Candidates must be able to project a favorable media *image*. The image is a composite of the candidate's words, mannerisms, appearance, personality, warmth, friendliness, humor, and ease in front of a camera. Policy positions have less to do with image than the candidate's ability to project personal qualities—leadership, compassion, strength, and character.

TABLE 6.2 WHEN IT COUNTS: WHERE THE PUBLIC LEARNS ABOUT PRESIDENTIAL CAMPAIGNS

Over time, newspapers and the nightly network news (ABC, CBS, NBC) have been declining as a source of presidential campaign news. In contrast, the Internet has risen rapidly as a source of campaign information.

	2004	2008	2012
Local TV news	42%	40%	32%
Cable news networks	38	38	36
Nightly network news	35	32	26
Daily newspaper	31	31	20
Internet	13	24	25
TV news magazines	25	22	—
Morning TV shows	20	22	16
National Public Radio	14	18	12
Talk radio	17	16	16
Cable political talk	14	15	15
Late-night talk shows	9	9	9
Religious radio	5	9	8
C-SPAN	8	8	—
Comedy TV shows	8	8	—

SOURCE: Adapted from Pew Research Center for the People & the Press, 2012. www.people-press.org.

name recognition
Public awareness of a candidate—whether people even know his or her name.

The Media and Candidate Selection

The media strongly influence the early selection of candidates. Media coverage creates **name recognition**, an essential quality for any candidate. Early media "mentions" of senators, governors, and other political figures as possible presidential contenders help sort out the field even before the election year begins. Conversely, media inattention can condemn aspiring politicians to obscurity.

Serious presidential campaigns now begin a year before the New Hampshire primary (or almost two years before the November presidential election). This early time period, "the invisible primary" (or money primary) is increasingly critical for campaigns.[20] Candidates must position themselves relative to competitors in their own party—build their name recognition, raise poll numbers, and build a campaign war chest. Inasmuch as campaign contributions are just beginning to come in, candidates have relatively little money to spend on paid advertising. They are forced to focus their efforts on attracting media attention by staging media events and issuing press releases. But from the media's perspective, campaign news is neither timely nor immediately relevant. Candidates must try to win media coverage by catering to the conflict and horse-race stories preferred by the media. Press releases and speeches focused on issues are most likely to be ignored.[21]

The media sort out the serious candidates early in a race. They even assign front-runner status, which may be either a blessing or a curse, depending on subsequent media coverage. In presidential primaries, the media play the *expectations game*, setting vote margins that the front-runner must meet in order to maintain *momentum*. If the front-runner does not win by a large enough margin, the media may declare the runner-up the "real" winner. This sorting out of candidates by the media influences not only voters, but—more important—financial contributors. The media-designated favorite is more likely to receive campaign contributions; financial backers do not like to waste money on losers. And as contributions roll in, the favorite can buy more television advertising, adding momentum to the campaign.[22]

The Media as Kingmakers

In the early months of a campaign, media coverage of candidates and their standing in public opinion polls tend to move together. Candidates who receive heavy media coverage usually do well in the polls. Good poll ratings create more media

6.1

6.2

6.3

6.4

6.5

6.6

6.7

6.8

media events
Staged activities designed to attract media attention.

horse-race coverage
Media coverage of electoral campaigns that concentrates on who is ahead and who is behind, and neglects the issues at stake.

coverage. Good poll ratings and increased media coverage inspire campaign contributions, which then allow candidates to buy television advertising to further increase their poll numbers. Media-sponsored public opinion polls play an important role in kingmaking. The CBS/*New York Times* poll, the NBC/Associated Press poll, the ABC/*Washington Post* poll, and the CNN/*USA Today* poll are widely reported; they become the benchmarks for voters, telling them who the winners and losers are.

The name of the game for candidates early in the race is *exposure*. Even appearances on entertainment shows, once considered "unpresidential," are now highly valued by political candidates. They vie to appear on cable talk shows, syndicated daytime programming like *The View*, and on late-night comedy talk shows.

Media Effects on the Campaign

Political candidates are aware of the importance of the media to their success. Their campaign managers must be "media-savvy" and they must hire media consultants early in the campaign. Candidates are advised to arrange daily newsworthy events to keep their name and image in the news. Television producers, reporters, and editors do not like to receive position papers on substantive issues or to present "talking heads"—shots only of the faces of speakers. Rather they prefer attention-getting, action-oriented, emotion-laden videotape. Candidates and their managers know this and so, to attract media attention, they often resort to **media events**—staged activities designed to polish the image of the candidate. Candidates arrange to appear at police conventions, at schools, at hazardous waste sites, on aircraft carriers, at flag factories, and so on in order to project an image on television of their concern for crime, education, the environment, national defense, patriotism, and the like.

The Media and the Horse Race

The media give election campaigns **horse-race coverage**: reporting on who is ahead or behind, what the candidates' strategies are, how much money they are spending, and, above all, what their current standing in the polls is. Such stories account for more than half of all television news coverage of an election. Additional stories are centered on *campaign* issues—controversies that arise on the campaign trail itself, including verbal blunders by the candidate—and *character* issues, such as the sex life of the candidate. In contrast, *policy* issues typically account for only about one-third of the television news stories in a presidential election campaign.

The Bad-News Bias

The media's bad-news bias is evident in election campaigns as well as in general news reporting. Negative stories about all presidential candidates usually outnumber positive stories. The media generally see their function in political campaigns as reporting on the weaknesses, blunders, and vulnerabilities of the candidates. It might be argued that exposing the flaws of the candidates is an important function in a democracy. But the media's negative reporting about candidates and generally skeptical attitude toward their campaign speeches, promises, and advertisements may contribute to political alienation and cynicism among voters.

The media focus intense scrutiny on the personal lives of candidates—their marriages, sex lives, drug or alcohol use, personal finances, past friendships, military service, club memberships, and other potential sources of embarrassment. Virtually any past error in judgment or behavior by a candidate is given heavy coverage. But the media defend their attention to personal scandal on the ground that they are reporting on the "character issue." They argue that voters must have information on candidates' character as well as on their policy positions.

☐ The Shrinking Sound Bite

Reporters and newsroom anchors dominate television broadcasting. They report roughly three-quarters of all campaign news themselves. The candidates are allocated less than 15 percent of the time devoted to campaign news stories. (Other sources—pundits, commentators, voters, and so forth—account for the remaining airtime.) The candidates themselves have very little direct contact with audiences in network news. The average **sound bite**—time allowed the candidates to speak on their own behalf—has shrunk to less than eight seconds!

sound bite
Concise and catchy phrase that attracts media coverage.

prior restraint
Government actions to restrict publication of a magazine, newspaper, or books on the grounds of libel, obscenity, or other legal violations prior to actual publication of the work.

☐ Paid Campaign Ads

Candidates cannot allow the news media to define them or their messages. Rather, they must endeavor to do so themselves, and of course they must try to define their opponents in negative terms. Television ads account for the largest portion of campaign spending. Nearly 1 million political commercials will be aired during a primary and general election cycle, for president, Congress, governorships, and state legislatures. Heavy costs are incurred in the production of ads as well as the purchase of broadcast time. Networks may charge $1 million or more for 30 seconds of nationwide prime-time advertising on a popular show.

The ad battle is the most visible element of an election campaign. Television advertising is most effective in motivating supporters to vote. Advertising can do so by creating a favorable image of the candidate, or more likely by creating a negative image of the opponent. But television ads run the risk of creating boredom and frustration among viewers who grow tired of the constant barrage of political ads. To counter these effects, advertising executives and their political consultants must develop interesting and captivating ads, and they must regularly develop new ads in the course of the campaign. Ads may change themes in response to polls or focus groups that indicate new or developing concerns among the electorate. And ads can also be changed to counter attacks from the opposition. As Election Day approaches, ads are more likely to "go negative," that is, to attack the opponent. And, with the emergence of Super PACs, the potential for unlimited negative attacks on candidates reached new heights in 2012.

Freedom Versus Fairness

6.6 Distinguish between freedom of the press and fairness of the press.

Complaints about the fairness of media are as old as the printing press. Most early newspapers in the United States were allied with political parties; they were not expected to be fair in their coverage. It was only in the early 1900s that many large newspapers broke their ties with parties and proclaimed themselves independent. And it was not until the 1920s and 1930s that the norms of journalistic professionalism and accuracy gained widespread acceptance.

The Constitution protects the *freedom* of the press; it was not intended to guarantee *fairness*. The 1st Amendment's guarantee of freedom of the press was originally designed to protect the press from government attempts to silence criticism. Over the years, the U.S. Supreme Court has greatly expanded the meaning of the free-press guarantee.

☐ No Prior Restraint

The Supreme Court has interpreted freedom of the press to mean that government may place no **prior restraint** on speech or publication (that is, before it is said or published). Originally, this doctrine was designed to prevent the government from closing

6.1

6.2

6.3

6.4

6.5

6.6

6.7

6.8

equal-time rule
Federal Communications Commission (FCC) requirement that broadcasters who sell time to any political candidate must make equal time available to opposing candidates at the same price.

libel
Writings that are false and malicious and intended to damage an individual.

slander
Oral statements that are false and malicious and intended to damage an individual.

down or seizing newspapers. Today, the doctrine prevents the government from censoring any news items. In the famous case of the Pentagon Papers, the *New York Times* and *Washington Post* undertook to publish secret information stolen from the files of the State Department and Defense Department regarding U.S. policy in Vietnam while the war was still going on. No one disputed the fact that stealing the secret material was illegal. What was at issue was the ability of the government to prevent the publication of stolen documents in order to protect national security. The Supreme Court rejected the national security argument and reaffirmed that the government may place no prior restraint on publication.[23] If the government wishes to keep military secrets, it must not let them fall into the hands of the American press.

☐ Press Versus Electronic Media

In the early days of radio, broadcast channels were limited, and anyone with a radio transmitter could broadcast on any frequency. As a result, interference was a common frustration of early broadcasters. The industry petitioned the federal government to regulate and license the assignment and use of broadcast frequencies.

The Federal Communications Commission (FCC) was established in 1934 to allocate broadcast frequencies and to license stations for "the public interest, convenience and necessity." The act clearly instructed the FCC: "Nothing in this Act shall be understood or construed to give the Commission the power of censorship." However, the FCC views a broadcast license and exclusive right to use a particular frequency as a *public trust*. Thus broadcasters, unlike newspapers and magazines, are licensed by a government agency and supposed to operate in the *public interest*.

☐ Decency

From time to time, the FCC has cracked down on "indecency" on radio and television, presumably doing so in the "public interest." Networks have been fined for the Super Bowl halftime "wardrobe malfunctions," and "shock-jocks" like Howard Stern have incurred millions of dollars in fines for themselves and their stations. Government suppression of "indecency" is constitutionally permitted over broadcast waves on the theory that these channels are limited, they belong to the public, and government licenses broadcasters. Otherwise, mere "indecency" that does not constitute "obscenity" is constitutionally protected by the 1st Amendment.

☐ The Equal-Time Requirement

The FCC requires radio and television stations that provide airtime to a political candidate to offer competing candidates the same amount of airtime at the same price. Stations are not required to give free time to candidates, but if stations choose to give free time to one candidate, they must do so for the candidate's opponents. But this **equal-time rule** does *not* apply to newscasts, news specials, or even long documentaries, nor does it apply to talk shows like *Piers Morgan*. Nor does it apply to presidential press conferences or presidential addresses to the nation, although the networks now generally offer free time for a "Democratic response" to a Republican president, and vice versa. A biased news presentation does not require the network or station to grant equal time to opponents of its views. And it is important to note that newspapers, unlike radio and television, have never been required to provide equal time to opposing views.

☐ Libel and Slander

Communications that wrongly damage an individual are known in law as **libel** (when written) and **slander** (when spoken). The injured party must prove in court that the communication caused actual damage and was either false or defamatory. A damaging falsehood or words or phrases that are defamatory (such as "Joe Jones is a rotten son of a bitch") are libelous and are not protected by the 1st Amendment from lawsuits seeking compensation.

Public Officials

Over the years, the media have sought to narrow the protection afforded public officials against libel and slander. In 1964, the U.S. Supreme Court ruled in the case of *New York Times v. Sullivan* that public officials did not have a right to recover damages for false statements unless they are made with "malicious intent."[24] The **Sullivan rule** requires public officials not only to show that the media published or broadcast false and damaging statements, but also to prove that they did so knowing that their statements were false and damaging or with "reckless disregard" for the truth or falsehood of their statements. The effect of the Sullivan rule is to free the media to say virtually anything about public officials. Indeed, the media have sought to expand the definition of "public officials" to "public figures"—that is, to include anyone they choose as the subject of a story.

Sullivan rule
Court guideline that false and malicious statements regarding public officials are protected by the 1st Amendment unless it can be proven they were known to be false at the time they were made or were made with "reckless disregard" for their truth or falsehood.

new media
Content and technology that result in the ability of individuals to actively and immediately share content generated in traditional media forms (text, image, sound, and video).

cyberculture
The emergent culture that results from computerization, networking, and use of new media.

"Absence of Malice"

The 1st Amendment protects the right of the media to be biased, unfair, negative, sensational, and even offensive. Indeed, even *damaging falsehoods* may be printed or broadcast as long as the media can show that the story was not deliberately fabricated by them with malicious intent; that is, if the media can show an "absence of malice."

Shielding Sources

The media argue that the 1st Amendment allows them to refuse to reveal the names of their sources, even when this information is required in criminal investigations and trials. Thus far, the U.S. Supreme Court has not given blanket protection to reporters to withhold information from court proceedings. However, a number of states have passed *shield laws* protecting reporters from being forced to reveal their sources.

Politics and the Internet

6.7 Evaluate the effects of the new media on politics.

The development of any new medium of communications invariably affects political life. Just as radio and, later, television reshaped politics in America, today the Internet is having its own unique impact on public affairs. The Internet provides a channel for *interactive mass participation* in politics. It is unruly and chaotic by design. It offers the promise of abundant and diverse information and the opportunity for increased political participation. It empowers everyone who can design a Web site to spread their views, whether their views are profound and public-spirited or hateful and obscene.

The New Media and Cyberculture

New media use digitization to transmit content. These media fill traditional roles of the "old media" to disseminate information and facilitate communication. But, unlike the old media, new media are not geographically bound; they transcend print, voice, or video; and the new media facilitate the development of content from nontraditional content providers. Most important, however, is that new media allow us to link and move across multiple sources of information, and allow the consumer of information to become an interactive user of information. New media facilitate **cyberculture**—content

cyberpolitics
The application of new media to campaign politics.

and social interactions arising from the use of new media—by diffusing content provision to large numbers of people, and devolving control of content selection to the user. New media and cyberculture significantly transformed campaigning and political journalism from the global level to the local level. The most prominent source of new media is the Internet, which has combined with other new media such as mobile devices to create rich, instant content communication that is broadly accessible.

It Started with Chaos by Design

During the Cold War, the RAND Corporation, a technological research think tank, proposed the Internet as a communications network that might survive a nuclear attack. It was deliberately designed to operate without any central authority or organization. Should any part of the system be destroyed, messages would still find their way to their destinations. The later development of the World Wide Web language allowed any connected computer in the world to communicate with any other connected computer. And introduction of the World Wide Web in 1992 also meant that users no longer needed computer expertise to communicate. By 1995, Americans were buying more computers than television sets and sending more e-mail than "snail mail." Since then, Internet usage has continued to mushroom (see Figure 6.4), and the political use of the Internet and related new media has exploded (see Table 6.3 for the political time line of the use of new media).

Cyberpolitics

Cyberpolitics is the application of new media to campaign politics. (The rate of change in new media is such that this chapter will be obsolete before you finish reading it.) Efforts to use new media in politics go back to the 1980s, when fax machines were used to disseminate political information from campaigns, to coordinate operations, and, in the case of the Chinese Tiananmen Square protests, to coordinate support from outside China to activists inside China. However, it was not until Internet browsers and the broad-based use of e-mail developed in the 1990s that the new media showed potential to be a player in politics.

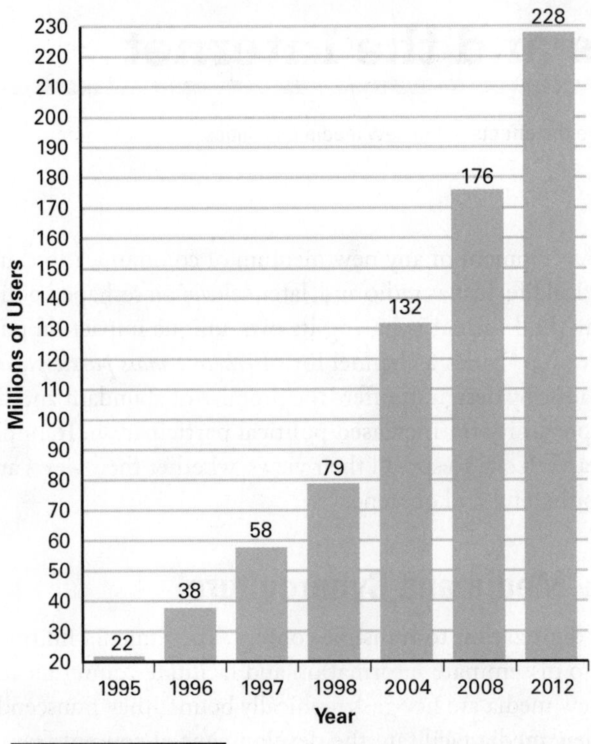

FIGURE 6.4 ONLINE AMERICA: GROWTH OF INTERNET USERS

Internet use has mushroomed over the last decade.

SOURCE: *Statistical Abstract of the United States*, 2012.

6.1
6.2
6.3
6.4
6.5
6.6
6.7
6.8

TABLE 6.3 THE POLITICAL NEW MEDIA TIME LINE

1996	msnbc.com news partnership created by Microsoft and General Electric's NBC subsidiary.
1997	FreeRepublic.com unveiled as a GOP Internet forum.
1998	MoveOn (moveOn.org) is created. *Drudge Report* (founded 1997) breaks the Bill Clinton/Monica Lewinsky story sat on by *Newsweek*, legitimizing Internet news. Drudge becomes top news aggregation site in America. Jesse Ventura wins the Minnesota governorship using an aggressive new media strategy. Paypal.com is founded. Google.com is founded.
1999	Al Gore, appearing on CNN, claims the initiative in creating the Internet, resulting in the first political Internet meme.
2000	John McCain raises a half-million dollars in 24 hours online after upsetting George Bush in the New Hampshire primary. Republicans pioneer microtargeted Internet advertising on political campaigns.
2000	The phrase "Netroots" enters the American lexicon.
2002	Markos Moulitas founds his blog, *Daily Kos.*
2003	Vermont governor Howard Dean uses the social network site Meetup.com to organize volunteers and activists. Arizona pioneers online voter registration.
2004	Online bloggers, starting at FreeRepublic.com, uncover the use of fraudulent memos in a CBS story about President Bush's national guard service. Dan Rather resigns.
2005	YouTube is created by three former PayPal employees. *The Huffington Post* is founded by Arianna Huffington (HuffPo later merges with AOL). Jack Kingston (R-GA-1) is the first member of Congress to have a blog.
2006	Ads campaign videos, and opposition research appear on YouTube. Conventional and new media become increasingly integrated. The microblogging application Twitter is unveiled by Jack Dorsey.
2007	The Barack Obama campaign makes extensive use of Facebook as an organizing tool to build an organizational base for the 2008 primaries. Ron Paul deploys the first "money bomb," raising over $4 million online in 24 hours. Politico.com is founded on the Internet and conventional media platforms. Fact-checking goes online as the *Saint Petersburg Times* creates Politifact.com.
2008	FiveThirtyEight.com makes political stats popular—and understandable. Obama surprises Hillary Clinton with a strong Super Tuesday primary performance, validating the meme. Obama campaign exploits mass texting and Facebook Connect, creates a Barack Obama app for the iPhone.
2009	GoogleBlast advertising is used for the first time in a major election in New York's Twentieth Congressional District.
2010	Smartphone apps such as Walking Edge connect street-level volunteers with databases and Google Maps to coordinate face-to-face contacting activities.
2012	Americans Elect, the $35 million online-based nominating experiment, fails to nominate a candidate for its bipartisan presidential ballot. The Sunlight Foundation's Politwoops starts recovering deleted congressional tweets (to the embarrassment of some members of Congress)
2014	Increased use of cyberattacks as a political tool and also a means of political protest. Revelation of expanded NSA Internet surveillance.

SOURCE: Steven Davy, 2010. "How Technology Changed American Politics in the Internet Age." *Mediashift.* http://www.pbs.org/mediashift/2010/04/how-technology-changed-american-politics-in-the-internet-age096.html; compiled by authors.

6.1
6.2
6.3
6.4
6.5
6.6
6.7
6.8

social media applications
Internet and new media applications that facilitate social coordination and interaction.

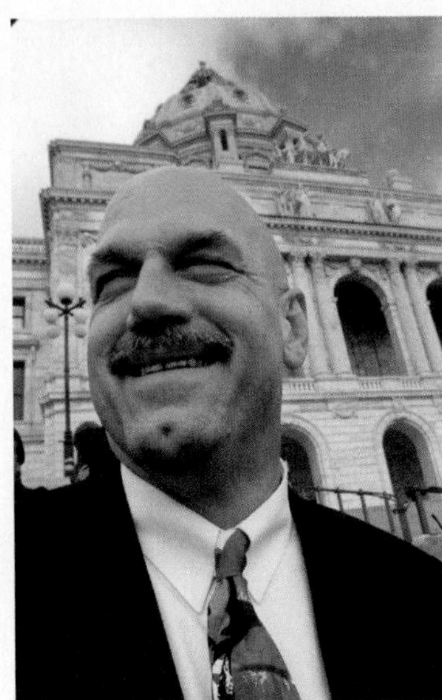

BODY POLITIC
Former professional wrestler Jesse "The Body" Ventura used an innovative new media campaign to win the 1998 election for Minnesota governor. Ventura, Angus King (Maine), and Lincoln Chaffee (R.I.) are the last three non-major party governors elected in the United States.

The First Cyberpolitics Success

The first major success by an Internet campaign was the 1998 Minnesota gubernatorial campaign. Running on the Reform Party ticket in a three-cornered race, former wrestler Jesse "The Body" Ventura won a low-cost, high turnout campaign. Ventura's campaign had strong appeal to independent and younger voters—and also demonstrated the first creative use of the Internet. Ventura's campaign, which spent just $300,000, kept an active, frequently updated Web site, and used a massive e-mail list to coordinate volunteers and promote events. Nine months before the election, Ventura endorsed the potential of the Internet, observing "It's tailor-made for my campaign ... It's reaching a huge amount of people at a very low price." His campaign director, Phil Madsen, observed that it was the mobilization, not the Web site, that was the key component of the Internet. They would create highly personalized events, draw in a few hundred people, and then post digital photos of the event within minutes of its end. People at the event went home and saw themselves online. Ventura's opponents ran conventional, old media campaigns and got caught flatfooted by Ventura's new-media blitz.

Innovation in the Twenty-First Century

The John McCain presidential campaign carried matters a step further in 2000. McCain, who was running an insurgency campaign against the establishment George W. Bush campaign, was able to translate his media appeal and some Internet savvy by his twenty-something Webmasters into a viable challenge. McCain's campaign was the first to actively and extensively use the Internet to collect credit card contributions. People who could not make the $500 to $5,000 or $50,000 donations that bought access to the Bush campaign could make a $10 or $50 donation on a credit card to McCain. And, unlike a donor check, which might take two weeks to clear, Internet money was immediately useable. McCain (and other candidates) also mimicked the Ventura campaign in using the Internet for coordinating tens of thousands of volunteers across numerous states. The George W. Bush campaign also used e-mail coordination and made creative use of targeted phone banking: Bush Webmaster Paul Ruffini (now a principal in Engage political communications) designed and implemented a Web-based program to coordinate 1.4 million volunteers.

In 2003, the Howard Dean campaign expanded on McCain's fund-raising and coordination efforts. Dean's was the first major campaign to make use of social media to coordinate campaign efforts and online video to disseminate content. Interested Dean activists started using Meetup and other **social media applications** (such as Slashdot and Scoop) designed to coordinate real-world meetings of people with similar interests. The campaign learned from the grassroots up, developing tools (DeanLink and Dean TV, an early YouTube style video-posting system) based on open source platforms in order to quickly set up community organizations and then allow them to adapt to their local needs. Howard Dean, in an interview during the campaign, told *Wired* magazine, "We fell into this by accident. I wish I could tell you we were smart enough to figure this out. But the community taught us. They seized the initiative through Meetup. They built our organization for us before we had an organization."[25]

By the time the 2006 campaign came around, Twitter had arrived as a communication tool. This permissive technology, which allows the transmission of brief messages (and later images and video), quickly emerged as a means for rapid event reporting for journalists and bloggers and a rapid-response vehicle for campaigns. By 2006, the conventional brick-and-mortar media, confronted with declining ratings and diminished print-copy readership, started to formally partner with new media sources. The highest profile evidence of this partnership was in 2007, when Cable News Network partnered with YouTube to sponsor a Democratic presidential debate.

Internet Fund-Raising Takes Off

The escalation of Internet fund-raising might just owe its success to Amazon.com and eBay. According to former Dean campaign strategist Joe Trippi, there was a limit to the ability to raise money online in 2000 because not enough Americans were comfortable using their credit card for online transactions. By 2004, the comfort with using credit online was sufficiently widespread to allow for dramatic short-term fund-raising from small-dollar donors. Howard Dean's efforts paved the way for online fund-raising by general election candidates in 2004. It also demonstrated how a nonconventional, insurgent candidacy could mobilize broad-based financial support. Former Libertarian candidate Ron Paul, seeking the GOP nomination in 2007, was largely discounted by the big money people of the GOP and by the mainstream and conservative media. When Paul deployed consecutive "**money bombs**" (intensive online fund-raising drives) in 2007, raising $4.3 million and $6 million, the financial potential of the Internet was fully demonstrated. Paul's efforts were later dwarfed by the online fund-raising prowess of the Obama campaign, but Paul did get there first. Now, texting and tweeting makes fund-raising that much easier, and donations can be made by just keying a text number and having a phone account debited—ask the Red Cross, which raised millions in disaster relief for Haiti and Japan via Twitter and texting.

money bombs
Large amounts of money raised in a brief period of time using only online resources.

"100 Million Cameras"

One of the major changes wrought by the Internet is online video. The development of high-quality, low-cost video production technologies fed into the ease of video dissemination through applications such as YouTube. Since 2008, candidates have used YouTube to announce candidacies, to roll out campaign advertising, and to take their case on issues directly to the public. Campaign events and candidate statements can be instantly captured, edited, and made available to the online public. This is a double-edged sword—candidates can immediately promote their successes, but conversely any suspicious or embarrassing candidate

The Game, the Rules, the Players

Old Media, New Science

Politics is full of numbers. In the last few years, the established media incorporated data visualization tools and other social science techniques into their coverage. One innovation is the media outlets moving to the Internet and absorbing "new media" outlets into their business model.

The two national papers of record in the United States are the *New York Times* and the *Washington Post*. These papers historically battled to cover major stories throughout the last half of the twentieth century. Their investigative teams, columnists, and editorial boards battled for the advantage in setting the debate on political coverage. In the twenty-first century, the new battle is for innovative, data-driven political coverage.

The *Washington Post* features homegrown talent that delves into the nuance of numbers and also outside bloggers. On the insure, Chris Cillizza redefined political coverage for the *Post* by bringing numbers to bear on critical races around the country in his blog *The Fix*. Analysis in *The Fix*, while data-driven, is also laced with both opinion and humor, making his reporting different from conventional reporters. The *Post* later acquired the political science blog *The Monkey Cage*, which applies data analysis and social science methods to current topics and controversies in American and global politics.

The *New York Times* hired data bloggers after the 2008 election, starting with Nate Silver's blog *FiveThirtyEight* (now hosted by ESPN). Silver used political science tools to slice into polling data and historical data to forecast presidential electoral votes, U.S. Senate seats, and the balance of control in Congress. Like Cillizza, he was not even 30 when he crashed the scene on election analysis. His forecasts were so powerful that in 2009, *Time* magazine named him one of the100 most influential people in the world, and in 2012 he was directly challenged on his accuracy by GOP leaders, including presidential nominee Mitt Romney. Silver called every state's vote correctly and also correctly forecast 31 of 33 U.S. Senate contests. Headed into the 2014 elections, Silver's forecasts were so accurate and so feared that Democrats used them as a vehicle to raise money from donors by invoking the prospect of a total GOP takeover of Congress.

QUESTIONS

1. Do you use data to make choices?
2. How often do you go to Internet-based sources instead of regular media outlets for information? Why?

activity can go straight to the Internet, because most mobile phone users have video capability. New media use for political information reached a critical mass in 2010. One in five voters actively used video applications like YouTube to seek political information.

☐ Political Web Sites Abound

The Internet is awash in political Web sites. The simple query "politics" on a standard search program can return well over a million matches. Almost all federal agencies, including the White House, Congress, the federal judiciary, and executive departments and agencies, maintain Web sites. Individual elected officeholders, including all members of Congress, maintain sites that include personal biographies, committee assignments, legislative accomplishments, issue statements, and press releases. The home pages of the Democratic and Republican parties offer political news, issue positions, opportunities to become active in party affairs, and invitations to send them money. No serious candidate for major public office lacks a Web site; these campaign sites usually include flattering biographies, press releases, and, of course, invitations to contribute financially to the candidates' campaigns. All major interest groups maintain Web sites—business, trade, and professional groups; labor unions; ideological and issue groups; women's, religious, environmental, and civil rights groups. Indeed, this virtual tidal wave of politics on the Internet may turn out to offer too much information in too fragmented a fashion, thereby simply adding to apathy and indifference.[26]

☐ Effecting Political Change Through New Media

The new media and cyberculture changed politics "from the bottom up" because of the proliferation of mobile electronic devices, increasingly sophisticated but easy-to-use applications, and rich online content. The entire world, and the sum of human knowledge, is at the fingertips of anyone with a smartphone or a touchpad. According to *US News & World Report*'s Mary Kate Cary, there are five significant changes to politics caused by new media.

1. "News you can choose." Fifty years ago, news consumers could get the local paper, wait for afternoon delivery of a national paper like the *New York Times*, or enjoy 30 minutes of local news and 30 minutes of national news from one of three network television broadcasts. The news was moderated, coordinated, and largely dispassionate. A small group of editors controlled what any individual could access as news. Now people can search for content, capture it for later consumption, and bring numerous editorial perspectives into comparison—or avoid some editorial perspectives all together.
2. "Share this." E-mail, listservs, chat boards, social media sites, and Twitter have emerged as a means to share news, good or bad. Long before people posted or clicked a "share" or a "one-+" to a story or a video, they sent links, attachments, and pasted copies of content to each other (conventional media outlets, having integrated to online, facilitate sharing in order to drive traffic). We tend to tweet what we like, politically, and we tend to retweet the tweets of like-minded people (see Figure 6.5).

   A tweet from the White House immediately lands in 1.7 million news feeds. When the 2011 East Coast earthquake struck northern Virginia, news of it went out over social media faster than the shockwave itself traveled up and down the East Coast (the Tweetquake). And related to "share this" is …
3. "Like it." Post it. Like it. Or critically comment on it. But expressing opinion is just a click away.
4. "Connect with others." Social media, Twitter, and texting make it possible to organize an event, build a protest, or throw together a rapid response to an unexpected political development. The costs of information dissemination have fallen to nearly zero—if you know who you want to contact.
5. "Donate now." Like sharing and liking, giving money to a political candidate is just a click away using an application or a text.

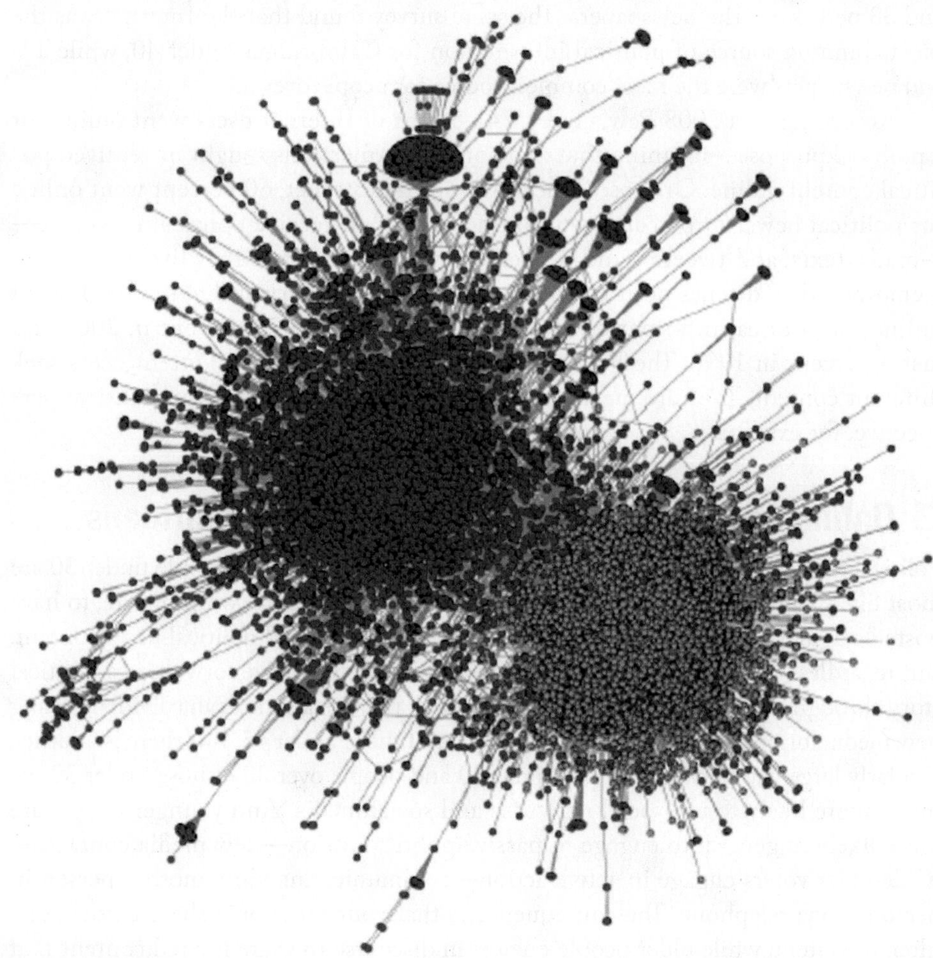

FIGURE 6.5 TWEETING PAST EACH OTHER?

Computer scientists at Indiana University studied the tweets of 45,000 Twitter users to graph the pattern and content of retweets—messages or stories that users passed on. Generally speaking, the Twitterverse is more left-leaning than right-leaning, with conservative hashtags like #TCOT (top conservative on twitter) being retweeted by conservatives and #P2 (a progressive hashtag) being retweeted by liberals. The Twitterverse is largely ideologically segregated but does have some ideological intersections.

SOURCES: Robert Lee Hotz, "Decoding Our Chatter." *Wall Street Journal,* October 1, 2011, accessed at online.wsj.com. Michael D. Conover, Bruno Goncalves, Jacob Ratkiewicz, Alessandro Flammini, and Filippo Menczer, 2011. "Predicting the Political Alignment of Twitter Users." White paper, Center for Complex Networks and Systems Research School of Informatics and Computing, Indiana University, Bloomington.

These changes are not just part of national campaigns or just for major offices. Campaigns for local political office and local referenda and bond issues have made use of these technologies for several years now. It is not just national campaigns that suffer from a lack of Internet presence—any contested election can only benefit from net savvy.

☐ Who Is Politically Online?

Precisely measuring the extent of Internet and new media political use is difficult. In 2010, Rasmussen Reports found that 37 percent of voters went to cable television for political news, 22 percent went to the broadcast networks, and 21 percent went to the Internet. Just 9 percent of respondents went to print sources first (Rasmussen uses computerized "robot" telephone calls to perform surveys of voters, another application of new media to collect content via a traditional medium). How much of the Internet source traffic is going to online versions of print sources is unknown. Two years before, ABC News/Facebook found that 70 percent of respondents put television (cable and broadcast) in their "top two" information sources, 26 percent said newspapers, and 23 percent said the Internet—and 40 percent of respondents in this survey said they used the Internet to get political content. And a 2011 Field Poll of California voters found that 56 percent went to television for political news, 44 percent to the Internet,

6.1

6.2

6.3

6.4

6.5

6.6

6.7

6.8

and 33 percent to the newspapers. The same survey found that the Internet was the most common source of political information for Californians under 40, while TV and newspapers were the most common source for people over 65.

According to a 2008 Pew survey, 74 percent of Internet users went online for a political purpose—meaning that a majority of Americans sought or received political content online. Of those Americans on the Internet, 60 percent went online for political news, 59 percent went online to send or receive political messages—e-mails, texts, and tweets—and 38 percent went online to either live chat or use a chat board to discuss politics. Out of all Americans surveyed, 44 percent went online for political information. This is an increase from 29 percent in 2004 and just 4 percent in 1996. The Pew report also found that online content users seek different content. They are more likely to seek content that affords a political perspective, for example.

□ Online Activity Is Dominated by Younger Americans

Political activities online are concentrated among younger voters. People under 30 are most likely to have engaged in political action using a social networking site, to have posted original political content, and to have used customized political news content. But regardless of their age, respondents are equally likely to have forwarded a political story through some form of new media. Overall, there is a significant divide in using new media for politics between those over 65 and those under 65. But there is another, similarly large gap between people under 30 and people over 30—those under 30 are much more likely to use social networks and social media. And younger people are more likely in general to engage in passive political action—new media contacts—while older voters engage in active action—communicating with another person in person or via telephone. The consequence is that younger people share textual, unfiltered content, while older people engage in discourse to share filtered content that they interpret when they share.

□ The Consequences of Media Platform Integration

The integration of historic Internet content and applications with handheld devices will only serve to expand the influence of new media–based content. Internet access penetrates four in five households. As of April 2010, 60 percent of U.S. households have broadband Internet access; in 2004, the share was 42 percent. But handheld devices are becoming almost universal, and the falling cost of high-capability devices places most of the tools of smartphones in the reach of most Americans. The number of wireless subscribers in the United States was 33.8 million in 1995, 109.5 million in 2000, 207.9 million in 2005, and 302.9 million by 2010 (including United States territories). Wireless-only households increased from 8.4 percent of households in 2005 to 26.6 percent by 2010.

□ Historic Significance of New Media

The new media elections of the latter part of the last decade mark the most significant transition of political campaigning via technology since the emergence of television as the dominant medium in 1960. Republican media consultant Bryan Merica told the *Los Angeles Times* that "what Obama did was show this is a tool we can use to not only fund-raise but win elections," referring to the use of social media to recruit, organize, and disseminate campaign messages. In 2010, conservative activists used the same social media tools (Facebook, Twitter, and texting) to build the Tea Party movement. Absent the application of these media tools, it is doubtful that the GOP could have refurbished its political brand so quickly.

All of these media tools, taken together, allow political candidates, officeholders, and message makers to bypass the filters of the established media outlets. The numbers of persons who consume this media are often smaller than the audiences of broadcast messages.

But they are also individuals who actively sought this content, meaning that they are the sort of high-interest consumers and users of political information sought by candidates.

The Financial Challenge

The one ongoing challenge arising from the new media is how to provide meaningful reporting inside a stable profit model. Publishers and television stations have created Web sites, phone apps, and tablet apps to put their product in front of users, but they continue to grapple with how to monetize the delivery of the news over these new platforms. As a consequence, staffing of established media outlets continues to decline.

So, What's a Journalist Anymore?

Once, not so long ago, it was easy to recognize a reputable journalistic source. Reputable sources were the network broadcast newscasts, the reporters for daily papers and national weekly magazines, and reporters for syndicates such as the Associated Press. Journalists had their content controlled by editors, who sought to separate entertainment and editorial content from reporting and analysis.

The rise of the new media has been accompanied by a decline in circulation and advertising revenue for traditional media outlets. Whereas the rise in new media has resulted in a diverse and growing body of professional and amateur content providers, traditional media outlets have engaged in ongoing rounds of staffing cuts and consolidation and sought to move to multimedia platforms to capture the new media audience. This has often lead traditional media outlets to partner with new media content providers—for example, the NBC affiliate in Washington DC gets some content from the writers at the snarky political blog Wonkette.com—or to seek high-end expert content for low cost—news outlets engage panels of experts to blog and comment on narrow areas of policy expertise.

As a consequence, "traditional" media outlets are increasingly offering content that is not developed by trained journalists. This new content often blends op-ed and analytical components, taking up space previously dedicated to straight reporting. And this content is not necessarily as closely scrutinized by editors or readily distinguished from "straight news."

New media have made every user a potential editor, and every blogger a potential reporter or pundit. The active engagement of the newest generation of voters with new media—using it, re-creating it, reshaping it, referring it—means that any story, video, blog post, or tweet is potentially just the start of a creative political act. However, the users and perpetrators of new media have discovered one of the challenges with creating original content—it is hard work, and your credibility and influence as a provider of new media content depend to no small extent on being right. What remains unresolved is how to manage the greater subjectivity of new media sources, and how laws designed to protect journalists will be applied to a growing body of new media content providers who have no formal code of professional ethics.

Internet Uncensored

The Internet allows unrestricted freedom of expression, from scientific discourses on particle physics and information on the latest developments in medical science, to invitations to join in paramilitary "militia" and offers to exchange pornographic photos and messages. Commercial sex sites outnumber any other category on the Web.

Congress unsuccessfully attempted to outlaw "indecent" and "patently offensive" material on the Internet with its Communications Decency Act of 1996. But the U.S. Supreme Court gave 1st Amendment protection to the Internet in 1997 in *Reno v. American Civil Liberties Union*.[27] The Court recognized the Internet as an important form of popular expression protected by the Constitution. Congress had sought to make it a federal crime to send or display "indecent" material to persons under 18 years of age (material describing or displaying sexual activities or organs in

6.1
6.2
6.3
6.4
6.5
6.6
6.7
6.8

information overload
Situation in which individuals are subjected to so many communications that they cannot make sense of them.

selective perception
Mentally screening out information or opinions with which one disagrees.

"patently offensive" fashion). But the Supreme Court reiterated its view that government may not limit the adult population to "only what is fit for children." The Court decision places the burden of filtering Internet messages on parents. Filtering software can be installed on home computers, but a 1st Amendment issue arises when it is installed on computers in public libraries.

Media Effects: Shaping Political Life

6.8 Assess the effects that the media have on public opinion and political behavior.

What effects do the media have on public opinion and political behavior? Let us consider media effects on (1) information and agenda setting, (2) values and opinions, and (3) behavior. These categories of effects are ranked by the degree of influence the media are likely to have over us. The strongest effects of the media are on our information levels and societal concerns. The media also influence values and opinions, but the strength of media effects in these areas is diluted by many other influences. Finally, it is most difficult to establish the independent effect of the media on behavior.

Information and Agenda-Setting Effects

The media strongly influence what we know about our world and how we think and talk about it. Years ago, foreign policy expert Bernard Cohen, in the first book to assess the effects of the media on foreign policy, put it this way: "The mass media may not be successful in telling people what to think, but the media are stunningly successful in telling their audience what to think about."[28]

However, **information overload** diminishes the influence of the media in determining what we think about. So many communications are directed at us that we cannot possibly process them all. A person's ability to recall a media report depends on repeated exposure to it and reinforcement through personal experience. For example, an individual who has a brother in a trouble spot in the Middle East is more likely to be aware of reports from that area of the world. But too many voices with too many messages cause most viewers to block out a great deal of information.

Information overload may be especially heavy in political news. Television tells most viewers more about politics than they really want to know. Political scientist Austin Ranney wrote: "The fact is that for most Americans, politics is still far from being the most interesting and important thing in life. To them, politics is usually confusing, boring, repetitious, and above all irrelevant to the things that really matter in their lives."[29]

Effects on Values and Opinions

The media often tell us how we *should* feel about news events or issues, especially those about which we have no prior feelings or experiences. The media can reinforce values and attitudes we already hold. However, the media seldom *change* our preexisting values or opinions. Media influence over values and opinions is reduced by **selective perception**, mentally screening out information or opinions we disagree with. People tend to see and hear only what they want to see and hear. For example, television news concentration on scandal, abuse, and corruption in government has not always produced the liberal, reformist values among viewers that media people expected. On the contrary, the focus of network executives on governmental scandals—Watergate, the Iran-Contra scandal, the sexual antics of politicians, and so on—has produced feelings

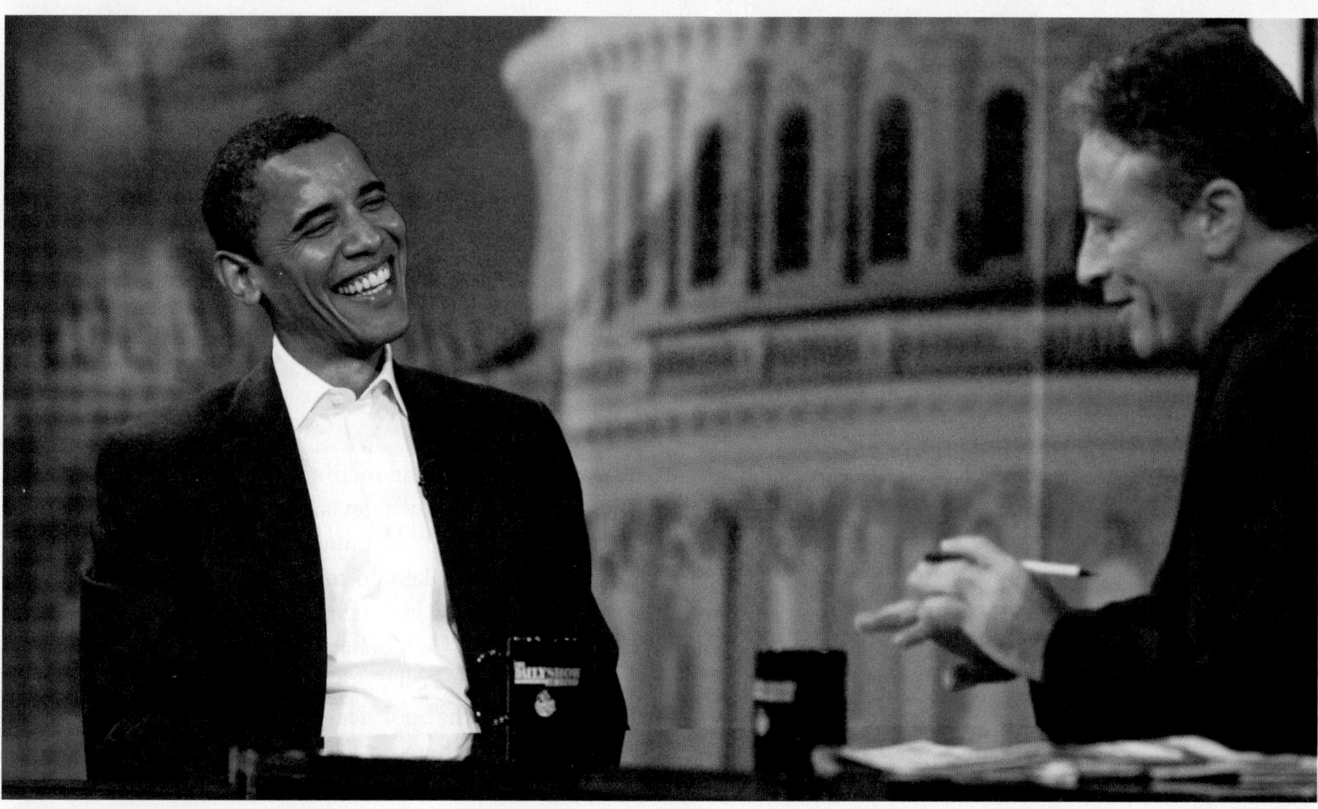

CAMPAIGNING ON LATE-NIGHT TV

Late-night television is now a popular campaign forum. Many viewers get their news from talk shows such as *The Daily Show* with Jon Stewart, pictured here with President Barack Obama in late 2007. Obama would later return to the show as president.

of general political distrust and cynicism toward government and the political system. These feelings have been labeled **television malaise**, a combination of social distrust, political cynicism, feelings of powerlessness, and disaffection from parties and politics that seems to stem from television's emphasis on the negative aspects of American life.

television malaise
Generalized feelings of distrust, cynicism, and powerlessness stemming from television's emphasis on the negative aspects of American life.

The media do not *intend* to create television malaise; they are performing their self-declared watchdog role. They expect their stories to encourage liberal reform of our political institutions. But the result is often alienation rather than reform.

□ Direct Effects on Public Opinion

Can the media change public opinion, and if so, how? For many years, political scientists claimed that the media had only minimal effects on public opinions and behavior. This early view was based largely on the fact that newspaper editorial endorsements seldom affected people's votes. But serious research on the effects of television tells a different story.

In an extensive study of 80 policy issues over 15 years, political scientists examined public opinion polls on various policy issues at a first point in time, then media content over a following interval of time, and finally public opinion on these same issues at the end of the interval. The purpose was to learn if media content—messages scored by their relevance to the issue, their salience in the broadcast, their pro/con direction, the credibility of the news source, and quality of the reporting—changed public opinion. Most people's opinions remained constant over time (opinion at the first point in time is the best predictor of opinion at the second point in time). However, when opinion did change, it changed in the direction supported by the media. "News variables alone account for nearly half the variance in opinion change." Other findings include the following:

- Anchors, reporters, and commentators have the greatest impact on opinion change. Television newscasters have high credibility and trust with the general public. Their opinions are crucial in shaping mass opinion.

6.1

6.2

6.3

6.4

6.5

6.6

6.7

6.8

- Independent experts interviewed by the media have a substantial impact on opinion, but not as great as newscasters themselves.
- A popular president can also shift public opinion somewhat. Unpopular presidents do not have much success as opinion movers, however.
- Interest groups on the whole have a slightly negative effect on public opinion. By pressing particular issues to forcefully, without room for discourse or compromise, the larger public does not respond sympathetically or even turns against the protesting group. Such cases include war protesters, animal rights advocates, and other demonstrators and protesters, even peaceful ones.[30]

☐ Effects on Behavior

Many studies have focused on the effects of the media on behavior: studies of the effects of TV violence, studies of the effects of television on children, and studies of the effects of obscenity and pornography.[31] Although it is difficult to generalize from these studies, television appears more likely to reinforce behavioral tendencies than to change them. For example, televised violence may trigger violent behavior in children who are already predisposed to such behavior, but televised violence has little behavioral effect on average children.[32] Nevertheless, we know that television advertising sells products. And we know that political candidates spend millions to persuade audiences to go out and vote for them on Election Day. Both manufacturers and politicians create name recognition, employ product differentiation, try to associate with audiences, and use repetition to communicate their messages. These tactics are designed to affect our behavior both in the marketplace and in the election booth.

Political ads are more successful in motivating a candidate's supporters to go to the polls than they are in changing opponents into supporters. It is unlikely that voters who dislike a candidate will be persuaded by political advertising to change their votes. But many potential voters are undecided, and the support of many others is dubbed "soft." Going to the polls on Election Day requires effort—people have errands to do, they may be tired, it may be raining. Television advertising is more effective with marginal voters.

A Constitutional Note

Can the FCC Ban Profanity from the Airwaves?

When the Bill of Rights was passed by the nation's first Congress, the 1st Amendment's reference to freedom of the press could hardly have envisioned radio, television, or the Internet. When radio broadcasting began in the 1920s, there was a scarcity of broadcast frequencies. Stations fought over frequencies and even jammed each other's programming. The industry welcomed the Federal Communications Act of 1934, which created the Federal Communications Commission (FCC) to license stations for the exclusive use of radio frequencies. The law stated that the use of a frequency was a "public trust" and that the FCC should ensure that it was used in "the public interest." Although technology has vastly multiplied radio and television channels, the FCC has continued to fine broadcasters for indecency or profanity. The Supreme Court has continued to uphold the powers of the FCC.[a]

Questions

1. What do you think are the community standards that should be used for television and radio broadcasting?
2. What makes the Internet different from the broadcast airwaves when it comes to regulating content?

[a] Reno v. American Civil Liberties Union, 521 U.S. 471 (1997).

Review the Chapter

The Power of the Media

6.1 Identify functions and components of the media, p. 176

It is only through the media that the general public comes to know about political events, personalities, and issues. Newsmaking—deciding what is or is not "news"—is a major source of media power. Media coverage not only influences popular discussion but also forces public officials to respond.

Sources of Media Power

6.2 Explain the sources of the media's power, p. 180

Media power also derives from the media's ability to set the agenda for public decision making—to determine what citizens and public officials will regard as "crises," "problems," or "issues" to be resolved by government.

The Business of the Media

6.3 Describe the business of the media, p. 183

The business of the media is to sell mass audiences to advertisers in order to make a profit for the owners.

The Politics of the Media

6.4 Assess how the politics of the media are shaped by their economic interests, professional environment, and ideological leanings, p. 184

The politics of the media are shaped by their economic interests in attracting readers and viewers. This interest largely accounts for the sensational, and negative aspects of news reporting. The professional environment of newspeople encourages an activist, watchdog role. The politics of most newspeople are liberal and Democratic.

Mediated Elections

6.5 Analyze the role of the media in shaping campaigns and elections, p. 192

Political campaigning is largely a media activity. The media have replaced the parties as the principal linkage between candidates and voters. But the media tend to report the campaign as a horse race, at the expense of issue coverage, and to focus more on candidates' character than on their voting record.

Freedom Versus Fairness

6.6 Distinguish between freedom of the press and fairness of the press, p. 195

The 1st Amendment guarantee of freedom of the press protects media from government efforts to silence or censor them and allows the media to be "unfair" when they choose to be. The Federal Communications Commission exercises modest controls over the electronic media, since the right to exclusive use of broadcast frequencies is a public trust. Public officials are provided little protection by libel and slander laws. The Supreme Court's Sullivan rule allows even damaging falsehoods to be written and broadcast as long as newspeople themselves do not deliberately fabricate lies with "malicious intent" or "reckless disregard."

Politics and the Internet

6.7 Evaluate the effects of the new media on politics, p. 197

The development of the Internet has provided for interactive mass participation in politics, blogging, political Web sites, and new sources of fund-raising opportunities. The new media increased the interactive and egalitarian qualities of news consumption.

Media Effects: Shaping Political Life

6.8 Assess the effects that the media have on public opinion and political behavior, p. 206

Media effects on political life can be observed in (1) information and agenda setting, (2) values and opinions, and (3) behavior—in that order of influence. The media strongly influence what we know about politics and what we talk about. The media are less effective in changing existing opinions, values, and beliefs than they are at creating new ones. Nevertheless, the media can alter opinions, based on the credibility of news anchors and reporters. Political ads are more important in motivating supporters to go to the polls, and in swinging undecided or "soft" voters, than in changing the minds of committed voters.

Learn the Terms

mass media, p. 176
narrowcasting, p. 180
fourth estate, p. 180
newsmaking, p. 181
agenda setting, p. 181
socialization, p. 182
soft news, p. 184
muckraking, p. 187
"feeding frenzy", p. 187
pundits, p. 189
name recognition, p. 193
media events, p. 194
horse-race coverage, p. 194
sound bite, p. 195
prior restraint, p. 195
equal-time rule, p. 196
libel, p. 196
slander, p. 196
Sullivan rule, p. 197
new media, p. 197
cyberculture, p. 197
cyberpolitics, p. 198
social media applications, p. 200
money bombs, p. 201
information overload, p. 206
selective perception, p. 206
television malaise, p. 207

Test Yourself

6.1 Identify functions and components of the media

The most common source for news in the United States is

a. the Internet
b. word of mouth
c. the national evening news
d. newspapers and magazines
e. local TV news

6.2 Explain the sources of the media's power.

Of the following potential characteristics of the media, which are historically true?

I. The media is a natural adversary of government
II. the content of the media always mirrors reality
III. media news outlets do not try to persuade, but merely presents facts
IV. the national government has historically controlled and moderated media content

a. Only I
b. Only I, II, and III
c. Only II, III, and IV
d. Only III
e. Only II and III

6.3 Describe the business of the media

The primary motivating force behind the media's endeavors is to

a. present the truth to its audiences
b. persuade people to buy advertised products
c. provide a public service
d. provide amusement to the masses
e. manipulate the political environment

6.4 Assess how the politics of the media are shaped by their economic interests, professional environment, and ideological leanings

Which of the following statements is true?

a. Talk radio has a liberal bias
b. Hollywood has a libertarian bias
c. The media is perceived as having a liberal bias
d. Fox News is perceived as having a liberal bias
e. Hollywood creates the perception that talk radio has a liberal bias

6.5 Analyze the role of the media in shaping campaigns and elections

The most common link between the candidates for major offices (president, governor, congressman or senator), and the voters is

a. the political party
b. the Internet and U.S. Postal Service
c. neighbors
d. personal contact
e. television

6.6 Distinguish between freedom of the press and fairness of the press.

The "Sullivan rule"

a. held that speech that was disloyal was not covered by the 1st Amendment
b. expanded the right of the press to publish materials about public officials
c. limited the right of the press to make damaging statements
d. upheld the right of the government to suppress obscene publications
e. Granted exclusive copyright on 'The Pentagon Papers' to New York Times.

6.7 Evaluate the effects of the new media on politics

Among the many effects of the New Media, the greatest is that they have

a. not really impacted political fund-raising
b. often been able to persuade political opponents to become political supporters
c. allowed unrestricted freedom of political expression
d. stopped the spread of untruthful bloggers
e. increased the sales of hard-copy news sources

6.8 Assess the effects that the media have on public opinion and political behavior

The media is effective in

a. the transmission of political values
b. providing political information
c. creating political values
d. counteracting political socialization by families
e. stimulating political behavior

Explore Further

SUGGESTED READINGS

Alterman, Eric. *What Liberal Media?* New York: Simon & Schuster, 2003. A contrarian argument that the media does *not* have a liberal bias but rather bends over backward to include conservative views.

Bennett, Lance W. *News: The Politics of Illusion*. New York: Longman, 2007. How presidents, Congress members, interest groups, and political activists try to get their messages into the news.

Fallows, James. *Breaking the News: How the Media Undermine American Democracy*. New York: Pantheon, 1996. An argument that today's arrogant, cynical, and scandal-minded news reporting is turning readers and viewers away and undermining support for democracy.

Gainous, Jason, and Kevin M. Wagner. *Tweeting to Power: The Social Media Revolution in American Politics*. New York: Oxford University Press, 2014. Examines the differing social media strategies of political candidates and lawmakers, and whether social media can disrupt elite-driven politics.

Goldberg, Bernard. *Bias: A CBS Insider Exposes How the Media Distort the News*. New York: Perennial, 2003. The title says it all.

Graber, Doris A. *Mass Media and American Politics*. 8th ed. Washington, D.C.: CQ Press, 2009. A wide-ranging description of media effects on campaigns, parties, and elections as well as on social values and public policies.

Patterson, Thomas E. *Out of Order*. New York: Random House, 1994. The antipolitical bias of the media poisons national election campaigns; policy questions are ignored in favor of the personal characteristics of candidates, their campaign strategies, and their standing in the horse race.

Prindle, David F. *Risky Business*. Boulder, Colo.: Westview Press, 1993. An examination of the politics of Hollywood, including its liberalism, activism, self-indulgence, and celebrity egotism.

Sabato, Larry J. *Feeding Frenzy: How Attack Journalism Has Transformed American Politics*. New York: Free Press, 1991. A strong argument that the media prefer to "employ titillation rather than scrutiny" and as a result produce "trivialization rather than enlightenment."

West, Darrell M. *Air Wars: Television Advertising in Election Campaigns*. 5th ed. Washington, D.C.: CQ Press, 2009. The evolution of campaign advertising from 1952 to 2008 and how voters are influenced by television ads.

SUGGESTED WEB SITES

Accuracy in Media **www.aim.org**
A self-described watchdog organization critical of liberal bias in the media.

American Journalism Review www.ajr.org
Features articles on current topics in print and television reporting, together with links to newspapers, television networks and stations, radio stations, and media companies.

The Annenberg Public Policy Center www.appcpenn.org
The Annenberg Center of the University of Pennsylvania conducts research on political use of the media, including the Internet.

The Center for Media and Public Affairs www.cmpa.com
Studies of news and entertainment media, including election coverage.

The Drudge Report www.drudgereport.com
Controversial site that links to stories not always carried by mainstream media. Links to all major media outlets.

Federal Communication Commission www.fcc.gov
Announcements and consumer information from the FCC.

The Monkey Cage http://www.washingtonpost.com/blogs/monkey-cage/Professional political scientists blog on contemporary politics.

National Association of Broadcasters www.nab.org
News and views of the media industry from their trade association.

Network Television www.cbsnews.com www.abcnews.com www.cnn.com www.msnbc.com www.foxnews.com
All major networks now maintain news sites on the Web.

Newspaper Web Sites www.usatoday.com www.nytimes.com www.washingtonpost.com www.wallstreetjournal.com
Virtually all major daily newspapers have Web sites that summarize each day's stories. For national news, the most frequently consulted sites are *USA Today, Wall Street Journal, New York Times, Washington Post.*

People for the American Way www.pfaw.org
Web site founded by Hollywood "liberals" to combat "right-wing" influence.

Pew Research Center for People & the Press www.people-press.org
Information and opinion polls on the media.

Politico www.politico.com
Favorite blog of political junkies, with links to multiple news articles and political commentaries.

7 Political Parties

Organizing Politics

They call him "The Natural." But, before Bill Clinton was the most popular Democratic politician in living memory, or the long-term governor he was just a young activist with a dream of public service. That career path presented both opportunities and challenges that allowed Clinton to touch many elements of the Democratic Party.

Clinton had grown up outside of Hot Springs, Arkansas, and attended Georgetown University in Washington, DC, on scholarship. He interned and clerked for Senator William Fulbright, and started to build broader connections in Democratic party circles.

Clinton attended Oxford on a Rhodes Scholarship, and was politically active against the Vietnam War. He also used political connections through Fulbright to avoid the draft by enrolling in the ROTC program at University of Arkansas. Clinton would later receive a 'high' draft number and didn't use his ROTC slot.

As a law student at Yale, Clinton and his girlfriend (and later wife) Hillary Rodham became involved in the campaign of George McGovern, an anti-war senator who would oppose Richard Nixon for president. They would move to Texas and serve as coordinators for McGovern (they lost Texas, but made friends with future filmmaker Steven Spielberg).

Clinton's decade of youthful journeying ended where he started, in Arkansas. He ran for Congress in 1974 in the 3rd congressional district and narrowly missed upsetting Republican John Paul Hammerschmidt. Two years later, he was elected attorney general. And then, in 1978, he was the Democratic nominee for governor. CBS's "60 minutes" observed in their narration over a story on Clinton that October, "This is Bill Clinton, Arkansas's attorney general. If everything goes right next month, he'll be elected governor. And the Democrats can't wait for him to grow up and run for president—he just 31 years old."

CONVENTIONS PRODUCE MEMORABLE MOMENTS The 2012 Democratic National Convention featured one of the finest political speeches ever, by former president Bill Clinton. Clinton's old-school speech often departed from the original script, but it brought Democratic partisans to their feet in response to "The Natural," as Clinton was nicknamed by political writer Joe Klein.

The Power of Organization

7.1 Show how the relationship between organization and political power explains political parties and interest groups.

political organizations
Parties and interest groups that function as intermediaries between individuals and government.

political parties
Organizations that seek to achieve power by winning public office.

party identification
Self-described identification with a political party, usually in response to the question, "Generally speaking, how would you identify yourself: as a Republican, Democrat, Independent, or something else?"

What is true of war is true of politics: in the struggle for power, organization grants advantage. Italian political scientist Gaetano Mosca put it succinctly: "A hundred men acting uniformly in concert, with a common understanding, will triumph over a thousand men who are not in accord and can therefore be dealt with one by one."[1] Thus politics centers on organization—on organizing people to win office and to influence public policy.

Political organizations—parties and interest groups—function as mediating institutions between the mass of individuals and the institutional structure of government. They organize individuals to give them power in selecting government officials—who governs—and in determining public policy—for what ends. Political scientist V. O. Key observed that political parties in democracies exist in three contexts: the party in the electorate, the party as organization, and the party in government. In the United States, **political parties** as organizations are more concerned with organizing the electorate to win public office than with influencing policy, whereas *interest groups* are more directly concerned with public policy and involve themselves with elections only to advance their policy interests (see Figure 7.1). In other words, parties and interest groups have developed an informal division of functions, with parties focusing on personnel and interest groups focusing on policy. Yet both organize individuals for more effective political action.

Party Voters

7.2 Assess the trends regarding party identification and loyalty of voters.

For the last eight decades, the Democratic Party has been traditionally able to claim to be the majority party among voters in the United States (see Figure 7.2). In opinion polls, those who "identify" with the Democratic Party generally outnumber those who "identify" with the Republican Party. (**Party identification** is determined by response to the question, "Generally speaking, how would you identify yourself: as a Republican, Democrat, Independent, or something else?") But the Democratic Party advantage among the voters has eroded over time, partly as a result of an ongoing increase in the number of people who call themselves Independents. Since the early 1990s, more voters have identified as Democratic than as Republican, but election outcomes have not been so decisively Democratic.

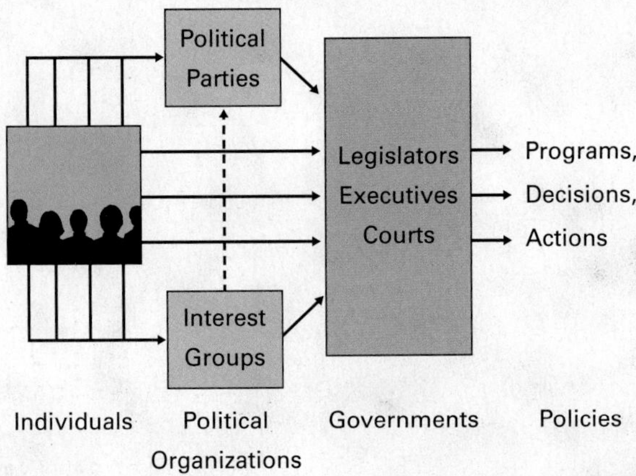

FIGURE 7.1 POLITICAL DEMOCRACY: ORGANIZATIONS AS INTERMEDIARIES

All political organizations function as intermediaries between individuals and government. Parties are concerned primarily with winning elected office; interest groups are concerned with influencing policy.

THE DONKEY AND THE ELEPHANT

The popular nineteenth-century cartoonist Thomas Nast is generally credited with giving the Democratic and Republican parties their current symbols: the donkey and the elephant. In *Harper's Weekly*'s 1870s cartoons, Nast critically portrayed the Democratic Party as a stubborn mule "without pride of ancestry nor hope of posterity." During this period of Republican Party dominance, Nast portrayed the Republican Party as an elephant, the biggest beast in the political jungle. Now both party symbols are used with pride.

☐ Realignment

Voting and party identification are relatively stable, but there are minor changes in voter preferences, often from election to election. There are also durable and lasting changes in voter preferences that help define political eras and the political status quo of those eras. Sudden, large, durable shifts in the electoral balance and the composition of the coalitions that support the major parties are called electoral **realignments**. Usually, realignments are associated with a sudden jolt or shock to the political system, usually surrounding an easy-to-understand issue like race relations or the economy. The existing parties and their issue positions are unable to accommodate the preferences of the groups in their coalition, and voters realign their party preferences. Most scholars agree that such party realignments occurred in the presidential elections of 1824 (Jackson, Democrats), 1860 (Lincoln, Republicans), 1896 (Bryan, Democrats), and 1932 (Roosevelt, Democrats). This

realignment
Long-term shift in social-group support for various political parties that creates new coalitions in each party.

FIGURE 7.2 PARTY IDENTIFICATION IN THE ELECTORATE

For many years, the Democratic Party enjoyed a substantial lead in party identification among voters. This Democratic lead eroded in the late 1960s as more people began to identify themselves as Independents.

SOURCE: Data from *National Election Studies*, University of Michigan, updated from Gallup Polls.

historical sequence gave rise to a theory that realigning elections occur every 36 years. As we will see, subsequent events frustrated the precision of this theory.

According to this theory, the election of 1968 should have been a realigning one. It is true that Richard Nixon's 1968 victory marked the beginning of a 24-year Republican era in presidential election victories that was broken only by Jimmy Carter in 1976. But there was relatively little shifting of the party loyalties of major social groups, and the Democratic Party remained the dominant party in the electorate and in Congress. Democratic Party loyalty eroded the next 30 years, but this erosion was not a classic party realignment.[2]

The Democratic Party still receives *disproportionate* support from Catholics, Jews, African Americans, less-educated and lower-income groups, blue-collar workers, union members, and big-city residents. The Republican Party still receives *disproportionate* support from Protestants, whites, more-educated and higher-income groups, white-collar workers, nonunion workers, and suburban and small-town dwellers. Disproportionate support does not mean these groups *always* give a majority of their votes to the indicated party, but only that they give that party a larger percentage of their votes than the party receives from the general electorate. This pattern of social-group voting and party identification has remained relatively stable over the years, even though the GOP has made some gains among many of the traditionally Democratic groups (see Figure 7.3).

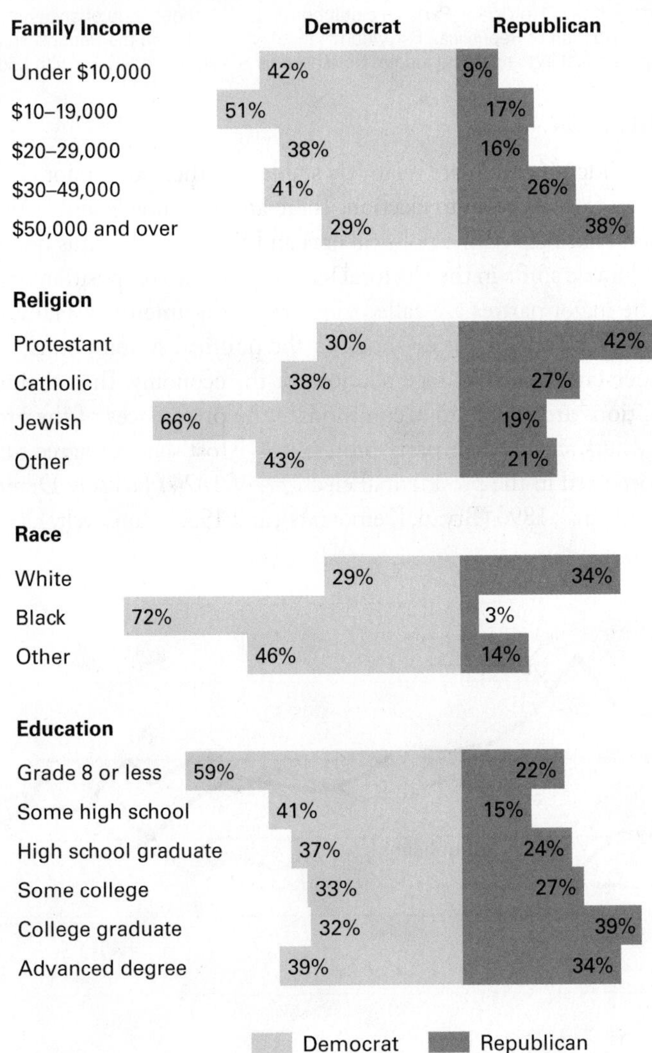

FIGURE 7.3 WHO BACKS WHOM?: SOCIAL-GROUP SUPPORT FOR THE DEMOCRATIC AND REPUBLICAN PARTIES

The Democratic Party draws disproportionate support from low-income, less-educated, Catholic, Jewish, and African American voters. The Republican Party relies more heavily on support from high-income, college-educated, white Protestant voters.

NOTE: Independents not shown.

SOURCE: Data from the 2010 National Election Studies, University of Michigan. Compiled by Professor Terri Towner, Oakland University.

The only major *shift* in social-group support has occurred among southern whites and white Protestant evangelical Christians. These groups shifted from heavily Democratic in party identification to a substantial Republican preference and have become the most loyal block of Republican voters in the United States.

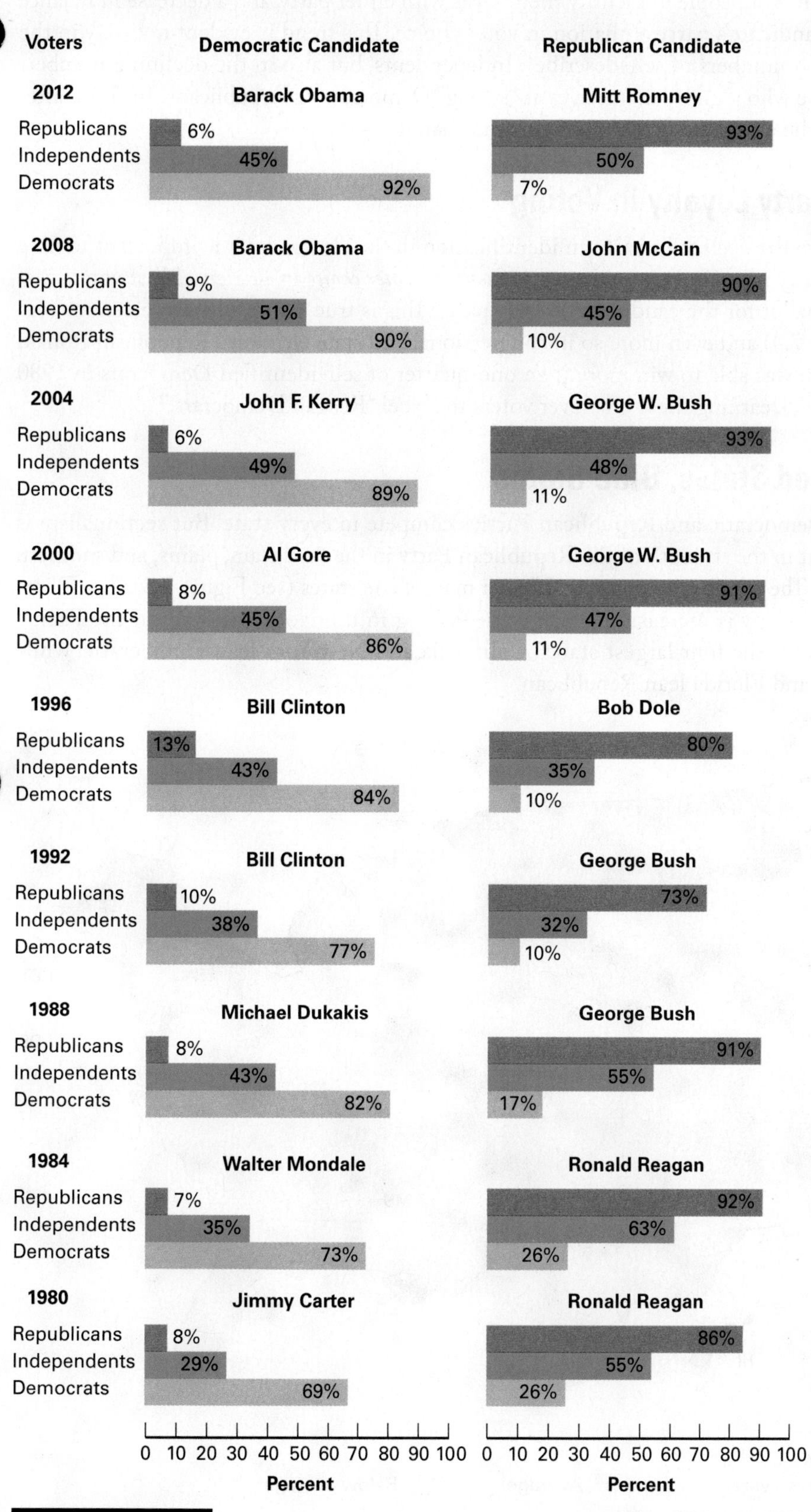

FIGURE 7.4 WHO VOTED HOW?: REPUBLICAN, DEMOCRATIC, AND INDEPENDENT VOTERS IN PRESIDENTIAL ELECTIONS

As the percentages here indicate, in recent years, registered Democrats have been more likely to "cross over" and vote for a Republican candidate for president than registered Republicans have been to vote for the Democratic presidential candidate.

SOURCE: *New York Times.*

dealignment
Declining attractiveness of the parties to the voters, a reluctance to identify strongly with a party, and a decrease in reliance on party affiliation in voter choice.

☐ Dealignment

What happened to party identifiers after the 1960s is dealignment. **Dealignment** describes the decline in attractiveness of the political parties to the voters, the growing reluctance of people to identify themselves with either party, and a decrease in reliance on a candidate's party affiliation in voter choice. This trend is evident not only in the growing numbers of self-described Independents, but also in the declining numbers of those who identify themselves as "strong" Democrats or Republicans. In short, after 1968, the electorate became less partisan than it once was.

☐ Party Loyalty in Voting

Despite the decline in partisan identification in the electorate, it is important to note that *party identification is a strong influence in voter choice in elections.* Most voters cast their ballot for the candidate of their party. This is true in presidential elections (see Figure 7.4) and even more so in congressional and state elections. Republican Ronald Reagan was able to win more than one-quarter of self-identified Democrats in 1980 and 1984, earning these crossover voters the label "Reagan Democrats."[3]

☐ Red States, Blue States

The Democratic and Republican Parties compete in every state. But sectionalism is evident in the strength of the Republican Party in the mountain, plains, and southern states. The result is a large red "L" on a map of the states (see Figure 7.5). The Democratic Party is increasingly bicoastal—strong in the Northeast and on the Pacific Coast. Of the four largest states, California and New York lean Democratic, while Texas and Florida lean Republican.

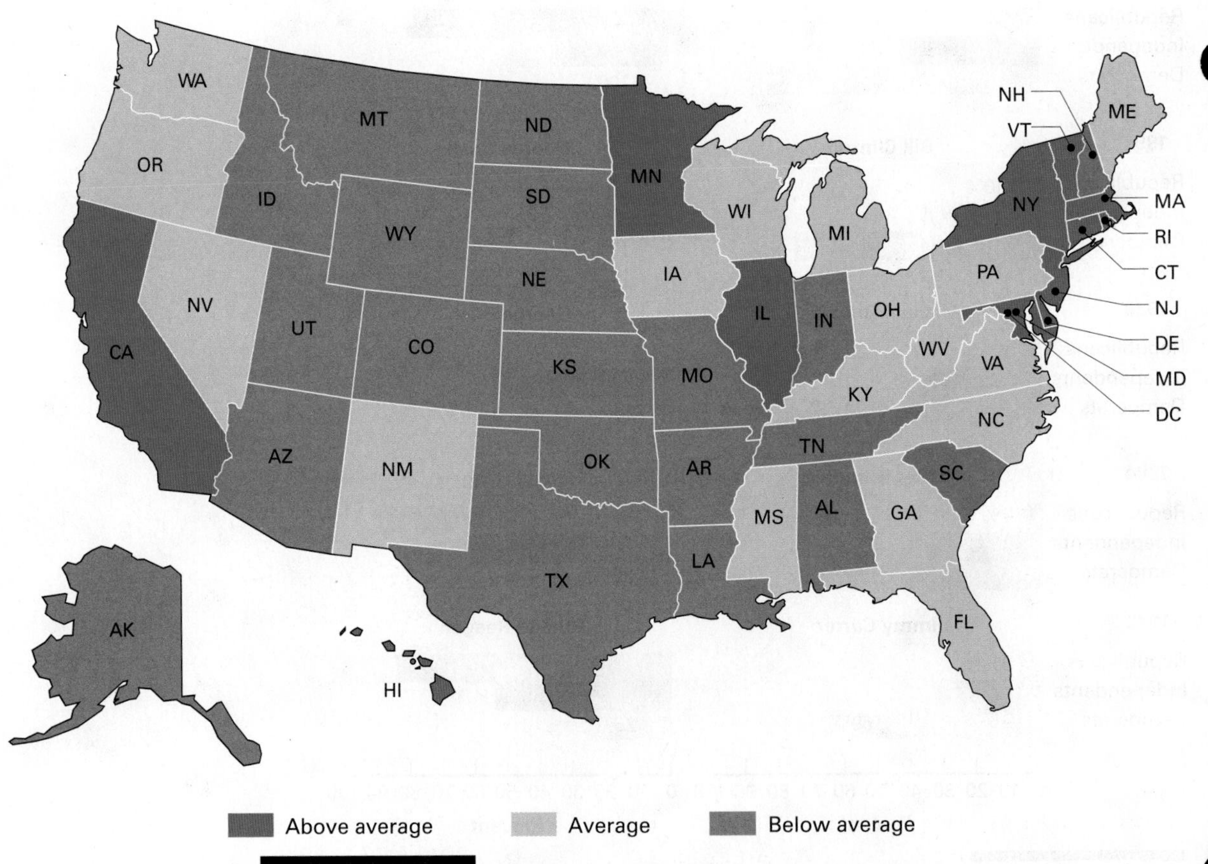

FIGURE 7.5 RED STATES, BLUE STATES

States with stronger than average Democratic identifiers are in blue, states with stronger than average Republican identifiers are in red, and states with average Republican and Democratic identifiers are in purple. The Democratic Party is strongest in the Northeast and on the West Coast. The GOP fares better in the southern and midwestern states.

SOURCE: Gallup.com, August 11, 2011; n = 170,000 likely voters surveyed between January and June 2011.

American Parties: A Historical Perspective

7.3 Trace changes in political parties over the course of American history.

Parties are *not* mentioned in the Constitution. Indeed, the nation's Founders regarded both parties and interest groups as "factions," citizens united by "some common impulse of passion, or of interest, adverse to the rights of other citizens, or to the permanent and aggregate interests of the community." The Founders viewed factions as "mischievous" and "dangerous."[4] Yet the emergence of parties was inevitable as people sought to organize themselves to exercise power over who governs (see Figure 7.6).

Political scientists and historians usually divide American political history into a series of eras or epochs, usually called "party systems." These eras are defined by an initial set of realigning elections that define the issues of debate and create lasting divisions of political identity in the electorate. Many of these issues—vested in race, economics, and culture—have remarkable durability in the American political debate. It is generally agreed that the 1824–28 election, which created the modern two-party system, was the first realigning era; the next era started in the late 1850s when the Republican Party emerged as the new, dominant major party in the north and the inability of politics to accommodate disputes led to the Civil War; the third great realignment was in the Gilded Age of the 1890s that resulted from economic distress and depression in the early part of the decade; the Great Depression coincided with the emergence of the New Deal Era (1928–36) and resulted in another significant and durable realignment of American party politics. Since the 1930s, several events—the 1960s, 1980, and 1990s—have been called "realigning" by pundits, politicians, and scholars.

Federalists
Those who supported the U.S. Constitution during the ratification process and who later formed a political party in support of John Adams's presidential candidacy.

Anti-Federalists
Those who opposed the ratification of the U.S. Constitution and the creation of a strong national government.

The Emergent Party System: Federalists and Democratic-Republicans

In his Farewell Address, George Washington warned the nation about political parties: "Let me . . . warn you in the most solemn manner against the baneful effects of the spirit of party generally."[5] As president, Washington stood above the factions that were coalescing around his secretary of the treasury, Alexander Hamilton, and around his former secretary of state, Thomas Jefferson. Jefferson had resigned from Washington's cabinet in 1793 to protest the fiscal policies of Hamilton, notably his creation of a national bank and repayment of the states' Revolutionary War debts with federal funds. Washington had endorsed Hamilton's policies, but so great was the first president's prestige that Jefferson and his followers directed their fire not against Washington but against Hamilton, John Adams, and their supporters, who called themselves **Federalists** after their leaders' outspoken defense of the Constitution during the ratification process. By the 1790s, Jefferson and Madison, together with many **Anti-Federalists** who had initially opposed the ratification of the Constitution, began calling themselves *Republicans* or *Democratic-Republicans*, terms that had become popular after the French Revolution in 1789.

Adams narrowly defeated Jefferson in the presidential election of 1796. This election was an important milestone in the development of the parties and the presidential election system. For the first time, two candidates campaigned as members of opposing parties, and candidates for presidential elector in each state pledged themselves as "Adams's men" or "Jefferson's men." By committing themselves in advance of the actual presidential vote, these pledged electors enabled voters in each state to determine the outcome of the presidential election.

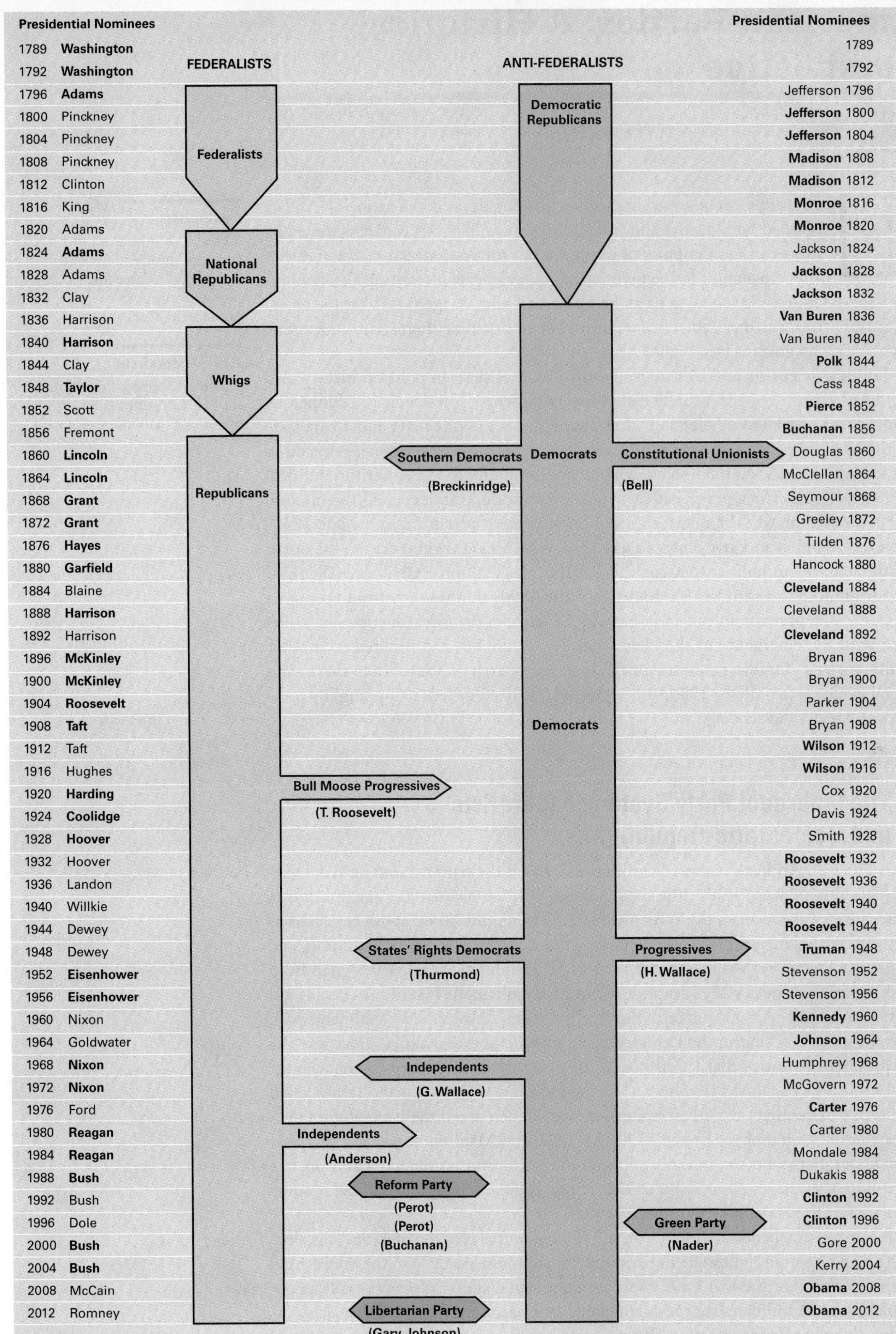
Presidential Nominees
1789 Washington
1792 Washington
1796 Adams
1800 Pinckney
1804 Pinckney
1808 Pinckney
1812 Clinton
1816 King
1820 Adams
1824 Adams
1828 Adams
1832 Clay
1836 Harrison
1840 Harrison
1844 Clay
1848 Taylor
1852 Scott
1856 Fremont
1860 Lincoln
1864 Lincoln
1868 Grant
1872 Grant
1876 Hayes
1880 Garfield
1884 Blaine
1888 Harrison
1892 Harrison
1896 McKinley
1900 McKinley
1904 Roosevelt
1908 Taft
1912 Taft
1916 Hughes
1920 Harding
1924 Coolidge
1928 Hoover
1932 Hoover
1936 Landon
1940 Willkie
1944 Dewey
1948 Dewey
1952 Eisenhower
1956 Eisenhower
1960 Nixon
1964 Goldwater
1968 Nixon
1972 Nixon
1976 Ford
1980 Reagan
1984 Reagan
1988 Bush
1992 Bush
1996 Dole
2000 Bush
2004 Bush
2008 McCain
2012 Romney
FEDERALISTS
Federalists
National Republicans
Whigs
Republicans
Bull Moose Progressives
(T. Roosevelt)
ANTI-FEDERALISTS
Democratic Republicans
Southern Democrats
(Breckinridge)
Democrats
Constitutional Unionists
(Bell)
Democrats
States' Rights Democrats
(Thurmond)
Progressives
(H. Wallace)
Independents
(G. Wallace)
Independents
(Anderson)
Reform Party
(Perot)
(Perot)
(Buchanan)
Green Party
(Nader)
Libertarian Party
(Gary Johnson)
Presidential Nominees
1789
1792
Jefferson 1796
Jefferson 1800
Jefferson 1804
Madison 1808
Madison 1812
Monroe 1816
Monroe 1820
Jackson 1824
Jackson 1828
Jackson 1832
Van Buren 1836
Van Buren 1840
Polk 1844
Cass 1848
Pierce 1852
Buchanan 1856
Douglas 1860
McClellan 1864
Seymour 1868
Greeley 1872
Tilden 1876
Hancock 1880
Cleveland 1884
Cleveland 1888
Cleveland 1892
Bryan 1896
Bryan 1900
Parker 1904
Bryan 1908
Wilson 1912
Wilson 1916
Cox 1920
Davis 1924
Smith 1928
Roosevelt 1932
Roosevelt 1936
Roosevelt 1940
Roosevelt 1944
Truman 1948
Stevenson 1952
Stevenson 1956
Kennedy 1960
Johnson 1964
Humphrey 1968
McGovern 1972
Carter 1976
Carter 1980
Mondale 1984
Dukakis 1988
Clinton 1992
Clinton 1996
Gore 2000
Kerry 2004
Obama 2008
Obama 2012

FIGURE 7.6 CHANGE AND CONTINUITY: THE AMERICAN PARTY SYSTEM, 1789–2012

Jefferson's Democratic-Republicans

Party activity intensified in anticipation of the election of 1800. Jefferson's Democratic-Republican Party first saw the importance of organizing voters, circulating literature, and rallying the masses to their causes. Many Federalists viewed this early party activity with disdain. The Federalists even tried to outlaw public criticism of the federal government by means of the Alien and Sedition Acts of 1798, which among other things made it a crime to publish false or malicious writings against the (Federalist) Congress or president or to "stir up hatred" against them. These acts directly challenged the articulated 1st Amendment guarantees of freedom of speech and the press. The Federalists went down to electoral defeat in 1800. Democratic-Republican electors won a **majority** (more than half the votes cast) in the Electoral College and swept to power in both houses of Congress (see *A Constitutional Note*: Political Parties and the Constitution). The election of 1800 was a landmark in American democracy—the first time that control of government passed peacefully from one party to another on the basis of an election outcome.

Jefferson's Democratic-Republican Party—later to be called the Democrats—was so successful that the Federalist Party never regained the presidency or control of Congress. The Federalists tended to represent merchants, manufacturers, and shippers who were concentrated in New York and New England. The Democratic-Republicans tended to represent agrarian interests, from large plantation owners to small farmers. In the mostly agrarian America of the early 1800s, the Democratic-Republican Party prevailed.[6] Jefferson easily won reelection in 1804, and his allies, James Madison and James Monroe, overwhelmed their Federalist opponents in subsequent presidential elections. Federalist opposition to the War of 1812 and threats of secession by some Federalists condemned the party to electoral oblivion. By 1820, the Federalist Party had ceased to exist; it seemed as if the new nation had ended party politics.

majority
Election by more than 50 percent of all votes cast in the contest.

plurality
Election by at least one vote more than any other candidate in the race.

Democratic Party
One of the main parties in American politics; it traces its origins to Thomas Jefferson's Democratic-Republican Party and acquired its current name under Andrew Jackson in 1828.

Whig Party
Formed in 1836 to oppose Andrew Jackson's policies; it elected presidents Harrison in 1840 and Tyler in 1848 but soon disintegrated over the issue of slavery.

The System of '24: Jacksonian Democrats and Whigs

With the demise of the Federalists, presidential candidates were largely nominated by state or regional caucuses, and in 1824 four candidates—William Crawford (Ga.) from the South, John Quincy Adams (Mass.) from New England, and Henry Clay (Ky.) and Andrew Jackson (Tenn.) from the "west"—vied for the presidency and splintered the party. Andrew Jackson won a **plurality** (at least one more vote than anyone else in the race) but not a majority of the popular and Electoral College vote, but he then lost to John Quincy Adams in a close decision by the factionalized House of Representatives led by outgoing speaker Clay. Jackson led his supporters to found a new party, the **Democratic Party**, to organize popular support for his 1828 presidential bid, which succeeded in ousting Adams.

Jacksonian ideas both *democratized* and *nationalized* the party system. Under Jackson, the Democratic Party began to mobilize voters on behalf of the party and its candidates. It pressed the states to lower or eliminate property qualifications for voting in order to recruit new Democratic Party voters. The electorate expanded from 365,000 voters in 1824 to well over a million in 1828 and over 2 million in 1840. The Democratic Party also pressed the states to choose presidential electors by popular vote rather than by state legislatures. Thus Jackson and his Democratic successor, Martin Van Buren, ran truly national campaigns directed at the voters in every state.

At the same time, Jackson's opponents formed the **Whig Party**, who took their name from American patriots of the Revolutions and also the English opposition party of the era. Like the English Whigs, who opposed the power of the king, the American Whigs charged "King Andrew" with usurping the powers of Congress and the people. The Whigs quickly adopted the Democrats' tactics of national campaigning and popular organizing—though the strength of the Whigs resided less in their party organization than in their network of strong, supportive newspapers. The Whigs twice gained the presidency and on two occasions each won control of the House and Senate; however, they never coalesced into a durable national majority party, in part because of internal tensions over the slavery issue.

7.1
7.2
7.3
7.4
7.5
7.6
7.7
7.8

Republican Party
One of the two main parties in American politics, it traces its origins to the antislavery and nationalist forces that united in the 1850s and nominated Abraham Lincoln for president in 1860.

battlefield sectionalism
The historic partisan division of the Democratic South and the Republican North arising from the Civil War.

The System of '60: Battlefield Sectionalism and Republican Dominance

Whigs and Democrats continued to share national power until the slavery conflict ignited the Civil War and destroyed the old party system. The Republican Party had formed in 1854 to oppose the spread of slavery to the western territories. By the election of 1860, the slavery issue so divided the nation that four sectional parties offered presidential candidates: Lincoln, the Republican; Stephen A. Douglas, the northern Democrat; John C. Breckinridge, the southern Democrat; and John Bell, the Constitutional Union Party candidate. No party came close to winning a majority of the popular vote, but Lincoln won in the Electoral College. (Had all of the popular votes of Lincoln's opponents been combined, he still would have carried a solid Electoral College majority.)

The new party system that emerged from the Civil War featured a victorious **Republican Party** that generally represented the northern industrial economy, and a struggling Democratic Party that generally represented a southern agricultural economy. The Democratic Party's ties to secession and antiwar groups in many northern and border South states doomed their presidential prospects from 1864 onward. Politics continued the divisions of the Civil War in what was called **battlefield sectionalism**—Democrats dominated politics in the Southern states, the "border" states like Kentucky, West Virginia, and Missouri, while Republicans were the first party in the west of the country. Democrats were only a political threat in the North in the largest urban centers. The Republican Party won every presidential election from 1860 to 1912 except for two victories by Democratic reformer and New York governor Grover Cleveland.

The System of '96: Gilded Age Realignment

A stock market crash and depression (the Panic of '93) had crippled the incumbent pro-business wing of the Democratic Party. Still, the Democratic Party offered a serious challenge in the election of 1896, while Republicans rallied to regain power in perhaps the most bitter presidential battle in history. The result of this "Gilded Age" realignment was a durable and lasting shift in the party affiliations of the nation's voters. The Democratic Party nominated William Jennings Bryan, a talented orator and a religious fundamentalist. Bryan sought to rally the nation's white "have-nots" to the Democratic Party banner, particularly the debt-ridden farmers of the South and West. Bryan's plan was to stimulate inflation (and thus enable debtors to pay their debts with "cheaper," less valuable dollars) through using plentiful, western-mined "free silver," rather than gold, as the monetary standard. Republicans sought to convince the nation that high tariffs, protection for manufacturers, and a solid monetary standard would lead to prosperity for industrial workers as well as the new tycoons. The Republican campaign, directed by Marcus Alonzo Hanna, attorney for John D. Rockefeller's Standard Oil Company, spent an unprecedented $16 million (current dollar equivalent: between $400 million and $3.5 billion) to elect Republican William McKinley. The battle produced one of the largest voter turnouts in history. The Republican Party solidified the loyalty of industrial workers, small-business owners, bankers, large manufacturers, and "congregationalist" Christians as well as black voters who respected "the party of Lincoln" and despised the segregationist practices of the southern Democratic Party. The "Bourbon" conservative pro-business wing of the Democratic party was effectively purged (except in the South). Democrats were left with a political base of southern whites, some plains states farmers, urban immigrants, and "liturgical" Christians who opposed efforts by government to regulate morality.

Republican Split, Democratic Win

Republicans won every presidential election from 1896 to 1928 except two, with landslide wins by McKinley (1896 and 1900), Theodore Roosevelt (1904), and William Howard Taft (1908). So great was the Republican Party's dominance in national elections that only a split among Republicans enabled the Democrats to capture the presidency. In 1912, Roosevelt (who became president following McKinley's assassination but did not run in 1908) sought to recapture the presidency from his former protégé, Republican William Howard Taft. At the **GOP** ("Grand Old Party," as the Republicans began labeling themselves) convention, party regulars rejected the unpredictable Roosevelt (TR) in favor of Taft, even though Roosevelt had won the few primary elections that had recently been initiated. TR launched a third, progressive party, the "Bull Moose," which actually outpolled the Republican Party in the 1912 election—the only time a third party has surpassed one of the two major parties in U.S. history. But the result was a victory for the Democratic candidate, former Princeton political science professor Woodrow Wilson. Following Wilson's two terms, Republicans reasserted their political dominance with strong victories by Warren G. Harding, Calvin Coolidge, and Herbert Hoover.

GOP
"Grand Old Party"—a popular label for the Republican Party.

New Deal
Policies of President Franklin D. Roosevelt during the Depression of the 1930s that helped form a Democratic Party coalition of urban working-class, ethnic, Catholic, Jewish, poor, and southern voters.

The System of '32: The New Deal Democratic Party

Economic crisis doomed the Democrats in 1896; it did the same to the Republicans in 1932. The promise of prosperity that empowered the Republican Party to hold its membership together faded in the light of the Great Depression. The U.S. stock market crashed in 1929; within four years, one-quarter of the labor force was unemployed. Having lost confidence in the nation's business and political leadership, in 1932, voters turned out incumbent Republican President Herbert Hoover in favor of Democrat Franklin D. Roosevelt, who promised the country a **New Deal**.

More than just bringing the Democrats to the White House, the Great Depression marked another party realignment. This time, traditionally Republican voting groups changed their affiliation and enabled the Democratic Party to dominate national politics for a generation. This realignment actually began in 1928, when Democratic presidential

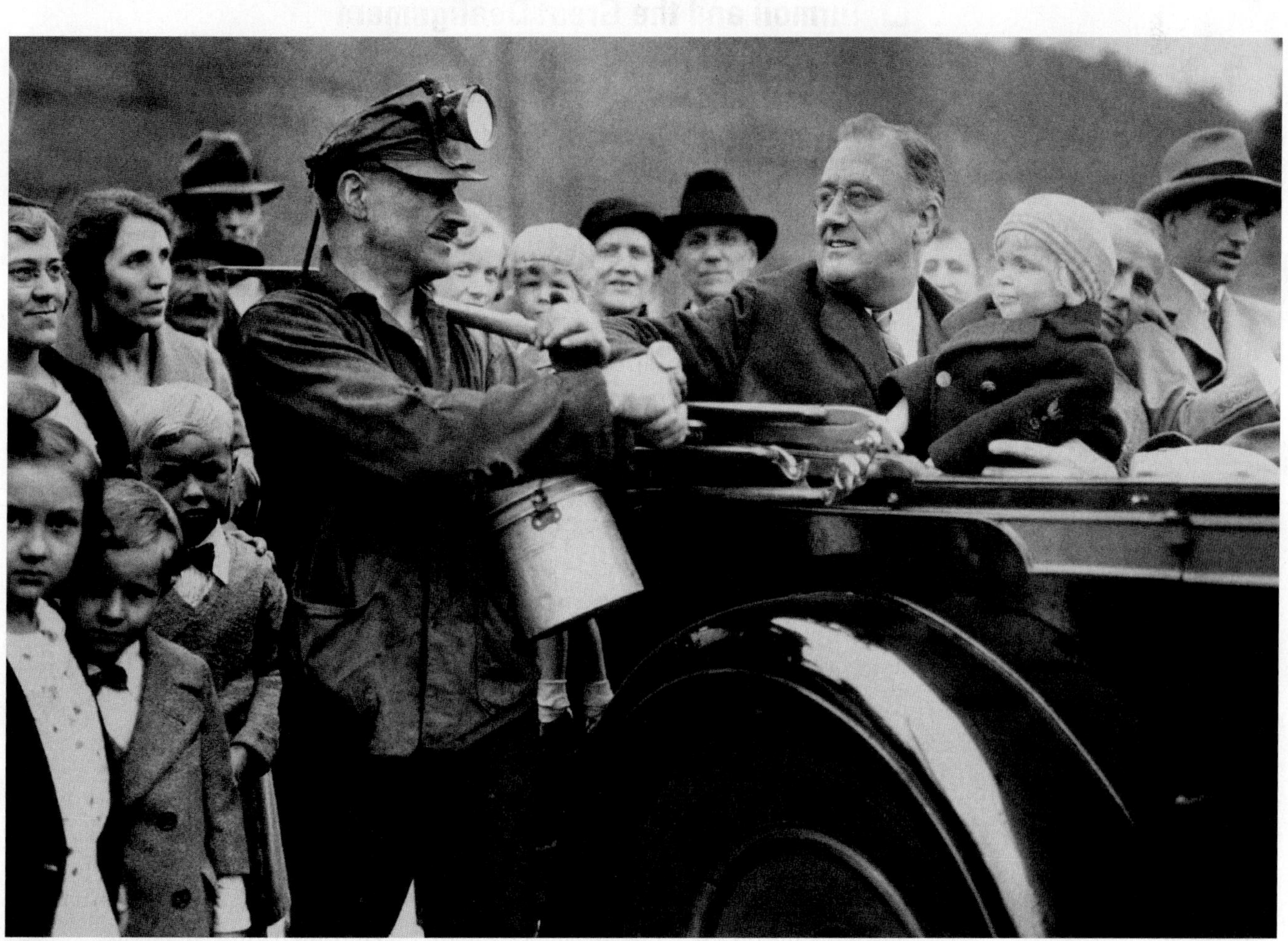

INSPIRING CONFIDENCE
Franklin Roosevelt campaigning among coal miners in West Virginia during the presidential election campaign of 1932. Roosevelt's optimism and "can-do" attitude in the face of the Great Depression helped cement the New Deal Democratic coalition that won him the presidency.

7.1

7.2

7.3

7.4

7.5

7.6

7.7

7.8

Fair Deal
Policies of President Harry Truman that extended Roosevelt's New Deal and maintained the Democratic Party's voter coalition.

Great Society
Policies of President Lyndon Johnson that promised to solve the nation's social and economic problems through government intervention.

candidate Al Smith, a Catholic, won many northern, urban, ethnic voters away from the Republican Party. By 1932, a majority New Deal Democratic coalition had been formed in American politics. It consisted of working classes and union members, especially in large cities; white ethnic groups who had previously aligned themselves with Republican machines; Catholics and Jews; African Americans, who ended their historic affiliation with the party of Lincoln to pursue new economic and social goals; poor people, who associated the New Deal with expanded welfare and Social Security programs; and southern whites, who had provided the most loyal block of Democratic voters since the Civil War, and who saw the potential of national wealth transfers into the South.

To be sure, this majority coalition had many internal factions, and it started to unravel not long after the death of FDR. Southern "Dixiecrats" walked out of the Democratic Party convention in 1948 to protest a party platform that called for an end to racial discrimination in employment; the "revolt of '48" cost Democrats four southern states in the election, but was insufficient to deny Harry Truman's reelection. The promise of a New Deal and Truman's successor, the **Fair Deal**—with its vast array of government supports for workers, elderly and disabled people, widows and children, and farmers—held the coalition together. Republican Dwight D. Eisenhower made inroads into this coalition by virtue of his personal popularity and the Republican Party's acceptance of most New Deal programs. But John F. Kennedy's "New Frontier" demonstrated the continuing appeal of the Democratic Party tradition. Lyndon Johnson's **Great Society** went further than the programs of any of his predecessors in government intervention in the economic and social life of the nation. Indeed, it might be argued that the Great Society laid the foundation for a political reaction that eventually destroyed the old Democratic coalition and led to yet another new party alignment.

☐ Turmoil and the Great Dealignment

The American political system underwent massive convulsions in the late 1960s. The civil rights revolution at home and an unpopular war in Vietnam strained the nation's political institutions, from the courts to Congress to the presidency. The damage was mainly to the national Democratic Party. The social tensions of integration and the economic impact of a changing global and domestic economy tore at two of the core components of the New Deal coalition: southern whites, and working class and unionized workers. The signing of the Civil Rights Act by President Lyndon Johnson compelled five Deep South states to vote for states' rights Republican Barry Goldwater—the second of three Deep South "bolts" from the party of Jefferson and Jackson since World War II.

When Lyndon Johnson announced his decision not to run for reelection in early 1968, the Democratic Party erupted in a battle that ultimately destroyed its majority support among presidential voters. At the 1968 Democratic Party convention in Chicago, Vice President Hubert Humphrey controlled a majority of the delegates inside the convention hall, but antiwar protesters dominated media coverage outside the hall. When Chicago police attacked unruly demonstrators with batons, the media broadcast to the world an image of the nation's turmoil. In the presidential campaign that followed, Humphrey and Republican Richard Nixon presented nearly identical positions supporting the U.S. military commitment in Vietnam while endorsing a negotiated, "honorable" settlement of the war. But the image of the Democratic Party became associated with the street protesters. Inside the convention hall, pressure from women and minorities led party leaders to adopt changes in the party's delegate-selection process for future conventions to assure better representation of these groups—at the expense of Democratic officeholders. The prospects for national Democrats was further diminished by Governor George Wallace (Ala.) running as an independent. Wallace, a segregationist Democrat and social conservative with strong populist appeal, won the electoral votes of five southern states and sufficiently fractured the vote in five others to allow Nixon to prevail with narrow pluralities.

In 1972, the Democratic Party convention followed a divisive nomination fight, conducted under new rules. The result was a convention that strongly reflected the views of antiwar protesters, civil rights advocates, feminist organizations, and liberal activists generally. The visibility of these activists, who appeared to be far more liberal than Democratic Party voters (and the electorate in general), allowed the Republican Party to portray the Democratic presidential nominee, George McGovern, as an unpatriotic liberal, willing to "crawl to Hanoi" and to sacrifice the nation's honor for peace. It also allowed the Republicans to characterize the new Democratic Party as soft on crime, tolerant of disorder, and committed to racial and sexual quotas in American life. Richard Nixon, never very popular personally, was able to win in a landslide in 1972. However, Nixon's coattails were short—Democrats maintained control of Congress, and would continue to do so for the rest of the decade.

The Watergate scandal and Nixon's forced resignation temporarily stemmed the tide of "the new Republican majority," and in 1976, moderate Republican President Gerald Ford was challenged for renomination by Governor Ronald Reagan (R-CA). Democrat Jimmy Carter's narrow victory over Ford in 1976 owed much to the latter's pardon of Nixon and also to Carter's ability to bring many southern whites back into the party fold while also holding on to the votes of southern blacks. By 1977, the party coalitions of both parties were in tatters; for 15 years, "independent" political identifiers had grown more numerous than supporters of either party. The partisan ties across levels of election—from president to congress to state offices and into local politics—had been weakened by the simultaneous decline of local party organizations across the United States, and the rise of several issues that cut across the lines of the party coalitions that emerged in the 1930s. Dealignment left large numbers of voters without coherent political moorings, and politicians developed political styles that were based more on their own personality than on party.

Reagan Coalition
Combination of economic and social conservatives, religious fundamentalists, and defense-minded anticommunists who rallied behind Republican President Ronald Reagan.

☐ Reagan '80 as Realignment

Under the leadership of Ronald Reagan, the Republican Party was able to assemble a majority coalition that dominated presidential elections in the 1980s, giving Reagan landslide victories in 1980 and 1984 and George H. W. Bush a convincing win in 1988. Reagan and the national GOP stepped into the dealigned political rubble of late 1970s politics and assembled a coherent idelogical coalition. The **Reagan Coalition** consisted of the following groups: economic conservatives concerned about high taxes and excessive government regulation, including business and professional voters who had traditionally supported the Republican Party; social conservatives concerned about crime, drugs, and racial conflict, including many Roman Catholic, white ethnic voters and union members who had traditionally voted Democratic; religious fundamentalists concerned about such issues as abortion and prayer in schools; southern whites concerned about racial issues, including affirmative action programs; and internationalists and anticommunists who wanted the United States to maintain a strong military force and to confront Soviet-backed Marxist regimes around the world. It is interesting to note that many of these groups were critical of the structure of FDR's New Deal Coalition—and that Reagan himself was a former "New Dealer."

Reagan held this coalition together in large part through his personal popularity and his infectious optimism about the United States and its future, and in part through economic success. Although sometimes at odds with one another, economic conservatives, religious fundamentalists, and internationalists could unite behind the "Great Communicator." Reagan's victory in 1980 also provided sufficient coattails to elect a Republican majority to the U.S. Senate for the first time in a generation and also to encourage Democratic conservatives in the Democrat-controlled House of Representatives to frequently vote with Republicans. As a result, Reagan got most of what he asked of Congress in his first term: cuts in personal income taxes, increased spending for national defense, and slower growth of federal regulatory activity. With the assistance of the Federal Reserve Board, inflation was brought under control. But Reagan largely failed to cut government spending as he had promised, and the result was a series of huge federal deficits. Reagan appointed conservatives to the Supreme Court and the federal judiciary, but no major decisions were reversed (including the *Roe v. Wade* decision, protecting abortion); social conservatives had to be content with the president's symbolic support. The social conservatives emerged as the fastest-growing component of the coalition, and would play a critical role in the creation of GOP success in the 1990s.

THE POWER OF UNITY

President Ronald Reagan created a Republican majority coalition in the 1980s by uniting Republican factions—economic conservatives, social conservatives, religious fundamentalists, and anticommunists—and adding many southern white Democrats.

During these years, the national Democratic Party was saddled with an unpopular image as the party of special-interests and executive failure. The key remaining loyal Democratic constituencies were African Americans and other minorities, government employees, union leaders, liberal intellectuals in the media and universities, feminist organizations, and environmentalists. Democratic presidential candidates Walter Mondale in 1984 and Michael Dukakis in 1988 were unable to appeal to centrist voters after running from the left in the party primaries. Republican Party strategists "defined" Mondale and Dukakis as liberal defenders of special-interests, using negative campaign advertising.

From 1968 to 1988, Democrats won just one presidential election. But they maintained control of the House of Representatives the whole time, held the U.S. Senate for all but six years, and continuously held more state governorships and state legislative seats than the Republicans. The party retained a strong leadership base on which to rebuild itself; part of this base moved to reassert Democratic competitiveness for the presidency. During the 1980s, Democratic leaders among governors and senators came together in the Democratic Leadership Council (DLC) to create a "new" Democratic Party closer to the center of the political spectrum. The chair of the Democratic Leadership Council was the young, energetic, and successful governor of Arkansas, Bill Clinton. The concern of the council was that the Democratic Party's traditional support for social justice and social welfare programs was overshadowing its commitment to economic prosperity. Many council members argued that a healthy economy was a prerequisite to progress in social welfare. Not all Democrats agreed with the council agenda. African American leaders (including the Reverend Jesse Jackson), as well as liberal and environmental groups, feared that the priorities of the council would result in the sacrifice of traditional Democratic Party commitments to minorities, poor people, and the environment.

In the short run, the centrist approach of the DLC would propel Bill Clinton to the presidency as a moderate. However, the DLC was not an opening act of a new, centrist Democratic party, but rather the last call before the emergence of an era of confrontational, polarized politics wherein voters and politicians sorted themselves into ideologically defined camps.

1992 to Today: The Era of Polarization

In the 1992 presidential election, Bill Clinton was in a strong position to take advantage of the faltering economy under George H. W. Bush, to stress the "new" Democratic Party's commitment to the middle class, and to avoid being labeled as a liberal defender of special interests. At the same time, he managed to rally the party's core activist groups—liberals, intellectuals, African Americans, feminists, and environmentalists. Many liberals in the party deliberately soft-pedaled their views during the 1992 election in order not to offend voters, hoping to win with Clinton and then fight for liberal programs later. Clinton won with 43 percent of the vote, to Bush's 38 percent. Independent Ross Perot, running on a platform of deficit reduction, led the polls for much of the summer and ultimately captured 19 percent of the popular vote, including many voters who were alienated from both the Democratic and Republican parties. Once in office, Clinton appeared to revert to liberal policy directions rather than to pursue the more moderate line he had espoused as a "new" Democrat. As Clinton's ratings sagged, the opportunity arose for a Republican resurgence.

A political earthquake shook Washington in the 1994 congressional elections. Republicans won the House of Representatives for the first time since 1954, regained control of the Senate, and captured a majority of the nation's governorships. Significant gains were made in the South; Republicans won a majority of the congressional seats for the first time since after the Civil War, and the Democratic Party collapsed as a viable electoral majority in most southern states.[7] The new Republican House Speaker, Newt Gingrich, tried to seize national policy leadership; Clinton was widely viewed as a failed president. But the Republicans quickly squandered their political opportunity. They had made many promises in a well-publicized "Contract with America"—a balanced federal budget, congressional term limits, tax cuts, welfare reform, and more—but they delivered little. Battles over a possible Balanced Budget Amendment, cuts in entitlement programs, and a controversial forced "government shutdown" largely backfired on Republicans and increased support for Clinton's incumbency. Clinton skillfully portrayed GOP leaders, especially Newt Gingrich, as "extremists" and himself as a responsible moderate prepared to trim the budget, reduce the deficit, and reform welfare, "while still protecting Medicare, Medicaid, education, and the environment." Clinton won reelection in 1996 over Dole and Perot, but still confronted a GOP Congress. Prosperity and a balanced budget allowed Clinton to weather the winds of sexual scandal to end his term with very high approval ratings. Meanwhile, in Congress, moderate lawmakers of both parties continued to retire or lose reelection; congressional voting became increasingly polarized.

A Nation Divided

The nation was more evenly divided in 2000 between the Democratic and Republican parties than perhaps at any other time in history. Democrat Al Gore won a narrow victory in the popular vote for president. But after a month-long legal battle for Florida's electoral votes, Republican George W. Bush, former Texas governor and son of the former President Bush, emerged as the winner, 271 electoral votes to 267. The Republican Party lost seats in the House, but retained a razor-thin margin of control of that body. In the Senate, the 2000 election created a historic 50–50 tie between Democrats and Republicans. The vote of the Senate's presiding officer, Republican Vice President Dick Cheney, would have given the GOP the narrowest of control of that body. But in 2001, Vermont's Republican Senator Jim Jeffords decided to switch his support to the Democratic Party, swinging control of the Senate to the Democrats. Four years later, the GOP consolidated its control over the White House, Senate, and House of Representatives. Republicans showed unexpected strength, especially on national security issues, and Bush won both the popular vote and the Electoral College vote. Turnout was high. Republicans added to their narrow controlling margins in both the House and the Senate.

WAR AND ECONOMIC UNCERTAINTY Republican electoral success ended in 2006. Hints of economic recession and the failure of the administration to address the aftermath of Hurricane Katrina led to polls suggesting that voters had lost confidence in President Bush.

What Do You Think?

The Appeal of the Republican and Democratic Parties

What explains partisanship among voters? What is it about the Republican and Democratic parties that appeals to voters? A Gallup survey asked Americans—after they identified themselves as Republicans or Democrats (or Independents who said they lean toward either party)—to explain in their own words just what it is about their chosen party that appeals to them most.

Republicans justify their allegiance to the GOP most often with a reference to the party's conservatism or conservative positions on moral issues. Beyond that, Republicans mention the party's conservative economic positions and its preference for smaller government.

In contrast to Republicans who mention conservatism as their rationale for identifying with the GOP, the proportion of Democrats who mention liberalism is comparatively small. Democrats are more likely to say that the Democratic Party appeals to them because it is for the working class, the middle class, or the "common man."

Q. What is it about the Republican Party that appeals to you most? (Asked of Republicans)

Conservative/more conservative (nonspecific)	26%
Conservative family/moral values	15
Overall platform/philosophy/policies (nonspecific)	12
Conservative on fiscal/economic issues	10
Favors smaller government	8
Favors individual responsibility/self-reliance	5
Always been a Republican	4
For the people/working people	3
Low taxes	3
Favor strong military	3
Pro-life on abortion	2

Q. What is it about the Democratic Party that appeals to you most? (Asked of Democrats)

For the middle class/working class/common man	25%
Social/moral issue positions	18
Overall platform/philosophy/policies (nonspecific)	14
Liberal/more liberal (nonspecific)	11
Help the poor	7
Always been a Democrat	5
Antiwar	3
Health care reform	2
Pro-environment/conservation	1

NOTE: "Other" and "no opinion" percentages not shown.

SOURCE: Gallup Poll, November 13, 2007. www.gallup.com.

Questions

1. How are Republican and Democratic partisans different in describing their party? How are they similar?
2. Are there any areas where Democrats and Republicans overlap in describing their parties?

War-weariness cost the GOP control of the House of Representatives and the Senate. Two years later, Democrats swept to total control of national government. War-weariness shaped the Democratic nomination fight, allowing Barack Obama to overhaul presumptive frontrunner Hillary Clinton for the nomination. The hints of economic instability detected in 2006 and 2007 became full-blown in 2008, as a plunge in housing values, a sharp decline in the stock market, emergency government takeovers of leading banks and investment houses, and Washington's $700 billion bailout of Wall Street all contributed to voter concern over the economy. Economic instability traditionally has helped Democratic candidates. And not since the Great Depression of the 1930s had Americans experienced so much economic anxiety as they did in 2008. Two years later, economic recovery had still not taken hold despite substantial infusions of government spending into the economy. Continuing high unemployment and a perceived failure of the Democrats in power to deal effectively with the sagging economy brought the GOP roaring back in the midterm congressional election. Obama's approval ratings approached the levels exhibited in the last year of his predecessor's administration. The Republican Party, declared all but dead after the 2008 election, was revitalized by an infusion of conservative activism mobilized under the banner of the Tea Party Movement. Republicans recaptured control of the House of Representatives and improved their numbers in the Senate.

The 2012 election was the most expensive and widely contested election in modern politics. Republicans had fully recovered from the 2008 election to challenge for the presidency behind Mitt Romney. The GOP continued to control the U.S. House, though a loss of seats reduced their majority from 242-193 to 234-201. In the Senate, expectations of a Republican takeover was derailed by flawed candidacies in Missouri, Connecticut, Indiana, Massachusetts, and Wisconsin and the failure to capitalize on opportunities in North Dakota and Montana. Republicans lost a net of two seats in the Senate and left Democrats in control.

The country continued to divide along partisan and racial lines. Once thought confined to the South, national voting for president became increasingly polarized by race. Republicans received an estimated 39% of the white vote for president and Congress, and an estimated 91% of all Republican votes came from Anglo whites. But the GOP was also becoming an increasingly regionalized party. Of the 23 Republican seats in the House and 45 in the Senate, nearly half in the Senate (22 of 45) and over 40% in the House came from the eleven-state South, which accounts for 32% of the total U.S. population. And, in an ironic reversal of roles, a majority of the Republican electoral votes came from the South, leading the party of Lincoln to depend more heavily on the old Confederacy for national political success.

Political Parties and Democratic Government

7.4 Outline the functions and perceptions of the two major American political parties, explain how the parties are financed, and assess their changing role in the electoral process.

olitical parties created democracy, and modern democracy is unthinkable save in terms of the parties."[8] Traditionally, political scientists have praised parties as indispensable to democratic government. They have argued that parties are essential for organizing popular majorities to exercise control over government. The development of political parties in all the democracies of the world testifies to the underlying importance of parties to democratic government. But political parties in the United States have lost their preeminent position as instruments of democracy. Other structures and organizations in society—interest groups, the mass media, independent campaign organizations, primary elections, social welfare agencies—now perform many of the functions traditionally regarded as prerogatives of political parties. Nevertheless, the Democratic and Republican parties remain important organizing structures for politics in the United States—and the only vehicle for ambitious politicians to seek and win public office.

"Responsible" Parties in Theory

In theory, political parties function in a democracy to organize majorities around broad principles of government in order to win public office and enact these principles into law. In the 1950s, the American Political Science Association (APSA) was asked by Congress to assess the American party and electoral system. The APSA came back with recommendations that promoted more "responsible" parties. So what should a "responsible" party do?

- Adopt a platform setting forth its principles and policy positions.
- Recruit candidates for public office who agree with the party's platform.
- Inform and educate the public about the platform.
- Organize and direct campaigns based on platform principles.
- Organize the legislature to ensure party control in policy making.
- Hold its elected officials responsible for enacting the party's platform.

If responsible, disciplined, policy-oriented parties competed for majority support, *if* they offered clear policy alternatives to the voters, and *if* the voters cast their ballots on the basis of these policy options, *then* the winning party would have a "policy mandate" from the people to guide the course of government. In that way, the democratic ideal of government by majority rule would be implemented.

7.1

7.2

7.3

7.4

7.5

7.6

7.7

7.8

What Do You Think?

Democratic and Republican Platforms: Can You Tell the Difference?

National Defense

A. "In our current fiscal environment, we must also make tough budgetary decisions across the board—and that includes within the defense budget."

B. "Severe, automatic, across-the-board cuts in defense spending over the next decade . . . would be a disaster for national security."

Health Care

A. "[H]istoric health care reform that provides economic security for families and enacted sweeping financial reform legislation"

B. "We agree with the four dissenting justices of the Supreme Court: 'In our view the entire Act before us is invalid in its entirety.' "

Abortion

A. "The Democratic Party strongly and unequivocally supports Roe v. Wade and a woman's right to make decisions regarding her pregnancy."

B. "We support a human life amendment to the Constitution and endorse legislation to make clear that the Fourteenth Amendment's protections apply to unborn children."

'God Talk'

A. We need a government that stands up for the hopes, values, and interests of working people, and gives everyone willing to work hard the chance to make the most of their God-given potential. (God is mentioned once in platform)

B. Reaffirm that our rights come from God, are protected by government, and that the only just government is one that truly governs with the consent of the governed. (God is mentioned ten times in platform)

Energy

A. "smart policies that lead to greater growth in clean energy generation and result in a range of economic and social benefits."

B. "The Republican Party is committed to domestic energy independence . . . Republicans advocate an all-of-the-above diversified approach, taking advantage of all our American God-given resources."

Immigration

A. "We need an immigration reform that creates a system for allocating visas that meets our economic needs, keeps families together, and enforces the law."

B. "State efforts to reduce illegal immigration must be encouraged, not attacked."

Other

A. "We support equal rights to democratic self-government and congressional representation for the citizens of our nation's capital."

B. "Congress should explore a greater role for private enterprise in appropriate aspects of the mail-processing system."

A. "The key is to make tough choices, in particular, pay-as-you-go budgetary rules."

B. "We call for a Constitutional amendment requiring a super-majority for any tax increase."

QUESTIONS

1. Look at the platform statements, and decide those you agree with, more or less. Which party are you closer to, based on their platforms?
2. George Wallace said you can't tell a dimes worth of difference between the major parties. Do the Democrats and Republicans look similar on any of these issues?

SOURCE: Excerpts from Democratic [A] and Republican [B] party platforms, 2012.

responsible party model
System in which competitive parties adopt a platform of principles, recruiting candidates and directing campaigns based on that platform and holding their elected officials responsible for enacting it.

median voter theorem
Two-party political systems tend to create centrist political parties who battle for decisive votes of moderate voters.

□ But Winning Prevails over Principle

Historically, the **responsible party model** never accurately described the American party system. America's major parties must appeal to tens of millions of voters in every section of the nation and from all walks of life, because they are at best loose coalitions of individuals and groups seeking to attract sufficient votes to gain control of government. *Winning has generally been more important than any principles or policies.*

If a major party is to acquire a majority capable of controlling the U.S. government, it cannot limit its appeal by relying on a single unifying principle. Instead, major American parties did not emphasize particular principles or ideologies so much as try to find a common ground of agreement among many different people. Each party appealed to a distinctive coalition of interests, and therefore each party expressed somewhat distinctive policy views.

This view on political parties is reflected in the **median voter theorem**. The median voter theorem holds that parties, in order to win, strive to attract the support of the large numbers of people near the center of public opinion. Generally, more votes are at the center of the ideological spectrum—the middle-of-the-road—than on the extreme liberal or conservative ends. Thus *no real incentive exists for vote-maximizing parties to take strong policy positions in opposition to each other* (see Figure 7.7).

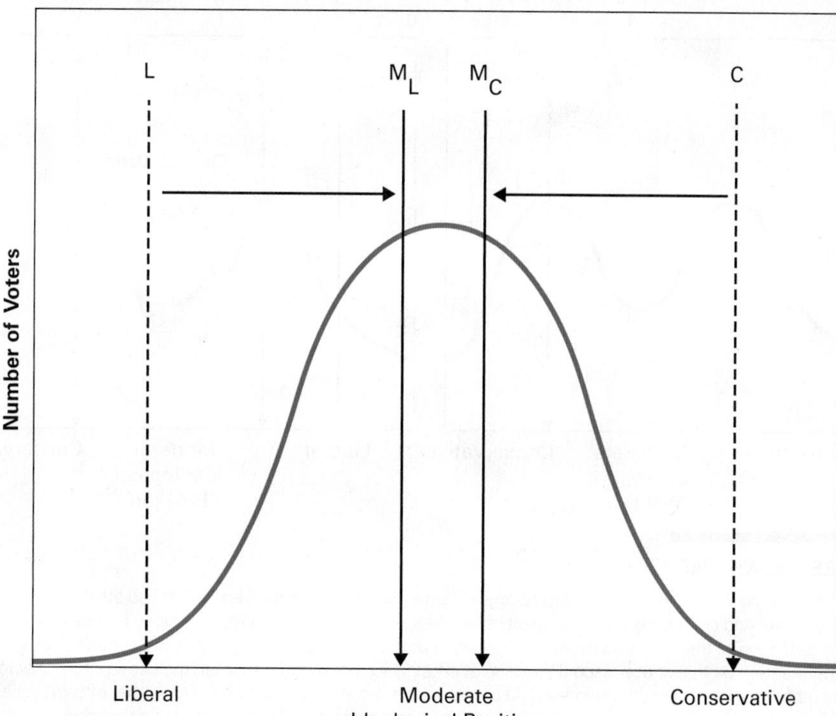

FIGURE 7.7 WHY PARTIES DRIFT TO THE CENTER

Why don't we have a party system based on principles, with a liberal party and a conservative party, each offering the voters a real ideological choice? Let's assume that voters generally choose the party closest to their own ideological position. If the liberal party (L) took a strong ideological position to the left of most voters, the conservative party (C) would move toward the center, winning more moderate votes, even while retaining its conservative supporters, who would still prefer it to the more liberal opposition party. Likewise, if the conservative party took a strong ideological position to the right of most voters, the liberal party would move to the center and win. So both parties must abandon strong ideological positions and move to the center, becoming moderate in the fight for support of moderate voters.

An alternative perspective emerged in the last three decades, the **wedge issue theorem**. The wedge issue approach was the foundation of political strategy of many southern Republicans, including the late Senator Jesse Helms (R-NC), former RNC chairman Lee Atwater (R-SC), and the architect of George Bush's electoral career, Karl Rove of Texas. Wedge issue theory posits that instead of moving as close to the center as possible, parties should instead stake out clear ideological ground and make their opponent's position on divisive issues look as unacceptable as possible and to activate their own base of ideological voters. The effect of the wedge issue approach is to demobilize ambivalent voters (and maybe weak supporters of the other party) by forcing centrist voters to make stark choices (see Figure 7.8). Under the assumptions of the wedge issue approach, the electorate looks quite different than under median voter.

wedge issue theorem
Political parties run on polarizing issues to mobilize their ideological base and force moderate voters to make stark choices or not vote.

party polarization
The tendency of the Democratic Party to take more liberal positions and the Republican Party to take more conservative positions on key issues.

Party and Ideology

Despite incentives for the parties to move to the center of the political spectrum, the Republican and Democratic parties are perceived by the public as ideologically separate. The electorate tends to perceive the Republican Party as conservative and the Democratic Party as liberal. The recent behavior of politicians and the self-perception of voters reinforce this perception, as voting has become more polarized. Democratic and Republican party activists have become more ideologically separate in recent years. And voters have become increasingly aware of this **party polarization**. Most voters now say that the Democratic Party is more liberal and the Republican Party is more conservative on a variety of high-profile issues, including government services and spending, government provision of health insurance, and government assistance

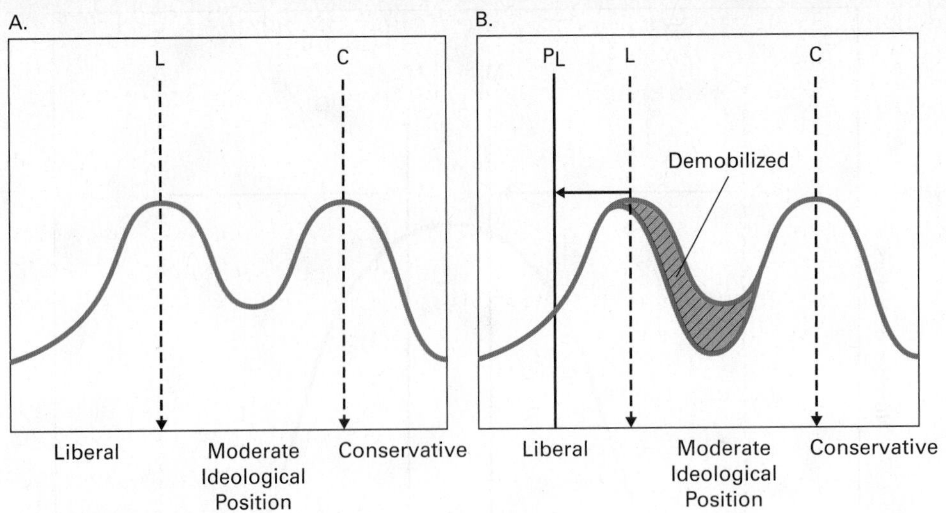

FIGURE 7.8 WHY PARTIES POLARIZE

But what if the conservative party (C) voters largely held a position on a critical issue that had strong emotional appeal (part A)? And complying with their position on the issue was necessary to win a party nomination? Being defined by the issue, the party's candidates might attempt to create the perception that the opposing party was far from the "center" on that critical issue (P^L), and attempt to force a wedge between the center of the electorate and the other party. Voters in the middle would confront a stark choice: choose one of the other of two parties defined by polar positions on the wedge issue, or (part B) stay home and don't vote (shaded demobilized area).

to African Americans and other minorities suffering historic discrimination.[9] And, among voters, Republicans describe themselves as conservatives far more often than as liberals. Democratic voters are more likely to identify themselves as liberals than as conservatives, although many like to think of themselves as moderates (see Table 7.1). This relationship between ideological self-identification and party self-identification is relatively stable over time.

For the last half century, the Democratic Party has been viewed as the more progressive major party. The Democratic Party includes liberals with strong views on social issues such as homosexuality, abortion, and environmental protection as well as reluctance to the use of military force. Yet another part of the Democratic coalition includes the people supportive of the role of government in providing a social safety net—efforts to provide jobs, help to the needy, and economic opportunity for all. The Republican Party tends to include defenders of the free enterprise system and opponents of government regulation, together with strongly religious people who hold traditional views on moral issues. The Republican Party also appeals to people strongly supportive of the military and an assertive foreign policy.

☐ The Erosion of Traditional Party Functions

Parties play only a limited role in campaign organization and finance. *Campaigns are generally directed by professional campaign management firms or by the candidates' personal organizations, not by parties.* Party organizations have largely been displaced in

TABLE 7.1 WHO VOTES FOR THE PARTIES? PARTY AND IDEOLOGY AMONG VOTERS

Self-identified liberals tend to vote Democratic, while conservatives tend to vote Republican.

	Democratic Voters	Republican Voters	Independent Voters	Total
Liberals	54%	4%	25%	28%
Moderates	29	13	42	28
Conservatives	17	82	32	43

SOURCE: Data from the 2008 and 2010 National Election Study. University of Michigan. Tabulations by Professor Terri Towner, Oakland University.

campaign activity by advertising firms, media consultants, pollsters, and others hired by the candidates themselves.

Most political candidates today are self-recruited. American political parties also play only a limited role in recruiting candidates for elected office. People initiate their own candidacies, first contacting friends and financial supporters. Often in state and local races, candidates contact party officials only as a courtesy, if at all.

The major American political parties cannot really control who their **nominee**—*the party's entry in a general election race—will be.* Rather, party **nominations** for most elected offices are won in **primary elections**. In a primary election, registered voters select who will be their party's nominee in the general election. Party leaders may endorse a candidate in a primary election and may even work to try to ensure the victory of their favorite, but the voters in that party's primary select the nominee. The infusion of ideological or single-issue voters into party primaries can defeat "insider" or "establishment" candidates.

Candidates usually communicate directly with voters through the mass media. Television has replaced the party organization as the principal medium of communication between candidates and voters. Candidates no longer rely much on party workers to carry their message from door to door. Instead, candidates can come directly into the voters' living rooms via television and the Internet.

Even if the American parties wanted to take stronger policy positions and to enact them into law, they would not have the means to do so. *American political parties have no way to bind their elected officials to the party platform or even to their campaign promises.* Parties have no strong disciplinary sanctions to use against members of Congress who vote against the party's policy position. The parties cannot deny them renomination. At most, the party's leadership in Congress can threaten the status, privileges, and pet bills of disloyal members. Party cohesion, where it exists, is more a product of likemindedness than of party discipline.

American political parties no longer perform social welfare functions—trading off social services, patronage jobs, or petty favors in exchange for votes. Traditional party organizations, or **machines**, especially in large cities, once helped immigrants get settled in, found **patronage** jobs in government for party workers, and occasionally provided aid to impoverished but loyal party voters. But government bureaucracies have replaced the political parties as providers of social services. Government employment agencies, welfare agencies, civil service systems, and other bureaucracies now provide the social services once undertaken by political machines in search of votes.

nominee
Political party's entry in a general election race.

nominations
Political party's selections of its candidates for public office.

primary elections
Elections to choose party nominees for public office; may be open or closed.

machines
Tightly disciplined party organizations, headed by a boss, that rely on material rewards—including patronage jobs—to control politics.

patronage
Appointment to public office based on party loyalty.

divided party government
One party controls the presidency while the other party controls one or both houses of Congress.

☐ Divided Party Government

Finally, to further confound the responsible party model, Americans seem to prefer **divided party government**—where one party controls the executive branch while the other party controls one or both houses of the legislative branch. Except for Kennedy, Johnson, and Carter, every president since World War II has confronted divided government at some point. From 1946 to 1990, American presidents faced a Congress in which the opposition party controlled one or both chambers about two-thirds of the time, while from 1992 to 2010 divided control and unified control were equally likely to occur.[10] It is noteworthy that American public opinion seems to prefer divided party government over unified party control, even though divided party control of government makes it difficult for either party to fully enact its platform. So, while divided government defies responsible party thinking, it is consistent with the countervailing institutional powers Madison incorporated into the Constitution.

☐ Party Finances

Parties as well as candidates raise hundreds of millions of dollars in every election year. At the national level, contributions to the parties go to the Democratic and

7.1

7.2

7.3

7.4

7.5

7.6

7.7

7.8

The Game, the Rules, the Players

Chairs of the DNC and RNC

Debbie Wasserman Schultz Democratic National Committee chairwoman U.S. Rep. Debbie Wasserman Schultz (D-FL) was born to campaign. In 1992, at age 26, she was elected to the Florida House of Representatives; she took over the seat of her boss, Peter Deutsch (who had been elected to Congress), to become the youngest woman to ever hold legislative office in Florida. Twelve years later, she won Deutsch's seat in the U.S. House. In 2011, President Obama tapped the lawmaker to take over the Democratic National Committee—a choice that was quickly ratified by the committee.

Wasserman Schultz trained to be a political professional. She earned a degree in political science from the University of Florida (UF) and pursued a master's degree at UF with a specialization in campaign management. She was active in campus politics, serving as student senate president and as an officer with the College Democrats. Her first job, as a legislative aide to Deutsch, came right after she got out of college. Florida lawmakers have limited staff resources, so a legislative aide takes on a prominent role in every aspect of the lawmaker's job. (Wasserman Schultz's career is indicative of the open nature of Florida politics—she moved to the Sunshine State from Long Island to go to college and lived in her legislative district for just three years before she was sent to the legislature.)

As a state lawmaker and member of Congress, Wasserman Schultz carved out a consistent liberal voting record that was usually in line with her heavily Democratic, Broward County–based constituency. She's pro-choice, pro-universal health care (she is also a breast cancer survivor), pro-education, and progressive on taxation. As a freshman in Congress, she was appointed to the powerful Steering and Policy Committee of the House Democratic Caucus. She was later named a deputy whip and currently sits on two "power" committees: Appropriations and Judiciary. Until the Democrats lost control of the House in 2010, she was ranked as the most powerful member of the Florida delegation in Congress, in part due to her fund-raising prowess and her influential committee positions.

A national party chair fills different roles, depending on the political situation in Washington. When the party is in the minority, the chairman often emerges as a major national spokesperson for the party. But when a party controls the presidency and Congress, the chairman's role is reduced in its public profile. The president is available as primary party leader, and the congressional leadership can also speak to party priorities for the majority. Debbie Wasserman confronted the challenge of being a party chair who must defend a president of her party while also serving as a member of the congressional minority. Many of her activities are consistent with an "insider" chairman who is focused on fund-raising (she is one of the most prolific fund-raisers in Washington), maintaining cohesion inside the party organization, and coordinating the party position with the White House. When the party chair emerges as a spokesperson, it is often to take an aggressive position opposite the Republican congressional caucuses.

Debbie Wasserman Schultz, chair of the Democratic National Committee.

QUESTIONS

1. **Describe the career ladder that Debbie Wasserman Schultz climbed.**
2. **How would her job as DNC chairwoman change if the Democrats did not hold the presidency?**

Reince Priebus

"What's a Reince Priebus?"—Stephen Colbert

"If you take all the vowels out of Reince Priebus, you are left with RNC PR BS."—Jon Stewart

Late-night hosts had a lot of fun with Reince Priebus. But Priebus, a young lawyer from Milwaukee, proved to be an effective chairman of the Republican

Reince Priebus, chair of the Republican National Committee.

(Continued)

(*Continued*)

National Committee. Priebus (R-WI) is a veteran of Wisconsin politics. His ascendency to the RNC chair coincided with the emergence of two other Wisconsinites—Governor Scott Walker and U.S. Rep. Paul Ryan—as prominent and sometimes controversial figures in the modern conservative movement. As RNC chairman, he moved aggressively to undo what was seen as a damaging tenure by his predecessor, Michael Steele.

Priebus started his political career as a teenage campaign volunteer. He later worked as a clerk in the Wisconsin Legislature in the early 1990s. He attended law school at the University of Miami and subsequently joined a politically prominent Milwaukee law firm. He unsuccessfully sought a state Senate seat in 2004, losing his only bid for public office. He was elected chair of the Wisconsin GOP in 2007 and played a prominent role in orchestrating the 2010 GOP takeover of Wisconsin's legislature and executive branch. He also served simultaneously as general counsel to the RNC—the head GOP lawyer.

Priebus was elected chairman of the RNC in early 2011, taking 97 of 168 votes on the seventh ballot (the RNC chairman is elected by a vote of RNC national committeemen, who are women and men elected from each state's party organization).

The choice of chairman was highly contentious. The incumbent chairman, Michael Steele, is the former lieutenant governor of Maryland and the first African American chairman of the RNC, and he sought a second term. However, he attracted substantial opposition because of his limited fund-raising success and spendthrift practices that had threatened to bankrupt the national organization (the RNC was $24 million in debt as of January 2011). Priebus promised a financially frugal operation that would emphasize fund-raising, voter mobilization, core conservative values, and coordination with movements such as the Tea Party. Within one year, he had righted the finances of the RNC and focused the message of the party on one goal—defeating President Obama in the 2012 election.

QUESTIONS

1. **Describe the career ladder that Reince Priebus has climbed.**
2. **How is his job and role different from that of his DNC counterpart, if at all?**

Republican National Committees and to the Democratic and Republican House and Senatorial Committees (see Table 7.2).

□ The Partisan Tilt of Campaign Contributions

Traditionally, the Republican Party was able to raise and spend more money in each election cycle than the Democratic Party. But the dollar differences have narrowed over the years. Perhaps more interesting are the differences in sources of support for each party. Broken down by sector (as in Table 7.3), the Democratic Party relies more heavily on lawyers and law firms, the entertainment industry (Hollywood), teachers

TABLE 7.2 WHERE'S THE MONEY?: PARTY FINANCES (IN MILLIONS)

Parties as well as candidates solicit campaign contributions. At the national level, contributions go to the Democratic and Republican National Committees and to the Democratic and Republican House and Senate Campaign Committees.

	2000	2004	2008	2012
Totals				
Democratic Party	$520	$731	$961	859
Republican Party	715	993	920	906
National Committees				
Dem. National Com.	260	311	260	292
Rep. National Com.	379	392	428	369
House Party Committees				
Dem. Cong. Camp. Com.	105	92	176	151
Nat'l Rep. Cong. Com.	145	186	118	135
Senate Party Committees				
Dem. Senatorial Camp. Com.	104	89	163	114
Nat'l Rep. Senatorial Camp. Com.	96	79	94	100

SOURCE: Center for Responsive Politics, www.opensecrets.org, 2012 data released November 5, 2012.

7.1
7.2
7.3
7.4
7.5
7.6
7.7
7.8

TABLE 7.3 WHO FINANCES THE PARTIES?: CONTRIBUTORS TO THE REPUBLICAN AND DEMOCRATIC PARTIES BY SECTOR

The Democratic Party relies more heavily on contributions from lawyers and law firms, TV, the movie and music industry, teacher and public employee unions, and industrial and building trade unions. The Republican Party relies more heavily on contributions from various business sectors.

Democratic Party	Republican Party
1. Lawyers/Law Firms	1. Securities & Investment
2. Securities & Investment	2. Real Estate
3. TV/Movies/Music	3. Misc Finance
4. Real Estate	4. Oil & Gas
5. Business Services	5. Business Services
6. Computers/Internet	6. Misc Manufacturing & Distributing
7. Education	7. Lawyers/Law Firms
8. Misc Finance	8. Health Professionals
9. Health Professionals	9. Misc Business
10. Misc. Business	10. Insurance
11. Non-Profit Institutions	11. Automotive
12. Printing & Publishing	12. Computers/Internet

SOURCE: Center for Responsive Politics. Candidate committees, miscellaneous, and "retired" excluded from this table. Data from 2012 presidential election.

and public-sector employee unions, and industrial and building trade unions. Business interests divide their contributions, but they tilt toward the Republican Party, notably the health care industry, insurance, manufacturing, oil and gas, automotive, and general and special contractors.

nonpartisan elections
Elections in which candidates do not officially indicate their party affiliation; often used for city, county, school board, and judicial elections.

caucus
Nominating process in which party members or leaders meet to nominate candidates or select delegates to conventions.

☐ Parties as Organizers of Elections

Despite the erosion of many of their functions, America's political parties survive as the principal institutions for organizing elections, by selecting nominees and providing a ballot position to seek office.[11] Party nominations organize electoral choice by narrowing the field of aspiring office seekers to the Democratic and Republican candidates. In the nineteenth century, this goal was accomplished using party caucuses and conventions. In the twentieth century, primaries became the predominant means of selecting general election candidates. Party conventions are still held in many states in every presidential year, but these conventions seldom have the power to determine the parties' nominees for public office.

Very few independents or third-party candidates are elected to high political office in the United States. **Nonpartisan elections**—elections in which there are no party nominations and all candidates run without an official party label—are common only in local elections, for city council, county commission, school board, judgeships, and so on. Only Nebraska has nonpartisan elections for its unicameral (one-house) state legislature.

☐ Early Party Conventions

Early party nominations were made by caucus or convention. The **caucus** was the earliest nominating process; party leaders (party chairs, elected officials, and "bosses") would simply meet several months before the election and decide on the party's nominee themselves. The early presidents—Thomas Jefferson, James Madison, James Monroe, and John Quincy Adams—were nominated by regional caucuses of members of Congress. Complaints about the exclusion of the people from this process led to nominations by convention—large meetings of delegates sent by local party organizations—starting in 1832. Andrew Jackson was the first president to be nominated by convention. The convention was considered more democratic than the caucus.

For nearly a century, party conventions were held at all levels of government—local, state, and national. City or county conventions included delegates from local **wards** and **precincts**, who nominated candidates for city or county office, for the state legislature, or even for the House of Representatives when a congressional district fell within the city or county. State conventions included delegates from counties, and they nominated governors, U.S. senators, and other statewide officers. State parties chose delegates to the Republican and Democratic national conventions every four years to nominate a president. Local and state parties still hold conventions, but most only select party officers and have no say over party nominees for public office.

wards
Divisions of a city for electoral or administrative purposes or as units for organizing political parties.

precincts
Subdivisions of a city, county, or ward for election purposes.

closed primaries
Primary elections in which voters must declare (or have previously declared) their party affiliation and can cast a ballot only in their own party's primary election.

open primaries
Primary elections in which a voter may cast a ballot in either party's primary election.

raiding
Organized efforts by one party to get its members to cross over in a primary and defeat an attractive candidate in the opposition party's primary.

Party Primaries

Primary elections have largely replaced conventions as the means of selecting major party nominees for public office[12]. Primary elections, introduced as part of the progressive reform movement of the early twentieth century, allow the party's *voters* to choose the party's nominee directly. The primary election was designed to bypass the power of party organizations and party leaders and to further democratize the nomination process. The reform succeeded, but also seriously weakened political parties, since candidates seeking a party nomination need only appeal to party *voters*—not *leaders*—for support in the primary election.[13]

Types of Primaries

There are some differences among the American states in how they conduct their primary elections. **Closed primaries** allow only voters who have previously registered as Democrats or Republicans (or in some states voters who choose to register as Democrats or Republicans on primary Election Day) to cast a ballot in their chosen party's primary. Closed primaries tend to discourage people from officially registering as Independents, even if they think of themselves as Independent, because people registered as Independents cannot cast a ballot in either party's primary.

Open primaries allow voters to declare on Election Day the party primary in which they wish to participate. Anyone, regardless of prior party affiliation, may choose to vote in either party's primary election. Voters simply request the ballot of one party or the other.[14] Open primaries provide opportunities for voters to cross over party lines and vote in the primary of the party they usually do not support. Opponents of open primaries have argued that these types of primary elections allow for **raiding**—organized efforts by one party to get its members to cross over to the opposition party's primary and vote strategically to defeat an attractive candidate and thereby improve the raiding party's chances of winning the general election. But there is little evidence to show that large numbers of voters actually behave in this fashion.

Louisiana is unique in its nonpartisan primary elections. All candidates, regardless of their party affiliation, run in the same primary election. If a candidate gets over 50 percent of the vote, he or she wins the office, without appearing on the general election ballot. If no one receives over 50 percent of the primary election votes, then the top two vote-getters, regardless of party, face each other in the general election. Louisiana uses a conventional closed-party primary with runoff to nominate candidates for congressional offices.[15]

Who's Getting What?

Is There a Sex Bias in Who the Parties Nominate?

Despite the high profile of women such as Sarah Palin and Michele Bachmann in Republican Party politics, women have problems getting nominated as Republicans. Experimental research shows that Republican voters are more likely to perceive both Republican and Democratic female candidates as less conservative than male candidates who otherwise share identical political profiles. In increasingly ideological party primaries, this makes it harder for women to win over some conservative voters. However, this same disadvantage—being perceived as moderate—works to the advantage of women who win a primary, because they have an easier time appealing to Independents and Democrats. In 2010, according to the Center for the American Woman in Politics, 36 women ran for the U.S. Senate—19 Democrats and 17 Republicans. Nine of the Democratic women won nomination (48 percent) compared to six Republicans (40 percent). Twenty-six women ran for governor—12 Democrats and 14 Republicans. Ten won nomination, five from each party. Four of those women faced off in woman-versus-woman contests in New Mexico and Oklahoma. In both instances, the Republican woman won. Also, 262 women ran for Congress in 2010—134 Democrats and 128 Republicans. Of those, 91 Democrats (67 percent) but 47 Republicans (37 percent) won their party nomination. Part of the dynamic is incumbency. For example, 54 of the Democrats and 15 Republicans were running as incumbents.

Questions

1. Why do you think it is harder for women to get nominated as Republicans?
2. Why do you think more women run for office as Democrats?

SOURCES: Center for the American Woman in Politics, www.cawp.rutgers.edu.

Richard E. Matland and David C. King. "Women as Candidates in Congressional Elections," in Cindy Simon Rosenthal, ed., *Women Transforming Congress.* Norman, Okla.: University of Oklahoma Press, 2003.

runoff primary
Additional primary held between the top two vote-getters in a primary where no candidate has received a majority of the vote.

California and Washington states use a variant of the Louisiana open primary, the "top-two" primary. Under the top-two system, voters choose candidates in the initial primary, and the top two finishers regardless of party go on to a general election. Nebraska also picks candidates for their nonpartisan Unicameral using this system.

Some states hold a **runoff primary** when no candidate receives a majority or a designated percentage of the vote in the party's first primary election. A runoff primary is limited to the two highest vote-getters in the first primary. Runoff elections are more common in the southern United States and in many municipal elections around the United States. In most states, only a plurality of votes is needed to win a party primary election.

□ Party Caucuses

Some state parties select their candidates, as well as their delegates to the national party conventions, in meetings of party members called caucuses. The best-known example is the Iowa presidential caucuses. Rather than going to the polls as in primary elections, caucus-goers in each party gather at set times and set locations in schools, churches, libraries, and recreation centers in their neighborhoods. They discuss party platforms, select county committee members, and, most important, in presidential years indicate their choice for their party's presidential nomination. Attending a caucus also requires a participant to declare his or her party affiliation and to openly indicate support for the candidate of his or her choice. Caucuses are more time-consuming than voting in primaries. There is conversation and debate, and sometimes several rounds of voting to make choices. Caucuses tend to be dominated by people with stronger partisan or ideological preferences, and benefit better-organized candidates—candidates who can persuade and assist supporters in making the extra effort to attend a caucus. In 2008, Barack Obama won most of the presidential caucus states because of his superior organization.

A Conflicting View

Thinking Reform: Do We Need Primaries?

Political parties mainly pick their nominees using primary elections. From local offices to delegates to presidential nominating conventions, the party primary is the method of choice in most states. But are parties good for American politics?

Party primaries were instituted to let voters pick candidates instead of party elites. Primaries allowed popular elections where no party competition existed. For a hundred years, primaries have become an increasingly common way of selecting nominees from dogcatcher to president.

But are primaries good for the parties? The voters who show up for party primaries are more ideological. As a result, party nominees have to appeal to the ideological extremes in their parties just to secure nomination, or be branded DINOs and RINOs (Democrat/Republican In Name Only). Some critics contend that this extreme control of the nominations contributes to party polarization.

Others think that ideological primaries lead to the nomination of extreme candidates who are too controversial to win a general election. In 2010 and 2012, several U.S. Senate contests that were important to Republicans were lost because the ideologically extreme Tea Party candidates turned off voters. These candidates were not controversial because they were conservative, but because of things they said. GOP candidates Richard Mourdock (Indiana) and Todd Akin (Missouri) made controversial statements regarding rape and abortion that swing voters found objectionable. Political analysts suggested that experienced, less-outrageous candidates chosen by a party nominating committee would have won.

An alternative for avoiding extreme candidates is to use an "open" primary where independents or even voters from the other party can vote in a party primary. This model, used in several states, does lead to the nomination of more moderate candidates in both political parties. But, critics contend that it undermines the concept of "political party" by taking control of choosing a party's candidates from its loyalists and leaders.

QUESTIONS

1. How important is it to you that a party control who it nominates? Do party leaders need more control, or less?
2. Do you think it is important for parties to nominate candidates who can see a perspective on issues other than that of their party's majority?

The Americans Elect Internet Primary

A new experiment was tried during the 2012 presidential election—a bipartisan, internet primary. Called 'Americans Elect,' the internet primary was designed to choose a bipartisan presidential ticket via a series of internet caucuses. The organization was created by former junk bond investor Peter Ackerman, who provided $5 million to start the organization in 2010, and by the end of 2011 had qualified the ballot for president in twelve states. The multi-round nominating process had relatively high thresholds for support of potential candidates for president—one had to have a thousand 'clicks' (votes) from ten different states to advance to the second round of the nominating process. No candidate nominated by the Americans Elect 'delegates' (360,000 registered online users) met this threshold, so the organization shut down its process. Americans Elect's failure demonstrates the limitation of an internet-only based mechanism in politics. The internet and social media revolutionized organizing, and even reinvigorated existing party organizations. But internet-only organizations are not yet capable of providing the organizational basis for a sustained and successful political party.

general election
Election to choose among candidates nominated by parties and/or Independent candidates who gained access to the ballot by petition.

General Elections

Following the parties' selections of their nominees, the **general election** (held in November, on the first Tuesday after the first Monday for presidential and most state elections) determines who will occupy elective office. Winners of the Democratic and Republican primary elections must face each other—and any Independent or third-party candidates—in the general election. Voters in the general election may choose any candidate, regardless of how they voted earlier in their party's primary or whether they voted in the primary at all.

Independent and minor-party candidates can get on the general election ballot, although the process is usually very difficult. Most states require independent candidates to file a petition with the signatures of several thousand registered voters. The number of signatures varies from state to state and office to office, but it may range up to 5 or 10 percent of *all* registered voters, a very large number that, in a big state especially, presents a difficult obstacle. The same petition requirements usually apply to minor parties, although some states automatically carry a minor party's nominee on the general election ballot if that party's candidate or candidates received a certain percentage (for example, 10 percent) of the vote in the previous general election.

Where's the Party?

7.5 Differentiate between the three political arenas in which the parties battle.

The Democratic and Republican parties are found in different political arenas (see Figure 7.9). As we noted at the beginning of this chapter, there is the party-in-the-electorate, the party-in-government, and the party as organization.

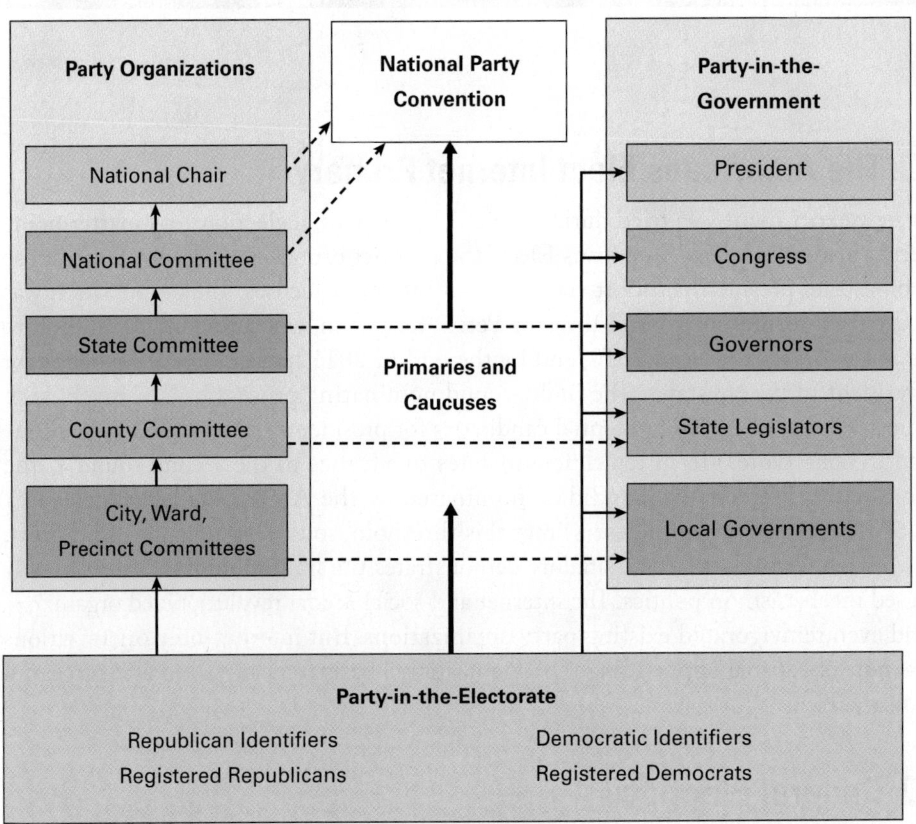

FIGURE 7.9 WHERE'S THE PARTY?

Even among Americans who strongly identify with a major party, there are differences among those who are strictly members of the party-in-the-electorate (voters), those who are members of the party-in-the-government (elected officials), and those who are members of the party organization (national and state party committee members).

Party-in-the-Electorate

The **party-in-the-electorate** is the voters who identify themselves as Democrats or Republicans and who tend to vote for the candidates of their party. The party-in-the-electorate has been in decline for four decades. Party loyalties among voters are weakening. Starting in the late 1960s, voters increasingly identified as independents, and since 2008, there has been an acceleration of voters eschewing party registration. **Ticket splitters** (who divide their votes between candidates of different parties for different offices in the same general election) increased from the 1960s through the 1990s, but since 1998, there has been an increase in coherent party-line voting among Democrats and Republicans.

party-in-the-electorate
Voters who identify themselves with a party.

ticket splitters
Persons who vote for candidates of different parties for different offices in a general election.

party-in-the-government
Public officials who were nominated by their party and who identify themselves in office with their party.

party organization
National and state party officials and workers, committee members, convention delegates, and others active in the party.

Party-in-the-Government

The second locus of party activity is the **party-in-the-government**—officials who received their party's nomination and won the general election. The party-in-the-government includes members of Congress, state legislators and local government officials, and elected members of the executive branch, including the president and governors. Party identification and loyalty among elected officeholders are generally stronger than party identification and loyalty among the party-in-the-electorate.

Within most legislatures, the parties have caucuses of their members. These caucuses organize the U.S. Senate and House of Representatives, and they organize most state legislatures as well. The majority party in the House meets in caucus to select the Speaker of the House as well as the House majority leader and whip. The minority party elects its own minority leader and whip. The majority party in the Senate elects the president pro tempore, who presides during the (frequent) absences of the vice president, as well as the Senate majority leader and whip. The minority party in the Senate elects its own minority leader and whip. Committee assignments in both the House and the Senate are allocated on a party basis; committee chairs are always majority-party members.

Party as Organization

Finally, there is the **party organization**—national and state party officials and workers, committee members, convention delegates, and others active in the party. The Democratic and Republican party organizations formally resemble the American federal system, with national committees; officers and staffs; and national conventions, 50 state committees, and more than 3,000 county committees with city, ward, and precinct levels under their supervision. State committees are not very responsive to the direction of the national committee; and in most states, city and county party organizations operate quite independently of the state committees. In other words, no real hierarchy of authority exists in American parties.

National Party Structure

The Democratic and Republican national party conventions possess *formal* authority over the parties. They meet every four years not only to nominate candidates for president and vice president but also to adopt a party platform, choose party officers, and adopt rules for the party's operation. Because the convention is a large body that meets for only three or four days, however, its real function is to ratify decisions made by national party leaders as well as to formally nominate presidential and vice presidential candidates.

The Democratic and Republican National Committees, made up of delegates from each state and territory, are supposed to govern party affairs *between* conventions. But the *real* work of the national party organizations is undertaken by the national party chairs and staff. The national chair is officially chosen by the national committee. If the party wins the presidency, the national chair usually serves as a liaison with the

Who's Getting What?

Coopting a Major Party: The Tea Party

The "Tea Party" protest movement seeks to evoke the image of the 1773 Boston Tea Party of the American Revolution and the early patriots' opposition to excessive taxation and repressive government. Growing from summer protests against health care reform, the "Taxed Enough Already" movement spawned the creation of diverse and competing organizations in several states, seeking to stake out ground as anti–large government grassroots organizations. Over time, they attracted a wide variety of people opposed to big government, Wall Street bailouts, stimulus spending, exploding deficits, and tax increases.

The Tea Party was not a product of the organized Republican Party. However, conservative Republican activists and operatives were involved in the creation of many Tea Party organizations, and in 2010 the Republican party primaries and Tea Party voters were a natural meeting place for two groups dedicated to the defeat of President Obama's agenda. Polling by the *Wall Street Journal* and NBC News just before the 2010 election showed just over a third of likely voters were Tea Party supporters, who favored Republicans 84 percent to 10 percent. By the end of the 2010 campaign, the House Republicans had a Tea Party Caucus—headed by Michele Bachmann (R-MN)—and many GOP candidates were openly running as Tea party candidates. Half of the 10 Tea Party–backed US Senate candidates won in the 2010 general elections, but less than a third of Tea Party–backed U.S. House candidates prevailed. Subsequent to the 2010 election and the polarizing 2011 and 2012 congressional sessions, Tea Party favorability fell off considerably among American voters.

The Tea Party created a basis of support around issues that were not receiving sufficient attention from the major parties. They gravitated into a major party organization, influenced nomination processes, and compelled Republican leadership in Congress to heed their concerns in legislation. The movement has proved insufficiently powerful to dominate the Republican Party, though they did claim a major leadership "scalp" with the primary defeat of Republican House Floor Leader Eric Cantor (R-VA).

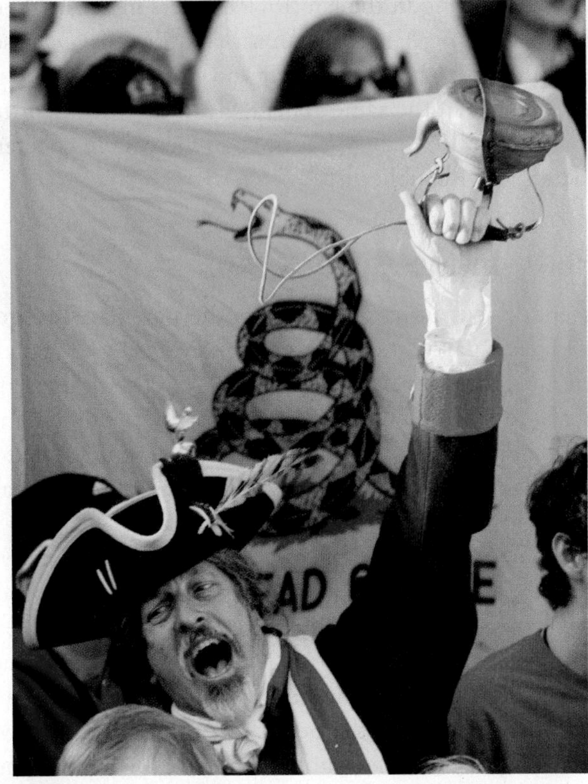

TEA PARTY

The use of durable symbols is one means of communicating ideas and values in politics. Here, a Tea Party supporter captures three strong symbols of the American Revolution—the tea kettle, the tricorner hat, and the 'Don't Tread on Me' flag of the early revolutionaries.

Questions

1. How has the Tea Party changed the Republican Party?
2. Does the Tea Party influence on the GOP create a polarizing political environment? Or did it arise from a polarizing political environment?

president for party affairs. If the party loses, the chair may be replaced before the next national convention. The national chair is supposed to be neutral in the party's primary battles, but when an incumbent president is seeking reelection, the national chair and staff lean very heavily in the president's favor.

☐ State Party Organizations

State party organizations consist of a state committee, a state chair who heads the committee, and a staff working at the state capital. Democratic and Republican state committees vary from state to state in composition, organization, and function. The state party chair is generally selected by the state committee, but this selection is often dictated by the party's candidate for governor. Membership on the state committee may range from about a dozen up to several hundred. The members may be chosen through party primaries or by state party conventions. Generally, representation on state committees is allocated by counties, but occasionally other units of government are recognized in state party organizations.

Most state party organizations maintain full-time staffs, including an executive director and public relations, fund-raising, and research people. These organizations help raise campaign funds for their candidates, conduct registration drives, provide advice and services to their nominees, and even recruit candidates to run in election districts and for offices where the party would otherwise have no names on the ballot. Services to candidates may include advertising and media consulting, advice on election-law compliance, polling, research (including research on opponents), registration and voter identification, mailing lists, and even seminars on campaign techniques.

convention
Nominating process in which delegates from local party organizations select the party's nominees.

presidential primaries
Primary elections in the states in which voters in each party can choose a presidential candidate for their party's nomination. Outcomes help determine the distribution of pledged delegates to each party's national nominating convention.

delegates
Accredited voting members of a party's national presidential nominating convention.

County Committees

The nation's 3,000 Republican and 3,000 Democratic county chairs probably constitute the most important building blocks in party organization in the nation. City and county party officers and committees are chosen in local primary elections; they cannot be removed by state or national party authorities.

National Party Conventions

7.6 Describe changes in the function of the national party conventions.

The Democratic and Republican parties are showcased every four years at the national party **convention**. The official purpose of these four-day, fun-filled events is the nomination of the presidential candidates and their vice presidential running mates. Yet the presidential choices have usually already been made in the parties' **presidential primaries** and caucuses earlier in the year. By midsummer, delegates who were pledged to cast their convention vote for one or another of the presidential candidates have already been selected. Not since 1952, when the Democrats took three convention ballots to select Adlai Stevenson as their presidential candidate, has convention voting gone beyond the first ballot.[16] The possibility exists that in some future presidential race no candidate will win a majority of delegates in the primaries and caucuses, and the result will be a *brokered* convention in which delegates will exercise independent power to select the party nominee. The last president selected by a "brokered" convention was Franklin Delano Roosevelt in 1932, who was chosen on the third ballot.

The Democratic and Republican national conventions are really televised party rallies, designed to showcase the presidential nominee, confirm the nominee's choice for a running mate, and inspire television viewers to support the party and its candidates in the forthcoming general election. Modern conventions are largely media events, carefully staged to present an attractive image of the party and its nominees. Party luminaries jockey for key time slots at the podium, and the party prepares slick videotaped commercials touting its nominee for prime-time presentation.

Convention Delegates

Convention **delegates** are generally party activists, ideologically motivated and strongly committed to their presidential candidates. Democratic delegates are much more *liberal* than Democratic voters, and Republican delegates are more *conservative*

7.1

7.2

7.3

7.4

7.5

7.6

7.7

7.8

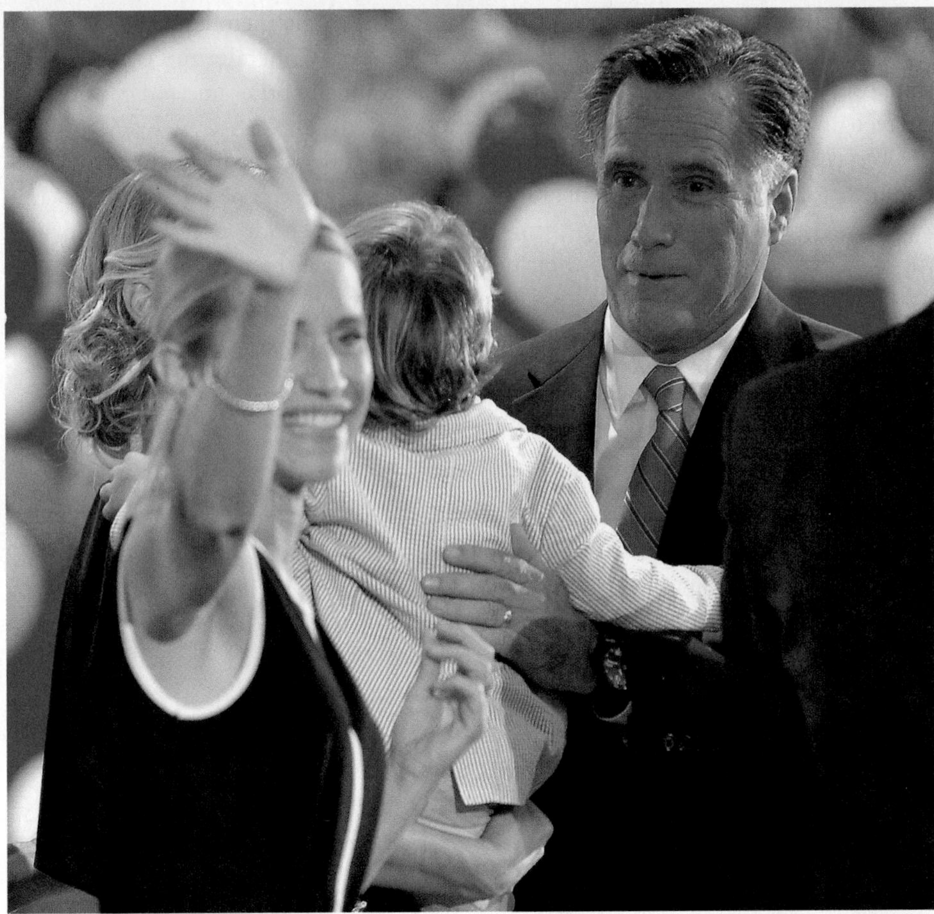

THE TRAPPINGS OF TRADITION

The balloon drop is a traditional, emotional end to a party nominating convention in the United States. The Romneys and Ryans celebrate the former Massachusetts governor's nomination for president amidst a balloon drop at the 2012 GOP convention.

than Republican voters (see Figure 7.10). There is a slight tendency for Democratic and Republican delegates to differ in social backgrounds; usually more African Americans, women, public employees, and union members are found among Democratic delegates than among Republican delegates. Many delegates are also involved in the organizational party as state or local officers or committee persons.

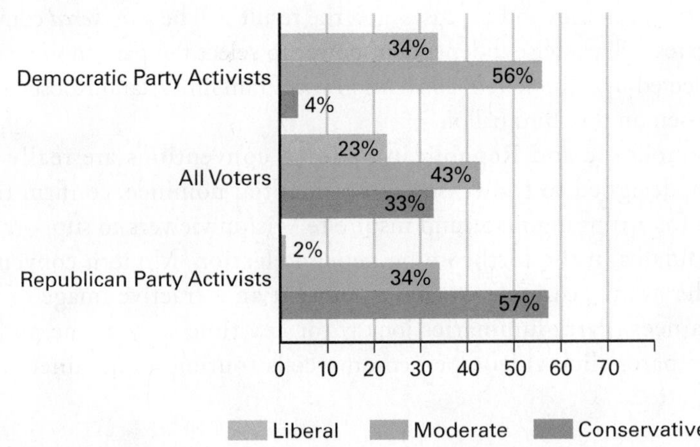

FIGURE 7.10 IDEOLOGIES OF PARTY ACTIVISTS COMPARED TO VOTERS

Democratic and Republican party activists (convention delegates in 2000) are far more likely to hold divergent liberal and conservative views than voters generally.

SOURCE: As reported in the *New York Times*, August 14, 2000.

Making Party Rules

National party conventions make rules for the party, including rules governing the selection of delegates at the next party convention. Democrats are especially likely to focus on delegate selection rules. In 1972, the Democratic Party responded to charges that African Americans, women, and other minorities were underrepresented among the delegates by appointing a special commission chaired by Senator George McGovern to "reform" the party. The McGovern Commission took "affirmative steps" to ensure that the next convention would include "goals" for the representation of African Americans, women, and other minorities among the delegates in proportion to their presence in the Democratic electorate. The effect of these reforms was to reduce the influence of Democratic officeholders (members of Congress, governors, state legislators, and mayors) at the convention and to increase the influence of ideologically motivated activists. Later rule changes eliminated the *unit vote*, in which all delegates from a state were required to vote with the majority of the state's delegation and which required that all delegates who were pledged to a candidate vote for that candidate unless *released* by the candidate.

Then, in the 1980s, the Democratic Leadership Council pressed the party to reserve some convention delegate seats for **superdelegates**—elected officials and party leaders not bound to one candidate—with the expectation that these delegates would be more moderate than the liberal party activists. The notion was that the superdelegates would inject more balanced, less ideological political judgments into convention deliberations, thus improving the party's chances of victory in the general elections. As a result, many Democratic senators, governors, and members of Congress now attend the convention as superdelegates. If presidential candidates fail to win a majority of delegates in the primaries and caucus, these superdelegates may control a nomination.

superdelegates
Delegates to the Democratic Party national convention selected because of their position in the government or the party and not pledged to any candidate.

platform
Statement of principles adopted by a political party at its national convention (specific portions of the platform are known as planks); a platform is not binding on the party's candidates.

Party Platforms

National conventions also write party platforms, setting out the party's goals and policy positions. Because a party's **platform** is not binding on its nominees, platform *planks* are largely symbolic, although they often provide heated arguments and provide distinct differences between the parties to present to voters.

Selecting a Running Mate

Perhaps the only suspense remaining in national party conventions centers on the presidential nominee's choice of a vice-presidential running mate. Even a presidential candidate who has decided on a running mate well in advance of the convention may choose to wait until the convention to announce the choice, otherwise there would be little real "news value" to the convention, and the television networks would give less coverage to it. By encouraging speculation about who the running mate will be, the candidate and the convention manager can sustain media interest.

The convention *always* accepts the presidential candidate's recommendation for a running mate. No formal rules require the convention to do so, but it would be politically unacceptable for the convention to override the first important decision of the party's presidential nominee. Convention delegates set aside any personal reservations they may have and unanimously endorse the presidential nominee's choice.

Campaign Kickoff

The final evening of the national conventions is really the kickoff for the general election campaign. The presidential nominee's acceptance speech tries to set the tone for the fall campaign. Party celebrities, including defeated presidential candidates, join hands at the podium as a symbol of party unity. Presidential and vice-presidential candidates, spouses, and families assemble under balloons and streamers, amid the happy noise and hoopla, to signal the start of the general election campaign. TV coverage helps provide the parties with small postconvention "bumps" in the polls—though such bumps rarely have a lasting effect on the campaign.[17]

Volunteers: The Life of the Party

Despite the perception that politics is a large-dollar profession, the operation of most Democratic and Republican parties is done on a limited budget. Instead, political party organizations run on the power of individuals committed to supporting and maintaining the party organization. State party organizations and some local organizations in heavily populated urban counties will have professional staffers, such as an executive director, a communications director, and support staff. Much of the expertise that supports the party is often subcontracted out, including polling, fund-raising, and communications costs such as design, printing, and mailings.

But in most local parties (and in some state parties) the work is done by volunteers. These volunteers will staff local and state party offices. They will work phone banks, contacting voters at election time, or calling potential party donors ("dialing for dollars") to raise money for the party operation. They will work distributing campaign literature on behalf of party candidates and deploying campaign signs in general elections. They help run local and state party meetings and conventions, and help set up other party events, such as fund-raisers. And they do so for no compensation. They serve as polling place workers, representing the party's interests in the conduct of fair elections. Unlike other forms of political activity, the barrier to participation as a volunteer is low; all you have to do is show up.

THE SPOUSE AS CANDIDATE

Michelle Obama speaks to the 2012 Democratic National Convention. Since 1992 when Hillary Clinton and Barbara Bush spoke at the national conventions supporting their husbands Bill and George, candidate spouses have been part of the convention lineup.

Volunteers are usually strong partisans, of all ages, who are drawn to the party for various reasons. Some are socialized to politics by their family. Others are drawn to the party because of an issue, a belief system, or a desire to be active in politics. They come into party politics through the Young Democrats or the College Republicans, or because they are in a union job where the union is active in the party. Sometimes, they come to politics through their church—a common experience among both white and African American evangelical Christians.

Volunteers are important. They cultivate interest in politics and develop an ongoing source of dedicated labor for the party and its candidates. Parties often develp campaign professionals and candidates from their volunteers. Future party leaders and convention delegates often start as volunteers, as do many local officeholders, state lawmakers, and federal officials.

third parties
Political parties that challenge the two major parties in an election.

ideological parties
Third parties that exist to promote an ideology rather than to win elections.

protest parties
Third parties that arise in response to issues of popular concern that have not been addressed by the major parties.

7.1 7.2 7.3 7.4 7.5 7.6 7.7 7.8

Third Parties in the United States

7.7 Evaluate the role of third parties within the U.S. electoral system.

Despite the cultural and electoral barriers to victory, **third parties**, more accurately called minor parties, are a common feature of American politics. These parties can be roughly classified by the role they play in the political system.

Ideological Parties

Ideological parties exist to promote an ideology rather than to win elections. They use the electoral process to express their views and to rally activists to their cause, and they measure success not by victory at the polls but by their ability to bring their names and their views to the attention of the American public. The socialist parties, which have run candidates in virtually every presidential election in this century, are prime examples of ideological parties in the United States.

Protest Parties

Protest parties arise around popular issues or concerns that the major parties have failed to address. An important historical example of a protest party is the Populist Party of the late 1800s. It arose as a protest by Midwestern farmers against eastern railroads, "trusts" and monopolies, and the gold standard. The Populists threatened to capture the wave of popular support for railroad regulation, cheap money, and antimonopoly legislation, and thus they endangered the established Democratic and Republican parties. But when the Democratic Party nominated William Jennings Bryan in 1896, the Populist Party officially endorsed Bryan and temporarily disappeared as a significant independent political organization. Populist ideas were set forth again in a new Progressive Party, which nominated Robert M. La Follette for president in 1924; the Democratic and Republican parties both nominated conservative candidates that year, helping La Follette win almost 17 percent of the popular vote.

Not all major protest movements have been accompanied by the formation of third parties. Indeed, protest leaders have often argued that a third-party effort distracts the movement from a more effective strategy of capturing control of one or both of the major parties. The labor-union-organizing movement of the 1930s and the civil rights and antiwar movements of the 1960s did not spark a separate third party but instead worked largely *within* the Democratic Party to advance their goals. The "Tea Party" protesters quickly evolved to work largely in the Republican Party.

The Game, the Rules, the Players

Republicans Rebound: The 2014 Midterm Elections

Thirty-year senate veteran Mitch McConnell (D-Ky.) overcame a major reelection challenge to lead the Republicans to a majority in the U.S. Senate.

Traditionally midterm elections have not proven very favorable to the party in the White House. And with President Barack Obama's approval ratings at a relatively weak 42 percent, prospects for congressional Democrats in 2014 were decidedly negative. To make matters worse for the Democrats in the Senate, 21 of the 36 seats to be elected were held by Democrats and only 15 by Republicans, thereby giving more targets to the GOP. Finally, Republican primary elections brought forth some very strong candidates; the GOP "establishment" worked to defeat more militant "Tea Party" challengers.

GOP Victories The House of Representatives was expected to remain Republican-controlled. The real battle was for control of the Senate. The Democrats went into the election with a 55 to 45 lead in that chamber (with two "independents" aligning themselves with the Democratic block). Republicans needed to hold on to all of their incumbents' seats, while capturing at least six Democratic-held seats. They succeeded in doing so. All GOP incumbents won, and Republicans won formerly Democratic seats in Arkansas, Colorado, Iowa, West Virginia, Montana, North Carolina, South Dakota, Alaska, and Louisiana. The new Senate would be controlled by a 54-seat Republican majority. The Republican leader, Mitch McConnell, after winning a spirited race for his own Kentucky seat, was set to become the new Majority Leader.

Republicans also expanded their majority in the House of Representatives. A fourteen to eighteen seat increase in the GOP's 223 seats promised to give Speaker John Boehner greater flexibility in dealing with rebellious Tea Party Republican members. Boehner will enjoy the largest House Republican majority in modern times.

Republicans were also successful in winning a majority of the nation's governorships. With the exception of Pennsylvania, GOP candidates won governorships in presidential swing states, Florida, Ohio, Michigan, Illinois, and Maryland. The key states of Wisconsin and Florida were hotly contested. Republican governor Scott Walker of Wisconsin had made a national name for himself in winning a recall election in 2012 after clashing with public employee unions over bargaining rights. Unions throughout the country poured millions of dollars into the race to defeat Walker, but he won easily in a traditionally Democratic state. Republican governor Rick Scott of Florida squeaked out a victory against former governor Charlie Crist. Crist had earlier served as Florida's Republican governor, but switched parties after his defeat in a Senate primary race by the popular Marco Rubio. Scott's approval ratings had been low throughout his tenure, but voters appeared to distrust the party "flip-flopper," Crist.

The Obama Factor Sagging in the polls and unwelcome by fellow Democrats in many competitive states across the country, Obama and his policies appeared to be partially responsible for the Democratic defeat. Obamacare remained problematic; many features, including coverage of prior conditions, were popular, but the individual mandate to purchase insurance and the increase in insurance costs were highly unpopular. Obama's "war on coal" (actually on all fossil fuels) hurt in Kentucky and West Virginia, and his opposition to the Keystone Pipeline hurt in Louisiana and elsewhere.

Obama had acquired an image of incompetence in dealing with a variety of domestic and foreign affairs. These included the initial website disaster in the rollout of Obamacare; the IRS targeting of conservative organizations; the release of five high-ranking terrorists in exchange for a suspected deserter; the misleading of the American people about the terrorist attack in Benghazi that killed the U.S. ambassador; incompetence in the administration of the Department of Veterans Affairs; the return of ISIS terrorists to Iraq and Syria following the U.S. complete withdrawal from Iraq; the Centers for Disease Control handling of the Ebola scare; the Snowden affair with revelations of widespread National Security Agency snooping; the Russian capture of the Crimea and their support for Russian separatists in the Ukraine.

Obama himself refused to accept the midterm elections as a referendum on his policies. While he

(Continued)

(*Continued*)

publicly expressed a willingness to compromise with the Republican Congress, in actual negotiations (when they were held at all) he refused to budge from this policy positions. And Obama's earlier pledge to bypass Congress on key issues such as immigration did not ingratiate him with congressional leaders. Opportunities for compromise may exist, notably on corporate taxes, trade authority, and infrastructure development, but it is uncertain whether Obama can deal with a newly energized Republican congressional leadership. Obama faces his final two years in the White House as a "lame duck," unlikely to get any of his priorities enacted into law.

Turnout Turnout appeared about average for a midterm election—approximately 35% of the voting age population, compared to 50–55% four presidential elections. Lower turnouts tend to increase the influence of highly partisan voters. Republicans are also somewhat more likely to vote than Democrats. High turnouts usually increase the influence of African-Americans and young people. Despite Democratic efforts at the "ground game"—efforts to increase turnout on Election Day—turnout was not much higher than previous midterm elections. Democrats had succeeded in most states in extending voting days, including Sundays to bring "souls to the polls" from African-American churches. Republicans had succeeded in various states in enacting voter photo ID requirements, believing that voter fraud gave Democratic candidates an edge.

Voter Discontent Polls signaled that voters were deeply pessimistic about the country with nearly 70 percent describing the economy as poor or not so good, and two-thirds believing that the country was "on the wrong track." Most voters cited the economy as their chief concern. Recovery from the Great Recession had been long and slow. Statistically the economy appeared relatively healthy (an unemployment rate below 6% and a GDP growth rate above 2%). But many voters did not "feel" that the economy had recovered. The nation's workforce had shrunk to historic lows, with many discouraged workers giving up looking for jobs (and therefore not counted as unemployed), while others chose to take early retirement or disability payments. Many others who lost jobs during recession found new jobs but at lower wages than they previously enjoyed. Real wages have declined in recent years.

☐ Single-Issue Parties

single-issue parties
Third parties formed around one particular cause.

splinter parties
Third parties formed by a dissatisfied faction of a major party.

Single-issue parties have frequently formed around a particular cause. Single-issue parties are much like protest parties, although somewhat narrower in their policy focus. The Greenback Party of the late 1800s shared with the Populists a desire for cheap inflated currency in order to ease the burden of debt and mortgage payments by farmers. But the Greenback Party focused on a single remedy: an end to the gold standard and the issuance of cheap currency—"greenbacks."

Perhaps the most persistent of minor parties over the years has been the Prohibition Party. It achieved temporary success with the passage of the 18th Amendment to the U.S. Constitution in 1919, which prohibited the manufacture, sale, or transportation of "intoxicating liquors," only to see its "noble experiment" fail and be repealed by the 21st Amendment.

Today, the Green Party provides an example of a single-issue party, with its primary emphasis on environmental protection. However, the Green Party itself contends that it is "part of the worldwide movement that promotes ecological wisdom, social justice, grassroots democracy and non-violence." Ralph Nader was the Green Party presidential candidate in 2000; he won about 2 percent of the vote. Nader's critics claimed that he helped Republican George W. Bush win that election by siphoning off votes from Democrat Al Gore.

☐ Splinter Parties

Finally, many third parties in American politics are really **splinter parties**, parties formed by a dissatisfied faction of a major party. Splinter parties may form around a particular individual, as did the Progressive (Bull Moose) Party of Theodore Roosevelt in 1912. As a popular former president, Teddy Roosevelt won more than 27 percent of the popular vote, outpolling Republican candidate William Howard Taft but allowing Democrat Woodrow Wilson to win the presidency.

7.1 7.2 7.3 7.4 7.5 7.6 7.7 7.8

Splinter parties also may emerge from an intense intraparty policy dispute. For example, in 1948, the States' Rights (Dixiecrat) Party formed in protest to the civil rights (fair employment practices) plank in the Democratic Party platform of that year and nominated Strom Thurmond for president. In 1968, George Wallace's American Independent Party won nearly 14 percent of the popular vote. Wallace attacked school desegregation and busing to achieve racial balance in schools as well as crime in the streets, welfare "cheats," and meddling federal judges and bureaucrats. He abandoned his third-party organization in 1972 to run in the Democratic presidential primary elections. Following some Democratic primary victories, he was shot and disabled for life.

☐ An Anti-Party Party

Many Americans feel disgusted with "politics as usual." They view both the Democratic and Republican parties as ineffective, unprincipled, and even corrupt. They represent a dealignment from the current party system; that is, they have no party loyalty and they usually describe themselves as "Independents." In 1992, Texas billionaire Ross Perot was able to mobilize many of these Independents into a third-party challenge to the two-party system. He spent nearly $100 million of his own money to build a nationwide organization, the Reform Party (originally called United We Stand) and to place his name on the ballot of all 50 states. Early in the campaign, his poll numbers mushroomed to 35 percent, higher than any other independent candidate's support in the history of modem polling. His political support came mostly from the center of the political spectrum—people who identified themselves as Independents. Perot participated in the first three-way presidential television debates and won 19 percent of the popular vote in the general election, the highest percentage won by a third-party candidate since Teddy Roosevelt in 1912. But he failed to win a single electoral vote. Perot ran again in 1996, but when his early poll numbers languished, he was excluded from the presidential debates. On Election Day, he won fewer than half of the votes (9 percent) that he had garnered four years earlier, and again failed to win any state's electoral votes. In 2000, the Reform Party imploded in a raucous convention, with rival factions almost coming to blows over control of the microphone. The party officially nominated conservative firebrand Pat Buchanan, but Buchanan's right-wing rhetoric attracted less

TABLE 7.4 OPPOSING THE TWO-PARTY SYSTEM: MODERN THIRD-PARTY PRESIDENTIAL VOTES

Independent and third-party presidential candidates have failed to win any electoral votes over the last 40 years.

Third-Party Presidential Candidates	Popular Vote (percentage)	Electoral Votes (number)
Theodore Roosevelt (1912), Progressive (Bull Moose) Party	27.4%	88
Robert M. La Follette (1924), Progressive Party	16.6	13
George C. Wallace (1968), American Independent Party	13.5	46
John Anderson (1980), Independent	6.6	0
Ross Perot (1992), Independent	18.9	0
Ross Perot (1996), Reform Party	8.5	0
Ralph Nader (2000), Green Party	2.7	0
Ralph Nader (2004), Independent	0.4	0
Ralph Nader (2008), Independent	0.4	0

than 1 percent of the voters. By 2004, many states had dropped the Reform Party from their ballots.

☐ Third-Party Prospects

In recent years, polls have reported that a majority of Americans favor the idea of a third party. But support for the *general* idea of a third party has never been matched by voter support for *specific* third-party or Independent presidential candidates (see Table 7.4).[18] Moreover, it is very difficult for a third party or Independent candidate to win electoral votes. Only Theodore Roosevelt, Robert M. La Follette, and George C. Wallace managed to win any electoral votes in the past century. The Reform Party, founded by billionaire Ross Perot in 1992, was the latest serious yet unsuccessful attempt to create a nationwide third party.

Why the Two-Party System Persists

7.8 Determine why the American two-party system has persisted.

The two-party system is deeply ingrained in American politics. Although third parties have often made appearances in presidential elections, no third-party candidate has ever won the Oval Office. (Lincoln's new Republican Party in 1860 might be counted as an exception, but it quickly became a major party.) Very few third-party candidates have won seats in Congress. Many other democracies have multiple-party systems, so the question arises as to why the United States has had a two-party system throughout its history.[19]

☐ Cultural Consensus

One explanation of the nation's continuing two-party system focuses on the broad consensus supporting the American political culture. The values of democracy, capitalism, free enterprise, individual liberty, religious freedom, and equality of opportunity are so widely shared that no party challenging these values has ever won much of a following. There is little support in the American political culture for avowedly fascist, communist, authoritarian, or other antidemocratic parties. Moreover, the American political culture includes a strong belief in the separation of church and state. Political parties with religious affiliations, common in European democracies, are absent from American politics. Socialist parties have frequently appeared on the scene under various labels—the Socialist Party, the Socialist Labor Party, and the Socialist Workers Party. But the largest popular vote ever garnered by a socialist candidate in a presidential election was the 6 percent won by Eugene V. Debs in 1912. In contrast, socialist parties have frequently won control of European governments.

On broad policy issues, most Americans cluster near the center. This general consensus tends to discourage multiple parties. There does not appear to be sufficient room for them to stake out a position on the ideological spectrum that would detach voters from the two major parties.

This cultural explanation blends with the influence of historical precedents. The American two-party system has gained acceptance through custom. The nation's first party system developed from two coalitions, Federalists and Anti-Federalists, and this dual pattern has been reinforced over two centuries.

7.1

7.2

7.3

7.4

7.5

7.6

7.7

7.8

proportional representation
Electoral system that allocates seats in a legislature based on the proportion of votes each party receives in a national election.

Winner-Takes-All Electoral System

Yet another explanation of the American two-party system focuses on the electoral system itself. Winners in presidential and congressional elections, as well as in state gubernatorial and legislative elections, are usually determined by a plurality, winner-takes-all vote. Even in elections that require a majority of more than 50 percent to win—which may involve a runoff election—only one party's candidate wins in the end. Because of the winner-takes-all nature of U.S. elections, parties and candidates have an overriding incentive to broaden their appeal to a plurality or majority of voters. Losers come away empty-handed. There is not much incentive in such a system for a party to form to represent the views of 5 or 10 percent of the electorate.

Americans are so accustomed to winner-takes-all elections that they seldom consider alternatives. In some countries, legislative bodies are elected by **proportional representation**, whereby all voters cast a single ballot for the party of their choice and legislative seats are then apportioned to the parties in proportion to their total vote in the electorate (see also *Compared to What?* More Proportional Representation? Ireland, Land of the STV.). Minority parties are assured of legislative seats, perhaps with as little as 10 or 15 percent of the vote. If no party wins 50 percent of the votes and seats, the parties try to form a coalition of parties to establish control of the government. In these nations, party coalition building to form a governing majority occurs *after* the election rather than *before* the election, as it does in winner-takes-all election systems.

Legal Access to the Ballot

Another factor in the American two-party system may be electoral system barriers to third parties. The Democratic and Republican nominees are automatically included on all general election ballots, but third-party and Independent candidates face difficult obstacles in getting their names listed. In presidential elections, a third-party candidate must meet the varied requirements of 50 separate states to appear on their ballots along with the Democratic and Republican nominees. These requirements often include filing petitions signed by up to 5 or 10 percent of registered voters. In addition, states require third parties to win 5 or 10 percent of the vote in the last election in order to retain their position on the ballot in subsequent elections. In 1980, Independent John Anderson gained access to the ballot in all 50 states, as did Independent Ross Perot in 1992. But just doing so required a considerable expenditure of effort and money that the major parties were able to avoid.

Compared to What?

More Proportional Representation? Ireland, Land of the STV

A criticism of American legislative elections is that the "winner take all" quality of single-member districts leaves some parties or groups without representation. A common method of election that is supposed to provide for more parties and more proportional representation is to use multimember districts with a "single, transferable vote" (STV). This is the system the Republic of Ireland uses to elect its parliament (the Dáil Éireann). As a result, in Ireland, six political parties plus independents all send representatives to the national legislature, compared to just two parties in the U.S.

How it works: The Republic of Ireland is divided among 44 parliamentary constituencies. Each constituency elects between three and five members of parliament (MPs), depending on how many people live in the constituency. Most of the parliament members come from the larger counties—for example, Dublin is divided into 11 constituencies and elects a total of 39 MPs. Voters cast ballots for individual candidates, who might or might not be members of parties.

Unlike in the U.S., though, where a voter casts one vote for a candidate to win, the Irish get to cast as many votes as there are seats to fill from the constituency, by ranking their preferences. So, if a district elects three members, they rank the available candidates from most acceptable to least acceptable.

If the number of votes a candidate receives from being in the "top 3" is greater than the total number of votes cast divided by 4 (seats to be filled +1), then they are elected. Any excess votes over this "threshold of inclusion" for a winning candidate are then reallocated to the next-preferred candidate on the list.

Party	Votes	Seats
Ruling Coalition		
Fine Gael	36.1%	69
Labour	19.5%	34
Oppositon		
Fianna Fail	17.5%	19
Sinn Fein	9.9%	14
People Before Profit	1.0%	1
Socialists	1.2%	1
Independents/Others	14.2%	27

If no one makes the threshold, then the lowest vote getter is eliminated and her or his votes are redistributed to the remaining, preferred candidates. This continues until enough candidates exceed the threshold of inclusion to fill the available seats in the constituency.

One result is that locally strong political parties that can't command a local majority can still win seats in the parliament. For example, Irish nationalist Sinn Fein party, which is historically the strongest advocate for ending Irish partition, is the fourth-largest vote-getting party in the Irish republic. But, despite being fourth everywhere and at best second in most counties, the party wins seats in areas like Dublin and Cork, even though it is not the majority party.

The other result is that no party can easily win control of government. Since 1989, no party has won a majority of the seats in parliament. Coalitions of two or more parties are required to organize the government and make law. So, in addition to the dominant center-left Fine Gael and center-right Fianna Fail parties, other parties such as the environmentalist Greens, the free-market Progressive Democrats, and the social-progressive Labour parties have all been part of governing majority coalitions.

Questions

1. Which parties are advantaged by the STV system in Ireland?
2. Do you think using a system like this in the United States would change party politics? How?

7.1

7.2

7.3

7.4

7.5

7.6

7.7

7.8

A Constitutional Note

Political Parties and the Constitution

Political parties had not yet formed in 1787 when the Founders met in Philadelphia to draft the Constitution. Indeed, George Washington and the other Founders believed that the new nation might be destroyed by the "baneful effects of the spirit of party." Nowhere in the Constitution do we find any reference to "parties." Indeed, the original Constitution called for presidential electors to cast two votes for president, with the candidate receiving the highest number becoming president and the candidate with the second-highest becoming vice president. But by 1800, parties had formed: the Federalists rallied around John Adams, the second president; and the Democratic-Republicans (often called Republicans, but not to be confused with today's Republican Party) supported Thomas Jefferson. Candidates for the Electoral College ran under these labels (or sometimes as just Adams's men or Jefferson's men). In the 1800 presidential election, the Democratic-Republican party won a majority of electors. But all of them had cast their votes for both Jefferson and his intended vice president, Aaron Burr. Thus Jefferson and Burr ended up with the same number of electoral votes, 73, for president. For a while, Burr considered challenging Jefferson for president, but in the end conceded the office. The incident illustrated the failure of the Founders to envision parties as central to the electoral process. Congress and the states were obliged to add the 12th Amendment to the Constitution by 1804 in order to separate "in distinct ballots" the persons voted for as president and vice president.

Question

1. Do you think party politics require us to consider additional changes to the Constitution, like we made in 1804?

Review the Chapter

The Power of Organization

7.1 Show how the relationship between organization and political power explains political parties and interest groups, p. 214

In the political arena, organization grants advantage. Political parties organize people in order to give them power in selecting government officials. Interest groups and political parties act as intermediaries between individuals and the government. Political parties compete for office and interest groups attempt to influence the making of public policy.

Party Voters

7.2 Assess the trends regarding party identification and loyalty of voters, p. 214

Dealignment refers to a decline in the attractiveness of the parties to voters, a growing reluctance of people to identify strongly with either party, and greater voter willingness to cross party lines. Despite dealignment, party identification remains a strong influence in voter choice.

American Parties: A Historical Perspective

7.3 Trace changes in political parties over the course of American history, p. 219

Political parties are not mentioned in the U.S. Constitution, yet they have played a central role in American political history. Major party realignments have occurred at critical points in American history, as major social groups shifted their political loyalties.

Political Parties and Democratic Government

7.4 Outline the functions and perceptions of the two major American political parties, explain how the parties are financed, and assess their changing role in the electoral process, p. 229

In theory, political parties are "responsible" organizations that adopt a principled platform, recruit candidates who support the platform, educate the public about it, direct an issue-oriented campaign, and then legislate and ensure that their candidates enact the party's platform. Political parties and candidates raise hundreds of millions of dollars each election year. Traditionally, the Republicans were able to raise more money than the Democrats but the gap between the two parties has narrowed in recent years. The Republicans usually have the support of the health care, insurance, manufacturing, and oil and gas interests, while the Democrats enjoy the support of teachers, union members, and the entertainment industries. American parties have lost many of their traditional functions. Party nominations are won by individual candidates in primary elections rather than through selection by party leaders. Most political candidates are self-selected: they organize their own campaigns. Television and new media have replaced the party as the principal means of educating the public. Party nominations are won in primary elections as earlier caucus and convention methods of nomination have largely disappeared. Primary elections in the various states may be open or closed and may or may not require run-off primaries. Primaries are also blamed for increased polarization of the parties. The nominees selected in each party's primary election then battle each other in the general election.

Where's the Party?

7.5 Differentiate between the three political arenas in which the parties battle, p. 240

The parties battle in three major arenas. The *party-in-the-electorate* refers to party identification among voters. The *party-in-government* refers to party identification and organization among elected officials. The *party organization* refers to party offices at the local, state, and national levels.

National Party Conventions

7.6 Describe changes in the function of the national party conventions, p. 243

Since presidential nominations are now generally decided in primary elections—with pledged delegates selected before the opening of the national conventions and with party platforms largely symbolic and wholly unenforceable on the candidates—the conventions have become largely media events designed to kick off the general election.

Third Parties in the U.S. System

7.7 Evaluate the role of third parties within the U.S. electoral system, p. 247

Opinion polls indicate that most Americans support the general idea of a third party, but throughout the twentieth century, no third-party candidate won very many votes.

Why the Two-Party System Persists

7.8 Determine why the American two-party system has persisted, p. 251

In the United States, many aspects of the political system—including cultural consensus, the winner-take-all electoral system, and legal restriction to ballot access—place major obstacles in the way of success for third parties and Independent candidates. Although never successful at gaining federal office in significant numbers, ideological, protest, single-issue, and splinter third parties have often been effective at getting popular issues on the federal agenda.

Learn the Terms

political organizations, p. 214
political parties, p. 214
party identification, p. 214
realignment, p. 215
dealignment, p. 218
Federalists, p. 219
Anti-Federalists, p. 219
majority, p. 221
plurality, p. 221
Democratic Party, p. 221
Whig Party, p. 221
Republican Party, p. 222
battlefield sectionalism, p. 222
GOP, p. 223
New Deal, p. 223
Fair Deal, p. 224
Great Society, p. 224
Reagan Coalition, p. 225
responsible party model, p. 230
median voter theorem, p. 230
wedge issue theorem, p. 231
party polarization, p. 231
nominee, p. 233
nominations, p. 233
primary elections, p. 233
machines, p. 233
patronage, p. 233
divided party government, p. 233
nonpartisan elections, p. 236
caucus, p. 236
wards, p. 237
precincts, p. 237
closed primaries, p. 237
open primaries, p. 237
raiding, p. 237
runoff primary, p. 238
general election, p. 239
party-in-the-electorate, p. 241
ticket splitters, p. 241
party-in-the-government, p. 241
party organization, p. 241
convention, p. 243
presidential primaries, p. 243
delegates, p. 243
superdelegates, p. 245
platform, p. 245
third parties, p. 247
ideological parties, p. 247
protest parties, p. 247
single-issue parties, p. 249
splinter parties, p. 249
proportional representation, p. 252

Test Yourself

7.1 Show how the relationship between organization and political power explains political parties and interest groups

Both political parties and interest groups

a. are interested in winning political office
b. are focused on ideology and policy
c. function as intermediaries between individuals and government
d. are bound by very formal divisions of functions
e. are indistinguishable in the modern political environment

7.2 Assess the trends regarding party identification and loyalty of voters.

When voters tend to fall away from identifying with any political party, this is called

a. dealignment
b. realignment
c. battlefield sectionalism
d. responsible party voting
e. deflection

7.3 Trace changes in political parties over the course of American history.

The present-day Democratic Party grew out of the

a. Federalists
b. Democratic-Republicans
c. Whigs
d. Anti-Whigs
e. The Official Monster Raving Loony Party

7.4 Outline the functions and perceptions of the two major American political parties, explain how the parties are financed, and assess their changing role in the electoral process.

A "responsible party" is expected to do which of the following functions?

I. Recruit candidates who agree with the party platform
II. Hold elected officials accountable
III. Adopt a platform stating the party principles
IV. Win office by compromising principles.

a. only IV
b. Only II and III
c. Only I and III
d. only I, II, and III
e. I, II, III, and IV

7.5 Differentiate between the three political arenas in which the parties battle.

The "real work" of the national party organization is undertaken by the

a. president of each party
b. governors of each state
c. Congress's Political Parties Committee
d. National Party Chairs and staff
e. volunteers

7.6 Describe changes in the function of the national party conventions

It would be correct to contend that, with respect to participants at party conventions

a. party convention delegates are not ideologically motivated
b. union members are more likely to be Democratic delegates rather than Republican delegates
c. Republican delegates tend to be more liberal than Republican voters
d. Democratic delegates tend to be more conservative than Democratic voters
e. The convention is largely dominated by broadcast networks

7.7 Evaluate the role of third parties within the U.S. electoral system.

Minority parties have a better chance of gaining some legislative seats in a

a. single-party system
b. a nonpartisan system
c. two-party system
d. super primary state
e. proportional representation system

7.8 Determine why the American two-party system has persisted.

An electoral system that allocates seats on the basis of the percentage of votes received is referred to as

a. single-member representation
b. a republic
c. a winner-takes-all system
d. proportional representation
e. an elitist system

Explore Further

SUGGESTED READINGS

Hershey, Marjorie. *Party Politics in America*. 13th ed. New York: Longman, 2008. An authoritative text on the American party system—party organizations, the parties-in-government, and the parties-in-the-electorate.

Downs, Anthony. *An Economic Theory of Democracy*. New York: Harper & Row, 1957. The classic work describing rational choice winning strategies for political parties and explaining why there is no incentive for vote-maximizing parties in a two-party system to adopt widely separate policy positions.

Hetherington, Marc J., and Bruce A. Larson. *Parties, Politics, and Public Policy in America*. 11th ed. Washington, D.C.: CQ Press, 2009. A comprehensive survey of American political parties, from the nominating process to campaign finance and the changing affiliations of voters.

Lowi, Theodore E., and Joseph Romange. *Debating the Two-Party System*. Boulder, Colo.: Rowman & Littlefield, 1997. Lowi argues that the two-party system is no longer adequate to represent the people of a diverse nation; Romange counters that two parties help unify the country and instruct Americans about the value of compromise.

Wattenberg, Martin P. *The Decline of American Political Parties, 1952–1992*. Cambridge, Mass.: Harvard University Press, 1994. An authoritative discussion of increasing negative attitudes toward the parties and the growing dealignment in the electorate.

White, John Kenneth, and Daniel M. Shen. *New Party Politics*. 2nd ed. Belmont, Calif.: Wadsworth, 2004. Historical approach to evolution of the American party system.

SUGGESTED WEB SITES

Center for Responsive Politics www.opensecrets.org
Source of information on campaign finances—contributors, recipients, PACs, lobbyists, and so forth.

Democratic Leadership Council/New Democrats Online http://www.dlc.org/
Moderate Democrats in the House and Senate set forth their views.

Democratic National Committee (DNC) www.democrats.org
News, press releases, policy positions, and so forth.

Franklin D. Roosevelt (FDR) Heritage Center http://www.fdrheritage.org/fdrbio.htm
Biography on FDR and information on the New Deal.

Libertarian Party www.lp.org
This site reflects the Libertarian Party's strong ideological commitments to individual liberty, free markets, and nonintervention in world affairs.

MoveOn www.moveon.org
Web site of the liberal political action committee.

The Polling Report www.pollingreport.com
Up-to-date polling information from a variety of polls on Democratic and Republican party preferences.

Reagan Library Page http://www.reaganfoundation.org/
This site is for the Reagan Presidential Library and celebrates Reagan's presidential achievements.

Reform Party www.reformparty.org
Information about founder Ross Perot and the principles of and news about the party.

Republican National Committee (RNC) www.rnc.org
GOP news, press releases, policy positions, and so forth.

8

Campaigns and Elections

Deciding Who Governs

Elected to the Nebraska legislature at 26 and state attorney general at age 32, Republican Jon Bruning's political career never lacked for money. In his first race for attorney general, he spent almost half a million dollars. In 2006 he was finance chair for GOP gubernatorial candidate Tom Osborne's campaign. In 2007, his brief US Senate campaign raised three-quarters of a million dollars, an amount which helped compel incumbent Republican U.S. Sen. Chuck Hagel to bow out of the race. Bruning deferred to former Governor Mike Johanns, but set his sights on running for the open Senate seat in 2012, left vacant by the retirement of Democratic U.S. Sen. Ben Nelson.

In 2012, Bruning and his main GOP primary opponent, state treasurer Don Stenberg, engaged in a bitter and negative campaign in which Bruning would hold a decided spending advantage—he raised and spent nearly $3.5 million in the campaign, compared to about $700,000 for Stenberg. Usually, spending the most money would be enough to win this kind of election. But Bruning lost—and so did Stenberg.

The winner, state lawmaker Deb Fisher, came from behind. Successful female candidates are not unusual in Nebraska; one in three elected officials are women, and the state elected women to the positions of governor and U.S. senator. But although Fisher trailed most polls, she enjoyed support from conservative favorite Sarah Palin. Critical to her victory, however, was a million-dollar expenditure by a Florida-based SuperPAC, attacking Bruning's ethics and finances. In 2014 Bruning again sought to move up, this time to the governor's mansion. And, again, he was the front-runner. But substantial SuperPAC money came in again and led to his narrow defeat in the 2014 GOP primary.

Money is a critical component in political campaigns. But spending the most money does not guarantee victory—the timing of spending, the intensity of a candidate's grassroots support, and the right message can combine with enough money to make a successful campaign.

8.1	8.2	8.3	8.4	8.5	8.6	8.7
Evaluate the role of elections in American democracy, p. 260	Characterize the various factors that motivate people to pursue a political career, p. 261	Explain the advantages of incumbency, p. 263	Identify the main components of campaign strategies, p. 265	Analyze the role of money in campaigns, identify the major sources of funding, assess the motivations of contributors, and evaluate efforts to regulate campaign finances, p. 271	Outline candidates' strategies for primary races and the general election, p. 281	Assess influences on voters' choices, p. 296

ONE AT A TIMIN' Alison Lundergan Grimes (D-KY) challenged U.S. Senate majority leader Mitch McConnell in one of the most closely watched campaigns of 2014.

Elections in a Democracy

8.1 Evaluate the role of elections in American democracy.

mandate
Perception of popular support for a program or policy based on the margin of electoral victory won by a candidate who proposed it during a campaign.

retrospective voting
Voting for or against a candidate or party on the basis of past performance in office.

Democratic government is government by "the consent of the governed." Elections give practical meaning to this notion of "consent." Elections allow people to choose among competing candidates and parties and to decide who will occupy public office. Elections give people the opportunity to pass judgment on current officeholders, either by reelecting them (granting continued consent) or by throwing them out of office (withdrawing consent).

In a representative democracy, elections function primarily to choose personnel to occupy public office—to decide "who governs." But elections also have an indirect influence on public policy, allowing voters to influence policy directions by choosing between candidates or parties with different policy priorities. Thus, elections indirectly influence "who gets what"—that is, the outcomes of the political process.

Elections as Mandates?

However, it is difficult to argue that elections serve as "policy mandates"—that is, that elections allow voters to direct the course of public policy. Frequently, election winners claim a **mandate**—overwhelming endorsement from the people—for their policies and programs. But for elections to serve as policy mandates, four conditions have to be met:

1. Competing candidates have to offer clear policy alternatives.
2. The voters have to cast their ballots on the basis of these policy alternatives alone.
3. The election results have to clearly indicate the voters' policy preferences.
4. Elected officials have to be bound by their campaign promises.[1]

As we shall see, *none* of these conditions is fully met in American elections. Often candidates do not differ much on policy questions, or they deliberately obscure their policy positions to avoid offending groups of voters. Voters themselves frequently pay little attention to policy issues in elections but rather vote along traditional party lines or group affiliations, or on the basis of the candidate's character, personality, or media image.

Moreover, even in elections in which issues seem to dominate the campaign, the outcome may not clearly reflect policy preferences. Candidates take stands on a variety of issues. It is never certain on which issues the voters agreed with the winner and on which issues they disagreed yet voted for the candidate anyway.

Finally, candidates often fail to abide by their campaign promises once they are elected. Some simply ignore their promises, assuming voters have forgotten about the campaign. Others point to changes in circumstances or conditions as a justification for abandoning a campaign pledge.

Retrospective Voting

Voters can influence future policy directions through **retrospective voting**—votes cast on the basis of the performance of incumbents, by either reelecting them or throwing them out of office.[2] Voters may not know what politicians will do in the future, but they can evaluate how well they performed in the past. When incumbent officeholders are defeated, it is reasonable to assume that voters did not like their performance and that newly elected officials should change policy course if they do not want to meet a similar fate in the next election. But it is not always clear what the defeated incumbents did in office that led to their ouster by the voters. Nor, indeed, can incumbents who won reelection assume that all of their policies are approved of by a majority of voters. Nevertheless, retrospective voting provides an overall judgment of how voters evaluate performance in office.

Prospective Voting

The opposite of retrospective voting is prospective voting—voting based on which party or candidate offers the best promises for the future.[3] Advocates of **prospective voting** contend that parties not in power are in a better position to offer incentives to voters than parties in power. Voters know what the incumbent party can provide, so all the challenging party has to do is offer a better promise. Evidence of purely prospective voting by voters is limited, and those studies indicate that prospective voting is informed by the past. This means that it is based on a *retrospective* assessment of candidates and parties.

prospective voting
Voting for or against a candidate or party on the expectations of their actions if they win.

professionalism
In politics, a reference to the increasing number of officeholders for whom politics is a full-time occupation.

Protection of Rights

Elections provide protection against official abuse. The long struggle for African American voting rights in the United States was premised on the belief that once black people acquired the right to vote, government would become more responsive to their concerns. In signing the Voting Rights Act of 1965, President Lyndon Johnson expressed this view: "The vote is the most powerful instrument ever devised by man for breaking down injustice and destroying the terrible walls which imprison men because they are different from other men."[4]

Power and Ambition

8.2 Characterize the various factors that motivate people to pursue a political career.

Personal ambition is a driving force in politics. Politics attracts people for whom *power*—the drive to shape the world according to one's own beliefs and values—and *celebrity*—the public attention, deference, name recognition, and social status that accompany public office—are more rewarding than money, leisure, or privacy.[5] "Political office today flows to those who want it enough to spend the time and energy mastering its pursuit. It flows in the direction of ambition—and talent."[6]

Communication Skills

Another important personal qualification is the ability to communicate with others. Politicians must know how to talk, and talk, and talk—to large audiences, in press conferences and interviews, on television, to reporters, to small groups of financial contributors, on the phone, at airports and commencements, to their staffs, on the floor of Congress or the state legislature. It matters less what politicians say than how they look and sound saying it. They must communicate sincerity, compassion, confidence, and good humor, as well as ideas.

Professionalism

Politics is increasingly characterized by **professionalism**. "Citizen officeholders"—people with business or professional careers who get into politics part time or for short periods of time—are being driven out of political life by career politicians—people who enter politics early in life as a full-time occupation and expect to make it their career. Politics increasingly demands all of a politician's time and energy. At all levels of government, from city council to state legislatures to the U.S. Congress, political work is becoming full-time and year-round.

8.1

8.2

8.3

8.4

8.5

8.6

8.7

careerism
In politics, a reference to people who started young working in politics, running for and holding public office, and who made politics their career.

Careerism

Professional political careers begin at a relatively early age. **Careerism** in politics begins when ambitious young people seek out internships and staff positions with members of Congress, with congressional committees, in state legislators' or governors' offices, in mayors' offices, or in council chambers. Others volunteer to work in political campaigns. Many find political mentors from whom they learn how to organize campaigns, contact financial contributors, and deal with the media. Soon they are ready to run for local office or the state legislature. Rather than challenge a strong incumbent, they may wait for an open seat to be created by retirement, by reapportionment, or by its holder seeking another office. Over time, running for and holding elective office become their career.

Lawyers in Politics

The prevalence of lawyers in politics is an American tradition. Among the 55 delegates to the Constitutional Convention in 1787, some 25 were lawyers. The political dominance of lawyers continues today, with lawyers filling about half of U.S. Senate seats and nearly half of the seats in the U.S. House of Representatives.

Lawyers dominate in politics because of the parallel skills required in law and politics. Lawyers represent clients, so they can apply their professional experience to represent constituents in Congress. Lawyers are trained to deal with statutory law, so they are assumed to be reasonably familiar with the United States Code (the codified laws of the U.S. government) when they arrive in Congress to make or amend these statutes. However, many lawyers go into politics because people interested in politics also go to law school. Involvement in politics can help build a legal practice by increasing the visibility of a lawyer, most of whom still refrain from advertising. And many government and political jobs are "lawyers only"—such as judges and prosecuting attorneys in federal, state, and local governments. Public service lawyers—U.S. attorneys at the Justice Department or state prosecutors—gain valuable experience and contacts for later use in either private law practice or politics.[7]

INSURGENCY?

Economics professor Daniel Brat spent about $100,000 to unseat Republican majority leader Eric Cantor in Virginia's 7th district. Cantor spent nearly $6 million in a losing effort. Brat exploited Tea Party connections and Cantor's lost connections to voters at home.

Careerists Versus Amateurs

Most officeholders who make it to Congress or the presidency are political careerists, and they typically have a record of service in state and local elective office or in campaign politics. The rare successful challengers who defeat incumbent congressmen and the frequent winners of open seat elections to Congress usually held prior office. Some members of Congress come to office with no prior political experience. These amateur politicians often have some other source of notoriety or celebrity. Political scientist David Canon calls it the "actors, athletes, and astronauts' effect"—many **amateurs** who win office were previously actors, such as Ronald Reagan or Arnold Schwarzenegger, who both went directly from actor to governor of California; former college or professional athletes, such as NFL Hall of Fame receiver Steve Largent and former quarterback Heath Shuler, who both went to Congress; or astronauts, like the first American to orbit the Earth, U.S. Senator John Glenn (D-OH), and U.S. Representative Jack Swigert (R-CO), who flew Apollo 13. Other amateurs are "pure" amateurs who lack celebrity or previous political experience. Pure win on rare occasions, and when they win, amateurs often have greater difficulty succeeding in Congress.[8]

amateurs
People who have not worked in politics or public service professions who run for public office.

incumbents
Candidates currently in office seeking reelection.

reelection rates
Percentages of incumbents running for reelection who are successful.

name recognition
Public awareness of a political candidate—whether they are familiar with his or her name.

The Advantages of Incumbency

8.3 Explain the advantages of incumbency.

In theory, elections offer voters the opportunity to "throw the rascals out." But in practice, voters seldom do so. **Incumbents**, people already holding public office, have a strong advantage when they seek reelection. The **reelection rates** of incumbents for *all* elective offices—city council, mayor, state legislature, governor, and especially Congress—are very high. Since 1950, more than 90 percent of all members of the House of Representatives who have sought reelection have been successful. The success rate of U.S. Senate incumbents is not as great, but it is still impressive; since 1950, more than 70 percent of senators seeking reelection have been successful.[9]

Why do incumbents usually win? So many people don't trust government—especially Congress—and hold politicians in low esteem. First of all, voters generally distinguish between Congress as an institution they distrust, and their own members of Congress, whom they trust and reelect. The result is popular members of Congress serving in an unpopular institution. The value of incumbency has been placed at as much as 10 percentage points, and this value comes from four major advantages that tend to enhance incumbents' chances of winning: name recognition, the quality of the competition, campaign contributions, and the resources of office.[10]

Name Recognition

Incumbents begin a campaign with greater **name recognition** than their challengers. Voters elected them before, and their name has become familiar to their constituents from their activities in office. Much of the daily work of all elected officials, especially members of Congress, is public relations—this includes speaking to groups, dealing with the media, and explaining policy to the public. Name recognition is a strategic advantage at the ballot box, especially if voters have little knowledge of policy positions or voting records. Voters tend to cast ballots for recognizable names over unknowns.

The Quality of Challengers

Senators lose more often than House members, because Senate challengers are more likely to have held high-visibility offices—for example, governor or member of Congress—before running for the Senate. Thus Senate challengers often enjoy some

8.1

8.2

8.3

8.4

8.5

8.6

8.7

challengers
In politics, a reference to people running against incumbent officeholders.

franking privilege
Free use of the U.S. mails granted to members of Congress to promote communication with constituents.

name recognition even before the campaign begins. Greater media attention to a statewide Senate race also helps move the challenger closer to the incumbent in public recognition. In contrast, House challengers are likely to have held less visible local or state legislative offices or to be political novices, and House races attract considerably less media attention than Senate races do. Ambitious local politicians can wait for a House seat to open up; Senate seats are fewer and come up for election less often, so ambitious politicians will take greater risks to get the seat.

Campaign Contributions

Incumbents have a strong advantage in raising campaign funds (see Table 8.1). Individuals and groups seeking access to those already in office are inspired to make contributions. **Challengers** have no immediate favors to offer; they must convince a potential contributor that they will win office and also that they are devoted to the interests of their financial backers.[11] In open seats, candidates with prior political experience are advantaged when raising money.

Contributing individuals and interest groups show a strong preference for incumbents over challengers. They do not wish to offend incumbent officeholders by contributing to their challengers; doing so risks both immediate retribution and future "freezing out" in the likely event of the challengers' defeat. Thus only when an incumbent has been especially hostile to an organization's interest, or in rare cases where an incumbent seems especially vulnerable, will an interest group support a challenger. Yet challengers need even larger campaign war chests than incumbents to be successful. Challengers must overcome the greater name recognition of incumbents, their many office resources, and their records of constituency service.

Resources of Office

Successful politicians use their offices to keep their names and faces before the public in various ways—public appearances, interviews, speeches, Web sites, twitter accounts, and press releases. Congressional incumbents make full use of the **franking privilege** (free use of the U.S. mails) to send self-promotional newsletters to tens of thousands of households in their district at taxpayers' expense. They travel on weekends to their district virtually year-round, using tax-funded travel allowances, to make local appearances, speeches, and contacts.

Members of Congress have large staffs working every day over many years with the principal objective of ensuring the reelection of their members. Indeed, Congress is structured as an "incumbent-protection society" organized and staffed to help guarantee the reelection of its members. Service to constituents occupies the energies of congressional office staffs both in Washington and in local district offices established for this purpose. Casework wins voters one at a time: tracing lost Social Security checks, ferreting out which federal loans voters qualify for and helping them with their applications, and performing countless other individual favors. These individual "retail-level" favors

TABLE 8.1 IN THE MONEY: INCUMBENT ADVANTAGE IN FUND-RAISING

Incumbent House and Senate members seeking reelection are able to raise much more than their challengers in campaign contributors.

	2006	2008	2010	2012
Senate				
Average Incumbent Raised	$11,317,025	8,740,153	10,782,810	$11,847,274
Average Challenger Raised	1,814,844	1,152,182	850,110	$1,360,844
House				
Average Incumbent Raised	1,270,855	1,356,481	1,364,380	$1,606,154
Average Challenger Raised	283,075	335,638	231,899	$267,364

SOURCE: Center for Responsive Politics; figures for 2004, 2006, 2008, 2010, and 2012 congressional elections.

are supplemented by larger-scale projects that experienced members of Congress can bring to their district or state (roads, dams, buildings, schools, grants, contracts) as well as undesirable projects (landfills, waste disposal sites, halfway houses) that they can keep out of their district. The longer incumbents have occupied the office, the more favors they have performed and the larger their networks of grateful voters—and the more voters who will indicate that they have personally met and been helped by the lawmaker.

campaign strategy

Plan for a political campaign, usually including a theme, an attempt to define the opponent or the issues, and an effort to coordinate images and messages in news broadcasts and paid advertising.

voter targeting

The use of voting record, polling, and market research data to identify and contact potential likely voters.

The Advantages of State and Local Incumbents

State legislators and local officeholders enjoy, on a smaller scale, similar perks of office as congresspeople, including greater name recognition than their opponents, connections to potential donors, and staff to help them deal with constituent requests. Many state lawmakers and local officials are elected without opposition or confront weak opponents.

Campaign Strategies

8.4 Identify the main components of campaign strategies.

Campaigning is largely a media activity, especially in presidential and congressional campaigns. Media campaigns are highly professionalized, relying on public relations and advertising specialists, professional fund-raisers, media consultants, and pollsters. Campaign management involves techniques like those employed in marketing commercial products. Professional media campaign management includes developing a **campaign strategy**: compiling computerized mailing lists and invitations for fund-raising events; selecting a campaign theme and developing a desirable candidate image; developing **voter targeting** lists and contacting strategies; monitoring the progress of the campaign with continual polling of the voters; producing video, audio, and print advertisements, signs, and bumper stickers; selecting clothing and hairstyles for the candidate; writing speeches and scheduling appearances; and even planning the victory party.

Selecting a Theme

Finding the right theme or "message" for a campaign is essential, and finding a theme for a candidate is like finding a theme for a product. A successful message is one that characterizes the candidate or the electoral choice confronting the voters. A campaign theme need not be controversial; indeed, it need not even focus on a specific issue. It might be as simple as "Faith, Family, and Freedom"—an attempt to "package" the candidate as being invested in traditional American values.

Modern media campaigns historically focus on candidates' personal qualities rather than on their stands on policy issues. Professional campaigns are based on the assumption that a candidate's "image" is the most important factor affecting voter choice. This image is largely devoid of issues, except in very general terms: for example, "stands up to the special interests," "fights for the taxpayer," or "cares about you."

This is not to say that issues do not matter. In party primaries, there are often litmus test issues that must be adhered to win nomination. Modern Republican candidates are expected to be pro-life on reproductive rights and pro-religion, and they confront relentless pressure to comply with the Grover Norquist antitax "pledge." Democratic candidates increasingly have to be pro-choice on reproductive rights, skeptical of critics of global climate change, and defenders of entitlement programs.

Even with issues on the table, ambiguity in a theme or message is often a winning strategy.[12] Voters tend to interpret ambiguous statements as agreement with their own views, and they often ascribe their views to candidates that they like for other reasons. In contrast, contradictory statements, even those made to different audiences, may hurt candidates, especially when contradictions are videotaped and shown side by side.

The Game, the Rules, the Players

"Just Folks"

Politicians are far from ordinary, but they almost always campaign as ordinary people. Candidates work public events, eating bad state fair food, drinking warm beer, and posing with animals, machines, and everyday people. They try to get recreation-type photo opportunities that people can relate to (Barack Obama playing in a pickup basketball game; George Bush operating a chainsaw) rather than activities they don't (John Kerry windsurfing in 2004). This "just folks" approach reflects a deeply ingrained egalitarian streak in American politics that had politicians in the nineteenth century emphasizing their log cabin origins.

Modern politicians sometimes take "just folks" campaigning to an extreme in order to build an image and separate themselves from the political pack. As governor of Massachusetts, Mike Dukakis rode the subway to work every day. Bob Graham spent much of his summer campaign doing "workdays," where he would perform a different person's job for an entire day. He continued this practice in his 8 years as governor and 18 years in the U.S. Senate, working as a cop, stevedore, construction worker, teacher, and baggage handler. Other politicians replicated Graham's gimmick over the years, though workdays are often elaborate photo ops.

Some "just folks" efforts fall flat. In 2012, multimillionaire and eventual GOP nominee Mitt Romney demonstrated an early and consistent flair for not relating to the concerns and economic life of ordinary people. He began with a $10,000 bet challenge to Texas Governor Rick Perry during the GOP primaries, and repeatedly reiterated in statements such as, "I don't care about the very poor." Romney's campaign subsequently corrected course with repeated efforts to show Romney as ordinary, though even these efforts proved condescending and superficial.

But "just folks" isn't always enough. Many Americans seek a candidate who is viewed as a fighter, someone who not only appreciates ordinary people and their problems, but also fights passionately for the interests of ordinary people. Such pugilistic, populist politicians are historically the staple of Democratic Party politics, but recently such candidates—and voters—have infiltrated the Republican Party as well. Political scientist V. O. Key said these fighters for "just folks" appealed to what was called the "hell-of-a-fellow" complex among the electorate: the fighter who stands against the polite hypocrisy of elites and captures politics as a moral struggle between people who work and people who take.

GEORGE BUSH, HECK OF A GUY

Despite being raised in a wealthy, distinguished political family, George W. Bush successfully cultivated an image as a Joe Six Pack everyman.

QUESTIONS

1. Are there other Americans archetypes that candidates seek to emulate, beyond the egalitarian "just folks"?
2. Do you find it persuasive when politicians try to be ordinary?

negative campaigning
Speeches, commercials, or advertising attacking a political opponent during a campaign.

Negative Campaigning: "Defining" the Opponent

A media campaign also seeks to "define" the opponent in negative terms. The original negative TV ad is generally identified as the 1964 "Daisy Girl" commercial, aired just once by the Lyndon B. Johnson presidential campaign (see *What Do You Think?* Dirty Politics). Negative ads can serve a purpose in exposing the record of an opponent. But **negative campaigning** risks an opponent's counterattack charges of "mudslinging," "dirty tricks," and "sleaze."

Research into the opponent's public and personal background ("oppo research") provides the data for negative campaigning. Previous speeches and writings can be mined for embarrassing or mean-spirited statements. The voting record of the opponent can be scrutinized for unpopular policy positions. Any evils that occurred during an opponent's term of office can be attributed to him or her, either directly ("She knew and conspired in it") or indirectly ("He should have known and done something about it"). Personal scandals or embarrassments can be developed as evidence of "character." If campaign managers fear that highly personal attacks on an opponent will backfire, they may choose to leak the information to reporters and try to avoid attribution of the story to themselves or their candidate.

Negative advertising is often blamed on television's dominant role in political campaigns. "The high cost of television means now that you have to go for the jugular."[13] A political consultant summarized the current rules of political engagement as follows:

1. Advertise early if you have the money.
2. Go negative early, often, and right through Election Day, if necessary.
3. Appeal to the heart and gut, rather than to the head.
4. Define your opponent to the voters before he or she can define him- or herself or you.
5. If attacked, hit back even harder.
6. It's easier to give voters a negative impression of your opponent than it is to improve their image of you.[14]

Smart candidates plan their campaign advertising to support three tracks of advertising: a positive track, to build the candidate's image; a negative track, to pull down the opponent; and a response track, to rebut the opponent's negative attacks. Generally speaking, each track requires distinct and separate advertisements.

focus group
In a political context, a small number of people brought together in a comfortable setting to discuss and respond to themes and issues, allowing campaign managers to develop and analyze strategies.

☐ Targeting Voters

Political campaigns for national, state, and local offices use sophisticated get-out-the-vote (GOTV) strategies to identify and mobilize voters. Since 2006, states have been required under the Help America Vote Act (HAVA) to construct and maintain accurate voter databases. Contractors convert these databases into repositories of information about the frequency with which voters vote, and marry those records with issue research, market research, and donor activities. Republicans have a national voting database called Voter Vault, and Democrats have the Voter Activation Network (the "VAN"). These databases allow candidates to develop survey samples, calling lists, and even door-to-door walking card lists to contact voters. These data also can be married with census and survey data to develop "micro-targeting" strategies to determine exactly which issues or images will activate different voters, based on their demographic profile and where they live.

☐ Using Focus Groups and Polling

Focus group techniques can help in selecting campaign themes and identifying negative characteristics in opponents. A **focus group** is a small group of people brought together to view videotapes, listen to specific campaign appeals, and respond to particular topics and issues. Media professionals then develop a campaign strategy around "hot-button" issues—issues that generate strong responses by focus groups—and avoid themes or issues that fail to elicit much interest.

The results of focus group work can then be tested in wider polling. Polling is a central feature of professional campaigning. Serious candidates for national and statewide offices almost always employ their own private polling firms, distinct from the national survey organizations that supply the media with survey data. Initial polling is generally designed to determine candidates' name recognition—the extent to which the voters recognize the candidates—and whatever positive and negative images are already associated with their names.

Campaign polling is highly professionalized, with telephone banks, trained interviewers, and computer-assisted-telephone-interviewing (CATI) software that records and tabulates responses instantly and sends the results to campaign managers. In well-financed campaigns, polling is continual throughout the campaign, so that

What Do You Think?

Dirty Politics

Political campaigning frequently turns ugly with vicious, personal negative advertising. It is widely believed that television's focus on personal character and private lives—rather than on policy positions and governmental experience—encourages negative campaigning. But vicious personal attacks in campaign politics predate television, and are nearly as old as the nation itself.

"If Jefferson is elected," proclaimed Yale's president in 1800, "the Bible will be burned and we will see our wives and daughters the victims of legal prostitution." In 1864, *Harper's Weekly* decried the "mudslinging" of the day, lamenting that President Abraham Lincoln was regularly referred to by his opponent as a "filthy storyteller, despot, liar, thief, braggart, buffoon, monster, Ignoramus Abe, robber, swindler, tyrant, fiend, butcher, and pirate." When Catholic Gov. Al Smith (D-NY) won the Democratic nomination in 1928, heartland Protestants were told, "If you vote for Al Smith you're voting against Christ and you'll all be damned," and opponents alleged that Smith would bring Pope Pius XI to Washington to rule America.

OBAMA GARB

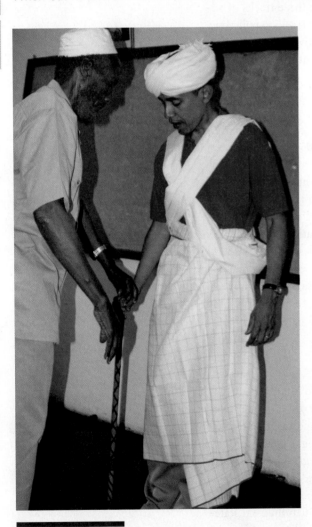

Senator Obama is dressed as a Somali Elder by Sheikh Mahmed Hassain (left), during his visit to Wajir in northeastern Kenya, near the Somali and Ethiopian borders, on August 27, 2006. Obama's deceased father, from whom he was estranged, was Kenyan.

Into the TV Age

Television's first memorable attack advertisement was the "Daisy Girl" commercial broadcast by Lyndon Johnson's presidential campaign in 1964 against his Republican opponent, Barry Goldwater. Although never mentioning Goldwater by name, the ad "defined" the Republican as a warmonger who would plunge the world into a nuclear holocaust. The ad opens with a small, innocent girl standing in an open field plucking petals from a daisy and counting, "1, 2, 3 . . . " When she reaches 9, an ominous adult male voice begins a countdown: "10, 9, 8 . . . " as the camera closes in on the child's face. At "zero," a mushroom cloud appears, reflected in her eyes, and envelops the screen. Lyndon Johnson's voice is heard: "These are the stakes."

"Attack ads" have multiplied in recent elections at all levels of government. 2004 Democratic presidential nominee John Kerry had volunteered for Vietnam after graduating from Yale. In four months as commander of a small "swift boat," he won a Silver Star, a Bronze Star, and three Purple Hearts. But an independent group, Swift Boat Veterans for the Truth, challenged the legitimacy of Kerry's medals in a series of TV ads. Later, the Swift Boat group redirected its attacks toward Kerry's post-Vietnam behavior as a leader in the Vietnam Veterans against the War. These ads, which placed a misrepresentative spin on Kerry's service and postwar activism, corresponded to a slight drop in Kerry's poll numbers, and gave rise to a new political phrase: *swiftboating*.

The Internet further facilitates dirty politics. The anonymity of the Net often inspires false and misleading postings. Perhaps the most offensive in 2008 was the recurring assertion that Barack Obama was a Muslim. These postings frequently referred to his middle name, Hussein, and later included a photo of him in African costume (from a 2006 trip to Kenya). The theme of Obama as "alien" continued throughout his first term and was still alive in the 2012 election, to the extent that a state court in Georgia took up a case of the president's eligibility for the presidential ballot.

Why Do Politicians Go Negative?

Put simply, negative advertising usually works. Controlled experiments indicate that targets of attack ads are rated less positively by people who have watched these ads. The downside is that negative advertising makes voters more cynical about politics and government in general. There is conflicting evidence about whether or not negative campaigning by opposing candidates reduces voter turnout.

Questions

1. If the government cannot regulate political speech, how can one eliminate negative campaigning?
2. Is negative campaigning really bad, if it informs voters?

SOURCES: Kathleen Hall Jamieson, *Dirty Politics; Deception, Distraction, and Democracy* (New York: Oxford University Press, 1992); also Stephen Ansolabehere et al., "Does Attack Advertising Demobilize the Electorate?" *American Political Science Review* 88 (December 1994): 829–38; Kim Fridkin Kahn and Patrick J. Kenney, " Do Negative Campaigns Mobilize or Suppress Turnout?" *American Political Science Review* 93 (December, 1999): 877–89; Robert A. Slayton. "When a Catholic Terrified the Heartland." *New York Times*, December 10, 2011.

managers can assess progress on a daily basis. Polls chart the candidate's progress and, perhaps more important, help assess the effectiveness of specific campaign themes. If the candidate appears to be gaining support, the campaign stays on course. But if the candidate appears to be falling in the polls, the campaign manager comes under intense pressure to change themes and strategies. As Election Day nears, the pressure increases on the trailing candidate to "go negative"—to launch even more scathing attacks on the opponent.

Incumbent Versus Challenger Strategies

Campaign strategies vary by the offices being sought, the nature of the times, and the imagination and inventiveness of the candidates' managers. But incumbency is perhaps the most important factor affecting the choice of a strategy. The challenger must attack the record of the incumbent, deplore current conditions in the city, state, or nation; and stress the need for change. Challengers are usually freer to take the offensive; incumbents must defend their record in office and either boast of accomplishments during their term or blame the opposition for blocking them. Challengers frequently opt for the "outsider" strategy, capitalizing on distrust and cynicism toward government.

News Management

News management is the key to the media campaign. News coverage of the candidates (earned media) is more credible in the eyes of viewers than paid advertisements. The campaign is planned to get the maximum favorable "free" exposure on the evening

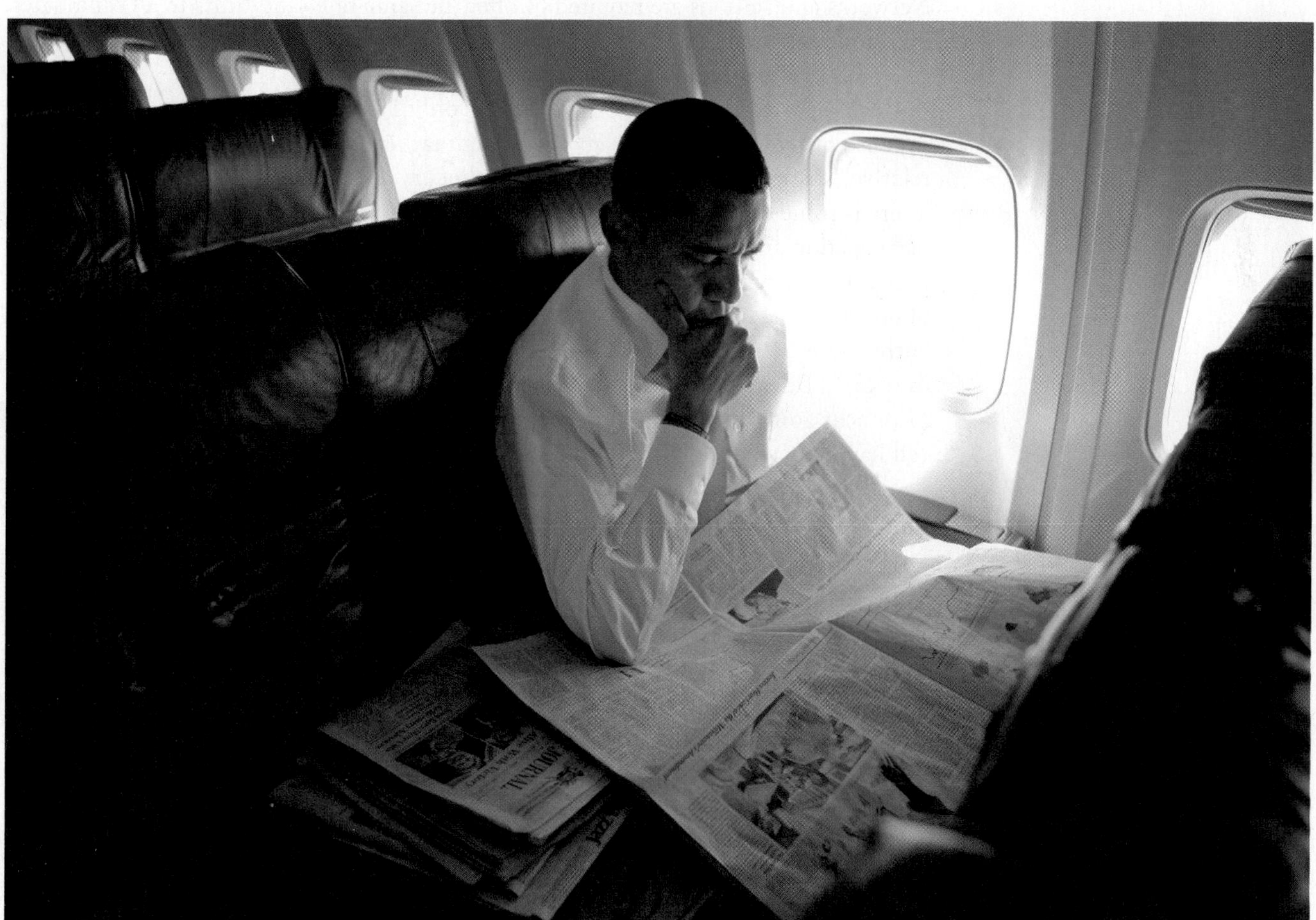

NEWS MANAGEMENT

Presidential candidate Barack Obama keeps up with the *New York Times* while traveling to a campaign stop in April 2008. Managing the news is the key to a modern media campaign.

photo ops
Staged opportunities for the media to photograph the candidate in a favorable setting.

sound bites
Concise and catchy phrases that attract media coverage.

news. Each day, a candidate must do something interesting and "newsworthy," that is, likely to be reported as news. Pictures are as important as words. Candidates must provide good **photo ops** for the media—opportunities where they can be photographed in settings or backgrounds that emphasize their themes. For example, if the theme is patriotism, then the candidate appears with war veterans, at a military base, or at a flag factory. If the theme is education, the candidate appears at a school; if crime control, then with police officers; if environmentalism, then in a wilderness area; if the economy, then at a closed factory or unemployment line or soup kitchen for the homeless.

Themes must be stated in concise and catchy **sound bites** that will register in the viewers' minds. Candidates now understand that the news media will select only a few seconds of an entire day of speech making for broadcast. The average length of a network news sound bite has shrunk from 45 to 7 seconds over the last 30 years. Thus, extended or serious discussion of issues during a campaign is sacrificed to the need for one-liners on the nightly news. Indeed, if a campaign theme cannot fit on a bumper sticker, it is too complex.

☐ Paid Advertising

Television "spot" ads must be prepared prior to and during the campaign. They involve employing expensive television advertising and production firms well in advance of the campaign and keeping them busy revising and producing new ads throughout the campaign to respond to changing issues or opponents' attacks. Commercial advertising is the most expensive aspect of the campaign. Heavy costs are incurred in the production of the ads and in the purchase of broadcast time. The Federal Communications Commission (FCC) does not permit television networks or stations to charge more than standard commercial rates for political ads, but these rates are already high. Networks and stations are required to offer the same rates and times to all candidates, but if one candidate's campaign treasury is weak or exhausted, an opponent can saturate broadcast airtime.

Paid spot ads on television are usually only 15 or 30 seconds long, owing to the expense of television time in many media markets. The result is that these ads pay relatively little attention to issues but rather try to appeal to the viewers' emotions. There is some evidence that simply showing enthusiasm for the candidate motivates participation and activates existing supporters to get out and vote, whereas appealing to fear is somewhat more effective in changing behavior, including swinging the votes of undecideds. However, advertising campaigns, whether they are directed at inspiring enthusiasm for the candidate or fear of a candidate's opponent, must be kept going over time. Bursts of emotion are likely to fade if the ad campaign does not keep the drumbeat going.[15] An accumulation of short spot ads, all aimed at the same theme, can have a meaningful impact on the course of an election.

Television ads are much maligned by scholars and commentators. And it is easy to identify particular ads that are silly, offensive, uninformative, and even misleading. Nevertheless, there is increasing evidence that paid political advertising does create a somewhat more attentive, more informed, and more-likely-to-vote citizenry. Moreover, paid ads appear to affect people with less political information and less interest in politics more than the better-informed and more active citizens. Thus campaign ads are often petty, sometimes offensive, and seldom uplifting. But they do serve an important political function.[16]

☐ Free Airtime

All candidates seek free airtime on news and talk shows, but the need to gain free exposure is much greater for underfunded candidates. They must go to extremes in devising media events, and they must encourage and participate in free televised debates. The debate format is particularly well suited for candidates who cannot match their opponents in paid commercial advertising. Thus, well-funded and poorly funded candidates may jockey over the number and times of public debates.

The Effects of Campaigning

Campaigns serve primarily to activate a candidate's supporters—to ensure that they go to the polls on Election Day. They serve secondarily to try to persuade undecideds to become supporters. Campaigns are designed to **mobilize** core supporters more than to persuade undecideds or opponents to vote for candidates. Undecideds must be both persuaded *and* mobilized to vote—a more difficult task than simply activating core supporters. Observers may wonder why candidates appear before partisan crowds, visit with supporters, and advertise in areas that appear to support them anyway. "Core party voters are more likely to receive and respond to campaign information, implying that successful campaigns are those that mobilize their supporters enough to translate their natural predispositions into actual votes."[17]

mobilize
In politics, to activate supporters to work for candidates and turnout on Election Day.

Campaign Finance

8.5 Analyze the role of money in campaigns, identify the major sources of funding, assess the motivations of contributors, and evaluate efforts to regulate campaign finances.

Getting elected to public office has never been more expensive. The professionalization of campaigning and the heavy costs of television advertising drive up the costs of running for office (see Figure 8.1). The presidential race in 2008 saw total campaign costs rise to almost $2 billion!

Congressional Costs

The typical winning campaign for a seat in the House of Representatives costs over $1.4 million. House members seeking to retain their seats must raise this amount *every two years*—about $2,500 a day, starting the day after the election. The typical winning campaign for a U.S. Senate seat costs over $7 million. But Senate campaign costs vary a great deal from state to state; Senate seats in the larger states may cost $25 million to $50 million or more. For example, multimillionaire Democrat Jon Corzine spent about $60 million of his *own* money in his successful bid for a U.S. Senate seat from New Jersey in 2002. The all-time record for personal contributions to one's own campaign is held by Michael Bloomberg, who reportedly spent $100 million in his 2009 race for mayor of New York City.

Spending for House seats also varies a great deal from one race to another. In nearly two-thirds of all House districts, one candidate (almost always the incumbent) outspends his or her opponent by a factor of 10 to 1 or more. Only about 16 percent of House campaigns are financially competitive; that is, neither candidate spends more than twice as much as his or her opponent. In the remaining 84 percent of House campaigns, one candidate spends more than twice as much as his or her opponent.[18]

Raising Campaign Cash

Fund-raising to meet the high costs of campaigning is the most important hurdle for any candidate for public office. Campaign funds come from a wide range of sources—small donors, big donors, interest group PACs of every stripe, labor unions, even taxpayers. In some cases, candidates pay their own way (or most of it). More typically, however, candidates for high public office—particularly incumbents—have become adept at running their campaigns using other people's money, not their own. More recently, a new actor has come onto the political stage—the SuperPACs, which are ostensibly independent committees that can raise and spend unlimited amounts of money for and against candidates (see *The Game, the Rules, the Players:* PACs, SuperPACs, and Corporations Made From People).

THE BILLIONAIRE MAYOR

Billionaire Michael Bloomberg funded his own independent campaign for mayor of New York in 2009. He reportedly spent $100 million of his own money, a record for a self-financed campaign.

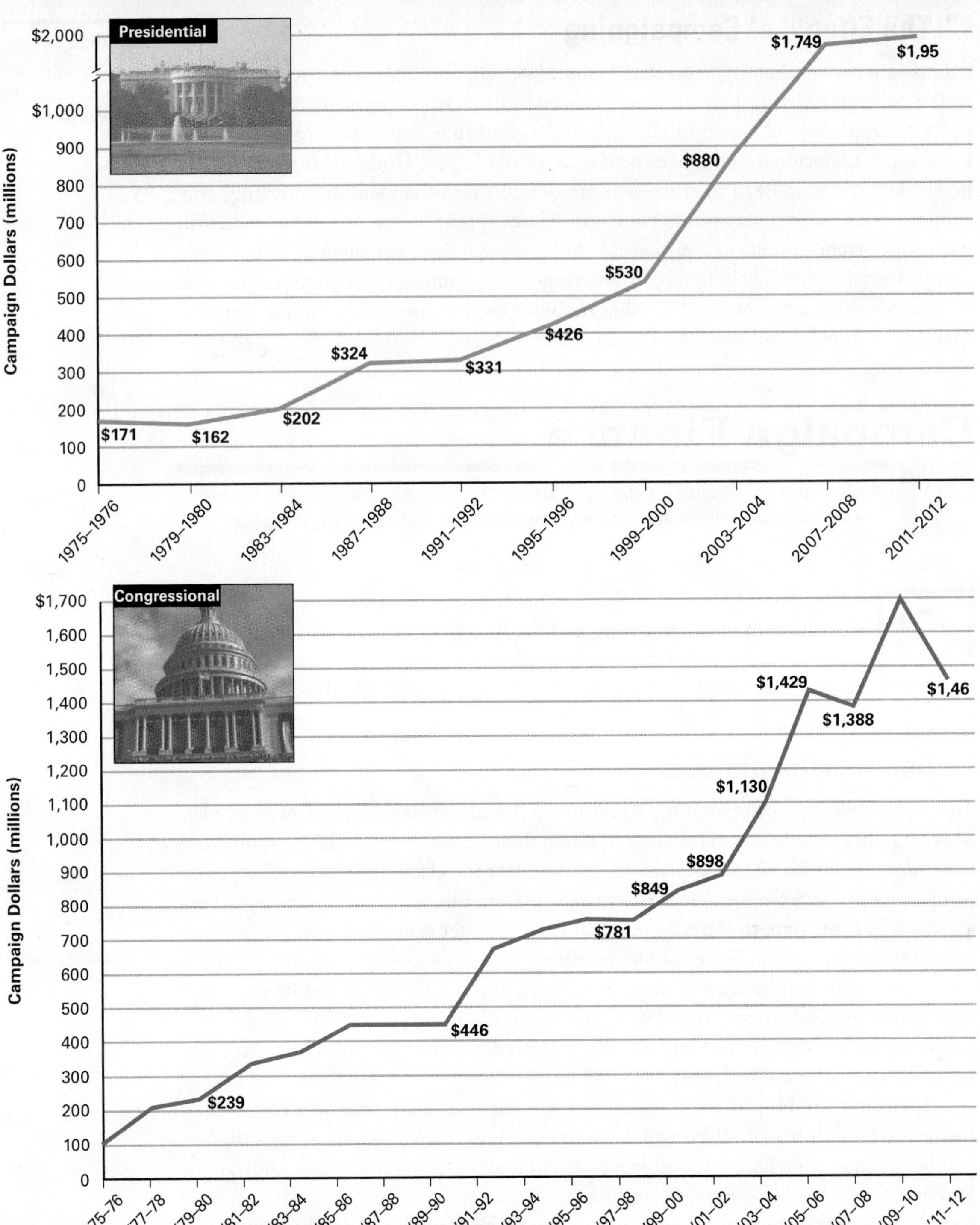

Note: Figures include campaign and party expenditures in primary and general elections, but exclude expenditures by independent groups.

FIGURE 8.1 SPARING NO EXPENSE: THE GROWING COSTS OF CAMPAIGNS

The costs of presidential and congressional campaigns now exceed $1.7 billion, and this figure does not include expenditures by independent groups.

SOURCE: Data from Center for Responsive Politics, www.opensecrets.org.

☐ Public Money

Presidential campaigns can be partly funded with taxpayer money through an income tax checkoff system. Each year, taxpayers are urged to check the box on their tax forms that authorizes $3 of their tax payment to go to the Federal Elections Commission for distribution to presidential candidates' campaigns as well as to political party conventions. However, taxpayers are becoming less and less willing to allow their tax monies to go into political campaigning (even though the $3 checkoff does not add to the

The Game, the Rules, the Players

PACs, SuperPACs, and Corporations Made from People

A **political action committee** (PAC) is an organization created to raise and spend and money in political campaigns. PACs are synonymous with big money in politics, special-interest influence, and, in the minds of many voters, corruption.

PACs were not widely used in national politics until the 1970s. When the Federal Election Campaign Act was passed by Congress, it led to the proliferation of two types of PACs: connected PACs, which are created by corporations, unions, trade associations, and other organized economic interests; and nonconnected PACs, which are created by ideological groups and politicians. Members of Congress sometimes create PACs in order to raise and give money to political allies and promote their own power.

There are limits on the amount of money a person can give to these traditional PACs, and also on the amount of money PACs can give to a candidate. But in 2010, a new creature emerged in the world of campaign finance: the SuperPAC. The SuperPACs brought even more money into politics. But there is a lot of confusion about what they are, and what they can do.

SuperPACs

SuperPACs are a special sort of PAC that can raise and then spend unlimited amounts of money. In 2010, a lawsuit called *Citizens United* made it possible for corporations and unions to directly spend their money advocating the election or defeat of candidates. Before that case, only individuals—actual human beings—could spend unlimited money advocating the election or defeat of a candidate.

The *Citizens United* case did not make it possible for individuals, corporations, or unions to directly give unlimited amounts of money directly to candidates or campaigns committees. The old direct contribution limits still apply.

And, *Citizens United* did not make it possible for SuperPACs to hide their donors. A related case that came after *Citizens United*, called *Speechnow.org v. Federal Election Commission*, resulted in that change. In this second lawsuit, a federal appeals court affirmed that limits cannot be placed on independent expenditures by PACs. But the court also held that it is not necessary for a PAC receiving donations as a 504c3 charitable organization to disclose its donors, if less than half of its donations are spend on electioneering. The great danger of this loophole is that it allows huge amounts of money—including foreign money—to enter and exit campaigns without any indication of who is trying to influence the election.

The litigation upheld the prohibition on coordinated efforts between groups spending money on independent expenditures, and the candidate benefiting from the expenditure. But there is a monstrous loophole in this rule: indirect, public communication from a candidate to a PAC is allowed, such as talking on television or through journalists. Speech rights allow candidates to call on SuperPACs to take action, and they do not prevent SuperPACs from listening. SuperPAC donors have to be disclosed by the PAC, but they do not have to do so until after an election. SuperPACs are often run by close friends, consultants, or former employees of the politicians they benefit. Therefore, noncoordination is primarily an illusion.

Why Was This Possible?

How did corporations and unions get in the position to spend so much money influencing elections? Until 2010, only individuals—living, breathing human beings—were considered "people" for the purpose of political action. But, in the nineteenth century, state and federal courts determined that corporations held certain 1st Amendment rights for the purpose of entering contracts. The federal courts in the *Citizens United* and *Speechnow.org* cases extended the concept of corporate citizenship to encompass political speech, so that speech rights for corporations and individuals were governed by the same logic.

A Light Touch

In 2011, comedic pundits Stephen Colbert and Jon Stewart created a soft-money Super PAC. The Colbert Super PAC laid bare the legal issues in campaign finance. Stephen Colbert went to the Federal Election Commission to establish his right to use his television program to promote his SuperPAC and to determine that his corporate employer, Viacom, could support those activities under what's called the media exemption. As long as the activities Viacom pays for take place only during Colbert's show, it is legal for them to do so.

QUESTIONS

1. **Do you think corporations are people?**
2. **Would you give money to a SuperPAC if you knew the money was not for serious political purposes?**
3. **If you were to propose a reform to the PAC system, what would it be?**

taxpayers' total taxes). Only about 11 percent of taxpayers currently check the box. The Presidential Election Campaign Fund has been in jeopardy of not having enough money to make its promised payments to the candidates and parties.

Presidential candidates may opt out of taxpayer-financed funding if they choose to do so. This allows them to spend as much money as they wish, but they receive no public money. (Democrat Barack Obama was so successful in raising cash in 2008 that

8.1
8.2
8.3
8.4
8.5
8.6
8.7

he declined federal funding. Republican John McCain faced a cash shortage and was obliged to accept federal money.) Nonetheless, all presidential candidates, and all candidates for Congress, must abide by federal campaign finance laws (see below).

☐ Small Donations

Millions of Americans participate in campaign financing, either by giving directly to candidates or the parties or by giving to political action committees, which then distribute their funds to candidates (see *Who's Getting What?* How the Internet Changed Campaign Fund-Raising). For members of Congress, small donors typically make up less than 20 percent of their campaign funds. The proportion is higher for presidential candidates. For donations under $200, contributors' names and addresses are recorded only by the candidates and parties, not passed along to the Federal Election Commission as part of the public record.

☐ Large Individual Donors

"Fat cats" are the preferred donors. These are the donors whose names are on the candidates' Rolodexes. They are the ones in attendance when the president, the Speaker of the House, or other top political dignitaries travel around the country holding fund-raisers. They are also the ones who are wined, dined, prodded, and cajoled in a seemingly ceaseless effort by the parties and the candidates to raise funds for the next election.

Who's Getting What?

How the Internet Changed Campaign Fund-Raising

At the National Level: Barack Obama raised more money for his presidential campaign in 2008 than any other candidate in history—until he ran for president in 2012. In 2008, Obama heavily outspent his opponents—Hillary Clinton in the Democratic primaries and John McCain in the general election. He declined public funding for his campaign and thereby avoided Federal Elections Commission spending limits. He raised more money through small contributions than any previous presidential contender. How did he do it?

Obama's extraordinary success in raising funds through the Internet is likely to change campaign fund-raising in future years. Obama reportedly raised $500 million from more than 3 million donors over the Internet.[a] About one-third of these donations came in amounts of less than $200. No previous presidential contender had ever raised so much money through such small donations.

Local Politics: In 2008, Sean Tevis, a software and information system architect from Lawrence, Kansas, filed to oppose incumbent Republican Representative Arlen Siegfreid in his predominantly Republican state legislative district. Most challengers for state legislative seats are lucky to raise $10,000 for their campaign; many of them self-finance and usually lose. Tevis lost, but not before he put on a clinic on how to raise money online. He very nearly defeated his incumbent opponent: he lost by less than 500 votes out of over 10,000 cast. Tevis ran a competitive challenge because he raised over $100,000 in a matter of weeks from over 5,000 online donors. Tevis crafted an online ad that mimicked Randall Munroe's geek-humor strip *xkcd*. The ad directed potential donors to a PayPal account and also described the regulatory limits on giving in Kansas elections. State and local candidates around the nation have subsequently mimicked Tevis's novel effort to raise cash from national constituencies. Similar strategies of online fund-raising have also extended to support noncandidate campaigns, such as the Occupy movement.

Instant Success: Asking for money via the Internet is much more timely and immediate than raising money through the mail or through events like dinners or concerts. Internet fund-raising is cheap; it does not entail significant costs. Internet solicitation is continuous; it does not require the candidate to spend time in personal appearances. Because it is so inexpensive, even small donations of $5 or $10 can be profitably solicited. And people making donations over the Internet can be tracked and solicited again and again throughout the campaign. New e-mail messages can be sent out as events occur that may inspire supporters to make repeat donations.

Questions

1. Is Internet fund-raising good for democracy? Are there possible abuses that might arise from Internet giving?
2. Do average voters benefit from the ability to make Internet donations? Why or why not?

[a]See David B. Magleby, "How Barack Obama Changed Presidential Campaigns," in Thomas R. Dye et al. *Obama: Year One* (New York: Longman, 2010).

☐ Candidate Self-Financing

Candidates for federal office also pump millions into their own campaigns. There are no federal restrictions on the amount of money individuals can spend on their own campaign.[19] Senate and House candidates frequently put $50,000 to $100,000 or more of their own money into their campaigns, through outright gifts or personal loans. (Candidates who loan themselves the money to run can pay themselves back later from outside contributions.)

issue ads
Ads that advocate policy positions rather than explicitly supporting or opposing particular candidates.

☐ Issue Ads

Issue ads advocate policy positions rather than explicitly advising voters to cast their ballots for or against particular candidates. But most of these ads leave little doubt about which candidate is being supported or targeted. There are no dollar limits on the size of contributions to sponsoring groups (often referred to as 527s from the section of the Internal Revenue code under which they operate).

☐ What Do Contributors "Buy"?

What does money buy in politics? A cynic might say that money can buy anything—for example, special appropriations for public works directly benefiting the contributor, special tax breaks, special federal regulations. Public opinion views big-money contributions as a major problem in the American political system. Scandals involving the direct (quid pro quo) purchase of special favors, privileges, exemptions, and treatments have been common enough in the past, and they are likely to continue in the future. But campaign contributions are rarely made in the form of a direct trade-off for a favorable vote. Such an arrangement risks exposure as bribery and may be prosecuted under the law. Campaign contributions are more likely to be made without any

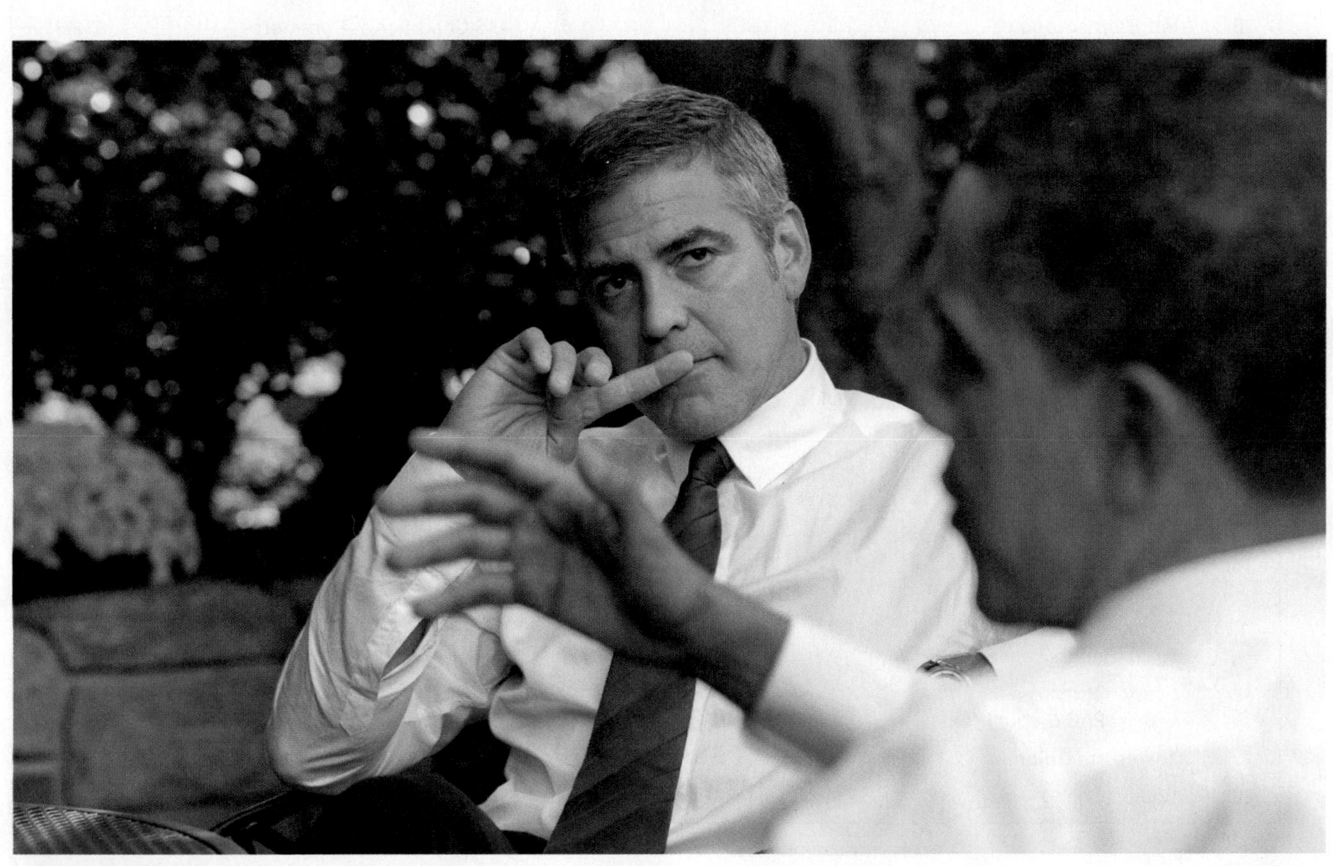

CELEBRITIES HELP RAISE FUNDS

Democratic and Republican candidates both benefit from celebrity fundraising. Actor George Clooney has been actively involved in fundraising for Democrats such as Barack Obama.

explicit quid pro quo but rather with a general understanding that the contributor has confidence in the candidate's good judgment on issues directly affecting the contributor. The contributor expects the candidate to be smart enough to figure out how to vote in order to keep the contributions coming in the future.

□ The Big-Money Contributors

Big-money contributors—businesses, unions, professional associations—pump millions into presidential and congressional elections. Union contributions are heavily weighted toward Democrats, as are the contributions of the trial lawyers. Businesses and business associations tend to split their contributions between the parties, but Republicans usually get the largest share (see Figure 8.2).

Direct Contributions					Independent Expenditures		
	PAC Name	**Total Amount (millions)**	**% Dem.**	**% Rep.**		**PAC Name**	**Total Amount (millions)**
1.	National Assn of Realtors	$3.9	44%	55%	1.	American Crossroads/Crossroads GPS (Republican)	$176.2
2.	National Beer Wholesalers Assn	$3.4	41%	59%	2.	Restore Our Future (Democratic)	$142.1
3.	Honeywell International	$3.2	41%	59%	3.	Priorities USA/Priorities USA Action	$65.2
4.	Operating Engineers Union	$3.2	84%	15%	4.	Majority PAC	$37.5
5.	National Auto Dealers Assn	$3.1	28%	72%	5.	Americans for Prosperity	$33.5
6.	Intl Brotherhood of Electrical Workers	$2.9	97%	2%	6.	US Chamber of Commerce	$32.3
7.	American Bankers Assn	$2.7	20%	80%	7.	House Majority PAC	$30.5
8.	AT&T Inc	$2.5	35%	65%	8.	American Future Fund	$24.5
9.	American Assn for Justice (Trial Lawyers)	$2.5	96%	3%	9.	Service Employees International Union	$19.6
10.	Credit Union National Assn	$2.5	47%	52%	10.	FreedomWorks	$19.6
11.	Blue Cross/Blue Shield	$2.4	35%	65%	11.	National Rifle Assn	$18.6
12.	Plumbers/Pipefitters Union	$2.4	94%	5%	12.	Club for Growth (Conservative anti-tax group)	$18.0
13.	American Fedn of St/Cnty/Munic Employees	$2.3	99%	1%	13.	American Fedn of St/Cnty/Munic Employees	$17.0
14.	Lockheed Martin	$2.3	41%	59%	14.	Winning Our Future	$17.0
15.	Machinists/Aerospace Workers Union	$2.2	98%	1%	15.	Americans for Job Security	$15.9
16.	American Federation of Teachers	$2.2	99%	0%	16.	Americans for Tax Reform	$15.8
17.	Senate Conservatives Fund (Republicans)	$2.1	0%	100%	17.	League of Conservation Voters	$13.9
18.	Every Republican is Crucial PAC (Republicans)	$2.1	0%	100%	18.	Ending Spending	$13.3
19.	Teamsters Union	$2.10	96%	4%	19.	Planned Parenthood	$11.9
20.	Boeing Co	$2.0	44%	56%	20.	American Action Network	$11.7

FIGURE 8.2 WHO GIVES WHAT?: TWENTY BIG INDEPENDENT SPENDERS IN 2012

SOURCE: Data from Center for Responsive Politics, www.opensecrets.org.

Buying Access to Policymakers

Large contributors expect to be able to call or visit and present their views directly to "their" officeholders. At the presidential level, major contributors who cannot get a meeting with the president expect to meet at least with high-level White House staff or cabinet officials. At the congressional level, major contributors usually expect to meet or speak directly with their representative or senator. Members of Congress boast of responding to letters, calls, or visits by any constituent, but contributors can expect a more immediate and direct response than noncontributors can. Lobbyists for contributing organizations routinely expect and receive a hearing from members of Congress.

political action committees (PACs)
Organizations that solicit and receive campaign contributions from corporations, unions, trade associations, and ideological and issue-oriented groups and their members, and then distribute these funds to political candidates.

Political Action Committees

Political action committees (PACs) are the most reliable source of money for reelection campaigns in Congress. Corporations and unions form PACs to seek contributions from managers and stockholders and their families, or union workers and their families. PACs are organized not only by corporations and unions but also by trade and professional associations, environmental groups, and liberal and conservative ideological groups. The wealthiest PACs are based in Washington, D.C. PACs are very cautious; their job is to get a maximum return on their contributions, winning influence and goodwill with as many lawmakers as possible in Washington. There's no return on their investment if their recipients lose at the polls; therefore most PACs—particularly business PACs—give most of their dollars to incumbents seeking reelection.

Individual Contributors

Most individual contributors are ideologically motivated. They make their contributions based on their perception of the ideological position of the candidate (or perhaps their perception of the candidate's opponent). They may make contributions to congressional candidates across the country who share their policy views. Liberal and conservative networks of contributors can be contacted through specialized mailing lists. Feminists have been effective in soliciting individual contributions across the country and funneling them very early in a campaign to women candidates through EMILY's List. Ideological contributors may only get the satisfaction of knowing that they are financially backing their cause in the political process. Some contributors simply enjoy the opportunity to be near and to be seen with high-ranking politicians. Politicians pose for photos with contributors, who later frame the photos and hang them in their office to impress their friends, associates, and customers. Contributors are disproportionately high-income, older people with strong partisan views (see Figure 8.3).

Buying Government Assistance

Many large contributors do business with government agencies. They expect any representative or senator they have supported to intervene on their behalf with these agencies, sometimes acting to cut red tape, ensure fairness, and expedite their cases, and other times pressuring the agencies for a favorable decision. Officials in the White House or the cabinet may also be expected to intervene on behalf of major contributors. There is little question raised when the intervention merely expedites consideration of a contributor's case, but pressure to bend rules or regulations to get favorable decisions raises ethical problems for officeholders. Corporations that do business with government agencies, and those that are heavily regulated by government agencies, may make contributions simply to "flex their muscles"—to signal bureaucrats that if they wished to do so, they could fight any agency's specific decisions.[20]

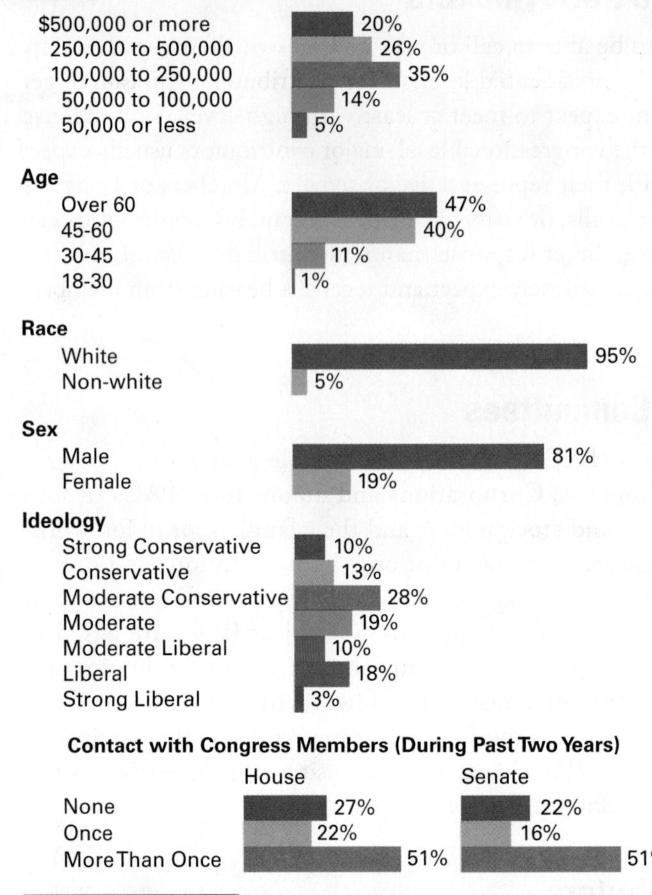

FIGURE 8.3 WHO'S GIVING?: CHARACTERISTICS OF INDIVIDUAL POLITICAL CONTRIBUTORS

Contributors to political campaigns generally are older and have higher incomes than most Americans. Whites and males contribute more than blacks and females, and conservatives contribute more than liberals.

SOURCE: John Green, Paul Herrnson, Lynda Powell, and Clyde Wilcox, "Individual Congressional Campaign Contributors," press release, June 9, 1998, Center for Responsive Politics, www.opensecrets.org. Reprinted by permission.

Federal Election Commission (FEC)

Agency charged with enforcing federal election laws and disbursing public presidential campaign funds.

Fund-Raising Chores

Fund-raising occupies more of a candidate's time than any other campaign activity. Candidates must personally contact as many individual contributors as possible. They work late into the evening on the telephone with potential contributors. Fund-raising dinners, cocktail parties, barbecues, fish fries, and so on, are scheduled nearly every day of a campaign. The candidate is expected to appear personally to "press the flesh" of big contributors. Movie and rock stars and other assorted celebrities may also be asked to appear at fund-raising affairs to generate attendance. Dinners may run to $2,300 a plate in presidential affairs, although often less in Senate or House campaigns. Tickets may be "bundled" to well-heeled individual contributors or sold in blocks to organizations. Lawmakers dial for dollars in the car going from event to event, making the most of the time available to fund the campaign.

Regulating Campaign Finance

The **Federal Election Commission (FEC)**, created in 1974, is responsible for enforcing limits on individual and organizational contributions to all federal elections, administering the public funding of presidential campaigns, and requiring full disclosure of all campaign financial activity in presidential and congressional elections. Enforcement of these federal election and campaign finance laws lies in the hands of the six-member FEC. Appointed by the president to serve staggered six-year terms, commission members are traditionally split three to three between Republicans and Democrats.

Limits on Contributions

The FEC now limits contributions to a candidate's campaign per election to $2,600 in direct individual contributions (in 2014) and $5,000 per election in organizational contributions. But there are many ways in which individuals and organizations can legally surmount these limits. Contributors may give a candidate $2,600 from each member of their family in a primary election and then another $2,600 per member in the general election. Organizations may generate much more than the $5,000 limit by bundling (combining) contributions from individual members.

soft money
Previously unregulated contributions to the parties, now prohibited; contributions to parties now limited.

Independent Organization Spending

Independent organizations can spend whatever they wish in order to promote their political views as long as these organizations do so "without cooperation or consultation with the candidate of his or her campaign." Finally, as noted, individuals may spend as much of their own money on their own campaigns as they wish.

Reporting

By law, every candidate for federal office must file periodic reports with the FEC detailing both the income and the expenditures of his or her campaign. Individual contributors who give an aggregate of $200 or more must be identified by name, address, occupation, and employer. All PAC and party contributions, no matter how large or small, must also be itemized. In addition, PACs themselves must file reports with the FEC at least four times a year, detailing both the contributions received by the PAC and the names of candidates and other groups that received the PAC's donations.

Campaign Finance Reform

In the 2000 Republican presidential primaries, U.S. Senator John McCain made campaign finance reform his principal issue. He surprised the Republican Party leaders by defeating George W. Bush in the New Hampshire primary that year. Bush and both Democratic and Republican leaders decided to jump on the campaign finance reform bandwagon, although with little real enthusiasm. In 2002, a somewhat reluctant Congress finally passed the Bipartisan Campaign Finance Reform Act.

Among other things, this act eliminated **soft-money** contributions to the parties; increased the individual contribution limit to candidates' campaigns from $1,000 to $2,000 (now $2,600); prohibited independent groups from coordinating their campaign spending with candidates or parties; and did not allow independent groups to mention the name of a candidate in their issue ads (see *A Conflicting View*: Eliminate Campaign Spending Limits).

But contributions to nonprofit independent groups remain unregulated. Big-money contributors who can no longer provide large amounts of cash to candidates or to parties *can* establish nonprofit independent groups to accept big contributions to enable them to produce and broadcast campaign advertisements.

The Supreme Court and Campaign Finance

The U.S. Supreme Court has recognized that limitations on campaign *contributions* help further a compelling government interest—"preventing corruption and the appearance of corruption" in election campaigns. But the Court has been reluctant to allow governments to limit campaign *expenditures*, because paying to express political views is necessary in the exercise of free speech. In an important early case, *Buckley v. Valeo* (1976), the Court held that limiting a candidate's campaign expenditures that are made from his own personal funds violated the 1st Amendment's guarantee of free speech.[21]

Later, when called upon to consider the constitutionality of the Bipartisan Campaign Reform Act (BCRA), the Court upheld limitations on contributions directly to federal candidates and to national parties. It also upheld limits on "soft-money" contributions to state and local parties, recognizing that these provisions were designed to prevent circumventions of valid prohibitions on campaign contributions.[22]

But still later, the Supreme Court reconsidered the BCRA's provisions limiting individual and organization electioneering communications. The Court distinguished between "express advocacy" on behalf of a candidate or party and "issue ads" that are *not* the functional equivalent of express advocacy. (These are ads, in other words, that do not urge viewers or listeners to vote for or against a particular candidate or party.) "When it comes to defining what speech qualifies as the functional equivalent of express advocacy, the Court should give the benefit of the doubt to speech, not censorship."[23] The effect of the decision is to permit political contributors to support organizations unaffiliated with a candidate or party, including nonprofit 527 organizations, that air television ads not expressly endorsing a candidate right up to Election Day.

Corporations, Unions, and *Citizens United*

In 2010, the Supreme Court struck down a long-standing prohibition on political expenditures from corporate and union treasuries. Previously, corporations and unions were obliged to create separate political action committees—PACs—to solicit separate funds from managers and stockholders and union members for political activity. But the Supreme Court held in a 5–4 decision that corporations and unions could spend money directly "for express advocacy or electioneering communications purposes."

A Conflicting View

Eliminate Campaign Spending Limits

Political speech is the heart of the 1st Amendment. Expenditures for political speech must be constitutionally protected. Spending money to broadcast one's political views, regarding candidates, issues, and public affairs generally, is an integral part of political speech. Speech must be heard by others to be effective, and in today's society this means spending money to again access to the mass media. Limitations on political spending in effect limit political speech and therefore violate the 1st Amendment's guarantee of freedom of speech. Any "undue influence" of money in politics is outweighed by the loss for democracy resulting from restrictions on free speech.

The Supreme Court was correct in its 2010 holding that corporations and unions could not be prohibited from engaging in political speech. The Court said, "Because speech is an essential mechanism for democracy—it is the means to hold officials out of both to the people—political speech must prevail against laws that would suppress it by design or inadvertence." The same reasoning applies to dollar limits placed upon individual and group contributions to federal candidates for public office. Individuals and groups should be permitted to contribute as much as they wish to their favored candidates.

It is true that individuals and organizations usually find ways to get around campaign finance laws in any case. The Supreme Court itself noted that "Political speech is so ingrained in this country's culture that speakers find ways around campaign finance laws." But there is no reason to evade these laws; they ought to be judged unconstitutional. "Restrictions on the amount of money a person or group can spend on political communication during a campaign . . . necessarily reduces the quantity of expression by restricting the number of issues discussed, the depth of their exploration, and the size of the audience reached."

The public's interest in combating corruption in politics can be satisfied by open disclosure laws—requiring candidates to disclose during the campaign the names of organizations and individuals that are contributing to their campaigns and the amounts of these contributions. Let the voters decide whether a candidate is supported by the "wrong" individuals or organizations, or whether a candidate is too heavily indebted to a particular contributor.

QUESTIONS

1. Is there too much money in politics? Or too little?
2. Do you think money is speech?

SOURCE: Quotations from *Citizens United v. FEC*, January 21, 2010.

"Political speech cannot be banned based on the speaker's corporate identity."[24] Corporations and unions are still prohibited from contributing directly to federal political candidates or directly to political parties ("soft money"). However, "Political speech is indispensable to democracy, and this is no less true because the speech comes from a corporation." The case started as an appeal by a conservative nonprofit corporation, Citizens United, of a ruling by the FEC preventing it from airing an anti–Hillary Clinton movie.

Critics of the decision complained that it will increase the influence of special-interest money in politics. President Barack Obama said, "It is a major victory for big oil, Wall Street banks, health insurance companies and the other powerful interests that marshal their power every day in Washington to drown out the voices of everyday Americans." It is not clear which party will benefit most from the Supreme Court's decision, although the decision generally drew praise from Republicans and criticism from Democrats.

The Presidential Campaign

8.6 Outline candidates' strategies for primary races and the general election.

The phrase *presidential fever* refers to the burning political ambition required to seek the presidency. The grueling presidential campaign is a test of strength, character, endurance, and determination. It is physically exhausting and mentally and emotionally draining. Every aspect of the candidates' lives—and the lives of their families—is subject to microscopic inspection by the news media. Most of this coverage is critical, and much of it is unfair. Yet candidates are expected to handle it all with grace and humor, from the earliest testing of the waters through a full-fledged campaign.

Media Mentions

Politicians with presidential ambitions may begin by promoting presidential *mentions* by media columnists and commentators. The media help identify "presidential timber" years in advance of a presidential race simply by drawing up lists of potential candidates, commenting on their qualifications, and speculating about their intentions. Mentions are likely to come to prominent governors or senators who start making speeches outside their states, who grab the media spotlight on a national issue, or who simply let it be known to the media "off the record" that they are considering a presidential race. Visiting early nomination states such as New Hampshire, Iowa, and South Carolina and giving speeches there is viewed as "testing the waters" and a signal of presidential ambitions.

Presidential Credentials

Political experience as vice president, governor, U.S. senator, or member of Congress not only inspires presidential ambition but also provides vital experience in political campaigning. However, virtually all presidential candidates testify that the presidential arena is far more challenging than politics at any other level. The experience of running for and holding high public office appears to be a political requirement for the presidency. Some presidential aspirants have tried to make a virtue of their lack of previous political office holding, no doubt hoping to attract support from the many Americans who disdain "politics as usual." But for over a century, no major party nominee for president has not previously held office as vice president, governor, U.S. senator, or member of Congress except World War II hero General Dwight D. Eisenhower.

The Game, the Rules, the Players

Mitt Romney, Republican Presidential Nominee

Mitt Romney was the candidate sent from central casting: tall, rich, good hair, big smile, successful in business, successful running the Olympics, and successful as a Republican governor in a Democratic state. His political history was centrist, built on problem solving. But, all that pragmatism made for problemsin his two campaigns for president.

This was no country for moderate men. Not if they are trying to win the GOP nomination for president.

Party politics had become ideologically polarized since the 1990s. Romney, who had been an independent during the Reagan Revolution of the 1980s; a pro-choice abortion candidate for the U.S. Senate in 1994, when the Republican Contract With America congress was swept into power, ushering in conservative lawmaking for a generation; and a governor of Massachusetts who oversaw an innovative health reform act; now sought the presidency in a party that saw Reagan as a messiah, and vilified Romney-style health care reform when it was twice proposed by Democratic presidents. He was a man out of step with his party.

The Political Inheritor

Mitt Romney is an inheritor in politics. His father, George W. Romney, was a successful automotive executive in Detroit, running Nash Motors (creator of the classic 'Rambler', and later called American Motors Corporation) and then serving three terms as governor of Michigan. The elder Romney was presumed to be a front-runner for president in 1968. His weak and disorganized campaign faltered, only remembered foran unfortunate gaffe regarding the Vietnam War (George Romney said U.S. military personnel had 'brainwashed' him regarding the success in southeast Asia). Romney would fade against Richard Nixon and Ronald Reagan in '68. After one term in Nixon's cabinet, he returned to private life as an elder in the Mormon Church.

Faith, Family, Career

Mitt Romney descends from a family of Mormon faith—the Church of Jesus Christ of Latter Day Saints (LDS). Young Mitt, raised in affluence in suburban Detroit, attended Cranbrook prep school, enrolled in Stanford University for a year, and then undertook a two-year Mormon mission to France. He returned to attend Brigham Young University, where he graduated in English with highest honors and gave the commencement address. He then enrolled at Harvard University where he received both an MBA degree and a law degree *cum laude* in 1975.

Romney's Harvard education propelled him immediately into management consulting. In 1977 he was hired by Bain & Company, where he became skilled at corporate turnarounds—taking over flagging companies and bringing them back to profitability. He then became head of a spinoff firm, Bain Capital,that invested in startup companies including Staples. Bain was a source of controversy, being perceived as a corporate raider. But because the firm also undertook leveraged buyouts of floundering companies and substantial corporate restructurings that were not hostile takeovers, this criticism is not necessarily valid. Romney's time at Bain is a source of contention, because as of 2012 it remained unclear whether Romney's corporate restructurings at Bain overall added or lost jobs for the economy.

Romney and his wife, Ann, have five sons. Ann suffers from multiple sclerosis, which is currently in remission, and is a skilled and attractive public speaker and campaigner. The Romneysare devout Mormons, regularly tithing (giving ten percent or more of their income) to the Church, possibly billions of dollars over time. Romney is an active religious leader, serving several years as a pastor for the Boston Mormon congregation. The Romney fortune is largely in blind trusts generating dividend income, estimated at as much as $21 million annually. Federal tax laws impose only a 15% tax on dividend income, keeping Romney's taxes low.

Politics & Civic Life

Romney turned his attention to politics in 1994 in an unsuccessful effort to unseat longtime incumbent Massachusetts Senator Edward M "Ted" Kennedy. Romney ran as a moderate Republican, but Kennedy blasted him for firing workers at a local plant owned by Bain. Although Romney gave Kennedy more competition than he had ever before experienced in Massachusetts politics, Romney lost 58 to 41 percent.

Romney left Bain in 1999 to serve as President of the Salt Lake City Committee for the 2002 Winter Olympic Games. He took over an organization deeply in debt and in danger of losing the Games altogether. He turned the Games into a stunning success. The experience led to a book, *Turnaround: Crisis Leadership and the Olympic Games*, and added to his reputation as a turnaround specialist.

In 2002 Romney set his sights on the governorship of Massachusetts. In an overwhelmingly Democratic state, Romney projected an image as a "moderate" with "pro-choice" and "progressive" views. He was elected by 50 percent of the vote to his Democratic opponent's 45 percent. As governor, Romney closed a huge budget gap through a combination of spending cuts, increased fees, and the closing of tax loopholes. But his signature accomplishment was the Massachusetts health reform law, later dubbed "Romneycare" by its critics. The law required all Massachusetts residents to buy health insurance or face a tax penalty. It established state subsidies for low-income persons unable to purchase health insurance on their own. It required businesses to offer health insurance to their employees.

Romney decided to forgo running for a second term as governor in 2006 in order to devote full time to a presidential bid. He chaired the Republican Governors Association, traveling the country and building a national political network. His presidential campaign

(*Continued*)

(*Continued*)

tried to capitalize on his business background, his leadership of the Olympics, and his experience as governor of Massachusetts. Despite heavy spending, Romney lost the Iowa caucuses to Mike Huckabee, a loss Romney attributed to the many evangelical Christians in that state who viewed Mormonism as heresy. He won the New Hampshire primary, but as the campaign evolved, he began to lose ground to eventual Republican nominee John McCain. In February he announced his withdrawal; he had spent over $100 million, including $45 million of his own money.

Romney the Nominee

After a failed presidential bid in 2008, Romney spent the next four years organizing, raising money, and repositioning himself as a 'severely conservative' candidate for president. Romney remained in a campaign mode leading up to the 2012 presidential election. He gave speeches on behalf of fellow Republican candidates and helped them to raise money in the 2010 congressional elections. He positioned himself as the leader going into the Republican presidential primaries.

His efforts paid off, as he was able to knit together a series of plurality wins in early Republican primaries while his more-conservative opponents imploded for various reasons. But, despite consistently winning based on the shadow argument that he was 'electable,'despite the flailing and incompetent performances of his opponents, Romney never quite captured the hearts of conservative Republican voters. On various occasions he trailed his GOP opponents—former Speaker of the House Newt Gingrich, House Member Michele Bachmann, Texas Gov. Rick Perry and businessman Herman Cain. In the end, his strongest challenger was former Pennsylvania Senator Rick Santorum, who attacked Romney as a phony conservative who flip-flopped on abortion, gay rights, and health care. Romney often appeared stiff and ill at ease before the camera, making several serious gaffes, and failing to connect personally with voters. Nonetheless, in April Santorum dropped out of the race citing Romney's financial and organizational advantages.

In the end, Mitt Romney prevailed, and surpassed his politically popular father. He came into the Republican National Convention as the consensus candidate. He survived a field of alternatives, all of whom challenged his truthfulness and his credentials to lead in politics. And, he assuaged the concerns of the two major components of the GOP base—evangelicals and Tea Partiers – who questioned his qualification to lead the charge against Barack Obama.

QUESTIONS

1. **How do Mitt Romney's life and background shape his political choices and opportunities?**
2. **What lessons from failure in 2008 does Mitt Romney take and use to succeed in 2012?**
3. **What are the major criticisms of Mitt Romney by his GOP primary opponents? Are they valid based on your reading?**

The Decision to Run

The decision to run for president involves complex personal and political calculations. Ambition to occupy the world's most powerful office must be weighed against the staggering costs—emotional as well as financial—of a presidential campaign.

Serious planning, organizing, and fund raising must begin at least two years before the general election. A staff must be assembled—campaign managers and strategists, fund-raisers, media experts, pollsters, issues advisers and speechwriters, lawyers and accountants—and supporters must be identified in key states throughout the nation. Paid and volunteer workers must be assembled (see Figure 8.4). Leaders among important interest groups must be contacted. A general campaign strategy must be developed, an organization put in place, and several millions of dollars in campaign contributions pledged in advance of the race. Often, the decision to run hinges on whether initial pledges of campaign contributions appear adequate. The serious presidential candidate must be able to anticipate contributions of $100 million or more for primary elections. Most of this work must be accomplished in the preprimary season—the months after Labor Day of the year preceding the election, and before the first primary election.

A Strategy for the Primaries

The road to the White House consists of two separate races: the primary elections and caucuses leading to the Democratic and Republican party nominations, and the general election. Each of these races requires a separate strategy. The primary race requires an appeal to party activists and the more ideologically motivated primary voters in key

8.1 8.2 8.3 8.4 8.5 8.6 8.7

states. The general election requires an appeal to the less partisan, less attentive, more ideologically moderate general election voters. Thus, the campaign strategy developed to win the nomination must give way after the national conventions to a strategy to win the November general election.

☐ Primary Campaigns

Primary campaigns come in different varieties. An incumbent president with no serious competition from within his own party can safely glide through his party's primaries, saving campaign money for the general election. In contrast, the party out of the White House typically goes through a rough-and-tumble primary (and preprimary) season, with multiple presidential aspirants. And when no incumbent president is running for reelection, both parties experience heavy party infighting among multiple presidential hopefuls.

Candidates strive during the preprimary season to win media attention, to climb the poll ratings, and raise campaign funds. Early front-runners must beware of stumbles and gaffes; they must be prepared for close scrutiny by the media; and they must expect to be the targets of their competitors. Not infrequently, early front-runners lose their momentum even before the first primary elections.

Primary voters are heavily weighted toward party activists, who are more ideologically motivated than the more moderate voters in general elections. Democratic primary voters are more liberal, and Republican primary voters are more conservative, than the voters in the November general election. Democratic primary voters include large numbers of the party's core constituents—union members, public employees, minorities, environmentalists, and feminists.

Presidential candidates must try to appeal not only to the ideological predispositions of their party's primary voters but also convince them of their "electability"—the likelihood that they can win the party's nomination and more important go on to win the presidential election. Often primary voters are torn between voting for their favorite candidate based on his or her ideological and issue positions and voting for the most electable candidate.

☐ The Iowa Caucuses

Iowa has traditionally held party caucuses even before the New Hampshire primary. Rather than going to the polls and casting ballots as in a primary election, Iowans gather at set times and at set locations in each of 1,700 precincts. At the Republican caucuses, a straw vote is taken indicating the voters' choice for presidential nominee. At Democratic caucuses participants divide into groups supporting their preferred presidential nominee. A "viability threshold" eliminates groups with too few members; these members are urged to realign in support of more viable candidates. Finally, a head count is taken which apportions delegates to the county convention and later district conventions. Delegates pledged to a presidential candidate seldom abandon their chosen candidate. The Iowa caucuses inspire retail politics, with presidential candidates shaking hands through small Midwestern towns and working fairs and other events. The Iowa parties have pledged to keep the Iowa caucuses at least one week ahead of the New Hampshire primary. The Iowa Democratic caucus electorate is usually more liberal than the national Democratic electorate, while the Republican caucus electorate is one of the more evangelical Christian electorates outside the South. Iowa has a poor record of picking nominees through 2012. In caucuses where no incumbent was in the party caucus, just three of eight Democratic winners and two of six Republican winners in Iowa won the party nomination.

☐ The New Hampshire Primary

The primary season begins in the winter snows of New Hampshire, traditionally the first state to hold a presidential primary election. New Hampshire is far more important *strategically* to a presidential campaign than it is in delegate strength. As a small state, New Hampshire supplies fewer than 1 percent of the delegates at the Democratic and Republican conventions. But the New Hampshire primary looms very large in media coverage and hence in overall campaign strategy. Although the popular Democratic Iowa party caucuses are held even earlier, New Hampshire is the nation's first primary, and the media begin speculating about its outcome and reporting early state-poll results months in advance.

The New Hampshire primary inspires **retail politics**—direct candidate contact with the voters. Presidential aspirants begin visiting New Hampshire in the year preceding the primary elections, speaking at town hall meetings, visiting with small groups, standing outside of supermarkets, walking through restaurants, greeting workers at factories and offices, and so on. These personal contacts bypass the media's filtering and interpreting of the candidate's personality and message. Retail politics is largely confined to New Hampshire, a small state and a year of preprimary time to reach voters personally. And there is some evidence that voters who actually meet candidates come away with a more favorable view of them.[25]

The "expectations" game is played with a vengeance in the early primaries. Media polls and commentators set the candidates' expected vote percentages, and the candidates and their spokespersons try to deflate these expectations. On election night, the candidates' **spin doctors** sally forth among the crowds of television and newspaper reporters to give a favorable interpretation of the outcome. The candidates themselves appear at campaign headquarters (and, they hope, on national television) to give the same favorable spin to the election results. But the media itself—particularly the television network anchors and reporters and commentators—interpret the results for the American people, determining the early favorites in the presidential horse race.

New Hampshire's electorate is far more moderate than Iowa's. Election rules allow independents to vote in either party's primary. As a consequence, the New Hampshire winner is often different from the Iowa winner, and usually a more moderate choice in both parties. But New Hampshire, like Iowa, does not always predict the outcome of the nomination fight. Since 1948, in nonincumbent races, 7 of 11 Republican New Hampshire winners went on to the nomination, but only 5 of 11 Democratic winners in New Hampshire did so.

What Iowa and New Hampshire provide is the initial *momentum* for the presidential candidates. "Momentum" is more than just a media catchword. The Democratic and Republican winners in these states have demonstrated their voter appeal, their "electability." Favorable results inspire more financial contributions and thus the resources needed to carry the fight into the next group of primary elections. Unfavorable results tend to dry up contributions; weaker candidates may be forced into an early withdrawal.

retail politics
Direct candidate contact with individual voters.

spin doctors
Practitioners of the art of spin control, or manipulation of media reporting to favor their own candidate.

front-end strategy
Presidential political campaign strategy in which a candidate focuses on winning early primaries to build momentum.

South Carolina Primary

South Carolina has held contested presidential primaries in both parties since the 1980s. The Saturday primary, held in advance of the late-winter Super Tuesday megaprimary, is always the "first in the South" contest. The South Carolina electorate is very different from the national electorate of either party. It is a foundational electorate composed of key components of both parties' coalitions. In the Democratic Primary, nearly half of all voters are African Americans and the white electorate; in the GOP, two-thirds of the voters are evangelical Christians. Until 2012, the winner of the GOP primary always won the Republican presidential nomination, and only one Democrat who won South Carolina (John Edwards in 2004) failed to win the nomination.

The Front-End Strategy

A **front-end strategy** places heavy emphasis on the results from Iowa and New Hampshire and other early primary states. This strategy involves spending all or most of the candidate's available resources—time, energy, and money—in these early states,

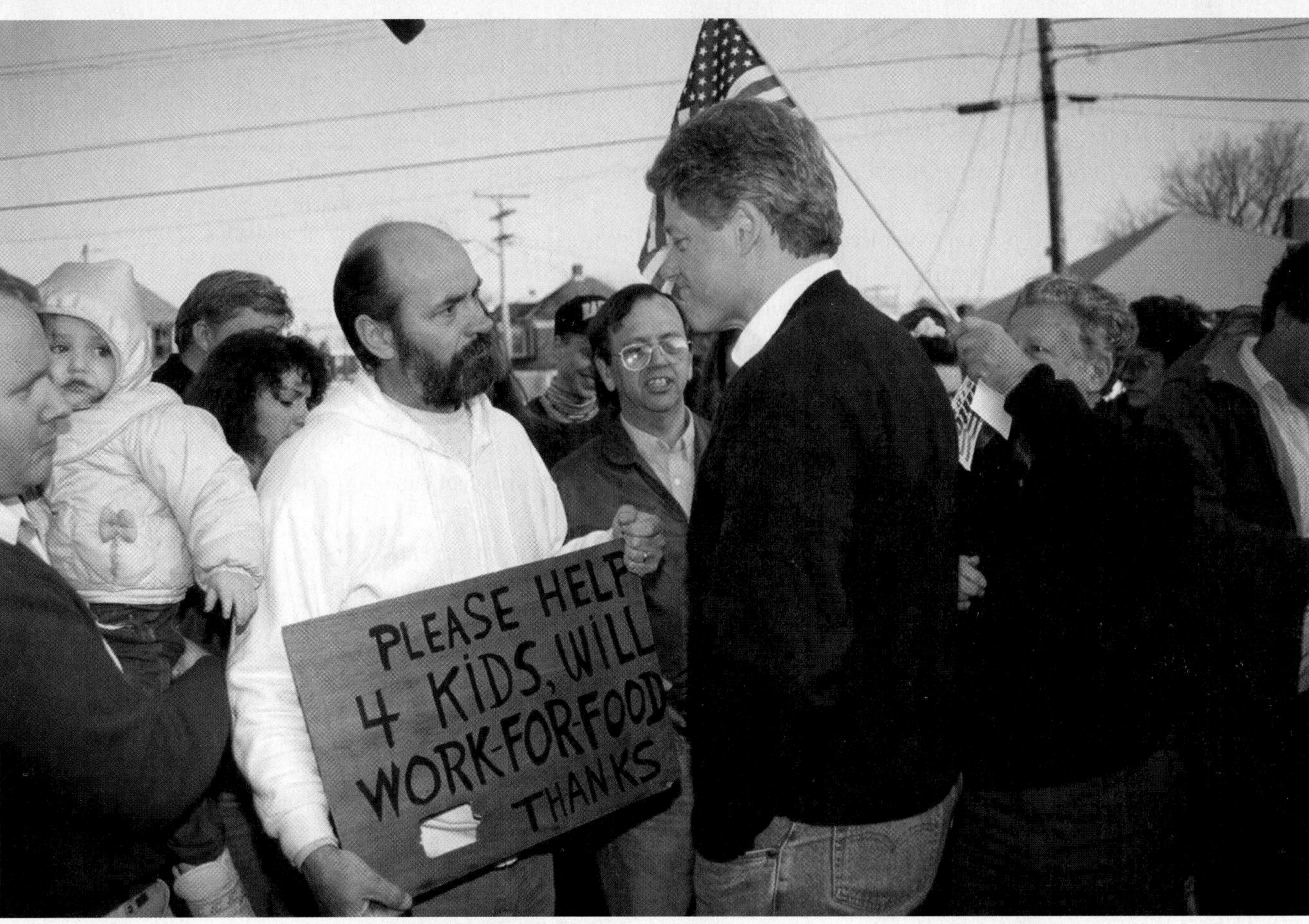

COMEBACK KID

Then Governor Bill Clinton aggressively worked the primary electorate in New Hampshire after damaging revelations of marital infidelity. His performance in the Granite State saved his campaign and eventually propelled him to the White House.

front-loading
The scheduling of presidential primary elections early in the year.

in the hopes that early victories will provide the momentum, in media attention and financial contributions, to continue the race.

Front-Loading Primaries

Traditionally, both the Democratic and Republican parties allowed Iowa and New Hampshire to be the first states in the nation to express their presidential preferences. But these states are atypical of the rest of the country, and resentment grew among other states regarding the influence exercised by these two small states. As early as 1988, southern governors and state legislative leaders sought to move the southern primaries to immediately follow New Hampshire, creating the "Super Tuesday" regional megaprimary. Over the next two decades, more states set their primaries earlier, and in 2008 and 2012, governors and state legislatures across the nation "**front-loaded**" their presidential primaries, pushing their dates earlier into January and February. Efforts by the Democratic and Republican National Committees sought to prevent a mad scramble among the states to be first in the nation in selecting convention delegates pledged to respective candidates. Both national party committees recognized the traditional first-in-the-nation positions of Iowa and New Hampshire, and they also approved of early selections by Nevada and South Carolina. But they sought to restrain all other states from making their selections earlier than the first Tuesday in February, including imposing delegate penalties on states that jumped the queue on primary order. In 2008, Florida and Michigan chose to jump the gun and hold primary elections in late January, and Florida did so again in 2012. The parties initially held to their effort to reduce the voting power of these states at conventions, but state leaders contended that the increased influence of an early voice in the nomination fight outweighed the loss of delegate power.

□ Big-State Strategy

Presidential aspirants who begin the race with widespread support among party activists, heavy financial backing, and strong endorsements from the major interest groups can focus their attention on the big-state primaries. A **big-state strategy** generally requires more money, more workers, and better organization than a front-end strategy. But the big states—California, New York, Texas, Florida, Pennsylvania, Ohio, and Michigan—have the most delegates. In the Republican Party, the big state strategy is more beneficial because many of the big states are "winner take all"—winning these states by small margins nonetheless guarantees a delegate windfall.

big-state strategy
Presidential political campaign strategy in which a candidate focuses on winning primaries in large states because of their high delegate counts.

swing states
States that are not considered to be firmly in the Democratic or Republican column.

□ Primary Debates

Voters pay attention to general election debates. But party primary debates often attract narrower audiences. But these debates can matter, though they take on a different character than the general election debates. Primary debates often involve many more candidates, so it is more challenging for a candidate to break out and distinguish him- or herself from the pack. Unlike the general election debates, which are supervised by a debate commission and have strictly enforced rules that limit rebuttal, interruption, and audience participation. Primary debates are usually staged by media outlets, political organizations, or the candidates themselves; the rules are often looser, so the events often lose their structure or devolve into crowd pandering. However, these debates matter. In 1980, Ronald Reagan resurrected his presidential campaign by asserting his right to be heard, roaring, "I am paying for this microphone" when a moderator attempted to shut him off in a New Hampshire debate. Barack Obama used the debates in 2007 and 2008 to directly challenge Hillary Clinton. And in 2012, Newt Gingrich and Mitt Romney resurrected flagging campaigns with widely viewed, aggressive debate performances that voters said were important to their vote choice.

□ The General Election Battle

Buoyed by the conventions—and often by postconvention bounces in the polls—the new nominees must now face the general electorate. Strategies in the general election are as varied as the imaginations of campaign advisers, media consultants, pollsters, and the candidates themselves. As noted earlier, campaign strategies are affected by the nature of the times and the state of the economy; by the incumbent or challenger status of the candidate; by the issues, conditions, scandals, or events currently being spotlighted by the media; and by the dynamics of the campaign itself as the candidates attack and defend themselves (see *The Game, the Rules, the Players*: Campaign '12—Obama Versus Romney).

□ Targeting the Swing States

In focusing on the most populous states, with their large electoral votes, candidates must decide which of these states are "winnable" and then direct their time, energy, and money to these **swing states**. Candidates cannot afford to spend too much effort in states that already seem to be solidly in their column, although they must avoid the perception that they are ignoring these strong bases of support. Neither can candidates waste much effort on states that already appear to be solidly in their opponent's column. So, the swing states receive most of the candidates' time, attention, and television advertising money.

□ Tarmac Politics

Waging a national campaign across several states and hundreds of media markets demands that politicians be constantly moving. Presidential candidates appear in several states in a single day, flying into an airport (or, if it is an incumbent president, an air force base), usually appearing on the runway tarmac for a quick event or interview, continuing on to a public rally or private fund-raising event, and then departing from the airport to the next destination. Tarmac politics, where candidates hop from airport to airport, are the norm not just in presidential politics, but are also common to gubernatorial and U.S. Senate campaigns in large states such as Florida, Texas, and California.

☐ The Presidential Debates

The nationally televised presidential debates are the central feature of the general election campaign. These debates attract more viewers than any other campaign event. Moreover, they enable a candidate to reach undecided voters and the opponent's supporters, as well as the candidate's own partisans. Even if issues are not really discussed in depth, people see how presidential candidates react as human beings under pressure, and even people who usually pay little attention to politics, may be drawn in by the drama of the confrontation.

Debates allow viewers an opportunity to see and hear candidates together and to compare their responses to questions as they stand side by side. The debates give audiences a better view of the candidates than they can get from 30-second commercial ads or 7-second news sound bites. Viewers can at least judge how the candidates react under pressure.

However, the debates emphasize candidate image over substantive policy issues. Candidates must appear presidential. They must appear confident, compassionate, concerned, and good humored. They must not appear uncertain or unsure of themselves, or aloof or out of touch with viewers, or easily upset by hostile questions. They must avoid verbal slips or gaffes or even unpolished or awkward gestures. They must remember that the debates are not really debates so much as joint press conferences in which the candidates respond to questions with rehearsed mini-speeches and practiced sound bites. Nominating primary debates have become increasingly common, and those debates often propel candidates toward the ideological base of the party. General election debates require candidates to exhibit appeal beyond the party base to win.

KENNEDY–NIXON Televised presidential debates began in 1960, when John F. Kennedy and Richard M. Nixon confronted each other on a bare stage before an America watching on black-and-white TV sets. Nixon was the vice president in the popular presidential administration of Dwight Eisenhower; he was also an accomplished college debate-team member. He prepared for the debates as if they were college debates, memorizing facts and arguments. But he failed to realize that image triumphs over substance on television. By contrast, Kennedy was handsome, cool, and confident; whatever doubts the American people may have had regarding his youth and inexperience were dispelled by his polished manner. Radio listeners tended to think that Nixon won, and debate coaches scored him the winner. But television viewers preferred the glamorous young Kennedy. The polls shifted in Kennedy's direction after the debate, and he won in a very close general election.

CARTER–FORD President Lyndon Johnson avoided debating in 1964, and Nixon, having learned his lesson, declined to debate in 1968 and 1972. Thus, televised presidential debates did not resume until 1976, when incumbent president Gerald Ford, perceiving he was behind in the polls, agreed to debate challenger Jimmy Carter. Ford made a series of verbal slips. Carter was widely perceived as having won the debate, and he went on to victory in the general election.

REAGAN–CARTER AND REAGAN–MONDALE It was Ronald Reagan who demonstrated the true power of television. Reagan had lived his life in front of a camera. It was the principal tool of both of his trades—actor and politician. In 1980, incumbent president Jimmy Carter talked rapidly and seriously about programs, figures, and

The Game, the Rules, the Players

Campaign '12—Obama Versus Romney

RIGHT VERSUS LEFT

The campaign between Mr. Obama and Mr. Romney was one of the most ideologically polarizing contests in modern political history. Here, the candidates meet before the first presidential debate in Denver.

The 2012 election was monumental. More money was spent on politics than had ever been spent on any American campaign, almost $2 billion for the presidency alone. The result was a solid reelection win for Barack Obama over challenger Mitt Romney and a continuation of divided government in Washington DC.

Incumbent presidents are usually reelected. When they fail, it is because they preside over a struggling economy. Barack Obama, elected on a promise of 'Change We Can Believe In' inherited an economic mess. After three years in office, the incumbent confronted the reality of running for reelection in the midst of an incomplete recovery and facing the full force of a hostile Republican congressional leadership adamant in their determination to defeat him for reelection. Early policy successes such as the Patient Protection and Affordable Care Act (PPACA, or 'Obamacare') and the Iraq withdrawal were swamped by ongoing concern about unemployment, energy prices, and rapidly growing deficit spending.

Obama's opponent, former Massachusetts Gov. Mitt Romney, provided a stark contrast to Obama. A moderate, career businessman with limited government experience, Romney had sought and lost the GOP nomination in 2008. He continued his campaign for four years, spending money and organizing to defeat a field of conservative opponents in the party primary. Romney repositioned from his pro-choice, pro-universal healthcare record as governor of Massachusetts, moving severely to the hard right on economic and social issues in order to placate the Tea Party and other conservative elements of the Republican base. He couldn't get to the right of the crowded GOP field, but won on a pragmatic argument: he was electable, his opponents were not.

The Long Campaign: The Obama campaign anticipated Romney as opponent well in advance of his

(*Continued*)

8.1

8.2

8.3

8.4

8.5

8.6

8.7

(Continued)

nomination. Campaign surrogates targeted Romney and his morphing political record for criticism. The Romney campaign responded by focusing his primary campaign on Mr. Obama, rather than on his primary opponents. The summer campaign showed a tight race. Mr. Obama was dogged by persistent unemployment above 8% and tepid economic growth.

The good news for the president came from the Supreme Court. In late June, a 5-4 majority led by conservative Chief Justice John Roberts mooted a major conservative criticism of the president's record by declaringthe constitutionality of the PPACA. This moved the repeal of Obamacare from the courts and back into the political realm, where Mitt Romney, an architect of a similar health care reform in Massachusetts, would now campaign on a promise to repeal what he had once created. This was one of several policy repositions by the Massachusetts Republican that reinforced the perception that he had no genuine political identity or belief system other than expedience.

The Republican National Convention in Tampa focused on the president's record of failure. Republicans sought to simultaneously reach out to women and Hispanics, while Romney sought to placate movement conservatives by choosing conservative congressman Paul Ryan of Wisconsin as his running mate. Democrats used their Charlotte convention to showcase their party diversity and to also bring back into the campaign party elder statesman Bill Clinton, who nearly overshadowed the incumbent president.

The Polarized Campaign: The election revealed the divisions that persist in American party politics. African American voters (13% of the electorate) voted overwhelmingly for President Obama, giving him 93% of their votes; Hispanics (10% of the electorate) supported Obama 71%–27%; and Asian Americans (3% of voters) supported Obama 73%–26%. Anglo whites still made up the vast majority of the voter turnout (72%), but only cast 38% of their ballots for Obama. White voter support for Obama was greatest in the Midwest, New England, and on the Pacific Coast, weakest in the west and the South.

Journalist Thomas Edsall notes that the electorate grows about 2% less white every election, which should result in a shift of about 1.7 points in the electorate towards the Democratic advantage. The Romney campaign engaged in extensive campaign appeals to Hispanic voters in particular, using Spanish language advertising to tout the 'migration' of his father George from Mexico to the United States and also to equate Obama with Latin-American socialists Fidel Castro and Hugo Chavez.

These divisions were not superficially racial. Instead, they reflected a growing difference in the perception of political philosophies of the major parties, their candidates, and the relative appeal to different groups. The growing states' rights perspective in the GOP in general attracted not just social and economic conservatives, but also racial conservatives and anti-immigration whites. The national Democratic Party was increasingly defined by diversity issues and associated with the expanded consumption of the economy by government. When Mitt Romney's campaign was hammed by criticism of the candidate's videotaped remarks, disparaging 47% of the American public as paying no taxes and only consuming government services and benefits, it only a subtext of the campaign: there were 'makers' and 'takers,' and Obama and the Democrats represented the takers. In the meantime, favorable economic indicators (unemployment fell below 8% for the first time in nearly four years) gave the president a boost in the closing weeks of the campaign, especially in battleground states like Ohio, Wisconsin, and Florida.

Six Scenarios: Going into the closing week of the campaign, six scenarios emerged for the election; all hinged on aspects of voter mobilization and the accuracy of the polls in measuring public support. Four of the six scenarios predicted an Obama victory. The most likely of these, which strictly followed survey research, indicated a solid Obama reelection (290 electoral votes to 248), with the South going to Mr. Romney. If the polls were biased beyond the margin of error, a solid Romney victory with 291 electoral votes emerged which immolated the electoral 'firewall' of Wisconsin, Minnesota, and Pennsylvania. However, if the Obama voter mobilization machine was fully effective, the Midwest would hold; Nevada and Colorado would vote Democratic; and Florida and Virginia would shift to the president's column resulting in a 332-206 victory. This last scenario was the one that emerged.

Despite a tepid recovery, President Obama was able to secure reelection. In part this was a result of sophisticated thinking among many Americans, who continued to ascribe more responsibility for economic woes to President Bush. President Obama also benefitted from strong support among voters who were concerned about health care, and also enjoyed support from voters who factored in his management of the response to the pre-election Superstorm Sandy that struck New Jersey and New York City (42% said hurricane response was 'important' in determining their vote and seven in ten of those voters supported Obama). But first and foremost, it was a product of four years of organization and mobilization, of expanded databasing and voter identification, and of the intensive use of phone-banking and personal contacting to mobilize voters of color, young voters (who went 60%–37% for Mr. Obama), and first-time voters.

QUESTIONS

1. How is race and ethnicity a factor in determing the outcome of the 2012 election?
2. Why did Mr. Obama win?

DO DEBATES MATTER?

President Barack Obama was criticized for his initial performance in debate against Mitt Romney. The poor showing caused polls to close, but did not cause Mr. Obama to lose reelection.

budgets. But Reagan was master of the stage; he was relaxed, confident, joking. He appeared to treat the president of the United States as an overly aggressive, impulsive younger man, regrettably given to exaggeration. When it was all over, it was clear to most viewers that Carter had been bested by a true professional in media skills.

However, in the first of two televised debates with Walter Mondale in 1984, Reagan's skills of a lifetime seemed to desert him. He stumbled over statistics and groped for words. Reagan's poor performance raised the only issue that might conceivably defeat him—his age. The president looked and sounded old. But in the second debate, Reagan laid the perfect trap for his questioners. When asked about his age and capacity to lead the nation, he responded with a serious dead-pan expression to a hushed audience and waiting America: "I want you to know that I will not make age an issue in this campaign. I am not going to exploit for political purposes [pause] my opponent's youth and inexperience." The studio audience broke into uncontrolled laughter. Even Mondale had to laugh. With a classic one-liner, Reagan buried the age issue and won not only the debate but also the election.

BUSH–DUKAKIS In 1988, Michael Dukakis ensured his defeat with a cold, detached performance in the presidential debates, beginning with the very first question. When CNN anchor Bernard Shaw asked, "Governor, if Kitty Dukakis were raped and murdered, would you favor an irrevocable death penalty for the killer?" The question demanded an emotional reply. Instead, Dukakis responded with an impersonal recitation of his stock position on law enforcement. Bush seized the opportunity to establish a more personal relationship with the viewers. Voters responded to Bush, electing him in an electoral college landslide.

CLINTON–BUSH–PEROT The three-way presidential debates of 1992 drew the largest television audiences in the history of presidential debates. In the first debate, Ross Perot's Texas twang and down-home folksy style stole the show. Chided by his opponents for having no governmental experience, he shot back, "Well, they have a point. I don't have any experience in running up a $4 trillion debt." But it was Bill Clinton's smooth performance in the second debate, with its talk-show format, that seemed to wrap up the election. Ahead in the polls, Clinton appeared at ease walking about the stage and responding to audience questions with sympathy and sincerity. By contrast, George Bush appeared stiff and formal, and somewhat ill at ease with the "unpresidential" format.

CLINTON–DOLE A desperate Bob Dole, running 20 points behind, faced a newly "presidential" Bill Clinton in their two 1996 debates. (Perot's poor standing in the polls led to his exclusion.) Dole tried to counter his image as a grumpy old man in the first encounter; his humor actually won more laughs from the audience than Clinton's. Dole injected more barbs in the second debate, complaining of "ethical problems in the White House." But Clinton remained cool and comfortable, ignoring the challenger and focusing on the nation's economic health. Viewers, most of whom were already in Clinton's court, judged him the winner of both debates.

BUSH–GORE Separate formats were agreed upon for three debates—the traditional podium, a conference table, and a town hall setting. Gore was assertive, almost to the point of rudeness, but both candidates focused on policy differences rather than on personal attacks. Viewers gave Gore the edge in these debates but found Bush more likable. Bush appeared to benefit more in the post-debate polls.

BUSH–KERRY Kerry prepared well for the three debates. He appeared tall, earnest, confident, well informed, and "presidential." He spoke forcefully, avoiding the qualifying clauses and lengthy sentences that had plagued his speeches in the past. Bush appeared uncomfortable, scowling at Kerry's answers, often repeating himself, and failing to "connect" with his audiences. Polls showed Kerry winning each debate.

OBAMA–McCAIN The debates magnified the contrasts: tall, young, and black versus short, old, and white. Obama, leading in the polls, had only to tie McCain, but he edged out the aging Senator in style and presence. McCain accused Obama of compiling "the most liberal voting record in the Senate." Obama shot back: "Mostly that's just me opposing George Bush's wrongheaded policies."

OBAMA–ROMNEY Three presidential debates were held between President Obama and Governor Romney in 2012, using the traditional formats: podium, town hall, and roundtable. Each debate produced a different result. Critics of debates say they don't really matter. In the first debate, Barack Obama seemed to take their word for it, appearing to be unfocused and mentally checked out. Gov. Romney made an aggressive case on domestic economic policy and was acclaimed the winner. Public opinion polls responded. The popular support and electoral vote projection lead that President Obama enjoyed coming out of the convention collapsed. Mr. Obama responded with effective and powerful performances in the second and third debates while largely placing Mr. Romney on defense, especially on issues of foreign policy. The later debates did not appreciably shift opinion in the battleground states in the same fashion as the first.

☐ Hitting the Talk Shows

Candidates know that more people watch entertainment talk shows than news shows. David Letterman, Jon Stewart, *The View*, and Jay Leno all have audiences that are as large or larger than *Meet the Press, Hardball, Hannity, The O'Reilly Factor*, and others. Moreover, entertainment hosts rarely ask policy questions, but rather toss "softball" queries about family, feelings, and personal qualities. Responding to these questions

PRESIDENT ELVIS

Bill Clinton was not the first modern presidential candidate to play an instrument for the public or to show up on a comedy show—Nixon did both. But Clinton's 1992 Arsenio Hall Show appearance captured the public's attention and defined Clinton as the fun, youthful candidate in the 1992 election.

"humanizes" the candidate. And these entertainment shows reach audiences who have relatively little political knowledge or awareness. This provides an opportunity for a candidate to actually win over undecideds and persuadable opposition voters with a likable personality, good humor, and a good rapport with the host.[26] Presidential candidates expend considerable effort to get themselves on as many entertainment talk shows as possible.

□ The Electoral College

The Constitution grants each state a number of electors equal to the number of its congressional representatives and senators combined (see map). Because representatives are apportioned to the states on the basis of population, the electoral vote of the states is subject to change after each 10-year census. No state has fewer than three electoral votes, because the Constitution guarantees every state two U.S. senators and at least one representative. The 23rd Amendment granted three electoral votes to the District of Columbia even though it has no voting members of Congress. So winning the presidency requires winning in states with at least 270 of the 538 total electoral votes.

Voters in presidential elections are actually choosing a slate of presidential electors pledged to vote for their party's presidential and vice presidential candidates. The names of electors seldom appear on the ballot, only the names of the candidates and their parties do. The slate that wins a *plurality* of the popular vote in a state (more than

8.1

8.2

8.3

8.4

8.5

8.6

8.7

Electoral College
The 538 presidential electors apportioned among the states according to their congressional representation (plus three for the District of Columbia) whose votes officially elect the president and vice president of the United States.

any other slate, not necessarily a majority) casts all of the state's vote in the Electoral College. (This "winner-take-all" system in the states is not mandated by the Constitution; a state legislature could allocate a state's electoral votes in proportion to the split in the popular vote, as happens in Nebraska and Maine. The winner-take-all system in the states helps ensure that the Electoral College produces a majority for one candidate.)

The **Electoral College** never meets at a single location; rather, electors meet at their respective state capitals to cast their ballots on about December 15, following the general election on the first Tuesday after the first Monday of November. The results are sent to the presiding officer of the Senate, the vice president, who in January presides over their count in the presence of both houses of Congress and formally announces the results. These procedures are usually considered a formality, but the U.S. Constitution does not *require* that electors cast their vote for the winning presidential candidate in their state. Occasionally "faithless electors" disrupt the process, although none has ever changed the outcome.

If no candidate wins a majority of electoral votes, the House of Representatives chooses the president from among the three candidates with the largest number of electoral votes, with each state casting *one* vote. The Constitution does not specify how House delegations should determine their vote, but by House rules, the state's vote goes to the candidate receiving a majority vote in the delegation.

Only two presidential elections have ever been decided formally by the House of Representatives. In 1800, Thomas Jefferson and Aaron Burr tied in the Electoral College because the 12th Amendment had not yet been adopted to separate presidential from vice presidential voting; all the Democratic-Republican electors voted for both Jefferson and Burr, creating a tie. In 1824, Andrew Jackson won the popular vote and more electoral votes than anyone else but failed to get a majority. The House chose John Quincy Adams over Jackson, causing a popular uproar and ensuring Jackson's election in 1828.

In addition, in 1876, Congress was called on to decide which electoral results from the southern states to validate; a Republican Congress chose to validate enough Republican electoral votes to allow Republican Rutherford B. Hayes to win, even though Democrat Samuel Tilden had won more popular votes. Hayes promised the Democratic southern states that in return for their acknowledgment of his presidential claim, he would end the military occupation of the South.

In 1888, the Electoral College vote failed to reflect the popular vote. Benjamin Harrison received 233 electoral votes to incumbent president Grover Cleveland's 168, even though Cleveland won about 90,000 more popular votes than Harrison. Harrison served a single lackluster term; Cleveland was elected for a second time in 1892, the only president to serve two nonconsecutive terms.

□ Getting the Electoral Vote

Presidential election campaigns must focus on the Electoral College. Big-state victories, even by very narrow margins, can deliver big electoral prizes. With a total of 538 electoral votes at stake, *the winner must garner victories in states that total a minimum of 270 electoral votes.*

In recent presidential elections, the Democratic candidates (Clinton in 1992 and 1996, Gore in 2000, Kerry in 2004, and Obama in 2008 and 2012) have won the northeastern states, including New York; the upper Midwestern states, including Michigan and Illinois; and, perhaps most important, the West Coast, including California (see Figure 8.5). Republican presidential candidates (Bush in 1992, Dole in 1996, Bush in 2000 and 2004, McCain in 2008, and Romney in 2012) have shown greater strength in the Great Plains and Rocky Mountain states and in the southeastern states (forming a Republican "L" on the Electoral College map). If these patterns continue in presidential elections, Democrats can depend on two of the four largest Electoral College vote states: California (54) and New York (29). Republicans must win in the other two: Texas (38) and Florida (29). The Electoral College battleground

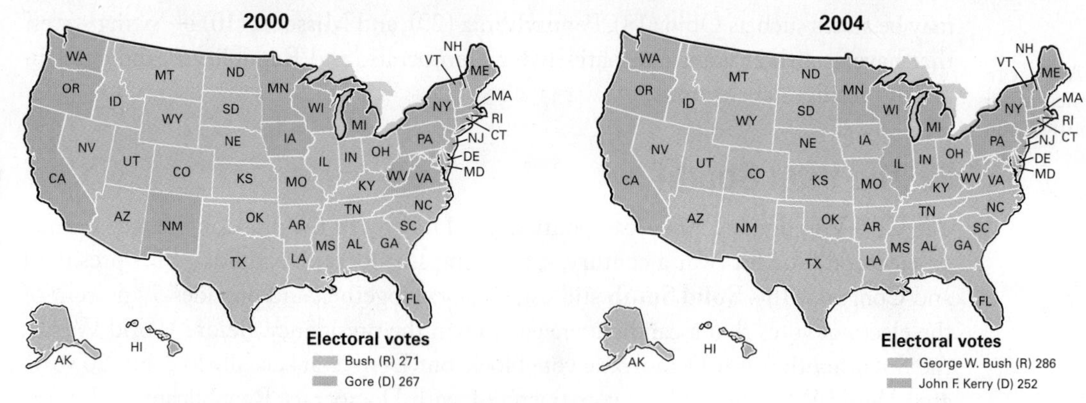

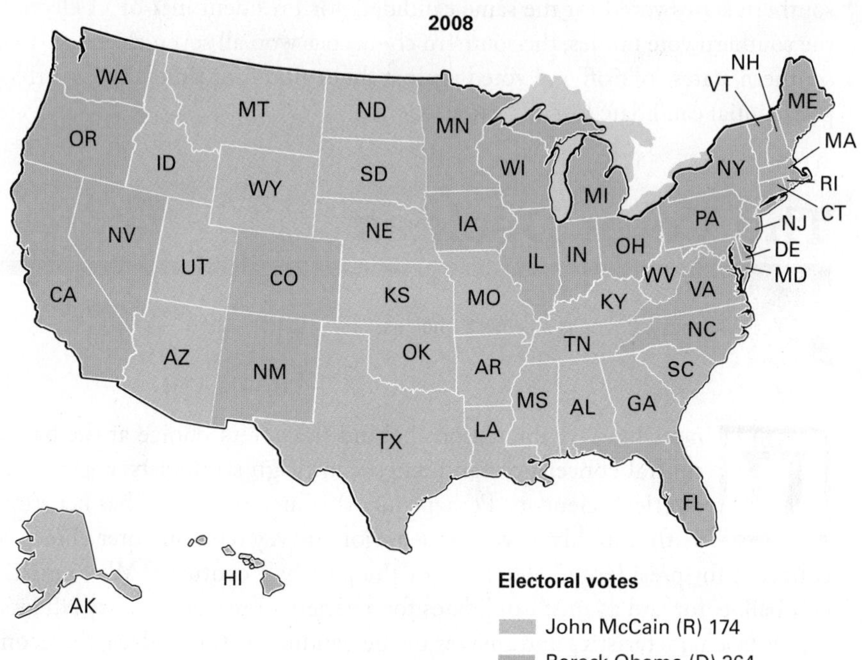

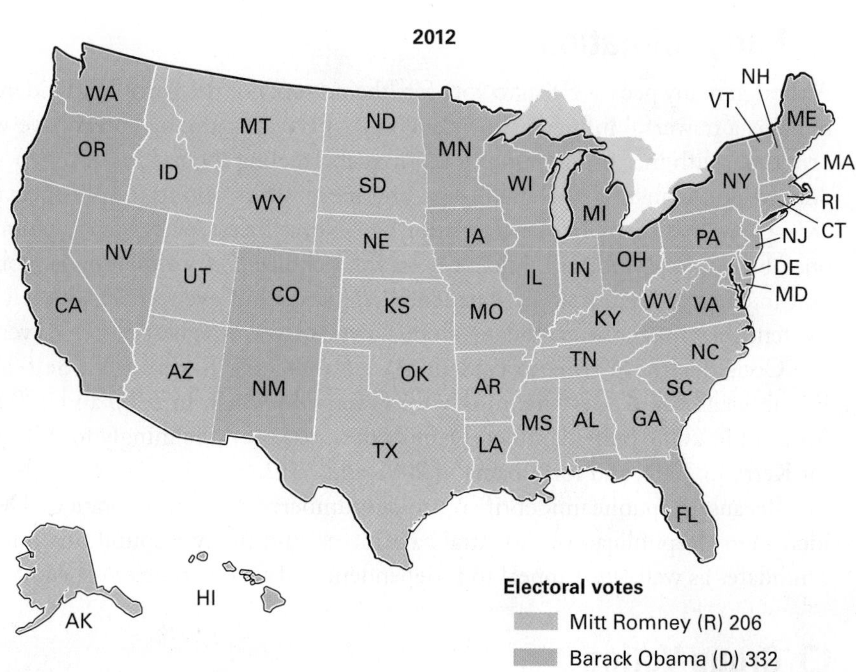

FIGURE 8.4 RED STATES, BLUE STATES

Electoral College votes by state in the past four presidential elections.

8.1

8.2

8.3

8.4

8.5

8.6

8.7

Solid South
An empirical theory of American politics stating that when the former Confederate states are unified and vote the same way, they determine who wins the presidency.

may be states such as Ohio (18), Pennsylvania (20), and Missouri (10) —"swing states" that have cast their votes alternatively for Democratic and Republican candidates in recent presidential elections.

☐ The Vital South?

The Civil War divided American politics. The 11 states of the old Confederacy formed an electoral bloc for over a century, supporting Democratic candidates for president and Congress. This **Solid South** still usually votes together, and provides 59 percent of the electoral votes that a candidate needs to win the presidency. Before World War II, the Solid South was a Democratic vote block, but Democrats usually lost. For 20 years after World War, the southern vote fractured, with Democrats, Republicans, and states' rights independents all winning support in Dixie. Since the 1970s, at least 10 of 11 southern states voted for the same candidate for President in 7 of 11 elections. When the southern vote unifies, the southern choice has won all seven elections. Two or more southern states split off and voted against the region four times. The South's preferred presidential candidate lost all four elections.

The Voter Decides

8.7 Assess influences on voters' choices.

Understanding the reasons behind the voters' choice at the ballot box is a central concern of candidates, campaign strategists, commentators, and political scientists. Perhaps no other area of politics has been investigated as thoroughly as voting behavior. Survey data on voter choice have been collected for presidential elections for the past half century.[27] We know that voters cast ballots for and against candidates for a variety of reasons—party affiliation, group interests, characteristics and images of the candidates themselves, the economy, and policy issues.[28] But forecasting election outcomes remains a risky business.

☐ Party Affiliation

Although many people claim to vote for "the person, not the party," party identification remains a powerful influence in voter choice. Party ties among voters have weakened over time, with increasing proportions of voters labeling themselves as Independents or only weak Democrats or Republicans, and more voters opting to split their tickets or cross party lines than did so a generation ago. Nevertheless, party identification remains one of the most important influences on voter choice. Party affiliation is more important in congressional than in presidential elections, but even in presidential elections the tendency to see the candidate of one's own party as "the best person" is very strong.

Consider these three presidential elections (see Figure 8.5). Self-identified Republicans voted overwhelmingly for George W. Bush in 2000 and 2004, and for McCain in 2008. Self-identified Democrats voted overwhelmingly for Gore in 2000, for Kerry in 2004, and for Obama in 2008 and 2012.

Because Republican identifiers are outnumbered in the electorate by Democratic identifiers, Republican presidential candidates, and many Republican congressional candidates as well, *must* appeal to Independent and Democratic crossover voters.

☐ Group Voting

We already know that various social and economic groups give disproportionate support to the Democratic and Republican parties. So it comes as no surprise that recent Democratic presidential candidates have received disproportionate support from

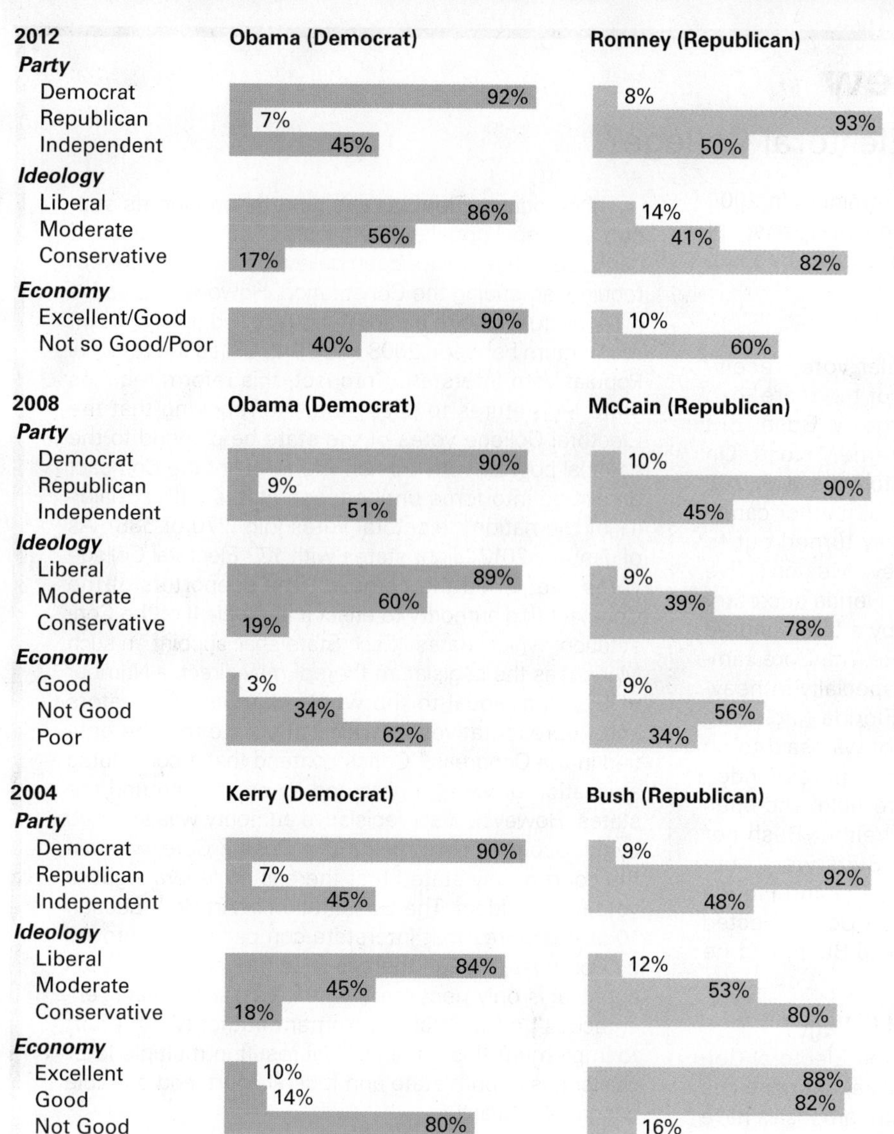

FIGURE 8.5 HOW WE VOTE: PARTY, IDEOLOGY, AND NATURE OF THE TIMES IN PRESIDENTIAL VOTING

Those who identify themselves as members of a major political party are highly likely to vote for the presidential candidates of their party. Likewise, those who identify themselves as liberals are more likely than average to vote for Democrats, and those who identify themselves as conservatives are more likely to vote for Republicans in presidential elections. In addition, voters who see the economic picture as better are more likely to vote for the incumbent, those who are concerned about the nation's economy are more likely to vote against the incumbent.

SOURCE: Election exit polls, Voter News Service.

African Americans, Catholics, Jews, the less-educated, and union workers; Republican presidential candidates have fared better among whites, Protestants, and more-educated voters (see Figure 8.6). That is, these groups have given a larger percentage of their vote to the Democratic or Republican candidates than the candidate received from the total electorate.

☐ Race and Gender Gaps

Among the more interesting group voting patterns is the serious *gender gap* affecting recent Republican candidates. Although Reagan won the women's vote in both 1980 and 1984, his vote percentages among men were considerably higher than among women. George H. W. Bush lost the women's vote in both 1988 and 1992. In 1996, the gender gap widened, with 54 percent of women voting for Clinton as opposed to only 38 percent for Dole; it continued in 2000, with

8.1

8.2

8.3

8.4

8.5

8.6

8.7

A Conflicting View

Should We Scrap the Electoral College?

Americans were given a dramatic reminder in 2000 that the president of the United States is *not* elected by nationwide *popular* vote, but rather by a majority of the *electoral votes* of the states.

Gore Wins but Loses

Al Gore won the nationwide popular vote, receiving about 500,000 more votes (out of the more than 100 million ballots cast) than George W. Bush. But the vote in several states was extremely close. On election night, Gore was reported to have won 262 electoral votes to Bush's 246—that is, neither candidate had the necessary 270. The key turned out to be Florida's 25 electoral votes. (New Mexico's five votes eventually went to Gore.) The Florida secretary of state declared Bush the winner by a few hundred votes out of 6 million cast in that state. The Gore campaign demanded *hand* recounts, especially in heavily Democratic counties in south Florida (including Palm Beach County, where the ballot was said to be confusing to voters). The Bush campaign responded that hand counts are subjective, unreliable, and open to partisan bias. For over a month neither Bush nor Gore would concede the election. Suits were initiated by both candidates in both federal and Florida state courts. Finally, the U.S. Supreme Court rejected Gore's appeal; Florida's votes went to Bush, and he was declared the winner.

What Would Replace the Electoral College?

Constitutional proposals to reform the Electoral College have circulated for nearly 200 years, but none has won widespread support. These reform proposals have included (1) election of the president by direct national popular vote; (2) allocation of each state's electoral vote in proportion to the popular vote each candidate received in the state; (3) allocation of electoral votes to winners of each congressional district and two to the statewide winners.

Democrats, Republicans, and Independents support a national popular vote for president, regardless of party. But it has always been believed that such a reform requires amending the Constitution. However, a creative proposal to expedite a popular vote picked up significant momentum between 2008 and 2012. Called the National Popular Vote Interstate Compact, this reform requires state legislatures to pass a statute requiring that the Electoral College votes of the state be pledged to the national popular vote winner. The terms of the Compact do not go into force until enough states with a majority of the nation's electoral votes join (270 of 538). As of January 2012, eight states with 132 Electoral College votes had joined the compact. The supporters of the Compact find authority to enact it in Article II of the Constitution, which states "Each State shall appoint, in such Manner as the Legislature thereof may direct, a Number of Electors, equal to the whole Number of Senators and Representatives to which the State may be entitled in the Congress." Critics contend that it constitutes a violation of voting rights and an end-run around the states. However, state legislative authority was affirmed by the Supreme Court in 2000 in *Bush v. Gore*, wherein the court plainly stated that there is no federal right to vote for president. The Constitution in Article I, Section 10 also requires that interstate compacts be approved by Congress, though there is legal precedent that such approval is only necessary when a state compact "encroaches" on federal government authority. An effort to implement this compact will result in multiple legal challenges in both state and federal court, and possible congressional action.

QUESTIONS

1. What arguments exist for getting rid of the Electoral College? For keeping it?
2. Think about your home state. Does it have more or less political clout under the Electoral College?

women giving Gore 54 percent of the vote as opposed to Bush's 43 percent. Again, in 2004, women gave Democrat Kerry 54 percent of their vote, and in 2008 they gave Obama 55 percent of their vote. African Americans have long constituted the most loyal group of Democratic voters, regularly giving the Democratic presidential nominee up to 90 percent or more of their vote. The overall Hispanic vote is Democratic, although a significant portion of Hispanics, notably Cuban Americans in Florida, vote Republican.

□ Candidate Image

In an age of direct communication between candidates and voters via television, the image of candidates and their ability to relate to audiences have emerged as important determinants of voter choice. Candidate image is most important in presidential contests, inasmuch as presidential candidates are personally more visible to the voter than candidates for lesser offices.[29]

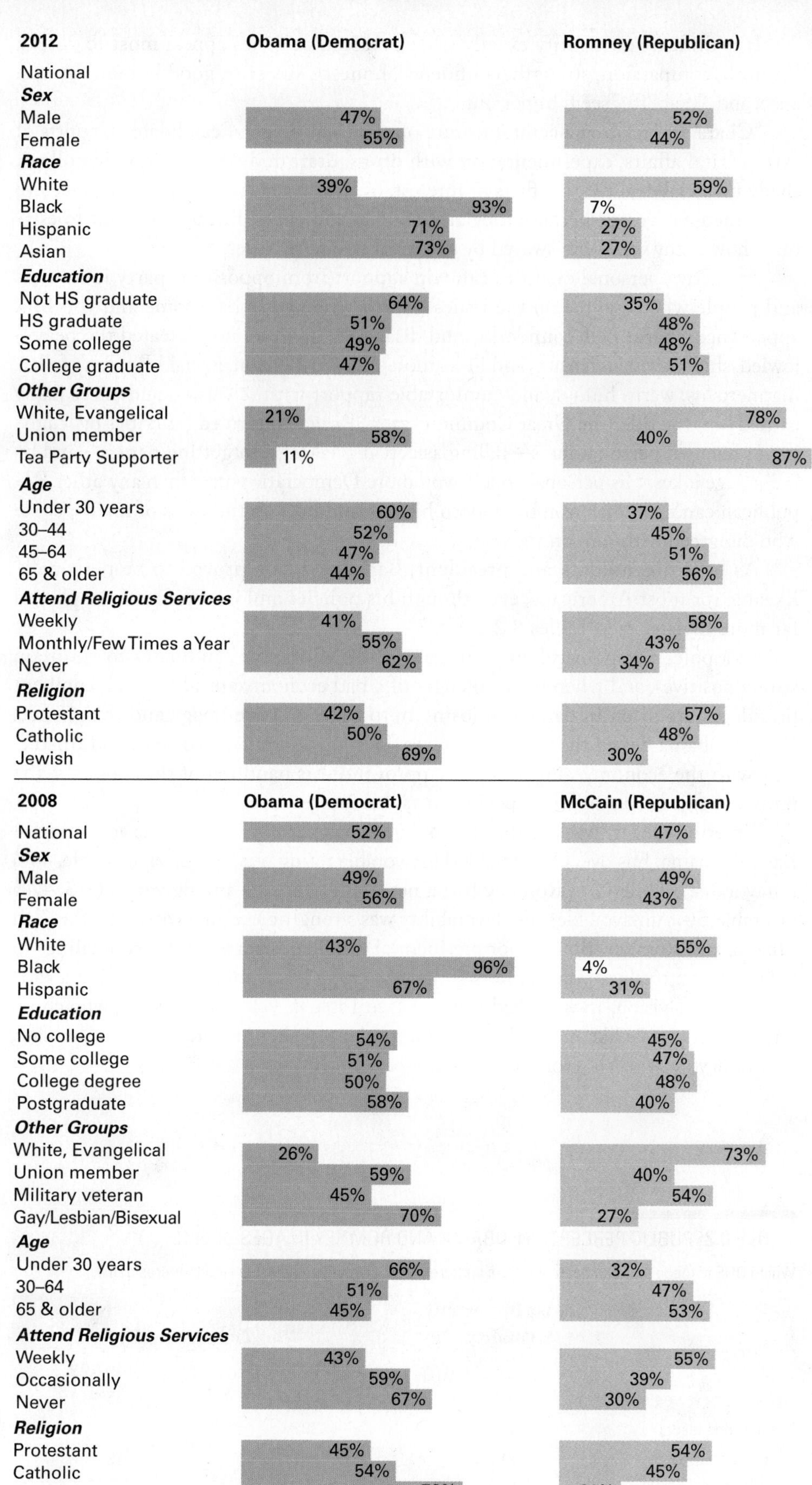

FIGURE 8.6 HOW WE VOTE: GROUP VOTING IN THE 2012 PRESIDENTIAL ELECTION

Democratic presidential candidates regularly do better among African American, Hispanic, lower income, and less-educated voters. The gender gap—men tending to vote Republican and women Democratic—first emerged in the Reagan years. Increasingly, white religious voters are casting their ballots for Republican candidates.

SOURCE: Election exit polls, Voter News Service.

It is difficult to identify exactly what personal qualities appeal most to voters. Warmth, compassion, strength, confidence, honesty, sincerity, good humor, appearance, and "likability" seem important.

"Character" is often a central feature of media coverage of candidates. Reports of extramarital affairs, experimentation with drugs, draft dodging, cheating in college, shady financial dealings, conflicts of interest, or lying or misrepresenting facts receive heavy media coverage because they attract large audiences. But it is difficult to estimate how many voters are swayed by so-called character issues.

Attractive personal qualities can win support from opposition-party identifiers and people who disagree on the issues. John F. Kennedy's handsome and youthful appearance, charm, self-confidence, and disarming good humor defeated the heavy-jowled, shifty-eyed, defensive, and ill-humored Richard Nixon. Ronald Reagan's folksy mannerisms, warm humor, and comfortable rapport with television audiences justly earned him the title "the Great Communicator." Reagan disarmed his critics by laughing at his own personal flubs—falling asleep at meetings, forgetting names—and by telling age jokes. His personal appeal won more Democratic voters than any other Republican candidate has won in modern history, and he won the votes of many people who disagreed with him on the issues.

As both a candidate and president, Barack Obama proved to be personally likeable for most Americans, even though his policies and job performance proved far more divisive (see Tables 8.2 and 8.3).

In a polarized political environment, it is difficult for candidates to maintain strong positives, and when the challenges of a bad economy are added in, incumbent presidents are often in danger of losing both their positive image and their office. Barack Obama defied those circumstances. Despite widespread concern and frustration with the economy, and strong disapproval of his handling of the economy, the president enjoyed an enduring positive personal image.

Entering the last week of the election, the Image Factor broke to the advantage of Barack Obama. His overall Favorable/Unfavorable rating was +7 (53% favorable, 46% unfavorable), while Gov. Romney had a net negative image among voters (−3, 47% favorable, 50% unfavorable), and favorability was strongly correlated with votes for both Obama and Romney. Both major presidential candidates stirred different qualities in voters. Among 'values' voters, voters seeking 'a strong leader,' and voters seeking a candidate with a 'vision,' most picked Romney (see Table 8.2). However, voters who chose 'cares about people like me' as their most important quality in a presidential candidate, over 80% voted for Mr. Obama.

TABLE 8.2 PUBLIC PERCEPTION: OBAMA AND ROMNEY IMAGES OF 2012

Which ONE of these four candidate qualities mattered most in deciding how you voted for president?

	Most Important Quality	Who They Voted For	
		Obama	**Romney**
Shares my values	27%	42%	55%
Is a strong leader	18%	38%	61%
Cares about people like me	21%	81%	18%
Has a vision for the future	29%	45%	54%

SOURCE: Election exit polls, Fox News, 2012.

TABLE 8.3 WHAT MATTERED MOST?: ISSUES THE VOTERS CARED ABOUT IN 2012

Relatively few voters cast their ballots strictly on the issue positions of the candidates. But voters cited these as the "most important" issues in 2012.

	Most Important Issue Facing the Country:	Who They Voted For	
		Obama	Romney
Foreign policy	5%	56%	33%
Federal budget deficit	15%	32%	66%
The economy	59%	47%	51%
Health care	18%	75%	24%

SOURCE: Election exit polls, Fox News, 2012.

☐ The Economy

Perhaps no other lesson has been as well learned by politicians: hard economic times hurt incumbents and favor challengers. Ever since the once-popular Republican incumbent Herbert Hoover was trounced by Franklin Roosevelt as the Great Depression of the 1930s deepened, politicians have understood that voters hold the incumbent party responsible for hard economic times. Fairly accurate predictions of voting outcomes in presidential elections can be made from models of the American economy. Economic conditions at election time—recent growth or decline in personal income, the unemployment rate, consumer confidence, and so on—are related to the vote given to the incumbent versus the challenger. The economy may not be the only important factor in presidential voting, but it is certainly a factor of great importance.[30] When voters punish politicians for the economy, it is usually the larger political environment they are responding to (sociotropic voting), rather than their own personal economic circumstances (egocentric voting).[31]

In 2012, the election was the issue on voters' minds; four years of recession and slow recovering weighed heavily. Three-quarters of voters said the economy was "not good" or "poor"; 59% said it as the most important issue facing the country. Voters who said the economy was their most important issue, a majority voted against President Obama, though 49% rated him better qualified to manage the economy. Economic assessments of the economy were related to candidate preference: 42% of Obama voters said the economy was excellent or good, compared to just 4% of Romney voters. Voters with other issue concerns such as health care voted overwhelming to reelect the incumbent president.

☐ Issue Voting

Casting one's vote exclusively on the basis of the policy positions of the candidates is rare. Most voters are unaware of the specific positions taken by candidates on the issues. Indeed, voters often believe that their preferred candidate agrees with them on the issues, even when this is not the case. In other words, voters project their own policy views onto their favorite candidate more often than they decide to vote for a candidate because of his or her position on the issues.

Nonetheless, campaigns often try to exploit "wedge issues" that may entice citizens to cross party lines and vote for the opposition candidate. A wedge issue is usually a hot-button issue, one that generates intense feelings. Many voters hold policy positions that conflict with their own party's candidate. Campaigns may try to win over some of these "persuadable" voters by appealing intensely to their held policy positions.[32]

8.1

8.2

8.3

8.4

8.5

8.6

8.7

A Constitutional Note

Corporations Are Made from People

Both Congress and the Supreme Court have confronted the issue of whether limiting campaign spending has the effect of limiting free speech. In 1976, in *Buckley v. Valeo,* the Supreme Court struck down Congress's limit on what an individual candidate or independent organization could spend to promote its own views in a campaign. "The First Amendment denies government the power to determine that spending to promote one's political views is ... excessive. In the free society ordained by our Constitution, it is not the government but the people who must retain control over the quantity and range of debate in a political campaign."[a] This decision means that wealthy individuals can spend unlimited amounts on their own campaigns, and independent organizations can spend unlimited amounts as long as their spending is independent of a candidate's campaign. However, the Supreme Court approved limits on *contributions* by individuals and organizations—distinguishing between contributions and expenditures. It approved the Federal Election Commission limits on individual and organizational contributions to political campaigns. Congress sought to remedy the many holes in the original Federal Election Campaign Act of 1974 in its Bipartisan Campaign Reform Act of 2002. It placed limits on "soft-money" contributions to political parties, most of which found its way into candidate campaigns. However, Congress did not challenge the Court's *Buckley* decision by trying to prevent individuals or nonprofit organizations from spending money to broadcast their views. Limiting spending for political broadcasting would "place substantial and direct restrictions on the ability of candidates, citizens, and associations to engage in protected political speech."[b] The result was the emergence of independent organizations, known as 527s, in subsequent elections. In 2010, the Supreme Court held that corporations and unions could not be prohibited from spending money "for express advocacy or electioneering purposes."[c]

Questions

1. Do you think corporations should enjoy full speech rights, like people?
2. Would you support a constitutional amendment to remove corporate personhood?

---

[a] *Buckley v. Valeo*, 424 U.S. 1 (1976).

[b] *McConnell v. Federal Election Commission*, 590 U.S. 93 (2003).

[c] *Citizens United v. F.E.C.*, January 21, 2010.

Review the Chapter

Elections in a Democracy

8.1 Evaluate the role of elections in American democracy, p. 260

Although winning candidates often claim a mandate for their policy proposals, in reality, few campaigns present clear policy alternatives to the voters, few voters cast their ballots on the basis of policy considerations, and the policy preferences of the electorate can seldom be determined from election outcomes.

Power and Ambition

8.2 Characterize the various factors that motivate people to pursue a political career, p. 261

Personal ambition for power and celebrity drives the decision to seek public office. Political entrepreneurship, professionalism, and careerism have come to dominate political recruitment; lawyers have traditionally dominated American politics

The Advantages of Incumbency

8.3 Explain the advantages of incumbency, p. 263

Incumbents begin campaigns with many advantages: name recognition, financial support, goodwill from services they perform for constituents, large-scale public projects they bring to their districts, and other resources of office.

Campaign Strategies

8.4 Identify the main components of campaign strategies, p. 265

Campaigning for office is largely a media activity, dominated by professional advertising specialists, fund-raisers, media consultants, and pollsters.

Campaign Finance

8.5 Analyze the role of money in campaigns, identify the major sources of funding, assess the motivations of contributors, and evaluate efforts to regulate campaign finances, p. 271

The professionalization of campaigning and the heavy costs of a media campaign drive up the costs of running for office. These huge costs make candidates heavily dependent on financial support from individuals and organizations. Fund-raising occupies more of a candidate's time than any other campaign activity. Campaign contributions are made by politically active individuals and organizations, including political action committees. Contributions are made in order to gain access to policymakers, or are ideologically motivated. The Federal Election Commission is responsible for enforcing the limits on campaign contributions to federal elections. Members are traditionally appointed in staggered terms by the president with three seats for Democrats and three seats for the Republicans. The recent emergence of SuperPACs has increased public skepticism about money in politics and increased the perception that a few big donors dominate politics.

The Presidential Campaign

8.6 Outline candidates' strategies for primary races and the general election, p. 281

Presidential primary strategies emphasize appeals to party activists and core supporters, including the more ideologically motivated primary voters. In a general election campaign, presidential candidates usually seek to broaden their appeal to moderate, centrist voters while holding on to their core supporters. Campaigns must focus on states where the candidate has the best chance for gaining the 270 electoral votes needed to win.

The Voter Decides

8.7 Assess influences on voters' choices, p. 296

Voter choice is influenced by party identification, group membership, perceived image of the candidates, and to a lesser extent, ideology and issue preferences.

Learn the Terms

mandate, p. 260
retrospective voting, p. 260
prospective voting, p. 261
professionalism, p. 261
careerism, p. 262
amateurs, p. 263
incumbents, p. 263
reelection rates, p. 263
name recognition, p. 263
challengers, p. 264
franking privilege, p. 264
campaign strategy, p. 265
voter targeting, p. 265
negative campaigning, p. 266
focus group, p. 267
photo ops, p. 270
sound bites, p. 270
mobilize, p. 271
issue ads, p. 275
political action committees (PACs), p. 277
Federal Election Commission (FEC), p. 278
soft money, p. 279
retail politics, p. 285
spin doctors, p. 285
front-end strategy, p. 285
front-loading, p. 286
big-state strategy, p. 287
swing states, p. 287
Electoral College, p. 294
Solid South, p. 296

Test Yourself

8.1 Evaluate the role of elections in American democracy

Voting for or against someone or a party on the basis of past performance is known as

a. prospective voting
b. *ex post facto* voting
c. Deterministic voting
d. performance voting
e. retrospective voting

8.2 Characterize the various factors that motivate people to pursue a political career

Of the following, what do actors, athletes, and astronauts *not* bring to a candidacy?

I. Experience with the media
II. Positive name recognition
III. Policy experience
IV. social status

a. Only I and III
b. Only II and III
c. Only III
d. I, II, III, and IV
e. Only II and IV

8.3 Explain the advantages of incumbency

Political incumbents enjoy which of the following advantages over challengers?

I. greater name recognition
II. the ability to raise money more easily
III. office resources

a. Only I and III
b. Only II and III
c. Only II
d. I, II, and III
e. Only III

8.4 Identify the main components of campaign strategies

Most campaign strategies provide for all of the following *except*

a. selecting a theme
b. defining the opponent
c. holding post-election evaluation sessions
d. coordinating advertising messages
e. Campaign strategies actually provide for all of the above

8.5 Analyze the role of money in campaigns, identify the major sources of funding, assess the motivations of contributors, and evaluate efforts to regulate campaign finances

Voter targeting, the process by which parties and candidates seek to identify potential voters

a. is growing more sophisticated because of the information we have about voters
b. is less important because of the increased use of television
c. doesn't work because voters lie
d. is largely under the control of the media
e. Doesn't work because voters preferences are transient

8.6 Outline candidates' strategies for primary races and the general election

The "front-end" strategy refers to

a. spin control
b. using overwhelming assets to assure victory
c. winning the early elections to build momentum
d. framing the story from the beginning
e. seizing control of the opposition message

8.7 Assess influences on voters' choices.

It would be accurate to say that Hispanics generally support the Democrats *except* for

a. Puerto Ricans in New York
b. Mexicans in California
c. Mexicans in the Rio Grande Valley
d. Angolans in Chicago
e. Cubans in Florida

Explore Further

SUGGESTED READINGS

Abramson, Paul R., John H. Aldrich, and David W. Rohde. *Change and Continuity in the 2008 Elections*. Washington, D.C.: CQ Press, 2009. An in-depth analysis of the 2008 presidential and congressional elections, assessing the impact of party loyalties, presidential performance, group memberships, and policy preferences on voter choice.

Cicero, Quintus. *How to Win an Election*. Princeton, NJ: Princeton University Press, 2012. No-nonsense advice to Roman orator and consular candidate Marcus Cicero, from his practical brother Quintus, on running a campaign. Still relevant after 2,000 years.

Ferrar-Myers, Victoria, and Diana Dwyre. *Limits and Loopholes: The Quest for Money, Free Speech and Fair Elections*. Washington, D.C.: CQ Press, 2007. A description of the passage of campaign finance legislation and subsequent court cases.

Fiorina, Morris P. *Retrospective Voting in American National Elections*. New Haven, Conn.: Yale University Press, 1981. Argues that retrospective judgments guide voter choice in presidential elections.

Flanigan, William H., and Nancy H. Zingale. *Political Behavior of the American Electorate*. 12th ed. Washington, D.C.: CQ Press, 2009. A comprehensive summary of the extensive research literature on the effects of party identification, opinion, ideology, the media, and candidate image on voter choice and election outcomes.

Halperin, Mark, and John Hellerman. *Double Down: Game Change 2012*. New York: Penguin, 2013. An inside look at the 2012 presidential campaign.

Iyengar, Shanto, and Stephen Ansolabehere. *Going Negative: How Political Advertisements Shrink and Polarize the Electorate*. New York: Free Press, 1996. The real problem with negative political ads is not that they sway voters to support one candidate over another, but that they reinforce the belief that all are dishonest and cynical.

Lewis-Beck, Michael S. *The American Voter Revisited*. An updated replication of the original *American Voter* (1960), confirming the influences of party, ideology, nature of the times, and issues on voter choice.

Rosenstone, Steven. *Forecasting Presidential Elections*. New Haven, Conn.: Yale University Press, 1985. A discussion of the models employed to forecast presidential election outcomes based on unemployment, inflation, and personal income statistics.

Sabato, Larry J., and Glenn R. Simpson. *Dirty Little Secrets: The Persistence of Corruption in American Politics*. New York: Random House Times Books, 1996. A political scientist and a journalist combine to produce a lurid report on unethical and corrupt practices in campaigns and elections.

SUGGESTED WEB SITES

Campaigns & Elections http://www.campaignsandelections.com/
The Web site of *Campaigns & Elections*, a magazine directed toward candidates, campaign managers, political TV advertisers, political consultants, and lobbyists.

Center for Responsive Politics www.opensecrets.org
The site of an organization devoted to the study of campaign finance laws, the role of money in elections, PACs, "soft money," and special-interest groups.

The Center for Voting and Democracy www.fairvote.org
A site with material on possible changes in the Electoral College.

Federal Election Commission www.fec.gov
The FEC Web site contains ample information on the important regulations and statutes relating to campaign finance.

Larry Sabato's Crystal Ball www.centerforpolitics.org/crystalball/
University of Virginia political scientist's web site providing national political analysis and prognostication.

Open Secrets www.opensecrets.org
The D.C.-based Center for Responsive Politics web site, dedicated to informing citizens about how money in politics affects their lives, empowering them with unbiased information, and advocating for a transparent and responsive government.

Dave's Political Atlas uselectionatlas.org
Dave Leip's web site provides historic and contemporary election results with pleasing maps and data downloads.

9

Interest Groups

Getting Their Share and More

Nineteenth-century lawyer, newspaper editor, and politician Gideon Tucker said "*No Man's life, liberty, or property is safe while the legislature is in session.*" Why? Because special interests may seek legislation that alters the tax code, creates a program, or condemns property for the public use—or, as Chief Justice John Marshall observed, "*the power to tax* involves the *power to destroy.*" That is, Tucker and Marshall would agree that the legislature can pick winners and losers based on whom they tax; how they tax; and what they choose to spend public money on.

Lobbyists, the professional traders of information and influence, shape legislation to benefit their clients. No one ever did so more creatively than Jack Abramoff, a former college Republican leader from a prominent financial sector family. In the early 1990s, after spending ten years in Hollywood making movies, Abramoff started lobbying on behalf of gaming Indian tribes. He fought and defeated federal legislation aimed at taxing Indian casinos, and he made extensive use of his connections to lawmakers and congressional staffers to advance his clients' agendas as well as his own. Abramoff was also one of the early architects of creating pseudo-grassroots organizations to pressure politics—what's called 'astroturfing.'

After six years in prison for conspiracy and fraud related to his lobbying activities, Abramoff wrote a best-selling book about the problems of influence peddling in politics. Among the reforms he argues for are financial and post-elective employment reform to keep former congressional staffers and members of congress from becoming lobbyists (a significant number of the 15,000 lobbyists in DC are one or the other).

Most lobbyists are not criminals, or bag men for interest groups. But the Jack Abramoff story was unsurprising because so much of the world economy flows through Washington's tax and regulation regime. For people who want to make a profit in big business, doing business with government requires them to have agents who can curry favor with lawmakers and staffers who craft the laws.

9.1 Explain the origins, functions, strengths, and weaknesses of the interest-group system in America, p. 308

9.2 Characterize the interests represented by organized interest groups lobbying in Washington, p. 311

9.3 Explain how interest-group leaders create and build organizations, p. 323

9.4 Describe the overall environment of lobbying in Washington and identify the main activities of lobbyists, p. 324

9.5 Outline the development, role, and structure of political action committees, p. 331

9.6 Assess the relationships between interest groups and bureaucratic agencies and identify ways in which interest groups seek to influence the federal court system, p. 334

9.7 Evaluate different positions on the consequences of interest groups for American democracy, p. 338

INFORMING ELITES Interest groups provide expertise on a variety of issues. They even supply witnesses and testimony to lawmakers who are making new policy.

Interest-Group Power

9.1 Explain the origins, functions, strengths, and weaknesses of the interest-group system in America.

interest groups
Organizations seeking to directly influence government policy.

majoritarianism
Tendency of democratic governments to allow the faint preferences of the majority to prevail over the intense feelings of minorities.

organizational sclerosis
Society encrusted with so many special benefits to interest groups that everyone's standard of living is lowered.

rganization is a means to power—to determining who gets what in society. Interest groups are organizations that seek to influence government policy. The 1st Amendment to the Constitution recognizes "the right of the people peaceably to assemble and to petition the government for a redress of grievances." Americans enjoy a fundamental right to organize themselves to influence government.

Electoral Versus Interest-Group Systems

The *electoral system* is organized to represent geographically defined constituencies—states and congressional districts in Congress. The *interest-group system* is organized to represent economic, professional, ideological, religious, racial, gender, and issue constituencies. In other words, the interest-group system supplements the electoral system by providing people with another avenue of participation. Individuals may participate in politics by supporting candidates and parties in elections, and also by joining **interest groups**, organizations that pressure government to advance their interests.[1]

Interest-group activity provides more *direct* representation of policy preferences than electoral politics. At best, individual voters can influence government policy only indirectly through elections. Elected politicians try to represent many different—and even occasionally conflicting—interests. But interest groups provide concentrated and direct representation of policy views in government.

Checking Majoritarianism

The interest-group system gives voice to special interests, whereas parties and the electoral system cater to the majority interest. Indeed, interest groups are often defended as a check on **majoritarianism**, the tendency of democratic governments to allow the faint preferences of a majority to prevail over the intense feelings of minorities. However, the interest-group system is frequently attacked because it obstructs the majority from implementing its preferences in public policy.

Concentrating Benefits While Dispersing Costs

Interest groups seek special benefits, subsidies, privileges, and protections from the government. The costs of these *concentrated* benefits are usually *dispersed* to all taxpayers, none of whom individually bears enough added cost to merit spending time, energy, or money to organize a group to oppose the benefit. Thus the interest-group system concentrates benefits to the few and disperses costs to the many. The system favors small, well-organized, homogeneous interests that seek the expansion of government activity at the expense of larger but less well-organized citizen-taxpayers. Over long periods of time, the cumulative activities of many special-interest groups, each seeking concentrated benefits to themselves and dispersed costs to others, result in what has been termed **organizational sclerosis**, a society so encrusted with subsidies, benefits, regulations, protections, and special treatments for organized groups that work, productivity, and investment are discouraged and everyone's standard of living is lowered. Political economists call this rent-seeking behavior, and believe it is a source of inefficiency in government and markets (See *Who's Getting What?* A Little Rent from My Friends).

Origins of Interest Groups

James Madison viewed interest groups—which he called "factions"—as a necessary evil in politics. He defined a faction as "a number of citizens, whether amounting to a majority or a minority of the whole, who are united and actuated by some common impulse of passion, or of interest, adverse to the rights of other citizens, or to the permanent and aggregate interests of the community." He believed that interest groups not only conflict with each other but, more important, also conflict with the common good. Nevertheless, Madison believed that the origin of interest groups was to be found in human nature—"a zeal for different opinions concerning religion, concerning government, and many other points"—and therefore impossible to eliminate from politics.[2]

social movements
Organized movements of persons who make "collective claims" on others.

Protecting Economic Interests

Madison believed that "the most common and durable source of factions, has been the various and unequal distribution of property." With genuine insight, he identified *economic interests* as the most prevalent in politics: "a landed interest, a manufacturing interest, a mercantile interest, a moneyed interest, with many lesser interests." From Madison's era to the present, businesspeople and professionals, bankers and insurers, farmers and factory workers, merchants and shippers have organized themselves to press their demands on government.

Advancing Social Movements

Social movements are organized movements of persons who make "collective claims" on others. They usually start out as large, informal groups of persons or organizations seeking specific social change. Sometimes social movements spawn durable interest groups; in other instances, movements harness the energy and resources of existing interest groups. However, unlike most interest groups, social movements are characterized by participation and claims of "ordinary people" rather than elites. Social movement claims are often directed *against* elites, or formal institutions with political or economic authority, or even other groups. There are numerous theories of social movements, though they all share common elements of a sense of systematic deprivation of a right, good, or service; a sense that there is an injustice arising from the depravation; and the ability to act as a mass in coordinated protest of the status quo. Further, social movement scholars connect social movements to democratic political systems in cultures that are also characterized by urbanization and literacy.

These movements are usually characterized by calls for reform of institutions by changing existing law. They often promote either traditional or progressive value sets, and more radical movements will seek to change the value set of society by creating new institutions or altering individual-level behavior. They can also seek to insulate traditional values and institutions from change. Social movements can therefore be conservative or progressive. Movements can start out as peaceful movements and then turn violent or as violent demonstrations that become peaceful.

Social movements are often component to the creation of political parties or transformation of durable party coalitions. Many of the enduring political debates in American politics are wrapped up in the ongoing social movements of the nineteenth and twentieth century. These movements left behind policies and institutions in the form of interest groups that continue to shape public policy and define the political parties. Abolitionist groups were formed before the Civil War to fight slavery. The National Association for the Advancement of Colored People (NAACP) emerged in 1909 to fight segregation laws and to rally public support against lynching and other violence against African Americans. Farm organizations emerged from the populist movement of the late nineteenth century to press demands for railroad rate regulation and easier credit terms. The small trade unions that workers formed in the nineteenth

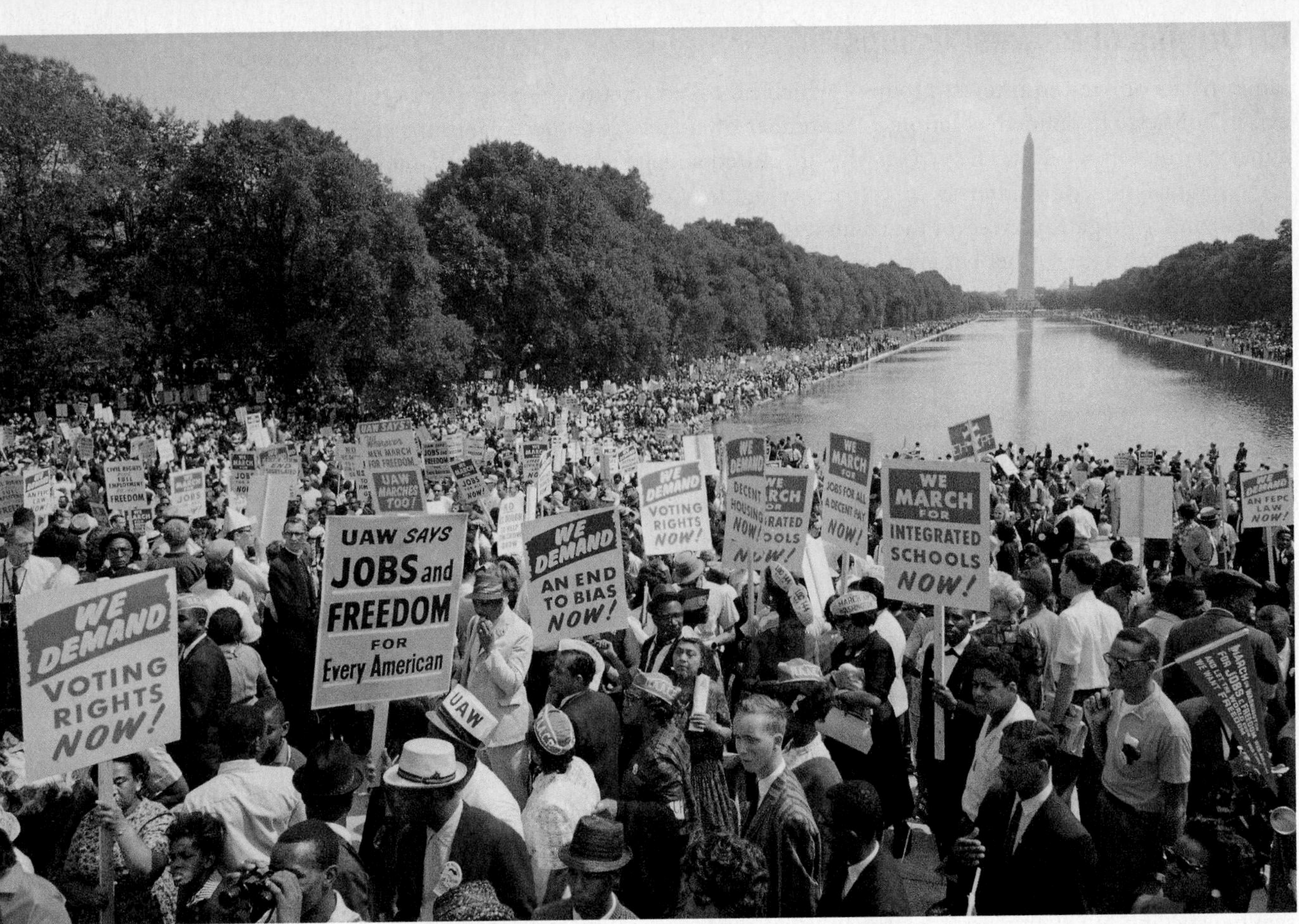

DEMOCRACY FOR THE MANY

Most Americans never take part in protests, but during the 1960s, effective protest reached its zenith with the civil rights marches. Every subsequent protest in the US takes its cues from these protests for equal treatment under the law.

century to improve their pay and working conditions gave way to large national unions in the 1930s as workers sought protection for the rights to organize, bargain collectively, and strike. The success of the women's suffrage movement led to the formation of the League of Women Voters in the early twentieth century, and a generation later the feminist movement inspired the National Organization for Women (NOW).

☐ Seeking Government Benefits

As government expands its activities, it creates more interest groups. Wars create veterans' organizations. The first large veterans' group—the Grand Army of the Republic—formed after the Civil War and successfully lobbied for bonus payments to veterans over the years. Today the American Legion, the Veterans of Foreign Wars, and the Vietnam Veterans of America engage in lobbying Congress and monitor the activities of the Department of Veterans Affairs. As the welfare state grew, so did organizations seeking to obtain benefits for their members, including the nation's largest interest group, the American Association of Retired Persons (AARP). Over time, organizations seeking to protect and expand welfare benefits for the poor also emerged. Federal grant-in-aid programs to state and local governments inspired the development of governmental interest groups—the Council of State Governments, the National League of Cities, the National Governors Association, the U.S. Conference of Mayors, and so on—so that it is not uncommon today to see state and local governments lobby the national government (cities, towns, and even counties lobby their state governments). Expanded government support for education led to political activity by the National Education Association, the American Federation of Teachers, the American Association of Land Grant Colleges and Universities, and other educational groups.

THE FIRST ADVOCACY GROUP

The Grand Army of the Republic was a fraternal organization of Civil War veterans. They lobbied congress for voting rights for black veterans, veterans' pensions, and influenced both political appointments and elections.

Responding to Government Regulation

As more businesses and professions came under government regulation in the twentieth century, more organizations formed to protect and further their interests, including such large and powerful groups as the American Medical Association (doctors), the American Bar Association (lawyers), and the National Association of Broadcasters (broadcasters). Indeed, the issue of regulation—whether of public utilities, interstate transportation, mine safety, medicines, or children's pajamas—always causes the formation of interest groups. Some form to demand regulation; others form to protect their members from regulatory burdens.

The Organized Interests in Washington

9.2 Characterize the interests represented by organized interest groups lobbying in Washington.

There are more than 1 million nonprofit organizations in the United States, several thousand of which are officially registered in Washington as lobbyists.[3] Trade and professional associations and corporations are the most common lobbies in Washington, but unions, public-interest

Who's Getting What?

A Little Rent from My Friends

Politics and economics are linked. Elections make government, and government can use taxes and regulations to change the economy. And, in politics, the economic concept of costs and benefits matter. Politicians like to win elections, and elections cost money. So, politicians often find themselves in relationships with economic interest groups who have money to spend on elections, and who have clients or members who are concerned about taxes and regulations.

Why Milk Is Cheap

Imagine that milk sells for seven dollars a gallon. But, because the government values cheap milk for families, it pays a subsidy to dairy producers to lower the cost of milk by four dollars a gallon. Then, it asks the dairies to also guarantee the price of milk in the long term. The producers agree, but only if some rules are put in place that makes it difficult for new dairies to start up and take advantage of the government's subsidies. This subsidy and the exclusion of other competitors make extra profits, instead of it coming from the dairy's efficiency.

In economics, this is a **rent**. A rent is payment for a good beyond the marginal cost of the factors that enter its production and supply. Because the government artificially limited the competitive supply of milk, and also inflated demand by subsidizing the price, it gave more wealth to the dairy than it would have captured in an open market for milk.

What Politicians Get

We can see rent seeking by interest groups and politicians in plain sight. In the United States, detailed campaign finance data shows the ties between economic interest groups—labor unions, corporations, and trade associations—and members of Congress. The congressmen and senators sit on specialized committees, and those committees control legislation that shapes taxes and the regulations for specific industries. Economic interest groups know who sits in Congress and who can influence laws passed affecting their industry.

So, industry groups use their political action committees and the individual donations of group members to fund the campaigns of influential lawmakers. In exchange, they get favorable rules or price supports. Lawmakers eagerly accept and solicit this money, which is the primary source of support for reelection campaigns. Challengers have a hard time getting money from these special-interest donors, because they have nothing to offer yet in terms of influence on laws. Only the incumbents can regularly capture these additional monies for campaigns.

QUESTIONS

1. Can you think of another example of rent seeking?
2. Is this practice a corrupting influence on Congress?
3. Are there good reasons to tolerate rent seeking in a democratic society?

SOURCES: Anne Krueger, "The Political Economy of the Rent-Seeking Society," *American Economic Review* 64(1974): 291–303.
Gordon Tullock, "The Welfare Costs of Tariffs, Monopolies, and Theft." *Western Economic Journal* 5(1967): 224–232.

rent
A payment for a good beyond the marginal cost of the factors that enter its production and supply.

environmental groups
Groups primarily concerned with issues of conservation or preservation of natural resources.

groups, farm groups, **environmental groups**, ideological groups, religious and civil rights organizations, women's groups, veterans and defense-related groups, groups organized around a single issue (for example, Mothers Against Drunk Driving), and even organizations representing state and local governments also recognize that they need to be "where the action is." Among this huge assortment of organizations, many of which are very influential in their highly specialized field, there are a number of well-known organized interests. Even a partial list of organized interest groups (see Table 9.1) demonstrates the breadth and complexities of interest-group life in American politics.

☐ Business and Trade Organizations

Traditionally, economic organizations have dominated interest-group politics in Washington. There is ample evidence that economic interests continue to play a major role in national policy making, despite the rapid growth over the last several decades of consumer and environmental organizations. Certainly in terms of the sheer number of organizations with offices and representatives in Washington, business and professional groups and occupational and trade associations are most numerous. More than half of the organizations with offices in Washington are business or trade associations, and all together these organizations account for about 75 percent of all of the reported lobbying expenditures.[4]

TABLE 9.1 MAJOR ORGANIZED INTEREST GROUPS, BY TYPE

Business	Business Roundtable; National Association of Manufacturers; National Federation of Independent Businesses; National Small Business Association; U.S. Chamber of Commerce
Trade	American Bankers Association; American Gas Association; American Hospital Association; American Iron and Steel Institute; American Petroleum Institute; American Truckers Association; Automobile Dealers Association; Edison Electric Institute; Home Builders Association; Motion Picture Association of America; National Association of Broadcasters; National Association of Realtors; Pharmaceutical Mfrs. of America
Professional	American Bar Association; American Medical Association; American Association for Justice (trial lawyers); National Education Association
Union	AFL-CIO; American Federation of State, County, and Municipal Employees; American Federation of Teachers; International Brotherhood of Teamsters; International Ladies' Garment Workers Union; National Association of Letter Carriers; United Auto Workers; United Postal Workers; United Steel Workers
Agricultural	American Farm Bureau Federation; National Cattlemen's Association; National Farmers Union; National Grange; National Milk Producers Federation; Tobacco Institute
Public Interest	Common Cause; Consumer Federation of America; Public Citizen; Public Interest Research Groups
Ideological	American Conservative Union; Americans for Constitutional Action (conservative); Americans for Democratic Action (liberal); Federalist Society (conservative); People for the American Way (liberal); MoveOn (liberal)
Women	League of Women Voters; National Organization for Women
Single Issue	Mothers Against Drunk Driving; NARAL Pro-Choice America; National Rifle Association; National Right to Life Committee; PETA; Planned Parenthood Federation of America; National Taxpayers Union
Environmental	Environmental Defense Fund; Friends of the Earth; Greenpeace; National Wildlife Federation; National Resources Defense Council; Nature Conservancy; Sierra Club; Union of Concerned Scientists; Wilderness Society; Zero Population Growth
Religious	American Israel Public Affairs Committee; Anti-Defamation League of B'nai B'rith; Christian Coalition; National Council of Churches; U.S. Catholic Conference
Civil Rights	American Civil Liberties Union; American Indian Movement; Gay Lesbian Alliance Against Discrimination; Mexican-American Legal Defense and Education Fund; National Association for the Advancement of Colored People; National Urban League; Southern Christian Leadership Conference
Age Related	AARP; National Committee to Preserve Social Security; Children's Defense Fund
Veterans	American Legion; Veterans of Foreign Wars; Vietnam Veterans of America
Defense	Air Force Association; American Security Council; Army Association; Navy Association
Government	National Association of Counties; National Conference of State Legislators; National Governors Association; National League of Cities; U.S. Conference of Mayors

9.1 9.2 9.3 9.4 9.5 9.6 9.7

trade associations
Interest groups composed of businesses in specific industries.

Business interests are represented, first of all, by large inclusive organizations, such as the U.S. Chamber of Commerce, representing thousands of local chambers of commerce across the nation; the National Association of Manufacturers; the Business Roundtable, representing the nation's largest corporations; and the National Federation of Independent Businesses, representing small business. Specific business interests are also represented by thousands of **trade associations**. These associations can closely monitor the interests of their specialized memberships. Among the most powerful of these associations are the American Bankers Association, the American Gas Association, the American Iron and Steel Institute, the National Association of Real Estate Boards, the American Petroleum Institute, and the National Association of Broadcasters. In addition, many individual corporations and firms achieve representation in Washington by opening their own lobbying offices or by hiring experienced professional lobbying, public relations, or law firms.

Professional Associations

Professional associations rival business and trade organizations in lobbying influence. The American Bar Association (ABA), the American Medical Association (AMA), and the National Education Association (NEA) are three of the most influential groups in Washington. For example, the ABA, which includes virtually all the nation's practicing attorneys, and its more specialized offspring, the American Association for Justice (trial lawyers), have successfully resisted efforts to reform the nation's tort laws.

Organized Labor

Labor organizations have declined in membership over the last several decades. The percentage of the private workforce belonging to unions has declined from about 37 percent in the 1950s to about 8 percent today (see Figure 9.1). The major industrial unions—for example, the United Steelworkers of America, United Automobile Workers, United Mine Workers—have shrunk in membership. Only the unions of government employees—for example, the American Federation of State, County, and Municipal Employees, the National Education Association—and some transportation and service workers unions—for example, the Teamsters Union, Service Employees International, International Brotherhood of Electrical Workers—have gained members in recent years.

Nevertheless, labor unions remain a major political influence in Congress and the Democratic Party. The AFL-CIO is a federation of 68 separate unions with more than

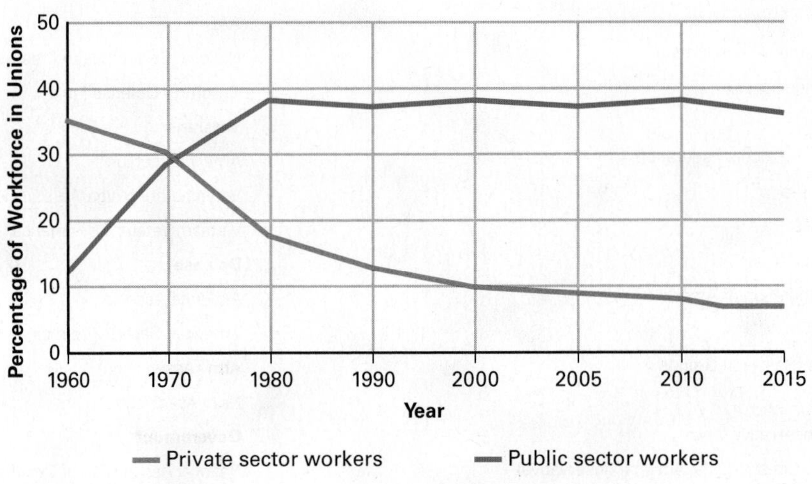

FIGURE 9.1 GOING PUBLIC: UNIONS AND THE AMERICAN WORKFORCE

Public employee unions, including teachers' unions, have remained strong over recent decades, while union membership in the private sector has declined.

SOURCE: *Statistical Abstract of the United States*, 2010.

13 million members. The AFL-CIO has long maintained a large and capable lobbying staff in Washington, and it provides both financial contributions and campaign services (registration, get-out-the-vote, information, endorsements) for members of Congress it favors. Many of the larger individual unions also maintain offices in Washington and offer campaign contributions and services.

Union influence is greatest among government employees, including teachers. About 38 percent of all public sector employees are unionized, primarily through the Service Employees International Union (SEIU); American Federation of State, County, and Municipal Employees (AFSCME); the National Education Association (NEA); the American Federation of Teachers (AFT); and the Teamsters Union.

Labor union political campaign contributions (see "PAC Power" in this chapter) remain a major source of union influence in Washington. The SEIU, AFSCME, NEA, Teamsters, United Auto Workers, United Steel Workers, Electrical Workers, Machinists, and Letter Carriers, as well as the AFL-CIO itself, are regularly ranked among the top contributors in congressional elections. Almost all union campaign contributions go to Democratic candidates.

SERVICE EMPLOYEES INTERNATIONAL UNION The 2.1-million-member Service Employees International Union (SEIU) is the nation's fastest-growing labor union. It focuses on organizing workers in the health care field, including employees of hospitals and nursing homes. It is also the largest property services union, including employees in building cleaning (janitors) and security. It competes with the American Federation of State, County, and Municipal Employees (AFSCME) in recruiting government employees.

WHERE UNIONS SURVIVE

The number of unionized private sector workers in the United States has declined dramatically in the last half-century, as manufacturing and skilled trades moved away from the United States. The bulk of union membership is in the new generation of unions, like the Service Employees International Union, which has heavy membership in health care and among government employees.

SEIU boasts that it supports "progressive" causes and candidates. It disaffiliated itself from the AFL-CIO presumably because that union federation was not aggressive enough in organizing low-paid workers or in the pursuit of a progressive policy agenda. Rather, the SEIU sees the Teamsters, Laborers Union, and United Farm Workers as its natural "change to win" allies.

The SEIU has been particularly active in the debate over health care reform. It would have preferred a Canadian-style single-payer government health system, but supported the "public option" as a politically viable alternative. It supports immigration reform, including legalization for taxpaying immigrants. SEIU is estimated to have spent $27 million in support of the election of President Obama, plus "boots on the ground" in the form of union volunteers at events and on the campaign trail.

Since the 2008 election, the SEIU has continued to be politically active as an organizing arm for progressive economic interests. The union is an ongoing source of financing for these efforts—according to SEIU's COPE PAC, there are 300,000 SEIU COPE members who give an average of $7 a month—$2.1 million—to the PAC. They have protested both governments and corporations over policy disputes. SEIU and other employee unions were active in the ongoing protests over conservative efforts to constrain public unions in Wisconsin, and they have participated in recall efforts directed at Wisconsin lawmakers and the Republican governor.

Farm Organizations

Even though the farm population of the United States has declined from about 25 percent of the total population in the 1930s to less than 3 percent today, farmers—especially large agricultural producers and corporate food processors—remain a very potent political force in Washington. Agricultural interests are organized both into large inclusive groups, such as the American Farm Bureau Federation and the National Grange, and into very effective specialized groups, such as the National Milk Producers and the National Cattlemen's Association. Small- and low-income farmers are represented by the National Farmers Union.

Women's Organizations

Women's organizations date back to the antislavery societies in pre–Civil War America. The first generation of feminists—Lucretia Mott, Elizabeth Cady Stanton, Lucy Stone, and Susan B. Anthony—learned to organize, hold public meetings, and conduct petition campaigns as abolitionists. After the Civil War, women were successful in changing many state laws that abridged the rights of married women and otherwise treated them as "chattel" (property) of their husbands. Women were also prominent in the Anti-Saloon League, which succeeded in outlawing prostitution and gambling in every state except Nevada and provided a major source of support for the 18th Amendment (Prohibition). In the early twentieth century, the feminist movement concentrated on obtaining the vote (suffrage) for women. Today the League of Women Voters—a broad-based organization that provides information to voters—backs registration and get-out-the-vote drives and generally supports measures seeking to ensure honesty and integrity in government.

Interest in feminist politics revived in the wake of the civil rights movement of the 1960s. New organizations sprang up to compete with the conventional activities of the League of Women Voters by taking a more activist stance toward women's issues. The largest of these organizations is the National Organization for Women (NOW), founded in 1966. In response to the progressive feminist movement in the 1970s, some conservative women's organizations emerged, often from the Christian conservative movement. The largest of these, Concerned Women for America, was formed in 1979 to oppose NOW by evangelist Beverly LaHaye, spouse of the author of the popular "*Left Behind*" series.

☐ Religious Groups

Churches and religious groups have a long history of involvement in American politics—from the pre–Civil War antislavery crusades, to the Prohibition effort in the early twentieth century, to the civil rights movement of the 1960s. The leadership for the historic Civil Rights Act of 1964 came from the Reverend Martin Luther King, Jr., and his Southern Christian Leadership Conference. Today religious groups span the political spectrum, from liberal organizations such as the National Council of Churches and Anti-Defamation League of B'nai B'rith, to conservative and fundamentalist organizations, such as the Christian Coalition, often referred to as the "religious right."

THE CHRISTIAN COALITION: ORGANIZING THE FAITHFUL Christian fundamentalists, whose religious beliefs are based on a literal reading of the Bible, have become a significant political force in the United States through effective organization. Perhaps the most influential Christian fundamentalist organization today is the Christian Coalition, with nearly 2 million active members throughout the country.

PULPIT FREEDOM SUNDAY

Under the 1954 Johnson Amendment, 501c3 tax-exempt organizations like churches cannot "participate in, or intervene in (including the publishing or distributing of statements), any political campaign on behalf of—or in opposition to—any candidate for public office." Since 2007, several ministers across the United States have challenged this rule by making openly political speeches in what is known as Pulpit Freedom Sunday.

9.1

9.2

9.3

9.4

9.5

9.6

9.7

public-interest groups
Interest groups that claim to represent broad classes of people or the public as a whole.

single-issue groups
Organizations formed to support or oppose government action on a specific issue.

Fundamentalist Christians are opposed to abortion, pornography, and homosexuality; they favor the recognition of religion in public life, including prayer in schools; and they despair at the decline of traditional family values in American culture, including the popular media. Until the 1970s, fundamentalist Protestant churches avoided politics, and instead concentrated evangelical efforts on saving individual souls. Their strength tended to be in the southern, rural, and poorer regions of the country. They were widely ridiculed in the national media.

In the 1960s, television evangelism emerged as a religious force in the United States. The Reverend Pat Robertson founded the Christian Broadcasting Network (CBN) and later purchased the Family Channel. But efforts by social conservatives to build a "moral majority" for political action largely failed, as did Robertson's presidential candidacy in 1988. But Robertson's campaign showed the organizing potential of evangelical Christians, and Robertson hired a twenty-something Republican organizer named Ralph Reed as the first director of the Christian Coalition. In the first six years of the Coalition's existence, Reed worked with social conservatives to promote evangelical Christians as candidates and organizational muscle in campaigns for local, state legislative, and congressional office.

Although officially nonpartisan, the Coalition became an important force in Republican politics; religious fundamentalists constitute between one-third and one-half of the party's core voter support in various states. The Christian Coalition does not officially endorse candidates, but its voter guides clearly indicate which candidates reflect the coalition's position on major issues. The political influence of the Christian Coalition in Republican politics, and the "religious right" generally, ensures that most GOP candidates for public office publicly express support for a "pro-family" agenda. This agenda includes a constitutional amendment allowing prayer in public schools; vouchers for parents to send their children to private, religious schools; banning late-term abortions as well as banning the use of taxpayer funds to pay for abortions; restrictions on pornography on cable television and the Internet; and opposition to human embryo research and human cloning.

☐ Public-Interest Groups

Public-interest groups claim to represent broad classes of people—consumers, voters, reformers, or the public as a whole. Groups with lofty-sounding names, such as Common Cause, Public Citizen, and the Consumer Federation of America, perceive themselves as balancing the narrow, "selfish" interests of business organizations, trade associations, unions, and other "special" interests. Public-interest groups generally lobby for greater government regulation of consumer products, public safety, campaign finance, and so on. Their reform agenda, as well as their call for a larger regulatory role for government, makes them frequent allies of liberal ideological groups, civil rights organizations, and environmental groups.[5]

Many public-interest groups were initially formed in the 1970s by "entrepreneurs" who saw an untapped "market" for the representation of these interests. Among the most influential public-interest groups are Common Cause, a self-styled "citizens' lobby," and the sprawling network of organizations created by consumer advocate Ralph Nader. Common Cause tends to focus on election-law reform, public financing of elections, and limitations on political contributions. The Nader network began as a consumer protection group focusing on auto safety but soon spread to encompass a wide variety of causes. Prominent among the Nader organizations are the campus-based Public Interest Research Groups (PIRGs).

☐ Single-Issue Groups

Like public-interest groups, **single-issue groups** appeal to principle and belief. But as their name implies, single-issue groups concentrate their attention on a single cause. They attract the support of individuals with a strong commitment to that cause.

The Game, the Rules, the Players

AARP: The Nation's Most Powerful Interest Group

AARP is the nation's largest and most powerful interest group, with more than 39 million members. AARP's principal interests are the Social Security and Medicare system programs, the nation's largest and most expensive entitlements.

Like many other interest groups, AARP has grown in membership not only by appealing to the political interests of retired people, but also by offering a wide array of material benefits. For a small annual fee, members are offered a variety of services, including discounted rates on home, auto, life and health insurance; discounted mail-order drugs, tax advisory services; discounted rates on hotels, rental cars, and so on; a newsletter, *The AARP Bulletin*; a semi-monthly magazine, *AAPP, The Magazine; VIVA,* for Hispanic members; and for baby boomers now reaching their 50s, *My Generation.*

The political power of senior citizens is so great that prospects for limiting current or even future increases in government benefits for the elderly are slim. President G. W. Bush's proposal to allow workers to invest part of their Social Security taxes in private accounts was defeated largely by the work of AARP. Social Security is said to be the "third rail of American politics—touch it and you're dead."

Critics of AARP argue that its lobbyists in Washington do not fairly represent the views of the nation's senior citizens, that few of its members know what its lobbying arm does at the nation's capital. AARP keeps its dues low, and consequently its membership high, through its business ties with insurance companies, its magazine advertising revenue, and commercial royalty revenues for endorsing products and services.

QUESTIONS

1. **Why is Social Security a "third rail" in politics?**
2. **It has been argued that the priorities of the AARP, and its clout 15 years ago, contribute to contemporary economic problems confronted by the United States. What do you think? How will AARP act in the current environment of budgetary austerity?**

SOURCE: Reprinted with permission from the April 1997 issue of *Reason Magazine,* Copyright 2000 by the Reason Foundation, 4315 S. Sepulveda Blvd., Suite 400, Los Angeles, CA 90034, www.reason.com.

Single-issue groups have little incentive to compromise their position. They exist for a single cause; no other issues really matter to them. They are by nature passionate and often shrill. Their attraction to members is the intensity of their beliefs.

Among the most vocal single-issue groups in recent years have been the organizations on both sides of the abortion issue. NARAL Pro-Choice America describes itself as "pro-choice" and opposes any restrictions on a woman's right to obtain an abortion. The National Right-to-Life Committee describes itself as "pro-life" and opposes abortion for any reason other than to preserve the life of the mother. Other prominent single-issue groups include the National Rifle Association (defending 2nd Amendment rights) and Mothers Against Drunk Driving (MADD).

ideological organizations
Interest groups that pursue ideologically based (liberal or conservative) agendas.

Ideological Groups

Ideological organizations pursue liberal or conservative agendas, often with great passion and considerable financial resources derived from true-believing contributors. The ideological groups rely heavily on computerized mailings to solicit funds from persons identified as holding liberal or conservative views. The oldest of the established ideological groups is the liberal Americans for Democratic Action (ADA), well known for its annual liberalism ratings of members of Congress according to their support for or rejection of programs of concern. The American Conservative Union (ACU) also rates members of Congress each year. Overall, Democrats do better on the liberal list and Republicans on the conservative list, although both parties include some Congress members who occasionally vote on the opposite side of the fence from the majority of their fellow party members (see Table 9.2). Other interest groups, such as the AFL-CIO, the National Taxpayers Union, and NARAL Pro-Choice America

TABLE 9.2 UNDER THE INFLUENCE?: IDEOLOGICAL INTEREST-GROUP RATINGS FOR U.S. SENATORS AND OBJECTIVE D-NOMINATE SCORES*

Ideological interest groups rate members of Congress according to their votes on issues deemed important to liberals and conservatives.

ACU	ADA	Nominate Scores**
American Conservative Union	**Americans for Democratic Action**	**Poole/Rosenthal Scores**
"Defenders of Liberty" (ACU = 100)	"Heroes" (ADA = 100)	**Ten Most Conservative**
Coburn, R-Okla	S. Brown, D-Ohio	Paul, Ky.
Cruz, R-Tex.	Cantwell, D-Wash.	Lee, Utah
Lee, R-	Coons, D-Del.	DeMint, S.C.
	Merkley, D-Ore.	Coburn, Okla.
	Murray, D-Wash.	R. Johnson, Wisc.
	Sanders, I-Vt.	Ensign, Nev.
	T. Udall, D-Colo.	Inhofe, Okla.
		Toomey, Penn.
		Vitter, La.
		Risch, Id.
"The Liberals" (ACU = 0)	**Zeroes (ADA = 0)**	**Ten Most Liberal**
Gillibrand, D-N.Y.	Burr, R-N.C.	Sanders, I-Vt.
Harkin, D-Iowa	Chambliss, R-Ga.	Durbin, D-Ill.
Hirono, D-Hawaii	Coburn, R-Okla.	Harkin, D-Iowa
Kaine, D-Va.	Cornyn, R-Tex.	Whitehouse, D-R.I.
Rockefeller, D-W.V.	DeMint, R-S.C.	S. Brown, D-Ohio
Sanders, I-Vt.	Graham, R-S.C.	Lautenberg, D-N.J.
Stabenow, D-Mich.	Hatch, R-Utah	Boxer, D-Calif.
	Inhofe, R-Okla.	Reed, D-R.I.
	Isakson, R-Ga.	Gillibrand, D-N.Y.
	R. Johnson, R-Wisc.	Franken, D-Minn.
	Kyl, R-Ariz.	
	McConnell, R-Ky.	
	Rubio, R-Fla.	
	Sessions, R-Ala.	
	Shelby, R-Ala.	

*ACU data are for 2013. ADA and Nominate data are for 2012.

**Nominate scores place lawmakers' roll call behavior into an objective "ideological space" by considering all roll call votes cast by members, rather than just certain roll call votes chosen by one interest group or another. The method is fully explained in Keith T. Poole and Howard Rosenthal in *Congress: A Political-Economic History of Roll Call Voting*. New York: Oxford University Press, 1997.

SOURCES: Americans for Democratic Action, www.adaction.org; American Conservative Union, www.conservative.org; D-Nominate scores from voteview.com.

also rate members of Congress, but these groups have a narrower focus than the ADA and ACU. Yet another prominent ideological group, People for the American Way, was formed by television producer Norman Lear to coordinate the efforts of liberals in the entertainment industry as well as the general public, but it issues no ratings.

☐ Environmental Groups

One of the most durable types of groups is environmental groups. Among the oldest of these are the Sierra Club (founded in 1892 by American naturalist John Muir and journalist Robert Underwood Johnson to protect Yosemite National Park); the National Geographic Society (founded in 1888); and the Audubon Society (founded in 1905), which is dedicated to nature conservation through education and local advocacy. In addition to these "old line" environmental organizations, a variety of organizations emerged in the twentieth century as environmental issues moved to the forefront of the national policy debate. Among the hundreds of organizations active in environmental policy are the Earth Policy Institute, the League of Conservation Voters, the National Resource Defense Council, People for the Ethical Treatment of Animals (PETA), the National Wildlife Federation; and the Ocean Conservancy. Also, two groups active on environmental issues are the National Rifle Association and Earth First (among other organizations involved in the antiglobalization social movement). The main difference between environmental groups is often over the ethics of environmentalism. The conservation groups view the purpose of environmental protection as protecting natural resources for the use of man (sometimes called "shallow ecology"). Preservation groups often emphasize a "deep ecology" approach that protects nature because of the innate value of nature itself.

9.1
9.2
9.3
9.4
9.5
9.6
9.7

□ Education Lobbies

Colleges, universities, and educational associations also lobby Congress. Significant amounts of federal research money flow into applied and basic research for hard sciences and behavioral sciences. Student financial aid and student loans pay tuition for students who enroll in universities. As indicated in Figure 9.2,

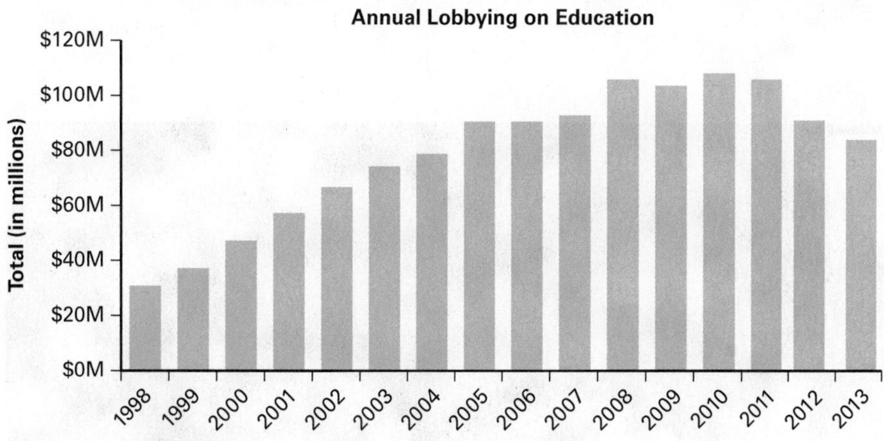

FIGURE 9.2 LOBBYING ISN'T JUST FOR BIG CORPORATIONS—IT'S ALSO FOR BIG EDUCATION

Many public and private colleges employ full-time professional lobbyists in Washington. In 2010, education entities spent over $107 million on lobbying.

SOURCE: Opensecrets.org.

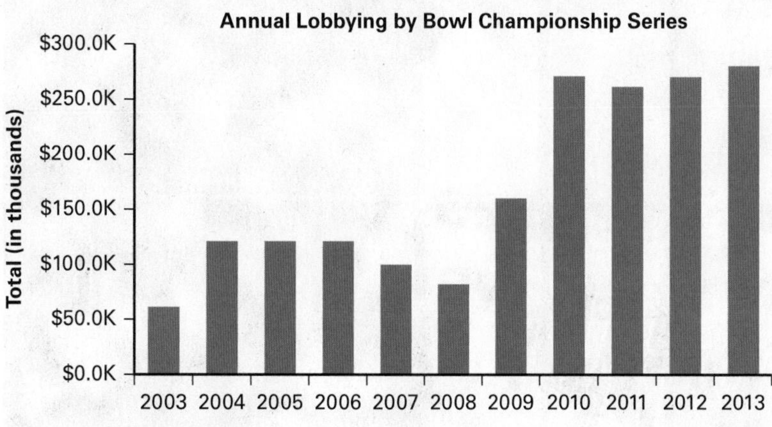

FIGURE 9.3 LOBBYING FOR FOOTBALL

The Bowl Championship Series spent over a half million dollars on lobbying in 2010–2011, mainly to preclude congressional intervention with the structure of the college football postseason.

SOURCE: Opensecrets.org.

higher education routinely expends over $100 million a year on lobbying activities, including lobbying by the NCAA and the Bowl Championship Series to lobby to keep lawmakers from interfering with their educationally based, economic enterprises (see Figure 9.3).

□ Government Lobbies

The federal government's grant-in-aid programs to state and local governments have spawned a host of lobbying efforts by these governments in Washington, D.C. Thus state- and local-government taxpayers foot the bill to lobby Washington to transfer federal taxpayers' revenues to states and communities. The National Governors Association occupies a beautiful marble building, the Hall of the States, in Washington, along with representatives of the separate states and many major cities. The National League of Cities and the National Association of Counties also maintain large Washington offices, as does the U.S. Conference of Mayors. The National Conference of State Legislators sends its lobbyists to Washington from its Denver headquarters. These groups pursue a wide policy agenda and often confront internal disputes. But they are united in their support for increased federal transfers of tax revenues to states and cities.

PROTEST AS ART

Creative protests can capture the attention of the media. Here, a People for the Ethical Treatment of Animals (PETA) member protests, in creative makeup, the caging and treatment of animals by performance circuses.

Leaders and Followers

9.3 Explain how interest-group leaders create and build organizations.

Organizations require leadership. And over time, leaders develop a perspective somewhat different from that of their organizations' membership. A key question in interest-group politics is how well organization leaders represent the views of their members.

interest-group entrepreneurs
Leaders who create organizations and market memberships.

free-riders
People who do not belong to an organization or pay dues, yet nevertheless benefit from its activities.

Interest-Group Entrepreneurs

People who create organizations and build membership in those organizations—**interest-group entrepreneurs**—have played a major role in strengthening the interest-group system in recent decades. These entrepreneurs help overcome a major obstacle to the formation of strong interest groups—the *free-rider* problem.

Free-riders are people who benefit from the efforts of others but do not contribute to the costs of those efforts. Not everyone feels an obligation to support organizations that represent their interests or views. Some people feel that their own small contribution will not make a difference in the success or failure of the organization's goals and, moreover, that they will benefit from any successes even if they are not members. Indeed, most organizations enroll only a tiny fraction of the people they claim to represent. The task of the interest-group entrepreneur is to convince people to join the organization, either by appealing to their sense of obligation or by attracting them through tangible benefits.

Marketing Membership

Interest-group entrepreneurs make different appeals for membership depending on the nature of the organization. Some appeal to passion or purpose: ideological (liberal or conservative) organizations, public-interest organizations committed to environmental or consumer protection or governmental reform, and single-issue organizations devoted to the support or opposition of a single policy issue (gun control, abortion, and so on). Entrepreneurs of these organizations appeal to people's sense of duty and commitment to the cause rather than to material rewards of membership.

Business, trade, and professional organizations usually offer their members tangible benefits in addition to lobbying on behalf of their economic interests. These benefits may include exclusive publications that provide access to business, trade, and national meetings that serve as social settings for the development of contacts, friendships, and business and professional relationships. Some offer select economic benefits such as discount travel and insurance, and credit cards.

It is generally easier to organize smaller, specialized economic interests than larger, general, noneconomic interests. People more easily recognize that their own membership is important to the success of a small organization, and economic interests are more readily calculated in dollar terms. Smaller organizations can also more easily mobilize their membership and monitor membership contributions to the cause of the group.

Large organizations with broad goals—such as advancing the interests of all veterans or all retired people or all automobile drivers—must rely even more heavily on tangible benefits to solicit members. AARP claims 39 million members, and the American Automobile Association has 28 million members, but most members have limited knowledge about the policy positions or lobbying activities of the organization. These members joined to receive specific benefits—magazines, insurance, travel tips, discounts. Leaders of these organizations may claim to speak for millions of members, but it is unlikely that these millions all share the policy views expressed by the leaders.

9.1
9.2
9.3
9.4
9.5
9.6
9.7

lobbyist
Person working to influence government policies and actions.

Organizational Democracy and Leader/Member Agreement

Most organized interest groups are run by a small group of leaders and activists. Few interest groups are governed democratically; members may drop out if they do not like the direction their organization is taking but rarely do they have the opportunity to directly challenge or replace the organization's leadership. Relatively few members attend national meetings, vote in organizational elections, or try to exercise influence within their organization. Thus the leadership may not always reflect the views of the membership, especially in large organizations that rely heavily on tangible benefits to recruit members. Leaders of these organizations enjoy considerable freedom in adopting policy positions and negotiating, bargaining, and compromising in the political arena.

The exception to this rule is the single-issue group. Because the strength of these groups is in the intensity of their members' beliefs, the leaders of such groups are closely tied to their members' views. They cannot bargain or compromise these views or adopt policy positions at variance with those of their members.

Class Bias in Membership

Americans are joiners. A majority of the population belong to at least one organization, most often a church. Yet membership in organized interest groups is clearly linked to socioeconomic status. Membership is greatest among professional and managerial, college-educated, and high-income persons.[6] As a consequence, it is middle class and elite values, rather than mass values, that are most often represented through organized interests.

The Washington Lobbyists

9.4 Describe the overall environment of lobbying in Washington and identify the main activities of lobbyists.

Washington is a labyrinth of interest representatives—lawyers and law firms; independent consultants; public and governmental relations firms; business, professional, and trade associations; and advocates of special causes. It is estimated that more than 15,000 people in Washington fit the definition of **lobbyist**, a person working to influence government policies and actions. This figure suggests that there are at least 28 lobbyists for every member of Congress. Roughly $1.5 *billion* is spent on direct lobbying activities *each year*[7]; this figure does *not* include political campaign contributions. The top spenders for direct lobbying are listed in Table 9.3.

Who Are the Lobbyists?

Lobbyists in Washington share a common goal—to influence the making and enforcing of laws—and common tactics to achieve this goal. Many lobbyists are the employees of interest-group organizations who devote all of their efforts to their sponsors.

Other lobbyists are located in independent law, consulting, or public relations firms that take on clients for fees. Independent lobbyists, especially law firms, are often secretive about whom they represent, especially when they represent foreign governments. Lobbyists frequently prefer to label their activities as "government relations," "public affairs," "regulatory liaison," "legislative counseling," or merely "representation." Some lobbying organizations rely heavily on their campaign contributions to achieve lobbying power; others rely on large memberships, and still others on politically active members who concentrate their attention on a narrow range of issues.

In reality, many independent lawyers and lobbyists in Washington are "fixers" who offer to influence government policies for a price. Many are former government officials—former Congress members, cabinet secretaries, White House aides, and the

TABLE 9.3 MONEY TALKS: TOP LOBBYING SPENDERS, 1998–2013

Direct spending on lobbying (not including campaign contributions) amounts to over $1 billion each year.

Rank	Organization	Total Spending
1	U.S. Chamber of Commerce	$1,018,910,680
2	General Electric	$297,960,000
3	American Medical Association	$295,057,500
4	American Hospital Association	$249,433,008
5	Pharmaceutical Research & Manufacturers of America	$246,386,420
6	National Association of Realtors	$245,760,858
7	AARP	$229,932,064
8	Blue Cross/Blue Shield	$220,956,832
9	Northrop Grumman	$202,685,253
10	Exxon Mobil	$193,022,742
11	Boeing	$183,432,310
12	Verizon Communications	$182,570,933
13	Edison Electric Institute	$180,356,789
14	Business Roundtable	$179,640,000
15	Lockheed Martin	$177,483,954
16	AT&T Inc.	$164,749,336
17	National Cable & Telecommunications Association	$155,650,000
18	Southern Companies	$155,070,694
19	Altria Group	$145,815,200
20	National Association of Broadcasters	$143,540,000

SOURCE: Center for Responsive Politics, www.opensecrets.org.

K Street
The primary location, in Washington, D.C., of many powerful lobbying organizations and interest groups.

like—who "know their way around." Their personal connections help to "open doors" to allow their paying clients to "just get a chance to talk" with top officials.

Lobbying firms are pleased to have people who know the lawmaking process from the inside and who can easily "schmooze" with their former colleagues. For example, former Speaker Newt Gingrich (R-GA) was never an actual lobbyist, but he nonetheless made millions of dollars advising a variety of interest groups on how to access Congress to get preferred policies. His experience is not unique—lobbying is a favorite occupation of former members; they can command much higher salaries as lobbyists than they did as Congress members.

Lobbyists do not emerge from the ether as fifty-something-year-old influence peddlers with grey hair and pockets full of PAC money. Some spend their entire careers in lobbying, starting work with a firm in an entry position as an analyst or assistant to a senior lobbyist. Others start as attorneys, and are associates and later partners in law firms that specialize in governmental relations. Other lobbyists are veteran congressional staffers or former executive agency officials who, after developing contacts and specializations in government, move over to **K Street** to work for a lobbying firm or an industry that lobbies government. And, still others start in some business or industry, and get involved in lobbying government through their firm's governmental relations office or through work with a trade association. The beginnings of all these careers often start with some internship or set of internships that creates an entry point to a more permanent career that leads to lobbying.

☐ The Think Tanks

Think tanks are nonprofit tax-free policy planning organizations that concentrate on policy development, rather than direct lobbying. Nonetheless, their reports, conferences, publications, and legislative testimony are central to the policy-making process in Washington. Certain think tanks—for example, the Council on Foreign

Relations, the Brookings Institution, the American Enterprise Institute, the Center for American Progress, and the Heritage Foundation—are influential in a wide range of key policy areas.

- **Council on Foreign Relations.** The CFR is the most influential foreign-policy organization in America, yet it denies that it exercises any control over U.S. foreign policy. Indeed, its bylaws declare "the Council shall not take any position on questions of foreign policy and no person is authorized to speak or purport to speak for the Council on such matters." But policy initiation and consensus building does not require the CFR to officially adopt the policy positions. Most major foreign-policy decisions are first aired in the CFR's prestigious publication *Foreign Affairs*.
- **The Brookings Institution.** The Brookings Institution has long been the dominant policy-planning group for American domestic policy, despite the growing number and influence of competing think tanks in recent years. The *New York Times* columnist and Harvard historian writing team, Leonard Silk and Mark Silk, described Brookings as the central locus of the Washington "policy network" where it does "its communicating: over lunch, whether informally in the Brookings cafeteria or at the regular Friday lunch around a great oval table . . . ; through consulting, paid or unpaid, for government or business at conferences, in the advanced studies program; and, over time, by means of the revolving door of government employment."[8] Brookings has inspired policy goals from the introduction of the first Budget of the United States Government in 1922, through the New Deal of the 1930s, and the Great Society of the 1960s, to the Clinton administration in the 1990s. It has been particularly influential in liberal Democratic administrations.
- **The American Enterprise Institute.** For many years, Republicans dreamed of a "Brookings Institution for Republicans." In the late 1970s that role was assumed by the American Enterprise Institute. But AEI tries to appeal to both Democrats and Republicans, who have doubts about big government. In confronting societal problems, the AEI gravitates toward market solutions, while Brookings tends to look for government solutions.
- **The Cato Institute.** The Cato Institute is a libertarian think tank founded in 1977 by libertarian politician Edward Crane and industrialist Charles Koch. Cato advocates policies based on market principles and limited government, and it has been critical of expansive executive authority under Republican and Democratic administrations. Cato also departs from most conservative think-tanks in its support for gay rights, liberal immigration policies, and defense of civil liberties. Cato invites occasional scrutiny for its strong financial ties to the Kochs and the influence of "Austrian school" economics in the organization (Austrian school economics eschews the statistical and mathematical foundations of mainstream economic study).
- **The Heritage Foundation.** Conservative ideologues have never been particularly welcome in the Washington establishment. Yet influential conservative business persons gradually came to understand that without an institutional base in Washington they could never establish a strong and continuing influence in the policy network. The result of their efforts was the Heritage Foundation, which was particularly influential during the Reagan administration.
- **The Center for American Progress.** On the left of the political spectrum is the newly influential Center for American Progress (CAP), the intellectual source of policy "change" in the Obama administration.[9] CAP is funded largely by George Soros, the billionaire sponsor of other flourishing left-liberal organizations. It was founded in 2003 by John Podesta, former chief of staff to President Clinton. It is designed to give the "progressive" movement the same ideological influence in the Obama administration as the Heritage Foundation exercised in the Reagan administration. CAP promises to engage in "a war of ideas with conservatives," and to be more active on behalf of progressive policies than the more scholarly Brookings Institution.

Regulation of Lobbies

The Constitution's 1st Amendment guarantee of the right "to petition the government for a redress of grievances" protects lobbying. But the government can and does regulate lobbying activities, primarily through disclosure laws. The Regulation of Lobbying Act requires lobbyists to register and to report how much they spend, but definitions of *lobbying* are unclear and enforcement is weak. Many large lobbying groups have never registered as lobbyists. These organizations claim that because lobbying is not their principal activity, they need not register under the law. In addition, financial reports of lobbyists grossly underestimate the extent of lobbying in Congress because the law requires reports of only money spent for *direct* lobbying before Congress, not money spent for public relations or grassroots mobilization of members to pressure Congress. Another weakness in the law is that it applies only to attempts to influence Congress; it does not regulate lobbying activities in administrative agencies or litigation in the courts.

Tax laws require nonprofit organizations to refrain from direct lobbying in order to retain their tax-free status. Under current tax law, individual contributions to nonprofit charitable and educational organizations are tax deductible, and the income of these organizations is tax free. But these organizations risk losing these tax preferences if a "substantial part" of their activities is "attempting to influence legislation." Thus, for example, Washington think tanks such as the Brookings Institution, the American Enterprise Institute, and the Heritage Foundation refrain from direct lobbying even though they make policy recommendations. But the line between public affairs "education" and "lobbying" is very fuzzy.

lobbying
Activities directed at government officials with the hope of influencing their decisions.

public relations
Building and maintaining goodwill with the general public.

Tightening Lobby Regulations

Recent scandals involving lobbyists (see "Lobbying Ethics" later in this chapter) have led to proposals to curtail gifts by lobbyists to Congress members, including paid vacations, dinners, flights, and so forth. Another reform proposal has been to eliminate "earmarking" of appropriations for specific projects that have been heavily lobbied. As a partial step toward reform, Congress now requires members who sponsor earmarks to be identified.

The Fine Art of Lobbying

Any activity directed at a government decision maker with the hope of influencing decisions is a form of **lobbying**. (The term arose from the practice of waiting in the lobbies of legislative chambers to meet and persuade legislators.) For organized interests, lobbying is continuous—in congressional committees, in congressional staff offices, at the White House, at executive agencies, at Washington cocktail parties. If a group loses a round in Congress, it continues the fight in the agency in charge of executing the policy, or it challenges the policy in the courts. The following year it resumes the struggle in Congress: it fights to repeal the offending legislation, to weaken amendments, or to reduce the agency's budget enough to cripple enforcement efforts.

Lobbying techniques are as varied as the imagination of interest-group leaders, but such activities generally fall into seven categories: (1) public relations; (2) access; (3) information; (4) grassroots mobilization; (5) protests and demonstrations; (6) coalition building; and (7) campaign support. In the real world of Washington power struggles, all these techniques may be applied simultaneously or innovative techniques may be discovered and applied at any time (see Figure 9.2).

Public Relations

Many interest groups actually spend more of their time, energy, and resources on **public relations**—developing and maintaining a favorable climate of opinion in the nation—than on direct lobbying of Congress. The mass media—television, Internet,

access
Meeting and talking with decision makers, a prerequisite to direct persuasion.

9.1
9.2
9.3
9.4
9.5
9.6
9.7

magazines, newspapers—are saturated with expensive ads by oil companies, auto companies, chemical manufacturers, trade associations, teachers' unions, and many other groups, all seeking to create a favorable image for themselves with the general public. These ads are designed to go well beyond promoting the sale of particular products; they portray these organizations as patriotic citizens, protectors of the environment, providers of jobs, defenders of family values, and supporters of the American way of life. Some groups have moved to increasingly sophisticated media production, including the creation of Internet-based video channels. Paid advertising and internally created video is less credible than news stories and media commentary, so interest groups generate a daily flood of press releases, media events, interviews, reports, and studies for the media. "Earned media" news stories appear to favor liberal public-interest groups.[10]

☐ Access

"Opening doors" is a major business in Washington. To influence decision makers, organized interests must first acquire **access** to them. Individuals who have personal contacts in Congress, the White House, or the bureaucracy (or who say they do) sell their services at high prices. Washington law firms, public relations agencies, and consultants—often former insiders—all offer their connections, along with their advice, to their clients. The personal prestige of the lobbyist, together with the group's perceived political influence, helps open doors in Washington.

Washington socializing is often an exercise in access. Lobbyists regularly pay hundreds, even thousands, of dollars per plate at fund-raising dinners for members of Congress. Lobbyists regularly provide dinners, drinks, travel, vacations, and other amenities to members of Congress, their families, and congressional staff, as well as to White House and other executive officials. Campaign donations also help open doors. These favors are rarely provided on a direct quid pro quo basis in exchange for votes. Rather, they are designed to gain access—"just a chance to talk."

Building personal relationships consumes much of a lobbyist's time (and the client's money). It is difficult to know how much this contributes to actual success in passing, defeating, or amending legislation. But, to quote one client: "I figured that half of the money I spend on lobbying is wasted. Trouble is, I don't know which half."[11]

☐ Information

Once lobbyists gain access, their knowledge and information become valuable resources to those they lobby. Members of Congress and their staff look to lobbyists for *technical expertise* on the issue under debate as well as *political information* about the group's position on the issue. Members of Congress must vote on hundreds of questions each year, and it is impossible for them to be fully informed about the wide variety of bills and issues they face. Consequently, many of them (and administrators in the executive branch as well) come to depend on trusted lobbyists.

Lobbyists also spend considerable time and effort keeping informed about bills affecting their interests. They must be thoroughly familiar with the "ins and outs" of the legislative process—the relevant committees and subcommittees, their schedules of meetings and hearings, their key staff members, the best moments to act, the precise language for proposed bills and amendments, the witnesses for hearings, and the political strengths and weaknesses of the legislators themselves. In their campaign to win congressional and bureaucratic support for their programs, lobbyists engage in many different types of activities. Nearly all testify at congressional hearings and make direct contact with government officials on issues that affect them. In addition, lobbyists provide the technical reports and analyses used by congressional staffs in their legislative research. Engaging in protest demonstrations is a less common activity, in part because it involves a high risk of alienating some members of Congress.

The Game, the Rules, the Players

The King of K Street

Most Americans know that the White House is on Pennsylvania Avenue. Far fewer know the other important street in Washington: K Street, which runs east to west just north of the White House and has the largest concentration of lobbyists in the capital (there are nearly 13,000 registered lobbyists in Washington, D.C.). So many lobbyists maintain offices there that "K Street" has become synonymous with big-money, special-interest lobbying. The map at left shows the location and lobbying expenditures of the top 10 firms in Washington. None are on K Street, but they do surround it.

Much of the lobbying that is done on behalf of special interests in the United States is not done by individual lobbyists, but by law firms and public relations firms that specialize in governmental affairs. Many organizations find that it is more beneficial to employ a "hired gun," with substantial access, than to try and navigate the corridors of power on their own. For a half century, both by reputation and by billings, the top lobbying firm in D.C. has been Patton Boggs, named for founding partner James R. Patton, Jr. and current senior partner Thomas Hale "Tommy" Boggs, Jr., who joined the firm in 1966.

Tommy Boggs has been called the "King of K Street" for decades, because no Washington lobbyist enjoys the access and trust afforded him. His parents, Hale and Lindy Boggs, were a Washington power couple in the 1960s and 1970s who were active in Democratic Party politics. Hale represented a New Orleans-based congressional district for three decades, and was majority leader when he died in a plane crash in 1973; Lindy took over the seat and landed on the Appropriations Committee in the U.S. House of Representatives. Tommy and his sister (journalist Cokie Roberts) grew up in the middle of Washington's social scene; speaker of the House Sam Rayburn was their babysitter, and their parents were friends of the Kennedys and the Johnsons. Boggs went to law school at Georgetown, then went to New Orleans to practice law before joining Patton's firm in 1966. After a failed run for Congress in 1970, Boggs focused on building a highly successful lobbying practice with close ties to the Democratic Party.

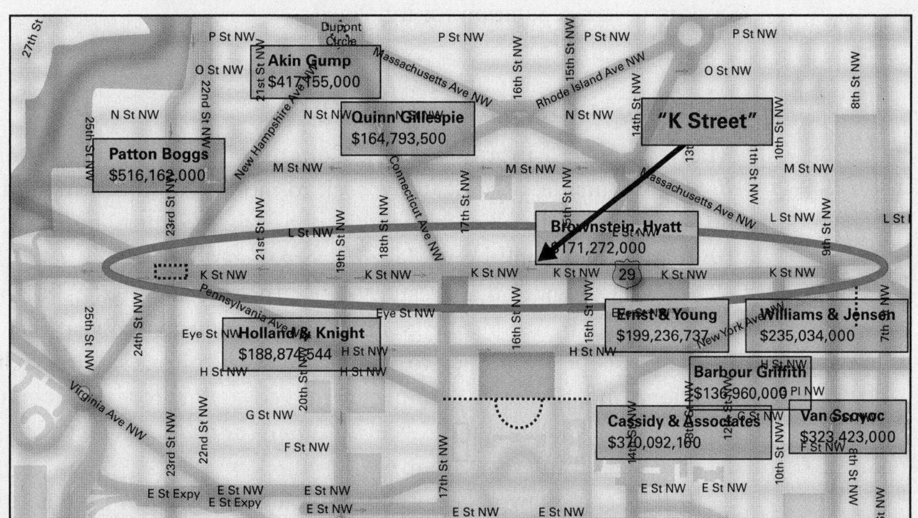

Lobbying Firm	Total	Address
Patton Boggs LLP	$516,162,000	2550 M Street
Akin, Gump et al.	$417,155,000	1333 NH Avenue NW
Cassidy & Associates	$370,092,100	700 13th Street NW
Van Scoyoc Associates	$323,423,000	101 Constitution Avenue
Williams & Jensen	$235,034,000	701 8th Street NW
Ernst & Young	$199,236,737	1101 New York Avenue NW
Holland & Knight	$188,874,544	2099 Pennsylvanie Avenue
Brownstein, Hyatt	$171,272,000	1350 I Street NW
Quinn Gillespie & Associates	$164,793,500	1133 Connecticut Avenue NW
Podesta Group	$157,270,000	1001 G Street NW

SOURCE: Opensecrets.org

(*Continued*)

9.1 9.2 9.3 9.4 9.5 9.6 9.7

(*Continued*)

Over the decades, Patton Boggs cultivated contacts and attracted a list of clients that included trial lawyers, insurance associations, and major corporations. His reputation and effectiveness was built on careful listening, and of trying to ascertain where the limits of all the players were in the negotiations over different policy proposals. Advocates of health care reform contend that it was Boggs who "killed" reform in the 1990s by insisting on the removal of malpractice reform from the Clinton reform proposal; the Clinton administration refused. When the legislation went to Congress, Boggs and his trial lawyer clients had one last opportunity to stop the bill, by calling their marker on almost $80 million in campaign monies directed to members of Congress. Boggs is a respectful listener, and years of trust and relationships were activated against the Clinton proposal, largely through the president's own party. Throughout every step of the legislative process the bill met resistence. It had its referral to a committee delayed; the referral to a subcommittee was stalled by Judiciary Chairman Jack Brooks; the marking up of the bill in committee cut away at the malpractice reform provisions—including embedding a killer provision that overturned past federal malpractice reforms. In a series of deft moves involving multiple lawmakers, the health care reform proposal was rendered unpalatable to a majority in Congress, based on years of advanced lobbying effort by The King of K Street.

QUESTIONS

1. Why does it make sense to use a "hired gun" lobbying firm?
2. Why is Tommy Boggs successful?
3. Do you think the K Street establishment is an elite system? Can it be penetrated by political outsiders?

grassroots lobbying
Attempts to influence government decision making by inspiring constituents to contact their representatives.

Experienced lobbyists develop a reputation for accurate information. Most successful lobbyists do not supply faulty information; their success depends on maintaining the trust and confidence of decision makers. A reputation for honesty is as important as a reputation for influence.

☐ Grassroots Mobilization

Many organized interests lobby Congress from both the *outside* and the *inside*. From the outside, organizations seek to mobilize **grassroots lobbying** of members of Congress by their constituents. Lobbyists frequently encourage letters and calls from "the folks back home." Larger organized interests often have local chapters throughout the nation and can mobilize these local affiliates to apply pressure when necessary. Lobbyists encourage influential local people to visit the office of a member of Congress personally or to make a personal phone call on behalf of the group's position. And, naturally, members are urged to vote for or against certain candidates, based on their policy stances (see *The Game, the Rules, the Players*: AARP: The Nation's Most Powerful Interest Group).

Experienced lawmakers recognize attempts by lobby groups to orchestrate "spontaneous" grassroots outpourings of cards and letters. Pressure mail is often identical in wording and content. Nevertheless, members of Congress dare not ignore a flood of letters and telegrams from home, for the mail shows that constituents are aware of the issue and care enough to sign their names.

☐ Protests and Demonstrations

Interest groups occasionally employ protests and demonstrations to attract media attention to their concerns and thereby apply pressure on officials to take action. For these actions to succeed in getting issues on the agenda of decision makers in Congress, in the White House, and in executive agencies, participation by the media, especially television, is essential. The media carry the message of the protest or demonstration both to the general public and directly to government officials.

Organized interest groups most often resort to protests and demonstrations when (1) they are frustrated in more traditional "inside" lobbying efforts; and/or (2) they wish to intensify pressure on officials at a specific point in time. Demonstrations typically attract media attention for a short time only. But media coverage of specific events can carry a clear message—for example, farmers driving tractors through Washington to protest farm conditions; motorcyclists conducting a giant "bike-in" to protest laws requiring helmets; cattle raisers driving steers down the Washington Mall to protest beef prices. The potential drawbacks to such activities are that the attention is short-lived and the group's reputation may be tarnished if the protest turns nasty or violent.

coalitions
A joining together of interest groups (or individuals) to achieve common goals.

bribery
Giving or offering anything of value in an effort to influence government officials in the performance of their duties.

political action committees (PACs)
Organizations that solicit and receive campaign contributions from corporations, unions, trade associations, and ideological and issue-oriented groups, and their members, and then distribute these funds to political candidates.

☐ Coalition Building

Interest groups frequently seek to build **coalitions** with other groups in order to increase their power. Coalitions tend to form among groups with parallel interests: for example, the National Organization for Women, the League of Women Voters, and NARAL Pro-Choice America on women's issues. Coalitions usually form temporarily around a single piece of legislation in a major effort to secure or prevent its passage.

☐ Campaign Support

Perhaps the real key to success in lobbying is the campaign contribution. Interest-group contributions not only help lobbyists gain access and a favorable hearing but also help elect people friendly to the group's goals. As the costs of campaigning increase, legislators must depend more heavily on the contributions of organized interests.

Most experienced lobbyists avoid making electoral threats. Amateur lobbyists sometimes threaten legislators by vowing to defeat them at the next election, but this tactic usually produces a hostile reaction among members of Congress. Legislators are likely to respond to crude pressures by demonstrating their independence and voting against the threatening lobbyist. Moreover, experienced members of Congress know that such threats are empty; lobbyists can seldom deliver enough votes to influence the outcome of an election.

☐ Lobbying Ethics

Experienced lobbyists also avoid offering a campaign contribution in exchange for a specific vote.[12] Crude "vote buying" (bribery) is illegal and risks repulsing politicians who refuse bribes. **Bribery**, when it occurs, is probably limited to very narrow and specific actions—payments to intervene in a particular case before an administrative agency; payments to insert a very specific break in a tax bill or a specific exemption in a trade bill; payments to obtain a specific contract with the government. Bribery on major issues is very unlikely; there is too much publicity and too many participants for bribery to be effective.

To the skeptical, "lobbying ethics" may seem to be an oxymoron. Lobbyists regularly send Congress members and even their staffs on expensive junkets around the world and entertain them back in Washington with golf outings, free meals at expensive restaurants, luxury skybox seats at sporting events, and a host of other perks. And, of course, they direct their clients' campaign contributions to Congress members who support their cause. Prudent lobbyists report these contributions and avoid any direct communications that would suggest that the contributions were made in exchange for a particular official action.

PAC Power

9.5 Outline the development, role, and structure of political action committees.

Organized interest groups channel their campaign contributions through **political action committees (PACs)**. PACs are organized by corporations, labor unions, trade associations, ideological and issue-oriented groups, and cooperatives and nonprofit corporations to solicit campaign contributions and distribute them to political candidates.

The Game, the Rules, the Players

So You Want to Be a Super-PAC

Political action committees sound ominous; Super-PACs doubly so. But, is it hard to make a Super-PAC? No! You can be in the "money is speech" business with just a few minutes effort and 49 cents to buy a first-class stamp. Here's how you do it:

First, your Super-PAC needs to have a raison d'être—a reason for being. Some exist to raise money to back a particular candidate, or to help a corporation or members of a union to raise and spend money in politics. Others advocate for or against an issue, like free religious exercise or gender awareness or taxing the collectable figurine industry. Your Super-PAC can be about just about anything.

Next, you need a name: Conventional PAC names often refer to the industry or interest they represent. "National Beer Wholesalers Association PAC" represents the distributors of beer, but they have a great nickname: Six-PAC. Super-PACs have names designed to evoke trust or aspirations, such as "The Faith Family Freedom Fund" or "Restore Our Future." They are also sufficiently vague as to not be readily identified as part of a narrow interest group. Be creative.

Then, do your paperwork. This is deceptively simple. To create a Super-PAC, you file a "statement of organization" with the Federal Election Commission (you can find the form here at http://www.fec.gov/pdf/forms/fecfrm1.pdf). Send the form back in with a cover letter indicating that you will function as a Super-PAC (the FEC has a sample for that, too, at http://www.fec.gov/pdf/forms/ie_only_letter.pdf). Mail the paperwork back to the Federal Election Commission at 999 E. St. NW, Washington, D.C. 20463. You'll need a stamp.

Finally, raise and spend lots of money. Anyone can give you money. Anyone. And, if you spend less than half of what you receive, you don't have to disclose who is backing you. It's your little secret. The only thing you can't do is make direct donations to political candidates, or coordinate with them. Now you are now in the "money is speech" business. Congratulations, Super-PAC!

QUESTIONS

1. If you had to create a Super-PAC, what would it be for?

SOURCES: www.fec.gov

Distributing PAC Money

Because PAC contributions are in larger lumps than individual contributions, PAC contributions often attract more attention from members of Congress. The PACs listed in Table 9.4 gave millions of dollars to finance the campaigns of their potential allies.

Most PACs use their campaign contributions to acquire access and influence with decision makers. Corporate, trade, and professional PAC contributions go overwhelmingly to incumbents, regardless of party. Leaders of these PACs know that incumbents are rarely defeated, and they do not wish to antagonize even unsympathetic members of Congress by backing challengers. However, ideological and issue-oriented PACs are more likely to allocate funds according to the candidates' policy positions and voting records. Labor PACs give almost all of their contributions to Democrats. Ideological and issue-oriented PACs give money to challengers as well as incumbents; in recent years, these groups collectively favored Democrats as women's, environmental, abortion rights, and elderly groups proliferated. (See *Who's Getting What?* EMILY's List.) Business, trade, and professional PACs usually split their contributions in order to ensure access to both Democrats and Republicans. For this last set of PACs, the bias isn't toward a party, but toward who is in power. Business, trade, and professional PACs give mainly to incumbents, not to challengers, and they tend to give heavily to the party with the majority in the House and Senate.

PAC money is less important in the Senate than in the House. PAC contributions account for about 35 percent of House campaign contributions; they account for only about 20 percent of Senate campaign contributions. Actually, PACs

TABLE 9.4 DEEP POCKETS: THE BIG MONEY PACS IN 2011–2012

Interest-group PAC contributions account for about 35 percent of House campaign contributions and 20 percent of contributions to Senate campaigns.

Rank	PAC Name	Total Amount	Dem Pct	Repub Pct
1	National Association of Realtors	$3,960,282	44%	55%
2	National Beer Wholesalers Association	$3,388,500	41%	59%
3	Honeywell International	$3,193,024	41%	59%
4	Operating Engineers Union	$3,186,387	84%	15%
5	National Auto Dealers Association	$3,074,000	28%	72%
6	International Brotherhood of Electrical Workers	$2,853,000	97%	2%
7	American Bankers Association	$2,736,150	20%	80%
8	AT&T Inc.	$2,543,000	35%	65%
9	American Association for Justice	$2,512,500	96%	3%
10	Credit Union National Association	$2,487,600	47%	52%
11	Blue Cross/Blue Shield	$2,401,398	35%	65%
12	Plumbers & Pipefitters Union	$2,395,150	94%	5%
13	American Federation of State, County, & Municipal Employees	$2,279,140	99%	1%
14	Lockheed Martin	$2,258,000	41%	59%
15	Machinists & Aerospace Workers Union	$2,173,500	98%	1%
16	American Federation of Teachers	$2,171,644	99%	0%
17	Senate Conservatives Fund	$2,113,229	0%	100%
18	Every Republican is Crucial PAC	$2,086,000	0%	100%
19	Teamsters Union	$2,053,410	96%	4%
20	Boeing	$2,044,000	44%	56%

SOURCE: Center for Responsive Politics, www.opensecrets.org.

contribute more *dollars* to the average senator than to the average House member. But because Senate campaigns cost so much more than House campaigns, PAC contributions are *proportionally* less. Senators must rely more on individual contributions than House members do.

☐ Payback

Representatives of organized interest groups say that their PAC contributions are designed to buy access—"a chance to talk"—with members of Congress, their staffs, and executives in the administration. Both interest groups and government officials usually deny that campaign contributions can "buy" support.

Nevertheless, the pattern of campaign contributions by major industries corresponds closely with the pattern of congressional voting on many key issues. Congress members who receive the largest PAC contributions from an industry group tend to vote in favor of that group's position. Congress members who oppose the industry's position generally receive far less.

Who's Getting What?

EMILY's List

Fund-raising is the greatest obstacle to mounting a successful campaign against an incumbent. And the most difficult problem facing challengers is raising money *early* in the campaign, when they have little name recognition and little or no standing in the polls.

EMILY's List is a politically adroit and effective effort to support liberal Democratic women candidates by infusing early *money* into their campaigns. EMILY stands for Early Money Is Like Yeast, because "it makes the dough rise." Early contributions provide the initial credibility that a candidate, especially a challenger, needs in order to solicit additional funds from individuals and organizations. EMILY is a fund-raising network of thousands of contributors, each of whom pays $100 to join and pledges to give at least $100 to two women from a list of candidates prepared by EMILY's leaders. Most of the contributors are professional women who appreciate EMILY's screening of pro-choice, liberal women candidates around the country.

EMILY's List was begun in 1985 by a wealthy heir to a founder of IBM, Ellen Malcolm. Women challengers for congressional races traditionally faced frustration in fund-raising. Incumbent male officeholders enjoyed a huge fund-raising advantage because contributors expected them to win and therefore opened their wallets to gain access and goodwill. EMILY's List has helped overcome defeatism among both women candidates and contributors.

EMILY's List supports only Democratic women candidates who are strong supporters of abortion rights. From 1990 to 2010, EMILY's List contributed nearly $24 million to women candidates, and the organization has disbursed more than $43 million since its inception. Of those dollars, 99 percent went to Democratic women candidates. When the list was founded, there were no

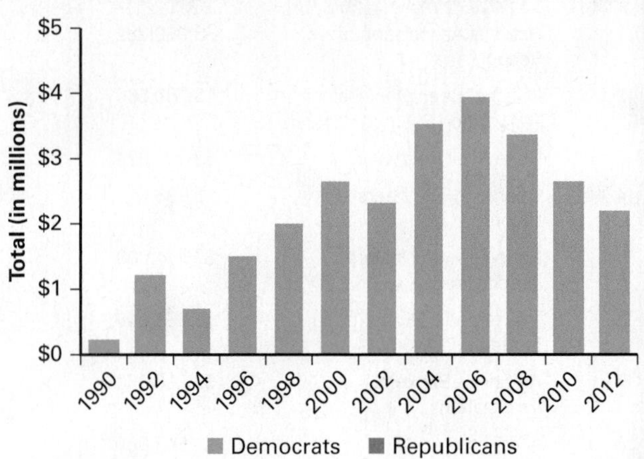

women in the Senate and only a very few in the House. In 2011, there were 17 women in the Senate and 75 in the House. The majority of these lawmakers were backed by EMILY's List. EMILY's List currently boasts of more than 100,000 members,

EMILY's List was an early supporter of Hillary Clinton in the 2008 Democratic presidential primary races, and in 2010, the organization took the position of actively opposing candidates backed by Sarah Palin's Sarah PAC.

QUESTIONS

1. Has EMILY's List succeeded in its mission of promoting women's representation?
2. About 41 percent of women regularly vote Republican. Do conservative women need an organization like EMILY's List?

Lobbying the Bureaucracy and the Courts

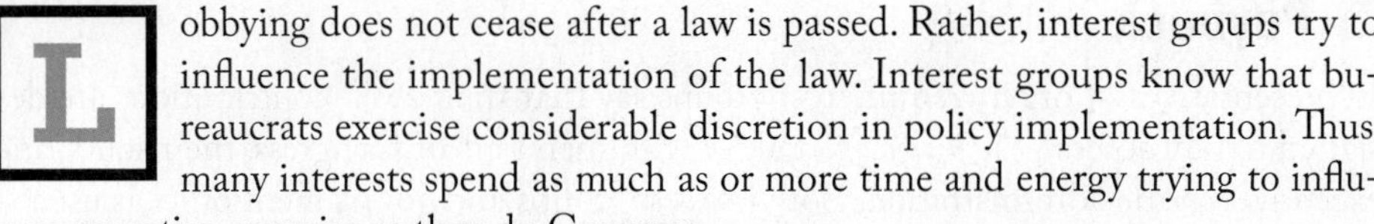
9.6 Assess the relationships between interest groups and bureaucratic agencies and identify ways in which interest groups seek to influence the federal court system.

Lobbying does not cease after a law is passed. Rather, interest groups try to influence the implementation of the law. Interest groups know that bureaucrats exercise considerable discretion in policy implementation. Thus, many interests spend as much as or more time and energy trying to influence executive agencies as they do Congress.

Lobbying the bureaucracy involves various types of activities, including monitoring regulatory agencies for notices of new rules and regulatory changes; providing reports, testimony, and evidence in administrative hearings; submitting contract and grant applications and lobbying for their acceptance; and monitoring the performance of executive agencies on behalf of group members.

Groups may try to influence the creation of a new agency to carry out the law or influence the assignment of implementation to an existing "friendly" agency. They may try to influence the selection of personnel to head the implementing agency.

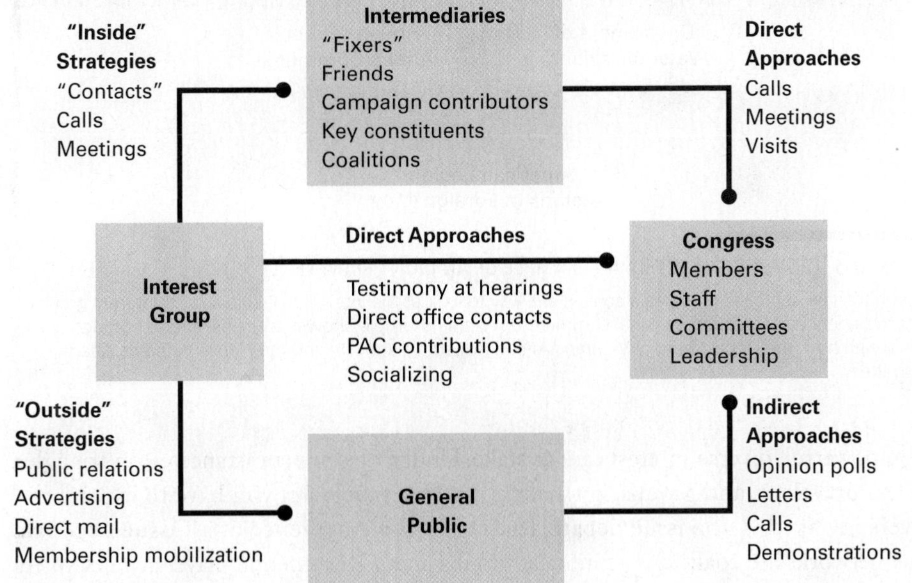

FIGURE 9.4 A GUIDE TO THE FINE ART OF LOBBYING

Interest groups seek to influence public policy both directly through lobbying and campaign contributions (inside strategy) and indirectly through public relations efforts to mold public opinion (outside strategy).

iron triangles
Mutually supportive relationships among interest groups, government agencies, and legislative committees with jurisdiction over a specific policy area.

They may lobby the agency to devote more money and personnel to enforcement of the law (or less, depending on a group's preference). They may argue for strict rules and regulations—or loose interpretations of the law—by the implementing agencies. Lobbyists frequently appear at administrative hearings to offer information. They often undertake to sponsor test cases of administrative regulations on behalf of affected members. In short, lobbying extends throughout the government.

Iron Triangles and Issue Networks

In general, interest groups strive to maintain close working relationships with the departments and agencies that serve their members or regulate their industries. Conversely, bureaucracies seek to nourish relationships with powerful "client" groups that are capable of pressuring Congress to expand their authority and increase their budgets. Both bureaucracies and interest groups seek close working relationships with the congressional committees that exercise jurisdiction over their policy function. Finally, members of Congress seek the political and financial support of powerful interest groups, and members also seek to influence bureaucrats to favor supportive interest groups.

The mutual interests of congressional committee members, organized groups, and bureaucratic agencies come together to form what have been labeled the "iron triangles" of American government. **Iron triangles** refer to stable relationships among interest groups, congressional committees, and administrative agencies functioning in the same policy area. Each of the three sides of these triangles depends on the support of the other two; their cooperation serves their own interests (see Figure 9.5).

In an iron triangle, bureaucracies, interest groups, and congressional committees "scratch each other's backs." Bureaucrats get political support from interest groups in their requests for expanded power and authority and increased budgetary allocations. Interest groups get favorable treatment of their members by the bureaucracy. Congressional committee members get political and financial support from interest groups, as well as favorable treatment for their constituents and contributors who are served or regulated by the bureaucracy.

Iron triangles are more likely to develop in specialized policy areas over which there is relatively little internal conflict. However, conflict, rather than cooperation, is more likely to characterize bureaucratic, congressional, interest-group relationships

9.1

9.2

9.3

9.4

9.5

9.6

9.7

issue networks
Coalitions of interest groups and governmental players who promote policy on a particular issue.

revolving doors
The movement of individuals from government positions to jobs in the private sector, using the experience, knowledge, and contacts they acquired in government employment.

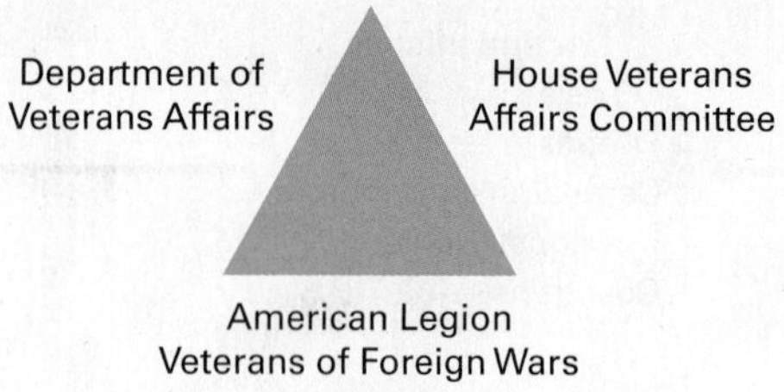

FIGURE 9.5 IT'S ALL CONNECTED: AN EXAMPLE OF AN IRON TRIANGLE

The iron triangle approach provides a convenient way to look at the interrelationship among interest groups, executive agencies, and congressional committees. As this example shows, veterans' interest groups work closely with both the Department of Veterans Affairs (executive agency) and the House Veterans Affairs Committee.

when powerful, diverse interests are at stake. Under these circumstances, iron triangles are less prevalent, and groups, lawmakers, and bureaucracies will have to expand the players involved in the issue debate, leading to the emergence of an **issue network**. Issue networks are coalitions of interest groups and governmental players who actively try to promote policy on a particular issue. Unlike the stable "plus-sum" relationships that characterize iron triangles, issue networks are often transient and do not sustain themselves beyond the resolution of the policy debate.

Agency Capture

The greatest fear of tightly coordinated action between lawmakers, agencies, and regulated interests is that of regulatory capture. When iron triangles emerge, all of the participants get benefits—lawmakers get reelection support, agencies get their budgets, and interest groups get preferred regulation. But is the public's interest served? When agencies regulate the targets of their policies in a manner that primarily (or only) benefits the regulated firm(s), the public interest is not served. The agency has become captive to the interests it is supposed to oversee. The economics literature is replete with examples of agency capture, including the Federal Communication Commission, the Securities and Exchange Commission, and the Nuclear Regulatory Commission. Under the watch of all these agencies (and others), there have been notable regulatory failures and instances of lax oversight that do not serve the public interest. The problem of agency capture is reinforced by "revolving door" movement between people who work for regulatory agencies and the firms and special interests they regulate.

Revolving Doors

It is not uncommon in Washington for people in a particular policy field to switch jobs, moving from a post in the government to a job in the private sector, or vice versa, or moving to different posts within the government. In one example, an individual might move from a job in a corporation (Pillsbury or General Mills) to the staff of an interest group (American Farm Bureau Federation), and then to the executive agency charged with implementing policy in the field (U.S. Department of Agriculture) or to the staff of a House or Senate committee with jurisdiction over the field (House Agricultural Committee or Senate Agriculture, Nutrition, and Forestry Committee). The common currency of moves within a network is both policy expertise and contacts within the field.

The term **revolving doors** is often used to criticize people who move from a government post (where they acquired experience, knowledge, and personal contacts) to a job in the private sector as a consultant, lobbyist, or salesperson. Defense contractors may recruit high-ranking military officers or Defense Department officials to help sell weapons to their former employers. Trade associations may recruit congressional staffers, White House staffers, or high-ranking agency heads as lobbyists, or these people may leave government service to start their own lobbying firms. Attorneys from the Justice Department, the Internal Revenue Service, and federal regulatory agencies may be recruited by Washington law firms to represent clients in dealings with their former employers.

Former members of Congress are considered the most viable commodity a lobby firm can offer their clients. The Center for Responsive Politics reports that 125 to 150 former Congress members are lobbyists, many of them among the highest paid in the profession. When asked, lobbyists themselves, especially former members of Congress, acknowledge that their success depends mostly on "schmoozing" with their former colleagues.[13]

Concern about revolving doors centers not only on individuals cashing in on their knowledge, experience, and contacts obtained through government employment, but also on the possibility that some government officials will be tempted to tilt their decisions in favor of corporations, law firms, or interest groups that promise these officials well-paid jobs after they leave government employment.

The Ethics in Government Act limits postgovernment employment in an effort to reduce the potential for corruption. Former members of Congress are not permitted to lobby Congress for one year after leaving that body. Former employees of executive agencies are not permitted to lobby their agency for one year after leaving government service, and they are not permitted to lobby their agency for two years on any matter over which they had any responsibility while employed by the government.

litigation
Legal dispute brought before a court.

amicus curiae
Person or group other than the defendant or the plaintiff or the prosecution that submits an argument in a case for the court's consideration.

☐ Lobbying the Courts

Interest groups play an important role in influencing federal courts. Many of the key cases brought to the federal courts are initiated by interest groups. Indeed, **litigation** is becoming a favored instrument of interest-group politics. Groups that oppose a new law or an agency's action often challenge it in court as unconstitutional or as violating the law. Interest groups bring issues to the courts by (1) supplying the attorneys for individuals who are parties to a case; (2) bringing suits to the courts on behalf of classes of citizens; or (3) filing companion **amicus curiae** (literally "friend of the court") arguments in cases in which they are interested.

The nation's most powerful interest groups all have legal divisions specializing in these techniques. The American Civil Liberties Union is one of the most active federal court litigants on behalf of criminal defendants. The early civil rights strategy of the National Association for the Advancement of Colored People (NAACP) was directed by its Legal Defense and Education Fund under the leadership of Thurgood Marshall. The NAACP chose to sponsor a suit by Linda Brown against the Board of Education in her hometown—Topeka, Kansas—in order to win the historic 1954 desegregation decision.[14] NARAL Pro-Choice America is active in sponsoring legal challenges to abortion restrictions. The Environmental Defense Fund and the Natural Resources Defense Council specialize in environmental litigation.

The special rules of judicial decision making preclude direct lobbying of judges by interest. Directly contacting federal judges about a case, letter writing, telephoning, and demonstrating outside of federal courtrooms are all considered inappropriate conduct. They inspire more resentment than support among federal judges. However, interest groups have been very active in direct lobbying of Congress over judicial appointments. Key interest groups supporting abortion rights—NARAL Pro-Choice America, People for the American Way, the National Organization for Women, and so on—have played a central role in confirmation battles.

THE AMERICAN CIVIL LIBERTIES UNION The American Civil Liberties Union (ACLU) is one of the largest and most active interest groups devoted to litigation. Its Washington offices employ a staff of several hundred people; it counts on some 5,000 volunteer lawyers across the country; and it has affiliates in every state and most large cities. The ACLU claims that its sole purpose is defense of civil liberty, that it has no other political agenda, that it defends the Communist Party and the Ku Klux Klan alike—not because it endorses their beliefs but because "the Bill of Rights is the ACLU's only client." And indeed on occasion it has defended the liberties of Nazis, Klansmen, and other right-wing extremists to express their unpopular views. But most ACLU work has involved litigation on behalf of liberal causes, such as abortion rights, resistance to military service, support for affirmative action, and opposition to the death penalty.

The ACLU was founded in 1920 by Roger Baldwin, a wealthy radical activist who opposed both capitalism and war. Baldwin graduated from Harvard University and briefly taught sociology at Washington University in St. Louis. He refused to be drafted during World War I and served a year's imprisonment for draft violation. In prison, Baldwin joined the Industrial Workers of the World (IWW, or the "Wobblies"), a radical labor union that advocated violence to achieve its goals. In the early 1920s, the ACLU defended socialists, "Bolsheviks," labor organizers, and World War I pacifists.

Later, the ACLU concentrated its efforts on the defense of 1st Amendment freedoms of speech, press, religion, and assembly. In the famous "Monkey Trial" of 1925, the ACLU helped defend schoolteacher John Scopes for having taught the theory of evolution in violation of Tennessee state law. In 1942, the ACLU stood alone in denouncing the round-up and internment of Japanese Americans. Later, it played a supporting role in the litigation efforts of the National Association for the Advancement of Colored People in the elimination of segregation; it defended Vietnam War protesters; it brought cases to court to ban prayer and religious exercise in public schools; it has opposed the death penalty and fought for abortion rights; and it defended the rights of people to burn the American flag as a form of symbolic speech.

Currently, the ACLU has a full agenda of cases and arguments. It is active in support of the detainees at the U.S. prison at Guantánamo Bay, Cuba, arguing that they should be given full constitutional rights. It continues its long opposition to capital punishment and defends many death row inmates. It is suing the state of Florida over racial differences in dropout rates. It supports affirmative action on university campuses across the country. It supports full recognition of same-sex marriages. It opposes the major provisions of the USA PATRIOT Act, including federal tracking of Internet communications, credit-card transactions, bank records, and other personal information of suspected terrorists.

Politics as Interest-Group Conflict

9.7 Evaluate different positions on the consequences of interest groups for American democracy.

olitics can be viewed as a struggle among interest groups over government policy. Interest groups, rather than individual citizens, can be viewed as the principal participants in American politics.

□ Pluralism as Democratic Politics

Pluralism is the idea that democracy can be preserved in a large, complex society through individual membership in interest groups that compete, bargain, and compromise over government policy. Individuals are influential in politics only when they act as part of, or on behalf of, groups. (Only leaders of organizations participate directly in policy making.) The group becomes the essential bridge between the individual and the government. Pluralists argue that interest-group politics is a natural extension of the democratic ideals of popular participation in government, freedom of association, and competition over public policy.

Pluralism portrays public policy at any given time as the equilibrium reached in the struggle among interest groups to influence policy (see Figure 9.6). This equilibrium is determined by the relative influence of interest groups. Changes in the relative influence of any interest group can be expected to result in changes in public policy; policy will move in the direction desired by the groups gaining in influence and away from the desires of groups losing influence.

According to this view of political life, government plays a passive role, merely "refereeing" group struggles. Public policy at any given moment represents the "equilibrium" point of the group pressures—the balance of competing interests. The job of politicians is to function as brokers of group interests, arranging compromises and balancing interests.

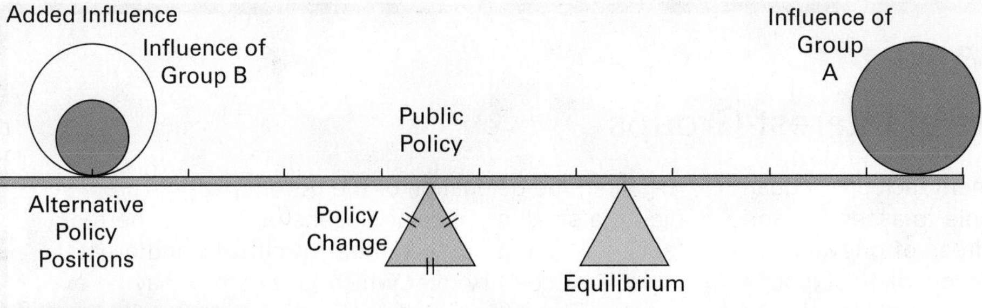

FIGURE 9.6 BALANCING ACT: UNDERSTANDING THE INTEREST-GROUP MODEL

According to pluralist theorists, policy in a democracy is the result of various special-interest groups "reaching equilibrium"—arriving at a compromise position that requires all parties to give up something but gives all parties something they wanted.

Balancing Group Power

Pluralism assumes that compromises *can* be arranged and that interests *can* be balanced in relatively stable fashion. It assumes that no single interest will ever become so dominant that it can reject compromise and proceed to impose its will on the nation without regard for the interests of other people. This assumption is based on several beliefs. The first is that interest groups act as a check on each other and that a system of *countervailing power* will protect the interests of all. For example, the power of big business will be checked by the countervailing power of big labor and big government.

A second belief is that *overlapping group membership* will tend to moderate the demands of particular groups and lead to compromise. Because no group can command the undivided loyalty of all its members, its demands will be less drastic and its leaders more amenable to compromise. If the leaders of any group go too far with their demands, those of its members who also belong to other groups endangered by these immoderate demands will balk.

A third belief is that radical programs and doctrinaire demands will be checked by the large, unorganized, but potentially significant *latent interest group* that is composed of Americans who oppose extremist politics.

Interest-Group Politics: How Democratic?

There are several problems with accepting pluralism as the legitimate heir to classic democratic theory. Democratic theory envisions public policy as the rational choice of *individuals* with equal influence who evaluate their needs and reach a majority decision with due regard for the rights of others. This traditional theory does not view public policy as a product of interest-group pressures. In fact, classic democratic theorists viewed interest groups and even political parties as intruders into an individualistic brand of citizenship and politics. Today, critics of pluralism charge that interest groups dominate the political arena, monopolize access to governmental power, and thereby restrict individual participation rather than enhance it.

Another assumption of pluralism is that group membership enhances the individual's influence on policy. But only rarely are interest groups democratically governed. Individuals may provide the numerical strength for organizations, but interest groups are usually run by a small elite of officers and activists. Leaders of corporations, banks, labor unions, medical associations, and bar associations—whose views and agendas often differ from those of their memberships—remain in control year after year. Very few people attend meetings, vote in organizational elections, or make their influence felt within their organizations.

Finally, pluralists hope that the power of diverse institutions and organizations in society will roughly balance out and prevent the emergence of a power monopoly. Yet inequality of power among organizations is commonplace. Examples abound of narrow, organized interests achieving their goals at the expense of the broader, unorganized public. Furthermore, producer interests, bound together by economic ties, usually dominate less well-organized consumer groups and groups based on noneconomic interests. Special interests seeking governmental subsidies, payments, and "entitlements" regularly prevail over the broader yet unorganized interests of taxpayers.

9.1

9.2

9.3

9.4

9.5

9.6

9.7

A Constitutional Note

Controlling the Effects of Interest Groups

The Constitution's 1st Amendment includes a guarantee of "the right of the people to assemble and petition their government for redress of grievances." The Constitution, then, protects the formation of groups and their right to lobby in Washington on behalf of their own interests. Yet the Founders worried about "the mischiefs of faction." James Madison, in *Federalist* No. 10, defined a faction as "a number of citizens, whether amounting to a majority or minority of the whole, who are united and actuated by some common impulse of passion, or interests, adverse to the rights of other citizens, or the permanent and aggregate interests of the community." But Madison also understood that "the latent causes of faction are thus sown in the nature of man." A faction could only be destroyed by destroying liberty itself, "by giving to every citizen the same opinions." According to Madison, a wiser and more practical approach would be to control the effects of faction by "first, the delegation of the government [in a republic] to a small number of citizens elected by the rest; secondly, the greater number of citizens and greater sphere of country over which [a republic] may be extended. The influence of factious leaders may kindle a flame within their particular States but will be unable to spread a general conflagration throughout the other States." Today, however, with national means of communication, interest groups are capable of doing exactly what Madison feared. They can mobilize mass opinion, intimidate elected representatives, and dominate the national political arena.

QUESTION

1. Is Madison's concept of "faction" adequate to explain a vast network of interest groups who petition government for favorable laws and regulations?

Review the Chapter

Interest-Group Power

9.1 Explain the origins, functions, strengths, and weaknesses of the interest-group system in America, p. 308

The interest-group system supplements the electoral system as a form of representation. The electoral system is designed to respond to broad majority preferences in geographically defined constituencies. The interest-group system represents narrower minority interests in economic, professional, ideological, religious, racial, gender, and issue constituencies. Interest groups originated to protect economic interests, to advance social movements, to seek government benefits, and to respond to government activity. As government has expanded into more sectors of American life, more interest groups have formed to influence government policy. The formation of interest groups is found in the social movement tradition of American politics.

The Organized Interests in Washington

9.2 Characterize the interests represented by organized interest groups lobbying in Washington, p. 311

Washington lobbying groups represent a wide array of organized interests. But business, trade, and professional associations outnumber labor union, women's, public-interest, single-issue, environmental, and ideological groups. When interests try to get special benefits for no real economic effort, this is called *rent-seeking*.

Leaders and Followers

9.3 Explain how interest-group leaders create and build organizations, p. 323

Interest-group formation has been aided in recent decades by entrepreneurs who create and build group memberships. They urge people to join organizations either by appealing to their sense of obligation or by providing an array of direct tangible benefits.

The Washington Lobbyists

9.4 Describe the overall environment of lobbying in Washington, and identify the main activities of lobbyists, p. 324

Most organized groups are dominated by small groups of leaders and activists. Few groups are governed democratically; members who oppose the direction of the organization usually drop out rather than challenge the leadership. Group membership and especially group leadership over-represent educated, upper-middle-class segments of the population. Lobbying activities include advertising and public relations, obtaining access to government officials, providing them with technical and political information, mobilizing constituents, building coalitions, organizing demonstrations, and providing campaign support. Bribery is illegal, and most lobbyists avoid exacting specific vote promises in exchange for campaign contributions.

PAC Power

9.5 Outline the development, role, and structure of political action committees, p. 331

Organized political action committees (PACs) proliferated following the 1974 "reform" of campaign finance laws. Most PAC money given to campaigns goes to incumbents; interest-group leaders know that incumbents are rarely defeated. SuperPAC money is usually provided by wealthy individuals and cannot be given directly to candidates.

Lobbying the Bureaucracy and the Courts

9.6 Assess the relationships between interest groups and bureaucratic agencies, and identify ways in which interest groups seek to influence the federal court system, p. 334

The mutual interests of organized groups, congressional committees, and bureaucratic agencies sometimes come together to form "iron triangles" of mutual support and cooperation in specific policy areas. In many policy areas, loose "policy networks" emerge among people who share an interest and expertise—although not necessarily opinions—about a policy and are in regular contact with each other. The "revolving door" problem emerges when individuals use the knowledge, experience, and contacts obtained through government employment to secure high-paying jobs with corporations, law firms, lobbying and consulting firms, and interest groups doing business with their old agencies. A consequence of revolving door practices is heightened prospects for agency capture and more rent seeking by special interests. Interest groups influence the nation's courts not only by providing financial and legal support for issues of concern to them but also lobbying Congress over judicial appointments.

Politics as Interest-Group Conflict

9.7 Evaluate different positions on the consequences of interest groups for American democracy, p. 338

Pluralism views interest-group activities as a form of democratic representation. For them, public policy balances group influence and a reasonable approximation of society's preferences. Competition among groups, overlapping group memberships, and latent interest groups all combine to ensure that no one group dominates the system.

Critics of pluralism warn that interest groups may monopolize power and restrict individual participation in politics rather than enhance it. They note that interest groups are not usually democratically governed, and their leaders are elites. They warn that accommodation rather than competition may characterize group interaction and that narrow producer interests tend to achieve their goals at the expense of broader consumer (taxpayer) interests.

The growing power of special interests, when combined with the declining power of parties and the fragmentation of government, causes gridlock and paralysis in policy making. The general public interest gets lost in the conflicting claims of special interests.

Learn the Terms

interest groups, p. 308
majoritarianism, p. 308
organizational sclerosis, p. 308
social movements, p. 309
rent, p. 312
environmental groups, p. 312
trade associations, p. 314
public-interest groups, p. 318
single-issue groups, p. 318
ideological organizations, p. 319
interest-group entrepreneurs, p. 323
free-riders, p. 323
lobbyist, p. 324
K Street, p. 325
lobbying, p. 327
public relations, p. 327
access, p. 328
grassroots lobbying, p. 330
coalitions, p. 331
bribery, p. 331
political action committees (PACs), p. 331
iron triangles, p. 335
issue networks, p. 336
revolving doors, p. 336
litigation, p. 337
amicus curiae, p. 337

Test Yourself

9.1 Explain the origins, functions, strengths, and weaknesses of the interest-group system in America

It would be accurate to maintain that

a. interest groups represent geographically defined constituencies and provide more direct representation of policy preferences than do political parties
b. parties represent geographically defined constituencies and provide more direct representation of policy preferences than do interest groups
c. interest groups represent various economic, ideological, and political constituencies and provide more direct representation of policy preferences than do political parties
d. parties represent various economic, ideological, and political constituencies and provide more direct representation of policy preferences than do interest groups
e. interest groups and parties cannot be differentiated

9.2 Characterize the interests represented by organized interest groups lobbying in Washington

Traditionally the ________ have dominated interest-group politics in America.

a. unions
b. business and trade organizations
c. ideologically oriented groups
d. single-issue groups
e. the churches

9.3 Explain how interest-group leaders create and build organizations

In general, it is easier to organize interest groups that are ________ and wish to pursue ___________.

a. smaller; broad goals
b. larger; broad goals
c. smaller; narrowly focused goals
d. larger; narrowly focused goals
e. ideological; rents

9.4 Describe the overall environment of lobbying in Washington and identify the main activities of lobbyists

In order to influence public policy, interest groups engage in which of the following behaviors?

I. presenting information to decision makers
II. mobilizing the "grass roots"
III. engaging in protests
IV. nominating candidates

a. I
b. I, II, III, and IV
c. I and IV
d. I, II, and III
e. I, II, and IV

9.5 Outline the development, role, and structure of political action committees

Political action committees are primarily interested in

a. organizing the electoral process
b. providing information to the candidates
c. soliciting and distributing campaign contributions
d. organizing protests and marches
e. increasing their membership

9.6 Assess the relationships between interest groups and bureaucratic agencies and identify ways in which interest groups seek to influence the federal court system

An "iron triangle" is

a. slang for the relationship between the Supreme Court, Congress, and Executive branches of government
b. a mutually beneficial relationship between the legislative committees, interest groups, and government agencies
c. just another name for an issue network
d. a situation where the local, state, and national governments all have concurrent jurisdiction
e. a conference committee that becomes locked up due to interest group influence

9.7 Evaluate different positions on the consequences of interest groups for American democracy

Adherents of pluralism believe that public policy making is primarily achieved

a. by a very small ruling elite at the top of society
b. by rent-seeking
c. by lobbying the bureaucracy
d. through the application of the principles of direct democracy
e. through conflict between competing interest groups

Explore Further

SUGGESTED READINGS

Abramoff, Jack. *Capitol Punishment: The Hard Truth About Washington Corruption from America's Most Notorious Lobbyist.* Washington, D.C.: WND Books, 2011. The subject of one of the most far-reaching corruption probes in Washington discusses the power plays and relationships inside K Street.

Baumgartner, Frank R., and Beth L. Leech. *Basic Interests: The Importance of Groups in Politics and in Political Science.* Princeton University Press, 1998. The first systematic analysis of interest group motivation and behavior to move beyond PAC analysis.

Frank R. Baumgartner, Jeffrey M. Berry, Marie Hojnacki, David C. Kimball, and Beth L. Leech. *Lobbying and Policy Change: Who Wins, Who Loses, and Why.* University of Chicago Press, 2009 A systematic examination of who wins and loses in lobbying efforts to effect policy change.

Berry, Jeffrey M. *The New Liberalism: The Rising Power of Citizen Groups.* Washington, D.C.: Brookings Institution Press, 1999. A description of the increasing number and activities of liberal interest groups in Washington and their success in defeating both business and conservative groups.

Berry, Jeffrey M., and Clyde Wilcox. *The Interest Group Society.* 5th ed. New York: Longman, 2009. Text coverage of organized interests, their relations with parties, PACs, "527s," and more.

Cigler, Allan J., and Burdett A. Loomis, eds. *Interest Group Politics.* 7th ed. Washington, D.C.: CQ Press, 2006. A collection of essays examining interest-group politics.

Goldstein, Kenneth M. *Interest Groups, Lobbying and Participation in America.* New York: Cambridge University Press, 2003. When and why people join interest groups, how they are recruited, and how groups try to influence legislation.

Herrnson, Paul S., Ronald G. Shaiko, and Clyde Wilcox. The *Interest Group Connection: Electioneering, Lobbying and Policy-Making.* 2nd ed. Washington, D.C.: CQ Press, 2004. Interest group activities in the electoral, legislative, judicial, and policy-making processes.

Lowi, Theodore J. *The End of Liberalism.* New York: Norton, 1969. The classic critique of "interest-group liberalism," describing how special interests contribute to the growth of government and the development of "clientism."

Olson, Mancur. *The Logic of Collective Action.* Cambridge, Mass.: Harvard University Press, 1965. A highly theoretical inquiry into the benefits and costs to individuals of joining groups and the obstacles (including the free-rider problem) to forming organized interest groups.

Olson, Mancur. *The Rise and Decline of Nations.* New Haven, Conn.: Yale University Press, 1982. Argues that, over time, the development of powerful special-interest lobbies has led to institutional sclerosis, inefficiency, and slowed economic growth.

Rozell, Mark J., Clyde Wilcox, and David Madland. *Interest Groups in American Campaigns.* Washington, D.C.: CQ Press, 2005. The role of interest groups in campaigns, including their adjustments to the Bipartisan Campaigns Reform Act of 2002 and the creation of "527s" to circumvent the act.

Vogel, Kenneth. *Big Money: 2.5 Billion Dollars, One Suspicious Vehicle, and a Pimp—on the Trail of the Ultra-Rich Hijacking American Politics.* New York: PublicAffairs. Gonzo journalism meets big money in this diagnosis of the American campaign finance system.

SUGGESTED WEB SITES

AARP www.aarp.org
The AARP site covers issues and provides information relevant to the concerns of citizens who are 50 years of age or older.

AFL-CIO www.aflcio.org
Home page of labor confederation; includes information on wages, unemployment, strikes, as well as news and press releases on union affairs.

American Farm Bureau Federation www.fb.org
The American Farm Bureau site reveals that the largest farm organization in America represents more than 5 million families in the 50 states and Puerto Rico.

American League of Lobbyists www.alldc.org
Lobbyists have their own Web site, one devoted to "ethical conduct" in the lobbying process and the "advancement of the lobbying profession."

American Medical Association www.ama-assn.org
Professional organization of doctors that both lobbies and publishes medical research in the prestigious *Journal of the American Medical Association* (JAMA).

Business Roundtable www.businessroundtable.org
Organization representing the largest U.S. corporations.

Children's Defense Fund www.childrensdefense.org
Advocacy organization for welfare programs; "the voice of children in America."

EMILY's List www.emilyslist.org
Political network for pro-choice Democratic women that raises early money for women candidates.

NAACP www.naacp.org
Oldest civil rights organization, working on behalf of African Americans.

National Organization for Women www.now.org
An organization of "feminist activists" concerned with abortion rights, lesbian rights, sexual harassment, affirmative action, and electing feminists.

National Rifle Association www.nra.org
The National Rifle Association site is devoted to opposing gun control legislation as well as employing the 2nd Amendment in its antigun control argument.

Public Citizen www.citizen.org
Organization founded by Ralph Nader; devotes its site to "protecting health, safety and democracy" as well as lobbying for "strong citizen and consumer protection laws."

U.S. Chamber of Commerce www.uschamber.com
Representing business, "3 million companies of all sizes."

10

Congress

Politics on Capitol Hill

Paul Ryan wasn't born with a silver spoon in his mouth. He grew up in Janesville, Wisconsin, the youngest of four kids. He attended a Catholic primary school and a public high school, playing sports and also working at the local McDonald's. When his father died during his high school years, Ryan received Social Security survivor's benefits, which were used to pay his way to Miami of Ohio University.

Through college, like many students, Ryan also worked, including a stint as salesman with the Chicago-based Oscar Mayer corporation. Ryan studied economics, and one of his professors helped him secure an internship with Wisconsin Senator Bob Kasten. He also once volunteered for a junior Cincinnati congressman named John Boehner, who would later become speaker of the U.S. House.

When he graduated in 1992, Ryan went to work for Kasten full-time. And, like many young DC staff, he was making a meager wage in one of the world's most expensive cities. He worked as a waiter and also as a fitness trainer (to this day, Ryan is a fitness buff). When his boss was defeated for reelection a few months after Ryan started on staff, he went over to a DC interest group as a speech writer where he would eventually work for the GOP's 1996 vice presidential nominee, Jack Kemp, before working briefly for another GOP senator.

In 1997, Ryan returned to Wisconsin, where he went to work for a family-owned company while also preparing to run for Congress in Wisconsin's open 1st congressional district. He won the primary and the general election to become one of the youngest members of Congress at age 27.

You never know where flipping burgers at McDonald's might get you eventually.

YOUNG GUN Paul Ryan emerged from the 2012 election as one of the most powerful and influential Republicans in the United States.

The Powers of Congress

10.1 Explain the sources of Congress's power.

The Constitution gives very broad powers to Congress. "All legislative Powers herein granted shall be vested in a Congress of the United States, which shall consist of a Senate and House of Representatives." *The nation's Founders envisioned Congress as the first and most powerful branch of government.* They equated national powers with the powers of Congress and gave Congress the most clearly specified role in national government.

Institutional Conflict

Yet over two centuries, the three separate branches of the national government—the Congress, the presidency and the executive branch, and the Supreme Court and federal judiciary—have struggled for power and preeminence in governing. This struggle for power among the separate institutions is precisely what the Founders envisioned. In writing the Constitution, they sought to create "opposite and rival interests" among the separate branches of the national government. "The constant aim," explained Madison, "is to divide and arrange the several offices in such a manner as that each may be a check on the other."[1] From time to time, first the Congress, then the presidency, and occasionally the Supreme Court have appeared to become the most powerful branch of government.

"The President Initiates, Congress Deliberates"

Throughout much of the twentieth century, Congress ceded leadership in national policy making to the president and the executive branch. Congress largely responded to the policy initiatives and spending requests originating from the president, executive

CONGRESS IN JOINT SESSION

President Barack Obama delivers the State of the Union address to a joint session of the Congress (House and Senate). Vice President Joe Biden and Speaker of the House John Boehner preside. Joint sessions are held in the House chamber; special guests are seated in the balconies.

agencies, and interest groups. Congress did not merely ratify or "rubber-stamp" these initiatives and requests; it played an independent role in the policy-making process. But this role was essentially a deliberative one, in which Congress accepted, modified, amended, or rejected the policies and budget requests initiated by the president and the executive branch.

It is easier for the Congress to obstruct the policy initiatives of the president than it is to assume policy leadership itself. Congress can defeat presidential policy proposals, deny presidential budget requests, delay or reject presidential appointments, investigate executive agencies, hold committee hearings to spotlight improprieties, and generally immobilize the executive branch. It can investigate and question nominees for the Supreme Court and the federal judiciary; it can legislate changes in the jurisdiction of the federal courts; and it can try to reverse court decisions by amending laws or the Constitution itself. The Congress can even threaten to impeach the president or federal judges. But these are largely reactive, obstructionist actions, usually accompanied by a great deal of oratory.

The design of the House chamber reflects the deliberative function of the Congress. The word Congress is a sixteenth-century term, taken from the Latin *con-* (together) and *gradus* (a step)—to take a step together. It stands in contrast to the eleventh-century, French-originating term *parlay* (to speak or talk), making the Parliament a place of speeches. The design of parliamentary bodies, like Great Britain's Westminster, places parties on opposite sides of a hall, making speeches in opposition and then dividing to vote. Latrobe's Hall of Congress arranges members in a semicircle, facing the "well" of the chamber where members speak to the entire body and engage the problem and each other.

Latrobe's Old Hall was only used for about 40 years. Though elegant, the semispherical ceiling created an odd acoustical effect. "As Members addressed the House, the sound of their voices echoed through the chamber. The high, curving wooden ceiling created a cacophony. Every noise reverberated throughout the room, and conversations occurring across the room could be heard with alarming clarity, hampering the orderly conduct of business." The disorderly acoustics and the doubling of the membership of the House from 107 members in 1802 to 234 members by 1853 prompted the need for a new chamber, completed in 1857. The "new" chamber is still in use, though the desks were replaced with benches in 1913. The Old Hall was turned into Statuary Hall and is part of the public tour of the Capitol building.

Dividing Congressional Power: House and Senate

Congress must not only share national power with the executive and judicial branches of government; it must also share power within itself. The framers of the Constitution took the advice of the nation's eldest diplomat, Benjamin Franklin: "It is not enough that your legislature should be numerous; it should also be divided.... One division should watch over and control the other, supply its wants, correct its blunders, and cross its designs, should they be criminal or erroneous."[2] Accordingly, the U.S. Congress is **bicameral**—composed of two houses (see Figure 10.1).

No law can be passed and no money can be spent unless both the House of Representatives and the Senate pass identical laws. Yet the House and the Senate have very different constituencies and terms. The House consists of 435 voting members, elected from districts within each state apportioned on the basis of equal population. (The average congressional district since the 2010 census has a population of about 708,000; the House also includes nonvoting delegates from Puerto Rico, the District of Columbia, Guam, the Virgin Islands, and American Samoa.) All House members face election every two years. The Senate consists of 100 members serving six-year terms, elected by statewide constituencies. Senate terms are staggered so that one-third of senators are elected every two years (see Table 10.1).

The House of Representatives, with its two-year terms, was designed to be more responsive to the American people. Representatives are fond of referring

bicameral
Any legislative body that consists of two separate chambers or houses; in the United States, the Senate represents 50 statewide voter constituencies, and the House of Representatives represents voters in 435 separate districts.

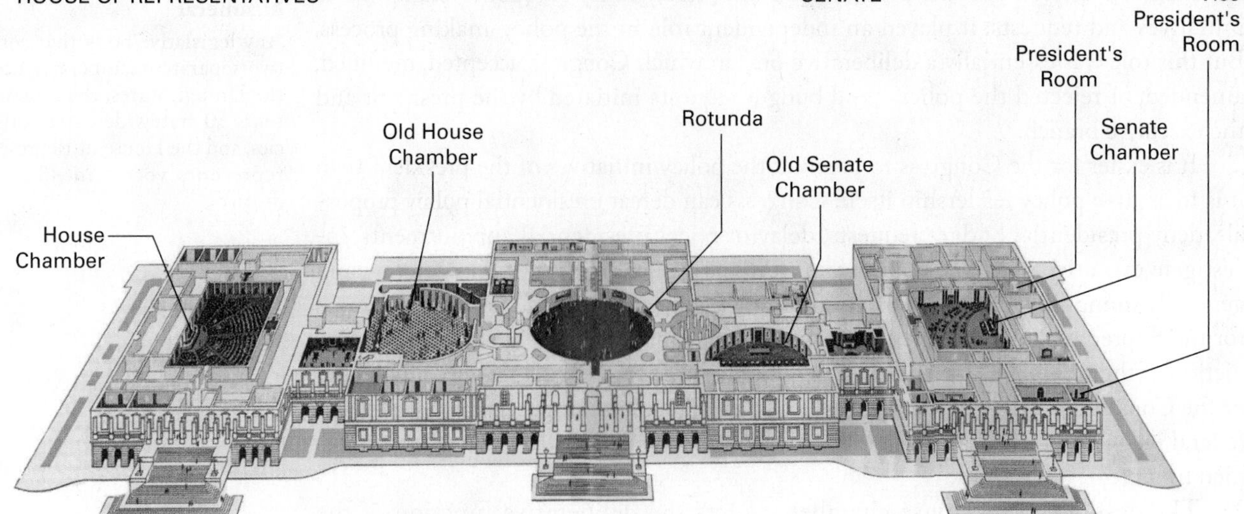

FIGURE 10.1 CORRIDORS OF POWER: CONGRESS

The architecture and floor plan of the Capitol Building in Washington reflect the bicameral division of Congress, with one wing for the House of Representatives and one for the Senate.

TABLE 10.1 COMPARING THE HOUSE AND SENATE

	House of Representatives	Senate
Terms	Two years	Six years
Members	435	100
Elections	All every two years	One-third every two years
Constituencies	Congressional districts	States
Unique powers	Originate tax bills	Advise and consent to (ratify) treaties by two-thirds vote
	Bring impeachment charges	Confirm appointments
		Try impeachment charges
Debate on bills	Limited by Rules Committee	Unlimited, except by unanimous consent or vote to close debate (three-fifths)
Member prestige	Modest; smaller personal staffs, fewer committee assignments	High; larger personal staffs, more committee assignments, always addressed as "Senator"
Leadership	Hierarchical, with speaker, majority and minority leaders and whips and committees, especially Rules, concentrating power	Less hierarchical, with each senator exercising more influence on leadership, committees, and floor votes
Committees	20 standing and select committees	20 standing and select committees
	Each member on about five committees	Each member on about seven committees
	Difficult to bypass	Easier to bypass

to their chamber as "the people's House," and the Constitution requires that all revenue-raising bills originate in the House. The Senate was designed to be a smaller, more deliberative body, with its members serving six-year terms. Indeed, the Senate is the more prestigious body. House members frequently give up their seats to run for the Senate; the reverse has seldom occurred. Moreover, the Senate exercises certain powers not given to the House: the power to ratify treaties and the power to confirm federal judges, ambassadors, cabinet members, and other high executive officials.

☐ Domestic Versus Foreign and Defense Policy

Congress is more powerful in domestic than in foreign and military affairs. It is freer to reject presidential initiatives in domestic policy areas such as welfare, health, education, the environment, and taxation. But Congress usually follows presidential leadership in foreign and defense policy even though constitutionally the president and Congress share power in these arenas. The president is "Commander in Chief" of the armed forces, but only Congress can "declare war." The president appoints and receives ambassadors and "makes treaties," but the Senate must confirm ambassadorial appointments and provide "advice and consent" to treaties. Historically presidents have led the nation in matters of war and peace.

The Vietnam experience inspired Congress to try to reassert its powers over war and peace. Military embarrassment, prolonged and indecisive fighting, and accumulating casualties—all vividly displayed on national television—encouraged Congress to challenge presidential war-making power. The War Powers Resolution of 1973, passed over the veto of President Richard Nixon, who was weakened by the Watergate scandal, sought to curtail the president's power to commit U.S. military forces to combat. But this legislation has not proven effective, and both Republican and Democratic presidents have continued to exercise war-making powers.

power of the purse
Congress's exclusive constitutional power to authorize expenditures by all agencies of the federal government.

oversight
Congressional monitoring of the activities of executive branch agencies to determine if the laws are being faithfully executed.

☐ The Power of the Purse

Congress's real power in both domestic and foreign (defense) policy centers on its **power of the purse**—its power over federal taxing and spending. Only Congress can "lay and collect Taxes, Duties, Imposts and Excises" (Article I, Section 8), and only Congress can authorize spending: "No Money shall be drawn from the Treasury, but in Consequence of Appropriations made by Law" (Article I, Section 9).

Congress jealously guards these powers. Presidents initiate taxing and spending policies by sending their budgets to the Congress each year. But Congress has the last word on taxing and spending. The most important bills that Congress considers each year are usually the budget resolutions setting ceilings on various categories of expenditures and the later appropriations bills authorizing specific expenditures. It is often in these appropriations bills that Congress exercises its greatest influence over national policy. Thus, for example, the Congress's involvement in foreign affairs centers on its annual consideration of appropriations for foreign aid, its involvement in military affairs centers on its annual deliberations over the defense appropriations bill, and so on.

☐ Oversight of the Bureaucracy

Congressional **oversight** of the federal bureaucracy is a continuing process by which Congress reviews the activities of the executive branch. The *formal* rationale of oversight is to determine whether the purposes of laws passed by Congress are being achieved by executive agencies and whether appropriations established by Congress are being spent as intended. Often the *real* purpose is to influence executive branch decisions, secure favorable treatment for friends and constituents, embarrass presidential appointees, undercut political support for particular programs or agencies, lay the political groundwork for budgetary increases or decreases for an agency, or simply enhance the power of congressional committees and subcommittees and those who chair them.

Oversight is carried out primarily through congressional committees and subcommittees. Individual senators and representatives can engage in a form of oversight simply by writing or calling executive agencies, but committees and their staffs carry on the bulk of oversight activity. Because committees and subcommittees specialize in particular areas of policy making, each tends to focus its oversight activities on particular executive departments and agencies. Oversight is particularly intense during budget hearings. Subcommittees of both the House and the Senate Appropriations Committees are especially interested in how money is being spent by the agencies they oversee.

10.1
10.2
10.3
10.4
10.5
10.6
10.7
10.8

advice and consent
The constitutional power of the U.S. Senate to reject or ratify (by a two-thirds vote) treaties made by the president.

confirmation
The constitutionally required consent of the Senate to appointments of high-level executive officials by the president and appointments of federal judges.

congressional hearings
Congressional committee sessions in which members listen to witnesses who provide information and opinions on matters of interest to the committee, including pending legislation.

congressional investigation
Congressional committee hearings on alleged misdeeds or scandals.

subpoena
A written command to appear before a court or a congressional committee.

contempt
Willful disobedience to, or open disrespect of, a court or congressional body.

perjury
Lying while under oath after swearing to tell the truth.

Senate Advice and Consent and Confirmation of Presidential Appointments

The Constitution provides that the president must obtain the **advice and consent** of the Senate for treaties "provided that two-thirds of the Senators present concur." In fact, the Senate has seldom provided "advice" to the president regarding treaties prior to their submission to the Senate for "consent." The president enjoys a high degree of autonomy over U.S. foreign policy. The process of treaty ratification begins when a president submits an already negotiated treaty to the Senate. Once submitted, treaties are referred to the Senate Foreign Relations Committee. That Committee cannot make changes in the treaty itself; it can either reject the treaty or forward it to the full Senate. The Senate itself cannot make changes in the formal treaty but must accept or reject it. Ratification requires a two-thirds vote. The Senate can, however, express its reservations to a treaty and/or instruct the president in how the treaty is to be interpreted.[3]

The Senate also exercises a special power over the president and the executive branch of government through its constitutional responsibility for approving presidential appointments of key executive officers, including Cabinet members, ambassadors, and other high officials.[4] And the Senate exercises a special power over the judicial branch through its constitutional responsibility for the **confirmation** of presidential appointments to the federal judiciary, including the Supreme Court.

Agenda Setting and Media Attention

Congressional hearings and investigations often involve agenda setting—bringing issues to the public's attention and placing them on the national agenda. For agenda-setting purposes, congressional committees or subcommittees need the assistance of the media. Televised hearings and investigations are perhaps the most effective means by which Congress can attract attention to issues as well as to itself and its members.

Hearings and investigations are similar in some ways, but hearings are usually held on a specific bill in order to build a record of both technical information (what the problem is and how legislation might be crafted to resolve it) and political information (who favors and who opposes various legislative options). In contrast, investigations are held on alleged misdeeds or scandals. Although the U.S. Supreme Court has held that there must be some "legislative purpose" behind a **congressional investigation**, that phrase has been interpreted very broadly indeed.[5]

The constitutional rationale for congressional investigations is that Congress is seeking information to assist in its lawmaking function. But from the earliest Congress to the present, the investigating powers of Congress have often been used for political purposes: to rally popular support for policies or programs favored by Congress; to attack the president, other high officials in the administration, or presidential policies or programs; to focus media attention and public debate on particular issues; or simply to win media coverage and popular recognition for members of Congress.

Congressional investigators have the legal power to **subpoena** witnesses (force them to appear), administer oaths, compel testimony, and initiate criminal charges for **contempt** (refusing to cooperate) and **perjury** (lying). These powers can be exercised by Congress's regular committees and subcommittees and by committees appointed especially to conduct a particular investigation.

Congress cannot impose criminal punishments as a result of its investigations; however, the information uncovered in a congressional investigation can be turned over to the U.S. Department of Justice, which may proceed with its own criminal investigation and perhaps indictment and trial of alleged wrongdoers in federal courts.

Congressional investigations have long been used as an opportunity for Congress to expose wrongdoing on the part of executive branch officials. The first congressional investigation (1792) examined why General Arthur St. Clair had been defeated by a tribal confederation of Miami and Shawnee Indians in Ohio; the Crédit Mobilier investigations (1872–73) revealed scandals in the Grant administration; the Select Committee on Campaign Practices, known universally as the "Watergate

Committee," exposed the activities of President Richard Nixon's inner circle that led to impeachment charges and Nixon's forced resignation; a House and Senate Joint Select Committee conducted the Iran-Contra investigation in the Reagan administration; the Senate Special Whitewater Committee investigated matters related to Bill and Hillary Clinton's real estate investments in Arkansas.

impeachment
Formal charges of wrongdoing brought against a government official, resulting in a trial and upon conviction removal from office.

apportionment
The allocation of legislative seats to jurisdictions based on population. Seats in the U.S. House of Representatives are apportioned to the states on the basis of their population after every 10-year census.

Impeachment and Removal

Potentially, Congress's most formidable power is that of impeaching and removing from office the president, other officers of the United States, and federal judges, including Supreme Court justices. Congress can do so only for "Treason, Bribery or other High Crimes and Misdemeanors." The House of Representatives has the sole authority to bring charges of **impeachment**, by a simple majority vote. Impeachment is analogous to a criminal indictment; it does not remove an officer but merely subjects him or her to trial by the Senate. Only the Senate, following a trial, can remove the federal official from office, and then only by a two-thirds vote.

Bill Clinton was the second president in the nation's history to be impeached by the U.S. House of Representatives. (Andrew Johnson was the first in 1867; after a one-month trial in the Senate, the "guilty" vote fell one short of two-thirds needed for Johnson's removal. President Richard Nixon resigned just prior to an impending impeachment vote in 1974.) The 1998 House impeachment vote split along partisan lines, with Republicans voting "yes" and Democrats voting "no." Two Articles of Impeachment were passed, one for perjury before a grand jury and one for obstruction of justice. In the subsequent Senate trial, only 45 senators (less than a majority and far less than the needed two-thirds) voted to convict President Clinton on the first charge, and only 50 voted to convict on the second.

Congressional Apportionment and Redistricting

10.2 Explain the processes of congressional apportionment and redistricting and assess how representative Congress is of the general population.

The Constitution states that "Representatives . . . shall be apportioned among the several states . . . according to their respective Numbers." It orders an "actual enumeration" (census) every 10 years. And it provides that every state shall have at least one representative, in addition to two senators, regardless of population. But the Constitution is silent on the size of the House of Representatives. Congress itself determines its own size; for more than a century, it allowed itself to grow to accommodate new states and population growth. In 1910 it fixed the membership of the House at 435.

The effect of doing so has been to expand the population of House districts over the years. Following the 2010 census, House districts have populations of about 710,000. It is sometimes argued that such large House constituencies prevent meaningful communication between citizens and their representatives. (The Framers originally envisioned House districts of no more than 30,000 people.) But expanding the size of the House would complicate its work, reduce the influence of individual members, require more procedural controls, and probably strengthen the power of party leaders.

Apportionment

Apportionment is the allocation of House seats to the states after each 10-year census. The Constitution does not specify a mathematical method of apportionment; Congress adopted a complex "method of equal proportion" in 1929, which so far has withstood court challenges. In 2012, political power continued to move south and west. Most of the gains in representatives are in the Southwest (+7), Texas (+4), and

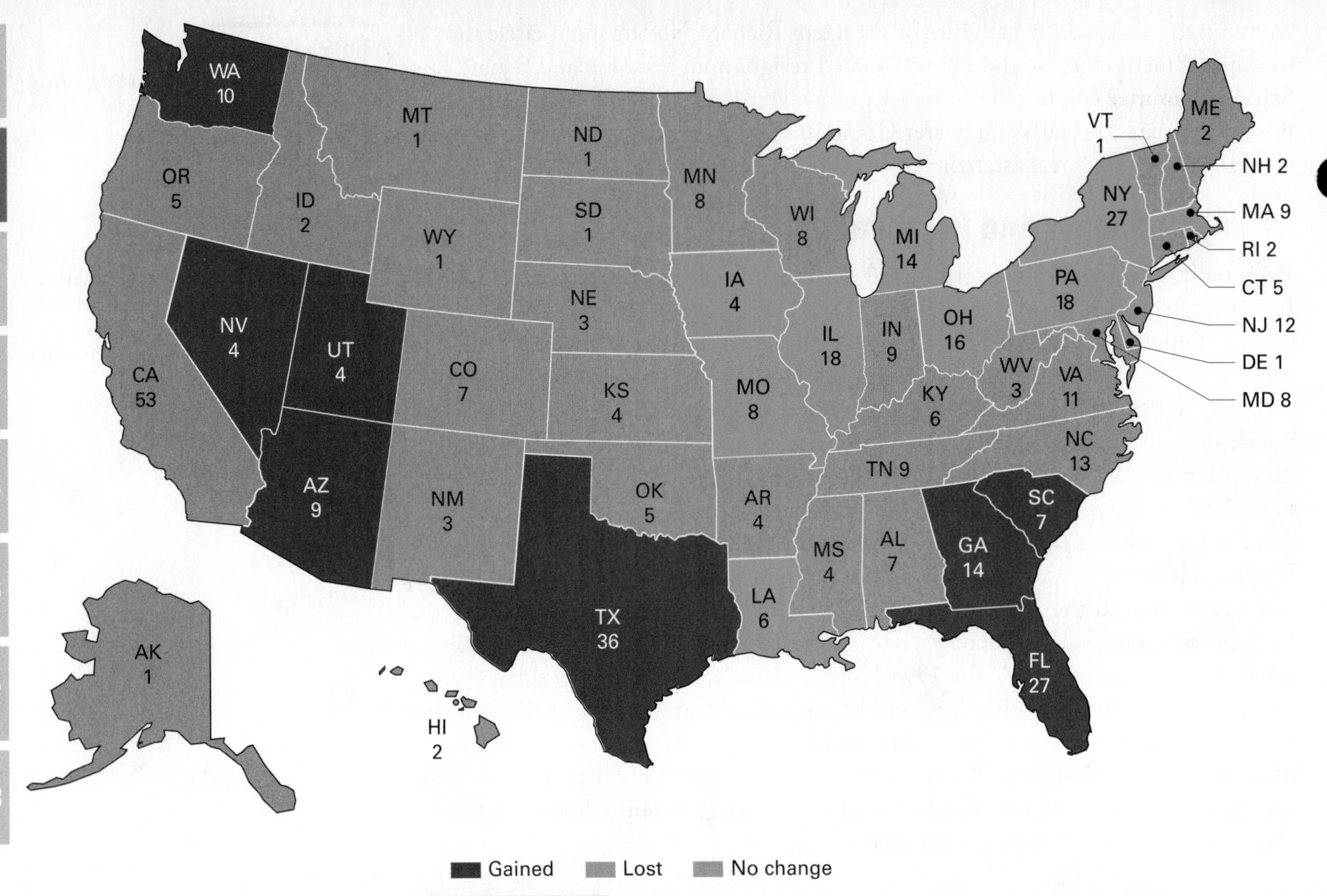

FIGURE 10.2 WINNERS AND LOSERS IN THE 2010 REAPPORTIONMENT

After the 2010 Census, seats in the U.S. House of Representatives were reapportioned among the states based on their population. Texas, the south Atlantic states, and the southwestern states west of the Rocky Mountains gained power in Congress and in the Electoral College.

malapportionment
Unequal numbers of people in legislative districts resulting in inequality of voter representation.

one person, one vote
The principle that legislative districts should have equal populations to ensure equal voting power of all individuals.

in the Deep South, Atlantic Coast states (+4) (see Figure 10.2). Seat losses are largely confined to the Northeast and the industrial Midwest. This is a continuation of a trend that has been underway for a half century (Figure 10.3).

☐ Malapportionment

Historically, state legislatures were notorious for their **malapportionment**—congressional (and state legislative) districts with grossly unequal numbers of people. In a district twice the size of the average district, the value of an individual's vote was heavily diluted. In Texas in 1962, a Dallas-based congressional district cast four times as many votes as some rural east Texas and south Texas districts.

☐ Enter the Supreme Court

Prior to 1962, the Supreme Court refused to intervene in apportionment, holding that this question belonged to the state legislatures and that the federal courts should avoid this "political thicket." So the Supreme Court's decision in the landmark case *Baker v. Carr* (1962) came as a surprise. The Court ruled that inequalities in voters' influence resulting from different-size districts violated the Equal Protection Clause of the 14th Amendment. The case dealt with a complaint about Tennessee's state legislative districts, but the Court soon extended its holding to congressional districts in a subsequent Georgia case.[6] "The conception of political equality from the Declaration of Independence to Lincoln's Gettysburg Address, to the 14th, 15th, 17th, and 19th Amendments, can mean only one thing—**one person, one vote**."[7]

The shift in the Supreme Court's policy raised a new question: How equal must districts be in order to guarantee voters "equal protection of the law"? The courts have ruled that only official U.S. Bureau of the Census figures may be used: estimated changes since the last census may *not* be used. In recent years, the courts have insisted on nearly exact mathematical equality in populations in congressional districts in a state. Even under perfect population apportionment, there are great discrepancies in votes cast across districts in a state. Recent litigation in Texas pursued citizen-based apportionment—thereby excluding both resident aliens and illegal immigrants from the equal population count.

redistricting
Drawing of legislative district boundary lines following each 10-year census.

"Actual Enumeration"

The U.S. Constitution is very specific in its wording: It calls for an "actual Enumeration" (Article I, Section 2) of the population in each 10-year census. However, the U.S. Bureau of the Census has considered the use of samples and estimates to correct what it perceives to be "undercounts." Undercounting is said to occur when certain populations are difficult to identify and count on an individual basis, populations such as recent non-English-speaking immigrants or residents of neighborhoods likely to mistake government census takers for law enforcement officers or other unwelcome government officials. Political leaders (usually Democrats) of states and cities with large immigrant and minority populations have favored the substitution of samples and estimates for actual head counts. However, the U.S. Supreme Court held in 1999 that the Census Act of 1976 prohibits sampling for purposes of apportioning House members among the states.[8] Congress may use sampling for determining the allocation of grant-in-aid funds if it wishes.

Redistricting

Redistricting refers to the drawing of boundary lines of congressional districts following the census. After each census, some states gain and others lose seats, depending on whether their populations have grown faster or slower than the nation's population. Population shifts *within* a state may force districting changes.

DRAWING THE LINES: THE ORIGINAL GERRYMANDER

The term *gerrymander* immortalizes Governor Elbridge Gerry (1744–1814) of Massachusetts, who in 1811 redistricted the state legislature to favor Democrats over Federalists. A district north of Boston was designed to concentrate, and thus "waste," Federalist votes. This political cartoon from the *Boston Gazette*, March 26, 1812, depicted the new district lines as a salamander, dubbing the process the "gerrymander."

10.1

10.2

10.3

10.4

10.5

10.6

10.7

10.8

gerrymandering
Drawing district boundary lines for political advantage.

cracking
Redistricting in which a strong minority is divided up and diluted to prevent it from electing a representative.

packing
Redistricting in which partisan voters are concentrated in a single district, "wasting" their majority vote and allowing the opposition to win by modest majorities in other districts.

Congressional district boundaries are usually drawn by state legislatures in each state; a state's redistricting act must pass both houses of the state legislature and win the governor's signature (or be passed over a gubernatorial veto). The U.S. Justice Department and the federal judiciary are also deeply involved in redistricting issues, particularly questions of whether or not redistricting disadvantages racial and linguistic minorities.

□ Gerrymandering

Gerrymandering is drawing district lines for political advantage (see Figure 10.3). The population of districts may be equal, yet the district boundaries are drawn in such a fashion as to grant advantage or disadvantage to parties and candidates. Gerrymandering has long been used by parties in control of state legislatures to maximize party seats in Congress (and state legislatures).

Gerrymandering, with the aid of sophisticated computer-mapping programs and data on past voting records of precincts, is a highly technical task. But consider a simple example where a city is entitled to three representatives and the eastern third of the city is Republican but the western two-thirds is Democratic (see Figure 10.3). If the Republicans could draw the district lines, they might draw them along a north–south direction to allow their party to win in one of the three districts. In contrast, if Democrats could draw the district lines, they might draw them along an east–west direction to allow their party to win all three districts by diluting the Republican vote. Such dividing up and diluting of a strong minority to deny it the power to elect a representative is called **cracking**. Often gerrymandering is not as neat as our example; district lines may twist and turn, creating grotesque patterns in order to achieve the desired effects. Another gerrymandering strategy—**packing**—is the heavy concentration of one party's voters in a single district in order to "waste" their votes and allow modest majorities of the party doing the redistricting to win in other districts.

□ Partisan Gerrymandering

Partisan gerrymandering does not violate federal court standards for "equal protection" under the 14th Amendment. There is no constitutional obligation to allocate seats "to the contending parties in proportion to what their anticipated statewide vote will be."[9] For several years, the Supreme Court threatened to intervene to correct partisan gerrymandering,[10] but in 2004 it finally decided that the issue was "nonjusticiable"—there were no "judicially manageable standards for adjudicating [party] claims." The Court decided that "'Fairness' is not a judicially manageable standard."[11] Parties are free to try to advantage themselves in redistricting, though efforts to find a judicially-manageable standard continue.

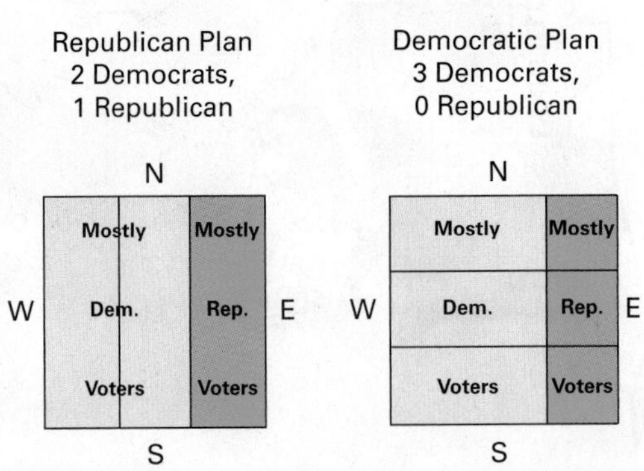

FIGURE 10.3 GERRYMANDERING MADE SIMPLE

Depending on how an area is divided into districts, the result may benefit one party or the other. In this example, dividing the area so one district has virtually all the Republicans gives that party a victory in that district while ceding the other two districts to the Democrats. In contrast, Democrats benefit when Republican voters are divided among the three districts so that their votes are splintered.

MAPPING DIVERSITY

Alabama lawmakers and staff examine proposed state legislative maps during the 2012 redistricting. The use of sophisticated computers to create districts to comply with the Voting Rights Act has made the Alabama legislature one of the most racially representative in the United States.

incumbent gerrymandering
Drawing legislative district boundaries to advantage incumbent legislators.

Racial Gerrymandering

Racial gerrymandering to disadvantage African Americans and other minorities violates both the Equal Protection Clause of the 14th Amendment and the Voting Rights Act of 1965. Until 2013 the Voting Rights Act specifies that redistricting in states with a history of voter discrimination or low voter participation must be "cleared" in advance with the U.S. Justice Department. This provision was overturned by the U.S. Supreme Court in the case *Shelby County v. Holder.*

Incumbent Gerrymandering

Yet another problem confronting state legislatures in redistricting is the preservation of incumbent Congress members, that is, **incumbent gerrymandering**. Incumbent gerrymandering means drawing district lines in such a way as to ensure that districts of incumbents include enough supporters of their party to provide a high probability of their reelection. But ensuring incumbents' security and maximizing the party's total number of seats are usually conflicting goals. It is not always possible to redraw district lines in such a way as to protect incumbents and at the same time ensure the largest number of party seats in a state. Incumbents want the largest number of their party's voters packed in *their* district, which robs other potentially competitive districts of party voters. Redistricting almost always confronts incumbents with new voters—voters who were previously in a different incumbent's district. As a result, incumbents usually have a somewhat more difficult reelection campaign following redistricting than in other elections.[12]

In 1982, Congress strengthened the Voting Rights Act by outlawing any electoral arrangement that has the effect of weakening minority voting power. This *effects test* replaced the earlier *intent test*, under which redistricting was outlawed

10.1
10.2
10.3
10.4
10.5
10.6
10.7
10.8

affirmative racial gerrymandering
Drawing district boundary lines to maximize minority representation.

only if boundaries were intentionally drawn to dilute minority political influence. In *Thornburg v. Gingles* (1986), the Supreme Court interpreted the effects test to require state legislatures to redistrict their states in a way that maximizes minority representation in Congress and the state legislatures.[13] The effect of this ruling was to require **affirmative racial gerrymandering**—the creation of predominantly African American and minority districts (labeled "majority-minority" districts) whenever possible. Following the 1990 census, redistricting in legislatures in states with large minority populations was closely scrutinized by the U.S. Justice Department and the federal courts. The result was a dramatic increase in African American and Hispanic representation in Congress (see Figure 10.7 later in this chapter).

The Supreme Court subsequently expressed constitutional doubts about bizarre-shaped districts based *solely* on race. In *Shaw v. Reno* (1993), Justice Sandra Day O'Connor wrote, "Racial gerrymandering, even for remedial purposes, may balkanize us into competing racial factions.... A reapportionment plan that includes in one district individuals who have little in common with one another but the color of their skin bears an uncomfortable resemblance to political apartheid"[14] (see Figure 10.4). Later, the Court held that the use of race as the "predominant factor" in drawing district lines is unconstitutional: "When the state assigns voters on the basis of race, it engages in the offensive and demeaning assumption that voters of a particular race, because of their race, think alike, share the same political interests and will prefer the same candidates at the polls."[15] But the Court has stopped short of saying that *all* race-conscious districting is unconstitutional.

☐ Partisanship Interacts with Race

Racial gerrymandering helps Republican congressional candidates. If African American voters are concentrated in heavily black districts, the effect is to "bleach" surrounding districts of Democratic-leaning black voters and thus improve the chances for Republican victories. Republican Party congressional gains in the South during the 1990s are partly due to racial gerrymandering.[16] In what has been described as a "paradox of representation," the creation of majority-minority districts brought more minority members to Congress, but it also led to a more conservative House of Representatives, as Republicans gained seats previously held by white liberal Democrats.[17]

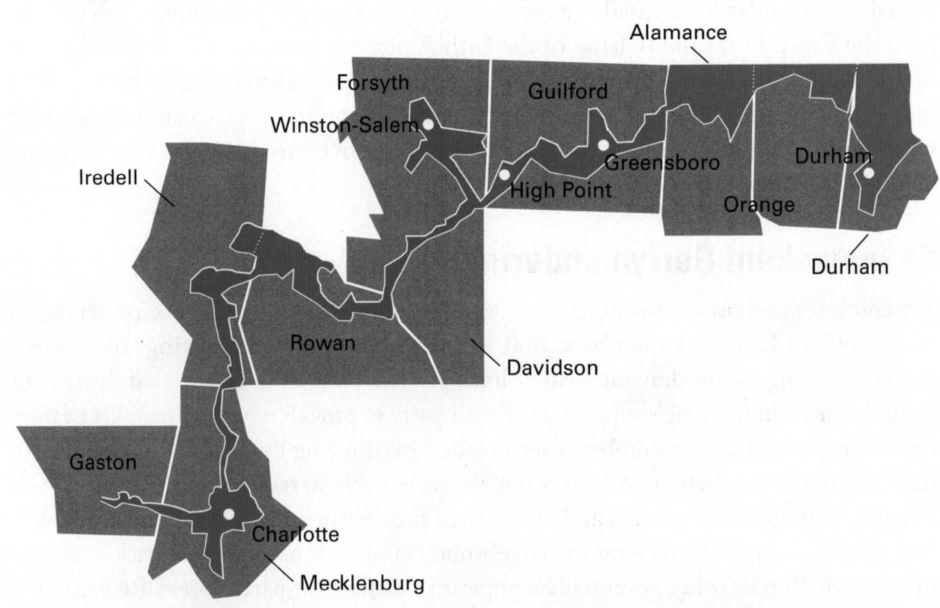

FIGURE 10.4 AFFIRMATIVE RACIAL GERRYMANDERING

North Carolina's Twelfth Congressional District was drawn up to be a "majority-minority" district by combining African American communities over a wide region of the state. The U.S. Supreme Court in *Shaw v. Reno* (1993) ordered a court review of this district to determine whether it incorporated any common interest other than race. The North Carolina legislature redrew the district in 1997, lowering its black population from 57 to 46 percent, yet keeping its lengthy connection of black voters from Charlotte to Greensboro.

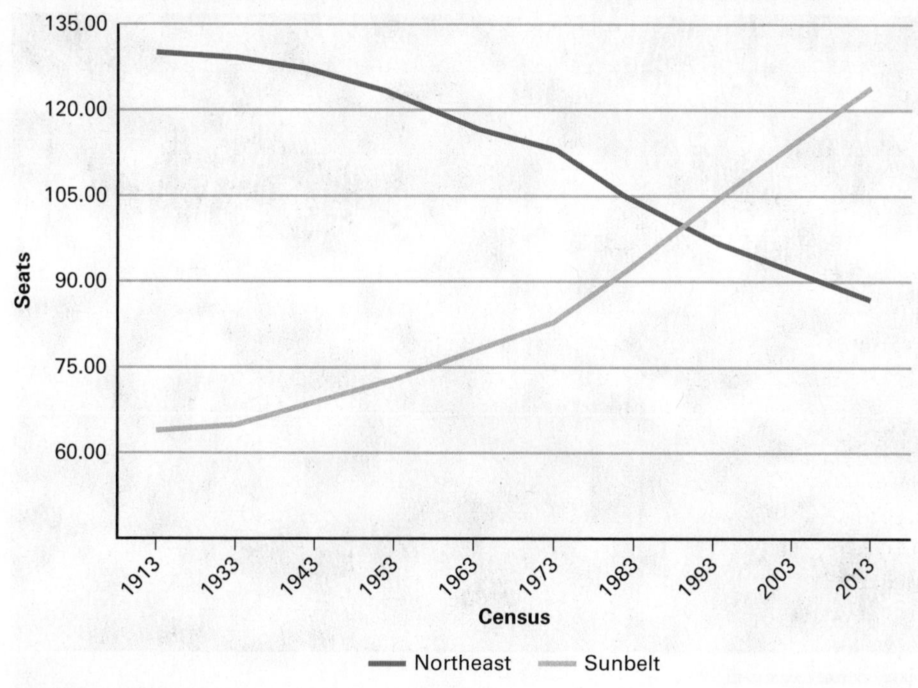

FIGURE 10.5 A CENTURY OF SUNBELT GAINS AND NORTHEASTERN DECLINE IN CONGRESS

In 1913, the industrial Northeast had over twice the votes in the U.S. House of Representatives as the Sunbelt states. Now, their relative power has reversed.

Life on Capitol Hill

10.3 Describe congressional elections and organization and characterize the working life of a member of Congress.

Members of Congress are independent political entrepreneurs—selling themselves, their services, and their personal policy views to the voters in 435 House districts and 50 states across the country. They initiate their own candidacies, raise most of their campaign funds from individual contributors, put together personal campaign organizations, and get themselves elected with relatively little help from their party. Their reelection campaigns depend on their ability to raise funds from individuals and interest groups and on the services and other benefits they provide to their constituents.

Who Runs for Congress?

Members of Congress come from a wide variety of backgrounds, ranging from acting and professional sports to medicine and the ministry. However, exceptionally high percentages of senators and representatives have prior experience in at least one of three fields—law, business, or public service. Members of Congress are increasingly career politicians, people who decided early in life to devote themselves to running for and occupying public office.[18] The many lawyers, by and large, are *not* practicing attorneys. Rather, the typical lawyer-legislator is a political activist with a law degree. These are people who graduated from law school and immediately sought public jobs—as federal or state prosecuting attorneys, as attorneys for federal or state agencies, or as staff assistants in congressional, state, or city offices. They used their early job experiences to make political contacts and learn how to organize a political campaign, find financial contributors, and deal with the media. Another group of Congress members are former businesspeople—not employees of large corporations, but people whose personal or family businesses brought them into close contact with government and their local community, in real estate, insurance, franchise dealerships, community banks, and so forth.

10.1

10.2

10.3

10.4

10.5

10.6

10.7

10.8

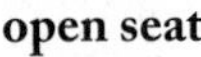

THE FRESHMAN CLASS

New members of the 112th Congress (elected in November 2010) pose in front of the U.S. Capitol. The group photo is a tradition for freshmen members.

open seat
Seat in a legislature for which no incumbent is running for reelection.

safe seats
Legislative districts in which the incumbent regularly wins by a large margin of the vote.

turnover
Replacement of members of Congress by retirement or resignation, by reapportionment, or (more rarely) by electoral defeat.

☐ Competition for Seats

Careerism in Congress is aided by the electoral advantages enjoyed by incumbents over challengers. Greater name recognition, advantages in raising campaign funds, and the resources of congressional offices all combine to limit competition for seats in Congress and to reelect the vast majority of incumbents. The result is an incumbent reelection percentage for House members that usually exceeds 90 percent. The average reelection rate for U.S. senators is more than 80 percent. Aspirants for congressional careers are well advised to wait for an **open seat**. Open seats in the House of Representatives are created when incumbents retire, die, or vacate the seat to run for higher. These opportunities occur on average in about 10 percent of House seats in each election. But every 10 years, reapportionment creates many new opportunities to win election to Congress. Reapportionment creates new seats in states gaining population, just as it forces out some incumbents in states losing population. Redistricting also threatens incumbents with new constituencies, where they have less name recognition, no history of casework, and perhaps no common racial or ethnic identification. Thus forced retirements and electoral defeats are more common in the first election following each 10-year reapportionment and redistricting of Congress.

☐ Winning Big

Not only do incumbent Congress members usually win, they usually also win big. Over 70 percent of House members win by margins of 60 percent or more or run unopposed. (In recent years, 10 to 18 percent of House members have had *no* opposition in the general election.) Senate races are somewhat more competitive. Senate challengers are usually people who have political experience and name recognition as members of the House, governors, or other high state officials. Even so, most Senate incumbents seeking reelection are victorious over their challengers. Most members of Congress, then, sit comfortably in **safe seats**—that is, they regularly win reelection by a large margin of the vote.

☐ Turnover

Despite a high rate of reelection of incumbents in Congress, about 15 percent of members arrive new to their jobs each session. **Turnover** occurs more frequently as a

The Game, the Rules, the Players

"Who Is Paul Ryan?"

Paul Ryan is one of the emerging leaders of the national Republican Party. Together with fellow Wisconsin Republicans Governor Scott Walker and RNC chairman Reince Priebus, Ryan has been at the forefront of the Generation X takeover of the Republican Party. In 2012, he was the GOP nominee for vice president. His name is one of several mentioned as a future presidential candidate.

Mr. Ryan was elected to the U.S. House in 1998 at age 28 from the 1st District in southern Wisconsin. He has spent all of his adult life in politics. He worked as a staff aide to Senator Bob Kasten, then for 1996 GOP vice presidential nominee Jack Kemp, and then as chief of staff to Senator Sam Brownback.

For the past several years, Ryan has carved out an area of expertise in budgeting and social services reform. In 2008 and 2009, Ryan advanced significant entitlement reform ("a Roadmap for America") in legislation that was bottled up in committee by the Democratic majority. At age 40, he became chairman of the powerful House Budget Committee. He reintroduced the Roadmap as part of the majority's federal budget, which passed out of the house on a party-line vote. The budget died in the Democratic Senate, but it created a budgetary "litmus test" that defined the GOP presidential nomination fight. In 2014, Ryan engaged a divisive discussion about the means by which social welfare services are delivered in the U.S., introducing a 200-page report condemning federal poverty programs as actually making poverty worse.

Ryan is a core fiscal conservative. But, his roll call voting record is not consistent with the new fiscal conservatism. Ryan supported both the TARP bailout and the bailout of Detroit automobile manufacturers in 2009. In 2013 he reached across the aisle (and chambers) to work with Democratic senator Patty Murray to craft the first bipartisan budget agreement in a generation.

Ryan's leadership role extends beyond budget matters. Together with former majority leader Eric Cantor (R-VA) and his successor as leader, Kevin McCarthy (R-CA), Ryan headed the "Young Guns" program, which targeted congressional races and recruited potential GOP candidates for open seats and Democratic-held districts. The defeat of 54 Democratic congressmen in 2010 is in part attributable to the efforts of Ryan, Cantor, and McCarthy—37 of the Republican challengers who won were previously state or local elected officials, most recruited through the Young Guns program.

Congressman Paul Ryan

Like many conservatives of his generation, Ryan says that Ayn Rand's books (*Atlas Shrugged, The Fountainhead*) inspired his entry into politics. His admiration for Rand has been a source of criticism from opponents and the media. Her writings promote a philosophy of "rational egoism," which rejects altruism and is popular among libertarian conservatives.

QUESTIONS

1. **Some political scientists describe a "ladder of ambition" that people climb to Congress. What are the rungs on Paul Ryan's career ladder?**
2. **How has Ryan influenced who else gets to Congress?**

result of retirement, resignation (sometimes to run for higher office), or reapportionment (and the loss of an incumbent's seat) than it does as a result of an incumbent's defeat in a bid for reelection. Roughly 10 percent of Congress members voluntarily leave office when their term expires.[19]

term limits
Limitations on the number of terms that an elected official can serve in office. The Constitution (Amendment XXII) limits the president to two terms. There are no limits on the terms of senators or representatives.

☐ Congressional Term Limits?

Public distrust of government helped to fuel a movement in the states to limit congressional terms. Several states attempted to limit their state's House members to four two-year terms and their senators to two six-year terms. Proponents of congressional **term limits** argued that career politicians become isolated from the lives and concerns of average citizens, that they acquire an "inside the Beltway" (the circle of highways that surround Washington) mentality. They also argued that term limits would increase competition, creating "open-seat" races on a regular basis and encouraging more people to seek public office.

Opponents of congressional term limits argued that they infringe on the voters' freedom of choice. If voters are upset with the performance of their Congress members, they can limit their terms by not reelecting them. But if voters wish to keep

ONE-TO-ONE POLITICS

Illinois Rep. Dan Lipinski discusses politics with a constituent in Chicago. The relationship with constituents is the most important one in Congress—the short term of office, the frank, and the use of periodic recesses are all designed to keep members in touch with the voters. Lipinski's father, Rep. Bill Lipinski, held the same seat in Congress from 1983 to 2005.

popular and experienced legislators in office, they should be permitted to do so. Opponents also argued that inexperienced Congress members would be forced to rely more on the policy information supplied them by bureaucrats, lobbyists, and staff people—thus weakening the institution of Congress.

But the U.S. Supreme Court ruled in 1995 that the states themselves cannot limit the terms of their members of Congress. "If the qualifications set forth in the text of the Constitution are to be changed, that text must be amended."[20] In a controversial 5–4 decision, the Court held that the Founders intended age, citizenship, and residency to be the *only* qualifications for members of Congress.

It is not likely that the necessary two-thirds of both houses of Congress will ever vote for a constitutional amendment to limit their own stay in office. Thus the Supreme Court's decision effectively killed the movement for congressional term limits.

☐ The Congressional Electorate

Congressional elections generally fail to arouse much interest among voters.[21] Indeed, only about 60 percent of the general public can name one U.S. senator from their state, and only about 40 percent can name both of their U.S. senators. Members of the House of Representatives fare no better: less than half of the general public can name their representative. But even constituents who know the names of their congressional delegation seldom know anything about the policy positions of these elected officials or about their votes on specific issues. Turnout in congressional *general elections* averages only about 35 percent in off-year (nonpresidential) elections. Turnout in congressional *primary elections* seldom exceeds 15 to 20 percent of persons eligible to vote. This lack of public attentiveness to congressional elections gives a great advantage to candidates with high name recognition, generally the incumbents (see *What Do You Think?* Why Do Voters Reelect Members of an Unpopular Congress?).

☐ Congressional Campaign Financing

Raising the $1–2 million it can take to win a House seat or the $5 to $50 million or more for a successful Senate campaign is a major job in and of itself. Even incumbents who face little or no competition still work hard at fund-raising, "banking" contributions against some future challenger. Large campaign chests, assembled well in advance of an election, can also be used to frighten off would-be challengers. Campaign funds can be used to build a strong personal organization back home, finance picnics and other festivities for constituents, expand the margin of victory, and develop a reputation for invincibility that may someday protect against an unknown challenger.[22]

Does money buy elections? In about 90 percent of all congressional races, the candidate who spends the most money wins. However, because most winning candidates are incumbents, the money probably reflects the expected political outcome rather than shaping it. But even in open-seat races, the candidate who spends the most money usually wins.

☐ Life in Congress

"All politics is local," declared former House Speaker Thomas P. "Tip" O'Neill, himself once the master of both Boston ward politics and the U.S. House of Representatives. Attention to the local constituency is the key to survival and success in congressional politics. If Congress often fails to deal responsibly with national problems, the explanation lies in part with the design of the institution. House members must devote primary attention to their districts and Senate members to their states. Only *after* their constituencies are served can they turn their attention to national policy making.

☐ The "Representativeness" of Congress

The Constitution requires only that members of the House of Representatives be (1) residents of the state they represent (they need not live in their congressional

What Do You Think?

Can Congress Get Anything Done?

A government cannot operate without a budget, revenue, or appropriations. But over the past thirty years, members of Congress have grown so polarized that they cannot agree on a budget or much of anything else. Polarization occurs when members of both parties move away from the moderate middle and share increasingly less common ground. Since 2001, Congress failed to pass a budget eight times, succeeding only in approving temporary budgets to keep government running. As the parties grow more polarized, Congress is less able to pass a permanent budget and the national debt increases.

What is political polarization? Polarization occurs when members of both political parties consistently vote along ideological lines. Political scientists track polarization because it has nearly doubled in the past thirty years, and it tends to impede the government's ability to function.

Is polarization related to greater annual debt? On a yearly basis, polarization is largely independent of the debt incurred by the United States—notice, for example, during the Clinton presidency how polarization grew even as debt decreased. However, as a long-term trend, both national debt and polarization in Congress do increase together.

Does polarization impede Congress's ability to create annual budgets? Yes. The more polarized Congress becomes, the more likely the disagreements over permanent budget solutions lead to temporary resolutions that barely stave off government shutdown.

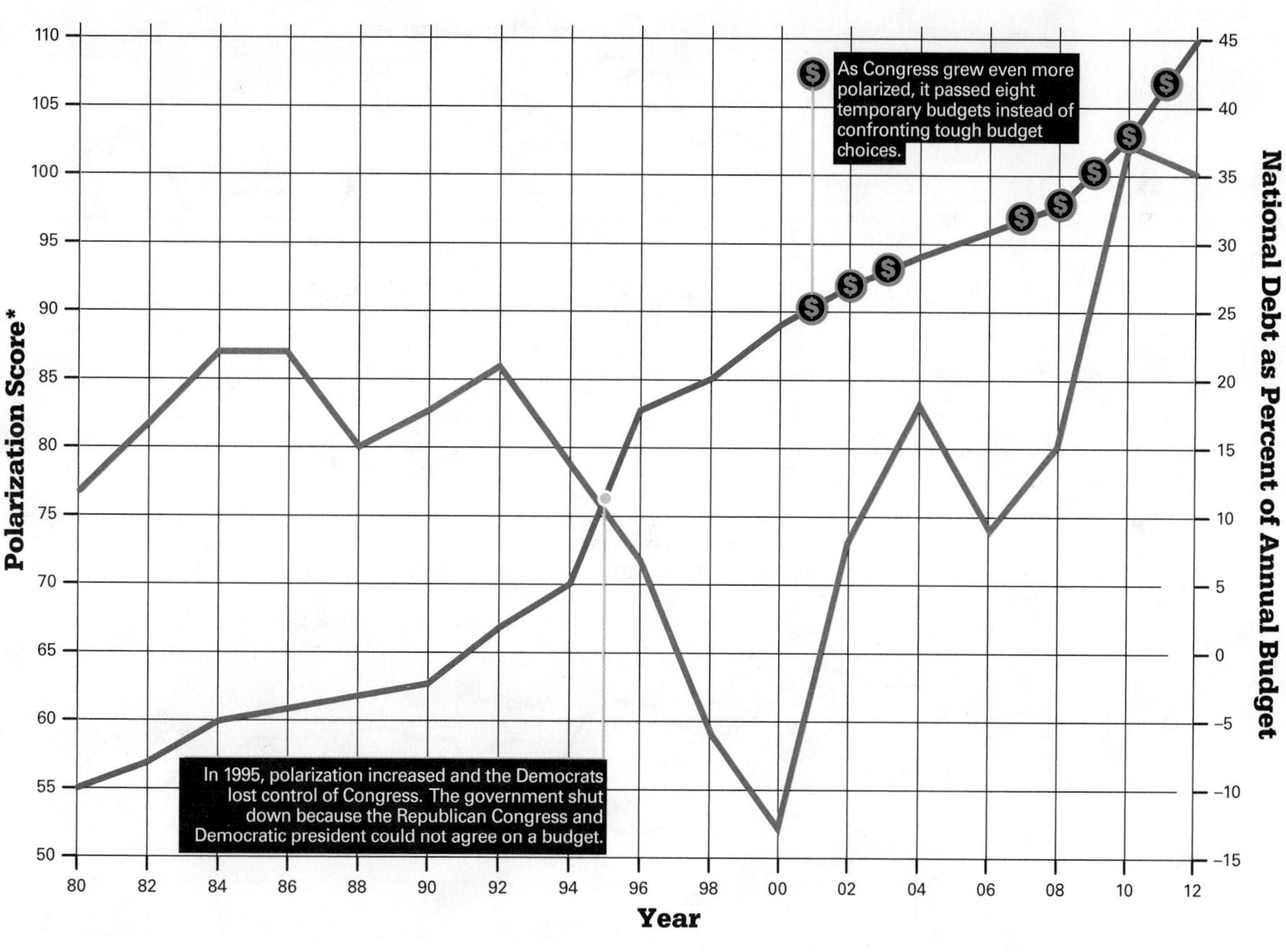

*Polarization is measured as the distance between the two parties' ideological scores as computed from data at Voteview.com.
SOURCE: Data from Voteview and the U.S. Government Accountability Office.

district, although virtually all do); (2) U.S. citizens for at least 7 years; and (3) at least 25 years old. Senators must also be residents of the state they represent, but they must be at least 30 years old and U.S. citizens for at least 9 years.

- **African Americans.** African Americans were first elected to Congress following the Civil War—seven black representatives and one black senator served in 1875. But with the end of Reconstruction, black membership in Congress fell to a single seat in the House from 1891 to 1955. Following the Civil Rights Act of 1964 and the Voting Rights Act of 1965, black membership in Congress rose steadily. Redistricting following the 1990 Census resulted in many new "majority-minority" congressional districts. After the 1992 elections, black membership in the House rose dramatically (see Figure 10.6), with most elected from predominantly African American districts.[23] As a result, although African Americans today make up a little more than 12 percent of the U.S. population, they make up about 9 percent of the House membership.

- **Hispanics.** Hispanics are the nation's largest minority, accounting for about 15 percent of the U.S. population. But Hispanic representation in the Congress lags considerably behind their population growth. Currently, only about 5 percent of House members are Hispanic, and three Hispanics serve in the U.S. Senate. The Voting Rights Act of 1965 protects "language minorities" as well as racial and ethnic minorities. Prior to the 1990 census and the creation of many court-ordered "majority-minority" congressional districts, very few Hispanics served in the Congress. But with the creation of new Hispanic majority districts, Hispanic representation began to increase in the House of Representatives. Most Hispanic House members come from California, Florida, and Texas.

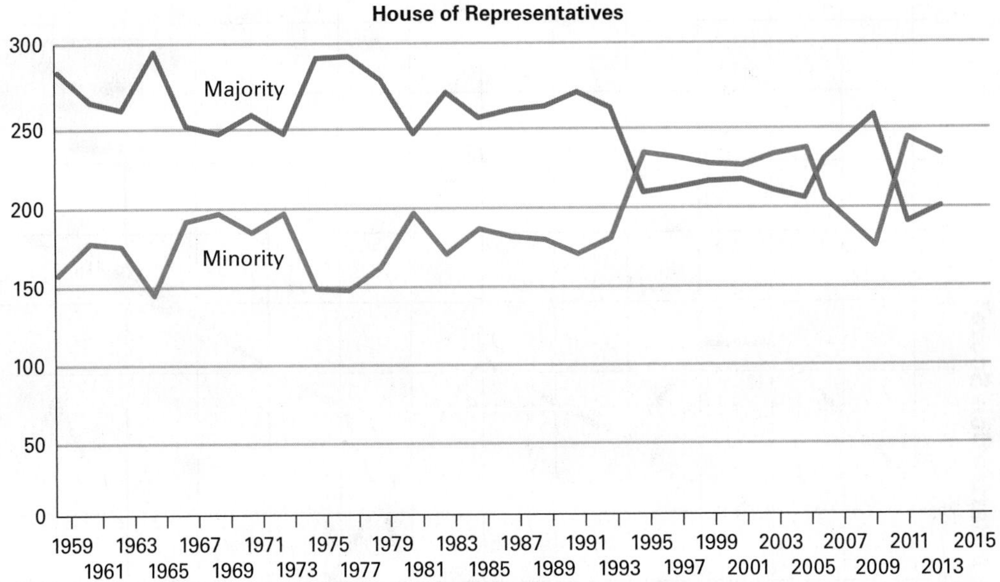

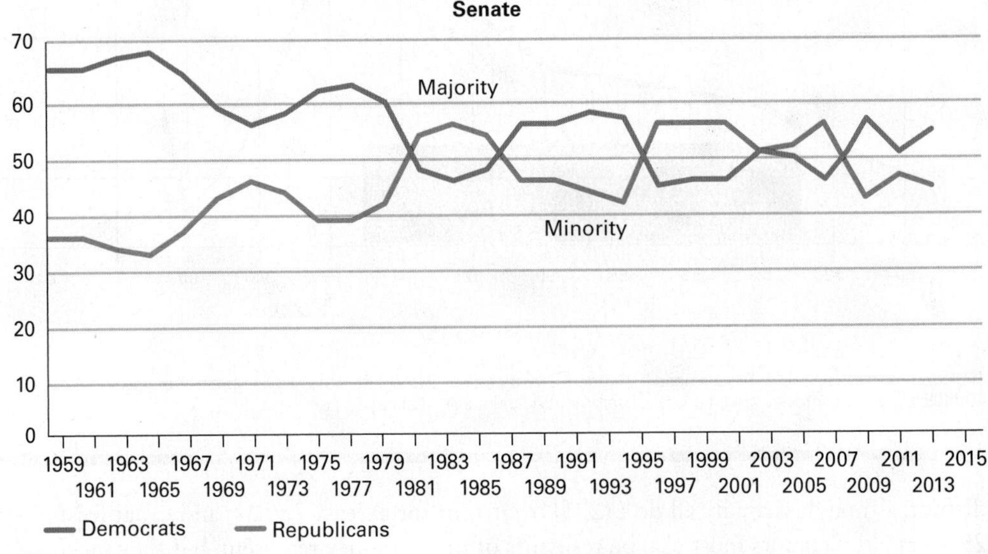

FIGURE 10.6 PARTIES ON CAPITOL HILL, PARTY CONTROL OF THE HOUSE AND SENATE

Except for two very brief periods, Democrats continuously controlled both the House of Representatives and the Senate for more than 40 years. The Democratic Party's "permanent" control of Congress was ended in 1994, when Republicans won majorities in both houses. Republicans usually held the House since, though often by narrow majorities.

- **Women.** Women have made impressive gains in both the House and the Senate in recent years. The "Year of the Woman" election in 1992 brought a significant increase in the number of women in the House of Representatives. Since then, women's representation in the House continued upward; 79 women served in the House in the 113th Congress (2013–2015), divided between 57 Democrats and 22 Republicans. In the Senate, 20 women served. California was represented by two Democratic women, Dianne Feinstein and Barbara Boxer. They were joined by 14 other Democratic women senators, and four Republican women senators. Although this is the largest delegation of women ever to serve together in the U.S. Senate, it is still only 17 percent of that body. The number of women in Congress has grown as a result of many factors, including strides that women have made in the workplace and other societal institutions. Yet stereotypes about women as politicians remain. Generally, voters view women as better able to handle "feminine" issues, such as health care, child care and education, but less able to handle "masculine" issues, including the economy and war. In the past, some women candidates tried to counter these stereotypes by emphasizing their toughness, especially on crime. But evidence suggests that women candidates can use female stereotypes to their advantage by focusing the campaign on gender-owned issues—health, welfare, education, and other compassion issues.[24]

☐ Congressional Staff

Congress is more than 535 elected senators and representatives. Congressional staff and other support personnel now total some 25,000 people. Each representative has a staff of 20 or more people, usually headed by a chief of staff or administrative assistant and including legislative assistants, communications specialists, constituent-service personnel, office managers, secretaries, and aides of various sorts. Senators frequently have staffs of 30 to 50 or more people, depending on the size of their state. All representatives and senators are provided with offices both in Washington and in their home districts and states. In addition, representatives receive more than $500,000 apiece for office expenses, travel, and staff; senators receive $2 million or more, depending on the size of their state's population. Overall, Congress spends more than $2 *billion* on itself each year.

Congressional staff people exercise great influence over legislation. Many experienced "Hill rats" have worked for the same member of Congress for many years. They become very familiar with "their" member's political strengths and vulnerabilities and handle much of the member's contacts with interest groups and constituents. Staff people, more than members themselves, move the legislative process—scheduling committee hearings, writing bills and amendments, and tracking the progress of such proposals through committees and floor proceedings. By working with the staff of other members of Congress or the staff of committees and negotiating with interest-group representatives, congressional staff are often able to work out policy compromises, determine the wording of legislation, or even outline "deals" for their member's vote (all subject to later approval by their member). With multiple demands on their time, members of Congress come to depend on their staff not only for information about the content of legislation but also for political recommendations about what position to take regarding it. Senior staff often move on to important policy positions with industry groups, think tanks, and lobbying firms.

☐ Support Agencies

In addition to the thousands of personal and committee staff who are supposed to assist members of Congress in research and analysis, four congressional support agencies provide Congress with information:

- The **Library of Congress** and its **Congressional Research Service** (CRS) are the oldest congressional support agencies. Members of Congress can turn to the Library of Congress for references and information. The CRS responds to direct requests of members for factual information on virtually any topic. It tracks major bills in Congress and produces summaries of each bill introduced. This information is available on computer terminals in members' offices.

10.1

10.2

10.3

10.4

10.5

10.6

10.7

10.8

Government Accountability Office
An arm of Congress that undertakes oversight of the operations and finances of executive agencies as well as performing policy research and evaluation.

home style
Activities of Congress members specifically directed at their home constituencies.

- The **Government Accountability Office** (GAO) has broad authority to oversee the operations and finances of executive agencies, to evaluate their programs, and to report its findings to Congress. Established as an arm of Congress in 1921, the GAO largely confined itself to financial auditing and management studies in its early years, but it has now expanded to more than 5,000 employees and undertakes a broad agenda of policy research and evaluation. Most GAO studies and reports are requested by members of Congress and congressional committees, but the GAO also undertakes some studies on its own initiative.
- The **Congressional Budget Office** (CBO) was created by the Congressional Budget and Impoundment Act of 1974 to strengthen Congress's role in the budgeting process. It was designed as a congressional counterweight to the president's Office of Management and Budget. The CBO supplies the House and Senate budget committees with its own budgetary analyses and economic forecasts, sometimes challenging those found in the president's annual budget.
- The **Government Printing Office** (GPO), created in 1860 as the publisher of the *Congressional Record*, now distributes over 20,000 different government publications in U.S. government bookstores throughout the nation.

□ Workload

Members of Congress claim to work 12- to 15-hour days: two to three hours in committee and subcommittee meetings; two to three hours on the floor of the chamber; three to four hours meeting with constituents, interest groups, other members, and staff in their offices; and two to three hours attending conferences, events, and meetings in Washington.[25] Members of Congress may introduce anywhere from 10 to 50 bills in a single session of Congress. Most bills are introduced merely to exhibit the member's commitment to a particular group or issue. Cosigning a popular bill is a common practice; especially popular bills may have 100 or 200 cosigners in the House of Representatives. Although thousands of bills are introduced, only 400 to 800 are passed in a session.[26]

□ Pay and Perks

Taxpayers can relate directly to what members of Congress spend on themselves, even while millions—and even billions—of dollars spent on government programs remain relatively incomprehensible. Taxpayer outrage over a 44 percent pay raise in 1991 and the use of automatic pay raises unless Congress voted to decline raises led to pay "reform," coupled with a stipulation that members of Congress would no longer accept honoraria from interest groups for their speeches and appearances, thus supposedly reducing members' dependence on outside income. Currently, automatic cost-of-living increases, also enacted by Congress, have raised members' pay to $174,000. House and Senate members receive the same pay. (Leaders of the House and Senate are paid a slightly higher salary than rank-and-file members.) Benefits, including retirement pay and health benefits, are very generous.

□ 27th Amendment

As the pay-raise debate raged in Washington, several states resurrected a constitutional amendment originally proposed by James Madison. Although passed by the Congress in 1789, it had never been ratified by the necessary three-quarters of the states. The 203-year-old amendment, requiring a House election to intervene before a congressional pay raise can take effect, was added as the 27th Amendment when ratified by 4 states (for a total of 39) in 1992.

□ Home Style

Members of Congress spend as much time politically cultivating their districts and states as they do legislating. **Home style** refers to the activities of senators and representatives in promoting their images among constituents and personally attending to constituents' problems and interests.[27] These activities include members' allocations of their personnel and staff resources to constituent services, members' personal appearances in the home district or state to demonstrate personal attention, and members' efforts to explain their Washington activities to the voters back home.

Casework

Casework is really a form of "retail" politics. Members of Congress can win votes one at a time by helping constituents on a personal level. Casework can involve everything from tracing lost Social Security checks and Medicare claims to providing information about federal programs, solving problems with the Internal Revenue Service, and assisting with federal job applications. Over time, grateful voters accumulate, giving incumbents an advantage at election time. Congressional staff do much of the actual casework, but letters go out over the signature of the member of Congress. Senators and representatives blame the growth of government for increasing casework, but it is also clear that members solicit casework, frequently reminding constituents to bring their problems to their member of Congress.[28]

casework
Services performed by legislators or their staff on behalf of individual constituents.

pork barreling
Legislation designed to make government benefits, including jobs and projects used as political patronage, flow to a particular district or state.

earmarks
Provisions in appropriation bills specifying particular projects for which federal money is to be spent.

franking privilege
Free mail service afforded members of Congress.

10.1 10.2 10.3 10.4 10.5 10.6 10.7 10.8

Pork Barrel and Earmarks

Pork barreling describes the efforts of senators and representatives to "bring home the bacon"—to bring federally funded projects, grants, and contracts that primarily benefit a single district or state to their home constituencies. Opportunities for pork barreling have never been greater: roads, dams, parks, and post offices are now overshadowed by redevelopment grants to city governments, research grants to universities, weapons contracts to local plants, "demonstration" projects of all kinds, and myriad other "goodies" tucked inside each year's annual appropriations bills.

Earmarks in these appropriations bills specify the particular project for which federal money is to be spent. Members of Congress understand the importance of supporting each other's earmarks, cooperating in the "incumbent-protection society." Even though earmarking and pork barreling add to the public's negative image of Congress as an institution, individual members gain local popularity for the benefits they bring to home districts and states. Reformers have long complained about earmarks; in 2009, they succeeded in obtaining a rule that earmarks must identify those members of Congress who sponsor them.

Pressing the Flesh

Senators and representatives spend a great deal of time in their home states and districts. Although congressional sessions last virtually all year, members of Congress find ways to spend more than 100 days per year at home.[29] It is important to be seen at home—giving speeches and attending dinners, fund-raising events, civic occasions, and so on. To accommodate this aspect of home style, Congress usually follows a Tuesday-to-Thursday schedule of legislative business, allowing members to spend longer weekends in their home districts. Congress also enjoys long recesses during the late summer and over holidays.

Puffing Images

To promote their images back home, members make generous use of their **franking privilege** (free mailing) to send their constituents newsletters, questionnaires, biographical material, and information about federal programs. Newsletters "puff" the accomplishments of the members; questionnaires are designed more to flatter voters than to assess opinions; and informational brochures tout federal services that members claim credit for providing and defending. Congress's penchant for self-promotion has also kept pace with the media and electronic ages. Congress now provides its members with television studios and support for making videotapes to send to local stations in home districts, and all members maintain Web sites on the Internet designed to puff their images.

Hill Styles and Home Styles

Members of Congress spend their lives "moving between two contexts, Washington and home, and between two activities, governing and campaigning."[30] They must regularly ask themselves how much time they should spend at home with their constituents versus how much time they should spend on lawmaking assignments in Washington. It is no surprise that freshman legislators spend more time in their districts; indeed, very few first-termers move their families to Washington. Long-term incumbents spend more time in Washington, but all Congress members spend more time at home in an election year.

Much of the time spent at home—with small groups of constituents, among contributors, in public speeches, and appearances on radio and television—is devoted to explaining issues and justifying the member's vote on them. "Often members defend their own voting record by belittling Congress—portraying themselves as knights errant battling sinister forces and feckless colleagues."[31]

Discretion

Lawmakers invest time and effort in cultivating constituency relationships in order to have the discretion to make tough decisions. Political economist Glenn Parker argues that, by building up "surpluses of votes" (or political capital) with constituents, lawmakers can later "spend" those votes to support a needed policy that is politically unpopular. Lawmakers can also use those surpluses to pursue policies that are interesting to them, but not to the constituency—like an agriculture-state lawmaker who is interested in some aspect of foreign policy. But, political capital can be overspent. A string of too many votes against the constituency's interests, or too much attention to policies that the constituents don't care about, can cost a lawmaker reelection.

Organizing Congress: Party and Leadership

Congress is composed of people who think of themselves as leaders, not followers. They got elected without much help from their party. Yet they realize that their

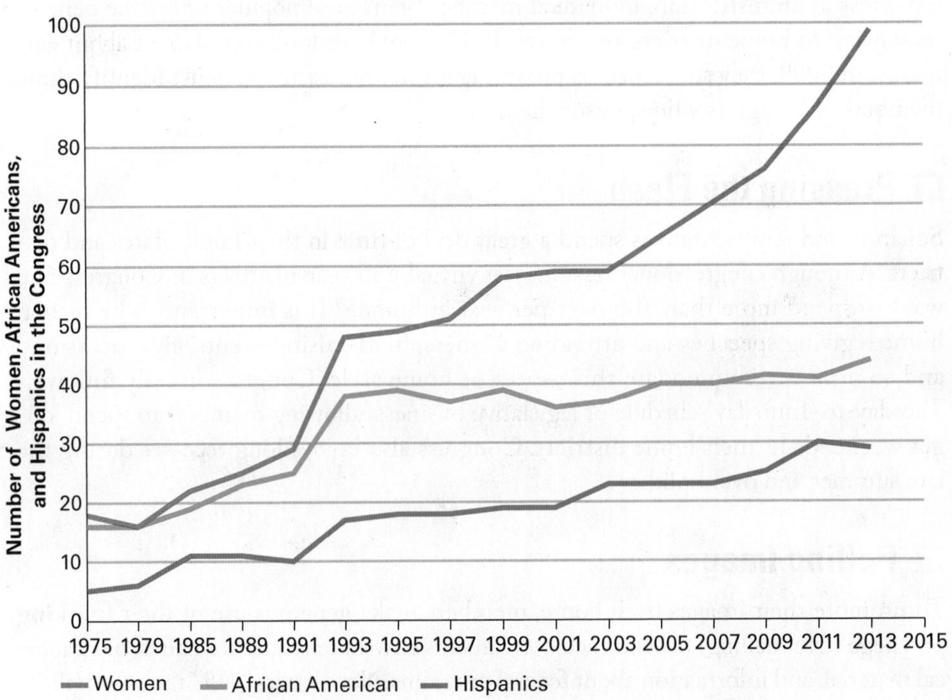

FIGURE 10.7 MINORITY VOICES: WOMEN, AFRICAN AMERICANS, AND HISPANICS IN THE CONGRESS

Although the Congress is still far short of "looking like America," in recent years, the number of African American, Hispanic, and female members has risen noticeably. Particularly impressive advances were made in the 1992 elections, following court-ordered creation of "majority-minority" districts.

chances of attaining their personal goals—getting reelected and influencing policy—are enhanced if they cooperate with each other.

Party Organizations in Congress

The Democratic and Republican party organizations within the House of Representatives and the Senate are the principal bases for organizing Congress (see Figure 10.7). The leadership of each house of Congress, although nominally elected by the entire chamber, is actually chosen by secret ballot of the members of each party at a "conference" or caucus (see Table 10.2).

The parties and their leaders do not choose congressional candidates, nor can they deny them renomination; all members of Congress are responsible for their own primary and general election success. But party leadership in each chamber can help incumbents achieve their reelection goals. Each party in the House and Senate sponsors a campaign committee that channels some campaign funding to party members seeking reelection.

Majority status confers great power on the party that controls the House and the Senate. The majority party chooses the leadership in each body, selects the chairs of every committee, and ensures that every committee has a majority of members from the majority party. In other words, if Democrats are in the majority in either the House or the Senate or both, Democrats will occupy all leadership positions, chair every committee, and constitute a majority of the members of every committee; of course, the Republicans enjoy the same advantages when they capture a majority of either body. Majority-party members in each house even take in more campaign contributions than minority members.[32]

TABLE 10.2 WHO OVERSEES WHAT?: COMMITTEES IN CONGRESS

Senate	
Agriculture, Nutrition, and Forestry	Homeland Security and Environmental Affairs
Appropriations	Indian Affairs Judiciary
Armed Services	Rules and Administration
Banking, Housing, and Urban Affairs	Small Business and Entrepreneurship
Budget	Veterans Affairs
Commerce, Science, and Transportation	Select Aging
Energy and Natural Resources	Select Ethics
Environment and Public Works	
Finance	Select Intelligence
Foreign Relations	
Health, Education, Labor and Pensions	
House	
Agriculture	Judiciary
Appropriations	Natural Resources
Armed Forces	Rules
Budget	Science, Space, and Technology
Energy and Commerce	Small Business
Education and the Workforce	
Ethics	
Financial Services	Transportation and Infrastructure
	Veterans Affairs
Homeland Security	Ways and Means
House Administration	Select Intelligence
International Relations	
Joint Committees	
Joint Economic Committee	Joint Committee on the Library
Joint Taxation	Commission on Security and Cooperation in Europe
Joint Committee on Printing	

Speaker of the House
Presiding officer of the House of Representatives.

majority leader
In the House, the majority-party leader and second in command to the Speaker, in the Senate, the leader of the majority party.

minority leader
In both the House and Senate, the leader of the opposition party.

whips
In both the House and Senate, the principal assistants to the party leaders and next in command to those leaders.

☐ In the House: "Mr. Speaker"

In the House of Representatives, the key leadership figure is the **Speaker of the House**, who serves as both presiding officer of the chamber and leader of the majority party. In the House, the Speaker has many powers. The Speaker decides who shall be recognized to speak on the floor and rules on points of order (with advice from the parliamentarian), including whether a motion or amendment is germane (relevant) to the business at hand. The Speaker decides to which committees new bills will be assigned and can schedule or delay votes on a bill. The Speaker appoints members of select, special, and conference committees and names majority-party members to the Rules Committee. And the Speaker controls both patronage jobs and office space in the Capitol. Although the norm of fairness requires the Speaker to apply the rules of the House consistently, the Speaker is elected by the majority party and is expected to favor that party.

☐ House Leaders and Whips

The Speaker's principal assistant is the **majority leader**. The majority leader formulates the party's legislative program in consultation with other party leaders and steers the program through the House. The majority leader also must persuade committee leaders to support the aims of party leaders in acting on legislation before their committees. Finally, the majority leader arranges the legislative schedule with the cooperation of key party members.

The minority party in the House selects a **minority leader** whose duties correspond to those of the majority leader, except that the minority leader has no authority over the scheduling of legislation. The minority leader's principal duty has been to organize the forces of the minority party to counter the legislative program of the majority and to pass the minority party's bills. It is also the minority leader's duty to consult ranking minority members of House committees and to encourage them to adopt party positions and to follow the lead of the president if the minority party controls the White House.

In both parties, **whips** assist leaders in keeping track of the whereabouts of party members and in pressuring them to vote the party line. Whips are also responsible for ensuring the attendance of party members at important roll calls and for canvassing their colleagues on their likely support for or opposition to party-formulated legislation. Finally, whips are involved regularly in the formation of party policy and the scheduling of legislation.

☐ In the Senate: "Mr. President"

The Constitution declares the vice president of the United States to be the presiding officer of the Senate. But vice presidents seldom exercise this senatorial responsibility, largely because the presiding officer of the Senate has very little power. Having only 100 members, the Senate usually does not restrict debate and has fewer scheduling constraints than the House. The only significant power of the vice president is the right to cast a deciding vote in the event of a tie on a Senate roll call. In the usual absence of the vice president, the Senate is presided over by a *president pro tempore*. This honorific position is traditionally granted by the majority party to one of its senior stalwarts. The job of presiding over the Senate is so boring that neither the vice president nor the president pro tempore is found very often in the chamber. Junior senators are often asked to assume the chore. Nevertheless, speeches on the Senate floor begin with the salutation "Mr. President," referring to the president of the Senate, *not* the president of the United States.

☐ Senate Majority and Minority Leaders

Senate leadership is actually in the hands of the Senate majority leader, but the Senate majority leader is not as powerful in that body as the Speaker is in the House. With fewer members, all of whom perceive themselves as powerful leaders, the Senate is less hierarchically organized than the House. The Senate majority leader's principal power is scheduling the business of the Senate and recognizing the first speaker in floor debate. To be effective in policy making, the majority leader must be skilled in interpersonal persuasion and communication. Moreover, in the media age, the Senate majority leader must also be a national spokesperson for the party, along with the Speaker of the House. The minority-party leader in the Senate represents the opposition in negotiations with the majority leader over Senate business.

☐ Career Paths Within Congress

Movement up the party hierarchy in each house is the most common way of achieving a leadership position.[33] The traditional succession pattern in the House is from whip to majority leader to Speaker. In the Senate, Republicans and Democrats frequently resort to election contests in choosing their party leaders, yet both parties have increasingly adopted a two-step succession route from whip to leader.[34]

☐ Leadership PACs

House and Senate leaders, and members who aspire to become leaders, often ingratiate themselves to their colleagues by distributing campaign funds to them. In recent years, *leadership PACs* have proliferated on Capitol Hill.

Party Fortunes in Congress

10.4 Evaluate the successes and failures of the two parties in Congress.

For 40 years (1954–94) Democrats enjoyed an advantage in congressional races; in fact, the Democratic Party was said to have a "permanent majority" in the House of Representatives (see Figure 10.6). The Republican victory in the congressional election of 1994 was widely described as a political "earthquake." It gave the GOP control of the House for the first time in four decades, as well as control of the Senate. Republicans remained in control of the House and the Senate (except for a brief period in 2001–2002) until the 2006 elections. Democrats strengthened their control in both houses in the 2008 elections. In 2010 Republicans won back their House majority, and maintained it in 2012. Democrats have maintained a Senate majority since the 2006 election.

☐ The Historic Democratic Party Dominance of Congress

The historic Democratic dominance of Congress was attributed to several factors. First, over those four decades more voters identified themselves with the Democratic Party than with the Republican Party. Party identification plays a significant role in congressional voting; it is estimated that 75 percent of those who identify themselves with a party cast their vote for the congressional candidate of their party.[35] Second, the Democratic advantage was buttressed by the fact that many voters considered local rather than national conditions when casting congressional votes. Voters may have wanted to curtail *overall* federal spending in Washington (a traditional Republican promise), but they wanted a member of Congress who would "bring home the bacon." Although both Republican and Democratic congressional candidates usually promised to bring money and jobs to their districts, Democratic candidates appeared more creditable on such promises because their party generally supported large domestic-spending programs. Finally, Democratic congressional candidates over those years enjoyed the many advantages of incumbency. It was thought that only death or retirement would dislodge many of them from their seats.

☐ The Republican "Revolution" of 1994–98

The sweeping Republican victory in 1994 surprised many analysts.[36] The GOP's capture of control of both houses of Congress for the first time in 40 years raised conservatives' hopes of a "revolution" in public policy. The new Republican House Speaker,

The Game, the Rules, the Players

Leader Versus Leader

Madam Speaker, Nancy Pelosi

Nancy Pelosi was the first woman in the history of the U.S. Congress to serve as Speaker of the House. Following the Democratic victory in the 2006 congressional elections, her Democratic colleagues in the House promoted her from minority leader, a post she had held since 2001, to Speaker. Pelosi returned to the minority leader's post in 2011; she is currently the second-longest serving party leader in the House ever, behind Democrat Sam Rayburn (1941–61). Pelosi has represented her San Francisco district since her first election to the Congress in 1987.

Pelosi comes from a highly political family. Her father, Thomas D'Alesandro, served five terms in Congress and later 12 years as mayor of Baltimore. Pelosi's brother also served as mayor of Baltimore. Young Nancy grew up in Washington and graduated from that city's Trinity College in 1962. She served as a congressional intern to her Maryland senator. She married Paul Pelosi, moved to his hometown of San Francisco, and raised five children. Prior to her election to Congress, she served on the National Democratic Committee. Her daughter Alexandra Pelosi is a documentary film maker (*Journeys with George, Diary of a Political Tourist*).

In her years in Congress, Pelosi built a solid liberal reputation, serving on the powerful Appropriations Committee. But Pelosi's real strength within the Democratic Party has long been her fund-raising ability. Her San Francisco district is the home of some of the party's wealthiest individual donors, and Democrats across the nation rely heavily upon money from California. Pelosi created her own leadership PAC and has handed out millions to her Democratic colleagues. She spends relatively little on her own reelection races in her heavily Democratic district. She is regularly reelected with an astonishing 80 percent of the vote.

Pelosi's reign as Speaker was described as especially hard driving. She was quoted as saying: "Tell them what you're going to do. Do it. And then tell them what you did." She had the responsibility for guiding the Obama agenda through the House. Republicans accused her of sidetracking their amendments and "ramming down the throat" of House members thousands of unread pages of legislation. The Republican capture of control of the House in the congressional elections of 2010 brought an end to her rule as Speaker.

Mr. Speaker, John Boehner

John Boehner assumed the speakership of the House after one of the most dramatic seat swings in American electoral history. Republicans picked up 63 seats to end unified Democratic control of the national government after just two years, and immediately set about opposing the fiscal agenda of the Obama administration. Boehner was elected to the House from Ohio in 1990, defeating scandal-plagued incumbent Buzz Lukens in the GOP primary in the Cincinnati-based 8th Congressional District. He has been reelected 10 times in the 8th, which includes suburban and rural townships between Cincinnati and Dayton. Elevated to Republican floor leader when the Republicans lost control of the House in 2007, Boehner became the third Republican speaker since 1995 and the first speaker from Ohio in 80 years.

As a freshman member of a group called "the Gang of Seven," Boehner challenged a variety of corrupt practices in the House, including the habit of members routinely overdrawing their House bank checking accounts, "dine-and-ditching" at the House restaurant, and converting office-purchased stamps to cash at the post office, an act of embezzlement. Boehner was an instrumental member of the 1994 GOP takeover of the House, helping author the "Contract with America" that led to Newt Gingrich's elevation to the speakership. In 1995, Boehner became the Republican Conference Chairman, a leadership position immediately behind the majority floor leader and the majority whip, but was ousted in 1998 by Representative J. C. Watts (R-OK). Boehner subsequently returned to the leadership as a committee chairman and later scored an upset election as Republican majority floor leader in February 2006, when he defeated majority whip (and acting floor leader) Roy Blount (R-MO) to succeed Tom DeLay (R-TX). (DeLay had been forced to resign Congress upon being indicted on money laundering charges.)

As speaker, Boehner inherited a raucous House. His leadership team of Eric Cantor (R-VA) and Kevin McCarthy (R-CA) are "movement" conservatives who have been actively involved in recruiting the current majority. A sizeable number of freshman lawmakers were elected with support from Tea Party voters in the Republican Primary. Boehner has to balance member demands when negotiating fiscal policy with the White House. The presence of a large, fiscally conservative caucus has allowed Boehner to take hard bargaining positions with the White House on a variety of issues, including deficit reduction, taxes, and new environmental legislation such as "cap and trade" emissions regulations. It has also presented difficulties for Boehner in constructing compromises that are generally conservative but too centrist for either Tea Party Republicans or progressive Democrats.

QUESTIONS

1. **Are John Boehner's and Nancy Pelosi's paths to power very different?**
2. **How do their past experiences shape their aspiration to power?**
3. **Do their past experiences shape their approaches to leadership?**

Newt Gingrich, was the acknowledged leader of the revolution, with Republican Senate Majority Leader Bob Dole in tow. The revolution fizzled out when Congress failed to successfully recommend either a constitutional amendment to impose congressional term limits, or a balanced budget amendment.

Republicans maintained their majority in 1996 and 1998 despite Bill Clinton's reelection and the subsequently unpopular impeachment effort directed at Clinton. Republicans had expected to benefit from Clinton's acknowledged sexual misconduct and the House impeachment investigation. But voters generally sided with Clinton. Speaker Gingrich subsequently resigned from Congress, and House GOP conference chairman John Boehner (R-OH) was ousted from the party leadership. The new speaker, Denny Hastert (R-IL) ushered in an era of low profile, highly partisan leadership that sought to anchor policy in the house on conservative principles. He would hold the speaker's gavel until the GOP lost the majority in the 2006 elections.

☐ An Era of Close Majorities in the Twenty-First Century

The congressional elections of 2000 reflected the close partisan division of the nation. Republicans barely held on to their majority in the House of Representatives, and produced a 50–50 tie in the Senate. The critical tie-breaking vote of Republican Vice President Dick Cheney was mooted when in May 2001, Vermont Republican Jim Jeffords declared himself an Independent, but gave his vote to the Democrats in the Senate, flipping control of the chamber and delivering control of the Senate floor and Senate committees to the opposition.

Democratic control was short-lived. The September 11, 2001, attacks sent George Bush's approval ratings skyrocketing, and the domestic political agenda was redefined in the context of terrorism and war. Republicans were cautious in their politicization of the conflict, but most of the rhetorical opposition to the growing drumbeat for war with Iraq in late 2002 came from Democratic politicians. President George W. Bush designated himself as "campaigner in chief," traveling about the country raising campaign money for Republican House and Senate candidates. His continuing high approval rating throughout 2002 made him a highly welcomed campaigner in districts and states across the nation. In his campaign stops, Bush talked about the war on terrorism and his need for "allies" in the Congress. President Bush appeared to influence just enough voters in key districts and states to reverse the historic pattern of presidential midterm congressional losses (Clinton and the Democrats pulled off the same feat in 1998). The GOP won back control of the U.S. Senate and strengthened its majority in the House of Representatives.

In 2004, President Bush again appeared to help GOP congressional candidates across the country. Republicans increased their control of the Senate from 51 to 55. They picked up several seats of retiring older-generation Southern Democrats and defeated the Democratic Senate floor leader for reelection in South Dakota. The 2004 election also made the Senate slightly more "diverse": African American Barack Obama was elected from Illinois, and Hispanic Mel Martinez was elected from Florida. In the House, Republicans also increased their margin of control. President Bush was quick to claim that winning the White House, the Senate, and the House of Representatives meant that the American People supported his "agenda" and that he had "political capital" he intended to expend. However, the war in Iraq rapidly eroded President Bush's popularity and led to the election of a Democratic-controlled House and Senate in the 2006 midterm congressional elections.

Republican congressional control had lasted 12 years. Democrats were anxious to advance their agenda. They failed to end the war in Iraq—the president is the commander in chief, so there was little Congress could do by itself to compel changes in strategy in Iraq other than engage in the politically risky move of cutting off funds for the war while American troops were in the field. The one major act of bipartisanship was the passage of the $700 billion Troubled Assets Recovery Program (TARP) during the closing weeks of the 2008 general election.

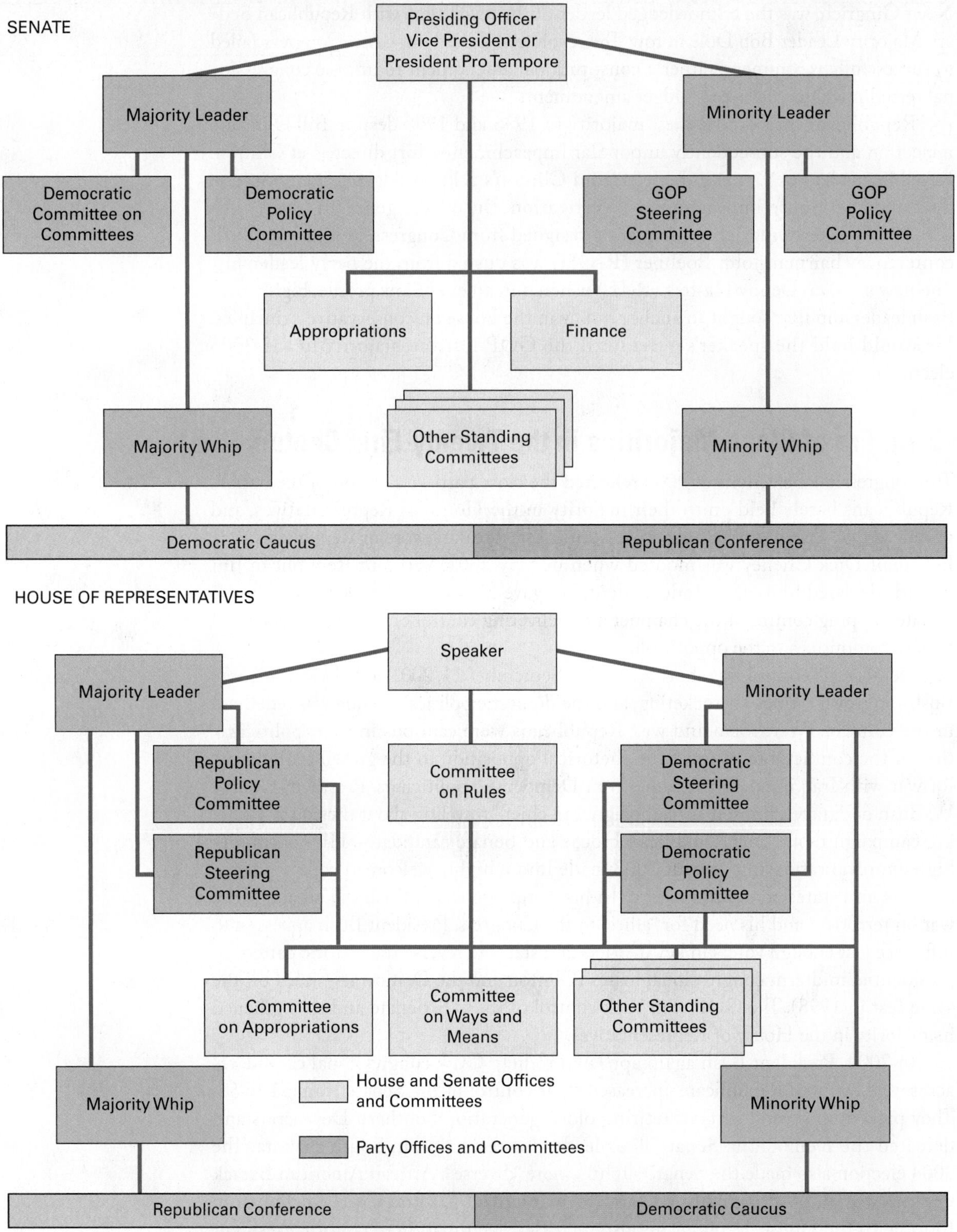

SENATE

Presiding Officer
Vice President or
President Pro Tempore

Majority Leader

Minority Leader

Democratic Committee on Committees

Democratic Policy Committee

GOP Steering Committee

GOP Policy Committee

Appropriations

Finance

Majority Whip

Other Standing Committees

Minority Whip

Democratic Caucus

Republican Conference

HOUSE OF REPRESENTATIVES

Speaker

Majority Leader

Minority Leader

Republican Policy Committee

Committee on Rules

Democratic Steering Committee

Republican Steering Committee

Democratic Policy Committee

Committee on Appropriations

Committee on Ways and Means

Other Standing Committees

House and Senate Offices and Committees

Party Offices and Committees

Majority Whip

Minority Whip

Republican Conference

Democratic Caucus

FIGURE 10.8 HOW IT WORKS: ORGANIZING THE CONGRESS

Aside from naming the Speaker of the House as head of that body's operations and the vice president as overseer of Senate deliberations, the Constitution is silent on the organization of Congress. Political parties have filled this gap: both majority and minority parties have their own leadership, which governs the appointment of members to the various committees, where much of the work of Congress actually takes place.

Democrats won unified control of government in 2008, including a 60-vote filibuster-proof majority in the Senate. Republicans cautioned voters that this outcome would give unchecked power to Democrats "Obama, Pelosi, and Reid"—referring to the new president, the Speaker of the House, and the Senate majority leader. United party government does not always ensure complete cooperation between the House, Senate, and White House—a lesson learned by the Obama administration, which

What Do You Think?

Why Do Voters Reelect Members of an Unpopular Congress?

Congress is the least popular branch of government. Public approval of Congress is well below that of the presidency and the Supreme Court. What accounts for this lack of popularity? The belief that members of Congress "spend more time thinking about their own political futures than they do in passing legislation" may contribute to this sentiment.

But public disapproval of Congress may also arise from a misunderstanding of democratic government. "People do not wish to see uncertainty, conflicting options, long debate, competing interests, confusion and compromised imperfect solutions.... They often see a patently unrealistic form of democracy."[a]

But in an apparent paradox, most voters *approve of their own* representative (see figure below), even while Congress itself is the object of popular distrust and ridicule. A majority of voters believe that their own representatives "deserve reelection." In late 2011, 33 percent of voters told Gallup they were seriously considering not sending their own representative back. Still, 90.7% of incumbents were reelected in 2012.

This apparent contradiction is explained in part by differing expectations: Americans expect Congress to deal with national issues, but they expect their own representatives to deal with local concerns and even personal problems. Members of Congress understand this concern and consequently devote a great deal of their time to constituent service. Indeed, many members of Congress try to dissociate themselves from Congress, attacking Congress in their own campaigns and contributing to negative images of the institution. Finally, the national news media are highly critical of Congress, but local news media frequently portray local members of Congress in a more favorable light.

QUESTIONS

1. Can you redesign Congress or congressional elections to make the institution more popular with the public?
2. If so, how so?
3. If not, why not?
4. Is it possible for Congress to be popular, given the issues it confronts?

[a]John R. Hibbing and Elizabeth Theiss-Morse. *Congress as Public Enemy.* Cambridge, Eng.: Cambridge University Press, 1995, p. 147. Also cited by Roger H. Davidson and Walter J. Oleszak. *Congress and Its Members.* 9th ed. Washington, D.C.: CQ Press, 2004, p. 487. Updated from Gallup.com.

Q. Do you approve of the way the U.S. Congress is handling its job?

Q. Do you approve or disapprove of the way the representative from your own congressional district is handling his or her job?

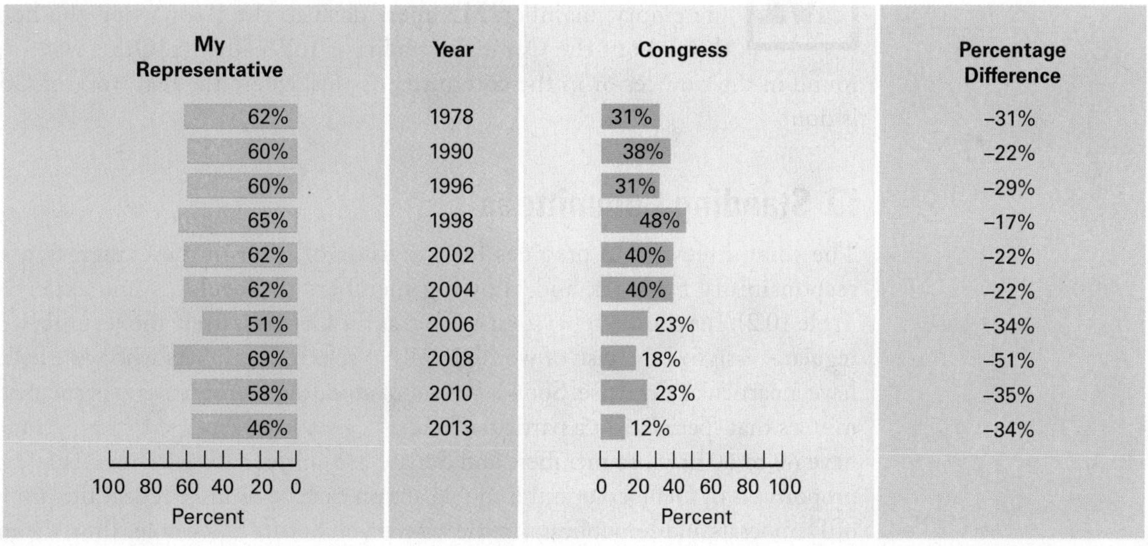

took 18 months to pass what was supposed to be the centerpiece legislative accomplishment of the term: health care reform. President Obama presented Congress with a lengthy legislative agenda, including a massive economic stimulus package, huge budget increases and increases in deficit spending, a comprehensive transformation of the nation's health care system, new regulations governing the nation's financial institutions, and a broad new "cap and trade" program in which the federal government would set overall national ceilings on carbon emissions. The president succeeded in getting many of his proposals enacted into law.

10.1

10.2

10.3

10.4

10.5

10.6

10.7

10.8

standing committee
Permanent committee of the House or Senate that deals with matters within a specified subject area.

ranking minority member
The minority-party committee member with the most seniority.

Democratic control of Congress and the White House seemed to inspire unity and discipline among Republicans. On key votes, the GOP was united in opposition to Obama-backed proposals; they complained bitterly that important legislation had been "rammed through" by the majority.

☐ Republican Resurgence

The midterm elections of 2014 reenergized the Republican Party. The GOP, already in control of the House of Representatives, reinforced their majority in that body to a number not seen in decades. More importantly, they captured control of the Senate, turning a 55–45 Democratic majority into a 54–46 Republican majority, a surprising pickup of nine seats. Republican control of both houses of Congress appeared to render President Barack Obama a "lame duck" for his final two years in office. Yet Obama remained defiant, promising again to do by executive order whatever Congress failed to do by law. But Republicans were now in a position to pass legislation and send it to the president's desk for signature or veto. The policy divisions between the parties, and between the president and Congress, promised to be more clearly defined through 2016.

In Committee

10.5 Characterize the legislative work of committees and assess the repercussions of committees for distribution of power in Congress.

Much of the real work of Congress is done in committee. The floor of Congress is often deserted; C-SPAN focuses on the podium, not the empty chamber. Members dash to the floor when the bell rings throughout the Capitol signaling a roll-call vote. Otherwise, they are found in their offices or in the committee rooms, where the real work of Congress is done.

☐ Standing Committees

The committee system provides for a division of labor in the Congress, assigning responsibility for work and allowing members to develop some expertise (see Table 10.2). The committee system is as old as the Congress itself: the very first Congress regularly assigned the task of wording bills to selected members who were believed to have a particular expertise. Soon a system of **standing committees**—permanent committees that specialize in a particular area of legislation—emerged. House committees have 40 to 60 or more members and Senate committees 15 to 25 members each. The proportions of Democrats and Republicans on each committee reflect the proportions of Democrats and Republicans in the House and Senate as a whole. Thus, the majority party has a majority of members on every committee, and every committee is chaired by a member of the majority party. The minority membership on each committee is led by the **ranking minority member**, the minority-party committee member with the most seniority.

The principal function of standing committees is the screening and drafting of legislation. With 8,000 to 10,000 or more bills introduced each session, the screening function is essential. The standing committees are the gatekeepers of Congress; less than 10 percent of the legislation introduced will pass the Congress. With rare exceptions, bills are not submitted to a vote by the full membership of the House or Senate without prior approval by the majority of a standing committee. Moreover, committees do not merely sort through bills assigned to them to find what they like.

Rather, committees—or more often their subcommittees—draft (write) legislation themselves. Committees may amend, rewrite, or write their own bills. Committees are "little legislatures" within their own policy jurisdictions. Each committee guards its own policy jurisdiction jealously; jurisdictional squabbles between committees are common.

□ The Pecking Order of Committees

The most powerful standing committees, and, therefore, the most sought-after committee assignments, are the Appropriations committees in the House and the Senate. These committees hold the federal purse strings, arguably Congress's most important power. These committees are closely followed in influence and desirability by the Ways and Means Committee in the House and the Senate Finance Committee; these committees must pass on all tax matters, as well as Social Security and Medicare financing. In the House, the Rules Committee is especially powerful, owing to its control over floor consideration of every bill submitted to the full House. The Senate Judiciary Committee is especially powerful because of its influence over all presidential nominees to the federal judiciary, including Supreme Court justices. The Senate Foreign Relations Committee is also a highly valued assignment. Perhaps the *least* desirable committee assignments are those on the Senate Ethics Committee and the House Standards of Official Conduct Committee; members of these ethics panels are obliged to sit in judgment of their own colleagues.

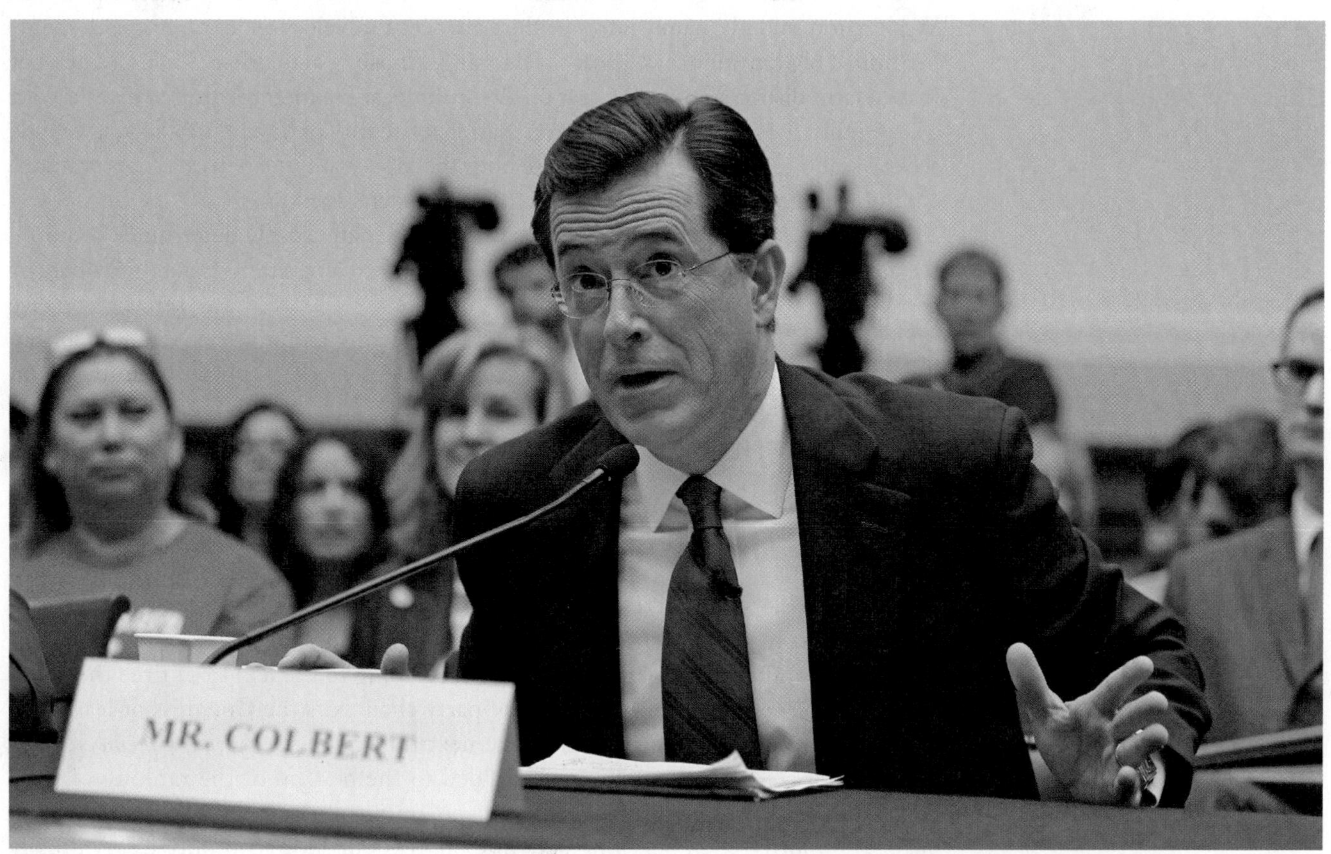

CELEBRITY TESTIMONY

A common scene the past decade has been celebrity entertainers testifying before Congress. Here, Stephen Colbert, host of the Colbert Report, testifies before a House Judiciary Subcommittee, on migrant worker conditions in the United States.

10.1

10.2

10.3

10.4

10.5

10.6

10.7

10.8

subcommittees

Specialized committees within standing committees; subcommittee recommendations must be approved by the full standing committee before submission to the floor.

seniority system

Custom whereby the member of Congress who has served the longest on the majority side of a committee becomes its chair and the member who has served the longest on the minority side becomes its ranking member.

Decentralization and Subcommittees

Congressional **subcommittees** within each standing committee further decentralize the legislative process. At present, the House has about 90 subcommittees and the Senate about 70 subcommittees, each of which functions independently of its full committee (see Table 10.2). Subcommittees have fixed jurisdictions (for example, the House International Relations Committee has subcommittees on Africa, Asia and the Pacific, international economic policy, international operations and human rights, and the Western Hemisphere); they meet and schedule their own hearings; and they have their own staffs and budgets. However, bills recommended by a subcommittee still require full standing-committee endorsement before being reported to the floor of the House or Senate. Full committees usually, but not always, ratify the decisions of their subcommittees.

Chairing a committee or subcommittee gives members of Congress the opportunity to exercise power, attract media attention, and thus improve their chances of reelection. Often committees have become "fiefdoms" over which their chairs exercise complete control and jealously guard their power. This situation allows a very small number of House and Senate members to block legislation. Many decisions are not really made by the whole Congress. Rather, they are made by subcommittee members with a special interest in the policy under consideration. Although the committee system may satisfy the desire of members to gain power, prestige, and reelection opportunities, it weakens responsible government in the Congress as a whole.

Committee Membership

Given the power of the committee system, it is not surprising that members of Congress have a very keen interest in their committee assignments. Members strive for assignments that will give them influence in Congress, allow them to exercise power in Washington, and ultimately improve their chances for reelection. For example, a member from a big city may seek a seat on Banking, Housing, and Urban Affairs, a member from a farm district may seek a seat on Agriculture, and a member from a district with a large military base may seek a seat on National Security or Veterans Affairs. Everyone seeks a seat on Appropriations, because both the House and the Senate Appropriations committees have subcommittees in each area of federal spending.[37]

Party leadership in both the House and the Senate largely determines committee assignments. These assignments are given to new Democratic House members by the Democratic Steering and Policy Committee; new Democratic senators receive their assignments from the Senate Democratic Steering Committee. New Republican members receive their committee assignments from the Republican Committee on Committees in both houses. The leadership generally tries to honor new members' requests and improve their chances for reelection, but because incumbent members of committees are seldom removed, openings on powerful committees are infrequent.

Seniority

Committee chairs are elected in the majority-party caucus. But the **seniority system** governs most movement into committee leadership positions. The seniority system ranks all committee members in each party according to the length of time they have served on the committee. If the majority-party chair exits the Congress or leaves the committee, that position is filled by the next *ranking majority-party member*. New members of a committee are initially added to the bottom of the ranking of their party; they climb the seniority ranking by remaining on the committee and accruing years of seniority. Members who stay in Congress but "hop" committees are usually placed at the bottom of their new committee's list.

The seniority system has a long tradition in the Congress. The advantage is that it tends to reduce conflict among members, who otherwise would be constantly engaged in running for committee posts. It also increases the stability of policy direction in committees over time. Critics of the system note, though, that the seniority system grants greater power to members from "safe" districts—districts that offer little

DEFENDING OBAMACARE

Health and Human Services Secretary Kathleen Sebelius appears before the Congress to testify on the implementation problems with the Patient Protection Affordable Care Act.

electoral challenge to the incumbent. (Historically in the Democratic Party, these districts were in the conservative South, and opposition to the seniority system developed among liberal northern Democrats. But in recent decades, many liberal Democrats gained seniority and the seniority system again became entrenched.) The seniority rule for selecting committee chairs has been violated on only a few notable occasions.

drafting a bill
Actual writing of a bill in legal language.

markup
Line-by-line revision of a bill in committee by editing each phrase and word.

Committee Hearings

The decision of a congressional committee to hold public hearings on a bill or topic is an important one. It signals congressional interest in a particular policy matter and sets the agenda for congressional policy making. Ignoring an issue by refusing to hold hearings on it usually condemns it to oblivion. Public hearings allow interest groups and government bureaucrats to present formal arguments to Congress. Testimony comes mostly from government officials, lobbyists, and occasional experts recommended by interest groups or committee staff members. Hearings are usually organized by the staff under the direction of the chair. Staff members contact favored lobbyists and bureaucrats and schedule their appearances. Committee hearings are regularly listed in the *Washington Post* and are open to the public. Indeed, the purpose of many hearings is not really to inform members of Congress but instead to gain publicity and rally public support behind an issue or a bill. The media are the real target audience of many public hearings, with committee members jockeying in front of the cameras for a "sound bite" on the evening news.

Markup

Once hearings are completed the committee's staff is usually assigned the task of writing a report and **drafting a bill.** The staff's bill generally reflects the chair's policy views. But the staff draft is subject to committee **markup**, a line-by-line consideration

discharge petition
Petition signed by at least 218 House members to force a vote on a bill within a committee that opposes it.

rule
Stipulation attached to a bill in the House of Representatives that governs its consideration on the floor, including when and for how long it can be debated and how many (if any) amendments may be appended to it.

closed rule
Rule that forbids adding any amendments to a bill under consideration by the House.

restricted rule
Rule that allows only specified amendments to be added to a bill under consideration by the House.

open rule
Rule that permits unlimited amendments to a bill under consideration by the House.

of the wording of the bill. Markup sessions are frequently closed to the public in order to expedite work. Lobbyists are forced to stand in the hallways, buttonholing members as they go into and out of committee rooms.

It is in markup that the detailed work of lawmaking takes place. Markup sessions require patience and skill in negotiation. Committee or subcommittee chairs may try to develop consensus on various parts of the bill, either within the whole committee or within the committee's majority. In marking up a bill, members of a subcommittee must always remember that the bill must pass both in the full committee and on the floor of the chamber. Although they have considerable freedom in writing their own policy preferences into law, especially on the details of the legislation, they must give some consideration to the views of these larger bodies. Consultations with party leadership are not infrequent.

Most bills die in committee. Some are voted down, but most are simply ignored. Bills introduced simply to reassure constituents or interest groups that a representative is committed to "doing something" for them generally die quietly. But House members who really want action on a bill can be frustrated by committee inaction. The only way to force a floor vote on a bill opposed by a committee is to get a majority (218) of House members to sign a **discharge petition.** Out of hundreds of discharge petition efforts, only a few dozen have succeeded.[38] The Senate also can forcibly "discharge" a bill from committee by simple majority vote; but because senators can attach any amendment to any bill they wish, there is generally no need to go this route.

On the Floor

10.6 Outline the process for a bill that has reached the floor and identify the obstacles to its passage.

A favorable "report" by a standing committee of the House or Senate places a bill on the "calendar." The word *calendar* is misleading, because bills on the calendar are not considered in chronological order and many die on the calendar without ever reaching the floor.

House Rules Committee

Even after a bill has been approved by a standing committee, getting it to the floor of the House of Representatives for a vote by the full membership requires favorable action by the Rules Committee. The Rules Committee acts as a powerful "traffic cop" for the House. In order to reach the floor, a bill must receive a rule from the Rules Committee. The Rules Committee can kill a bill simply by refusing to give it a rule. A **rule** determines when the bill will be considered by the House and how long the debate on the bill will last. More important, a rule determines whether amendments from the floor will be permitted and, if so, how many. A **closed rule** forbids House members from offering any amendments and speeds up consideration of the bill in the form submitted by the standing committee. A **restricted rule** allows certain specified amendments to be considered. An **open rule** permits unlimited amendments. Most key bills are brought to the floor of the House with fairly restrictive rules. In recent sessions, about three-quarters of all bills reaching the floor were restricted, and an additional 10 to 15 percent were fully closed. Only a few bills were open.[39]

Killer Amendments

Sometimes conflicts over legislation cannot be resolved in committee. Attempts to advance hostile amendments increase when Congress is more polarized. In a polarized Congress, therefore, it is more important to the majority to maintain control of the debate and the amendments that can be offered. Hostile amendments that are designed to significantly alter the intent of legislation to guarantee failure on final passage are called **"killer" amendments**. Killer amendments exploit "wedges" on an issue that force members to vote for the amendment for fear of constituency backlash. There have been just 26 killer amendments placed on legislation in the past half century, but they account for one-fifth of all final passage failures on legislation referred out of the Rules Committee.[40]

"killer" amendments
An amendment to a piece of legislation that is designed to ensure the defeat of the bill on final vote.

☐ Senate Floor Traditions

The Senate has no rules committee, but relies instead on a **unanimous consent agreement** negotiated between the majority and minority leader to govern consideration of a bill. The unanimous consent agreement generally specifies when the bill will be debated, what amendments will be considered, and when the final vote will be taken. However, as the name implies, a single senator can object to a unanimous consent agreement and thus hold up Senate consideration of a bill. Senators do not usually do so, because they know that a reputation for obstructionism will imperil their own favorite bills at a later date. Once accepted, a unanimous consent agreement is binding on the Senate and cannot be changed without another unanimous consent agreement. To get unanimous consent, Senate leaders must consult with all interested senators. Unanimous consent agreements have become more common in recent years as they have become more specific in their provisions.

unanimous consent agreement
Negotiated by the majority and minority leaders of the Senate, it specifies when a bill will be taken up on the floor, what amendments will be considered, and when a vote will be taken.

The Senate cherishes its tradition of unrestricted floor debate. Senators may speak as long as they wish or even try to **filibuster** a bill to death by talking nonstop and tying up the Senate for so long that the leadership is forced to drop the bill in order to go on to other work. Senate rules also allow senators to place a "hold" on a bill, indicating their unwillingness to grant unanimous consent to its consideration. Debate may be ended only if *60* or more senators vote for **cloture**, a process of petition and voting that limits the debate. A cloture vote requires a petition signed by 16 senators; two days must elapse between the petition's introduction and the cloture vote. If cloture passes, then each senator is limited to one hour of debate on the bill. But getting the necessary 60 votes for cloture is often difficult (see *What Do You Think*? Should Senate Actions Be Thwarted by Filibusters?).

filibuster
Delaying tactic by a senator or group of senators, using the Senate's unlimited debate rule to prevent a vote on a bill.

cloture
Vote to end debate—that is, to end a filibuster—which requires a three-fifths vote of the entire membership of the Senate.

Senate floor procedures also permit unlimited amendments to be offered, even those that are not germane to the bill. A **rider** is an amendment to a bill that is not germane to the bill's purposes.

rider
Amendment to a bill that is not germane to the bill's purposes.

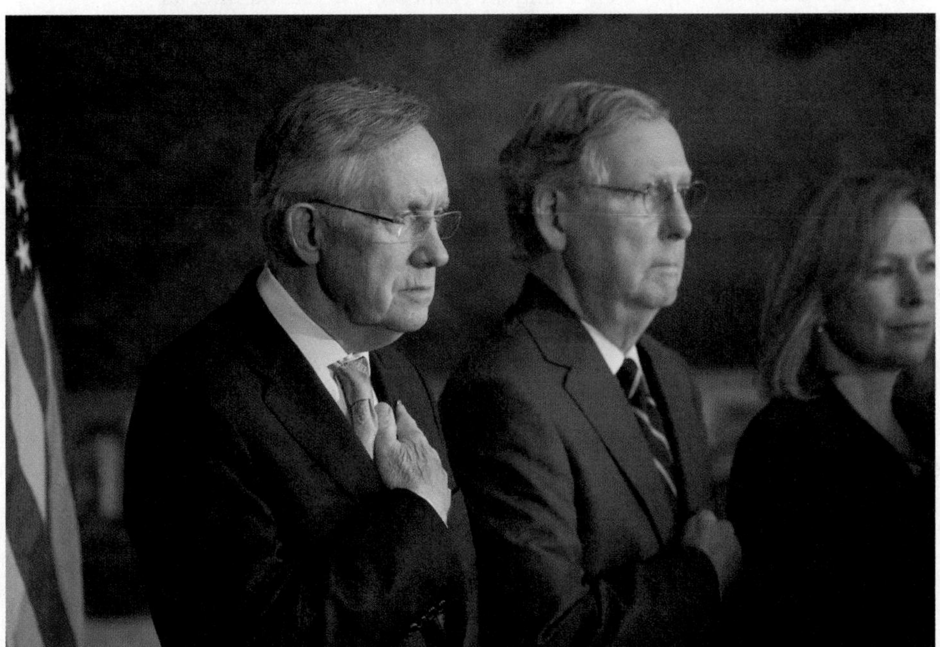

RUNNING THE FLOOR
Senate floor leaders Sen. Harry Reid (D-Nev.) and Mitch McConnell (R-Ky.)

What Do You Think?

Should Senate Actions Be Thwarted by Filibusters?

On March 6, 2013, Sen. Rand Paul (R-KY) took to the floor of the Senate to speak on the nomination of John Brennan to be head of the Central Intelligence Agency. Paul spoke expansively, starting at just after lunch and not ending for nearly 13 hours. His speech brought attention to the controversial use of unmanned drones by the Obama administration.

Four hours into his speech, it transformed into a filibuster. Senate Majority Leader Harry Reid (D-NV) sought unanimous consent to end debate and vote on Brennan's nomination. Senator Paul objected, and his speech continued, supported by friendly senators who asked him supporting questions, often several minutes in length. It would be the ninth-longest speech in U.S. Senate history. Such a filibuster might not happen again. Eight months later, the Senate majority voted to get rid of filibusters on executive and judicial nominations.

The Origin of the Filibuster

From the earliest days of the Senate the idea of "unlimited debate" was enshrined in its rules and customs. A procedural decision by the senate's presiding officer, Vice President Aaron Burr, left no need to "move the previous question" in Senate procedure. In doing so, Burr accidentally left open the ability of a single senator to block a vote by speaking and refusing to yield.

For over a century, the "filibuster" was honored as "insurance against the will of a majority of states being imposed over the wishes of a minority of states." Liberals and progressives in the Senate came to loathe the filibuster rule. President Woodrow Wilson persuaded the Senate to adopt a "cloture rule," which called for cutting off debate with a two-thirds vote of senators present and voting. For decades afterward, liberals in both parties sought to completely eliminate the filibuster, as it became an important tool of opponents of civil rights legislation. (The Civil Rights Act of 1964 was passed only after a successful cloture vote ended a southern filibuster.) In 1975, the Senate lowered the vote requirement for cloture to 60—that is, three-fifths rather than two-thirds.

The Path to the "Nuclear Option"

Since 2000, filibusters became more common. Partisanship in the Senate intensified. Democrats and Republicans both regularly threaten filibusters to stop legislation and nominations they oppose. This means that controversial Bills, judicial nominees, or executive appointments could not get through the Senate without 60 votes, rather than a simple majority of 51.

Through 2013, 168 presidential nominees had ever been filibustered. During the Obama administration, a record 82 were filibustered—nearly half ever. Frustrated with GOP delaying tactics on nominations and lacking the 60 votes to invoke "cloture," the Democratic majority changes the rule for ending debate on nominees so that just 51 votes were required.

It was called the "nuclear option." Senate Democrats had used the filibuster to thwart judicial nominees submitted by Republican President George W. Bush. They argued against threats by the then-majority Republicans to eliminate the filibuster rule for judicial nominations. A temporary truce was fashioned, and the filibuster was saved. No such truce was available in November 2013, and now the filibuster remains only for legislation and confirmation of Supreme Court nominees.

Polling data show Americans support the filibuster rule. When asked by CNN in 2005, "As you may know, the filibuster is a Senate procedure which has been used to prevent the Senate from passing controversial legislation or confirming controversial appointments by the president, even if a majority of senators support that action. A vote of at least 60 senators out of 100 is needed to end a filibuster. Do you favor or oppose the use of the filibuster in the U.S. Senate?" the response from the public was 56 percent in favor, 39 percent opposed.

The Longest Filibusters of the Senate, as of January 2014:
1. Sen. Strom Thurmond (D-S.C.) (1957): 24 hours, 18 minutes
2. Alphonse D'Amato (1986): 23:30
3. Sen. Wayne Morse (I-Ore.) (1953): 22:26
4. Sen. Robert La Follette (R-Wis.) (1908): 18:23
5. Sen. William Proxmire (D-Wis.) (1981): 16:12
6. Huey P. Long (1935): 15:30
7. Alphonse D'Amato (1992): 15:14
8. Robert Byrd (1964): 14:13
9. Rand Paul (2013): 12:52

QUESTIONS

1. How does the filibuster work?
2. How has the filibuster been changed over time?
3. Do you trust the majority of either party enough to give it a Senate without a filibuster?

SOURCES: *The Polling Report* (2009). www.pollingreport.com; Robert Schlesinger. "Poll Shows Few Americans Understand Senate Filibuster Rules." *U.S. News & World Report*, January 29, 2010, accessed at http://www.usnews.com/opinion/blogs/robert-schlesinger/2010/01/29/poll-shows-few-americans-understand-senate-filibuster-rules.

These Senate traditions of unlimited debate and unrestricted floor amendments give individual senators considerably more power over legislation than individual representatives enjoy. In the last two decades, senators have increasingly used **holds** to stop legislation. A hold happens when a senator informs his party floor leader that a piece of legislation should not be brought up to the floor for consideration, or the senator will filibuster the bill. Holds are not formally recognized in Senate rules, but they place the majority leader "on notice" that a filibuster could happen if the senate tries to move on the legislation.

hold
An informal request by a senator to his party's leader that a piece of legislation not be brought to the floor for consideration.

roll-call vote
Vote of the full House or Senate at which all members' individual votes are recorded and made public.

conference committees
Meetings between representatives of the House and Senate to reconcile differences over provisions of a bill passed by both houses.

Floor Voting

The key floor votes are usually on *amendments* to bills rather than on their final passage. Indeed, "killer amendments" are deliberately designed to defeat the original purpose of the bill. Other amendments may water down the bill so much that it will have little policy impact. Thus the true policy preferences of senators or representatives may be reflected more in their votes on amendments than their vote on final passage. Members may later claim to have supported legislation on the basis of their vote on final passage, even though they earlier voted for amendments designed to defeat the bill's purposes.

Members may also obscure their voting records by calling for a voice vote—simply shouting "aye" or "nay"—and avoiding recording of their individual votes. In contrast, a **roll-call vote** involves the casting of individual votes, which are reported in the *Congressional Record* and are available to the media and the general public. Electronic voting machines in the House allow members to insert their cards and record their votes automatically. The Senate, truer to tradition, uses no electronic counters.

Conference Committees

The Constitution requires that both houses of Congress pass a bill with identical wording. However, many major bills pass each house in different forms, not only with different wording but sometimes with wholly different provisions. Occasionally the House or the Senate will resolve these differences by reconsidering the matter and passing the other chamber's version of the bill. But about 15 percent of the time, serious differences arise and bills are assigned to **conference committees** to reach agreement on a single version for resubmission to both houses. Conference committees are temporary, with members appointed by the leadership in each house, usually from among the senior members of the committees that approved the bills.

Conference committees can be very powerful. Their final bill is usually (although not always) passed in both houses and sent to the president for approval. In resolving differences between the House and the Senate versions, the conference committee makes many final policy decisions. Although conference committees have considerable leeway in striking compromises, they focus on points of disagreement and usually do not change provisions already approved by both houses. Figure 10.9 summarizes the lawmaking process.

Decision Making in Congress

10.7 Assess the influences on congressional decision making.

How do senators and representatives decide how they will vote on legislation? From an almost limitless number of considerations that go into congressional decision making, a few factors recur across a range of voting decisions: party loyalty, presidential support or opposition, constituency concerns, interest-group pressures, and the personal values and ideologies of members themselves.

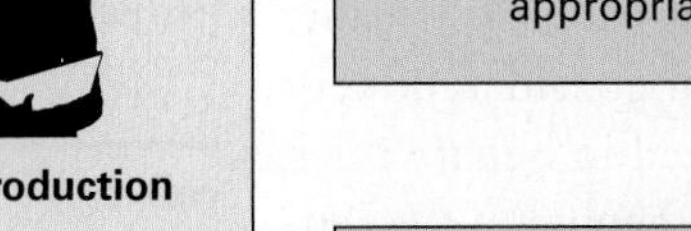

	HOUSE	SENATE
Bill Introduction	Bill is introduced and assigned to a committee, which refers it to the appropriate subcommittee.	Bill is introduced and assigned to a committee, which refers it to the appropriate subcommittee.
Subcommittee Hearings	**Subcommittee** Subcommittee holds hearings and "marks up" the bill. If the bill is approved in some form, it goes to the full committee.	**Subcommittee** Subcommittee holds hearings, debates provisions and "marks up" the bill. If a bill is approved, it goes to the full committee.
Committee Action	**Committee** Full committee considers the bill. If the bill is approved in some form, it is "reported" to the full House and placed on the House calendar.	**Committee** Full committee considers the bill. If the bill is approved in some form, it is "reported" to the full Senate and placed on the Senate calendar.
Floor Action	**Rules Committee** Rules Committee issues a rule to govern debate on the floor. Sends it to the full House. **Full House** Full House debates the bill and may amend it. If the bill passes and it is in a form different from the Senate version, it must go to a conference committee.	**Leadership** Majority and minority leaders negotiate "unanimous consent" agreements scheduling full Senate debate and vote on the bill. **Full Senate** Full Senate debates the bill. Senate may amend it. If the bill passes and is in a form different from the House version, it must go to a conference committee.
Conference Action	**Conference Committee** Conference committee of senators and representatives meets to reconcile differences between bills. When agreement is reached, a compromise bill is sent back to both the House and the Senate.	
Presidential Decision	**President** President signs or vetoes the bill. Congress can override a veto by a two-thirds majority vote in both the House and Senate.	

FIGURE 10.9 RUNNING THE GAUNTLET: HOW A BILL BECOMES A LAW

This diagram depicts the major hurdles a successful bill must overcome in order to be enacted into law. Few bills introduced travel this full path; less than 10 percent of bills introduced are passed by Congress and sent to the president for approval or veto. Bills fail at every step along the path, but most die in committees and subcommittees, usually from inaction rather than from being voted down.

Party Voting

Party appears to be the most significant influence on congressional voting. **Party votes** are roll-call votes on which a majority of voting Democrats oppose a majority of voting Republicans. Traditionally, party votes occurred on roughly *half* of all roll-call votes in Congress. Partisanship in Congress, as reflected in the percentage of party votes, rose during the 1990s but may be moderating somewhat today.

Party unity is measured by the percentage of Democrats and Republicans who stick by their party on party votes. Party unity for both the Democratic and Republican parties has remained at fairly constant levels (85–95 percent) in both the House and the Senate over the past 10 years. This is higher than in previous decades, when party unity was regularly 50–60 percent in both the House and Senate. Greater party unity suggests increased partisan polarization in Congress.

party votes
Majority of Democrats voting in opposition to a majority of Republicans.

party unity
Percentage of Democrats and Republicans who stick with their party on party votes.

bipartisanship
Agreement by members of both the Democratic and the Republican parties.

divided party government
One party controls the presidency while the other party controls one or both houses of Congress.

Sources of Partisanship

Why do Democrats and Republicans in Congress vote along party lines? First of all, the Democratic Party has become more liberal and the Republican Party has become more conservative over the years. Conservative Democrats, once very common in southern politics, are rapidly disappearing. At the same time, the ranks of liberal Republicans, mostly from the Northeast, have thinned. Second, the decline in voter turnout, especially in primary elections, has added to the importance of well-organized and ideologically motivated groups. In primary elections, Republicans must be more concerned with pleasing conservative activists (e.g., the Christian Coalition, National Right-to-Life Committee, National Rifle Association, and so on), and Democrats must be more concerned with pleasing liberal groups (National Education Association; American Federation of State, County, and Municipal Employees; Sierra Club; and so on). And third, the rising costs of campaigning make members ever more dependent upon the financial support of these interests.

Conflict between the parties occurs frequently on domestic social and economic issues—welfare, housing and urban affairs, health, business regulation, taxing, and spending. Traditionally, **bipartisanship** was the goal of both presidents and congressional leaders on foreign and defense policy issues. Since the Vietnam War, however, Democrats in the Congress have been more critical of U.S. military involvements (and defense spending in general) than have Republicans.

Presidential Support or Opposition

Presidential influence in congressional voting is closely tied to party lines. Presidents almost always receive their greatest support from members of their own party. Both Democratic and Republican presidents can usually depend on 80 percent or more of their party's members in Congress to support their position. When the president's party controls both houses of Congress, the result should be fairly smooth sailing for the president's agenda. In contrast, policy gridlock is often associated with **divided party government**—either a Democratic president and a Republican-controlled House or Senate, or a Republican president and a Democratic-controlled House or Senate.

Presidents often "go over the heads" of Congress, using the media to appeal directly to the people to support presidential programs and force Congress to act. The president has better access to the media than Congress has. But such threats and appeals can only be effective when (1) the president himself is popular with the public, and (2) the issue is one about which constituents can be made to feel intensely.

Presidents can also threaten to veto legislation. This threat, expressed or implied, confronts congressional leaders, committee chairs, and sponsors of a bill with several options. They must decide whether to (1) modify the bill to overcome the president's objections; (2) try to get two-thirds of both houses to commit to overriding the

The Game, the Rules, the Players

Rise of the Hispanic Conservatives: Marco Rubio and Ted Cruz

The growing Hispanic population has the attention of Democrats and Republicans. As Hispanics grow in the electorate, so to do Hispanic politicians. Most Hispanic politicians are Democrats, but the most prominent recent Hispanic officeholders are conservative Republicans. Two of the most prominent are Marco Rubio (R-FL) and Ted Cruz (R-TX). Both are Cuban Americans, the children of expatriate Cuban exiles who fled Cuba in the 1950s, and are known to have presidential ambitions.

Senator Marco Rubio was born in 1971; he attended the University of Florida and then law school in Miami. After working for the first Cuban member of Congress, Miami's Ileana Ros-Lehtinen, Rubio was elected as a city commissioner. He then went on to the Florida House of Representatives, where he became the first Cuban speaker of any state legislature. As speaker, he innovated the "idearaiser" approach to rebranding modern conservatism and published a book, *100 Innovative Ideas for Florida's Future.* In 2009, when Rubio sought an open U.S. Senate seat held by retiring senator Mel Martinez, he attracted the support of Tea Party conservatives, and defeated establishment Governor Charlie Crist and Democratic U.S. Rep. Kendrick Meek in the general election.

Rubio's ascension initially resembled the emergence in 2004 of Illinois state senator Barack Obama as a national figure. Rubio is frequently mentioned among Republican presidential contenders. But his support of Immigration reform has hurt him among conservative Republicans who refer to it as "amnesty."

Ted Cruz traveled a different path in politics. Born in Canada in 1970 to his Texan parents, Cruz went to high school in Katy; he attended Princeton and Harvard Law (with Barack Obama) and was founder of the *Harvard Latino Law Review.* He later clerked for Chief Justice William Rehnquist. From 2003 to 2008, he served as solicitor general of Texas. In 2011, Cruz announced for the U.S. Senate seat opened up by the retirement of fellow Republican Kay Bailey Hutchison. Cruz defeated the establishment Republican front-runner, Lieutenant Governor David Dewhurst, in a runoff election, winning 57 percent to 43 percent despite Dewhurst's substantial financial advantage.

As a lawmaker, Cruz has been more visible and more effective—or disruptive—than Rubio. Cruz has repeatedly bucked leadership and his own caucus to push a conservative fiscal agenda. He played a strong role in forcing the government shutdown of 2013, in order to force a defunding of the Affordable Care Act and to call attention to profligate government spending.

Like Rubio, Cruz has presidential ambitions and has spent time stumping the early primary states of Iowa and South Carolina and speaking to conservative groups such as the Conservative Political Action Conference.

The Republicans need Hispanics. Hispanic voters are a potentially important voting block for both parties. They typically vote Democratic, but according to the Gallup Poll, half of Hispanics identify as independents but only one in eight claim to be Republicans.

QUESTIONS

1. **Describe the differences in the career paths to the U.S. Senate for Marco Rubio and Ted Cruz.**
2. **Do you think that high-profile Hispanic leaders will help Republicans win more Hispanic vote? Why or why not?**
3. **What do the victories of Ted Cruz and Marco Rubio, over "establishment" Republicans, tell us about the changing Republican Party?**

constituency
The votes in a legislator's home district.

threatened veto; or (3) pass the bill and dare the president to veto it, and then make a political issue out of the president's opposition. Historically, fewer than 5 percent of vetoes have been overridden by the Congress. Unless the president is politically very weak (as Richard Nixon was during the Watergate scandal), Congress cannot count on overriding a veto. If members of Congress truly want to address an important problem and not just define a political issue, they must negotiate with the White House to write a bill the president will sign.

☐ Constituency Influence

Constituency influence in congressional voting is most apparent on issues that attract media attention and discussion and generate intense feelings among the general public. If many voters in the home state or district know about an issue and have intense feelings about it, members of Congress are likely to defer to their constituents' feeling, regardless of the position of their party's leadership or even their own personal feelings. Members of Congress from *safe seats* seem to be just as attuned to the interests of their constituents as members from competitive seats.

Constituencies may also exercise a subtle influence by conditioning the personal views of members. Many members were born, raised, and continue to live in the towns they represent; over a lifetime, they have absorbed and internalized the views of their communities. Moreover, some members of Congress feel an obligation to represent their constituents' opinions even when they personally disagree.

However, members of Congress have considerable latitude in voting against their constituents' opinions if they choose to do so. Constituents, as noted earlier, lack information about most policy issues and the voting records of their senators and representatives. Even when constituents know about an issue and feel strongly about it, members can afford to cast a "wrong" vote from time to time. A long record of home style politics—casework, pork barreling, visits, public appearances, and so on—can isolate members of Congress from the wrath generated by their voting records. Only a long string of "wrong" votes on issues important to constituents is likely to jeopardize an incumbent.

trustees
Legislators who feel obligated to use their own best judgment in decision making.

delegates
Legislators who feel obligated to present the views of their home constituents.

Interest-Group Influence

Inside the Washington Beltway, the influence of interest groups, lobbyists, and fundraisers on members of Congress is well understood. This influence is seldom talked about back home or on the campaign trail, except perhaps by challengers. Lobbyists have their greatest effects on the *details* of public policy. Congressional decisions made in committee rooms, at markup sessions, and around conference tables can mean billions of dollars to industries and tens of millions to individual companies. Pressures from competing interest groups can be intense as lobbyists buttonhole lawmakers and try to win legislative amendments that can make or break business fortunes. One of the most potent tools in the lobbyist's arsenal is money. The prohibitive cost of modern campaigning has dictated that dollars are crucial to electoral victory, and virtually all members of Congress spend more time than they would like courting it, raising it, and stockpiling it for the next election.

Voters may be wrong when they think that all members of Congress are crooks, but they are not far off the mark when they worry that their own representatives may be listening to two competing sets of constituents—the real constituents back home in the district and the "cash constituents" who come calling in Washington.[41]

Personal Values

It was the eighteenth-century English political philosopher Edmund Burke, himself a member of Parliament, who told his constituents; "You choose a member indeed; but when you have chosen him, he is not a member of Bristol, but he is a member of *Parliament*." Burke defended the classic notion of representatives as **trustees** who feel obligated to use their own best judgment about what is good for the nation as a whole. In this theory, representatives are not obligated to vote the views of their constituents. This notion contrasts with the idea of representatives as **delegates** who feel obligated to vote according to the views of "the folks back home" regardless of their own personal viewpoint. Most legislators *claim* to be trustees, perhaps because of the halo effect generated by the independence implied in the term.

Democratic political philosophers have pondered the merits of trustee versus delegate representation over the centuries, but the question only rarely arises in actual congressional deliberations. In many cases, members' own personal views and those of their constituents are virtually identical. Even when legislators perceive conflicts between their own views and those of their constituents, most attempt to find a compromise between these competing demands rather than choose one role or another exclusively.[42] The political independence of members of Congress—their independence from party, combined with the ignorance of their constituents about most policy issues—allows members to give great weight to their own personal ideologies in voting.

WHIPPING VOTES FOR THE MAJORITY

Now in the Senate, former Representative Roy Blunt (R-Mo) had the job of lining up support for legislation ('whipping votes') on behalf of his leadership team.

Congressional Customs, Norms, and Ethics

10.8 Outline the customs and norms of Congress and evaluate the mechanisms for ensuring ethical behavior in Congress.

Over time, institutions develop customs and norms of behavior to assist in their functioning. These are not merely quaint and curious folkways; they promote the purposes of the institution. Congressional customs and norms are designed to help members work together, to reduce interpersonal conflict, to facilitate bargaining and promote compromise.

Civility

Traditionally, members of Congress understood that uncivil behavior—expressions of anger, personal attacks on character, ugly confrontations, flaming rhetoric—undermined the lawmaking function. Indeed, civility was encouraged by the long-standing custom of members of Congress referring to each other in elaborately courteous terms: "my distinguished colleague from Ohio," "the honorable representative from Pennsylvania," and the like. By custom, even bitter partisan enemies in Congress were expected to avoid harsh personal attacks on each other. The purpose of this custom was to try to maintain an atmosphere in which people who hold very different opinions can nevertheless function with some degree of decorum. Unfortunately, many of these customs and norms of behavior are breaking down. Individual ambition and the drive for power and celebrity have led to a decline in courtesy, cooperation, and respect for traditional norms. One result is that it has become increasingly difficult for Congress to reach agreement on policy issues. Another result is that life in Congress is increasingly tedious, conflict-filled, and unpleasant (see *A Conflicting View*: Congress Can Act Responsibly on Occasion).

The Demise of the Apprenticeship Norm

Years ago, "the first rule"[43] of congressional behavior was that new members were expected to be seen but not heard on the floor, to be studious in their committee work, and to be cooperative with party leaders. But the institutional norm of apprenticeship has been swept aside as increasingly ambitious and independent senators and representatives arrive on Capitol Hill. Today new members of Congress feel free to grab the spotlight on the floor, in committee, and in front of television cameras. "The evidence is clear, unequivocal, and overwhelming: the [apprenticeship] norm is simply gone."[44] Nevertheless, experienced members are more active and influential in shaping legislation than are new members.[45]

Specialization and Deference

The committee system encourages members of Congress to specialize in particular policy areas. Even the most independent and ambitious members can perceive the advantage of developing power and expertise in an area especially relevant to their constituents. Traditionally, members who developed a special expertise and accumulated years of service on a standing committee were deferred to in floor proceedings. These specialists were "cue givers" for party members when bills or amendments were being voted on. Members are still likely to defer to specialized committee members when the issues are technical or complicated, or when the issue is outside of their own area of policy specialization, but deference is increasingly rare on major public issues.

A Conflicting View

Do Scandals Really Hurt?

From time to time politicians get in trouble. They take bribes. Or, they get involved in sexual relationships with workers, interns, or prostitutes. Perhaps they are caught using illegal drugs, or stealing from the public.

There are numerous examples. No fewer than 20 scandals involving congressmen have been made public since 2001. The scandals include money laundering and racketeering (Rep. Rick Renzi, R-AZ, three years in prison); drunk driving (Sen. Mike Crapo, R-ID—six-month suspended sentence); cocaine possession (Rep. Trey Radel, R-Fla., one year probation); fraud (Rep. Jesse Jackson Jr., D-IL, one year in prison); bribery (Rep. William Jefferson, D-LA, 13 years in prison); and tax evasion (Sen. Ted Stevens, R-Alaska, charges later dismissed).

Some scandals are more far reaching. Lobbyist Jack Abramoff created one of the most complex and far-reaching mechanism for directing gifts and benefits to politicians. Abramoff was one of the architects of the "K Street Project," which created a "pay-to-play" system where campaign money and other benefits including postelective employment flowed from lobbyists to congressional staffers and members of Congress. Former majority leader Tom DeLay (R-TX) was the only elected official formally caught up in the probe that led to the conviction of Abramoff and several congressional staff.

Most members who get caught up in scandals resign office. In the examples mention here, all but one resulted in the politician quitting office. Only Senator Stevens and Rep. Jefferson sought reelection, and both later lost because of their scandals.

Scandals have electoral consequences. In 1992 twenty-four members of the House were defeated for reelection because of a scandal involving the US House bank. Two years later, powerful Congressman Dan Rostenkowski (D-Ill.), was defeated for reelection in 1994 because he was involved in an embezzlement and money laundering scandal involving the U.S. House post office.

When an incumbent has a scandal, voters are less likely to vote for them in the next election. Some get beat. Others are merely weakened. Election analysts say scandals cause a "brand crisis" for incumbents. They lose votes, and also attract other people to vote against them. This damage is usually greatest immediately after a scandal. But even if a member survives the first reelection after a scandal, they may not be in the clear. The damage can endure for up to four years before a politician recovers.

QUESTIONS

1. Does a sex scandal or a financial scandal make you less likely to vote for a politician? Which one concerns you more?
2. Are you more concerned about misconduct of politicians in their personal life, even if it is criminal conduct, or misconduct in office? Why?

Bargaining

Bargaining is central to the legislative process. Little could be achieved if individual members were unwilling to bargain with each other for votes both in committees and on the floor. A willingness to bargain is a longstanding functional norm of Congress.

Members of Congress are not expected to violate their consciences in the bargaining process. On the contrary, members respect one another's issues of conscience and receive respect in return. On most issues, however, members can and do bargain their support. "Horse trading" is very common in committee work. Members may bargain in their own personal interest, in the interests of constituents or groups, or even in the interests of their committee with members of other committees. Because most bargaining occurs in a committee setting, it is seldom a matter of public record. The success and reputation of committee chairs largely depend on their ability to work out bargains and compromises.

Bargaining can assume different forms. Explicit trade-offs such as "If you vote for my bill, I'll vote for yours" are the simplest form of bargaining, but implicit understandings may be more common. Members may help other members in anticipation of receiving reciprocal help at some future unspecified time. Moreover, representatives who refuse to cooperate on a regular basis may find little support for their own bills. Mutual "back scratching" allows members to develop a reservoir of IOUs for the future. Building credit is good business for most members; one can never tell when one will need help in the future.

10.1

10.2

10.3

10.4

10.5

10.6

10.7

10.8

A Conflicting View

Congress Can Act Responsibly on Occasion

Congress is not always mired in partisanship, squabbling, and gridlock. On occasion, it acts responsibly in the national interest. Indeed, consider the following congressional landmarks in U.S. history:

Louisiana Purchase (1803)

President Thomas Jefferson offered to purchase from France nearly 830,000 square miles between the Mississippi and the Rockies for $15 million—about three cents an acre. There is no constitutional provision authorizing the federal government to buy foreign territory, but the Senate, accepting Jefferson's broad interpretation of the Constitution, approved the purchase. The House appropriated the money to consummate the deal. On December 29, 1803, the United States took possession of North America's heartland, doubling the nation's size with territory that would eventually comprise 13 states.

Homestead Act (1862)

This Civil War–era legislation allowed any family head or adult male to claim 160 acres of government land for a $10 registration fee and a promise to live there continuously for five years. It opened up the midwestern United States for immediate settlement. The act drew thousands of English, Irish, Germans, Swedes, Danes, Norwegians, and Czechs to the United States, pushing settlement farther west.

Social Security Act (1935)

The act was designed to secure "the men, women, and children of the nation against certain hazards and vicissitudes of life," explained President Franklin Roosevelt. The act's best-known measure is the social insurance system that provides monthly checks to the elderly.

National Labor Relations Act (1935)

By declaring that workers had a right to join unions and bargain collectively with employers for pay raises and improved working conditions, the act spurred the growth of the nation's major industrial unions. Labor's Magna Carta also provided workers with the legal weapons to improve plant conditions and protect themselves from employer harassment.

G.I. Bill of Rights (1944)

The G.I. Bill of Rights, known officially as the Serviceman's Readjustment Act of 1944, offered to pay tuition for college or trade education to ex–World War II servicemen. It also mandated that they receive up to $500 a year for tuition, books, and supplies. Nearly 8 million veterans took advantage of this first G.I. Bill, and American higher education expanded rapidly as a result. Veterans also made use of the bill's guaranteed mortgages and low interest rates to buy new homes in the suburbs, inspiring a housing boom.

Truman Doctrine (1947) and NATO (1949)

The Truman Doctrine initiated U.S. resistance to expansion of the Soviet Union into Western Europe following World War II, and the NATO treaty has provided the framework for European security for half a century. Truman declared to a joint session of Congress, "I believe that it must be the policy of the United States to support free people who are resisting attempted subjugation by armed minorities or by outside pressures."

Federal Highway Act (1956)

President Dwight D. Eisenhower was right when he said, "More than any single action by the government since the end of the war, this one would change the face of America." The most expensive public-works project in U.S. history, the highway act built the 41,000-mile nationwide interstate highway system.

Civil Rights Act of 1964

Only Congress could end racial segregation in privately owned businesses and facilities. It did so by an overwhelming vote of both houses in the Civil Rights Act of 1964. Injustices endure, but the end of segregated restaurants, theaters, and drinking fountains provided new opportunities for African Americans and helped change white attitudes. In addition, Title VII of the act prohibits gender discrimination and serves as the legal bulwark for women's rights.

Voting Rights Act of 1965

President Lyndon B. Johnson signed this act in the same room in the Capitol where Abraham Lincoln had penned the Emancipation Proclamation. This legislation guaranteed all Americans the most fundamental of all rights—the right to vote. Between the 1964 and 1968 presidential elections, black voter registration increased 50 percent across the nation, even in the reluctant Southern states, giving African Americans newfound political clout.

Medicare and Medicaid (1965)

Congress amended the Social Security Act of 1935 to provide for national health insurance for the aged (Medicare) and for the poor (Medicaid). In 2003 (28 years later) Congress added prescription drug coverage to Medicare.

QUESTIONS

1. Are there any examples given where, when congress acts responsibly, they make government smaller?
2. What issue do you think Congress should be acting on, to be responsible, but doesn't? What is it? Why?

Bargaining requires a certain kind of integrity. Members of Congress must stick to their agreements. They must not consistently ask too high a price for their cooperation. They must recognize and return favors. They must not renege on promises. They must be trustworthy.

Conference-committee bargaining is essential if legislation acceptable to both houses is to be written. Indeed, it is expected that conferees from each house will bargain and compromise their differences. "Every House-Senate conference is expected to proceed via the methods of 'give and take,' 'trading back and forth,' 'pulling and hauling,' 'horse-trading and compromise,' 'splitting the difference,' etc."[46]

logrolling
Bargaining for agreement among legislators to support each other's favorite bills, especially projects that primarily benefit individual members and their constituents.

10.1

10.2

10.3

10.4

10.5

10.6

10.7

10.8

☐ Logrolling

Logrolling is mutual agreement to support projects that primarily benefit individual members of Congress and their constituencies. Logrolling is closely associated with pork-barrel legislation. Yet it can occur in virtually any kind of legislation. Even interest-group lobbyists may logroll with each other, promising to support each other's legislative agendas.

☐ Leader–Follower Relations

Because leaders have few means of disciplining members, they must rely heavily on their bargaining skills to solicit cooperation and get the work of Congress accomplished. Party leaders can appeal to members' concerns for their party image among the voters. Individual majority members want to keep their party in the majority—if for no other reason than to retain their committee and subcommittee chairs. Individual minority members would like their party to win control of their house in order to assume the power and privileges of committee and subcommittee chairs. Party leaders must appeal to more than partisanship to win cooperation, however.

To secure cooperation, leaders can grant—or withhold—some tangible benefits. A member of the House needs the Speaker's support to get recognition, to have a bill called up, to get a bill scheduled, to see to it that a bill gets assigned to a preferred

Who's Getting What?

Slicing a Shrinking Pie

Congress is incapable of balancing its budget. In Republican hands, Congress has cut taxes while increasing spending. In Democratic hands, Congress has increased spending while not increasing taxes. Both parties have a half-century-long history of contributing to the national debt.

The core tension in the budget process for Congress involves four parts:

(1)Taxes: Republicans want to cut them, Democrats want to raise them.

(2) Entitlements: There are government programs that people contribute money to now that they must be allowed to participate in, by law, in the future. Liberals want to expand them; conservatives want to cut them. These are the bulk of the federal budget.

(3) Defense spending: The United States has the largest defense budget in the world. Liberals want to cut it; conservatives want to increase it.

(4) The debt: Should you borrow from the future to pay for today's government?

Congress and the White House are engaged in a battle for moral and fiscal supremacy on these issues. The result has been deadlock since 2011. The creation of a Joint Select Committee on Deficit Reduction in the summer of 2011 failed to find a solution to this problem, but instead only delayed a crisis until 2013. Then, automatic, across-the-board cuts in government programs created by the committee (called the sequester) set up a series of confrontations, but did not lead to a solution. Government spent the next two years operating with less money, running 90 days at a time on a series of continuing resolutions.

QUESTIONS

1. How should Congress decide where to make budget cuts?
2. Do you think it is morally defensible to borrow money to pay for government?

10.1

10.2

10.3

10.4

10.5

10.6

10.7

10.8

gridlock
Political stalemate between the executive and legislative branches arising when one branch is controlled by one major political party and the other branch by the other party.

committee, to get a good committee assignment, and to help a bill get out of the Rules Committee, for example.

Party leaders may also seek to gain support from their followers by doing favors that ease their lives in Washington, advance their legislative careers, and help them with their reelection. Favors from party leaders oblige members to respond to leaders' requests at a later time. Members themselves like to build up a reservoir of good feeling and friendship with the leadership, knowing that eventually they will need some favors from the leadership.

☐ Gridlock

Congress is often criticized for legislative **gridlock**—the failure to enact laws, including appropriations acts, that are widely perceived to have merit. Indeed, much of the popular frustration with Congress relates to gridlock arising from policy and budgetary stalemates. Research has suggested that the following factors contribute to congressional gridlock:[47]

- Divided party control of the presidency and Congress
- Divided party control of the House and Senate
- Greater ideological polarization (liberal versus conservative) of the parties
- In the Senate, the willingness of members to filibuster against a bill, requiring 60 votes to overcome the opposition

In contrast, the factors that appear to lessen gridlock and encourage significant legislative accomplishment include:

- Unified party control of the presidency, House, and Senate
- Larger numbers of moderates among Democrats and Republicans in Congress (as opposed to larger numbers of strong liberals and strong conservatives)
- Overwhelming public support for new legislation

Note that the constitutional structure of American government—separation of powers and checks and balances, as well as bicameralism—plays a major role in gridlock, as does the American two-party system (see *Compared to What?* The Parliamentary System). Overcoming gridlock requires a willingness of members of both parties in both houses of Congress, as well as the White House, to bargain and compromise over legislation. And it requires strong public opinion in support of congressional action.

☐ Congressional Ethics

Although critics might consider the phrase *congressional ethics* to be an oxymoron, the moral climate of Congress today is probably better than in earlier eras of American history. Nevertheless, Congress as an institution has suffered from well-publicized scandals that continue to prompt calls for reform.

☐ Ethics Rules

Congress has an interest in maintaining the integrity of the institution itself and the trust of the people. Thus Congress has established its own rules of ethics. These rules include the following:

- **Financial disclosure.** All members must file personal financial statements each year.
- **Honoraria.** Members cannot accept fees for speeches or personal appearances.
- **Campaign funds.** Surplus campaign funds cannot be put to personal use.
- **Gifts.** Members may not accept gifts worth more than $50 (with annual increases in these amounts for inflation).

Compared to What?

The Parliamentary System

The parliamentary system of government evolved over centuries in Great Britain, and many countries have emulated the British model. Indeed, most of the democracies in the world today are parliamentary systems.

In a parliamentary system, power is concentrated in the legislature. The executive heads—cabinet ministers—are members of the parliament (MPs) and chosen by the majority party in that body. (If no party wins a majority in the parliament, then a coalition of parties must agree on who will serve as prime minister and who will serve in the cabinet.) The head of the majority party is the nation's prime minister; the prime minister serves as both chief executive and chief legislator. The prime minister (PM) and the cabinet are referred to as "the government." Most parliamentary systems have a head of state, often a figurehead, either a president elected by the parliament or a hereditary monarchy as in Great Britain.

There is no real separation of powers in a parliamentary system. The government remains in power as long as it commands a majority in the parliament. Only a parliamentary vote of no-confidence can oust a government from power, an unlikely event inasmuch as the government is composed of the majority party members of the parliament. The government can call new elections for parliament whenever it wishes; but by constitutional tradition in Great Britain elections must be held at least every five years.

What are the advantages of a parliamentary system? It is easier to pass legislation. The party in power controls both the government and the parliament itself. Any legislation that is introduced by the government must pass the parliament; a defeat would constitute a vote of no-confidence. There is no real possibility of legislative–executive gridlock. Another advantage is that an unpopular government can be ousted at any time. There is no need to wait up to four years to rid the nation of an unpopular chief executive. The majority party itself can replace the prime minister, or members of the majority can desert their party, forcing a new election. Finally, parliaments tend to have a more adversarial style of debate in open sessions of the parliament. Parliamentary debates are more fun than sessions of the U.S. House of Representatives or Senate.

Among the disadvantages of a parliamentary system is that the head of the government is not directly elected by the people, as in the U.S. presidential system. Rather, the prime minister is designated by the majority party in the parliament. The voters may know in advance of an election who heads the contending parties and vote for the party with the preferred leader, but voters do not directly elect the prime minister.

From the American perspective, perhaps the most serious criticism is that a parliamentary system offers no real checks and balances. Legislative and executive powers are concentrated in the majority party in the parliament. The fact that Great Britain has an unwritten constitution, a constitution that can be changed by the parliament itself, further concentrates power in a single body. (Great Britain has a largely ceremonial House of Lords, but parliamentary powers are concentrated in the House of Commons.)

QUESTIONS

1. Do you think Congress should be able to be dissolved and then subject to special elections when it fails to do its job?
2. Do you trust Congress enough to give it absolute legislative and executive authority in the United States? Why or why not?

- **Free travel.** Members may not accept free travel from private corporations or individuals for more than four days of domestic travel and seven days of international travel per year. (Taxpayer-paid "junkets" to investigate problems at home or abroad or attend international meetings are not prohibited.)
- **Lobbying.** Former members may not lobby Congress for at least one year after retirement.

But these limited rules have not gone very far in restoring popular trust in Congress.

☐ Gray Areas: Services and Contributions

Congress members are expected to perform services for their political contributors. However, a direct *quid pro quo*—receiving a financial contribution specifically for the performance of official duty—is illegal. Few Congress members would be so foolish as to openly state a price to a potential contributor for a specific service, and most contributors know not to state a dollar amount that would be forthcoming if the member performed a particular service for them. But what if the contribution

10.1

10.2

10.3

10.4

10.5

10.6

10.7

10.8

censure
Public reprimand for wrongdoing, given to a member standing in the chamber before Congress.

and the service occur close together? A Senate Ethics Committee once found a close relationship between a service and a contribution to be an "impermissible pattern of conduct [that] violated established norms of behavior in the Senate ... [and] was improper and repugnant."[48] But the Ethics Committee offered little in the way of a future guidance in handling services for campaign contributors.

Gray Areas: Investment Income

When people with access to nonpublic information about a company—corporate directors, officers, or major stockholders—make stock or bond trades based on such information without disclosing it, it is called "insider trading." Such trading is illegal under the Securities and Exchange Act of 1909 and the Insider Trading and Securities Fraud Enforcement Act of 1988. But, because the Securities and Exchange Commission has determined that "insider trading" laws do not apply to members of Congress or their staff who come into possession of such information, lawmakers have been able to use information gleaned from congressional service to trade in stocks and make profits that exceed normal market performance.[49]

In late 2011, media attention focused on these practices. The response in Congress was to hold hearings on the previously-stalled H.R. 1148, "Stop Trading on Congressional Knowledge Act," which passed into law in 2012. The new law prohibits lawmakers and senior staff from profiting off of the non-public information they obtain via their official positions, through the stock market.

Expulsion

The Constitution gives Congress the power to discipline its own members. "Each House may... punish its Members for disorderly Behaviour, and, with the Concurrence of two thirds, expel a Member." But the Constitution fails to define *disorderly behavior*. It seems reasonable to believe that criminal conduct falls within the constitutional definition of disorderly behavior. Bribery is a criminal act: it is illegal to solicit or receive anything of value in return for the performance of a government duty.

But no U.S. Senator has been expelled from Congress since the Civil War. Bob Packwood (R-OR) resigned his Senate seat in 1995 after the Ethics Committee recommended his expulsion for sexual harassment of congressional staff. Several House members have been expelled. Representative Michael Myers (D-PA) was expelled for taking bribes in an FBI sting operation in 1980. (The sting also resulted in two other House members and a senator resigning rather than face expulsion; three other representatives were defeated for reelection.) Representative James A. Traficant (D-OH) was expelled in 2002 following his conviction on 10 federal corruption charges. Several House members have resigned rather than face expulsion, usually involving financial misconduct or sexual misconduct: Representative Randy Cunningham (R-CA) resigned in 2005 after pleading guilty to charges of accepting $2.4 million in bribes from lobbyists, and Representative Tom Foley (R-FL) resigned his seat in 2006 after sexually explicit messages to teenage congressional pages came to light. More recently, Representatives Anthony Weiner (D-NY) and Christopher Lee (R-NY) resigned amid Internet-based sex scandals involving, respectively, photo-texting of the member's genitalia and a Craigslist solicitation for sex, and Representative David Wu (D-OR) resigned after revelations of an inappropriate sexual relationship with the daughter of a donor. Some members, however, refuse to give in to scandal.

Censure

A lesser punishment in the Congress than expulsion is official **censure**. Censured members are obliged to "stand in the well" and listen to the charges read against them. It is supposed to be a humiliating experience and fatal to one's political career. In 1983 two members of Congress, Barney Frank (D-MA) and Gerry Studds (D-MA), were censured for sexual misconduct with teenage congressional pages. Both were obliged to "stand in the well." Charles Rangel (D-NY), then chairman of the powerful Ways and Means Committee, was censured in 2010 for numerous ethical violations related to questionable business dealings and misuse of office. Rangel, when asked to speak on his coming censure, observed "I know in my heart I am not going to be judged by this Congress. I'll be judged by my life in its entirety." He was the twenty-third member of Congress ever censured.

Lesser forms of censure include a public reprimand or admonition by the Ethics Committee expressing disapproval of the Congress member's behavior. And the Ethics Committee may also order a member to repay funds improperly received.

A Constitutional Note

Congress as the First Branch

The Founders believed that the Congress would be the first and most powerful branch of government. Thus, Article I establishes the Congress, describes its structure, and sets forth its powers. Note that its powers are the enumerated powers of the national government. Following the English precedent of two houses of the legislature, a House of Commons and a House of Lords, the Founders created two separate houses, a House of Representatives and a Senate. They did so in part as a result of the Connecticut Compromise, which balanced large population states in the House with the small population states' demands for equality in the Senate. But the Founders also wanted a Senate elected by state legislatures, not the people, "as a defense to the people against their own temporary errors and delusions." The Founders believed that the Senate would balance the interests and numerical superiority of common citizens with the property interests of the less numerous landowners, bankers, and merchants, who they expected to be sent to the Senate by the state legislatures. This defense against "temporary errors and delusions" of the people was strengthened by different lengths of tenure for the House and Senate. All House members were elected every two years, but Senate members were elected for six-year terms, with one-third of the Senate elected every two years. The longer terms of the Senate were designed to protect senators from temporary popular movements. Not until the 17th Amendment was ratified in 1913, over a century later, were senators directly elected by the people. In short, the original Constitution of 1787 was careful to limit the role of the people in lawmaking.

QUESTIONS

1. Since 2009, Tea Party activists have called for a return to the indirect election of U.S. Senators, in order to create some popular distance between senators and voters. What do you think of repealing the 17th Amendment to allow state legislatures to elect U.S. senators?
2. Is the two-year term for members of the House of Representatives too short? Why?

Review the Chapter

The Powers of Congress

10.1 Explain the sources of Congress's power, p. 346

The Congress represents local and state interests in policy making. The Senate's constituencies are the 50 states, and the House's constituencies are 435 separate districts. Both houses of Congress, but especially the House of Representatives, wield power in domestic and foreign affairs primarily through the "power of the purse."

Congressional powers include oversight and investigation. These powers are exercised primarily through committees. Although Congress claims these powers are a necessary part of lawmaking, their real purpose is usually to influence agency decision making, to build political support for increases or decreases in agency funding, to lay the political foundation for new programs and policies, and to capture media attention and enhance the power of members of Congress.

Congressional Apportionment and Redistricting

10.2 Explain the processes of congressional apportionment and redistricting and assess how representative Congress is of the general population, p. 351

Congress is gradually becoming more "representative" of the general population in terms of race and gender. Redistricting, under federal court interpretations of the Voting Rights Act, has increased African American and Hispanic representation in Congress. And women have significantly increased their presence in Congress in recent years. Nevertheless, women and minorities do not occupy seats in Congress proportional to their share of the general population.

Life on Capitol Hill

10.3 Describe congressional elections and organization and characterize the working life of a member of Congress, p. 357

Members of Congress are independent political entrepreneurs. They initiate their own candidacies, raise their own campaign funds, and get themselves elected with very little help from their party. Members of Congress are largely career politicians who skillfully use the advantages of incumbency to stay in office. Incumbents outspend challengers by large margins. Interest-group political action committees and individual contributors strongly favor incumbents. Congressional elections are seldom focused on great national issues but rather on local issues and personalities and the ability of candidates to "bring home the bacon" from Washington and serve their constituents. If Congress fails to pay attention to national and international issues, it is in part due to their focus on issues of importance to the local constituency. Slowly, the institution is becoming more representative of minorities and women. Once elected to Congress, members are provided with an office, a staff, and the assistance of many support agencies like the Congressional Budget Office, Government Accounting Office, Government Printing Office, and the Library of Congress. Benefits include free mailing privileges, a generous retirement plan, and excellent medical insurance. Members of Congress spend as much time on "home style" activities—promoting their images back home and attending to constituents' problems—as they do legislating. Casework wins votes one at a time, gradually accumulating political support back home, and members often support each other's "pork-barrel" products. Enhancing the image among voters buys discretion for lawmakers in doing their job. Despite the independence of members, the Democratic and Republican Party structures in the House and Senate remain the principal bases for organizing Congress. Party leaders in the House and Senate generally control the flow of business in each house, assigning bills to committees, scheduling or delaying votes, and appointing members to committees. But leaders must bargain for votes; they have few formal disciplinary powers. They cannot deny renomination to recalcitrant members.

Party Fortunes in Congress

10.4 Evaluate the successes and failures of the two parties in Congress, p. 369

Congress as an institution is not very popular with the American people. Scandals, pay raises, perks, and privileges reported in the media have hurt the image of the institution. Nevertheless, individual members of Congress remain popular with their districts' voters.

In Committee

10.5 Characterize the legislative work of committees and assess the repercussions of committees for distribution of power in Congress, p. 374

The real legislative work of Congress is done in committee. Standing committees screen and draft legislation; with rare exceptions, bills do not reach the floor without approval by a majority of a standing committee. The committee and subcommittee system decentralizes power in Congress. The system satisfies the desires of members to gain power, prestige, and electoral advantage, but it weakens responsible government in the Congress as a whole. All congressional committees are chaired by members of the majority party. Seniority is still the major determinant of power in Congress.

On the Floor

10.6 Outline the process for a bill that has reached the floor and identify the obstacles to its passage, p. 378

In order to become a law, a bill must win committee approval and withstand debate in both houses of Congress. The rules attached to a bill's passage in the House can significantly help or hurt its chances. Bills passed with differences in the two houses must be reworked in a conference committee composed of members of both houses and then passed in identical form in both.

Decision Making in Congress

10.7 Assess the influences on congressional decision making, p. 381

In deciding how to vote on legislation, Congress members are influenced by party loyalty, presidential support or opposition, constituency concerns, interest-group pressures, and their own personal values and ideology. Party majorities oppose each other on roughly half of all roll-call votes in Congress. Presidents receive the greatest support in Congress from members of their own party.

Congressional Customs, Norms, and Ethics

10.8 Outline the customs and norms of Congress, and evaluate the mechanisms for ensuring ethical behavior in Congress, p. 386

The customs and norms of Congress help reduce interpersonal conflict, facilitate bargaining and compromise, and make life more pleasant on Capitol Hill. They include the recognition of special competencies of members, a willingness to bargain and compromise, mutual "back scratching" and logrolling, reciprocity, and deference toward the leadership. But traditional customs and norms have weakened over time as more members have pursued independent political agendas. And partisanship and incivility in Congress have risen in recent years. Congress establishes its own rules of ethics. The Constitution empowers each house to expel its own members for "disorderly conduct" by a two-thirds vote, but expulsion has seldom occurred. Some members have resigned to avoid expulsion; others have been officially censured yet remained in Congress.

Learn the Terms

bicameral, p. 347
power of the purse, p. 349
oversight, p. 349
advice and consent, p. 350
confirmation, p. 350
congressional hearings, p. 350
congressional investigation, p. 350
subpoena, p. 350
contempt, p. 350
perjury, p. 350
impeachment, p. 351
apportionment, p. 351
malapportionment, p. 352
one person, one vote, p. 352
redistricting, p. 353
gerrymandering, p. 354
cracking, p. 354
packing, p. 354
incumbent gerrymandering, p. 355
affirmative racial gerrymandering, p. 356
open seat, p. 358
safe seats, p. 358
turnover, p. 358
term limits, p. 359
Government Accountability Office, p. 364
home style, p. 364
casework, p. 365
pork barreling, p. 365
earmarks, p. 365
franking privilege, p. 365
Speaker of the House, p. 368
majority leader, p. 368
minority leader, p. 368
whips, p. 368
standing committee, p. 374
ranking minority member, p. 374
subcommittees, p. 376
seniority system, p. 376
drafting a bill, p. 377
markup, p. 377
discharge petition, p. 378
rule, p. 378
closed rule, p. 378
restricted rule, p. 378
open rule, p. 378
"killer" amendments, p. 379
unanimous consent agreement, p. 379
filibuster, p. 379
cloture, p. 379
rider, p. 379
hold, p. 381
roll-call vote, p. 381
conference committees, p. 381
party votes, p. 383
party unity, p. 383
bipartisanship, p. 383
divided party government, p. 383
constituency, p. 384
trustees, p. 385
delegates, p. 385
logrolling, p. 389
gridlock, p. 390
censure, p. 392

Test Yourself

10.1 Explain the sources of Congress's power.

The most important source of Congress's power stems from its authority to

a. ratify treaties
b. confirm presidential appointments
c. declare war
d. authorize the expenditure of federal funds
e. remove the president from office without cause

10.2 Explain the processes of congressional apportionment and redistricting and assess how representative Congress is of the general population.

When redistricting results in partisan voters being so concentrated that much of their vote is wasted, it is called

a. packing
b. splintering
c. chubbing
d. ticket splitting
e. transfer voting

10.3 Describe congressional elections and organization and characterize the working life of a member of Congress.

The largest source of candidates for political office comes from which of the following occupations?

a. agriculture and real estate
b. medicine, journalism, and public relations
c. public service and law
d. business
e. former athletes

10.4 Evaluate the successes and failures of the two parties in Congress.

Since the 1994 elections, it is most typically the case that

a. the Democrats control the majority of seats in the House of Representatives and the Senate
b. the Republicans control the majority of seats in the House of Representatives and the Senate
c. the Democrats control the majority of seats in the House of Representatives and the Republicans control the Senate
d. the Republicans control the majority of seats in the House of Representatives and the Democrats control the Senate
e. neither party has usually had majority control of either chamber.

10.5 Characterize the legislative work of committees and assess the repercussions of committees for distribution of power in Congress.

When lawmakers cultivate political capital and vote surpluses with voters, they do so to

a. acquire discretion to make tough decisions and pursue policies
b. to ensure reelection without facing a tough opponent
c. travel
d. impress their colleagues and acquire institutional prestige
e. continue to engage in earmarking and pork barreling

10.6 Outline the process for a bill that has reached the floor and identify the obstacles to its passage.

A bill that has passed but has different wording in the House and Senate versions is sent to

a. the House Rules Committee
b. the president for final determination
c. both the House and Senate Reconciliation Committee
d. the Senate Reconciliation Committee
e. a conference committee

10.7 Assess the influences on congressional decision making.

Gridlock in Congress is in part a result of

a. unified party control of the presidency and Congress
b. greater ideological polarization of the parties
c. unified party control of the House and Senate
d. the willingness of House members to filibuster
e. the decline of party polarization

10.8 Outline the customs and norms of Congress and evaluate the mechanisms for ensuring ethical behavior in Congress.

Of the following norms of behavior in Congress, which one has been weakened the least since the 1960s?

a. Specialization
b. Apprenticeship
c. Civility
d. Seniority
e. Institutional loyalty

Explore Further

SUGGESTED READINGS

Bullock, Charles S. III. 2010. *Redistricting: The Most Political Activity in America.* Lanham, Md: Rowman & Littlefield Press. Describes the law, politics, and mechanics or redistricting and reapportionment.

Davidson, Robert H., Walter J. Oleszek, and Frances E. Lee. *Congress and Its Members.* 11th ed. Washington, D.C.: CQ Press, 2007. Authoritative text on Congress covering the recruitment of members, elections, home styles and Hill styles, leadership, decision making, and relations with interest groups, presidency, and courts. Emphasizes tension between lawmaking responsibilities and the desire to be reelected.

Fenno, Richard F. *Home Style.* Boston: Little, Brown, 1978. The classic description of how attention to constituency by members of Congress enhances their reelection prospects. Home style activities, including casework, pork barreling, travel and appearances back home, newsletters, and surveys, are described in detail.

Gaddie, Ronald Keith, and Charles S. Bullock III. *Elections to Open Seats in the U.S. House: Where the Action Is.* Lanham, Md.: Rowman & Littlefield Press. Comprehensive study of the most competitive elections for Congress, including case studies and historical analysis as well as simulations of a totally term-limited congressional election.

Herrnson, Paul S. *Congressional Elections: Campaigning at Home and in Washington.* 5th ed. Washington, D.C.: CQ Press, 2007. Interviews with candidates, campaign aides, and political consultants to paint a comprehensive portrait of congressional campaigns.

Jacobson, Gary C. *The Politics of Congressional Elections.* 7th ed. New York: Longman, 2009. Coverage of congressional campaigns and elections with reference to questions of responsibility and representation.

Jones, Charles O. *Separate but Equal Branches: Congress and the Presidency.* 2nd ed. Washington, D.C.: CQ Press, 1999. Presidential–congressional relations under Johnson; Nixon; Ford; Carter; Reagan; Bush, Sr., and Clinton.

Mann, Thomas and Norman Ornstein, *The Broken Branch: How Congress Is Failing America and How to Get It Back on Track.* New York: Oxford University Press, 2006; and *It's Even Worse Than It Looks* (New York: Basic Books, 2012). How the congresses of the early twenty-first century have failed to provide functional government, and recommendations for how to fix Congress.

Oleszek, Walter J. *Congressional Procedures and Policy Processes.* 7th ed. Washington, D.C.: CQ Press, 2007. The definitive work on congressional rules, procedures and traditions and their effect on the course and content of legislation.

Ornstein, Norman J., Thomas E. Mann, and Michael J. Malbin. *Vital Statistics on Congress.* Washington, D.C.: CQ Press, 2008. Published biennially. Excellent source of data on members of Congress, congressional elections, campaign finance, committees and staff, workload, and voting alignments.

Sinclair, Barbara. *Unorthodox Lawmaking.* 3rd ed. Washington, D.C.: CQ Press, 2007. A description of the various detours and shortcuts a major bill is likely to take in Congress, including case studies.

Stathis, Stephen W. *Landmark Legislation 1774–2002.* Washington, D.C.: CQ Press, 2003. A summary of major congressional legislation over 225 years, in a single volume.

SUGGESTED WEB SITES

Congressional Budget Office www.cbo.gov

The Web site of the CBO is an excellent source of data on federal finances, economic projections, and the budgetary process.

Congressional Quarterly (CQ) www.cq.com

The *Congressional Quarterly Weekly Report* provides the most comprehensive coverage of events in Congress, including key issues, House and Senate roll-call votes, backgrounds of members, and political and election information. The CQ Press is a major publisher of books on politics and government.

Dave's Redistricting App http://gardow.com/davebradlee/redistricting/

A redistricting simulator that uses real census data and electoral data to allow anyone to redraw local, state, and congressional districts for every state in the union.

Government Accountability Office www.gao.gov

The GAO Web site provides the latest reports evaluating government programs and spending.

Library of Congress http://thomas.loc.gov

The Thomas system allows the tracing of bills from their introduction, through the committee system, floor schedule vote, and so on.

Roll Call www.rollcall.com

This online magazine covers a variety of current topics about Congress but is especially strong on stories dealing with running for Congress and/or campaign financing.

U.S. House of Representatives www.house.gov

Official Web site of the House, with a schedule of floor and committee actions, legislative information, and links to every Representative's Web site and every committee Web site.

U.S. Senate www.senate.gov

Official Senate Web site, with floor and committee schedules, Senate news, and links to each senator's Web site.

11

The President

White House Politics

In late March 2012, Barack Obama made his first presidential visit to Oklahoma. Mr. Obama had not been to Oklahoma since 2007, when he had passed through on a fundraising tour. There was little reason for Obama to be in Oklahoma—the state had not voted for him in the 2008 presidential primary, and in the subsequent general election he lost every county in the state. Earlier that same March, he garnered just 57 percent of the presidential primary vote against four non-entities. Barack Obama was not popular in Oklahoma.

Still, Obama came. He flew into Tinker Air Force Base, then, the next day, made a speech on domestic energy production at the Cushing oil distribution hub. The southern leg of the Keystone pipeline would originate at Cushing, but it was the northern leg of the Keystone expansion that was being held up by the Obama administration and which was causing difficulties with Republicans and energy-oriented voters and elites. Environmentalists and green energy advocates wanted to stop Keystone, while pro-oil and domestic consumption advocates wanted Keystone speeded up.

As Obama finished his speech and continues what would be a four-day, four state tour to illuminate energy policy, he was approached by a Tulsa-based reporter who told the president she was born in the same hospital as him in Hawaii. Mr. Obama did not miss a beat. He smiled, and making light of efforts to challenge his legitimacy as president, quipped "do you have your birth certificate?"

11.1 Identify the powers and responsibilities of the president, p. 400

11.2 Identify the powers granted to the president by the Constitution, p. 404

11.3 Assess the sources of the president's political power and analyze how presidents' personality and policy positions impact their approval ratings, p. 410

11.4 Outline the responsibilities and powers of the president as the nation's chief executive, p. 418

11.5 Analyze the factors affecting the success of the president as the chief legislator and lobbyist, p. 423

11.6 Assess the role of the president as a global leader, p. 427

11.7 Trace the expansion of presidential powers as Commander in Chief, p. 431

11.8 Characterize the roles and responsibilities of the vice president, p. 435

THE SYMBOLIC POLITICS OF THE PRESIDENCY Presidents are uniquely positioned to use their office to draw attention to issues. Here, President Barack Obama discusses energy policy in front of the Cushing oil distribution hub in Cushing, Oklahoma.

11.1

11.2

11.3

11.4

11.5

11.6

11.7

11.8

Presidential Power

11.1 Identify the powers and responsibilities of the president.

Americans look to their president for "greatness." The presidency embodies the popular "great man" view of history and public affairs—attributing progress in the world to the actions of particular individuals. Great presidents are those associated with great events: George Washington with the founding of the nation, Abraham Lincoln with the preservation of the Union, Franklin D. Roosevelt with the nation's emergence from economic depression and victory in World War II (see *What Do You Think?* How Would You Rate the Presidents?). People tend to believe that the president is responsible for "peace and prosperity" as well as for "change." They expect their president to present a "vision" of America's future and to symbolize the nation.

The Symbolic President

The president *is* the American government for most people. People expect the president to act decisively and effectively to deal with national problems. They expect the president to be "compassionate"—to show concern for problems confronting individual citizens. The president, while playing these roles, is the focus of public attention and the nation's leading celebrity—for example, presidents are routinely named as the most admired people in the country by the public during their incumbency. Presidents receive more media coverage than any other person in the nation, for everything from their policy statements to their favorite foods to their dogs and cats.

Managing Crises

In times of crisis, the American people look to their president to take action, to provide reassurance, and to protect the nation and its people. It is the president as the only nationally elected member of government—not Congress or the courts—who

SHOWING CONCERN IN A CRISIS

Crisis management is a key presidential responsibility. People look to the president for reassurance in times of national tragedy, and to exercise strong executive judgment in critical events. Here, President Kennedy speaks to the nation at the height of the Cuban Missile Crisis, October 22, 1962, as customers in a department store look on.

What Do You Think?

How Would You Rate the Presidents?

From time to time, historians have been polled to rate U.S. presidents (see table below). The survey ratings given to the presidents have been remarkably consistent. Abraham Lincoln, George Washington, and Franklin Roosevelt are universally recognized as the greatest American presidents. It is more difficult for historians to rate recent presidents; their views are influenced by their own (generally liberal and reformist) political views. Richard Nixon once commented, "History will treat me fairly. Historians probably won't."

Historians may tend to rank activist presidents, who led the nation through war or economic crisis higher than passive presidents who guided the nation in peace and prosperity. Initially, Dwight Eisenhower, who presided in the relatively calm 1950s, was ranked low by historians. But later, after comparing his performance with those who came after him, his steadiness and avoidance of war raised his ranking dramatically.

Public opinion on great presidents is influenced by recent events. A 2011 Gallup Poll of 1,015 adults asked them, "Who do you regard as the greatest United States president?" Respondents placed the two most popular recent presidents—Ronald Reagan and Bill Clinton—first and third respectively, with Lincoln in between. Washington was fifth, and FDR was sixth.

QUESTIONS

1. What makes presidents "great," in your opinion?
2. Why do you think that experts and the general public have different opinions about who are "great" presidents?

Arthur M. Schlesinger, Jr. (1962)

Great
1. Lincoln
2. Washington
3. F. Roosevelt
4. Wilson
5. Jefferson

Near Great
6. Jackson
7. T. Roosevelt
8. Polk
9. Truman (tie)
10. J. Adams
11. Cleveland

Average
12. Madison
13. J. Q. Adams
14. Hayes
15. McKinley
16. Taft
17. Van Buren
18. Monroe
19. Hoover
20. B. Harrison
21. Arthur
22. Eisenhower (tie)
23. A. Johnson

Below Average
24. Taylor
25. Tyler
26. Fillmore
27. Coolidge
28. Pierce
29. Buchanan

Failure
30. Grant
31. Harding

Robert Murray (1982)

Presidential Rank
1. Lincoln
2. F. Roosevelt
3. Washington
4. Jefferson
5. T. Roosevelt
6. Wilson
7. Jackson
8. Truman
9. J. Adams
10. L. Johnson
11. Eisenhower
12. Polk
13. Kennedy
14. Madison
15. Monroe
16. J. Q. Adams
17. Cleveland
18. McKinley
19. Taft
20. Van Buren
21. Hoover
22. Hayes
23. Arthur
24. Ford
25. Carter
26. B. Harrison
27. Taylor
28. Tyler
29. Fillmore
30. Coolidge
31. Pierce
32. A. Johnson
33. Buchanan
34. Nixon
35. Grant
36. Harding

Arthur M. Schlesinger, Jr. (1996)

Great
1. Lincoln
2. Washington
3. F. Roosevelt

Near Great
4. Jefferson
5. Jackson
6. T. Roosevelt
7. Wilson
8. Truman
9. Polk

High Average
10. Eisenhower
11. J. Adams
12. Kennedy
13. Cleveland
14. L. Johnson
15. Monroe
16. McKinley

Average
17. Madison
18. J. Q. Adams
19. B. Harrison
20. Clinton
21. Van Buren
22. Taft
23. Hayes
24. G. H. W. Bush
25. Reagan
26. Arthur
27. Carter
28. Ford

Below Average
29. Taylor
30. Coolidge
31. Fillmore
32. Tyler

Failure
33. Pierce
34. Grant
35. Hoover
36. Nixon
37. A. Johnson
38. Buchanan
39. Harding

Federalist Society (2000)

Great
1. Washington
2. Lincoln
3. F. Roosevelt

Near Great
4. Jefferson
5. T. Roosevelt
6. Jackson
7. Truman
8. Reagan
9. Eisenhower
10. Polk
11. Wilson

Above Average
12. Cleveland
13. Adams
14. McKinley
15. Madison
16. Monroe
17. L. Johnson
18. Kennedy

Average
19. Taft
20. J. Q. Adams
21. G. H. W. Bush
22. Hayes
23. Van Buren
24. Clinton
25. Coolidge
26. Arthur

Below Average
27. B. Harrison
28. Ford
29. Hoover
30. Carter
31. Taylor
32. Grant
33. Nixon
34. Tyler
35. Fillmore

Failure
36. A. Johnson
37. Pierce
38. Harding
39. Buchanan

CSPAN (2009)
1. Lincoln
2. Washington
3. F. Roosevelt
4. T. Roosevelt
5. Truman
6. Kennedy
7. Jefferson
8. Eisenhower
9. Wilson
10. Reagan
11. L. Johnson
12. Polk
13. Jackson
14. Monroe
15. Clinton
16. W. McKinley
17. J. Adams
18. G. H .W. Bush
19. J. Q. Adams
20. Madison
21. Cleveland
22. Ford
23. Grant
24. Taft
25. Carter
26. Coolidge
27. Nixon
28. Garfield
29. Taylor
30. B. Harrison
31. Van Buren
32. Arthur
33. Hayes
34. Hoover
35. Tyler
36. G. W. Bush
37. Fillmore
38. Harding
39. W. Harrison
40. Pierce
41. A. Johnson
42. Buchanan

Gallup All-Time (2011)
1. Reagan
2. Lincoln
3. Clinton
4. Kennedy
5. Washington
6. F. Roosevelt
7. Obama
8. T. Roosevelt
9. Truman
10. G. W. Bush
11. Jefferson
12. Carter
13. Eisenhower
14. G. H. W. Bush
15. Scattering

Gallup Modern (2011)
1. Kennedy
2. Reagan
3. Clinton
4. Eisenhower
5. Obama
6. G. H. W. Bush
7. Carter
8. G. W. Bush
9. L. Johnson
10. Ford
11. Nixon

NOTE: These ratings result from surveys of scholars ranging in number from 55 to 950.

SOURCES: Arthur Murphy, "Evaluating the Presidents of the United States," *Presidential Studies Quarterly* 14 (1984): 117–26; Arthur M. Schlesinger, Jr., "Rating the Presidents: Washington to Clinton," *Political Science Quarterly* 112 (1997): 179–90; CSPAN Historians Presidential Leadership Survey (2009), www.c-span.org/presidentialsurvey; "Federalist Society—*The Wall Street Journal* Survey on Presidents (2000)," http://www.gallup.com/poll/146183/Americans-Say-Reagan-Greatest-President.aspx; www.opinionjournal.com/hail/rankings.html

11.1

11.2

11.3

11.4

11.5

11.6

11.7

11.8

is expected to speak on behalf of the American people in times of national triumph and tragedy. The president gives expression to the nation's pride in victory. The nation's heroes are welcomed; its scientists, writers, and poets are recognized; and its championship sports teams are feted in the White House Rose Garden.

The president also gives expression to the nation's sadness in tragedy and strives to help the nation go forward. How presidents respond to crises often defines their place in history. Franklin D. Roosevelt raised public morale during the Great Depression of the 1930s by reassuring Americans that "the only thing we have to fear is fear itself." Later he led the nation into war following the Japanese attack on Pearl Harbor, December 7, 1941, "a day which will live in infamy." When the *Challenger* spaceship disintegrated before the eyes of millions of television viewers in 1986, Ronald Reagan gave voice to the nation's feelings about the disaster: "I want to say something to the schoolchildren of America who were watching the live coverage of the shuttle's take-off. I know it is hard to understand, but sometimes painful things like this happen. The future doesn't belong to the faint-hearted. It belongs to the brave." George W. Bush found a voice for his foundering presidency amidst the rubble of the World Trade Center after the 9/11 attacks, telling first responders, "I can hear you. The rest of the world hears you. And the people who knocked these buildings down will hear all of us soon."

Providing Policy Leadership

Presidents exert policy leadership two ways: as the executive who sets an agenda and as a partisan leader who attempts to get his preferred policies enacted through the legislative process.

The president is expected to set policy priorities for the nation. Most policy initiatives originate in the White House and various departments and agencies of the executive branch and then are forwarded to Congress with the president's approval. Presidential programs are submitted to Congress in the form of messages, including the president's annual State of the Union Address, and in the budget of the United States government, which the president presents each year to Congress.

As a political leader, the president is expected to mobilize political support for policy proposals. It is not enough for the president to send policy proposals to Congress. The president must mobilize public opinion, lobby members of Congress, and win legislative battles. To avoid being perceived as weak or ineffective, presidents must get as much of their legislative programs through Congress as possible.

Managing the Economy

The public holds the president responsible for maintaining a healthy economy. Presidents are blamed for economic downturns, whether or not governmental policies had anything to do with market conditions. Presidents crash on the rocks of economic distress, whether it is economic recession, economic depression, an unemployment crisis, or an inflationary spiral. Herbert Hoover in 1932, Gerald Ford in 1976, Jimmy Carter in 1980, and George H. W. Bush in 1992—all incumbent presidents defeated for reelection during recessions—learned the hard way that the general public holds the president responsible for hard economic times. When incumbent presidents are not up for election, their party is often punished for hard times—such as John McCain's 2008 loss. Presidents must have an economic "game plan" to stimulate economy growth while limiting inflation—and they must have a successful plan to win reelection.

Managing the Government

The ultimate responsibility for implementation—in the words of the Constitution, "to take Care that the Laws be faithfully executed"—rests with the president. As the chief executive of a mammoth federal bureaucracy with 2.8 million civilian employees, the president is responsible for implementing policy, that is, for achieving policy goals.

Policy making does not end when a law is passed. Policy implementation involves issuing orders, creating organizations, recruiting and assigning personnel, disbursing funds, overseeing work, and evaluating results. Most government policy decisions do not carry the president's imprimatur—but the media and the public will characterize the actions of "the Bush Justice Department" or the "Obama EPA" as being extensions of the president's policy preferences.

☐ The Global President

History and the Constitution give the United States one voice in international affairs—the president's voice. The president is invested with treaty-making authority; the receiving and appointment of ambassadors; and the conduct of war as

	Vice-President	Governor	US Senate	Congress	State Legislator	General
George Washington				■	■	■
John Adams	■			■	■	
Thomas Jefferson	■	■		■	■	
James Madison				■	■	
James Monroe		■	■	■	■	
John Quincy Adams		■			■	
Andrew Jackson			■	■		■
Martin Van Buren	■	■	■		■	
William H. Harrison			■	■	■	
John Tyler		■	■	■	■	
James K. Polk		■		■	■	
Zachary Taylor						■
Millard Fillmore	■			■	■	
Franklin Pierce			■	■	■	
James Buchanan			■	■	■	
Abraham Lincoln				■	■	
Andrew Johnson	■	■	■	■	■	
Ulysses S. Grant						■
Rutherford B. Hayes		■		■		
James A. Garfield				■	■	
Chester A. Arthur	■					
Grover Cleveland		■				
Benjamin Harrison			■			
William McKinley		■		■		
Theodore Roosevelt	■	■			■	
William H. Taft						
Woodrow Wilson		■				
Warren G. Harding			■		■	
Calvin Coolidge	■	■			■	
Herbert Hoover						
Franklin D. Roosevelt		■			■	
Harry S. Truman	■		■			
Dwight D. Eisenhower						■
John F. Kennedy			■	■		
Lyndon B. Johnson	■		■	■		
Richard M. Nixon	■		■	■		
Gerald Ford	■			■		
James E. Carter		■			■	
Ronald Reagan		■				
George H. W. Bush	■			■		
William J. B. Clinton		■				
George W. Bush		■				
Barack H. Obama			■		■	

FIGURE 11.1 HOW DO I BECOME PRESIDENT?

So you want to be president? Well, the pathway to power is pretty narrow, difficult to navigate, and while many dream of the job, very few will get there. Every American president has been a man. No woman has ever won a major party nomination, and only two (Sarah Palin and Geraldine Ferraro) have ever been on a major party ticket. The office most often used as a stepping stone to the presidency is governor (18 presidents were previously governor), and it is preferable to become governor before you turn 50. U.S. senators often aspire to the presidency; 15 have served but very few have gotten there directly from the Senate (just 3 since 1900). Thirteen vice presidents have been president. And half the presidents either served in a state legislature or as a congressional representative (22 each). No private citizen has been elevated to the presidency without public service as either a cabinet officer (two) or as a successful general (three).

Commander in Chief of the armed forces of the United States. Efforts by Congress to speak on behalf of the nation in foreign affairs and to limit the war-making power of the president have been generally unsuccessful.

Constitutional Powers of the President

11.2 Identify the powers granted to the president by the Constitution.

Popular expectations of presidential leadership far exceed the formal constitutional powers granted to the president. Compared with the Congress, the president has only modest constitutional powers (see Table 11.1).

Who Is Eligible to Be President?

To become president, the Constitution specifies that a person must be a natural-born citizen at least 35 years of age and a resident of the United States for 14 years.

Initially, the Constitution put no limit on how many terms a president could serve. George Washington set a precedent for a two-term maximum that endured until Franklin Roosevelt's decision to run for a third term in 1940 (and a fourth term in 1944). In reaction to Roosevelt's lengthy tenure, Congress proposed the 22nd

TABLE 11.1 MODEST FORMAL POWERS: THE CONSTITUTIONAL POWERS OF THE PRESIDENT

The formal constitutional powers of the president are very modest, especially compared to popular expectations of presidential leadership.

Chief Executive
Implement policy: "take Care that the Laws be faithfully executed" (Article II, Section 3)
Supervise executive branch of government
Appoint and remove executive officials (Article II, Section 2)
Prepare executive budget for submission to Congress (by law of Congress)
Chief Legislator
Initiate policy: "give to the Congress Information of the State of the Union, and recommend to their Consideration such Measures as he shall judge necessary and expedient" (Article II, Section 3)
Veto legislation passed by Congress, subject to override by a two-thirds vote in both houses
Convene special session of Congress "on extraordinary Occasions" (Article II, Section 3)
Chief Diplomat
Make treaties "with the Advice and Consent of the Senate" (Article II, Section 2)
Exercise the power of diplomatic recognition: "receive Ambassadors" (Article II, Section 3)
Make executive agreements (by custom and international law)
Commander in Chief
Command U.S. armed forces: "The president shall be Commander in Chief of the Army and Navy" (Article II, Section 2)
Appoint military officers
Chief of State
"The executive Power shall be vested in a President" (Article II, Section 1)
Grant reprieves and pardons (Article II, Section 2)
Represent the nation as chief of state
Appoint federal court and Supreme Court judges (Article II, Section 2)

Amendment, ratified in 1951, which officially restricts the president to two terms (or one full term if a vice president must complete more than two years of the previous president's term).

□ Presidential Succession

Until the adoption of the 25th Amendment in 1967, the Constitution had said little about presidential succession, other than designating the vice president as successor to the president "in Case of the Removal, . . . Death, Resignation, or Inability" and giving Congress the power to decide "what Officer shall then act as President" if both the president and vice president are removed. The Constitution was silent on how to cope with serious presidential illnesses. It contained no provision for replacing a vice president. The incapacitation issue was more than theoretical: James A. Garfield lingered months after being shot in 1881; Woodrow Wilson was an invalid during his last years in office (1919–20); Dwight Eisenhower suffered major heart attacks in office; and Ronald Reagan was in serious condition following an assassination attempt in 1981.

The 25th Amendment stipulates that when the vice president and a majority of the cabinet notify the Speaker of the House and the president pro tempore of the Senate in writing that the president "is unable to discharge the powers and duties of his office," then the vice president becomes *acting* president. To resume the powers of office, the president must then notify Congress in writing that "no inability exists." If the vice president and a majority of cabinet officers do not agree that the president is capable of resuming office, then Congress "shall decide the issue" within 21 days. A two-thirds vote of both houses is required to replace the president with the vice president.

The disability provisions of the amendment have never been used, but the succession provisions have been. The 25th Amendment provides for the selection of a new vice president by presidential nomination and confirmation by a majority vote of

What Do You Think?

Should Presidents Have Term Limits?

The 22nd Amendment to the Constitution limits a president to two terms in office or 10 years, total. The amendment was adopted in 1951. It had been advanced by Republican lawmakers in 1947 who believed that Franklin Delano Roosevelt's violation of the two-term precedent set by George Washington was, in the words of FDR's 1944 opponent Thomas Dewey, "the most dangerous threat to our freedom ever proposed." (FDR served 13 years as president.)

Term limits creates a constraint on the reelected president. The president will not stand on the ballot again, so using his popularity to advance policy goals is constrained. Political opponents focus on delaying a president's agenda, in the hope of electing a different president in a couple of years while waiting out the "lame duck." It is also possible that term limits make a president a bit too free. Without the constraint of reelection, the president can make unpopular choices and use the powers of his office to stall or stop initiatives preferred by Congress and the public.

Some observers say the president needs a longer term of office, freed of the demands of reelection. If a president were elected for either six or eight years, they could then govern freed of the need to face the voters again. Skeptics of this approach say it leaves the president too far removed from popular control, and could lead to either an instant lame duck or alternatively a dictator.

Other critics say that the problem isn't term limits but the election calendar. A president is elected for four years, then faces a reelection for four more years. A third of the Senate is elected every two years, as is the entire House of Representatives. So, a president goes about his first term with all of the House and much of the Senate focused on electioneering rather than governing. After the first several months of the first term, the president is caught up in the midterm election in order to maintain support in Congress. Then, after the midterm, the president is in a reelection battle. Perhaps if senators and congressmen had longer terms (say eight years and four years), we could have fewer elections and presidents could focus on governing.

QUESTIONS

1. Do presidents need term limits? Why?
2. Should presidents have longer terms in office? Why?

impeachment
Equivalent of a criminal charge against an elected official; removal of the impeached official from office depends on the outcome of a trial.

both houses of Congress. When Vice President Spiro Agnew resigned in the face of bribery charges in 1973, President Richard Nixon nominated the Republican leader of the House, Gerald Ford, as vice president; and when Nixon resigned in 1974, Ford assumed the presidency and made Nelson Rockefeller, governor of New York, his vice president. Thus Gerald Ford's two-year tenure in the White House marked the only time in history when the man serving as president had not been elected to either the presidency or the vice presidency. (If the offices of president and vice president are both vacated, then Congress by law has specified the next in line for the presidency as the Speaker of the House of Representatives, followed by the president pro tempore of the Senate, then the cabinet officers, beginning with the secretary of state.)

Impeachment

The Constitution grants Congress the power of **impeachment** over the president, vice president, and "all civil Officers of the United States" (Article II, Section 4). Technically, impeachment is a charge similar to a criminal indictment brought against an official. The power to bring charges of impeachment is given to the House of Representatives. The power to try all impeachments is given to the Senate, and "no Person shall be convicted without the Concurrence of two thirds of the Members present" (Article I, Section 3). Impeachment by the House and conviction by the Senate only remove an official from office; a subsequent criminal trial is required to inflict any other punishment.

The Constitution specifies that impeachment and conviction can only be for "Treason, Bribery, or other High Crimes and Misdemeanors." These words indicate that Congress is not to impeach presidents, federal judges, or any other officials simply because Congress disagrees with their decisions or policies. Indeed, the phrase implies that only serious criminal offenses, not political conflicts, can result in impeachment. Nevertheless, politics was at the root of the impeachment of President Andrew Johnson in 1867. Johnson was a Southern Democrat who had remained loyal to the Union. Lincoln had chosen him as vice president in 1864 as a gesture of national unity. A Republican House impeached him on a party-line vote, but after a month-long trial in the Senate, the "guilty" vote fell one short of the two-thirds needed for removal.[1]

And partisan politics played a key role in the House impeachment and later Senate trial of Bill Clinton (see *The Game, the Rules, the Players:* Sex, Lies, Politics, and Impeachment).

Presidential Pardons

The Constitution grants the president the power to "grant Reprieves and Pardons." This power derives from the ancient right to appeal to the king to reverse errors of law or justice committed by the court system. It is absolute: the president may grant pardons to anyone convicted of a *federal* crime for any reason. The most celebrated use of the presidential pardon was President Ford's blanket pardon of former President Nixon "for all offenses against the United States which he, Richard Nixon, has committed or may have committed or taken part in." Ford defended the pardon as necessary to end "the bitter controversy and divisive national debate," but his actions may have helped cause his defeat in the 1976 election.

FORD PARDONS NIXON

President Richard Nixon and Vice-President Gerald Ford. After Nixon's resignation during the Watergate scandal, new President Ford pardoned Nixon for any crimes he might have committed as president. The power to pardon is absolute, but Ford's approval rating plummeted.

Executive Power

The Constitution declares that the "executive Power" shall be vested in the president, but it is unclear whether this statement grants the president any powers that are not specified later in the Constitution or given to the president by acts of Congress. In other words, does the grant of "executive Power" give presidents constitutional authority to act as they deem necessary *beyond* the actions specified elsewhere in the Constitution or specified in laws passed by Congress?

The Game, the Rules, the Players

Sex, Lies, Politics, and Impeachment

Two presidents have been impeached by the US House—Bill Clinton (1998–99) and Andrew Johnson (1867). President Richard Nixon resigned just ahead of an impeachment vote in 1974. All three cases were built around some violation of the law, though critics of the respective impeachments contend that all were politically motivated.

Andrew Johnson was impeached over a violation of the Tenure of Office Act—the act was passed to set up a confrontation between Johnson and Congress, who were in dispute over the Reconstruction of the South after the Civil War. Nixon was subject to a year-long investigation of illegal activities by the Committee to Reelect the President (CREEP) and actions to cover up those activities. Bill Clinton's impeachment stemmed from sex.

In 1998, an Independent Counsel (Kenneth Starr) appointed by a federal court reported that Bill Clinton had engaged in perjury, obstruction of justice, witness tampering, and "abuse of power," centered around an inappropriate sexual relationship with a White House college intern, Monica Lewinsky. The Starr Report described the relationship in graphic and lurid detail. The House vote to impeach Clinton on December 19, 1998 (228 to 205), was largely along partisan lines, with all but five Republicans voting "yes" and all but five Democrats voting "no." And the vote in Clinton's Senate "trial" on February 12, 1999, was equally partisan. Even on the strongest charge—that Clinton had tried to obstruct justice—the Senate failed to find the president guilty. Removing Clinton failed to win even a majority of Senate votes, far less than the required two-thirds. All 45 Democrats were joined by 5 Republicans to create a 50–50 tie vote that left Clinton tarnished, but still in office.

Most Americans believed the president had a sexual affair in the White House and subsequently lied about it; however, they also *approved* of the way Clinton was performing his job as president. Indeed, the public appeared to rally around the president following the allegations of sexual misconduct.

Various explanations have been offered for this apparent paradox—a public that believed the president had had an affair in the White House and lied about it, yet gave the president the highest approval ratings of his career. Many Americans believe that private sexual conduct is irrelevant to the performance of public duties—Bill Clinton's promiscuous behavior is therefore not unique in the minds of many voters. Others argue, however, that private character counts in presidential performance; indeed, that it is a prerequisite for public trust. The president, in this view, performs a symbolic role that requires dignity, honesty, and respect. The acceptance of a president's adulterous behavior, according to one commentator, lowers society's standards of behavior. "The president's legacy . . . will be a further vulgarization and demoralization of society."[a]

But does engaging in extramarital sex and lying about it meet the Constitution's standard for impeachment—"Treason, Bribery, or other High Crimes and Misdemeanors"? Despite pious rhetoric in Congress about the "search for truth," "impartial investigation," and "unbiased constitutional judgment," the impeachment process, whatever the merits of the charges against a president, is *political*, not judicial.

QUESTIONS

1. **Perjury—knowingly giving false testimony in a sworn legal proceeding—is a criminal offense. But does the Constitution envision more serious misconduct to result in the removal of a president?**
2. **Should the power of impeachment be removed from the Congress? Why or why not?**

[a]Gertrude Himmelfarb, "Private Lives, Public Morality," *New York Times*, February 9, 1998.

Contrasting views on this question have been offered over two centuries. President Abraham Lincoln, defending his suspension of the Writ of Habeas Corpus during the Civil War, stated that the circumstances of emergency granted the executive potentially unlimited power to preserve the Union and constitutional government, even if those actions might violate the constitution. Lincoln claimed that extraordinary circumstances guided the expansion of executive power ("I claim not to *have* controlled *events*, but confess plainly that *events have* controlled *me*.").

President William Howard Taft provided the classic narrow interpretation of executive power: "The president can exercise no power which cannot be fairly and reasonably traced to some specific grant of power or justly implied and included within such express grant as proper and necessary to its exercise."[2] Theodore Roosevelt, Taft's bitter opponent in a three-way race for the presidency in 1912, expressed a view closer to Lincoln, but circumscribed by the Constitution: "My belief was that it was not only his right but his duty to do anything that the needs of the nation demanded, unless such action was forbidden

A Conflicting View

Watergate: The Limits of the Imperial Presidency?

In his 1973 book *The Imperial Presidency*, historian Arthur Schlesinger, Jr. argued that the presidency had grown too powerful. The institution had increased through a series of foreign policy crises, starting in the Civil War, then the Spanish American War and two World Wars. These expansions of power caused the presidency to reach beyond its constitutional powers in domestic politics as well. The imperial presidency, and the application of those beliefs, reached an apex in the Nixon administration—and the explosion of the imperial Nixon presidency in the Watergate scandal almost coincident to the American withdrawal from Vietnam crippled the moral and political authority of the presidency for the rest of the 1970s.

Richard Nixon is the only president ever to resign the office, thereby escaping certain impeachment by the House of Representatives and a certain guilty verdict in trial by the Senate. Yet Nixon's first term as president included a number of historic successes. He negotiated the first strategic nuclear arms limitation treaty, SALT I, with the Soviet Union. He changed the global balance of power in favor of the Western democracies by opening relations with the People's Republic of China. He withdrew U.S. troops from Vietnam, negotiated a peace agreement, and ended one of America's longest and bloodiest wars. But his remarkable record is forever tarnished by his failure to understand the limits of presidential power. Nixon and his men believed in the expansive powers of the president beyond the Constitution, and Nixon, after leaving office, told interviewer David Frost, "When the President does it, that means it is not illegal."

Nixon lived in the shadow of political inadequacy. No electoral victory was enough, and Nixon and his team set out in 1972 to ensure a successful reelection. On the night of June 17, 1972, five men with burglary tools and wiretapping devices were arrested in the offices of the Democratic National Committee in the Watergate Building in Washington. Also arrested were E. Howard Hunt, Jr., G. Gordon Liddy, and James W. McCord, Jr., all employed by the Committee to Reelect the President (CREEP). All pleaded guilty and were convicted. There is no evidence that Nixon himself ordered or had prior knowledge of the break-in, he discussed with his chief of staff, H. R. Haldeman, and White House advisers John Ehrlichman and John Dean the advisability of payoffs to buy the defendants' silence. Nixon hoped his landslide electoral victory in November 1972 would put the matter to rest.

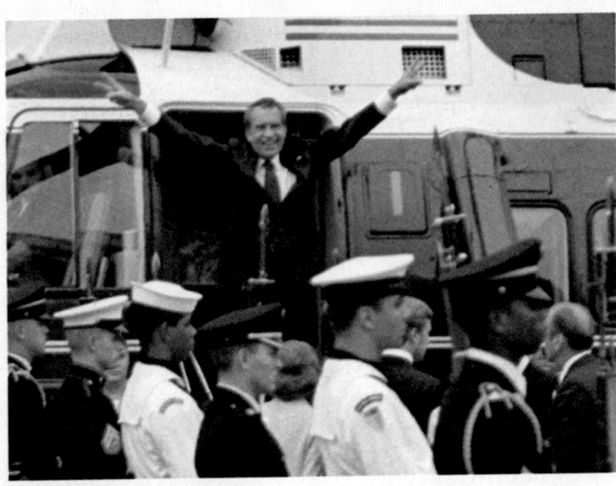

Richard Nixon is the only president ever to resign the office. He did so in 1974 to avoid impeachment following the Watergate scandal. He is shown here leaving the White House for the last time aboard the presidential helicopter Marine One.

A series of sensational revelations in the *Washington Post* kept the story alive. Using an inside source known only as Deep Throat (later revealed to be FBI associate director Mark Felt), Bob Woodward and Carl Bernstein, investigative reporters for the *Post*, alleged that key members of Nixon's reelection committee, including its chairman, former Attorney General John Mitchell, and White House staff were actively involved in the break-in and, more important, in the subsequent attempts at a cover-up.

In February 1973, the U.S. Senate formed a Special Select Committee on Campaign Activities—the "Watergate Committee"—to delve into Watergate and related activities. The committee's nationally televised hearings enthralled millions of viewers with lurid stories of "the White House horrors." John Dean broke with the White House and testified before the committee that he had earlier warned Nixon that the cover-up was "a cancer growing on the presidency." Then, in a dramatic revelation, the committee learned that President Nixon maintained a secret tape-recording system in the Oval Office. Hoping that the tapes would prove or disprove charges of Nixon's involvement in the cover-up, the committee issued a subpoena to the White House. Nixon refused to comply, arguing that the constitutional separation of powers gave the president an "executive privilege" to withhold his private conversations from Congress. The U.S. Supreme Court, voting 8 to 0 in *United States v. Richard M. Nixon*, ordered Nixon to turn over the tapes. Committee members interpreted them as confirming Nixon's involvement in the payoffs and cover-up. Informed by congressional leaders of his own party that impeachment by a majority of the House and removal from office by two-thirds of the Senate were assured, on August 9, 1974, Richard Nixon resigned his office.

On September 8, 1974, new President Gerald R. Ford pardoned former President Nixon "for all offenses against the United States which he, Richard Nixon, has committed or may have committed or taken part in" during his presidency. Upon his death in 1994, Nixon was eulogized for his foreign policy successes; however, his presidency heightened the scrutiny of every one of his successors in the use of executive prerogative, and it also confirmed the worse fears of the Imperial presidency.

QUESTIONS

1. Was Nixon's presidency really "imperial"? Why or why not?
2. How would the Watergate affair have turned out if Congress had not had the power of impeachment?

Schlesinger, Arthur M., Jr., *The Imperial Presidency*, Boston: Houghton Mifflin Company, 1973.

by the Constitution or by the laws."[3] Although the constitutional question has never been fully resolved, history has generally sided with those presidents who have taken an expansive view of their powers (see also *A Conflicting View:* Watergate: The Limits of the Imperial Presidency?).

executive privilege
Right of a president to withhold from other branches of government confidential communications within the executive branch; although posited by presidents, it has been upheld by the Supreme Court only in limited situations.

Some Historical Examples

U.S. history is filled with examples of presidents acting independently, beyond specific constitutional powers or laws of Congress. The most notable include:

- George Washington issued a Proclamation of Neutrality during the war between France and Britain following the French Revolution, thereby establishing the president's power to make foreign policy.
- Thomas Jefferson, who prior to becoming president argued for a narrow interpretation of presidential powers, purchased the Louisiana Territory despite the fact that the Constitution contains no provision for the acquisition of territory, let alone authorizing presidential action to do so.
- Andrew Jackson ordered the removal of federal funds from the national bank and removed his secretary of the treasury from office, establishing the president's power to *remove* executive officials, a power not specifically mentioned in the Constitution.
- Abraham Lincoln, asking, "Was it possible to lose the nation yet preserve the Constitution?" established the precedent of vigorous presidential action in national emergencies: he blockaded southern ports, declared martial law in parts of the country, and issued the Emancipation Proclamation—all without constitutional or congressional authority.
- Franklin D. Roosevelt, battling the Great Depression during the 1930s, ordered the nation's banks to close temporarily. Following the Japanese attack on Pearl Harbor in 1941, he ordered the incarceration without trial of many thousands of Americans of Japanese ancestry living on the West Coast.

Checking Presidential Power

President Harry Truman believed that "the president has the right to keep the country from going to hell" and was willing to use means beyond those specified in the Constitution or authorized by Congress. In 1952, while U.S. troops were fighting in Korea, steelworkers at home were threatening to strike. Rather than cross organized labor by forbidding the strike under the terms of the Taft-Hartley Act of 1947 (which he had opposed), Truman chose to seize the steel mills by executive order and continue their operations under U.S. government control. The U.S. Supreme Court ordered the steel mills returned to their owners, however, acknowledging that the president may have inherent powers to act in a national emergency but arguing that Congress had provided a legal remedy, however distasteful to the president. Thus, the president can indeed act to keep the country from "going to hell," but if Congress has already acted to do so, the president must abide by the law.[4]

Executive Privilege

Over the years, presidents and scholars have argued that the Constitution's establishment of a separate executive branch of government entitles the president to **executive privilege**—the right to keep confidential communications from other branches of government. Public exposure of internal executive communications would inhibit the president's ability to obtain candid advice from subordinates and would obstruct the president's ability to conduct negotiations with foreign governments or to command military operations.

But Congress has never recognized executive privilege. It has frequently tried to compel the testimony of executive officials at congressional hearings. Presidents have regularly refused to appear themselves at congressional hearings and have frequently

11.1

11.2

11.3

11.4

11.5

11.6

11.7

11.8

Watergate
The scandal that led to the forced resignation of President Richard M. Nixon. Adding "-gate" as a suffix to any alleged corruption in government suggests an analogy to the Watergate scandal.

impoundment
Refusal by a president to spend monies appropriated by Congress; outlawed except with congressional consent by the Budget and Impoundment Control Act of 1974.

deferrals
Items on which a president wishes to postpone spending.

rescissions
Items on which a president wishes to cancel spending.

refused to allow other executive officials to appear or divulge specific information, citing executive privilege. The federal courts have generally refrained from intervening in this dispute between the executive and legislative branches. However, the Supreme Court has ruled that the president is not immune from court orders when illegal acts are under investigation. In *United States v. Nixon* (1974), the U.S. Supreme Court acknowledged that although the president might legitimately claim executive privilege where military or diplomatic matters are involved, such a privilege cannot be invoked in a criminal investigation. The Court ordered President Nixon to surrender tape recordings of White House conversations between the president and his advisers during the **Watergate** scandal.[5] Subsequent presidents have made similar claims to executive privilege, and vice president Dick Cheney once made the unique claim that the vice president's office is not bound by information requests directed at the executive branch because it is also part of the legislature as presiding officer of the Senate.

☐ Presidential Impoundment

The Constitution states that "no Money shall be drawn from the Treasury, but in Consequence of appropriations made by Law" (Article I, Section 9). Clearly the president cannot spend money *not* appropriated by Congress. But the Constitution is silent on whether the president *must* spend all of the money appropriated by Congress for various purposes. Presidents from Thomas Jefferson onward frequently refused to spend money appropriated by Congress, an action referred to as **impoundment**. But taking advantage of a presidency weakened by the Watergate scandal, the Congress in 1974 passed the Budget and Impoundment Control Act, which requires the president to spend all appropriated funds. The act does provide, however, that presidents may send Congress a list of specific **deferrals**—items on which they wish to postpone spending—and **rescissions**—items they wish to cancel altogether. Congress by *resolution* (which cannot be vetoed by the president) may restore the deferrals and force the president to spend the money. Both houses of Congress must approve a rescission; otherwise the government must spend the money.

☐ Responsibility to the Courts

The president is not "above the law"; that is, his conduct is not immune from judicial scrutiny. The president's official conduct must be lawful; federal courts may reverse presidential actions found to be unconstitutional or violative of laws of Congress. And presidents are not immune from criminal prosecution; they cannot ignore demands to provide information in criminal cases. However, the Supreme Court has held that the president has "absolute immunity" from civil suits "arising out of the execution of official duties."[6] In other words, the president cannot be sued for damages caused by actions or decisions that are within his constitutional or legal authority.

But can the president be sued for *private* conduct beyond the scope of his official duties? In 1997, the U.S. Supreme Court rejected the notion of presidential immunity from civil claims arising from actions outside of the president's official duties.[7]

Political Resources of the President

11.3 Assess the sources of the president's political power and analyze how presidents' personality and policy positions impact their approval ratings.

The real sources of presidential power are not found in the Constitution. Political scientist Richard Neustadt argued that the president's power is the *power to persuade*. As Harry Truman put it, "I sit here all day trying to persuade people to do things they ought to have sense enough to do without my persuading them. . . . That's all the powers of the president amount to."[8]

The president's political resources are potentially very great. The nation looks to the president for leadership, for direction, for reassurance. The president is the focus of public and media attention. The president has the capacity to mobilize public opinion, to communicate directly with the American people, and to employ the symbols of office to advance policy initiatives in both foreign and domestic affairs.

The Reputation for Power

A reputation for power is itself a source of power. Presidents must strive to maintain the image of power in order to be effective. A president perceived as powerful, especially by the national media, can exercise great influence abroad with foreign governments and at home with the Congress, interest groups, and the executive bureaucracy. A president perceived as weak, unsteady, bumbling, or error prone will soon become unpopular and ineffective.

Presidential Popularity

Presidential popularity with the American people is a political resource. Popular presidents cannot always transfer their popularity into foreign policy successes or legislative victories, but popular presidents usually have more success than unpopular presidents.

Presidential popularity is regularly tracked in national opinion polls. For more than 40 years, national surveys have asked the American public: "Do you approve or disapprove of the way _______ is handling his job as president?" (see Figures 11.2 and 11.3). Analyses of variations over time in these poll results suggest some generalizations about presidential popularity (see Figure 11.2).

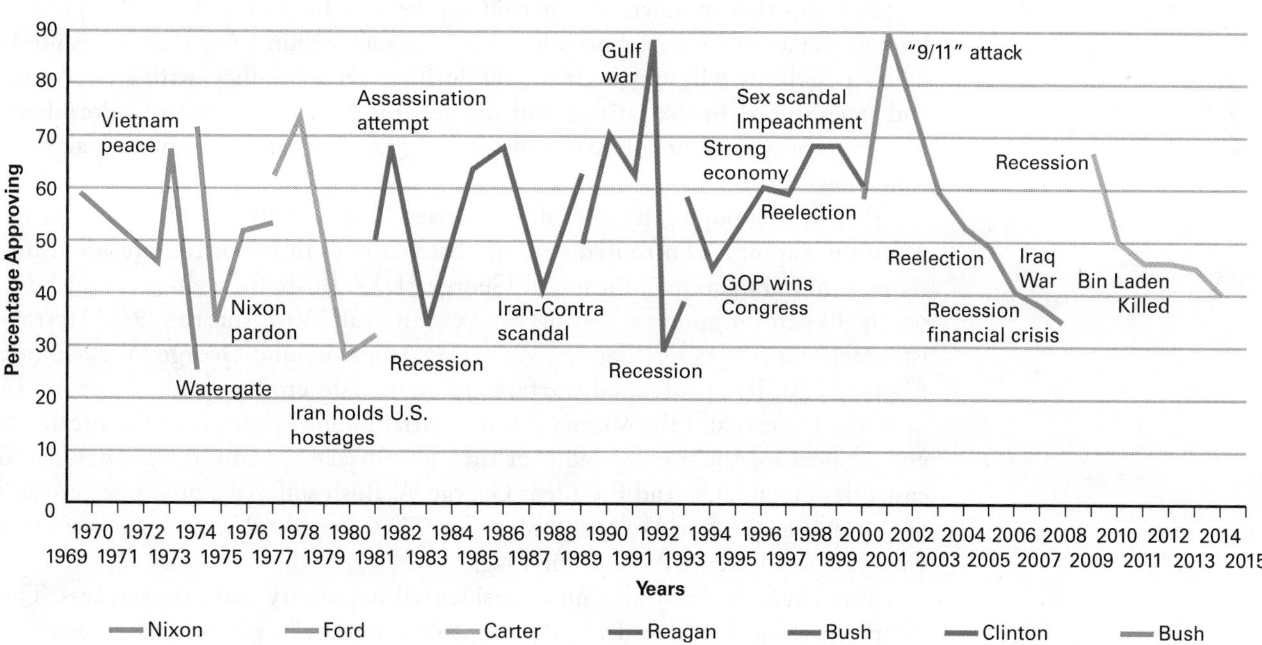

FIGURE 11.2 THE BATTLE FOR PUBLIC APPROVAL: PRESIDENTIAL POPULARITY OVER TIME

Americans expect a great deal from their presidents and are quick to give these leaders the credit—and the blame—for major events in the nation's life. In general, public approval (as measured by response to the question, "Do you approve or disapprove of the way _______ is handling the job of president?") is highest at the beginning of a new president's term in office and declines from that point. Major military conflicts generally raise presidential ratings initially but can cause dramatic decline if the conflict drags on. In addition, public approval of the president is closely linked to the nation's economic health. When the economy is in recession, Americans tend to take a negative view of the president.

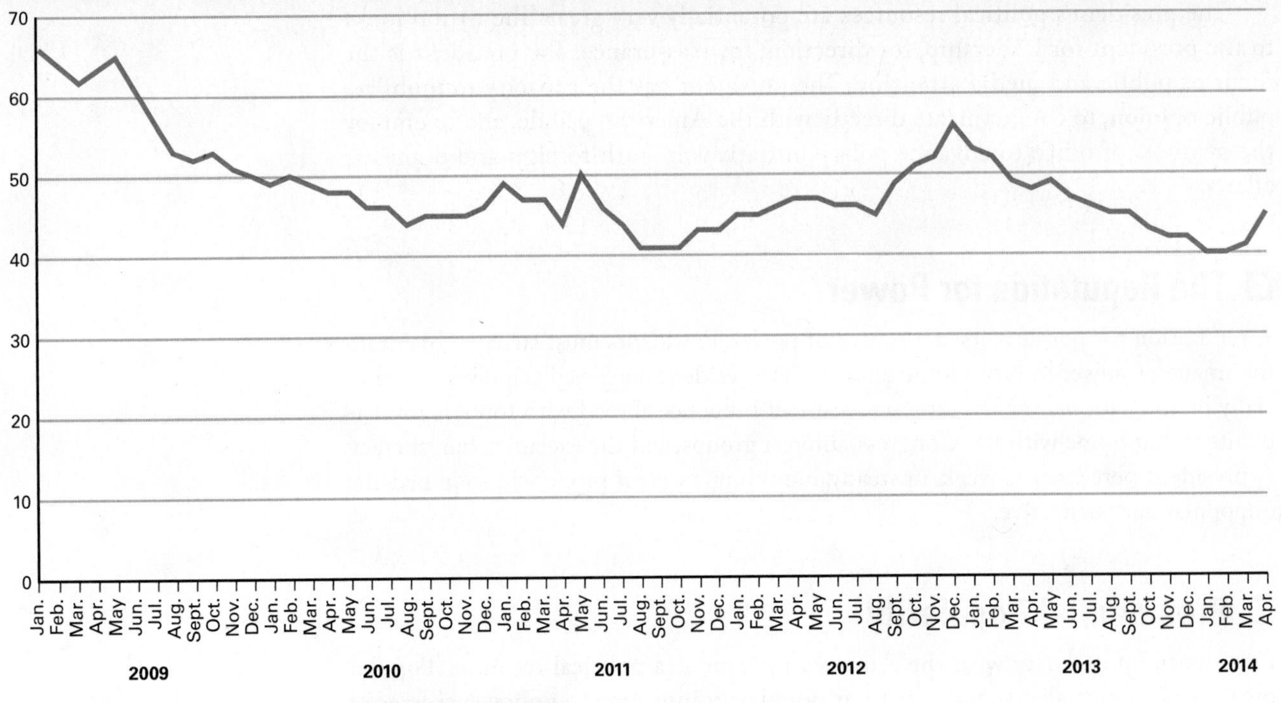

FIGURE 11.3 BARACK OBAMA'S APPROVAL RATINGS

President Obama began his term in office with high approval ratings, but over time, his approval rating dropped to under 50 percent.

SOURCE: Various polls reported in *The Polling Report*, www.pollingreport.com.

Presidential popularity is usually high at the beginning of a president's term of office, but this "honeymoon" period can be very brief. The American public's high expectations for a new president can turn sour within a few months. A president's popularity will vary a great deal during a term in office, with sharp peaks and steep valleys in the ratings. But the general trend is downward.[9] Presidents usually recover some popularity at the end of their first term as they campaign for reelection.

Presidential popularity rises during crises. People "rally 'round the president" when the nation is confronted with an international threat or the president initiates a military action.[10] President George H. W. Bush, for example, registered nearly 90 percent approval during the Persian Gulf War. And the "9/11" terrorist attacks on America rallied the American people behind George W. Bush (see Figure 11.3). But prolonged warfare and stalemate erode popular support. In both the Korean and the Vietnam wars, initial public approval of the president and support for the war eroded over time as military operations stalemated and casualties mounted.[11] And President George W. Bush suffered a prolonged erosion of approval as the Iraq War continued (see *The Game, the Rules, the Players*: Does Congress Really Rally Around the Flag?).

Major scandals *may* also hurt presidential popularity and effectiveness. The Watergate scandal produced a low of 22 percent approval for Nixon just prior to his resignation. Reagan's generally high approval ratings were blemished by the Iran-Contra scandal hearings in 1987, although he ultimately left office with a high approval rate. But highly publicized allegations of sexual improprieties against President Clinton in early 1998 appeared to have the opposite effect; Clinton's approval ratings went *up*. The Clinton scandal demonstrated that the public can differentiate between private conduct and performance in office—polling indicated intense disapproval of the president's personal conduct, while approval for his official conduct in office remained high.

Finally, economic recessions erode presidential popularity. Every president in office during a recession has suffered loss of popular approval, including President Reagan during the 1982 recession. But no president suffered a more precipitous decline in approval ratings than George H. W. Bush, whose popularity plummeted from its Gulf War high of 89 percent in 1991 to a low of 37 percent in only a year, largely as a result of recession. His son's approval rating sank below 30 percent during the recession and financial crisis that engulfed the nation in 2008.

White House press corps
Reporters from both print and broadcast media assigned to regularly cover the president.

☐ Access to the Media

The president dominates the news more than any other single person. All major television networks, newspapers, and newsmagazines have reporters (usually their most experienced and skilled people) covering the "White House beat." The presidential press secretary briefs these reporters daily, but the president also may appear in person in the White House pressroom at any time. Presidents regularly use this media access to advance their programs and priorities.[12]

The **White House press corps** is an elite group of reporters assigned to cover the president. It includes the prestige press—the *New York Times*, *Washington Post*, *Wall Street Journal*, *Time*, *Newsweek*, *U.S. News & World Report*—as well as the television networks—ABC, CBS, NBC, CNN, FOX, and even the foreign press. Indeed, more than 1,800 journalists have White House press credentials. Fortunately, however, not all show up at once (there are only 48 seats in the White House briefing room, and attendance at press

THE WHITE HOUSE PRESS CORPS

The White Press Corps keeps constant vigil on the president, covering both substantive and symbolic events. Recent presidents hold relatively few White House press conferences, preferring instead to travel to town halls outside of Washington, where questions are easier to handle than those coming from knowledgeable White House reporters.

What Do You Think?

Are There Keys to the Presidency?

Historian Allan Lichtman's claims that there are 13 factors that determine who wins the presidency. If a candidate scores eight of these factors (called keys) positively, he wins the popular vote.

There are two types of keys. Some of the keys look the same to anyone who looks at them. These are called "objective keys." Others look different depending on who does the looking, and are called "subjective keys."

Objective Keys

- Party mandate: After the midterm elections, does the president's party hold more seats than four years before?
- Incumbency: Is an incumbent president running for reelection?
- Short-term economy: The economy is not in recession during the election campaign.
- Third Party: There is no significant third-party challenge.
- Long-term economy: Real per capita economic growth during the president's term is better than the previous two presidential terms.

Somewhat Subjective Keys

- Contest in the party: The party of the president does not have a serious battle for the nomination.
- Foreign/military failure: The president hasn't had a major failure in foreign or military affairs.
- Foreign/military success: The president has had a major victory in foreign or military affairs.
- Policy change: The president has achieved major changes in national policy.
- Social unrest: There is no sustained social unrest during the term.
- Scandal: The incumbent administration is untainted by major scandal.

Highly Subjective Keys

- Incumbent charisma: The incumbent party's candidate is charismatic or a national hero.
- Challenger charisma: The challenging party's candidate is not charismatic or a national hero.

Evaluating Success: How do the keys do when predicting elections? Pretty darn good. Starting in 1984, and in every election since, the presidential candidate who scored on at least eight of the keys went on to win the presidency. Many of these elections were very close. In these eight elections, the winning candidate had less than 50 percent of the vote three times, and only exceeded 53.5 percent of the popular vote once (Mr. Reagan in 1984). One incumbent was beaten, and the White House changed parties three times.

QUESTIONS

1. Looking back at the last election, do the "keys" to the presidency explain the result?
2. What about looking forward to the next election? Who ought to win based on the keys?
3. Are the issues or candidate qualities that mattered to you represented in the "keys"?

"JFK, Ronald Reagan, Bill Clinton, and Barack Obama were all considered 'charmers'— inspirational speakers whose style was as persuasive as their content."

conferences is usually about 300). The great majority of daily newspapers have no Washington correspondents, but instead rely on national news services, such as the Associated Press.

Formal press conferences are a double-edged sword for the president. They *can* help mobilize popular support for presidential programs. Presidents often try to focus attention on particular issues, and they generally open press conferences with a policy statement on these issues. But reporters' questions and subsequent reporting often refocus the press conference in other directions. Often the lead media story emerging from a press conference has nothing to do with the president's purpose in holding the conference. The president cannot control questions or limit the subject matter of press conferences.

Presidents may also use direct television addresses from the White House. (President Reagan made heavy use of national prime-time television appeals to mobilize support for his programs; he was exceptionally successful in generating telephone calls, wires, and letters to Congress in support of his programs.) However, there is some evidence that with the multiplication of channels available to the public, presidential addresses may have less impact today on public opinion than in previous years. Television ratings for presidential addresses have been declining, and in reaction some broadcast networks have declined to cover presidential addresses.[13] Even the State of the Union Address attracts fewer viewers than in the past. Nonetheless, presidents continue to receive more television and press coverage than any other political figure. And a combination of national speeches, press conferences, speeches to various groups around the country, and media interviews, together with public appearances by members of their administrations, can move public opinion in the president's direction.[14]

☐ Institutional Power

A different argument for presidential power is that it does not arise from personal persuasion, but from the growth of institutional tools and powers that make the president stronger relative to Congress.[15]

The institutional power approach to the presidency argues that power is the ability to move an agenda through Congress. When presidents are successful in Congress, they have power. Presidents are increasingly institutionally powerful because they have more legal ability to act unilaterally. Most constitutional powers enjoyed by presidents are reactive—vetoing legislation, for example—and in almost all interactions with Congress, presidents don't get the last-mover advantage. Vetoes can be overridden; appointments and treaties can be rejected.

Modern presidents obtained a variety of powers to act unilaterally. Component to these powers are two features that give them power: they get to move first and thereby set the status quo for other institutions to react to; and they are unitary actors, and do not have to build coalitions within the institution of the presidency. Institutional growth allows "presidents [to] simply set public policy and dare others to counter." This power is invested in the growth of executive power through agreement and orders.

United States v. Curtiss-Wright (1936) established executive agreements as having the force because of the sole authority of the executive in areas of foreign policy (Curtiss-Wright sold 15 machine guns to Bolivia in violation of an executive agreement). *United States v. Pink* (1942) affirmed that executive agreements effectively have the same force as treaties. And *United States v. Belmont* (1937) extended the authority under executive agreements to encompass executive orders. President Roosevelt seized Russian financial assets in response to the Soviets reneging on American-held debts. The court equated his executive order with federal law. This extension of unilateral executive powers has led presidents to increasingly use these powers—agreements and orders—to pursue policy. They are able to issue directives that affect executive agencies, and which have a ripple effect throughout society. For example, Franklin Roosevelt and Harry Truman substantially advanced civil rights in the United States through executive orders that mandated integration of the federal workforce and the armed forces, respectively, 20 years before the Civil Rights Act of 1964. Richard Nixon made the EPA as an executive agency

BURDENS OF THE OVAL OFFICE

The presidency is an around the clock job, and the Oval Office is the most powerful symbol of the presidency. Here, President Barack Obama confers on the phone with Indian Prime Minister Manmohan Singh on a Saturday afternoon.

via executive order. Bill Clinton dramatically increased public health policy through executive orders despite the failure of his health care reform legislation.

In all of these executive moves, and others involving the president as first mover, Congress could only react. And, because the president has the power of the veto, he can sustain executive order/agreement policy with the support of a minority in one chamber of Congress. So, perhaps, the president's powers extend beyond mere persuasion?

Personality Versus Policy

A president with an engaging personality—warmth, charm, and good humor—can add to his political power. And, of course, a president who seems distant, uncaring, or humorless can erode his political resources. (Richard Nixon's seeming mean-spiritedness contributed to the collapse of his approval ratings during the Watergate scandal; Jimmy Carter's often cold and distant appearance failed to inspire much popular support for his programs; and George H. W. Bush appeared to be uncaring about the economic circumstances of ordinary Americans.) The public evaluates presidents as much on style as on policy substance.[16] (Perhaps no other president in recent times enjoyed so much personal popularity as Ronald Reagan.) If the public thinks the president understands and cares about their problems, they may be willing to continue to approve of the job he is doing despite policy setbacks. In other words, the public evaluates the president by how much they like him as a person. (President Bill Clinton's likability kept his public approval ratings high during the sex scandal and impeachment effort.) Yet, as we have seen, public approval ratings of presidents can rise or fall based on wars and crises, scandals, and economic prosperity or recession, even while their personal style remains unaltered.

Party Leadership

Presidents are leaders of their party, but this role is hardly a source of great strength. It is true that presidents select the national party chair, control the national committee and its Washington staff, and largely direct the national party convention. Incumbent presidents can use this power to help defeat challengers *within* their own parties. President Ford used this power to help defeat challenger Ronald Reagan in 1976; President Carter used it to help defeat challenger Ted Kennedy in 1980; and President George H. W. Bush used it against challenger Pat Buchanan in 1992. But the role of party leader is of limited value to a president in relations with Congress because the parties have few direct controls over their members.

Nevertheless, presidents enjoy much stronger support in Congress from members of their own party than from members of the opposition party. Some of the president's party support in Congress is a product of shared ideological values and policy positions. But Republican Congress members do have some stake in the success of a Republican president, as do Democratic members in the success of a Democratic president. Popular presidents may produce those few extra votes that make the difference for party candidates in close congressional districts.

Policy Leadership

Presidents feel an obligation to exercise policy leadership—develop a policy agenda, present it to the Congress, sell it to the American people, and lobby it through to success. Presidents are less likely than most politicians to pander to public opinion. Rather, they expect to be able to shape public opinion themselves.[17] (See *Who's Getting What?* Big Government, and Some "Change" on the Side?)

Nevertheless, there are times when presidents prudently decide to follow public opinion, rather than try to change it. First of all, presidents who are approaching a reelection contest become more responsive to public opinion. They are less likely to go off into new policy directions or to support unpopular policies. Generally, presidents present their policy initiatives at the beginning of their terms. This period usually corresponds to a president's high public approval rating. Indeed, throughout a presidential

Who's Getting What?

Big Government, and Some "Change" on the Side?

President Barack Obama's policy initiatives during his two terms in office required a vast expansion of the size and power of government, and huge spending increases. The president ran promising "change" to Americans; was this what they expected?

Wall Street Bailout

The Emergency Economic Stabilization Act of 2008 was supported by then-President George W. Bush, the Democratic leadership in Congress, and presidential candidates Barack Obama and John McCain. Opinion polls showed that most Americans opposed a "Wall Street bailout." The act gave the Treasury Department unprecedented power to bail out the nation's financial institutions. The Troubled Asset Relief Program (TARP) allocated over $700 billion to aid banks, insurance companies, and investment firms that held mortgage-backed "toxic assets." General Motors was later added to the list of corporations receiving government assistance. Critics noted that by accepting ownership shares in banks and corporations, the government was tilting toward "socialism." The automotive corporations receiving bailout funds returned to profitability, and the TARP program did return a profit.

The "Stimulus" Package

A massive economic "stimulus" plan was President Obama's principal response to the recession. Spending increases and tax cuts of $787 billion made it the largest single fiscal policy measure in U.S. history. It was financed with unprecedented new debt. Republicans complained that the spending had little to do with creating jobs, but instead only increased liberal government involvement in domestic policy areas. By the end of 2011, job recovery continued to the point where the number of jobs created nearly offset the number lost during the first 18 months of the Obama administration—even as government jobs were eliminated. Total job recovery from the onset of the recession in 2008 was achieved in 2014.

Health Care Reform

President Obama's comprehensive health care reform program promised to transform one-sixth of the nation's economy. At the center of the reform is an individual mandate that all Americans acquire basic health insurance. Federally supervised health insurance exchanges were created in the states to negotiate with insurance companies to provide affordable insurance. Private insurers will no longer be permitted to deny insurance for preexisting conditions or to drop coverage when patients get sick. The president failed in his efforts to get a government-run insurance program, a "public option," included in the legislation. The Congressional Budget Office estimated the cost of PPACA at nearly $1 trillion. The program substantially increased health insurance coverage, especially in states that created their own health insurance exchanges.

Greater Financial Regulation

New regulation and oversight of the nation's financial institutions is designed to avoid future financial crises. A new agency has been created to protect consumers from predatory and deceptive credit card and mortgage loan practices. New authority is granted to the Federal Reserve to intervene when banks, insurance companies, and investment firms considered "too big to fail" face financial difficulties. Critics charged that the government was being authorized to "take over" the nation's financial system.

Cap and Trade

President Obama proposed a new carbon emission ceiling and trading program known as "cap and trade." The federal government would set a total amount of emission allowances, that is, a national "cap" (or ceiling) on carbon emissions. The government then allocates or auctions off to polluting industries and firms tradable emissions allowances (a similar program has been used to manage SO_2 emissions in the U.S. since 1990). Industries are given or sold allowances to pollute; these allowances can then be bought and sold. The system encourages innovation by individual firms; if they reduce their emissions, they can sell their allowances to other firms. The cost of the program will be borne by all energy users, passed on by industries in the form of price increases. Cap and trade passed the Republican-controlled House in 2012, but stalled in the U.S. Senate.

Redistributing Wealth via the Tax Code

Barack Obama campaigned on a promise to lower taxes on the middle class, which he defined as 95 percent of taxpayers. He also pledged to raise taxes on upper-income Americans, which he defined as families earning $250,000 a year or more. The Bush tax cuts expired at the end of 2010 and were extended to 2013. In early 2013, the *American Taxpayer Relief Act of 2012* locked in the marginal rates for most earners, while increasing the top marginal tax rate from 35 to 39.6 percent for people making over $400,000 a year.

National Defense Authorization Act

The government's expansion is not just in terms of size or expenditures. One of the major promises of the Obama administration was to close down the terrorist detention facility at Guantánamo Bay, Cuba. This campaign promise, embraced by libertarians and antiwar activists, was not realized. Instead, the National Defense Authorization Act of 2011, signed by President Obama, authorizes the detention of American citizens suspected of terrorist acts without the benefit of habeas corpus to challenge their detention.

As government expands across a broad range of policy areas, it grows in size and complexity. As government spending increases, the nation goes deeper into debt. Americans increasingly are looking to government, however, rather than to themselves to resolve their problems. In an earlier era, President Ronald Reagan set the tone of American politics: "Government is not the solution. Government is the problem." Under President Obama's vision of "change," government becomes the solution.

QUESTIONS

1. How many of these expansions of government originated in the Obama administration?
2. Of these expansions of government, how many are in response to the fiscal crisis of 2008?

executive orders
Formal regulations governing executive branch operations issued by the president.

term, the higher their approval rating, the more likely they are to present new policy directions and even to take unpopular policy positions. In contrast, presidents experiencing low approval ratings are much less likely to present new policy initiatives or to pursue unpopular policies.[18]

Chief Executive

11.4 Outline the responsibilities of the president as the nation's chief executive.

The president is the chief executive of the nation's largest bureaucracy: 2.7 million civilian employees, 60 independent agencies, 15 departments, and the large Executive Office of the President. The formal organizational chart of the federal government places the president at the head of this giant structure. But the president cannot command this bureaucracy in the fashion of a military officer or a corporation president. When Harry Truman was preparing to turn over the White House to Dwight Eisenhower, he predicted that the general of the army would not understand the presidency: "He'll sit here and say 'Do this! Do that!' and nothing will happen. Poor Ike—it won't be a bit like the army. He'll find it very frustrating." Truman vastly underestimated the political skills of the former general, but the crusty Missourian clearly understood the frustrations confronting the nation's chief executive. The president does not command the executive branch of government but rather stands at its center—persuading, bargaining, negotiating, and compromising to achieve goals.

The Constitutional Executive

The Constitution is vague about the president's authority over the executive branch. It vests executive power in the presidency and grants the president authority to appoint principal officers of the government "by and with the Advice and Consent of the Senate." Under the Constitution, the president may also "require the Opinion, in writing, of the principal Officer in each of the executive Departments, upon any Subject relating to the Duties of their respective Offices." This awkward phrase presumably gives the president the power to oversee operations of the executive departments. Finally, and perhaps most important, the president is instructed to "take Care that the Laws be faithfully executed."

At the same time, Congress has substantial authority over the executive branch. Through its lawmaking abilities, Congress can establish or abolish executive departments and regulate their operations. Congress's "power of the purse" allows it to determine the budget of each department each year and thus to limit or broaden or even "micromanage" the activities of these departments. Moreover, Congress can pressure executive agencies by conducting investigations, calling administrators to task in public hearings, and directly contacting agencies with members' own complaints or those of their constituents.

Executive Orders

Presidents frequently use **executive orders** to implement their policies. Executive orders might direct specific federal agencies to carry out the president's wishes, or direct all federal agencies to pursue the president's preferred course of action. Presidential executive orders derive from the vague constitutional language of Article II granting "executive power" to the president. Presidents regularly issue 50 to 100 executive orders each year. Research suggests that Democratic presidents issue more orders than Republican presidents; presidents issue executive orders to circumvent

Congress but only when they believe Congress will not overturn their orders; and presidents issue more executive orders when they are seeking reelection.[19]

Every president since George Washington issued executive orders. The most-far-reaching occurred during wartime, including Abraham Lincoln's Emancipation Proclamation in 1863. Until 1952 there were no clear rules on what limited the president's use of executive orders. But in that year the Supreme Court held that President Harry Truman's seizing the nation's steel mills during the Korean War in order to avert a strike was unconstitutional. The order failed to follow an Act of Congress that addressed strikes that created a national emergency. Since then, presidents generally cite laws under which they say they are acting when issuing executive orders.[20]

In 2014 President Barack Obama declared his intention to circumvent Congress with executive orders if Congress failed to act as he wished. He ordered the Immigration and Naturalization Service to not enforce immigration laws by deporting children brought to the United States illegally by their parents, after Congress failed to pass a "DREAM Act" to authorize such action. He changed the effective dates of portions of his own health care reform bill (PPACA) following failures in the rollout of the program. And, he ordered an increase in the federal minimum wage that would be paid by federal contractors.

□ Appointments

Presidential power over the executive branch derives in part from the authority to appoint and remove top officials. Presidents shape policy by careful attention to top appointments—cabinet secretaries, agency heads, and White House staff—by selecting people who share the president's policy views and who have the personal qualifications to do an effective job. Political considerations weigh heavily: unifying the president's party; garnering interest-group support; rewarding loyalty; achieving a balance of racial, ethnic, and gender representation.[21] The appointment power gives the president some control over the executive branch. The president only appoints 3,000 of the executive branch's 2.7 million civilian employees. Cabinet secretaries and heads of independent regulatory agencies require congressional confirmation. The White House staff is chosen without the approval of Congress. Most executive branch employees are recruited, paid, and protected under civil service laws and are not easily removed by the president.

Presidents have limited power to remove the heads of independent regulatory agencies. Congress sets the terms of these officials. For example, Federal Communications Commission members are appointed for 5 years, while Federal Reserve Board members, responsible for the nation's money supply, enjoy the longest term of any executive officials—14 years. Congress's sets term length for regulatory agencies to insulate those quasi-judicial agencies from "political" influence.

□ Recess Appointments

Vacancies in judicial and executive branch offices subject to presidential appointment can be temporarily filled when the Senate is not in session, and must be confirmed by the end of the next session of Congress. Recess appointments were traditionally made when Congress was part-time and the Senate was out of session for extended periods of time. In the last two decades, parties opposite the President's have used Senate procedures to forestall or delay confirming presidential appointees. Presidents Clinton, G. W. Bush, and Obama all made controversial recess appointments to significant executive and judicial positions. Obama even went forward with recess appointments when the U.S. Senate was in "gavel session"—the Senate would convene for five minutes then immediately adjourn in order to prevent the president from making recess appointments. These appointments were challenged before the Supreme Court. In 2014 the Court unanimously ruled in *NLRB v. Noel Canning*, 572 U.S. ____ (2014) that the president could not make recess appointments even when the Senate was out of town and open only in a gavel session.

11.1

11.2

11.3

11.4

11.5

11.6

11.7

11.8

cabinet
The heads (secretaries) of the executive departments together with other top officials accorded cabinet rank by the president; only occasionally does it meet as a body to advise and support the president.

□ Budget

Presidential authority also derives from the president's role in the budgetary process. The Constitution makes no mention of the president with regard to expenditures; rather, it grants the power of the purse to Congress. Indeed, for nearly 150 years, executive departments submitted their budget requests directly to the Congress without first submitting them to the president. But with the passage of the Budget and Accounting Act in 1921, Congress established the Office of Management and Budget (OMB) (originally named the Bureau of the Budget) to assist the president in preparing an annual Budget of the United States Government for presentation to the Congress. The president's budget is simply a set of recommendations to Congress. Congress must pass appropriations acts before the president or any executive department or agency may spend money. Congress can and frequently does alter the president's budget recommendations.

□ The Cabinet

The **cabinet** is not mentioned in the U.S. Constitution; it has no formal powers. It consists of the secretaries of the 15 executive departments and others the president may designate, including the vice president, the administrator of the Environmental Protection Agency, the director of the Office of Management and Budget, the director of National Drug Control Policy, and the special trade representative. According to custom, cabinet officials are ranked by the date their departments were created (see Table 11.2). Thus the secretary of state is the senior cabinet officer, followed by the secretary of the treasury. They sit next to the president at cabinet meetings; heads of the newest departments sit at the far ends of the table.

The cabinet rarely functions as a decision-making body. Cabinet officers in the United States are powerful because they head giant administrative organizations. The secretary of state, the secretary of defense, the secretary of the treasury, the attorney general, and, to a lesser extent, the other departmental secretaries are all people of power and prestige. But seldom does a strong president hold a cabinet meeting to decide important policy questions. More frequently, presidents know what they want and hold cabinet meetings only to help promote their views.

The Constitution requires that "officers of the United States" be confirmed by the Senate. In the past, the Senate rarely rejected a presidential cabinet nomination; the traditional view was that presidents were entitled to pick their own people and even make their own mistakes. In recent years, however, the confirmation process has become more partisan and divisive, with the Senate conducting lengthy investigations

TABLE 11.2 THE CABINET DEPARTMENTS

By custom, the 15 executive departments are ranked by their dates of creation.

Department	Created	Department	Created
State	1789	Health and Human Services‡	1953
Treasury	1789	Housing and Urban Development	1965
Defense*	1947	Transportation	1966
Justice	1789	Energy	1977
Interior	1849	Education	1979
Agriculture†	1889	Veterans Affairs	1989
Commerce	1913	Homeland Security	2002
Labor	1913		

*Formerly the War and Navy Departments, created in 1789 and 1798, respectively.

†Agriculture Department created in 1862, made part of cabinet in 1889.

‡Originally Health, Education, and Welfare; reorganized in 1979, with the creation of a separate Department of Education.

THE CABINET

President Obama meeting with his cabinet. The president calls his cabinet together to explain and promote his views, not to decide issues. Cabinet secretaries usually sit nearer to the president based on seniority, with the Secretary of State seated closest.

and holding public hearings on presidential cabinet nominees. The intense public scrutiny and potential for partisan attacks, together with financial disclosure and conflict-of-interest laws, may be discouraging some well-qualified people from accepting cabinet posts.

National Security Council (NSC)

"Inner cabinet" that advises the president and coordinates foreign, defense, and intelligence activities.

The National Security Council

The **National Security Council (NSC)** is really an "inner cabinet" created by law in 1947 to advise the president and coordinate foreign, defense, and intelligence activities. The president is chair, and the vice president, secretary of state, secretary of defense and secretary of the treasury are participating members. The chair of the Joint Chiefs of Staff and the director of central intelligence serve as advisers to the NSC. The president's national security adviser also sits on the NSC and heads its staff. The purposes of the council are to advise and coordinate policy; but in the Iran-Contra scandal in 1987, a staff member of the NSC, Lt. Col. Oliver North, undertook to *implement* security policy by directly channeling funds and arms to Nicaraguan "contras" fighting a communist-dominated government. Various investigative committees strongly recommended that the NSC staff confine itself to an advisory role.

White House Staff

Today, presidents exercise their powers chiefly through the White House staff. This staff includes the president's closest aides and advisers. Over the years, the White House staff has grown from Roosevelt's small "brain trust" of a dozen advisers to several hundred people.

Senior White House staff members are trusted political advisers, often personal friends or long-time associates of the president. Some enjoy office space in the White House itself and daily contact with the president (see Figure 11.4). Appointed without

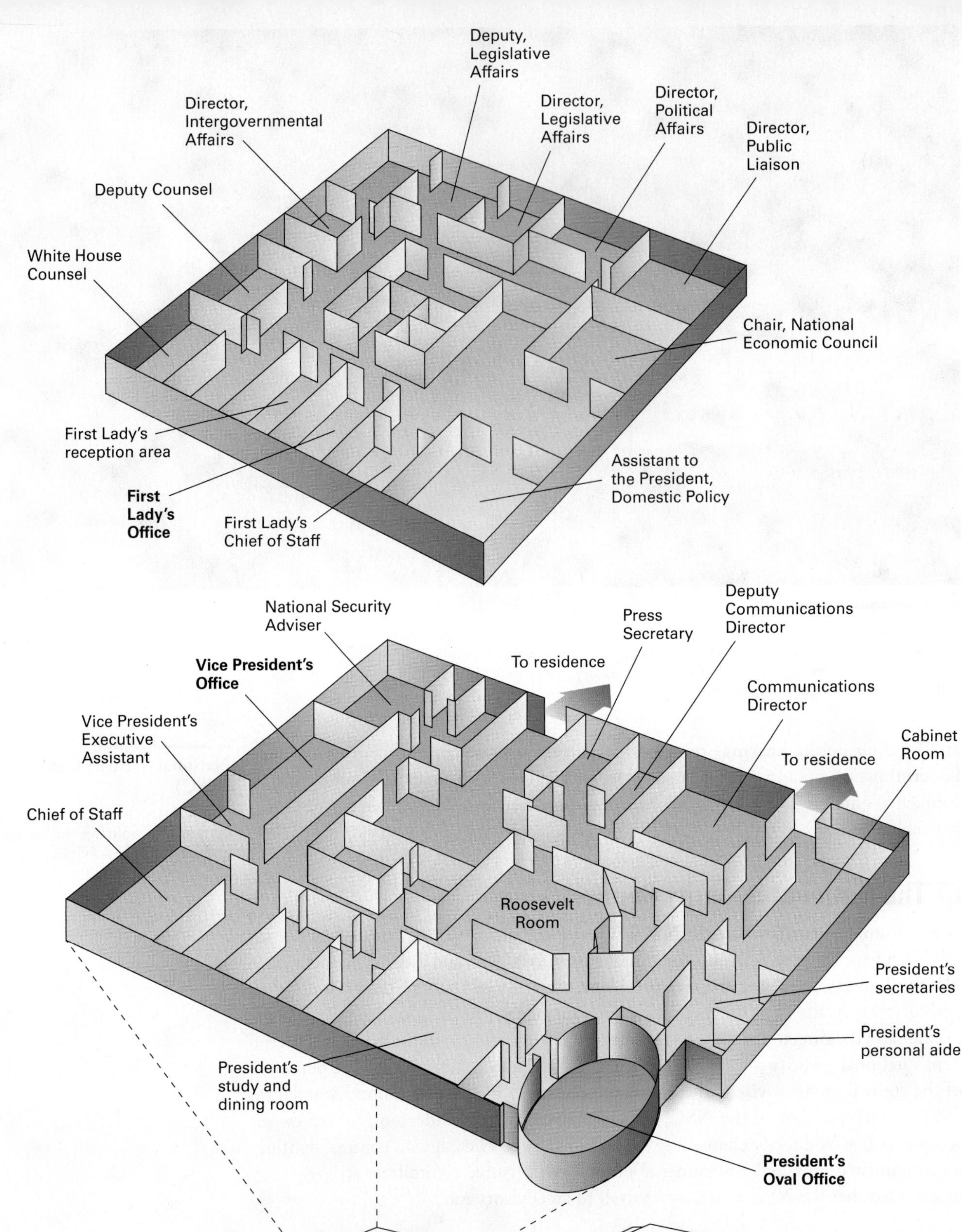

FIGURE 11.4 CORRIDORS OF POWER: THE WHITE HOUSE WEST WING

Presidents allocate office space in the White House according to their own desires. An office located close to the president's is considered an indication of the power of the occupant. This diagram shows the office assignments during the Clinton administration.

Senate confirmation, they are loyal to the president alone, not to departments, agencies, or interest groups. Their many tasks include the following:

- Providing the president with sound advice on everything from national security to congressional affairs, policy development, and electoral politics.
- Monitoring the operations of executive departments and agencies and evaluating the performance of key executive officials.
- Setting the president's schedule, determining whom the president will see and call, where and when the president will travel, and where and to whom the president will make personal appearances and speeches.
- Above all, protecting their boss and steering the president away from scandal, political blunders, and errors of judgment.

The senior White House staff normally includes a chief of staff, the national security adviser, a press secretary, the counsel to the president (an attorney), a director of personnel (patronage appointments), and assistants for political affairs, legislative liaison, and domestic policy. Staff organization depends on each president's personal taste. Some presidents have organized their staffs hierarchically, concentrating power in the chief of staff. Others have maintained direct contact with several staff members.

Chief Legislator and Lobbyist

11.5 Analyze the factors affecting the success of the president as the chief legislator and lobbyist.

The president has the principal responsibility for the initiation of national policy. Indeed, about 80 percent of the bills considered by Congress originate in the executive branch. Presidents have a strong incentive to fulfill this responsibility: the American people hold them responsible for anything that happens in the nation during their term of office, whether or not they have the authority or capacity to do anything about it.

Policy Initiation

The Founders understood that the president would be involved in policy initiation. The Constitution requires the president to "give to the Congress Information of the State of the Union," to "recommend to their Consideration such Measures as he shall judge necessary and expedient" (Article II, Section 3). "On extraordinary Occasions" the president may call a recessed Congress into special session. Each year, the principal policy statement of the president comes in the State of the Union message to Congress. It is followed by the president's Budget of the United States Government, which sets forth the president's programs with price tags attached. Many other policy proposals are developed by executive departments and agencies, transmitted to the White House for the president's approval or "clearance," and then sent to Congress.

Congress may not accept all or even most of the president's proposals. Indeed, from time to time it may even try to develop its own legislative agenda in competition with the president's. But the president's legislative initiatives usually set the agenda of congressional decision making. As one experienced Washington lobbyist put it, "Obviously when the president sends up a bill, it takes first place in the queue. All other bills take second place."[22]

THE STATE OF THE UNION

Originally a minor function handled by correspondence, the State of the Union Address has evolved into a major policy and political speech.

White House Lobbying

Presidents do not simply send their bills to Congress and then await the outcome. The president is also expected to be the chief lobbyist on behalf of the administration's

11.1

11.2

11.3

11.4

11.5

11.6

11.7

11.8

honeymoon period
Early months of a president's term in which his popularity with the public and influence with the Congress are generally high.

bills as they make their way through the legislative labyrinth. The White House staff includes "legislative liaison" people—lobbyists for the president's programs. They organize the president's legislative proposals, track them through committee and floor proceedings, arrange committee appearances by executive department and agency representatives, count votes, and advise the president on when and how to "cut deals" and "twist arms."

Presidents are not without resources in lobbying Congress. They may exchange many favors, large and small, for the support of individual members. They can help direct "pork" to a member's district, promise White House support for a member's pet project, and assist in resolving a member's problems with the bureaucracy. Presidents also may issue or withhold invitations to the White House for prestigious ceremonies, dinners with visiting heads of state, and other glittering social occasions—an effective resource because most members of Congress value the prestige associated with close White House "connections."[23]

The president may choose to "twist arms" individually—by telephoning and meeting with wavering members of Congress. Arm twisting is generally reserved for the president's most important legislative battles. There is seldom time for a president to contact individual members of Congress personally about many bills in various stages of the legislative process—in subcommittee, full committee, floor consideration, conference committee, and final passage—in both the House and the Senate. Instead, the president must rely on White House staff for most legislative contacts and use personal appeals sparingly.

President Barack Obama has relied more on an "outside strategy" for lobbying Congress, rather than direct efforts at "twisting arms" or "cutting deals" with individual members. Obama boosted his legislative proposals in speeches and town meetings across the country in attempts to rally the grassroots. Even some of his supporters complained that he leaves to Congress many of the details of bills, as well as the negotiations and compromises needed to pass legislation. The result was the empowerment of congressional committee chairs and Senate Majority Leader Harry Reid and the (then) Speaker of the House Nancy Pelosi, and, it has been argued, the consequence was unpopular legislation and a loss of control of the House in the midterm election.

The Honeymoon

The **honeymoon period** at the very start of a president's term offers the best opportunity to get the new administration's legislative proposals enacted into law. Presidential influence in Congress is generally highest at this time both because the president's personal popularity is typically at its height and because the president can claim the recent election results as a popular mandate for key programs. Sophisticated members of Congress know that votes cast for a presidential candidate are not necessarily votes cast for that candidate's policy positions. But election results signal to members of Congress, in a language they understand well, that the president is politically popular and that they must give the administration's programs careful consideration. President Lyndon Johnson succeeded in getting the bulk of his Great Society program enacted in the year following his landslide victory in 1964. Ronald Reagan pushed through the largest tax cut in American history in the year following his convincing electoral victory over incumbent president Jimmy Carter in 1980. Bill Clinton was most successful with the Congress during his first year in office, in 1993, even winning approval for a major tax increase as part of a deficit-reduction package. George W. Bush succeeded in getting a tax cut through Congress in his first six months in office. Both Democrat Clinton and Republican Bush benefited from having their party control the Congress during their first months in office. And Democrat Barack Obama enjoyed Democratic control of the House and Senate in his first years in office. His overall success rate in Congress exceeded any previous president, but declined when Republicans captured the U.S. House.

Presidential "Box Scores"

gridlock
Political stalemate between the executive and legislative branches arising when one branch is controlled by one major political party and the other branch by the other party.

How successful are presidents in getting their legislation through Congress? *Congressional Quarterly* regularly compiles "box scores" of presidential success in Congress—percentages of presidential victories on congressional votes on which the president took a clear-cut position. The measure does not distinguish between bills that were important to the president and bills that may have been less significant. But viewed over time (see Figure 11.5), the presidential box scores provide interesting insights into the factors affecting the president's legislative success.

The most important determinant of presidential success in Congress is party control. Presidents are far more successful when they face a Congress controlled by their own party. Democratic presidents John F. Kennedy and Lyndon Johnson enjoyed the support of Democratic-controlled Congresses and posted average success scores over 80 percent. Jimmy Carter was hardly a popular president, but he enjoyed the support of a Democratic Congress and an average of 76.8 percent presidential support. Republican presidents Richard Nixon and Gerald Ford fared poorly with Democratic-controlled Congresses. Republican president Ronald Reagan was very successful in his first term when he faced a Democratic House and a Republican Senate, but after Democrats took over both houses of Congress, his success rate plummeted. During the Reagan and first Bush presidencies, divided party control of government (Republicans in the White House and Democrats controlling one or both houses of Congress) was said to produce **gridlock**, the political inability of the government to act decisively on the nation's problems. President Bill Clinton's achievements when Democrats controlled the Congress (1993–94) contrasted with his dismal record in dealing with Republican-controlled Congresses (1995–99). Likewise, President George W. Bush was very successful when Republicans controlled Congress, but his success evaporated after Democrats gained control. Barack Obama's record success rate in his first two years can be attributed to heavy Democratic margins in both Houses. The Republican

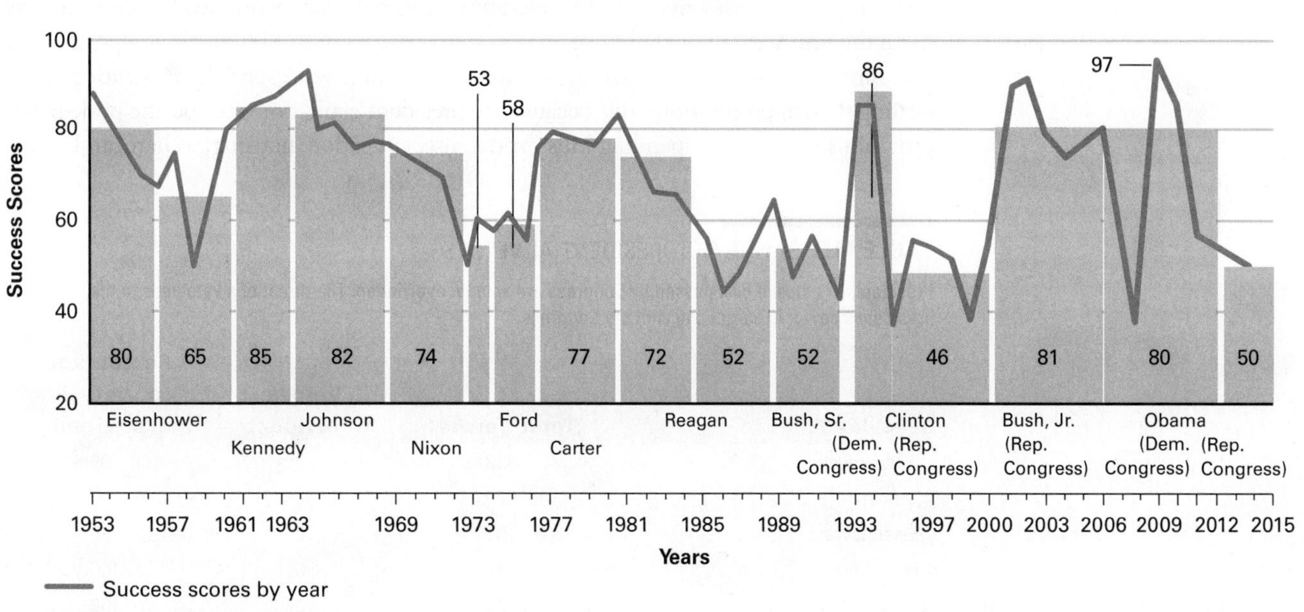

FIGURE 11.5 BOX SCORES: PRESIDENTIAL SUCCESS IN CONGRESS

Presidential "box scores"—the percentage of times that a bill endorsed by the president is enacted by Congress—are closely linked to the strength of the president's party in Congress. For example, both Dwight D. Eisenhower and Ronald Reagan benefited from having a Republican majority in the Senate in their first terms and suffered when Democrats gained control of the Senate in their second terms. Democratic control of both houses of Congress resulted in high box scores for Democratic presidents John Kennedy, Lyndon Johnson, and Jimmy Carter. Clinton was very successful in his first two years, when the Democrats controlled Congress, but when the Republicans won control following the 1994 midterm election, his box score plummeted. When George W. Bush enjoyed a Republican Congress, he succeeded in passing over 80 percent of his bills; however, his success fell dramatically with the election of a Democratic Congress. Presidents succeed most often in their first year in office—the "honeymoon" period. This was true of Barack Obama; he enjoyed a record success rate in his first year, and had continued success in 2010; but his congressional success fell off dramatically with the election of a Republican-controlled House of Representatives.

11.1

11.2

11.3

11.4

11.5

11.6

11.7

11.8

veto
Rejection of a legislative act by the executive branch; in the U.S. federal government, overriding of a veto requires a two-thirds majority in both houses of Congress.

pocket veto
Effective veto of a bill when Congress adjourns within 10 days of passing it and the president fails to sign it.

override
Voting in Congress to enact legislation vetoed by the president; requires a two-thirds vote in both the House and Senate.

line-item veto
Power of the chief executive to reject some portions of a bill without rejecting all of it.

capture of the House in 2010 promised gridlock—and while President Obama had a generally successful scorecard, it paled compared to his first two years.

☐ The Veto Power

The **veto** is the president's most powerful weapon in dealing with Congress. The veto is especially important to a president facing a Congress controlled by the opposition party. Even the *threat* of a veto enhances the president's bargaining power with Congress.[24] Confronted with such a threat, congressional leaders must calculate whether they can muster a two-thirds vote of both houses to override the veto.

To veto a bill passed by Congress, the president sends to Congress a veto message specifying reasons for not signing it. If the president takes no action for 10 days (excluding Sundays) after Congress has passed a bill, the bill becomes law without the president's signature. However, if Congress has adjourned within 10 days of passing a bill and the president has not signed it, then the bill does not become law; this outcome is called a **pocket veto**.

A bill returned to Congress with a presidential veto message can be passed into law over the president's opposition by a two-thirds vote of both houses. (A bill that has received a pocket veto cannot be overridden because the Congress is no longer in session.) In other words, the president needs only to hold the loyalty of more than one-third of *either* the House or the Senate to sustain a veto. If congressional leaders cannot count on the votes to **override**, they are forced to bargain with the president. "What will the president accept?" becomes a key legislative question.

The president's bargaining power with Congress has been enhanced over the years by a history of success in sustaining presidential vetoes. From George Washington to Barack Obama, more than 96 percent of all presidential vetoes have been sustained (see Table 11.3).

☐ Line-Item Veto Power Denied

For many years, presidents, both Democratic and Republican, petitioned Congress to give them the **line-item veto**, the ability to veto some provisions of a bill while accepting other provisions. The lack of presidential line-item veto power was especially frustrating when dealing with appropriations bills because the president could not veto specific pork-barrel provisions from major spending bills for defense, education, housing, welfare, and so on.

TABLE 11.3 SAYING NO: PRESIDENTIAL VETOES

Presidential vetoes of bills passed by Congress are seldom overridden. The threat of a veto adds to the president's power in bargaining with the Congress.

President	Total Vetoes*	Vetoes Overridden	Percentage of Vetoes Sustained
F. Roosevelt	633	9	99%
Truman	250	12	95
Eisenhower	181	2	99
Kennedy	21	0	100
L. Johnson	30	0	100
Nixon	43	5	90
Ford	66	12	85
Carter	31	2	94
Reagan	78	8	91
G. H. W. Bush	46	1	98
Clinton	37	2	95
G. W. Bush	8	1	88
Obama (2009–14)	2	0	100

*Regular vetoes plus pocket vetoes.

SOURCE: Harold W. Stanley and Richard G. Niemi, *Vital Statistics on American Politics, 1999–2000*. Washington, D.C.: CQ Press, 2000, p. 256. Updated by authors.

Finally, in 1996, Congress granted the president authority to "cancel" spending items in any appropriation act and any limited tax benefit. Such cancellation would take effect immediately unless blocked by a special "disapproval bill" passed by Congress.

However, opponents of the line-item veto successfully challenged its constitutionality, arguing that it transfers legislative power—granted by the Constitution only to Congress—to the president. The U.S. Supreme Court agreed: "There is no provision in the Constitution that authorizes the president to enact or amend or repeal statutes." The line-item veto, the Court said, "authorizes the president himself to elect to repeal laws, for his own policy reasons" and therefore violates the law-making procedures set forth in Article I of the Constitution.[25]

Global Leader

11.6 Assess the role of the president as a global leader.

The president of the United States is the leader of the world's largest and most powerful democracy. During the Cold War, the president of the United States was seen as the leader of the "free world." The threat of Soviet expansionism, the huge military forces of the Warsaw Pact, and Soviet-backed guerrilla wars around the world all added to the global role of the American president as the defender of democratic values. In today's post–Cold War

THE SPECIAL RELATIONSHIP

The president is recognized throughout the world as the American "head of state"; this power aids him in dominating American foreign and defense policy making. The American relationship with Great Britain is especially important. Here, President Obama and British Prime Minister David Cameron take in an NCAA basketball game.

11.1

11.2

11.3

11.4

11.5

11.6

11.7

11.8

diplomatic recognition
Power of the president to grant or withhold "legitimacy" to or from a government of another nation (to declare or refuse to declare it "rightful").

treaty
A formal agreement with another nation (bilateral) or nations (multilateral) signed by the president and consented to by the Senate by a two-thirds vote.

world, Western Europe and Japan are formidable economic competitors and no longer routinely defer to American political leadership. But if a new stable world order based on democracy and self-determination is to emerge, the president of the United States must provide the necessary leadership.

Global leadership is based on a president's powers of persuasion—and on the ability to deliver, whether it be promise or threat.[26] Presidents are more persuasive when the American economy is strong, when American military forces are perceived as ready and capable, and when the president is seen as having the support of the American people and Congress. America's allies as well as its enemies perceive the president as the controlling force over U.S. foreign and military policy. Only occasionally do they seek to bypass the president and appeal to the Congress or to American public opinion.

Presidents sometimes prefer their global role to the much more contentious infighting of domestic politics. Abroad, presidents are treated with great dignity as head of the world's most powerful state. In contrast, at home presidents must confront hostile and insulting reporters, backbiting bureaucrats, demanding interest groups, and contentious members of Congress.

☐ Foreign Policy

As the nation's chief diplomat, the president has the principal responsibility for formulating U.S. foreign policy. The president's constitutional powers in foreign affairs are relatively modest. Presidents have the power to make treaties with foreign nations "with the Advice and Consent of the Senate." Presidents may negotiate with nations separately or through international organizations such as the North Atlantic Treaty Organization (NATO) or the United Nations, where the president determines the U.S. position in that body's deliberations. The Constitution also empowers the president to "appoint Ambassadors, other public Ministers, and Consuls" and to "receive Ambassadors." This power of **diplomatic recognition** permits a president to grant or withhold legitimacy to or from ruling groups around the world (to declare or refuse to declare them "rightful"). Despite controversy, President Franklin Roosevelt officially recognized the communist regime in Russia in 1933, Richard Nixon recognized the communist government of the People's Republic of China in 1972, and Carter recognized the communist Sandinistas' regime in Nicaragua in 1979. To date, all presidents have withheld diplomatic recognition of the Castro government in Cuba.

Presidents have expanded on these modest constitutional powers to dominate American foreign policy making. In part, they have done so as a product of their role as Commander in Chief. Military force is the ultimate diplomatic language. During wartime, or when war is threatened, military and foreign policy become inseparable. The president must decide on the use of force and, equally important, when and under what conditions to order a cease-fire or an end to hostilities.

Presidents have also come to dominate foreign policy as a product of the customary international recognition of the head of state as the legitimate voice of a government. Although nations may also watch the words and actions of the American Congress, the president's statements are generally taken to represent the official position of the U.S. government.

☐ Treaties

Treaties the president makes "by and with the Advice and Consent of the Senate" are legally binding upon the United States. The Constitution specifies that "all Treaties made . . . under the Authority of the United States, shall be the supreme Law of the Land, and the Judges in every State shall be bound thereby" (Article VI). Thus **treaty** provisions are directly enforceable in federal courts.

Although presidents may or may not listen to "advice" from the Senate on foreign policy, no formal treaty is valid unless "two-thirds of the Senators present concur" to its ratification. Although the Senate has ratified the vast majority of treaties, presidents must be sensitive to Senate concerns. The Senate defeat of the Versailles Treaty in 1920, which formally ended World War I and established the League of Nations,

11.1
11.2
11.3
11.4
11.5
11.6
11.7
11.8

Compared to What?

Parliaments, Ministers, and No Confidence

Most parliamentary democracies separate the head of government role from the head of state role, typically filled by a president or monarch. The role of the head of state is usually a unifying role and invested mainly with symbolic powers. Lawmaking and policy powers are invested in the head of government.

The executive in the United States is elected separate from the legislature, but the president of the United States still acts as a head of government as well as a head of state. The presidential cabinet is selected by the president, but confirmed by the Senate. No one may serve in the executive branch and as a lawmaker as well.

In parliamentary democracies, the head of government—often called first minister, prime minister, or chancellor—comes from the legislative majority. This first minister is assisted by a cabinet of ministers, chosen from among the members of parliament to lead executive departments. These cabinet members continue to be voting members of the lawmaking body. The minority party often has a "shadow" cabinet made up of members of the minority who mirror the cabinet minister roles of the majority.

Parliamentary governments do not necessarily receive fixed terms of office. Usually, parliaments are expected to hold elections every four or five years. Elections can be called earlier by the head of government to take advantage of political circumstances. (Margaret Thatcher did so in 1983 after successfully winning the Falklands War against Argentina.) Or if the government loses an important policy vote in parliament (called a vote of no confidence), the parliament is dissolved and new elections are called. For example, since the emergence of the modern British parliament in the eighteenth century, there have been 11 successful no confidence votes that felled prime ministers. So, if the government fails on economic policy or in war, it is possible that there will be a loss of support in the parliament that will cause the government to fall.

QUESTION

1. The president of the United States has a four-year term. Should Congress, or the public, be able to call for votes of no confidence in the president before the presidential term ends?

prompted Presidents Roosevelt and Truman to include prominent Democratic and Republican members of the Senate Foreign Relations Committee in the delegations that drafted the United Nations Charter in 1945 and the NATO Treaty in 1949.

executive agreements
Agreements with other nations signed by the president of the United States but less formal (and hence potentially less binding) than a treaty because it does not require Senate confirmation.

Executive Agreements

Over the years, presidents have come to rely heavily on **executive agreements** with other governments rather than formal treaties. An executive agreement signed by the president of the United States has much the same effect in international relations as a treaty. However, an executive agreement does not require Senate ratification. Presidents have asserted that their constitutional power to execute the laws, command the armed services, and determine foreign policy gives them the authority to make agreements with other nations and heads of state *without* obtaining approval of the U.S. Senate. However, unlike treaties, executive agreements do not supersede laws of the United States or of the states with which they conflict, but they are otherwise binding on the United States.

The use of executive agreements in important foreign policy matters was developed by President Franklin Roosevelt. Prior to his administration, executive agreements had been limited to minor matters. But in 1940, Roosevelt agreed to trade 50 American destroyers to England in exchange for the use of naval bases in Newfoundland and the Caribbean. Roosevelt was intent on helping the British in the struggle against Nazi Germany, but before the Japanese attack on Pearl Harbor in 1941, isolationist sentiment in the Senate was too strong to win a two-thirds ratifying vote for such an agreement. Toward the end of World War II, Roosevelt at the Yalta Conference and Truman at the Potsdam Conference negotiated secret executive agreements dividing the occupation of Germany between the Western Allies and the Soviet Union.

Congress has sometimes objected to executive agreements as usurping its own powers. In the Case Act of 1972, Congress required the president to inform it of all executive agreements within 60 days, but the act does not limit the president's power to make agreements. It is easier for Congress to renege on executive agreements than on treaties that the Senate has ratified. In 1973, President Nixon signed an executive agreement

SECRET AGREEMENTS

The "Big Three," comprised of Prime Minister Winston Churchill of Great Britain (right), Marshal Josef Stalin of the Soviet Union (left), and a gravely ill President Franklin Roosevelt (middle), traveled to Yalta, a port on Russia's Crimean peninsula, and negotiated secret executive agreements dividing Germany among the Allies in 1945. Germany remained divided until 1989, when protesters tore down the Berlin Wall and the Soviet Union under Mikhail Gorbachev acquiesced in the unification of Germany under a democratic government.

with South Vietnamese President Nguyen Van Thieu pledging that the United States would "respond with full force" if North Vietnam violated the Paris Peace Agreement that ended American participation in the Vietnam War. But when North Vietnam re-invaded South Vietnam in 1975, Congress rejected President Gerald Ford's pleas for renewed military aid to the South Vietnamese government, and Ford knew that it had become politically impossible for the United States to respond with force.

☐ Intelligence

The president is responsible for the intelligence activities of the United States. Presidents have undertaken intelligence activities since the founding of the nation. During the Revolutionary War, General George Washington nurtured small groups of patriots living behind British lines who supplied him with information on Redcoat troop movements.[27] Today, the Director of National Intelligence (DNI) is appointed by the president (subject to Senate confirmation) and reports directly to the president.

The DNI coordinates the activities of the "intelligence community." Some elements of the intelligence community—the Central Intelligence Agency, the Defense Intelligence Agency, the National Security Agency, the National Reconnaissance Office, and the National Geospacial Intelligence Agency—deal exclusively with intelligence collection, analysis and distribution. Other elements of the intelligence community are located in the Department of Defense, Department of Homeland Security, Federal Bureau of Investigation, Department of State, Department of Energy, and Department of the Treasury. Indeed, the fragmentation of the intelligence community may be its principal weakness.[28]

☐ The Central Intelligence Agency

The CIA provides intelligence on national security to the president, the DNI, the National Security Council, and other top Washington decision makers. The CIA is responsible for (1) assembly, analysis, and dissemination of intelligence information from all agencies in the intelligence community; (2) collection of human intelligence from abroad; (3) with specific "presidential findings," the conduct of **covert actions**, including paramilitary special operations.

covert actions
Secret intelligence activities outside U.S. borders undertaken with specific authorization by the president; acknowledgment of U.S. sponsorship would defeat or compromise their purpose.

Covert actions refer to activities in support of the national interest of the United States that would be ineffective if their sponsorship were made public. For example, one of the largest covert actions ever undertaken by the United States was the support, for nearly 10 years, of the Afghan rebels fighting Soviet occupation of their country during the Afghanistan War (1978–88). Public acknowledgment of such aid would have assisted the Soviet-backed regime in Afghanistan to claim that the rebels were not true patriots but rather "puppets" of the United States. The rebels themselves did not wish to acknowledge U.S. aid publicly, even though they knew it was essential to the success of their cause. Hence Presidents Carter and Reagan aided the Afghan rebels through covert action.

Covert action is, by definition, secret. And secrecy spawns elaborate conspiracy theories and flamboyant tales of intrigue and deception. In fact, most covert actions consist of routine transfers of economic aid and military equipment to pro-U.S. forces that do not wish to acknowledge such aid publicly. Although most covert actions would have widespread support among the American public if they were done openly, secrecy opens the possibility that a president will undertake to do by covert action what would be opposed by Congress and the American people if they knew about it.

In the atmosphere of suspicion and distrust engendered by the Watergate scandal, Congress passed intelligence oversight legislation in 1974 requiring a written "presidential finding" for any covert action and requiring that members of the House and Senate Intelligence Committees be informed of all covert actions. The president does not have to obtain congressional approval for covert actions; but Congress can halt such actions if it chooses to do so.

Commander in Chief

11.7 Trace the expansion of presidential powers as Commander in Chief.

Global power derives primarily from the president's role as Commander in Chief of the armed forces of the United States. Presidential command over the armed forces is not merely symbolic; presidents may issue direct military orders to troops in the field. As president, Washington personally led troops to end the Whiskey Rebellion in 1794; Abraham Lincoln issued direct orders to his generals in the Civil War; Lyndon Johnson personally chose bombing targets in Vietnam; and George H. W. Bush personally ordered the 1991 Gulf War cease-fire after 100 hours of ground fighting. All presidents, whether they are experienced in world affairs or not, soon learn after taking office that their influence throughout the world is heavily dependent upon the command of capable military forces.

☐ War-Making Power

Constitutionally, war-making power is divided between the Congress and the president. Congress has the power "to declare war," but the president is the "Commander in Chief of the Army and Navy of the United States."

In reality, however, presidents have exercised their powers as Commander in Chief to order U.S. forces into military action overseas on many occasions—from John Adams's ordering of U.S. naval forces to attack French ships (1798–99), to Harry

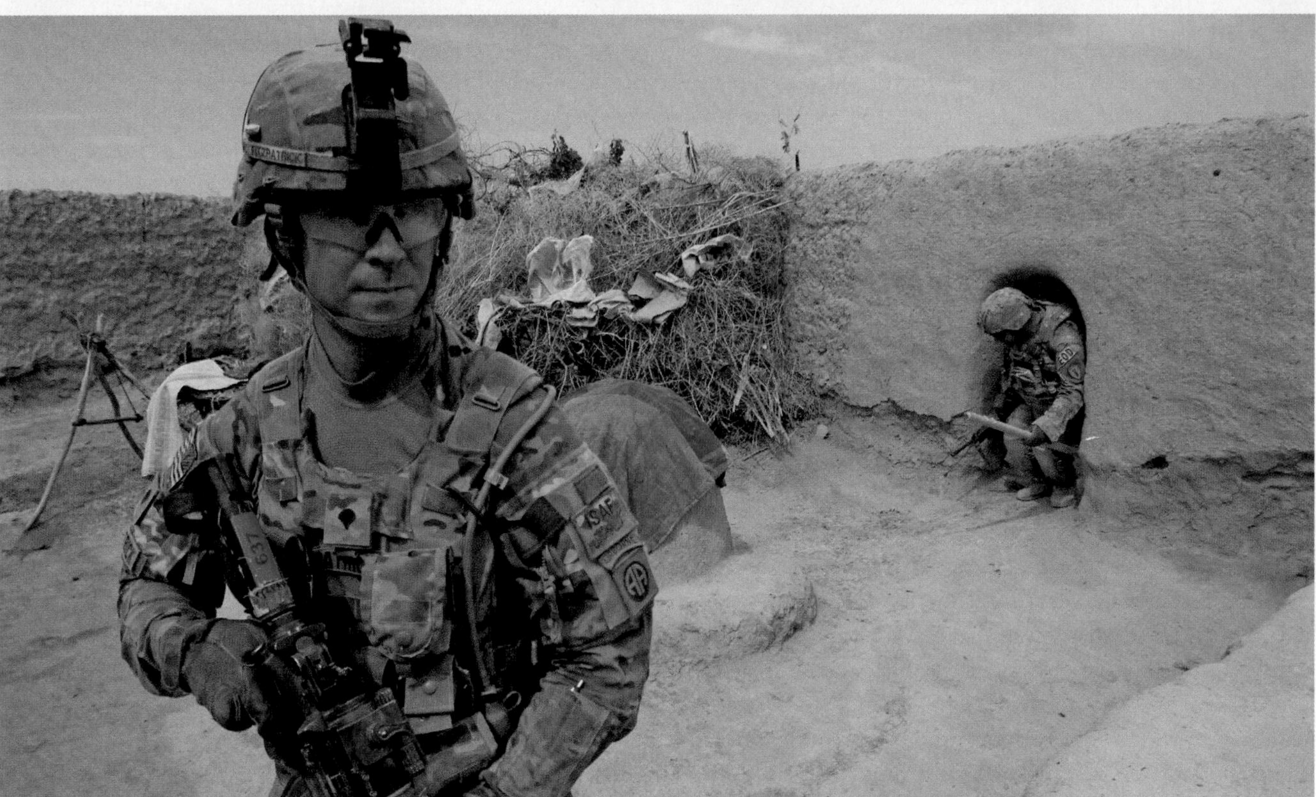

CENTRAL ASIA WOES

Afghanistan has been a central concern of every American president since Jimmy Carter. American troops entered Afghanistan in 2001 and have been there since, engaged in the United States' longest ongoing war.

Truman's decision to intervene in the Korean War (1951–53), to Lyndon Johnson's and Richard Nixon's conduct of the Vietnam War (1965–73), to George H. W. Bush's Operation Desert Storm (1991), to Bill Clinton's interventions in Bosnia and Kosovo (1998–99), to George W. Bush's military actions in Afghanistan (2001) and Iraq (2003). President Barack Obama's withdrawal of U.S. military forces in Iraq and increase in troops in Afghanistan were both made under his power as Commander in Chief. The Supreme Court has consistently refused to hear cases involving the war powers of the president and Congress.[29]

Thus, although Congress retains the formal power to "declare war," in modern times wars are seldom "declared." Instead, they begin with direct military actions, and the president, as Commander in Chief of the armed forces, determines what those actions will be. Historically, Congress accepted the fact that only the president has the information-gathering facilities and the ability to act with the speed and secrecy required for military decisions during periods of crisis. Not until the Vietnam War was there serious congressional debate over whether the president has the power to commit the nation to war.

War Powers Resolution

In the early days of the Vietnam War, the liberal leadership of the nation strongly supported Democratic President Lyndon Johnson's power to commit the nation to war. By 1969, however, many congressional leaders had withdrawn their support of the war. With a new Republican president, Richard Nixon, and a Democratic Congress, congressional attacks on presidential policy became much more partisan.

Antiwar members of Congress made several attempts to end the war by cutting off money for U.S. military activity in Southeast Asia. Such legislation only passed after President Nixon announced a peace agreement in 1973, however. It is important to note that Congress has *never* voted to cut off funds to support American armies while they were in the field.

Congress also passed the **War Powers Resolution**, designed to restrict presidential war-making powers, in 1973. (President Nixon vetoed the bill, but the Watergate affair undermined his support in Congress, which overrode his veto.) The act has four major provisions:

War Powers Resolution
Bill passed in 1973 to limit presidential war-making powers; it restricts when, why, and for how long a president can commit U.S. forces and requires notification of and, in many cases, approval by Congress.

1. In the absence of a congressional declaration of war, the president can commit armed forces to hostilities or to "situations where imminent involvement in hostilities is clearly indicated by the circumstances" only:
   - To repel an armed attack on the United States or to forestall the "direct and imminent threat of such an attack."
   - To repel an armed attack against U.S. armed forces outside the United States or to forestall the threat of such attack.
   - To protect and evacuate U.S. citizens and nationals in another country if their lives are threatened.
2. The president must report promptly to Congress the commitment of forces for such purposes.
3. Involvement of U.S. forces must be no longer than 60 days unless Congress authorizes their continued use by specific legislation.
4. Congress can end a presidential commitment by resolution, an action that does not require the president's signature.

The unilateral commitment of American forces to support actions against the Gaddaffi regime in Libya evoked concerns from Democrats and Republicans alike that the president had exceeded his war powers. However, despite threats to invoke the War Powers Act against the president, no action was forthcoming.

Presidential Noncompliance

The War Powers Resolution raises constitutional questions. A Commander in Chief clearly can order U.S. forces to go anywhere. Presumably, Congress cannot constitutionally

The Game, the Rules, the Players

Does Congress Really Rally Around the Flag?

In times of international crisis or war, public opinion often coalesces in support of the president. Criticism from the press declines, and criticism from Congress and the opposition party declines (or even disappears). Almost no members of Congress opposed the United States's entry into World War II, Vietnam, or the invasion of Afghanistan to respond to the 9/11 attacks. During the buildup to the Iraq War, Congressional opposition to President Bush did emerge, while supporters of the president routinely equated supporting the president with patriotism.

Legislators from the major parties have a history of criticism of the president's use of force. Abraham Lincoln's own party asked him to appear before a congressional committee to explain his conduct in the Civil War. In 1812 and 1845, significant congressional opposition to U.S. declarations of war came from Federalists and Whigs. Before the United States's entry into World War I, several lawmakers—including Republicans with German constituents—opposed the declaration. During the buildup to the United States's entry into World War II, several votes on administration proposals to change the Neutrality Act attracted significant opposition, as did the Lend-Lease bill to send aid to Great Britain. More recently, Republicans during the Clinton administration and Democrats during the Bush administration voted against authorizations for the use of force in areas such as Bosnia, Kosovo, and Iraq, and GOP congressional criticism of presidential conduct of war increased with the election of a Democrat as president in 2008.

When rally effects happen in Congress, they usually take place immediately after a crisis. Then, congressional criticism of (and opposition to) administration policy in war can revert back to conventional party politics.

QUESTIONS

1. Should members of Congress refrain from criticizing presidents during a time of war?
2. As Commander in Chief, should the president be accountable to Congress for the conduct of war?
3. Is opposing a president during time of war unpatriotic? Why?

command troops, yet that is what the act attempts to do by specifying that troops must come home if Congress orders them to do so or if Congress simply fails to endorse the president's decision to commit them. No president—Democrat or Republican—can allow Congress to usurp this presidential authority. Thus, since the passage of the War Powers Resolution, presidents have continued to undertake military actions on their own initiative.

Politically, it is often important for the president to show the world, and especially enemies of the United States, that he has congressional support for going to war. For this reason, presidents have asked Congress for resolutions in support of using military means to achieve specific goals. President George H. W. Bush asked for and received (by a close vote) a resolution of support to use military force to oust Iraqi forces from Kuwait in 1991. President George W. Bush won strong support for a congressional resolution in 2002 to allow him to use military force to make Saddam Hussein comply with U.N. resolutions. Both presidents claimed that they had the constitutional authority as Commander in Chief to use military force even *without* such resolutions. But politically such resolutions strengthen the president when he chooses to use military force.

☐ Presidential Use of Military Force in Domestic Affairs

Democracies are generally reluctant to use military force in domestic affairs. Yet the president has the constitutional authority to "take Care that the Laws be faithfully executed" and, as Commander in Chief of the armed forces, can send them across the nation as well as across the globe. The Constitution appears to limit presidential use of military forces in domestic affairs to protecting states "against domestic Violence" and only "on Application of the [state] Legislature or the [state] Executive (when the Legislature cannot be convened)" (Article IV, Section 4). Although this provision would seem to require states

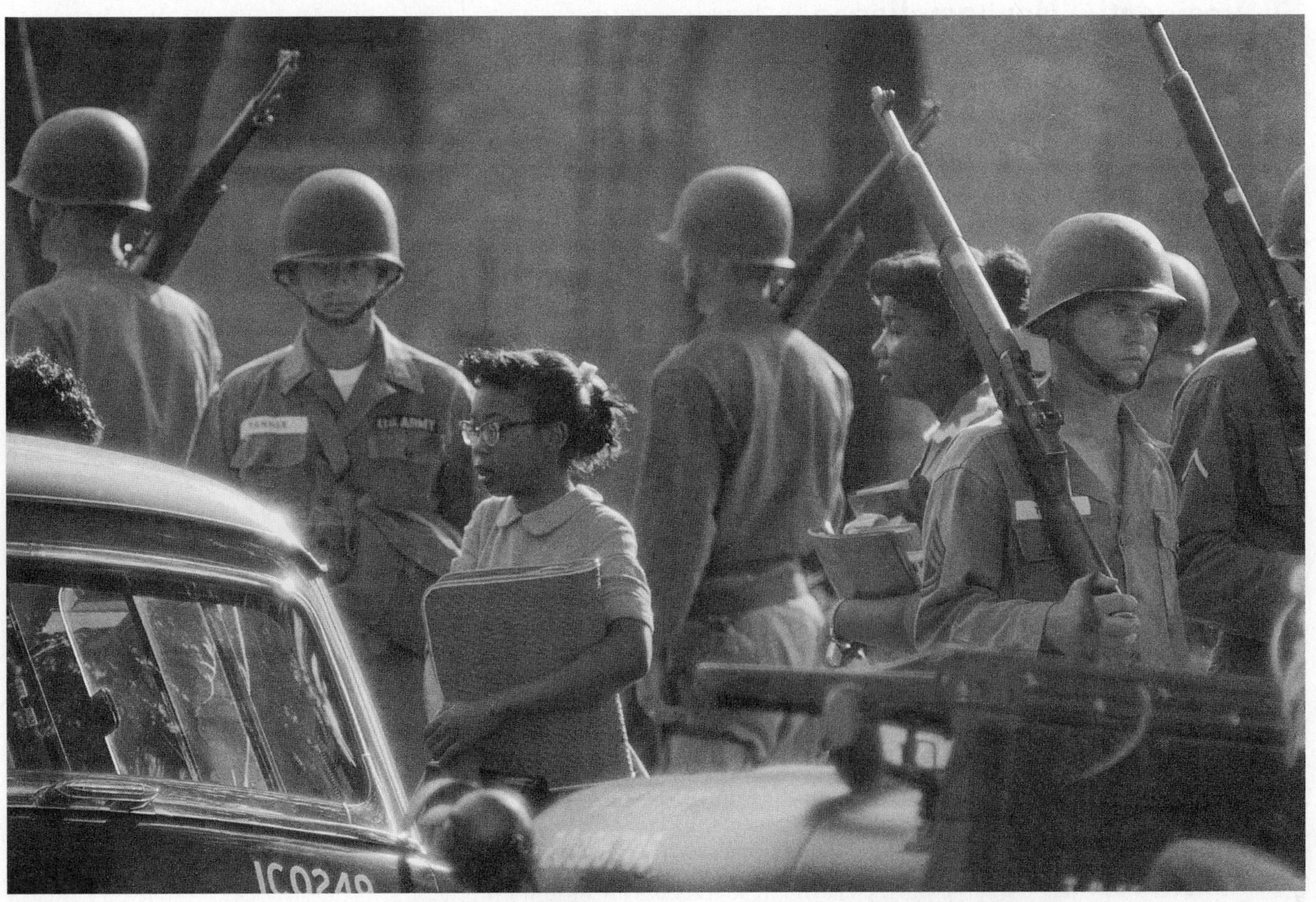

U.S. TROOPS HAVE BEEN USED TO ENFORCE FEDERAL LAW

U.S. soldiers watch as African-American children go to school on October 3, 1957, in Little Rock, Arkansas. President Eisenhower federalized the Arkansas National Guard and also deployed the 101st Airborne Division to enforce the desegregation order in Little Rock.

themselves to request federal troops before they can be sent to quell domestic violence, historically, presidents have not waited for state requests to send troops when federal laws, federal court orders, or federal constitutional guarantees are being violated. The Posse Comitatus Act (18 USC 1385) only requires that the actions of uniformed U.S. forces maintain order in a fashion that originates in the Constitution or in an act of Congress.

Relying on their constitutional duty to "faithfully execute" federal laws and their command over the nation's armed forces, presidents have used military force in domestic disputes since the earliest days of the Republic. Perhaps the most significant example of a president's use of military force in domestic affairs was Dwight Eisenhower's 1957 dispatch of U.S. troops to Little Rock, Arkansas, to enforce a federal court's desegregation order. In this case, the president acted directly *against* the expressed wishes of the state's governor, Orval Faubus, who had posted state units of the National Guard at the entrance of Central High School to prevent the admission of black students, which had been ordered by the federal court. Eisenhower officially called Arkansas's National Guard units into federal service, took personal command of them, and then ordered them to leave the high school. He then replaced the Guard units with U.S. federal troops under orders to enforce desegregation. Eisenhower's action marked a turning point in the struggle over school desegregation. The Supreme Court's historic desegregation decision in *Brown v. Board of Education of Topeka* might have been rendered meaningless had not the president chosen to use military force to secure compliance.

The Vice-Presidential Waiting Game

11.8 Characterize the roles and responsibilities of the vice president.

Historically, the principal responsibility of the vice president is to be prepared to assume the responsibilities of the president. Eight vice presidents have become president following the death of their predecessor. But vice presidents have not always been well prepared: Harry Truman, who succeeded Franklin Roosevelt while World War II still raged, had never even been informed about the secret atomic bomb project.

Political Selection Process

The political process surrounding the initial choice of vice-presidential candidates does not necessarily produce the persons best qualified to occupy the White House. It is, indeed, a "crap shoot"[30]; if it produces a person well qualified to be president, it is only by luck. Candidates may *claim* that they select running mates who are highly qualified to take over as president, but this claim is seldom true.

Vice-presidential candidates were historically chosen to give political "balance" to the ticket, in order to attract voters who might otherwise desert the party or stay home. Democratic presidential candidates sought to give ideological and geographical balance to the ticket. Northern liberal presidential candidates (Adlai Stevenson, John Kennedy) selected southern conservatives (John Sparkman, Estes Kefauver, Lyndon Johnson) as their running mates. In the past, the Democratic ticket has been balanced by sex (Mondale/Ferraro in 1984); to balance geography (Dukakis/Bentsen returned to the New England/South formula in 1988); and on personality—dour and serious John Kerry ran with cheerful, enthusiastic, and outgoing North Carolinian John Edwards in 2004. Bill Clinton sought a different kind of balance: Al Gore's military service in Vietnam and his unimpeachable family life helped offset reservations about Clinton's avoidance of the draft and his past marital troubles. Barack Obama chose an experienced foreign policy running mate in Joe Biden.

The Game, the Rules, the Players

Scranton Joe

Joe Biden, war consigliere? Barack Obama won the Democratic Party nomination as a 47-year-old, first-term U.S. senator. In choosing Senator Joe Biden (D-DE) as his running mate, Obama balanced the ticket with experience in Washington and foreign-policy expertise. Biden, who had spent nearly four decades in the Senate, was an ideal choice for vice president as *consigliere*—a term for "counselor" popularized by the character Tom Hagan in Mario Puzo's book *The Godfather*.

Biden had first won his Senate seat in 1972 as an anti–Vietnam War candidate. He was just 30 years old, the minimum age the Constitution specifies for a member of the Senate. He went on to serve over three decades in the Senate, including prestigious posts as chairman of the Judiciary Committee and chairman of the Foreign Relations Committee. He had sought unsuccessfully to be the Democratic presidential nominee himself, even declaring that Obama was not "ready" for the presidency and would need "on-the-job training." Moreover, Biden had voted for the war in Iraq. But his liberal voting record paralleled that of Obama's, and his long service in the Senate and his knowledge of foreign affairs provided a balance to Obama's relative newness to national politics. Whatever differences Obama and Biden may have had in the past were set aside in order to present a balanced Democratic ticket in 2008.

As "veep," Biden initially assumed the role of senior advisor many had envisioned. Biden worked with Democrats on Capitol Hill to move the president's legislative agenda—a difficult task given the sometimes chaotic approach to advancing policy by the Obama Administration in its first year. He also traveled extensively to Iraq and Afghanistan and took on a prominent voice in occasional opposition to Secretary of State Clinton in matters of foreign policy (Biden is former chair of the Senate Foreign Relations Committee). Some observers have described his role as "contrarian," as the critical voice against which sentiment for policy is tested. In 2010, he also assumed the traditional role of partisan campaign bulldog, taking to the stump for Democratic candidates and lashing out, often in colorful fashion, against Republicans in Congress.

Despite talk that Biden might be "dumped" from the ticket in 2012, he continued as the president's running mate. Similar rumors were directed at Bush vice president (and consigliere) Dick Cheney in 2004, and at Eisenhower's veep, Richard Nixon, in 1956. Only one modern president successfully changed vice-presidential running mates: Franklin Roosevelt replaced John Nance Garner with Henry Wallace in 1940, and then replaced Wallace with Harry Truman in 1944.

QUESTIONS

1. **What balancing qualities did Joe Biden bring to the presidential ticket in 2008?**
2. **Biden and Cheney were in their sixties when they became vice president—generally considered too old to have presidential ambitions. Why do you think a politician "settles" for the vice presidency given little hope of otherwise becoming president?**

VEEPS: THE GREAT WAITERS

Vice-President Joe Biden (D) leaves a media event featuring his Chinese counterpart Xi Jingping. Vice-presidents often conduct diplomatic and ceremonial functions in addition to their formal duties as president of the Senate. Fourteen presidents of the United States were previously vice-president.

Republican presidential candidates sought to accommodate either the conservative or moderate wing of their party in their vice-presidential selections. Moderate Eisenhower chose conservative Nixon in 1952. Conservative Ronald Reagan turned to his moderate primary opponent George H. W. Bush in 1980, who in 1988 tapped conservative Dan Quayle. But in 2000, George W. Bush chose to add *experience* to the ticket by choosing Dick Cheney, secretary of defense in his father's administration. In 2008, McCain added excitement to the Republican ticket in a surprise move by selecting Alaska Governor Sarah Palin, social conservative and mother of five children. McCain garnered some initial electoral benefit in picking the charismatic Palin, but the subsequent campaign proved that the choice was of limited benefit to the presidential candidate.

□ Vice-Presidential Roles

Presidents determine what role their vice presidents will play in their administration. Constitutionally, the only role given the vice president is to preside over the Senate and to vote in case of a tie in that body. Presiding over the Senate is so tiresome that vice presidents perform it only on rare ceremonial occasions, but they have occasionally cast important tie-breaking votes. If the president chooses not to give the vice president much responsibility, the vice presidency becomes what its first occupant, John Adams, described as "the most insignificant office that ever the invention of man contrived or his imagination conceived." One of Franklin Roosevelt's three vice presidents, the salty Texan John Nance Garner, put it more pithily, saying that the job "ain't worth a bucket of warm spit" (reporters of that era may have substituted "spit" for Garner's actual wording).

The political functions of vice presidents are more significant than their governmental functions. Vice presidents are obliged to support their president and the administration's policies. But sometimes a president will use the vice president to launch strongly partisan political attacks on opponents while the president remains "above" the political squabbles and hence more "presidential." Richard Nixon served as a partisan "attack dog" for Eisenhower and then gave Spiro Agnew this task in his own administration. The attack role also allows the vice president to help cement political support for the president among highly partisan ideologues. Vice presidents are also useful in campaign fund-raising. Large contributors expect a personal touch; the president cannot be everywhere at once, so the vice president is frequently a guest at political fund-raising events. Presidents also have traditionally sent their vice presidents to attend funerals of world leaders and placed them at the head of governmental commissions.

□ Carving a Role Out

Vice presidents themselves strive to play a more significant policy-making role, often as senior presidential adviser and confidant. Recent presidents have encouraged the development of the vice presidency along these lines. Walter Mondale, the first modern vice president to perform this function, had an office in the White House next to the president's, had access to all important meetings and policy decisions, and was invited to lunch privately each week with President Carter. Vice President Al Gore was routinely stationed behind President Clinton during major policy pronouncements. Clinton reportedly gave great weight to Gore's views on the environment, on cost savings in government, and on information technology. Gore also spoke out aggressively in defense of Clinton's policies. Thus, the senior advisory role is becoming institutionalized over time—and it has been an important role in the Bush and Obama administrations.

Politically ambitious vice presidents are obliged to play a torturous waiting game. They can use their time in office to build a network of contacts that can later be tapped for campaign contributions, workers, and support in their own race for the presidency, should they decide to run. But winning the presidency following retirement of their former boss requires a delicate balance. They must show loyalty to the president in order to win the president's endorsement and also to help ensure that the administration in which they participated is judged a success by voters. At the same time, vice

A Constitutional Note

How Broad Is the "Executive Power"?

The Constitution states that "The executive Power shall be vested in a President of the United States of America" (Article II). The Constitution also gives the president specific powers; for example, "to take care that the laws be faithfully executed"; to appoint and remove executive officials; "to give to the Congress information on the State of the Union and recommend to their Consideration such Measures as he shall judge necessary and expedient"; to veto legislation passed by Congress, subject to override by a two-thirds vote of both houses; to convene special sessions of Congress; to make treaties "with the Advice and Consent of the Senate"; to receive ambassadors; to grant pardons; to appoint federal court and Supreme Court judges, subject to Senate confirmation; and to serve as Commander in Chief of the armed forces. And the Congress may by law add to the president's powers. But does the Constitution's general grant of "executive power" give the president any powers that are not specified later in the Constitution or given to the president by acts of Congress? Most presidents have asserted a general "executive power," or, as Theodore Roosevelt said, "My belief was that it was not only his right but his duty to do anything that the needs of the nation demanded, unless such action was forbidden by the Constitution or by the laws." But when the Congress has addressed a problem by law, the president is obliged to follow the law, whether he likes it or not.[a] Closely related to the question of executive power is the question of "executive privilege." Can a president withhold information from the Congress or the courts to preserve confidentiality within the executive branch? The Supreme Court has acknowledged a constitutional protection for the "president's need for complete candor and objectivity from advisers" and for "military, diplomatic, or sensitive national security secrets."[b] But the president cannot withhold information from the courts in a criminal investigation not related to defense or diplomacy, as Richard Nixon found to his dismay in the Watergate affair.

QUESTIONS

1. Once executive power has expanded beyond the powers conferred in the Constitution, can it be constrained?
2. What guarantee does Congress, the courts, or the public have that presidents will comply with the constitutional and legal constraints on their powers?

[a] *Youngstown Sheet & Tube Co. v. Sawyer*, 343 U.S. 579 (1952).
[b] *United States v. Nixon*, 418 U.S. 683 (1974).

presidents must demonstrate that they have independent leadership qualities and a policy agenda of their own to offer voters. This dilemma becomes more acute as their boss's term nears its end.

Only a few sitting vice presidents have won election to the White House: John Adams (1797), Thomas Jefferson (1801), Martin Van Buren (1837), and George H. W. Bush (1988). In addition, four vice presidents won election in their own right after entering the Oval Office as a result of their predecessors' death: Theodore Roosevelt (1901), Calvin Coolidge (1923), Harry Truman (1945), and Lyndon Johnson (1963). Only one nonsitting former vice president has been elected president: Richard Nixon (1968, after losing to Kennedy in 1960). Thus, out of the 48 men who served the nation as vice president through 2008, only 9 were ever elected to higher office.

Review the Chapter

Presidential Power

11.1 Identify the powers and responsibilities of the president, p. 400

As head of the government, the president is expected to set forth policy priorities for the nation, to manage the economy, to mobilize political support for the administration's programs in Congress, to manage the giant federal bureaucracy, and to recruit people for policy-making positions in both the executive and judicial branches of government.

Constitutional Powers of the President

11.2 Identify the powers granted to the president by the Constitution, p. 404

Popular expectations of presidential leadership far exceed the formal constitutional powers of the president: chief administrator, chief legislator, chief diplomat, Commander in Chief, and chief of state. The vague reference in the Constitution to "executive Power" has been used by presidents to justify actions beyond those specified elsewhere in the Constitution or in laws of Congress. Presidents, unlike other Federal constitutional officers, are term-limited by the Constitution.

Political Resources of the President

11.3 Assess the sources of the president's political power and analyze how presidents' personality and policy positions impact their approval ratings, p. 410

It is the president's vast political resources that provide the true power base of the presidency. These include the president's reputation for power, personal popularity with the public, access to the media, and party leadership position. The institutional basis of presidential power has grown in the last century. Presidential popularity and power are usually the highest at the beginning of the term of office. Presidents are more likely to be successful in Congress during this honeymoon period. Presidents' popularity also rises during crises, especially during international threats and military actions. But prolonged indecision and stalemate erode popular support, as do scandals and economic recessions.

Chief Executive

11.4 Outline the responsibilities and powers of the president as the nation's chief executive, p. 418

As chief executive, the president oversees the huge federal bureaucracy. Presidential control of the executive branch is exercised through executive orders, appointments and removals, and budgetary recommendations to Congress. But the president's control of the executive branch is heavily circumscribed by Congress, which establishes executive departments and agencies, regulates their activities by law, and determines their budgets each year.

Chief Legislator and Lobbyist

11.5 Analyze the factors affecting the success of the president as the chief legislator and lobbyist, p. 423

Presidents are expected not only to initiate programs and policies but also to shepherd them through Congress. Presidential success scores in Congress indicate that presidents are more successful early in their term of office. Presidents who face a Congress controlled by the opposition party are far less successful in winning approval for their programs than presidents whose party holds a majority.

The veto is the president's most powerful weapon in dealing with Congress. The president needs to hold the loyalty of only one more than one-third of either the House or the Senate to sustain a veto. Few vetoes are overridden. The threat of a veto enables the president to bargain in Congress for more acceptable legislation.

Global Leader

11.6 Assess the role of the president as a global leader, p. 427

During the long years of the Cold War, the president of the United States was the leader of the "free world." In the post–Cold War world, the president is still the leader of the world's most powerful democracy and is expected to exercise global leadership on behalf of a stable world order.

Commander in Chief

11.7 Trace the expansion of presidential powers as Commander in Chief, p. 431

The global power of presidents derives primarily from this presidential role as Commander in Chief. Constitutionally, war-making power is divided between Congress and the president, but historically it has been the president who has ordered U.S. military forces into action. In the War Powers Resolution, Congress tried to reassert its war-making power after the Vietnam War, but the act has failed to restrain presidents. Presidents have also used the armed forces in domestic affairs to "take Care that the Laws be faithfully executed."

The Vice-Presidential Waiting Game

11.8 Characterize the roles and responsibilities of the vice president, p. 435

The principal responsibility of the vice president is to be prepared to assume the responsibilities of the president. However, the selection of the vice president is dominated more by political concerns than by consideration of presidential qualifications. Aside from officially presiding over the U.S. Senate, vice presidents perform whatever roles are assigned to them by the president. Few sitting vice-presidents are elected president, but many eventually served as president.

Learn the Terms

impeachment, p. 406
executive privilege, p. 409
Watergate, p. 410
impoundment, p. 410
deferrals, p. 410
rescissions, p. 410
White House press corps, p. 413
executive orders, p. 418
cabinet, p. 420
National Security Council (NSC), p. 421
honeymoon period, p. 424
gridlock, p. 425
veto, p. 426
pocket veto, p. 426
override, p. 426
line-item veto, p. 426
diplomatic recognition, p. 428
treaty, p. 428
executive agreements, p. 429
covert actions, p. 431
War Powers Resolution, p. 433

Test Yourself

11.1 Identify the powers and responsibilities of the president.

The president is expected to be responsible for all of the following *except*

a. presiding over the Senate in case of a tie vote
b. administering the federal bureaucracy
c. expressing the nation's sentiments during a time of crisis
d. presenting the State of the Union Address each year
e. Actually, the president is expected to be responsible for all these things

11.2 Identify the powers granted to the president by the Constitution.

The right of the executive branch to withhold confidential communications from the other branches of government is known as

a. administrative censure
b. executive privilege
c. the national security exception
d. executive classification prerogative
e. cloture

11.3 Assess the sources of the president's political power and analyze how presidents' personality and policy positions impact their approval ratings.

The Institutional Power of the president increased because of all of these reasons EXCEPT

a. Foreign policy crises created an Imperial presidency
b. The Supreme Court recognized many unilateral executive orders as having force of law
c. The president's role in the budget increased with the professionalization of the executive branch
d. Congress became weak
e. The loss of the right of pardon

11.4 Outline the responsibilities and powers of the president as the nation's chief executive.

Formal regulations governing the executive branch operations are known as

a. presidential directives
b. executive directives
c. presidential orders
d. executive orders
e. executions

11.5 Analyze the factors affecting the success of the president as the chief legislator and lobbyist.

The main source of national policy initiatives is the

a. cabinet
b. president
c. Congress
d. Federal Bureaucracy
e. the courts

11.6 Assess the role of the president as a global leader.

The office that is responsible for the overall coordination of the intelligence activities of the United States government is the

a. Defense Intelligence Agency (DIA)
b. Central Intelligence Agency (CIA)
c. National Security Agency (NSA)
d. Director of National Intelligence (DNI)
e. The office of the Vice President (VPOTUS)

11.7 Trace the expansion of presidential powers as Commander in Chief.

The legislation passed after the Vietnam War, which attempted to limit the war-making powers of the president, was the

a. The Neutrality Act
b. Executive Defense Restrictions Amendment
c. Armed Forces Deployment Resolution
d. Defense Appropriations Act
e. War Powers Resolution

11.8 Characterize the roles and responsibilities of the vice president.

The Constitution stipulates that the vice president is to

a. prepare himself for the presidency
b. represent the government at funerals of dignitaries
c. preside over the Senate
d. preside over the cabinet in the absence of the president
e. stay in the country at all times

Explore Further

Barber, James David. *The Presidential Character: Predicting Performance in the White House*. 4th ed. New York: Longman, 2009. Barber's original thesis that a president's performance in office is largely a function of active/passive and positive/negative character; includes classifications of twentieth-century presidents through Reagan.

Edwards, George C., and Stephen J. Wayne. *Presidential Leadership*. 8th ed. Belmont, Calif.: Wadsworth, 2010. Comprehensive text covering nomination and election of the president, relations with the public, the media, the bureaucracy, Congress and the courts.

Jacobson, Gary C. *A Divider, Not a Uniter*. New York: Longman, 2008. Poll data showing that George W. Bush accelerated the polarization of the American people along party lines.

Pfiffner, James P. *The Modern Presidency*. 6th ed. Belmont, CA: Wadsworth, 2011. Text coverage of institutional relationships between the president and the public, the White House staff, the executive branch, Congress, the intelligence community, and so on.

Milkus, Stanley, and Michael Nelson. *The American Presidency: Origins and Development, 1776–2011*. 5th ed. Washington, D.C.: CQ Press, 2011. A comprehensive history of the presidency that argues that the institution is best understood by examining its development over time; it describes the significant presidential actions in the early days of the Republic that shaped the office as well as the modern era in which the president has replaced Congress and the political parties as the leading instrument of popular rule.

Nelson, Michael, ed. *The Presidency and the Political System*. 10th ed. Washington, D.C.: CQ Press, 2013. Essays on the presidency up to and including Barack Obama.

Neustadt, Richard E. *Presidential Power*. New York: Wiley, 1960. The classic argument that the president's power is the power to persuade, and that the formal constitutional powers of the presidency provide only a framework for the president's use of persuasion, public prestige, reputation for power, and other personal attributes to exercise real power.

Pika, Joseph A., and John Maltese. *The Politics of the Presidency*. 7th ed. Washington, D.C.: CQ Press, 2009. An overview of the institution of the presidency, including George W. Bush as a wartime president.

Schultz, Jeffrey D. *Presidential Scandals*. Washington, D.C.: CQ Press, 1999. An historical survey of scandals in presidential administrations, from George Washington to Bill Clinton.

Skowronek, Stephen. 2011. *Presidential Leadership in Political Time,* 2nd ed. Lawrence: University of Kansas press, 2011.

SUGGESTED WEB SITES

American Presidents www.americanpresidents.org
Biographical facts and key events in the lives of all U.S. presidents.

Cabinet www.whitehouse.gov/government/cabinet.html
The White House site provides the names of the current president's cabinet as well as those individuals with "cabinet-rank" status.

Center for the Study of the Presidency www.thepresidency.org
Studies of the presidency and publication of the scholarly journal *Presidential Studies Quarterly*.

Central Intelligence Agency www.cia.gov
The CIA site provides information about the agency's mission, organization, values, press releases, and congressional testimony along with employment possibilities.

Defense Link www.defense.gov
Official site of the U.S. Department of Defense, with news and links to the U.S. Army, Navy, Air Force, and Marine Corps Web sites and other defense agencies and commands.

National Security Council www.whitehouse.gov/nsc
Site provides brief history of NSC plus new releases dealing with national security.

State Department www.state.gov
Official site includes news, travel warnings, http://www.state.gov/s/l/treaty/tif/index.htm
Complete list of all treaties of the United States in force as of January 1, 2000.

The White House www.whitehouse.gov
This official White House site provides up-to-date information or news about the current president's policies, speeches, appointments, proclamations, and cabinet members.

12

The Bureaucracy

Bureaucratic Politics

atherine Mitchell was a physician with the Veterans' Administration Health System in Phoenix. Arizona is a popular place for military retirees and individuals otherwise separated from the service. As a consequence, there's a lot of demand for VA services, and Dr. Mitchell ran an important program—the Iraq and Afghanistan Post-Deployment Center.

What she saw in trying to run her facility was a failed system where a lack of money and inadequate staff made it impossible to provide needed health care to deserving veterans. So, she complained to the Inspector General, and instead of getting help, she was investigated and placed on involuntary administrative leave. Was it intimidation by the VA?

Hers was not the only story of this sort. Other "whistle-blowers"—people who make (supposedly confidential) reports of administrative wrongdoing—reported that they had been hazed, harassed, transferred, or had their personnel records altered. Some reported disruptions in their pay for no reason.

The Veterans Administration came under extreme scrutiny in 2014 for general failures in their health care system. Veterans reported excessively long waits for appointments—often several months—as well as lost and otherwise mishandled records. Whistle-blower complaints about poor staffing, violations of procedure in handling patients, and other administrative violations appeared to be ignored.

Dr. Mitchell and other whistle-blowers got the attention of Congress, where members held hearings and also advanced legislation to provide the VA with more resources and alternative ways of delivering services to suffering vets.

12.1 Assess the nature, sources, and extent of bureaucratic power, p. 444

12.2 Describe the types of agencies in the federal bureaucracy and the extent and purposes of the bureaucracy, p. 448

12.3 Trace changes over time in the size and composition of the bureaucracy and assess the repercussions for democracy, p. 456

12.4 Explain how the bureaucracy is staffed, to whom it is accountable, and how accountability is affected by politics and bureaucratic culture, p. 460

12.5 Outline the budgetary process and evaluate the advantages and disadvantages of the current system, p. 462

12.6 Outline the growth of federal regulation, p. 469

12.7 Evaluate the cost of federal regulation, p. 472

12.8 Summarize the constraints that Congress can place on the bureaucracy, p. 472

VETERANS' WOES Many veterans have confronted medical, financial, and emotional challenges. Here an Atlanta veteran protests the foreclosure of his home.

Bureaucratic Power

12.1 Assess the nature, sources, and extent of bureaucratic power.

bureaucracy
Departments, agencies, bureaus, and offices that perform the functions of government.

chain of command
Hierarchical structure of authority in which command flows downward; typical of a bureaucracy.

division of labor
Division of work among many specialized workers in a bureaucracy.

impersonality
Treatment of all persons within a bureaucracy on the basis of "merit" and of all "clients" served by the bureaucracy equally according to rules.

Political conflict does not end after a law has been passed by Congress and signed by the president. The arena for conflict merely shifts from Capitol Hill and the White House to the **bureaucracy**—to the myriad departments, agencies, and bureaus of the federal executive branch that implement the law. Despite the popular impression that policy is decided by the president and Congress and merely implemented by the federal bureaucracy, in fact, policy is also made by the bureaucracy. Indeed, it is often remarked that, "implementation is the continuation of policy making by other means." The Washington bureaucracy is a major base of power in the American system of government—independent of Congress, the president, the courts, and the people. Indeed, controlling the bureaucracy has become a major challenge of democratic government.

The Nature of Bureaucracy

"Bureaucracy" has become a negative term equated with red tape,[1] paper shuffling, duplication of effort, waste and inefficiency, impersonality, senseless regulations, and unresponsiveness to the needs of "real" people. But bureaucracy is really a form of social organization found not only in governments but also in corporations, armies, schools, and many other societal institutions. The German sociologist Max Weber described bureaucracy as a "rational" way for society to organize itself that has the following characteristics: a **chain of command** (hierarchical structure of authority in which command flows downward); a **division of labor** (work divided among many specialized workers in an effort to improve productivity); and **impersonality** (all persons within the bureaucracy treated on "merit" principles, and all "clients" served by the bureaucracy treated equally according to rules; all activities undertaken according to rules; records maintained to assure rules are followed).[2] Thus, according to Weber's definition, General Motors and IBM, the U.S. Marine Corps, the U.S. Department of Education, and all other institutions organized according to these principles are "bureaucracies."

The Growth of Bureaucratic Power

Bureaucratic power has grown with advances in technology and increases in the size and complexity of society. There are a variety of explanations for this growth of power.

- **Needed Expertise and Technological Advances.** Congress and the president do not have the time, energy, or expertise to handle the details of policy making. A related explanation is that the increasing complexity and sophistication of technology require technical experts ("technocrats") to actually carry out the intent of Congress and the president. Neither the president nor the 535 members of Congress can look after the myriad details involved in environmental protection, occupational safety, air traffic control, or thousands of other responsibilities of government. So the president and Congress create bureaucracies, appropriate money for them, and authorize them to draw up detailed rules, regulations, and "guidelines" that actually govern the nation. Bureaucratic agencies receive only vague and general directions from the president and Congress. Actual governance is in the hands of the Environmental Protection Agency, the Occupational Safety and Health Administration, the Federal Aviation Administration, and hundreds of similar agencies (see Figure 12.1).

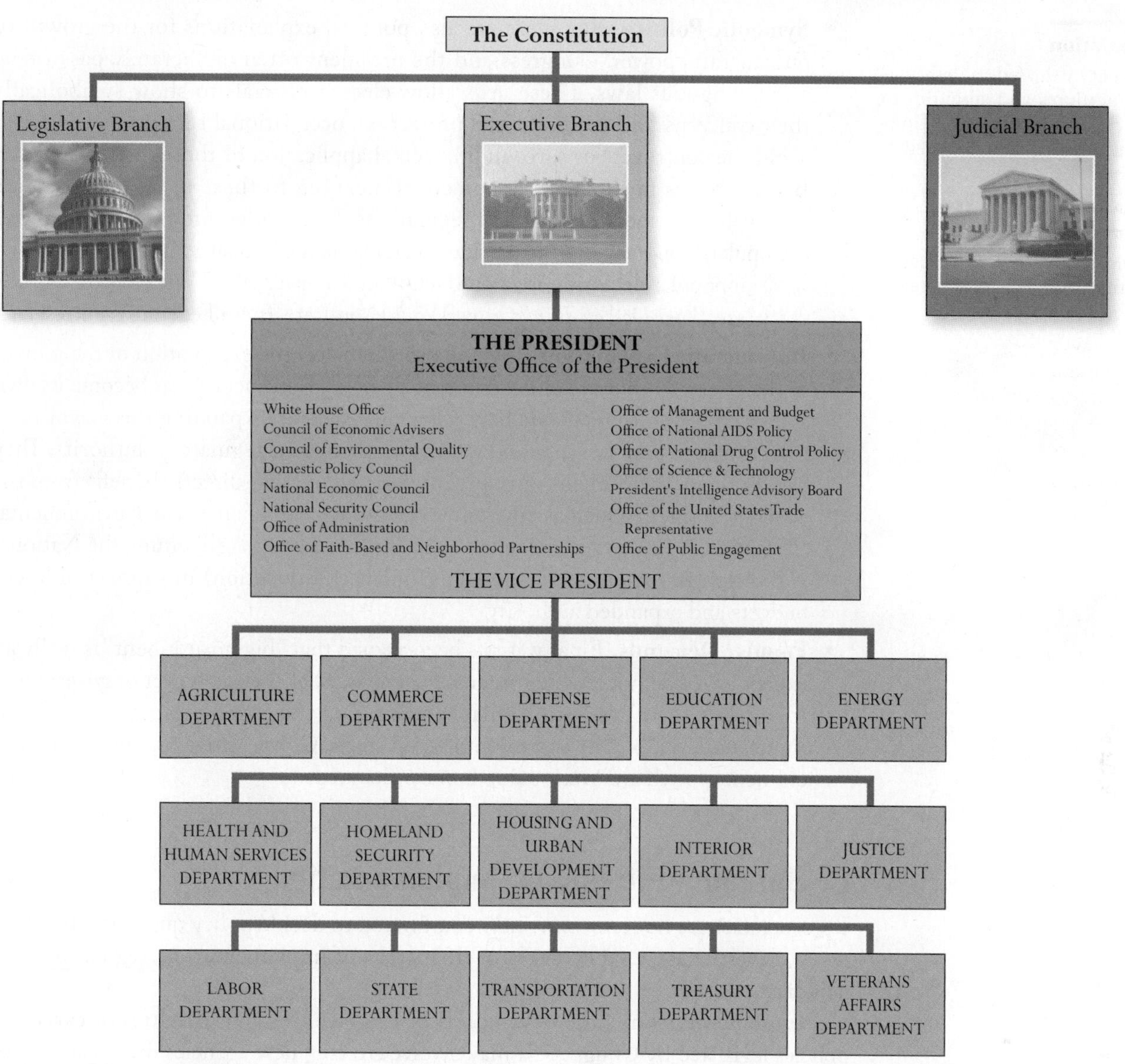

INDEPENDENT AGENCIES, COMMISSIONS, AND GOVERNMENT CORPORATIONS

Advisory Council on Historic Preservation	Federal Communications Commission (FCC)	National Aeronautics and Space Administration (NASA)	Office of Special Counsel
African Development Foundation	Federal Deposit Insurance Corporation (FDIC)	National Archives and Records Administration (NARA)	Office of the National Counterintelligence Executive
AMTRAK (National Railroad Passenger Corporation)	Federal Election Commission (FEC)	National Capital Planning Commission	Overseas Private Investment Corporation
Central Intelligence Agency (CIA)	Federal Housing Finance Board	National Council on Disability	Panama Canal Commission
Commission on Civil Rights	Federal Labor Relations Authority	National Credit Union Administration (NCUA)	Peace Corps
Commodity Futures Trading Commission	Federal Maritime Commission	National Endowment for the Arts	Pension Benefit Guaranty Corporation
Consumer Product Safety Commission (CPSC)	Federal Mediation and Conciliation Service	National Endowment for the Humanities	Postal Regulatory Commission
Corporation for National and Community Service	Federal Mine Safety and Health Review Commission	National Labor Relations Board (NLRB)	Railroad Retirement Board
Defense Nuclear Facilities Safety Board	Federal Reserve System	National Mediation Board	Securities and Exchange Commission (SEC)
Election Assistance Commission	Federal Retirement Thrift Investment Board	National Science Foundation (NSF)	Selective Service System
Environmental Protection Agency (EPA)	Federal Trade Commission (FTC)	National Transportation Safety Board	Small Business Administration (SBA)
Equal Employment Opportunity Commission (EEOC)	General Services Administration (GSA)	Nuclear Regulatory Commission (NRC)	Social Security Administration (SSA)
Export-Import Bank of the United States	Institute of Museum and Library Services	Occupational Safety and Health Review Commission	Tennessee Valley Authority
Farm Credit Administration	Inter-American Foundation	Office of Government Ethics	U.S. Trade and Development Agency
	International Broadcasting Bureau (IBB)	Office of Personnel Management	United States Agency for International Development
	Merit Systems Protection Board		United States International Trade Commission
			United States Postal Service (USPS)

FIGURE 12.1 THE FEDERAL BUREAUCRACY

Although the president has constitutional authority over the operation of the executive branch, Congress creates departments and agencies and appropriates their funds, and Senate approval is needed for presidential appointees to head departments.

12.1

12.2

12.3

12.4

12.5

12.6

12.7

12.8

implementation
Development by the federal bureaucracy of procedures and activities to carry out policies legislated by Congress, it includes regulation as well as adjudication.

regulation
Development by the federal bureaucracy of formal rules for implementing legislation.

- **Symbolic Politics.** But there are also political explanations for the growth of bureaucratic power. Congress and the president often deliberately pass vague and ambiguous laws. These laws allow elected officials to show symbolically their concerns for environmental protection, occupational safety, and so on, yet avoid the controversies surrounding actual application of those lofty principles. Bureaucracies must then give practical meaning to these symbolic measures by developing specific rules and regulations. If the rules and regulations prove unpopular, Congress and the president can blame the bureaucrats and pretend that these unpopular decisions are a product of an "ungovernable" Washington bureaucracy (see *What Do You Think?* How Would You Rate These Federal Agencies?).
- **Bureaucratic Explanation.** There is also a bureaucratic explanation of the growth in the size and influence of government agencies. Bureaucracy has become its own source of power. Bureaucrats have a personal stake in expanding the size of their own agencies and budgets and adding to their own regulatory authority. They can mobilize their "client" groups (interest groups that directly benefit from the agency's programs, such as environmental groups on behalf of the Environmental Protection Agency, farm groups for the Department of Agriculture, the National Education Association for the Department of Education) in support of larger budgets and expanded authority.
- **Popular Demands.** Finally, it has been argued that "big government" is really an expression of democratic sentiments. People want to use the power of government to improve their lives—to regulate and develop the economy, to guarantee civil rights, to develop their communities, and so on. Conservative opponents of government growth are overlooking popular demands.[3]

☐ Bureaucratic Power: Implementation

Bureaucracies are not *constitutionally* empowered to decide policy questions. But they do so, nevertheless, as they perform their tasks of implementation, regulation, and adjudication.

Implementation is the development of procedures and activities to carry out policies legislated by Congress. It may involve creating new agencies or bureaus or assigning new responsibilities to old agencies. It often requires bureaucracies to translate laws into operational rules and regulations and usually to allocate resources—money, personnel, offices, supplies—to the new function. All of these tasks involve decisions by bureaucrats, decisions that drive how the law will actually affect society. In some cases, bureaucrats delay the development of regulations based on a new law, assign enforcement responsibility to existing offices with other higher priority tasks, and allocate few people with limited resources to the task. In other cases, bureaucrats act forcefully in making new regulations, insist on strict enforcement, assign responsibilities to newly created aggressive offices with no other assignments, and allocate a great deal of staff time and agency resources to the task. Interested groups have a strong stake in these decisions, and they actively seek to influence the bureaucracy.

☐ Bureaucratic Power: Regulation

Regulation involves the development of formal rules for implementing legislation. The federal bureaucracy publishes about 80,000 pages of rules in the *Federal Register* each year. The Environmental Protection Agency (EPA) is especially active in developing regulations governing the handling of virtually every substance in the air, water, or ground. The rule-making process for federal agencies is prescribed by an Administrative Procedures Act, first passed in 1946 and amended many times. Generally, agencies must:

- Announce in the *Federal Register* that a new regulation is being considered.
- Hold hearings to allow interested groups to present evidence and arguments regarding the proposed regulation.

What Do You Think?

How Would You Rate These Federal Agencies?

Americans are familiar with only a few federal agencies. But among the fairly well-known agencies, the Center for Disease Control, the FBI, and the space agency NASA win majorities in national polls rating them as "excellent" or "good." In contrast, majorities rate the Environmental Protection Agency, the tax-collecting Internal Revenue Service, and the Food and Drug Administration as "only fair" or "poor." In past years, the Federal Reserve Board was highly rated; however, following the financial crisis in 2008, popular regard for the overseer of the nation's banking system plummeted and continues to remain low.

QUESTIONS

1. Most Americans do not have direct contact with most federal agencies. That said, do you think they can give informed opinions on the job agencies do?
2. Examine the agencies that rate closer to excellent versus the ones that rate closer to poor. Do the low or highly rated agencies have anything in common?

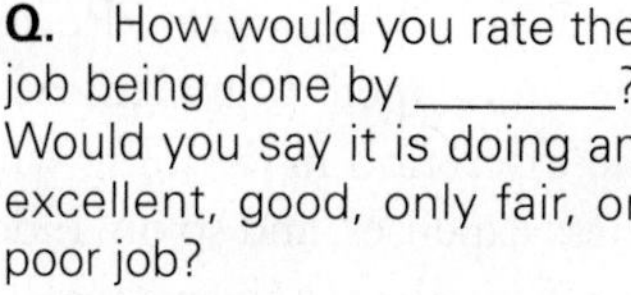

Q. How would you rate the job being done by ________? Would you say it is doing an excellent, good, only fair, or poor job?

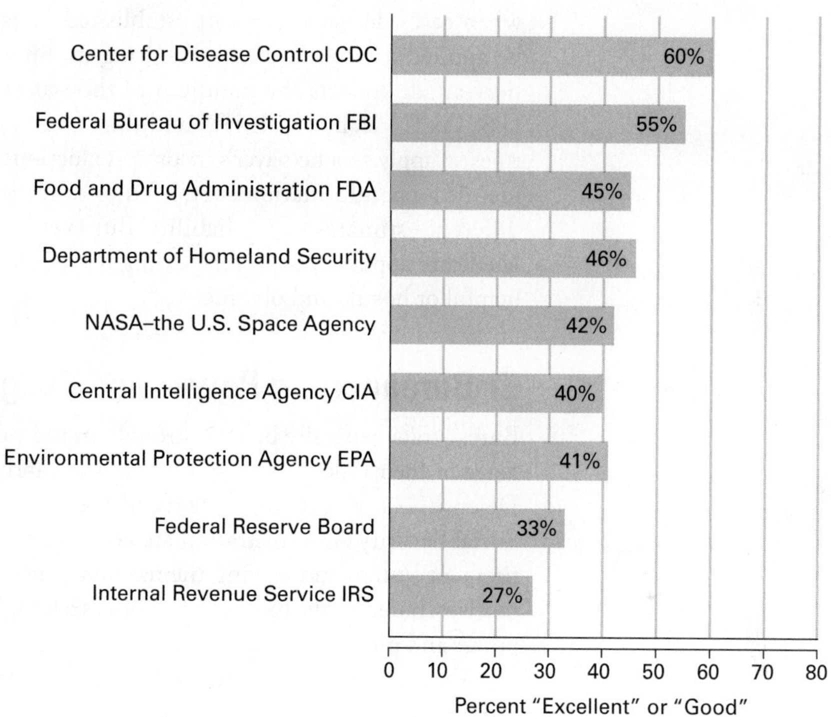

SOURCE: Gallup Opinion Poll, May 20–21, 2013.

- Conduct research on the proposed regulation's economic and environmental impacts.
- Solicit "public comments" (usually the arguments of interest groups).
- Consult with higher officials, including the Office of Management and Budget.
- Publish the new regulation in the *Federal Register.*

adjudication
Decision making by the federal bureaucracy as to whether an individual or organization has complied with or violated government laws and/or regulations.

Regulatory battles are important because formal regulations that appear in the *Federal Register* have the effect of law. Congress can amend or repeal a regulation only by passing new legislation and obtaining the president's signature. Controversial bureaucratic regulations often remain in place because Congress is slow to act, because key committee members block corrective legislation, or because the president refuses to sign bills overturning the regulation.

☐ Bureaucratic Power: Adjudication

Adjudication involves bureaucratic decisions about individual cases. Rule making resembles the legislative process, and adjudication resembles the judicial process.

12.1
12.2
12.3
12.4
12.5
12.6
12.7
12.8

budget maximization
Bureaucrats' tendencies to expand their agencies' budgets, staff, and authority.

discretionary funds
Budgeted funds not earmarked for specific purposes but available to be spent in accordance with the best judgment of a bureaucrat.

In adjudication, bureaucrats decide whether a person or firm is failing to comply with laws or regulations and, if so, what penalties or corrective actions are to be applied. Regulatory agencies and commissions—for example, the National Labor Relations Board, the Federal Communications Commission, the Equal Employment Opportunity Commission, the Federal Trade Commission, the Securities and Exchange Commission—are heavily engaged in adjudication. Their elaborate procedures and body of previous decisions closely resemble the court system. Losers may appeal to the federal courts, but the record of agency success in the federal courts discourages many appeals.

Bureaucratic Power: Administrative Discretion

Much of the work of bureaucrats is administrative routine—issuing Social Security checks, printing forms, delivering the mail. Routines are repetitive tasks performed according to established rules and procedures. Yet bureaucrats almost always have some discretion in performing even the most routine tasks. Discretion is greatest when cases do not exactly fit established rules, or when more than one rule might be applied to the same case, resulting in different outcomes. The Internal Revenue Service administers the hundreds of thousands of rules developed to implement the U.S. Tax Code, but each IRS auditing agent has wide discretion in deciding which rules to apply to a taxpayer's income, deductions, business expenses, and so on. Indeed, identical tax information submitted to different IRS offices almost always results in different estimates of tax liability. But even in more routine tasks, from processing Medicare applications to forwarding mail, individual bureaucrats can be friendly and helpful or hostile and obstructive.[4]

Bureaucratic Power and Budget Maximization

Bureaucrats generally believe strongly in the value of their programs and the importance of their tasks. Senior military officers and civilian officials of the Department of Defense believe in the importance of a strong national defense, and top officials in the Social Security Administration are committed to maintaining the integrity of the retirement system and serving the nation's senior citizens. Beyond these public-spirited motives, bureaucrats, like everyone else, seek higher pay, greater job security, and added power and prestige for themselves.

These public and private motives converge to inspire bureaucrats to seek to expand the powers, functions, and budgets of their departments and agencies. Rarely do bureaucrats request a reduction in authority, the elimination of a program, or a decrease in their agency's budget. Rather, over time, **budget maximization**—expanding the agency's budget, staff, and authority as much as possible—becomes a driving force in government bureaucracies. This is especially true of discretionary funds. **Discretionary funds** are those that bureaucrats have flexibility in deciding how to spend, rather than money committed by law to specific purposes.[5] Thus, bureaucracies continually strive to add new functions, acquire more authority and responsibility, and increase their budgets and personnel. Bureaucratic expansion is just one of the reasons that government grows over time.

The Federal Bureaucracy

12.2 Describe the types of agencies in the federal bureaucracy and the extent and purposes of the bureaucracy.

The federal bureaucracy—officially part of the executive branch of the U.S. government—consists of about 2.8 million civilian employees (plus 1.4 million persons in the armed forces) organized into 15 cabinet departments, more than 60 independent agencies, and a large Executive Office

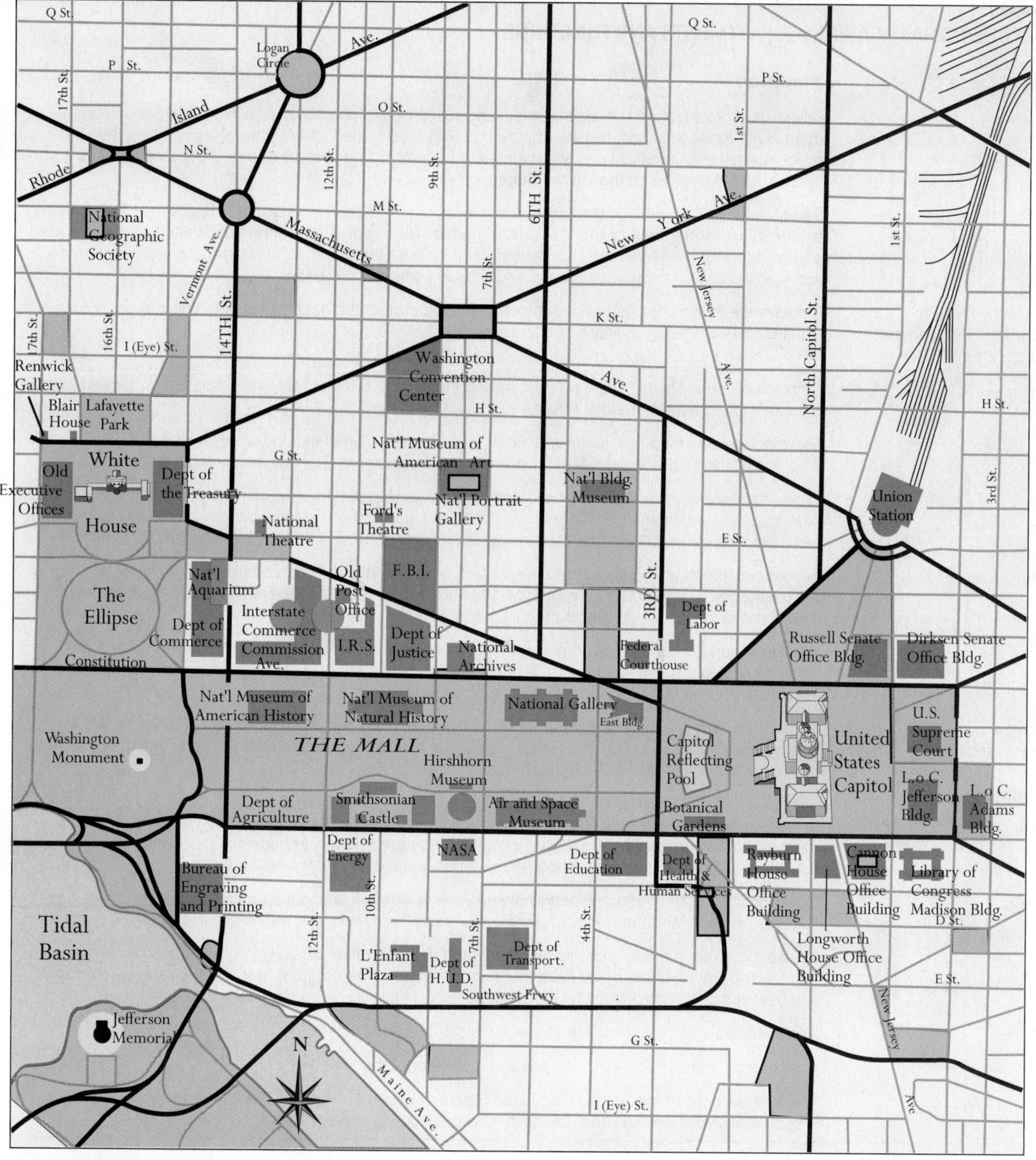

FIGURE 12.2 THE CAPITOL, WHITE HOUSE, AND BUREAUCRACY CORRIDORS OF POWER

This map shows the Capitol, the White House, and the major departments of the federal bureaucracy in Washington, D.C.

of the President (see Figure 12.2). The expenditures of *all* governments in the United States—the federal government, the 50 state governments, and some 89,000 local governments—now amount to over $5 *trillion* (roughly one-third of the U.S. gross domestic product, or GDP, of $15 *trillion*). About $3.8 *trillion* a year (about 25 percent of GDP)—is spent by the *federal* government. Government spending in the United States remains relatively modest compared to that of many nations (see *Compared to What?* The Size of Government in Other Nations).

□ Cabinet Departments

Cabinet departments employ about 60 percent of all federal workers (see Table 12.1). Each department is headed by a secretary (with the exception of the Justice Department, which is headed by the attorney general), who is appointed by the president and

TABLE 12.1 WHO DOES WHAT?: CABINET DEPARTMENTS AND FUNCTIONS

Department and Date Created	Function
State (1789)	Advises the president on the formation and execution of foreign policy; negotiates treaties and agreements with foreign nations; represents the United States in the United Nations and in more than 50 major international organizations and maintains U.S. embassies abroad; issues U.S. passports and, in foreign countries, visas to the United States.
Treasury (1789)	Serves as financial agent for the U.S. government; issues all payments of the U.S. government according to law; manages the debt of the U.S. government by issuing and recovering bonds and paying their interest; collects taxes owed to the U.S. government; collects taxes and enforces laws on alcohol, tobacco, and firearms and on customs duties; manufactures coins and currency.
Defense (1947: formerly the War Department, created in 1789, and the Navy Department, created in 1798)	Provides the military forces needed to deter war and protect the national security interest; includes the Departments of the Army, Navy, and Air Force.
Justice (1789)	Enforces all federal laws, including consumer protection, antitrust, civil rights, drug, and immigration and naturalization; maintains federal prisons.
Interior (1849)	Has responsibility for public lands and natural resources, for American Indian reservations, and for people who live in island territories under U.S. administration; preserves national parks and historical sites.
Agriculture (1889)	Works to improve and maintain farm income and to develop and expand markets abroad for agricultural products; safeguards standards of quality in the food supply through inspection and grading services; administers rural development, credit, and conservation programs; administers food stamp program.
Commerce (1913)	Encourages the nation's international trade, economic growth, and technological advancement; conducts the census; provides social and economic statistics and analyses for business and government; maintains the merchant marine; grants patents and registers trademarks.
Labor (1913)	Oversees working conditions; administers federal labor laws; protects workers' pension rights; sponsors job training programs; keeps track of changes in employment, price, and other national economic indicators.
Health and Human Services (1953 as Health, Education, and Welfare; reorganized with Education as a separate department in 1979)	Administers social welfare programs for the elderly, children, and youths; protects the health of the nation against impure and unsafe foods, drugs, and cosmetics; operates the Centers for Disease Control; funds the Medicare and Medicaid programs.
Housing and Urban Development (1965)	Is responsible for programs concerned with housing needs, fair housing opportunities, and the improvement and development of the nation's communities; administers mortgage insurance programs, rental subsidy programs, and neighborhood rehabilitation and preservation programs.
Transportation (1966)	Is responsible for the nation's highway planning, development, and construction; also urban mass transit, railroads, aviation, and the safety of waterways, ports, highways, and oil and gas pipelines.
Energy (1977)	Is responsible for the research, development, and demonstration of energy technology; marketing of federal electric power; energy conservation; the nuclear weapons program; regulation of energy production and use; and collection and analysis of energy data.
Education (1979)	Administers and coordinates most federal assistance to education.
Veterans Affairs (1989)	Operates programs to benefit veterans and members of their families.
Homeland Security (2002)	Prevents terrorist attacks within the United States, reduces the vulnerability of the nation to terrorism, and minimizes the damage and assists in recovery from terrorist attacks.

SOURCE: *The United States Government Manual,* Washington, D.C.: Government Printing Office, annual.

must be confirmed by the Senate. Each department is hierarchically organized; each has its own organization chart.

Cabinet status confers great legitimacy on a governmental function and prestige on the secretary, thus strengthening that individual's voice in the government. Therefore the elevation of an executive agency to cabinet level often reflects political considerations as much as or more than national needs. Strong pressures from "client" interest groups (groups principally served by the department), as well as presidential and congressional desires to pose as defenders and promoters of particular interests, account for the establishment of all of the newer departments. President Woodrow Wilson appealed to the labor movement in 1913 when he separated out a Department of Labor from the earlier business-dominated Department of Commerce and Labor. In 1965, President Lyndon Johnson created the Department of Housing and Urban Development to demonstrate his concern for urban problems. Seeking support from teachers and educational administrators, President Jimmy Carter created a separate Department of Education in 1979 and changed the name of the former Department of Health, Education, and Welfare to the Department of Health and Human Services (perhaps finding the phrase "human services" more politically acceptable than "welfare"). President Ronald Reagan tried, and failed, to "streamline" government by abolishing the Department of Education. But Reagan himself added a cabinet post, elevating the Veterans Administration to the Department of Veterans Affairs in an attempt to ingratiate himself with veterans. President George W. Bush created a new Department of Homeland Security in 2002 in response to the "9/11" terrorist attacks on America and the threat of future attacks directly on the soil of the United States.

Cabinet Department Functions

The relative power and prestige of each cabinet-level department is a product not only of its size and budget but also of the importance of its function. By custom, the "pecking order" of departments—and therefore the prestige ranking of their secretaries—is determined by their year of origin. Thus the Departments of State, Treasury, Defense (War), and Justice, created by the First Congress in 1789, head the protocol list of departments. Overall, the duties of the 15 cabinet-level departments of the executive branch cover an enormous range—everything from providing mortgage insurance to overseeing the armed forces of the United States (see Table 12.1).

Cabinet Appointments

The Constitution requires that "Officers of the United States" be confirmed by the Senate. In the past, the Senate rarely rejected a presidential cabinet nomination; the

Compared to What?

The Size of Government in Other Nations

How does the size of the public sector in the United States compare with the size of the public sector in other economically advanced, democratic countries? There is a great deal of variation in the size of government across countries. Government spending exceeds one-half of the total output of Sweden, Denmark, Netherlands, Finland, Germany, Italy, Austria, Belgium, and France. The high level of government spending in these countries primarily reflects greater public-sector involvement in the provision of housing, health care, retirement insurance, and aid to the unemployed. The sizes of the public sectors in Japan and Canada are only slightly higher than that of the United States.

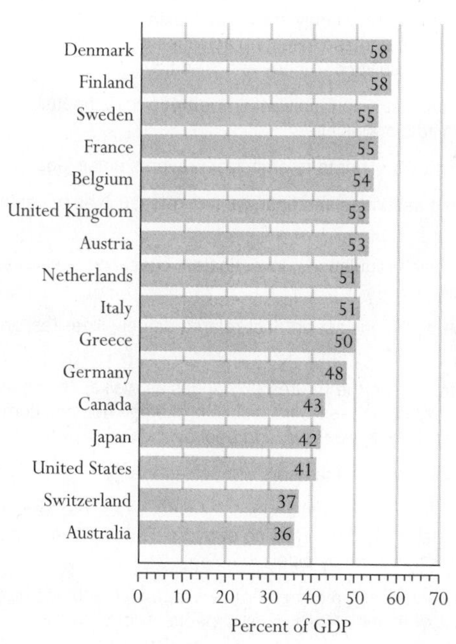

Recent analysis of 35 developed countries reveals that government consumption of a country's productivity increases with the growth of the retiree population, more urbanization, and more equality in the distribution of wealth. Governments have more transfer payments when there is more free trade, more democratization, and greater regulation of the economy. So, economic forces drive the government consumption of a nation's wealth, but political and social forces drive the aggressive use of wealth transfers.

QUESTION

1. Why do you think government growth and democracy grow together? If so, when we promote democracy around the world, do we promote the growth of government and government consumption?

SOURCES: United States Census Bureau, *Statistical Abstract of the United States, 2012*, Table 1360, at page 863. Boris Gramc. "Factors in the Size of Government in Developed Countries." *Prague Economic Papers* 2 (2002): 130–142.

traditional view was that presidents were entitled to pick their own people and even make their own mistakes. In recent years, however, the confirmation process has become more partisan and divisive, with the Senate conducting lengthy investigations and holding public hearings on presidential cabinet nominees. In 1989, the Senate rejected President Bush's nomination of John Tower as secretary of defense in a partisan battle featuring charges that the former Texas senator was a heavy drinker. The intense public scrutiny and potential for partisan attacks, together with financial disclosure and conflict-of-interest laws, may discourage some well-qualified people from accepting cabinet posts.

□ Independent Regulatory Commissions

Independent regulatory commissions differ from cabinet departments in their function, organization, and accountability to the president. Their function is to *regulate* a sector of society—transportation, communications, banking, labor relations, and so on (see Table 12.2). These commissions are empowered by Congress both to make and enforce rules, and they thus function in a legislative and judicial fashion. To symbolize their impartiality, many of these organizations are headed by *commissions,* usually with 5 to 10 members, rather than by a single secretary. Major policy decisions are made by majority vote of the commission. Finally, these agencies are more independent of the president than are cabinet departments. Their governing commissions are appointed by the president and confirmed by the Senate in the same fashion as cabinet

TABLE 12.2 WHO DOES WHAT? MAJOR REGULATORY BUREAUCRACIES

Commission	Date Created	Primary Functions
Federal Communications Commission	1934	Regulates interstate and foreign communications (FCC) by radio, television, wire, and cable.
Food and Drug Administration (FDA)	1930	Sets standards of safety and efficacy for foods, drugs, and medical devices.
Federal Home Loan Bank	1932	Regulates savings and loan associations that specialize in making home mortgage loans.
Federal Maritime Commission	1961	Regulates the waterborne foreign and domestic offshore commerce of the United States.
Federal Reserve Board (FRB)	1913	Regulates the nation's money supply by making monetary policy, which influences the lending and investing activities of commercial banks and the cost and availability of money and credit.
Federal Trade Commission (FTC)	1914	Regulates business to prohibit unfair methods of competition and unfair or deceptive acts or practices.
National Labor Relations Board (NLRB)	1935	Protects employees' rights to organize; prevents unfair labor practices.
Securities and Exchange Commission (SEC)	1934	Regulates the securities and financial markets (such as the stock market).
Occupational Safety and Health Administration (OSHA)	1970	Issues workplace regulations; investigates, cites, and penalizes for noncompliance.
Consumer Product Safety Commission (CPSC)	1972	Protects the public against product-related deaths, illnesses, and injuries.
Commodity Futures Trading Commission	1974	Regulates trading on the futures exchanges as well as the activities of commodity exchange members, public brokerage houses, commodity salespersons, trading advisers, and pool operators.
Nuclear Regulatory Commission (NRC)	1974	Regulates and licenses the users of nuclear energy.
Federal Energy Regulatory Commission (formerly the Federal Power Commission)	1977	Regulates the transportation and sale of natural gas, the transmission and sale of electricity, the licensing of hydroelectric power projects, and the transportation of oil by pipeline.
Equal Employment Opportunity Commission (EEOC)	1964	Investigates and rules on charges of racial, gender, and age discrimination by employers and unions, in all aspects of employment.
Environmental Protection Agency (EPA)	1970	Issues and enforces pollution control standards regarding air, water, solid waste, pesticides, radiation, and toxic substances.
Federal Elections Commission (FEC)	1975	Administers and enforces federal campaign finance laws.

SOURCE: FirstGov, www.firstgov.gov/agencies.

secretaries, but their terms are fixed; they cannot be removed by the president.[6] These provisions are designed to insulate regulators from direct partisan or presidential pressures in their decision making.

A few powerful regulatory agencies remain inside cabinet departments. The most notable are the Food and Drug Administration (FDA), which remains in the Department of Health and Human Services and has broad authority to prevent the sale of drugs not deemed by the agency to be both "safe" and "effective"; the Occupational Health and Safety Administration (OSHA) in the Department of Labor, with authority to make rules governing any workplace in America; and the most powerful government agency of all, the Internal Revenue Service in the Treasury Department, with its broad authority to interpret the tax code, maintain records on every American, and investigate and punish alleged violations of the tax code.

☐ Independent Agencies

Congress has created a number of independent agencies outside of any cabinet department. Like cabinet departments, these agencies are hierarchically organized with a single head—usually called an "administrator"—who is appointed by the

What Do You Think?

Environment, or Economy?

While campaigning for president in 2011, former House Speaker Newt Gingrich (R-GA) advanced the "red meat notion" to antiregulation Iowa Republicans that the Environmental Protection Agency (EPA) ought to be abolished (a red meat issue is one that is designed to spark the ideological hunger of the audience). Environmental regulation becomes unpopular during periods of economic decline and uncertainty, and the EPA is a traditional target of limited-government conservatives. The EPA is more expansive in the development and implementation of environmental regulations under Democratic administrations (or less hindered than when Republicans are in power), and the Obama EPA was behaving true to form, pursuing expanded regulatory authority on a variety of issues related to air quality and carbon emissions.

But does the public want to protect the environment, or protect jobs?

With which of these statements about the environment and the economy do you most agree—protection of the environment should be given priority, even at the risk of economic growth, or economic growth should be given priority, even if the environment suffers to some extent?

QUESTIONS

1. Given the choice between more jobs or less pollution, which would you choose?
2. Do you think that there would be less resistance to environmental regulation in a healthy economy? Why or why not?

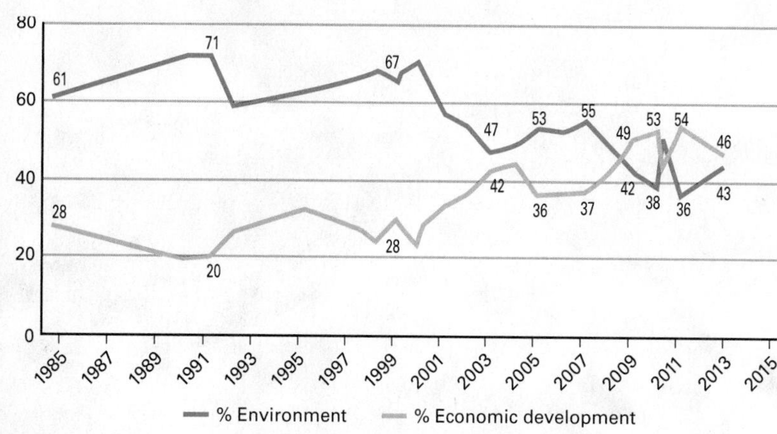

SOURCES: Gallup Opinion Poll, March 28, 2011, accessed at www.gallup.org; see also E. Elliott, J. L. Regens, and B. J. Seldon, 1996. Exploring Variation in Public Support for Environmental Protection. *Social Science Quarterly* 76(1): 41–52.

12.1
12.2
12.3
12.4
12.5
12.6
12.7
12.8

president and confirmed by the Senate. Administrators have no fixed terms of office and can be dismissed by the president; thus they are independent only insofar as they report directly to the president rather than through a cabinet secretary. Politically, this independence ensures that their interests and budgets will not be compromised by other concerns, as may occur in agencies located within departments.

One of the most powerful independent agencies is the Environmental Protection Agency (EPA), which is responsible for implementing federal legislation dealing with clean air, safe drinking water, solid waste disposal, pesticides, radiation, and toxic substances. The EPA establishes and enforces comprehensive and complex standards for thousands of substances in the environment. It enjoys the political support of influential environmental interest groups, including the Environmental Defense Fund, Friends of the Earth, the National Audubon Society, the National Wildlife Federation, the Natural Resources Defense Council, the Sierra Club, and the Wilderness Society. The EPA started as an independent agency that would act as a primary implementing authority of federal policy. However, the scope of activities regulated by the EPA led the agency to develop coordinated relationships with state environmental agencies to implement most federal programs.

☐ The "Fed"

The Federal Reserve System is the most independent of all federal government agencies. The function of the Fed is to regulate the supply of money and thereby avoid both inflation and recession. The Federal Reserve System is independent of either the president and Congress. Its seven-member board of governors is appointed for *14-year terms.* Members are appointed by the president, with the consent of the Senate, but they may not be removed from the board except for "cause." No member has ever been removed since the creation of the board in 1913. The chairman of the board serves only a four-year term, but the chairman's term overlaps that of the president so that new presidents cannot immediately name their own chair (see *The Game, the Rules, the Players:* Janet Yellen Managing the Nation's Money).

THE U.S. COAST GUARD AT WORK

The U.S. Coast Guard icebreaker Cutter Healy breaks ice near Point Barrow, Alaska. Economic development near the Arctic Circle makes this little known and underfunded mission very important. Often government agencies engage in a variety of tasks that are unseen, but critical to the function of American society.

□ Government Corporations

Government corporations are created by Congress to undertake independent commercial enterprises. They resemble private corporations in that they typically charge for their services. Like private corporations, they too are usually governed by a chief executive officer and a board of directors, and they can buy and sell property and incur debts.

Presumably, government corporations perform a service that the private enterprise system has been unable to carry out adequately. The first government corporation was the Tennessee Valley Authority, created by President Franklin Roosevelt

12.1
12.2
12.3
12.4
12.5
12.6
12.7
12.8

The Game, the Rules, the Players

Janet Yellen: Managing the Nation's Money

Janet Yellen is the 15th chair of the Board of Governors of the Federal Reserve System. Yellen was nominated by President Barack Obama and confirmed by the U.S. Senate in 2014. She previously served as vice chair from 2010 to 2014. It is Yellen's job to guide the "Fed" in managing the nation's money supply to avoid both inflation and recession. She is the first woman to head the world's largest reserve bank.

Yellen is from Brooklyn, New York, and grew up in Bay Ridge. She graduated *summa cum laude* from Pembroke College (Brown University) in 1967 and then earned her PhD in economics from Yale in 1971 where she studied with Nobel Prize winners James Tobin and Joseph Stiglitz. She served on the faculty at Harvard, the London School of Economics, and Berkeley.

Like many of her predecessors, Yellen moved between the academy and public service. She worked as an economist at the Fed in the 1970s, then later returned to Washington, first as a member of the Federal Reserve System's Board of governors, and then as a chair of President Bill Clinton's Council of Economic Advisers. Before returning to the Fed as vice chair in 2010, she was president of the Federal Reserve Bank of San Francisco.

Yellen was a potentially controversial pick to lead the Fed. She was the first Democratic nominee for chair of the Federal Reserve since Paul Volcker in 1979. And, her writings and observations about issues of investment bubbles and inflation disturbed critics in both parties. In particular, monetarists were concerned that Yellen's intellectual emphasis on fighting unemployment would lead her to be a "loose-money" chair who would not tighten the money supply to keep down consumer inflation. Three years before the collapse of the U.S. housing bubble that set off the Great Recession, Yellen had dismissed concerns about the bubble, contending that it would feel like a "good-sized bump in the road."

Her nomination in October 2013 was delayed nearly four months as the Congress and President Obama fought over budget and deficit issues. She was confirmed in January 2014. The 56–26 confirmation vote in the Senate was the closest Fed chair confirmation ever.

The housing bubble turned out to be more than a bump in the road. Yellen's predecessor, Ben Bernanke, had worked with the Bush administration and, together with Treasury Secretary Henry Paulson, developed the $700 billion Wall Street bailout plan hurriedly passed by Congress in 2008. Bernanke argued that the bailout was essential in avoiding a deep recession—and it was a policy consistent with the loose-money philosophy attached to his successor, who continues to maintain low interest rates.

These same policies are the primary source of criticism of the Fed by hard-money conservatives. When Bernanke started at the Fed, he enjoyed strong "trust" numbers. This trust had disappeared by 2013, especially among conservatives and low-earners. His successor Yellen enjoyed no honeymoon with the public—over 40 percent of the public expressed no confidence in the new chair, according to the Gallup poll.

QUESTIONS

1. Do you think the Federal Reserve is a political institution? Or an economic institution? Why?
2. How do you think Janet Yellen's sex matters in her running of the Fed, if at all?

SOURCE: Gallup Poll, April 14, 2011; April 17, 2009; May 10, 2005; accessed at www.gallup.org.

12.1

12.2

12.3

12.4

12.5

12.6

12.7

12.8

spoils system
Selection of employees for government agencies on the basis of party loyalty, electoral support, and political influence.

during the Depression to build dams and sell electricity at inexpensive rates to impoverished citizens in the mid-South. In 1970, Congress created Amtrak to restore railroad passenger service to the United States. While ridership has increased, competition with government-supported air and highway travel has forced Amtrak to continually seek federal subsidies to maintain operations. The U.S. Post Office had originally been created as a cabinet-level department, but in 1971 it became the U.S. Postal Service, a government corporation with a mandate from Congress to break even. But competition from e-mail and private delivery services, such as UPS and FedEx, has cut into Postal Service revenue and forced it to borrow from the U.S. Treasury to offset deficits.

Contractors and Consultants

How has the federal government grown enormously in power and size, yet kept its number of employees at roughly the same level in recent years? The answer is found in the spectacular growth of private firms that live off federal contracting and consulting fees. Nearly one-fifth of all federal government spending flows through private contractors: for supplies, equipment, services, leases, and research and development. An army of scientists, economists, education specialists, management consultants, transportation experts, social scientists, and others are scattered across the country in universities, think tanks, consulting firms, and laboratories. Many are concentrated in the "beltway bandit" firms surrounding Washington, D.C.

The federal grant and contracting system is enormously complex; an estimated 150,000 federal contracting offices in nearly 500 agencies oversee thousands of outside contractors and consultants.[7] Although advertised bidding is sometimes required by law, most contracts and grants are awarded without competition through negotiation with favored firms or "sole source contracts" with organizations believed by bureaucrats to be uniquely qualified. Even when federal agencies issue public requests for proposals (RFPs), often a favored contractor has been alerted and advised by bureaucrats within the agency about how to win the award.

Bureaucracy and Democracy

12.3 Trace changes over time in the size and composition of the bureaucracy and assess the repercussions for democracy.

Traditionally, conflict over government employment centered on the question of partisanship versus competence. Should the federal bureaucracy be staffed by people politically loyal to the president, the president's party, or key members of Congress? Or should it be staffed by nonpartisan people selected on the basis of merit and protected from "political" influence?

The Spoils System

Historically, government employment was allocated by the **spoils system**—selecting employees on the basis of party loyalty, electoral support, and political influence. Or, as Senator William Marcy said in 1832, "They see nothing wrong in the rule that to the victors belong the spoils of the enemy."[8] The spoils system is most closely associated with President Andrew Jackson, who viewed it as a popular reform of the earlier tendency to appoint officials on the basis of kinship and class standing. Jackson sought to bring into government many of the common people who had supported him. Later in the nineteenth century, the bartering and sale of government jobs became so scandalous and time-consuming that presidents complained bitterly about the task. When President James Garfield was shot and killed in 1881 by a disgruntled job seeker, the stage was set for reform.

The Merit System

The **merit system**—government employment based on competence, neutrality, and protection from partisanship—was introduced in the Pendleton Act of 1883. The act created the Civil Service Commission to establish a system for selecting government personnel based on merit, as determined by competitive examinations. In the beginning, "civil service" coverage included only about 10 percent of total federal employees. Over the years, however, more and more positions were placed under civil service, primarily at the behest of presidents who sought to "freeze in" their political appointees. By 1978, more than 90 percent of federal employees were covered by civil service or other merit systems.

merit system
Selection of employees for government agencies on the basis of competence, with no consideration of an individual's political stance and/or power.

The civil service system established a uniform General Schedule (GS) of job grades from GS 1 (lowest) to GS 15 (highest), with an Executive Schedule added later for top managers and pay ranges based on an individual's time in the grade. Each grade has specific educational requirements and examinations. College graduates generally begin at GS 5 or above; GS 9 through GS 12 are technical and supervisory positions; and GS 13, 14, and 15 are midlevel management and highly specialized positions. The Executive Schedule (the "supergrades") are reserved for positions of greatest responsibility. In 2014 general schedule annual pay ranged from roughly \$18,000–23,000 (GS–1) to \$25,000–32,000 (GS–4). For grades 5–8, up to \$50,000; for grades 9–15 from \$42,000 to \$130,000. Executive schedule positions range in salary up to \$202,000.

About two-thirds of all federal civilian jobs come under the General Schedule system, with its written examinations and/or training, experience, and educational requirements. Most of the other one-third of federal civilian employees are part of the "excepted services"; they are employed by various agencies that have their own separate merit systems, such as the Federal Bureau of Investigation, the Central Intelligence Agency, the U.S. Postal Service, and the State Department Foreign Service. The military also has its own system of recruitment, promotion, and pay.

SPOILED ROTTEN?

During the administration of Andrew Jackson, the spoils system was perhaps more overt than at any other time in the history of the U.S. federal government. Jackson claimed he was trying to involve more of the "common folk" in the government, but his selection of advisers on the basis of personal friendship rather than qualifications sometimes caused him difficulties.

Political Involvement

Congress passed the Hatch Act in 1939, a law that prohibited federal employees from engaging in partisan political activity, including running for public office, soliciting campaign funds, or campaigning for or against a party or candidate. It also protected federal merit system employees from dismissal for partisan reasons. But over the years, many federal employees came to believe that the Hatch Act infringed on their rights as citizens. In 1993, a Democratic-controlled Congress repealed major portions of the Hatch Act, allowing civil servants to hold party positions and involve themselves in political fund-raising and campaigning. They still may not be candidates for public office in partisan elections, or solicit contributions from subordinate employees or people who do business with—or have cases before—their agencies.

The Problem of Responsiveness

The civil service system, like most other "reforms," eventually created problems at least as troubling as those in the system it replaced. First of all, there is the problem of a *lack of responsiveness* to presidential direction. Civil servants, secure in their protected jobs, can be less than cooperative toward their presidentially appointed department or agency heads. They can slow or obstruct policy changes with which they personally disagree. Each bureau and agency develops its own "culture," usually in strong support of the governmental function or client group served by the organization. Changing the culture of an agency is extremely difficult, especially when a presidential administration is committed to reducing its resources, functions, or services. Bureaucrats' powers of policy obstruction are formidable: they can help mobilize interest-group support against the president's policy; they can "leak" damaging information to sympathizers in Congress or the media to undermine the president's policy; they can delay and/or "sabotage" policies with which they disagree.

12.1
12.2
12.3
12.4
12.5
12.6
12.7
12.8

A Conflicting View

The IRS And Suspicious Tea

Does the Internal Revenue Service have any business being in campaign politics? Does the very important function of that agency—collecting revenue—require it to have a special distance from rancorous partisan debates?

Taxation is a weighty power. Justice John Marshall summarized the successful argument of attorney Daniel Webster in the *McCulloch v. Maryland* case as "the power to tax involves the power to destroy." Taxation removes value from a person or their property, under the penalty of prison or the confiscation of property. There have long been allegations of the use of tax authorities to harass political enemies. In 2013, these allegations were tied to the Obama administration in the seemingly arbitrary use of IRS power to favor some groups over others in determining the tax status of groups involved in political action.

More tax-exempt groups are being created to engage in campaign politics. The 2010 *Citizens United* and *SpeechNOW*.org decisions expanded the ability of corporations, unions, and charitable entities to spend money on political messages. Soon after the decision, there was an explosion of applications to create more tax-exempt 501(c)(4) organizations. These organizations could funnel money from large-dollar donors into campaign activities, all the while not divulging who were the donors. Many of these organizations had been organized by conservatives affiliated with the emerging Tea Party movement. And, these acts of organizing and attempting to operate under these new rules for tax-exempt organizations brought them into direct contact with the Internal Revenue Service.

The IRS

The IRS is a universally loathed, often feared institution. It was created with a single purpose, collecting taxes from the people. In any given year the IRS will process almost 175,000,000 tax returns for individuals, joint filer, and corporations, and collect trillions of dollars of taxes.

It is typically among the least-popular government agencies. It is the one agency of government that is supposed to make universal contact with all Americans, and it does so for a single, unpleasant purpose. The IRS takes money, and, when people avoid paying taxes, it uses its substantial powers to seize property and to seek criminal penalties. Just over a quarter of Americans think the IRS does its job well.

The IRS's job requires it to have broad powers of investigation, audit, and prosecution. It has a powerful regulatory function, determining the tax-exempt status of not-for-profit and charitable organizations. This last function also gives the IRS a powerful role in American political campaigns, because the tax status of organizations dictate the scope of activities they can engage in under federal election law.

Scrutinizing Activist Groups

From April 2010 to April 2012, the IRS engaged in an intensive investigation of certain groups applying for 501(c)(4) status. The groups were chosen based on words in their names ("tea party" or "Israel" or "occupy" or "progressive" for example); the issue they wanted to advocate (like taxes or debt); and their educational purpose, such as informing people about the Constitution or Obamacare. Then, at several IRS offices but most notably the Cincinnati office, decisions were placed on hold for applications from conservative-sounding groups using terms such as "Tea" or "9/12" or "patriots" or "liberty" (the Ohio Liberty Coalition is one example). Applications for progressive and liberal groups using terms like "occupy" or "liberal" or "equality" were processed more quickly, and the groups were then able to function in the campaign environment.

Many of these groups, whether liberal or conservative, were flagged for additional scrutiny by IRS screeners (screeners are individuals who review and make recommendations regarding the group applications). In many instances, requests for additional information or documentation were made of the groups, including but not limited to the names of their donors; the amount of money received; and the names of organizations providing education, training, or services to the applicant group. Some groups were explicitly asked if they had support or ties to the conservative activist groups or foundations funded by the Koch brothers of Wichita, Kansas.

Congress Responds

Some groups singled out for special scrutiny by the IRS complained to members of Congress. Inquiries in 2012, 2013, and 2014 headed by Rep. Darrell Issa (R-CA) focused on the activities of the IRS Exempt Organizations division and its director, Lois Lerner. In 2013, an audit by the Treasury Department's inspector general concluded that the IRS had applied inappropriate criteria, and that employees conducting the screenings displayed "defiance" toward their superiors, ignorance of tax law, and created an "appearance of impropriety" through the extreme scrutiny, burdensome questions, and time delays directed toward conservative groups. In her appearances before the House Committee on Oversight and Government Reform, Ms. Lerner did not cooperate with investigators and instead invoked her 5th Amendment rights against self-incrimination.

QUESTIONS

1. Should a taxation agency have the ability to regulate campaign spending?
2. Is the use of an agency to your political advantage unethical, or just politics?

The Problem of Productivity

Perhaps the most troublesome problem in the federal bureaucracy has involved *productivity*—notably the inability to improve job performance because of the difficulties in rewarding or punishing civil servants. "Merit" salary rewards have generally proven ineffective in rewarding the performance of federal employees. More than 99 percent of federal workers regularly receive annual "merit" pay increases. Moreover, over time, federal employees have secured higher grade classifications and hence higher pay for most of the job positions in the General Schedule. This "inflation" in GS grades, combined with regular increases in salary and benefits, has resulted in many federal employees enjoying higher pay and benefits than employees in the private sector performing similar jobs.

At the same time, very poor performance often goes largely unpunished. Once hired and retained through a brief probationary period, a federal civil servant cannot be dismissed except for "cause." Severe obstacles to firing a civil servant result in a rate of dismissal of about one-tenth of 1 percent of all federal employees (see Table 12.3). It is doubtful that only such a tiny fraction are performing unsatisfactorily. A federal executive confronting a poorly performing or nonperforming employee must be prepared to spend more than a year in extended proceedings to secure a dismissal. Often, costly substitute strategies are devised to work around or inspire the resignation of unsatisfactory federal employees—assigning them meaningless or boring tasks, denying them promotions, transferring them to distant or undesirable locations, removing secretaries or other supporting resources, and the like.

Civil Service Reform

Presidents routinely try to remedy some of the problems in the system. The Civil Service Reform Act of 1978, initiated by President Jimmy Carter, replaced the Civil Service Commission with the Office of Personnel Management (OPM) and made the OPM responsible for recruiting, examining, training, and promoting federal employees. Unlike the Civil Service Commission, the OPM is headed by a single director responsible to the president. The act also sought to (1) streamline procedures through which individuals could be disciplined for poor performance; (2) establish merit pay for middle-level managers; and (3) create a Senior Executive Service (SES) composed of about 8,000 top people designated for higher Executive Schedule grades and salaries who also might be given salary bonuses, transferred among agencies, or demoted, based on performance.

But like many other reforms, this act failed to resolve the major problems—the responsiveness and productivity of the bureaucracy. No senior executives were fired, demoted, or involuntarily transferred. The bonus program proved difficult to implement: there are few recognized standards for judging meritorious work in public service, and bonuses often reflect favoritism as much as merit. Because the act created a separate Merit Systems Protection Board to hear appeals by federal employees from dismissals, suspensions, and demotions, rates of dismissal for all grades have not changed substantially from earlier days.

TABLE 12.3 FIRING A BUREAUCRAT: WHAT IS REQUIRED TO DISMISS A FEDERAL EMPLOYEE

Very few federal civil servants are ever dismissed from their jobs.

- Written notice at least 30 days in advance of a hearing to determine incompetence or misconduct.
- A statement of cause, indicating specific dates, places, and actions cited as incompetent or improper.
- The right to a hearing and decision by an impartial official, with the burden of proof falling on the agency that wishes to fire the employee.
- The right to have an attorney and to present witnesses in the employee's favor at the hearing.
- The right to appeal any adverse action to the Merit Systems Protection Board.
- The right to appeal any adverse action by the board to the U.S. Court of Appeals.
- The right to remain on the job and be paid until all appeals are exhausted.

12.1

12.2

12.3

12.4

12.5

12.6

12.7

12.8

TABLE 12.4 DIVERSITY IN THE BUREAUCRACY: MINORITIES IN FEDERAL EMPLOYMENT

Minorities are not well represented at the higher levels of the federal bureaucracy.

	Percentage White, Non-Hispanic	Percentage African American	Percentage Hispanic
Overall, 2006	67.8%	17.2%	7.5%
Overall, 2010	66.1	18.2	8.0
By pay grade			
GS 1–4, 2006	56.7	23.9	8.9
GS 1–4, 2010	58.9	22.7	8.1
GS 5–8	58.6	25.1	9.0
GS 5–8, 2010	58.5	25.0	9.0
GS 9–11	67.2	16.7	9.4
GS 9–11, 2010	65.8	18.3	8.7
GS 12–13	73.8	13.8	5.8
GS 12–13, 2010	70.0	14.7	7.8
GS 14–15	79.2	9.7	4.1
GS 14–15, 2010	75.8	11.4	4.5
Executive, 2006	85.2	6.4	3.7
Executive, 2010	78.7	6.4	4.1
U.S. Population	66.0	13.2	16.0

SOURCE: Office of Personnel Management. *Statistical Data Mart (SDM),* Table 1–5. 2012, www.opm.gov.

NOTE: Table excludes Native Americans, Alaska Natives, and Asian and Pacific Islanders.

☐ Bureaucracy and Representation

In addition to the questions of responsiveness and productivity, there is also the question of the representativeness of the federal bureaucracy. About 17 percent of the total federal civilian workforce is African American, and 7.5 percent is Hispanic. However, a close look at *top* bureaucratic positions reveals far less diversity. As Table 12.4 shows, only 6.4 percent of federal "executive" positions (levels GS 16–18) are filled by African Americans, and only 4.1 percent by Hispanics. Thus the federal bureaucracy is *un*representative of the general population in its top executive positions.

Bureaucratic Politics

12.4 Explain how the bureaucracy is staffed, to whom it is accountable, and how accountability is affected by politics and bureaucratic culture.

To whom is the federal bureaucracy really accountable? The president, Congress, or itself? Article II, Section 2, of the Constitution places the president at the head of the executive branch of government, with the power to "appoint Ambassadors, other public Ministers and Consuls, Judges of the Supreme Court, and all other Officers of the United States . . . which shall be established by Law." Appointment of these officials requires "the Advice and Consent of the Senate"—that is, a majority vote in the Senate. The Constitution also states that, "the Congress may by Law vest the Appointment of such inferior Officers, as they think proper, in the President alone." If the bureaucracy is to be made accountable to the president, we would expect the president to directly appoint *policy-making* executive officers. But it is difficult to determine exactly how many positions are truly "policy making."

Presidential "Plums"

The president retains direct control over about 3,000 federal jobs. Many of these jobs are considered policy-making positions. They include presidential appointments authorized by law—cabinet and subcabinet officers, judges, U.S. marshals, U.S. attorneys, ambassadors, and members of various boards and commissions. The president also appoints a large number of "Schedule C" jobs throughout the bureaucracy, described as "confidential or policy-determining" in character. Each new administration goes through many months of high-powered lobbying and scrambling to fill these posts. Applicants with congressional sponsors, friends in the White House, or a record of loyal campaign work for the president compete for these "plums." Political loyalty must be weighed against administrative competence.[9]

Rooms at the Top

The federal bureaucracy has "thickened" at the top, even as total federal employment has declined. Over time, departments and agencies have added layers of administrators, variously titled "deputy secretary," "undersecretary," "assistant secretary," "deputy assistant secretary," and so on. Cabinet departments have become top-heavy with administrators, and the same multiplication of layers of executive management has occurred in independent agencies as well.[10]

Whistle-Blowers

The question of bureaucratic responsiveness is complicated by the struggle between the president and Congress to control the bureaucracy. Congress expects federal agencies and employees to respond fully and promptly to its inquiries and to report candidly on policies, procedures, and expenditures. **Whistle-blowers** are federal employees (or employees of a firm contracting with the government) who report government waste, mismanagement, or fraud to the media or to congressional committees or who "go public" with their policy disputes with their superiors. Congress generally encourages whistle-blowing as a means of getting information and controlling the bureaucracy, but the president and agency heads whose policies are under attack are often less kindly disposed toward whistle-blowers.[11] In 1989, Congress passed the Whistleblower Protection Act, which established an independent agency to guarantee whistle-blowers protection against unjust dismissal, transfer, or demotion.

whistle-blowers
Employees who expose waste, fraud or mismanagement in government or government contracting.

Agency Cultures

Over time, every bureaucracy tends to develop its own "culture"—beliefs about the values of the organization's programs and goals and close associations with the agency's client groups and political supporters. Many government agencies are dominated by people who have been in government service most of their lives, and most of these people have worked in the same functional field most of their lives. They believe their work is important, and they resist efforts by either the president or Congress to reduce the activities, size, or budget of their agency. Career bureaucrats tend to support enlargement of the public sector—to enhance education, welfare, housing, environmental and consumer protection, and so on. Bureaucrats not only share a belief in the need for government expansion but also stand to benefit directly from increased authority, staffing, and funding as government takes on new and enlarged responsibilities. (See *Who's Getting What?* How Much Money Does the Government Waste?)

"Reinventing" Government

Reformers lament "the bankruptcy of bureaucracy"—the waste, inefficiency, impersonality, and unresponsiveness of large government organizations. They decry "the routine tendency to protect turf, to resist change, to build empires, to enlarge one's sphere of control, to

outsourcing
Government contracting with private firms to perform public services.

protect projects and programs regardless of whether or not they are any longer needed."[12] Many bureaucratic reform efforts have foundered, from Hoover Commission studies in the Truman and Eisenhower years to the Grace Commission work in the Reagan administration. More recently, in the 1990s, President Bill Clinton assigned a "reinventing government" task to Vice President Al Gore. Gore produced a report designed to put the "customer" (U.S. citizen) first, to "empower" government employees to get results, to cut red tape, to introduce competition and a market orientation wherever possible, and to decentralize government decision making.[13] Very little of the Gore agenda was accomplished.

Outsourcing

The federal government is increasingly **outsourcing** its work—contracting to private companies for work formerly done by U.S. employees. As various departments across the government—from the Department of Defense to the National Park Service—have turned projects over to private businesses, the number of federal jobs has also declined, from 3.1 million in 1992 to 2.8 million in 2010. Among the advantages of outsourcing are: private firms bid competitively for contracts, likely resulting in lower costs for the U.S. government—and therefore the American taxpayer. In addition, the private sector has fewer rules and regulations in comparison with operations within the departments and agencies of the federal government. Businesses may be able to undertake and complete projects faster and more efficiently than can governmental organizations. But outsourcing has its disadvantages—in many ways, simply the reverse of its advantages. The low-cost bidder may be a foreign-owned company. Should the U.S. government be concerned about which companies get its contracts, and where the employees of those companies live? Also, the private sector may be less accountable than the public sector. Work being done by for-profit companies may cut corners and be less reliable than that being done by the government itself.

Presidential Initiative

Presidents can create some new agencies by executive order. Often Congress gives presidents the authority to reorganize agencies by legislation. But presidents have also acted on their own to create new agencies. Indeed, one study concludes that presidents have created about 40 percent of all new agencies[14]—perhaps the most famous was President Kennedy's Peace Corps. Of course, Congress has the last word, inasmuch as the continuation of a presidentially created agency requires funding and Congress controls the purse strings. It can end an agency's existence by cutting off its funds.

The Budget

12.5 Outline the budgetary process and evaluate the advantages and disadvantages of the current system.

OMB

The president's power over the budget expanded dramatically with the creation of this agency, which only exists to prepare a budget that fits executive priorities. Here, then-budget director Jack Lew presents the proposed FY 2012 budget.

he federal government's annual budget battles are the heart of the political process. Budget battles decide who gets what and who pays the cost of government. The budget is the single most important policy statement of any government.

The president is responsible for submitting the annual *Budget of the United States Government*—with estimates of revenues and recommendations for expenditures—for consideration, amendment, and approval by the Congress. But the president's budget reflects the outcome of earlier bureaucratic battles over who gets what. Despite highly publicized wrangling between the president and Congress each year—and occasional declarations that the president's budget is "DOA" (dead on arrival)—final congressional appropriations rarely deviate by more than 2 or 3 percent from the original presidential budget. Thus, the president and the Office of Management and Budget in the Executive Office of the President have real budgetary power.

Who's Getting What?

How Much Money Does the Government Waste?

Americans are markedly cynical about the amount of waste in government spending. On average, Americans believe that 50 cents of every tax dollar that goes to the federal government in Washington are wasted. This figure is higher than in previous years (when the mean number of cents believed to be wasted ranged from 38 to 45), perhaps as a result of the increased spending in the Obama administration. State and local government are perceived to be somewhat less wasteful than the government in Washington.

But it is difficult to determine how much money the government actually wastes. What is "waste" to one person may be a necessary and vital government function to another—and it also reflects the often limited knowledge of the public about what government does, and at what level of government it does it.

Q. Of every tax dollar that goes to (the federal government, your state government, your local government) how many cents of each dollar would you say are wasted?

Mean number of cents of each dollar wasted	1982	2003	2011
Federal government	45¢	46¢	51¢
State government	38	38	42
Local government	34	36	38

Job Description	Positions	Average Pay (2011$)	% Increase Since 2006
Physician	30,953	184,395	67.70%
Dentist	2,145	143,084	46.90%
Design patent examiner	100	120,298	36.20%
Securities compliance examiner	149	141,012	25.10%
Customs and border protection	20,502	74,017	16.90%
Cemetery administration	116	82,810	13.80%
Patent examiner	7,180	103,625	12.40%
Writer and editor	1,419	85,851	9.10%
Border patrol enforcement	21,291	69,731	8.90%
Worker's compensation claims examiner	1,139	86,608	8.60%
Passport and visa examiner	1,472	68,845	8.30%
Nuclear materials courier	338	63,321	7.60%
Financial analyst	1,490	104,269	7.50%
Pharmacist	9,149	107,556	7.10%
Plant protection technician	1,086	32,109	7.00%
Financial manager	1,390	125,480	6.10%
Dental hygienist	612	54,235	6.00%
Civil rights analyst	65	106,783	5.80%
Fishery biologist	2,558	84,132	5.80%
Foreign agricultural affairs	167	129,638	5.00%

(*Continued*)

12.1
12.2
12.3
12.4
12.5
12.6
12.7
12.8

(Continued)

The General Accountability Office (GAO) of the U.S. Congress has the authority to audit the operations and finances of federal agencies. The GAO has often found fraud and mismanagement of government operations that come to 10 percent or more of the spending of the agencies that it has reviewed. This suggests the possibility that $380 billion of the federal government's $3.8 trillion budget is being wasted. Independent government commissions that studied federal government operations, such as the Grace Commission during the Reagan administration in the 1980s, put an even higher figure on government waste: more than 20 percent of government spending.

Despite frequent pledges by presidents and Congress to end waste and inefficiency in the federal government, it has proven difficult if not impossible to do so. Many programs that have been identified as having a great deal of waste and fraud are also politically very popular. Medicare, for example—which has been found to pay for unnecessary tests and procedures, for needless medical equipment, and for overpriced drugs—is a very popular program. Promises to eliminate waste in Medicare usually stir concerns, especially among senior citizens. Economic stimulus bills regularly include many wasteful projects, but these same projects meet Congress members' demands for pork-barrel projects that bring contracts and jobs to their districts around the country.

Are Federal Employees Paid Too Much?

Federal employees earn higher average salaries than private-sector workers in similar jobs. Federal workers earned an average salary of $67,691 in 2008 for occupations that are found in both government and the private sector. The average pay for the same mix of jobs in the private sector was $60,048. Moreover, the salary figures did not include the value of health, pension, and other benefits, which averaged $40,785 per federal employee versus $9,882 per private worker.[a] And pay is going up. The starting pay for a government car mechanic in 2011 is nearly $47,000, up over 20 percent from 2006. For a lawyer, the average starting pay is just over $100,000—up over 25 percent from five years before. As a consequence, government service has become increasingly attractive for young Americans entering the work force. And existing federal workers are less inclined to retire or quit to go to the private sector.

However, salaries at the top of the federal government—department secretaries, agency and bureau heads—rarely match the top salaries in business firms, some of which have payouts of $1 million or more. And the private sector was found to pay higher-than-government salaries for a select group of high-skilled occupations, including lawyers. Many federal occupations—for example, air traffic controllers, tax collectors, FBI agents—have no direct equivalent in the private sector.

Increased federal pay is not the same across all government jobs. The table on page 487 reports the top-20 pay-gaining jobs in federal service since 2006.

QUESTIONS

1. Look at the perceived waste in government, based on the levels of government. Do we tend to perceive waste in in levels of government we distrust?
2. Do you think government wastes money? Or does it underestimate demand for the services it creates?

[a]Data from U.S. Bureau of Economic Analysis as reported in *USA Today*, March 4, 2010; and in *USA Today*, December 26, 2011.

SOURCES: Gallup poll, September 19, 2011, www.gallup.com; General Accountability Office, *Federal Evaluation Issues* (Washington, D.C.: 1989); *President's Private Sector Survey on Cost Control* (Grace Commission). Washington, D.C.: Government Printing Office, 1984.

☐ Office of Management and Budget

The Office of Management and Budget (OMB) has the key responsibility for budget preparation. In addition to this major task, OMB has related responsibilities for improving the organization and management of the executive agencies, coordinating the extensive statistical services of the federal government, and analyzing and reviewing proposed legislation.[15]

Preparation of the budget begins when OMB, after preliminary consultations with the executive agencies and in accord with presidential policy, develops targets or ceilings within which the agencies are encouraged to build their requests (see Figure 12.3). Budget materials and instructions then go to the agencies, with the request that the forms be completed and returned to OMB. This request is followed by about three months of arduous work by agency budget officers, department heads, and the "grassroots" bureaucracy in Washington, D.C., and out in the field. Budget officials at the bureau and departmental levels check requests from the smaller units, compare them with previous years' estimates, hold conferences, and make adjustments. The heads of agencies are expected to submit their completed requests to OMB by July or August.

	WHO	WHAT	WHEN
 **Presidential budget making**	President and OMB	OMB presents long-range forecasts for revenues and expenditures to the president. President and OMB develop general guidelines for all federal agencies. Agencies are sent guidelines and forms for their budget requests.	January February March
	Executive agencies	Agencies prepare and submit budget requests to OMB.	April May June July
	OMB and agencies	OMB reviews agency requests and holds hearings with agency officials.	August September October
	OMB and president	OMB presents revised budget to president. President and OMB write budget message for Congress.	November December January
	President	President presents budget for the next fiscal year to Congress.	February
 **Congressional budget process**	CBO and congressional committees	CBO reviews taxing and spending proposals and reports to House and Senate budget committees.	February-April
	Congress; House and Senate budget committees	Committees present first concurrent resolution, which sets overall total for budget outlays in major categories. Full House and Senate vote on resolution. Committees are instructed to stay within Budget Committee's resolution.	May June
	Congress; House and Senate appropriations committees and budget committees	Appropriations committees and subcommittees draw up detailed appropriations bills and submit them to budget committees for second concurrent resolution. The full House and Senate vote on "reconciliations" and second (firm) concurrent resolution.	July August September
	Congress and president	House and Senate pass various appropriations bills (nine to sixteen bills, by major functional category, such as "defense"). Each is sent to president for signature. (If successfully vetoed, a bill is revised and resubmitted to the president.)	September October
 **Executive budget implementation**	Congress and president	Fiscal year for all federal agencies begins October 1. If no appropriations bill for an agency has been passed by Congress and signed by the president, Congress must pass and the president sign a continuing resolution to allow the agency to spend at last year's level until a new appropriations bill is passed. If no continuing resolution is passed, the agency must officially cease spending government funds and must officially shut down.	After October 1

FIGURE 12.3 HOW IT WORKS: THE BUDGET PROCESS

Development, presentation, and approval of the federal budget for any fiscal year take almost two full years. The executive branch spends more than a year on the process before Congress even begins its review and revision of the president's proposals. The problems of implementing the budgeted programs then fall to the federal bureaucracy.

12.1
12.2
12.3
12.4
12.5
12.6
12.7
12.8

fiscal year
Yearly government accounting period, not necessarily the same as the calendar year. The federal government's fiscal year begins October 1 and ends September 30.

budget resolution
Congressional bill setting forth target budget figures for appropriations to various government departments and agencies.

authorization
Act of Congress that establishes a government program and defines the amount of money it may spend.

appropriations act
Congressional bill that provides money for programs authorized by Congress.

obligational authority
Feature of some appropriations acts by which an agency is empowered to enter into contracts that will require the government to make payments beyond the fiscal year in question.

outlays
Actual dollar amounts to be spent by the federal government in a fiscal year.

Although these requests usually remain within target levels, occasionally they include some "overceiling" items (requests above the suggested ceilings). With the requests of the spending agencies at hand, OMB begins its own budget review, including hearings at which top agency officials support their requests as convincingly as possible. Frequently OMB must say "no," that is, reduce agency requests. On rare occasions, dissatisfied agencies may ask the budget director to take their cases to the president.

☐ The President's Budget

In December, the president and the OMB director devote much time to the key document, *The Budget of the United States Government (The Budget),* which by now is approaching its final stages of assembly. Each budget is named for the **fiscal year** in which it *ends.* The federal fiscal year begins on October 1 and ends the following September 30. (Thus *The Budget of the United States Government Fiscal Year* 2014 begins October 1, 2013, and ends September 30, 2014.) Although the completed document includes a revenue plan with general estimates for taxes and other income, it is primarily an expenditure budget. In late January, the president presents Congress with *The Budget* for the fiscal year beginning October 1. After the budget is in legislative hands, the president may recommend further alterations as needed.

☐ Relevant Congressional Committees

The Constitution gives Congress the authority to decide how the government should spend its money: "No money shall be drawn from the Treasury, but in Consequence of Appropriations made by Law" (Article I, Section 9). The president's budget is sent initially to the House and Senate Budget Committees, which rely on their own bureaucracy, the Congressional Budget Office (CBO), to review the president's budget. Then these committees draft a first **budget resolution** (due May 15) setting forth target goals for specific appropriations and revenue measures. If proposed spending exceeds the targets in the budget resolution, the resolution comes back to the floor in a reconciliation measure. A second budget resolution (due September 15) sets binding budget figures. The two budget resolutions are often folded into a single measure to avoid arguing the same issues twice.

Congressional approval of each year's spending is usually divided into 13 separate appropriations bills, each covering separate broad categories of spending (for example, defense, labor, commerce). Appropriations bills are drawn up by the House and Senate Appropriations Committees acting as overseers of agencies in their appropriations bills. Each committee has about 10 largely independent subcommittees, each reviewing the requests of a particular agency. Specific appropriations bills are taken up by the subcommittees in hearings. Departmental officers answer questions on the conduct of their programs and defend their requests for the next fiscal year; lobbyists and other witnesses testify. Although committees and subcommittees have broad discretion in allocating funds to the agencies they monitor, they must stay within overall totals set forth in the second budget resolution adopted by Congress.

☐ Appropriations Acts

It is important to distinguish between appropriations and authorization. An **authorization** is an act of Congress that establishes a government program and defines the amount of money it may spend. Authorizations may be for one or several years. An authorization does not actually provide the money that has been authorized; only an **appropriations act** can do that. Appropriations acts, which are usually for a single fiscal year, are almost always *less* than authorizations; deciding how much less is the real function of the Appropriations Committees and subcommittees. (By its own rules, Congress cannot appropriate money for programs it has not already authorized.)

Appropriations acts include both obligational authority and outlays. **Obligational authority** permits a government agency to enter into contracts that will require the government to make payments beyond the fiscal years in question. **Outlays** must be spent in the fiscal year for which they are appropriated.

Continuing Resolutions

All appropriations acts *should* be passed by both houses and signed by the president into law before the start of the fiscal year. Congress rarely meets this deadline, so the government usually finds itself beginning a new fiscal year without a budget. Constitutionally, any U.S. government agency for which Congress does not pass an appropriations act may not draw money from the Treasury and is obliged to shut down. To get around this problem, Congress usually adopts a **continuing resolution** that authorizes government agencies to keep spending money for a specified period at the same level as in the previous fiscal year.

A continuing resolution is supposed to grant additional time for Congress to pass—and the president to sign—appropriations acts. But occasionally this process has broken down in the heat of political combat over the budget: the time period specified in a continuing resolution has expired without agreement on appropriations acts or even on a new continuing resolution.

continuing resolution
Congressional bill that authorizes government agencies to keep spending money for a specified period at the same level as in the previous fiscal year; passed when Congress is unable to enact final appropriations measures by October 1.

incremental budgeting
Method of budgeting that focuses on requested increases in funding for existing programs, accepting as legitimate their previous year's expenditures.

SHUTDOWNS

In theory the failure of Congress to pass appropriations acts or a continuing resolution should result in the shutting down of any or all federal agencies. In the past, some funding gaps have occurred that temporarily shut down various agencies. But in 1994 during a bitter battle between Democratic President Bill Clinton and a Republican-controlled Congress, the federal government was technically "shut down" for several weeks. Thousands of government employees were furloughed, though emergency personnel and active-duty military were exempted. Again, in 2013 a shutdown occurred for 16 days when a Republican-controlled House battled President Obama over the budget. Republicans insisted on cutting funds for the Patient Protection and Affordable Care Act ("Obamacare"). The Democratic-controlled Senate and President Obama refused to accept such a budget. Public opinion blamed congressional Republicans for the shutdown, and the House was forced to accept a continuing resolution that still funded Obamacare. Key government functions (military, Veterans Affairs, Social Security, air traffic control, etc.) were unaffected. The House later passed a bill providing back pay to all affected federal employees.

The Politics of Budgeting

Budgeting is very political. Being a good "bureaucratic politician" involves (1) cultivating a good base of support for requests among the public at large and among interests served by the agency; (2) developing attention, enthusiasm, and support for one's program among top political figures and congressional leaders; (3) winning favorable coverage of agency activities in the media; and (4) following strategies that exploit opportunities.

Budgeting Is "Incremental"

The most important factor determining the size and content of the budget each year is last year's budget. Decision makers generally use last year's expenditures as a *base;* active consideration of budget proposals generally focuses on new items and requested increases over last year's base. The budget of an agency is almost never reviewed as a whole. Agencies are seldom required to defend or explain budget requests that do *not* exceed current appropriations; but requested increases *do* require explanation and are most subject to reduction by OMB or Congress.

The result of **incremental budgeting** is that many programs, services, and expenditures continue long after there is any real justification for them. When new needs, services, and functions arise, they do not displace older ones but rather are *added* to the budget. Budget decisions are made incrementally because policy makers do not have the time, energy, or information to review every dollar of every budget request every year. Nor do policy makers wish to refight every political battle over existing programs

12.1
12.2
12.3
12.4
12.5
12.6
12.7
12.8

A Conflicting View

Bureaucratic Regulations Are Suffocating America

"The regulations are much tougher in a free market because you cannot commit fraud, you cannot steal, you cannot hurt people ... in a true free market, in a Libertarian society you cannot do that, you have to be responsible." Rep. Ron Paul (R-TX), candidate for president, on *The Daily Show,* September 26, 2011.

Today, bureaucratic regulations of all kinds—environmental controls, workplace safety rules, municipal building codes, government contracting guidelines—have become so numerous, detailed, and complex that they are stifling initiative, curtailing economic growth, wasting billions of dollars, and breeding popular contempt for law and government.

Consider, for example, the Environmental Protection Agency's rules and regulations, now *32 volumes* of fine print. Under one set of rules, before any land on which "toxic" waste was once used can be reused by anyone for any purpose, it must be cleaned to near perfect purity. The dirt must be made cleaner than soil that has never been used for anything. The result is that most new businesses choose to locate on virgin land rather than incur the enormous expense of cleaning dirt, and a great deal of land previously used by industry sits vacant while new land is developed.

These and similar examples of "the death of common sense" in bureaucratic regulations are set forth by critic Philip K. Howard, who argues, "We have constructed a system of regulatory law that basically outlaws common sense."[a]

The explosive growth in federal regulations in the last two decades has added heavy costs to the American economy. The costs of regulations do not appear in the federal budget; rather, they are paid for by businesses, employees, and consumers. Indeed, politicians prefer a regulatory approach to the environment, health, and safety precisely because it forces costs on the private sector—costs that are largely invisible to voters and taxpayers. Yet as the costs of regulation multiply for American businesses, the prices of their products rise in world markets.

How large is the regulatory bill? Proponents of a regulatory activity usually object to estimating its cost. Politicians who wish to develop an image as protectors of the environment, of consumers, of the disabled, and so on, do not want to call attention to the costs of their legislation. Only recently has the Office of Management and Budget (OMB) even attempted to estimate the costs of federal regulatory activity. Overall, regulatory activity costs Americans between $300 billion (OMB estimate) and $1 trillion a year (Center for Competitive Enterprise Institute estimate), an amount equal to over one-quarter of the total federal budget.

Regulation also places a heavy burden on innovations and productivity. The costs and delays in winning permission for a new product tend to discourage invention and to drive up prices. For example, new drugs are difficult to introduce in the United States because the Food and Drug Administration (FDA) typically requires up to 10 years of testing. Western European nations are many years ahead in their number of life-saving drugs available; they speak of the "drug lag" in the United States. Critics charge that if aspirin were proposed for marketing today, it would not be approved by the FDA, though medical research in the 1960s and 1970s established the basic mechanisms of aspirin's effects, which were not known when it was introduced to the market in the nineteenth century by the firm Bayer AG.

Which Worries You More?

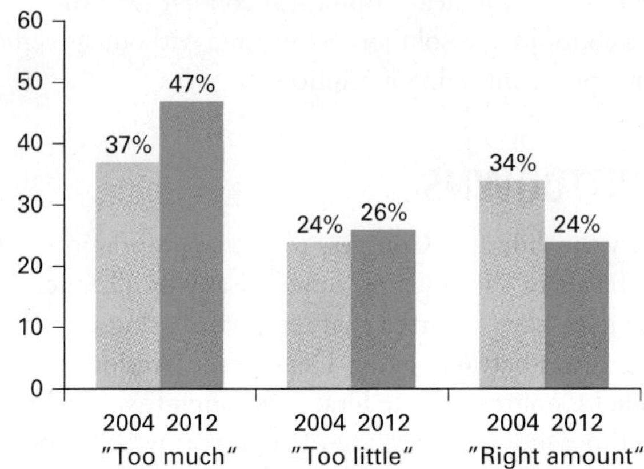

Which of the following do you most agree with: The federal government should become more involved in regulating and controlling business, the federal government should become less involved in regulating and controlling business, or things are right about the way they are?

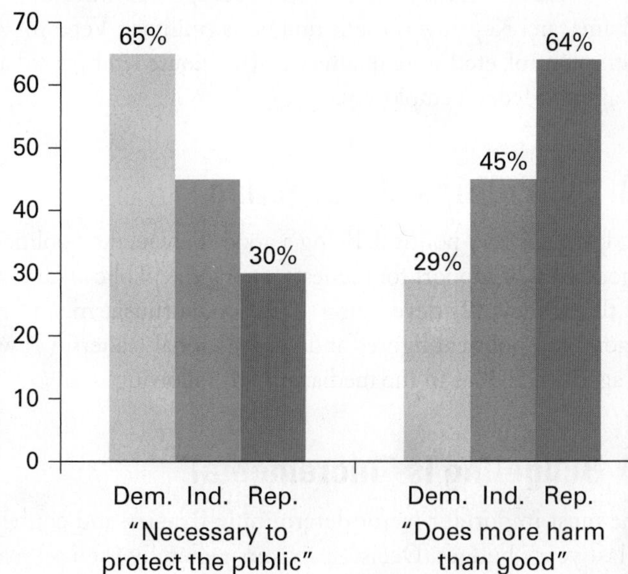

QUESTIONS

1. Do you trust firms in the marketplace to create safe products without public regulation?
2. Can the public effectively sanction a firm that "cheats" on the public, as Representative Paul describes?
3. What is an example of a needless regulation that you would like to see abolished?

[a]Philip K. Howard, *The Death of Common Sense: How Law Is Suffocating America.* New York: Random House, 1995, pp. 10–11.

every year. So they generally accept last year's base spending level as legitimate and focus attention on proposed increases for each program.

Reformers have proposed "sunset" laws requiring bureaucrats to justify their programs every five to seven years or else the programs go out of existence, as well as **zero-based budgeting** that would force agencies to justify every penny requested—not just requested increases. In theory, sunset laws and zero-based budgeting would regularly prune unnecessary government programs, agencies, and expenditures and thus limit the growth of government and waste in government (see *Who's Getting What?* How Much Money Does the Government Waste?). But in reality, sunset laws and zero-based budgeting require so much effort in justifying already accepted programs that executive agencies and legislative committees grow tired of the effort and return to incrementalism.

The "incremental" nature of budgetary politics helps reduce political conflicts and maintain stability in governmental programs. As bruising as budgetary battles are today, they would be much worse if the president or Congress undertook to review the value of *all* existing expenditures and programs each year. Comprehensive budgetary review would "overload the system" with political conflict by refighting every policy battle every year.

zero-based budgeting
Method of budgeting that demands justification for the entire budget request of an agency, not just its requested increase in funding.

program budgeting
Identifying items in a budget according to the functions and programs they are to be spent on.

☐ Budgeting Is Nonprogrammatic

Budgeting is *nonprogrammatic* in that an agency budget typically lists expenditures under ambiguous phrases: "personnel services," "contractual services," "travel," "supplies," "equipment." It is difficult to tell from such a listing exactly what programs the agency is spending its money on. Such a budget obscures policy decisions by hiding programs behind meaningless phrases. Even if these categories are broken down into line items (for example, under "personnel services," the line-item budget might say, "John Doaks, Assistant Administrator, $85,000"), it is still next to impossible to identify the costs of various programs.

For many years, reformers have called for budgeting by programs. **Program budgeting** would require agencies to present budgetary requests in terms of the end products they will produce or at least to allocate each expense to a specific program. However, bureaucrats are often unenthusiastic about program budgeting; it certainly adds to the time and energy devoted to budgeting, and many agencies are reluctant to describe precisely what it is they do and how much it really costs to do it. Moreover, some political functions are best served by *non*program budgeting. Agreement comes more easily when the items in dispute can be treated in dollars instead of programmatic differences. Congressional appropriations committees can focus on increases or decreases in overall dollar amounts for agencies rather than battle over even more contentious questions of which individual programs are worthy of support.

Congressional Constraints on the Bureaucracy

12.6 Outline the growth of federal regulation.

Bureaucracies are unelected hierarchical organizations, yet they must function within democratic government. To wed bureaucracy to democracy, ways must be found to ensure that bureaucracy is responsible to the people. Controlling the bureaucracy is a central concern of democratic government. The federal bureaucracy is responsible to all three branches of government—the president, the Congress, and the courts. Although the president is the nominal head of the executive agencies, Congress—through its power to create or eliminate and fund or fail to fund these agencies—exerts its full share of control. Most of the structure

12.1
12.2
12.3
12.4
12.5
12.6
12.7
12.8

of the executive branch of government (see Figure 12.1) is determined by laws of Congress. Congress has the constitutional power to create or abolish executive departments and independent agencies, or to transfer their functions, as it wishes. Congress can by law expand or contract the discretionary authority of bureaucrats. It can grant broad authority to agencies in vaguely written language, thereby adding to the power of bureaucracies, which can then determine themselves how to define and implement their own authority. In contrast, narrow and detailed laws place constraints on the bureaucracy.

In addition to specific constraints on particular agencies, Congress has placed a number of general constraints on the entire federal bureaucracy. Among the more important laws governing bureaucratic behavior are the following:

- **Administrative Procedures Act (1946).** Requires that agencies considering a new rule or policy give public notice in the *Federal Register,* solicit comments, and hold public hearings before adopting the new measures.
- **Freedom of Information Act (1966).** Requires agencies to allow citizens (and the media) to inspect all public records, with some exceptions for intelligence, current criminal investigations, and personnel actions (see Figure 12.4).
- **Privacy Act (1974).** Requires agencies to keep confidential the personal records of individuals, notably their Social Security files and income tax records.

☐ Senate Confirmation of Appointments

The U.S. Senate's power to confirm presidential appointments gives it some added influence over the bureaucracy.[16] It is true that once nominated and confirmed, cabinet secretaries and regulatory commission members can defy the Congress; only the president can remove them from office. Senators usually try to impress their own views

Attention: Freedom of Information/Privacy Request Name and Address of Agency

This is a request under the Freedom of Information Act, 5 U.S.C. Sec.552

I request a copy of the following documents be provided for me.

____

____

I am aware that if my request is denied I am entitled to know the grounds for this denial and make an administrative appeal.

I am willing to pay fees for this request up to a maximum of $_____. If you estimate that fees will exceed this limit, please inform me first.

Thank you for your prompt attention.

Signature

Address

____

____

____

FIGURE 12.4 HOW TO USE THE FREEDOM OF INFORMATION ACT

The Freedom of Information Act (FOIA) of 1966 requires agencies of the federal government to provide any member of the public records of the agencies. As amended by the Privacy Act of 1974, individuals can obtain their personal records held by government agencies and are given the right to correct information that is inaccurate. The FOIA does not apply to Congress, the federal courts, state and local government agencies (unless a state has a similar law), military plans and weapons, law enforcement investigations, records of financial institutions, or records which would invade the privacy of others. An agency must respond within 10 days to an FOIA request, but it may charge fees for the costs of searching for the documents and duplicating them.

A good request must "reasonably describe" the records that are being sought; it must be specific enough that an agency employee will be able to locate the records within a reasonable amount of time.

on presidential appointees seeking confirmation, however. Senate committees holding confirmation hearings often subject appointees to lengthy lectures on how the members believe their departments or agencies should be run. In extreme cases, when presidential appointees do not sufficiently reflect the views of Senate leaders, their confirmation can be held up indefinitely or, in very rare cases, defeated in a floor vote on confirmation.

casework
Services performed by legislators and their staffs on behalf of individual constituents.

☐ Congressional Oversight

Congressional oversight of the federal bureaucracy is a continuing activity. Congress justifies its oversight activities on the grounds that its lawmaking powers require it to determine whether the purposes of the laws it passed are being carried out. Congress has a legitimate interest in communicating legislative *intent* to bureaucrats charged with the responsibility for implementing laws of Congress. But often oversight activities are undertaken to influence bureaucratic decision making. Members of Congress may seek to secure favorable treatment for friends and constituents, try to lay the political groundwork for increases or decreases in agency appropriations, or simply strive to enhance their own power or the power of their committees or subcommittees over the bureaucracy.

Oversight is lodged primarily in congressional committees and subcommittees whose jurisdictions generally parallel those of executive departments and agencies. However, all too frequently, agencies are required to respond to multiple committee inquiries in both the House and the Senate.

☐ Congressional Appropriations

The congressional power to grant or to withhold the budget requests of bureaucracies and the president is perhaps Congress's most potent weapon in controlling the bureaucracy. Spending authorizations for executive agencies are determined by standing committees with jurisdiction in various policy areas, such as armed services, judiciary, education, and labor, and appropriations are determined by the House and Senate Appropriations Committees and, more specifically, their subcommittees with particular jurisdictions. These committees and subcommittees exercise great power over executive agencies. The Defense Department, for example, must seek *authorizations* for new weapons systems from the House and Senate Armed Services Committees and *appropriations* to actually purchase these weapons from the House and Senate Appropriations Committees, especially their Defense Appropriations subcommittees.

☐ Congressional Investigation

Congressional investigations offer yet another tool for congressional oversight of the bureaucracy. Historically, congressional investigations have focused on scandal and wrongdoing in the executive branch. Occasionally, investigations even produce corrective legislation, although they more frequently produce changes in agency personnel, procedures, or policies. Investigations are more likely to follow media reports of waste, fraud, or scandal than to uncover previously unknown problems. In other words, investigations perform a political function for Congress—assuring voters that the Congress is taking action against bureaucratic abuses. Studies of routine bureaucratic performance are likely to be undertaken by the Government Accountability Office (GAO), an arm of Congress and frequent critic of executive agencies. GAO may undertake studies of the operations of executive agencies on its own initiative but more often responds to requests for studies by specific members of Congress.

☐ Casework

Perhaps the most frequent congressional oversight activities are calls, letters, and visits to the agencies by individual members of Congress seeking to influence particular actions on behalf of themselves or their constituents. A great deal of congressional **casework** involves intervening with executive agencies on behalf of constituents.[17] Executive

TSA SCREENING

Deemed necessary as part of the War on Terrorism, the one-size-fits all screenings by TSA have been a source of ongoing public frustration.

departments and agencies generally try to deal with congressional requests and inquiries as favorably and rapidly as the law allows. Pressure from a congressional office will lead bureaucrats to speed up an application, correct an error, send information, review a case, or reinterpret a regulation to favor a client with congressional contacts. But bureaucrats become very uncomfortable when asked to violate established regulations on behalf of a favored person or firm. The line between serving constituents and unethical or illegal attempts to influence government agencies is sometimes very difficult to discern.

Interest Groups and Bureaucratic Decision Making

12.7 Evaluate the cost of federal regulation.

Interest groups understand that great power is lodged in the bureaucracy. Indeed, interest groups exercise an even closer oversight of bureaucracy than do the president, Congress, and courts, largely because their interests are directly affected by day-to-day bureaucratic decisions. Interest groups focus their attention on the particular departments and agencies that serve or regulate their own members or that function in their chosen policy field. For example, the American Farm Bureau Federation monitors the actions of the Department of Agriculture; environmental lobbies—such as the National Wildlife Federation, the Sierra Club, and the Environmental Defense Fund—watch over the Environmental Protection Agency as well as the National Park Service and U.S. Forest Service. The American Legion, Veterans of Foreign Wars, and Vietnam Veterans "oversee" the Department of Veterans Affairs. Thus specific groups come to have a proprietary interest in "their" specific departments and agencies. Departments and agencies understand that their "client" groups have a continuing interest in their activities.

Many bureaucracies owe their very existence to strong interest groups that successfully lobbied Congress to create them. The Environmental Protection Agency owes its existence to the environmental groups, just as the Equal Employment Opportunity Commission owes its existence to civil rights groups. Thus many bureaucracies nourish interest groups' support to aid in expanding their authority and increasing their budgets.

Interest groups can lobby bureaucracies directly by responding to notices of proposed regulations, testifying at public hearings, and providing information and commentary. Or interest groups can lobby Congress either in support of bureaucratic activity or to reverse a bureaucratic decision. Interest groups may also seek to "build fires" under bureaucrats by holding press conferences, undertaking advertising campaigns, and soliciting media support for agency actions. Or interest groups may even seek to influence bureaucracies through appeals to the federal courts.

Judicial Constraints on the Bureaucracy

12.8 Summarize the constraints that Congress can place on the bureaucracy.

udicial oversight is another source of restraint on the bureaucracy. Bureaucratic decisions are subject to review by the federal courts. Federal courts can even issue *injunctions* (orders) to an executive agency *before* it issues or enforces a regulation or undertakes a particular action. Thus the judiciary poses a check on bureaucratic power.

☐ Judicial Standards for Bureaucratic Behavior

Historically, the courts have stepped in when agency actions have violated laws passed by Congress, when agencies have exceeded the authority granted them under the laws, when the agency actions have been adjudged "arbitrary and unreasonable," and when agencies have failed in their legal duties under the law. The courts have also restrained the bureaucracy on procedural grounds—ensuring proper notice, fair hearings, rights of appeal, and so on. In short, appeals to the courts must cite failures of agencies to abide by substantive or procedural laws.

Judicial oversight tends to focus on (1) whether agencies are acting beyond the authority granted them by Congress; and (2) whether they are abiding by rules of procedural fairness. It is important to realize that the courts do not usually involve themselves in the *policy* decisions of bureaucracies. If policy decisions are made in accordance with the legal authority granted agencies by Congress, and if they are made with procedural fairness, the courts generally do not intervene.

☐ Bureaucrats' Success in Court

Bureaucracies have been very successful in defending their actions in federal courts.[18] Individual citizens and interest groups seeking to restrain or reverse the actions or decisions of executive agencies have been largely *unsuccessful.* What accounts for this success? Bureaucracies have established elaborate administrative processes to protect their decisions from challenge on procedural grounds. Regulatory agencies have armies of attorneys, paid for out of tax monies, who specialize in these narrow fields of law. It is very expensive for individual citizens to challenge agency actions. Corporations and interest groups must weigh the costs of litigation against the costs of compliance before undertaking a legal challenge of the bureaucracy. Excessive delays in court proceedings, sometimes extending to several years, add to the time and expense of challenging bureaucratic decisions.

A Constitutional Note

Congress and the Budget

The Constitution places "the power of the purse" firmly in the hands of Congress: "No money shall be drawn from the Treasury, but in Consequence of Appropriations made by Law" (Article I, Section 9). Congress has multiple means of controlling the bureaucracy. It can create, eliminate, or reorganize agencies, and it can alter their functions and rules of operation as it sees fit. And the Senate can confirm or withhold confirmation of presidential appointments. In the exercise of these powers, Congress can hold hearings, conduct investigations, and interrogate executive officials. But the power over appropriations for departments and agencies remains the most important instrument of congressional control over the bureaucracy. The president, of course, is head of the executive branch, and the Constitution charges him to "take care that the laws be faithfully executed" (Article II, Section 3). Prior to 1921, executive departments and agencies submitted their budgets directly to the Congress with very little presidential input or control. But the Budget and Accounting Act of that year established a Bureau of the Budget, which later was placed in the White House, directly under the president. The act required all executive agencies to submit their budgets to the Bureau of the Budget, now called the Office of Management and Budget (OMB), and to the president. The president and OMB draw up *The Budget of the United States Government* each year for submission to Congress. The Budget Committees of the House and Senate by resolution set overall totals for budget outlays in major categories. These committees are under no obligation to follow the president's budget recommendations. Later, the Appropriations Committees and subcommittees of each house write up specific appropriations bills. If it wishes, Congress can ignore items in the president's budget and appropriate whatever funds to whatever agencies it chooses. The Appropriations Committees of the House and Senate jealously guard Congress's "power of the purse."

QUESTIONS

1. Do you think the president should be allowed a veto over parts of a budget? Alternatively, do you think the Constitution should be amended to remove the executive veto, allowing the president no say over the setting of the budget?
2. Both budget "agencies" are invested in the executive (Office of Management and Budget) and legislative branch (Congressional Budget Office, General Accountability Office), respectively. Do we need a new "independent agency" to review and score budgetary priorities and revenue forecasts?

Review the Chapter

Bureaucratic Power

12.1 Assess the nature, sources, and extent of bureaucratic power, p. 444

Bureaucratic power has grown with increases in the size of government, advances in technology, and the greater complexity of modern society. Congress and the president do not have the time, resources, or expertise to decide on the details of policy across the wide range of social and economic activity in the nation. Bureaucracies must draw up the detailed rules and regulations that actually govern the nation. Often laws are passed for their symbolic value; bureaucrats must give practical meaning to these laws. And the bureaucracy itself is now sufficiently powerful to get laws passed adding to its authority, size, and budget.

Policy implementation is the development of procedures and activities and the allocation of money, personnel, and other resources to carry out the tasks mandated by law. Implementation includes regulation—the making of detailed rules based on the law—as well as adjudication—the application of laws and regulations to specific cases. Bureaucratic power increases with increases in administrative discretion.

The Federal Bureaucracy

12.2 Describe the types of agencies in the federal bureaucracy and the extent and purposes of the bureaucracy, p. 448

The federal bureaucracy consists of 2.8 million civilian employees in 15 cabinet departments and more than 60 independent agencies, as well as a large Executive Office of the President. Federal employment is not growing, but federal spending is growing rapidly.

Today, federal spending amounts to 25 percent of GDP, and federal, state, and local government spending combined amounts to 35 percent of GDP.

Bureaucracy and Democracy

12.3 Trace changes over time in the size and composition of the bureaucracy and assess the repercussions for democracy, p. 456

Bureaucracies usually seek to expand their own powers, functions, and budgets. Most bureaucrats believe strongly in the value of their own programs and the importance of their tasks. And bureaucrats, like everyone else, seek added power, pay, and prestige. Bureaucratic expansion contributes to the growth of government.

Historically, political conflict over government employment centered on the question of partisanship versus competence. Over time, the "merit system" replaced the "spoils system" in federal employment, but the civil service system raised problems of responsiveness and productivity in the bureaucracy. Civil service reform efforts have not really resolved these problems.

Bureaucratic Politics

12.4 Explain how the bureaucracy is staffed, to whom it is accountable, and how accountability is affected by politics and bureaucratic culture, p. 460

The president's control of the bureaucracy rests principally on the powers to appoint and remove policy-making officials, to recommend increases and decreases in agency budgets, and to recommend changes in agency structure and function.

But the bureaucracy has developed various means to insulate itself from presidential influence. Bureaucrats have many ways to delay and obstruct policy decisions with which they may disagree. Whistle-blowers may inform Congress or the media of waste, mismanagement, or fraud. A network of friends and professional associates among bureaucrats, congressional staffs, and client groups helps create a "culture" within each agency and department. The bureaucratic culture is highly resistant to change.

The Budget

12.5 Outline the budgetary process and evaluate the advantages and disadvantages of the current system, p. 462

Budget battles over who gets what begin in the bureaucracy as departments and agencies send their budget requests forward to the president's Office of Management and Budget. OMB usually reduces agency requests in line with the president's priorities. The president submits spending recommendations to Congress early each year in *The Budget of the United States Government*. Congress is supposed to pass its appropriations acts prior to the beginning of the fiscal year, October 1, but frequently falls behind schedule. Most budgeting is incremental, in that last year's agency expenditures are usually accepted as a base and attention is focused on proposed increases. Incrementalism saves time and effort and reduces political conflict by not requiring agencies to justify every dollar spent, only proposed increases each year. Nonprogrammatic budgeting also helps reduce conflict over the value of particular programs. The result, however, is that many established programs continue long after the need for them has disappeared.

Congressional Constraints on the Bureaucracy

12.6 Outline the growth of federal regulation, p. 469

Congress can exercise control over the bureaucracy in a variety of ways: by creating, abolishing, or reorganizing departments and agencies; by altering their authority and functions; by requiring bureaucrats to testify before congressional committees; by undertaking investigations and studies through the Government Accountability Office; by intervening directly on behalf of constituents; by instructing presidential nominees in Senate confirmation hearings and occasionally delaying or defeating nominations; and especially by withholding or threatening to withhold agency appropriations or by writing very specific provisions into appropriations acts.

Interest Groups and Bureaucratic Decision Making

12.7 Evaluate the cost of federal regulation, p. 472

Interest groups also influence bureaucratic decision making directly by testifying at public hearings and providing information and commentary, and indirectly by contacting the media, lobbying Congress, and initiating lawsuits.

Judicial Constraints on the Bureaucracy

12.8 Summarize the constraints that Congress can place on the bureaucracy, p. 472

Judicial control of the bureaucracy is usually limited to determining whether agencies have exceeded the authority granted them by law or have abided by the rules of procedural fairness. Federal bureaucracies have a strong record of success in defending themselves in court.

Learn the Terms

bureaucracy, p. 444
chain of command, p. 444
division of labor, p. 444
impersonality, p. 444
implementation, p. 446
regulation, p. 446
adjudication, p. 447
budget maximization, p. 448
discretionary funds, p. 448
spoils system, p. 456
merit system, p. 457
whistle-blowers, p. 461
outsourcing, p. 462
fiscal year, p. 466
budget resolution, p. 466
authorization, p. 466
appropriations act, p. 466
obligational authority, p. 466
outlays, p. 466
continuing resolution, p. 467
incremental budgeting, p. 467
zero-based budgeting, p. 469
program budgeting, p. 469
casework, p. 471

Test Yourself

12.1 Assess the nature, sources, and extent of bureaucratic power.

Bureaucratic power stems from which of the following powers:

I. develop formal rules
II. adjudicate individual cases
III. use administrative discretion

a. Only I
b. Only I & III
c. Only II
d. I, II, & III
e. Only II & III

12.2 Describe the types of agencies in the federal bureaucracy and the extent and purposes of the bureaucracy.

Which of the following can it be said to be true of the Federal government bureaucracy?

a. federal bureaucracy consists of about 2.8 million civilian employees
b. the federal government spends about 50 percent of the nation's GDP
c. the senior and most important cabinet office is the Department of the Interior
d. legislation is crafted by agencies and take effect unless Congress otherwise passes a law to the contrary
e. Agencies are exempt from executive orders.

12.3 Trace changes over time in the size and composition of the bureaucracy and assess the repercussions for democracy.

Historically, government employment was based on party loyalty, political support, and friendship. This was known as

a. the compadre system
b. the spoils system
c. the patronage system
d. the merit system
e. The Borda method

12.4 Explain how the bureaucracy is staffed, to whom it is accountable, and how accountability is affected by politics and bureaucratic culture.

Government contracting with private firms to perform public services is known as

a. privatization
b. private-public partnerships
c. socialism
d. outsourcing
e. cooptation

12.5 Outline the budgetary process and evaluate the advantages and disadvantages of the current system.

A method of budgeting that tries to review the entire budget of an agency (not just the requested changes) is

a. management by objective budgeting
b. incremental budgeting
c. zero-based budgeting
d. nonprogrammatic budgeting
e. rescission

12.6 Outline the growth of federal regulation.

The agency that is responsible for conducting studies of the federal bureaucratic performance is the

a. Office of Management and Budget
b. Congressional Budget Office
c. General Accountability Office
d. Office of the Comptroller
e. The Federal Reserve

12.7 Evaluate the cost of federal regulation.

In an effort to influence the bureaucracy, interest groups may perform which of the following activities

I. hold press conferences and create media events
II. lobby the bureaucracy directly
III. testify at public hearings
IV. institute potential rules through private action

a. Only II
b. Only I & II
c. Only I & IV
d. I, II, III, IV
e. Only I, II, & III

12.8 Summarize the constraints that Congress can place on the bureaucracy.

The courts become involved in agency actions when they

I. violate congressional legislation
II. have exceeded the authority granted to them
III. have engaged in activities that have been determined to be arbitrary
IV. the issue is only constitutional

a. Only I & II
b. Only II
c. Only I & IV
d. I, II, III, IV
e. Only I, II, & III

Explore Further

Gormley, William T., and Steven J. Balla. *Bureaucracy and Democracy: Accountability and Performance*. 2nd ed. Washington, D.C.: CQ Press, 2007. Administrative theory and approaches to bureaucratic relationship in a democracy.

Henry, Nicholas. *Public Administration and Public Affairs*. 11th ed. New York: Longman, 2010. Authoritative introductory textbook on public organizations (bureaucracies), public management, and policy implementation.

Howard, Philip K. *The Death of Common Sense: How Law Is Suffocating America*. New York: Random House, 1995. Outrageous stories of bureaucratic senselessness coupled with a plea to allow bureaucrats flexibility in achieving the purposes of laws and holding them accountable for outcomes.

Kettl, Donald F., and James W. Fesler. *The Politics of the Administrative Process*. 4th ed. Washington, D.C.: CQ Press, 2008. Introduction to bureaucracy and public administration, including a case appendix with illustrations complementing each chapter.

Kerwin, Cornelius M. *Rulemaking: How Government Agencies Write Law and Make Policy*. 4th ed. Washington, D.C.: CQ Press, 2010. Argues that rulemaking actually defines the laws of Congress and describes the political activity surrounding rulemaking.

Neiman, Max. *Defending Government: Why Big Government Works*. New York: Longman, 2000. A spirited defense of big government as a product of people's desire to improve their lives.

O'Rourke, P. J. *Parliament of Whores: A Lone Humorist Tries to Explain the Entire U.S. Government*. New York: Grove Press, 1991. Former *Rolling Stone* White House correspondent takes an ironic look at how the problem with government is, evidently, us.

Osborne, David, and Ted Gaebler. *Reinventing Government*. New York: Addison-Wesley, 1992. The respected manual of the "reinventing government" movement, with recommendations to overcome the routine tendencies of bureaucracies and inject "the entrepreneurial spirit" into them.

Pressman, Jeffrey L., and Aaron Wildavsky. *Implementation*. Berkeley, Calif: University of California Press, 1973. The classic case study of "how great expectations in Washington are dashed in Oakland: or, why it's amazing that federal programs work at all, this being a saga of the Economic Development Administration as told by two sympathetic observers who seek to build morals on a foundation of ruined hopes."

Schick, Allen. *The Federal Budget: Politics, Policy, Process*. 3rd ed. Washington, D.C.: Brookings Institution, 2007. A comprehensive explanation of the federal budgetary process.

Smith, Robert W., and Thomas D. Lynch. *Public Budgeting in America*. 5th ed. New York: Longman, 2004. Standard text describing public budget processes, behaviors, and administration.

Wildavsky, Aaron, and Naomi Caiden. *New Politics of the Budgetary Process*. 5th ed. New York: Longman, 2004. An updated version of Wildavsky's classic book on how budgetary decisions are really made.

Wilson, James Q. *Bureaucracy: What Government Agencies Do and Why They Do It*. New York: Basic Books, 1989. In the author's words, "an effort to depict the essential features of bureaucratic life in the government agencies of the United States." Examining what really motivates middle-level public servants, Wilson argues that congressional attempts to "micromanage" government activities hamper the ability of bureaucrats to do their jobs.

SUGGESTED WEB SITES

American Society for Public Administration www.aspa.net
Organization of scholars and practitioners in public administration. Site includes information on careers, job listings, and so on.

Amtrak www.amtrak.com
The Amtrak Web site provides valuable information about trip planning, reservations, train schedules, and train fares.

Center for Public Integrity www.publicintegrity.org
Reform organization committed to "exposing" corruption, mismanagement, and waste in government.

Code of Federal Regulations www.law.cornell.edu/cfr
All 50 titles of federal regulations can be found at the Cornell Law School site.

Fed World www.fedworld.gov
Run by the U.S. Commerce Department, this site contains information about federal/state–local agency links, government jobs, IRS forms, Supreme Court decisions, and the vast array of governmental services.

Federal Reserve System www.federalreserve.gov
This Federal Reserve System site covers general information about "Fed" operations, including monetary policy, reserve bank services, international banking, and supervisory and regulatory functions.

First Gov www.firstgov.gov
Official Web portal to all federal departments and agencies, information on government benefits, agency links, and so forth.

Food and Drug Administration www.fda.gov
The Food and Drug Administration site is a reflection of the agency's mission "to promote and protect the public health by helping safe and effective products reach the market in a timely way."

Internal Revenue Service www.irs.gov
The tax-collecting IRS is potentially the most powerful of all government agencies, with financial records on every tax-paying American.

Occupational Safety and Health Administration www.osha.gov
This site covers new information directly related to OSHA's mission "to ensure safe and healthful workplaces in America."

Office of Management and Budget (OMB) www.omb.gov
The OMB site includes all budget documents and information on regulatory oversight.

USA Jobs www.usajobs.gov
This site is the official source for federal employment information.

13

Courts
Judicial Politics

Obamacare was dead. That was supposed to be the story. When the Supreme Court took up the challenges to the Affordable Care Act, the two most likely outcomes were that the five Republican-appointed justices on the Court, led by Chief Justice John Roberts, would line up against the four Democrats and strike down the centerpiece of healthcare reform. The key to the other scenario, everyone knew, was for Justice Anthony Kennedy, the Reagan-appointed Republican who sometimes voted with the left, to line up with the liberals. Kennedy was the key.

Well, it didn't matter where Justice Kennedy landed. The Supreme Court upheld the Affordable Care Act, and they didn't do it with Justice Kennedy, who voted to overturn the Act. Instead, Chief Justice Roberts lined up with the court liberals to uphold the key provision of the Act, the individual mandate, which Roberts termed a 'tax.' His opinion, however, also found common language with the dissenting conservatives to argue that the Commerce Clause, a key component of congressional power, wasn't unlimited and was not applied here. He upheld the health care bill as a tax while limiting congressional power under the Commerce Clause.

It was a neat trick, one apparently designed to restore political integrity to a Court badly scarred by the decision in the 2000 presidential election and also the *Citizen's United* campaign finance case. And, some critics have argued, Roberts appears to have penned both the opinion of the Court and the dissenting opinion, placing himself on both sides of the issue and inviting conservative criticism of the very conservative Chief Justice.

The Federal Courts and judges are unique among Federal actors. They are appointed for life, and enjoy substantial powers to enforce and interpret the law. This makes the courts, and especially the Supreme Court, actors who are uniquely situated to consider politics outside of the influence of elections or short-term politics. It can also lead to judicial acts that are often politically unpopular and which shape the larger political environment.

13.1 Assess the basis for and use of judicial power, p. 480

13.2 Compare and contrast the philosophies of judicial activism and judicial restraint, p. 483

13.3 Outline the structure and jurisdiction of the federal courts, p. 486

13.4 Characterize the "special rules" of judicial decision making, p. 491

13.5 Assess the role of politics in the judicial selection process, p. 494

13.6 Outline the decision-making process of the Supreme Court and areas in which the Court has been active, p. 500

13.7 Assess the role of politics and ideology in Supreme Court decision making, p. 503

13.8 Evaluate checks on Supreme Court power, p. 507

Innovative laws, such as the Patient Protection Affordable Care Act, are often challenged in court. The most significant make their way here, to the U.S. Supreme Court.

Judicial Power

13.1 Assess the basis for and use of judicial power.

"There is hardly a political question in the United States which does not sooner or later turn into a judicial one."[1] This observation, made in 1835 by French diplomat and traveler Alexis de Tocqueville, is even more accurate today. It is the Supreme Court and the federal judiciary, rather than the president or Congress, that has taken the lead in deciding many of the most heated issues of American politics. It has undertaken to:

- Eliminate racial segregation and decide about affirmative action.
- Ensure separation of church and state and decide about prayer in public schools.
- Determine the personal liberties of women and decide about abortion.
- Define the limits of free speech and free press and decide about obscenity, censorship, and pornography.
- Ensure equality of representation and require legislative districts to be equal in population.
- Define the rights of criminal defendants, prevent unlawful searches, limit the questioning of suspects, and prevent physical or mental intimidation of suspects.
- Protect private homosexual acts between consenting adults from criminal prosecution.
- Decide the life-or-death issue of capital punishment.

Courts are "political" institutions. Like Congress, the president, and the bureaucracy, courts decide who gets what in American society. Judges do not merely "apply" the law to specific cases. Years ago, former Supreme Court Justice Felix Frankfurter explained why this mechanistic theory of judicial objectivity fails to describe court decision making.

> The meaning of "due process" and the content of terms like "liberty" are not revealed by the Constitution. It is the Justices who make the meaning. They read into the neutral language of the Constitution their own economic and social views. . . . Let us face the fact that five Justices of the Supreme Court are the molders of policy rather than the impersonal vehicles of revealed truth.[2]

Constitutional Power of the Courts

The Constitution grants "the judicial Power of the United States" to the Supreme Court and other "inferior Courts" that Congress may establish. The Constitution guarantees that the Supreme Court and federal judiciary will be politically independent: judges are appointed, not elected, and hold their appointments for life (barring commission of any impeachable offenses). It also guarantees that their salaries will not be reduced during their time in office. The Constitution goes on to list the kinds of cases and controversies that the federal courts may decide. Federal judicial power extends to any case arising under the Constitution and federal laws and treaties, to cases in which officials of the federal government or of foreign governments are a party, and to cases between states or between citizens of different states.

Interpreting the Constitution: Judicial Review

The Constitution is the "supreme Law of the Land" (Article VI). Judicial power is the power to decide cases and controversies and, in doing so, to decide what the Constitution and laws of Congress really mean. This authority—together with the guaranteed independence of judges—places great power in the Supreme Court and the federal judiciary.

Indeed, because the Constitution takes precedence over laws of Congress as well as state constitutions and laws, it is the Supreme Court that ultimately decides whether Congress, the president, the states, and their local governments have acted constitutionally.

The power of **judicial review** is the power to invalidate laws of Congress or of the states that conflict with the U.S. Constitution. Judicial review is not specifically mentioned in the Constitution but has long been inferred from it. Even before the states had approved the Constitution, Alexander Hamilton wrote in 1787 that "limited government . . . can be preserved in practice no other way than through the medium of courts of justice, whose duty it is to declare all acts contrary to the manifest tenor of the Constitution void."[3] But it was the historic decision of *Marbury v. Madison* (1803)[4] that officially established judicial review as the most important judicial check on congressional power (see *The Game, the Rules, the Players*: John Marshall and Early Supreme Court Politics). Writing for the majority, Chief Justice Marshall constructed a classic statement in judicial reasoning as he proceeded step by step to infer judicial review from the Constitution's Supremacy (Article VI) and Judicial Power (Article III, Section 1) clauses:

judicial review
Power of the courts, especially the Supreme Court, to declare laws of Congress, laws of the states, and actions of the president unconstitutional and invalid.

- The Constitution is the supreme law of the land, binding on all branches of government: legislative, executive, and judicial.
- The Constitution deliberately establishes a government with limited powers.
- Consequently, "an act of the legislature repugnant to the Constitution is void." If this were not true, the government would be unchecked and the Constitution would be an absurdity.
- Under the judicial power, "It is emphatically the province and duty of each of the judicial departments to say what the law is."
- "So if a law be in opposition to the Constitution . . . the court must determine which of these conflicting rules governs the case. This is the very essence of judicial duty."
- "If, then, the courts are to regard the Constitution, and the Constitution is superior to any ordinary act of the legislature, the Constitution, and not such ordinary act, must govern the case to which they both apply."
- Hence, if a law is repugnant to the Constitution, the judges are duty bound to declare that law void in order to uphold the supremacy of the Constitution.

Judicial Review of State Laws

The power of the federal courts to invalidate *state* laws and constitutions that conflict with federal laws or the federal Constitution is easily defended. Article VI states that the Constitution and federal laws and treaties are the supreme law of the land, "any Thing in the Constitution or Laws of any State to the Contrary notwithstanding." Indeed, the Constitution specifically obligates state judges to be "bound" by the Constitution and federal laws and to give these documents precedence over state constitutions and laws in rendering decisions. Federal court power over state decisions is probably essential to maintaining national unity: 50 different state interpretations of the meaning of the Constitution or of the laws and treaties of Congress would create unimaginable confusion. Thus, the power of federal judicial review over state constitutions, laws, and court decisions is seldom questioned.

The Supreme Court has used its power of judicial review more frequently to invalidate state laws than laws of Congress. Some of these decisions had impact far beyond the individual states on trial. For example, the historic 1954 decision in *Brown v. Board of Education of Topeka*, declaring segregation of the races in public schools to be unconstitutional, struck down the laws of 21 states.[5] The 1973 *Roe v. Wade* decision, establishing the constitutional right to abortion, struck down antiabortion laws in more than 40 states.[6] In 2003, the Court again struck down the laws of more than 40 states by holding that private homosexual acts by consenting adults were protected by the Constitution.[7]

LANDMARK CASE
Linda Brown (front, right) in her classroom in Topeka, taken at about the time of the *Brown v. Board of Education* decision. Brown was refused admittance to a white elementary school, and her family was one of the plaintiffs in the case.

The Game, the Rules, the Players

John Marshall and Early Supreme Court Politics

John Marshall was a dedicated Federalist. A prominent Virginia lawyer, he was elected a delegate to Virginia's Constitution-ratifying convention, where he was instrumental in winning his state's approval of the document in 1788. Later Marshall served as secretary of state in the administration of John Adams (1797–1801), where he came into conflict with Adams's vice president, Thomas Jefferson.

In the election of 1800, Jefferson's Democratic-Republicans crushed Adams's Federalist Party. But Adams, taking advantage of the fact that his term of office would not expire until the following March,[a] sought to pack the federal judiciary with Federalists. The lame duck Federalist majority in the Senate confirmed the appointments, and John Marshall was sworn in as chief justice of the Supreme Court on February 4, 1801. However, he continued to serve as secretary of state at the request of President Adams. Many of these "midnight appointments" came at the very last hours of Adams's term of office, while Marshall simultaneously served as chief justice and ran the State Department.

When Marshall left his position at the State Department on March 3, several of these commissions were still undelivered. Jefferson and the Democratic-Republicans were enraged over this last-minute Federalist chicanery, so when Jefferson assumed office, he ordered his new secretary of state, James Madison, not to deliver the remaining commissions. William Marbury, one of the disappointed Federalist appointees, brought a lawsuit to the Supreme Court, asking it to issue a writ of mandamus ("we command") to James Madison, ordering him to do his duty and deliver the valid commission. (Jefferson and Marshall were cousins and had little liking for each other).

The Judiciary Act of 1789, which established the federal court system, had included a provision granting original jurisdiction to the Supreme Court to issue writs of mandamus. The case, therefore, came directly to new Chief Justice John Marshall, who had failed to deliver the commission in the first place. (Today, we expect justices who are personally involved in a case to "recuse" themselves—that is, not to participate in that case, allowing the other justices to make the decision—but Marshall's actions were typical of his time.)

John Marshall realized that if he issued a direct order to Madison to deliver the commission, Madison would probably ignore it. The Court had no way to enforce such an order, and Madison had the support of President Jefferson. Issuing the writ would create a constitutional crisis in which the Supreme Court would most likely lose power. But if the Court failed to pronounce Madison's actions unlawful, it would lose legitimacy. The new Democratic-Republican majority fired a warning shot at the Court by passing the Judiciary Act of 1802, which largely repealed the previous Act, and canceling the Supreme Court's June 1802 session in order to forestall a court challenge.

Marshall resolved his political dilemma with a brilliant judicial ploy. Writing for the majority in *Marbury v. Madison*, he announced that Madison was wrong to withhold the commission but that the Supreme Court could not issue a writ of mandamus because Section 13 of the Judiciary Act of 1789, which gave the Court *original* jurisdiction in the case, was unconstitutional. Giving the Supreme Court *original* jurisdiction conflicted with Article III, Section 2, of the Constitution, which gives the Supreme Court original jurisdiction only in cases affecting "Ambassadors, other public Ministers and Consuls, and those in which a State shall be a Party." "In all other Cases," the Constitution states that the Court shall have appellate jurisdiction. Thus Section 13 of the Judiciary Act was unconstitutional. However, other parts of the Act, including provisions that reduced the size of the Court and which returned the justices to riding circuit, were upheld by Marshall.

By declaring part of an act of Congress unconstitutional, Marshall accomplished multiple political objectives. He avoided a showdown with the executive branch that would undoubtedly have weakened the Court. He left Jefferson and Madison with no Court order to disobey. At the same time, Marshall forced Jefferson and the Democratic-Republicans to acknowledge the Supreme Court's power of judicial review—the power to declare an act of Congress unconstitutional. (To do otherwise would have meant acknowledging Marbury's claim.) Thus, Marshall sacrificed Marbury's commission to a greater political goal, enhancing the Supreme Court's power.

Sometimes scholars and pundits will argue that Marshall *created* judicial review in the *Marbury* case. This is not true. Alexander Hamilton, writing as *Publius* in *The Federalist,* No. 78, discussed the application of judicial review:

> The interpretation of the laws is the proper and peculiar province of the courts. A constitution is, in fact, and must be regarded by the judges, as a fundamental law. It therefore belongs to them to ascertain its meaning, as well as the meaning of any particular act proceeding from the legislative body. If there should happen to be an irreconcilable variance between the two, that which has the superior obligation and validity ought, of course, to be preferred; or, in other words, the Constitution ought to be preferred to the statute, the intention of the people to the intention of their agents. Nor does this conclusion by any means suppose a superiority of the judicial to the legislative power. It only supposes that the power of the people is superior to both; and that where the will of the legislature, declared in its statutes, stands in opposition to that of the people, declared in the Constitution, the judges ought to be governed by the latter rather than the former.

QUESTIONS

1. How do the politics of the day enter this case?
2. Did the high court have the power of judicial review prior to *Marbury*?
3. Why is legitimacy important to appellate courts?

[a]Not until the adoption of the 20th Amendment in 1933 was the president's inauguration moved up to January.

Judicial Review of Laws of Congress

Judicial review is potentially the most powerful weapon in the hands of the Supreme Court. It enables the Court to assert its power over Congress, the president, and the states and to substitute its own judgment for that of other branches of the federal government and the states. However, the Supreme Court has been fairly restrained in its use of judicial review to void acts of Congress. Prior to the Civil War, the Supreme Court invalidated very few laws of any kind. Since that time, however, the general trend has been for the U.S. Supreme Court to strike down more *state* laws as unconstitutional. In contrast, the Court has been relatively restrained in its rejection of *federal* laws; over two centuries, the Court has struck down fewer than 150 of the more than 60,000 laws passed by Congress.

Some laws overturned by the Supreme Court have been very important. In *Buckley v. Valeo* (1976),[8] the Court struck down provisions of the Federal Election Campaign Act that had limited the amount individuals could spend to finance their own campaigns or express their own independent political views. In *United States v. Morrison* (2000), the Supreme Court struck down Congress's Violence Against Women Act[9] as an unconstitutional expansion of the interstate commerce power and an invasion of powers reserved to the states. Overall, however, the Supreme Court's use of judicial review against Congress has been restrained.

statutory laws
Laws made by act of Congress or the state legislatures, as opposed to constitutional law.

Judicial Review of Presidential Actions

The Supreme Court has only rarely challenged presidential power. The Court has overturned presidential policies both on the grounds that they conflicted with laws of Congress and on the grounds that they conflicted with the Constitution. In *Ex parte Milligan* (1866),[10] for example, the Court held (somewhat belatedly) that President Abraham Lincoln could not suspend the writ of habeas corpus in rebellious states during the Civil War. In *Youngstown Sheet & Tube Co. v. Sawyer*, in 1952,[11] it declared President Harry Truman's seizure of the nation's steel mills during the Korean War to be illegal. In 1974, it ordered President Richard Nixon to turn over taped White House conversations to the special Watergate prosecutor, leading to Nixon's forced resignation.[12] And in 1997, the Court held that President Bill Clinton was obliged to respond to a civil suit even while serving in the White House.[13]

Interpreting Federal Laws

The power of the Supreme Court and the federal judiciary does not rest on judicial review alone. The courts also make policy in their interpretation of **statutory laws**—the laws of Congress. Frequently, Congress decides that an issue is too contentious to resolve. Members of Congress cannot themselves agree on specific language, so they write, sometimes deliberately, vague, symbolic language into the law—words and phrases like "fairness," "equitableness," "good faith," "good cause," and "reasonableness"—effectively shifting policy making to the courts by giving courts the power to read meaning into these terms.

Activism Versus Self-Restraint

13.2 Compare and contrast the philosophies of judicial activism and judicial restraint.

Supreme Court Justice Felix Frankfurter once wrote: "The only check upon our own exercise of power is our own sense of self-restraint. For the removal of unwise laws from the statute books, appeal lies not to the courts but to the ballot and to the processes of democratic government."[14]

13.1

13.2

13.3

13.4

13.5

13.6

13.7

13.8

judicial self-restraint
Self-imposed limitation on judicial power by judges deferring to the policy judgments of elected branches of government.

original intent
Judicial philosophy under which judges attempt to apply the values of the Founders to current issues.

judicial activism
Making of new law through judicial interpretations of the Constitution.

Judicial Self-Restraint

The idea behind **judicial self-restraint** is that judges should not read their own philosophies into the Constitution and should avoid direct confrontations with Congress, the president, and the states whenever possible. The argument for judicial self-restraint is that federal judges are not elected by the people and therefore should not substitute their own views for the views of elected representatives. The courts should defer to the judgments of the other branches of government unless there is a clear violation of constitutional principle. The benefit of the doubt should be given to actions taken by elected officials. Courts should only impose remedies that are narrowly tailored to correct specific legal wrongs. As Justice Sandra Day O'Connor argued in her Senate confirmation hearings, "The courts should interpret the laws, not make them . . . I do not believe it is a function of the Court to step in because times have changed or social mores have changed."[15]

Wisdom Versus Constitutionality

A law may be unwise, unjust, or even stupid and yet still be constitutional. One should not equate the wisdom of a law with its constitutionality, and the Court should decide only the constitutionality and not the wisdom of a law. Justice Oliver Wendell Holmes once lectured a younger colleague, 61-year-old Justice Harlan Stone, on this point:

> Young man, about 75 years ago I learned that I was not God. And so, when the people . . . want to do something I can't find anything in the Constitution expressly forbidding them to do, I say, whether I like it or not, "Goddamn it, let 'em do it."[16]

However, the actual role of the Supreme Court in the nation's power struggles suggests that the Court indeed often equates wisdom with constitutionality. People frequently cite broad phrases in the 5th and 14th Amendments establishing constitutional standards of "due process of law" and "equal protection of the laws" when attacking laws they believe are unfair, unwise, or unjust. Most Americans have come to believe that unwise laws must be unconstitutional. If so, then the courts must be the final arbiters of fairness, wisdom, and justice.

Original Intent

Should the Constitution be interpreted in terms of the intentions of the Founders or according to the morality of society today? Most jurists agree the Constitution is a living document, that it must be interpreted by each generation in the light of current conditions, and that to do otherwise would soon render the document obsolete. But in interpreting the document, whose values should prevail—the values of the judges or the values of the Founders? The doctrine of **original intent** takes the values of the Founders as expressed in the text of the Constitution and attempts to apply these values to current conditions. Defenders of original intent argue that the words in the document must be given their historical meaning and that meaning must restrain the courts as well as the legislative and executive branches of government. That is, the Supreme Court should not set aside laws made by elected representatives unless they conflict with the original intent of the Founders. Judges who set aside laws that do not accord with their personal views of today's moral standards are simply substituting their own morality for that of elected bodies. Such decisions lack democratic legitimacy because there is no reason why judges' moral views should prevail over those of elected representatives.

Judicial Activism

However, the doctrine of original intent carries little weight with proponents of judicial activism. The idea behind **judicial activism** is that the Constitution is a living document whose strength lies in its flexibility, and judges should shape constitutional meaning to fit the needs of contemporary society. The argument for judicial activism is that viewing the Constitution as a broad and flexible document saves the nation from having to pass dozens of new constitutional amendments to accommodate changes in society. Instead, the courts need to give contemporary interpretations to constitutional phrases, particularly general phrases such as "due process of law" (5th Amendment), "equal protection of the laws" (14th Amendment), "establishment of religion" (1st Amendment), and "cruel and unusual punishment" (8th Amendment). Courts have the responsibility to review the actions of other branches of government vigorously, to strike down unconstitutional acts, and to impose far-reaching remedies for legal wrongs whenever necessary.

stare decisis
Judicial precept that the issue has already been decided in earlier cases and the earlier decision need only be applied in the specific case before the bench; the rule in most cases, it comes from the Latin for "the decision stands."

precedent
Legal principle that previous decisions should determine the outcome of current cases; the basis for stability in law.

☐ *Stare Decisis*

Conflicts between judicial activism and judicial self-restraint are underscored by questions of whether to let past decisions stand or to find constitutional support for overturning them. The principle of ***stare decisis***, which means the issue has already been decided in earlier cases, is a fundamental notion in law. Reliance on **precedent** gives stability to the law; if every decision were new law, then no one would know what the law is from day to day. Yet the Supreme Court has discarded precedent in many of its most important decisions: *Brown v. Board of Education* (1954), which struck down laws segregating the races; *Baker v. Carr* (1962), which guaranteed equal representation in legislatures; *Roe v. Wade* (1973), which made abortion a constitutional right; and many other classic cases; and *Bush v. Gore* (2000), in which it looked past the traditional deference to completing state judicial proceedings before intervening to decide the 2000 presidential election.[17] Former Justice William O. Douglas, a defender of judicial activism, justified disregard of precedent as follows:

> The decisions of yesterday or of the last century are only the starting points. . . . A judge looking at a constitutional decision may have compulsions to revere the past history and accept what was once written. But he remembers above all else that it is the Constitution which he swore to support and defend, not the gloss which his predecessors may have put on it. So he comes to formulate his own laws, rejecting some earlier ones as false and embracing others. He cannot do otherwise unless he lets men long dead and unaware of the problems of the age in which he lives do his thinking for him.[18]

☐ Rules of Restraint

Even an activist Supreme Court adheres to some general rules of judicial self-restraint, however, including the following:

- The Court will pass on the constitutionality of legislation only in an actual case; it will not advise the president or Congress on constitutional questions.
- The Court will not anticipate a question on constitutional law; it does not decide hypothetical cases.
- The Court will not formulate a rule of constitutional law broader than that required by the precise facts to which it must be applied.
- The Court will not decide on a constitutional question if some other ground exists on which it may dispose of the case.
- The Court will not decide on the validity of a law if the complainants fail to show that they have been injured by the law.
- When doubt exists about the constitutionality of a law, the Court will try to interpret the law so as to give it a constitutional meaning and avoid the necessity of declaring it unconstitutional.
- Complainants must have exhausted all remedies available in lower federal courts or state courts before the Supreme Court will accept review.
- The Court will invalidate a law only when a constitutional issue is crucial to the case and is substantial, not trivial.

- Occasionally, the Court defers to Congress and the president, classifies an issue as a political question, and refuses to decide it. The Court has generally stayed out of foreign and military policy areas.
- If the Court holds a law unconstitutional, it will confine its decision to the particular section of the law that is unconstitutional; the rest of the statute stays intact.

Structure and Jurisdiction of Federal Courts

13.3 Outline the structure and jurisdiction of the federal courts.

The federal court system consists of three levels of courts—the Supreme Court, the Courts of Appeals, and the district courts—together with various special courts (see Figure 13.1). Only the Supreme Court is established by the Constitution, although the number of justices is determined by Congress. Article III authorizes Congress to establish such "inferior Courts" as it

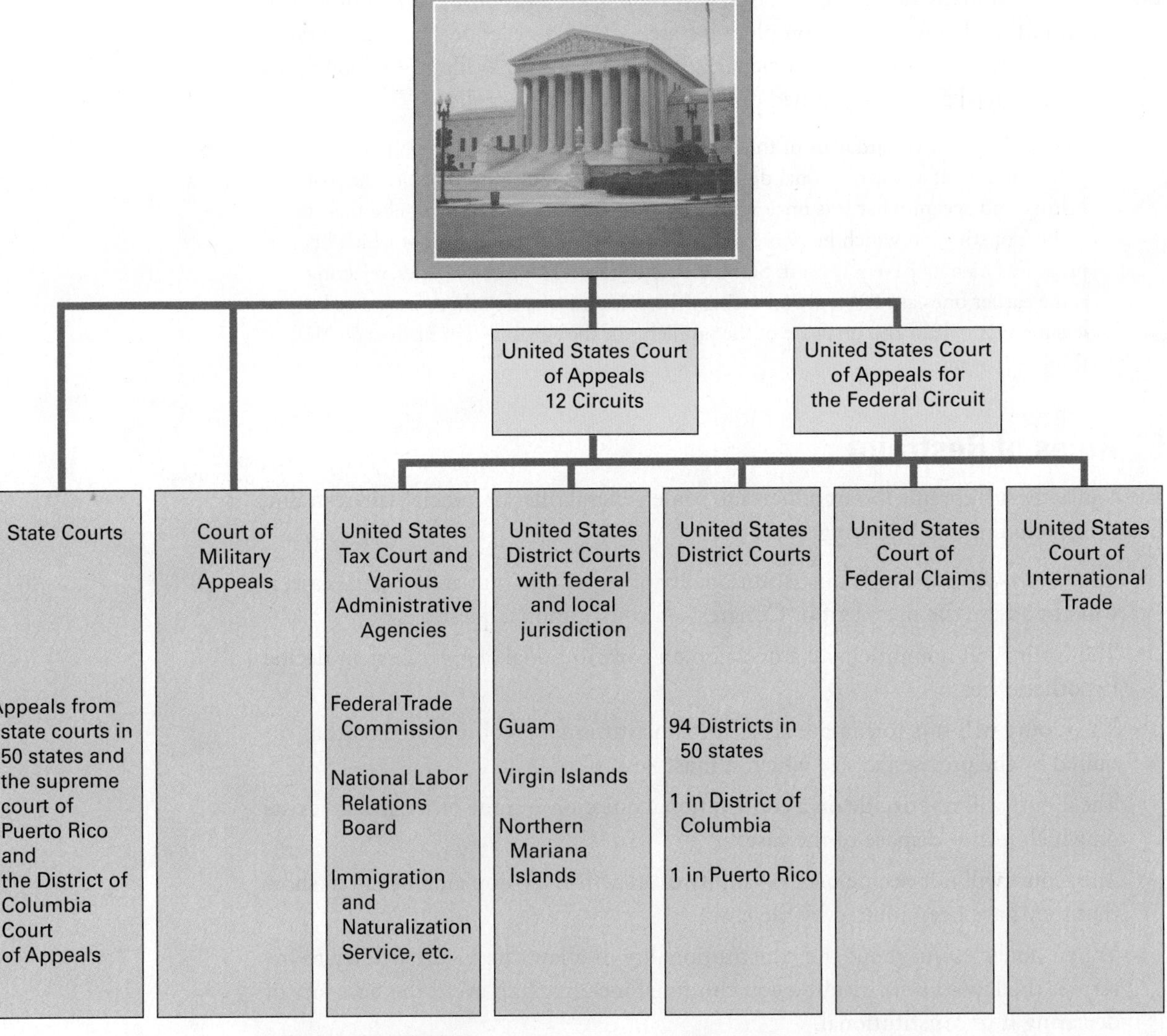

FIGURE 13.1 STRUCTURE OF FEDERAL COURTS

The federal court system of the United States is divided into three levels: the courts of original jurisdiction (state courts, military courts, tax courts, district courts, claims courts, and international trade courts); the U.S. Courts of Appeals, which hear appeals from all lower courts except state and military panels; and the U.S. Supreme Court, which can hear appeals from all sources.

deems appropriate. Congress has designed a hierarchical system with a U.S. Court of Appeals divided into 12 regional circuit courts, a federal circuit, and 94 district courts in the 50 states and one each in Puerto Rico, the U.S. Virgin Islands, Guam, the Northern Marianas, and the District of Columbia. Table 13.1 describes their **jurisdiction** and distinguishes between **original jurisdiction**—where cases are begun, argued, and initially decided—and **appellate jurisdiction**—where cases begun in lower courts are argued and decided on **appeal**.

The Supreme Court is the "court of last resort" in the United States, but it hears only a very small number of cases each year. In a handful of cases, the Supreme Court has original jurisdiction; these concern primarily disputes between states (or states and residents of other states), disputes between a state and the federal government, and disputes involving foreign dignitaries. However, most Supreme Court cases are appellate decisions involving cases from state supreme courts or cases tried first in a U.S. district court.

jurisdiction
Power of a court to hear a case in question.

original jurisdiction
Refers to a particular court's power to serve as the place where a given case is initially argued and decided.

appellate jurisdiction
Particular court's power to review a decision or action of a lower court.

appeal
In general, requests that a higher court review cases decided at a lower level. In the Supreme Court, certain cases are designated as appeals under federal law; formally, these must be heard by the Court.

☐ District Courts

District courts are the original jurisdiction trial courts of the federal system. Each state has at least one district court, and larger states have more (New York, for example, has four). There are about 800 federal district judges, each appointed for life by the president and confirmed by the Senate. The president also appoints a U.S. marshal for each district to carry out orders of the court and maintain order in the courtroom. District courts hear criminal cases prosecuted by the Department of Justice as well as civil cases. As trial courts, the district courts make use of both **grand juries** (called to hear evidence and, if warranted, to indict a defendant by bringing formal criminal charges) and **petit** (regular) **juries** (which determine guilt or innocence). District courts may hear 270,000 civil cases in a year and 70,000 criminal cases.

district courts
Original jurisdiction trial courts of the federal system.

grand juries
Juries called to hear evidence and decide whether defendants should be indicted and tried.

petit (regular) juries
Juries called to determine guilt or innocence.

☐ Courts of Appeals

Federal **circuit courts** (see Figure 13.2) are appellate courts. They do not hold trials or accept new evidence but consider only the records of the trial courts and oral or written arguments (**briefs**) submitted by attorneys. Federal law guarantees everyone the right to appeal, so the Courts of Appeal have little discretion in this regard. Appellate judges themselves estimate that more than 80 percent of all appeals are frivolous—that is, without any real basis. There are more than a hundred circuit judges, each appointed for life by the president subject to confirmation by the Senate. Normally, these judges serve together on a panel to hear appeals. More than 90 percent of the cases decided by the Court of Appeals end at this level. Further appeal to the Supreme Court is not automatic; it must be approved by the Supreme Court itself. Because the Supreme Court hears very few cases, in most cases the decision of the circuit court becomes law.

circuit courts
The 12 appellate courts that make up the middle level of the federal court system.

briefs
Documents submitted by an attorney to a court, setting out the facts of the case and the legal arguments in support of the party represented by the attorney.

TABLE 13.1 WHO DECIDES WHAT?: JURISDICTION OF FEDERAL COURTS

Supreme Court of the United States	United States Courts of Appeals (Circuit Courts)	United States District Courts
Appellate jurisdiction (cases begin in a lower court); hears appeals, at its own discretion, from: 1. Lower federal courts 2. Highest state courts Original jurisdiction (cases begin in the Supreme Court) over cases involving: 1. Two or more states 2. The United States and a state 3. Foreign ambassadors and other diplomats 4. A state and a citizen of a different state (if begun by the state)	No original jurisdiction; hear only appeals from: 1. Federal district courts 2. U.S. regulatory commissions 3. Certain other federal courts	Original jurisdiction over cases involving: 1. Constitution of the United States 2. Federal laws, including federal crimes 3. Civil suits under the federal law 4. Civil suits between citizens of states where the amount exceeds $75,000 5. Admiralty and maritime cases 6. Bankruptcy cases 7. Review of actions of certain federal administrative agencies 8. Other matters assigned to them by Congress

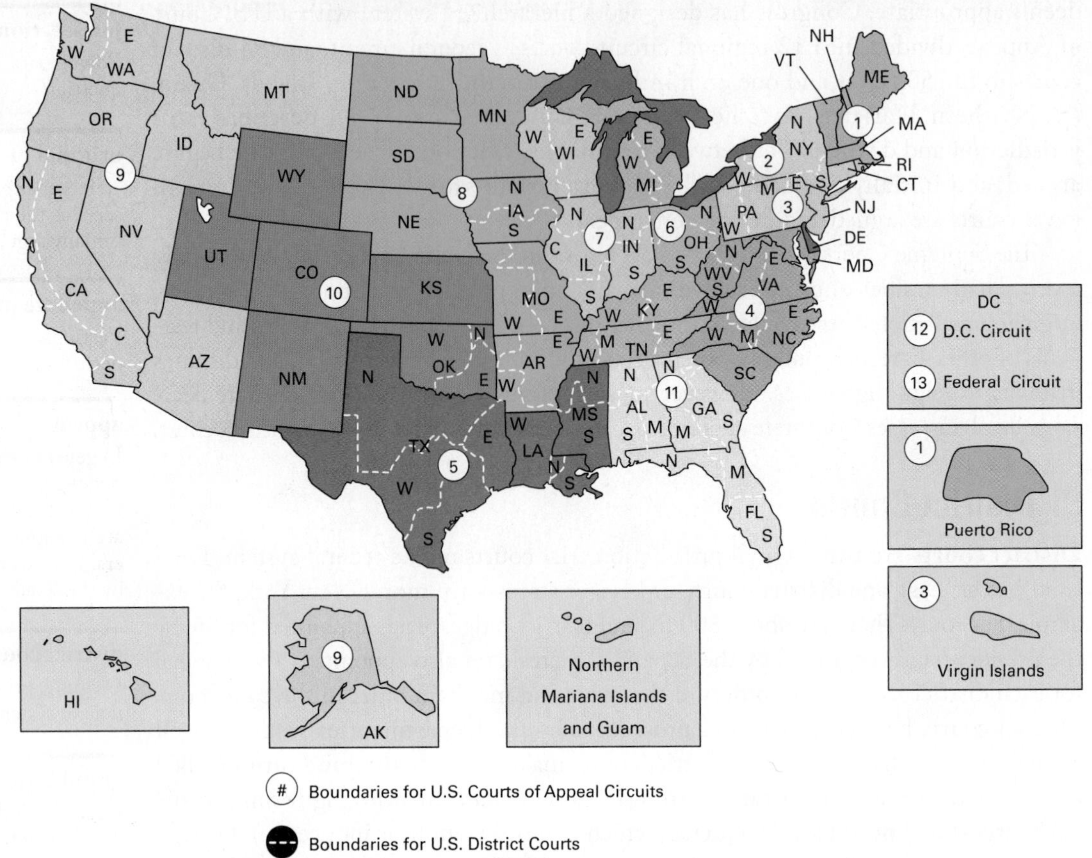

FIGURE 13.2 GEOGRAPHY OF THE FEDERAL COURT SYSTEM

For administrative convenience, the U.S. District Courts are organized into 12 circuits (regions), plus the Federal Circuit (Washington, D.C.). Within each region, circuit court judges form panels to hear appeals from district courts. U.S. Circuit Courts of Appeals are numbered. U.S. District Courts are named for geographical regions of the states (East, West, North, South, Middle), for example, U.S. District Court for Northern California.

Supreme Court

The Supreme Court of the United States is the final interpreter of all matters involving the Constitution and federal laws and treaties, whether the case began in a federal district court or in a state court. Appeals to the U.S. Supreme Court may come from a state court of last resort (usually a state's supreme court) or from lower federal courts. The Supreme Court determines whether to accept an appeal and consider a case. It may do so when there is a "substantial federal question" presented in a case or when there are "special and important reasons," or it may reject a case—with or without explaining why.

In the early days of the Republic, the size of the Supreme Court fluctuated to as many as 10 justices, but since 1869 it has remained at nine: the Chief Justice and eight associate justices. The Supreme Court is in session each year from October through June, hearing oral arguments, accepting written briefs, conferring, and rendering opinions.

Appeals from State Courts

Each of the 50 states maintains its own courts. The federal courts are not necessarily superior to those courts; state and federal courts operate independently. State courts have original jurisdiction in most criminal and civil cases. Because the U.S. Supreme Court has appellate jurisdiction over state supreme courts as well as over lower federal courts, the Supreme Court oversees the nation's entire judicial system, but the great bulk of cases begin and end in the state court systems. The federal courts do not interfere once a case has been started in a state court except in very rare circumstances. And Congress has stipulated that legal disputes between citizens of different states must involve $75,000 or more to be heard in federal courts. Moreover, parties to cases in state courts must "exhaust their remedies"—that is, appeal their case all the way through the state court system—before

A Conflicting View

Tort Reform: America Is Drowning Itself in a Sea of Lawsuits

America is threatening to drown itself in a sea of lawsuits. There are 15 million lawsuits filed in the United States every year. Most are civil suits, where one person seeks to recover money from another person, corporation, or government, either due to a contractual obligation or because of some physical, emotional, reputational, or financial injury. There are more than 805,000 lawyers in the United States (compared to about 650,000 physicians). These lawyers are in business, and their business is litigation. Generating business means generating lawsuits. And just as businesses search for new products, lawyers search for new legal principles on which to bring lawsuits. They seek to expand legal liability for civil actions—that is, to expand the definition of civil wrongdoings, or torts.

Unquestionably, the threat of lawsuits is an important safeguard for society, compelling individuals, corporations, and government agencies to behave responsibly toward others. Because victims require compensation for *actual* damages incurred by the wrongdoing of others, liability laws protect all of us. When someone sues over a "civil duty" (rather than over a contract) it is called a **tort claim**. When 79-year-old Stella Liebeck spilled a scalding cup of "to-go" coffee from an Albuqueque McDonald's restaurant in 1992, she had to go to the hospital for eight days and undergo skin grafts. She subsequently sued McDonald's, and won a seven-figure verdict. This is an example of a tort claim.

But we need to consider the social costs of frivolous lawsuits, especially those brought without any merit but initiated in the hope that individuals or firms will offer a settlement just to avoid the expenses of defending themselves. Legal expenses and excessive jury awards leveled against corporations increase insurance premiums for businesses and service providers. The Insurance Information Institute estimates that the overall cost of civil litigation in America is many times more than that of other industrial nations, perhaps amounting to over 2 percent of our nation's GDP. For example, the risk of lawsuits forces physicians to practice "defensive medicine," ordering expensive tests, multiple consultations with specialists, and expensive procedures, not because they are adjudged medically necessary, but rather to protect themselves from the possibility of a lawsuit. Insurance premiums have risen sharply for physicians seeking malpractice insurance, as have premiums for recreation facilities, nurseries and day-care centers, motels, and restaurants.

Tort reform is an area of legislation dedicated to limiting either the circumstances under which one can sue, the amount of financial compensation (**damages**) someone can receive, or the circumstances under which someone is responsible for attorneys' fees in an unsuccessful lawsuit. Progressives often say tort reform is a pro-business issue designed to limit liability of businesses and intimidate litigants with the threat of attorneys fees should they lose. Conservatives will argue that tort reform is necessary to fix a legal system and insurance system that is abused by lawyers and some plaintiffs.

Reforming the nation's liability laws presents major challenges to the political system. The reform movement can count on support from some normally powerful interest groups—insurance companies, manufacturers, drug companies, hospitals, and physicians. Appeals of tort claims to the U.S. Supreme Court often scramble the ideological foundation of the Court (*BMW v. Gore* 517 U.S. 559 (1996)), and legislation dealing with federal tort reform has attracted support of liberal and conservative lawmakers in Congress. But legal reform is an anathema to the legal profession itself, notably the powerful American Association for Justice (formerly the Association of Trial Lawyers). And lawyers compose the single largest occupational background of Congress members—indeed, of politicians generally.

QUESTIONS

1. What are the barriers to implementing tort reform?
2. What are the primary social and economic benefits of tort reform?
3. Does tort reform needlessly limit the common law right to sue when one is injured by another party? Why or why not?

the federal courts will hear an appeal. Appeals from state supreme courts go directly to the U.S. Supreme Court and not to a federal district or circuit court. Such appeals are usually made on the grounds that a "federal question" is involved in the case—that is, a question has arisen regarding the application of the Constitution or a federal law.

tort claim
When someone sues over a "civil duty" rather than over a contract.

damages
Financial compensation one can receive for an injury.

☐ Federal Cases

Some 10 million civil and criminal cases are begun in the nation's courts each year (see *A Conflicting View*: Tort Reform: America Is Drowning Itself in a Sea of Lawsuits). About 267,000 (less than 3 percent) of the cases are begun in the federal courts. About 8,000 are appealed to the Supreme Court each year, but only about 125 of them are openly argued and decided by signed opinions. The Constitution "reserves" general police powers to the states. That is, civil disputes and most crimes—murder,

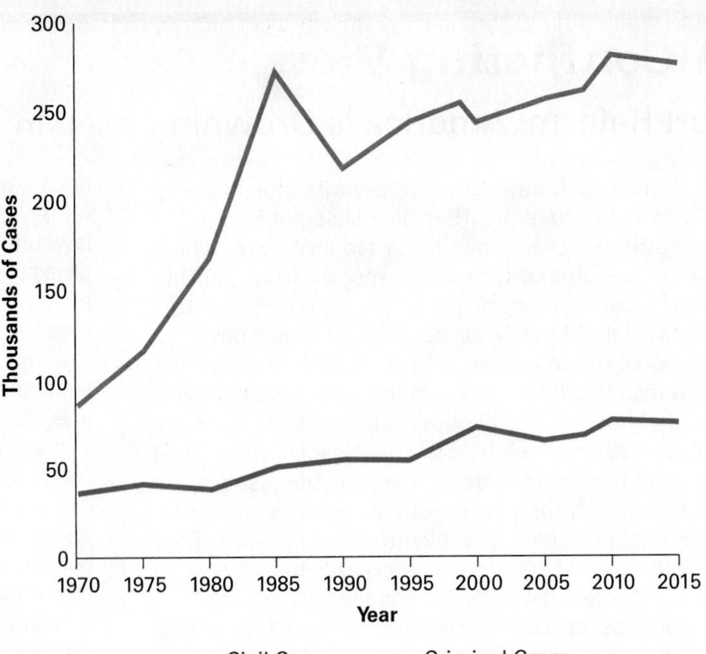

FIGURE 13.3 OVERWORKED?: CASELOADS IN FEDERAL COURTS

Caseloads in the federal courts place a heavy burden on prosecutors and judges. Increases in civil suits in the federal courts are the result of more plaintiffs insisting on taking their cases to the federal level both originally and on appeal. Increases in criminal cases are the result of Congress's decision to make more crimes—especially drug-related crimes—federal offenses and to pursue such criminals more vigorously.

robbery, assault, and rape—are normally state offenses rather than federal crimes and thus are tried in state and local courts.

Federal court caseloads have risen over the years (see Figure 13.3), in part because more civil disputes are being brought to federal courts. In addition, the U.S. Justice Department is prosecuting more criminal cases, as federal law enforcement agencies—such as the Federal Bureau of Investigation (FBI), Drug Enforcement Administration (DEA), Internal Revenue Service (IRS), and Bureau of Alcohol, Tobacco, Firearms, and Explosives (ATF)—have stepped up their investigations. Most of this recent increase is attributable to enforcement of federal drug laws.

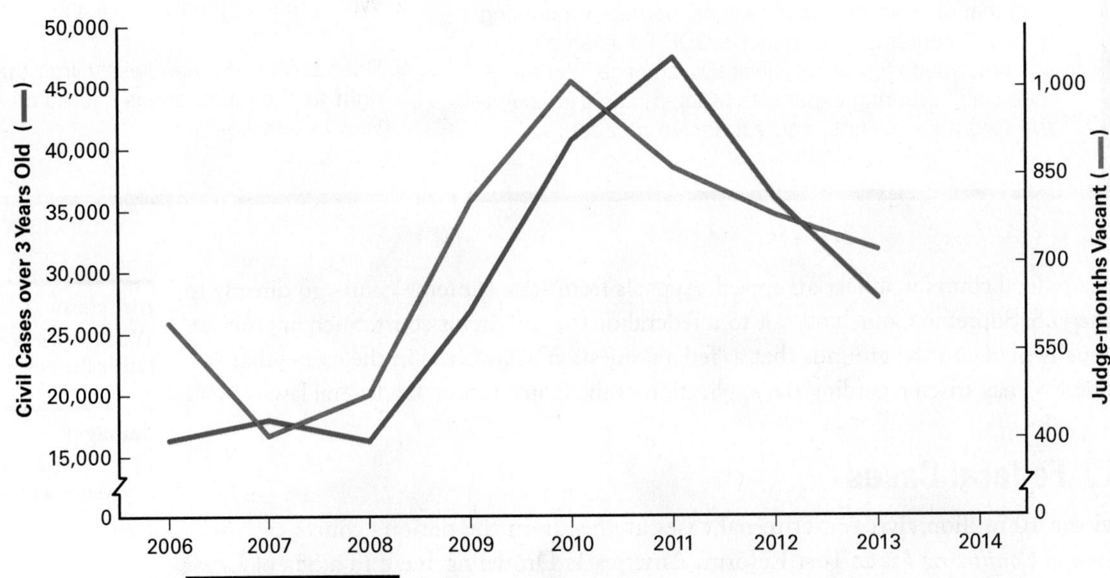

FIGURE 13.4 EMPTY ROBES AND CASE OVERLOAD

As more and more federal judgeships sat vacant the backlog of civil cases in the United States dramatically increased. Filling judicial vacancies since 2010 has reduced the civil case backlog considerably.

SOURCE: Federal Court Management Statistics, March 2014. www.uscourts.gov.

Traditionally, federal crimes were offenses directed against the U.S. government, its property, or its employees or involved the crossing of state lines. Over the years, however, Congress has greatly expanded the list of federal crimes so that federal and state criminal court jurisdictions often overlap, as they do, for example, in most drug violations.

The Special Rules of Judicial Decision Making

13.4 Characterize the "special rules" of judicial decision making.

Courts are political institutions that resolve conflict and decide about public policy. But unlike Congress, the presidency, and the bureaucracy, the courts employ highly specialized rules in going about their work.

☐ Cases and Controversies

Courts do not initiate policy but rather wait until a case or controversy is brought to them for resolution. A case must involve two disputing parties, one of which must have incurred some real damage as a result of the action or inaction of the other. They do *not* issue policy declarations or decide hypothetical cases. Rather, the courts wait until disputing parties bring a case to them that requires them to interpret the meaning of a law or determine its constitutionality in order to resolve the case. Only then do courts render opinions.

The vast majority of cases do *not* involve important policy issues. Courts determine the guilt or innocence of criminal defendants. Courts enforce contracts and award damages to victims of negligence in **civil cases**. And courts render these decisions on the basis of established law. Only occasionally do courts make significant policy decisions.

☐ Adversarial Proceedings

Underlying judicial decision making is the assumption that the best way to decide an issue is to allow two disputing parties to present arguments on each side. Judges in the United States do not investigate cases, question witnesses, or develop arguments themselves (as they do in some European countries). This **adversarial system** depends on quality of argument on each side, which means it often depends on the capabilities of attorneys. There is no guarantee that the adversarial process will produce the best policy outcomes.

☐ Standing

To bring an issue into court as a case, individuals or firms or interest groups must have **standing**; that is, they must be directly harmed by a law or action. People cannot "go to court" simply because they do not like what the government is doing. Merely being taxpayers does not entitle people to claim that they are damaged by government actions.[19] Individuals or firms automatically have standing when they are prosecuted by the government for violation of laws or regulations. Thus, one way to gain standing in order to challenge the legality of a regulation or the constitutionality of a law is to violate the regulation or law and invite the government to prosecute.

To sue the government, plaintiffs must show they have suffered financial damages, loss of property, or physical or emotional harm as a direct result of the government's action. (The party initiating a suit and claiming damages is the **plaintiff**; the party against whom a suit is brought is the **defendant**.) The ancient legal doctrine of **sovereign immunity** means that one cannot sue the government without the

civil cases
Noncriminal court proceedings in which a plaintiff sues a defendant for damages in payment for harm inflicted.

adversarial system
Method of decision making in which an impartial judge or jury or decision maker hears arguments and reviews evidence presented by opposite sides.

standing
Requirement that the party who files a lawsuit have a legal stake in the outcome.

plaintiff
Individual or party who initiates a lawsuit or complaint.

defendant
Party against whom a criminal or civil suit is brought.

sovereign immunity
Legal doctrine that individuals can sue the government only with the government's consent.

13.1

13.2

13.3

13.4

13.5

13.6

13.7

13.8

class action suits
Cases initiated by parties acting on behalf of themselves and all others similarly situated.

contingency fee
Fee paid to attorneys to represent the plaintiff in a civil suit and receive in compensation an agreed-upon percentage of damages awarded (if any).

remedies and relief
Orders of a court to correct a wrong, including a violation of the Constitution.

government's consent. But by law, the U.S. government allows itself to be sued in a wide variety of contract and negligence cases. A citizen can also personally sue to force government officials to carry out acts that they are required by law to perform or for acting contrary to law. The government does not allow suits for damages as a result of military actions.

☐ Class Action Suits

Class action suits are cases brought into court by individuals on behalf of not only themselves but also of all other persons "similarly situated." That is, the party bringing the case is acting on behalf of a "class" of people who have suffered the same damages from the same actions of the defendant. One of the most famous and far-reaching class action suits was *Brown v. Board of Education of Topeka* (1954). The plaintiff, Linda Brown of Topeka, Kansas, sued her local board of education on behalf of herself and all other black pupils who were forced to attend segregated schools, charging that such schools violated the Equal Protection Clause of the 14th Amendment. When she won the case, the Court's ruling affected not only Linda Brown and the segregated public schools in Topeka but also all other black pupils similarly situated across the nation.

Class action suits have grown in popularity. These suits have enabled attorneys and interest groups to bring multimillion-dollar suits against corporations and governments for damages to large numbers of people, even when none of them has individually suffered sufficient harm to merit bringing a case to court. For example, an individual overcharged by an electric utility would not want to incur the expense of suing for the return of a few dollars. But if attorneys sue the utility on behalf of a large number of customers similarly overcharged, the result may be a multimillion-dollar settlement from which the attorneys can deduct their hefty fees.

☐ Legal Fees

Going to court requires financial resources. Criminal defendants are guaranteed an attorney, without charge if they are poor, by the 6th Amendment's guarantee of "Assistance of Counsel."[20] However, persons who wish to bring a *civil* suit against individuals, corporations, or governments must still arrange for the payment of legal fees. The most common arrangement is the **contingency fee**, in which plaintiffs agree to pay expenses and share one-third or more of the money damages with their lawyers if the case is won. If the case is lost, neither plaintiffs nor their lawyers receive anything for their labors. Lawyers do not usually participate in such arrangements unless the prospects for winning the case are good and the promised monetary reward is substantial. Civil suits against the government have increased since Congress enacted a law requiring governments to pay the attorneys' fees of citizens who successfully bring suit against public officials for violation of their constitutional rights.

☐ Remedies and Relief

Judicial power has vastly expanded through court determination of **remedies and relief**. These are the orders of a court following a decision that are designed to correct a wrong. In most cases, judges simply fine or sentence criminal defendants to jail or order losing defendants in civil suits to pay monetary damages to the winning plaintiffs. In recent years, however, federal district court judges have issued sweeping orders to governments to correct constitutional violations. For example, a federal district judge took over operation of the Boston public schools for more than 10 years to remedy *de facto* (an existing, although not necessarily deliberate, pattern of) racial segregation. A federal district judge ordered the city of Yonkers, New York, to build public housing in white neighborhoods. A federal district judge took over the operation of the Alabama prison system to ensure proper prisoner treatment. A federal district judge ordered the Kansas City, Missouri, school board to increase taxes to pay for his desegregation plan.[21]

independent counsel ("special prosecutor")

A prosecutor appointed by a federal court to pursue charges against a president or other high official. This position was allowed to lapse by Congress in 1999 after many controversial investigations by these prosecutors.

□ Independent Counsels?

The Ethics in Government Act of 1978 (passed in the wake of the Watergate scandal) granted federal courts the power, upon request of the attorney general, to appoint an **independent counsel,** or **"special prosecutor"**, to investigate and prosecute violations of federal law by the president and other high officials. This act was challenged in the U.S. Supreme Court as a transferal of executive power ("to take care that the laws be faithfully executed"—Article II) to the judicial branch of government in violation of the separation of powers in the U.S. Constitution. But the Court upheld the law, noting that the attorney general, an executive branch official appointed by the president, had to request the judiciary to appoint the independent counsel.[22]

Whatever the original intent of the act, special prosecutors were often accused of *bringing politics into the criminal justice system.* Indeed, special prosecutor Kenneth Starr's dogged pursuit of Bill and Hillary Clinton (in "Whitewater" real estate deals and later the Monica Lewinsky sex scandal) was deemed a "witch hunt" by friends of the president. The First Lady linked Starr to "a vast right-wing conspiracy" trying to reverse the outcome of two presidential elections .

Congress allowed the independent counsel law to lapse in 1999. Democrats, infuriated by Starr's investigations, joined Republicans, who had earlier complained when Reagan and Bush administration officials were the targets of prosecution, in killing the act. Getting rid of the law, said its opponents, will help to "decriminalize" politics in Washington.

THE ROBERTS COURT

Once the bastion of white male Protestants, the Supreme Court is now more racially and gender diverse than ever, with two racial/ethnic minorities and three women. The Protestants are gone—six of the justices are Roman Catholic, three are Jewish.

13.1
13.2
13.3
13.4
13.5
13.6
13.7
13.8

The Politics of Selecting Judges

13.5 Assess the role of politics in the judicial selection process.

litmus test
In political terms, a person's stand on a key issue that determines whether he or she will be appointed to public office or supported in electoral campaigns.

senatorial courtesy
Custom of the U.S. Senate with regard to presidential nominations to the judiciary to defer to the judgment of senators from the president's party from the same state as the nominee.

The Constitution specifies that all federal judges, including justices of the Supreme Court, shall be appointed by the president and confirmed by a majority vote of the Senate. Judicial recruitment is a political process: presidents almost always appoint members of their own party to the federal courts. More than 80 percent of federal judges have held some political office prior to their appointment to the court. More important, political philosophy now plays a major role in the selection of judges. Thus the appointment of federal judges has increasingly become an arena for conflict between presidents and their political opponents in the Senate.

The Politics of Presidential Selection

Presidents have a strong motivation to select judges who share their political philosophy. Judicial appointments are made for life. The Constitution stipulates that federal judges "shall hold their Offices during good Behaviour." A president cannot remove a judge for any reason, and Congress cannot impeach judges just because it dislikes their decisions.

This independence of the judiciary has often frustrated presidents and Congresses. Presidents who have appointed people they thought were liberals or conservatives to the Supreme Court have been surprised sometimes by the decisions of their appointees. An estimated one-quarter of the justices of the Supreme Court have deviated from the political expectations of the presidents who appointed them.[23]

It is important to recognize that presidents' use of political criteria in selecting judges has a democratic influence on the courts. Presidents can campaign on the pledge to make the courts more liberal or conservative through their appointive powers, and voters are free to cast their ballots on the basis of this pledge.

Political Litmus Test

Traditionally, presidents and senators have tried to discern where a Supreme Court candidate fits on the continuum of liberal activism versus conservative self-restraint. Democratic presidents and senators usually prefer liberal judges who express an activist philosophy. Republican presidents usually prefer conservative judges who express a philosophy of judicial self-restraint. Until very recently, both the president and the Senate denied using any political "litmus test" in judicial recruitment. A **litmus test** generally refers to recruitment based on a nominee's stand on a single issue. Since the Supreme Court ruling on *Roe v. Wade* (1973), however, the single issue of abortion has come to dominate the politics of judicial recruitment.

The Politics of Senate Confirmation

All presidential nominations for the federal judiciary, including the Supreme Court, are sent to the Senate for confirmation. The Senate refers them to its powerful Judiciary Committee, which holds hearings, votes on the nomination, and then reports to the full Senate, where floor debate may precede the final confirmation vote.

The Senate's involvement in federal district judgeships traditionally centered on the practice of **senatorial courtesy**. If senators from the president's party from the same state for which an appointment was being considered disapproved of a nominee, their Senate colleagues would defeat the nomination. But if the president and senators from that party agreed on the nomination, the full Senate, even if controlled by the opposition, customarily confirmed the nomination. During the Reagan–Bush years,

What Do You Think?

Should Supreme Court Nominees Reveal Their Views on Key Cases Before the Senate Votes to Confirm Them?

U.S. Senators on the Judiciary Committee, questioning presidents' Supreme Court nominees, have traditionally been frustrated by the refusal of nominees to comment on issues that are likely to come before the Court in future cases. The nominees have argued that giving specific opinions may impinge upon their judicial impartiality when faced with specific cases. A true judicial approach requires that they examine specific facts in a case, listen to the arguments on both sides, and confer with their colleagues on the Court before rendering an opinion. They should not approach cases with preconceived opinions. Thus, when asked if he supported *Roe v. Wade*, John Roberts simply stated that the case was now precedent in constitutional law and entitled to "due respect." "I should stay away from issues that may come before the court again."

But Democratic Senator (later vice president) Joseph R. Biden, Jr., insisted that Roberts could at least discuss his views about abortion and the right of privacy, as well as other general legal views. "Without any knowledge of your understanding of the law, because you will not share it with us, we are rolling the dice with you, judge."

In her Senate testimony in 2009, Justice Sonia Sotomayor followed the precedent of other nominees to the Supreme Court in declining to take positions on issues that were likely to come before the Court. However, her long record as a federal district judge and later a judge on the Court of Appeals clearly indicated her activist judicial philosophy. As an Appeals Court judge she had ruled against the New Haven Connecticut firefighters who had been denied promotion because African Americans had not performed well on a promotion exam. The Supreme Court later overruled her in a close 5 to 4 decision. So the Democratic-controlled Senate had good reason to believe that she would join the liberal bloc on the Court.

Polls reveal that the general public wants to know the Supreme Court nominee's views on important issues.

Q. When the Senate votes on a nominee for the U.S. Supreme Court, should it consider only that person's legal qualifications and background, or, along with legal background, should the Senate also consider how that nominee might vote on major issues the Supreme Court decides?

Legal Background Only	Issues Too	Unsure
36%	51%	10%

SOURCES: Congressional Quarterly Weekly Report, September 19, 2005, p. 2497; *New York Times*, September 14, 2005.

QUESTIONS

1. Do you think the Senate should consider how a nominee might vote on major issues the Supreme Court decides?
2. Has the existence of issue "litmus tests" like the abortion question made judicial candidates needlessly vague? Why or why not?

however, partisan divisions between these Republican presidents and Senate Democrats eroded the tradition of senatorial courtesy.

Supreme Court nominations have always received close political scrutiny in the Senate. (See *What Do You Think?* Should Supreme Court Nominees Reveal Their Views on Key Cases Before the Senate Votes to Confirm Them?) Over the last two centuries, the Senate has rejected or refused to confirm about 20 percent of presidential nominees to the high court (see Table 13.2). In the past, most senators believed that presidents deserved to appoint their own judges; the opposition party would get its own opportunity to appoint judges when it won the presidency. Only if the Senate found some personal disqualification in a nominee's background (for example, financial scandal, evidence of racial or religious bias, judicial incompetence) would a nominee likely be rejected. But publicity and partisanship over confirmation of Supreme Court nominees have increased markedly in recent years.[24]

Filibustering Court Nominees

The Constitution requires only a majority vote of the Senate to "advise and consent" to a presidential nominee for a federal court judgeship, including a seat on the Supreme Court. However, recent partisan battles over nominees have centered on the Senate's filibuster rule and the 60 votes required for cloture to end a filibuster.[25] President George W. Bush suffered several key defeats of judicial nominees for seats on the U.S. Court of Appeals by failing to get 60 votes to end filibusters over these nominations. All of his nominations were qualified from a judicial point of view, but all were considered too conservative by leading Democrats in the Senate. Republicans

13.1

13.2

13.3

13.4

13.5

13.6

13.7

13.8

TABLE 13.2 SENATE CONFIRMATION VOTES ON SUPREME COURT NOMINATIONS SINCE 1950

Nominee	President	Year	Vote
Earl Warren	Eisenhower	1954	NRV[a]
John Marshall Harlan	Eisenhower	1955	71–11
William J. Brennan	Eisenhower	1957	NRV
Charles Whittaker	Eisenhower	1957	NRV
Potter Stewart	Eisenhower	1959	70–17
Byron White	Kennedy	1962	NRV
Arthur Goldberg	Kennedy	1962	NRV
Abe Fortas	Johnson	1965	NRV
Thurgood Marshall	Johnson	1967	69–11
Abe Fortas[b]	Johnson	1968	Withdrawn[c]
Homer Thornberry	Johnson	1968	No action
Warren Burger	Nixon	1969	74–3
Clement Haynsworth	Nixon	1969	Defeated 45–55
G. Harrold Carswell	Nixon	1970	Defeated 45–51
Harry Blackmun	Nixon	1970	94–0
Lewis Powell	Nixon	1971	89–1
William Rehnquist	Nixon	1971	68–26
John Paul Stevens	Ford	1975	98–0
Sandra Day O'Connor	Reagan	1981	99–0
William Rehnquist[b]	Reagan	1986	65–33
Antonin Scalia	Reagan	1986	98–0
Robert Bork	Reagan	1987	Defeated 42–58
Douglas Ginsburg	Reagan	1987	Withdrawn
Anthony Kennedy	Reagan	1988	97–0
David Souter	Bush, Sr.	1990	90–9
Clarence Thomas	Bush, Sr.	1991	52–48
Ruth Bader Ginsburg	Clinton	1993	96–3
Stephen G. Breyer	Clinton	1994	87–9
John G. Roberts, Jr.	Bush, Jr.	2005	78–22
Harriet Miers	Bush, Jr.	2005	Withdrawn
Samuel Alito, Jr.	Bush, Jr.	2005	58–42
Sonia Sotomayor	Obama	2009	68–31
Elena Kagan	Obama	2010	63–37

[a]No recorded vote.

[b]Elevation to chief justice.

[c]Nomination withdrawn after Senate vote failed to end filibuster against nomination; vote was 45 to 43 to end filibuster.

SOURCE: *Congressional Quarterly's Guide to the U.S. Supreme Court*, 4th ed. (Washington, D.C.: CQ Press, 2004); updated by the author.

threatened to try to end the filibuster rule for judicial nominations. They argued that the Constitution itself specifies a "majority vote of the Senate," not a three-fifths vote for confirmation. But ending the filibuster rule, even for only judicial nominations, would challenge a sacred tradition of the Senate. (Some senators referred to it as the "nuclear option.") A compromise in 2005 allowed some Republican appellate court nominees to be confirmed. The Democrats chose *not* to filibuster the Supreme Court nominations of John Roberts or Samuel Alito, and Republicans did not filibuster the nomination of Sonia Sotomayor or Elena Kagan. In the previous Congress, majority Senate Democrats eliminated the filibuster on all judges except Supreme Court nominees. Whether this rule change survives a change in party control is unknown.

Who Is Selected?

What background and experiences are brought to the Supreme Court? Despite often holding very different views on the laws, the Constitution, and their interpretation, the justices of the U.S. Supreme Court tend to share a common background of education at the nation's most prestigious law schools and prior judicial experience.

Federal district judges are usually recommended by a judicial selection committee set up by the U.S. senators in their state or by the senators themselves through more informal mechanisms, but the president picks the judge. Appellate nominees sit on circuits with jurisdiction in several states. Senators in the circuit will have input on appellate openings, and seats on the circuit courts are informally viewed as "belonging" to one state or another, but the president picks the judge. Political ties are important in advancing a potential nomination. Choose your party and your friends with care.

Bar associations assess the suitability of candidates for the bench. Generally speaking, there is an expectation of at least 12 years in legal practice, preferably with substantial courtroom experience—state judge, state or federal prosecutor, or extensive trial practice. Nominees to the appeals court usually have a strong academic background—teaching law school and publishing law review articles and books (many district and appeals judges continue to teach at law schools while on the bench). It helps to have clerked for a federal judge either while in law school or soon after law school (clerkships tend to go to the best law students, usually from the better law schools). Judges often hire clerks from their alma mater.

There is a personal dimension. "Character" and "reputation" matter when choosing judges, so in addition to the political connections you develop, how you behave will matter. Lawyers who pass the bar exam are members of the bar and officers of the court; they are held to a higher standard of behavior than other citizens. According to the ABA's Standing Committee on judicial nominations, they consider a potential judge's "compassion, decisiveness, open-mindedness, courtesy, patience, freedom from bias, and commitment to equal justice under the law." If you are nominated for a federal judgeship, the ABA (and the FBI) will engage in extensive background interviews to assess your worthiness to sit on the bench. They will look into your finances, and into your criminal record.

It isn't a job one gets into for the money. Federal district judges are paid $169,300 a year, appellate judges $179,500, and the justices of the Supreme Court make $208,100. This is far more money than most Americans earn; but it is far less than most experienced, successful lawyers earn in private practice. If you position yourself to become a federal judge, the odds are you will be leaving a position at a major law school or in private practice that pays more money.

☐ Law Degrees

There is no constitutional requirement that Supreme Court justices be attorneys, but every person who has ever served on the high court has been trained in law. Moreover, most of the justices have attended one or another of the nation's most prestigious law schools (see Table 13.3).

☐ Judicial Experience

Historically, most Supreme Court justices have been federal or state court judges. All of the justices sitting today have come from the U.S. Court of Appeals. Many justices have served some time as U.S. attorneys in the Department of Justice early in their legal careers. Relatively few have held elected political office, but one chief justice—William Howard Taft—previously held the nation's highest elected post, the presidency.

☐ Age

Most justices have been in their fifties when appointed to the Court. Presumably this is the age at which people acquire the necessary prominence and experience to bring themselves to the attention of the White House and Justice Department as potential candidates. At the same time, presidents seek to make a lasting imprint on the Court, and candidates in their fifties can be expected to serve on the Court for many more years than older candidates with the same credentials.

TABLE 13.3 THE SUPREME COURT: BACKGROUND OF THE JUSTICES

Justice	Age at Appointment	President Who Appointed	Law School	Position at Time of Appointment	Years as a Judge Before Appointment
Antonin Scalia	50	Reagan (1986)	Harvard	U.S. Court of Appeals	4
Anthony M. Kennedy	51	Reagan (1988)	Harvard	U.S. Court of Appeals	12
Clarence Thomas	43	Bush, Sr. (1991)	Yale	U.S. Court of Appeals	2
Ruth Bader Ginsburg	60	Clinton (1993)	Columbia	U.S. Court of Appeals	13
Stephen G. Breyer	56	Clinton (1994)	Harvard	U.S. Court of Appeals	14
John G. Roberts, Jr., Chief Justice	50	Bush, Jr. (2005)	Harvard	U.S. Court of Appeals	2
Samuel A. Alito, Jr.	55	Bush, Jr. (2005)	Yale	U.S. Court of Appeals	15
Sonia Sotomayor	55	Obama (2009)	Yale	U.S. Court of Appeals	17
Elena Kagan	50	Obama (2010)	Harvard	Solicitor General	0

What Do You Think?

Do We Need Term Limits for Judges?

Federal judges are appointed for life, subject only to a condition of "good behavior" in office. A complaint directed at the federal judiciary is that the judges are too independent and are not accountable to the public. Terms such as "activist" are leveled at judges who make decisions politicians don't like. One possible solution advanced by critics is to require term limits on judges. A related solution is to require an age limit on judges and mandate retirement at, say, age 70.

It is possible to remove a federal judge through impeachment, or a panel of judges can determine that a federal judge is disabled and unable to continue on the bench. Impeachment of federal judges is rare—two federal judges have been impeached since 2009—and impeachment is usually reserved for illegal or unethical conduct.

The alternative to life tenure is to use some sort of "retention" system where judges are reviewed and then subject to reappointment and reconfirmation. Many states elect judges for long terms, say six or eight years, or have a judicial commission recommend an appointee to the governor. That appointee is then subject to periodic "retention" election before the voters.

At the national level, several retention-style remedies have been suggested for the federal appeals courts. It has been suggested that on the Supreme Court a new justice be appointed every two years, with only the nine newest justices sitting on every case, and the older justices making themselves available in cases of absence, disability, or vacancy on the court. Long terms of 8, 12, or 18 years have been suggested, with the opportunity for presidential reappointment and reconfirmation.

Is there really an age and tenure problem? If you look at the 11 federal appeals courts, the average tenure of the 134 judges is 13 years. Over a third have been on the bench less than 8 years, and only about 30 percent have been there for more than 16 years. Of judges named by the last two two-term presidents of the twentieth century (Reagan and Clinton) most are gone. Since Reagan left office in 1989, two of his three original Supreme Court nominees are still on the bench. But, of his 83 appellate judges appointed, 57 have retired, as have 268 of the 295 district judges he appointed. For Mr. Clinton, who left office in 2001, his two Supreme Court nominees and 41 of his 66 appellate judges remain, but 184 of the 305 district court judges he named have left the bench. The judiciary is largely a product of the presidents of the twenty-first century.

Defenders of life tenure contend that it is the bulwark of ensuring that legislatures do not run roughshod over the rights of the minority. In *Federalist 78*, Alexander Hamilton observed, "The independence of the judges may be an essential safeguard against the effects of occasional ill humors in the society. These sometimes extend no farther than to the injury of the private rights of particular classes of citizens, by unjust and partial laws . . . the firmness of the judicial magistracy is of vast importance in mitigating the severity and confining the operation of such laws. It not only serves to moderate the immediate mischiefs of those which may have been passed, but it operates as a check upon the legislative body in passing them."

QUESTIONS

1. How would you design a system to pick judges for less than life, but still limit their terms?
2. Look up a news article on limiting judge terms. What assumptions does the writer make? Is their goal political?

Race and Gender

No African American had ever served on the Supreme Court until President Lyndon Johnson's appointment of Thurgood Marshall in 1967. A Howard University Law School graduate, Marshall had served as counsel for the National Association for the Advancement of Colored People Legal Defense Fund and had personally argued the historic *Brown v. Board of Education* case before the Supreme Court in 1954. He

The Game, the Rules, the Players

"A Wise Latina on the Bench"

Justice Sonia Sotomayor was the first of two justices named to the Supreme Court by President Barack Obama (the other is Elena Kagan). Sotomayor was a pathbreaker, only the third woman and first Latina named to the high court.

In nominating her to the U.S. Supreme Court, President Obama proclaimed: "Judge Sonia Sotomayor has lived the American dream." She grew up in a public housing project in the South Bronx after her family moved to New York from Puerto Rico during World War II. Her father died when she was nine years old and her mother, a nurse, raised her and her younger brother (now a physician in Syracuse, New York). Young Sonia was diagnosed with diabetes as a child and began taking daily insulin injections. She excelled in school and graduated as valedictorian at the academically rigorous Cardinal Spellman High School. She was rewarded with a full scholarship to Princeton University, where she graduated Phi Beta Kappa in 1976. She also engaged in political activism at Princeton, charging that the University had failed to provide courses in Puerto Rican history and politics or to actively recruit Latino faculty. Sotomayor attended Yale Law School, again on a full scholarship, and she served as editor of the *Yale Law Journal*. She graduated from law school in 1979 and was admitted to the New York Bar in 1980.

Sotomayor began her legal career as an assistant district attorney in New York. She was married in 1976 and divorced in 1983; she has no children. After five years as a prosecutor, she entered private practice, and in 1991 she was nominated to the U.S. District Court for the Southern District of New York by Republican President George H. W. Bush. Her first notable decision was in *Silverman v. Major League Baseball Player Relations Committee, Inc.*, in which she enjoined baseball owners from using replacement players to break the 1994 strike. The decision effectively ended the strike and brought back baseball. Bill Clinton nominated her to the Court of Appeals for the Second Circuit in 1997. Republican senators expressed concern at that time about her liberal leanings, so her confirmation was temporarily held up. She was confirmed in 1998 on a 67–29 Senate vote.

Her long judicial record and subsequent behavior on the Court indicate that she is a strong member to the liberal bloc on the high court. She delivered the opinion of the Court on 15 occasions in her first two years, and also filed 10 dissenting opinions, including a powerful dissenting opinion in *Berghuis v. Thompkins* 560 US _____ (2010), in which the majority narrowed the Miranda protections of criminal suspects: "Today's decision turns Miranda upside down. Criminal suspects must now unambiguously invoke their right to remain silent—which, counterintuitively, requires them to speak. At the same time, suspects will be legally presumed to have waived their rights even if they have given no clear expression of their intent to do so." But on a Court that is perceived to be ideologically divided, "liberal" Justice Sotomayor has nonetheless voted with the most conservative justices at least 70 percent of the time.

In hearings before the Senate Judiciary Committee, she was questioned about this statement she made at a Berkeley Law School lecture in 2001: "I would hope that a wise Latina woman with the richness of her experience would more often than not reach a better conclusion than a white male who hasn't lived that life." In addressing the Senate question, she testified that a judge must always follow the law regardless of personal background (in effect contradicting her earlier controversial statement).

JUSTICE SONIA SOTOMAYOR

As President Obama's first Supreme Court appointee, Justice Sotomayor brought unique cultural experiences to the high court.

QUESTIONS

1. What are the key personal experiences of Justice Sotomayor? The key professional experiences?
2. How have her experiences shaped her as a judge?
3. Do you think experience and judgment changed her perception of the relative importance of these early experiences?

13.1

13.2

13.3

13.4

13.5

13.6

13.7

13.8

writ of certiorari

Writ issued by the Supreme Court, at its discretion, to order a lower court to prepare the record of a case and send it to the Supreme Court for review. Most cases come to the Court as petitions for writs of certiorari.

rule of four

At least four justices must agree to hear an appeal (writ of certiorari) from a lower court in order to get a case before the Supreme Court.

served as solicitor general of the United States under President Lyndon Johnson before his elevation to the high court. Upon Marshall's retirement in 1991, President George H. W. Bush sought to retain minority representation on the Supreme Court, yet at the same time to reinforce conservative judicial views, with his selection of Clarence Thomas.

No woman had served on the Supreme Court prior to the appointment of Sandra Day O'Connor by President Ronald Reagan in 1981. O'Connor was Reagan's first Supreme Court appointment. Although a relatively unknown Arizona state court judge, she had the powerful support of Arizona Republican Senator Barry Goldwater and Stanford classmate Justice William Rehnquist. The second woman to serve on the high court, Ruth Bader Ginsburg, had served as an attorney for the American Civil Liberties Union while teaching at Columbia Law School and had argued and won several important gender discrimination cases. President Jimmy Carter appointed her in 1980 to the U.S. Court of Appeals; President Bill Clinton elevated her to the Supreme Court in 1993.

Sonia Sotomayor is the third woman and the first Hispanic to serve on the Supreme Court. In her early years, she had been active on behalf of the Puerto Rican Legal Defense and Education Fund. She had compiled a lengthy judicial record on the federal district court and the Court of Appeals and her activist judicial philosophy was well known. She heard appeals in more than 3,000 cases and wrote 380 opinions. She brings more judicial experience to the Supreme Court than any justice in modern times. (See *The Game, the Rules, the Players*: "A Wise Latina on the Bench")

In contrast, Elena Kagan comes to the Supreme Court with no bench experience. She is a Princeton graduate, an Oxford scholar, and a magna cum laude graduate of Harvard Law School. Following graduation in 1986 and two years of private practice, she joined the faculty of the University of Chicago Law School. Later she went on to serve in the Clinton White House as a legal counselor. She returned to Harvard Law School in 1999, and in 2003 she became the dean. She was pulled back into government service in 2009 as President Barack Obama's solicitor general.

Supreme Court Decision Making

13.6 Outline the decision-making process of the Supreme Court and areas in which the Court has been active.

The Supreme Court sets its own agenda: it decides what it wants to decide. Of the more than 8,000 requests for hearings that come to its docket each year, the Court issues opinions on only about 125 cases. Another 150 or so cases are decided *summarily* (without opinion) by a Court order either affirming or reversing the lower court decision. The Supreme Court refuses to rule at all on the vast majority of cases that are submitted to it. Thus, the rhetorical threat to "take this all the way to the Supreme Court" is usually an empty one. It is important, however, to realize that a refusal to rule also creates law by allowing the decision of the lower court to stand. That is why the U.S. Circuit Courts of Appeals are powerful bodies.

Setting the Agenda: Granting Certiorari

Most cases reach the Supreme Court when a party in a case appeals to the Court to issue a **writ of certiorari** (literally to "make more certain"), a decision by the Court to require a lower federal or state court to turn over its records on a case.[26] To "grant certiorari"—that is, to decide to hear arguments in a case and render a decision—the Supreme Court relies on its **rule of four**: four justices must agree to do so. Deciding which cases to hear takes up a great deal of the Court's time.

What criteria does the Supreme Court use in choosing its policy agenda—that is, in choosing the cases it wishes to decide? The Court rarely explains why it accepts or rejects cases, but there are some general patterns. First, the Court accepts cases involving issues that the justices are interested in. The justices are clearly interested in the area of 1st Amendment freedoms—speech, press, and religion. Members of the Court are also interested in civil rights issues under the Equal Protection Clause of the 14th Amendment and the civil rights laws and in overseeing the criminal justice system and defining the Due Process Clauses of the 5th and 14th Amendments.

In addition, the Court seems to feel an obligation to accept cases involving questions that have been decided differently by different Circuit Courts of Appeals. The Supreme Court generally tries to see to it that "the law" does not differ from one circuit to another. Likewise, the Supreme Court usually acts when lower courts have made decisions clearly at odds with Supreme Court interpretations in order to maintain control of the federal judiciary. Finally, the Supreme Court is more likely to accept a case in which the U.S. government is a party and requests a review, especially when an issue appears to be one of overriding importance to the government. In fact, the U.S. government is a party in almost half of the cases decided by the Supreme Court.

amicus curiae
Literally, "friend of the court"; a person, private group or institution, or government agency that is not a party to a case but participates in the case (usually through submission of a brief) at the invitation of the court or on its own initiative.

solicitor general
Attorney in the Department of Justice who represents the U.S. government before the Supreme Court and any other courts.

☐ Hearing Arguments

Once the Supreme Court places a case on its decision calendar, attorneys for both sides submit written briefs on the issues. The Supreme Court may also allow interest groups to submit **amicus curiae** (literally, "friend of the court") briefs. This process allows interest groups direct access to the Supreme Court. In the affirmative action case of *University of California Regents v. Bakke* (1978),[27] the Court accepted 59 *amicus curiae* briefs representing more than 100 interest groups. The U.S. government frequently submits amicus curiae arguments in cases in which it is not a party. In cases where the U.S. government becomes involved, the **solicitor general** of the United States is responsible for presenting the government's arguments to the court, both in cases in which the government is a party and in cases in which the government is merely an amicus curiae.

Oral arguments before the Supreme Court are a time-honored ritual of American government. They take place in the marble "temple"—the Supreme Court building across the street from the U.S. Capitol in Washington, D.C. The justices, clad in their black robes, sit behind a high "bench" and peer down at the attorneys presenting their arguments. Arguing a case before the Supreme Court is said to be an intimidating experience. Each side is usually limited to either a half hour or an hour of argument, but justices frequently interrupt with their own pointed questioning. Court watchers sometimes try to predict the Court's decision from the tenor of the questioning. Oral argument is the most public phase of Supreme Court decision making, but no one really knows whether these arguments ever change the justices' minds.

☐ In Conference

The actual decisions are made in private conferences among the justices. These conferences usually take place on Wednesdays and Fridays and cover the cases argued orally during the same week. The chief justice presides, and only justices (no law clerks) are present. It is customary for the chief justice to speak first on the issues, followed by each associate justice in order of seniority. A majority must decide which party wins or loses and whether a lower court's decision is to be affirmed or reversed.

☐ Writing Opinions

The *written* opinion determines the actual outcome of the case (votes in conference are not binding). When the decision is unanimous, the chief justice traditionally

A Conflicting View

The Roberts Doctrine? Equal Sovereignty

In the case *Shelby County v. Holder*, Chief Justice John Roberts wrote for the majority of the Court in striking down a part of the Voting Rights Act of 1965 that compels some states (but not others) to submit changes of state election laws to the federal government for approval. The provision of the law was created in 1965, and it assumed, correctly at the time, that some states would act in bad faith in conducting elections, in order to deny black voters their voting rights.

In striking down the test the law applied to decide if a state was covered or not, Justice Roberts observed that the law "employed extraordinary measures to address an extraordinary problem . . . a drastic departure from basic principles of federalism. And §4 of the Act applied that requirement only to some States—an equally dramatic departure from the principle that all States enjoy equal sovereignty."

The assumption under equal sovereignty is that the states were initially invested with sovereignty won in the war for independence. Some sovereignty is ceded to the national government when creating in the Constitution "an indestructible Union composed of indestructible States" according to the Supreme Court in *Texas v. White* (74 U.S. 700 1868).

Roberts starts with an assumption in previous cases that the relationship between the national government and the states requires equality of treatment of the states in the same way that equality of treatment is required of *individuals* by the government. When distinctions are made by Congress in attempting to regulate the state, then, truly "extraordinary" circumstances are required to upset the equality guaranteed by federalism.

Critics of Roberts' doctrine, led by Justice Ginsberg, content that the requirement of "equal sovereignty" doesn't exist in the way Roberts describes. According to Ginsberg and the minority in *Shelby County*, it was meant to apply only to the process of admitting states to the Union. Extending the equal sovereignty principle "outside its proper domain . . . is capable of much mischief," including placing unanticipated constraints on the ability of Congress to exercise its power to regulate the states using the 14th Amendment's enforcement clause. Others contend that Roberts has used the power of the Court to radically alter the relationship of the states to the national government in a way that undoes decades of legal precedent.

QUESTIONS

1. Should the Court or the Congress determine the relationsip between the national government and the states?
2. Has Justice Roberts engaged in judicial activism? Or did he restore the balance of federalism in creating his doctrine?

majority opinion
Opinion in a case that is subscribed to by a majority of the judges who participated in the decision.

concurring opinion
Opinion by a member of a court that agrees with the result reached by the court in the case but disagrees with or departs from the court's rationale for the decision.

dissenting opinion
Opinion by a member of a court that disagrees with the result reached by the court in the case.

writes the opinion. In the case of a split decision, the Chief Justice may take on the task of writing the **majority opinion** or assign it to another justice in the majority. If the Chief Justice is in the minority, the senior justice in the majority makes the assignment. Writing the opinion of the Court is the central task in Supreme Court policy making. Broadly written opinions may effect sweeping policy changes; narrowly written opinions may decide a particular case but have very little policy impact. The reasons cited for the decision become binding law, to be applied by lower courts in future cases. Yet despite the crucial role of opinion writing in Court policy making, most opinions are actually written by law clerks who are only recent graduates of the nation's prestigious law schools. The justices themselves read, edit, correct, and sometimes rewrite drafts prepared by clerks, but clerks may have a strong influence over the position taken by justices on the issues.

A draft of the opinion is then circulated among members of the majority. Any majority member who disagrees with the reasoning in the opinion, and thus disagrees with the policy that is proposed, may either negotiate changes in the opinion with others in the majority or write a concurring opinion. A **concurring opinion** agrees with the decision about which party wins the case but sets forth a different reason for the decision, proposing, in effect, a different policy position.

Justices in the minority often agree to present a **dissenting opinion**. The dissenting opinion sets forth the views of justices who disagree with both the decision and the majority reasoning. Dissenting opinions do not have the force of law. They are written both to express opposition to the majority view and to appeal to a future Court to someday modify or reverse the position of the majority. Occasionally, the Court is unable to agree on a clear policy position on particularly vexing questions. If the majority is strongly divided over the reasoning behind their decision and as many as four justices dissent altogether from the decision, lower courts will lack clear guidance and future cases will be decided on a case-by-case basis, depending on multiple factors occurring in each case. The absence of a clear opinion of the Court, supported by a unified majority of the justices, invites additional cases, keeping the issue on the Court's agenda until such time (if any) as the Court establishes a clear policy on the issue.

Politics and the Supreme Court

13.7 Assess the role of politics and ideology in Supreme Court decision making.

The political views of Supreme Court justices have an important influence on Court decisions. Justices are swayed primarily by their own ideological views; but public opinion, the president's position, and the arguments of interest groups all contribute to the outcome of cases.

Liberal and Conservative Voting Blocs

Although liberal and conservative voting blocs on the Court are visible over time, on any given case particular justices may deviate from their perceived ideological position. Many cases do not present a liberal–conservative dimension. Each case presents a separate set of facts, and even justices who share a general philosophy may perceive the central facts of a case differently. Moreover, the liberal-versus-conservative dimension sometimes clashes with the activist-versus-self-restraint dimension. Although we generally think of liberals as favoring activism and conservatives, self-restraint, occasionally those who favor self-restraint are obliged to approve of legislation that violates their personal conservative beliefs because opposing it would substitute their judgment for that of elected officials. So ideological blocs are not always good predictors of voting outcomes on the Court.

Over time, the composition of the Supreme Court has changed, as has the power of its various liberal and conservative voting blocs (see Table 13.4). The liberal bloc, headed by Chief Justice Earl Warren, dominated Court decision making from the mid-1950s through the end of the 1960s. The liberal bloc gradually weakened following

TABLE 13.4 HOW THEY VOTE: LIBERAL AND CONSERVATIVE BLOCS ON THE SUPREME COURT*

	The Warren Court 1968	The Burger Court 1975	The Rehnquist Court 2004	The Roberts Court 2015
Liberal	Earl Warren Hugo Black William O. Douglas Thurgood Marshall William J. Brennan Abe Fortas	William O. Douglas Thurgood Marshall William J. Brennan	John Paul Stevens Ruth Bader Ginsburg Stephen G. Breyer David Souter	Ruth Bader Ginsburg Stephen G. Breyer Sonia Sotomayor Elena Kagan
Moderate	Potter Stewart Byron White	Potter Stewart Byron White Lewis Powell Harry Blackmun	Anthony Kennedy Sandra Day O'Connor	Anthony Kennedy
Conservative	John Marshall Harlan	Warren Burger William Rehnquist	William Rehnquist Antonin Scalia Clarence Thomas	John Roberts Samuel Alito Antonin Scalia Clarence Thomas

*All blocs have been designated by the author.

13.1
13.2
13.3
13.4
13.5
13.6
13.7
13.8

President Richard Nixon's appointment of Warren Burger as Chief Justice in 1969, but not all of Nixon's appointees joined the conservative bloc; Justice Harry Blackmun and Justice Lewis Powell frequently joined in voting with the liberal bloc. Among Nixon's appointees, only William Rehnquist consistently adopted conservative positions. President Gerald Ford's only appointee to the Court, John Paul Stevens, began as a moderate and drifted to the liberal bloc. As a result, the Burger Court, although generally not as activist as the Warren Court, still did not reverse any earlier liberal holdings.

President Ronald Reagan, who had campaigned on a pledge to restrain the liberal activism of the Court, tried to appoint conservatives. His first appointee, Sandra Day O'Connor, turned out to be less conservative than expected, especially on women's issues and abortion rights. When Chief Justice Burger retired in 1986, Reagan seized on the opportunity to strengthen the conservative bloc by elevating Rehnquist to Chief Justice. Reagan also appointed Antonin Scalia, another strong conservative, to the Court. Reagan added Anthony Kennedy to the Court in 1988, hoping to give Rehnquist and the conservative bloc the opportunity to form a majority. Had President Reagan succeeded in getting the powerful conservative voice of Robert Bork on the Court, it is possible that many earlier liberal decisions, including *Roe v. Wade*, would have been reversed. But the Senate rejected Bork; David Souter, the nominee ultimately confirmed, eventually drifted toward the liberal bloc.

Liberals worried that the appointment of conservative Clarence Thomas as a replacement for the liberal Thurgood Marshall would give the conservative bloc a commanding voice in Supreme Court policy making. But no solid conservative majority emerged. Justices Rehnquist, Scalia, and Thomas were considered the core

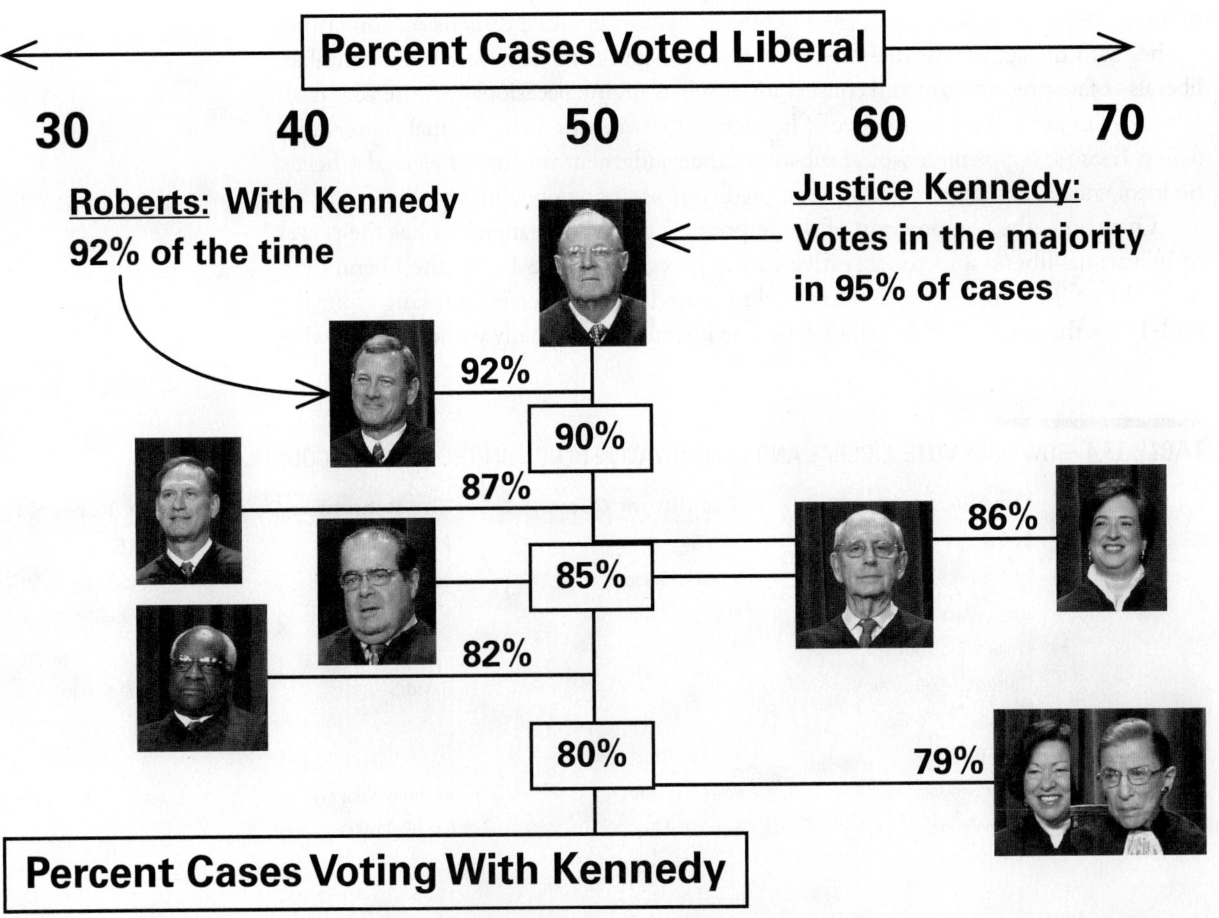

FIGURE 13.5 IS THE SUPREME COURT REALLY DIVIDED?

In the 2013 term, the Court issued 75 opinions, and over 50 were voted in the majority at least 70 percent of the time. No justice voted liberal over 71 percent of the time or less than 39 percent of the time. Justice Kennedy voted liberal half the time, and was in the majority in all but four cases, including all ten 5–4 decisions handed down by the court. Every justice voted with Kennedy at least 79 percent of the time.

of the conservative bloc, but they had to win over at least two of the more moderate justices in order to form a majority in a case. President Bill Clinton's appointees, Ruth Bader Ginsburg and Stephen G. Breyer, consistently supported liberal views on the Supreme Court. Liberalism on the Court—as measured by pro-individual rights decisions against the government in civil liberties cases, pro-defendant decisions in criminal cases, and pro-women and minorities decisions in civil rights cases—has declined significantly since the 1960s.[28]

The appointment of John Roberts as chief justice and Samuel Alito as associate justice in 2005 added a strong and learned voice to the conservative bloc (see *The Game, the Rules, the Players:* John Roberts, Chief Justice). Liberals have been refreshed with the appointments of Justices Elena Kagan and Sonia Sotomayor. The consequence, however, is an often moderated Court. Justice Kennedy swings from the left bloc to right bloc of justices in his voting, and is most often in the majority. The most recent terms have witnessed the justices coming to consensus on all but a few especially controversial cases, and the ideological blocs have moderated, often coalescing around Kennedy.

U.S. solicitor general
The U.S. government's chief legal counsel, presenting the government's arguments in cases in which it is a party or in which it has an interest.

☐ Public Opinion

"By all arguable evidence of the modern Supreme Court, the Court appears to reflect public opinion about as accurately as other policy makers."[29] And indeed, on the liberal–conservative dimension, it can be argued that Supreme Court decisions have generally followed shifts in American public opinion. However, the Court appears to lag behind public opinion. It is doubtful that the justices read opinion polls; their jobs do not depend on public approval ratings. Rather, it is more likely that the justices, whose nomination and confirmation depended on an elected president and Senate, generally share the views of those who put them on the bench. Thus public opinion affects the Court only indirectly, through the nomination and confirmation process.

☐ Presidential Influence

Even after a president's initial appointment of a Justice to the High Court, a president may exercise some influence over judicial decision making. The Office of the **U.S. Solicitor General** is charged with the responsibility of presenting the government's (the president's) views in cases not only to which the U.S. government is a party, but also in cases in which the president and the attorney general have a strong interest and present their arguments in amicus curiae briefs. The Solicitor General's Office, in both Democratic and Republican presidential administrations, has compiled an enviable record in Supreme Court cases. When representing federal agencies that are parties to cases, the solicitors general have won two-thirds of their cases before the Supreme Court over the years. And in cases where the solicitor general has offered an amicus curiae brief, the government's position has prevailed in about three-quarters of the cases. In contrast, the states have won fewer than half of the cases before the Supreme Court in which a state has been a party.

☐ Interest-Group Influence

Interest groups have become a major presence in Supreme Court cases. First of all, interest groups (for example, Planned Parenthood, National Association for the Advancement of Colored People, American Civil Liberties Union) sponsor many cases themselves. They find persons they believe to be directly damaged by a public policy, initiate litigation on their behalf, and provide the attorneys and money to pursue these cases all the way to the Supreme Court. Second of all, it is now a rare case that comes to the Court without multiple amicus curiae briefs filed by interest groups.

How influential are interest groups in Supreme Court decisions? Certainly, interest groups have a significant influence in bringing issues before the Supreme Court through their sponsorship of cases. It is unlikely that the Court would have acted when it did on many key issues from racial segregation in 1954 (*Brown v. Board of Education* sponsored

The Game, the Rules, the Players

John Roberts, Chief Justice

John Roberts has set about molding the Constitution to fit his legal philosophy views. He earns the ire or praise of the left or the right, depending on the day and the decision. Decisions coming from the high court surrounding the Obama administration's health care reforms, voting rights, same-sex marriage, and campaign finance have proved controversial. All came from Roberts's pen.

Roberts graduated from a Catholic high school in Indiana first in his class and as the captain of the football team. After one year at Sacred Heart University, he transferred to Harvard, where he majored in history and graduated summa cum laude and Phi Beta Kappa in 1976. He went on to Harvard Law School and served as editor of the *Harvard Law Review*. He then clerked for Supreme Court Justice William Rehnquist.

He served in the Reagan administration as a special assistant to the attorney general and later associate counsel in the White House. Roberts was deputy solicitor general to the first President Bush, and argued some 39 cases for the government before the Supreme Court. President George H. W. Bush nominated him for the U.S. Court of Appeals in 1992, but Congress adjourned without confirming the nomination. During the Clinton years, Roberts was partner in a Washington law firm. In 2003, he was renominated to the U.S. Court of Appeals by President George W. Bush and confirmed by the U.S. Senate. In 2005 Roberts was elevated to chief justice when, during his nomination and confirmation for associate justice, Chief Justice William H. Rehnquist passed away. He was calm and collected during the highly partisan questioning by the Senate Judiciary Committee. Following the custom of nominees to decline to say how they might vote on specific issues before the high court, he nonetheless stated that *Roe v. Wade* "is settled law of the land." That was not enough to win over many Democrats, including Senators Schumer and Kennedy. Yet Roberts was confirmed by a Senate vote of 78 senators to 22.

CHIEF JUSTICE JOHN ROBERTS

Named Chief Justice in 2005 to succeed his mentor William Rehnquist, Roberts has managed a court that is increasingly defined by ideological differences among the justices.

As chief justice, he occasionally takes the lead in delivering the opinion of the Court. From 2005 to 2013, Roberts penned just 58 majority opinions, and very few dissents or concurrences. In his decisions on the high court, Roberts reflects the moderate to conservative views that he expressed in Senate committee hearings. He voted to uphold the ban on partial-birth abortions enacted by Congress, but gave no indication that he might vote to reverse *Roe v. Wade*.

Relatively early in his tenure, Roberts surprised some observers by siding with the liberal four justices in a property seizure case, *Jones v. Flowers* (547 U.S. 240 2006), which reversed a previous Supreme Court decision by requiring the state to achieve contact with a property owner before selling his or her seized property to collect back taxes. In *Hollingsworth v. Perry*, he penned the majority opinion for an unusual majority (Roberts, Scalia, Ginsberg, Breyer, Kagan) holding that appellants had no standing to challenge the federal court decision overturning the California's same-sex marriage ban. His authorship with four conservative justices of the controversial 2010 *Citizens United* case and its assertion that corporations are people for the purpose of political speech might be his least popular decision.

Roberts's strongest bid for political independence for himself and the Court was in the *Patient Protection and Affordable Care Act Cases*, a consolidation of lawsuits dealing with the Obama adminstration's health reform policies. In the primary case, *National Federation of Independent Business v. Sebelius* (567 U.S. ________ 2012), Roberts broke from the conservatives and sided with the four liberal justices to uphold the act. As chief, he assigned the opinion to himself, and wrote a defense of the law's health care mandate as a tax. He also explained how Congress's commerce clause powers did not apply to the Act, and that Congress had limited power under the commerce clause. This view was shared by the four dissenting conservative justices.

Sometimes, with Justice Roberts, the controversy lags. In 2009 he held together a diverse coalition in *NAMUDNO v. Holder*, 557 U.S. ______ (2009), when a local government in Texas challenged the implementation and constitutionality of the Voting Rights Act (VRA). Progressives feared the Court would overturn the Act, but Roberts's opinion limited the case to the issues of implementation and never reached the constitutional question. But the kernel of critics' fears was in the decision. Four years later, when the Supreme Court heard another challenge to the VRA in *Shelby County v. Holder*, Roberts wrote the opinion that struck down a critical provision of the law. It was the first reversal of a major congressional voting rights law since the end of Reconstruction.

QUESTIONS

1. **What are the key personal experiences of Justice Roberts? The key professional experiences?**
2. **How have his experiences shaped him as a judge?**

by the NAACP) to abortion in 1992 (*Planned Parenthood v. Casey* sponsored by Planned Parenthood) in the absence of interest-group activity. And interest-group *amicus curiae* briefs are now mentioned (cited) in about two-thirds of the written decisions of the Court. However, these briefs may not have much *independent* effect on decisions, that is, they may not have convinced the justices to decide a case one way or another. Several studies have found that interest-group briefs have had very little effect on Supreme Court decisions.[30]

Checking Court Power

13.8 Evaluate checks on Supreme Court power.

any people are concerned about the extent to which we now rely on a nonelected judiciary to decide key policy issues rather than depending on a democratically elected president or Congress.

Legitimacy as a Restraint on the Judiciary

Court authority derives from legitimacy rather than force. By that we mean that the courts depend on their authority being seen as rightful, on people perceiving an obligation to abide by court decisions whether they agree with them or not. The courts have no significant force at their direct command. Federal marshals, who carry out the orders of federal courts, number only a few thousand. Courts must rely primarily on the executive branch for enforcement of their decisions.

Today, most Americans believe that Supreme Court decisions are authoritative statements about the Constitution and that people have an obligation to obey these decisions whether they agree with them or not.[31] Thus public opinion constrains other public officials—from the president, to governors, to school superintendents, to law enforcement officials—to obey Supreme Court decisions.[32] Their constituents do not hold them personally responsible for unpopular actions ordered by the Supreme Court or federal judges. On the contrary, their constituents generally expect them to comply with court decisions.

Compliance with Court Policy

Federal and state court judges must apply Supreme Court policies when ruling on cases in their own courts. Occasionally, lower courts express their disagreement with the Supreme Court in an opinion, even when they feel obliged to carry out the High Court's policy. At times, lower federal and state courts try to give a narrow interpretation to a Supreme Court decision with which they disagree. But judges who seek to defy the Supreme Court face the ultimate sanction of reversal on appeal by the losing party. Professional pride usually inspires judges to avoid reversals of their judgments by higher courts even though a long record of reversals is not grounds for impeachment or removal of a federal judge.

Public officials who defy Supreme Court rulings risk lawsuits and court orders mandating compliance. Persons injured by noncompliance are likely to file suit against noncomplying officials, as are interest groups that monitor official compliance with the policies they support. These suits are expensive, time-consuming, and potentially embarrassing to government officials and agencies. Once a court order is issued, continued defiance can result in fines and penalties for contempt of court.

The president of the United States is subject to federal court orders. Historically, this notion has been challenged: early presidents believed they were separate and at least co-equal to the courts and that their own determination about the legality or constitutionality of their own acts could not be overturned by the courts. President Andrew Jackson could—and did—say: "John Marshall has made his decision. Now let him enforce it," expressing the view that the president was not obliged to enforce court decisions he disagreed with.[33] But in the course of 200 years, the courts—not the president—have gained in legitimacy as the final authority on the law and the

Constitution. Today, a president who openly defied the Supreme Court would lose any claims to legitimacy and would risk impeachment by Congress.

The case of Richard Nixon illustrates the weakness of a modern president who would even consider defying the Supreme Court. When Nixon sought to invoke executive privilege to withhold damaging tapes of White House conversations in the Watergate investigation, federal district judge John Sirica rejected his claim and ordered that the tapes be turned over to the special prosecutor in the case. In arguments before the Supreme Court, Nixon's lawyers contended that the president would not have to comply with a Supreme Court decision to turn over the tapes. Yet when the Court ruled unanimously against him, Nixon felt bound to comply and released tapes that were very damaging to his cause. But Nixon understood that refusal to abide by a Supreme Court decision would most assuredly have resulted in impeachment. Under the circumstances, compliance was the better of two unattractive choices.

□ Presidential Influence on Court Policy

The president and Congress can exercise some restraint over the Court's power through the checks and balances built into the Constitution. Using the office's powers of appointment, presidents have effectively modified the direction of Supreme Court policy and influenced lower federal courts as well. Certainly presidents must await the death or retirement of Supreme Court justices and federal judges, and presidents are constrained by the need to secure Senate confirmation of their appointees. However, over time presidential influence on the courts can be significant. During their combined 12 years in the White House, Ronald Reagan and his successor George H. W. Bush were able to fill 70 percent of federal district and appellate court judgeships and six of nine Supreme Court positions with their own appointees. As noted earlier, however, their appointees did not always reflect these presidents' philosophies in rendering decisions. Nevertheless, the federal courts tilted in a somewhat more conservative direction. President Bill Clinton's appointments generally strengthened liberal, activist impulses throughout the federal judiciary, and George W. Bush's appointees generally supported a conservative, restrained judiciary. Predictably, President Obama's appointees have reflected a strong, liberal activist philosophy.

□ Congressional Checks on the Judiciary

The Constitution gives Congress control over the structure and jurisdiction of federal district and appellate courts, but congressional use of this control has been restrained. Only the Supreme Court is established by the Constitution; Article III gives Congress the power to "ordain and establish . . . inferior" courts. In theory, Congress could try to limit court jurisdiction to hear cases that Congress did not wish it to decide. Congress has used this power to lighten the federal courts' workload; for example, Congress has limited the jurisdiction of federal courts in cases between citizens of different states by requiring that the dispute involve more than $75,000. But Congress has never used this power to change court policy—for example, by removing federal court jurisdiction over school prayer cases or desegregation cases. Indeed, federal courts would probably declare unconstitutional any congressional attempt to limit their power to interpret the Constitution by limiting jurisdiction.

Likewise, although Congress could, in theory, expand membership on the Supreme Court, the custom of a nine-member Supreme Court is now so deeply ingrained in American government that "court packing" is politically unthinkable. Franklin Roosevelt's unsuccessful 1937 attempt to expand the Supreme Court was the last serious assault on the size of its membership.

A more common congressional constraint on the Supreme Court is amending statutory laws to reverse federal court interpretations of these laws that Congress believes are in error. Thus when the Supreme Court decided that civil rights laws did not mandate a cutoff of *all* federal funds to a college upon evidence of discrimination in a single program but only the funds for that program,[34] Congress amended its own laws to require the more sweeping remedy. Although members of Congress frequently berate the Court for what they see as misreading of the laws, all Congress needs to do to reverse a Court interpretation of those laws is to pass amendments to them.

Constitutional amendment is the only means by which Congress and the states can reverse a Supreme Court interpretation of the Constitution itself. After the Civil War, the 13th Amendment abolishing slavery reversed the Supreme Court's *Dred Scott* decision (1857) that slavery was constitutionally protected. The 16th Amendment (1913) gave Congress the power to impose an income tax, thus reversing the Supreme Court's earlier decision in *Pollock v. Farmer's Loan*[35] holding income taxes unconstitutional (1895). But recent attempts to reverse Supreme Court interpretations of the Constitution by passing constitutional amendments on the issues of prayer in public schools, busing, and abortion have all failed to win congressional approval. The barriers to a constitutional amendment are formidable: a two-thirds vote of both houses of Congress and ratification by three-quarters of the states. Thus, for all practical purposes, the Constitution is what the Supreme Court says it is.

Congress can impeach federal court judges, but only for "cause" (committing crimes), not for their decisions. Although impeachment is frequently cited as a constitutional check on the judiciary, it has no real influence over judicial policy making. Only five federal court judges have ever been impeached by the House, convicted by the Senate, and removed from office, although two others were impeached and another nine resigned to avoid impeachment. In 1989, Federal District Court Judge Alcee Hastings became the first sitting judge in more than 50 years to be impeached, tried, and found guilty by Congress. He was convicted by the Senate of perjury and conspiracy to obtain a $150,000 bribe; however, a federal district court judge later ruled that he should have been tried by the full Senate, not a special committee of the Senate. Hastings declared the ruling a vindication; in 1992, he won a congressional seat in Florida, becoming the first person ever to become a member of the House after being impeached by that same body. Even criminal convictions do not ensure removal from office, although judges have resigned under fire.

A Constitutional Note

The Power of Judicial Review

Nowhere in the Constitution do we find any mention of the power of "judicial review." It is true that the Constitution's Supremacy Clause (Article VI, Section 2) makes the Constitution and national laws and treaties "the supreme law of the land, anything in the Constitution or laws of any *state* to the contrary notwithstanding." The Founders clearly believed that federal court power over state decisions was essential to maintaining national unity. But at the *national* level, why should an appointed court's interpretation of the Constitution prevail over the views of an elected Congress and an elected president? All are pledged to uphold the Constitution. The answer is that the Framers distrusted popular majorities and elected officials subject to their influence. So the Framers deliberately insulated the courts from popular majorities; by appointing judges for life terms, they sought to ensure their independence. Alexander Hamilton viewed the federal courts as a final bulwark against threats to principle and property. Writing in *The Federalist*, No. 78, in late 1787, he said: "Limited government . . . can be preserved in practice no other way than through the medium of courts of justice, whose duty it is to declare all acts contrary to the manifest tenor of the Constitution void." But it was not until the case of *Marbury v. Madison* in 1803 that John Marshall first assumed the power of judicial review. He argued persuasively that (1) the Constitution is declared "the supreme law of the land," and national as well as state laws must be congruent with it; (2) Article III gives the Supreme Court the "judicial power," which includes the power to interpret the meaning of laws and, in case of conflict between laws, to decide which law shall prevail; and (3) the courts are sworn to uphold the Constitution, so they must declare void any law that conflicts with the Constitution. Despite the logic of the argument, judicial review—the ability of an unelected judiciary, serving for life, to invalidate laws of Congress and actions of the president—would appear to be an undemocratic feature of the Constitution.

QUESTIONS

1. What components of the Constitution establish judicial review, according to Hamilton?
2. Is judicial review undemocratic?
3. Can you think of any way for Congress and the president to reverse a Court's application of judicial review?

Review the Chapter

Judicial Power

13.1 Assess the basis for and use of judicial power, p. 480

The power of judicial review is the power to invalidate laws of Congress or of the states that the federal courts believe conflict with the U.S. Constitution. This power is not specifically mentioned in the Constitution but was derived by Chief Justice John Marshall from the Supremacy Clause and the meaning of judicial power in Article III.

The Supreme Court has been fairly restrained in its use of judicial review with regard to laws of Congress and actions of presidents; it has more frequently overturned state laws. The federal courts also exercise great power in the interpretation of the laws of Congress, especially when statutory language is vague.

Activism Versus Self-Restraint

13.2 Compare and contrast the philosophies of judicial activism and judicial restraint, p. 483

Arguments over judicial power are reflected in the conflicting philosophies of judicial activism and judicial self-restraint. Advocates of judicial restraint argue that judges must not substitute their own views for those of elected representatives and the remedy for unwise laws lies in the legislature, not the courts. Advocates of judicial activism argue that the courts must view the Constitution as a living document, and its meaning must fit the needs of a changing society.

Structure and Jurisdiction of Federal Courts

13.3 Outline the structure and jurisdiction of the federal courts, p. 486

The federal judiciary consists of three levels of courts—the Supreme Court, the U.S. Courts of Appeals, and the U.S. District Courts. The district courts are trial courts that hear both civil and criminal cases. The courts of appeals are appellate courts and do not hold trials but consider only the record of trial courts and the arguments (briefs) of attorneys. More than 90 percent of federal cases end in appeals courts. The Supreme Court can hear appeals from state high courts as well as lower federal courts. The Supreme Court hears only about 200 cases a year.

The Special Rules of Judicial Decision Making

13.4 Characterize the "special rules" of judicial decision making, p. 491

Courts function under general rules of restraint that do not bind the president or Congress. The Supreme Court does not decide hypothetical cases or render advisory opinions. The principle of stare decisis, or reliance on precedent, is not set aside lightly.

The Politics of Selecting Judges

13.5 Assess the role of politics in the judicial selection process, p. 494

The selection of Supreme Court justices and federal judges is based more on political considerations than legal qualifications. Presidents almost always appoint judges from their own party, and presidents increasingly have sought judges who share their ideological views. However, because of the independence of judges once they are appointed, presidents have sometimes been disappointed in the decisions of their appointees. In addition, Senate approval of nominees has become increasingly politicized, with problems most evident when different parties control the White House and the Senate. The justices of the U.S. Supreme Court tend to share a common background of education at the nation's most prestigious law schools. Most appointees have experience as federal court judges; Elena Kagan is the first justice in many years to lack judicial experience. Today, one African American and three women serve on the Supreme Court.

Supreme Court Decision Making

13.6 Outline the decision-making process of the Supreme Court and areas in which the Court has been active, p. 500

The Supreme Court sets its own agenda for policy making, usually by granting or withholding certiorari. Generally, four justices must agree to grant certiorari for a case to be decided by the Supreme Court. The Supreme Court has been especially active in policy making in interpreting the meaning of the 14th Amendment's guarantee of "equal protection of the laws," as well as of the civil rights and voting rights acts of Congress. It has also been active in defining the meaning of freedom of press, speech, and religion in the 1st Amendment and "due process of law" in the 5th Amendment.

The federal courts are active in overseeing government regulatory activity. But federal courts have generally left the areas of national security and international relations to the president and Congress. In addition, the Court tends to accept cases involving questions decided differently by different courts of appeal, cases in which lower courts have challenged Supreme Court interpretations, and cases in which the U.S. government is a party and it requests review.

Politics and the Supreme Court

13.7 Assess the role of politics and ideology in Supreme Court decision making. p. 503

The Supreme Court risked its reputation for political impartiality when it intervened in the 2000 presidential election. The Court issued a decision that in effect gave Florida's 25 electoral votes to George W. Bush and thus winning him a majority in the Electoral College.

Liberal and conservative blocs on the Supreme Court can be discerned over time. Generally, liberals have been judicial activists and conservatives have been restraintists. Today, a moderate bloc appears to hold the balance of power.

Checking Court Power

13.8 Evaluate checks on Supreme Court power, p. 507

Court power derives primarily from legitimacy rather than force. Most Americans believe that Supreme Court decisions are authoritative statements about the Constitution and people have an obligation to obey these decisions whether they agree with them or not. Although early presidents thought of themselves as constitutional coequals with the Supreme Court and not necessarily bound by Court decisions, today it would be politically unthinkable for a president to ignore a court order.

There are very few checks on Supreme Court power. Presidents may try to influence Court policy through judicial nominations, but once judges are confirmed by the Senate, they can pursue their own impulses. Congress has never used its power to limit the jurisdiction of federal courts in order to influence judicial decisions.

Only by amending the Constitution can Congress and the states reverse a Supreme Court interpretation of its meaning. Congress can impeach federal judges only for committing crimes, not for their decisions.

Learn the Terms

judicial review, p. 481
statutory laws, p. 483
judicial self-restraint, p. 484
original intent, p. 484
judicial activism, p. 484
stare decisis, p. 485
precedent, p. 485
jurisdiction, p. 487
original jurisdiction, p. 487
appellate jurisdiction, p. 487
appeal, p. 487
district courts, p. 487
grand juries, p. 487
petit (regular) juries, p. 487
circuit courts, p. 487
briefs, p. 487
tort claim, p. 489
damages, p. 489
civil cases, p. 491
adversarial system, p. 491
standing, p. 491
plaintiff, p. 491
defendant, p. 491
sovereign immunity, p. 491
class action suits, p. 492
contingency fee, p. 492
remedies and relief, p. 492
independent counsel ("special prosecutor"), p. 493
litmus test, p. 494
senatorial courtesy, p. 494
writ of certiorari, p. 500
rule of four, p. 500
amicus curiae, p. 501
solicitor general, p. 501
majority opinion, p. 502
concurring opinion, p. 502
dissenting opinion, p. 502
U.S. solicitor general, p. 505

Test Yourself

13.1 Assess the basis for and use of judicial power.

The power of the Supreme Court to declare a law passed by Congress or one of the states unconstitutional is known as

a. constitutional evaluation
b. constitutional review
c. judicial evaluation
d. *stare decisis*
e. judicial review

13.2 Compare and contrast the philosophies of judicial activism and judicial restraint.

The rule of *stare decisis*

a. greatly expands the decision-making freedom of the Justices
b. is based on statutory law
c. is based on following precedent and thus limits the decision-making power of the Justices
d. rejects common law
e. only applies in Louisiana under the *Code Napoleon*

13.3 Outline the structure and jurisdiction of the federal courts.

A trial court of original jurisdiction in the federal system consists of which of the following elements?

I. a court that only hears appeals of district court decisions in order to determine if due process was followed
II. determined solely by Article III of the Constitution
III. a court that hears and weighs evidence in order to reach an original decision in a civil or criminal case

a. I, II, & III
b. Only I
c. Only III
d. Only II
e. Only I & III

13.4 Characterize the "special rules" of judicial decision making.

The idea of sovereign immunity involves

a. diplomatic immunity for foreign dignitaries
b. the idea that the government cannot be sued without its consent
c. the idea that the sovereign nations back their currencies with hard assets
d. the old belief that royalty was immune to the laws
e. the divine right of kings, much like the executive pardon power

13.5 Assess the role of politics in the judicial selection process.

The *litmus test* that has come to dominate the recruitment process in judicial selection revolves around the case of

a. *Brown v. Board of Education*
b. *Roe v. Wade*
c. *Marbury v. Madison*
d. *Regents of the University of California v. Bakke*
e. *In re Calipari*

13.6 Outline the decision-making process of the Supreme Court and areas in which the Court has been active.

At least ________ Justices must agree to hear a case before they will issue a ________, which is the way most cases reach the Supreme Court.

a. four; writ of certiorari
b. five; writ of mandamus
c. six; writ of certiorari
d. four; writ of habeas corpus
e. the chief; a writ of certiorari

13.7 Assess the role of politics and ideology in Supreme Court decision making.

The Roberts Court is viewed as a '5-4' court. The "swing vote" on the court today is considered to be ________ because he/she is often the deciding vote between the conservatives and liberal voting blocs.

a. Antonin Scalia
b. John Roberts
c. Anthony Kennedy
d. Ruth Bader Ginsburg
e. Ron Artest

13.8 Evaluate checks on Supreme Court power.

The case of *Marbury v. Madison* is notable because it resulted in the court articulating its power of ________ over acts of Congress.

a. judicial oversight
b. *a priori* review
c. *ex post facto* oversight
d. judicial review
e. veto

Explore Further

SUGGESTED READINGS

Baum, Lawrence. *The Supreme Court*. 10th ed. Washington, D.C.: CQ Press, 2009. Readable introduction to the Supreme Court as a political institution, covering the selection and confirmation of judges, the nature of the issues decided by courts, the process of judicial decision making, and the impact of Supreme Court decisions.

Bork, Robert H. *Coercing Virtue*. Washington, D.C.: AEI Press, 2003. An argument that judges, rather than legislators, are making and repealing law and deciding cases with partisan and ideological subjectivity.

Carp, Robert A., Ronald Stidham, and Kenneth L. Manning. *Judicial Process in America*. 8th ed. Washington, D.C.: CQ Press, 2010. Comprehensive coverage of the America judicial system at all levels.

Carter, Lief H., and Tom Burke. *Reason in Law*. New York: Longman, 2009. Examines the relationship between law and politics, and uses case studies to explore how judicial decisions are the product of "thoughtful judges of judging."

Epstein, Lee, and Thomas G. Walker. *Constitutional Law for a Changing America: Institutional Power and Constraints*. 7th ed. Washington, D.C.: CQ Press, 2010. Commentary and selected excerpts from cases dealing with the structure and powers of government.

Johnson, Charles, and Danette Buickman. *Independent Counsel: The Law and the Investigations*. Washington, D.C.: CQ Press, 2001. A comprehensive history of the independent counsel law and the investigations conducted under it since 1978, from Watergate to Whitewater.

McClosky, Robert G. *The American Supreme Court*. 4th ed. Rev. by Sanford Levinson. Chicago: University of Chicago Press. 2005. Classic work on the Supreme Court's role in constructing the Constitution, with updates to latest cases.

Neubauer, David W., and Stephen S. Weinhold. *Judicial Politics: Law, Courts, and Politics in the United States*. 5th ed. Belmont, Calif.: Wadsworth, 2010. Introduction to the judicial process with controversial cases in each chapter.

U.S. Supreme Court decisions are available at most public and university libraries as well as at law libraries in volumes of

United States Reports. Court opinions are cited by the names of the parties, for example, *Brown v. Board of Education of Topeka*, followed by a reference number such as 347 U.S. 483 (1954). The first number in the citation (347) is the volume number; "U.S." refers to *United States Reports*; the subsequent number is the page on which the decision begins; the year the case was decided is in parentheses.

SUGGESTED WEB SITES

American Bar Association (ABA) www.abanet.org
ABA news and views; information for law students.

FindLaw for Students http://stu.findlaw.com
Law school information for schools A–Z, state bar information, job listings, law school rankings, and so forth.

LawInfo www.lawinfo.com
Web site offering legal documents, legal help guides, attorney references, and so forth.

Southern Poverty Law Center www.splcenter.org
Civil rights law firm opposing death penalty, hate groups, display of religion in public places, and so forth.

Southeastern Legal Foundation www.southeasternlegal.org
Public interest law firm advocating limited government, individual freedom, and the free enterprise system.

Supreme Court Cases www.law.cornell.edu
This Cornell Law School's Legal Information Institute site contains up-to-date information about important legal decisions rendered by federal and state courts along with an exhaustive online law library available to researchers.

United States Courts www.uscourts.gov
The goal of this site is "to function as a clearinghouse for information from and about the Judicial Branch of the U.S. government." The site covers the U.S. Supreme Court, U.S. Courts of Appeals, U.S. District Courts, and U.S. Bankruptcy Courts.

Supreme Court of the United States www.supremecourtus.gov
Official site provides recent decisions, case dockets, oral arguments, and public information.

14

Politics and Personal Liberty

Where do you have privacy? When do you have the ability to stop government authority from intruding on you and your space? The answer is possibly nowhere if the circumstances warrant. Residents in Boston saw the balance between security versus privacy and process after the 2013 Boston Marathon bombing.

On April 15 two improvised explosive devices were detonated near the finish line of the Boston Marathon, killing three individuals and injuring scores. Within minutes, law enforcement was collecting information from surveillance cameras and individual camera phones. State and federal officials shut down Boston's airspace. By April 18 they had pieced together an image of the bombing suspects and released it. The bombers were identified as Tamerlan and Dzhokhar Tsarnaev. A manhunt began.

The brothers Tsarnaev were on the run. At one point they led police on a moving, shooting, bomb-tossing car chase straight out of the movies. They finally abandoned their stolen car west of Cambridge. A ping off of one of their electronic devices was isolated by police, who then identified a grid of several blocks of Watertown, Massachusetts, divided it into quadrants, and then executed a search. Governor Deval Patrick asked a million Massachusetts residents to shelter in place.

One brother, Tamerlan, died in a shootout with police around midnight April 19th. Later that morning, reverse-911 calls were used to again order a shelter in place. Armored, heavily armed police began a house-to-house search, evacuating residents and searching houses for the fugitive bombers. No warrants were served. Videos of police frog-marching residents from their home made their way to the Internet, outraging some libertarians.

Ultimately, the Tsarnaevs were not found in anyone's home. Instead the surviving brother was apprehended in part because Watertown resident David Henneberry, on hearing the shelter-in-place

14.1 Outline the Founders' views on individual liberty and trace the expansion of the Bill of Rights, p. 516

14.2 Differentiate the two aspects of freedom of religion, p. 517

14.3 Assess the extent of and limits on freedom of speech and the press and trace the evolution of the Supreme Court's view of obscenity, p. 524

14.4 Identify protections granted under the right to privacy, p. 534

14.5 Outline the right to assembly and petition and limitations on this right, p. 536

14.6 Describe the protection of property rights and related Court decisions, p. 538

14.7 Explain the Supreme Court's interpretation of the right to bear arms, p. 540

14.8 Identify the constitutional rights of criminal defendants and assess the consequences of their implementation, p. 542

ROBOCOP Increasingly militarized police were put on full display during the Watertown hunt for the Boston Marathon bomber.

call, did what many Americans did—the opposite. He went outside to check his boat and discovered that a wounded Dzhokhar Tsarnaev was hiding inside his craft, the *Slipaway II*. He called the authorities.

An ongoing issue in the post-9/11 security era is the extent to which fundamental liberties are surrendered for security. Civil libertarians are increasing concerned that invasive electronic observation, warrantless searches, and public image profiling are all component to an increased erosion of individual liberties.

Power and Individual Liberty

14.1 Outline the founders' views on individual liberty and trace the expansion of the Bill of Rights.

To the authors of the Declaration of Independence, individual liberty was inherent in the human condition. It was not derived from governments or even from constitutions. Rather, governments and constitutions existed to make individual liberty more secure.

> We hold these truths to be self-evident, that all men are created equal, that they are endowed by their Creator with certain unalienable Rights, that among these are Life, Liberty and the pursuit of Happiness. That to secure these rights, Governments are instituted among Men, deriving their just powers from the consent of the governed.

The authors of the Bill of Rights (the first 10 amendments to the Constitution) did *not* believe that they were creating individual rights, but rather that they were recognizing and guaranteeing rights that belonged to individuals by virtue of their humanity. These freedoms—of person, property, and conscience—are deemed fundamental and universal. However, a government can only guarantee them within the scope of its constituted power. We cannot guarantee liberties for human beings beyond our borders.

Authority and Liberty

To avoid the brutal life of a lawless society, where the weak are at the mercy of the strong, people form governments and endow them with powers to secure peace and self-preservation. People voluntarily relinquish some of their individual freedom to establish a government that is capable of protecting them from their neighbors as well as from foreign aggressors. This government must be strong enough to maintain its own existence or it cannot defend the rights of its citizens.

But what happens when a government becomes too strong and infringes on the liberties of its citizens? How much liberty must individuals surrender to secure an orderly society? This is the classic dilemma of free government: people must create laws and governments to protect their freedom, but the laws and governments themselves restrict freedom. In the American case, the assumption is that rights can only be relinquished and infringed upon via some due process.

Democracy and Personal Liberty

Democracy, defined only as a *decision-making process*—widespread popular participation and rule by majority—offers little protection for individual liberty. Democracy must be informed by *substantive values*—a recognition of the dignity of all individuals and their equality under law. Otherwise, some people, particularly those Madison termed in the *Federalist Papers* "the weaker party, or an obnoxious individual," would be vulnerable to deprivations of life, liberty, or property simply by decisions of majorities. The "great object" of the Constitution, according to James Madison, was to preserve popular government yet at the same time to protect individuals from "unjust" majorities. The former is achieved through the use of cumbersome and interdependent institutions. The latter is achieved by the adoption of the Bill of Rights, passed by the First Congress in September 1789 and then sent to the states for ratification. The Bill of Rights explicitly articulate limits on governmental power over the individual, placing personal liberty beyond the reach of government (see Table 14.1).[1] Each individual's rights to life, liberty, and property; due process of law; and equal protection of the law are not subject to majority vote. Or, as Supreme Court Justice Robert Jackson once declared, "One's right to life, liberty, and property, to free speech, a free press, freedom of worship and assembly, and other fundamental rights may not be submitted to vote: they depend on the outcome of no elections."[2]

incorporation
In constitutional law, the application of almost all of the Bill of Rights to the states and all of their subdivisions through the 14th Amendment.

Nationalizing the Bill of Rights

The Bill of Rights begins with the words "*Congress* shall make no law . . ." indicating that it was originally intended to limit only the powers of the federal government. The Bill of Rights was added to the Constitution because of fear that the *federal* government might become too powerful and encroach on individual liberty. But what about encroachments by state and local governments and their officials?

The 14th Amendment includes the words "No *State* shall . . ."; its provisions are directed specifically at states. Initially, the U.S. Supreme Court rejected the argument that the 14th Amendment's Privileges or Immunities Clause[3] and the Due Process Clause[4] incorporated the Bill of Rights. But beginning in the 1920s, the Court handed down a long series of decisions that gradually brought about the **incorporation** of almost all of the protections of the Bill of Rights into the "liberty" guaranteed against state actions by the Due Process Clause of the 14th Amendment. In *Gitlow v. New York* (1925), the Court ruled that "freedom of speech and of the press—which are protected by the First Amendment from abridgment by Congress—are among the fundamental personal rights and liberties protected by the due process clause of the 14th Amendment from impairment by the states."[5] Over time, the Court applied the same reasoning in incorporating almost all provisions of the Bill of Rights into the 14th Amendment's Due Process Clause—including, most recently, the 2nd amendment. States and all of their subdivisions—cities, counties, townships, school districts, and so forth—are bound by the Bill of Rights.

Freedom of Religion

14.2 Differentiate the two aspects of freedom of religion.

Americans are a very religious people. Belief in God and church attendance are more widespread in the United States than in any other advanced industrialized nation. Although many early American colonists came to the new land to escape religious persecution, they frequently established their own government-supported churches and imposed their own religious beliefs on others. Puritanism was the official faith of colonial Massachusetts, and Virginia officially established the Church of England. Only two colonies (Maryland and Rhode Island) provided for full religious freedom. To lessen conflict among the states, the Framers impeded the new national government from establishing an official religion or interfering with religious exercises.[6] The very first words of the 1st Amendment set forth *two* separate prohibitions on government: "Congress shall make no law respecting an *establishment of religion*, or prohibiting the *free exercise* thereof." Taken together the Free Exercise Clause and the Establishment Clause guarantee separate religious freedoms.

14.1
14.2
14.3
14.4
14.5
14.6
14.7
14.8

TABLE 14.1 HOW ARE WE PROTECTED?: RIGHTS UNDER THE CONSTITUTION

The Bill of Rights

The first 10 amendments to the Constitution of the United States, passed by the First Congress of the United States in September 1789 and ratified by the states in December 1791.

Amendments	Protections
1st Amendment: Religion, Speech, Press, Assembly, Petition	
Congress shall make no law respecting an establishment of religion, or prohibiting the free exercise thereof; or abridging the freedom of speech, or of the press; or the right of the people peaceably to assemble, and to petition the Government for a redress of grievances.	Prohibits government establishment of religion. Protects the free exercise of religion. Protects freedom of speech. Protects freedom of the press. Protects freedom of assembly. Protects the right to petition government "for a redress of grievances."
2nd Amendment: Right to Bear Arms	
A well-regulated Militia, being necessary to the security of a free State, the right of the people to keep and bear Arms, shall not be infringed.	Protects the right of people to bear arms and states to maintain militia (National Guard) units.
3rd Amendment: Quartering of Soldiers	
No Soldier shall, in time of peace, be quartered in any house, without the consent of the Owner, nor in time of war, but in manner to be prescribed by law.	Prohibits forcible quartering of soldiers in private homes in peacetime, or in war without congressional authorization.
4th Amendment: Searches and Seizures	
The right of the people to be secure in their persons, houses, papers, and effects, against unreasonable searches and seizures, shall not be violated, and no Warrants shall issue, but upon probable cause, supported by Oath or affirmation, and particularly describing the place to be searched, and the persons or things to be seized.	Protects against "unreasonable searches and seizures." Requires warrants for searches of homes and other places where there is a reasonable expectation of privacy. Judges may issue search warrants only with "probable cause," and such warrants must be specific regarding the place to be searched and the things to be seized.
5th Amendment: Grand Juries, Double Jeopardy, Self-Incrimination, Due Process, Protection Against Government Takings of Property	
No person shall be held to answer for a capital, or otherwise infamous crime, unless on a presentment or indictment of a Grand jury, except in cases arising in the land or naval forces, or in the Militia, when in actual service in time of War or public danger; nor shall any person be subject for the same offence to be twice put in jeopardy of life or limb, nor shall be compelled in any criminal case to be a witness against himself, nor be deprived of life, liberty, or property without due process of law; nor shall private property be taken for public use, without just compensation.	Requires that, before trial for a serious crime, a person (except military personnel) must be indicted by a grand jury. Prohibits double jeopardy (trial for the same offense a second time after being found innocent). Prohibits the government from forcing any person in a criminal case to be a witness against himself or herself. Prohibits the government from taking life, liberty, or property, "without due process of law." Prohibits government from taking private property without paying "just compensation."
6th Amendment: Fair Trial	
In all criminal prosecutions, the accused shall enjoy the right to a speedy and public trail, by an impartial jury of the State and district wherein the crime shall have been committed, which district shall have been previously ascertained by law, and to be informed of the nature and cause of the accusation, to be confronted with the witnesses against him, to have compulsory process for obtaining witnesses in his favor, and to have the Assistance of Counsel for his defense.	Requires that the accused in a criminal case be given the right to a speedy and public trial, and thus prohibits prolonged incarceration without trial or secret trials. Requires that trials be by jury and take place in the district where the crime was committed. Requires that the accused be informed of the charges, have the right to confront witnesses, have the right to force supporting witnesses to testify, and have the assistance of counsel.
7th Amendment: Trial by Jury in Civil Cases	
In Suits at common law, where the value in controversy shall exceed twenty dollars, the right of trial by jury shall be preserved, and no fact tried by a jury shall be otherwise re-examined in any Court of the United States, than according to the rules of the common law.	Reserves the right to a jury trial in civil cases. Limits the degree to which factual questions decided by a jury may be reviewed by another court.
8th Amendment: Bail, Fines, and Punishment	
Excessive bail shall not be required, nor excessive fines imposed, nor cruel and unusual punishments inflicted.	Prohibits excessive bail. Prohibits excessive fines. Prohibits cruel and unusual punishment.
9th Amendment: Unspecified Rights Retained by People	
The enumeration in the Constitution, of certain rights, shall not be construed to deny or disparage others retained by the people.	Protection of unspecified rights (including privacy) that are not listed in the Constitution. The Constitution shall not be interpreted to be a complete list of rights retained by the people.
10th Amendment: Rights Reserved to the States	
The powers not delegated to the United States by the Constitution, nor prohibited by it to the States, are reserved to the States respectively, or to the people.	States retain powers that are not granted by the Constitution to the national government or prohibited by it to the states.

(Continued)

Rights in the Text of the Constitution	
Several rights were written into the text of the Constitution in 1787 and thus precede in time the adoption of the Bill of Rights.	
Article I, Section 9: Habeas Corpus, Bills of Attainder, and Ex Post Facto Laws	
The privilege of the Writ of Habeas Corpus shall not be suspended, unless when in Cases of Rebellion or Invasion, the public Safety may require it. No Bill of Attainder or ex post facto Law shall be passed.	Habeas corpus prevents imprisonment without a judge's determination that a person is being lawfully detained. Prohibition of bills of attainder prevents Congress (and states) from deciding people guilty of a crime and imposing punishment without trial. Prohibition of ex post facto laws prevents Congress (and states) from declaring acts to be criminal that were committed before the passage of a law making them so.
13th and 14th Amendments	
The Bill of Rights begins with the words "Congress shall make no law . . . " indicating that it initially applied only to the *federal* government. Although states had their own constitutions that guarantee many of the same rights, for more than a century the Bill of Rights did not apply to state and local governments. Following the Civil War, the 13th, 14th, and 15th (voting rights) Amendments were passed, restricting *state* governments and their local subdivisions. But not until many years later did the U.S. Supreme Court, in a long series of decisions, apply the Bill of Rights against the states.	
13th Amendment	
Neither slavery nor involuntary servitude, except as a punishment for crime whereof the party shall have been duly convicted, shall exist within the United States, or any place subject to their jurisdiction.	Prohibits slavery or involuntary servitude except for punishment by law; applies to both governments and private citizens.
14th Amendment	
All persons born or naturalized in the United States, and subject to the jurisdiction thereof, are citizens of the United States and of the State wherein they reside. No State shall make or enforce any law which shall abridge the privileges or immunities of citizens of the United States; nor shall any State deprive any person of life, liberty, or property, without due process of law; nor deny to any person within its jurisdiction the equal protection of the laws.	Protects "privileges and immunities of citizenship." Prevents deprivation of life, liberty, or property "without due process of law"; this phrase incorporates virtually all of the rights specified in the Bill of Rights. Prevents denial of "equal protection of the laws" for all persons.

Free Exercise of Religion

The **Free Exercise Clause** prohibits government from restricting religious beliefs or practices. Although the wording of the 1st Amendment appears absolute ("Congress shall make *no* law . . ."), the U.S. Supreme Court has never interpreted the phrase to protect any conduct carried on in the name of religion. In the first major decision involving this clause, the Court ruled in 1879 that polygamy could be outlawed by Congress in Utah Territory even though some Mormons argued that it was part of their religious faith. The Court distinguished between belief and behavior, saying that "Congress was deprived of all legislative power over mere opinion [by the 1st Amendment], but was left free to reach actions which were in violation of social duties."[7] The Court employed the Free Exercise Clause to strike down an attempt by a state to prohibit private religious schools and force all children to attend public schools.[8] This decision protects the entire structure of private religious schools in the nation.

Free Exercise Clause
Clause in the 1st Amendment to the Constitution that prohibits government from restricting religious beliefs and practices that do not harm society.

Later, the Supreme Court elaborated on its distinction between religious belief and religious practice. *Beliefs* are protected absolutely. Religious *practices* are not, so governmental restrictions on religious exercise can be enacted for valid secular purposes such as public health, safety, or welfare.[9] The Free Exercise Clause does *not* confer the *right* to practice human sacrifice or even the ceremonial use of illegal drugs.[10] Individuals must comply with valid and neutral laws even if these laws restrict religious practices.

The Supreme Court has continued to face many difficulties in applying its "valid secular test" to specific infringements of religious freedom. When Amish parents refused to allow their children to attend school beyond the eighth grade, Wisconsin argued that its universal compulsory school attendance law had a valid purpose: the education of children. Amish parents argued that high school exposed their children to worldly influences and values contrary to their religious beliefs. The Supreme Court sided with the Amish, deciding that their religious claims outweighed the legitimate interests of the state in education.[11] When a Florida city attempted to outlaw the Santeria (a mix of Catholicism and voodoo) practice of slaughtering animals in religious ceremonies, the Supreme Court held that the city's ordinance was "not neutral" and "targeted" a particular religious ceremony and was therefore unconstitutional.[12] In 2014 the Supreme Court held that closely-held corporations could petition to forego providing contraceptives as part of the health benefits package under Obamacare based on the religious objections of the owners.

The Game, the Rules, the Players

Are We One Nation "Under God"?

For over 100 years, the Pledge of Allegiance has been recited in public school rooms at the beginning of each day. In 1954, at the height of the Cold War, Congress added the words "under God" after "one nation," to emphasize that the United States acknowledged spiritual values in contrast to "godless communism." President Dwight D. Eisenhower, upon signing the bill, said it would strengthen "those spiritual weapons which forever will be our country's most powerful resource in peace and war."

As early as 1943, the Supreme Court declared that public school pupils could not be *required* to recite the pledge. The opinion was widely praised as an expression of our constitutional freedoms: "If there is any fixed star in our constitutional constellation, it is that no official, high or petty, can prescribe what shall be orthodox in politics, nationalism, religion, or other matters of opinion, or force citizens to confess by word or act their faith therein."[a] Pupils who did not wish to take the pledge were free to stand silent in the classroom while the pledge was being recited.

The Supreme Court was called upon to review the phrase "under God" in 2002 when the father of a public school pupil argued that these words constituted an establishment of religion by an instrument of the government. He argued that the pledge with "under God" constituted "a ritual proclaiming that there is a God" and therefore violated the Establishment Clause of the 1st Amendment. The Words "under God" asserted monotheism and possibly offended atheists, the nonreligious, and others who did not wish to swear an oath of allegiance to a monotheistic deity.

The U.S. Court of Appeals for the Ninth Circuit agreed that the words "under God" were not neutral and representted a swearing of allegiance to monotheism. The effect of this appeals court's opinion was to remove the words "under God" from the Pledge.

However, subsequently it was revealed that the father (who was divorced) did not have custody over his daughter, and that the custodial mother did not wish her daughter to bring suit over this issue. The Supreme Court, therefore, dismissed the case on this technicality and avoided the substantive issue of whether or not the words "under God" in the Pledge of Allegiance violated the Establishment Clause.[b]

It can be argued that these words do not refer to any specific religion or deity but simply acknowledge the nation's spiritual heritage. References to God have long been part of our national identity. Our coins invoke the blessing "In God We Trust," chaplains are provided for the Armed Forces, prayers open the sessions of both chambers of Congress as well as the Supreme Court itself. A strong majority (84 percent) of Americans support the inclusion of the words "under God" in the Pledge of Allegiance—an inclusion made in the 1950s at the height of the Cold War. The Supreme Court recently affirmed that prayers by volunteer chaplains before public meetings is not establishment, when it upheld by a 5-4 vote this practice in the town of Greece, New York.

Two approaches to overcoming the state-church separation involve broadening the context of the religious information or expression. In pushing for creationism in school curricula, concepts such as "creation science" and "intelligent design" are developed by religious advocates as alternatives to evolutionary science. Or, important components of Christian belief systems like the Ten Commandments are placed in a historic context (as examples of law giving or cultural heritage) to permit their display in government buildings. These approaches lead to unexpected results, such as non-Christian religious displays in the public space that are either mocking or offensive. In some states, Ten Commandment monuments or creche displays at Christmas have invited protest displays, including parades of the Pastafarian Church of the Flying Spaghetti Monster, displays of Festivus Poles, and efforts by Hindus and Satanists to attempt to erect monuments to their belief systems on grounds where Ten Commandment monuments are present.

QUESTIONS

1. **Should government be able to recognize or invoke the concept of "God"?**
2. **Are the means through which government invokes God coercive? Do they violate your conscience? What about someone else's conscience?**

[a] *West Virginia Board of Education v. Barnette*, 319 U.S. 624 (1943).

[b] *Elk Grove United School District v. Newdow*, 542 U.S. 277 (2004).

SOURCES: Philip Goodchild. 2007. *The Theology of Money*. Norwich: Canterbury Press.
Mark A. Noll. 2001. *God and Mammon: Protestants, Money, and the Market, 1790–1860*. New York: Oxford.

The Supreme Court has often upheld government actions that were challenged as infringements of religious freedom. The Court approved an Internal Revenue Service action revoking the tax-exempt status of Bob Jones University, which forbade interracial dating or marriage among its students. The school argued that its rule was based on religious belief, but the Court held that the government had "an overriding interest in eradicating racial discrimination in education."[13] The Court upheld an Oregon law prohibiting possession of peyote (a hallucinogenic drug made from cactus plants) against claims of a Native American church that its use was a religious sacrament.[14] The Court also upheld a U.S. Air Force dress code regulation that prevented orthodox Jews from wearing a yarmulke while in uniform, holding that "the mission of the military . . . [including fostering] obedience, unity, commitment and esprit de corps" overrides the individual freedom that would protect civilians from such a government regulation.[15]

☐ Congress Overruled

Congress attempted to expand upon the Free Exercise Clause with its Religious Freedom Restoration Act in 1993. Congress was dissatisfied with the Supreme Court's willingness to approve of restrictions on religious practices, restrictions that were part of a valid and neutral law. So Congress mandated that:

> Government shall not substantially burden a person's exercise of religion even if that burden results from a rule of general applicability . . . [unless the government can show that the burden] is in furtherance of a compelling government interest; and is the least restrictive means of furthering that compelling government interest.

Most religious groups praised the act. It had near unanimous support in the Congress. But the Supreme Court decided that the act was an unconstitutional effort by Congress to usurp the power of the courts to interpret the meaning of the Constitution:

> When the court has interpreted the Constitution, it has acted within the province of the judicial branch which embraces the duty to say what the law is . . . the Act contradicts vital principles necessary to maintain separation of powers and the federal balance.[16]

So it is the Supreme Court and not the Congress that has the final say regarding the meaning of the Free Exercise Clause—indeed, of the Constitution.

CORPORATIONS AND RELIGIOUS EXERCISE

The Hobby Lobby Corporation is a privately held company whose owners are deeply committed Christians. In 2014 the Court ruled that, under the Religious Freedom Restoration Act, they could use their religious convictions as a basis for not providing employees' contraception under the Affordable Care Act. The Court did not state that the corporation enjoyed religious freedom in the same manner as a person.

14.1

14.2

14.3

14.4

14.5

14.6

14.7

14.8

Establishment Clause
Clause in the 1st Amendment to the Constitution that is interpreted to require the separation of church and state.

wall-of-separation doctrine
The Supreme Court's interpretation of the No Establishment Clause that laws may not have as their purpose aid to one religion or aid to all religions.

Lemon test
To be constitutional, a law must have a secular purpose; its primary effect must neither advance nor inhibit religion; and it must not foster excessive government entanglement with religion.

No Establishment of Religion

Various meanings have been ascribed to the 1st Amendment's **Establishment Clause**.

- The first meaning—what the writers of the Bill of Rights had in mind—is that it merely prohibits the government from officially recognizing and supporting a national church, like the Church of England in that nation.
- A second meaning is somewhat broader: the government may not prefer one religion over another or demonstrate favoritism toward or discrimination against any particular religion, but it might recognize and encourage religious activities in general.
- The most expansive meaning is that the clause creates "a wall of separation between church and state" that prevents government from endorsing, aiding, sponsoring, or encouraging any or all religious activities.

The phrase "separation of church and state" does *not* appear in the Constitution. It was first used by Thomas Jefferson in a letter to a Baptist Church in 1802 assuring them that the federal government would not establish a national church. The current meaning derives from a 1947 decision by Justice Hugo Black, who, writing for the Supreme Court majority, gave the following definition of the **wall-of-separation doctrine**:

> Neither a state nor the Federal Government can set up a church. Neither can pass laws which aid one religion, aid all religions, or prefer one religion over another. Neither can force nor influence a person to go to or to remain away from church . . . or force him to profess a belief or disbelief in any religion. . . . No tax in any amount, large or small, can be levied to support any religious activities or institutions, whatever they may be called, or whatever form they may adopt to teach or practice religion.[17]

Although the Supreme Court has generally voiced its support for the wall-of-separation doctrine, on several occasions it has permitted cracks to develop in the wall. In allowing public schools to give pupils regular releases from school to attend religious instructions given outside of the school, Justice William O. Douglas wrote that the state and religion need not be "hostile, suspicious or even unfriendly."[18]

What Constitutes "Establishment"?

It has proven difficult for the Supreme Court to reconcile this wall-of-separation interpretation of the 1st Amendment with the fact that religion plays an important role in the life of most Americans. Public meetings, including sessions of the Congress, often begin with prayers;[19] coins are inscribed with the words "In God We Trust"; and the armed forces provide chaplains for U.S. soldiers.

The Supreme Court has set forth a three-part **Lemon test** for determining whether a particular law constitutes "establishment" of religion and thus violates the 1st Amendment. To be constitutional, a law affecting religious activity:

- Must have a secular purpose.
- As its primary effect, must neither advance nor inhibit religion.
- Must not foster "an excessive government entanglement with religion."[20]

Using this three-part test, the Supreme Court held that it was unconstitutional for a state to pay the costs of teachers' salaries or instructional materials in parochial schools. The justices argued that this practice would require excessive government controls and surveillance to ensure that funds were used only for secular instruction and thus involved "excessive entanglement between government and religion."

However, the Court has upheld the use of tax funds to provide students attending church-related schools with nonreligious textbooks, lunches, transportation, sign-language interpreting, and special education teachers. And the Court has upheld a state's granting of tax credits to parents whose children attend private schools, including religious schools.[21] The Court has also upheld government grants of money to church-related colleges and universities for secular purposes.[22] The Court has ruled that if public

SEPARATION ANXIETY

A Menorah-lighting ceremony celebrating Chanukah on public property near the White House. The Supreme Court is divided over whether such public displays violate the Establishment Clause of the 1st Amendment, which is interpreted as requiring the separation of church and state.

buildings are open to use for secular organizations, they must also be opened to use by religious organizations.[23] And the Court has held that a state institution (the University of Virginia) not only can but must grant student activity fees to religious organizations on the same basis as it grants these fees to secular organizations.[24]

The Supreme Court has upheld tax exemptions for churches on the grounds that "the role of religious organizations as charitable associations, in furthering the secular objectives of the state, has become a fundamental concept in our society."[25] It held that schools must allow after-school meetings on school property by religious groups if such a privilege is extended to nonreligious groups.[26] Deductions on federal income tax returns for church contributions are also constitutional. The Supreme Court allows states to close stores on Sundays and otherwise set aside that day, as long as there is a secular purpose—such as "rest, repose, recreation and tranquility"—in doing so.[27]

But the Court has not always acted to "accommodate" religion. In a controversial case, the Court held that a Christmas nativity scene sitting alone on public property was an official "endorsement" of Christian belief and therefore violated the Establishment Clause. However, if the Christian display was accompanied by a Menorah, a traditional Christmas tree, Santa Claus and reindeer, it would simply be "taking note of the season" and not an unconstitutional endorsement of religion.[28] And in another case, the Supreme Court held that a Louisiana law requiring the teaching of "creationism" along with evolution in the public schools was an unconstitutional establishment of a religious belief.[29]

Critics of the Supreme Court have complained of inconsistencies and contradictions in its consideration of cases involving the Establishment Clause. The Court has made some extremely fine distinctions in considering whether the public display of the Ten Commandments is or is not an establishment of religion. The Court held that a law requiring the posting of the 10 Commandments in every classroom in Kentucky was unconstitutional, but a monument to the 10 Commandments on the grounds of the Texas state capital was merely "an acknowledgment of our nation's heritage."[30] (See also *The Game, the Rules, the Players:* Are We One Nation "Under God"?)

Prayer in the School

The Supreme Court's most controversial interpretation of the Establishment Clause involved the question of prayer and Bible-reading ceremonies conducted by public schools. The practice of opening the school day with prayer and Bible-reading ceremonies was once widespread in American public schools. To avoid the denominational aspects of these ceremonies, New York State's Board of Regents substituted the following nondenominational prayer, which it required to be said aloud in each class in the presence of a teacher at the beginning of each school day: "Almighty God, we acknowledge our dependence upon Thee, and we beg Thy blessings upon us, our parents, our teachers, and our country." New York argued that this brief prayer did not violate the Establishment Clause, because the prayer was denominationally neutral and because student participation in the prayer was voluntary. However, in *Engel v. Vitale* (1962), the Supreme Court stated that "the constitutional prohibition against laws respecting an establishment of a religion must at least mean in this country it is no part of the business of government to compose official prayers for any group of the American people to recite as part of a religious program carried on by government." The Court pointed out that making prayer voluntary did not free it from the prohibitions of the Establishment Clause, and that clause prevented the *establishment* of a religious ceremony by a government agency regardless of whether the ceremony was voluntary.[31]

One year later, in the case of *Abington Township v. Schempp*, the Court considered the constitutionality of Bible-reading ceremonies in the public schools. Here again, even though the children were not required to participate, the Court found that Bible reading as an opening exercise in the schools was a religious ceremony. The justices went to some trouble in the majority opinion to point out that they were not "throwing the Bible out of the schools." They specifically stated that the *study* of the Bible or of religion, when presented objectively and as part of a secular program of education, did not violate the 1st Amendment; however, religious *ceremonies* involving Bible reading or prayer established by a state or school did.[32]

"Voluntary" Prayer

State efforts to encourage "voluntary prayer" in public schools have also been struck down by the Supreme Court as unconstitutional. When the state of Alabama authorized a period of silence for "meditation or voluntary prayer" in public schools, the Court ruled that this action was an "establishment of religion." The Court said the law had no secular purpose, that it conveyed "a message of state endorsement and promotion of prayer," and that its real intent was to encourage prayer in public schools.[33] In a stinging dissenting opinion, Justice William Rehnquist noted that the Supreme Court itself opened its session with a prayer and that both houses of Congress opened every session with prayers led by official chaplains paid by the government. In 1992, the Court held that invocations and benedictions at public high school graduation ceremonies were an unconstitutional establishment of religion.[34] And in 2000, the Court ruled that student-led "invocations" at football games were unconstitutional. A Texas school district that allowed students to use its public address system at football games "to solemnize the event" was violating the Establishment Clause. "The Constitution demands that schools not force on students the difficult choice between whether to attend these games or to risk facing a personally offensive religious ritual."[35] (See *The Game, the Rules, the Players*: Are We One Nation "Under God"?)

State Vouchers to Attend Religious Schools

Another important issue arising under the Establishment Clause is the granting of educational vouchers to parents to spend at any school they choose, including religious schools. State governments redeem the vouchers submitted by schools by paying specific amounts for each student enrolled. When Ohio initiated a "Scholarship Program" that provided tuition aid to certain students in the Cleveland City School District who could choose to use this aid to attend either public or private or religious schools of their parents' choosing, opponents challenged the program in federal court, arguing that it "advanced a religious mission" in violation of the Establishment Clause. Although parents could use the vouchers to send their children to other public schools or nonreligious private schools, over 90 percent of the students participating in the scholarship program were enrolled in religiously affiliated schools. In 2002, the U.S. Supreme Court held (in a narrow 5–4 decision) that the program did *not* violate the Constitution.[36] The Court reasoned that the program was neutral with respect to religion and provided assistance directly to citizens who, in turn, directed this aid to religious schools wholly as a result of their own independent private choices. The incidental advancement of a religious mission is reasonably attributed to the individual recipients, not the government, "whose role ends with the distribution of benefits."

Freedom of Speech and the Press

14.3 Assess the extent of and limits on freedom of speech and the press and trace the evolution of the Supreme Court's view of obscenity.

lthough the 1st Amendment is absolute in its wording ("Congress shall pass no law . . . abridging the freedom of speech"), the Supreme Court has never been willing to interpret this statement as a protection of *all* speech. What kinds of speech does the 1st Amendment protect from government control, and what kinds of speech may be constitutionally prohibited?

Clear and Present Danger Doctrine

The classic example of speech that can be prohibited was given by Justice Oliver Wendell Holmes in 1919: "The most stringent protection of free speech would not protect a man in falsely shouting 'fire' in a theater and causing a panic."[37] Although Holmes recognized that the government may prevent speech that creates a serious and immediate danger to society, he objected to government attempts to stifle critics of its policies, such as the Espionage Act of 1917 and the Sedition Act of 1918. The Sedition Act prohibited, among other things, speech that was meant to discourage the sale of war bonds and "disloyal" speech about the government, the Constitution, the military forces, or the flag of the United States. In the case of *Gitlow v. New York*, the majority supported the right of the government to curtail any speech that "tended to subvert or imperil the government," but Holmes dissented, arguing that "every idea is an incitement. It offers itself for belief and if believed it is acted on unless some other belief outweighs it."[38] Unless the expression of an idea created a *serious and immediate danger*, Holmes argued that it should be tolerated and combated or defeated only by the expression of better ideas. Holmes's standard for determining the limits of free expression became known as the **clear and present danger doctrine**. Government should not curtail speech merely because it *might tend* to cause a future danger: "The question in every case is whether the words used are used in such circumstances and are of such a nature as to create a clear and present danger that they will bring about the substantive evils that Congress has a right to prevent."[39] Holmes's argument inspired a long struggle in the courts to strengthen constitutional protections for speech and press.

Although Holmes was the first to use the phrase "clear and present danger," it was Justice Louis D. Brandeis who later developed the doctrine into a valuable constitutional principle that the Supreme Court gradually came to adopt. Brandeis explained that the doctrine involved two elements: (1) the clearness or seriousness of the expression, and (2) the immediacy of the danger flowing from the speech. With regard to immediacy he wrote,

> No danger flowing from speech can be deemed clear and present, unless the incidence of the evil apprehended is so imminent that it may befall before there is opportunity for full discussion. If there be time to expose through discussion the falsehood and fallacies, to avert the evil by the processes of education, the remedy to be applied is more speech, not enforced silence.

And with regard to seriousness he wrote,

> Moreover, even imminent danger cannot justify resort to prohibition [of speech] . . . unless the evil apprehended is relatively serious. Prohibition of free speech and assembly is a measure so stringent that it would be inappropriate as the means for averting a relatively trivial harm to society. . . . There must be the probability of serious injury to the State.[40]

clear and present danger doctrine
Standard used by the courts to determine whether speech may be restricted; only speech that creates a serious and immediate danger to society may be restricted.

preferred position
Refers to the tendency of the courts to give preference to the 1st Amendment rights to speech, press, and assembly when faced with conflicts.

Preferred Position Doctrine

Over the years, the Supreme Court has given the 1st Amendment freedoms of speech, press, and assembly a special **preferred position** in constitutional law. These freedoms are especially important to the preservation of democracy. If speech, press, or assembly are prohibited by government, the people have no way to correct the government through democratic processes. Thus the burden of proof rests on the *government* to justify any restrictions on speech, writing, or assembly.[41] In other words, any speech or writing is presumed constitutional unless the government proves that a serious and immediate danger would ensue if the speech were allowed.

The Cold War Challenge

Despite the Supreme Court's endorsement of the clear and present danger and preferred position doctrines, in times of perceived national crisis the courts have been willing to permit some government restrictions of speech, press, and assembly. At the

14.1

14.2

14.3

14.4

14.5

14.6

14.7

14.8

freedom of expression
Collectively, the 1st Amendment rights to free speech, press, and assembly.

symbolic speech
Actions other than speech itself but protected by the 1st Amendment because they constitute political expression.

A THREAT OF VIOLENCE

The Supreme Court ruled in 2003 that cross burning was meant to intimidate and was therefore not protected as symbolic speech by the 1st Amendment.

outbreak of World War II, just prior to the United States's entry into that world conflict, Congress passed the Smith Act, which stated,

> It shall be unlawful for any person to knowingly or willfully advocate, abet, advise, or teach the duty, necessity, desirability, or propriety of overthrowing or destroying any government in the United States by force or violence, or by the assassination of any officer of any such government.

Congress justified its action in terms of national security, initially as a protection against fascism during World War II, then later as a protection against communism in the early days of the Cold War.

In 1949, the Department of Justice prosecuted Eugene V. Dennis and 10 other top leaders of the Communist Party of the United States for violation of the Smith Act. A jury found them guilty of violating the act, and the party leaders were sentenced to jail terms ranging from one to five years. In 1951, the case of *Dennis v. United States* came to the Supreme Court on appeal. In upholding the conviction of the Communist Party leaders, the Court seemed to abandon Brandeis's idea that "present" meant "before there is opportunity for full discussion."[42] It seemed to substitute clear and *probable* for clear and *present*.

Since that time, however, the Supreme Court has returned to a policy closer to the original clear and present danger doctrine. As the Cold War progressed, Americans grew to view communism as a serious threat to democracy, but not a *present* danger. The overthrow of the American government advocated by communists was not an incitement to *immediate* action. A democracy must not itself become authoritarian to protect itself from authoritarianism. In later cases, the Supreme Court held that the mere advocacy of revolution, apart from unlawful action, is protected by the 1st Amendment.[43] It struck down federal laws requiring communist organizations to register with the government,[44] laws requiring individuals to sign "loyalty oaths,"[45] laws prohibiting communists from working in defense plants,[46] and laws stripping passports from Communist Party leaders.[47] In short, once the perceived Cold War crisis began to fade, the Supreme Court reasserted the 1st Amendment rights of individuals and groups.

Symbolic Speech

The 1st Amendment's guarantees of speech, press, and assembly are broadly interpreted to mean **freedom of expression**. Political expression encompasses more than just words. For example, when Mary Beth Tinker and her brothers were suspended for wearing black armbands to high school to protest the Vietnam War, they argued that the wearing of armbands constituted **symbolic speech** protected by the 1st Amendment. The Supreme Court agreed, noting that the school did not prohibit all wearing of symbols but instead singled out this particular expression for disciplinary action.[48]

The Supreme Court continues to wrestle with the question of what kinds of conduct are symbolic speech protected by the 1st Amendment and what kinds of conduct are outside of this protection. Symbolic speech, like speech itself, cannot be banned just because it offends people. "If there is only one bedrock principle underlying the First Amendment, it is that the Government may not prohibit the expression of an idea simply because society finds the idea itself offensive or disagreeable."[49] The Court held that flag burning was "symbolic speech"[50] and therefore protected by the 1st Amendment. In contrast, cross burning was "a form of intimidation and a threat of impending violence"[51] and therefore not protected by the 1st Amendment.

Speech and Public Order

The Supreme Court has wrestled with the question of whether speech can be prohibited when it stirs audiences to public disorder, not because the speaker urges lawless action but because the audience reacts with hostility. Can a speaker be arrested because of the *audience's* disorderly behavior? In an early case, the Supreme

Court fashioned a *fighting words doctrine*, to the effect that words that "ordinary men know are likely to cause a fight" may be prohibited.[52] But later the Court saw that this doctrine could create a huge constitutional hole in the 1st Amendment guarantee of free speech. Authorities could curtail speech simply because it met with audience hostility. The Court recognized that "speech is often provocative and challenging. It may . . . have profound unsettling effects. . . . That is why freedom of speech, while not absolute, is nevertheless protected against censorship."[53] The Court has held that the 1st Amendment protects the use of profane words when used to express an idea: "One man's vulgarity may be another's lyric."[54] And the Court has consistently refused to allow government authorities to use prior restraint to ban speech that might create a disturbance.

The Supreme Court has held that reasonable restrictions can be placed on the manner and places of protests. Students may conduct protests on designated places on campus or places that do not interrupt the educational process. Cities can require permits for parades as long as they do not discriminate in the issuance of permits. Authorities cannot selectively ban some protests and parades but not others; authorities cannot regulate the content of signs or speech. The Court most recently held that a state-mandated 35-foot "buffer zone" between abortion protesters and a clinic in Massachusetts limited speech too broadly. The Court did not strike down the use of buffer zones, which it had previously endorsed at distances as great as 100 feet.[55]

☐ Campus Speech

Many colleges and universities have undertaken to ban speech that is considered racist, sexist, homophobic, or otherwise "insensitive" to the feelings of women and minorities. Varieties of "speech codes," "hate codes," and sexual harassment regulations that prohibit verbal expressions raise serious constitutional questions, especially at state-supported colleges and universities. The 1st Amendment includes insulting or offensive racist or sexist words or comments in its protection (see *Who's Getting What?* Political Correctness Versus Free Speech on Campus). Many of these college and university regulations would not withstand a judicial challenge if students or faculty undertook to oppose them in federal court.

☐ Hate Speech and Hate Crimes

"Hate" speech is usually defined as hostile or prejudicial attitudes expressed toward another person's or group's characteristics, notably sex, race, ethnicity, religion, or sexual orientation. Banning hate speech is now common at colleges and universities, in business employment and sports enterprises, on radio and television, and in the press. But do *government* prohibitions on hate speech violate the 1st Amendment?

Historically, the Supreme Court viewed prohibitions on offensive speech as unconstitutional infringements of 1st Amendment freedoms. "The remedy to be applied is more speech, not enforced silence."[56]

The Supreme Court was called upon to review prohibitions on hate speech in 1992 when the city of St. Paul, Minnesota, enacted an ordinance prohibiting any communication that "arouses anger, alarm, or resentment among others on the basis of race, color, creed, religion, or gender." The ordinance defined such expressions as "disorderly conduct" and made them misdemeanors punishable by law. But the Supreme Court, in a unanimous decision, struck down the city's effort to prohibit expressions only because they cause "hurt feelings, offense, or resentment." Speech expressing racial, gender, or religious intolerance is still speech, and it is protected by the 1st Amendment.[57]

However, the Supreme Court is willing to recognize that bias-motivated crimes—crimes intentionally directed at a victim because of his or her race, religion, disability, national origin, or sexual orientation—may be more heavily punished than the same crimes inspired by other motives. The Court held that a criminal defendant's "abstract beliefs, however obnoxious to most people, may not be taken into consideration by a

14.1
14.2
14.3
14.4
14.5
14.6
14.7
14.8

Who's Getting What?

Political Correctness Versus Free Speech on Campus

Universities have a very special responsibility to protect freedom of expression. The free and unfettered exchange of views is essential to the advancement of knowledge—the very purpose of universities. For centuries universities have fought to protect academic freedom from pressures arising from the world *outside* of the campus—governments, interest groups, financial contributors—arguing that the university must be a protected enclave for free expression of ideas. But today's threat to academic freedom arises from *within* universities—from efforts by administrations, faculty, and campus groups to suppress ideas, opinions, and language that are not "politically correct" (PC). PC activists seek to suppress opinions and expressions they consider to be racist, sexist, "homophobic," or otherwise "insensitive" to specified groups.[a]

Speech Codes

The experience at the University of Michigan with its "Policy on Discrimination and Discriminatory Harassment" illustrates the battles occurring on many campuses over 1st Amendment rights. In 1988, a series of racial incidents on campus prompted the university to officially ban "any behavior verbal or physical" that "stigmatized" an individual "on the basis of race, ethnicity, religion, sex, sexual orientation, creed, national origin, ancestry, age, marital status, handicap, or Vietnam era veteran status" or that created "an intimidating, hostile, or demeaning environment for educational pursuits." A published guide provided examples of banned activity, which included the following:

- A male student makes remarks in class like "women just aren't as good in this field as men."
- Jokes about gay men and lesbians.
- Commenting in a derogatory way about a particular person or group's physical appearance or sexual orientation, or their cultural origins, or religious beliefs.

WIZARD OF SPEECH

It is difficult to ban unpopular speech. Former American Nazi and Ku Klux Klansman David Duke got his start giving white supremacy speeches at Louisiana State University's Free Speech Alley in the 1970s.

Free Speech

In 1989, "John Doe," a psychology graduate student studying gender differences in personality traits and mental functions, filed suit in federal court requesting that the University of Michigan policy be declared a violation of the 1st Amendment. (He was permitted by the court to remain anonymous because of fear of retribution.) He was joined in his complaint against the university by the American Civil Liberties Union.

In its decision, the court acknowledged that the university had a legal responsibility to prevent racial or sexual discrimination or harassment. However, it did not have a right to

> establish an anti-discrimination policy which had the effect of prohibiting certain speech because it disagreed with ideas or messages sought to be conveyed. . . . Nor could the University proscribe speech simply because it was found to be offensive, even gravely so, by large numbers of people. . . . These principles acquire a special significance in the University setting, where the free and unfettered interplay of competing views is essential to the institution's educational mission. . . . While the Court is sympathetic to the University's obligation to ensure educational opportunities for all of its students, such efforts must not be at the expense of free speech.[b]

It seems ironic that students and faculty now must seek the protection of the federal courts from attempts by universities to limit speech. Traditionally, universities themselves fought to protect academic freedom. Academic freedom included the freedom of faculty and students to express themselves in the classroom, on the campus, and in writing, on controversial and sensitive topics, including race and gender. It was recognized that students often express ideas that are biased or ill informed, immature, or crudely expressed. But students were taught that the remedy for offensive language or off-color remarks or ill-chosen examples was more enlightened speech, not the suppression of speech.

QUESTIONS

1. Do you have a right to not be offended?
2. Do speech codes promote, or inhibit, meaningful conversations about important subjects?
3. Does your college have a speech code? What does it say?

[a]Dinesh D'Souza. *Illiberal Education: The Politics of Race and Sex on Campus* (New York: Vintage Books, 1992).
[b]*John Doe v. University of Michigan*, 721 F. Supp. 852 (1989).

sentencing judge."[58] But a defendant's *motive* for committing a particular criminal act has traditionally been a factor in sentencing, and a defendant's verbal statements can be used to determine motive.

commercial speech
Advertising communications given only partial protection under the 1st Amendment to the Constitution.

Commercial Speech

Do 1st Amendment freedoms of expression apply to commercial advertising? The Supreme Court has frequently asserted that **commercial speech** is protected by the 1st Amendment. The Court held that states cannot outlaw price advertising by pharmacists[59] or advertising for services by attorneys[60] and that cities cannot outlaw posting "For Sale" signs on property, even in the interests of halting white flight and promoting racially integrated neighborhoods. Advertising is the "dissemination of information" and is constitutionally protected;[61] but advertising rights are not absolute. The public's interest in receiving true or correct information is balanced against the expression rights of the advertiser. This "balancing of interests" approach thus allows the Federal Communications Commission to regulate the contents of advertising on radio and television and even to ban advertising for certain products such as cigarettes, and the Federal Trade Commission to enforce "truth" in advertising by requiring commercial packages and advertisers to prove all claims for their products.

Libel and Slander

Libel and slander have never been protected by the 1st Amendment against subsequent punishment. Once a communication is determined to be libelous or slanderous, it is outside of the protection of the 1st Amendment. The courts have traditionally defined "libel" as a "damaging falsehood." However, if plaintiffs are public officials, they must prove that the statements made about them are not only false and damaging but also "made with actual malice"—that is, with knowledge that they are false or with "reckless disregard" of the truth—in order to prove libel.[62] (See also *Who's Getting What?* Political Correctness Versus Free Speech on Campus.)

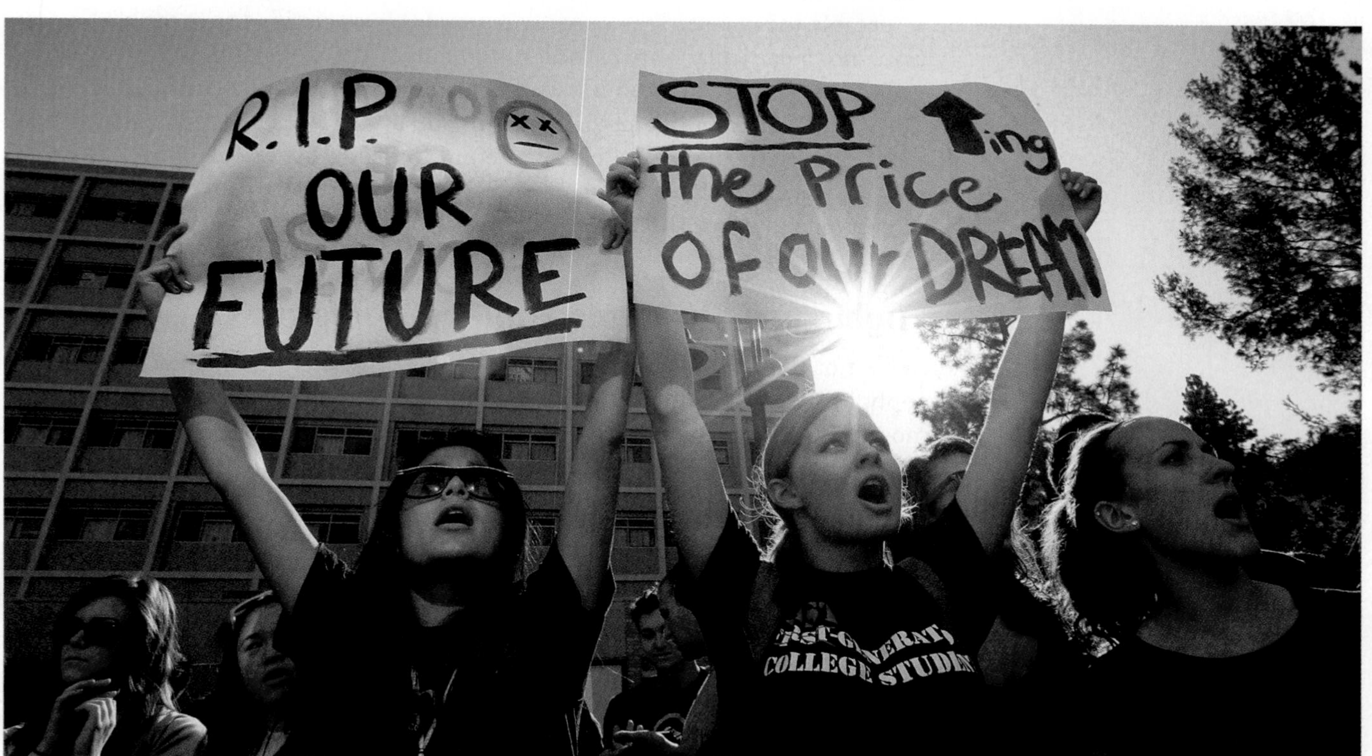

STUDENT PROTEST

UCLA students protest a tuition hike, November, 2009. The University of California Board of Regents raised tuition and cut spending in an effort to close the state's huge budget deficit.

14.1
14.2
14.3
14.4
14.5
14.6
14.7
14.8

EYE OF THE BEHOLDER

The Supreme Court recognizes "local community standards" in determining what is, or is not, obscene. Here, tourists walk past adult entertainment lounges in New Orleans' historic Vieux Carré.

Obscenity and the Law

Obscene materials of all kinds—words, publications, photos, videotapes, films—are *not* protected by the 1st Amendment. Most states ban the publication, sale, or possession of obscene material, and Congress bans its shipment in the mails. Because obscene material is not protected by the 1st Amendment, it can be banned without even an attempt to prove that it results in antisocial conduct. In other words, it is not necessary to show that obscene material would result in a clear and present danger to society, the test used to decide the legitimacy of *speech*. In order to ban obscene materials, the government need only prove that they are *obscene*.

Defining "obscenity" has confounded legislatures and the courts for years, however. State and federal laws often define pornography and obscenity in such terms as "lewd," "lascivious," "filthy," "indecent," "disgusting"—all equally as vague as "obscene." "Pornography" is simply a synonym for "obscenity." *Soft-core pornography* usually denotes nakedness and sexually suggestive poses; it is less likely to confront legal barriers. *Hard-core pornography* usually denotes explicit sexual activity. After many fruitless efforts by the Supreme Court to come up with a workable definition of "pornography" or "obscenity," a frustrated Justice Potter Stewart wrote the now-famous quote in 1974, "I shall not today attempt further to define [hard-core pornography]. . . . But *I know it when I see it*."[63]

Slackening Standards: *Roth v. United States*

The Court's first comprehensive effort to define "obscenity" came in *Roth v. United States* (1957). Although the Court upheld Roth's conviction for distributing pornographic magazines through the mails, it defined "obscenity" somewhat narrowly: "Whether to the average person applying contemporary community standards, the dominant theme of the material, taken as a whole, appeals to prurient interests."[64]

Note that the material must be obscene to the *average* person, not to children or particular groups of adults who might be especially offended by pornography. The standard is "contemporary," suggesting that what was once regarded as obscene might be acceptable today. Later, the *community standard* was clarified to mean the "society at large," not a particular state or local community.[65] The material must be "considered as a whole," meaning that even if a work includes some obscene material, it is still acceptable if its "dominant theme" is something other than "prurient." The Court added that a work must be "utterly without redeeming social or literary merit" in order to be judged obscene.[66] The Court never really said what a "prurient" interest was but reassured everyone that "sex and obscenity are not synonymous."

Tightening Standards: *Miller v. California*

The effect of the Roth decision, and the many and varied attempts by lower courts to apply its slippery standards, tended to limit law enforcement efforts to combat pornography during the 1960s and 1970s. The Supreme Court itself came under ridicule when it was reported that the justices had set up a movie room in the basement of the Supreme Court building to view films that had been brought before them in obscenity cases.[67]

So the Supreme Court tried again, in *Miller v. California* (1973), to give law-enforcement officials some clearer standards in determining obscenity. Although the Court retained the "average person" and "contemporary" standards, it redefined "community" to mean the *local* community rather than the society at large. It also defined "prurient" as "patently offensive" representations or descriptions of "ultimate sex acts, normal or perverted, actual or simulated," as well as "masturbation, excretory functions, and lewd exhibition of the genitals." It rejected the earlier requirement that the work had to be "utterly without redeeming social value" in order to be judged obscene, and it substituted instead "lacks serious literary, artistic, political, or scientific value."[68]

The effect of the Supreme Court's *Miller* standards has been to increase the likelihood of conviction in obscenity–pornography cases. It is easier to prove that a work lacks serious value than to prove that it is utterly without redeeming merit. Moreover, the *local community standard* allows prosecution of adult bookstores and X-rated video stores in some communities, while allowing the same stores to operate in other communities. The Supreme Court has also upheld local ordinances that ban nudity in public places, including bars and lounges. The Court rejected the argument that nude dancing was "expressive" conduct.[69]

Porn on the Internet

The emergence of new technologies challenges courts in the application of 1st Amendment principles. The Internet allows users to gain access to information worldwide, from bomb-making instructions and sex conversations to obscene video; interactive, live-action sex sites; and even child pornography. Many commercial access services ban obscene messages and exclude sites with sexually offensive commentary. Software programs that screen out pornographic content are readily available to consumers. Nonetheless, despite the efforts to limit and screen pornographic content on the Internet, pornography is a $100-billion worldwide industry, largely driven by U.S.-made content. Can *government* try to ban such material from the Internet without violating 1st Amendment freedoms?

Congress tried unsuccessfully to ban "indecent" and "patently offensive" communications from the Internet in its Communications Decency Act of 1996. Proponents of the law cited the need to protect children from pornography. But in 1997, the Supreme Court held the act unconstitutional: "Notwithstanding the legitimacy and importance of the Congressional goal of protecting children from harmful materials, we agree that the statute abridges freedom of speech protected by the 1st Amendment." Government cannot limit Internet messages "to only what is fit for children." The Supreme Court agreed with the assertion that "as the most participatory form of mass speech yet developed, [the Internet] deserves the highest protection from government intrusion."[70]

Child Pornography

In 1982, the U.S. Supreme Court struck a hard blow against child pornography—the "dissemination of material depicting children engaged in sexual conduct regardless of whether the material is obscene."[71] Such material includes any visual depiction of children performing sexual acts or lewdly exhibiting their genitals. The Court reasoned that films or photographs of sexual exploitation and abuse of children were "intrinsically related" to criminal activity; such material was evidence that a crime has been committed. Thus the test for *child* pornography was much stricter than the standards set for obscene material. It is not necessary to show that the sexual depiction of children is "obscene" (under the *Miller* standards) in order to ban such material; it is only necessary to show that children were used in the production of the material.

But what if the images of children involved in sexual activity are produced by means other than using real children, such as the use of youthful-looking adults or computer-imaging technology? In the Child Pornography Prevention Act of 1996, Congress tried to prohibit "any visual depiction, including any photograph, film, video, picture, or computer or computer-generated image … [that] is, or appears to be, of a minor engaging in sexually explicit conduct." Congress did not construct this act to meet the *Miller* standards; it prohibited *any* depictions of sexually explicit activity by children, whether or not they contravened community standards or had serious redeeming value. (Other countries have different standards. For example, in France, it is illegal to use underage actors in sexually explicit roles, but the film itself is not illegal.)

But the Supreme Court, in a highly controversial (6–3) decision, held that there was an important distinction between actual and virtual child pornography. Virtual child pornography and adults posing as minors do not directly involve the exploitation or abuse of children. The Court held that the congressional definition of child

14.1
14.2
14.3
14.4
14.5
14.6
14.7
14.8

prior restraint
Government actions to restrict publication of a magazine, newspaper, or books on grounds of libel, obscenity, or other legal violations prior to actual publication of the work.

pornography was overly broad; the mere assertion that such material might encourage pedophiles to seduce children was not sufficient to prohibit it. "The First Amendment requires a more precise restriction."[72]

In January 2011, MTV premiered *Skins,* an American adaptation of a racy BBC series that dealt with casual sex, casual drug use, eating disorders, and the social pressures of a group of dysthymic teenagers. The show took the added step of using teenage actors to portray teenagers, rather than older actors who looked younger, and like the BBC series, it was developed by a young production and writing team. And, it showed a lot of skin and plenty of sex. As a consequence, the group Parents Television Council trained its guns on MTV, urging a (successful) sponsor boycott of *Skins.* The group also urged an investigation of whether the nudity and simulated sex in *Skins* by teenage actors violated American child porn laws. Ultimately, the American marketplace decided about *Skins;* the audience fell by two-thirds from the January premiere, leading MTV to cancel the show in June, stating "*Skins* is a global television phenomenon that, unfortunately, didn't connect with a U.S. audience as much as we had hoped."

Freedom of the Press

Democracy depends on the free expression of ideas. Authoritarian regimes either monopolize the media or subject them to strict licensing and censorship of their content. The idea of a free and independent press is deeply rooted in the evolution of democratic government.

No-Prior-Restraint Doctrine

Long before the Bill of Rights was written, English law protected newspapers from government restrictions or licensing prior to publication—a practice called **prior restraint**. This protection, however, does not mean that publishers are exempt from *subsequent punishment* for libelous, obscene, or other illegal publications. Prior restraint is more dangerous to free expression because it allows the government to censor the work prior to publication and forces the defendants to *prove* that their material should *not* be censored. In contrast, subsequent punishment requires a trial in which the government must prove that the defendant's published materials are unlawful.

In *Near v. Minnesota* (1931), a muckraking publication that accused local officials of trafficking with gangsters was barred from publishing under a Minnesota law that prohibited the publication of a "malicious, scandalous or defamatory newspaper." The Supreme Court struck down the law as unconstitutional, affirming the *no-prior-restraint doctrine*. The doctrine is not absolute. Chief Justice Charles Evans Hughes noted that prior government censorship might be constitutional "if publication … threatened the country's safety in times of war."[73]

Yet the question of whether or not the government can restrain publication of stories that present a serious threat to national security remains unanswered. For example, can the government restrain the press from reporting in advance on the time and place of an impending U.S. military action, thereby warning an enemy and perhaps adding to American casualties? In the most important case on this question, *New York Times v. United States* (1971), the Supreme Court upheld the right of the newspaper to publish secret documents that had been stolen from State Department and Defense Department files. The material covered U.S. policy decisions in Vietnam, and it was published while the war was still being waged. But five separate (concurring) opinions were written by justices in the majority as well as two dissenting opinions. Only two justices argued that government can *never* restrain any publication, regardless of the seriousness or immediacy of the harm. Others in the majority cited the government's failure to show proof in this case that publication "would surely result in direct, immediate, and irreparable damage to our nation or its people."[74] Presumably, if the government had produced such proof, the case might have been decided differently. The media interpret the decision as a blanket protection to publish anything they wish regardless of harm to government or society.

☐ Film Censorship

The no-prior-restraint doctrine was developed to protect the print media—books, magazines, newspapers. When the motion picture industry was in its infancy, the Supreme Court held that films were "business, pure and simple" and were not entitled to the protection of the 1st Amendment.[75] But as films grew in importance, the Court gradually extended 1st Amendment freedoms to cover motion pictures.[76] However, the Supreme Court has not given the film industry the same strong no-prior-restraint protection it has given the press. The Court has approved government requirements for prior submission of films to official censors, as long as (1) the burden of proof that the film is obscene rests with the censor; (2) a procedure exists for judicial determination of the issue; and (3) censors are required to act speedily.[77] To avoid government-imposed censorship, the motion picture industry first adopted its own system of rating films:

G: suitable for all audiences

PG: parental guidance suggested

PG-13: parental guidance strongly suggested for children under 13

R: restricted to those 17 or older unless accompanied by a parent or guardian

NC-17: no one under 17 admitted

Some city governments have sought to restrict showing of NC-17 films, and their restrictions have been upheld by the Courts.[78]

☐ Radio and Television Censorship

The Federal Communications Commission was created in 1934 to allocate broadcast frequencies and to license stations. The exclusive right to use a particular frequency is a "public trust." Thus, broadcasters, unlike newspapers and magazines, are licensed by the government and subject to government rules. Although the 1st Amendment protects broadcasters, the Supreme Court has recognized the special obligations that may be imposed on them in exchange for the exclusive right to use a broadcast frequency. "No one has a First Amendment right to a license or to monopolize a radio frequency; to deny a station license because 'the public interest' requires it, is not a denial of free speech."[79] Thus, the Court has upheld FCC-imposed "equal time" and "fairness" rules against broadcasters, even while striking down government attempts to impose the same rules on newspapers.[80]

☐ Media Claims for Special Rights

The news media make various claims to special rights arising out of the 1st Amendment's guarantee of a free press. Reporters argue, for example, that they should be able to protect their news sources and are not obliged to give testimony in criminal cases when they have obtained evidence in confidence. However, the only witnesses the Constitution exempts from compulsory testimony are defendants themselves, who enjoy the 5th Amendment's protection against "self-incrimination." The Supreme Court has flatly rejected reporters' claims to a privilege against compulsory testimony. "We cannot seriously entertain the notion that the First Amendment protects a newsman's agreement to conceal the criminal conduct of his source, or evidence thereof, on the theory that it is better to write about a crime than to do something about it."[81]

Despite these rulings, reporters regularly boast of their willingness to go to jail to protect sources, and many have done so. But the media have also pressured the nation's legislatures for protection. Congress has passed the Privacy Protection Act, which sharply limits the ability of law-enforcement officials to search press offices, and many states have passed **shield laws** specifically protecting reporters from giving testimony in criminal cases.

shield laws
Laws in some states that give reporters the right to refuse to name their sources or to release their notes in court cases; may be overturned by the courts when such refusals jeopardize a fair trial for a defendant.

Privacy, Abortion, and the Constitution

14.4 Identify protections granted under the right to privacy.

right of "privacy" is not expressly provided for anywhere in the Constitution. But does the word *liberty* in the 1st and 14th Amendments include a constitutional right to privacy?

Finding a Right to Privacy

The U.S. Supreme Court found a right of privacy in the Constitution when it struck down a Connecticut law prohibiting the use of contraceptives in 1965. Estelle Griswold had opened a birth control clinic on behalf of the Planned Parenthood League of that state and was distributing contraceptives in violation of the state statute prohibiting their use. She challenged the constitutionality of the statute, even though there is no direct reference to birth control in the Bill of Rights. The Supreme Court upheld Griswold's challenge, finding a right of privacy, according to Justice William O. Douglas, in the "penumbras formed by the emanations from" the 1st, 3rd, 4th, 5th, 9th, and 14th Amendments. "Various guarantees create a zone of privacy. . . . Would we allow the police to search the sacred precincts of marital bedrooms for telltale signs of the use of contraceptives? The very idea is repulsive to the notion of privacy surrounding the marriage relationship." In concurrent opinions, other justices found the right of privacy in the 9th Amendment: "The enumeration in the Constitution of certain rights, shall not be construed to deny or disparage others retained by the people."[82]

Roe v. Wade

The fact that *Griswold* dealt with reproduction gave encouragement to groups advocating abortion rights. In 1969, Norma McCorvey sought an abortion in Texas but was refused by doctors who cited a state law prohibiting abortion except to save a woman's life. McCorvey challenged the Texas law in federal courts on a variety of constitutional grounds, including the right to privacy. McCorvey became "Jane Roe," and the case became one of the most controversial in the Supreme Court's history.[83]

The Supreme Court ruled that the constitutional right of privacy as well as the 14th Amendment's guarantee of "liberty" included a woman's decision to bear or not to bear a child. The Court held that the word *person* in the Constitution did *not* include the unborn child; therefore, the 5th and 14th Amendments' guarantee of "life, liberty, or property" did not protect the "life" of the fetus. The Court also ruled that a state's power to protect the health and safety of the mother could not justify any restriction on abortion in the first three months of pregnancy. Between the third and sixth months of pregnancy, a state could set standards for abortion procedures in order to protect the health of women, but a state could not prohibit abortions. Only in the final three months could a state prohibit or regulate abortion to protect the unborn.

Rather than end the political controversy over abortion, *Roe v. Wade* set off a conflagration. Congress defeated efforts to pass a constitutional amendment restricting abortion or declaring that life begins at conception. However, when Congress banned the use of federal funds under Medicaid (medical care for the poor) for abortions except to protect the life of a woman, the Supreme Court upheld the ban, holding that there was no constitutional obligation for governments to *pay* for abortions.[84]

Reaffirming *Roe v. Wade*

Abortion has become such a polarizing issue that "pro-choice" and "pro-life" groups are generally unwilling to search out a middle ground—it is the defining American political issue for three decades. The Supreme Court has chosen a policy of affirming a woman's right to abortion while upholding modest restrictions, as evidenced by the Court's ruling in *Planned Parenthood of Pennsylvania v. Casey* (1992).[85]

In this case, the Supreme Court considered a series of restrictions on abortion enacted by Pennsylvania: physicians must inform women of risks and alternatives; women must wait 24 hours after requesting an abortion before having one; and the parents of minors must be notified. It struck down a requirement that spouses be notified. Later, the court struck drawn a parental notification law that did not provide an exception for a judge to withhold notification when it would not be in the best interest of the minor.

Justice Sandra Day O'Connor took the lead in forming a moderate, swing bloc on the Court. Her majority opinion strongly reaffirmed the fundamental right of abortion, both on the basis of the 14th Amendment and on the principle of *stare decisis*. But the majority also upheld states' rights to protect any fetus that reached the point of "viability." The Court went on to establish a new standard for constitutionally evaluating restrictions: they must not impose an "undue burden" on women seeking abortion or place "substantial obstacles" in her path. All of Pennsylvania's restrictions met this standard and were upheld—except spousal notification.

"Partial-Birth Abortion"

An abortion procedure known as "intact dilation and evacuation" or "partial-birth abortion" has been the object of prohibitions by a number of states and by Congress itself. This procedure, which is used in very few abortions, involves partial delivery of the fetus feet first, then vacuuming out the brain and crushing the skull to ease complete removal. A Nebraska law banning the procedure was declared an unconstitutional "undue burden" on a woman's right to abortion by the Supreme Court in 2002; the Nebraska law failed to make an exception to save the life of the mother. In response, Congress passed a ban on partial-birth abortions in 2003, and President George W. Bush signed it into law. (Earlier bans passed by Congress had been vetoed by President Bill Clinton.) Congress provided an exception—allowing the method if it is necessary to save a mother's life. The Supreme Court upheld this congressional prohibition on partial-birth abortions, recognizing that government "has the power to restrict abortions after viability if the law contains exceptions for pregnancies endangering the woman's life or health."[86]

Sexual Conduct

"Liberty gives substantial protection to adult persons in deciding how to conduct their lives in matters pertaining to sex." This Supreme Court ruling in *Lawrence v. Texas* (2003) struck down a state law against homosexual sodomy. The ruling overturned an earlier case in which the Court held that the Constitution granted no "fundamental right to homosexuals to engage in acts of consensual sodomy."[87] Rather, the Supreme Court decided that "The liberty protected by the Constitution allows homosexual persons the right to choose to enter upon relationships in the confines of their homes and their own private lives and still retain their dignity as free persons."[88]

Other Private Activities

How far does the right of privacy extend? The Supreme Court appears to have left this question open to argument. In 1969, the Court held that privacy may be constitutionally protected where there is a "reasonable expectation of privacy," notably in one's own

14.1

14.2

14.3

14.4

14.5

14.6

14.7

14.8

home. The Court overturned a criminal conviction for the "mere private possession of obscene material," that is, the possession and viewing of pornography at home.[89]

A Right to Die?

In most states, for most of the nation's history, it has been a crime to help another person commit suicide. Michigan's prosecution of Dr. Jack Kevorkian for publicly participating in physician-assisted suicides launched a nationwide debate on the topic. More important, a group of physicians in Washington, along with their gravely ill patients, filed suit in federal court seeking a declaration that their state's law banning physician-assisted suicide violated the "liberty" guaranteed by the 14th Amendment. They argued that mentally competent, terminally ill patients had the "right to die"; that is, they had a privacy right to request and receive aid in ending their life. They relied on the Supreme Court's previous rulings on abortion, contending that Washington's law placed an undue burden on the exercise of a privacy right. But the U.S. Supreme Court held that there is no *constitutional right* to physician-assisted suicide.[90] The Court implied that if the laws governing the practice are to be changed, they must be changed by legislatures, not by reinterpreting the Constitution.

Patients have a right to refuse treatment, even if by so doing they ensure their own deaths. Life-sustaining procedures can be ended at the request of a family member only if there is "clear and convincing evidence" that the patient would not want these procedures.[91] Most states now recognize "living wills" in which people express their wishes while still of sound mind. The absence of a living will, and disputes within the family over what a comatose patient would wish, can cause prolonged and bitter court fights.

Freedom of Assembly and Petition

14.5 Outline the right to assembly and petition and limitations on this right.

The 1st Amendment guarantees "the right of the people peaceably to assemble, and to petition the government for redress of grievances." The right to organize political parties and interest groups derives from the right of assembly. And freedom of petition protects most lobbying activities.

The Right of Association

Freedom of assembly includes the right to form and join organizations and associations. In an important case during the early civil rights movement, the state of Alabama attempted to harass the National Association for the Advancement of Colored People by requiring it to turn over its membership lists to authorities. The Supreme Court held the state's action to be an unconstitutional infringement of the freedom of association.[92] In the 1960s, the Supreme Court struck down attempts by governments to regulate the Communist Party by requiring membership registration, or penalizing individuals for party membership, or by removing party members from privileges other citizens enjoy.[93]

Freedom of association, like freedom of speech and press, is not absolute. Large national organizations, with no firm ideological views, can be forced to abide by antidiscrimination laws. The Court expressly held that the United States Jaycees and later the Rotary Club could not discriminate on the basis of sex. These large, nonideological, nonreligious, nonpolitical groups are granted less protection than "expressive" groups.[94]

"Expressive" groups, including religious organizations, are free to limit participation to persons who subscribe to their views. Antidiscrimination laws, including those protecting homosexuals, cannot force an organization to accept participation by individuals who do not share its expressed views. In a well-publicized case, the Supreme Court held that the right of association protected the organizers of Boston's St. Patrick's Day parade from being forced by law to include the "Irish-American Gay, Lesbian and Bisexual Group of Boston."[95] And in another well-publicized case, the Supreme Court held that the Boy Scouts are not obliged to accept gays as scouts: "The forced inclusion of an unwanted person in a group infringes the group's freedom of expressive association if the presence of that person affects in a significant way the group's ability to advocate public or private viewpoints."[96]

In another important freedom of association case, the Supreme Court held that California's blanket primary law, a statute that extended participation in party primary elections to all registered voters regardless of their political party affiliation, was unconstitutional.[97] The Court struck down the law, holding that it forced political parties to associate with those who do not share their beliefs.

The Supreme Court has also protected the right of students to form organizations. "First Amendment rights … are available to teachers and students. It can hardly be argued that either teachers or students shed their constitutional rights at the school house gate."[98] Attempts by a college or university to deny official recognition to a student organization based on its views violates the right of association.

Protests, Parades, and Demonstrations

Freedom of assembly includes the right to peacefully protest, parade, and demonstrate. Authorities may, within reasonable limits, enact restrictions regarding the "time, place, and manner" of an assembly so as to preserve public order, smooth traffic flow, freedom of movement, and even peace and quiet. But these regulations cannot be

SIT-DOWN STRIKE

United Auto Workers union members staged an extended strike in the GM tool and die plant in Flint, Michigan, in the winter of 1936–37. The strike succeeded in part because state authorities used police and troops to prevent strikebreakers from disrupting the strike. Such protests are not protected by constitutional assembly rights.

14.1

14.2

14.3

14.4

14.5

14.6

14.7

14.8

takings clause
The 5th Amendment's prohibition against government taking of private property without just compensation.

eminent domain
The action of a government to take property for public use with just compensation even if the owner does not wish to sell.

unevenly applied to groups with different views. Thus authorities may require a permit to parade, but they cannot deny a permit to a group because of the nature of their views or content of their message. For example, the Supreme Court held that city authorities in Skokie, Illinois, acted unconstitutionally in prohibiting the American Nazi Party from holding a march in that city even though it was populated with large numbers of Jewish survivors of the Holocaust.[99]

Picketing

Assemblies of people have a high potential for creating a public disturbance. Parades block traffic and litter the streets; loudspeakers assault the ears of local residents and bystanders; picket lines may block the free passage of others. Although the right of assembly is protected by the 1st Amendment, its exercise involves conduct as well as expression, and therefore it is usually subject to greater government regulation than expression alone. The Court has generally upheld reasonable use of public property for assembly, but it has not forced *private* property owners to accommodate speeches or assemblies. Airport terminals, shopping malls, and other open forums, which may or may not be publicly owned, have posed problems for the courts.

Freedom of assembly has been tested by opponents of abortion who picket abortion clinics, hoping to embarrass and dissuade women from entering them. Generally, the courts have allowed limits on these demonstrations to ensure that people can move freely in and out of the clinics. Freedom of assembly does not include the right to block access to public or private buildings. And when abortion opponents demonstrated at the residence of a physician who performed abortions, the Supreme Court upheld a local ordinance barring assemblies in residential neighborhoods.[100] Physically obstructing access to buildings almost always violates state or local laws, as does the threat or use of force by picketers. The Supreme Court made a distinction between a "fixed buffer zone," prohibiting assembly around a building entrance, and a "floating buffer zone" (of 15 feet), prohibiting demonstrators from approaching individuals in public places. The "fixed" zone was held to be a constitutional limit on assembly but the "floating" zone was held to be an unconstitutional limit on free speech.[101] In 1994, Congress passed a federal law guaranteeing access to abortion clinics, arguing that the federal government should act to guarantee a recognized constitutional right.

Protecting Property Rights

14.6 Describe the protection of property rights and related Court decisions.

The 5th Amendment provides specific protection for private property against government confiscation: "nor shall private property be taken for public use without just compensation." This **takings clause** recognizes that occasionally governments—federal, state, or local—may be obliged to take property from private owners for public uses, for example, streets, roads, public buildings, parks and the like. But the Founders wanted to be certain that even these "takings" from private owners would have some constitutional protection. Taking land from private owners who do not wish to sell it to the government is known as **eminent domain**. The 5th Amendment's takings clause guarantees that the taking of private property by the government for public use can only be done with just compensation being paid to the owner. Usually, a city or state tries to purchase land from the owners in a mutually agreed transaction. But if the owners do not wish to sell or do not agree with the government's offered price, the issue is determined by a court in eminent domain proceedings. In these proceedings, a city

Who's Getting What?

What Gets Took in a Taking?

A person works hard, earns some money, establishes a credit rating, and then buys a home. Or a commercial property. Or maybe some land. The person has a title that is filed with the state that indicates that he or she owns the property. Then a local government (or state, or national) comes along and indicates that the property is needed for some other purpose, and exercises eminent domain to compel that person to sell them the property. This seizure of private property, with compensation but without the owner's consent, is usually called a taking. In some parts of the United States, it's called appropriation.

The legal exercise of eminent domain was codified in Europe in the senas *dominium eminens*, and it represents the assumption that all private property can be appropriated for the use of the state to serve civil society. Those uses can include actions to provide for national defense, local policing, or the creation of public infrastructure like roads, canals, bridges, and public facilities. The expectation is that when the state makes a taking, the property owner will be fairly compensated.

In the United States, takings and property rights are explicitly addressed in the 5th Amendment, which states "nor shall private property be taken for public use, without just compensation"; since 1897, the "takings clause" has been interpreted to apply to state and local governments as well as the national government.

The first problem with takings arises over defining "public use." National government takings are constrained by the exercise of their enumerated powers; state and local governments have greater latitude. So state and local government must only show "public benefit" from the taking, rather than pursuit of a specific and enumerated power. In *Kelo v. City of New London* (2005), the U.S. Supreme Court upheld by a 5–4 vote the right of a municipality to take a property in order to allow a private developer to redevelop the property. The concept of "public purpose" was broadly defined to include private development that would create more jobs and increase the tax revenue base of the city. This unpopular decision led to a wave of state and local initiatives and legislation to constrain governments taking authority. The second issue in takings is determining "just compensation." Compensation is usually based on the fair market value of the property, rather than the economic potential of the property if developed.

Another issue that arises with eminent domain is effective takings. An effective taking (or regulatory taking) is when legislation or regulatory rules prevent a property owner from engaging in certain economic activities. So, for example, if someone owned property in a wetland, the Clean Water Act might prevent that person from engaging in some economic activities that would damage the wetland or pollute the waters adjacent to the wetland. The Supreme Court has wavered on the issue of effective takings, but generally sides with the state's authority. In *Lucas v. South Carolina Coastal Commission*, a regulatory action only becomes a taking when the regulation removes "all economically-beneficial uses of the property." This is consistent with the Supreme Court's historic view that the actual value of a property defines compensation, rather than the speculative value. Similarly, the loss of some speculative economic activity that does not remove all possible economic value is required for a regulatory taking.

The exercise of police action by the state to take property does not constitute a taking. Property seized as forfeiture for not paying taxes, or because the property was used in a criminal enterprise, does not require the state to compensate the owner.

QUESTIONS

1. What's the difference between a physical taking and an "effective" (or regulatory) taking?
2. Does the broad interpretation of "public use" allow governments to pick economic winners and lowers through takings?
3. After reading this box, do you have more or less confidence in your property rights? Why?

or state must go to court and show that the land is needed for a legitimate public purpose; the court will then establish a fair price (just compensation) based on testimony from the owner, the city or state, and impartial appraisers (see also *Who's Getting What?* What Gets Took in a Taking?).

☐ Public Use

Takings under eminent domain are valid only when the property is to be put to "public use." But what constitutes a "public use"? Traditionally, public use referred to goods that served the general public, including schools, highways, public buildings, public memorials, and other facilities open to the public generally. Over time, however, the public use clause was given expanded meaning. Eminent domain was used in urban renewal projects to eliminate slums and blighted areas of a city.

The Right to Bear Arms

14.7 Explain the Supreme Court's interpretation of the right to bear arms.

The 2nd Amendment to the U.S. Constitution states: "A well regulated Militia, being necessary to the security of a free State, the right of the people to keep and bear Arms, shall not be infringed." The militia tradition came to the United States from England, and is one of two common law traditions that can place an abled-body man under arms for the good of the state. One is the *posse comitatus*, which mobilizes to apprehend fugitives; the other is the *fyrd*, which was organized to protect a locality against external invasion. The fyrd evolved into the militia, and a household obligation of militia service was the ability to provide and bear arms.

Bearing Arms

The origins of the 2nd Amendment reveals the concern of colonists with attempts by despotic governments to confiscate the arms of citizens and render them helpless to resist tyranny. James Madison wrote in *The Federalist*, No. 46, that "the advantage of being armed which the Americans possess over the people of almost every other nation, forms a barrier against the enterprise of [tyrannical] ambition."[102] The 2nd Amendment was adopted with little controversy; most state constitutions at the time, like Pennsylvania's, declared that "the people have a right to bear arms for the defense of themselves and the state." Early American political rhetoric was filled with praise for an armed citizenry able to protect its freedoms by force if necessary—implicitly including, in the view of many contemporary and subsequent commentators, the state itself.

An Individual Right

But many constitutional scholars argued over the years that the 2nd Amendment protected only the collective right of the states to form militias—that is, their right to maintain National Guard units. They focused on the qualifying phrase "a well-regulated Militia, being necessary to the security of a free State." But after years of controversy, the Supreme Court finally decided the issue in 2008: "The Second Amendment protects an individual right to possess a firearm unconnected with service in a militia, and to use that arm for traditionally lawful purposes, such as self defense within the home."[103] A District of Columbia law prohibiting the possession of handguns violated "the ancient right of individuals to keep and bear arms for self-defense." But the Court went on to warn that "Like most rights the Second Amendment right is not unlimited" and that reasonable restrictions on guns may be constitutional. In 2011, the Court extended the 14th Amendment application of the Bill of Rights to include 2nd Amendment rights (see *What Do You Think?* Guns on Campus).

New controls on guns are a common policy demand following highly publicized murders or assassination attempts. The Federal Gun Control Act of 1968 was a response to the assassinations of Senator Robert F. Kennedy and Martin Luther King, Jr., in that year, and efforts to legislate additional restrictions occurred after attempts to assassinate presidents Gerald Ford and Ronald Reagan. Today, various federal gun control laws include the following:

- A ban on interstate and mail-order sales of handguns
- Prohibition of the sale of firearms to convicted felons
- A requirement that all firearms *dealers* be licensed by the federal Bureau of Alcohol, Tobacco, Firearms, and Explosives
- Requirements that manufacturers record the serial number of all firearms and that dealers record all sales
- Restrictions of private ownership of automatic weapons and military weapons.

What Do You Think?

Guns on Campus

Are guns allowed on your campus? Should they be? For a half decade, since the massacres at Virginia Tech and Northern Illinois, a debate has raged in legislatures and on college campuses about the ability of students or faculty to be armed on campus.

There are two difficult questions in the debate over guns on campus. On the antiguns side: does banning concealed-carry by a student or faculty member render them more vulnerable to violent attack? On the pro-gun side: do guns on campus create a hostile environment or create more danger if a violent situation emerges?

A pro-concealed-carry-on-campus Facebook group attracted several thousand supporters, and creative student protests, such as the "empty holster movement," seek to bring attention to the issue. Fifteen legislatures introduced campus carry legislation, and in Mississippi and Wisconsin, such legislation eventually passed. Administration is generally resistant to allowing guns on campus, and many campuses interpret the new laws as giving them discretion to ban guns.

Critics fear violence from undisciplined or unstable, gun-wielding students or faculty, like Dr. Amy Bishop, who killed three colleagues at the University of Alabama-Hunstville, or a chilled student–faculty relationship based on the perception that there are guns in the classroom. Campus police indicate that bringing more guns on campus makes it more difficult to identify criminal shooters. As one campus safety director has stated, "It isn't like a guy with a [concealed-carry] permit is wearing a white hat. In a violent situation, when we see a gun on campus, we see a threat." Advocates like Amanda Carpenter of Reno, Nevada, point out that despite claims of campus safety, there are violent robberies and rapes that might be prevented if potential victims were armed. "Had I been carrying that night . . . I know I would have been able to stop my rape."[a]

QUESTIONS

1. Does your college have a campus weapons policy?
2. Do you think a "reasonable prohibition" policy can be used to exclude firearms and other weapons from campuses?
3. If guns are allowed on campuses, should they be allowed in other public facilities, such as courthouses, state capitol buildings, or public schools? Why or why not?

[a]Rachel Wiseman (2011, October 9). "Students: Campaign for Right to Carry Concealed Guns on Campuses Gains Traction," *Chronicle of Higher Education*.

Finally, there is the *Brady Law* requirement for a five-day waiting period for the purchase of a handgun. (The law was named for James S. Brady, former press secretary to President Ronald Reagan, who was severely wounded in the 1981 attempted assassination of the president.) Handgun dealers must send police agencies a form completed by the buyer; police agencies have five days to make certain the purchaser is not a convicted felon.

GUN LAWS AND CRIME There is no systematic evidence that gun control laws reduce violent crime. If we compare violent crime rates in jurisdictions with very restrictive gun laws (for example, New York, Massachusetts, New Jersey, Illinois, and the District of Columbia, all of which prohibit the possession of unlicensed handguns by citizens) to crime rates in jurisdictions with very loose controls, we find no difference in rates of violent crime that cannot be attributed to social conditions.[104]

THE 2ND AMENDMENT The Supreme Court ruled in 2008 that the 2nd Amendment right to bear arms was an individual right, not merely the collective right of the states to maintain militia (National Guard) units.[105] The Court specifically ruled that a total prohibition on the possession of handguns was unconstitutional and that individuals had a constitutional right to possess arms "for traditionally lawful purposes, such as self defense within the home." (The Court also held that a trigger-lock requirement "makes it impossible for citizens to use arms for the core lawful purpose of self-defense and is hence unconstitutional.") But the Court went on to indicate that certain reasonable prohibitions on guns were constitutional: prohibitions on carrying concealed weapons, prohibitions on the possession of firearms by felons and the mentally ill, and prohibitions on the carrying of firearms in sensitive places such as schools and government

14.1 14.2 14.3 14.4 14.5 14.6 14.7 14.8

writ of habeas corpus
Court order directing public officials who are holding a person in custody to bring the prisoner into court and explain the reasons for confinement; the right to habeas corpus is protected by Article I of the Constitution.

buildings, or laws imposing conditions and qualifications on the commercial sale of arms.

Two years later, when addressing a challenge to a set of Chicago handgun ordinances (*McDonald v. Chicago*, 561 U.S. 3025, 130 S.Ct. 3020 (2010)), the US Supreme Court further held that the individual right to bear arms was also binding on the states.[106] This decision, while lauded by 2nd amendment advocates and many Tea Party conservatives, in fact, finds its authority in the ability of the national government to regulate the states through the 14th Amendment. This is the most significant extension of the application of the Bill of Rights through the 14th Amendment since *Roe v. Wade* in 1973.

Rights of Criminal Defendants

14.8 Identify the constitutional rights of criminal defendants and assess consequences of their implementation.

hile society needs the protection of the police, it is equally important to protect society from the police. Arbitrary searches and arrests, imprisonment without trial, forced confessions, beatings and torture, secret trials, tainted witnesses, excessive punishments, and other human rights violations are all too common throughout the world. The U.S. Constitution limits the powers of the police and protects the rights of the accused (see Table 14.2).

The Guarantee of the Writ of Habeas Corpus

One of the oldest and most revered rights in English common law is the right to obtain a **writ of habeas corpus**, which is a court order directing public officials who are holding a person in custody to bring the prisoner into court and explain the reasons for confinement. If a judge finds that the prisoner is being unlawfully detained, or finds insufficient evidence that a crime has been committed or that the prisoner could have committed it, the judge must order the prisoner's release. Thus, the writ of habeas corpus is a means to test the legality of any imprisonment (see *What Do You Think?* Habeas on the Battlefield?).

The writ of habeas corpus was considered so fundamental to the Framers of the Constitution that they included it in the original text of Article I: "The privilege of the Writ of Habeas Corpus shall not be suspended, unless when in Cases of Rebellion or Invasion the public Safety may require it." Despite the qualifying phrase, the Supreme Court has never sanctioned the suspension of the writ of habeas corpus, even during wartime. President Abraham Lincoln suspended the writ of habeas corpus in several areas during the Civil War, but in the case of *Ex parte Milligan* (1866), the Supreme Court ruled that the president had acted unconstitutionally.[107] (With the war over, however, the Court's decision had no practical effect.) Again, in 1946, the Supreme Court declared that the military had had no right to substitute military courts for ordinary courts in Hawaii during World War II, even though Hawaii was in an active theater of war.[108] State courts cannot issue writs of habeas corpus to federal officials, but federal judges may issue such writs to state officials whenever there is reason to believe that a person is being held in violation of the Constitution or laws of the United States.

The Writ of Habeas Corpus looms as one of the great advances in the law. According to the writ, the power of a king over his subjects was not absolute—it had to be exercised with cause. If the king, or an officer of the crown, detained a subject of the crown, a writ of habeas corpus compelled that the prisoner be produced before the court. The court would then determine if sufficient proof was provided by the

TABLE 14.2 INDIVIDUAL RIGHTS IN THE CRIMINAL JUSTICE PROCESS

Rights	Process
4th Amendment: Protection Against Unreasonable Searches and Seizures Warranted searches for sworn "probable cause." Exceptions: consent searches, safety searches, car searches, and searches incident to a valid arrest.	**Investigation by Law-Enforcement Officers** Expectation that police act lawfully.
5th Amendment: Protection against Self-Incrimination Miranda rules **Habeas Corpus** Police holding a person in custody must bring that person before a judge with cause to believe that a crime was committed and the prisoner committed it.	**Arrest** Arrests based on warrants issued by judges and magistrates. Arrests based on crimes committed in the presence of law enforcement officials. Arrests for "probable cause."
8th Amendment: No Excessive Bail Defendant considered innocent until proven guilty; release on bail and amount of bail depends on seriousness of crime, trustworthiness of defendant, and safety of community.	**Hearing and Bail** Preliminary hearing in which prosecutor presents testimony that a crime was committed and probable cause for charging the accused.
5th Amendment: Grand Jury (Federal) Federal prosecutors (but not necessarily state prosecutors) must convince a grand jury that a reasonable basis exists to believe the defendant committed a crime and he or she should be brought to trial.	**Indictment** Prosecutor, or a grand jury in federal cases, issues formal document naming the accused and specifying the charges.
6th Amendment: Right to Counsel Begins in investigation stage, when officials become "accusatory"; extends throughout criminal justice process. Free counsel for indigent defendants.	**Arraignment** Judge reads indictment to the accused and ensures that the accused understands charges and rights and has counsel. Judge asks defendant to choose a plea: Guilty, *nolo contendere* (no contest), or not guilty. If defendant pleads guilty or no contest, a trial is not necessary and defendant proceeds to sentencing.
6th Amendment: Right to a Speedy and Public Trial Impartial jury. Right to confront witnesses. Right to compel favorable witnesses to testify.	**Trial** Impartial judge presides as prosecuting and defense attorneys present witnesses and evidence relevant to guilt or innocence of defendant and make arguments to the jury. Jury deliberates in secret and issues a verdict.
4th Amendment: Exclusionary Rule Illegally obtained evidence cannot be used against defendant.	**Sentencing** If the defendant is found not guilty, the process ends. Defendants who plead guilty or no contest and defendants found guilty by jury are sentenced by fine, imprisonment, or both by the judge. Sentences imposed must be commensurate to the crimes committed.
8th Amendment: Protection Against Cruel and Unusual Punishments **5th Amendment: Protection Against Double Jeopardy** Government cannot try a defendant again for the same offense.	**Appeal** Defendants found guilty may appeal to higher courts for reversal of verdict or a new trial based on errors made anywhere in the process.

authorities to hold the subject for trial. It is a simple, efficient check on abuse of power by the state.

So is the writ free from politics? The simple answer is "no." Political scientist Justin Wert, writing about the "not-so-great Writ of Liberty," sees it as a political product. Conflict over the use of the writ is intertwined with the application of fugitive slave laws before the Civil War; habeas was also used to seek resolution of slave ownership disputes. Congress has suspended habeas in times of insurrection, and the Courts and Congress have both expanded the scope of application of the writ after wars. Access to the writ has been denied to groups of Americans in time of foreign conflict, such as interred Japanese Americans during World War II. And the Court has at various times sought to aggressively expand habeas rights and acted to constrain habeas, and, most recently, sought to apply habeas rights to individuals who are beyond the borders of the United States. In all these instances, change did not occur in a vacuum—it was a function of a larger politics.

There have been historic political debates and actions of state and national government that preceded the emergency situations or historic law suits that allowed the high court to hold forth on habeas rights. The legal issues surrounding the *Dred Scott* case are habeas issues arising from American fugitive slave laws. These issues were the focus of state and federal court litigation and political debate for three decades before. Similarly, the innovations in policy embodied in the USA PATRIOT Act were not

A Conflicting View

Habeas on the Battlefield?

The United States has held 6,000 or more "enemy combatants" captured on the battlefields of Afghanistan and Iraq for many years. Some are held at the U.S. base in Guantánamo Bay, Cuba.

Prisoners of war (POWs)—uniformed members of the military forces of a nation detained after combat—have never been entitled to constitutional protection. (The U.S. held tens of thousands of German and Japanese prisoners of war during World War II.) They are entitled only to "humane treatment" under the Geneva Accords. During World War II, the U.S. courts rejected repeated habeas petitions by German POWs.

"Detainees" from the war on terrorism are not officially prisoners of war, inasmuch as they are not uniformed soldiers of any nation. As military detainees, they were not given lawyers or access to courts or, in many cases, even identified by name.

But in 2004, the Supreme Court held that enemy combatants captured on the battlefield and "imprisoned in territory over which the United States exercises an exclusive jurisdiction and control" are entitled to constitutional rights including habeas corpus—the right to bring their case to U.S. courts. "The fact that petitioners are being held in military custody is immaterial."[a]

In response, President George W. Bush created special military tribunals to hear the cases of the detainees. Initially, Congress was not asked to authorize these tribunals. Rather, the president cited his power as Commander-in-Chief in wartime to do so. But the Supreme Court held in 2006 that without congressional authorization, the president had exceeded his authority in creating the military tribunals.[b]

Following this decision, President Bush asked Congress for legislative authorization to establish "military commissions" to try "any alien unlawful enemy combatant." Congress passed the Military Commissions Act in October 2006, with voting on final passage largely along party lines—Republicans in favor and Democrats opposed. The new Act applied to aliens, not citizens, and only to "unlawful" enemy combatants (in contrast to lawful prisoners of war who are "regular forces of a state"). It specifically prohibited habeas corpus appeals to U.S. courts. Military commissions were to function under their own procedural rules—rules that did not necessarily afford full constitutional protections for defendants.

But in a controversial 5–4 decision, the Supreme Court held that detainees at Guantánamo "have the constitutional privilege of habeas corpus"—access to federal courts to challenge their detention as enemy combatants. Congress and the president cannot deny them the fundamental right of habeas corpus. Although the Constitution recognizes that habeas corpus can be suspended "in cases of Rebellion or Invasion," this Suspension Clause does not apply to the prisoners at Guantánamo. "Some of the petitioners had been in custody for six years with no definitive judicial determination as to the legality of their detention. Their access to the writ [of habeas corpus] is a necessity to determine the lawfulness of their status, even if, in the end, they do not obtain the relief they seek."[c] In a stinging dissent, Justice Scalia wrote: "Today, for the first time in our Nation's history, the Court confers a constitutional right to habeas corpus on alien enemies detained abroad by military forces in the course of an ongoing war. . . . It will almost certainly cause more Americans to be killed."

QUESTIONS

1. How is the right of habeas for detained alien enemy combatants different from how we treat prisoners of war?
2. Do we need to create a new category of legal detention for irregular combatants?

[a] *Rasul v. Bush*, 542 U.S. 466 (2004).
[b] *Hamdan v. Rumsfeld*, 548 U.S. 557 (2006).
[c] *Boumediene v. Bush*, June 12, 2008.

bill of attainder
Legislative act inflicting punishment without judicial trial; forbidden under Article I of the Constitution.

novel, but had been unsuccessfully pursued as policy by Democratic and Republican attorney generals long before the post-9/11 passage of the act.

Congress extended the authority of the executive to detain American civilians indefinitely in December 2011. The National Defense Authorization Act of 2012 includes two provisions, sub-sections 20121 and 1022, which affirm previous authority under the post-9/11 Authorization for Use of Military Force. But, critics contend that the new law allows the president to detain civilians on US soil, even through arrest by the armed forces. The law was challenged in 2012 by the American Civil Liberties Union.

The Prohibition of Bills of Attainder and Ex Post Facto Laws

Like the guarantee of habeas corpus, protection against bills of attainder and ex post facto laws was considered so fundamental to individual liberty that it was included in the original text of the Constitution. A **bill of attainder** is a legislative act inflicting punishment without judicial trial. An **ex post facto law** is a retroactive criminal law that works against the accused—for example, a law that makes an act criminal after the act is committed or a law that increases the punishment for a crime and applies it retroactively.

ex post facto law
Retroactive criminal law that works against the accused; forbidden under Article I of the Constitution.

search warrant
Court order permitting law-enforcement officials to search a location in order to seize evidence of a crime; issued only for a specified location, in connection with a specific investigation, and on submission of proof that "probable cause" exists to warrant such a search.

Unreasonable Searches and Seizures

Individuals are protected by the 4th Amendment from "unreasonable searches and seizures" of their private "persons, houses, papers, and effects." The 4th Amendment lays out specific rules for searches and seizures of evidence: "No warrants shall issue, but upon probable cause, supported by Oath or affirmation, and particularly describing the place to be searched, and the persons or things to be seized." Judges can only issue a **search warrant** based on the probable cause that someone has committed a crime. The indiscriminate searching of whole neighborhoods or groups of people prevented by the 4th Amendment's requirement that the place to be searched must be specifically described in the warrant, though such searches have happened, most notably after the Boston marathon bombing in 2013. The things to be seized must be described in the warrant. This prevents "fishing expeditions" into an individual's home and personal effects on the possibility that some evidence of unknown illegal activity might crop up. The only exception is if police, in the course of a valid search for a specified item, find other items whose very possession is a crime—for example, illicit drugs.

The courts permit police to undertake "reasonable" searches *without* a warrant: in connection with a valid arrest; to protect the safety of police officers; to obtain evidence in the immediate vicinity and in the suspect's control; to preserve evidence in danger of being immediately destroyed; and searches with the consent of a suspect. Most police searches are warrantless under one or another of these conditions. The Supreme Court has also allowed car searches and searches of open fields without warrants. The requirement of "probable cause" has been very loosely defined; an anonymous informant's tip qualifies as "probable cause" to make a search, seizure, or arrest.[109] And if the police, while making a warranted search see evidence of a crime "in plain view," they may seize such evidence without further authorization.[110] And the Court recently approved "no-knock searches," reversing a long tradition of requiring police to knock and identify themselves before breaking into a home. The Court has held that merely stopping a car for a traffic violation does not give police an excuse to search the car for drugs.[111] And, trained police dog searches of the exterior of a residence require a warrant.

Examinations of your body can require a warrant. An individual cannot be compelled to provide a blood sample without a warrant. However, a DNA cheek swab can be taken from a person in police custody. DNA swabs have been likened to fingerprints by the Supreme Court.

Wiretapping and Electronic Surveillance

The Supreme Court views wiretapping and electronic surveillance as a search and seizure within the meaning of the 4th Amendment; such law enforcement techniques require "probable cause" and a warrant. The government may not undertake to eavesdrop where a person has "a reasonable expectation of privacy" without first showing probable cause and obtaining a warrant. Congress has also enacted a law prohibiting federal agents from intercepting a wire, oral, or electronic communication without first obtaining a warrant (see *The Game, the Rules, the Players*: When Is Your Privacy Not Yours?).

POLICE POWERS
Police in Philadelphia search for a suspect wanted in a shooting. The exercise of police powers by the state is the oldest enduring issue in America. When the police can enter your home, detain you, and how they arrest you is one of the main sources of amending the Constitution, through the Bill of Rights.

FISA and Domestic Surveillance

In the Foreign Intelligence Surveillance Act of 1978 (FISA), Congress created a special FISA court to oversee the collection of electronic intelligence within the United States. It requires all intelligence agencies, including the National Security Agency, which is responsible for the collection of electronic intelligence, to obtain warrants upon

14.1
14.2
14.3
14.4
14.5
14.6
14.7
14.8

Who's Getting What?

When Is Your Privacy Not Yours?

Americans take privacy for granted, even when we readily give it up. People recoil at the constant resetting of the privacy controls on Facebook and grouse about corporations that sell consumer information to market researchers—though we readily provide those data in order to have convenient transactions, and consent to a loss of privacy.

The cocoon of privacy is not impenetrable, especially in the world of new media. Social media, your phone records, e-mail, and our electronic devices are all subject to search. And our privacy rights fall off as our control over our space is lessened. Privacy is based, in part, on the 'seal' of your home being sacred and only violated for a warrant search. It is found in the assumption that those thoughts in your mind are your own. But when you go in the public space, you make your person, the car you might drive, and the possessions you might carry potentially subject to search. As we put information out into the electronic environment, these words, pictures, thoughts, and patterns of movement are also possibly subject to examination.

How secure is your privacy in new media?

E-Mail and Text Messages at Work

In 2003, Ontario, California, police Sergeant Jeff Quon sued his department and the police chief because department supervisors read sexually explicit text messages between Quon, his wife, and his girlfriend (a police dispatcher) that were on Quon's digital pager. Internal affairs subsequently disciplined Quon and other officers, leading to the litigation.

The problem was that the pager wasn't Quon's personal property; it was issued to him by the police department. The department informally billed officers for texting overages and subsequently requested transcripts of texts for officers who routinely incurred substantial text costs, in order to determine if their text character limit was too low. Quon had signed a policy statement that limited personal use of the device and indicated that the city reserved the right to "monitor and log all network activity ... with or without notice." A federal appeals court held that Quon's 4th Amendment rights had been violated. The city appealed to the U.S. Supreme Court, and on June 10, 2010, the Court unanimously ruled that because the digital pager belonged to the employer, not the employee, there was no expectation of privacy in personal communications using the device (*City of Ontario v. Quon*, 560 U.S. ___ (2010)).

Digital privacy advocates were outraged. But the decision was actually quite narrow. Justice Kennedy accepted as "given" that Quon had a "reasonable expectation of privacy" in his text messages over the pager, and that the review of them constituted a government search much the same as a physical search of an employee workspace. However, the search was reasonable because it occurred in the routine conduct of a reasonable policy implementation, namely determining if there was the need for higher texting limits. Employers *can* create policies that limit your privacy on company-owned devices and computers; however, there is a reasonable expectation of privacy in your working space that extends into your personal effects and also your electronic workspace.

Can the Cops Look in My Phone?

Can the cops look in your cell phone? Until 2014, the answer was probably "yes." In a 1969 case, *Chimel v. California*, a person under arrest could be searched without warrant including "the area into which he might reach." *United States v. Robinson* then delineated a rule searches to preserve the safety of the officer. Law enforcement viewed cell phones and smart devices as just another personal effect, like cigarettes or a wallet. State courts and federal appeals courts disagreed on whether smart devices were something different. In *Riley v. California*, 573 U.S. _____ (2014), the Court unanimously held that it is unconstitutional to conduct a warrantless search and seizure of digital contents of a cell phone during an arrest, determining that the contents of the phone constituted no threat to an officer, and that arguments regarding vulnerabilities of the contents to "digital wiping" were specious. As Justice Roberts observed in writing for the majority, "Modern cell phones are not just another technological convenience. With all they contain and all they may reveal, they hold for many Americans 'the privacies of life'." One need not comply with a law enforcement request to examine a personal electronic device.

Illegally Intercepted Communications

An illegally intercepted cell phone conversation can be shared if it "involves matters of significant public interest," i.e., protecting the public or enforcing the law in the name of protecting the public. And the police can access the GPS tracking devices in your phone—information the Federal Communications Commission *requires* service providers to furnish in order to track the location of 911 calls. However, they cannot necessarily access your GPS data in the process of a criminal investigation.

Can the Police Come into My House for My Computer?

The police cannot *just* enter your home to search your computer or portable device. That requires a warrant. In the process of conducting a warranted search of a particular crime, if the computer or portable device is not specified but evidence is likely on the computer, then they can search your computer. They can also copy the content of the computer or device. Any object in plain view—including a device or a computer—can also be taken and then searched once a warrant is obtained. If you consent to a search, then you surrender the right to not have items searched. You do not have to turn over passwords on encryption keys, though a court might order you to provide data in an unencrypted format. Also, e-mail searches require a warrant—unless the e-mail is more than six months old and stored on a third-party server.

(*Continued*)

(*Continued*)

Always remember that you have the right to see and examine a warrant. You always have the right to request counsel. And you have no obligation to cooperate in an investigation or to say anything.

"Big Teacher" Might Be Watching You—But He Shouldn't Be, Right?

In 2010, a group of high school students in suburban Philadelphia sued their school district. The students were provided with school-owned MacBooks under what was called the "One-to-One" initiative. What they didn't know was that school officials, using software called Theft Track, activated and used the webcams to observe the students at home and then, using a software called LANrev, snapped and transmitted more than 66,000 images of thousands of students' behavior at home, while also erasing any trace of their activity on the machine (classic spyware activity). Then, a student named Blake Robbins was disciplined for undisclosed behavior at home. The undisclosed behavior was revealed in webcam snaps (including a snap of Robbins in his bed), but presumably violated school policies. The FBI and the local DA investigated, but found no criminal intent in the actions of the school district administrators. Robbins and two other students subsequently sued the school district in civil court for violating their privacy (*Robbins v. Lower Merion School District*). In litigation, it was discovered that the school district actively sought to conceal its surveillance activities. The district settled for $610,000.

QUESTIONS

1. Are your rights to privacy in your electronic devices broader or narrower than you thought?
2. Even if you are innocent and "have nothing to fear," is a search of your electronic devices discomforting to you? Why?

a showing that the surveillance is required for investigation of possible attacks upon the nation. The FISA court is secret, and the persons under surveillance are not notified.

Following the 9/11 attacks, President Bush authorized the National Security Agency to intercept *international* calls to and from Americans—calls involving known or suspected terrorists—without a FISA warrant. The president claimed that he had inherent constitutional powers as Commander in Chief to gather intelligence during war or armed conflict and that the United States is currently at war with international terrorists. Opponents of warrantless surveillance argue that the president is bound by the FISA Act, which specifically requires court warrants for surveillance within the United States, including international calls.

PUBLIC SURVEILLANCE

A ceiling-mounted video surveillance camera keeps an eye on subway riders in New York, March, 2010. Video cameras are now nearly universal in public places.

14.1

14.2

14.3

14.4

14.5

14.6

14.7

14.8

indictment
Determination by a grand jury that sufficient evidence exists to warrant trial of an individual on a felony charge; necessary before an individual can be brought to trial.

grand jury
Jury charged only with determining whether sufficient evidence exists to support indictment of an individual on a felony charge; the grand jury's decision to indict does not represent a conviction.

Congress and the president reached a compromise with the FISA Amendments Act of 2008. This act allows the government to undertake warrantless surveillance of suspected terrorists for seven days before obtaining a FISA warrant. It allows wiretapping of international calls and intercepts of international e-mails. It removes requirements for detailed descriptions of the information sought in a request for a FISA warrant. It protects telecommunications companies from lawsuits for "past or future cooperation" with the government in electronic surveillance. It denies the president's claim that his war powers supersedes FISA laws.[112]

Drug Testing

"Unreasonable" drug testing violates the 4th Amendment. But the Supreme Court has held that it is reasonable to impose mandatory drug testing on railroad workers, federal law-enforcement agents, and even students participating in athletics.[113] However, when the state of Georgia enacted a law requiring drug testing for candidates for public office, the Court found it to be an "unreasonable" search in violation of the 4th Amendment.[114] Apparently mandatory drug testing in occupations affecting public safety and drug testing in schools to protect children are reasonable, while suspicionless drug testing of the general public is not.

Arrests

The Supreme Court permits *arrests without warrants* (1) when a crime is committed in the presence of an officer; and (2) when an arrest is supported by "probable cause" to believe that a crime has been committed by the person apprehended.[115] However, the Court has held that police may not enter a home to arrest its occupant without either a warrant for the arrest or the consent of the owner.[116] And, while awaiting a search warrant, police can only detain someone in the immediate area to be searched.

Indictment

The 5th Amendment requires that an **indictment** be issued by a **grand jury** before a person may be brought to trial on a felony offense. This provision protects against unreasonable, harassing prosecutions by the government. In principle, a grand jury is supposed to determine whether the evidence submitted to it by prosecutors is sufficient to place a person on trial. In practice, grand juries spend little time deliberating on most cases. Neither defendants nor their attorneys are permitted to testify before grand juries without the prosecution's permission. Thus, the prosecutor controls the information submitted to grand juries and instructs them in their duties. In almost all cases, grand juries accept the prosecution's recommendations with little or no discussion. Thus grand juries, whose hearings are secret, provide little check on federal prosecutors.

Self-Incrimination and the Right to Counsel

Freedom from self-incrimination had its origin in English common law; it was originally designed to prevent persons from being tortured into confessions of guilt. It is also a logical extension of the notion that individuals should not be forced to contribute to their own prosecution, that the burden of proof rests on the state. The 5th Amendment protects people from both physical and psychological coercion.[117] It protects not only accused persons at their own trial but also witnesses testifying in trials of other persons, civil suits, congressional hearings, and so on. Thus "taking the Fifth" has become a standard phrase in our culture: "I refuse to answer that question on the grounds that it might tend to incriminate me." The protection also means that judges, prosecutors, and juries cannot use the refusal of people to take the stand at their own trial as evidence of guilt. Indeed, a judge or attorney is not even permitted to imply this to a jury, and a judge is obligated to instruct a jury not to infer guilt from a defendant's refusal to testify.

It is important to note that individuals may be forced to testify when they are not themselves the object of a criminal prosecution. Government officials may also extend a **grant of immunity from prosecution** to a witness in order to compel testimony. Under a grant of immunity, the government agrees not to use any of the testimony against the witness; in return, the witness provides information that the government uses to prosecute others who are considered more dangerous or more important than the immune witness. Because such grants ensure that nothing the witnesses say can be used against them, immunized witnesses cannot refuse to answer under the 5th Amendment.

The Supreme Court under Chief Justice Earl Warren greatly strengthened the 5th Amendment protection against self-incrimination and the right to counsel in a series of rulings in the 1960s:

- *Gideon v. Wainwright (1963)*: Equal protection under the 14th Amendment requires that free legal counsel be appointed for all indigent defendants in all criminal cases.[118]
- *Escobedo v. Illinois (1964)*: Suspects are entitled to confer with counsel as soon as police investigation focuses on them or once "the process shifts from investigatory to accusatory."[119]
- *Miranda v. Arizona (1966)*: Before questioning suspects, a police officer must inform them of all their constitutional rights, including the right to counsel (appointed at no cost to the suspect if necessary) and the right to remain silent. Although suspects may knowingly waive these rights, the police cannot question anyone who at any point asks for a lawyer or declines "in any manner" to be questioned. If the police commit an error in these procedures, the accused goes free, regardless of the evidence of guilt.[120]

grant of immunity from prosecution
Grant by the government to an individual of freedom from prosecution on a particular charge in return for testimony by that individual that might otherwise be self-incriminating.

exclusionary rule
Rule of law that evidence found in an illegal search or resulting from an illegally obtained confession may not be admitted at trial.

bail
Release of an accused person from custody in exchange for promise to appear at trial, guaranteed by money or property that is forfeited to court if defendant does not appear.

☐ The Exclusionary Rule

Illegally obtained evidence and confessions may not be used in criminal trials. If police find evidence of a crime in an illegal search or if they elicit statements from suspects without informing them of their rights to remain silent or to have counsel, the evidence or statements produced are not admissible in a trial. This **exclusionary rule** is one of the more controversial procedural rights that the Supreme Court has extended to criminal defendants. The rule is also unique to the United States: in Great Britain evidence obtained illegally may be used against the accused, although the accused may bring charges against the police for damages.

The rule provides *enforcement* for the 4th Amendment guarantee against unreasonable searches and seizures, as well as the 5th Amendment guarantee against compulsory self-incrimination and the guarantee of counsel. Initially applied only in federal cases, in *Mapp v. Ohio* (1961) the Supreme Court extended the exclusionary rule to all criminal cases in the United States.[121] A *good faith exception* is made "when law enforcement officers have acted in objective good faith or their transgressions have been minor."[122] And police are *not* prohibited from tricking a suspect into giving them incriminating evidence.[123] But the exclusionary rule is frequently attacked for the high price it extracts from society—the release of guilty criminals. Why punish society because of the misconduct of police? Why not punish police directly, perhaps with disciplinary measures imposed by courts that discover errors, instead of letting guilty persons go free?

☐ Bail Requirements

The 8th Amendment says only that "*excessive* bail shall not be required." This clause does not say that pretrial release on **bail** will be available to all. The Supreme Court has held that "in our society liberty is the norm, and detention prior to trial or without trial is the carefully limited exception." Pretrial release on bail can be denied on the basis of the seriousness of the crime (bail is often denied in murder cases), the

14.1

14.2

14.3

14.4

14.5

14.6

14.7

14.8

trustworthiness of the defendant (bail is often denied when the prosecution shows that the defendant is likely to flee before trial), or, in a more controversial exception, when release would threaten "the safety of any other person or the community."[124] If the court does not find any of these exceptions, it must set bail no higher than an amount reasonably calculated to ensure the defendant's later presence at trial.

Most criminal defendants cannot afford the bail money required for pretrial release. They must seek the services of a bail bondsman, who charges a heavy fee for filing the bail money with the court. The bail bondsman receives all of the bail money back when the defendant shows up for trial. But even if the defendant is found innocent, the bail bondsman retains the charge fee. (Thus the system is said to discriminate against poor defendants who cannot afford the bondsman's fee.) The failure of a criminal defendant to appear at his or her trial is itself a crime and subjects the defendant to immediate arrest as well as forfeiture of bail. Most states authorize bail bondsmen to find and arrest persons who have "jumped bail," return them to court, and thereby recover the bail money.

☐ Fair Trial

The original text of the Constitution guaranteed jury trials in criminal cases, and the 6th Amendment went on to correct weaknesses the Framers saw in the English justice system at that time—closed proceedings, trials in absentia (where the defendant is not present), secret witnesses, long delays between arrest and trial, biased juries, and the absence of defense counsel. Specifically, the 6th Amendment guarantees the following:

- The right to a speedy and public trial. ("Speedy" refers to the time between arrest and trial, not the time between the crime itself and trial,[125] but the Supreme Court has declined to set a specific time limit that defines "speedy."[126])
- An impartial jury chosen from the state or district where the crime was committed.
- The right to confront (cross-examine) witnesses against the accused.
- The right of the accused to compel (subpoena) favorable witnesses to appear.
- The right of the accused to be represented by counsel.

Over the years, the courts have elaborated on these elements of a fair trial so that today trial proceedings follow a rigidly structured format. First, attorneys make opening statements. The prosecution describes the crime and how it will prove beyond a reasonable doubt that the defendant committed it. The defense attorney argues either that the crime did not occur or that the defendant did not do it. Next, each side, again beginning with the prosecution, calls witnesses who first testify on "direct examination" for their side, then are cross-examined by the opposing attorney. Witnesses may be asked to verify evidence that is introduced as "exhibits." Defendants have a right to be present during their own trials (although an abusive and disruptive defendant may be considered to have waived his or her right to be present and be removed from the courtroom).[127] Prosecution witnesses must appear in the courtroom and submit to cross-examination (although special protection procedures, including videotaped testimony, may be used for children).[128] Prosecutors are obliged to disclose any information that might create a reasonable doubt about the defendant's guilt,[129] but the defendant may not be compelled to disclose incriminating information.

After all of the witnesses offered by both sides have been heard and cross-examined, prosecution and defense give their closing arguments. The burden of proof "beyond a reasonable doubt" rests with the prosecution; the defense does not need to prove that the accused is innocent, only that reasonable doubt exists regarding guilt.

Juries must be "impartial": they must not have prejudged the case or exhibit bias or prejudice or have a personal interest in the outcome. Judges can dismiss jurors for "cause." During jury selection, attorneys for the prosecution and defense are allowed a fixed number of "peremptory" challenges of jurors (although they cannot do so on the basis of race or gender).[130] Jury selection is often regarded by attorneys as the key to the outcome of a case; both sides try to get presumed sympathetic people on the

The Game, the Rules, the Players

Here's Looking at Your Mail, Kid

The National Security Agency (NSA) is the premier communications intelligence agency in the world. It was created in 1952 to break the communication codes of potential adversaries and to protect the communications of the United States.

This function was not new—previous organizations in the U.S. government had been engaged in cryptography and communications surveillance since 1917, when America entered World War II. The nearly universal scope and increased sophisticated of electronic communications increased the need and opportunity for NSA to engage in communication surveillance. Historically, the NSA had been forbidden from spying within the United States.

After the al Qaeda attacks in September 2001, the NSA implemented a program called the President's Surveillance Program ("the Program"). The Program was not revealed until 2005, when the *New York Times* reported that the communications of about 1,000 persons in the country had been monitored without a warrant, by executive order. A year later, it was learned that the NSA had data on the phone calls of tens of millions of Americans.

Had the NSA gone too far?

Americans had no idea. The NSA was collecting data on every phone call in the country. The agency was also using sophisticated software to trace and access 1.7 billion emails every day. All of this data fed what was called a "data mining operation" to identify potential patterns of email and phone traffic that might be related to security threats.

No warrants were issued.

The NSA achieved this goal by intercepting electronic communications as they traveled through the fiber optic networks of the United States. When a call or email hit a junction in the system, software would copy the content. The message then continued forward, with one copy going to the NSA's server farm for storage, and the original continuing to the recipient. Then the data were available for the NSA to use for potential data mining. These techniques are based on complex algorithm applications and are used to try and tease out potential threats from the chaos of our data transmissions.

Until 2013, the public was unaware of the scope of NSA activities. The leaks by government contractor Edward Snowden of the existence of a program called PRISM blew open public debate. PRISM collected all data and traffic from nine Internet providers throughout the United States and the world and included spying on leaders of other nations. Snowden fled the United States.

The response of the American public in the summer of 2013 was decidedly critical. Nearly 53 percent of Americans disapproved of the surveillance activities while just 37 percent approved. Republicans (63 percent) and Independents (56 percent) were far more critical of the program than Democrats (40 percent disapproved, 49 percent approved). But a lot of this is just politics. When the public was polled about the original data mining program in 2006 during the Republican Bush administration, 72 percent of Republicans approved and 22 percent disapproved, while among Democrats, 20 percent approved and 76 percent disapprove.

So, when it comes to the NSA and privacy, what the public thinks depends on whether their party is in power.

QUESTIONS

1. **Should the government be spying on American citizens?**
2. **Should the government be bound by warrants when observing communications?**

jury. In well-publicized cases, judges may "sequester" a jury (keep them in a hotel away from access to the mass media) in order to maintain impartiality. Judges may exclude press or television to prevent trials from becoming spectacles if they wish.[131] By tradition, English juries have had 12 members; however, the Supreme Court has allowed 6-member juries in non-death-penalty cases.[132] Also by tradition, juries should arrive at a unanimous decision. If a jury cannot do so, judges declare a "hung" jury and the prosecutor may schedule a retrial. Only a "not guilty" prevents retrial of a defendant. Traditionally, it was believed that a lack of unanimity raised "reasonable doubt" about the defendant's guilt. But the Supreme Court has permitted nonunanimous verdicts in some cases.[133]

plea bargaining
Practice of allowing defendants to plead guilty to lesser crimes than those with which they were originally charged in return for reduced sentences.

Plea Bargaining

Few criminal cases actually go to trial. More than 90 percent of criminal cases are plea bargained. In **plea bargaining**, the defendant agrees to plead guilty and waives the right to a jury trial in exchange for concessions made by the prosecutor, perhaps the dropping of more serious charges against the defendant or a pledge to seek a reduced sentence or

14.1

14.2

14.3

14.4

14.5

14.6

14.7

14.8

The Game, the Rules, the Players

Litigators for the Powerless at the ACLU

The mission of the American Civil Liberties Union (ACLU) is to "defend and preserve the individual rights and liberties guaranteed to every person in this country by the Constitution and laws of the United States."

Formed in 1920 at the height of America's first great anticommunist "Red Scare" (which bore no small similarities to current "anti-Islamist" rhetoric), the ACLU has brought historic cases that protected broad-based civil liberties of the ordinary and also the politically unpopular. In the last century, the ACLU has challenged mandated teaching of Biblical creationism in the 1920s and interracial marriage bans in the 1960s. They repeatedly brought or supported litigation establishing the right to privacy and defending the rights of the accused. The ACLU has defended opponents of liberty, including cases protecting the political rights of unpopular groups such as the Ku Klux Klan and the American Nazi Party. During the last decade, the ACLU actively worked against increasingly invasive government surveillance while also taking on the critical issue of "sagging" laws as a form of racial profiling. The ACLU is heavily dependent on outside counsel and academics to help advance their agenda.

At the top, the current president of the ACLU, Susan Herman, has worked with the organization since she was a law student at NYU in the early 1970s. As a faculty member at the Brooklyn Law College, she continued to work with the organization as an attorney and advocate. In 2008, she was elected president of the ACLU after previously serving as general counsel for the organization and also spending two decades on the national board. In an era of increasing concern about terrorism, security, and individual liberty, Herman, an expert in criminal procedure, has authored books and law review articles on terrorism, due process rights, and the USA PATRIOT Act.

QUESTIONS

1. **It is often alleged that the ACLU is a 'leftist' organization. Do they confine their defense of civil liberties to only people who agree with them?**
2. **Do you think the national security environment of the 2000s contributed to the rise of the ACLU president Susan Herman? Why?**
3. **Do you think we should defend the speech rights of 'hate' groups? Why?**

fine. Some critics of plea bargaining view it as another form of leniency in the criminal justice system that reduces its deterrent effects. Other critics view plea bargaining as a violation of the Constitution's protection against self-incrimination and guarantee of a fair jury trial. Prosecutors, they say, threaten defendants with serious charges and stiff penalties in order to force a guilty plea. Still other critics see plea bargaining as an "under-the-table" process that undermines respect for the criminal justice system.

Yet it is vital to the nation's court system that most defendants plead guilty. The court system would quickly break down from overload if any substantial proportion of defendants insisted on jury trials.

Double Jeopardy

The Constitution appears to bar multiple prosecutions for the same offense: "Nor shall any person be subject for the same offense to be twice put in jeopardy of life or limb" (5th Amendment). But very early, the Supreme Court held that this clause does not protect an individual from being tried a second time if jurors are deadlocked and cannot reach a verdict in the first trial (a "hung" jury).[134] Moreover, the Supreme Court has held that federal and state governments may separately try a person for the same offense if it violates both federal and state laws.[135] Thus, in the well-publicized Rodney King case in 1992, in which police officers were videotaped beating King, a California court found the officers not guilty of assault; however, the U.S. Justice Department later won convictions against the officers in a federal court for violating King's civil rights. Finally, a verdict of guilt or innocence in a criminal trial does not preclude a civil trial in which plaintiffs (private citizens) sue for damages inflicted by the accused. Thus, O. J. Simpson was found not guilty of murder in a criminal trial but was later found to be responsible for the deaths of two people in a civil trial. Civil courts, of course, can only impose monetary awards; they cannot impose criminal penalties.

Compared to What?

The Death Penalty Around the World

More than half of the world's countries have now abolished the death penalty. Amnesty International, a worldwide organization opposed to the death penalty, reports that 59 countries currently retain the death penalty, but only 25 of them actually carried out executions in 2008. All European countries have abolished the death penalty. In the Americas, only one nation, the United States, continues to employ the death penalty on a regular basis. (Some Caribbean nations, including Trinidad and Tobago, the Bahamas, Cuba, and Jamaica, also continue its use.) Mexico prohibits the death penalty and will not extradite persons facing the death penalty in other countries, including the United States. The first modern national ban on the death penalty was in Venezuela, which ended the practice in 1863; since 2001, another 24 countries have outlawed the death penalty. In 2008, the United Nations General Assembly passed a resolution calling for a general moratorium on executions around the world. According to Amnesty International, some of the recent trends in the use of capital punishment include:

"Four countries in the G20 executed in 2010: China, Japan, Saudi Arabia and the USA.

36 of the 53 Member States of the African Union are abolitionist in law or practice.

Four of the 54 Member States of the Commonwealth [of Nations, the successor states to the old British Empire] executed in 2010: Bangladesh, Botswana, Malaysia and Singapore. More than 11,000 people remain on death row in Commonwealth countries.

3 of the 10 Member States of the Association of Southeast Asian Nations executed in 2010.

21 of the 192 Member States of the UN carried out executions in 2010."

QUESTION

1. Do you think the death penalty should remain legal in the United States?

SOURCE: Data from Amnesty International. "Death Sentences and Executions, 2010." www.amnesty.org.

☐ The Death Penalty

Perhaps the most heated debate in criminal justice policy today concerns capital punishment. Opponents of the death penalty argue that it violates the prohibition against "cruel and unusual punishments" in the 8th Amendment to the Constitution. They also argue that the death penalty is applied unequally. A large proportion of those executed have been poor, uneducated, and nonwhite. In contrast, many Americans feel that justice demands strong retribution for heinous crimes—a life for a life. A mere jail sentence for a multiple murderer or rapist-murderer seems unjust compared with the damage inflicted on society and the victims. In many cases, a life sentence means less than 10 years in prison under the current early-release and parole policies in many states. Convicted murderers have been set free, and some have killed again (see *Compared to What?* The Death Penalty Around the World).

☐ Prohibition Against Unfair Application

Prior to 1971, the death penalty was officially sanctioned by about half of the states. Federal law also retained the death penalty. However, no one had actually suffered the death penalty since 1967 because of numerous legal tangles and direct challenges to the constitutionality of capital punishment.

In *Furman v. Georgia* (1972), the Supreme Court ruled that capital punishment, *as then imposed*, violated the 8th and 14th Amendment prohibitions against cruel and unusual punishment and due process of law. The justices' reasoning in the case was very complex. Only Justices William J. Brennan and Thurgood Marshall declared that capital punishment itself is cruel and unusual. The other justices in the majority felt that death sentences had been applied unfairly; some individuals received the death penalty for crimes for which many others received much lighter sentences. These justices left open the possibility that capital punishment would be constitutional if it was specified for certain kinds of crime and applied uniformly.[136]

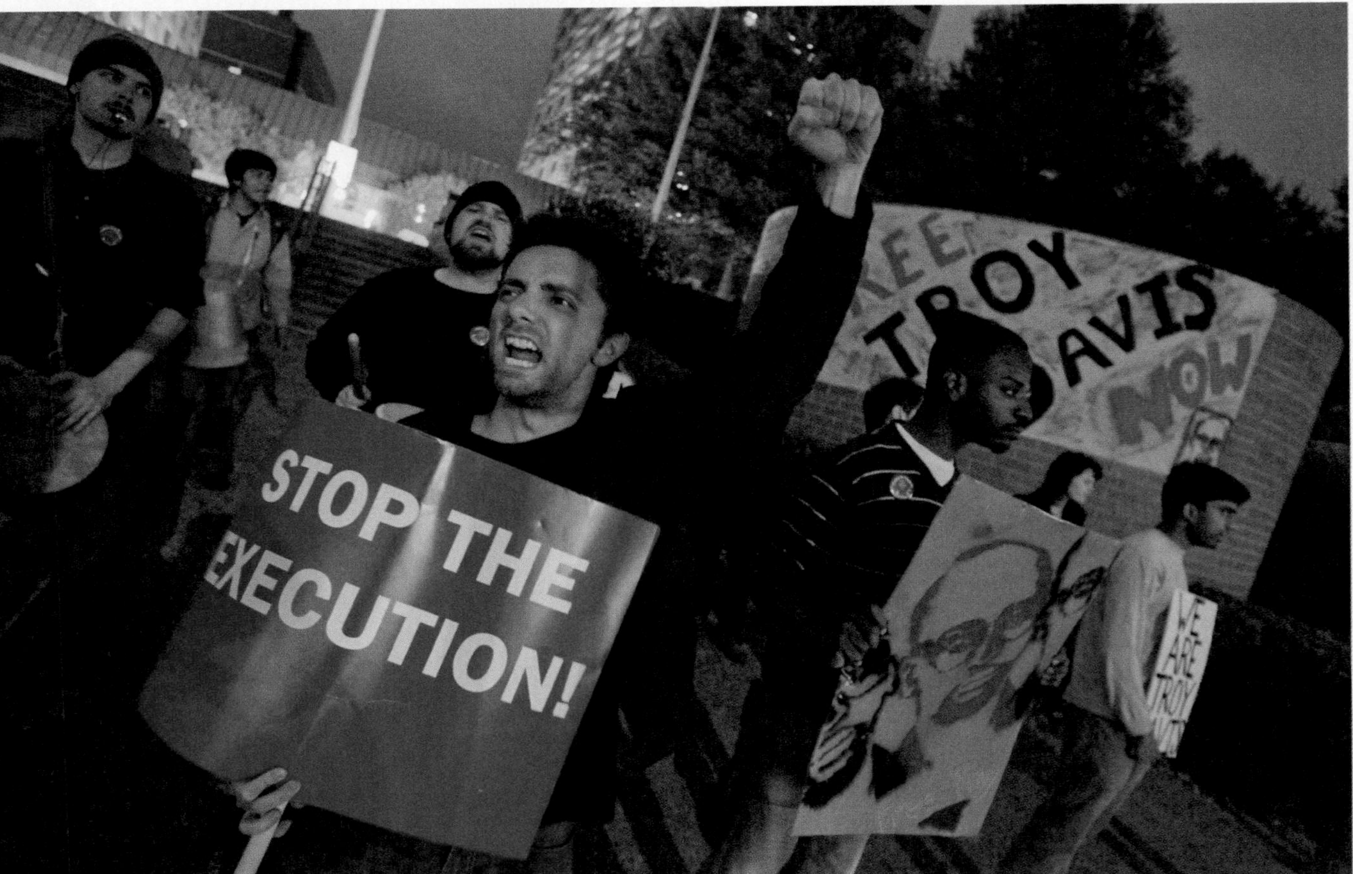

EXECUTION WHEN GUILT IS IN DOUBT

Demonstrators opposed to the execution of Georgia death row inmate Troy Davis protest in front of the state pardon and parole board, September 21, 2011. The American public largely supports the death penalty, though a growing source of opposition is the belief that the justice system is flawed and convicts innocent persons.

After this decision, a majority of states rewrote their death penalty laws to try to ensure fairness and uniformity of application. Generally, these laws mandate the death penalty for murders committed during rape, robbery, hijacking, or kidnapping; murder of prison guards; murder with torture; and multiple murders. They call for two trials to be held—one to determine guilt or innocence and another to determine the penalty. At the second trial, evidence of "aggravating" and "mitigating" factors must be presented; if there are aggravating factors but no mitigating factors, the death penalty may be imposed.

☐ Death Penalty Reinstated

The revised death penalty laws were upheld in a series of cases that came before the Supreme Court in 1976. The Court concluded that "the punishment of death does *not* invariably violate the Constitution." The majority decision noted that the Framers of the Bill of Rights had accepted death as a common penalty for crime. Although acknowledging that the Constitution and its amendments must be interpreted in a dynamic fashion, reflecting changing moral values, the Court's majority noted that most state legislatures have been willing to reenact the death penalty and hundreds of juries have been willing to impose that penalty. Thus, "a large proportion of American society continues to regard it as an appropriate and necessary criminal sanction." Moreover, the Court held that the social purposes of retribution and deterrence justify the use of the death penalty; this ultimate sanction is "an expression of society's moral outrage at particularly offensive conduct."[137]

The Court reaffirmed that *Furman v. Georgia* struck down the death penalty only where it was invoked in "an arbitrary and capricious manner." A majority of the justices upheld the death penalty in states where the trial is a two-part proceeding, provided that during the second part the jury is given relevant information and standards for deciding whether to impose the death penalty. The Court approved the consideration of "aggravating and mitigating circumstances." Later, the Court held that the jury, not a judge acting alone, must find aggravating circumstances in order to impose the death sentence.[138] The Court also called for automatic review of all death sentences by state supreme courts to ensure that none is imposed under the influence of passion or prejudice, that aggravating factors are supported by the evidence, and that the sentence is not disproportionate to the crime. The court disapproved of state laws making the death penalty mandatory in all first-degree murder cases, holding that such laws were "unduly harsh and unworkably rigid." The Court has held that executions of the mentally retarded are "cruel and unusual punishments" prohibited by the 8th Amendment, and that the 8th Amendment prohibits executions of offenders who were under age 18 when their crimes were committed.[139]

☐ Racial Bias

The death penalty has been challenged as a violation of the Equal Protection Clause of the 14th Amendment because of racial bias in the application of the punishment. White murderers are just as likely to receive the death penalty as black murderers. However, some statistics show that if the *victim* is white, there is a greater chance that the killer will be sentenced to death than if the victim is black. Nevertheless, the U.S. Supreme Court has ruled that statistical disparity in the race of victims by itself does not bar the use of the death penalty in all cases. There must be evidence of racial bias against a particular defendant in order for the Court to reverse a death sentence.[140]

A Constitutional Note

The Origins of the Bill of Rights

The Constitution that emerged from the Philadelphia Convention of 1787 did not include a Bill of Rights. This was a particularly glaring omission, because the idea of a bill of rights was popular at the time, and most constitutions contain one. The Founders certainly believed in limited government, and they did write a few liberties into the body of the Constitution, including protection against bills of attainder and ex post facto laws, the guarantee of the writ of habeas corpus, a limited definition of treason, and the guarantee of jury trials. But they dismissed the notion of a written Bill of Rights as unnecessary, claiming that the national government, as a government of only enumerated powers, could not exercise any powers not expressly delegated to it. And the power to infringe on free speech or press or otherwise restrain liberty was not among the enumerated powers. It was therefore not necessary to specifically deny the new government the power to interfere with individual liberty. But this logic was unconvincing to Anti-Federalist opponents of the new Constitution; they wanted much firmer written guarantees of liberty in the Constitution. So Federalist supporters of the Constitution made a solemn promise to add a Bill of Rights as amendments to the Constitution in order to help secure votes for its ratification. Thus, the fundamental guarantees of liberty in the Bill of Rights were political concessions made to win support for the Constitution itself. True to their word, supporters of the Constitution, including James Madison, secured the congressional passage of 12 amendments in the very first Congress to be convened under the new Constitution. Ten of these amendments—the Bill of Rights—were ratified by the states by 1791.

QUESTIONS

1. Reflecting on this chapter, who was more right about the need to enumerate certain rights in the Constitution—the Federalists, or the Anti-Federalists? Why?
2. Has the national government been constrained in the exercise of powers not explicitly delegated to it?

Review the Chapter

Power and Individual Liberty

14.1 Outline the founders' views on individual liberty and trace the expansion of the Bill of Rights, p. 516

Laws and government are required to protect individual liberty, yet laws and governments themselves restrict liberty. To resolve this dilemma, constitutions seek to limit governmental power over the individual. In the U.S. Constitution, the Bill of Rights is designed to place certain liberties beyond the reach of government.

Initially, the Bill of Rights applied against only the federal government, not state or local governments. But over time, the Bill of Rights was nationalized, as the Supreme Court applied the Due Process Clause of the 14th Amendment to all governments in the United States.

Freedom of Religion

14.2 Differentiate the two aspects of freedom of religion, p. 517

Freedom of religion encompasses two separate restrictions on government: government must not establish religion or prohibit its free exercise. Although the wording of the 1st Amendment is absolute ("Congress shall make no law ..."), the Supreme Court has allowed some restrictions on religious practices that threaten health, safety, or welfare.

The Supreme Court's efforts to maintain "a wall of separation" between church and state have proven difficult and controversial. The Court's banning of prayer and religious ceremony in public schools more than 30 years ago remains politically unpopular today.

Freedom of Speech and the Press

14.3 Assess the extent of and limits on freedom of speech and the press, and trace the evolution of the Supreme Court's view of obscenity, p. 524

The Supreme Court has never adopted the absolutist position that all speech is protected by the 1st Amendment. The Court's clear and present danger doctrine and its preferred position doctrine recognize the importance of free expression in a democracy, yet the Court has permitted some restrictions on expression, especially in times of perceived national crisis.

The Supreme Court has placed obscenity outside the protection of the 1st Amendment, but it has encountered considerable difficulty in defining "obscenity."

Freedom of the press prevents government from imposing prior restraint (censorship) on the news media except periodically in wartime, when it has been argued that publication would result in serious harm or loss of life. The Supreme Court has allowed greater government authority over radio and television than over newspapers, on the grounds that radio and television are given exclusive rights to use specific broadcast frequencies.

Privacy, Abortion, and the Constitution

14.4 Identify protections granted under the right to privacy, p. 534

The right to privacy encompasses protections for such things as the use of contraceptives, the ability to obtain an abortion, and sexual conduct and other activities performed in one's own home. The Supreme Court has not, however, extended this protection to physician-assisted suicide.

Freedom of Assembly and Petition

14.5 Outline the right to assembly and petition and limitations on this right, p. 536

The 1st Amendment guarantee of the right of assembly and petition protects the organization of political parties and interest groups. It also protects the right of people to peacefully protest, parade, and demonstrate. Governments may, within reasonable limits, restrict these activities for valid reasons but may not apply different restrictions to different groups based on the nature of their views.

Protecting Property Rights

14.6 Describe the protection of property rights and related Court decisions, p. 538

The 5th Amendment provides specific protection for private property against government confiscation "without just compensation." The taking of property from owners who do not wish to sell it is called eminent domain. The Court has allowed the use of eminent domain to serve the public interest, but has also allowed the states to create more restrictive definitions of what constitutes "public use."

Right to Bear Arms

14.7 Explain the Supreme Court's interpretation of the right to bear arms, p. 540

The 2nd Amendment guarantees "the right of the people to keep and bear arms." The Supreme Court has held that this is an individual right, and not just a collective right of the states to maintain National Guard units.

Rights of Criminal Defendants

14.8 Identify the constitutional rights of criminal defendants and assess the consequences of their implementation, p. 542

The Constitution includes a number of important procedural guarantees in the criminal justice system: the writ of habeas corpus; prohibitions against bills of attainder and ex post facto laws; protection against unreasonable searches and seizures; protection against self-incrimination; guarantee of legal counsel; protection against excessive bail; guarantee of a fair public and speedy trial by an impartial jury; the right to confront witnesses and to compel favorable witnesses to testify; and protection against cruel or unusual punishment.

The Supreme Court's exclusionary rule helps enforce some of these procedural rights by excluding illegally obtained evidence and self-incriminating statements from criminal trials. In the 1960s, Court interpretations of the 4th and 5th Amendments strengthened the rights of criminal defendants. Police procedures adjusted quickly, and today there is little evidence that procedural rights greatly hamper law enforcement.

Few criminal cases go to trial. Most are plea bargained, with the defendant pleading guilty in exchange for reduced charges and/or a lighter sentence. Although this practice is frequently criticized, without plea bargaining, the nation's criminal court system would break down from case overload.

The Supreme Court has ruled that the death penalty is not a "cruel and unusual punishment," but the Court has insisted on fairness and uniformity of application.

Learn the Terms

incorporation, p. 517
Free Exercise Clause, p. 519
Establishment Clause, p. 522
wall-of-separation doctrine, p. 522
Lemon test, p. 522
clear and present danger doctrine, p. 525
preferred position, p. 525
freedom of expression, p. 526
symbolic speech, p. 526
commercial speech, p. 529
prior restraint, p. 532
shield laws, p. 533
takings clause, p. 538
eminent domain, p. 538
writ of habeas corpus, p. 542
bill of attainder, p. 544
ex post facto law, p. 545
search warrant, p. 545
indictment, p. 548
grand jury, p. 548
grant of immunity from prosecution, p. 549
exclusionary rule, p. 549
bail, p. 549
plea bargaining, p. 551

Test Yourself

14.1 Outline the Founders' views on individual liberty and trace the expansion of the Bill of Rights.

The founders believed that individual liberty was

a. derived from the Bill of Rights
b. granted by the sovereign
c. conditioned upon the consent of the governed
d. derived from the legality of governmental authority
e. inherent in the human condition

14.2 Differentiate the two aspects of freedom of religion.

To be constitutional a law dealing with religious beliefs must have

a. a devoutly held religious basis
b. as its main intention the advancement of religious activities
c. the least amount of entanglement possible with the government
d. reasonable provisions that inhibit religious activities
e. an established state church

14.3 Assess the extent of and limits on freedom of speech and the press and trace the evolution of the Supreme Court's view of obscenity.

Speech that presents society with a "serious and immediate danger" may be curtailed. This is known as the

a. "preferred position" doctrine
b. doctrine of original intent
c. "clear and present danger" doctrine
d. Sullivan Doctrine
e. Cody Doctrine

14.4 Identify protections granted under the right to privacy.

The right to privacy

a. is expressly protected by the Constitution
b. may be deduced from many sources in the Constitution
c. protects physician-assisted suicide
d. was first enunciated in *Roe v. Wade*
e. does not exist until the 14th amendment

14.5 Outline the right to assembly and petition and limitations on this right.

Freedom of assembly includes the right to

I. protest
II. demonstrate
III. join organizations
IV. Engage in the destruction of private property

a. Only I & IV
b. Only II
c. Only I and III
d. I, II, and III
e. I, II, III & IV

14.6 Describe the protection of property rights and related Court decisions.

The action of a government to take property for public use with just compensation is called ________.

a. civic taking
b. eminent domain
c. public purpose
d. sovereign immunity
e. default

14.7 Explain the Supreme Court's interpretation of the right to bear arms.

In 2010, the Supreme Court ruling that struck down a city of Chicago handgun ordinance:

a. extended the application of the 2nd Amendment to the states
b. found that handgun ownership was not protected by the 2nd Amendment
c. found the 2nd Amendment protected the right of states to maintain National Guards
d. the "right to bear arms" apply only to the states
e. just to show the Obama administration it could do so

14.8 Identify the constitutional rights of criminal defendants and assess the consequences of their implementation.

All of the following preserve the rights of criminal defendants *except*

a. guarantee of the writ of habeas corpus
b. prohibition of ex post facto laws
c. search warrants required in connection with all valid arrests
d. consultation with legal counsel
e. *Amicus* briefs

Explore Further

SUGGESTED READINGS

Burwell v. Hobby Lobby, 573 U.S. ___ (2014). A 'closely held corporation' is one where a majority of the stock is held by five or fewer individuals.

Domino, John C. *Civil Rights and Liberties in the 21st Century.* New York: Longman, 2010. Comprehensive text with landmark rulings on civil liberties.

Epstein, Lee, and Thomas G. Walker. *Constitutional Law for a Changing America: Rights, Liberties and Justice.* 7th ed. Washington, D.C.: CQ Press, 2010. An authoritative text on civil liberties and the rights of the criminally accused. It describes the political context of Supreme Court decisions and provides key excerpts from the most important decisions.

Garrow, David. *Liberty and Sexuality: The Right to Privacy and the Making of* Roe v. Wade. New York: Macmillan, 1994. Historical account of the background and development of the right to privacy and abortion.

Kobylka, Joseph F. *The Politics of Obscenity.* Westport, Conn.: Greenwood Press, 1991. Comprehensive review of Supreme Court obscenity decisions, arguing that the *Miller* case in 1973 was a turning point away from a more permissive to a more restrictive approach toward sexually oriented material. It examines the litigation strategies of the American Civil Liberties Union and other groups in obscenity cases.

Lewis, Anthony. *Gideon's Trumpet.* New York: Random House, 1964. The classic story of Clarence Gideon and how his handwritten habeas corpus plea made its way to the U.S. Supreme Court, resulting in the guarantee of free legal counsel for poor defendants in felony cases.

Savage, David. *The Supreme Court and Individual Rights.* 4th ed. Washington, D.C.: CQ Press, 2004. An overview of individual rights—freedom of ideas, political participation, due process and criminal rights, equal rights, and personal liberties.

Shiell, Timothy C. *Campus Hate Speech on Trial.* Lawrence, Kans.: University of Kansas Press, 1998. Traditional academic values emphasizing the free exchange of ideas are being sacrificed on campus by anti–hate speech codes.

Sullivan, Harold J. *Civil Rights and Liberties: Provocative Questions and Evolving Answers.* 2nd ed. New York: Longman, 2004. Contemporary issues in civil liberties discussed in a question-and-answer format.

Wert, Justin J. *Habeas Corpus in America: The Politics of Individual Rights.* Lawrence, Kan.: University of Kansas Press, 2011. Explores the evolution of the Great Writ and the impact of political forces throughout time on its interpretation and application.

SUGGESTED WEB SITES

American Civil Liberties Union (ACLU) www.aclu.org
This American Civil Liberties Union Web site provides ample information about the ACLU as an organization and the issues it deals with.

Americans United for Separation of Church and State www.au.org
Organization advocating elimination of religious activity from public life.

Anti-Defamation League of B'nai B'rith www.adl.org
Organization opposing anti-Semitism and securing justice for the Jewish people.

Brady Campaign www.bradycampaign.org
The nation's leading gun control organization, with facts, legislation, and a "report card" on each state.

Bureau of Alcohol, Tobacco, Firearms, and Explosives www.atf.gov
Federal agency responsible for regulation of alcohol, tobacco, firearms, and explosives; site includes publications on gun crimes.

Bureau of Justice Statistics www.ojp.usdoj.gov/bjs
Federal statistics on jails, prisons, probation, and capital punishment. Click to capital punishment for numbers of executions and persons under sentence of death.

Christian Coalition www.cc.org
Organization dedicated to "take America back" from the "judicial tyranny" that would remove religion from public life.

First Amendment Center www.firstamendmentcenter.org
Vanderbilt University center provides sources of information on 1st Amendment issues.

Internet Freedom www.netfreedom.org
Organization opposed to all forms of censorship and content regulation on the Internet.

National Association of Scholars www.nas.org
Advocacy organization opposing speech codes and other PC violations of individual freedom on campuses.

National Coalition to Abolish the Death Penalty www.ncadp.org
This site provides information about public policies, institutions, and individuals that collectively work toward the "unconditional rejection of capital punishment."

National Right to Life Committee www.nric.org
Leading antiabortion organization with information on current legislation and court cases.

Pro-Choice America www.prochoiceamerica.org
Formerly the National Abortion Rights Action League (NARAL), with information on current legislation and court cases.

Right to Keep and Bear Arms www.rkba.org
Organizations advocating self-defense rights with information on legislation, court cases, and related matters.

15

Politics and Civil Rights

Equal treatment under the law is the ideal of American politics—that all persons stand before the law, and are treated the same regardless of race, creed, color, or national origin. Now this notion has extended to the topic of sexual identity, resulting in a dramatic change in public policy and public opinion.

In 2007, longtime companions Edith Windsor and Thea Spyer were married in a civil ceremony in Canada. They had lived together as a romantic couple for 40 years, and after Canada legalized same-sex marriages in its Civil Marriage Act of 2005, the couple traveled there to marry. The two women returned to their home state of New York, where they lived together until Thea passed away two years later. Edith was her sole heir and filed for the federal estate exemption as a surviving spouse. The IRS denied her claim, citing Section 3 of the Defense of Marriage Act of 1996 (DOMA), which defined marriage as between a man and a woman. Edith Windsor paid $363,053 in estate taxes.

The next year, Edith sued the United States seeking a refund because DOMA treated heterosexual couples different from "other similarly situated couples without justification." She had difficulty finding counsel. Several gay rights groups refused to take the case. Finally, an attorney with a New York City law firm that had unsuccessfully sued to allow same-sex couples to marry in New York State took the case, assisted by the American Civil Liberties Union.

The Obama administration agreed with Edith and her lawyers and refused to defend the law. Instead, the U.S. House of Representatives through its Bipartisan Legal Advisory Group (BLAG) defended the law. Edith won in federal district court, which ruled that DOMA violated her 5th Amendment rights to due process. The Federal Appeals Court affirmed the district court's decision and BLAG appealed to the U.S. Supreme Court. A year later the Court, in a 5–4 decision written by Justice Kennedy, affirmed the lower court ruling and struck down Section 3 of DOMA, stating that the law served to "demean the couple, whose moral and sexual choices the Constitution protects."

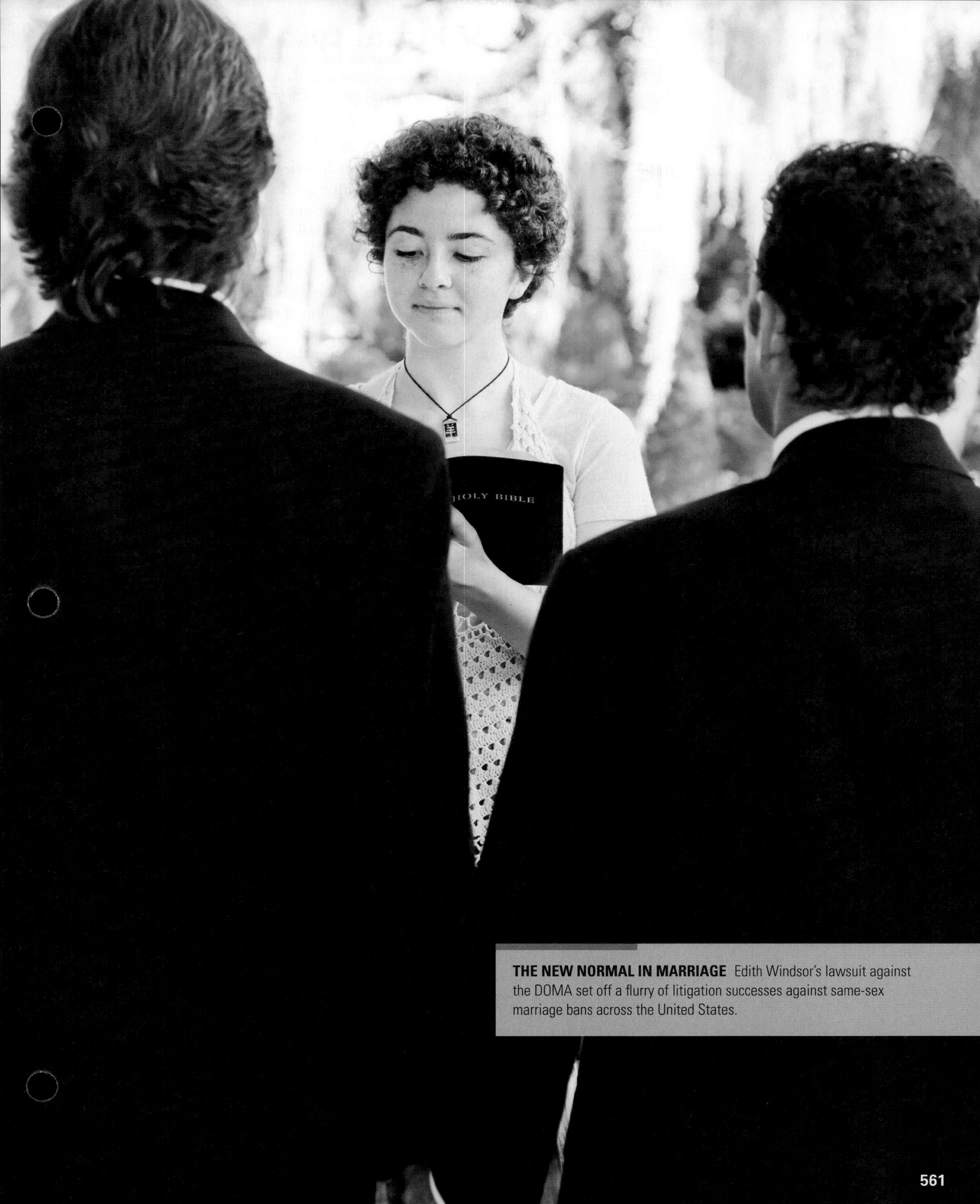

THE NEW NORMAL IN MARRIAGE Edith Windsor's lawsuit against the DOMA set off a flurry of litigation successes against same-sex marriage bans across the United States.

15.1
15.2
15.3
15.4
15.5
15.6
15.7
15.8
15.9

The Irony of Equality

15.1 Assess the role that politics played over the centuries in America's quest for equality and analyze how the Constitution was interpreted to first justify and then attack slavery and segregation.

Equality has been the central issue of American politics throughout the history of the nation. It is the issue that sparked the nation's only civil war, and it continues today to be the nation's most vexing political concern.

Conflict begins over the very definition of "equality." Although Americans agree in the abstract that everyone is equal, they disagree over what they mean by "equality." Traditionally, equality meant "equality of *opportunity*": an equal opportunity to develop individual talents and abilities and to be rewarded for work, initiative, merit, and achievement. Over time, the issue of equality has shifted to "equality of *results*": an equal sharing of income and material rewards. With this shift in definition has come political conflict over the question of what, if anything, government should do to narrow the gaps between rich and poor, men and women, blacks and whites, and all other groups in society. The other shift has been from a civil rights debate dominated by the legal status and concerns of African Americans to a far-reaching debate about discrimination and policies concerning linguistic minorities, women, and sexual identity minorities.

The nation's long struggle over equality has produced a number of constitutional and legal milestones in civil rights. These are summarized in Table 15.1. Much of the politics of civil rights centers on the development and interpretation of these guarantees of equality.

Slavery, Segregation, and the Constitution

In penning the Declaration of Independence in 1776, Thomas Jefferson affirmed that "All men are created equal." Yet from 1619, when the first slaves were brought to Jamestown, Virginia, until 1865, when the 13th Amendment to the Constitution outlawed the practice, slavery was a way of life in most of the American states. Africans were captured, enslaved, transported to America, bought and sold, and used as personal property.

Slavery and the Constitution

The Constitution of 1787 recognized and protected slavery in the United States. Article I stipulated that slaves were to be counted as three-fifths of a person for purposes of representation and taxation; it also prohibited any federal restriction on the importation of slaves until 1808. Article IV even guaranteed the return of escaped slaves to their owners. The Founders were aware that the practice of slavery contradicted their professed belief in "equality." This contradiction caused them some embarrassment, and they avoided the word *slave* in favor of the euphemism "person held to Service or Labour" in writing the Constitution.

Supreme Court Chief Justice Roger Taney, ruling in the notorious case of *Dred Scott v. Sandford* in 1857, reflected the racism that prevailed in early America:

> They had for more than a century before been regarded as beings of an inferior order, and altogether unfit to associate with the white race, either in social or political relations; and so far inferior, that they had no rights which the white man was bound to respect; and that the negro might justly and lawfully be reduced to slavery for his benefit.[1]

Taney's decision in this case interpreted the Constitution in terms of the *original intent* of the Founders. The ruling upheld slavery and the constitutional guarantee given slave owners for the return of slaves escaping to nonslave states.

TABLE 15.1 TOWARD EQUALITY: GUARANTEES OF CIVIL RIGHTS

13th Amendment (1865)	Neither slavery nor involuntary servitude, except as a punishment for crime whereof the party shall have been duly convicted, shall exist within the United States, or any place subject to their jurisdiction.
14th Amendment (1868)	No State shall make or enforce any law which shall abridge the privileges or immunities of citizens of the United States; nor shall any State deprive any person of life, liberty, or property, without due process of law; nor deny to any person within its jurisdiction the equal protection of the laws.
15th Amendment (1870)	The rights of the citizens of the United States to vote shall not be denied or abridged by the United States or by any State on account of race, color, or previous condition of servitude.
19th Amendment (1920)	The right of the citizens of the United States to vote shall not be denied or abridged by the United States or by any State on account of sex.
Civil Rights Acts of 1866, 1871, and 1875	Acts passed by the Reconstruction Congress following the Civil War. The Civil Rights Act of 1866 guaranteed newly freed persons the right to purchase, lease, and use real property. The Civil Rights Act of 1875 outlawed segregation in privately owned businesses and facilities, but in the Civil Rights Cases (1883), the Supreme Court declared the act an unconstitutional expansion of federal power, ruling that the 14th Amendment limits only "State" actions. Other provisions of these acts were generally ignored for many decades. But the Civil Rights Act of 1871 has been revived in recent decades; the act makes it a federal crime for any person acting under the authority of state law to deprive another of rights protected by the Constitution.
Civil Rights Act of 1957	The first civil rights law passed by Congress since Reconstruction. It empowers the U.S. Justice Department to enforce voting rights, established the Civil Rights Division in the Justice Department, and created the Civil Rights Commission to study and report on civil rights in the United States.
Civil Rights Act of 1964	A comprehensive enactment designed to erase racial discrimination in both public and private sectors of American life. Major titles of the act: I. outlaws arbitrary discrimination in voter registration and expedites voting rights suits; II. bars discrimination in public accommodations, such as hotels and restaurants, that have a substantial relation to interstate commerce; III. and IV. authorize the national government to bring suits to desegregate public facilities and schools; V. extends the life and expands the power of the Civil Rights Commission; VI. provides for withholding federal funds from programs administered in a discriminatory manner; VII. establishes the right to equality in employment opportunities.
Civil Rights Act of 1968	Prohibits discrimination in the advertising, financing, sale, or rental of housing, based on race, religion, or national origin and, as of 1974, sex. A major amendment to the act in 1988 extended coverage to the handicapped and to families with children.
Voting Rights Act	Enacted by Congress in 1965 and renewed and expanded over the years, this law sought to eliminate restrictions on voting were used to discriminate against blacks and other minority groups. Amendments in 1975 (1) required bilingual ballots in all states; (2) required prior approval by the Justice Department —"preclearance"— of any election law changes in states covered by the act; (3) extended legal protection of voting rights to Hispanic Americans, Asian Americans, and American Indians. The 1982 act provides that *intent* to discriminate need not be proven if the *results* demonstrate otherwise. The U.S. Supreme Court reviewed the act in 2013 and found that the coverage formula for the Justice Department's preclearance authority was outdated. (It was based on 1972 voting data.) The Court upheld the other sections of the Act.

abolition movement
Social movement before the Civil War whose goal was to abolish slavery throughout the United States.

Civil War, Emancipation, and Reconstruction

A growing number of Americans, especially members of the **abolition movement**, disagreed with Taney. In 1860, internal party divisions over the slavery issue led to a four-way race for the presidency and the election of Abraham Lincoln. Although personally opposed to slavery, Lincoln had promised during the campaign not to push for abolition where it existed. Many Southern leaders were unconvinced, however, and on December 20, 1860 (three months before Lincoln's inauguration), South Carolina became the first state to secede from the Union, touching off the Civil War.

The Civil War was the nation's bloodiest war. (Combined deaths of Union and Confederate forces matched the nation's losses in World War II, even though the nation's population in 1860 was one-fifth the population in 1940.) Very few families during the Civil War did not experience a direct loss from that conflict. As casualties

15.1

15.2

15.3

15.4

15.5

15.6

15.7

15.8

15.9

Emancipation Proclamation
Lincoln's 1862 Civil War declaration that all slaves residing in rebel states were free. It did not abolish all slavery; that would be done by the 13th Amendment in 1865.

Reconstruction
The post–Civil War period when the Southern states were occupied by federal troops and newly freed African Americans occupied many political offices and exercised civil rights.

mounted, northern Republicans joined abolitionists in calling for emancipating (freeing) the slaves simply to punish the Rebels. They knew that much of the South's power depended on slave labor. Lincoln also knew that if he proclaimed that the war was being fought to free the slaves, military intervention by the British on behalf of the South was less likely. Accordingly, on September 22, 1862, Lincoln issued his **Emancipation Proclamation**. Claiming his right as commander in chief of the army and navy, he declared that, as of January 1, 1863, "all persons held as slaves within any State, or designated part of a State, the people whereof shall then be in rebellion against the United States, shall be then, thenceforward, and forever free."

The Emancipation Proclamation freed slaves in the seceding states, and the 13th Amendment in 1865 abolished slavery everywhere in the nation. But freedom did not mean civil rights. The post–Civil War Republican Congress attempted to "reconstruct" Southern society. The 14th Amendment, ratified in 1868, made "equal protection of the laws" a command for every state to obey. The 15th Amendment, passed in 1869 and ratified in 1870, prohibited federal and state governments from abridging the right to vote "on account of race, color, or previous condition of servitude." In addition, Congress passed a series of civil rights laws in the 1860s and 1870s guaranteeing the newly freed slaves protection in the exercise of their constitutional rights. Between 1865 and the early 1880s, the success of **Reconstruction** was evident in widespread black voting throughout the South, the presence of many blacks in federal and state offices, and the admission of blacks to theaters, restaurants, hotels, and public transportation.[2]

Who's Getting What?

The Impact of the Voting Rights Act

The Voting Rights Act (VRA) of 1965 identified seven states—Alabama, Georgia, Louisiana, Mississippi, North Carolina, South Carolina, Virginia—for special coverage. These states used tests to qualify to vote, had very low voter participation, and also the highest percentages of African American residents. Under the VRA, any change in election laws would have to be approved by the U.S. attorney general to be sure that minority voters were not discriminated against.

One consequence of this law is an increase in the number of black officeholders in these states. In 1964, there was just one African American elected to the nearly 1,200 state legislative seats in the seven VRA states, even though blacks constituted over a quarter of all citizens in these states. Black representation has climbed slowly but steadily, to 7 percent of seats in 1980, 13 percent by 1990, and 23 percent by 2012.

This part of the law was overturned in 2013 by the Supreme Court.

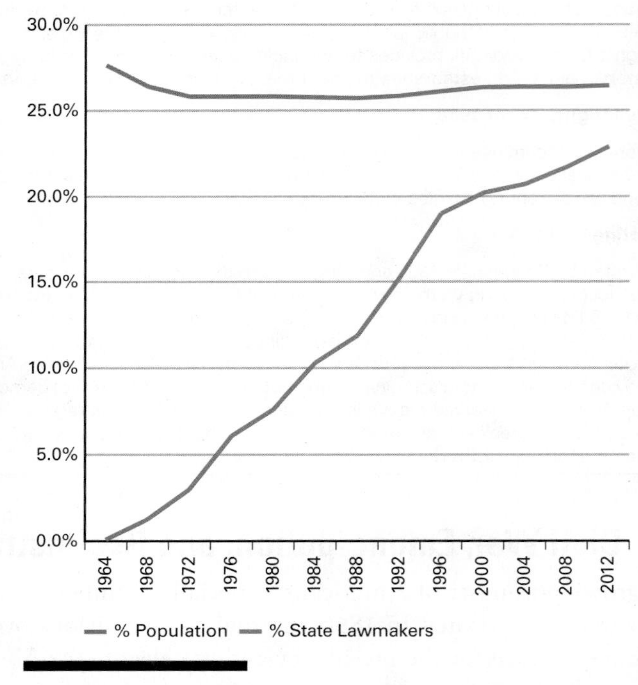

African American population and state legislators in the seven Voting Rights Act states

QUESTIONS

1. Describe the change in black representation compared to the black share of the population.
2. Do you think that overturning of part of the Voting Rights Act will diminish black representation in these states?

SOURCE: Officeholder data collected by authors; black population data from various editions of the U.S. Census.

The Imposition of Segregation

Political support for Reconstruction policies soon began to erode; within a decade Americans became weary of the race issue in the South after decades of debate, war, and Reconstruction. In the Compromise of 1877, the national government agreed to end military occupation of the South, give up its efforts to rearrange Southern society, and lend tacit approval to white supremacy in that region. In return, the Southern states pledged their support to the Union, accepted national supremacy, and agreed to permit the Republican presidential candidate, Rutherford B. Hayes, to assume the presidency, although the Democratic candidate, Samuel Tilden, had received more popular votes in the disputed election of 1876.

As white Southerners regained political power and blacks lost the protection of federal forces, the Supreme Court moved to strike down Reconstruction laws. In the Civil Rights Cases of 1883, the Supreme Court declared federal civil rights laws preventing discrimination by private individuals to be unconstitutional.[3] By denying Congress the power to protect blacks from discrimination by businesses and individuals, the Court paved the way for the imposition of segregation as the prevailing social system of the South. In the 1880s and 1890s, white Southerners imposed segregation in public accommodations, housing, education, employment, and almost every other sector of private and public life. By 1895, most Southern states had passed laws *requiring* racial segregation in education and in public accommodations—more than 90 percent of the African American population lived in the South, making Jim Crow nearly universal to the black American experience.

Segregation became the social instrument by which African Americans were "kept in their place"—that is, denied social, economic, educational, and political equality. In many states, **Jim Crow** followed them throughout life: birth in segregated hospital wards, education in segregated schools, residence in segregated housing, employment in segregated jobs, eating in segregated restaurants, and burial in segregated graveyards. Segregation was enforced by a variety of public and private sanctions, from lynch mobs to country club admission committees. But government was the principal instrument of segregation in both the Southern and the border states of the nation. (For a look at the political reactions of African Americans to segregation, see *The Game, the Rules, the Players:* African American Politics in Historical Perspective.)

Jim Crow
Second-class-citizen status conferred on blacks by Southern segregation laws; derived from a nineteenth-century song-and-dance act (usually performed by a white man in blackface) that stereotyped blacks.

separate but equal
Ruling of the Supreme Court in the case of *Plessy v. Ferguson* (1896) to the effect that segregated facilities were legal as long as the facilities were equal.

Early Court Approval of Segregation

Segregation was imposed despite the 14th Amendment's guarantee of "equal protection of the laws." In the 1896 case of *Plessy v. Ferguson*, the Supreme Court upheld state laws requiring segregation. Although segregation laws involved state action, the Court held that segregation of the races did not violate the Equal Protection Clause of the 14th Amendment as long as people in each race received equal treatment. Schools and other public facilities that were **separate but equal** were constitutional, the Court ruled.

> The object of the amendment was undoubtedly to enforce the absolute equality of the two races before the law, but in the nature of things it could not have been intended to abolish distinctions based upon color, or to enforce social—as distinguished from political—equality, or a commingling of the two races upon terms unsatisfactory to either. Laws permitting, and even requiring, their separation in places where they are liable to be brought into contact do not necessarily imply the inferiority of either race to the other, and have been generally, if not universally, recognized as within the competency of the state legislatures in the exercise of their police power.[4]

The effect of this decision was to give constitutional approval to segregation; the decision was not reversed until 1954.

The Game, the Rules, the Players

African American Politics in Historical Perspective

Many early histories of Reconstruction paid little attention to the political responses of African Americans to the imposition of segregation. But there were at least three distinct types of response: accommodation to segregation; the formation of a black protest movement and resort to legal action; and migration out of the South (to avoid some of the worst consequences of white supremacy) coupled with political mobilization of black voters in large Northern cities. Political economist Albert Otto Hirschman refers to this as "exit, voice, and loyalty." Given a choice of alternatives when there is decay in the quality of policy provided or of organizational quality, people in the group can leave (exit), they can protest and attempt to create a better outcome, or they can mitigate their effort to change things and accept the status quo.

Accommodation

The foremost African American advocate of accommodation to segregation was well-known educator Booker T. Washington (1856–1915). Washington enjoyed wide popularity among both white and black Americans. An adviser to two presidents (Theodore Roosevelt and William Howard Taft), he was highly respected by white philanthropists and government officials. In his famous Cotton States' Exposition speech in Atlanta in 1895, Washington assured whites that blacks were prepared to accept a separate position in society: "In all things that are purely social we can be as separate as the fingers, yet one as the hand in all things essential to mutual progress."[a]

Washington's hopes for black America lay in a program of self-help through education. He himself had attended Hampton Institute in Virginia, where the curriculum centered around practical trades for African Americans. Washington obtained some white philanthropic support in establishing his own Tuskegee Institute in Tuskegee, Alabama, in 1881. His first students helped build the school. Early curricula at Tuskegee emphasized immediately useful vocations, such as farming, teaching, and blacksmithing. One of Tuskegee's outstanding faculty members, George Washington Carver, researched and developed uses for Southern crops. Washington urged his students to stay in the South, acquire land, and build homes, thereby helping eliminate ignorance and poverty.

Protest

While Booker T. Washington was urging African Americans to make the best of segregation, a small group was organizing in support of a declaration of black resistance and protest that would later rewrite American public policy. The leader of this group was W. E. B. Du Bois (1868–1963), a historian and sociologist at Atlanta University. In 1905, Du Bois and a few other black intellectuals met in Niagara Falls, Canada, to draw up a platform intended to "assail the ears" and sear the consciences of white Americans. The Niagara Statement listed the major injustices perpetrated against African Americans since Reconstruction: the loss of voting rights, the imposition of Jim Crow laws and segregated public schools, the denial of equal job opportunities, the existence of inhumane conditions in Southern prisons, the exclusion of blacks from West Point and Annapolis, and the federal government's failure to enforce the 14th and 15th Amendments. Out of the Niagara meeting came the idea of a nationwide organization dedicated to fighting for African Americans, and on February 12, 1909, the one hundredth anniversary of Abraham Lincoln's birth, the National Association for the Advancement of Colored People (NAACP) was founded.

Du Bois himself was on the original board of directors of the NAACP, although a majority of the early board members and financial contributors were white. Du Bois was also the NAACP's first director of research and the editor of its magazine, *Crisis*. The NAACP began a long and eventually successful campaign to establish black rights through legal action. Over the years, this organization brought hundreds of court cases at the local, state, and federal court levels on behalf of African Americans denied their constitutional rights.

Migration and Political Mobilization: Voice or Exit?

World War I provided an opportunity for restive blacks in the South to escape the worst abuses of white supremacy by migrating en masse to Northern cities. Between 1916 and 1918, an estimated half million African Americans moved north to fill the labor shortage caused by the war effort. Most arrived in large Northern cities only to find more poverty and segregation, but at least they could vote, and they did not encounter laws requiring segregation in public places.

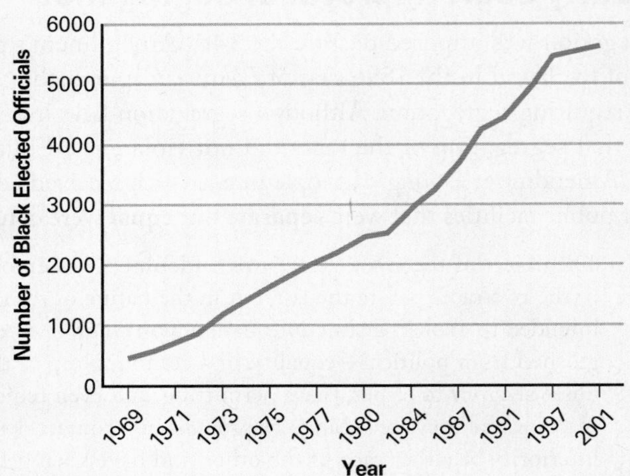

GROWING BLACK REPRESENTATION

Since the implementation of the Voting Rights Act in the 1960s, the number of black elected officials in the South has grown dramatically. (Data from Charles S. Bullock III and Ronald Keith Gaddie, 2009. The Triumph of Voting Rights in the South. Norman, Okla., The University of Oklahoma Press)

(*Continued*)

[a]Quoted in Henry Steele Commager, ed., 1967. *The Struggle for Racial Equality*. New York: Harper & Row, p. 19.

(*Continued*)

The progressive "ghettoization" of African Americans—their migration from the rural South to the urban North and their increasing concentration in central cities—had profound political as well as social implications. The ghetto provided an environment conducive to political mobilization. As early as 1928, African Americans in Chicago were able to elect one of their own to the U.S. House of Representatives. The election of Oscar de Priest, the first black member of Congress from the North, signaled a new turn in American urban politics by announcing to white politicians that they would have to reckon with the black vote in Northern cities. The black neighborhoods would soon provide an important element in a new political coalition that was about to take form in the 1930s: the Democratic Party of Franklin Delano Roosevelt.

The increasing concentration of African Americans in large, politically competitive, "swing" states provided black voters with new political power—not only to support the Democratic Party coalition in national politics but also to elect African Americans to public office. Once the Voting Rights Act was fully implemented, the ability of black votes to project political power and elect representatives was more pronounced in the South than anywhere else.

QUESTIONS

1. **What are the main differences in the approaches of Booker T. Washington and W. E. B. DuBois to issues of civil rights?**
2. **Do you think migration and voting were more effective tools in advancing African Americans toward full participation in the economic and political life of the United States?**

Equal Protection of the Laws

15.2 Differentiate the various meanings of equal protection of the laws.

he initial goal of the civil rights movement was to eliminate segregation laws, especially segregation in public education. Only after this battle was well under way could the civil rights movement turn to the fight against segregation and discrimination in all sectors of American life, *private* as well as *governmental.*

The Strange National Career of Jim Crow

"Jim Crow" laws are usually remembered as laws in former Confederate states that separated blacks and whites in the public space, the economy, and in personal relations. However, Jim Crow was insidious and diverse in its application across the United States. Over half of the states outside the South had some sort of Jim Crow law that applied to African Americans, American Indians, or Asians. Some examples:

In 1865, the Arizona territory passed a statute prohibiting marriage between whites and "Negroes, mulattoes, Indians, Mongolians." The statute was amended in 1901. Indians were removed from the statute in 1942. The entire statute was repealed in 1962.

In California, the influx of Chinese labor prompted a variety of statutory and state constitutional changes. The state (or localities) imposed prohibitions on Chinese employment, education, housing, and intermarriage (which also extended to blacks and Japanese), and in the nineteenth century required black and American Indian children to attend separate schools. Until 1926, Chinese immigrants were banned for life from voting by the state constitution.

The state of Maine required a voter to be able to read the Constitution in English. Maryland segregated all passenger trains. Nebraska banned interracial marriage with Africans and Asians and maintained segregated public schools. North Dakota kept Indian children segregated from whites in public schools.

In Oklahoma, the state required telephone companies to segregate public phones. Oklahoma was also the first state to enter the Union (in 1907) with constitutionally mandated, segregated schools.

15.1
15.2
15.3
15.4
15.5
15.6
15.7
15.8
15.9

All of these laws are now gone, and in the minds of the contemporary public, Jim Crow lingers as a peculiar legacy of the South. But bans on school integration and mixed race marriage in particular were widespread beyond the South, giving Jim Crow a national reach. These widespread bans are part of the American national racial history, and indicate a far more pervasive impact of segregation beyond the South.

The NAACP and the Legal Battle

The National Association for the Advancement of Colored People (NAACP) and its Legal Defense and Education Fund led the fight to abolish lawful segregation. As chief legal counsel to the fund, Thurgood Marshall (later the first African American to sit on the U.S. Supreme Court) began a long legal campaign to ensure equal protection of the law for African Americans. Initially, the NAACP's strategy focused on achieving the "equal" portion of the separate-but-equal doctrine. Segregated facilities, including public schools, were seldom "equal," even with respect to physical conditions, teachers' salaries and qualifications, curricula, and other tangible factors, and southern states failed to live up even to this standard. In a series of cases, Marshall and other NAACP lawyers convinced the Supreme Court to act when segregated facilities were clearly unequal. For example, the Court ordered the admission of individual blacks to white public universities where evidence indicated that separate black institutions were inferior or nonexistent.[5]

But Marshall's goal was to prove that segregation *itself* was inherently unequal whether or not facilities were equal in all tangible respects—a reversal of the *Plessy* case. In 1952, Marshall led a team of NAACP lawyers in a suit to admit Linda Brown to the white public schools of Topeka, Kansas, one of the few segregated school systems where white and black schools were equal with respect to buildings, curricula, teachers' salaries, and other tangible factors. In choosing the *Brown* suit, the NAACP sought to prevent the Court from simply ordering the admission of black pupils because tangible facilities were not equal and to force the Court to review the doctrine of segregation itself.

Brown v. Board of Education of Topeka

On May 17, 1954, the Court rendered its historic decision in the case of *Brown v. Board of Education of Topeka*:

> Segregation of white and colored children in public schools has a detrimental effect upon the colored children. The impact is greater when it has the sanction of law, for the policy of separating the races is usually interpreted as denoting the inferiority of the Negro group. A sense of inferiority affects the motivation of a child to learn. Segregation with the sanction of law, therefore, has a tendency to retard the educational and mental development of Negro children and to deprive them of some of the benefits they would receive in a racially integrated school system. Whatever may have been the extent of psychological knowledge of the time of *Plessy v. Ferguson*, this finding is amply supported by modern authority. Any language in *Plessy v. Ferguson* contrary to this source is rejected. . . . We conclude that in the field of public education the doctrine of "separate but equal" has no place. Separate educational facilities are inherently unequal.[6]

The Supreme Court decision in *Brown* was symbolically very important. Although it would be many years before any significant number of black children would attend previously all-white schools in the South, the decision by the nation's highest court stimulated black hopes and expectations. Indeed, *Brown* started the modern civil rights movement. As the African American psychologist Kenneth Clark wrote, "This [civil rights] movement would probably not have existed at all were it not for the 1954 Supreme Court school desegregation decision, which provided a tremendous boost to the morale of blacks by its clear affirmation that color is irrelevant to the rights of American citizens."[7]

Enforcing Desegregation

The *Brown* ruling struck down the laws of 21 states as well as congressional laws segregating the schools of the District of Columbia (see Figure 15.1).[8] Such a far-reaching exercise of judicial power was bound to meet with difficulties in enforcement, and the Supreme Court was careful not to risk its own authority. It did not order immediate national desegregation, but instead asked state and local authorities under federal court supervision to proceed with "all deliberate speed" in desegregation.[9] For more than 15 years, state and school districts in the South waged a campaign of resistance to desegregation. Delays in implementing school desegregation continued until 1969, when the Supreme Court rejected a request by Mississippi officials for further delay, declaring that all school districts were obligated to end their dual school systems "at once" and "now and hereafter" to operate only integrated schools.[10]

Federal district judges enjoy wide freedom in fashioning remedies for past or present discriminatory practices by governments. If a federal district court anywhere in the United States finds that any actions by governments or school officials have contributed to racial imbalances (for example, drawing school district attendance lines in order to separate black and white pupils), the judge may order the adoption of a desegregation plan to overcome racial imbalances produced by official action. A large number of cities came under federal district court orders to improve racial balances in their schools through busing.

In the 1971 case of *Swann v. Charlotte-Mecklenburg County Board of Education* (1971), the Supreme Court approved several techniques to correct historic segregation, including the use of racial balance requirements in schools and the assignments of pupils to schools based on race; "close scrutiny" by judges of schools that are predominantly of one race; redrawing school attendance zones as well as "clustering" or "grouping" of schools to achieve racial balance; and, most prominently, court-ordered busing of pupils to achieve racial balance.[11] The Court was careful to note that racial imbalance in schools is not itself grounds for ordering these remedies unless it is also shown that some present or past governmental action contributed to the imbalance.

De Facto Segregation

However, in the absence of any past or present governmental actions contributing to racial imbalance, states and school districts are not required by the 14th Amendment to integrate their schools. For example, where central-city schools are predominantly

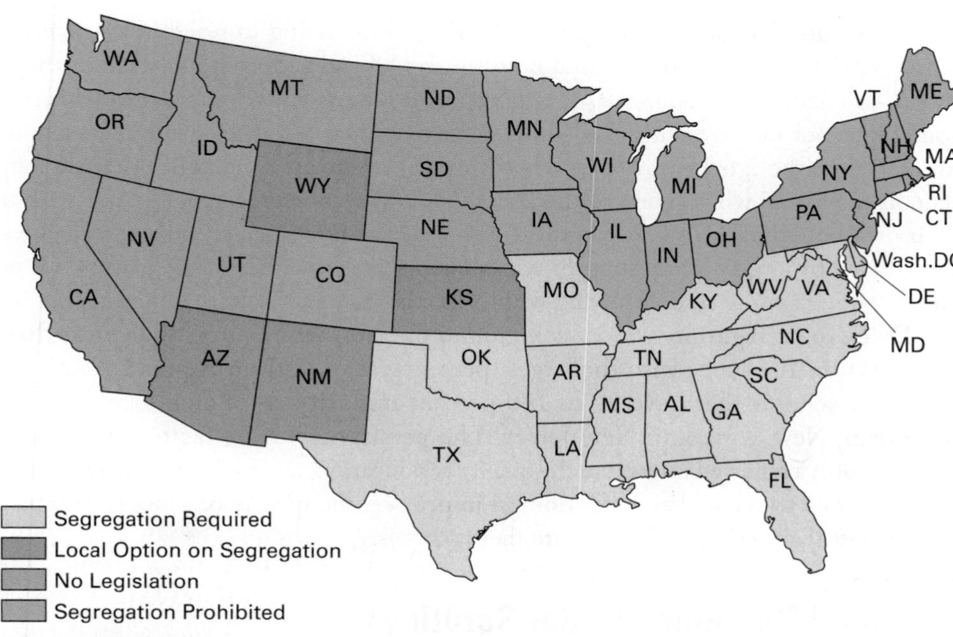

FIGURE 15.1 SEGREGATION LAWS IN THE UNITED STATES IN 1954

Segregation of the races in public schools was widespread in 1954 before the historic *Brown* decision deciding it was unconstitutional.

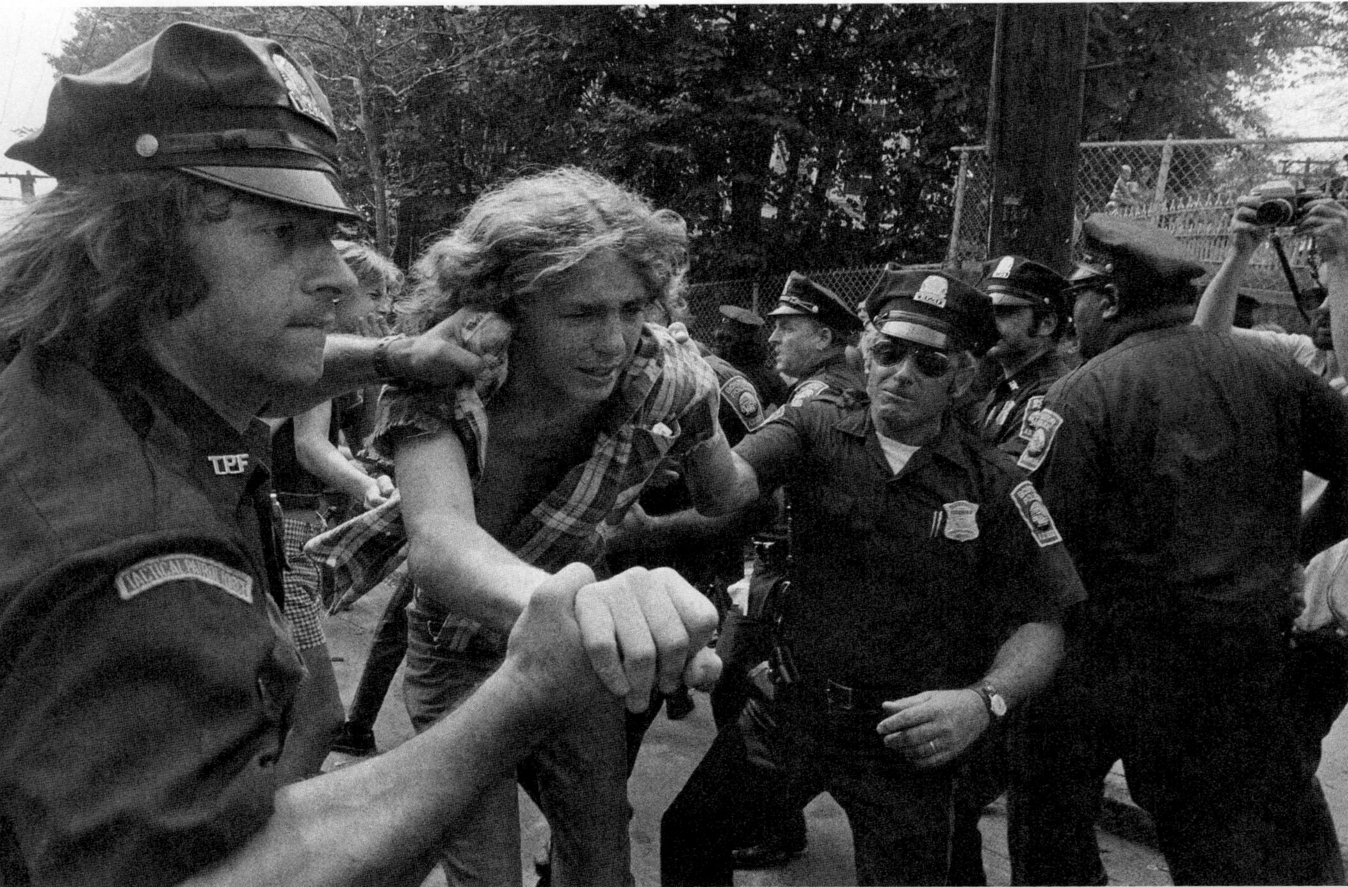

NORTH AND SOUTH

Although the first conflicts over integration in the public schools erupted in the segregated Southern states, Northern cities later became the focus of unrest over school integration. When federal judges ordered the busing of schoolchildren outside their neighborhoods in order to achieve racial balances citywide, parents and politicians in some Northern cities responded with a ferocity equal to earlier Southern protests. In Boston, many parents initially boycotted a busing order in 1974, refusing to send their children to school at all or establishing private schools and even attacking busloads of minority children arriving at formerly white schools.

de facto segregation
Racial imbalances not directly caused by official actions but rather by residential patterns.

black and suburban schools are predominantly white owing to residential patterns, cross-district busing is not required unless some official action brought about these racial imbalances. Thus, in 1974, the Supreme Court threw out a lower federal court order for massive busing of students between Detroit and 52 suburban school districts.[12] Although Detroit city schools were 70 percent black and the suburban schools almost all white, none of the area school districts segregated students within their own boundaries. This important decision means that largely black central cities surrounded by largely white suburbs will remain segregated in practice because there are not enough white students living within the city boundaries to achieve integration.

De facto segregation is more common in the Northern metropolitan areas than in the South. The states with the largest percentages of African American students attending schools that have 90 to 100 percent minority enrollments are Illinois, Michigan, New York, and New Jersey. The persistence of de facto segregation, together with a renewed interest in the quality of education, has caused many civil rights organizations to focus their attention on improving the quality of schools in urban areas rather than trying to desegregate these schools.

Racial Balancing Under Scrutiny

Racial balancing in public schools is coming under increasing Supreme Court scrutiny. With regard to schools with a history of segregation (mainly Southern schools), the Supreme Court has begun to address the question of when desegregation has been

TABLE 15.2 NONSOUTHERN STATES THAT SEGREGATED SCHOOLS OR PROHIBITED INTERRACIAL MARRIAGE AT SOME TIME AFTER THE CIVIL WAR

Segregation was not just a southern activity. In the century between the end of the Civil War and the striking down of Jim Crow laws across the United States, all eleven southern states segregated their schools and banned interracial marriage. But another 26 states adopted one or both of these policies too. Of these, twelve segregated schools and banned interracial marriage; six only segregated schools; and eight only banned interracial marriage.

Segregated Schools	Interracial Marriage Ban	Segregated Schools & Interracial Marriage Ban	
	In the South		
		Alabama	North Carolina
		Arkansas	South Carolina
		Florida	Tennessee
		Georgia	Texas
		Louisiana	Virginia
		Mississippi	
	Outside the South		
Kansas	Colorado	Arizona	Montana
Maryland	Maine	California	Nevada
Missouri	Nebraska	Connecticut	North Dakota
New Mexico	Oregon	Illinois	Ohio
Pennsylvania	Rhode Island	Indiana	Oklahoma
West Virginia	South Dakota	Kentucky	Wyoming
	Utah		
	Washington		

NOTE: Data collected by authors.

achieved and therefore when racial balancing plans can be abandoned. In the 1990s, the Court began to free school districts from direct court supervision and court-ordered racial balancing. When the last vestiges of state-sanctioned discrimination have been removed "as far as practicable," the Supreme Court has allowed lower federal courts to dissolve racial balancing plans even where imbalance due to residential patterns continue to exist.[13] The Supreme Court has also held that racial classifications by governments for whatever purpose are subject to "strict scrutiny" by the courts. This means that racial classifications must be "narrowly tailored" to achieve a "compelling government interest."

The Civil Rights Acts

15.3 Outline major civil rights legislation.

The early goal of the civil rights movement was to eliminate discrimination and segregation practiced by *governments*, particularly states and school districts. When the civil rights movement turned to *private* discrimination—discrimination practiced by private owners of restaurants, hotels, motels, and stores; private employers, landlords, and real estate agents; and others who were not government officials—it had to take its fight to Congress. *The Constitution does not govern the activities of private individuals*. Only Congress at the national level could outlaw discrimination in the private sector. Yet prior to 1964, Congress had been content to let the

nonviolent direct action
Strategy used by civil rights leaders such as Martin Luther King, Jr., in which protesters break "unjust" laws openly but in a "loving" fashion in order to bring the injustices of such laws to public attention.

courts struggle with the question of civil rights. New political tactics and organizations were required to put the issue of equality on the agenda of Congress.

Martin Luther King, Jr., and Nonviolent Direct Action

Leadership in the struggle to eliminate discrimination and segregation from private life was provided by a young African American minister, Martin Luther King, Jr. Under King, the civil rights movement developed and refined political techniques for use by American minorities, including **nonviolent direct action**. Nonviolent direct action is a form of protest that involves breaking "unjust" laws in an open way while embracing affirmative emotions rather than hostile confrontation. The purpose of nonviolent direct action is to call attention—to "bear witness"—to the existence of injustice. In the words of Martin Luther King, Jr., such civil disobedience "seeks to dramatize the issue so that it can no longer be ignored."

King formed the Southern Christian Leadership Conference (SCLC) in 1957 to develop and direct the growing nonviolent direct action movement. During the next few years, the SCLC overshadowed the older NAACP in leading the fight against segregation. Where the NAACP had developed its strategy of court litigation to combat discrimination by *governments*, now the SCLC developed nonviolent direct action tactics to build widespread popular support and to pressure Congress to outlaw discrimination by *private businesses*.

The year 1963 was perhaps the most important for nonviolent direct action. The SCLC focused its efforts in Birmingham, Alabama, where King led thousands of marchers in a series of orderly and peaceful demonstrations. When police attacked the marchers with fire hoses, dogs, and cattle prods—in full view of national television

SPEAKING UP FOR EQUALITY

In the civil rights march of 1963, more than 200,000 people marched peacefully on Washington, D.C., to end segregation. It was here that Martin Luther King, Jr., delivered his famous "I Have a Dream" speech.

cameras—millions of viewers around the country came to understand the injustices of segregation. The Birmingham action set off demonstrations in many parts of the country. The theme remained one of nonviolence, and it was usually whites rather than blacks who resorted to violence in these demonstrations.

The culmination of King's nonviolent philosophy was a huge yet orderly march on Washington, D.C., held on August 28, 1963. More than 200,000 blacks and whites participated in the march, which was endorsed by many civic leaders, religious groups, and political figures. The march ended at the Lincoln Memorial, where Martin Luther King, Jr., delivered his most eloquent appeal, titled "I Have a Dream." Congress passed the Civil Rights Act of 1964 by better than a two-thirds favorable vote in both houses; it won the overwhelming support of both Republican and Democratic members of Congress.

Martin Luther King, Jr., "I Have a Dream"

If a man hasn't discovered something he will die for, he isn't fit to live.[14]

For Martin Luther King, Jr. (1929–68), civil rights was something to die for, and before he died for the cause, he would shatter a century of Southern segregation and set a new domestic agenda for the nation's leaders. King's contributions to the development of nonviolent direct action won him international acclaim and the Nobel Peace Prize.

King's father was the pastor of one of the South's largest and most influential African American congregations, the Ebenezer Baptist Church in Atlanta, Georgia. Young Martin was educated at Morehouse College in Atlanta and received a Ph.D. in religious studies at Boston University. Shortly after beginning his career as a Baptist minister in Montgomery, Alabama, in 1955, a black woman, Rosa Parks, refused to give up her seat to whites on a Montgomery bus, setting in motion a year-long bus boycott in that city. Only 26 years old, King was thrust into national prominence as the leader of that boycott, which ended in the elimination of segregation on the city's buses. In 1957, King founded the Southern Christian Leadership Conference (SCLC) to provide encouragement and leadership to the growing nonviolent protest movement against segregation.

Perhaps the most dramatic application of nonviolent direct action occurred in Birmingham, Alabama, in the spring of 1963. Thousands of African Americans, ranging from schoolchildren to senior citizens, marched in protest. Although the demonstrators conducted themselves in a nonviolent fashion, police and firefighters attacked the demonstrators with fire hoses, cattle prods, and police dogs, all in clear view of national television cameras. Thousands of demonstrators were dragged off to jail, including King. (It was at this time that King wrote his "Letter from Birmingham Jail," explaining and defending nonviolent direct action.) Pictures of police brutality flashed throughout the nation and the world, touching the consciences of many white Americans.

King was also the driving force behind the most massive application of nonviolent direct action in U.S. history: the great "March on Washington" in August 1963, during which more than 200,000 black and white marchers converged on the nation's capital. The march ended at the Lincoln Memorial, where King delivered his most eloquent appeal, titled "I Have a Dream," in which he eloquently articulated his abiding belief in the Amercan Creed, that all men are created equal. It was in the wake of the March on Washington that President John F. Kennedy sent to Congress a strong civil rights bill that would be passed after his death—the Civil Rights Act of 1964. That same year, King received the Nobel Peace Prize.

White racial violence in the early 1960s, including murders and bombings of black and white civil rights workers, shocked and disgusted many whites in both the North and the South. In 1963, Medgar Evers, the NAACP's state chair for Mississippi, was shot to death by a sniper as he entered his Jackson home. That same year, a bomb killed four young black girls attending Sunday school in Birmingham. On the evening of April 3, 1968, King spoke to a crowd in Memphis, Tennessee. His speech, which some say foreshadowed his imminent assassination by paraphrasing Moses's message to the Israelites that he would not enter "the promised land," affirmed his determination that equal civil rights we be attained, that he had no fear of any man.[15] The next night, April 4, 1968, the world's leading exponent of nonviolence was killed by an assassin's bullet as he stood on a hotel balcony in Memphis.

The Civil Rights Act of 1964

Signed into law on July 4, 1964, the Civil Rights Act of 1964 ranks with the Emancipation Proclamation, the 14th Amendment, and the *Brown* case as one of the most important steps toward full equality for all minorities, including African Americans. Among its most important provisions are the following:

> *Title II*: It is unlawful to discriminate against or segregate persons on the grounds of race, color, religion, or national origin in any public accommodation, including hotels, motels, restaurants, movies, theaters, sports arenas, entertainment houses, and other places that offer to serve the public. This prohibition extends to all business establishments whose operations affect interstate commerce or whose discriminatory practices are supported by state action.
>
> *Title VI*: Each federal department and agency is to take action to end discrimination in all programs or activities receiving federal financial assistance in any form. This action may include termination of financial assistance to persistently discriminatory agencies.
>
> *Title VII*: It is unlawful for any employer or labor union to discriminate against any individual in any fashion in employment because of the individual's race, color, religion, sex, or national origin. The Equal Employment Opportunity Commission is established to enforce this provision by investigation, conference, conciliation, persuasion, and, if need be, civil action in federal court.

The Civil Rights Act of 1968

For many years "fair housing" had been considered the most sensitive area of civil rights legislation. Prospects for a fair housing law were poor at the beginning of 1968. However, when Martin Luther King, Jr., was assassinated on April 4 of that year, the mood of Congress and the nation changed dramatically. Congress passed a fair housing law as tribute to the slain civil rights leader. The Civil Rights Act of 1968 prohibited discrimination in the sale or rental of a dwelling to any person on the basis of race, color, religion, or national origin.

Equality: Opportunity Versus Results

15.4 Distinguish between equality of opportunity and equality of results and trace the Court's evolving attitude toward affirmative action.

Although the gains of the civil rights movement were immensely important, these gains were primarily in *opportunity* rather than in *results*. The civil rights movement of the 1960s did not bring about major changes in the conditions under which most African Americans lived in the United States. Racial politics today center around the *actual* inequalities between blacks and whites in incomes, jobs, housing, health, education, and other conditions of life. These politics are influenced by deep cultural and philosophical differences between most racial minorities and most Anglo whites.

Continuing Inequalities

The issue of inequality today is often posed as differences in the "life chances" of blacks and whites and Hispanics (see Table 15.3). The average income of a black family is 62 percent of the average white family's income. The average Hispanic family's

TABLE 15.3 ASSESSING EQUALITY: MINORITY "LIFE CHANCES" IN AMERICA

Equality of opportunity is not the same as equality of results. Differences remain between white and minority "life chances," for example, in income, poverty, unemployment, and education.

Median Income of Families				
	1980	**1990**	**2000**	**2012**
White	$47,560	$51,734	$53,029	$57,009
Black	27,519	30,033	33,676	33,321
Hispanic	31,952	32,837	34,442	39,005
Asian				69,636
Percentage of Persons Below Poverty Level				
	1980	**1990**	**2000**	**2012**
White	10.2%	10.7%	9.5%	15.0%
Black	32.5	31.9	22.5	27.2
Hispanic	25.7	28.1	21.5	25.6
Asian				11.7
Unemployment Rate				
	1980	**1990**	**2000**	**2012**
White	6.3%	4.8%	2.6%	7.2%
Black	14.3	11.4	5.4	13.8
Hispanic	10.1	8.2	4.4	10.3
Asian			2.7	5.9
Education: Percentage of Persons over 25 Who Have Completed High School				
	1970	**1980**	**1990**	**2012**
White	55%	69%	79%	91%
Black	31	51	66	92
Hispanic	32	44	51	70
Asian				93
Education: Percentage of Persons over 25 Who Have Completed College				
	1970	**1980**	**1990**	**2012**
White	11%	17%	22%	36%
Black	4	8	11	26
Hispanic	4	8	9	17
Asian				58

SOURCE: U.S. Bureau of the Census, www.census.gov/2012. Bureau of Labor Statistics www.bls.gov/2012.

income is 68 percent of the average white family's income. Nearly 25 percent of all black families live below the recognized poverty line, whereas 11 percent of white families do so. The black unemployment rate is more than twice as high as the white unemployment rate.

African American and Hispanic minorities have improved their economic condition in recent years. However, the income *disparity* between whites and minorities has remained about the same (see Figure 15.2). This income gap remains despite a significant narrowing of differences in educational levels between whites and minorities.

The civil rights movement opened up new opportunities for African Americans. But equality of *opportunity* is not the same as equality of *results*.

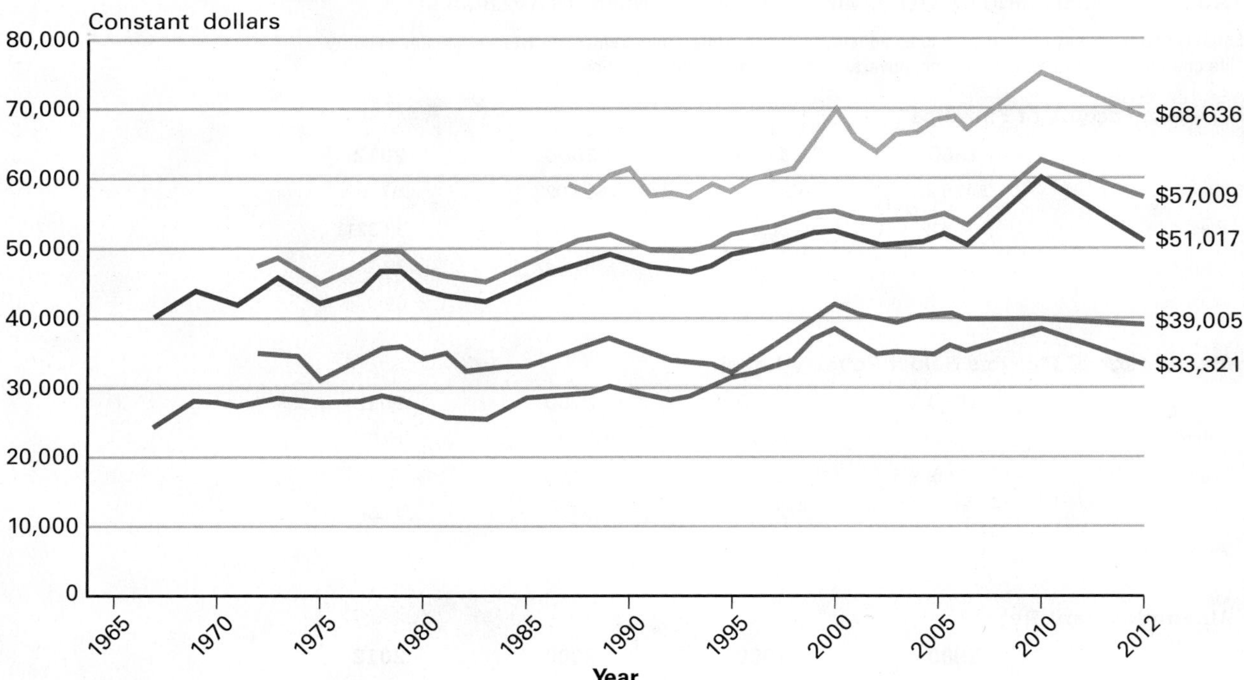

FIGURE 15.2 INCOME INEQUALITIES BY RACE AND ETHNIC GROUP

Disparities among racial and ethnic groups in America provide evidence of continuing inequalities. Real (inflation-adjusted) income has risen slowly over 40 years, but disparities remain.

SOURCE: U.S. Census Bureau, *Current Population Reports P60-245 Income, Poverty, and Health Insurance Coverage in the United States: 2012.* 1968 to 2010 Annual Social and Economic Supplements.

affirmative action
Any program, whether enacted by a government or by a private organization, whose goal is to overcome the results of past unequal treatment of minorities and/or women by giving members of these groups preferential treatment in admissions, hiring, promotions, or other aspects of life.

quota
Provision of some affirmative action programs in which specific numbers or percentages of positions are open only to minorities and/or women.

Policy Choices

What public policies should be pursued to achieve equality in America? Is it sufficient that government eliminate discrimination, guarantee equality of opportunity, and apply color-blind standards to both blacks and whites? Or should government take **affirmative action** to overcome the results of past unequal treatment of blacks—preferential or compensatory treatment to assist black applications for university admissions and scholarships, job hiring and promotion, and other opportunities for advancement in life?

Shifting Goals in Civil Rights Policy

The equal-opportunity, nondiscrimination approach began with President Harry Truman's decision to desegregate the armed forces in 1948 and carried through to Title VI and Title VII of the Civil Rights Act of 1964, which eliminated discrimination in federally aided projects and private employment. Gradually, however, the goal of the civil rights movement shifted from the traditional aim of equality of opportunity through nondiscrimination alone to affirmative action involving the establishment of "goals and timetables" to achieve greater equality of results between blacks and whites. While avoiding the term **quota**, the notion of affirmative action tests the success of equal opportunity by observing whether blacks achieve admissions, jobs, and promotions in proportion to their numbers in the population.

Affirmative Action

Affirmative action programs were initially developed in the federal bureaucracy. Federal executive agencies were authorized by the Civil Rights Act of 1964 to develop "rules and regulations" for desegregating any organization or business receiving

Who's Getting What?

The Stonewall Riots

"The Stonewall" is a bar on Christopher Street, between 4th Street and Waverly in the Greenwich Village neighborhood of New York City. On the morning of June 28, 1969, a NYPD raid on homosexual hangouts in Greenwich Village resulted in the first instance of active resistance to prosecuting homosexuals. These are known as the Stonewall Riots, which mark the beginning of the modern gay rights movement in the United States.

After World War II, Greenwich Village emerged as the center of an artistic and lifestyle counterculture in the United States, and also proved attractive to gay Americans. Efforts by New York City to shut down gay bars met with limited success; bars such as the Stonewall were run by organized crime, who tempered police vigilance with bribery. The Stonewall was one of the most "openly" gay bars, and it operated to a known clientele following procedures like a Prohibition-era speakeasy or a Southern "bottle club."

About 200 patrons were in Stonewall when it was raided. Police secured the premises and then proceeded to follow their established procedure for identifying the sex of patrons (the Stonewall had a separate "queen" bar in back for cross-dressers). The cross-dressers refused to cooperate, prompting the police to use more aggressive tactics while awaiting transport for the detained patrons.

Nondetained patrons refused to disperse, and as rumors spread that patrons in the bar were being beaten, a lesbian woman resisting arrest was struck by a billy club; her plea for assistance resulted in the crowd throwing bottles and bricks. The police, having experienced antiwar violence and race rioting in New York City in recent years, responded with violence; efforts to use fire hoses to quell the rioters proved ineffective. Inside the Stonewall, someone set fire to the front bar stand, while outside, cars were overturned. The NYPD called for tactical weapons backup—the forerunner of SWAT—and sought to reassert control. Police and rioters pursued each other through the streets of Greenwich Village. Calm prevailed by dawn on the 28th, but rioting began again that night and continued until 4:00 A.M. on Sunday.

THE STONEWALL INN

Previous gay rights protests had been held for nearly a decade, mainly in New York, L.A., Chicago, and San Francisco, and Stonewall wasn't the first violent resistance to police authority against nonstraights—that distinction belongs to the 1966 Compton Café riot, which involved resistance by transgendered men against the police. And the riots at Stonewall were not just a reaction to state repression. They also represented a rebellion against the quiet, conformist approach to gay rights advanced by groups such as Mattachine. The conservative, nearly philosophical approach to protest and recognition was overwhelmed by openly gay, openly identified groups that refused to minimize sexuality in their organizations or their movement. But Stonewall is a watershed; subsequently, the movement for gay rights was not governed by quiet, assimilative strategies but by demands for open recognition in society and under the law.

The marginalization of gays in the United States in many ways outpaced racial and ethnic segregation. Homosexuals were deemed to be security threats by the State Department; classified as sociopaths by the American Psychiatric Association from 1952–73; and tracked by federal authorities and denied employment in government and the military. Even the post office took on a role in enforcing antihomosexual policy.

By the mid-twentieth century, deeply rooted and secreted organizations, such as the Mattachine Society and its spinoff, ONE, Inc., sought to organize for gay rights and assimilation, but with limited success and in fear of legal persecution. The first major success of the gay rights movement was a federal court challenge to the refusal of the U.S. Postal Service to mail *ONE* magazine's October 1954 issue, which featured an article on homosexuals in heterosexual marriages. The post office and the FBI termed the issue "obscene," and a federal district court and the 9th Circuit U.S. Court of Appeals agreed, siding with the government.

The case was appealed to the U.S. Supreme Court. The Court took up the case and, relying on the precedent in *Roth v. United States*, reversed the lower courts on a 5–4 vote and issued an order that recognized homosexual press rights. The decision in *One, Inc. v. Olesen* 355 US 371 (1958) was one of the shortest in Supreme Court history, reading in its entirety, "The petition for writ of certiorari is granted and the judgment of the United States Court of Appeals for the Ninth Circuit is reversed."

QUESTIONS

1. How does the pre-Stonewall gay rights movement compare to the approach to civil rights for blacks espoused by Booker T. Washington?
2. Once violence erupts in most protest movements, sympathy is lost for the rioting group. Yet, since Stonewall, sympathy and support for gay rights has grown in the United States. Why do you think this is the case?

Bakke case
U.S. Supreme Court case challenging affirmative action.

federal funds. In 1965, President Lyndon B. Johnson signed Executive Order 11246, requiring all federal agencies and businesses contracting with the federal government to practice affirmative action. In 1972, the U.S. Office of Education issued guidelines that mandated "goals" for university admissions and faculty hiring of minorities and women. The Equal Employment Opportunity Commission (EEOC), established by the Civil Rights Act of 1964, is responsible for monitoring affirmative action programs in private employment.

Affirmative Action in the Courts

The constitutional question posed by affirmative action programs is whether they discriminate against whites in violation of the Equal Protection Clause of the 14th Amendment. A related question is whether affirmative action programs discriminate against whites in violation of the Civil Rights Act of 1964, which prohibits discrimination "on account of race," not just discrimination against blacks. Clearly, these are questions for the Supreme Court to resolve.

The *Bakke* Case

In the absence of a history of racial discrimination, the Supreme Court has been willing to scrutinize affirmative action programs to ensure that they do not directly discriminate against whites. In *University of California Regents v. Bakke* (1978), the Supreme Court struck down a special admissions program for minorities at a state medical school on the grounds that it excluded a white applicant because of his race and violated his rights under the Equal Protection Clause.[16] Allan Bakke applied to the University of California Davis Medical School two consecutive years and was rejected; in both years, black applicants with significantly lower grade point averages and medical aptitude test scores were accepted through a special admissions program that reserved 16 minority places in a class of one hundred.[17] The University of California did not deny that its admissions decisions were based on race. Instead, it argued that its racial classification was "benign," that is, designed to assist minorities. The special admissions program was designed to (1) "reduce the historical deficit of traditionally disfavored minorities in medical schools and the medical profession"; (2) "counter the effects of societal discrimination"; (3) "increase the number of physicians who will practice in communities currently underserved"; and (4) "obtain the educational benefits that flow from an ethnically diverse student body."

The Supreme Court held that these objectives were legitimate and that race and ethnic origin *may* be considered in reviewing applications to a state school without violating the 14th Amendment's Equal Protection Clause. However, the Court also held that a separate admissions program for minorities with a specific *quota* of openings that were unavailable to white applicants *did* violate the Equal Protection Clause. The university was ordered to admit Bakke to its medical school and to eliminate the special admissions program. It recommended that California consider an admissions program developed at Harvard, which considered disadvantaged racial or ethnic background as a "plus" in an overall evaluation of an application but did not set numerical quotas or exclude any person from competing for all positions. Supporters of affirmative action predictably emphasized the Supreme Court's willingness to allow minority status to be considered a positive factor; opponents, the Supreme Court's unwillingness to allow quotas that exclude whites from competing for some positions. Because **Bakke** had "won" the case, many observers felt that the Supreme Court was not going to permit racial quota systems.

Affirmative Action as a Remedy for Past Discrimination

The Supreme Court has continued to approve of affirmative action programs where there is evidence of past discriminatory practices. In *United Steelworkers of America v. Weber* (1979), the Supreme Court approved a plan developed by a private employer and a union to reserve 50 percent of higher paying, skilled jobs for minorities.

What Do You Think?

Affirmative Action

Americans generally support the notion of 'affirmative action.' A 2013 poll found 58 percent of Americans saying they favor 'affirmative action programs for racial minorities,' including 51 percent of whites, 76 percent of blacks, and 69 percent of Hispanics:

Q. Do you generally favor of oppose affirmative action programs for racial minorities?

	Favor %	Oppose %
National adults	58	37
Whites	51	44
Blacks	76	20
Hispanics	69	25

However, Americans are less likely to support affirmative action in college admissions because the question raises potential consequences of such programs—admitting some minority students who would otherwise not be admitted on their merits alone:

Q. Which comes closer to your view about evaluating students for admission into a college or universities—applicants should be admitted solely on the basis of merit, even if that results in few minority students being admitted, (or) an applicant's racial and ethnic background should be considered to help promote diversity on college campuses, even if that means admitting some minority students who otherwise would not be admitted?

	Favor %	Oppose %
National adults	67	28
Whites	75	22
Blacks	44	48
Hispanics	59	31

These views have remained fairly stable over time, including differences between whites, blacks, and Hispanics.

SOURCE: Gallup, June 13-July 5 2013, at www.gallup.com.

CHALLENGING AFFIRMATIVE ACTION

Barbara Grutter and Jennifer Gratz contested the affirmative action policies of the University of Michigan. The Supreme Court rejected Grutter's challenge, holding that the law school's admission policy was "narrowly tailored" to achieve a "compelling interest"—diversity. But the high court upheld Gratz's claim that making race the "decisive factor" in undergraduate admissions was unconstitutional.

The Court held that "employers and unions in the private sector [are] free to take such race-conscious steps to eliminate manifest racial imbalances in traditionally segregated job categories. We hold that Title VII does not prohibit such . . . affirmative action plans." According to the Court, it would be "ironic indeed" if the Civil Rights Act were used to prohibit voluntary private race-conscious efforts to overcome the past effects of discrimination.[18] In *United States v. Paradise* (1987), the Court upheld a rigid 50 percent black quota system for promotions in the Alabama Department of Safety, which had excluded blacks from the ranks of state troopers prior to 1972 and had not promoted any blacks higher than corporal prior to 1984. In a 5–4 decision, the majority stressed the long history of discrimination in the agency as a reason for upholding the quota system. Whatever burdens imposed on innocent parties were outweighed by the need to correct the effects of past discrimination.[19]

set-aside program
Program in which a specified number or percentage of contracts must go to designated minorities.

☐ Cases Questioning Affirmative Action

However, the Supreme Court has continued to express concern about whites who are directly and adversely affected by government action solely because of their race. In *Firefighters Local Union 1784 v. Stotts* (1984), the Court ruled that a city could not lay off white firefighters in favor of black firefighters with less seniority.[20] In *City of Richmond v. Crosen Co.* (1989), the Supreme Court held that a minority **set-aside program** in Richmond, Virginia, which mandated that 30 percent of all city construction

strict scrutiny
Supreme Court holding that race-based actions by governments can be done only to remedy past discrimination or to further a "compelling" interest and must be "narrowly tailored" to minimize effects on the rights of others.

diversity
Term in higher education that refers to racial, gender, and ethnic representation among students and faculty.

contracts must go to "blacks, Spanish-speaking, Orientals, Indians, Eskimos, or Aleuts," violated the Equal Protection Clause of the 14th Amendment.[21]

☐ Strict Scrutiny

The Supreme Court has also held that racial classifications in law must be subject to "**strict scrutiny**." This means that race-based actions by government—any disparate treatment of the races by federal, state, or local public agencies—must be found necessary to remedy past proven discrimination, or to further clearly identified, legitimate, and "compelling" government interests. Moreover, race-based actions must be "narrowly tailored" and "least restrictive" so as to minimize adverse effects on rights of other individuals. In striking down a federal construction contract set-aside program for small businesses owned by racial minorities, the Court expressed skepticism about governmental racial classifications: "There is simply no way of determining what classifications are 'benign' and 'remedial' and what classifications are in fact motivated by illegitimate notions of racial inferiority or simple racial politics."[22]

In addition, the Supreme Court has held that "classifying and assigning school children according to a binary conception of race is an extreme approach in light of this Court's precedents and the nation's history of using race in public schools." The Court held that Seattle's voluntary student assignment plan that relied on race to determine which schools students could attend violated the Equal Protection Clause of the 14th Amendment. Seattle had never segregated by law. It struck down a similar Louisville plan that had succeeded a court-ordered desegregation plan where the last vestiges of legal segregation were eliminated. The Court held that, under either circumstance, narrow tailoring requires "serious good faith consideration of workable race-neutral alternatives." Racial diversity may be a "compelling interest" in higher education, but in public schools, assignment of pupils *must* be made on a nonracial basis. "Dividing people by race is inherently suspect because such classifications promote notions of racial inferiority and lead to a politics of racial hostility."[23]

☐ Affirmative Action and "Diversity" in Higher Education

Most colleges and universities in the United States—public as well as private—identify "**diversity**"—a term that refers to racial, gender, and ethnic representation in the student body and faculty—as an institutional goal. University administrators argue that students benefit when they interact with others from different cultural heritages. There is some evidence that students admitted under policies designed to increase diversity do well in their postcollege careers. And there are claims that racial and ethnic diversity promotes self-esteem and broadens students' understanding of the historic differences of Americans while promoting intelligent conversation. But despite numerous efforts to develop scientific evidence that racial or ethnic diversity on the campus improves learning, no definitive conclusions have emerged. Educational research on this topic is clouded by political and ideological conflict. There is no evidence that racial diversity does in fact promote the expression of ideas on the campus or change perspectives or viewpoints of students.

☐ Diversity as a Constitutional Question

The U.S. Supreme Court has held that the Equal Protection Clause of the 14th Amendment requires that racial classifications be subject to "strict scrutiny."[24] The Court held in 2003 that diversity may be a compelling government interest because it "promotes cross-racial understanding, helps to break down racial stereotypes, and enables [students] to better understand persons of different races." This opinion was written by Justice Sandra Day O'Connor in a case involving the University of Michigan Law School's affirmative action program. In a 5–4 decision, O'Connor, writing for the majority, said the Constitution "does not prohibit the law school's narrowly tailored use of race in admissions decisions to further a compelling interest in obtaining the educational benefits that flow from a diverse student body."[25]

However, in a case involving the University of Michigan's affirmative action program for *undergraduate admissions*, the Supreme Court held that the admissions policy was "not narrowly tailored to achieve respondents' asserted interest in diversity" and therefore violated the Equal Protection Clause of the 14th Amendment. The Court again recognized that diversity may be a compelling interest, but *rejected an affirmative action plan that made race the decisive factor* for even minimally qualified minority applicants. Yet the Supreme Court restated its support for limited affirmative action programs that use race as a "plus" factor, the position the court has held since the *Bakke* case in 1978.[26]

☐ Race-Neutral Approaches to Diversity

There is a variety of ways in which diversity can be achieved without using racial preferences in the admission of students. Under President George W. Bush the U.S. Department of Education recommended (1) preferences based on socioeconomic status; (2) recruitment outreach efforts targeted at students from traditionally low-performing schools; and (3) admission plans for students who finish at the top of their high school classes without regard to SAT or ACT scores.[27] Texas and Florida currently give preference to students who stand at or near the top of their class in each of the states' high schools. Both states officially abandoned racial preferences. Yet currently both states enroll roughly the same numbers of minorities in their colleges and universities that they did before abandoning racial preferences.

☐ The Absence of a Clear Constitutional Principle

No clear rule of law or constitutional principle tells us exactly what is permissible and what is prohibited in the way of racially conscious laws and practices. Nevertheless, over time, some general tendencies in Supreme Court policy can be identified. Affirmative action programs are *more likely to be found constitutional* when

- They are adopted in response to a past proven history of discrimination.
- They do not absolutely bar whites or ban them from competing or participating.

Compared to What?

Discrimination and the Romani in Europe

One of the most distinct minority groups in Europe are the nomadic Roma, sometimes derisively called "gypsies." There are approximately 10 million of these persons, whose ancestors originated in India. The countries with the largest percentage of Roma are Bulgaria (over 10 percent), Slovakia (9.2 percent), and Romania (8.3 percent), located in central and southern Europe.

Romani are historically persecuted throughout the world, in no small part due to their lack of assimilation to local culture, or the perception that they are criminal and untrustworthy as a class. Among the recent policies pursued by modern states are forced assimilation (France), sterilization (Czechoslovakia), expulsion and repatriation (several states, most recently Germany and France), public banning of Romani music and culture (Romania), and eradication and acts of genocide (Albania, Nazi Germany). Romani have responded to these acts with resistance and sometimes armed violence.

How the EU and its constituent states deal with Antiziganism (discrimination and racism directed against Roma) is a growing issue in Europe. According to Amnesty International, the Roma confront systematic discrimination across Europe. The EU has documented the systematic segregation of Romani children in European schools that offer low-quality education. Roma are arrested at a far higher rate than other ethnics, leading to complaints of selective and discriminatory enforcement.

The European Union is attempting to formulate policy to deal with Roma discrimination. Among the initiatives being undertaken in member states are efforts at job training, reintegration of Romani students into schools, and the creation of liaison and assistance officers to assist Romani in dealing with government and the dominant local culture. Nonetheless, many Romani still confront violence and systematic discrimination.

QUESTION

1. How does the Romani discrimination experience compare to that of blacks or Hispanics in the United States?

SOURCE: European Commission, *Improving the Tools for the Social Inclusion and Non-discrimination of Roma in the EU—Summary and Selected Projects* (2010).

- They serve a clearly identified, legitimate, and "compelling governmental interest."
- They are "narrowly tailored" to achieve the government's compelling interest and represent the "least restrictive" means of doing so.

It is important to note that the Supreme Court has never adopted the color-blind doctrine, first espoused by Justice Harlan in his *dissent* from *Plessy v. Ferguson*, that "Our Constitution is color-blind, and neither knows nor tolerates classes among the citizens." If the Equal Protection Clause required the laws of the United States and the states to be truly color-blind, then no racial guidelines, goals, or quotas would be tolerated. Occasionally, this view has been expressed in recent minority dissents (see *A Conflicting View*: The Constitution Should Be Color-Blind).

Civil Rights Initiatives in the States

National rethinking of affirmative action was inspired by a citizens' initiative placed on the ballot in California by popular petition and approved by 54 percent of the state's voters in 1996. The California Civil Rights Initiative added the following phrase to that state's constitution:

> Neither the state of California nor any of its political subdivisions or agents shall use race, sex, color, ethnicity or national origin as a criterion for either discriminating against, or granting preferential treatment to, any individual or group in the operation of the State's system of public employment, public education or public contracting.[28]

A Conflicting View

The Constitution Should Be Color-Blind

In 1896 a single voice spoke out against all racial classifications—Supreme Court Justice John Harlan opposing segregation: "Our Constitution is color-blind and neither knows nor tolerates classes among the citizens." He was *dissenting* from the Supreme Court's majority opinion in the infamous *Plessy v. Ferguson* case, which approved the segregationist "separate but equal" doctrine. Martin Luther King, Jr., had a dream that where people might be not "judged by the color of their skin but by the content of their character." Can that dream be made a reality?

Over time, the civil rights movement shifted its focus from *individual rights* to *group benefits*. Affirmative action programs classify people by group membership, thereby challenging the widely held belief that people be judged on individual attributes such as character and achievement, rather than their group. Racial and gender preferences are encountered in hiring and promotion practices in private and public employment and in college and university admissions, scholarships, and recruitment.

Affirmative action divides Americans into two classes—those who enjoy legally mandated preferential treatment and those who do not. Some early supporters of affirmative action have come to view race-conscious programs as no longer necessary. They argue that disadvantages in society today are based more on class than on race. If preferences are to be granted at all, in their view, they should be based on economic disadvantage, not race.

Misgivings are also expressed by some African American scholars, claiming unfair stigmatizing of the supposed beneficiaries of affirmative action through negative stereotyping of blacks as unable to advance on merit alone, and thereby doing more harm than good. African American economist Glenn Loury claims that proponents of affirmative action have an inferiority complex: "When blacks say we have to have affirmative action, please don't take it away from us, it's almost like saying, you're right, we can't compete on merit. But I know that we can compete." Conservative columnist William Bennett claims that "affirmative action has not brought us what we want—a color-blind society. It has brought us an extremely color conscious society. In our universities we have separate dorms, separate social centers. What's next—water fountains? That's not good and everybody knows it."

QUESTIONS

1. Is it enough to "level a playing field," given historic discrimination?
2. Do you think you can express your political opinions on race freely on campus?

SOURCE: Quotations reported in *Newsweek*, February 13, 1996.

The key words are "or granting preferential treatment to. . . ." Opponents argued that a constitutional ban on preferential treatment of minorities and women eliminates affirmative action programs in government, prevents governments from acting to correct historic racial or gender imbalances, and denies minorities and women the opportunity to seek legal protections in education and employment. Opponents challenged the California Civil Rights Initiative in federal courts, arguing that by preventing minorities and women from seeking preferential treatment under law, the initiative violated the Equal Protection Clause of the 14th Amendment. But a Circuit Court of Appeals held, and the U.S. Supreme Court affirmed, that "[A] ban on race or gender preferences, as a matter of law or logic does not violate the Equal Protection Clause in any conventional sense . . . Impediments to preferential treatment do not deny equal protection."[29] The Court reasoned that the Constitution allows some race-based preferences to correct past discrimination, but it does not prevent states from banning racial preferences altogether.

Following success in California, the organizer of that initiative, former California Board of Regents member Ward Connerly, created a nationwide organization to advance similar efforts in other states. The American Civil Rights Institute was instrumental in winning a constitutional amendment banning racial preferences in the state of Washington in 1998. Later, the threat of a ballot initiative in Florida caused Governor Jeb Bush to ban race-based preferences in state universities and state contracting by executive order in 2000. And in 2006, voters in Michigan approved an initiative banning racial preferences by a margin of 58 to 42 percent. This Michigan Civil Rights Initiative was opposed by the state's political leadership, including both the Democratic and Republican candidates for governor. (The initiative was spearheaded by Jennifer Gratz, who had earlier prevailed in her Supreme Court case against the University of Michigan's affirmative action program in undergraduate admissions.) In 2010 voters in Arizona approved an initiative banning racial, ethnic, or sexual preferences in state and local government contracting, employment, and education (including universities) with a 60 percent margin of the vote. Supporters of racial preferences in affirmative action programs have generally sought to keep initiatives banning racial preferences from appearing on state ballots. These initiatives have won voter approval in most of the states where they have appeared. Some argue that these ballot measures are misleading because they are labeled "civil rights initiatives," while the key phrase "or granting preferential treatment to" is buried in the wording of the initiatives. Court challenges to these initiatives abound in states where they have appeared and in states where initiative signatures have been sought.

Hispanics in America

15.5 Characterize the Hispanics in the United States demographically and politically.

Hispanics—a term the U.S. Census Bureau uses to refer to Mexican Americans, Puerto Ricans, Cubans, and others of Spanish-speaking ancestry and culture—are now the nation's largest minority (see Table 15.4). The largest Hispanic subgroup is Mexican Americans. Some are descendants of citizens who lived in the Mexican territory annexed to the United States in 1848, but most have come to the United States in accelerating numbers in recent years. The largest Mexican American populations are found in Texas, Arizona, New Mexico, and California. Puerto Ricans are the second-largest Hispanic subgroup. Cubans make up the third-largest subgroup; many are refugees or descendants of refugees from Fidel Castro's Cuba and live mainly in South Florida. Each of these

TABLE 15.4 THE CHANGING FACE OF AMERICA

The Census for 2010 included over 50 million Hispanics, the nation's largest minority group

	Number (000)	Percent of Population (%)
Whites[a]	196,670	63.7
Hispanics	50,325	16.3
African Americans	38,901	12.6
Asians	14,819	4.8
All other[b]	12,349	4.0
Total Population	308,745	100.0

[a]White alone, not of Hispanic origin.

[b]Includes American Indian, Alaska Native, Hawaiian and Pacific Islander, and persons identified as being of two or more races.

SOURCE: *Statistical Abstract of the United States* 2012–13, p.23.

Hispanic groups has encountered a different experience in American life. Indeed, some evidence indicates that these groups identify themselves separately, rather than as Hispanics as a single group.[30]

If all Hispanics are grouped together for statistical comparisons, their median family income level is below that of whites (see Table 15.3 on page 604). Hispanic poverty and unemployment rates are also higher than those of whites. The percentage of Hispanics completing high school and college education is well below that of both whites and blacks, suggesting language or other cultural obstacles in education. Yet within these overall racial comparisons, there are wide disparities among subgroups as well as among individuals.

The Game, the Rules, the Players

César Chávez, Mobilizing Latino Farmworkers

César Chávez mobilized America's Latino farmworkers for political and economic advancement. Chávez was a self-educated farmworker from California. He was recruited in the 1950s by the Community Service Organization, a Latino civil rights group, to lead a campaign to encourage Mexican Americans to register and vote. He would later co-found the union that became the United Farm Workers (UFW).

Starting in 1965 Chávez and the UFW led a five-year strike of California grape pickers that attracted national attention. It ended with the first labor agreement between the California growers and the union. Chávez also won the passage of the California Agricultural Labor Relations Act, which recognized the collective bargaining rights of the state's farmworkers. He and the UFW opposed illegal immigration as a threat to the wages and working conditions of farmworkers, and he backed President Reagan's Immigration Reform Act of 1986 that offered amnesty to undocumented aliens.

Chávez died in 1993, at the age of 66. President Bill Clinton posthumously awarded Chávez the Presidential Medal of Freedom.

QUESTION

1. Are you surprised that Mexican American immigrants historically supported immigration reform and opposed illegal immigration? Why?

Mexican Americans

For many years, agricultural business encouraged immigration of Mexican farm laborers willing to endure harsh conditions for low pay. Many came to the United States as *indocumentados*—undocumented, or illegal, aliens. In the Immigration Reform Act of 1986, Congress offered amnesty to all undocumented workers who had entered the United States prior to 1982.

Economic conditions in Mexico and elsewhere in Central America continue to fuel immigration, legal and illegal, to the United States. But with lower educational levels, average incomes of Mexican American families in the United States are lower and the poverty rate is higher than the general population. Although Mexican Americans have served as governors of Arizona and New Mexico and have won election to the U.S. Congress, their political power does not yet match their population percentages. Mexican American voter turnout is lower than other ethnic groups, perhaps because many are resident aliens or illegal immigrants not eligible to vote, or perhaps because of cultural factors that discourage political participation.[31]

Puerto Ricans

Residents of Puerto Rico are American citizens because Puerto Rico is a commonwealth of the United States. Puerto Rico's commonwealth government resembles that of a state, with a constitution and elected governor and legislature, but the island has no voting members of the U.S. Congress and no electoral votes for president. As citizens, Puerto Ricans can move anywhere in the United States; many have immigrated to New York City, and there is a next-generation migration into central Florida.

Puerto Ricans have not fared as well economically as other Hispanic groups within the United States: Puerto Ricans have lower median family incomes and higher poverty percentages, in part perhaps because of lower workforce participation. One explanation centers on the history of access to federal welfare programs on the island and the resulting social dependency it fostered among some Puerto Rican families.[32]

Puerto Ricans have long debated whether to remain a commonwealth of the United States, apply for statehood, or seek complete independence from the United States. As citizens of a commonwealth, Puerto Ricans pay no U.S. income tax (although their local taxes are substantial) while receiving all the benefits that U.S. citizens are entitled to—Social Security, welfare assistance, food stamps, Medicaid, Medicare, and so forth. If Puerto Rico chose to become a state, its voters could participate in presidential and congressional elections, but its taxpayers would not enjoy the same favorable cost–benefit ratio they enjoy under commonwealth status. Some Puerto Ricans also fear that statehood would dilute the island's cultural identity and force English on them as the national language, even though there is no legally mandated official language of the United States.

As a state, Puerto Rico would have two U.S. senators and perhaps six U.S. representatives. The island's majority party, the Popular Democratic Party, is closely identified with the Democratic Party, so most of these new members would likely be Democrats. But the island's New Progressive Party, identified with the Republican Party, supports statehood, and many GOP leaders believe their party should appeal to Hispanic voters. If Puerto Ricans were to choose independence, a new constitution for the Republic of Puerto Rico would be drawn up by the islanders themselves.

Only Congress can admit a new state, but Congress is unlikely to act without the full support of Puerto Ricans themselves. Several nonbinding referenda votes have been held in Puerto Rico over the years. Opinion today appears to be closely divided, with commonwealth status edging out statehood by a small margin; independence has never received more than one percent of the vote.

15.1
15.2
15.3
15.4
15.5
15.6
15.7
15.8
15.9

Cuban Americans

Many Cuban Americans, especially those in the early waves of refugees from Castro's revolution in 1959, were skilled professionals and businesspeople, and they rapidly set about building Miami into a thriving economy. Although Cuban Americans are the smallest of the Hispanic subgroups, today they are better educated and enjoy higher incomes than the others. They are well organized politically and have succeeded in electing Cuban Americans to statewide and congressional offices in Florida.

Organizing for Political Activity

For many decades, American agriculture encouraged Mexican American immigration, both legal and illegal, to labor in fields as *braceros*. Most of these migrant farmworkers lived and worked under very difficult conditions; they were paid less than minimum wages for back-breaking labor. Farmworkers were not covered by the federal National Labor Relations Act and therefore not protected in the right to organize labor unions. But civil rights activity among Hispanics, especially among farmworkers, grew during the 1960s under the leadership of César Chávez and his United Farm Workers union. Chávez organized a national boycott of grapes from California vineyards that refused to recognize the union or improve conditions. The boycott finally ended in a union contract with the growers and later a California law protecting the right of farmworkers to organize unions and bargain collectively with their employers. More important, the movement galvanized Mexican Americans throughout the Southwest to engage in political activity.[33]

However, inasmuch as many Mexican American immigrants were noncitizens, and many were *indocumentados* (undocumented residents of the United States), the voting strength of Mexican Americans never matched their numbers in the population. The Immigration Reform and Control Act of 1986 granted amnesty to illegal aliens living in the United States in 1982. But the same act also imposed penalties on employers who hired illegal aliens. The effect of these threatened penalties on many employers was to make them wary of hiring Hispanics, especially as permanent employees. At the same time, industries in need of cheap labor—agriculture, health and hospitals, restaurants, clothing manufacturers, and so on—continued to encourage legal and illegal immigration to fill minimum and even subminimum wage level jobs with few if any benefits.

Hispanic Political Power

The Voting Rights Act of 1965, as later amended and as interpreted by the Supreme Court, extends voting rights protections to "language minorities," including Hispanics. But Mexican American voter turnout remains relatively weak. Various explanations have been advanced for the lower voter participation of Mexican Americans. Language barriers may still discourage some voters, even though ballots in many states are now available in Spanish. Illegal immigrants, of course, cannot vote. And lower education and income levels are associated with lower voter turnout.

Nonetheless, Hispanic political power is increasing overtime. Projections of the Hispanic population in the United States suggest that will rise (from 16.3 percent in 2010) to over 22 percent by 2030. The spec proportion of all presidential voters rose from 7.4 percent in 2008 to 8.4 percent in 2012, even only about half of the eligible Hispanic voters went to the polls. (See figure 15.4.)

Overall, most Hispanic voters identify with the Democratic Party. Mexican Americans in the southwestern states and Puerto Ricans in New York have traditionally supported Democratic candidates. And a strong anti-Communist heritage among Cuban Americans fostered a Republican voting tradition in Florida. (This Republican

THE IMMIGRANT BATTLE

Feelings run high over immigration reform at a 2006 meeting of the National Council of La Raza. The NCLA is the nation's largest Hispanic civil rights organization.

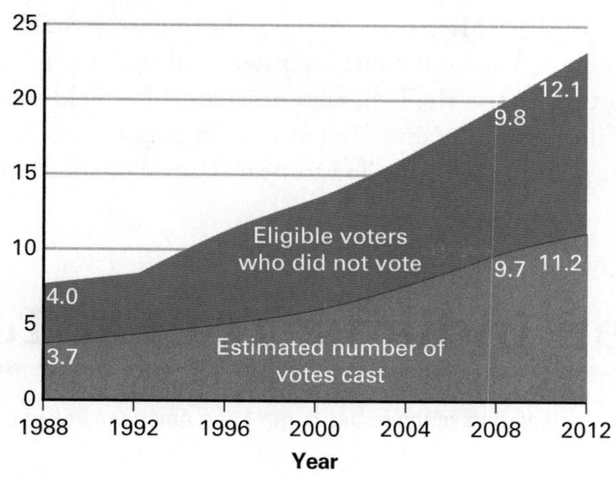

FIGURE 15.3 LATINO PARTICIPATION IN PRESIDENTIAL ELECTIONS, 1988–2012

A record 11.2 million Latinos voted in the 2012 presidential election, but Latinos' voter turnout rate continues to lag other groups significantly, according to an analysis of new Census Bureau data by the Pew Research Center. Overall, 48 percent of Hispanic eligible voters turned out to vote in 2012, down from 49.9 percent in 2008. By comparison the 2012 voter turnout rate among African Americans was 66.6 percent and among Anglo whites was 64.1 percent.

tradition in Florida is changing as more Hispanics in the state are coming from Central and South America and younger Cubans are less concerned with the Castro regime in the country of their parents' origin.)

While supporting the Democratic Party, Hispanics are generally conservative on social issues (opposing abortion and same-sex marriage, favoring government vouchers to pay a parochial school tuitions), but liberal on economic values (favoring government of vision of Health Insurance for all, favoring larger federal government with many services).[34]

Hispanics have been elected governors of Arizona, Nevada, New Mexico, and Florida. (Currently Brian Sandoval serves as governor of Nevada and Susanna Martinez as governor of New Mexico; both are Republicans. And in the U.S. Senate, Republican Ted Cruz represents Texas and Republican Marco Rubio represents Florida.) The social conservatism of Hispanics may provide an opening for the Republican Party. But passing immigration reform is necessary to the future success of the GOP with Hispanic voters, and probably necessary for the future of the GOP itself in presidential elections.

Most Hispanics today believe that they confront less prejudice and discrimination than their parents. Nonetheless, in 1994 California voters approved a referendum, Proposition 187, that would have barred welfare and other benefits to persons living

TABLE 15.5 PARTY VERSUS IDEOLOGY AMONG HISPANICS

	%
Party	
Democrat	51
Republican	18
Ideology	
Conservative	54
Liberal	39

SOURCE: www.hispanicvoters2012.com

15.1 15.2 15.3 15.4 15.5 15.6 15.7 15.8 15.9

15.1
15.2
15.3
15.4
15.5
15.6
15.7
15.8
15.9

in the state illegally. Most Hispanics oppose the measure, believing that it was motivated by prejudice. (A federal court later declared major provisions of Proposition 187 unconstitutional. And the U.S. Supreme Court has held that a state may not bar the children of illegal immigrants from attending public schools.[35]) The bitterness lingering from that political fight has led to near demise of the Republican Party of California.

American Indians: Trail of Tears

15.6 Trace the historical roots of the issues confronting American Indians.

Christopher Columbus, having erred in his estimate of the circumference of the globe, believed he had arrived in the Indian Ocean when he first came to the Caribbean. He mistook the Arawaks there for people of the East Indies, calling them *Indios*, and this Spanish word passed into English as "Indians"—a word that came to refer to all American Indian peoples. But at the time of the first European contacts, these peoples had no common ethnic identity; hundreds of separate cultures and languages were thriving in the Americas. Although estimates vary, most historians believe 7 to 12 million people lived in the land that is now the United States and Canada; 25 million more lived in Mexico; and as many as 60 to 70 million in all lived in the Western Hemisphere, a number comparable to Europe's population at the time.

In the centuries that followed, the American Indian population of the Western Hemisphere was devastated by warfare, by famine, and, most of all, by epidemic diseases brought from Europe. Overall, the Native population fell by 90 percent, the greatest known human disaster in world history. By 1910, only 210,000 American Indians lived in the United States. Their population has slowly recovered to the current 2.8 million (less than 1 percent of the U.S. population). Roughly half live on reservations and trust lands, the largest of which is the Navajo and Hopi enclave in the southwestern United States (see Figure 15.4). The most notable exception is Oklahoma, where over 320,000 American Indians are resident but only 5 percent live on reservations.

The Trail of Broken Treaties

In the Northwest Ordinance of 1787, Congress, in organizing the western territories of the new nation, declared, "The utmost good faith shall always be observed toward the Indians. Their lands and property shall never be taken from them without their consent." The Intercourse Act of 1790 declared that public treaties between the United States government and the independent Native nations would be the only legal means of obtaining Indian land. Congress has full constitutional authority to regulate all interactions with the American Indian tribes.

As president, George Washington forged a treaty with the Creeks: in exchange for land concessions, the United States pledged to protect the boundaries of the Creek nation and to allow the Creeks themselves to punish all violators of their laws within these boundaries. This semblance of legality was reflected in hundreds of treaties that followed. (Indeed, in recent years some American Indian nations have successfully sued in federal court for reparations and return of lands obtained in violation of the Intercourse Act of 1790 and subsequent treaties.) Yet Native lands were constantly invaded by whites. The resulting Native resistance typically led to wars that ultimately resulted in great loss of life among warriors and their families and the further loss of Native land. The cycle of invasion, resistance, military defeat, and further land concessions continued for 100 years.

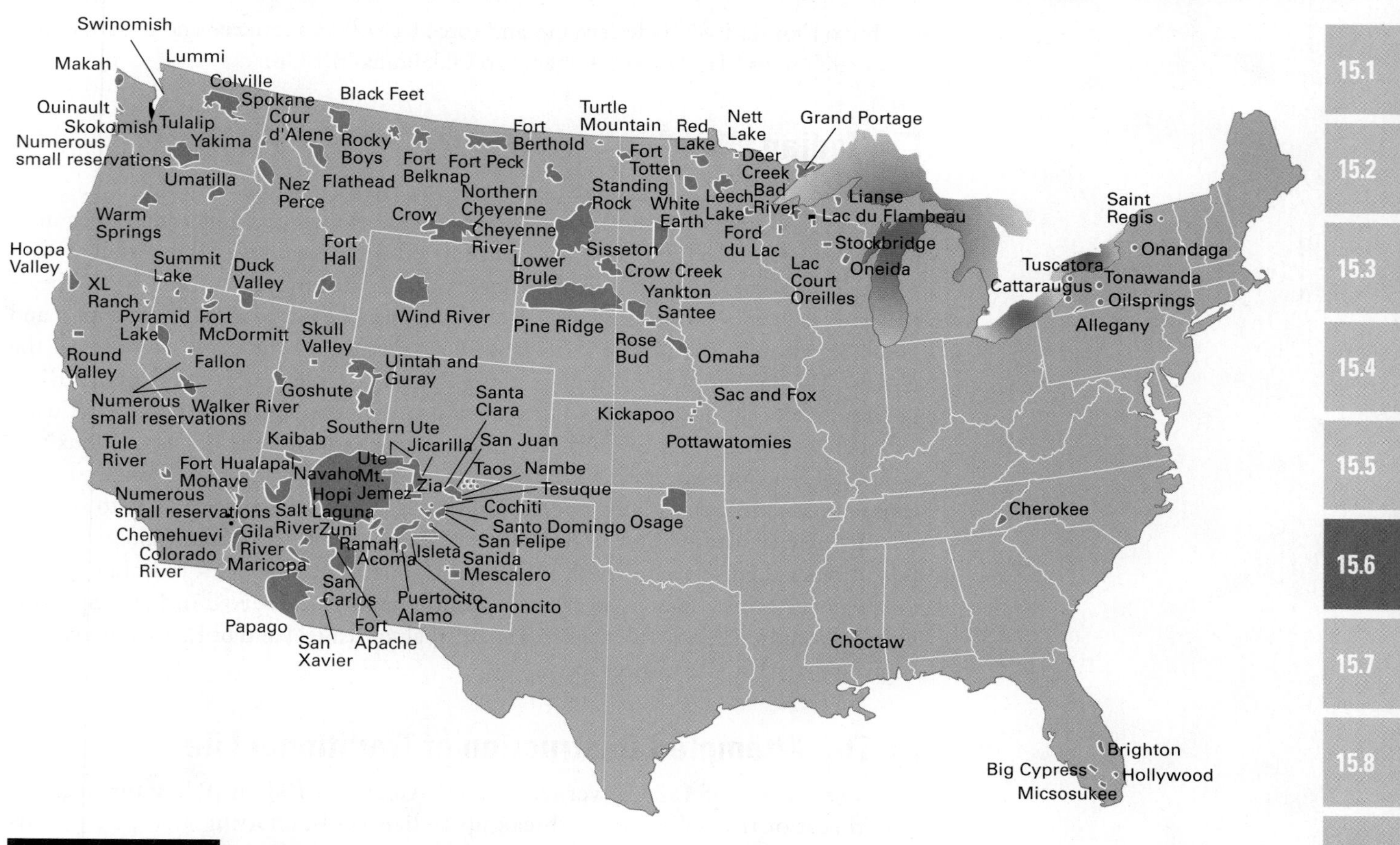

FIGURE 15.4 AMERICAN INDIAN PEOPLES

This map shows the locations of the principal American Indian reservations in the United States. Tribal governments officially govern these reservations. (Alaska Natives, including Aleuts and Eskimos, live mostly in 200 villages widely scattered across rural Alaska; 12 regional American Indian corporations administer property and mineral rights on behalf of Native peoples in that state.)

"Indian Territories"

Following the purchase of the vast Louisiana Territory in 1803, President Thomas Jefferson sought to "civilize" the Natives by promoting farming in "reservations" that were located west of the Mississippi River. But soon, peoples who had been forced to move from Ohio to Missouri were forced to move again to survive the relentless white expansion. President James Monroe designated as "Indian territory" most of the Great Plains west of the Missouri River. Native peoples increasingly faced three unattractive choices: assimilation, removal, or extinction.

In 1814, the Creeks, encouraged by the British during the War of 1812 to attack American settlements, faced an army of Tennessee volunteer militia led by Andrew Jackson. At the Battle of Horseshoe Bend, Jackson's cannon fire decimated the Creek warriors. In the uneven Treaty of Fort Jackson, the Creeks, Choctaws, and Cherokees were forced to concede millions of acres of land.

By 1830, the "Five Civilized Tribes" of the southeastern United States (Cherokees, Chickasaws, Choctaws, Creeks, and Seminoles) had ceded most but not all of their lands. When gold was discovered on Cherokee land in northern Georgia in 1829, whites invaded their territory. Congress, at the behest of President Andrew Jackson, passed the Removal Act, ordering the forcible relocation of the Indians to Oklahoma Indian Territory. The Cherokees tried to use the whites' law to defend their land, bringing their case to the U.S. Supreme Court. When Chief Justice John Marshall held the Cherokees were a "domestic dependent nation" that could not be forced to give up its land, President Jackson replied scornfully, "John Marshall has made his decision. Now let him enforce it." He sent a 7,000-strong army to pursue Seminoles into

15.1

15.2

15.3

15.4

15.5

15.6

15.7

15.8

15.9

the huge Florida Everglades swamp and forced 16,000 Cherokees and other peoples on the infamous "Trail of Tears" march to Oklahoma in 1838.

"Indian Wars"

The "Indian Wars" were fought between the Plains nations and the U.S. Army between 1864 and 1890. Following the Civil War, the federal government began to assign boundaries to each nation and authorized the Bureau of Indian Affairs (BIA) to "assist and protect" Indians on their "reservations." But the reservations were repeatedly reduced in size until subsistence by hunting became impossible. Malnutrition and demoralization of the Native peoples were accelerated by the mass slaughter of the buffalo. The best-known event of the long war occurred at the Little Bighorn River in Montana on June 25, 1876, where Lieutenant Colonel George Armstrong Custer led elements of the U.S. Seventh Cavalry to annihilation at the hands of Sioux and Cheyenne warriors led by chiefs Crazy Horse, Sitting Bull, and Gall. Renewed army campaigns against the Plains peoples followed. Crazy Horse was forced to surrender. In 1881, destitute Sioux under Chief Sitting Bull returned from exile in Canada to surrender themselves to reservation life. Among the last peoples to hold out were the Apaches, whose famous warrior Geronimo finally surrendered in 1886. Sporadic fighting continued until 1890, when a small, malnourished band of Lakota Sioux were wiped out at Wounded Knee Creek.

The Attempted Destruction of Traditional Life

The Dawes Act of 1887 governed federal American Indian policy for decades. The thrust of the policy was to break up Indian lands, allotting acreage for individual homesteads in order to assimilate Natives into the white agricultural society. Farming was to replace hunting, and traditional Native customs were to be shed for English language and schooling. But this effort to destroy culture never really succeeded. Although Native peoples lost more than half of their 1877 reservation land, few lost their communal ties or accumulated much private property. Life on the reservations was often desperate. Natives suffered the worst poverty of any group in the United States, with high rates of infant mortality, alcoholism, and other diseases. The Federal Bureau of Indian Affairs (BIA), notoriously corrupt and mismanaged, encouraged dependency and regularly interfered with religious affairs and customs. The main benefit of the Dawes commission was the creation of tribal enrollment, which fixes the lineage of subsequent descendants of the tribes.

Citizenship

The adoption of the 14th amendment in 1868 did not fix citizenship on the American Indians. Section 1 of the Amendment states, "All persons born or naturalized in the United States, and subject to the jurisdiction thereof, are citizens of the United States and of the State wherein they reside." As members of an indigenous people of limited sovereignty, Indians were not eligible for citizenship in the same fashion as the newly freed slaves. However, in 1924, the Indian Citizenship Act made American Indians citizens. Sponsored by Ohio Rep. Homer Snyder, the act conferred citizenship on native-born American Indians without affecting their citizenship status in the Indian nations. Several states banned Indian voting, and it was 1948 before Indians were able to vote in elections in all of the United States, when Arizona and New Mexico changed their state laws.

The New Deal

The New Deal under President Franklin D. Roosevelt came to American Indians in the form of the Indian Reorganization Act of 1934. This act sought to restore Native tribal structures by recognizing these nations as instruments of the federal government.

Landownership was restored, and elected Native tribal councils were recognized as legal governments. Efforts to force assimilation were largely abandoned. The BIA became more sensitive to Native culture and began employing American Indians in larger numbers. Yet the BIA remained "paternalistic," frequently interfering in tribal "sovereignty."

☐ The American Indian Movement

The civil rights movement of the 1960s inspired a new activism among American Indian groups. The American Indian Movement (AIM) was founded in 1968 and attracted national headlines by occupying Alcatraz Island in San Francisco Bay. Violence flared in 1972, when AIM activists took over the site of the Wounded Knee battle and fought with FBI agents. Several Native nations succeeded in federal courts and in Congress at winning back lands and/or compensation for lands taken from them in treaty violations.

☐ American Indians Today

The U.S. Constitution (Article I, Section 8) grants Congress the full power "to regulate Commerce . . . with the Indian Tribes." States are prevented from regulating or taxing Native peoples or extending their courts' jurisdiction over them unless authorized by Congress. The Supreme Court recognizes American Indians "as members of quasi-sovereign tribal entities"[36] with powers to regulate their own internal affairs, establish their own courts, and enforce their own laws, all subject to congressional supervision. Thus, for example, many Native peoples chose to legalize gambling, including casino gambling, on reservations in states that otherwise prohibited the activity. Those living off reservations have the same rights and responsibilities as other citizens. The Voting Rights Act of 1965 protects Indians in the same manner as other race and language minorities.

States and tribes have engaged in conflict over numerous policies, including fishing rights, casino gaming, and battles over surface water rights. Tribes and pueblos have moved into a variety of business enterprises—casinos are best known, but tribes are also involved in environmental cleanup, telecommunications, manufacturing, distribution, resorts, and health care.

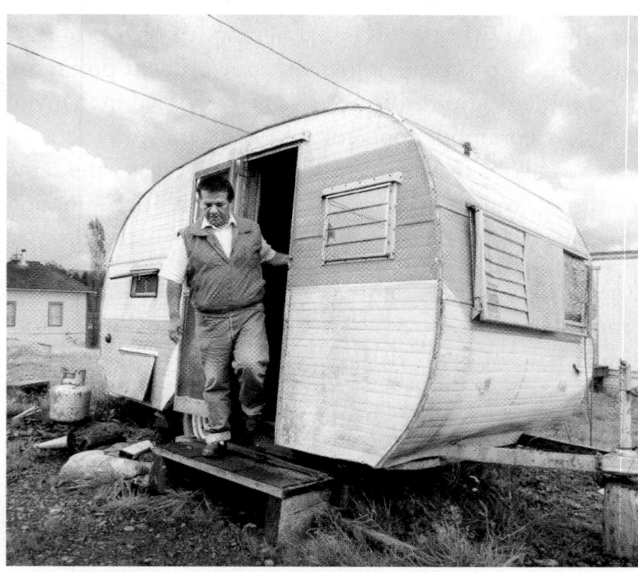

POVERTY IN INDIAN COUNTRY

Poverty is more pronounced on American Indian reservations than in nearly any other part of the United States

Tribes in the United States usually operate under one of two systems: a principal chief/council model (such as the Cherokee or the Chickasaw); or a business council alone model (such as the Wind River reservation or Shoshone and Arapaho tribes).

The business success of some tribes has further enhanced the importance of the governing councils. For example, the Cherokee Business Council is the governing body of the second-largest U.S. tribe, the Cherokee Nation. The council has 17 members, including 15 elected from districts inside the physical boundaries of the nation in northeastern Oklahoma, and two other members elected at-large to represent Cherokee living outside the nation. The principal chief is elected by a popular vote. Elections are high-dollar propositions, and involve major political consultants and modern campaign techniques, such as direct mail, phone-banking, and sometimes even litigation over election procedures.

The Bureau of Indian Affairs in the Department of the Interior continues to supervise reservation life, and American Indians enrolled as members of nations and living on reservations are entitled to certain benefits established by law and treaty. Nevertheless, these peoples remain the poorest and least healthy in the United States, with high incidences of infant mortality, suicide, and alcoholism. Approximately half of all American Indians live below the poverty line—largely among the half of Indians living on reservations.

The Rights of Disabled Americans

15.7 Assess the legal protections offered to disabled Americans.

Disabled Americans were *not* among the classes of people protected by the landmark Civil Rights Act of 1964. Throughout most of the nation's history, little thought was given to making public or private buildings or facilities accessible to blind, deaf, or mobility-impaired people.[37] Not until the Education of Handicapped Children Act of 1975 did the federal government mandate that the nation's public schools provide free education to handicapped children.

Americans with Disabilities Act

The Americans with Disabilities Act (ADA) of 1990 is a sweeping law that prohibits discrimination against disabled people in private employment, government programs, public accommodations, and telecommunications. The act is vaguely worded in many of its provisions, requiring "reasonable accommodations" for disabled people that do not involve "undue hardship." This means disabled Americans do not have exactly the same standard of protection as minorities or women, who are protected from discrimination *regardless* of hardship or costs. Specifically, the ADA includes the following protections:

- **Employment.** Disabled people cannot be denied employment or promotion if, with "reasonable accommodation," they can perform the duties of the job. Reasonable accommodation need not be made if doing so would cause "undue hardship" on the employer.
- **Government programs.** Disabled people cannot be denied access to government programs or benefits. New buses, taxis, and trains must be accessible to disabled persons, including those in wheelchairs.
- **Public accommodations.** Disabled people must enjoy "full and equal" access to hotels, restaurants, stores, schools, parks, museums, auditoriums, and the like. To achieve equal access, owners of existing facilities must alter them "to the maximum extent feasible"; builders of new facilities must ensure that they are readily accessible to disabled persons unless doing so is structurally impossible.

- **Communications.** The Federal Communications Commission is directed to issue regulations that will ensure telecommunications devices for hearing- and speech-impaired people are available "to the extent possible and in the most efficient manner."

Mental and Learning Disabilities

The ADA protects the rights of people with learning and psychiatric disabilities as well as physical disabilities. The U.S. Equal Employment Opportunity Commission has received almost as many complaints about workplace discrimination against the mentally disabled as it has received from people claiming back injuries. But it is far more difficult for employers to determine how to handle a depressed or anxiety-ridden employee than an employee with a visible physical disability. How can employers distinguish uncooperative employees from those with psychiatric disorders?

The American Council on Education reports that following the passage of ADA, the percentage of students in colleges and universities claiming a "learning disability" jumped from 3 to 10 percent.[38] A decision by the U.S. Department of Education that "attention deficit disorder" is covered by the ADA has resulted in another significant rise in students claiming disabilities. Rising rates of autism and Asperger's syndrome present related challenges to colleges and universities. Colleges and universities are required to provide special accommodations for students with disabilities, including tutors, extra time on examinations, oral rather than written exams, and the like.

ENABLING THE DISABLED

The most recent Americans to pressure Congress and the courts for protection of rights long denied them are the nation's disabled citizens. In 1990, disability rights activists succeeded in getting Congress to pass the Americans with Disabilities Act, which mandates the removal of many barriers that have kept handicapped people from working, traveling, and enjoying leisure activities.

15.1 15.2 15.3 15.4 15.5 15.6 15.7 15.8 15.9

Gender Equality and the Politics of Sexual Orientation

15.8 Determine how the 14th Amendment has been interpreted regarding gender equality and describe the policy issues arising from sexual orientation.

The historical context of the 14th Amendment implies its intent to guarantee equality for newly freed slaves, but the wording of its Equal Protection Clause applies to "any person." Thus, the text of the 14th Amendment could be interpreted to bar any gender differences in the law, in the fashion proposed in the failed Equal Rights Amendment. But the Supreme Court has not interpreted the Equal Protection Clause to give the same level of protection to gender equality as to racial equality. In 1873, the Supreme Court specifically rejected arguments that this clause applied to women, and the Court once upheld a state law banning women from practicing law, arguing that "the natural and proper timidity and delicacy which belongs to the female sex evidently unfits it for many of the occupations of civil life. . . . The paramount destiny and mission of women are to fulfill the noble and benign offices of wife and mother. This is the law of the Creator."[39]

Early Feminist Politics

The earliest active feminist organizations grew out of the pre–Civil War antislavery movement, where the first generation of feminists—including Lucretia Mott, Elizabeth Cady Stanton, Lucy Stone, and Susan B. Anthony—learned to organize, hold public meetings, and conduct petition campaigns. After the Civil War, women were successful in changing many state laws that abridged the property rights of married women and otherwise treated them as "chattel" (property) of their husbands. By the early 1900s, activists were also successful in winning some protections for women in the workplace, including state laws limiting women's hours of work, working conditions, and physical demands. At the time, these laws were regarded as "progressive."

The most successful feminist efforts of the 1800s centered on protection of women in families. The perceived threats to women's well-being were their husbands' drinking, gambling, and consorting with prostitutes. Women led the Anti-Saloon League,

15.1
15.2
15.3
15.4
15.5
15.6
15.7
15.8
15.9

Equal Rights Amendment (ERA)
A proposed constitutional amendment, passed by Congress but never ratified by three-quarters of the states, that would have explicitly guaranteed equal rights for women.

Title IX
A provision in the Federal Education Act forbidding discrimination against women in college athletic programs.

succeeded in outlawing gambling and prostitution in every state except Nevada, and provided the major source of moral support for the 18th Amendment (Prohibition).

In the early twentieth century, the feminist movement concentrated on women's suffrage—the drive to guarantee women the right to vote. The early suffragists employed mass demonstrations, parades, picketing, and occasional disruption and civil disobedience—tactics similar to those of the civil rights movement of the 1960s. The culmination of their efforts was the 1920 passage of the 19th Amendment to the Constitution: "The right of citizens of the United States to vote shall not be denied or abridged by the United States or by any State on account of sex." The suffrage movement gave rise to the League of Women Voters; in addition to women's right to vote, the League has sought protection of women in industry, child welfare laws, and honest election practices.

Judicial Scrutiny of Gender Classifications

In the 1970s, the Supreme Court became responsive to arguments that sex discrimination might violate the Equal Protection Clause of the 14th Amendment. In *Reed v. Reed* (1971), it ruled that sexual classifications in the law "must be reasonable and not arbitrary, and must rest on some ground of difference having fair and substantial relation to . . . important governmental objectives."[40] This is a much more relaxed level of scrutiny than the Supreme Court gives to racial classification in the law. Subsequent to *Reed*, a proposed **Equal Rights Amendment** to the U.S. Constitution was passed by Congress in 1972 but never ratified by the states. Had it been ratified by the necessary 38 states, it would have eliminated most, if not all, gender differences in the law.

The Supreme Court continues to wrestle with the question of whether some gender differences can be recognized in law. The question is most evident in laws dealing with sexual activity and reproduction. The Court has upheld statutory rape laws that make it a crime for an adult male to have sexual intercourse with an underage female, regardless of her consent: "We need not to be medical doctors to discern that young men and young women are not similarly situated with respect to the problems and the risks of sexual intercourse. Only women may become pregnant, and they suffer disproportionately the profound physical, emotional and psychological consequences of sexual activity."[41]

Women's participation in military service, particularly combat, raises even more controversial questions regarding permissible gender classifications. The Supreme Court appears to have bowed out of this particular controversy. In upholding Congress's draft registration law for men only, the Court ruled that "the constitutional power of Congress to raise and support armies and to make all laws necessary and proper to that end is broad and sweeping."[42] Congress and the Defense Department are responsible for determining assignments for women in the military.

Title IX

Most sports fans don't know a lot about civil rights law. But odds are that they have heard of **Title IX**, the amendment to the Civil Rights Act of 1964 that extends the nondiscrimination guarantees in education beyond racial and ethnic categories to also encompass sex. It was not designed as "sports legislation," but the increase in women's athletic opportunities in high schools and colleges is the most visible consequence of the law.

In the 1970s there were worries that Title IX would adversely affect men's sports. John Tower, the senior senator from Texas, introduced an amendment in 1974 to exempt "revenue sports" (football) from Title IX. It did not pass; a substitute, the Javits Amendment, inserted language to make "reasonable provisions" for the "nature of particular sports." A year later, the federal government published the rules governing Title IX, and colleges and universities were given three years to comply. Athletics continued to avoid full coverage. A court decision in *Grove City College v. Bell* (465 U.S. 555 (1984)) held that only programs directly receiving federal funding were subject to Title IX, so if athletics at a school didn't receive federal funding, athletics was not covered by Title IX. However, Congress amended the law in 1988 to correct the Court's decision. A 1994 amendment requires athletic programs to collect and

WOMEN IN COMBAT Lee Ann Hester is the first woman decorated for valor for combat in close action, winning the Silver Star in Iraq in 2005.

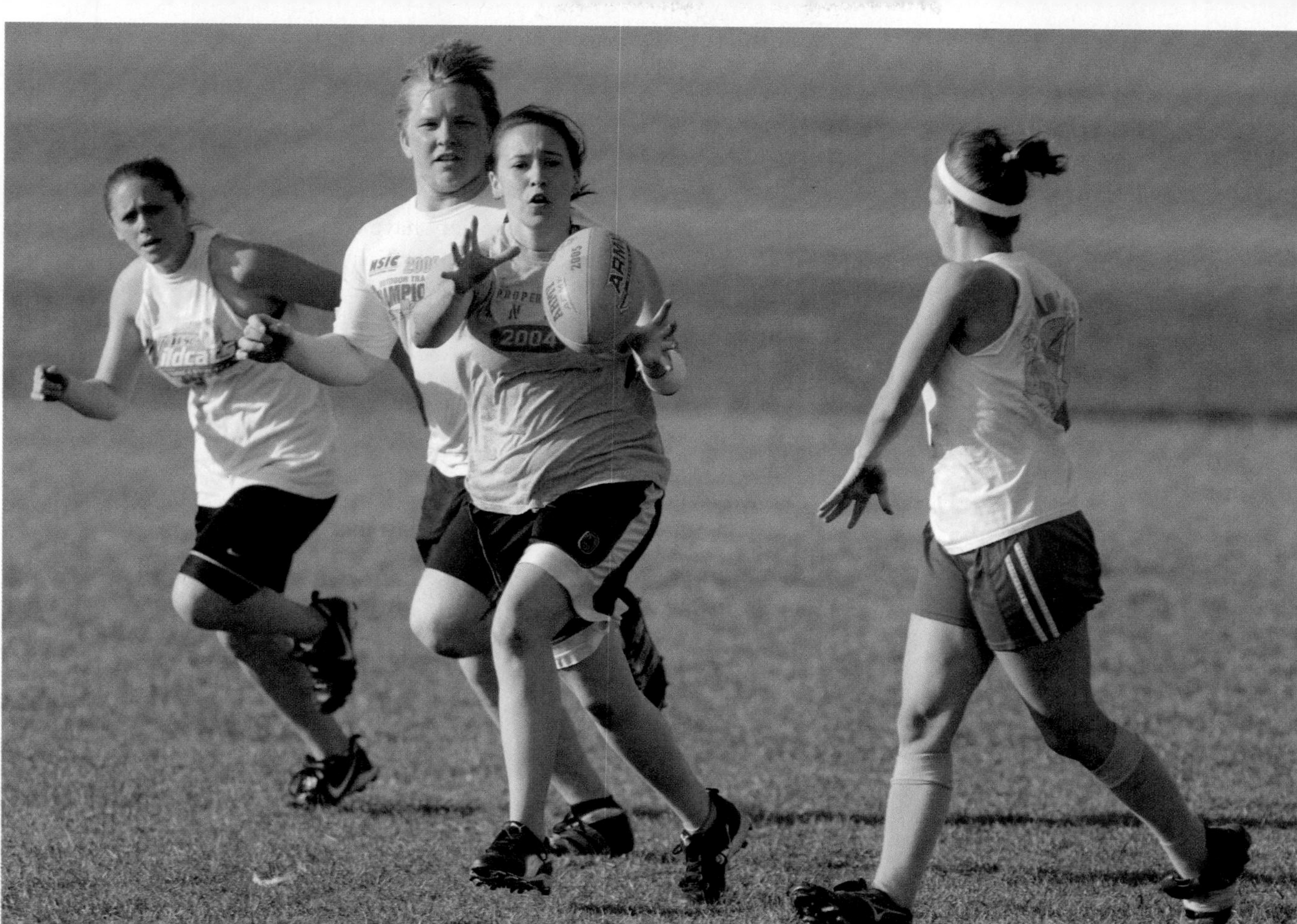

TITLE IX IN ACTION

A variety of women's sports have grown in popularity on college campuses thanks to Title IX, including crew and, pictured here, rugby.

disclose information on roster sizes, recruiting budgets, scholarships, and coaches' salaries for men's and women's sports.

To demonstrate compliance with Title IX, an institution must meet at least one of three prongs of a test for compliance:

1. Athletic participation "opportunities" are substantially proportionate to the student (undergraduate) enrollment.
2. There is demonstrated, continual expansion of athletic opportunities for the underrepresented sex. For example, an institution has added additional sports for women.
3. There is "full and effective accommodation" of the athletic interests and ability of underrepresented sex.

Critics of Title IX often note that, if fully implemented, it would hurt football. But in order to keep football, which often pays the bills in many athletic programs, a reduction has occurred in other men's sports, such as wrestling, cross-country track, and swimming. In contrast women's sports have thrived: estimates of the increase in women's high school (900 percent) and college (450 percent) sports since 1972 stand as evidence of the success of Title IX. A market for women's athletics has followed. The results of Title IX have been impressive. In 2011, there were more than 170,000 female student athletes, a dramatic increase over the 30,000 when the law was passed in 1972. Women's teams in the National Collegiate Athletic Association rose from about 4,800 to over 18,000, slightly more than the number of men's teams according the the NCAA.[44] However, while women make up 54 percent of college undergraduate students, the female share of athletes is only 45 percent. Val Ackerman, the first

15.1
15.2
15.3
15.4
15.5
15.6
15.7
15.8
15.9

woman president of USA Basketball, observes that Title IX "accelerated the creation of women's sports organizations and has fueled the development of women's sports in every way."[44,45]

Gender Equality in the Economy

As cultural views of women's roles in society have changed and economic pressures on family budgets have increased, women's participation in the labor force has risen. Today women comprise over 47 percent of the nation's total workforce. The gap between women's and men's participation in the nation's workforce is closing over time. With the movement of women into the workforce, feminist political activity has shifted toward economic concerns—gender equality in education, employment, pay, promotion, and credit.

Gender Equality in Civil Rights Laws

Title VII of the Civil Rights Act of 1964 prevents sexual (as well as racial) discrimination in hiring, pay, and promotions. The Equal Employment Opportunity Commission, the federal agency charged with eliminating discrimination in employment, has established guidelines barring stereotyped classifications of "men's jobs" and "women's jobs." The courts have repeatedly struck down state laws and employer practices that differentiate between men and women in hours, pay, retirement age, and so forth.

The Federal Equal Credit Opportunity Act of 1974 prohibits sex discrimination in credit transactions. Federal law prevents banks, credit unions, savings and loan associations, retail stores, and credit card companies from denying credit because of sex or marital status. However, these businesses may still deny credit for a poor or nonexistent credit rating, and some women who have always maintained accounts in their husband's name may still face credit problems if they apply in their own name.

A Constitutional Note

The 14th Amendment

The Constitution of 1787 not only recognized slavery by counting slaves as three-fifths of a person for apportionment of representatives and direct taxes (Article I, Section 2) but also protected slavery by requiring states to return escaped slaves to their owners (Article IV, Section 2). (The Founders appear to have been embarrassed by the word *slave* and employed the euphemism "person held to service or labor.") Following the Civil War, the 13th Amendment prohibited slavery, and the 15th Amendment prohibited states from denying the right to vote on account of race, color, or previous condition of servitude. But it was the 14th Amendment that eventually became the basis of the civil rights movement in America and the source of the most important guarantees of equality:

> No State shall make or enforce any law which shall abridge the privileges or immunities of citizens of the United States; nor shall any state deprive any person of life, liberty, or property, without due process of law; nor deny to any person within its jurisdiction the equal protection of the laws.

What are the meanings of words such as "liberty," "due process of law," and "equal protection of the laws"? Constitutionally, the history of the civil rights movement centers around definitions of these terms, as does the history of the women's movement.

QUESTIONS

1. The Civil War changed American society and led to the changes in the Constitution embodied in the 14th Amendment. Should we consider the 14th Amendment a "reframing" of the Constitution?
2. Does this mean that we need to limit our reference to the "intent of the Framers" of the original, unamended Constitution?
3. Can their intentions be honored in a nation so fundamentally disrupted by the social changes wrought by the Civil War and described in this chapter?
4. Do the meanings of liberty, due process, and equal protection mean the same thing that they did in the nineteenth century?

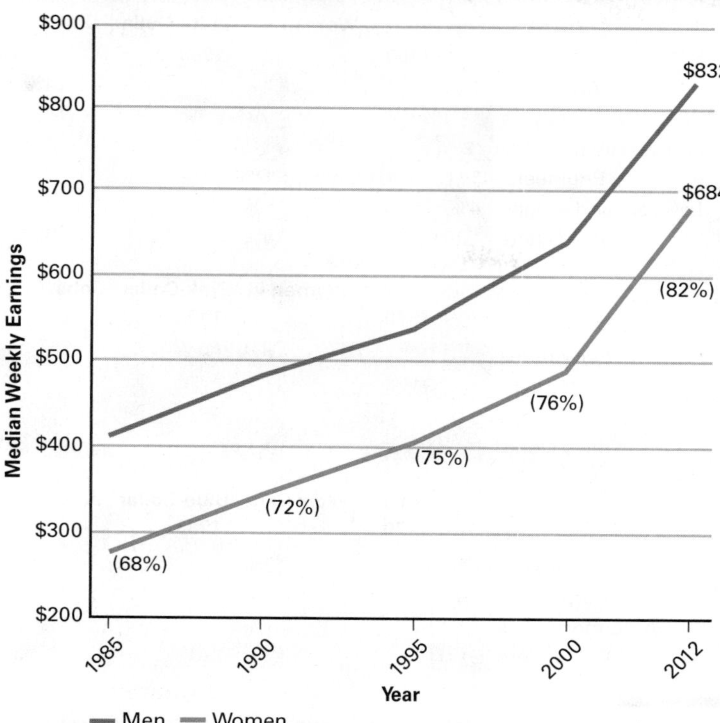

FIGURE 15.5 THE EARNINGS GAP: MEDIAN WEEKLY EARNINGS OF MEN AND WOMEN

The continuing "earnings gap" between men and women reflects a division in the labor market between traditionally male higher paying occupations and traditionally female lower paying positions.

NOTE: Figures in parentheses indicate the ratio of women's to men's median weekly earnings of full time workers.

SOURCE: Bureau of Labor Statistics, www.bls.gov.

The Earnings Gap

Despite protections under federal laws, women continue to earn substantially less than men do. Today, women, on average, earn about 82 percent of what men do (see Figure 15.5). This earnings gap has been closing very slowly: in 1985, women earned an average 68 percent of men's earnings. The earnings gap is not primarily a product of **direct discrimination**: women in the same job with the same skills, qualifications, experience, and work record are not generally paid less than men, and such direct discrimination has been illegal since the Civil Rights Act of 1964. Rather, the earnings gap is primarily a product of a division in the labor market between traditionally male and female jobs, with lower salaries paid in traditionally female occupations.

direct discrimination
Now illegal practice of differential pay for men versus women even when those individuals have equal qualifications and perform the same job.

comparable worth
Argument that pay levels for traditionally male and traditionally female jobs should be equalized by paying equally all jobs that are "worth about the same" to an employer.

The Dual Labor Market and "Comparable Worth"

The existence of a "dual" labor market, with male-dominated "blue-collar" jobs distinguishable from female-dominated "pink-collar" jobs, continues to be a major obstacle to economic equality between men and women. These occupational differences result from cultural stereotyping, social conditioning, and training and education—all of which narrow the choices available to women. Although significant progress has been made in reducing occupational sex segregation (see Figure 15.6), many observers nevertheless doubt that sexually differentiated occupations will be eliminated in the foreseeable future.

As a result of a growing recognition that the wage gap is more a result of occupational differentiation than direct discrimination, some feminist organizations have turned to a new approach—the demand that pay levels in various occupations be determined by **comparable worth** rather than by the labor market. Comparable

15.1
15.2
15.3
15.4
15.5
15.6
15.7
15.8
15.9

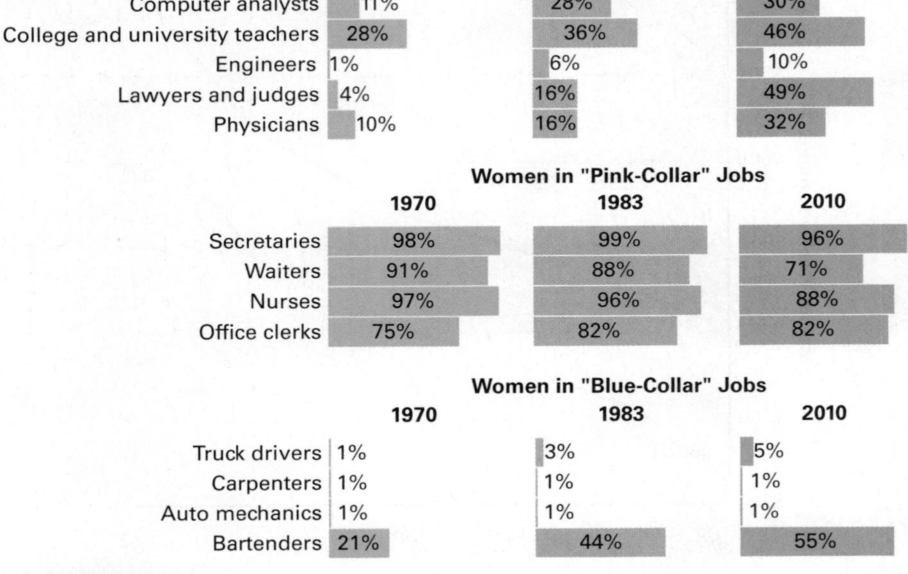

FIGURE 15.6 WHERE WOMEN WORK: GENDER DIFFERENTIATION IN THE LABOR MARKET

Most of the earnings gap between men and women in the U.S. labor force today is the result of the different job positions held by the two sexes. Although women are increasingly entering "white-collar" occupations long dominated by men, they continue to be disproportionately concentrated in "pink-collar" service positions. "Blue-collar" jobs have been the most resistant to change, remaining a male bastion, although women bartenders now outnumber men.

SOURCE: *Statistical Abstract of the United States*, 2012–2013, pp. 383–86.

glass ceiling
"Invisible" barriers to women rising to the highest positions in corporations and the professions.

worth goes beyond paying men and women equally for the same work and calls for paying the same wages for jobs of comparable value to the employer. Advocates of comparable worth argue that governmental agencies or the courts should evaluate traditionally male and female jobs to determine their "worth" to the employer, perhaps by considering responsibilities, effort, knowledge, and skill requirements. Jobs adjudged to be "comparable" would be paid equal wages. Government agencies or the courts would replace the labor market in determining wage rates.

The "Glass Ceiling"

Overall about 20% of the nation's top corporate elites—presidents and directors of the 500 largest corporations—are women. This is a considerable advance over 1972 when fewer than 5% of top corporate and financial leadership positions were occupied by women. Women have made even greater advances in higher education, where today over 25% of president and trustees of major universities are women. The barriers to women's advancement to top positions in the corporate and financial worlds are often very subtle, giving rise to the phrase **glass ceiling**. In explaining "why women aren't getting to the top," one observer argues that "at senior management levels, competence is assumed. What you're looking for is someone who fits, someone who gets along, someone you trust. Now, that's subtle stuff. How does a group of men feel that a woman is going to fit? I think it's very hard." Or, as a woman bank executive says, "The men just don't feel comfortable."[46] Finally, it is important to note that affirmative action efforts by governments—notably the EEOC—are directed primarily at entry-level positions rather than senior management posts.

Sexual Harassment

Sexual harassment on the job is also a violation of Title VII. But it is not always clear what kind of behavior constitutes "sexual harassment." The Supreme Court has defined it as:

> Unwelcome sexual advances, requests for sexual favors, and other verbal or physical conduct of a sexual nature constitute sexual harassment when (1) submission to such conduct is made either explicitly or implicitly a term or condition of an individual's employment; (2) submission to or rejection of such conduct by an individual is used as the basis for employment decisions affecting such individual; or (3) such conduct has the purpose or effect of unreasonably interfering with an individual's work performance or creating an intimidating, hostile, or offensive working environment.[47]

There are no great difficulties in defining sexual harassment when jobs or promotions are conditional on the granting of sexual favors. But several problems arise in defining a "hostile working environment." This phrase may include offensive utterances, sexual innuendoes, dirty jokes, the display of pornographic material, and unwanted proposals for dates. First, it would appear to include speech, and hence raise 1st Amendment questions regarding how far speech may be curtailed by law in the workplace. Second, the definition depends more on the subjective feelings of the individual employee about what is "offensive" and "unwanted" than on an objective standard of behavior easily understood by all. Justice Sandra Day O'Connor wrestled with the definition of a "hostile work environment" in *Harris v. Forklift* in 1993. She held that a plaintiff need not show that the utterances caused psychological injury but that a "reasonable person," not just the plaintiff, must perceive the work environment to be hostile or abusive. Presumably a single incident would not constitute harassment; rather, courts should consider "the frequency of the discriminatory conduct," "its severity," and whether it "unreasonably interferes with an employee's work performance."[48]

Politics and Sexual Orientation

15.9 Assess the advances in the treatment of same-sex rights through legislation and litigation.

The political movement on behalf of gay and lesbian rights is often traced back to the 1969 Stonewall riots in New York City, where gays confronted police in an effort to halt harassment. Since that time, gays have made considerable strides in winning public acceptance of their lifestyle and in changing public policy. Discrimination based on sexual orientation is not prohibited in *federal* civil rights acts (a bill to do so passed the Senate in 2013 but was not taken up by the House). But over the years, many states and cities have enacted laws prohibiting discrimination against homosexuals. Nonetheless, many gay issues remain on the nation's political agenda.

Privacy Rights

Historically, "sodomy" was defined as "an act against the laws of human nature" and criminalized in most states. As late as 1986, the U.S. Supreme Court upheld a Georgia law against sodomy, holding that "the Constitution does not confer a fundamental right upon homosexuals to engage in sodomy."[49] But the Supreme Court reversed its position in 2003 in *Lawrence v. Texas*, holding that consenting adults "engaged in sexual practices common to a homosexual lifestyle . . . are entitled to respect for their private lives. . . . Their right to liberty under the Due Process Clause gives them the full right to engage in their conduct without intervention of the government."[50] The Court noted that since its earlier decision, most of the states had repealed their laws against sodomy. *Lawrence v. Texas* is a landmark decision that is likely to affect every type of civil case involving sexual orientation.

However, the Court has refused to interfere with private or religious organizations that ban avowed homosexuals. In *Boy Scouts of America v. Dale* (2000), the Court upheld a Boy Scout prohibition against homosexuals becoming scout leaders.[51]

15.1

15.2

15.3

15.4

15.5

15.6

15.7

15.8

15.9

☐ Defense of Marriage Act

Congress passed a Defense of Marriage Act (DOMA) in 1996, declaring that marriages between a man and a woman and that " no state... Shall be required to give effect to any public act, record, or judicial proceeding of any other state respecting a relationship between persons of the same sex that is treated as a marriage." DOMA was designed to circumvent the Full Faith and Credit Clause of Article IV of the U.S. Constitution that requires each state to recognize the "public acts, records, judicial proceedings of every other state." (Article IV does, however, include a provision that Congress may "prescribe the manner in which such acts, records, and proceedings shall be proved, and the effect thereof.") DOMA reflected the prevailing view at the time that same-sex marriage should not be recognized in the states. DOMA also prevented the federal government from recognizing same-sex marriages.

The U.S. Supreme Court reviewed DOMA in 2013 in a landmark decision, *Windsor v. United States*. The case arose from a challenge to federal estate tax laws that deny equal treatment to same-sex marriages. (In arguments before the Court, rather than defend a federal law as customary, Atty. Gen. Eric Holder on behalf of the Obama administration argued with the plaintiffs that DOMA violated the U.S. constitution.) In a complex 5–4 decision, the court held that the federal government cannot discriminate in its own programs and laws against same-sex couples. The decision did *not* strike down same-sex marriage in other nations and the states. Indeed, the decision appeared to uphold the power of the states to determine marriage laws. But the court held that legally married same-sex couples must be treated equally under federal law. The effect of the decision is to require greater scrutiny by the courts of the possible discriminatory effects of laws placing prohibitions on same-sex marriages.

☐ Ending "Don't Ask, Don't Tell"

Upon taking office in 1993, President Bill Clinton announced his intention to overturn the military's long-standing ban on gays serving in the armed forces. Gay-rights groups had donated heavily to the Clinton campaign. But military professionals strongly objected to this change, and veterans groups criticized the plan. Clinton was obliged to compromise on the issue, and the policy of "Don't Ask, Don't Tell" emerged. The policy was that the military would no longer inquire into the sexual orientation of service personnel or recruits as long as they did not make their orientation public.

Congress authorized the president to end "Don't Ask, Don't Tell" in 2011, if he certified that doing so would not adversely affect military preparedness. President Barack Obama quickly did so, thereby ending the policy and allowing gays and lesbians to serve openly in the military.

☐ Same-Sex Marriage

A majority of states ban same-sex marriage, by either state laws or state constitutional provisions. Many of these prohibitions came about as a result of popular initiative and referendum in the states.[52]

While several states had earlier sanctioned "civil unions" between same-sex couples, thereby granting them the benefits given under law to married couples, it was not until 2003 at the Massachusetts Supreme Court's rule that same-sex couples had the right to *marriage* under the Massachusetts state constitution. In 2011 the state of New York passed into law a law authorizing same-sex marriage. In 2012, Maryland and Washington voters approved referenda legalizing same-sex marriage, and Minnesota voters rejected a ban on same-sex marriage.

As of 2013, 14 states (California, Connecticut, Delaware, Iowa, Maine, Maryland, Massachusetts, Minnesota, New Hampshire, New Jersey, New York, Rhode Island, Vermont, and Washington) as well as the District of Columbia, issued marriage licenses to same-sex couples.

Various federal and state courts have overturned the implementation of bans on same-sex marriage. Judicial support for such marriages was encouraged by the U.S.

Supreme Court's decision in 2012 in *Windsor v. United States* striking down federal laws that discriminated against same-sex marriages legally conducted in states (see below). The decision protects same-sex couples in federal bankruptcy, a state, tax, immigration, and employment laws, and in all federal benefit programs including Social Security and Medicaid.

☐ AIDS

The gay rights movement was threatened in the early 1980s by the spread of the HIV virus and the deadly disease, acquired immune deficiency syndrome, or AIDS. Gay men were identified as one of the high-risk groups in the United States. The medical consensus was that the disease is spread through a sexual activity especially prevalent among male homosexuals as well as through the sharing of contaminated needles among intravenous drug users and through blood transfusions. Casual contact (touching, kissing, using common utensils, etc.) does not transmit the disease. But the gay rights movement was successful in its campaign to convince Americans that "anyone could get AIDS," and over time, it won the sympathy and support of the American public. Funding for AIDS research rose dramatically. The Center for Disease Control (CDC) gave priority to the search for antidotes to the virus, and at the same time, instituted a public education effort aimed at changing sexual behavior. Gay organizations across the nation distributed material describing safe sex practices. Over time, deaths from AIDS declined and the feared epidemic was held in check.

☐ State Laws

Much of the conflict over gay rights occurs at the state level—in referenda, legislative enactments, and court decisions—yielding a complex mosaic of laws involving sexual orientation throughout the nation. Among the issues confronting the states:

- **Adoption**. Should gay and lesbian couples be allowed to adopt children?
- **Hate Crimes**. Should hate crime laws also protect homosexuals?
- **Health**. Should health insurance companies be required to extend benefits to homosexual spouses?
- **Employment**. Should laws against job discrimination be extended to protect homosexuals?
- **Housing**. Should laws against discrimination in housing be extended to protect homosexuals?
- **Marriage**. Should gay and lesbian couples be allowed to marry?
- **Civil Unions**. Should gay and lesbian couples be allowed to legally form civil unions giving them many of the rights of married couples?

State laws differ on each of these issues, although recent changes have generally benefited gays and lesbians.[53]

☐ Same-Sex Politics

The sexual identity movement includes a loose coalition of groups, including Lesbian Gay Bisexual and Transgender Centers (LGBT); National Gay and Lesbian Task Force; Queer Nation; AIDS Coalition to Unleash Power (ACT-UP); and the Gay Lesbian Alliance Against Defamation (GLAAD). Many of these groups have affiliates in colleges, universities, and communities across the country.

The goals of the movement have evolved over the years from initially seeking protection against government restrictions on private behavior; to later seeking government protection of gays and lesbians from discrimination; to still later seeking societal approval of homosexuality as a morally equivalent alternative lifestyle.[54] Over time, public opinion has become much more supportive of gay and lesbian goals.

Review the Chapter

The Irony of Equality

15.1 Assess the role that politics played over the centuries in America's quest for equality and analyze how the Constitution was interpreted to first justify and then attack slavery and segregation, p. 562

The original Constitution of 1787 recognized and protected slavery. Not until after the Civil War did the 13th Amendment (1865) abolish slavery. But the 14th Amendment's guarantee of "equal protection of the laws" and the 15th Amendment's guarantee of voting rights were largely ignored in Southern states after the federal government's Reconstruction efforts ended. Segregation was held constitutional by the U.S. Supreme Court in its "separate but equal" decision in *Plessy v. Ferguson* in 1896.

The NAACP led the long legal battle in the federal courts to have segregation declared unconstitutional as a violation of the Equal Protection Clause of the 14th Amendment. Under the leadership of Thurgood Marshall, a major victory was achieved in the case of *Brown v. Board of Education of Topeka* in 1954.

Equal Protection of the Laws

15.2 Differentiate the various meanings of equal protection of the laws, p. 567

The struggle over school desegregation continues even today. Federal courts are more likely to issue desegregation orders (including orders to bus pupils to achieve racial balance in schools) in school districts where present or past actions by government officials contributed to racial imbalances. Courts are less likely to order desegregation where racial imbalances are a product of residential patterns.

The Civil Rights Acts

15.3 Outline major civil rights legislation, p. 571

The courts could eliminate *governmental* discrimination by enforcing the 14th Amendment of the Constitution, but only Congress could end private discrimination through legislation. Martin Luther King, Jr.'s campaign of nonviolent direct action helped bring remaining racial injustices to the attention of Congress. Key legislation includes the Civil Rights Act of 1964, which bans discrimination in public accommodations, government-funded programs, and private employment; the Voting Rights Act of 1965, which authorizes strong federal action to protect voting rights; and the Civil Rights Act of 1968, which outlaws discrimination in housing.

Equality: Opportunity Versus Results

15.4 Distinguish between equality of opportunity and equality of results and trace the Court's evolving attitude toward affirmative action, p. 574

Today, racial politics center around continuing inequalities between blacks and whites in the areas of income, jobs, housing, health, education, and other conditions of life. Should the government concentrate on "equality of opportunity" and apply "color-blind" standards to both blacks and whites? Or should government take "affirmative action" to assist blacks and other minorities to overcome the results of past unequal treatment?

Generally the Supreme Court is likely to approve of affirmative action programs when these programs have been adopted in response to a past proven history of discrimination, when they are narrowly tailored so as not to adversely affect the rights of individuals, when they do not absolutely bar whites from participating, and when they serve clearly identified, compelling, and legitimate government objectives.

Even though there is scant definitive evidence to support the claim that diversity on college campuses improves learning, universities have approved affirmative action programs that take race into consideration when deciding who to admit as a student and who to hire as a professor. But the Court has held that the use of racial classifications in the acceptance process would be given "strict scrutiny."

Hispanics in America

15.5 Characterize the Hispanics in the United States demographically and politically, p. 583

Economic conditions in Mexico and other Spanish-speaking nations of the Western Hemisphere continue to fuel large-scale immigration, both legal and illegal, into the United States. Hispanics (Latinos) are now the nation's largest minority group. Hispanic political power is on the rise.

While their vote does not yet match their population percentage, the Hispanic proportion of presidential voters is increasing. Most Hispanics vote Democratic, and the future of the Republican Party is jeopardized if it fails to respond to Hispanic concerns, including immigration reform. Hispanics have won election to governorships and the U.S. Senate.

American Indians: Trail of Tears

15.6 Trace the historical roots of the issues confronting American Indians, p. 588

Since the arrival of the first Europeans on this continent, American Indian peoples have experienced cycles of invasion, resistance, military defeat, and land concessions. Today, American Indian peoples collectively remain the poorest and least healthy of the nation's ethnic groups.

The Rights of Disabled Americans

15.7 Assess the legal protections offered to disabled Americans, p. 592

The Americans with Disabilities Act of 1990 prohibits discrimination against disabled persons in private employment, government programs, public accommodations, and communications.

Gender Equality

15.8 Determine how the 14th Amendment has been interpreted regarding gender equality and describe the policy issues arising from sexual orientation, p. 593

The Equal Protection Clause of the 14th Amendment applies to "any person," but traditionally, the Supreme Court has recognized gender differences in laws. Nevertheless, in recent years, the Court has struck down gender differences where they are unreasonable or arbitrary and unrelated to legitimate government objectives.

Gender discrimination in employment has been illegal since the passage of the Civil Rights Act of 1964. Nevertheless, differences in average earnings of men and women persist, although these differences have narrowed somewhat over time. The earnings gap appears to be mainly a product of lower pay in occupations traditionally dominated by women and higher pay in traditionally male occupations. Although neither Congress nor the courts have mandated wages based on comparable worth of traditional men's and women's jobs in private employment, many governmental agencies and some private employers have undertaken to review wage rates to eliminate gender differences.

The Equal Protection Clause does not bar government from treating persons in various income classes differently. However, governments must treat every individual in a class equally, and the classifications must not be "arbitrary" or "unreasonable." The poor cannot demand benefits or services as a matter of constitutional rights; however, once government establishes a social welfare program by law, it must provide equal access to all persons "similarly situated."

Politics and Sexual Orientation

15.9 Assess the advances in the treatment of same-sex rights through legislation and litigation, p. 599

The Supreme Court has held that consenting adults engaging and practices, calm into a homosexual lifestyle are entitled to the rights of privacy. Yet various other gay rights issues remain unsettled. Job discrimination against gays is *not* yet prohibited by federal civil rights laws, but many states prohibit such discrimination.

President Obama ended the Clinton era policy of "Don't Ask, Don't Tell", thereby allowing gays and lesbians to serve openly in the military.

A majority of states continue to ban same-sex marriage. While several states had earlier sanctioned "civil unions" between same-sex couples, in 2002 Massachusetts became the first state to rule that same-sex couples had the right to *marriage*. An increasing number of states are now coming to recognize same-sex marriage. Congress passed a Defense of Marriage Act in 1996, declaring that marriage is between a man and a woman and that federal laws could not recognize same-sex marriages. But the U.S. Supreme Court held that this Act was an unconstitutional denial of equal treatment to same-sex couples, and that the federal government could not discriminate against them in its own programs and laws. But the decision did *not* strike down same-sex marriage prohibitions in the states. Nonetheless, the effect of the decision is to require greater scrutiny by the courts of the possible discriminatory effects of prohibitions on same-sex marriage.

Learn the Terms

abolition movement, p. 563
Emancipation Proclamation, p. 564
Reconstruction, p. 564
Jim Crow, p. 565
separate but equal, p. 565
de facto segregation, p. 570
nonviolent direct action, p. 572
affirmative action, p. 576
quota, p. 576
Bakke case, p. 578
set-aside program, p. 579
strict scrutiny, p. 580
diversity, p. 580
Equal Rights Amendment (ERA), p. 594
Title IX, p. 594
direct discrimination, p. 597
comparable worth, p. 597
glass ceiling, p. 598

Test Yourself

15.1 Assess the role that politics played over the centuries in America's quest for equality and analyze how the Constitution was interpreted to first justify and then attack slavery and segregation.

Perhaps the main debate in America today about equality centers around

a. equality of opportunity versus equality before the law
b. equality before the law versus equal access to health care
c. equality of results versus equal opportunity
d. genetic equality versus legal equality
e. legality of results

15.2 Differentiate the various meanings of equal protection of the laws.

Racial imbalances that are not caused by governmental action but by residential patterns

a. are "restrictive covenants"
b. are unconstitutional
c. are evidence of "de facto segregation"
d. have resulted in most of the affirmative action programs
e. no longer occur

15.3 Outline major civil rights legislation.

A method that Martin Luther King, Jr., advocated using for the elimination of discrimination was

a. the development of an Afro-centric culture
b. establishing a separate republic for African Americans in parts of Mississippi and Louisiana
c. nonviolent direct action
d. the development of "black power"
e. stare decisis

15.4 Distinguish between equality of opportunity and equality of results and trace the Court's evolving attitude toward affirmative action.

In the case of the *University of California Board of Regents v. Bakke* the Supreme Court held that an admissions program

a. with racial quotas was constitutional
b. which took race into consideration was constitutional
c. with set-asides was constitutional
d. which did not take race into consideration violated the 14th Amendment
e. must include a voter registration opportunity for resident students

15.5 Characterize the Hispanics in the United States demographically and politically.

Today the largest minority group in America is

a. African Americans
b. Hispanic Americans
c. Asian Americans
d. Multiracial Americans
e. we can't be sure

15.6 Trace the historical roots of the issues confronting American Indians.

American Indians are distinct from other minorities in the US because

I. they were the first to get a guarantee of voting rights
II. casinos
III. they are also members of domestic nations of limited sovereignty

a. I and III only
b. I, II, and III
c. III only
d. II only
e. I and III only

15.7 Assess the legal protections offered to disabled Americans.

The landmark legislation that protects disabled Americans is the

a. Disabled Accommodations Act
b. Handicapped Recovery Act
c. Americans with Disabilities Act
d. Handicapped Employment Act
e. Civil Rights Act of 1957

15.8 Determine how the 14th Amendment has been interpreted regarding gender equality and describe the policy issues arising from sexual orientation.

Some of the early concerns of the first feminists revolved around

I. property rights
II. women's suffrage
III. concerns about their husbands' drinking

a. Only I
b. Only II
c. Only I and III
d. I, II, and III
e. Only III

Explore Further

SUGGESTED READINGS

Bowen, William G., and Derek Curtis Bok. *The Shape of the River*. Princeton, N.J.: Princeton University Press, 1999. An argument by two university presidents that preferential treatment of minorities in admissions to prestigious universities has led to the subsequent success in life by the beneficiaries of the preferences.

Fox-Genovese, Elizabeth. *Feminism Is Not the Story of My Life*. New York: Doubleday, 1995. Critique of radical feminism for failing to understand the central importance of marriage and motherhood in women's lives, and a discussion of how public policy could ease the clashing demands of work and family on women.

Fraga, Louis R., John A. Garcia, Rodney Hero, and Michael Jones-Correa. *Latinos in the New Millennium*. New York: Cambridge University Press 2013. A comprehensive profile of Latinos in the U.S., covering demographics, politics, values, identities, policy preferences, etc.

Garcia, F. Chris, and Gabriel Sanchez. *Hispanics and the U.S. Political System: Moving into the Mainstream.* New York: Longman, 2007. A description of the growing influence of Hispanics both as voters and politicians.

LeMay, Michael. *Perennial Struggle: Race, Ethnicity and Minority Group Relations in the United States*, 3rd ed. New York: Longman, 2009. A description and assessment of minority group strategies—accommodation, separatism, radicalism—in coping with their political and economic status.

McDonald, Laughlin. *American Indians and the Fight for Voting Rights.* Norman, Okla.: University of Oklahoma Press, 2011. One of the ACLU's leading lawyers describes and analyzes the efforts to pursue full voting rights for American Indians in the United States.

Thernstrom, Stephen, and Abigail Thernstrom. *America in Black and White*. New York: Simon & Schuster, 1997. Information-rich analysis tracing social and economic progress of African Americans and arguing that gains in education and employment were greater *before* the introduction of affirmative action programs.

Thomas R. Dye, *Who's Running America? The Obama Reign*, Boulder, CO: Paradigm Press, 2013.

Walton, Hanes, and Robert C. Smith. *American Politics and the African-American Quest for Freedom*. 6th ed. New York: Pearson 2012. Comprehensive text arguing the profound influence that African Americans have on American politics.

Windsor V. United States, June 26, 2013.

SUGGESTED WEB SITES

ADA Home Page www.usdoj.gov/crt/ada
Federal agency site with guide to disability rights laws.

American Council on Education www.acenet.edu
Information on a wide range of educational issues, including diversity, testing, and admissions.

American Indian Movement www.aimovement.org
Advocacy organization for American Indians, with news and views on treaties and treaty violations.

Brown Matters www.brownmatters.org
Chronology of *Brown v. Board of Education*, 1957.

Bureau of Indian Affairs http://www.bia.gov
Government agency with responsibility for administration of 562 federally recognized tribal governments in the United States.

The Center for Individual Rights www.cir-usa.org
Advocacy organization opposing racial preferences.

U.S. Equal Employment Opportunity Commission (EEOC) www.eeoc.gov
Federal EEOC site with information on what constitutes discrimination by age, disability, race, ethnicity, religion, and gender; on how to file a charge; and guidance for employers.

Feminist.Com www.feminist.com
Web site promoting women's business development, with information and advice.

FIRE: Foundation for Equal Rights in Education www.thefire.org
Advocacy organization defending individual rights on campus and opposing racial preferences.

The King Center http://thekingcenter.com
Biography of MLK, Jr., together with news and information from the Atlanta King Center.

National Council of La Raza www.nclr.org
Issue positions, programs, and news dedicated to improving the life experiences of Hispanic Americans.

Mexican American Legal Defense League www.maldef.org
Advocacy and litigation on behalf of Latinos, with information on cases dealing with immigration rights.

NAACP Legal Defense Fund www.naacpldf.org
Founded in 1940 by Thurgood Marshall to provide legal assistance to poor African Americans. Originally affiliated with the NAACP, now a separate organization.

The National Collegiate Athletic Association The governing body of amateur collegiate athletics and a primary organization promoting Title IX compliance www.NCAA.org

National Organization for Women (NOW) www.now.org
Advocacy organization for feminist activists working to protect abortion rights, end discrimination against women, and "eradicate racism, sexism, and homophobia."

Pew Hispanic Center www.pewhispanic.org
Research and surveys on the U.S. Hispanic population.

U.S. Commission on Civil Rights www.usccr.gov
National clearinghouse on information regarding discrimination based on race, color, religion, sex, age, disability, or national origin. Publishes reports, findings, and recommendations.

U.S. Department of Justice, Civil Rights Division www.usdoj.gov/crt
Responsible for enforcement of U.S. civil rights laws. Site includes information on cases.

16

Politics and the Economy

In a letter dated September 6, 1789, Thomas Jefferson wrote James Madison to discuss a notion of generational obligation. He argued that people are constrained, morally and ethically, to not incur any debt for which their own generation cannot pay. Jefferson's point is still relevant today in the circles of deficit hawks and sound money advocates who dislike Keynesian deficit policies and fear that current fiscal policy hinders future generations.

In his five-page letter, Jefferson argues from actuarial data that each generation limit its borrowing to no longer than nineteen years to repay. Any obligation beyond that transfers the obligation to pay beyond the capacity of the generation contracting the debt, and binds the generation that had no voice in assuming the debt:

> [S]uppose Louis XV and his contemporary generation had said to the money-lenders of Genoa, give us money that we may eat, drink, and be merry in our day; and on condition you will demand no interest till the end of 19 years you shall then for ever after receive an annual interest of 125/8 percent. The money is lent on these conditions, is divided among the living, eaten, drank, and squandered. Would the present generation be obliged to apply the produce of the earth and of their labour to replace their dissipations?

He then asked Madison, in his new Constitution, to contain a clause "that neither the legislature, nor the nation itself, can validly contract more debt than they may pay within their own age, or within the term of 19 years?"

Jefferson was a horrible manager of his personal finances and died in debt. But he also argued, ironically, that constitutions themselves need to be crafted by the living generation, because "They are masters too of their own persons, and consequently may govern them as they please."

Contemporary politicians and activists often try to legitimate their politics through the Founders. For anti-deficit libertarians and Tea Party activists, Jefferson's discourse with Madison has found new light as a vehicle to legitimate balanced budgets and support the return to the "sound money" gold standard.

16.1	16.2	16.3	16.4	16.5	16.6
Compare politics and economics as decision-making systems, p. 608	Describe the role that fiscal and monetary policy play in economic decision making, p. 608	Identify the different ways of assessing the strength of the economy, p. 611	Describe the relationships between government spending, deficits, and the national debt, p. 614	Analyze the various kinds of taxes and how they distribute the tax burden, p. 619	Trace changes in tax policies under different administrations in recent decades, p. 624

THE GREAT RECESSION After the banking crisis of 2008, it took nearly six years for the American economy to fully recover.

16.1

16.2

16.3

16.4

16.5

16.6

political economy
The relationships between governments and markets.

fiscal policy
Economic policies involving taxing, spending, and deficit levels of the national government.

monetary policy
Economic policies involving the money supply, interest rates, and banking activity.

Politics and Economics

16.1 Compare politics and economics as decision-making systems.

Earlier, we observed that one of America's foremost political scientists, Harold Lasswell, defined "politics" as "who gets what, when, and how." One of America's foremost economists, Paul Samuelson, defined "economics" as "deciding what shall be produced, how, and for whom."[1]

The similarity between these definitions is based on the fact that both the political system and the economic system provide society with the means for deciding about the production and distribution of goods and services. The political system involves *collective* decisions—choices made by communities, states, or nations—and relies on government coercion through laws, regulations, taxes, and so on to implement them. A free-market economic system involves *individual* decisions—choices made by millions of workers and consumers and thousands of firms—and relies on *voluntary exchange* through buying, selling, borrowing, contracting, and trading to implement them. Both politics and markets function to transform popular demands into goods and services, to allocate costs, and to distribute goods and services.

One of the key questions in any society is how much to rely on government versus the marketplace to provide goods and services. This question of the proper relationship between governments and markets—that is, between politics and economics—is the subject of **political economy**. The United States is primarily a free-market economy, but the federal government increasingly influences economic activity (see *The Game, the Rules, the Players*: How Washington Dealt with the Financial Crisis).

Economic Decision Making

16.2 Describe the role that fiscal and monetary policy play in economic decision making.

Economic decision making involves both fiscal and monetary policy. **Fiscal policy** refers to the taxing, spending, and borrowing activities of the national government. Fiscal policy making takes place within the same system of separated powers and checks and balances that governs other areas of federal policy making, with both Congress and the president sharing responsibility.

Monetary policy refers to decisions regarding the supply of money in the economy, including private borrowing, interest rates, and banking activity. Monetary policy is a principal responsibility of the powerful and independent Federal Reserve Board. Congress established the Federal Reserve Board in 1913, and its power rests on congressional legislation. Congress could, if it wished, reduce its power or even abolish the Fed. No serious effort has ever been undertaken to do so, though actors as diverse as the progressive Occupy movement and conservative libertarians such as Ron Paul have called for this step.

Congress, the President, and Fiscal Policy

The Constitution of the United States places all taxing, borrowing, and spending powers in the hands of Congress. Article I grants Congress the "Power to lay and collect Taxes, Duties, Imposts and Excises, to pay the Debts and provide for the common Defence and general Welfare of the United States," and "to borrow Money on the Credit of the United States." It also declares that "No Money shall be drawn from the

The Game, the Rules, the Players

How Washington Dealt with the Financial Crisis

For years, Americans lived on easy credit. Families ran up credit card debt and borrowed heavily for cars, tuition, and especially mortgages. Mortgage lenders approved loans for borrowers without fully examining their ability to pay. Federally chartered corporations, Fannie Mae and Freddie Mac, encouraged mortgage loans to low-income and minority home buyers. Some mortgages were "predatory," with initial low payments followed by steep upward adjustable rates. To make matters worse, banks and financial institutions bundled "subprime" mortgages together and sold them as "derivatives." Risk was largely ignored. Banks, insurers, and lenders all assumed that housing prices would inevitably rise.

But eventually the bubble burst. Housing prices fell dramatically. Homeowners found themselves holding "upside-down" mortgages—mortgages that exceeded the value of their homes. Many were unable or unwilling to meet their mortgage payments. Foreclosures and delinquencies spiraled upward. Investors who held mortgage-backed securities began to incur heavy losses. Investment banks and mortgage insurers including Fannie Mae and Freddie Mac found themselves in serious financial trouble. The stock market plummeted.

Wall Street Bailout

In 2008, the credit crunch ballooned into Wall Street's biggest crisis since the Great Depression. Hundreds of billions of dollars in mortgage-related investments went bad, and the nation's leading investment banks and insurance companies sought the assistance of the Treasury Department and the Federal Reserve System. As the hemorrhaging continued, it was soon clear that the nation was in danger of tumbling into a deep recession. In September, President Bush sent the secretary of the Treasury, accompanied by the Federal Reserve chairman, to Congress to plead for a massive $700 billion bailout of banks, insurance companies, and investment firms that held mortgage-backed "illiquid assets." They argued that a full-blown depression might result if the federal government failed to intervene in financial markets. House and Senate Democratic and Republican leaders, and even the presidential candidates—Barack Obama and John McCain—all supported the bill. But polls show that most Americans opposed a "Wall Street bailout." Congress members were being asked by their leaders to ignore the folks back home. After an initial House "No" vote that stunned Washington, Congress was eventually persuaded to approve the Emergency Economic Stabilization Act of 2008.

Treasury's TARP

The Treasury Department was given unprecedented power to bail out the nation's financial institutions. The program was named the Troubled Asset Relief Program (TARP). The nation's leading banks, insurance companies, and financial institutions were given TARP funds. In exchange, these institutions were expected to modify home mortgages that were in danger of default, to help mortgage borrowers refinance their loans at lower interest rates, and to loosen credit in an effort to jump-start the economy. But most of all, the TARP funds ensured the continued stability of the nation's financial system.

Fed Response

In addition to the TARP bailouts, the Federal Reserve Board made a dramatic decision to pump over $1.5 trillion into the nation's financial system in order to unlock mortgage, credit card, college, and auto lending. The Fed lowered its own discount rate (the rate it charges member banks to borrow money from the system) to near zero, to encourage banks to make loans. But low-interest rates and easy credit cannot guarantee that banks will lend money or that businesses and individuals will borrow money. As recession deepened in early 2009, President Barack Obama and Congress sought to provide additional economic stimulus.

The Economic Stimulus Package

A massive economic stimulus package, officially the American Recovery and Reinvestment Act of 2009, became the centerpiece of President Barack Obama's early policy agenda. Its combination of spending increases and tax cuts totaled $757 billion—the largest single fiscal policy measure in American history. It was written in record time by a Democratic-controlled Congress; House Republicans were unanimous in opposition, and only three Republican senators supported the bill. The stimulus package consisted of roughly two-thirds spending and one-third tax rebates. Democrats in Congress used the package to increase spending in a wide variety of domestic programs—in education, Medicaid, unemployment compensation, food stamps, health technology, child tax credits, disability payments, higher education grants, renewable energy subsidies, and rail and transit transportation—as well as traditional spending for highways and bridges. Republicans complained that much of the spending had little to do with stimulating the economy but rather increased government involvement in liberal policy areas favored by Democrats. Republicans argued that tax cuts should be the principal approach to stimulating the economy.

Financial Overhaul

In an effort to prevent a repeat of the financial crisis, Congress passed a sweeping overhaul of the nation's financial regulations in 2010. Included in the overhaul were new regulations to restrict derivatives, stricter capital requirements for banks, new powers to seize financial institutions on the brink of bankruptcy, a new council of regulators to monitor the fiscal system for major risks, and a new consumer protection agency to monitor consumer credit. The Federal Reserve retained its powers over monetary policy. But critics blasted the bill for failing to reform Freddie Mac and Fannie Mae, the federal corporations that were partly responsible for the crisis.

QUESTIONS

1. **Of the various programs enacted by the Bush and Obama administrations, which appear to have succeeded, in your informed opinion?**
2. **What are the main areas of criticism of the Obama Administration policies: That they spent money? That they spent money on relief for the poor and economically dislocated? Or that they spent money on firms believed to be part of the cause of the financial meltdown?**

16.1

16.2

16.3

16.4

16.5

16.6

Federal Reserve Board (the Fed)
Independent agency of the executive branch of the federal government charged with overseeing the nation's monetary policy.

inflation
Rise in the general level of prices; not just the prices of some products.

recession
Decline in the general level of economic activity.

Treasury, but in Consequence of Appropriations made by Law." For nearly 150 years, the power to spend was interpreted in a limited fashion: Congress could only spend money to perform powers specifically enumerated in Article I, Section 8, of the Constitution. But the Supreme Court has since ruled that the phrase "to pay the Debts and provide for the common Defence and general Welfare" may be broadly interpreted to authorize congressional spending for any purpose that serves the general welfare. Thus, today there are no constitutional limits on Congress's taxing and spending power. Congress's borrowing power has always been unlimited constitutionally; *there is no constitutional requirement for a balanced budget.*

The Constitution gives the president no formal powers over taxing and spending or borrowing, stating only that the president shall "... recommend to [Congress's] Consideration such Measures as he shall judge necessary and expedient" (Article II, Section 3). From this meager constitutional grant of power, however, presidents have gradually acquired leadership over national economic policy. The principal instrument of executive economic policy making is the Budget of the United States Government, which the president submits annually to Congress. The budget sets forth the president's recommendations for spending for the forthcoming fiscal year; revenue estimates, based on existing taxes or recommendations for new or increased tax levels; and estimates of projected deficits and the need for borrowing when, as has usually been the case of late, spending recommendations exceed revenue estimates.

□ The Fed and Monetary Policy

Most economically advanced democracies have central banks, whose principal responsibility is to regulate the supply of money, both currency in circulation and bank deposits. And most of these democracies have found it best to remove this responsibility from the direct control of elected politicians. Politicians everywhere are sorely tempted to inflate the supply of money in order to fund projects and programs with newly created money instead of new taxes. Nations pay for this approach with a general rise in prices and a reduction in goods and services available to private firms and individuals—inflation. Indeed, nations whose control of the money supply has fallen victim to irresponsible governments have experienced inflation rates of 500 to 1,000 percent per year, which is to say that their money became worthless.

The Federal Reserve System of the United States is largely independent of either the president or Congress. Its independent status is a result not only of law but also of its structure. It is run by a seven-member board of governors who are appointed by the president, with the consent of the Senate, for *14-year* terms. Members may not be removed from the board except for "cause"; no member has ever been removed since the creation of the board in 1913. The board's chair serves only a four-year term, but the chair's term overlaps that of the president, so that new presidents cannot immediately name their own chair.

The task of the **Federal Reserve Board (the Fed)** is to regulate the money supply and by so doing to help avoid both inflation and recession. The Fed oversees the operation of the nation's 12 Federal Reserve Banks, which actually issue the nation's currency, called "Federal Reserve Notes." The Federal Reserve Banks are bankers' banks; they do not directly serve private citizens or firms. They hold the deposits, or "reserves," of banks; lend money to banks at "discount rates" that the Fed determines; buy and sell U.S. Government Treasury bonds; and assure regulatory compliance by private banks and protection of depositors against fraud. The Fed determines the reserve requirements of banks and otherwise monitors the health of the banking industry. The Fed also plays an important role in clearing checks throughout the banking system.

The Fed's influence over the economy is mainly through monetary policy—increasing or decreasing the supply of money and hence largely determining interest rates. When **inflation recession** threatens, the Fed typically acts to expand ("ease") the supply of money and lower interest rates by (1) lowering the reserve requirement of banks and thereby increasing the amount of money they have to loan out; or (2) lowering the discount rate and thereby the cost of borrowing by banks; or (3) selling off government bonds in "open market operations," thereby increasing the funds banks can lend to individuals and businesses. When **inflation** threatens, the Fed typically acts to limit ("tighten") the money supply and increase interest rates by taking the opposite of each action just described.

Although it is the Fed that makes monetary policy, voters typically hold the president responsible for recessions. Hence presidents frequently try to persuade the independent Fed into lowering interest rates, especially in an election year, believing a temporary stimulus to help win the election is worth whatever inflationary effects it might create after the election.

gross domestic product (GDP)
Measure of economic performance in terms of the nation's total production of goods and services for a single year, valued in terms of market prices.

economic cycles
Fluctuations in real GDP growth followed by contraction.

unemployment rate
Percentage of the civilian labor force who are not working but who are looking for work or waiting to return to or to begin a job.

Measuring the Performance of the American Economy

16.3 Identify the different ways of assessing the strength of the economy.

Underlying the power of nations and the well-being of their citizens is the strength of their economy—their total productive capacity. The United States produces about $17 *trillion* worth of goods and services in a single year for its 310 million people—more than $50,000 worth of output for every person.

JANET YELLEN
As the new Federal Reserve chair, Yellen has been polarizing as a 'loose money' advocate who will not put the brakes on inflation.

Economic Growth

Gross domestic product (GDP) is a widely used measure of the performance of the economy.[2] GDP is a nation's total production of goods and services for a single year valued in terms of market prices. It is the sum of all the goods and services that people have been willing to pay for, from wheat production to bake sales, machine tools to maid service, aircraft manufacturing to bus rides, automobiles to chewing gum. GDP counts only final purchases of goods and services (that is, it ignores the purchase of steel by car makers until it is sold as a car) to avoid double counting in the production process. GDP also excludes financial transactions (such as the sale of bonds and stocks) and income transfers (such as Social Security, welfare, and pension payments) that do not add to the production of goods and services. Although GDP is expressed in current dollar prices, it is often recalculated in constant dollar terms to reflect real values over time, adjusting for the effect of inflation. GDP estimates are prepared each quarter by the U.S. Department of Commerce; these figures are widely reported and closely watched by the business and financial community.

Growth in real (constant dollar) GDP measures the performance of the overall economy. Economic recessions and recoveries are measured as fluctuations or swings in the growth of GDP. For example, a recession is usually defined as negative GDP growth in two or more consecutive quarters. Historical data reveal that periods of economic growth have traditionally been followed by periods of contraction, giving rise to the notion of **economic cycles** (see Figure 16.1).

Unemployment

From a political standpoint, the **unemployment rate** may be the most important measure of the economy's performance (see *The Game, the Rules, the Players*: "It's the Economy, Stupid"). The unemployment rate is the percentage of the civilian labor force that

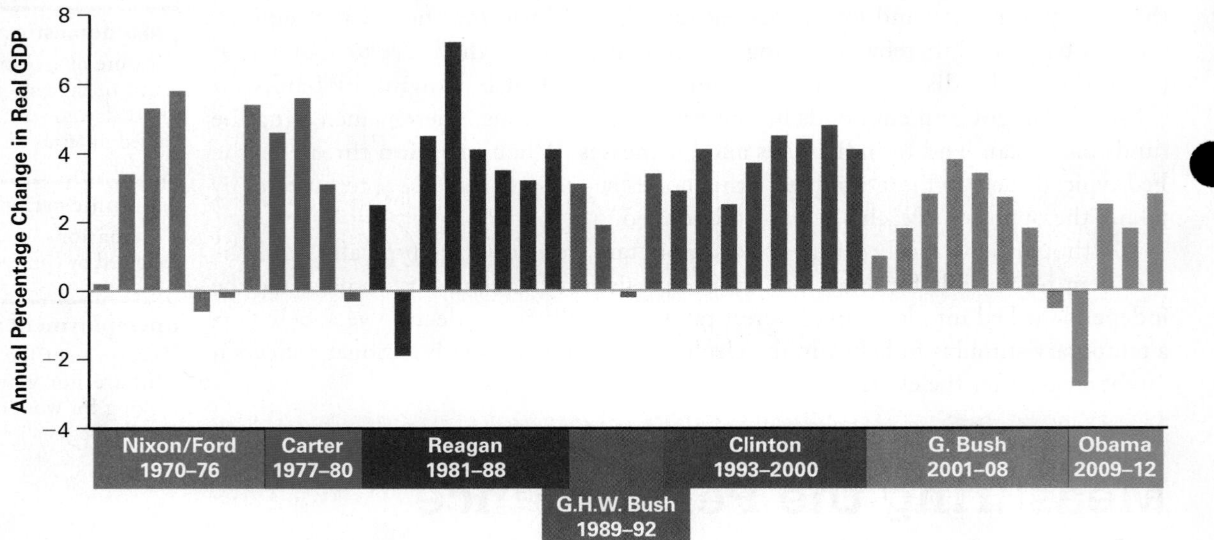

FIGURE 16.1 ECONOMIC GROWTH IN AMERICA

Periods of economic growth are reflected here as increases in the annual percent change in the GDP. Recessions are shown as negative (below zero) GDP growth. The recession that began in 2008 was the worst in over 50 years.

SOURCE: Data from Bureau of Economic Analysis, 2013, www.bea.gov.

are looking for work or waiting to return to or begin a job. Unemployment is different from not working; people who have retired or who attend school and people who do not work because of sickness, disability, or unwillingness are not considered part of the labor force and so are not counted as unemployed. People who are so discouraged about finding a job that they have quit looking for work are also not counted in the official unemployment rate. The unemployed do include people who have been terminated from their last job or temporarily laid off from work as well as people who voluntarily quit and those who have recently entered or reentered the labor force and are now seeking employment.

The unemployment rate is measured each month by the U.S. Department of Labor. It does so by contacting a random sample of more than 50,000 households in many locations throughout the country. Trained interviewers ask a variety of questions to determine how many (if any) members of the household are either working or have a job but did not work at it because of sickness, vacation, strike, or personal reasons (employed); or whether they have no job but are available for work and actively seeking a job (unemployed). The unemployment rate fluctuates with the business cycle, reflecting recessions and recoveries (see Figure 16.2). Generally, unemployment lags behind GDP growth, going down only after the recovery has begun. Following years of economic growth in the 1990s, the nation's unemployment rate fell to near record lows, below 5 percent. But the economic recession beginning in 2008 pushed unemployment back up to above 10 percent.

☐ Inflation

Inflation erodes the value of the dollar because higher prices mean that the same dollars can now purchase fewer goods and services. Thus inflation erodes the value of savings, reduces the incentive to save, and hurts people who are living on fixed incomes. When banks and investors anticipate inflation, they raise interest rates on loans in order to cover the anticipated lower value of repayment dollars. Higher interest rates, in turn, make it more difficult for new or expanding businesses to borrow money, for home buyers to acquire mortgages, and for consumers to make purchases on credit. Thus inflation and high interest rates slow economic growth.

The Game, the Rules, the Players

"It's the Economy, Stupid"

The pointed political advice, "It's the economy, stupid," is generally attributed to James Carville, campaign consultant to Democrat Bill Clinton during the 1992 presidential race against incumbent Republican George H. W. Bush. The perceived performance of the economy during the election year is an excellent predictor of presidential voting outcomes. When the economy is prosperous, voters reward the incumbent presidential party. When the economy sours, they vote the incumbent party out of the White House.

Indeed, the percentage vote for the incumbent party's candidate can be predicted reasonably well from responses to the survey question, whether business conditions have improved or gotten worse over the previous year. When a majority of people surveyed in presidential elections from 1980 through 2008 said the economy had gotten "worse," the candidate of the party occupying the White House lost. When a majority of people said the economy was "the same" or "better" than the previous year, the candidate of the incumbent party won the election. The only exception was the presidential election of 2000, where the candidate of the incumbent Democratic Party, Al Gore, lost to the Republican challenger, George W. Bush, despite a strong economy. According to the economic voter theses, Al Gore "should" have won and won easily, not just barely won the popular vote (and lost in the Electoral College).

JAMES CARVILLE The coiner of the phrase "it's the economy, stupid," 1992 Clinton operative James Carville has staunchly defended the Obama administration's economic policies in the media.

In the 2008 presidential campaign, the economic meltdown of mid-September led an already pessimistic public to get even more negative in its evaluation of the economy. Republican John McCain's slim chances were demolished by the financial crises. Democrat Barack Obama won the election with 53 percent of the vote, although this outcome was somewhat less than predicted by the economic thesis.

Interestingly, it is not the voters' own personal economic well-being that affects their vote but rather the voters' perception of *general* economic conditions. People may report that their own financial situation is good, but vote against the incumbent party when they perceive the general economy as poor. Media attention to the economy during the campaign signals voters about the state of the economy, and increased media attention focuses voters' attention on the economy.

The 2012 election campaign largely focused on the economy. Voters consistently rated the economy their top concern, and the shallow recovery from the 2008–2009 recession was a source of finger-pointing and blame by both parties. Democrats criticized Republicans for obstructing President Obama's policies in the Congress, while Republicans criticized the administration for tepid job growth, excessive deficit spending, and high taxes.

By the last month of the 2012 presidential campaign, the economy appeared to be recovering. The unemployment rate fell below 8 percent for the first time in four years. The stock market doubled in value from the bottom of the 2009 crash. Obama was reelected, but his margin of victory (51 percent) was not as great as in 2008 (53 percent).

QUESTIONS

1. **When you vote, do you vote on the economy?**
2. **Do you think your opinion and vote is shaped by your own experiences or by your perception of the larger economic environment?**

SOURCE: See Robert S. Erickson, "The American Voter and the Economy, 2008"; Thomas M. Holbrook, "Economic Considerations and the 2008 Presidential Election"; and Michael S. Lewis-Beck and Richard Nadeau, "Obama and the Economy 2008," in *P.S. Political Science & Politics* 42 (July 2009): 467–84.

☐ Recession

Economists define a recession as two or more quarters of negative economic growth, that is, declines in the gross domestic product. (In politics, a recession is often proclaimed when the economy only slows its growth rate or when unemployment rises.) Recessions also entail a rise in unemployment and declines in consumer spending and capital investment. In some recessions, prices decline as well—"deflation."

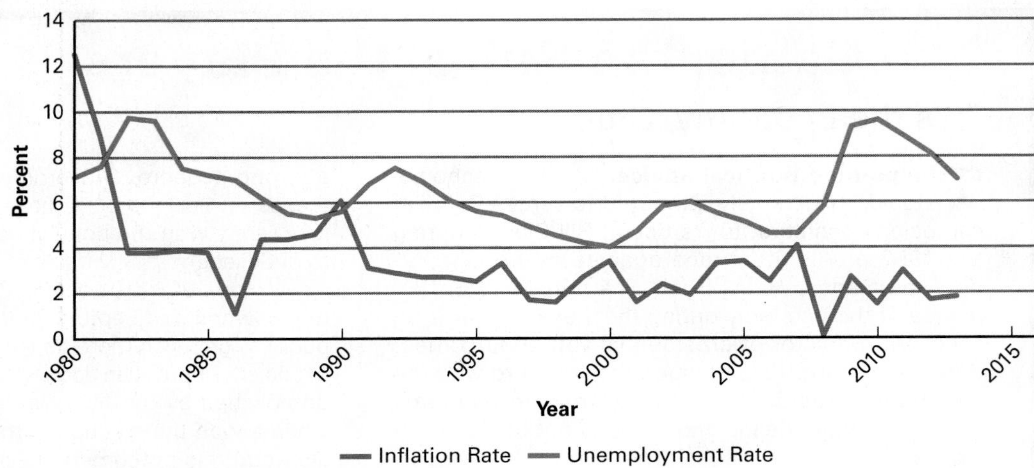

FIGURE 16.2 UNEMPLOYMENT AND INFLATION IN AMERICA

The nation suffered higher unemployment rates during the relatively mild recessions of 1975 and 1982. But unemployment rose to over 10 percent in 2009, the worst job market in many decades, before gradually declining over the next three years.

SOURCE: Data from Bureau of Labor Statistics, 2013, www.bls.gov.

Government Spending, Deficits, and Debt

16.4 Describe the relationships between government spending, deficits, and the national debt.

mandatory spending
Spending for program commitments made by past congresses.

entitlement programs
Social welfare programs that provide classes of people with legally enforceable rights to benefits.

indexing
Tying of benefit levels in social welfare programs to the general price level.

in-kind (noncash) benefits
Benefits of a social welfare program that are not cash payments, including free medical care, subsidized housing, and food stamps.

he expenditures of all governments in the United States—federal, state, and local governments combined—today amount to over 35 percent of GDP. The federal government itself spends more than $3.7 trillion each year—about 23 percent of GDP.

"Mandatory" Spending

Much of the growth of federal government spending over the years is attributed to **mandatory spending** items in the federal budget. These "uncontrollables" are budget items committed to by past policies of Congress that are not easily changed in annual budget making. Sources of mandatory spending include the following:

- **Entitlement programs**. Federal programs that provide classes of people with a legally enforceable right to benefits are called **entitlement programs**. Entitlement programs account for more than half of all federal spending, including Social Security, Medicare and Medicaid, food stamps, federal employees' retirement pensions, and veterans' benefits (see Figure 16.3). These entitlements are benefits that past Congresses have pledged the federal government to pay. Entitlements are not really uncontrollable. Congress can always amend the basic laws that established them, but doing so is politically difficult and might be regarded as abandonment of a public trust. As more people become "entitled" to government benefits—for example, as more people reach retirement ages and claim Social Security benefits, federal spending increases.
- **Indexing of benefits**. Another reason that spending increases each year is that Congress has authorized automatic increases in benefits to match inflation. Benefits under such programs as Social Security are tied to the Consumer Price Index. This **indexing** pushes up the cost of entitlement programs each year.
- **Increasing costs of in-kind benefits**. Rises in the cost of major **in-kind (noncash) benefits**, particularly the medical costs of Medicaid and Medicare, also guarantee

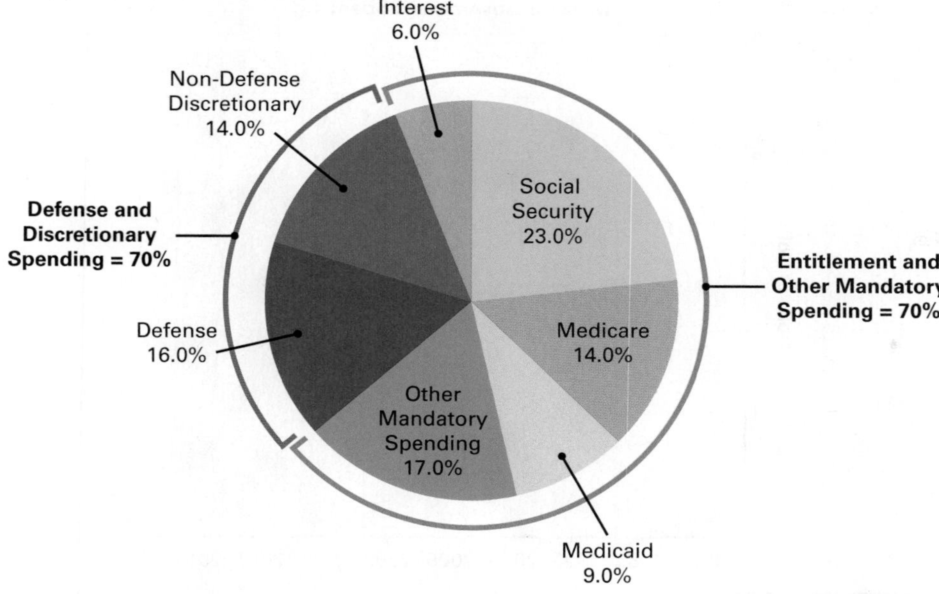

FIGURE 16.3 WHO GETS WHAT?: FEDERAL BUDGET SHARES

Mandatory spending—spending commitments in existing laws, notably Social Security, Medicare, Medicaid, and other entitlements, plus interest on the national debt—accounts for about 70 percent of the federal budget. Discretionary spending, including defense, accounts for only about 30 percent of the budget.

SOURCE: *Budget of the United States Government,* 2015.

growth in federal spending. These in-kind benefit programs have risen faster in cost than cash benefit programs.

- **Interest on the national debt.** The federal government has a long history of deficit spending. As these annual deficits accumulate, the total national debt increases. Interest payments on the national debt rise accordingly.

discretionary spending
Spending for programs not previously mandated by law.

deficits
Imbalances in the annual federal budget in which spending exceeds revenues.

national debt
Total debt accumulated by the national government over the years.

"Discretionary" Spending

Washington policymakers consider spending that is not previously mandated by law to be **discretionary**. Almost 40 percent of the federal budget is officially designated as discretionary, but this includes spending for national defense. Nondefense discretionary spending is less than 20 percent of the budget. It includes everything from national parks to federal prisons, from highways to air travel.

Exploding Deficits

The series of Obama administration budgets called for massive new government spending and huge federal **deficits**. For many years, federal government spending rose more or less incrementally (see Figure 16.4). But in 2009, federal spending rose by almost $1 trillion from the previous year, the largest single year-to-year increase in history. That same year, federal revenues declined; the extra spending was financed through a $1.7 trillion deficit, the largest annual deficit in history (see Figure 16.5). The bulk of these increases in spending and deficit levels can be attributed to the nation's fiscal crisis and government efforts designed to offset recession. But high levels of deficits and federal spending are projected to continue into the foreseeable future, barring a significant departure in government spending or an unexpected influx of new tax revenue.

The Debt Burden

The accumulated annual federal deficits—that is, expenditures exceeding revenues each year—add up to the nation's **national debt**. This debt in 2012 was over $16 trillion

Massive Government Spending
Trillions of Dollars
4
3
2
1
0.3
0.9
1.5
1.8
2.5
3.9
3.7
3.8
3.9
1975
1985
1995
2000
2005
2009
2010
2012
2015

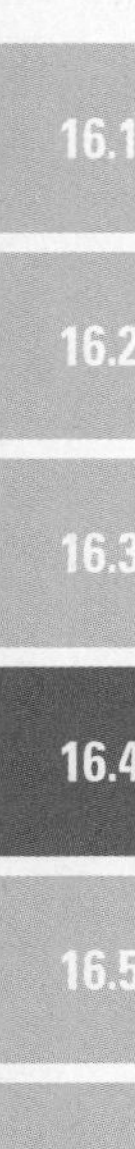

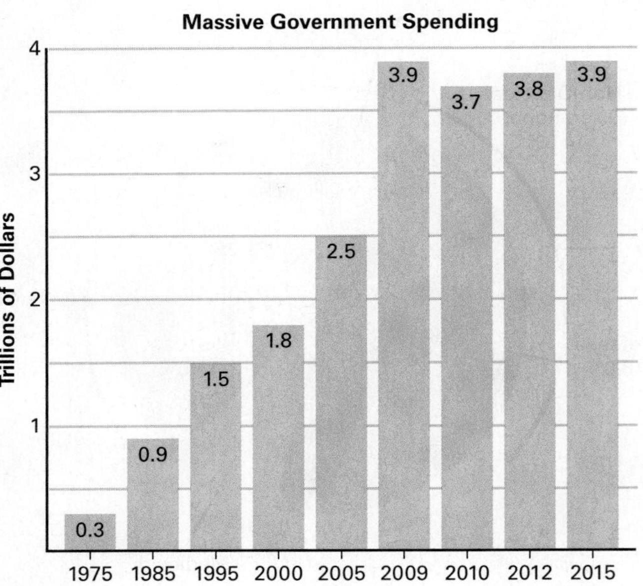

FIGURE 16.4 MASSIVE GOVERNMENT SPENDING

Obama's budgets have called for nearly $4 trillion in government spending each year ($3.9 in 2015).

SOURCE: *Budget of the United States Government*, 2013.

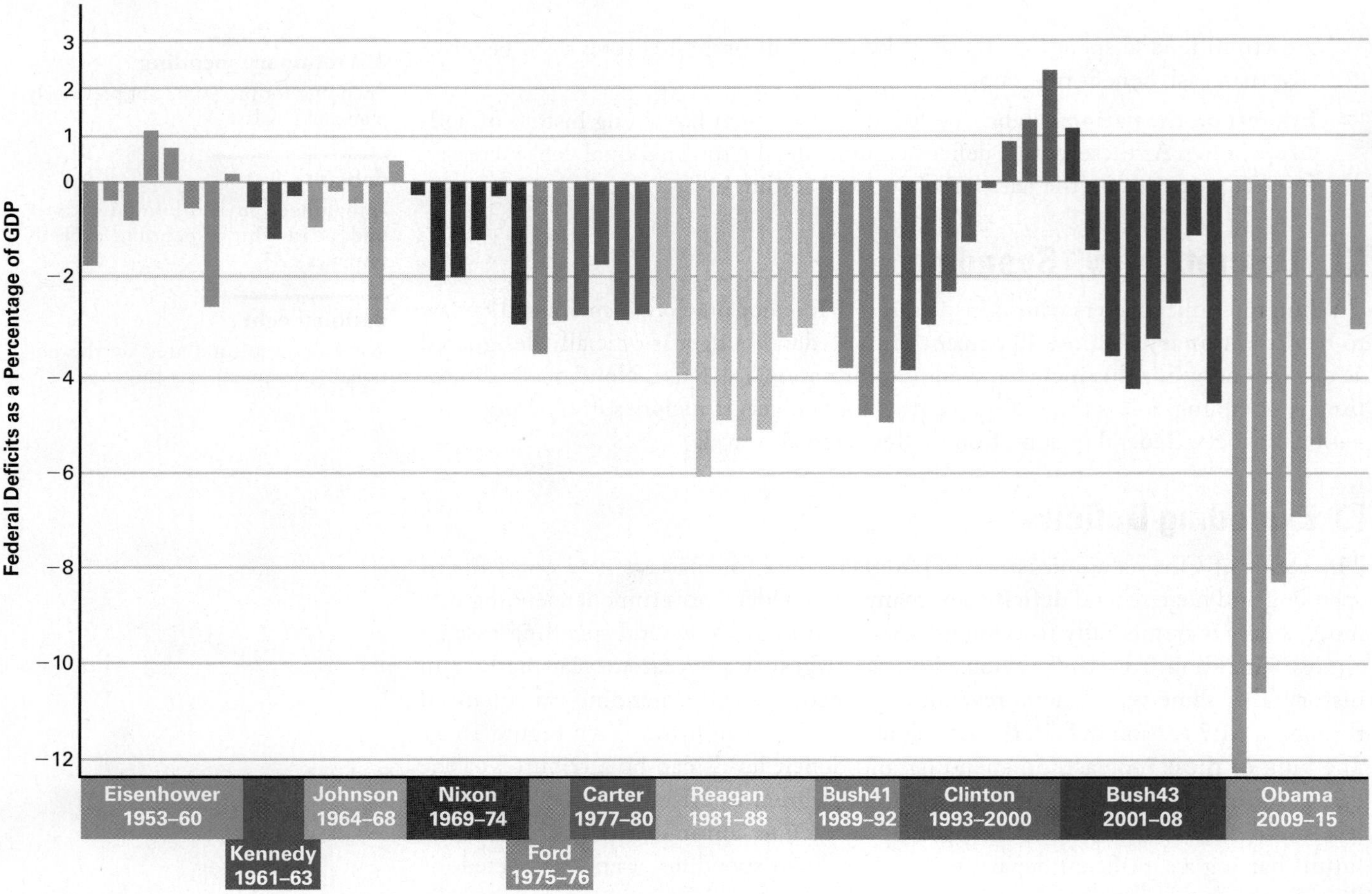

Federal Deficits as a Percentage of GDP
3
2
1
0
−2
−4
−6
−8
−10
−12
Eisenhower 1953–60
Kennedy 1961–63
Johnson 1964–68
Nixon 1969–74
Ford 1975–76
Carter 1977–80
Reagan 1981–88
Bush41 1989–92
Clinton 1993–2000
Bush43 2001–08
Obama 2009–15

FIGURE 16.5 FEDERAL DEFICITS THROUGH THE YEARS

This figure shows annual federal deficits as percentages of the GDP. In only 4 of the last 40 years (1998–2001) has the federal government not incurred a deficit. Deficits in the Obama administration have ballooned to levels unprecedented since World War II.

SOURCE: *Budget of the United States Government*, 2015.

($50,000 for every man, woman, and child in the nation). In only 4 of the last 40 years (1998–2001), has the federal government *not* incurred a deficit.

The national debt is owed mostly to U.S. banks and financial institutions and private citizens who buy Treasury bonds. But an increasing share of the debt is owed to foreign banks and governments, including China. As old debt comes due, the U.S. Treasury Department sells new bonds to pay off the old; that is, it continues to "roll over" or "float" the debt.

Interest payments on the national debt comes from current taxes. These payments divert money away from *all* other government programs. Even if the federal government manages to balance future budgets, interest payments will remain obligations of the children and grandchildren of the current generation of policymakers and taxpayers. In effect, policymakers today are shifting the burden of government to future generations.

☐ The Debt Ceiling

Congress by law sets a ceiling for the national debt. This ceiling forbids the U.S. Treasury Department from exceeding this dollar limit. The ceiling must be increased periodically to accommodate the nation's growing debt.

Usually Congress does this with little fanfare, but by 2011 a Republican-controlled House of Representatives threatened *not* to raise the debt ceiling unless the Obama administration agreed to cuts in federal spending. The Treasury secretary warned that the government could not meet its financial obligations if Congress failed to raise the debt ceiling. In that event, the failure to raise the debt ceiling might even result in a first-ever default on U.S. bonds that were coming due. After tense negotiations, Congress agreed in the Budget Control Act of 2011 to raise the debt ceiling in exchange for modest spending cuts and the promise that a bipartisan "supercommittee" of Congress would recommend ways to further reduce the deficits. But the supercommittee dissolved itself in November 2011 after failing to reach any sort of agreement to adress debt and deficit reduction.

☐ Budget Gridlock and Government "Shut Down"

The Constitution states that "no money shall be drawn from the Treasury, but in Consequence of Appropriations made by Law" (Art. I, Sect. 9). In theory the failure of Congress to pass appropriations acts, or to authorize continuing spending in "continuing resolution," would require all government spending to cease, in effect causing a government "shutdown." But in practice federal government shutdowns have only been partial, affecting only "nonessential" services.

The federal government shut down in 2013 when the Republican-controlled House of Representatives and Democratic President Barack Obama deadlocked over spending for fiscal year 2014. The House insisted that the continuing resolution for that year exclude funding for the President's signature domestic program, "Obamacare." "Defunding" Obamacare became a top priority, especially among conservative Republican lawmakers. But the Democratic-controlled Senate refused to pass the House resolution, and President Obama promised to veto it even if the Senate were to do so. President Obama declared that he would not negotiate over the extension of the debt ceiling. Negotiations collapsed between all of the parties, and the government officially shut down on October 1.

President Obama succeeded in placing the blame for the shutdown on the House Republicans. He closed the Statue of Liberty, canceled White House tours, furloughed a reported 800,000 federal employees, ordered the U.S. Park Service to fence off the World War II Memorial in Washington, and generally sought to convince the public that the GOP was doing great damage to the nation. The House responded by passing a series of separate appropriations for the National Parks Service, the National Institutes of Health, the Food and Drug Administration, the National Guard and Reserves, veterans benefits, food stamps, and Head Start. But the president rejected all of these specific bills, and the Democratic-controlled Senate, led by Majority Leader Harry Reid, refused to vote with any of them.

A CONTRASTING VIEW

WE SHOULD PASS A BALANCED BUDGET AMENDMENT TO THE CONSTITUTION

A balanced budget amendment to the U.S. Constitution would limit federal government to an amount equal to or less than the revenue it receives each year. There would be exceptions, whereby Congress could spend more in times of war or recession or national emergency, if approved by a supermajority in both the House and Senate. The wording of proposed amendments varies. One simple version: "Outlays of the United States for any fiscal year shall not exceed receipts to the United States for that year, unless 3.5 (or 2/3) of the whole number of both houses of Congress shall provide for a specific excess of outlays of revenues."

The Economics of It. A balanced budget amendment challenges Kenynesian economics, which teaches that federal spending and borrowing should counter economic cycles. The federal government should borrow money during recessions to stimulate the economy, and pay the debt off during upturns to hold down inflation. But politicians are loath to give up federal deficits, in either good times or bad, by either reducing spending or increasing taxes. It is easier to spend now, increase deficits, and place the burden of debt on future generations. Obligating taxpayers of tomorrow, our children and grandchildren, to pay for spending today may be morally indefensible, but it is politically attractive. Proponents of a balanced budget argue that only a constitutional amendment can protect future generations against the self-interested politicians. Or as one Congress member put it: "If you don't tie our hands, we'll keep stealing."

But even proponents of an amendment recognize that wars, recession, or national emergencies can cause temporary imbalances of outlays over receipts. So most proposals for a balanced budget amendment include exceptions approved by majorities in both houses, that is a three-fifths or two-thirds vote.

One Vote Short. Any constitutional amendment requires a two-thirds vote of both the House and Senate, as well as ratification by three-quarters of the states. The states appear ready to ratify a balanced budget amendment if Congress can send it to them. Indeed, several states have petitioned Congress to pass such an amendment. In 1997 a balanced budget amendment fell one vote short in the U.S. Senate of the required two-thirds. This vote was inspired by the 1994 midterm Republican congressional election victory and pledge in the Republican "Contract with America" to pass the amendment. But the narrow defeat appeared to set back the balanced budget amendment movement for more than a decade.

Renewed Efforts. U.S. Senator Orin Hatch (R-UT) is a longtime advocate of the balanced budget amendment. In 2010 he renewed his effort by proposing an amendment that: (1) mandates the total outlays for any fiscal year cannot exceed revenues; (2) requires the president to submit a balanced budget to Congress each year; and (3) waives these requirements if there is a formal declaration of war, or a military conflict threatening national security, or if two-thirds of both the House and Senate approves.

The Hatch proposal goes further in limiting Congress's fiscal powers. It would cap federal spending at 20 percent of GDP, and would require a two-thirds vote of both houses to raise taxes. The Hatch proposal would allow four years following notification by the necessary three-quarters of the states before taking effect. The purpose of the delay is to allow time for the federal government to adjust its fiscal policies.

A constitutional amendment does not require the president's signature. But achieving a three-fifths or two-thirds majority in both chambers of Congress requires bipartisan support. Democrats must join with Republicans if the balanced budget amendment to the Constitution is ever to pass.

QUESTIONS

1. Would you support a balanced budget amendment? Why or why not?
2. Go to the website of your member of Congress or Senator. Have they expressed an opinion about a balanced budget amendment? What is it?

All polls show increasing public disapproval of the Republican Party, House Republicans began to fight among themselves—"moderate" Republicans breaking with conservative "Tea Party" Republicans over continuing the shut down. Initially the Republican leadership in the House and Senate (including House Speaker John Boehner and Senate Majority Leader Mitch McConnell) conceded to the President and voted to approve a continuing resolution that preserved funding for Obamacare. The shutdown ended October 16, 2013, with the Republican Party in disarray.

☐ The "Sequester"

The Budget Control Act of 2011 also contained a provision referred to as the "sequester"—automatic, across the board spending reductions in discretionary in defense spending. The sequestration excluded mandatory programs, including Social Security and Medicare. Democratic and Republican congressional negotiators as well as President Obama originally believed that the cuts involved in the sequester were so drastic that the "super committee" would be forced to come up with a more reasonable deficit reduction plan. But Congress, the President, and the "super committee" failed to reach any agreement.

The sequester which remained in place through 2013 and actually made modest cuts in government spending. It affected a wide variety of discretionary domestic programs, but its greatest impact was on the United States military. The Defense Department was obliged to cut funding for training, maintenance, and new replacement weapons acquisition.

Democrats in Republicans finally came together in late 2013 to agree on a budget that would last through 2014 and effectively end the sequester. The compromise was worked out by the Republican Chairman of the House Budget Committee, Paul D. Ryan of Wisconsin, and Senate Budget Committee Chairwoman Democrat Patty Murray of Washington. The compromise exceeds the spending limits set by the sequester (limits in the budget control act of 2011), but it promises to end the continuing threat of a government shutdown. Overall, it appeared to be a victory for congressional Democrats, and President Barack Obama promptly signed it into law.

individual income tax
Taxes on individuals' wages and other earned income, the primary source of revenue for the U.S. federal government.

The Tax Burden

16.5 Analyze the various kinds of taxes and how they distribute the tax burden.

The tax burden in the United States is modest compared to burdens in other advanced democracies (see *Compared to What?* Tax Burdens in Advanced Democracies). Federal revenues are derived mainly from (1) individual income taxes, (2) corporate income taxes, (3) Social Security payroll taxes, (4) estate and gift taxes, and (5) excise taxes and custom duties.

Individual Income Taxes

The **individual income tax** is the federal government's largest source of revenue (see Figure 16.6). Following tax cuts enacted by Congress in 2001 and 2003, individual incomes are taxed at seven rates: 10, 15, 25, 28, 33, 35, and 39.6 percent.

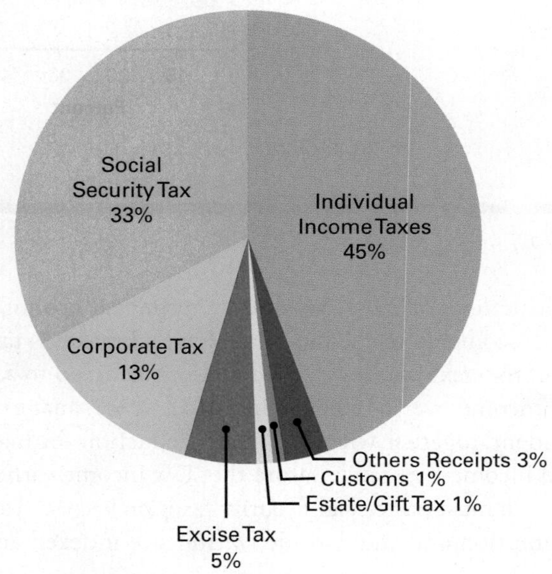

FIGURE 16.6 WHERE THE MONEY COMES FROM: SOURCES OF FEDERAL INCOME

Individual income taxes make up the largest portion of the federal government's revenues (43 percent). The government also relies heavily on the second largest source of its revenues, Social Security taxes.

SOURCE: *Budget of the United States Government,* 2014.

Compared to What?

Tax Burdens in Advanced Democracies

Americans complain a lot about taxes. But from a global perspective, overall tax burdens in the United States are relatively low (see figure). Tax revenues in the United States amount to about 29 percent of the gross domestic product (GDP). U.S. taxes are well below the burdens imposed in Sweden, Denmark, and other nations with highly developed welfare systems.

QUESTIONS

1. Do we need more taxes? Why?
2. Pick a country from the list and see how it raises revenue from taxes. How do we compare to that country in terms of indicators of economic and social health: child poverty, mortality rate, health coverage?

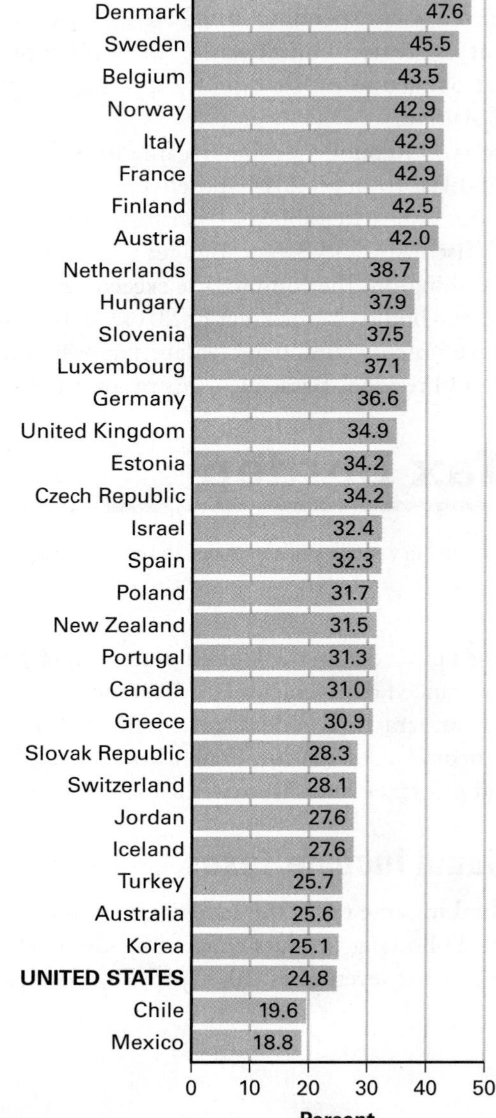

SOURCE: OECD. www.oecd.org, 2013

Tax rates are structured as marginal rates, a term that economists use to mean "additional." That is, income up to the top of the lowest bracket is taxed at 10 percent; additional income in the next bracket is taxed at 15 percent, up to a top marginal rate of 39.6 percent on income over $450,000 (in 2013). A personal exemption for each taxpayer and dependent, together with a standard deduction for married couples and a refundable earned income tax credit, ensure that low income earners pay no income tax. (However, they still must pay Social Security taxes on wages.) Tax brackets, as well as the personal exemption and standard deduction, are indexed annually to protect against inflation.

The income tax is automatically deducted from the paychecks of employees. This "withholding" system is the backbone of the individual income tax. There is no withholding of nonwage income such as dividends on investments, but taxpayers with such income must file a "Declaration of Estimated Taxes" and pay this estimate in quarterly installments. Before April 15 of each year, all income-earning Americans must report their taxable income for the previous year to the Internal Revenue Service on its 1040 Form.

Americans are usually surprised to learn that half of all personal income is not taxed. To understand why, we must know how the tax laws distinguish between *adjusted gross income* (an individual's total money income minus expenses incurred in earning that income) and *taxable income* (that part of adjusted gross income subject to taxation). Federal tax rates apply only to *taxable* income.

Tax expenditures are tax revenues lost to the federal government because of exemptions, exclusions, deductions, and special treatments in tax laws. Federal government revenues from individual and business income taxes would be substantially higher were it not for special provisions in tax laws that enable taxpayers to avoid paying taxes on often substantial sums of income. Although each of these "loopholes" supposedly has a larger social goal behind it (for example, the deductibility of mortgage interest is supposed to stimulate the purchase and construction of homes, keeping up the value of those assets for current homeowners and keeping the construction industry employed), critics charge that many cost far more than they are worth to society. These are the major tax expenditures in federal tax law:

- Personal exemptions for taxpayer, spouse, and children
- Deductibility of mortgage interest on homes
- Deductibility of property taxes on first and second homes
- Deferral of capital gains on home sales
- Deductibility of charitable contributions
- Credit for child-care expenses
- Tax-free deposits for educational savings accounts
- Exclusion of employer contributions to pension plans and medical insurance
- Partial exclusion of Social Security benefits
- Exclusion of interest on public-purpose state and local bonds
- Deductibility of state and local income taxes
- Accelerated depreciation of machinery, equipment, and structures
- Deductible contributions to IRAs and 401(K) retirement plans, and accrued interest and profits in these plans. (But taxes must be paid when cash is taken from these plans.)

There is a continual struggle between proponents of special tax exemptions to achieve social goals and those who believe the tax laws should be simplified and social goals met by direct government expenditures. Much of the political infighting in Washington involves the efforts of interest groups to obtain exemptions, exclusions, deductions, and special treatments in tax laws.[3]

In addition to these multiple means of **tax avoidance** (legal means), an "underground economy" that facilitates **tax evasion** (illegal means of dodging taxes) costs the federal government many billions of dollars. The federal Internal Revenue Service itself estimates that it is losing about $300 billion per year in revenue due to the failure of people to report income and pay taxes on it. Independent estimates of the size of the underground economy are much higher, perhaps $500 billion, or 15 percent of all taxes due.[4] Many citizens receive cash for goods and services they provide, and it simply does not occur to them to report these amounts as income in addition to the wage statements they receive from their employer. Many others receive all or most of their income from cash transactions; they have a strong incentive to underreport their income. And, of course, illegal criminal transactions such as drug dealing are seldom reported on personal income tax forms. As tax rates rise, hiding income becomes more profitable.

tax expenditures
Revenues lost to the federal government because of exemptions, exclusions, deductions, and special-treatment provisions in tax laws.

tax avoidance
Taking advantage of exemptions, exclusions, deductions, and special treatments in tax laws (legal).

tax evasion
Hiding income and/or falsely claiming exemptions, deductions, and special treatments (illegal).

Capital Gains and Dividend Taxation

Individuals not only pay taxes on earned income—wages, salaries, tips, and profits from their businesses—but also on *capital gains*—profits from the sale of personally owned assets, including homes, furnishings, stocks, and bonds. Losses from these sales may be used to offset gains. Any net gain it is taxed at a rate of 15% (unless the asset was held less than one year, whereupon the gain is taxed at ordinary income tax rates). For most individuals this capital gains tax rate is considerably lower than the rate assessed on ordinary earned income.

The dividends from stocks are also taxed at a lower rate than earned income. For most dividend recipients the rate is 15%, the same as for capital gains. (For families earning $450,000 or more the dividend rate rises to 20%.)

Why should income earned from money investments be taxed at a lower rate than income earned from work? Preferential tax treatment for dividends and capital gains a appeals to a wide variety of interests, especially a Wall Street brokerage houses and investment firms and the wheel estate industry. It's significantly reduces the tax burden on high income taxpayers—the most likely to have incomes from investments. A central reform in the Reagan Tax Reform Act of 1986 was the elimination of preferential treatment for income from capital Investments. But over time, both Republican and Democratic presidents and congresses have worked to reduce taxes on dividends and capital gains. In 2003 Republicans and Congress, following President George W Bush's lead, succeeded in lowering the dividend and capital gains tax rate to 15%. President Obama campaigned to raise these rates, the succeeded only in getting a 20% rates imposed on high income earners in 2013.

Many investors argue that a tax on dividends amounts to double taxation, because the corporations issuing the dividends have already been taxed on their overall corporate income. Another argument centers on the negative effect of taxes on capital gains and dividends on the accumulation of capital needed for economic growth.

The dispute over preferential treatment for dividends and capital gains was highlighted by billionaire Warren Buffett, who observed that his effective tax rate (about 16%) was well above that of his secretary. Buffett receives most of his income from investments. He urged his friend President Obama to adopt a "Buffet rule" requiring all high income individuals to pay at least 30% of their income in federal taxes.

AMT and the EITC

To further complicate tax laws, an alternative minimum tax (AMT) requires taxpayers to compute a separate AMT tax in addition to their "regular" income tax. Taxpayers are then required to pay eight whichever taxes higher. The AMT tax allows *no* deductions for personal exemptions or state or local taxes, and it limits deductions for home mortgages, medical expenses, and other items. The AMT imposes a 25 to 20% are eight on this adjusted income.

The AMT was designed to ensure that high income tax payers with many exclusions and deductions would pay a minimum tax it was originally passed by Congress in 1969 an applied only to the highest income taxpayers. But over time inflation has pushed many middle-class taxpayers into the grasp of the AMT. Congress has periodically raised the income amount that qualifies individuals for the imposition of the AMT.

The Earned Income Tax Credit (EITC) has become a major source of Federal support for low income families. The EITC was enacted in 1975 to provide an incentive to low income workers. The credit does more than eliminate the burden of income taxes on low income people; rather it results in a "refund" check for those who qualify in claim the credit. In 2013 families with two or more children incomes below

$51,567 qualify for the credit; the maximum check from the Federal government was $5372. The EITC may be thought of as a "negative income tax."

Many taxpayers deliberately "over withhold" taxes from their paychecks, in effect giving the federal government a no interest loan. Their reward is a return of their own money the following year. Overwithholding, together with the EITC, ensures that most middle and low income taxpayers receive a government's checked each new year the political effect is to lessen opposition to income taxation.

incidence
Actual bearer of a tax burden.

Corporate Income Taxes

The corporate income tax provides only about 13 percent of the federal government's total revenue. The tax is set at 35 percent of net corporate income profits. However, corporations find many ways of reducing their taxable income—often to zero. The result is that many very large corporations pay little in taxes. Religious, charitable, and educational organizations, as well as labor unions, are exempt from corporate income taxes except for income they may derive from "unrelated business activity."

Who really bears the burden of the corporate income tax? Economists differ over whether the corporate income tax is "shifted" to consumers or whether corporations and their stockholders bear its burden. The evidence on the **incidence**—that is, who actually bears the burden—of this tax is inconclusive.[5]

Social Security Taxes

The second largest source of federal revenue is the Social Security and Medicare tax. It is withheld from paychecks as the "FICA" deduction, an acronym that helps hide the true costs of Social Security and Medicare from wage earners. The total tax is 15.3 percent. The Social Security tax is 12.4 percent and the Medicare tax is 2.9 percent. All wage income is subject to the Medicare tax, but wage income above a certain level, $113,700 in 2013, is not subject to the Social Security tax.

Only *wage* income is subject to FICA tax; profits, dividends, interest, rents, and capital gains are not.

Taxes collected under FICA are earmarked (by Social Security number) for the account of each taxpayer. Workers thus feel they are receiving benefits as a right rather than as a gift of the government. However, less than 15 percent of the benefits being paid to current recipients of Social Security can be attributed to their prior contributions. Current taxpayers are paying more than 85 percent of the benefits received by current retirees.

"Can't we put in something about rich white guys don't have to pay taxes?"

DON'T TAX YOU, DON'T TAX ME
The Federal Tax Code has always offered privileges to those who influence how it is written.

Today, a majority of taxpayers pay more in Social Security taxes than income taxes. If we assume that the employer's share of the tax actually comes out of wages that would otherwise be paid to the employee, then more than 75 percent of all taxpayers pay more in Social Security taxes than in income taxes. (For 2011 and 2012, the employee contribution of payroll taxes was temporarily reduced by 2 percentage points, resulting in about a thousand-dollar-a-year tax cut per worker, on average. This tax break was ended in 2013.)

Estate and Gift Taxes

Taxation of property left to heirs is one of the oldest forms of taxation in the world. Federal estate taxes levy a tax rate that rises to 40 percent. Estates worth less than $5 million per person or $10 million for couples (indexed in future years for inflation) are exempt. Because taxes at death otherwise could be avoided by simply giving estates to heirs while the giver is still alive, a federal gift tax is also levied on anyone who gives gifts in excess of $14,000 annually. Gifts to spouses and charitable contributions are exempt.

16.1

16.2

16.3

16.4

16.5

16.6

progressive taxation
System of taxation in which higher-income groups pay a larger percentage of their incomes in taxes than do lower-income groups.

regressive taxation
System of taxation in which lower-income groups pay a larger percentage of their incomes in taxes than do higher-income groups.

proportional (flat) taxation
System of taxation in which all income groups pay the same percentage of their income in taxes.

Opponents of the estate tax refer to it as a "death tax." They argue that people who work hard and want to pass on the fruits of their labor to their children should not be punished for doing so. Opponents succeeded in the American Taxpayer Relief Act of 2012 in reducing the estate tax rate from 55 to 40 percent and increasing the exemption from $1 million to $5 million. Supporters argue that estate taxes are fair because, unlike other taxes, the person who acquires an inheritance did not work for it. Estate taxes do not directly target economic activity.

Excise Taxes and Custom Duties

Federal excise taxes on the consumption of liquor, tobacco, gasoline, telephones, air travel, and other so-called luxury items, together with customs taxes on imports, provide about 5 percent of total federal revenues.

Tax Politics

16.6 Trace changes in tax policies under different administrations in recent decades.

The politics of taxation centers on the question of who actually bears the heaviest burden of a tax—especially which income groups must devote the largest proportion of their income to taxes. **Progressive taxation** requires high-income groups to pay a larger percentage of their incomes in taxes than low-income groups. **Regressive taxation** takes a larger share of the income of low-income groups. **Proportional (flat) taxation** requires all income groups to pay the same percentage of their income in taxes. Note that the *percentage of income* paid in taxes is the determining factor. Most taxes take more money from the rich than the poor, but a progressive or regressive tax is distinguished by the percentages of income taken from various income groups.

The Argument for Progressivity

Progressive taxation is generally defended on the principle of ability to pay; the assumption is that high-income groups can afford to pay a larger *percentage* of their incomes in taxes at no more of a sacrifice than that required of lower-income groups to devote a smaller proportion of their income to taxation. This assumption is based on what economists call *marginal utility theory* as it applies to money; each additional dollar of income is slightly less valuable to an individual than preceding dollars. For example, a $5,000 increase in the income of an individual already earning $100,000 is considered to be less valuable than a $5,000 increase to an individual earning only $10,000 or to an individual with no income at all. Hence, it is argued that added dollars of income can be taxed at higher rates without violating equitable principles.

The Argument for Proportionality

Opponents of progressive taxation generally assert that equity can only be achieved by taxing everyone at the same percentage of their income, regardless of the size of their income. Progressivity penalizes initiative, enterprise, and the risk taking necessary to create new products and businesses. It also reduces incentives to expand and develop the nation's economy. Highly progressive taxes curtail growth and make everyone poorer (see *A Conflicting View*: We Should Enact a Flat Tax).

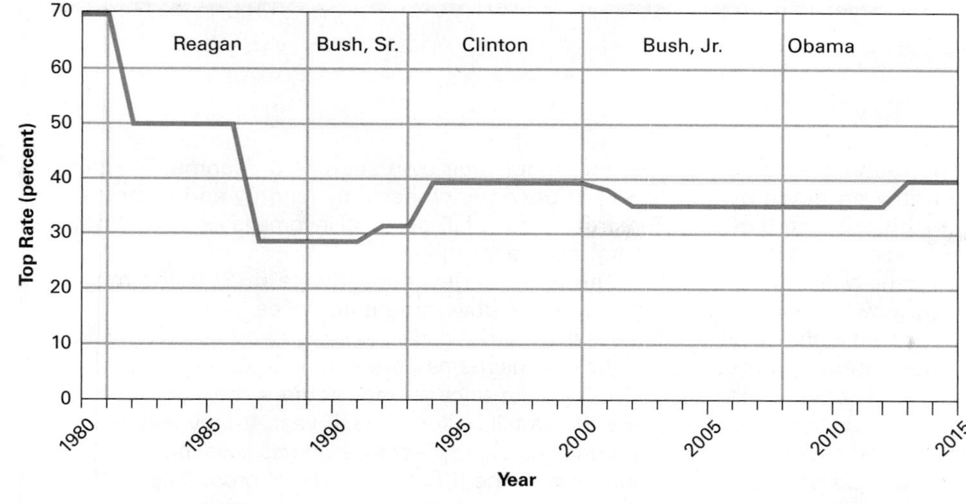

FIGURE 16.7 TOP PERSONAL INCOME TAX RATES, BY PRESIDENT

The top marginal personal income tax rate fell dramatically during the Reagan administration, then began to creep upward again under Presidents Bush and Clinton. George W. Bush lowered the top rate in 2001 and again in 2003, but these tax cuts remain controversial. President Obama succeeded in raising the top marginal rate back to 39.6 percent in 2013.

☐ Reagan's Reductions in Progressivity

The most dramatic change in federal tax laws occurred during the Reagan years (see Figure 16.7). The top marginal tax rate fell from 70 percent when President Reagan took office to 28 percent following enactment of tax reform in 1986. The Tax Reform Act of 1986 also reduced 14 rate brackets to only 2 rate brackets, 15 and 28 percent.

☐ Bush and Clinton Rate Increases

At the Republican national convention in 1988, presidential nominee George H. W. Bush made a firm pledge to American voters that he would veto any tax increases passed by the Democratic-controlled Congress: "Read my lips! No new taxes." Yet in a 1990 budget summit with Democratic congressional leaders, President Bush agreed to add a top marginal rate of 31 percent to the personal income tax. Breaking his solemn pledge on taxes contributed heavily to Bush's defeat in the 1992 presidential election.

Proposals to "soak the rich" are always politically very popular. President Clinton pushed Congress to raise the top marginal tax rates to 39.6 percent for families earning $250,000.

☐ Bush Tax Cuts

George W. Bush came into office vowing *not* to make the same mistake as his father, raising tax rates in an effort to compromise with the Democrats. On the contrary, Bush was strongly committed to lowering taxes. He argued that tax cuts would revive the economy. He believed that federal deficits were the result of slow economic growth; tax reductions might temporarily add to deficits, but eventually the economic

A Conflicting View

We Should Enact a Flat Tax

More than a hundred years ago, Supreme Court Justice Stephen J. Field, in striking down as unconstitutional a progressive income tax enacted by Congress, predicted that such a tax would lead to class wars: "Our political contests will become a war of the poor against the rich, a war constantly growing in intensity and bitterness."[a] But populist sentiment in the early twentieth century—the anger of Midwestern farmers toward Eastern rail tycoons and the beliefs of impoverished Southerners that they would never have incomes high enough to pay an income tax—helped secure the passage of the 16th Amendment to the U.S. Constitution. The federal income tax passed by Congress in 1914 had a top rate of 7 percent; less than 1 percent of the population had incomes high enough to be taxed. Today the top rate is 39.6 percent (actually over 42 percent when mandated phaseouts of deductions are calculated); about half of the population pays income taxes.

The current income tax progressively penalizes all the behaviors that produce higher incomes—work, savings, investment, and initiative. And whenever incomes are taxed at different rates, people will figure out ways to take advantage of the differential. They will hire lawyers, accountants, and lobbyists to find or create exemptions, exclusions, deductions, and preferential treatments for their own sources of income. The tax laws will become increasingly lengthy and complex. Today about half of all personal income is excluded from federal income taxation.

The Internal Revenue Service (IRS) is the most intrusive of all government agencies, overseeing the finances of every tax-paying citizen and corporation in America. It maintains personal records on more than 100 million Americans and requires them to submit more than a billion forms each year. It may levy fines and penalties and collect taxes on its own initiative; in disputes with the IRS, the burden of proof falls on the taxpayer, not the agency. Its 110,000 employees spend $8 billion per year reviewing tax returns, investigating taxpayers, and collecting revenue. Americans pay an additional $30 billion for the services of tax accountants and preparers, and they waste some $200 billion in hours of record keeping and computing their taxes.

We should replace the current federal income tax system with a simple flat tax that could be calculated on a postcard. The elimination of all exemptions, exclusions, deductions, and special treatments, and the replacement of current progressive tax rates with a flat 19 percent tax on all forms of income, even excluding family incomes under $25,000, would produce just as much revenue as the current complicated system. It would sweep away the nation's army of tax accountants and lawyers and lobbyists and increase national productivity by relieving taxpayers of millions of hours of record keeping and tax preparation. A flat tax could be filed on a postcard form (see figure). Removing progressive rates would create incentives to work, save, and invest in America. It would lead to more rapid economic growth and improve efficiency by directing investments to their most productive uses rather than to tax avoidance. It would eliminate current incentives to underreport income, overstate exemptions, and avoid and evade taxation. Finally, by exempting a generous personal and family allowance, the flat tax would be made fair.

Form 1 — Individual Wage Tax — 2000

Your first name and initial (if joint return, also give spouse's name and initial)	Last name	Your social security number
Home address (number and street including apartment number or rural route)		Spouse's social security number
City, town, or post office, state, and ZIP code		Your occupation
		Spouse's occupation

1	Wages and salary	1
2	Pension and retirement benefits	2
3	Total compensation (*line 1 plus line 2*)	3
4	Personal allowance	
	(a) 0–$16,500 for married filing jointly	4a
	(b) 0–$9,500 for single	4b
	(c) 0–$14,000 for single head of household	4c
5	Number of dependents, not including spouse	5
6	Personal allowances for dependents (*line 5 multiplied by $4,500*)	6
7	Total personal allowances (*line 4 plus line 6*)	7
8	Taxable compensation (*line 3 less line 7, if positive; otherwise zero*)	8
9	Tax (*19% of line 8*)	9
10	Tax withheld by employer	10
11	Tax due (*line 9 less line 10, if positive*)	11
12	Refund due (*line 10 less line 9, if positive*)	12

QUESTIONS

1. What are the benefits of a flat tax? The costs?
2. In 1981, Ronald Reagan passed tax reform that reduced the number of tax brackets to two; subsequently, the number of brackets expanded. Can you institute a flat tax and avoid having indexing reinstated?

[a] *Pollock v. Farmer's Loan*, 158 U.S. 601 (1895).

growth inspired by lower taxes would increase government revenues and eliminate deficits.[6]

Bush moved the Republican-controlled Congress to lower the top marginal rate to 35 percent, and restructure rates through six brackets—10, 15, 25, 28, 33, and 35 percent. And the Bush 2003 tax package also contained a variety of new credits and special treatments:

> *Dividends*: Corporate stock dividends are taxed at a low 15 percent rather than at the same rate as earned income. During the Bush Administration, the president and Republicans in Congress initially proposed eliminating all taxes on dividends. They argued that corporations already paid taxes on corporate profits, and inasmuch as dividends come out of profits, taxing them as personal income amounted to "double taxation." They also recognized that nearly one-half of all American families now own stock or mutual funds, and they hoped that this new tax break would be politically popular.
>
> *Marriage penalty*: For married couples, the new law made the standard personal deduction twice that of a single person. This change corrected a flaw in the tax law that had long plagued married persons filing joint returns.
>
> *Child tax credit*: The per child tax credit was raised to $1,000 (from $600). This was a politically popular change supported by many Democrats as well as Republicans.
>
> *Capital gains*: Finally, the Bush tax package chipped away again at the tax on capital gains—profits from the sale of investments held at least 1 year. The capital gains tax was reduced from 20 to 15 percent.

The Bush tax cuts were scheduled to expire at the end of 2010, but were extended for two years until the end of 2012.

GROVER NORQUIST

Author of the Tax Pledge, Norquist has made use of George H. W. Bush's broken pledge "Read my lips, no new taxes" to compel conservative politicians to sign on to never voting for a tax increase.

Redistributing Income

Barack Obama campaigned on a promise to lower taxes on the middle class, which he defined as 95 percent of taxpayers. He also pledged to raise taxes on upper-income Americans, which he defined as families earning $250,000 a year or more. This combination of changes in taxation would make the tax code more progressive, in effect redistributing income among Americans.

But the top 5 percent of income earners in the United States already pay over half of all federal income taxes (see *Who's Getting What?* Who Pays the Income Tax?). The top 1 percent pays over a third of these taxes. And almost all federal income taxes are paid by the upper half of income earners.

President Obama urged Congress to allow the Bush tax cuts to expire, thus raising the top marginal tax rate from 35 percent to 39.6 percent. He also recommended a phaseout of deductions, including charitable contributions and mortgage payments, for high-income families. Republican critics charged that any increase in taxes in a weak economy would further depress buying power, discourage investment, and slow or reverse economic recovery.

Following the Republican victory in the midterm congressional elections in 2010, Republicans in Congress united behind the notion of extending the Bush tax cuts to "every taxpayer," including those who paid the top rate. The issue threatened gridlock and an inability of Congress to act in time to stave off the tax increases schedules to begin in January 2011. The issue fell to the Democratic-controlled "lame-duck" Congress in December to resolve.

But when Republicans captured control of the House of Representatives in the midterm elections of 2010, Obama's quest for tax increases appeared doomed. Indeed, virtually all House Republicans signed a pledge, initiated by Grover Norquist, president of Americans for Tax Reform, not to increase taxes or impose any new taxes on the American people. Acrimonious negotiations continued in Washington over the next several years.

The "Fiscal Cliff"

The United States faced a "fiscal cliff" at the end of 2012 when a series of previously enacted laws was set to expire. The scheduled expiration of the Bush tax cuts would have raised the top personal income tax rate back to 39.6 percent, raised taxes on dividends and capital gains, lowered the child tax credit, and reimposed the marriage penalty. The "sequestration" called for in the Budget Control Act of 2011 was set to take effect. And the new debt ceiling was looming, with the resulting threat to curtail U.S. payments on its debts.

After long and tedious negotiations, Congress came to a year-and agreement—the American Taxpayer Relief Act of 2012. Among its more important provisions are:

- Increasing the top tax rate. It permanently increased the top income tax rate from 35 to 39.6 percent on incomes over $400,000 ($450,000 for married couples).
- Raising capital gains and dividends taxes. It raised the tax rate on capital gains and dividends from 15 to 20 percent for individuals with incomes above $400,000 ($450,000 for married couples). It retains the 15 percent rate for taxpayers below that income level. It capped a new 3.5 surtax on investment income for individuals with incomes over $200,000 (250,000 for married couples).
- Reinstating the personal exemption. It reinstated the Bush-era personal exemption, but phased out itemized exemptions for taxpayers with incomes over $200,000 ($300,000 for married couples).
- Maintaining estate tax exemption. It maintained the estate tax exemption of $5 million, indexed in future years for inflation. The estate tax rate was set of 40 percent.

Who's Getting What?

Who Pays the Income Tax?

The federal income tax is highly progressive. Progressive rates, together with the personal and standard deductions for families and the earned income tax credit for low-income earners, combined to remove most of the income tax burden on middle- and low-income Americans. Indeed, the lower half of the nation's taxpayers pay less than 4 percent of total income taxes paid to the federal government (see figure).

The top 50 percent of income earners pay virtually all of the nation's personal income tax. Indeed, the top 10 percent of income earners pay about 71 percent of all of the income taxes collected by the federal government, and the top 1 percent pay over a third of all income taxes. These figures do not include payroll taxes that are paid at a flat rate, by wage earners on the first $113,700 (in 2013) of wage and salary income. They also do not include capital gains taxes on investments. And, they do not include the variety of consumption taxes and property taxes people pay to state and local governments.

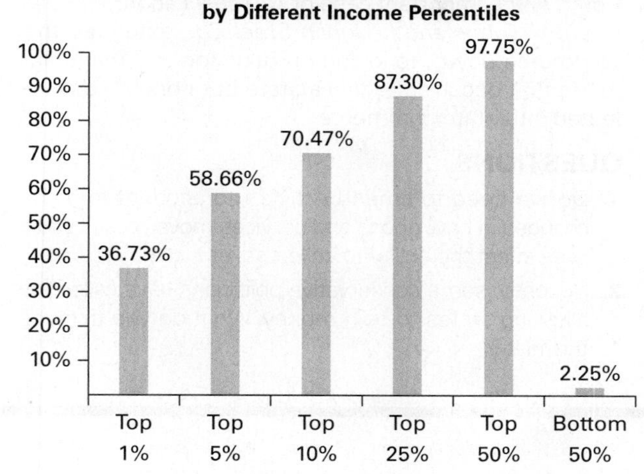

QUESTIONS

1. Does concentrating the tax debate only on personal income taxes create a bias in our understanding of individual tax burdens?
2. If we eliminated the income tax, how would you pay for government?

SOURCES: Joint Economic Committee, U.S. Congress, April 2007. National Tax Foundation from U.S. Internal Revenue Service, 2009.

- Setting a permanent AMT threshold. It raised the AMT threshold to $50,600 ($78,780 for married couples). The threshold was permanently indexed to inflation.

But this Act failed to resolve the long-standing budget crisis. It did not result in a budget for 2013 or 2014 or even promised a continuing resolution for these years. It did not end the "sequestration." Nor did it resolve a recurring issue of the debt ceiling. These issues would continue to gridlock in Washington (see "Budget Gridlock and Government 'Shut Down'" earlier in the chapter).

16.1
16.2
16.3
16.4
16.5
16.6

A Constitutional Note

The Constitution and Private Property

The protection of private property was one of the principal motives in convening the Constitutional Convention of 1787. Among the powers set forth in Article I, Section 8, are the "power to lay and collect taxes, duties, imposts, and excises"; "to borrow money"; "to regulate commerce with foreign nations and among the several states and with the Indian Tribes"; "to establish ... uniform rules of bankruptcy"; "to coin money, regulate the value thereof"; "to provide for the punishment of counterfeiting." And among the powers specifically denied to the states in Section 10 are the powers to "coin money; emit Bills of Credit; make any Thing but Gold and Silver Coin a Tender in Payment of Debts; pass any ... Law impairing the Obligation of Contracts...." In addition, the Constitution of 1787 created what we call today a *common market or free trade area* among the states: "No state shall ... lay any Imports or Duties on Imports or Exports...." This prevents states taxing goods or services moving across state lines or from taxing foreign commerce. In short, the Constitution places power over the economy in the hands of the national government and prevents the states from interfering with commerce. However, for well over a century, the Supreme Court interpreted the Interstate Commerce Clause narrowly to include only the regulation of goods and services that actually moved across state lines. It was not until 1937 that the Court, in the important case of *National Labor Relations Board v. Jones and Loughlin Steel Co.*, extended the commerce power to include production and manufacturing that occurred *within* a state but nonetheless affected interstate commerce.

QUESTIONS

1. Do we need to amend Article I to account for how changes in how goods and services move across state lines affect the ability to collect taxes?
2. Recently, some conservative politicians have called for allowing states to coin money. What do you think of this idea?

Review the Chapter

Politics and Economics

16.1 Compare politics and economics as decision-making systems, p. 608

The similarity of the definition of *economics* ("deciding what shall be produced, how and for whom") and *politics* ("deciding who gets what, when and how") reflects the fact that both systems provide society with a means for deciding about the production and distribution of goods and services.

Economic Decision Making

16.2 Describe the role that fiscal and monetary policy play in economic decision making, p. 608

Fiscal policy—decisions about government taxing, spending, and deficits or surpluses—is decided in the president's budget recommendations and in the appropriations acts passed by Congress. Monetary policy is largely decided by the independent Federal Reserve Board.

Measuring the Performance of the American Economy

16.3 Identify the different ways of assessing the strength of the economy, p. 611

The performance of the economy can be measured by GDP growth and the unemployment and inflation rates. Politically, the unemployment rate may be the most important of these measures of economic performance.

Government Spending, Deficits, and Debt

16.4 Describe the relationships between government spending, deficits, and the national debt, p. 614

Annual federal budget deficits over the years have led to a national debt of more than $7 trillion, an amount equal to $50,000 for every person in the country. Arguments between Republicans and Democrats and President Obama over how to deal with deficits have led to government gridlock and even a temporary "shutdown" of the federal government.

The Tax Burden

16.5 Analyze the various kinds of taxes and how they distribute the tax burden, p. 619

Tax politics centers on the question of who actually bears the burden of a tax. The individual income tax, the largest source of federal government revenue, is progressive, with higher rates levied at higher-income levels. Progressive taxation is defended on the ability-to-pay principle. But half of all personal income, and a great deal of corporate income, is untaxed, owing to a wide variety of exemptions, exclusions, deductions, and special treatments on tax laws. These provisions are defended in Washington by a powerful array of interest groups.

Tax Politics

16.6 Trace changes in tax policies under different administrations in recent decades, p. 624

The Reagan administration reduced top-income tax rates from 70 to 28 percent, believing high rates discouraged work, savings, and investment, and thereby curtailed economic growth. However, George H. W. Bush agreed to an increase in the top rate to 31 percent. Bill Clinton pushed Congress to raise the top rates to 39.6 percent. George W. Bush succeeded in getting two tax cut bills through Congress in 2001 and 2003. The bills lowered the top marginal income tax rate to 35 percent and lowered the capital gain rate to 15 percent.

In late 2012, President Obama succeeded in getting Congress to raise the top marginal income tax back up to 39.6 percent for high-income earners.

Learn the Terms

political economy, p. 608
fiscal policy, p. 608
monetary policy, p. 608
Federal Reserve Board (the Fed), p. 610
inflation, p. 610
recession, p. 610
gross domestic product (GDP), p. 611
economic cycles, p. 611
unemployment rate, p. 611
mandatory spending, p. 614
entitlement programs, p. 614
indexing, p. 614
in-kind (noncash) benefits, p. 614
discretionary spending, p. 615
deficits, p. 615
national debt, p. 615
individual income tax, p. 619
tax expenditures, p. 621
tax avoidance, p. 621
tax evasion, p. 621
incidence, p. 623
progressive taxation, p. 624
regressive taxation, p. 624
proportional (flat) taxation, p. 624

Test Yourself

16.1 Compare politics and economics as decision-making systems.

It would be accurate to say that the political system involves ________ decision making and that the economic system involves ________ decision making.

a. individual; individual
b. collective; collective
c. collective; individual
d. individual; collective
e. coercive; punitive

16.2 Describe the role that fiscal and monetary policy play in economic decision making.

Decisions about taxing, spending, and borrowing at the national level are known as

a. fiscal policy
b. Keynesian policy
c. monetary policy
d. reserve policy
e. Constitutional interpretation

16.3 Identify the different ways of assessing the strength of the economy.

Measures of the performance of the nation's economy include

I. unemployment rate
II. Gross Domestic Product
III. inflation rate
IV. Social security COLAs

a. Only I and III
b. Only II
c. I, II, III, IV
d. Only I, II, and III
e. Only IV

16.4 Describe the relationships between government spending, deficits, and the national debt.

Spending for program commitments made by previous Congresses is

a. discretionary spending
b. mandatory spending
c. entitlement spending
d. guaranteed spending
e. deficit spending

16.5 Analyze the various kinds of taxes and how they distribute the tax burden.

More people pay this tax than any other federal tax

a. estate tax
b. Social Security tax
c. individual income tax
d. excise tax
e. tea tax

16.6 Trace changes in tax policies under different administrations in recent decades.

A tax that takes a smaller share of the income of high-income tax payers is a

a. progressive tax
b. proportional tax
c. flat tax
d. regressive tax
e. excise tax

Explore Further

Boortz, Neil, and John Linder. 2009. *The Fair Tax Book.* New York: William Morrow. An Atlanta-based conservative radio host and a former Georgia congressman argue for abolishing the income tax and replacing it with a 23 percent transaction and sales tax.

Estimates by Office of Management and Budget for 2013. www.omb.gov.

Green, Mark, and Michele Jolin, eds. *Change for America.* New York: Basic Books, 2009. A comprehensive policy agenda—"progressive blueprint"—for the Obama administration.

Jacobs, Laurence R., and Theda S. Skocpol, eds. *Inequality and American Democracy.* New York: Russell Sage Foundation, 2005. A series of essays describing increasing inequality in America and its political and social consequences.

Lehne, Richard. *Government and Business: American Political Economy in Comparative Perspective*, 3rd. ed. Washington, DC: CQ Press, 2012. America's response to worldwide economic turmoil.

Miller, Roger LeRoy, David K. Benjamin, and Douglas C. North. *The Economic of Public Issues,* 18th ed. New York: Pearson, 2014. Short essays applying economic principles to a variety of public issues.

Sowell, Thomas. *Basic Economics: A Citizen's Guide to the Economy 4th*. New York: Basic Books, 2010. Introduction to economics with an emphasis on public policy. No jargon or equations.

Tax Foundation. *Putting a Face on America's Tax Returns: A Chart Book,* 2nd ed. Washington, DC: Tax Foundation, 2013.

Wolff, Edward N. *Top Heavy* (updated edition). New York: Century Foundation, 2002. The study of the increasing inequality of wealth in United States and an argument for taxing financial wealth (bank accounts, stocks, bonds, property, houses, cars, and so on) as well as income.

SUGGESTED WEB SITES

Bureau of Economic Analysis www.bea.gov

Source of official economic statistics, listed A–Z.

Bureau of Labor Statistics www.bls.gov

The U.S. Department of Labor's Bureau of Labor Statistics site contains monthly information about the nation's employment rate plus a wealth of supporting data.

Center on Budget and Policy Priorities www.cbpp.org

Research on budget issues, including effects on low income families.

The Concord Coalition www.concordcoalition.org

Nonpartisan advocacy organization promoting fiscal responsibility and a balanced federal budget.

Council of Economic Advisors (CEA) www.whitehouse.gov/cea

Official CEA site, with latest Economic Report of the President and timely economic indicators.

Federal Reserve System www.federalreserve.gov

Official site of the Fed, with data on money supply, interest rates, and banking regulation.

Internal Revenue Service (IRS) www.irs.gov

Official IRS site, with downloadable tax forms, information on tax laws, and tax statistics.

National Taxpayers Union www.ntu.org

Advocacy organization for taxpayers "to keep what they have earned," with policy papers and data on tax burdens.

Organization for Economic Cooperation and Development (OECD) www.oecd.org.

International organization that provides cross-national data on economic growth, taxation, etc.

Tax Foundation Advocacy www.taxfoundation.org

Organization devoted to making the public "tax conscious," with information, "fiscal facts," and "tax freedom day."

World Trade Organization (WTO) www.wto.org

Official WTO site, with trade agreements, including General Agreement on Tariffs and Trade (GATT).

17 Politics and Social Welfare

he United States spends over $100 billion a year on food assistance programs such as food stamps—or, about $2,400 a year per recipient. The use of food stamps has increased since 2008, and although conservative critics of the program do not argue against providing food assistance, they do contend that there is fraud and abuse in SNAP (the food stamp program) that amounts to between 1 percent and 3 percent of the program's funds.

This fraud seems to stem from changes in the technology used to distribute this food assistance. SNAP benefits are not distributed using paper coupons anymore; instead, a card similar to a debit card is issued to recipients. This paperless system improves the efficiency of transactions for the consumer, the retailer, and the USDA; it allows transactions to be tracked, and the USDA can easily deactivate a lost, stolen, or sold card once it is reported. Utilizing these cards is similar to other consumer transactions and removes the stigma previously associated with drawing upon social welfare benefits. However, this ease of use has also contributed to ease of fraud.

The USDA is investigating instances of SNAP recipients selling their benefit cards, including sales on eBay. But in order for such fraud to work, retailers have to be complicit, for example exchanging benefit cards for cash, or accepting cards for purchases from people ineligible to receive benefits. And since the USDA does not require any identification to use a SNAP benefit card, such fraud cannot be enforced at the cash register. The social safety net is an established policy arena for the American government. But, much like voting rights, it finds itself under assault from critics who point to corruption and fraud in the system. In a period of prolonged economic downturn and recovery, social programs provide an important safety net for Americans. But, are the concerns about fraud driven by a desire to run better programs? Or to simply shut down those programs in the name of fiscal austerity and ideological preference?

FOOD IN A SNAP Nearly 45 million Americans qualified for the needs-based Supplemental Nutrition Assistance Program in 2012.

transfer payments
Direct payments (either in cash or in goods and/or services) by governments to individuals as part of a social welfare program, not as a result of any service or contribution rendered by the individual.

poverty line
Official standard regarding what level of annual cash income is sufficient to maintain a "decent standard of living"; those with incomes below this level are eligible for most public assistance programs.

means-tested spending
Spending for benefits that is distributed on the basis of the recipient's income.

Power and Social Welfare

17.1 Assess the importance of social welfare policy.

Social welfare policy largely determines who gets what from government—who benefits from government spending on its citizens and how much they get. This vast power has made the federal government a major *redistributor* of income from one group to another—from the working population to retirees, from the employed to the unemployed, from taxpayers to poor people. Direct payments to individuals—Social Security, welfare, pension, and other **transfer payments**—now account for about 60 percent of all federal government outlays.

When most Americans think of social welfare programs, they think of poor people. An estimated 45 to 50 million people in the United States (12 to 15 percent of the population) have incomes below the official **poverty line**—that is, their annual cash income falls below what is required to maintain a decent standard of living (see Figure 17.1). Experimentation with the poverty level to adjust for market variations in food and housing costs can result in higher levels of estimated poverty. As of 2012, the official poverty level for a family of four in the United States was $23,482 a year.

But poor people are *not* the principal beneficiaries of social welfare spending. Most social welfare spending, including the largest programs—Social Security and Medicare—goes to the *non*poor (see Figure 17.2). Less than one-third of federal social welfare spending is **means-tested spending**—that is, distributed on the basis of the recipient's income. The middle classes, not the poor, are the major beneficiaries of the nation's social welfare system.

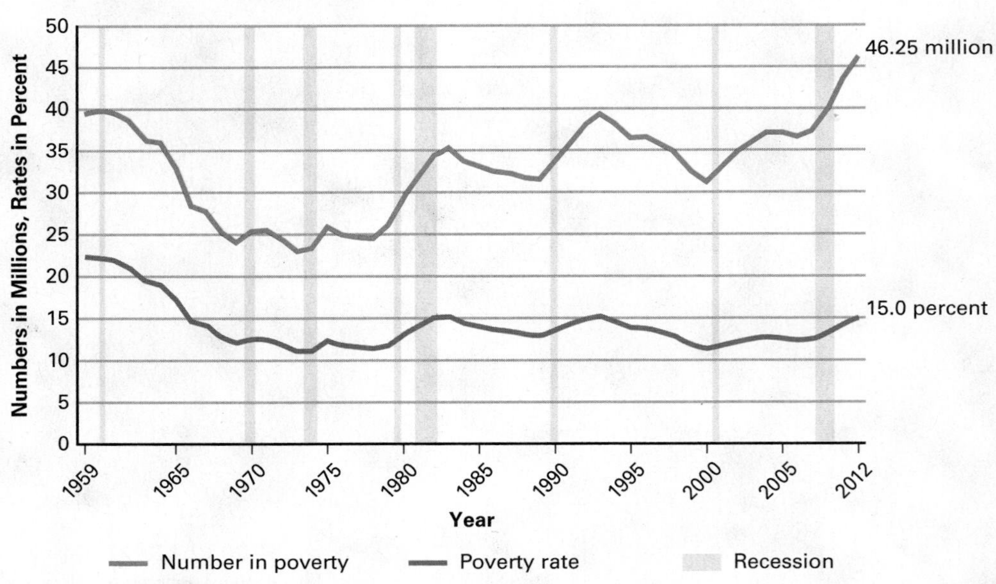

FIGURE 17.1 AMERICA'S POOR: THE RATE AND NUMBER

Approximately 15 percent of Americans lives below the *official* poverty level. Poverty rises during recessions.

SOURCE: www.census.gov/hhes/poverty00/2012.

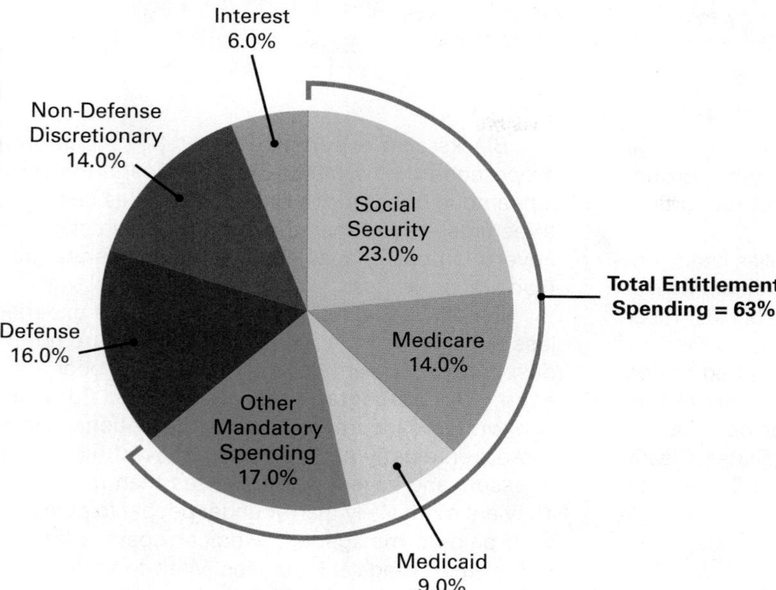

FIGURE 17.2 WHO'S ENTITLED?

Social welfare entitlement programs take up over 67 percent of the federal government's budget. But most of these payments go to the nonpoor.

SOURCE: *Budget of the United States Government*, 2015.

Poverty in the United States

17.2 Characterize the extent of poverty in the United States and identify correlates.

How much poverty really exists in the United States? It depends on how you define the term *poverty*. The official definition used by the federal government focuses on the cash income needed to maintain a "decent standard of living." The official poverty line is only a little more than one-third of the median income of all American families. It takes into account the effects of inflation, rising each year with the rate of inflation.

Temporary Poverty

Poor people are often envisioned as a permanent "underclass" living most of their lives in poverty. But most poverty is not long term. Tracing poor families over time presents a different picture of the nature of poverty from the "snapshot" view taken in any 1 year. For example, over the last decade, 11 to 15 percent of the nation's population has been officially classified as poor in any one year. However, only *some* poverty is persistent: about 6 to 8 percent of the population remains in poverty for more than five years. Thus, about half of the people who are counted as poor are experiencing poverty for only a short period of time. For these temporary poor, welfare is a "safety net" that helps them through hard times.

Persistent Poverty

However, about half of the people on welfare rolls at any one time are *persistently poor*, that is, likely to remain on welfare for five or more years. For these people, welfare is a more permanent part of their lives.

Who's Getting What?

Who Are the Poor?

Poverty occurs in many kinds of families and in all races and ethnic groups. However, some groups experience poverty (low income) in greater proportions than the national average (see figure).

Poverty is most common among families headed by women. The incidence of poverty among these families is five times greater than that for married couples. These women and their children constitute over two-thirds of all of the persons living in poverty in the United States. About one of every five children in the United States lives in poverty. These figures describe what has been labeled the "feminization of poverty" in the United States. Clearly, poverty is closely related to family structure. The disintegration of the traditional husband–wife family is the single most influential factor contributing to poverty today.

Percentage Living Below the Poverty Level

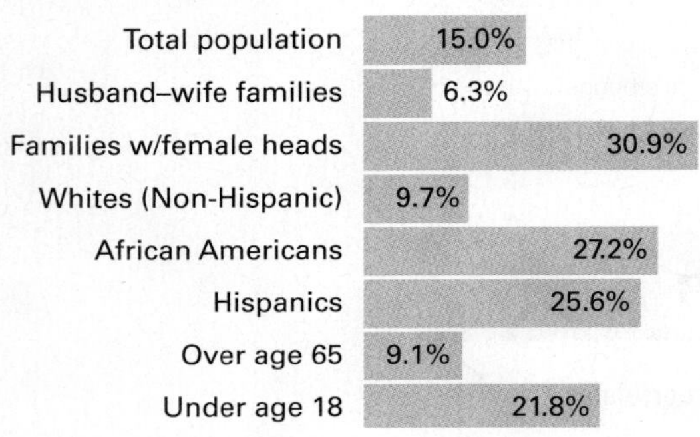

SOURCE: U.S. Bureau of the Census, 2012.

Blacks also experience poverty in much greater proportions than whites. Over the years, the poverty rate among blacks in the United States has been almost three times higher than the poverty rate among whites. Poverty among Hispanics is also significantly greater than among whites.

In contrast, elderly people in America experience less poverty than the nonaged. The aged are not poor, despite the popularity of the phrase "the poor and the aged." The percentage of persons over 65 years of age with low incomes is *below* the national average. Moreover, elderly people are much wealthier in terms of assets and have fewer expenses than the nonaged. They are more likely than younger people to own homes with paid-up mortgages. Medicare pays a large portion of their medical expenses. With fewer expenses, elderly people, even with relatively smaller cash incomes, experience poverty differently from the way a young mother with children experiences it. Continuing increases in Social Security benefits over the years are largely responsible for this singular "victory" in the war against poverty.

QUESTIONS

1. Should we have different standards for poverty based on whether someone is young or old?
2. If poverty is related to race and ethnicity, should we target poverty policies based on race and ethnicity?

underclass
People who have remained poor and dependent on welfare over a prolonged period of time.

Because they place a disproportionate burden on welfare resources, persistently poor people pose serious questions for social scientists and policymakers. Prolonged poverty and welfare dependency create an **underclass** that suffers from many social ills—teen pregnancy, family instability, drugs, crime, alienation, apathy, and irresponsibility.[1] Government educational, training, and jobs programs, as well as many other social service efforts, fail to benefit many of these people.

☐ Family Structure

Poverty and welfare dependency are much more frequent among female-headed households with no husband present than among husband–wife households (see *Who's Getting What?* Who Are the Poor?). Traditionally, "illegitimacy" was held in check by powerful religious and social structures. But these structures weakened over time and the availability of welfare cash benefits, food stamps, medical care, and government housing removed much of the economic hardship once associated with unwed motherhood. Indeed, it was sometimes argued that government welfare programs, however well meaning, ended up perpetuating poverty and social dependency. This argument inspired welfare reform in 1996 (see "Politics and Welfare Reform" later in this chapter).

☐ The "Truly Disadvantaged"

The nation's largest cities have become the principal location of many of the social problems confronting our society—poverty, homelessness, racial tension, drug abuse,

HOMELESS IN AMERICA

Some "street people" are unable to benefit from social welfare programs due to alcoholism, drug abuse, mental illness, or other disabilities that cause them to fall through the social welfare safety net.

delinquency, and crime. These problems are all made worse by their concentration in large cities.

Why has the inner city become the locus of social problems? Some observers argue that changes in the labor market from industrial goods–producing jobs to professional, financial, and technical service–producing jobs have increasingly divided the labor market into low-wage and high-wage sectors.[2] The decline in manufacturing jobs, together with a shift in remaining manufacturing jobs and commercial (sales) jobs to the suburbs, has left inner-city residents with fewer and lower paying job opportunities. The rise in joblessness in the inner cities has in turn increased the concentration of poor people, added to the number of poor single-parent families, and increased welfare dependency.

Social Welfare Policy

17.3 Outline the major social welfare programs in the United States.

Public welfare has been a recognized responsibility of government in English-speaking countries for many centuries. As far back as the Poor Relief Act of 1601, the English Parliament provided workhouses for the "able-bodied poor" (the unemployed) and poorhouses for widows and orphans, elderly and handicapped people.[3] Today, nearly one-third of the U.S. population receives some form of government benefits: Social Security, Medicare or Medicaid, disability insurance, unemployment compensation, government employee

17.1

17.2

17.3

17.4

17.5

17.6

17.7

17.8

The Game, the Rules, the Players

Making Policy at the Street Level

Sometimes power does not require climbing a hierarchy. There is substantial power to make public policy and to effect change in positions that are at the "street level"—first responders, case workers, parole officers, social workers, public health care workers, and policy analysts who try to evaluate how well policies work. Some jobs in these careers are initially accessible with less than a college degree and require the ability to follow procedures, quickly evaluate the needs of a person seeking help from government, and often implement a necessary policy against the wishes of the target of the policy. Many street-level implementors have undergraduate degrees and sometimes advanced degrees in sociology, public health, social work, or public administration. The jobs are often emotionally demanding, and not especially well compensated, but they do attract individuals who are dedicated to applying government to the task of improving individual lives. These jobs, and the programs they are attached to, are often perceived to be bastions for liberals, because of the progressive-era origins of welfare state policies in the United States.

QUESTIONS

1. Who are "street level" implementors you've encountered in your life? Were they capable at their jobs?
2. Have you considered a position in public service? Why or why not?

social insurance
Social welfare programs to which beneficiaries have made contributions so that they are entitled to benefits regardless of their personal wealth.

public assistance
Those social welfare programs for which no contributions are required and only those defined as low-income are eligible; includes food stamps, Medicaid, and Family Assistance.

entitlements
Benefits of social welfare programs for which individuals are eligible by law.

Social Security
Social insurance program composed of the Old Age and Survivors Insurance program, which pays benefits to retired workers who have paid into the program and their dependents and survivors, and the Disability Insurance program, which pays benefits to disabled workers and their families.

retirement, veterans' benefits, food stamps, school lunches, job training, public housing, or cash public assistance payments. More than half of all families in the United States include at least one person who receives a government check. Thus, the "welfare state" now encompasses a very large part of our society.

The major social welfare programs can be classified as either **social insurance** or **public assistance**. This distinction is an important one that has on occasion become a major political issue. If the beneficiaries of a government program are required to have made contributions to it before claiming any of its benefits, and if they are entitled to the benefits regardless of their personal wealth—as in Social Security and Medicare—then the program is said to be financed on the social insurance principle. If the program is financed out of general tax revenues, and if recipients are required to show that they are poor before claiming its benefits—as in Temporary Assistance to Needy Families, Supplemental Security Income, and Medicaid—then the program is said to be financed on the public assistance principle. Public assistance programs are generally labeled as "welfare."

Entitlements

Entitlements are government benefits for which Congress has set eligibility criteria—age, income, retirement, disability, unemployment, and so on. Everyone who meets the criteria is "entitled" by law to the benefit, either by established legal right or by legislation.

Most of the nation's major entitlement programs were launched either in the New Deal years of the 1930s under President Franklin D. Roosevelt (Social Security; unemployment compensation; Aid to Families with Dependent Children, now called Temporary Assistance to Needy Families; and Aid to Aged, Blind, and Disabled, now called Supplemental Security Income) or in the Great Society years of the 1960s under President Lyndon B. Johnson (food stamps, Medicare, Medicaid).

Social Security

Begun during the Depression (1935), **Social Security** is now the largest of all entitlements; it comprises two distinct programs. The Old Age and Survivors Insurance program provides monthly cash benefits to retired workers and their dependents and to survivors of insured workers. The Disability Insurance program provides monthly cash benefits for disabled workers and their dependents. An automatic, annual cost-of-living adjustment (COLA) for both programs matches any increase in the annual inflation rate. The program is funded by a payroll tax (FICA) on employers and employees. Retirees can begin receiving benefits at age 62 (full benefits at age 66), regardless of their personal wealth or income.

THE ORIGINS OF FEDERAL WELFARE PROGRAMS

Most of America's social welfare programs began in either the Great Depression of the 1930s or the War on Poverty in the 1960s. At the outset of the Depression, millions of unemployed Americans, like these New Yorkers in a bread line, had only private charities to turn to for survival.

Unemployment Compensation

Unemployment compensation temporarily replaces part of the wages of workers who lose their jobs involuntarily and helps stabilize the economy during recessions. The U.S. Department of Labor oversees the system, but states administer their own programs, with latitude within federal guidelines to define weekly benefits and other program features. Benefits are funded by a combination of federal and state unemployment taxes on employers.

Supplemental Security Income (SSI)

Supplemental Security Income (SSI) is a means-tested, federally administered income assistance program that provides monthly cash payments to needy elderly (65 or older), blind, and disabled people. A loose definition of "disability"—including alcoholism, drug abuse, and attention deficiency among children—has led to a rapid growth in the number of SSI beneficiaries.

Family Assistance (TANF)

Family Assistance, officially Temporary Assistance to Needy Families (formerly AFDC, or Aid to Families with Dependent Children), is a grant program to enable the states to assist needy families. States now operate the program and define "need"; they set their own benefit levels and establish (within federal guidelines) income and resource limits. The federal government mandates a two-year limit on benefits, a five-year lifetime limit, and other requirements (see "Politics and Welfare Reform" later in this chapter).

Food Stamps (SNAP)

The **Food Stamp program**, officially called SNAP (Supplemental Nutrition Assistance Program), provides low-income household members with coupons that they can redeem for enough food to provide a minimal nutritious diet. The program is overseen by the federal government but administered by the states.

Earned Income Tax Credit (EITC)

The **Earned Income Tax Credit (EITC)** is designed to assist the working poor. It provides larger refunds than taxpayers actually paid during the previous tax year. Thus the EITC is in effect a "negative" income tax. It was originally passed by a Democratic-controlled Congress and signed by Republican President Gerald Ford in 1975. Over the years, EITC payments have increased substantially. However, the program benefits only those who apply for the credit when filing their income tax (see *Who's Getting What?* Are You Eligible for the Earned Income Tax Credit?).

Medicaid

Medicaid is a joint, federal–state program providing health services to low-income Americans. Women and children receiving benefits under TANF automatically qualify for Medicaid, as does anyone who gets cash assistance under SSI. States can also offer Medicaid to the "medically needy"—those who face crushing medical costs but whose income or assets are too high to qualify for SSI or Family Assistance, including pregnant women and young children not receiving Family Assistance. Medicaid also pays for long-term nursing home care, but only after beneficiaries have used up virtually all of their savings and income.

unemployment compensation
Social insurance program that temporarily replaces part of the wages of workers who have lost their jobs.

Supplemental Security Income (SSI)
Public assistance program that provides monthly cash payments to the needy elderly (65 or older), blind, and disabled.

Family Assistance (TANF)
Public assistance program that provides monies to the states for their use in helping needy families with children.

Food Stamp program (SNAP)
Public assistance program that provides low-income households with coupons redeemable for enough food to provide a minimal nutritious diet.

Earned Income Tax Credit (EITC)
Tax refunds in excess of tax payments for low-income workers.

Medicaid
Public assistance program that provides health care to the poor.

17.1
17.2
17.3
17.4
17.5
17.6
17.7
17.8

Who's Getting What?

Are You Eligible for the Earned Income Tax Credit?

Can you receive the federal earned income tax credit (EITC)? It depends on your income, your marital status, and whether you have kids. You must have a Social Security Number. You must have earned income, but investment income of less than $2,950. You must be a citizen or legal resident, but you cannot appear as a dependent child on someone else's taxes. And you can't make much money. If you are single with no children, you must earn less than $13,000 a year—or, if married and filing jointly, less than $16,000 a year. If you are married and have two or more children, the EITC is available for people making less than $42,000 a year.

QUESTION

1. The earned income tax credit results in over 40 percent of Americans paying no federal income taxes. Do you think we should eliminate these credits so all Americans contribute to paying for government through taxed income?

Senior Power

17.4 Explain the reasons for and consequences of the political strength of older Americans.

Senior citizens are the most politically powerful age group in the population. They constitute 28 percent of the voting-age population, but, more important, because of their high voter turnout rates, they constitute more than one-third of the voters on Election Day. Persons over age 65 average a 68 percent turnout rate in presidential elections and a 61 percent rate in congressional elections. By comparison, those aged 18 to 21 have a turnout rate of 36 percent in presidential elections and 19 percent in congressional elections, so the voting power of senior citizens is twice that of young people. Moreover, seniors are well represented in Washington; AARP is the nation's largest organized interest group. No elected officials can afford to offend seniors, and seniors strongly support generous Social Security benefits.

The Aged in the Future

The baby boom from 1945 to 1960 produced a large generation of people who crowded schools and colleges in the 1960s and 1970s and encountered stiff competition for jobs in the 1980s. During the baby boom, women averaged 3.5 births during their lifetime. Today, the birthrate is only 1.4 births per woman, less than the 2.1 figure required to keep the population from declining. (Current U.S. population growth is a product of immigration.) The baby-boom generation began retiring in 2010, and by 2030, its members will constitute more than 80 million people, 20 percent of the population (see Figure 17.3). Changes in lifestyle—less smoking, more exercise, better weight control—may increase the aged population even more. Medical advances may also extend life expectancy.

The Generational Compact

The Framers of the Social Security Act of 1935 created a "trust fund" with the expectation that a reserve would be built up from social insurance taxes paid by working persons. The reserve would earn interest, and the interest and principal would be used in later years to pay benefits. In theory, Social Security is an insurance program. (Payments are recorded by name and Social Security number.) Many people believe that they get back what they paid during their working years. Reality, however, has proven much different.

Social Security is actually financed on a pay-as-you-go system, rather than a reserve system. Today, the income from all social insurance premiums (taxes) pays for current Social Security benefits. This generation of workers is paying for the benefits of the last generation, and this generation must hope that its future benefits will be

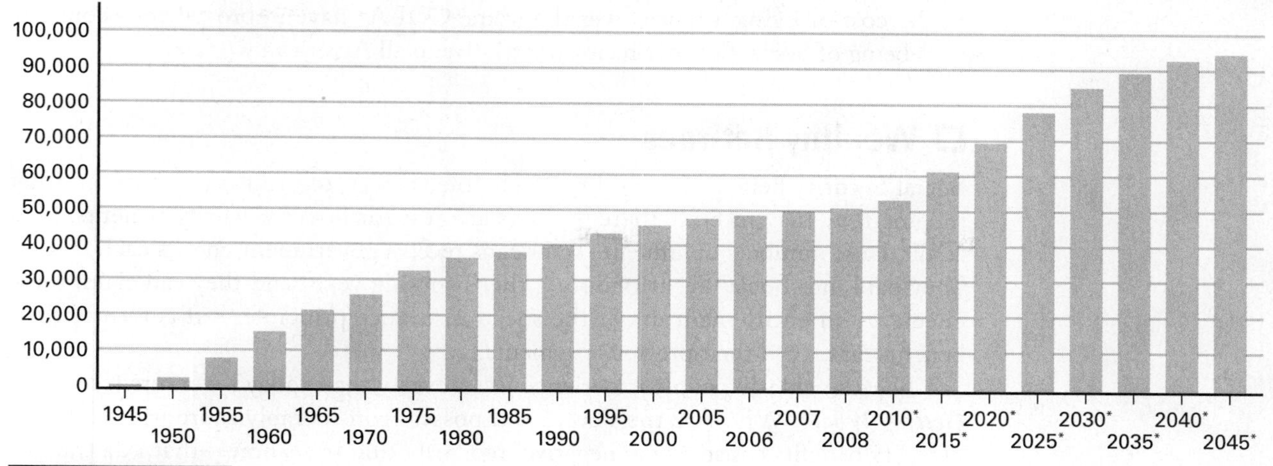

FIGURE 17.3 THE AGING OF AMERICA: THE GROWING NUMBER OF SOCIAL SECURITY BENEFICIARIES

Tens of thousands of Old-Age, Survivors, and Disability Insurance (OASDI) enrollees, 1945–2045. As the "baby boom" generation (persons born from 1945 to 1960) ages, the burden on the Social Security system increases.

*Projected number.

SOURCE: "2009 Annual Report of the Board of Trustees, Federal Old-Age and Survivors Insurance and Disability Insurance Trust Funds." Social Security Administration, May 2009.

financed by the next generation of workers. Taxing current workers to pay benefits to current retirees may be viewed as a compact between generations. Each generation of workers in effect agrees to pay benefits to an earlier generation of retirees and expects the next generation will pay for its retirement.

dependency ratio
In the Social Security system, the number of recipients as a percentage of the number of contributing workers.

COLAs
Annual cost-of-living adjustments mandated by law in Social Security and other welfare benefits.

The Rising Dependency Ratio

Because current workers must pay for the benefits of current retirees and other beneficiaries, the **dependency ratio** becomes an important component of evaluating the future of Social Security. The dependency ratio for Social Security is the number of recipients as a percentage of the number of contributing workers. Americans are living longer and increasing the dependency ratio. A child born in 1935, when the Social Security system was created, could expect to live only to age 61, four years *less* than the retirement age of 65. The life expectancy of a child born in 2010 is 78 years, 13 years *beyond* the average retirement age. In the early years of Social Security, there were 10 workers supporting each retiree—a dependency ratio of 10 to 1. But today, as the U.S. population has grown older—due to lower birthrates and longer life spans—the dependency ratio is closer to two workers for each retiree.

Social Security Taxes

Social Security taxes are levied on workers' earnings. Combined Social Security and Medicare taxes amount to 15.3 percent of wage earnings. (The Social Security tax is 12.4 percent and the Medicare tax is 2.9 percent.) Half is paid directly by the employer, and half is deducted from the employees' check as the FICA deduction. All wage income is subject to the Medicare tax, but wage income above a certain level—$113,700 in 2013—is not subject to Social Security taxes. This wage cap increases every year.

Cost-of-Living Increases

Currently, the annual Social Security cost-of-living adjustments (**COLAs**) are based on the Consumer Price Index, which estimates the cost of all consumer items each year. These costs include home buying, mortgage interest, child rearing, and other costs that many retirees do not confront. Moreover, most workers do not have the same protection against inflation as retirees; average wage rates do not always match increases in the cost of living. Hence, over the years, COLAs have improved the economic well-being of Social Security recipients relative to all American workers.

☐ Wealthy Retirees

Social Security benefits are paid to *all* eligible retirees, regardless of whatever other income they may receive. There is no means test for Social Security benefits. As a result, large numbers of affluent Americans receive government checks each month. They paid into Social Security during their working years, and they can claim these checks as an entitlement under the social insurance principle. But currently their benefits far exceed their previous payments.

Because elderly people experience less poverty than today's workers (see *Who's Getting What?*: Who Are the Poor?) and possess considerably more wealth, Social Security benefits constitute a "negative" redistribution of income—that is, a transfer of income from poorer to richer people. The elderly are generally better off than the people supporting them.

☐ "Saving" Social Security

The Social Security system appears to be adequately financed for the next few years. (In 1983, a National Commission on Social Security Reform, appointed by President Reagan, recommended an increase in Social Security taxes and a gradual increase in the retirement age from 65 to 67 beginning in 2000. Congress adopted these recommendations.) But with the aging of the population and the resulting increases in the dependency ratio expected in the twenty-first century, Social Security will become a heavy burden on working Americans.

"Saving" Social Security is a popular political slogan in Washington. But agreement on exactly how to reform the system continues to evade lawmakers. In theory, Congress could reform Social Security by limiting COLAs to the true increases in the cost of living for retirees, or it could introduce means tests to deny benefits to high-income retirees. But politically these reforms are very unlikely. Another reform frequently recommended is to allow American workers to deposit all or part of their Social Security payroll tax into an individual retirement account to buy securities of their own choosing. But such a plan would expose those individuals to the risk of bad investment decisions.

Politics and Welfare Reform

17.5 Analyze the role of politics in welfare reform.

Americans confront a clash of values in welfare policy. Americans are a generous people; they believe government should aid those who are unable to take care of themselves, especially children, disabled people, and elderly people. But Americans are worried that welfare programs encourage dependency, undermine the work ethic, and contribute to illegitimate births and the breakup of families. Although social insurance programs (Social Security, Medicare, and unemployment compensation) are politically popular and enjoy the support of large numbers of active beneficiaries, public assistance programs (Family Assistance, SSI, Medicaid) are less popular. A variety of controversies surround welfare policy in the United States.

☐ Conflict Over What Causes Poverty

Americans have different ideas about what causes poverty (see Table 17.1). Some attribute poverty to characteristics of individuals—drug use, declining moral values,

TABLE 17.1 PUBLIC OPINION: WHAT CAUSES POVERTY?

Americans have different ideas about what causes poverty.

Question: For each of the following, please tell me if this is a major cause of poverty, a minor cause of poverty, or not a cause at all.

	Major	Minor	Not a Cause	Don't Know
Drug abuse	70%	24%	5%	2%
Medical bills	58	32	7	2
Decline in moral values	57	29	12	3
Too many part-time or low-wage jobs	54	32	10	4
Too many single parents	54	32	12	2
Poor people lacking motivation	52	35	9	4
Poor public schools	47	38	13	4
The welfare system	46	37	11	7
A shortage of jobs	34	41	23	2

SOURCE: Kaiser Family Foundation, poll reported in Public Agenda, 2007, www.publicagenda.org.

Temporary Assistance to Needy Families

Welfare reform program replacing federal cash entitlement with grants to the states for welfare recipients.

lack of motivation. Others blame the economy—too many part-time and low-wage jobs and a shortage of good jobs. Still others place blame on the welfare system itself. Indeed, prior to welfare reform in 1996, some scholars argued that government itself was a major cause of poverty—that social welfare programs destroyed incentives to work, encouraged teenage pregnancies, and made people dependent on government handouts.[4] They argued that the combination of cash payments, food stamps, Medicaid, and housing assistance unintentionally discouraged people from forming families, taking low-paying jobs, and, perhaps, with hard work and perseverance, gradually pulling themselves and their children into the mainstream of American life.

There is little doubt that poverty and welfare dependency are closely related to family structure. As noted earlier, poverty is much more frequent among female-headed households with no husband present than among husband–wife households. As births to unmarried women rose, poverty and social dependency increased. (In 1970, only 11 percent of births were to unmarried women; by 2011, this figure had risen to 41 percent of all births before starting to decline.[5] The troubling question was whether the welfare system ameliorated some of the hardships confronting unmarried mothers and their children, or whether it actually contributed to social dependency by mitigating the consequences of unmarried motherhood. For example, were teenage pregnancies more common because teenagers knew that government benefits were available to young mothers and their children?

Reforming Family Assistance

A political consensus grew over the years that long-term social dependency had to be addressed in welfare policy. The fact that most nonpoor mothers work convinced many *liberals* that welfare mothers had no special claim to stay at home with their children. And many *conservatives* acknowledged that some transitional assistance—education, job training, continued health care, and day care for children—might be necessary to move welfare mothers into the workforce.

Although President Clinton had once promised "to end welfare as we know it," it was the Republican-controlled Congress elected in 1994 that proceeded to do so. The Republican-sponsored welfare reform bill ended the 60-year-old federal "entitlement" for low-income families with children—the venerable AFDC program. In its place, the Republicans devised a "devolution" of responsibility to the states through federal block grants—**Temporary Assistance to Needy Families**—lump sum allocations to the states for cash welfare payments, with benefits and eligibility requirements decided by the states. Conservatives in Congress imposed tough-minded "strings" to state aid, including a two-year limit on continuing cash benefits and a five-year lifetime limit;

What Do You Think?

Did Welfare Reform Work?

Welfare reform, officially called Temporary Assistance to Needy Families, was passed by Congress in 1996; its provisions took effect in 1997. By early 1998, the Clinton administration, as well as Republican congressional sponsors of welfare reform, was declaring it a success.

The number of cash welfare recipients in the nation has dropped below 5 million—the lowest number in more than 25 years. Only about 2 percent of Americans are now on cash welfare—the smallest proportion since 1970.

All states have now developed work programs for welfare recipients. Applicants for welfare benefits are now generally required to enter job-search programs, undertake job training, and accept jobs or community service positions.

However, although nearly everyone agrees that getting people off welfare rolls and onto payrolls is the main goal of reform, there are major obstacles to the achievement of this goal. First of all, a substantial portion (perhaps 25 to 40 percent) of long-term welfare recipients have handicaps—physical disabilities, chronic illnesses, learning disabilities, alcohol or drug abuse problems—that prevent them from holding a full-time job. Many long-term recipients have no work experience (perhaps 40 percent), and two-thirds did not graduate from high school. Almost half have three or more children, making day-care arrangements a major obstacle. It is unlikely that any counseling, education, job training, or job placement programs could ever succeed in getting these people into productive employment.

Early studies of people who left the welfare rolls following welfare reform suggest that over half and perhaps as many as three-quarters have found work, although most at minimum or near-minimum wages.[a]

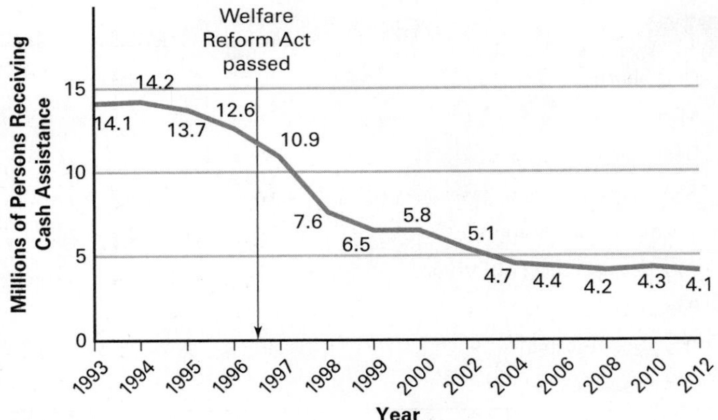

QUESTIONS

1. Do you think most Americans clearly understand what welfare programs are?
2. Are there practical, structural obstacles to moving people from welfare to work? Or are these just consequences of life that must be dealt with by all Americans?

[a] *Governing* (April 1999), pp. 21–26.

a "family cap" that would deny additional cash benefits to women already on welfare who bear more children; the denial of cash welfare to unwed parents under 18 years of age unless they live with an adult and attend school. President Clinton vetoed the first welfare reform bill passed by Congress in early 1996, but as the presidential election neared, he reversed himself and signed the Welfare Reform Act, establishing the Temporary Assistance to Needy Families program. Food stamps, SSI, and Medicaid were continued as federal "entitlements" (see *What Do You Think?* Did Welfare Reform Work?).

☐ SNAP Dependency

While TANF was reducing dependency on family cash assistance, SNAP (food stamps) became America's fastest-growing social welfare program. As recently as 2000, only 17 million Americans received food stamps. But by 2012 roughly 50 million people did so. The average benefit per person also doubled in these years.

SNAP is financed by the U.S. Department of Agriculture (USDA). It is that department's largest and most expensive program. USDA has encouraged states to relax eligibility requirements for SNAP, and it has pursued aggressive advertising and outreach programs to recruit recipients. The predictable result has been greater family dependency on food stamps. SNAP is at the center of debate as Congress considers each year's misnamed "farm bill," the appropriations act for USDA.

Soaring Disability

Social Security Disability Insurance (SSDI) was originally created as a safety net for severely disabled workers. It was added to the Social Security Act of 1935 in 1956. For years it remained a relatively modest component of Social Security. As late as 1990 there were only about 30 million recipients, defined as "workers unable to engage in any substantial gainful activity by reason of any medically determinable physical or mental impairment which can be expected to result in death or can be expected to last for a continuous period of not less than 12 months." By 2012 disability recipients soared to over 80 million. A large legal establishment ("disability advocates") has grown to initiate and pursue disability claims. Unlike unemployment compensation, which is now fixed in duration, disability benefits go on for a lifetime.

The Minimum Wage

Significant numbers of people who work part-time or even full-time still fall below the poverty level. These "working poor" may comprise as much as 1 in 10 of the nation's workers. A federal minimum wage was first enacted by the Fair Labor Standards Act of 1937 at $0.25 per hour. Today the federal minimum wage is $7.25, and several states and cities have set their own higher minimum wage (Seattle recently set a minimum wage of $15 per hour), and President Obama set, via executive order, a minimum wage for national government contractors at $10.10 per hour.

The current federal minimum wage results in an annual income of only about $15,000, well below the poverty level. Proponents of increasing the minimum wage argue that no worker can support a family (or oneself) on the minimum wage. Opponents argue that most minimum-wage workers are teenagers, part-time workers, or persons just entering the labor force with no skills. Raising the minimum wage would eliminate many of these entry-level jobs and the accompanying work experience needed to get ahead in life.

Extended Unemployment

Originally unemployment compensation was designed as a "temporary and partial" replacement of wages for involuntarily unemployed workers. But in recent years Congress has extended unemployment payments to well beyond the 26 weeks that had been established as the maximum length of compensation. Indeed, at one point Congress had extended benefits to 99 weeks (over two years) to accommodate the long-term unemployed. Nationwide, benefits average about $350 per week. Critics of extensions note that beneficiaries tend to find jobs near the end of their compensation period, suggesting that compensation encourages people to remain unemployed.

Health Care in America

17.6 Compare the United States and other nations on health care expenditures and measures of health care and describe the nation's major health care programs.

The United States spends more of its resources on health care than any other nation (see *Compared to What?* Health and Health Care Costs in Advanced Democracies). Nevertheless, the United States ranks well below other advanced democracies in key measures of the health of its people such as life expectancy and infant death rate.

The Health of Americans

Historically, most reductions in death rates have resulted from public health and sanitation improvements, including immunizations, clean public water supplies, sanitary

Compared to What?

Health and Health Care Costs in Advanced Democracies

Americans spend more than any other nation in the world for health care (see figure). Few people object to heavy spending for health care if they get their money's worth. But cross-national comparisons of health statistics indicate that Americans on the average are less healthy than citizens in other advanced democracies. The United States ranks *below* many other advanced nations in life expectancy and infant death rates—two commonly used measures of national health.

The United States offers some of the most advanced and sophisticated medical care in the world, attracting patients from the countries that rank well ahead of it in various health measures. The United States is the locus of some of the most advanced medical research, attracting medical researchers from throughout the world. But the high quality of medical care available in the United States, combined with the poor health statistics of the general public, suggests that the nation's health care problems center more on access to care and education and prevention of health problems than on the quality of care available.

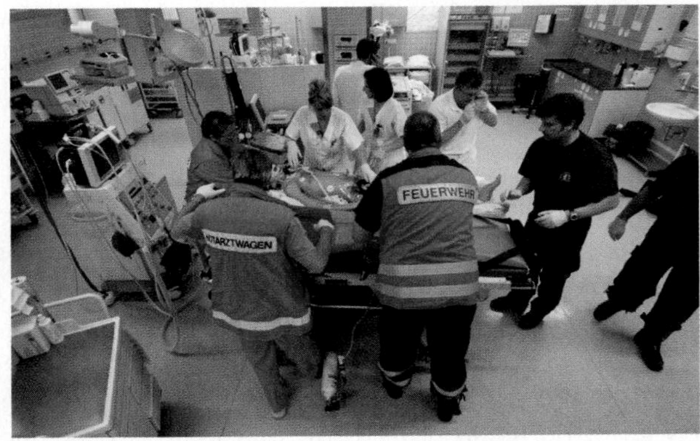

QUESTION

1. When marketplaces create disparities that result in costs to society, it is called a "market failure." Given the disparity between the overall standard of American health care and the access to basic health care, has the market failed in health care?

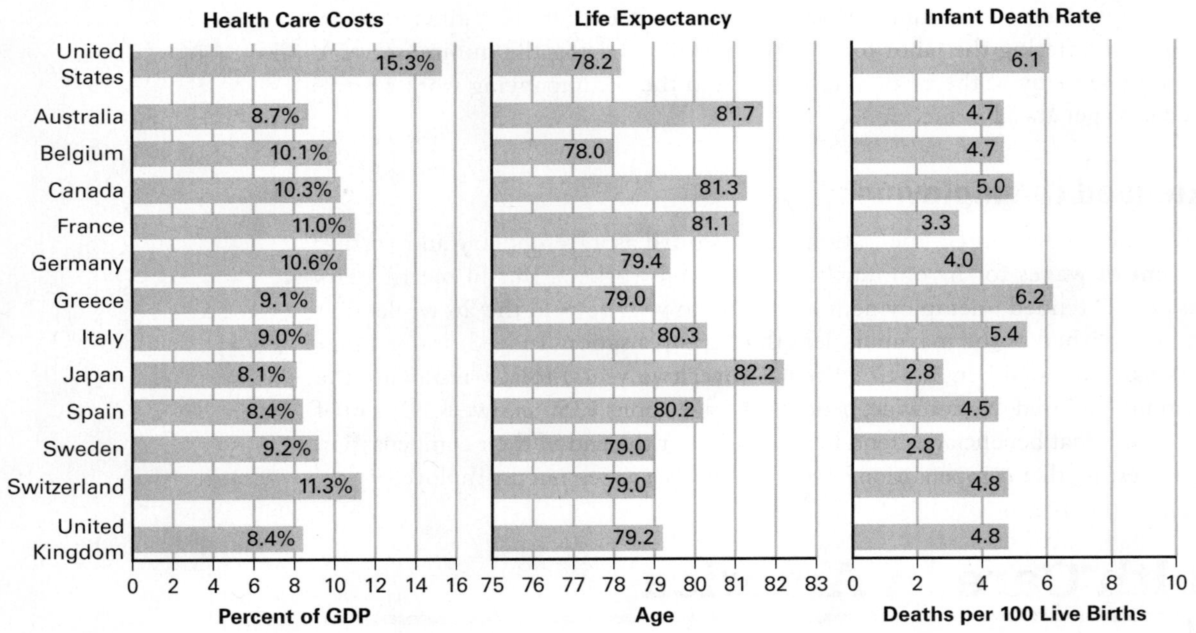

SOURCE: *Statistical Abstract of the United States, 2012*, pp. 824, 827.

sewage disposal, improved diets, and increased standards of living. Many of the leading causes of death today, including heart disease, cancer, and stroke, are closely linked to heredity, personal habits, and lifestyles (smoking, eating, drinking, exercise, stress), and the physical environment—factors over which doctors and hospitals have no direct control. Thus, some argue that the greatest contribution to better health is likely to be found in altered personal habits and lifestyles rather than in more medical care. Thanks to improved health care habits as well as breakthroughs in medical technology, Americans are living longer than ever before.

CAMPAIGNING FOR OBAMACARE

President Obama campaigned long and hard for his national healthcare reform bill Obamacare. Here he is speaking at a town hall meeting in Portsmouth, NH, on August 11, 2009. Congress finally enacted the Patient Protection and Affordable Care Act of 2010 that transformed health care in America.

Health Care Costs

No system of health care can provide as much as people will use. Anyone whose health and life may be at stake will want the most thorough diagnostic testing, the most constant care, the most advanced treatment. Sworn to preserve life, doctors, too, want the most advanced diagnostic and treatment facilities available for their patients. Under conditions of uncertainty in a medical situation—and there is always some uncertainty—physicians are trained to seek more consultations, run more tests, and try new therapeutic approaches. Any tendency for doctors to limit testing and treatment is countered by the threat of malpractice suits; it is always easier to order one more test or procedure than to risk even the tiniest chance that failing to do so will some day be cause for a court suit. So in the absence of restraints, both patients and doctors will push up the costs of health care. Currently, health care costs appear to have stabilized at about 15 percent of the nation's GDP.

Medicare
Social insurance program that provides health care insurance to elderly and disabled people.

Medicare

Medicare is a two-part program that helps elderly and disabled people pay acute-care (as opposed to long-term-care) health costs. Hospital insurance (Part A) helps pay the cost of hospital inpatient and skilled nursing care. Anyone 65 or older who is eligible for Social Security is automatically eligible for Part A benefits. Also eligible are people under 65 who receive Social Security disability or railroad retirement disability and people who have end-stage kidney disease. Part A is financed primarily by the 1.45 percent payroll tax collected with Social Security (FICA) withholding. Supplemental Medical Insurance (Part B) is an optional add-on taken

17.1
17.2
17.3
17.4
17.5
17.6
17.7
17.8

Medicaid
Federal aid to the states to provide health insurance for low-income persons.

SCHIP
Federal grants to the states to extend health insurance to children of low-income families.

by virtually all those covered by Part A. It pays 80 percent of covered doctor and outpatient charges. Small monthly premiums are deducted from Social Security benefit checks to finance it.

Medicaid

The federal government provides funds under **Medicaid** to enable states to provide medical services for low-income persons. Unlike Medicare, Medicaid is a welfare program designed for needy persons; no prior contributions are required, and the recipients of Medicaid services are generally welfare recipients. Each state operates its own Medicaid program. Medicaid is the costliest of all public assistance programs. States must pay about 45 percent of Medicaid costs, with the federal government paying the remainder. Medicaid is the most rapidly growing item in the budgets of most states.

SCHIP

Under the State Children's Health Insurance Program (**SCHIP**), the federal government provides grants to the states to extend health insurance to children who would not otherwise qualify for Medicaid. The program is generally targeted toward families with incomes below 200 percent of the poverty level. However, each state may set its own eligibility limits, and each state has flexibility in the administration of the program.

Obama's Health Care Transformation

17.7 Describe the key provisions of the Patient Protection and Affordable Care Act of 2010.

President Barack Obama and a Democratic-controlled Congress acted to transform health care in America with the comprehensive Patient Protection and Affordable Care Act of 2010. National health care had been attempted unsuccessfully by past presidents, including Franklin D. Roosevelt, Harry Truman, and Bill Clinton. According to President Obama, "Moving to provide all Americans with health insurance is not only a moral imperative, but it is also essential to a more effective and efficient healthcare system."[6]

Stimulus to Change

A major stimulus to health reform was to extend coverage to all Americans. About 85 percent of the nation's population was covered by either government or private health insurance. Government covered about 27 percent of the nation's population—through Medicare for the aged, Medicaid for the poor, and other government programs, including military and veterans' care. Private insurance covered about 58 percent of population (see Figure 17.4).

But about 15 percent of the U.S. population—an estimated 45 million Americans—had *no* medical insurance. These included workers and their dependents whose employers did not offer a health insurance plan, as well as unemployed people who were not eligible for Medicare or Medicaid. People who lacked health insurance frequently postponed or went without needed medical care or they were denied medical care by hospitals and physicians in all but emergency situations. Confronted with serious illness, they might impoverish themselves in order to become eligible for Medicaid. Any unpaid medical bills had to be absorbed by hospitals or shifted to paying patients and their insurance companies.

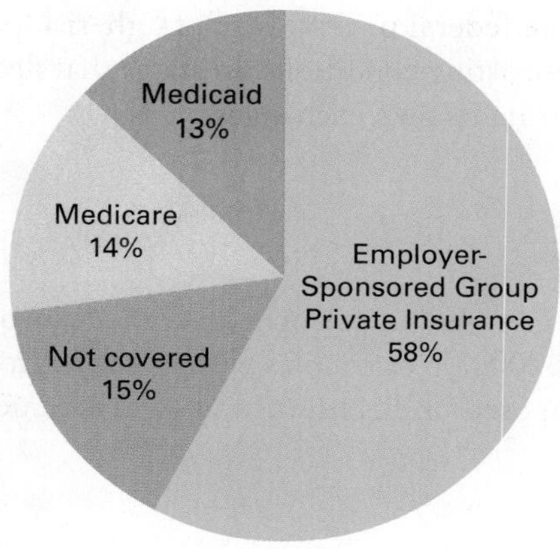

FIGURE 17.4 HEALTH COVERAGE AND THE UNINSURED IN 2008

SOURCE: *Statistical Abstract of the United States, 2008*, p.107

The Patient Protection and Affordable Care Act—Obamacare

America's health care system will continue to rely primarily on private health insurance companies. However, private insurers will no longer be permitted to deny insurance for preexisting conditions, or to drop coverage when patients get sick, or to place lifetime limits on coverage. Dependent children under age 26 can be covered under their parents' insurance plan. These particular reforms faced no serious opposition in Congress.

Patient Protection and Affordable Care Act—Obamacare
Comprehensive transformation of America's healthcare system requiring all Americans to obtain health insurance.

individual mandate
A requirement that every American purchase health insurance or face a tax penalty.

But many provisions in the 2,500-page bill stirred intense controversy. Republicans in both the House of Representatives and the Senate were unanimous in their opposition to the overall bill. Its many provisions include the following:

Individual Mandate

Every American is required to purchase health insurance or face a tax penalty up to 2.5 percent of their household income. The Internal Revenue Service is charged with enforcing this individual mandate.

Employer Mandate

Employers with 50 or more workers are obliged to provide health insurance to their employees. Companies that fail to do so will face substantial fines. Small businesses are offered tax credits for offering their employees health insurance.

Medicaid Expansion

State Medicaid eligibility is expanded to include all individuals with incomes up to 133 percent of the federal poverty level. The federal government will initially fund this expansion, but eventually the states must do so themselves. The federal government, however, cannot deny all Medicaid funding to states which choose not to comply with the expansion.[7]

Health Insurance Exchanges

The federal government will assist states in creating "exchanges" or marketplaces where individuals can purchase health insurance from private companies. Health plans offered through the exchanges must meet federal requirements, including coverage for preventative care. Federal subsidies will be available for individuals who earn between

17.1
17.2
17.3
17.4
17.5
17.6
17.7
17.8

"public option"
A government-run nonprofit health insurance agency that would compete with private insurers; rejected by Congress.

133 and 400 percent of the federal poverty level. High-risk pools will be created to cover individuals with pre-existing conditions. In states that decline to participate, the federal government will create its own exchanges.

Taxes

A surtax of 3.8 percent is imposed on personal investment income of individuals with adjusted gross income of $200,000 or couples with adjusted gross income of $250,000 or more. New fees are imposed on health insurance companies and on brand-name drug manufacturers.

No "Public Option"

Congress rejected President Obama's proposed "**public option**"—a government-run nonprofit health insurance agency that would compete with private insurers. The president had argued that a public option was necessary "to keep them honest" by offering reasonable coverage at affordable prices. But critics warned that the public option threatened a "government takeover" of the nation's health care system. Over time, private insurance companies would lose out to the public program, eventually creating a single national health insurance system or "socialized medicine." Liberals in Congress were disappointed when the public option was dropped from the bill.

Challenges to Obamacare

17.8 Describe the challenges to Obamacare and the Supreme Court decision upholding it.

Republicans in Congress were unanimously opposed to the Patient Protection and Affordable Care Act of 2010 – "Obamacare." They promised to repeal it, if possible, or if not, to obstruct its implementation. Attorneys General in twenty-six states and the National Federation of Independent Business brought suit in federal court challenging the constitutionality of the Act.

The Constitutionality of the Individual Mandate

At the heart of Obamacare is the requirement that every American must obtain health insurance. The health-insurance industry itself strongly supports this provision; it generates customers including younger and healthier people. It also enables insurers to accept the risks of covering people with costly preexisting conditions. The Supreme Court decided to hear the case in 2012 even though the individual mandate was not scheduled to go into effect until 2014.

Chief Justice John Roberts wrote the majority, 5 to 4, opinion in this important case.[8] He first determined that the individual mandate *cannot* be upheld under Congress's power to regulate interstate commerce allowing Congress to command people to buy a product—health insurance—would open a vast new domain of federal power. The Founders gave Congress the power to *regulate* commerce not to *compel* it. Ignoring this distinction would undermine the principle that the federal government is a government of limited and enumerated powers.

However, Roberts concluded that the individual mandate is actually a tax, and as such it is a constitutional exercise of Congress's power to "lay and collect taxes" (Art. 1 Sect. 8). The Act itself refers to a "penalty" for noncompliance. But Roberts held that "every reasonable construction must be resorted to, in order to save a statute from unconstitutionality." He reasoned that the individual mandate can be interpreted as a tax on those who choose to go without insurance. He observed that the tax is administered and collected by the Internal Revenue Service.

STATE COMPLIANCE WITH MEDICAID EXPANSION The Act authorizes the Secretary of Health and Human Services to withdraw existing Medicaid funds from any state that refuses to participate in the Act's expansion of the program, However, Roberts held that this provision of the Act "runs counter to this nation's system of federalism." The threatened loss of *all* Medicaid funds leaves the states with no real option but to acquiesce in Medicaid expansion. To be constitutional under the spending clause of the Constitution, states must voluntarily accept the terms of the program. States cannot be compelled to participate in a federal program.

IRS ENFORCEMENT Americans who do not purchase health insurance by 2014 are subject to a fine to be levied by the IRS at tax time. The Act authorizes the IRS to determine who is not in compliance, to levy fines, and to withhold the fines from tax refunds. Opponents in Congress seek to prevent the IRS from enforcing the law, perhaps by "defunding" the cost of administration. But President Obama has pledged to veto any attempt to weaken the individual mandate or its enforcement.

STATE PARTICIPATION IN EXCHANGES States are authorized by the Act to create health insurance exchanges to provide coverage for individuals and small businesses by pooling them into larger groups to buy insurance from private companies. States can refuse to participate, which might complicate the administration of the Act. But the federal government is authorized to step in where the states fail to create these exchanges.

IMPLEMENTATION Initially the implementation of Obamacare was chaotic. Despite years to prepare, the website portal designed to enroll millions of new customers was a disaster. Prospective enrollees could not access the website or get it to accept their applications. Even completed applications were not forwarded to insurance companies. The president subsequently extended enrollment deadlines for individuals and small businesses, and gave big businesses an additional year to comply.

"RATIONING" CARE Health care reform will expand health insurance coverage to virtually all Americans. About 35 million more people will be brought into the nation's health insurance system. But critics fear that this influx of patients will overload doctors and hospitals, leading to long waits and perhaps "rationing" of care. Government limits on physicians' fees may cause doctors to turn away Medicare, Medicaid, and government-subsidized patients.

NO TORT REFORM Health care reform largely fails to contain the nation's burgeoning health care costs. Congress failed to include any provision for the reform of medical malpractice litigation. Lawsuits against physicians, hospitals, and insurers are a major cause of increased health care costs. Physicians must pay exorbitant fees for malpractice insurance. More importantly, physicians are inspired by fear of lawsuits to order numerous tests and procedures not necessary for good medical practice. Tort reform would pay for the actual lifetime cost of medical errors but place a cap on "pain and suffering" damages.

17.1
17.2
17.3
17.4
17.5
17.6
17.7
17.8

A Constitutional Note

Rights Versus Entitlements

The Constitution *limits* government. It does not oblige the government to provide any benefits or services to people, such as education, welfare, Social Security, medical care, and so on. Constitutionally speaking, there is no *right* to these benefits. The states, for example, are not obliged by the Constitution to provide public education; the national government is not obliged by the Constitution to provide Social Security or Medicare. These governments do so as a matter of legislation, not as a mandate of the U.S. Constitution. (Of course, if the national or state governments decide to provide such services, they must provide them equally to all persons "similarly situated," that is, they cannot discriminate but must provide "equal protection of laws" under the 14th Amendment.) Political rhetoric often claims a right to an education, or to Social Security, or to medical care, or to other important programs. But there are no such rights set forth in the Constitution. Although politically unthinkable, states could abolish public education altogether; Congress could abolish Social Security or Medicare.

However, governments over time have provided benefits and services that people have come to depend upon. The laws granting these benefits set eligibility requirements—age, income, disability, unemployment, and so forth. Everyone who meets these requirements is said to be *entitled* to these benefits by law—that is to say, the statute by title mandates these benefits. Indeed, we have come to refer to these benefits as *entitlements*. But it is important to distinguish between *rights*—limits on government power to protect individuals—and *entitlements*—benefits that governments have enacted for persons who meet specific requirements.

QUESTIONS

1. Is the term "entitlement" as described here the same as most people probably understand it?
2. How is a right different from an entitlement?

Review the Chapter

Power and Social Welfare

17.1 Assess the importance of social welfare policy, p. 636

Social welfare policy largely determines who gets what from government: over half of the federal budget is now devoted to "human resources." The major redistributor of income from group to group is the federal government.

Poverty in the United States

17.2 Characterize the extent of poverty in the United States and identify correlates, p. 637

The poor are *not* the principal beneficiaries of social welfare spending. Only about one-third of all federal social welfare spending is means tested. Most social welfare spending, including the largest programs—Social Security and Medicare—goes to the middle class.

About 11 to 15 percent of the U.S. population falls below the annual cash income level that the federal government sets as its official definition of poverty.

Poverty is temporary for many families, but some poverty is persistent—lasting five years to a lifetime. Prolonged poverty and welfare dependency create an "underclass" beset by many social and economic problems. Poverty is most frequent among families headed by single mothers.

Social Welfare Policy

17.3 Outline the major social welfare programs in the United States, p. 639

Nearly one-half of all American families receives some form of government payments or benefits. Entitlements are government benefits for which Congress has set eligibility criteria by law. Social Security and Medicare are the largest entitlement programs. The elderly are entitled to these benefits regardless of their income or wealth.

Senior Power

17.4 Explain the reasons for and consequences of the political strength of older Americans, p. 642

Senior citizens are politically powerful; they vote more often than younger people and they have powerful lobbying organizations in Washington. Social Security is the largest single item in the federal budget. Yet proposals to modify Social Security or Medicare benefits are politically dangerous.

Politics and Welfare Reform

17.5 Analyze the role of politics in welfare reform, p. 644

Public assistance programs, including Family Assistance, Supplemental Security Income, and food stamps, require recipients to show that they are poor in order to claim benefits.

Welfare reform in 1996 replaced federal entitlements to cash payments with block grants to the states. It also set time limits on welfare enrollment.

Health Care in America

17.6 Compare the United States and other nations on health care expenditures and measures of health care, and describe the nation's major healthcare programs, p. 647

Americans spend more on health care than citizens of any other nation, yet we rank below many other nations in life expectancy and infant death rates. Medicare provides health insurance for the aged, and Medicaid covers the poor, and the SCHIP programs in the states cover poor children.

Obama's Health Care Transformation

17.7 Describe the key provisions of the Patient Protection and Affordable Care Act of 2010, p. 650

President Obama and a Democratic Congress brought about massive transformation of the nation's health care system in the Patient Protection and Affordable Care Act of 2010. This act includes a requirement that health insurance companies no longer be permitted to deny insurance for preexisting conditions or to drop coverage when patients get sick. More controversial provisions include an "individual mandate" that all citizens acquire health insurance, mandated employer insurance for large companies, health insurance exchanges in the states, and a tax penalty for noncompliance. Republicans in Congress united against the bill.

Challenges to "Obamacare"

17.8 Describe the challenges to "Obamacare" and the Supreme Court decision upholding it, p. 652

Twenty-six states and the Federation of Independent Business brought suit in federal court challenging the constitutionality of the individual mandate, as well as Medicaid expansion, in the Patient Protection and Affordable Care Act. Chief Justice John Roberts, writing the majority opinion for a divided (5—4) Supreme Court, held that the individual mandate was constitutional under Congress's taxing power. He also held that the threat to withdraw all Medicaid funds from states that did not agree to expand their programs was unconstitutional under the nation's system of federalism. Republican opponents of the Act promised to repeal it if possible, or if not, to encourage states to refuse to participate in Medicaid expansion or the creation of health insurance exchanges. Critics fear that the Act will eventually lead to a "rationing" of medical care, and that the failure to include tort reform will force medical care costs upward. The initial implementation of the Act was chaotic when the government web portal malfunctioned.

Learn the Terms

transfer payments, p. 636
poverty line, p. 636
means-tested spending, p. 636
underclass, p. 638
social insurance, p. 640
public assistance, p. 640
entitlements, p. 640
Social Security, p. 640
unemployment compensation, p. 641
Supplemental Security Income (SSI), p. 641
Family Assistance, p. 641
Food Stamp program, p. 641
Earned Income Tax Credit (EITC), p. 641
Medicaid, p. 641
dependency ratio, p. 643
COLAs, p. 643
Temporary Assistance to Needy Families, p. 645
Medicare, p. 649
Medicaid, p. 650
SCHIP, p. 650
Patient Protection and Affordable Care Act—Obamacare, p. 651
individual mandate, p. 651
"public option", p. 652

Test Yourself

17.1 Assess the importance of social welfare policy.

Approximately ______ percent of Americans were living below the poverty line in 2012.

a. 6–10%
b. 12–15%
c. 18–22%
d. 30–33%
e. 33–38%

17.2 Characterize the extent of poverty in the United States and identify correlates.

The percentage of individuals who live below the government's poverty line would be highest among which group?

a. African Americans
b. female-headed households
c. the elderly
d. Hispanics
e. Anglo whites

17.3 Outline major social welfare programs in the United States.

Approximately ______ percent of the United States' population receives some form of benefit from the federal government.

a. 20
b. 25
c. 33
d. 50
e. 67

17.4 Explain reasons for and consequences of the political strength of older Americans.

The most politically powerful age group is

a. 30- to 40-year-olds
b. 40- to 50-year-olds
c. 50- to 60-year-olds
d. 65 and older
e. 18-30 year olds

17.5 Analyze the role of politics in welfare reform.

Americans are in conflict over what causes poverty. Many believe that it is caused by

a. a weak economy
b. individual characteristics of the recipients
c. the welfare system itself
d. a, b, and c
e. not a, b, or c

17.6 Compare the United States and other nations on health care expenditures and measures of health care, and describe the nation's major healthcare programs.

Medicare was enacted in 1965 to provide health insurance for which of the following groups?

I. the poor
II. the aged
III. children
a. Only I
b. Only II
c. Only III
d. I, II, and III
e. II and III

17.7 Describe the key provisions of the Patient Protection and Affordable Care Act of 2010.

Congress rejected President Obama's proposal for:

a. requiring all Americans purchase insurance
b. establishing a government run health insurance agency
c. insurance companies to cover preexisting conditions
d. requiring large employers to provide health insurance to their employees.
e. Both a and c only

17.8 Describe the challenges to "Obamacare" and the Supreme Court decision upholding it.

Opponents criticize PPACA for its failure to

a. expand Medicaid beyond the poverty level
b. provide enforcement for the individual mandate
c. protect physicians from medical malpractice suits
d. provide health insurance exchanges
e. provide a mandate for universal coverage

Explore Further

SUGGESTED READINGS

Altman, Nancy J. *The Battle for Social Security*. New York: Wiley, 2005. An overview of the history and partisan battles over Social Security, from its beginning under Franklin D. Roosevelt to George W. Bush's proposals to privatize part of the system.

DiNitto, Diana M., and Linda K. Cummins. *Social Welfare Politics and Policy*. 7th ed. New York: Pearson, 2011. A comprehensive overview of social welfare programs—Social Security, Medicare, SSI, cash assistance, Medicaid, food stamps, and so on—and the political controversies surrounding them.

Jacobs, Lawrence K., and Theda Skocpol. *Healthcare Reform in American Politics.* New York: Oxford Press, 2010. An overview of the passage of the Patient Protection and Affordable Care Act of 2010.

Miller, Roger LeRoy, Daniel K. Benjamin, and Douglass C. North. *The Economics of Public Issues*, 18th ed. New York: Pearson, 2014. Sound economic commentary on a wide variety of public issues.

Murray, Charles. *Losing Ground*. 10th American ed. New York: Basic Books, 1994. Controversial, classic thesis, first put forth in 1984, that government social welfare programs, by encouraging social dependence, had the unintended and perverse effect of slowing and even reversing earlier progress in reducing poverty, crime, ignorance, and discrimination. Often cited as the inspiration for welfare reform.

Schiller, Bradley R. *The Economics of Poverty and Discrimination*. 10th ed. New York: Longman, 2008. Leading text on poverty and welfare in America.

Weissert, Carol S., and William G. Weissert. *Governing Health: The Politics of Health Policy*. 4th ed. Baltimore, Md.: Johns Hopkins University Press, 2012. Health care policy making, including the roles of Congress, the president, interest groups, and the bureaucracy.

Wilson, William Julius. *The Truly Disadvantaged*. Chicago: University of Chicago Press, 1987. Classic thesis that the growth of the underclass is primarily a result of the decline of manufacturing jobs and their shift to the suburbs, and the resulting concentration of poor, jobless, isolated people in the inner city.

SUGGESTED WEB SITES

AARP Social Security www.aarp.org/socialsecurity
AARP's Social Security Center site provides information about the Social Security system, including such items as the system's future solvency and a tutorial on how the system works.

Centers for Disease Control www.cdc.gov
Official site for health information and statistics.

Food Stamp Program www.fns.usda.gov/snap
This U.S. Department of Agriculture's Food Stamp program site contains information about application procedures, recipient eligibility guidelines, and other relevant subjects.

Institute for Research on Poverty www.irp.wisc.eduu
University of Wisconsin Institute leads in research on extent and causes of poverty.

Medicare www.medicare.gov
Official government site explaining eligibility, plan options, appeals, and so forth.

National Center for Children in Poverty www.nccp.org
Columbia University Center with studies and data on children in poverty.

Social Security Online www.ssa.gov
Find out all about your Social Security benefits.

Social Security Reform www.socialsecurity.org
CATO Institute think tank urges private investment of Social Security premiums.

18

Politics and National Security

It is said that politics is war by other means. So, too, war can be seen as a tool of politics, diplomacy, or even justice. The American military is the most expensive and widely deployed in the world, and has fought three major wars in the Middle East and central Asia since 1991. But not all of our combat deployments are large-scale. Since the end of the Cold War, American ground combat troops have been deployed for action to Afghanistan, Bosnia, East Timor, Georgia, Haiti, Iraq, Kuwait, Liberia, Macedonia, Pakistan, the Philippines, Saudi Arabia, Serbia, Somalia, Sudan, Yemen, and in late 2011, Uganda.

The intervention in Uganda was ordered by President Obama to help battle Joseph Kony, leader of the Lord's Resistance Army—six months before widespread knowledge of his atrocities went viral with Invisible Children's KONY 2012 video. About one-hundred special operations combat advisors were sent to Uganda to assist the Ugandan military in their ongoing war against Kony, who has engaged in a terror campaign including rape, murder, and kidnapping since 1991. Kony and his organization had been designated terrorists and a terror organization by the United States since 2001, and in 2005 an International Court warrant was issued for Kony.

The use of selective special operations forces to conduct similar missions has a long history in the U.S. military. U.S. combat advisors worked in Vietnam as early as 1955, the beginning of a twenty-year military presence in the country.

The decision to pursue Kony received support across the aisle from both parties, including critics of the administration. The mission is largely humanitarian in purpose; other than some mineral resources and recent oil discoveries, there is little strategic value to Uganda. With a low life expectancy rate, a high HIV infection rate, and a history of strongman government, Uganda is a poor candidate for a stable, democratic regime.

U.S. MILITARY ADVISORS Since 2011, U.S. soldiers have worked with the Ugandan personnel who are pursuing international fugitive and insurgent Joseph Kony.

collective security
Attempt to bring order to international relations by all nations joining together to guarantee each other's "territorial integrity" and "independence" against "external aggression."

Soviet Union
The Union of Soviet Socialist Republics (USSR), consisting of Russia and its bordering lands and ruled by the communist regime in Moscow; officially dissolved in 1991.

Power Among Nations

18.1 Describe the ways in which nations have attempted to bring order to international politics.

International politics, like all politics, is a struggle for power. The struggle for power is global; it involves all the nations and peoples of the world, whatever their goals or ideals. As the distinguished political scientist Hans Morgenthau once observed,

> Whatever the ultimate aims of international politics, power is always the immediate aim. Statesmen and peoples may ultimately seek freedom, security, prosperity or power itself. They may define their goals in terms of a religious, philosophic, economic, or social ideal. . . . But whenever they strive to realize their goal by means of international politics, they are striving for power.[1]

The struggle for power among nations has led to many attempts to bring order to the international system.

Collective Security

Originally, **collective security** meant that *all* nations would join together to guarantee each other's "territorial integrity and existing political independence" against "external aggression" by any nation. This was the idea behind the League of Nations, established in 1919. However, opposition to international involvement was so great in the United States after World War I that, after a lengthy debate, the Senate refused to enroll the United States in the League of Nations. More important, the League of Nations failed to deal with acts of aggression by the Axis Powers—Germany, Japan, and Italy—in the 1930s. During that decade, Japan invaded Manchuria, Italy invaded Ethiopia, and Germany dismembered Czechoslovakia. Finally, when Germany invaded Poland in 1939, World War II began. Japan bombed the U.S. Navy base at Pearl Harbor on December 7, 1941, and the United States joined in the war. World War II cost more than 40 million lives, both civilian and military.

Formation of the United Nations

Even after World War II, the notion of collective security remained an ideal of the victorious Allied Powers. The Charter of the United Nations, signed in 1945, provided for the following organization:

- The Security Council, with 11 member nations, 5 of them being permanent members—the United States, the **Soviet Union** (whose membership is now held by Russia), Britain, France, and China—and each having the power to veto any action by the Security Council.
- The General Assembly, composed of all the member nations, each with a single vote.
- The Secretariat, headed by a secretary general with a staff at United Nations headquarters in New York. The current secretary general is Ban Ki-moon of South Korea.
- Separate organizations to handle specialized affairs—for example, the Economic and Social Council, the Trusteeship Council, and the International Court of Justice at The Hague in the Netherlands.

The Security Council has the "primary responsibility" for maintaining "international peace and security." The General Assembly has authority over "any matter affecting the peace of the world," although it is supposed to defer to the Security Council when the council has already taken up a particular security matter. No nation has a veto in the General Assembly; every nation has one vote regardless of its size or power. Most resolutions can be passed by a majority vote.

The United Nations in the Cold War

The United Nations (UN) proved largely ineffective during the long Cold War confrontation between the communist nations, led by the Soviet Union, and the Western democracies, led by the United States. The UN grew from its original 51 member nations to 150 (193 in 2012), but many of those nations were headed by authoritarian regimes of one kind or another. The Western democracies were outnumbered in the General Assembly, and the Soviet Union frequently used its veto to prevent action by the Security Council. Anti-Western and antidemocratic speeches became common in the General Assembly.

During the Cold War, the UN was overshadowed by the confrontation of the world's two **superpowers**: the United States and the Soviet Union. Indeed, international conflicts throughout the world—in the Middle East, Africa, Latin America, Southeast Asia, and elsewhere—were usually influenced by some aspect of the superpowers' struggle.

STANDING TALL?

The UN building in New York City symbolizes the hope that nations can resolve problems through collective action. However, the United Nations has achieved only limited success in the worldwide war on terror.

The UN Today

Following the disintegration of the Soviet Union in 1991, Russia inherited its UN Security Council seat. Many of the regional conflicts in the world were no longer "proxy" wars between superpowers. Over the years, the UN has sent blue-helmeted "peacekeeping" forces to monitor cease-fires in many troubled areas of the world. Yet the United Nations and its Security Council must rely on "the last remaining superpower," the United States, to take the lead in enforcing its resolutions. However, a top-heavy bureaucracy at UN headquarters in New York, together with scandal and inefficiency in UN spending, has eroded support for the UN in the United States.

superpowers
Refers to the United States and the Soviet Union after World War II, when these two nations dominated international politics.

regional security
Attempt to bring order to international relations during the Cold War by creating regional alliances between a superpower and nations of a particular region.

North Atlantic Treaty Organization (NATO)
Mutual-security agreement and joint military command uniting the nations of Western Europe, initially formed to resist Soviet expansionism.

Regional Security—NATO

The general disappointment with the United Nations as a form of collective security gave rise as early as 1949 to a different approach, **regional security**. In response to aggressive Soviet moves in Europe, the United States and the democracies of Western Europe created the **North Atlantic Treaty Organization (NATO)**. In the NATO treaty, 15 Western nations agreed to collective regional security: they agreed that "an armed attack against one or more [NATO nations] ... shall be considered an attack against them all." The United States made a specific commitment to defend Western Europe in the event of a Soviet attack. A joint NATO military command was established (with Dwight D. Eisenhower as its first commander) to coordinate the defense of Western Europe.

After the formation of NATO, the Soviets made no further advances into Western Europe. The Soviets themselves, in response to NATO, drew up the Warsaw Pact, a comparable treaty with their own Eastern European satellite nations. But for many years, the real deterrent to Warsaw Pact expansion was not the weak NATO armies, but rather the pledge of the United States to use its strategic nuclear bomber force to inflict "massive retaliation" on the Soviet Union itself in the event of an attack on Western Europe.

The Warsaw Pact disintegrated following the dramatic collapse of the communist governments of Eastern Europe in 1989. Former Warsaw Pact nations—Poland, Hungary, Romania, Bulgaria, and East Germany—threw out their ruling communist regimes and demanded the withdrawal of Soviet troops from their territory. The Berlin Wall was dismantled in 1989, and Germany was formally reunified in 1990, bringing together the 61 million prosperous people of West Germany and the 17 million less affluent people of East Germany. A unified Germany continued as a member of NATO. The Communist Party was ousted from power in Moscow, and the Soviet Union collapsed in 1991.

NATO Expansion

The United States and its Western European allies agree that NATO continues to play an important role in the security of Europe. Indeed, the continued deployment of some level of U.S. troops to NATO is widely considered to be reassurance that the United States remains committed to this security.

In recent years, NATO has made the key decision to expand its security protections to the newly democratic nations of Eastern Europe. Three nations—Poland, Hungary, and the Czech Republic—were admitted to NATO in 1998. At that time, Russia strongly objected to NATO expansion, viewing it as an incursion of Western powers in the East and a threat to Russia's security. A NATO–Russia Council was created in 2002 to calm Russian fears about NATO's intentions. In 2004, seven additional countries—Bulgaria, Estonia, Latvia, Lithuania, Romania, Slovakia, and Slovenia—were admitted to membership. All of these nations were formerly under the domination of the Soviet Union. NATO now has 26 members (see Figure 18.1).

☐ NATO and Ethnic Conflicts in the Balkans

Traditionally, NATO forces were never deployed outside of Western Europe. Yet ethnic wars in the former communist nation of Yugoslavia, and the media coverage of the hardships endured by the people there, inspired NATO to intervene and deploy

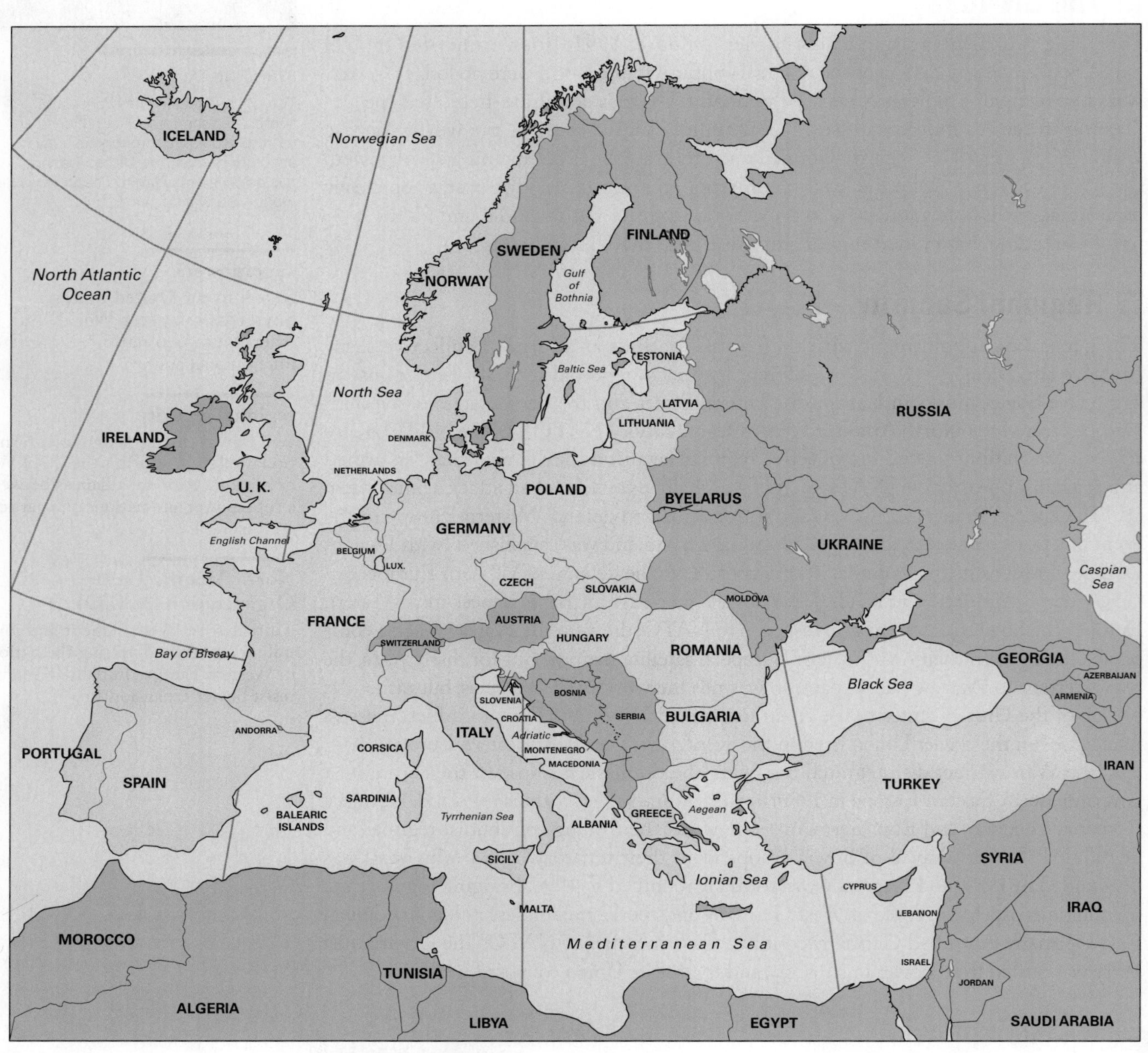

FIGURE 18.1 NATO NATIONS OF EUROPE*

NATO was originally created to protect the nations of Western Europe from Soviet expansion; the collapse of the Soviet Union in 1991 has led to the expansion of NATO into Eastern European nations formerly dominated by the old Soviet Union.

*NATO members United States and Canada not shown.

troops to Bosnia in 1995 to halt conflict raging among Serbs, Croats, and Muslims. The United States provided about one-third of the ground troops deployed in Bosnia as "peacekeepers."

NATO again acted militarily to halt ethnic conflict in Kosovo in 1999. NATO's objective was to force Serbian troop withdrawal from the largely Muslim province. NATO relied exclusively on bombing from the air to force the Serbian withdrawal. Despite some controversy, even among NATO nations, as well as denunciations from Russia and China, NATO aircraft and missiles hit targets in both Kosovo and Serbia itself. (Even the Chinese embassy in the Serbian capital of Belgrade was bombed, apparently by mistake.) Eventually, Serbian troops were withdrawn from Kosovo; they were replaced by NATO troops (and a small contingent of Russian troops).

NATO in Afghanistan

In 2003, NATO created an International Security Assistance Force, officially under UN auspices, "to assist the Islamic Republic of Afghanistan in creating a stable and secure environment for the people of Afghanistan." Some 37 nations contributed troops to this Force, but the United States contributed the largest number (see "The War in Afghanistan" later in this chapter).

Cold War
Political, military, and ideological struggle between the United States and the Soviet Union following the end of World War II and ending with the collapse of the Soviet Union's communist government in 1991.

Truman Doctrine
U.S. foreign policy, first articulated by President Harry S. Truman, that pledged the United States to "support free peoples who are resisting attempted subjugation by armed minorities or by outside pressures."

containment
Policy of preventing an enemy from expanding its boundaries and/or influence, specifically the U.S. foreign policy vis-à-vis the Soviet Union during the Cold War.

The Legacy of the Cold War

18.2 Outline the major events of the Cold War and assess its legacy.

or more than 40 years following the end of World War II, the United States and the Soviet Union confronted each other in the protracted political, military, and ideological struggle known as the **Cold War**.

Origins

During World War II, the United States and the Soviet Union joined forces to eliminate the Nazi threat to the world. The United States dismantled its military forces at the end of the war in 1945, but the Soviet Union, under the brutal dictatorship of Josef Stalin, used the powerful Red Army to install communist governments in the nations of Eastern Europe in violation of wartime agreements to allow free elections. Stalin also ignored pledges to cooperate in a unified allied occupation of Germany; Germany was divided, and in 1948 Stalin unsuccessfully tried to oust the United States, Britain, and France from Berlin in a yearlong "Berlin Blockade." Former British Prime Minister Winston Churchill warned the United States as early as 1946 that the Soviets were dividing Europe with an "Iron Curtain." When Soviet-backed communist forces threatened Greece and Turkey in 1947, President Harry S. Truman responded with a pledge to "support free people who are resisting attempted subjugation by armed minorities or by outside pressures," a policy that became known as the **Truman Doctrine**.

Containment

The United States had fought two world wars to maintain democracy in Western Europe. The new threat of Soviet expansionism and communist world revolution caused America to assume world leadership on behalf of the preservation of democracy. In an influential article in the Council on Foreign Relations' journal *Foreign Affairs*, the State Department's Russia expert George F. Kennan called for a policy of **containment**:

> It is clear that the main element of any United States policy toward the Soviet Union must be that of a long-term, vigilant containment of Russian expansive tendencies. . . .[2]

18.1

18.2

18.3

18.4

18.5

18.6

Marshall Plan
U.S. program to rebuild the nations of Western Europe in the aftermath of World War II in order to render them less susceptible to communist influence and takeover.

Korean War
Communist North Korea invaded noncommunist South Korea in June 1950, causing President Harry S. Truman to intervene militarily, with UN support. General Douglas MacArthur defeated the North Koreans, but with China's entry into the war, a stalemate resulted. An armistice was signed in 1953, with Korea divided along nearly original lines.

Cuban Missile Crisis
The 1962 confrontation between the Soviet Union and the United States over Soviet placement of nuclear missiles in Cuba.

To implement the containment policy, the United States first initiated the **Marshall Plan**, named for Secretary of State George C. Marshall, to rebuild the economies of the Western European nations. Marshall reasoned that *economically* weak nations were more susceptible to communist subversion and Soviet intimidation. The subsequent formation of NATO provided the necessary *military* support to contain the Soviet Union.

The Korean War

The first military test of the containment policy came in June 1950, when communist North Korean armies invaded South Korea. President Truman assumed that the North Koreans were acting on behalf of their sponsor, the Soviet Union. The Soviets had already aided Chinese communists under the leadership of Mao Zedong in capturing control of mainland China in 1949. The United States quickly brought the Korean invasion issue to the Security Council. With the Soviets boycotting this meeting because the Council had refused to seat the new communist delegation from China, the Council passed a resolution calling on member nations to send troops to repel the invasion.

America's conventional (nonnuclear) military forces had been largely dismantled after World War II. Moreover, President Truman insisted on keeping most of the nation's forces in Europe, fearing that the Korean invasion was a diversion to be followed by a Soviet invasion of Western Europe. But General Douglas MacArthur, in a brilliant amphibious landing at Inchon behind North Korean lines, destroyed a much larger enemy army, captured the North Korean capital, and moved northward toward the Chinese border. Then in December 1950, disaster struck American forces as a million-strong Chinese army entered the conflict. Chinese troops surprised the Americans, inflicting heavy casualties, trapping entire units, and forcing U.S. troops to beat a hasty retreat. General MacArthur urged retaliation against China, but Truman sought to keep the war "limited." When MacArthur publicly protested political limits to military operations, Truman dismissed the popular general. The **Korean War** became a bloody stalemate.

Dwight Eisenhower was elected president in 1952 in large measure because he promised to "go to Korea" to end the increasingly unpopular war. He also threatened to use nuclear weapons in the conflict, but eventually agreed to a truce along the original border between North and South Korea. Communist expansion in Korea was "contained," but at a high price: the United States lost more than 38,000 men in the war.

The Cuban Missile Crisis

The most serious threat of nuclear holocaust during the entire Cold War was the **Cuban Missile Crisis**. In 1962, Soviet Premier Nikita Khrushchev sought to secretly install medium-range nuclear missiles in Cuba in an effort to give the Soviet Union nuclear capability against U.S. cities. In October 1962, intelligence photos showing Soviet missiles at Cuban bases touched off a 13-day crisis. President Kennedy rejected advice to launch an air strike to destroy the missiles before they could be activated. Instead, he publicly announced a naval blockade of Cuba, threatening to halt Soviet missile-carrying vessels at sea by force if necessary. The prospect of war appeared imminent; U.S. nuclear forces went on alert. Secretly, Kennedy proposed to withdraw U.S. nuclear missiles from Turkey in exchange for Soviet withdrawal of nuclear missiles from Cuba. Khrushchev's agreement to the deal appeared to the world as a backing down; Kennedy would be hailed for his statesmanship in the crisis, while Khrushchev would soon lose his job.

The Vietnam War

When communist forces led by Ho Chi Minh defeated French forces at the battle of Dien Bien Phu in 1954, the resulting Geneva Accords divided that country into North Vietnam, with a communist government, and South Vietnam, with a U.S.-backed government. When South Vietnamese communist (Vietcong) guerrilla forces threatened the South Vietnamese government in the early 1960s, President Kennedy sent a force of more than 12,000 advisers and counterinsurgency forces to assist in every aspect of training and support for the Army of the Republic of Vietnam (ARVN) in South Vietnam and authorized a gradual increase in air strikes against North Vietnam. Washington committed more than 500,000 troops to a war of attrition, a war in which U.S. firepower was expected to inflict sufficient casualties on the enemy to force a peace settlement. But over time, the failure to achieve any decisive military victories eroded popular support for the **Vietnam War**.

Vietnam War
War between noncommunist South Vietnam and communist North Vietnam from 1956 to 1975, with increasing U.S. involvement, ending with U.S. withdrawal in 1973 and communist victory in 1975. The war became unpopular in the United States after 1968 and caused President Johnson not to run for a second term.

On January 31, 1968, the Vietnamese holiday of Tet, Vietcong forces blasted their way into the U.S. embassy compound in Saigon and held the courtyard for six hours. The attack was part of a massive, coordinated Tet offensive against all major cities of South Vietnam. U.S. forces responded and inflicted very heavy casualties on the Vietcong. By any military measure, the Tet offensive was a "defeat" for the enemy and a "victory" for U.S. forces. Yet the Tet offensive was Hanoi's greatest *political* victory. Television pictures of bloody fighting in Saigon and Hue seemed to mock President Johnson's promises of an early end to the war.

On March 31, 1968, President Johnson went on national television to make a dramatic announcement: he halted the bombing of North Vietnam and asked Hanoi for peace talks, concluding, "I shall not seek, and I will not accept, the nomination of my party for another term as your president." Formal peace talks opened in Paris on May 13.

A COSTLY CAMPAIGN

The Vietnam War inflicted more than 58,000 battle deaths on U.S. forces. Units of army infantry and Marines slogged through the jungles of Southeast Asia for more than eight years. The Paris Peace Accord, signed in 1973, was ignored by the communist regime in Hanoi; The 1975 invasion of South Vietnam by the North prompted a sudden evacuation of all U.S. personnel from Saigon. Here, sailors dump an Army helicopter off the deck of the the USS Okinawa to make room for additional evacuation aircraft.

18.1
18.2
18.3
18.4
18.5
18.6

The new president, Richard Nixon, and his national security adviser, Henry Kissinger, knew the war must be ended, but they sought to end it "honorably." Even in the absence of a settlement with the communists in Vietnam, Nixon began the withdrawal of U.S. troops under the guise of "Vietnamization" of the war effort. Unable to persuade Hanoi to make even the slightest concession at Paris, President Nixon sought to demonstrate American strength and resolve. In December 1972, the United States unleashed a devastating air attack directly on Hanoi for the first time. Critics at home labeled Nixon's action "the Christmas bombing," but when negotiations resumed in Paris in January, the North Vietnamese quickly agreed to peace on the terms that Kissinger and Le Duc Tho had worked out earlier.

The South Vietnamese government lasted two years after the agreement. In early 1975, Hanoi decided that the Americans would not "jump back in" and therefore "the opportune moment" was at hand for a new invasion. President Gerald Ford's requests to Congress for emergency military aid to the South Vietnamese fell on deaf ears. Saigon (now Ho Chi Minh City) fell to the North Vietnamese in April 1975, and the United States abandoned hundreds of thousands of loyal Vietnamese who had fought alongside the Americans for years.[3] The spectacle of U.S. Marines using their rifle butts to keep desperate Vietnamese from boarding helicopters on the roof of the U.S. embassy "provided a tragic epitaph for twenty-five years of American involvement in Vietnam."[4]

☐ The Vietnam Syndrome

America's humiliation in Vietnam had lasting national consequences. The United States suffered more than 58,000 battle deaths and missing-in-action among the 2.8 million U.S. personnel who served in Vietnam. A new isolationism permeated American foreign policy following defeat in Vietnam. The slogan "No More Vietnams" was used to oppose any U.S. military intervention, whether or not U.S. vital interests were at stake. Disillusionment replaced idealism. American leaders had exaggerated the importance of Vietnam; now Americans were unwilling to believe their leaders when they warned of other dangers.

☐ Rebuilding America's Defenses

The decision to rebuild Western military forces and reassert international leadership on behalf of democratic values gained widespread support in the Western world in the early 1980s. President Ronald Reagan, British Prime Minister Margaret Thatcher, French President François Mitterrand, and German Chancellor Helmut Kohl all pledged to increase their defense efforts and all held fast against a "nuclear freeze" movement that would have locked in Soviet superiority in European-based nuclear weapons.

The Reagan defense buildup extended through 1985—with increases in defense spending, improvements in strategic nuclear weapons, and, perhaps more important, the rebuilding and reequipping of U.S. conventional forces. The American and NATO defense buildup, together with the promise of a new, expensive, and technologically sophisticated race for ballistic missile defenses, forecast heavy additional strains on the weak economy of the Soviet Union. Thus, in 1985, when new Soviet President Mikhail Gorbachev came to power, the stage was set for an end to the Cold War.

Gorbachev announced reductions in the size of the Soviet military and reached agreements with the United States on the reduction of nuclear forces. More important, in 1988, he announced that the Soviet Union would no longer use its military forces to keep communist governments in power in Eastern European nations. This stunning announcement, for which he received the Nobel Peace Prize in 1990, encouraged opposition democratic forces in Poland (the Solidarity movement), Czechoslovakia, Hungary, Bulgaria, Romania, and East Germany. Gorbachev refused to intervene to halt the destruction of the Berlin Wall in 1989, despite pleas by the East German hardline communist leader Erich Honecker.

☐ The Collapse of Communism

When hardliners in the Communist Party, the military, and the KGB attempted the forcible removal of Gorbachev in August 1991, democratic forces rallied to his support. Led by Boris Yeltsin, the first elected president of the Russian Republic, thousands of demonstrators took to the streets; Soviet military forces stood aside. Yeltsin emerged as the most influential leader in the nation. The failed coup hastened the demise of the Communist Party. The party lost legitimacy with the peoples of Russia and the other republics.

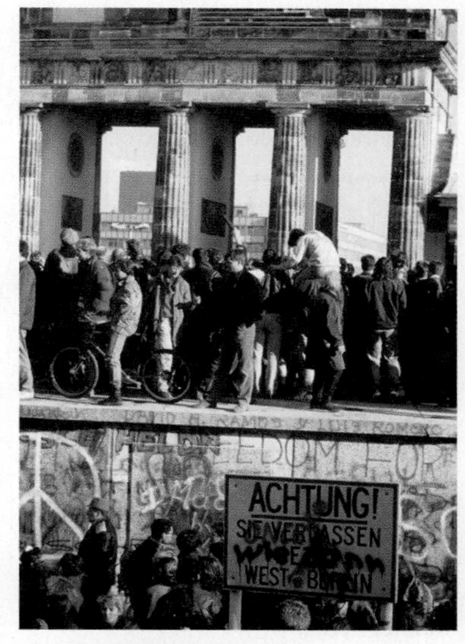

REUNIFYING BERLIN

The fall of the Berlin Wall and the demise of the Soviet Union ushered in a short-lived hope that the United States might be able to pull back from global defense commitments.

☐ The Disintegration of the Soviet Union

Strong independence movements in the republics of the Soviet Union emerged as the authority of the centralized Communist Party in Moscow waned. Lithuania, Estonia, and Latvia—nations that had been forcibly incorporated into the Soviet Union in 1939—led the way to independence in 1991. Soon all 15 republics of the Soviet Union declared their independence, and the Union of Soviet Socialist Republics officially ceased to exist after December 31, 1991. The red flag with its hammer and sickle atop the Kremlin was replaced with the flag of the Russian Republic.

☐ Russia After Communism

The transition from a centralized state-run economy to free markets turned out to be more painful for Russians than expected. Living standards for most people declined, alcoholism and death rates increased, and even average life spans shortened. Ethnic conflict and political separatism, especially in the largely Muslim province of Chechnya, added to Russia's problems. Yeltsin was able to overcome these political challenges and win reelection as president in 1996. But corruption, embezzlement, graft, and organized crime continued to undermine democratic reforms. Poor health eventually forced Yeltsin

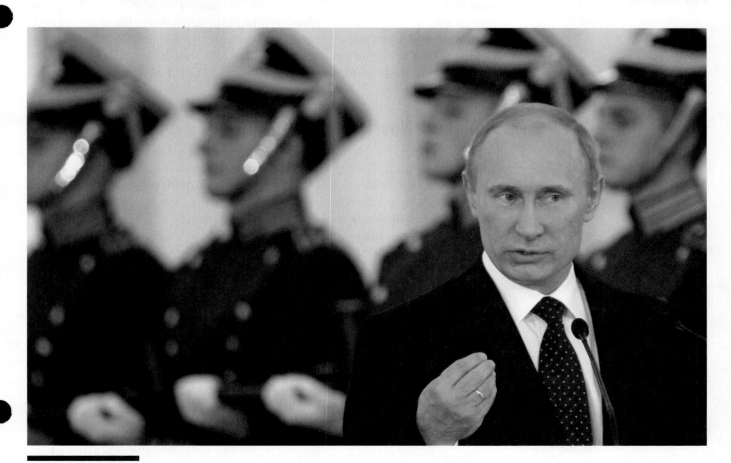

RUSSIA'S STRONGMAN

Russian President Vladimir Putin remains a popular figure in his country despite charges of election fraud.

to turn over power to Vladimir Putin, who himself won election as president of Russia in 2000. Putin became a popular leader among Russians despite his recentralization of power and weakening of democratic institutions. Putin's protégé, Dmitry Medvedev, assumed the presidency of Russia in 2008; Putin occupied the post of prime minister. Putin again assumed the presidency in 2012. He has retained his popularity among the Russian people.

Nuclear Threats

18.3 Trace the evolution of the nuclear weapons policies of the United States.

Nuclear weaponry has made the world infinitely more dangerous. During the Cold War, the nuclear arsenals of the United States and the Soviet Union threatened a human holocaust. Yet, paradoxically, the very destructiveness of nuclear weapons caused leaders on both sides to exercise extreme caution in their relations with each other. Scores of wars, large and small, were fought by different nations during the Cold War years, yet American and Soviet troops never engaged in direct combat against each other.

☐ Deterrence

To maintain nuclear peace during the Cold War, the United States relied primarily on the policy of **deterrence**. Deterrence is based on the notion that a nation can dissuade a *rational* enemy from attacking by maintaining the capacity to destroy the enemy's homeland even *after* the nation has suffered a well-executed surprise attack by the enemy. Deterrence assumes that the worst may happen—a surprise first strike against a nation's nuclear forces. It emphasizes **second-strike capability**—the ability of a nation's forces to survive a surprise attack by the enemy and then to inflict an unacceptable level of destruction on the enemy's homeland. Deterrence is really a *psychological* defense against attack; no effective physical defense against a ballistic missile attack exists even today.

☐ Limiting Nuclear Arms: SALT

The United States and the Soviet Union engaged in negotiations over nuclear arms control for many years. The development of reconnaissance satellites in the 1960s made it possible for each nation to monitor the strategic weapons possessed by the other. Space photography made cheating on agreements more difficult and thus opened the way for both nations to seek stability through arms control.

Following the election of Richard Nixon as president in 1968, the United States, largely guided by former Harvard professor Henry Kissinger (national security adviser to the president and later secretary of state), began negotiations with the Soviet Union over strategic nuclear arms. In 1972, the two nations concluded two and a half years of Strategic Arms Limitation Talks (SALT) about limiting the nuclear arms race. The agreement, **SALT I**, consisted of a treaty limiting antiballistic missiles (ABMs) and an agreement placing a numerical ceiling on offensive missiles. In the **ABM Treaty**, both nations pledged *not* to build ballistic missile defenses. This meant that the populations of both nations in effect would be held hostage against a first strike by either nation.

SALT I was the first step forward on the control of nuclear arms; both sides agreed to continue negotiations. After seven years of difficult negotiations, the United States and the Soviet Union produced the lengthy and complicated **SALT II** treaty in 1979. It set an overall limit on "strategic nuclear launch vehicles"—ICBMs, SLBMs, bombers, and long-range cruise missiles—at 2,250 for each side. It also limited the number of missiles that could have multiple warheads (MIRVs). But when the Soviet Union invaded Afghanistan in 1979, President Carter withdrew the SALT II treaty

deterrence
U.S. approach to deterring any nuclear attack from the Soviet Union by maintaining a second-strike capability.

second-strike capability
Ability of a nation's forces to survive a surprise nuclear attack by the enemy and then to retaliate effectively.

SALT I
First arms limitation treaty between the United States and the Soviet Union, signed in 1972, limiting the total number of offensive nuclear missiles; it included the ABM Treaty that reflected the theory that the population centers of both nations should be left undefended.

ABM Treaty
A formal treaty in 1972 between the United States and the Soviet Union in which each side agreed not to build or deploy antiballistic missiles.

SALT II
Lengthy and complicated treaty between the United States and the Soviet Union, agreed to in 1979 but never ratified by the U.S. Senate, that set limits on all types of strategic nuclear launch vehicles.

from Senate consideration. However, President Carter, and later President Reagan, announced that the United States would abide by the provisions of the unratified SALT II treaty as long as the Soviet Union did so.

Reducing Nuclear Arms: START

In negotiations with the Soviets, the Reagan administration established three central principles of arms control—reductions, equality, and verification. The new goal was to be *reductions* in missiles and warheads, not merely limitations on future numbers and types of weapons, as in previous SALT talks. To symbolize this new direction, President Reagan renamed the negotiations the Strategic Arms *Reduction* Talks, or START.

The **START I** Treaty signed in Moscow in 1991 by Presidents George H. W. Bush and Mikhail Gorbachev was the first agreement between the nuclear powers that actually resulted in the reduction of strategic nuclear weapons. The START I Treaty reduced the total number of deployed strategic nuclear delivery systems to no more than 1,600, a 30 percent reduction from the SALT II level.

A far-reaching **START II** agreement, signed in 1993 by U.S. President George H. W. Bush and Russian President Yeltsin, promised to eliminate the threat of a first-strike nuclear attack by either side. Its most important provision was the agreement to eliminate all multiwarhead (MIRVed) land-based missiles. START II also called for the reduction of overall strategic warheads to 3,500.

START I
First treaty between the United States and the Soviet Union that actually reduced the strategic nuclear arms of the superpowers, signed in 1991.

START II
A treaty between the United States and Russia eliminating all multiwarhead land missiles and reducing nuclear weapons stockpiles; signed in 1993.

The New START Treaty

The New START Treaty was negotiated by Russian President Dimitry Medvedev and U.S. President Barack Obama in Prague, Czech Republic, in 2010. It follows reductions in strategic nuclear weapons agreed upon by Russian President Vladimir Putin and U.S. President George W. Bush in Moscow in 2002.

The New START Treaty reduces overall nuclear warheads for each side to 1,550. Each side is allowed a combination of 700 missile silos and bombers. Each side can determine for itself the composition of its strategic forces—long-range bombers, land-based missiles, submarine-based missiles—consistent with these limits. The effect of the New START Treaty, together with earlier reductions in strategic nuclear weapons, is to reduce the nuclear arsenals of the former adversaries by 87 percent from Cold War levels (see Figure 18.2). Both sides resolved to seek even deeper cuts in nuclear weapons, but no agreement was reached on the development of ballistic missile defense systems.

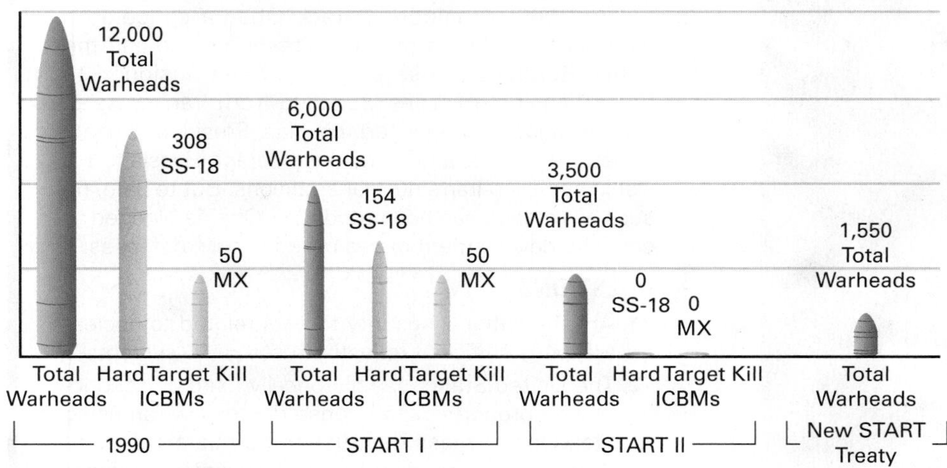

FIGURE 18.2 REDUCING NUCLEAR ARMS

Implementation of the START II Treaty and the new START Treaty will reduce the total number of warheads in both the United States and Russia by over 87 percent from Cold War levels and will completely eliminate hard-target-kill ICBMs.

A Conflicting View

We Should Defend Ourselves Against a Ballistic Missile Attack

Ever since the terrible nuclear blasts at Hiroshima and Nagasaki in Japan in 1945, the world has avoided nuclear war. Peace has been maintained by deterrence—by the threat of devastating nuclear attacks that would be launched in retaliation to an enemy's first strike. But in 1983, President Ronald Reagan urged that instead of deterring war through fear of retaliation, the United States should seek a technological defense against nuclear missiles.

> Our nuclear retaliating forces have deterred war for forty years. The fact is, however, that we have no defense against ballistic missile attack .... In the event that deterrence failed, a president's only recourse would be to surrender or to retaliate. Nuclear retaliation, whether massive or limited, would result in the loss of millions of lives. . . .[a]

"Star Wars"

Reagan's Strategic Defense Initiative (SDI) was a research program designed to explore means of destroying enemy nuclear missiles in space before they could reach their targets. Following President Reagan's initial announcement of SDI in March 1983, the press quickly labeled the effort "Star Wars." In theory, a ballistic missile defense (BMD) system could be based in space, orbiting over enemy missile-launching sites. Should an enemy missile get through the space-based defense, a ground-based BMD system would attempt to intercept warheads as they reentered the atmosphere and approached their targets. SDI included research on laser beams, satellite surveillance, computerized battle-management systems, and "smart" and "brilliant" weapons systems. SDI under President Reagan was a very ambitious program with the goal of creating an "impenetrable shield" that would protect not only the population of the United States but the population of our allies as well.

TESTING AN ABM

A sea-based ABM successfully intercepted a falling satilite in 2008.

Protection Against Nuclear Terrorism

The end of the Cold War refocused SDI away from defense against a massive Russian missile attack to more limited yet more likely threats. Today, the principal nuclear threats are missiles launched by terrorists or a "rogue state." These threats are considered "nondeterrable" because terrorists and terrorist states ignore retaliatory threats. President George H. W. Bush redirected SDI toward defending against more limited yet potentially devastating missile attacks.

The success of the Patriot antiballistic missile in destroying short-range Iraqi SCUD missiles during the Gulf War in 1991 demonstrated that enemy missiles could be intercepted in flight. (The Patriot is a ground-based "tactical" weapon designed to protect specific military targets.) However, developing an effective antiballistic missile that can intercept and destroy another missile in space proved to be more difficult, although not impossible.

The Future of BMDs

As a Reagan-era initiative, partisanship has tended to cloud the debate over BMDs. In 1993, President Clinton announced the termination of the separate SDI organization, but he reassured the nation that research would continue on the ground-based ballistic missile defenses. President George W. Bush notified the Russians in 2002 that the United States was withdrawing from provisions of the ABM Treaty of 1972 that prohibited the development, testing, or deployment of new ballistic missile defense systems.

President George W. Bush announced a limited deployment of sea-based and ground-based missile interceptors and advanced Patriot missiles in 2004. The president envisioned an incremental growth of an antiballistic missile capability that would be directed at potential attacks from terrorist states. Currently, the United States has a limited BMD system based in Alaska, presumably to defend against missiles from North Korea.

In 2009, President Barack Obama canceled a planned deployment of BMD sites in Poland and the Czech Republic; these sites had been designed to defend against missiles launched from Iran. Russian leaders vigorously opposed this plan. President Obama hoped that cancellation would encourage Russia to assist in curtailing Iran's nuclear ambitions. But to date, no such assistance has been rendered. Obama pledged to continue development of sea-based missile defenses.

QUESTIONS

1. Are the national security threats related to nuclear weapons sufficient to justify costly BMD systems?
2. The United States has historically used a "second-strike," proportional response doctrine when using weapons of mass destruction. Is this a sufficient deterrent when dealing with potential, nuclear rogue states or nonstate nuclear actors?

[a]President Ronald Reagan, *The President's Strategic Defense Initiative*, The White House, January 3, 1985.

Nuclear Terrorism

Even as the threat of a large-scale nuclear attack recedes, the threats arising from "nondeterrable" sources are increasing. Today, the principal nondeterrable threats are missiles launched by terrorist nations, notably North Korea and Iran. Over time, global nuclear and ballistic missile proliferation steadily increases the likelihood of these types of threats. Terrorist attacks are considered "nondeterrable" because the threat of nuclear retaliation is largely meaningless.

Defending against terrorist missile attacks requires the development and deployment of **ballistic missile defense (BMD)** systems, weapons capable of detecting, intercepting, and destroying ballistic missiles while they are in flight. At present there is no defense against a ballistic missile attack on American cities (see *A Conflicting View*: We Should Defend Ourselves Against a Ballistic Missile Attack).

ballistic missile defense (BMD)
Weapons systems capable of detecting, intercepting, and destroying missiles in flight.

terrorism
Title 22 of the U.S. Code, Section 2656 (d): "The term 'terrorism' means premeditated, politically motivated violence perpetrated against noncombatant targets by subnational groups or clandestine agents, usually intended to influence an audience."

The War on Terrorism

18.4 Describe the nature of terrorism and the U.S. response to terrorism.

Terrorism is a political act. The deliberate targeting of civilians, the infliction of widespread destruction, and the resulting media portrayals of the pain and suffering of victims are designed to call attention to political grievances and to instill fear in people. (The Latin root of the term *terrere* means "to frighten.") The horror of terrorist acts and their unpredictability add to public fear—people can neither anticipate nor prepare for tragedies inflicted upon them. Terrorists hope to undermine the confidence of people in their government to protect them, and so they will conclude that submission to the terrorists' demands is preferable to living in a continuing climate of anxiety and uncertainty.

Global Terrorism

Global terrorism has evolved over the years into highly sophisticated networks operating in many countries. Prior to the attacks on New York's World Trade Center and the Pentagon on September 11, 2001, most Americans thought of terrorism as foreign. Terrorist acts on American soil had been rare; the most destructive attack—the Oklahoma City bombing of a federal building in 1995—had been carried out by domestic terrorists. But the 9/11 attacks were on an unprecedented scale and revealed a sophisticated global plot against America.

A loose-knit network of terrorist cells (al-Quaeda) organized by a wealthy Saudi Arabian, Osama bin Laden, was engaged in global terrorism. Al-Qaeda's political grievances included America's support of Israel in Middle East conflicts and an American presence in Islamic holy lands, notably Saudi Arabia. Several nations share these grievances and, more important, provided support and haven to al-Qaeda and similar terrorist organizations. The principal base of support and sanctuary for al-Qaeda was the repressive and violent Taliban regime of Afghanistan.

Declaring War on Terrorism

On the evening of September 11, President George W. Bush spoke to the American people from the Oval Office in a nationally televised address:

> The pictures of airplanes flying into buildings, fires burning, huge structures collapsing, have filled us with disbelief, terrible sadness, and a quiet, unyielding anger. These mass murders were intended to frighten our nation into chaos and retreat. But they failed; our country is strong .... These deliberate and deadly attacks were more than acts of terror. They were acts of war.

The Game, the Rules, the Players

The Use of Force: Operation Desert Storm

Saddam Hussein's invasion of Kuwait on August 2, 1990, was apparently designed to restore his military prestige after an indecisive war against Iran; to secure additional oil revenues to finance the continued buildup of Iraqi military power; and to intimidate (and perhaps invade) Saudi Arabia and the Gulf states, thereby securing control over a major share of the world's oil reserves.

The Iraqi invasion met with a surprisingly swift response by the United Nations, with Security Council resolutions condemning the invasion, demanding an immediate withdrawal, and imposing a trade embargo and economic sanctions. President George H. W. Bush immediately set to work to stitch together a coalition military force that would eventually include 30 nations. Early on, the president described the U.S. military deployment as "defensive," but he soon became convinced that neither diplomacy nor an economic blockade would dislodge Saddam from Kuwait and so ordered the military to prepare an "offensive" option.

The top U.S. military commanders—including the chair of the Joint Chiefs of Staff, General Colin Powell, and the commander in the field, General Norman Schwarzkopf—had been field officers in Vietnam, and they were resolved not to repeat the mistakes of that war. They were reluctant to go into battle without the full support of the American people. If ordered to fight, they wanted to employ overwhelming and decisive military force; they wanted to avoid the gradual escalation, protracted conflict, target limitations, and political interference in the conduct of the war that had characterized the U.S. military's efforts in Vietnam. Accordingly, they presented the president with a plan that called for a very large military buildup involving nearly 500,000 troops. Coalition forces also included British and French heavy armored units, and Egyptian, Syrian, Saudi, and other Arab forces.

From Baghdad, CNN reporters Bernard Shaw and Peter Arnett were startled on the night of January 16 when Operation Desert Storm began with an air attack on key installations in the city. Iraqi forces were also surprised, despite the prompt timing of the attack; Saddam had assured them that the United States lacked the resolve to fight.

The success of the coalition air force was spectacular. American TV audiences saw videotapes of laser-guided bombs entering the doors and air shafts of enemy bunkers. Civilian damage was lower than in any previous air war. After five weeks of air war, intelligence estimated that nearly half the Iraqi tanks and artillery in the field had been destroyed, demoralized troops were hiding in deep shelters, and the battlefield had been isolated and "prepared" for ground operations.

General Schwarzkopf's plan for the ground war emphasized deception and maneuver. While Iraqi forces prepared for attacks from the south and the east coast, he sent heavily armed columns in a "Hail Mary" play—a wide sweep to the west, outflanking and cutting off Iraqi forces in the battle area. On the night of February 24, the ground attack began. Marines breached ditches and minefields and raced directly to the Kuwait airport; army helicopter air assaults lunged deep into Iraq; armored columns raced northward across the desert to outflank Iraqi forces and then attack them from the west, while a surge in air attacks kept Iraqi forces holed up in their bunkers. Iraqi troops surrendered in droves, highways from Kuwait City became a massive junkyard of Iraqi vehicles, and Iraqi forces that tried to fight were quickly destroyed. After 100 hours of ground fighting, President George H. W. Bush ordered a cease-fire.

The United States had achieved a decisive military victory quickly and with remarkably few casualties. The president resisted calls to expand the original objectives of the war and go on to capture Baghdad, to destroy the Iraqi economy, to encourage Iraq's disintegration as a nation, or to kill Saddam, although it was expected that his defeat would lead to his ouster. Although the war left many political issues unresolved, it was the most decisive military outcome the United States had achieved since the end of World War II.[a] President Bush chose to declare victory and celebrate the return of American troops.

QUESTION

1. Do you think the relative ease with which the U.S. military defeated conventional forces in the field in the first and second Gulf War created, among the American public, unrealistic expectations about warfare?

[a]See Harry G. Summers, Jr., *On Strategy II: A Critical Analysis of the Gulf War.* New York: Dell, 1992.

The president outlined a broad "response to terrorism" to be fought both at home and abroad through diplomatic, military, financial, investigative, homeland security, and humanitarian means. He warned that the new war on terrorism would require a long-term sustained effort. It would require Americans to accept new restrictions on their lives, including an Airport Security Act federalizing security at U.S. airports and instituting new strict security measures, and a USA PATRIOT Act (Provide Appropriate Tools Required to Intercept and Obstruct Terrorism) expanding the authority of the attorney general and federal law-enforcement agencies to fight domestic terrorism. It would require the creation of a new Department of Homeland Security designed to coordinate many federal, state, and local law-enforcement agencies charged with responsibility for dealing with acts of terror.

☐ Afghanistan—Operation Enduring Freedom

The military phase of the war on terrorism began October 7, 2001, when U.S. Air Force and Navy aircraft began attacks on known al-Qaeda bases in Afghanistan, and U.S. Special Forces organized and led anti-Taliban fighters, including several tribal groups, in a campaign against the Taliban regime. A coalition of nations participated in Operation Enduring Freedom; some, including Britain and Canada, contributed troops, while others, including Pakistan, Saudi Arabia, and Uzbekistan, informally allowed U.S. forces to base operations on their territory. Kabul, the capital of Afghanistan, was occupied by anti-Taliban forces on November 13, 2001 (see "The War in Afghanistan" later in this chapter).

☐ Asymmetrical Warfare

Traditionally, the United States structured its military tactics and forces to confront conventional threats—national armies with heavy armor, tanks and artillery, mechanized infantry, and combat aircraft. During the Cold War, U.S. forces were designed to confront heavy Soviet armor and artillery in Central Europe, in a manner similar, albeit more violent, to the armies that fought in World War II. The Gulf War in 1991 demonstrated the superiority of American forces in large-scale conventional operations.

But the war on terror required the United States to reshape its military planning to confront unconventional (or asymmetrical) wars—lightly armed, irregular enemy forces engaging in tactics such as ambushes, hidden explosives, suicide bombings, and hostage takings. America's enemies are fully aware of the overwhelming firepower of conventional U.S. military forces. Consequently they seek to minimize U.S. advantage in firepower in a variety of ways. They choose terrain that inhibits the use of conventional tank, artillery, and air power—jungles and mountains where these conventional forces cannot operate as effectively as in open country. They also choose built-up urban areas where civilian populations inhibit U.S. forces from employing their full firepower. They avoid direct confrontations with large American units, blending in with the population and seeming to disappear in the presence of U.S. combat forces.

The War in Iraq

18.5 Explain the reasons for the U.S. military intervention in Iraq and assess the progress and outcome of that intervention.

At the end of the Gulf War in 1991, the Iraqi regime of Saddam Hussein agreed to destroy all of its chemical and biological weapons and to end its efforts to acquire nuclear weapons. United Nations inspectors were to verify Iraqi compliance with these conditions. But Saddam's regime refused to cooperate; in 1998, he ordered the inspectors out of the country. Over a

18.1
18.2
18.3
18.4
18.5
18.6

What Do You Think?

When Should the United States Use Military Force?

All modern presidents have acknowledged that the most agonizing decisions they have made were to send U.S. military forces into combat. These decisions cost lives. The American people are willing to send their sons and daughters into danger—and even to see some of them wounded and killed—but *only* if a president convinces them that the outcome "is worth dying for." A president must be able to explain why they lost their lives and to justify their sacrifice.

Only to Protect Vital Interests?

The U.S. military learned many bitter lessons in its long bloody experience in Vietnam. Among those lessons was what became known as the Powell Doctrine, advanced by then chair of the Joint Chiefs of Staff, General Colin Powell:

- The United States should commit its military forces only in support of vital national interests.
- If military forces are committed, they must have clearly defined military objectives—the destruction of enemy forces and/or the capture of enemy-held territory.
- Any commitment of U.S. forces must be of sufficient strength to ensure overwhelming and decisive victory with the fewest possible casualties.
- Before committing U.S. military forces, there must be some reasonable assurances that the effort has the support of the American people and their representatives in Congress.
- The commitment of U.S. military forces should be a last resort, after political, economic, and diplomatic efforts have proven ineffective.

These guidelines for the use of military force are widely supported within the U.S. military itself.[a] Contrary to Hollywood stereotypes, military leaders are extremely reluctant to go to war when no vital interest of the United States is at stake, where there are no clear-cut military objectives, without the support of Congress or the American people, or without sufficient force to achieve speedy and decisive victory with minimal casualties. They are wary of seeing their troops placed in danger merely to advance diplomatic goals, or to engage in "peacekeeping," or to "stabilize governments," or to "show the flag." They are reluctant to undertake humanitarian missions while being shot at. They do not like to risk their soldiers' lives under "rules of engagement" that limit their ability to defend themselves.

In Support of Important Political Objectives?

In contrast to military leaders, political leaders and diplomats often reflect the view that "war is a continuation of politics by other means"—a view commonly attributed to nineteenth-century German theorist of war Karl von Clausewitz. Military force may be used to protect interests that are important but not necessarily vital. Otherwise, the United States would be rendered largely impotent in world affairs. A diplomat's ability to achieve a satisfactory result often depends on the expressed or implied threat of military force. The distinguished international political theorist Hans Morgenthau wrote, "Since military strength is the obvious measure of a nation's power, its demonstration serves to impress others with that nation's power."[b]

Currently, American military forces must be prepared to carry out a variety of missions in addition to the conduct of conventional war:

- Demonstrating U.S. resolve in crisis situations.
- Demonstrating U.S. support for democratic governments.
- Protecting U.S. citizens living abroad.
- Peacemaking among warring factions or nations.
- Peacekeeping where hostile factions or nations have accepted a peace agreement.
- Providing humanitarian aid often under warlike conditions.
- Assisting in an international war against drug trafficking.

In pursuit of such objectives, recent U.S. presidents have sent troops to Lebanon in 1982 to stabilize the government (Reagan), to Grenada in 1983 to rescue American medical students and restore democratic government (Reagan), to Panama in 1989 to oust drug-trafficking General Manuel Antonio Noriega from power and to protect U.S. citizens (Bush, Sr.); to Somalia in 1992–93 to provide emergency humanitarian aid (Bush, Sr., and Clinton); to Haiti in 1994 to restore constitutional government (Clinton) and again to Haiti in 2004 (Bush, Jr.); and to Bosnia and Kosovo in 1999–2000 (Clinton) for peacekeeping among warring ethnic factions.

QUESTIONS

1. Do you think that vital economic interests are the only reason to justify the use of military force?
2. Given the dramatic expansion of diverse democratic regimes around the world, does the United States need to continue to defend democracy, or use promoting democracy as a basis for using military force?

[a]See Caspar W. Weinberger, "The Uses of Military Force." Arlington Va.: American Forces Information Services Survey, 1985, pp. 2–11.
[b]Morgenthau, *Politics among Nations*, p. 80.

12-year period, Iraq violated at least a dozen UN resolutions. Following a U.S. military buildup in the region in late 2002, Saddam allowed UN inspectors to return, but continued to obstruct their work. On March 19, 2003, after giving Saddam a 48-hour warning to leave Iraq, the United States and Great Britain launched air strikes designed to eliminate Saddam and his top command.

□ Counterinsurgency

Counterinsurgency includes military, paramilitary, political, economic, and psychological actions designed to defeat guerilla forces. The fight against terrorist organizations in the Middle East and Africa inspired the U.S. military to develop a counterinsurgency (COIN) capability. Much of the work in doing so is attributed to General David Petraeous, former commander of U.S. forces in Iraq and Afghanistan.

Originally, COIN doctrine called for:

- An expansion in the size of the Army and the Marine Corps in recognition of the need for more 'boots on the ground.'
- the transformation of a division-sized Army into one organized in Brigade Command Teams (roughly one-third the size of a division).
- heavier reliance on Army Reserve and National Guard units (many reserve and guard units perform multiple tours of duty in Iraq and Afghanistan).
- The introductions of new equipment, including mine-resistant and ambush protection vehicles (MAPVs) and unmanned aerial vehicles (UAVs or drones) capable of both reconnaissance and attack missions.
- An overhaul of counterinsurgency doctrine to shift operations away from 'enemy-centric' armed conflict and toward a 'population-centric' approach emphasizing political goals and the importance of social and cultural factors in military operations.

Yet some military leaders remain resistant to the new emphasis on counterinsurgency. They argue that the true lesson of Afghanistan and Iraq is that U.S. forces should avoid protracted commitments to 'peacekeeping' and 'nationbuilding' and instead undertake only those military operations that promise rapid, decisive results. Moreover, the emphasis on counterinsurgency may adversely affect America's capability to confront an attack by the large conventional forces of North Korea on South Korea. And it may also inhibit U.S. forces if they are ever confronted with a conventional war with a major Mideast adversary like Iran.

The United States withdrawal from Iraq and Afghanistan (see below) has tended to deemphasize counterinsurgency within the military. Nonetheless, the United States pledges itself toward "achieving our core goal of disrupting, dismantling and defeating al-Qaeda and preventing Afghanistan from ever being a safe haven again."

□ The Drawdown

The Obama military strategy now calls for a reduction in the "overall capacity" of U.S. forces. Officially the intent is to have forces that are 'smaller, leaner, agile, and flexible.' The reduction is in part justified by the withdrawal of conventional U.S. forces from Iraq and Afghanistan. But the drawdown goes beyond the forces previously committed to those countries. Current forces remain close to postwar levels (see Table 18.1). The impact of the drawdown is being felt primarily in the readiness of forces. Flight training has been reduced for pilots, large-scale maneuvers for ground units have been canceled, and fewer ships are available for immediate deployment. Future weapons programs have been drawn out or shelved altogether.

The drawdown is occurring despite the Obama Administration's announced "pivot to Asia"—"a rebalancing toward the Asian-Pacific region." The states objective

18.1
18.2
18.3
18.4
18.5
18.6

TABLE 18.1 U.S. MILITARY FORCE LEVELS

	1990	2000	2012
Active duty military personnel (in millions)	2.1	1.4	1.4
Army divisions	18	10	10 (45 BCT)
Navy carrier battle groups	15	12	11
Marine expeditionary forces	3	3	3
Air Force fighter wings	24	12	(10 AEFs)

SOURCE: Author compilation of data from various editions of International Institute of Strategic Studies, *The Military Balance*. London: IISS.
NOTE: BCT = Brigade Combat Team; AEF = Aerospace Expeditionary Forces. The Army maintains ten active duty divisions. However, the Army has been reorganized into 45 Brigade Combat Teams (BCTs). Each BCT includes about 3,500 soldiers. BCTs may be armored (tanks), mechanized infantry, airborne (paratroopers), air assault (helicopters), or Stryker (combined arms). The Air Force has been reorganized into ten Aerospace Expeditionary Forces (AEFs). Each AEF combines bomber, fighter, attack, refueling, and reconnaissance aircraft.

of the pivot to Asia is to strengthen strategic relationships with Japan, South Korea, the Philippines, India, and other Southeast Asian nations, against the growing power of China in the region.

☐ Stretched Too Thin?

The U.S. Military forces are currently deployed in more than 120 countries around the world. These deployments include South Korea, Afghanistan, Qatar, Bahrain, Saudi Arabia, Kuwait, Bosnia, Kosovo, the Philippines, Japan, Cuba (Guantanamo), Colombia, Honduras, and the NATO countries, including Great Britain, Germany, Italy, Ireland, and Turkey.

Over the years, U.S. military forces have been assigned increasing numbers of missions—war-fighting, peacekeeping, nationbuilding, counterinsurgency, and humanitarian aid. Yet force levels have remained minimal. Experience has taught the U.S. military that casualties can be kept low only when overwhelming military force is employed quickly and decisively. Lives are lost when minimal forces are sent into combat, when they have inadequate air combat support, or when they are extended over too broad a front. Current numbers of Army and Air Force combat units, and the limited transport and support services available to the military, are inadequate to meet two major regional conflicts simultaneously—the historic two-and-a-half war doctrine. Potential regional foes—for example, Iran and North Korea—deploy modern heavy armor and artillery forces. Both appear to be nuclear capable. The United States is not prepared to fight wars in the Middle East and on the Korean Peninsula at the same time.

☐ Operation Iraqi Freedom

At different times, President George W. Bush stated the purposes of "Operation Iraqi Freedom" as (1) the elimination of Iraq's weapons of mass destruction, (2) a "regime change" for Iraq to end the threat that Saddam posed for his neighbors and to free the Iraqi people from his oppressive rule, and (3) to ensure that Saddam would not harbor or assist terrorist organizations. But President Bush and Secretary of State Colin Powell failed to secure UN Security Council approval for military action. Among the permanent members of the Security Council, only the British, with the strong support of Prime Minister Tony Blair, were prepared to offer significant military support for the war against Saddam. Public opinion in America supported military action, but public opinion in Europe opposed it. (In contrast, see *Compared to What?* World Opinion About the United States.) France and Germany led the diplomatic opposition; Turkey refused to let U.S. troops use its territory to attack Iraq; and the United States was obliged to rely primarily on Kuwait, Qatar, and the other smaller Gulf states for regional support.

American and British soldiers and Marines took just 21 days to sweep the 350 miles from the Kuwait border to downtown Baghdad. The British 3rd Armored

Division, with Australian support, captured the port city of Basra; the U.S. 3rd Infantry Division moved up the west side of the Euphrates River; and the U.S. 1st Marine Division moved up the east side. Special Operations Forces, together with elements of the 101st Airborne Division, joined Kurdish forces in northern Iraq. Special Operations Forces also acted quickly to secure Iraq's oil fields and prevent their destruction. At first, progress was hindered by the requirement that soldiers wear heavy chemical protection gear and carry decontamination equipment. But neither chemical nor biological weapons were used against U.S. forces. The advance on Baghdad was speeded up, and the city was captured with precious few casualties.

□ The Occupation of Iraq

The American occupation of Iraq started out poorly, and worsened over time. Planning for a postwar Iraq appeared nonexistent. The U.S. administrator for Iraq, Paul Bremmer, began by dismissing the entire Iraqi Army, sending thousands of well-armed, unemployed young men into the streets. The United States promised to restore infrastructure—water, electricity, roads—yet Bremmer pursued a policy of dismissing virtually all Iraqi managers and technicians on the grounds that they had been Baathists (Saddam's ruling party members). Later, the United States would be obliged to begin recruiting and training an Iraqi army and police force and bringing in U.S. contract workers, managers, and technicians. Bremmer was fired after one year.[5]

THE "FLASH" PATCH OF THE 3RD INFANTRY DIVISION

Along with the 1st Marine Division, this unit was at the tip of the spear of the drive toward Baghdad in 2003.

Soon, Iraqi street mobs that had earlier torn down Saddam's statue began demonstrations against the American presence. An insurgent movement seemed to surprise Secretary of Defense Donald Rumsfeld. He steadfastly refused to send additional U.S. troops to Iraq to handle the insurgency and insisted that a new Iraqi government could eventually recruit and train enough troops to contain the insurgency. No weapons of mass destruction were found despite an intensive search. Saddam himself was captured and turned over to the Iraqis, who conducted a bizarre trial and executed him.

□ Civil War

The population of Iraq is composed of three major factions: the Kurds, who occupy most of northeastern Iraq; the Shiites, who occupy most of southern Iraq; and the Sunnis, who occupy central Iraq. Baghdad itself is divided between Sunni and Shiite neighborhoods. The Sunnis have long dominated Iraq. Saddam's family was Sunni. Yet the Shiites are the largest faction, accounting for more than half of the total population of Iraq. Over the years, the Kurds have fought for a separate Kurdistan, an outcome strongly opposed by neighboring Turkey.

Iraq gradually disintegrated into a bloody civil war, with Sunni and Shiite forces committing atrocities against each other. By 2006, most of the violence in Iraq was occurring among various factions; thousands of Iraqis were victims of sectarian killings. The Shiites, the majority of Iraq's population, gained power for the first time in more than 1,000 years. Above all, the Shiites are interested in preserving that power. The Sunnis fear displacement and the loss of their traditional position of power in Iraq. The Kurds seek at a minimum quasi-independence and control over the oil resources in their region. The Shiites also seek control over oil resources in southern Iraq. But the areas with the largest Sunni population lack oil resources, so the Sunnis fight to maintain control of all of Iraq. Today, corruption remains rampant throughout the country; the judiciary is weak; oil production is down.

□ The Insurgency

Attacks on U.S. forces and Iraqi army and police grew in intensity and deadliness, month after month. Most attacks against Americans came from disaffected Sunni Arabs, including former elements of Saddam's regime. Al-Qaeda was responsible for a portion of the violence, including the more spectacular suicide attacks, truck bombs, and attacks on religious and political targets. The insurgency raised the flag of "Jihad"

Compared to What?

World Opinion About the United States

Overall, world opinion about the United States remains positive. In 28 of 38 nations surveyed by the Pew Research Center, more than half of the persons interviewed expressed a favorable view of the United States. The highest ratings were found in Europe, Latin America, and the Asian Pacific region. But evaluations in predominantly Muslim nations were decidedly negative. Ratings of the United States were particularly high in Israel.

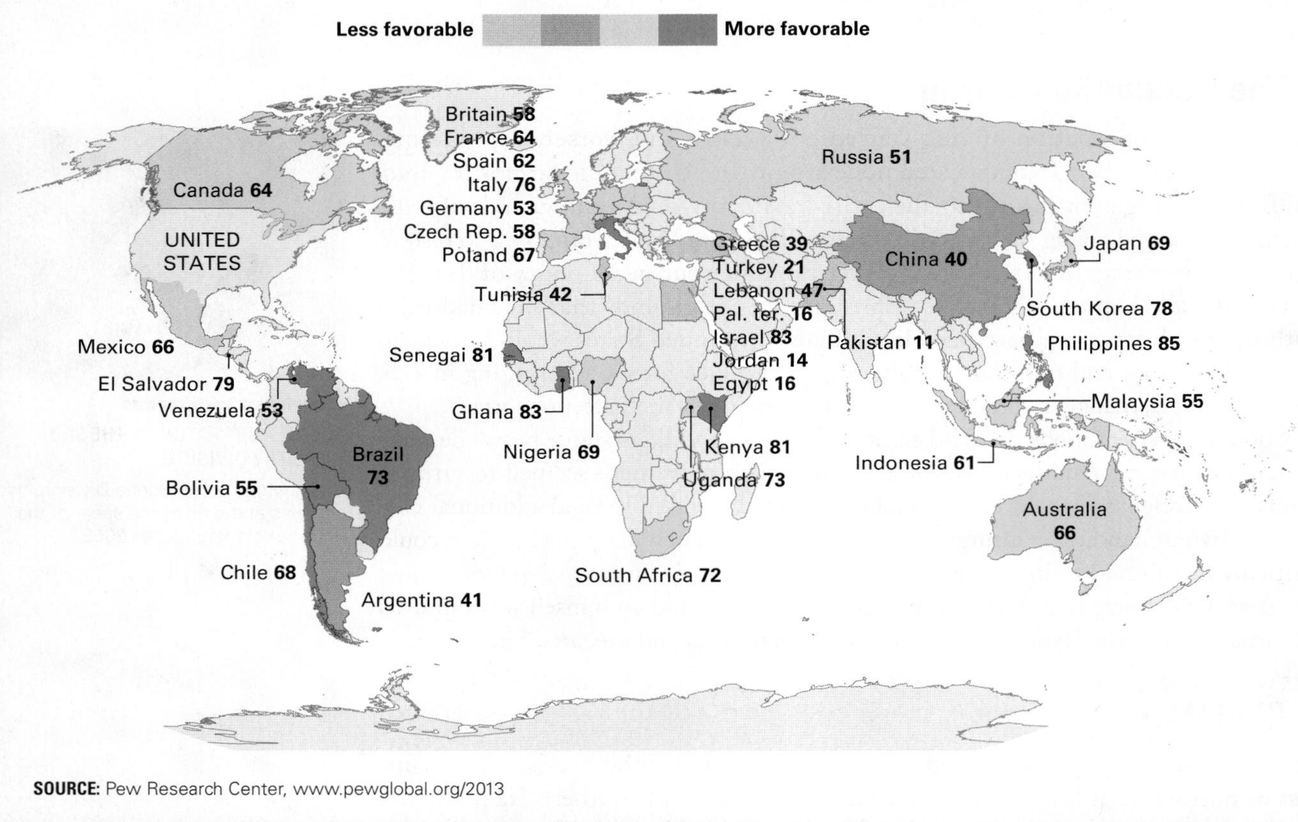

SOURCE: Pew Research Center, www.pewglobal.org/2013

and brought in thousands of Islamic radical foreign fighters. The Shiites organized their own militia, the strongest being the Mahdi Army, with as many as 60,000 fighters led by Moqtada al-Sadr. Large areas of Iraq came under the control of one or another of these insurgent groups.

American military forces suffered a gruesome toll in lives and limbs. By 2010, over 4,000 American troops had been killed, many from "improvised explosive devices." U.S. Army and Marine forces approached the "breaking point." Nearly every Army and Marine combat unit, and several National Guard and Reserve units, were rotated into Iraq more than once. The strain on U.S. forces worldwide became clearly evident, with both personnel and equipment wearing down.

☐ The "Surge"

The sweeping Democratic victory in the congressional elections of 2006 was widely attributed to popular disaffection with the war in Iraq. Democrats gained control of both the House and the Senate. Many of their supporters expected them to end the war by cutting off funds for the prosecution of the war. At a minimum, opponents of the war wanted Congress to set a timetable for the reduction of U.S. troops in Iraq. But when staring directly at the prospect of cutting off funds for troops in the field, Congress blinked. Resolutions to end the war or to force U.S. troop reductions failed.

Instead, President Bush announced a "surge" in troop strength designed to improve security in Iraq and allow the Iraqi government to reach "benchmarks" in resolving civil strife. The "surge" involved increasing U.S. troop levels in Iraq from roughly 138,000 to 160,000. In January 2007, the president appointed a new commander for Iraq, General David Petraeus.

Petraeus reported to Congress that the "surge" was working, that progress was being made in stabilizing Iraq and in training Iraqi forces, that U.S. troop levels could be reduced to presurge levels, but that some U.S. forces might be needed in Iraq for 10 years or more. He argued that a timetable for troop reductions would be counterproductive.

Loss of Public Support

It had become clear that the American public no longer supported the war and wanted U.S. troops withdrawn from Iraq as soon as possible. There was frustration over the failure of the Iraqi government to make progress in resolving sectarian differences. International opinion opposed the continuation of U.S. military occupation of Iraq. Years after the start of the war, violence continued and there was no end in sight. The U.S. military was weakened overall by the stresses placed upon it by the fighting in Iraq.

Shortly after the war in Iraq began, most Americans thought Iraq was worth going to war over. Indeed, this opinion climbed to 76 percent immediately following the capture of Baghdad. As American casualties mounted and the previously accomplished mission was unrealized, mass opinion in support of the war declined rapidly. By late 2004, the majority of Americans believed it was "not worth going to war" over Iraq (see Figure 18.3). Moreover, a majority of Americans came to believe that President Bush and leaders of his administration had "deliberately misled" the public about whether Iraq had possessed weapons of mass destruction.

Withdrawal of U.S. Forces

In the presidential campaign of 2008, Barack Obama pledged to end the war in Iraq "responsibly." He warned against "an occupation of undetermined length, with undetermined costs and undetermined consequences." Upon taking office in January 2009, Obama ordered the U.S. military to plan for a phased withdrawal of American combat forces from Iraq. The U.S. military was ordered to "redeploy" combat brigades at a pace of one to two per month over a 16-month period, ending in the summer of 2010. A "residual force" was to remain in Iraq to conduct targeted counterterrorism missions and protect American diplomatic personnel. But the Iraqi government, headed by Prime Minister Nuri al-Maliki, refused to grant immunity to U.S. troops in Iraq,

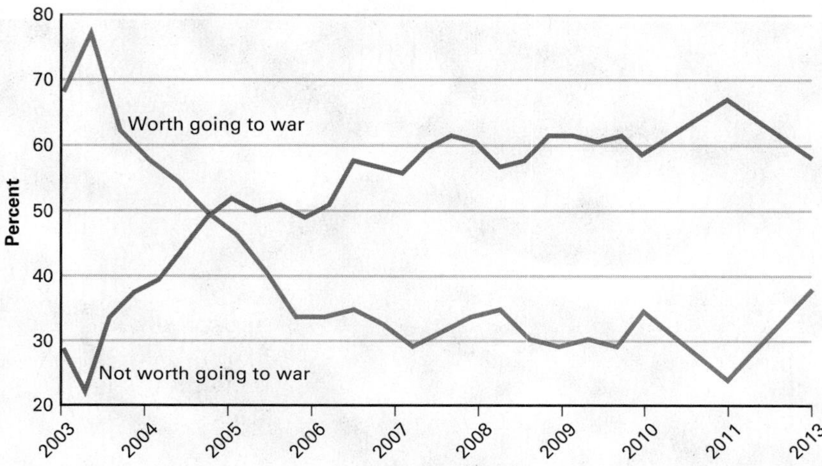

FIGURE 18.3 CHANGING PUBLIC OPINION ABOUT THE WAR IN IRAQ

Support for the war in Iraq among the American people declined over time.

SOURCE: Various polls as reported in *The Polling Report*, www.pollingreport.com

18.1

18.2

18.3

18.4

18.5

18.6

a necessary condition for their continued presence in that country. President Obama ordered all remaining U.S. troops to leave Iraq by the end of 2011.

The American public remains unconvinced that military intervention in Iraq was worth the heavy price paid: over 4,500 American service members killed and 35,000 wounded. Sporadic violence continues in Iraq and the future of democracy in that embattled country remains in doubt.

The War in Afghanistan

18.6 Explain the war in Afghanistan and assess its progress.

It was the Taliban regime in Afghanistan that provided al-Qaeda with safe haven. And it was al-Qaeda that was responsible for the September 11, 2001, attacks on the New York World Trade Center and the Pentagon. On October 7, 2001, U.S. Air Force and Navy aircraft began attacks on al-Qaeda bases in Afghanistan. U.S. Special Operations Forces aided the anti-Taliban fighters in that country, and Kabul, the capital, fell to these forces on November 13, 2001.

ISAF

United States and NATO created an International Security Assistance Force (ISAF) in 2002 to conduct comprehensive counterinsurgency operations, to support the development of the Afghan National Security Forces, and to provide a secure environment for the development of a legitimate government in Afghanistan. A meeting in Bonn, Germany, of various Afghan political and military groups produced general agreement on the installation of a new government in Kabul, headed by Hamid Karzai. The Karzai government exercises less than full control over Afghanistan's various tribal chiefs (or "warlords"), who exercise substantial independent power throughout the country.

Obama's War

While campaigning for president in 2008, Senator Barack Obama drew a sharp distinction between the war in Iraq and the war in Afghanistan. Iraq, he claimed, had diverted America's attention away from the greater dangers posed by al-Qaeda and

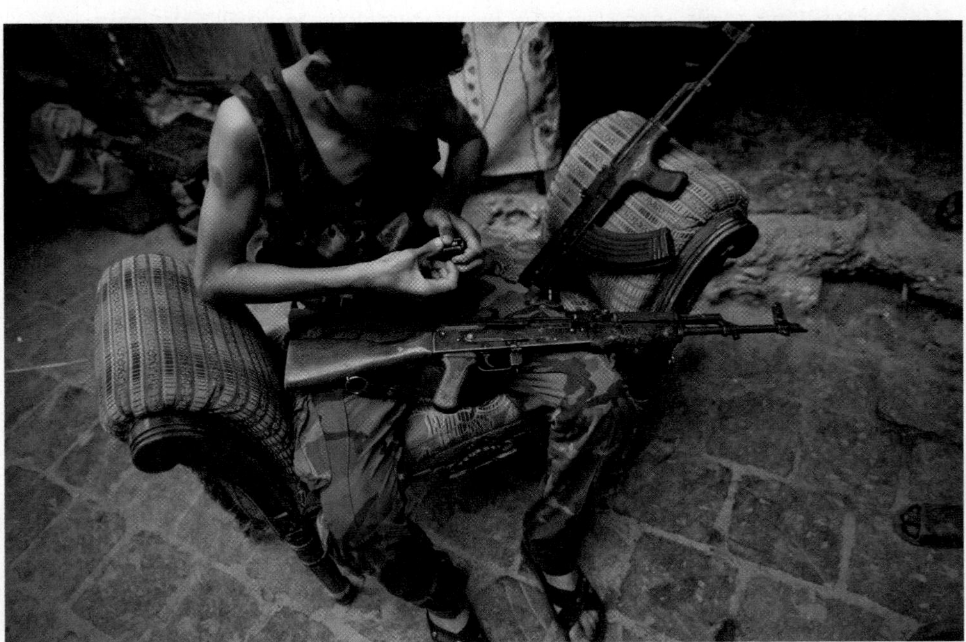

Taliban forces in Afghanistan. Shortly after entering the White House, President Obama ordered a strategic review of the situation in Afghanistan and neighboring Pakistan. The review concluded that the situation was "increasingly perilous," with al-Qaeda and its Taliban allies controlling large sections of both Afghanistan and Pakistan. Additional combat brigades were to be sent to the region as well as thousands of trainers for Afghanistan army and police forces.

Afghanistan became the Obama administration's principal military effort. In December 2009, President Obama ordered a substantial increase in U.S. combat forces in Afghanistan. Yet, at the same time, he pledged that "our troops will begin to come home" in the summer of 2011. Afghan government in 2011, with a view to completing the transition by 2014.

☐ Counterinsurgency Operations

The announced goal of the U.S. policy is to "disrupt, dismantle, and defeat" Al Qaida in both Afghanistan and Pakistan. The policy suggests that al-Qaeda will no longer find safe haven across the border in Pakistan. Economic and military aid to Pakistan is to be contingent upon that country's commitment to its own security and its willingness to "confront violent extremists." Afghanistan will offer a test of the U.S. military's concept of asymmetrical (counterinsurgency) warfare.

☐ Limited Objectives

U.S. policy recognizes that Afghanistan's 25 million people are divided along ethnic lines. The central government in Kabul exercises little control over a country the size of Texas. U.S. strategy appears to be to win over local tribes and leaders, including Taliban forces that are not allied to al-Qaeda. The objective of U.S. policy is not necessarily to bring Western-style democracy to Afghanistan, but rather to ensure that the country does not become a safe haven fort al-Qaeda and its terrorist allies.

In an Afghanistan–Pakistan Security Review in 2011, the Obama Administration attempted to clarify the overall goal of the mission in that area: "It is not to defeat every last threat to the security of Afghanistan, because it is the Afghans who must secure their country. And it is not nation building, because it is the Afghans who must

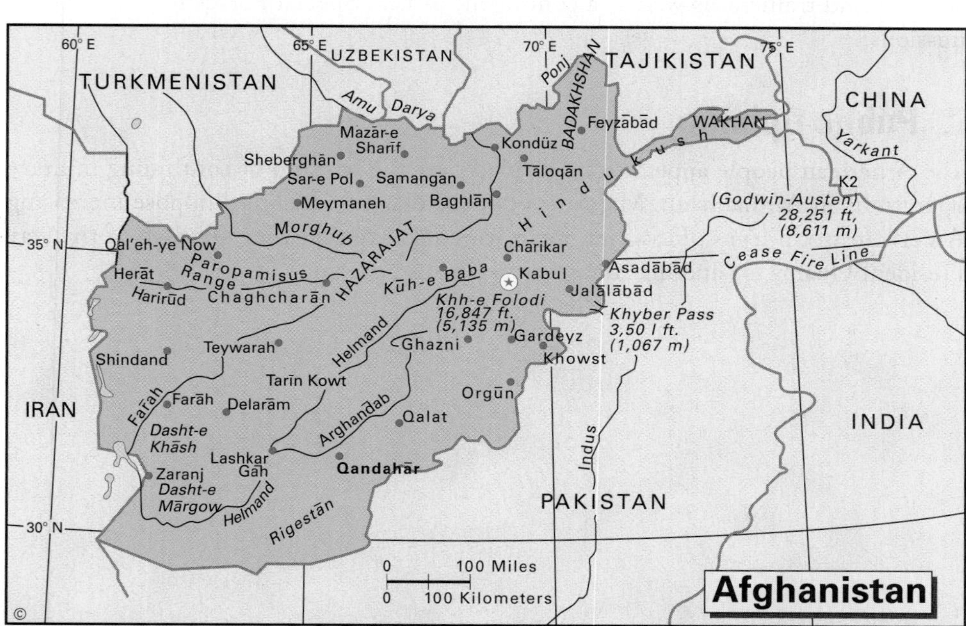

FIGURE 18.4 BATTLING IN ROUGH TERRAIN

Afghanistan presents difficult terrain for U.S. counterinsurgency operations. The Taliban and al-Qaeda are largely concentrated in the mountainous areas along the Pakistan border. They often retreat into Pakistan to regroup and rearm.

18.1

18.2

18.3

18.4

18.5

18.6

A Constitutional Note

Congress Versus the Commander in Chief

The Constitution of 1787 divided war-making powers between the Congress and the president. Article I, Section 8, states that "Congress shall have Power ... to provide for the common Defense ... to declare War ... to raise and support Armies ... to provide and maintain a Navy ... to make Rules for the Government and Regulation of the land and naval forces." However, Article II, Section 2, states that "the President shall be the Commander in Chief of the Army and Navy of the United States." But today, wars are not "declared"; instead, they begin with military action, and the president is responsible for the actions of the Armed Forces of the United States. Presidents have sent U.S. troops beyond the borders of the United States in military actions on more than 200 occasions. In contrast, Congress has formally declared war only five times: the War of 1812, the Mexican War in 1846, the Spanish–American War in 1898, World War I in 1917, and World War II in 1941. Congress did *not* declare war in the Korean War (1950–53), the Vietnam War (1965–73), the Persian Gulf War (1991), or the wars in Afghanistan (2002–) or Iraq (2003–). While presidents asked for the support of Congress in these wars, no formal declarations of war were ever made. The Supreme Court has consistently refused to hear cases involving the war powers of the president and Congress.

QUESTIONS

1. Should Congress be more aggressive in checking the discriminate use of military force by presidents? Why or why not?
2. Why do you think the Supreme Court hesitates to interfere with presidential and congressional war powers?

build their nation. Rather, we are focused on disrupting, dismantling, and defeating al-Qaeda in Afghanistan and Pakistan, and preventing its capacity to threaten America and our allies in the future."[6]

☐ NATO Exit

The leaders of NATO met in Chicago in 2012 and endorsed an exit strategy. ISAF forces handed over command of combat missions to Afghan forces in 2013, while shifting their own forces to a support role of advising and training Afghans. Most U.S. and other NATO forces are to be withdrawn by the end of 2014. A U.S.-Afghanistan Strategic Partnership Agreement envisions a continued presence of U.S. military advisors and trainers, as well as a contingent of U.S. Special Forces for antiterrorist missions.

☐ Public Opinion

The American people appear to be divided over the wisdom of continuing military operations in Afghanistan. Majorities oppose the war itself and oppose increasing American troop levels. However, majorities also say that they approve of the way President Obama is handling "the situation in Afghanistan."

Review the Chapter

Power Among Nations

18.1 Describe the ways in which nations have attempted to bring order to international politics, p. 660

There is no world government capable of legislating and enforcing rules of international politics. But various efforts to stabilize relations among nations have been attempted, including the balance-of-power system of alliances in the eighteenth and nineteenth centuries, the collective security arrangements of the League of Nations and the United Nations in the twentieth century, and the regional security approach of the North Atlantic Treaty Organization.

The Legacy of the Cold War

18.2 Outline the major events of the Cold War and assess its legacy, p. 663

The United Nations was largely ineffective during the Cold War, the confrontation between the Western democracies led by the United States and communist bloc nations led by the Soviet Union. During these years, the Western nations relied principally on the strength of the North Atlantic Treaty Organization (NATO) to deter war in Europe.

For nearly 50 years, the Cold War largely directed U.S. foreign and defense policy. The United States sought to contain Soviet military expansionism and world communist revolutionary forces in all parts of the globe. U.S. involvement in the Korean and Vietnam wars grew out of this containment policy.

The end of the Cold War followed the ouster of communist governments in Eastern Europe in 1989, the unification of Germany in 1990, the collapse of the Warsaw Pact communist military alliance in 1991, and the dissolution of the Soviet Union in 1991. Russia has inherited most of the nuclear weapons and military forces of the former Soviet Union as well as its seat on the UN Security Council.

Nuclear Threats

18.3 Trace the evolution of the nuclear weapons policies of the United States, p. 668

During the Cold War years, U.S. and Soviet military forces never engaged in direct combat against each other, although many "proxy" conflicts took place throughout the world. The most serious threat of nuclear war occurred during the Cuban Missile Crisis in 1962.

To maintain nuclear peace, the United States relied primarily on the policy of deterrence—dissuading the Soviets from launching a nuclear attack by maintaining survivable second-strike forces capable of inflicting unacceptable levels of destruction in a retaliatory attack.

In 1970, President Richard Nixon and National Security Adviser Henry Kissinger began negotiations with the Soviet Union with a view to limiting the nuclear arms race. These Strategic Arms Limitation Talks produced the SALT I agreement in 1972, and later, under President Jimmy Carter, the SALT II agreement in 1979. Both agreements set limits on future strategic weapons development but failed to reduce existing weapons stockpiles.

President Ronald Reagan renamed the negotiations START, emphasizing the goal of reductions in weapons rather than limitations, and stressing equality and verification. The START I (1991) and START II (1993) Treaties called for reducing nuclear arsenals by two-thirds from Cold War levels.

The New START Treaty negotiated in 2010 calls for further reductions in nuclear warheads. Terrorist states that acquire nuclear weapons may not be deterred from using them by the threat of retaliation. Ballistic missile defenses (BMDs)—missiles designed to intercept and destroy enemy missiles in flight—offer the possibility of protecting the United States and its allies from nuclear terrorism.

The War on Terrorism

18.4 Describe the nature of terrorism and the U.S. response to terrorism, p. 671

Following the Vietnam War, many military leaders argued that U.S. forces should be used only to protect vital American interests, only in support of clearly defined military objectives, only with sufficient strength to ensure decisive victory with the fewest possible casualties, only with the support of the American people and Congress, and only as a last resort.

Recent presidents, however, have used military forces to carry out a variety of missions in addition to conventional war, including peacekeeping, antiterrorist, and humanitarian activities. They have argued that the risks were worth taking in light of the importance of the goals.

The threat posed by terrorist groups throughout the world inspired the U.S. military to design counterinsurgency strategies to confront unconventional (or asymmetrical) wars. The United States remains committed to the goal of "disrupting, dismantling, and defeating al-Qaeda."

The Obama administration now calls for a reduction in the overall capacity of U.S. forces. The intent is to have forces that are "smaller, leaner, agile, and flexible." But North Korea and Iran both deploy large conventional armies. The United States is not prepared to fight wars in the Middle East and the Korean peninsula simultaneously.

The War in Iraq

18.5 Explain the reasons for the U.S. military intervention in Iraq and assess the progress and outcome of that intervention, p. 673

Following the Gulf War, Iraq violated a dozen or more UN resolutions calling on that country to destroy chemical and biological weapons and to open their weapons sites for inspection. Saddam Hussein's refusal led to Operation Iraqi Freedom in 1991. Saddam Hussein was apprehended and regime change was accomplished; however, the occupation of Iraq was poorly executed. No weapons of mass destruction were found. Over time a majority of Americans came to believe that the war in Iraq was "not worth fighting." Following a surge in U.S. forces in Iraq, violence in that country appeared to subside. President Obama ran for office pledging to end the war in Iraq in a "responsible manner." He ordered all remaining U.S. troops to leave that country by the end of 2011. The United States suffered over 4,500 American service members killed and 35,000 wounded in Iraq.

The War in Afghanistan

18.6 Explain the war in Afghanistan and assess its progress, p. 680

The military phase of America's war on terrorism began October 7, 2001, when U.S. aircraft began attacks on al-Qaeda bases in Afghanistan, and U.S. special forces organized and led Afghan fighters to oust the Taliban regime that had harbored terrorists.

The United States was aided by its NATO allies. A prolonged counterinsurgency war followed. Taliban and al-Qaeda frequently retreated into Pakistan to regroup and rearm. President Obama stated that the objective of U.S. policy in Afghanistan was not necessarily to bring democracy to that country, but rather to ensure that it does not again become a safe haven for terrorists. Obama increased U.S. forces in Afghanistan in 2012, but at the same time announced that U.S. and other NATO forces would be withdrawn by the end of 2014.

Learn the Terms

collective security, p. 660
Soviet Union, p. 660
superpowers, p. 661
regional security, p. 661
North Atlantic Treaty Organization (NATO), p. 661
Cold War, p. 663
Truman Doctrine, p. 663
containment, p. 663
Marshall Plan, p. 664
Korean War, p. 664
Cuban Missile Crisis, p. 664
Vietnam War, p. 665
deterrence, p. 668
second-strike capability, p. 668
SALT I, p. 668
ABM Treaty, p. 668
SALT II, p. 668
START I, p. 669
START II, p. 669
ballistic missile defense (BMD), p. 671
terrorism, p. 671

Test Yourself

18.1 Describe the ways which nations have attempted to bring order to international politics.

In international politics all nations seek the goal of

a. power
b. social justice
c. order and the rule of law
d. freedom and democracy
e. hegemony

18.2 Outline major events of the Cold War and assess its legacy.

The most serious threat of a nuclear holocaust during the Cold War was probably during

a. the Korean War
b. the Vietnam War
c. the fall of the Berlin wall
d. the Cuban Missile Crisis
e. the Suez Crisis

18.3 Trace the evolution of the nuclear weapons policies of the United States.

The Powell Doctrine, advanced by General Colin Powell recommended the use of military force, under what of the following conditions?

I. only in support of U.S. vital interests
II. to demonstrate U.S. support for democratic governments
III. to assist in humanitarian aid
IV. for redress of historic colonial grievences

a. Only I
b. Only II
c. I, II, and IV
d. I, II, and III
e. I and IV

18.4 Describe the nature of terrorism and the U.S. response to terrorism.

Terrorism is a violent political act which is distinguished by its willingness to

a. use weapons of mass destruction
b. achieve publicity of alleged wrongs
c. consciously target civilians
d. use suicide "martyrs"
e. Use organized and regularized military tactics in the open

18.5 Explain the reasons for the U.S. military intervention in Iraq and assess the progress and outcome of that intervention.

Public opinion polling on the war in Iraq revealed that it

a. was never very popular
b. was supported (at least initially) by three-quarters of the public
c. never attained the support of 50 percent of the people
d. held the support of over 50 percent of the public since 2005
e. could justify a return to combat action in Iraq

18.6 Explain the war in Afghanistan and assess its progress.

The Obama Administration's approach to the war in Afghanistan was to do which of the following

a. increase U.S. military forces in that country without commiting to withdrawal
b. begin a withdrawal of U.S. forces in 2014 without increasing troop commitments
c. only disrupt, dismantle, and defeat al-Qaeda
d. increase U.S. military forces in that country, begin a withdrawal of U.S. forces in 2014, and disrupt, dismantle, and defeat Al Qaida
e. increase U.S. military forces in that country and disrupt, dismantle, and defeat al-Qaeda, without commiting to withdrawal

Explore Further

SUGGESTED READINGS

Banks, William C., Renee deNevers, and Mitchel B. Wallerstein. *Combatting Terrorism Strategies and Approaches*. Washington, D.C.: CQ Press, 2007. Comprehensive description of a variety of counterterrorism strategies, including law enforcement, diplomacy, and military action.

Clausewitz, Karl von. *On War*. Edited and translated by Michael Howard and Peter Paret. Princeton, N.J.: Princeton University Press, 1984. The classic theory of war and military operations, emphasizing their political character; first published in 1832.

Hastedt, Glenn P. *American Foreign Policy: Past, Present, Future*. 8th ed. New York: Longman, 2011. A foreign policy text that deals with national security issues within the broader context of foreign policy.

International Institute for Strategic Studies. *The Military Balance*. London: International Institute for Strategic Studies, published annually. Careful description of the military forces of more than 160 countries; this book is considered the most authoritative public information available.

Gottleib, Stuart. *Debating Terrorism and Counterterrorism*, 2nd ed. Washington, DC: CQ Press, 2013. Pro and con arguments over nature of terrorism and methods of combating it.

Hook, Stephen W., and John Spanier. *American Foreign Policy Since World War II*. 18th ed. Washington, D.C.: CQ Press; 2009. Updated version of classic text on American foreign policy, concluding with "A World of Trouble."

Nacos, Brigitte L. *Terrorism and Counterterrorism*. 2nd ed. New York: Longman, 2008. Terrorism's causes, actors, and strategies as well as counterterrorism responses.

Snow, Donald M. *National Security for a New Era*. 4th ed. New York: Longman, 2011. Comprehensive text examining U.S. national security issues following the end of the Cold War and 9/11.

Summers, Harry G., Jr. *On Strategy II: A Critical Analysis of the Gulf War*. New York: Dell, 1992. Analysis of the Gulf War based on Clausewitz's classic principles of war. The strategic decisions leading to victory in the Gulf contrast markedly with the decisions in Vietnam that led to defeat, a topic covered in Summers's groundbreaking first book, *On Strategy: A Critical Analysis of the Vietnam War* (New York: Dell, 1984).

US Department of Defense. *Sustaining US Global Leadership: Priorities for 21st Century Defense*, 2012.

SUGGESTED WEB SITES

American Security Council http://www.ascfusa.org
Organization providing summary information on national security threats.

CIA-Terrorism https://www.cia.gov/news-information/cia-the-war-on-terrorism/
Reports, news, and facts regarding terrorism.

CIA World Factbook www.cia.gov/library/publications/the-world-factbook
Nations listed A–Z with geography, people, economy, government, military, and so on.

Cuban Crisis www.cubacrisis.net
The October 1962 nuclear missile crisis described day to day, with photos.

Department of Defense www.defense.gov/top-issue
Official Defense Department site link to information on Afganistan and Iraq.

Korean War Project Organization www.koreanwar.org
Dedicated to the memory of sacrifices of Americans in Korea, with links to battles, units, and memorials.

NATO www.nato.int
The official "North Atlantic Treaty Organization" site contains basic facts about the alliance, current NATO news and issues, and important NATO policies.

State Department www.state.gov
This U.S. Department of State Web site contains background notes on the countries and regions of the world.

Terrorism Research Center www.terrorism.com
The "Terrorism Research Center" Web site is dedicated to "informing the public of the phenomena of terrorism and information warfare." It contains news, analytical essays on terrorist issues, and many links to other terrorism materials and research sources.

United Nations www.un.org
This United Nations site contains basic information about the world body's mission, member states, issues of concern, institutions, and accomplishments.

The **Declaration** of Independence

Drafted mainly by Thomas Jefferson, this document, adopted by the Second Continental Congress and signed by John Hancock and fifty-five others, outlined the rights of man and the rights to rebellion and self-government. It declared the independence of the colonies from Great Britain, justified rebellion, and listed the grievances against George III and his government. What is memorable about this famous document is not only that it declared the birth of a new nation, but that it set forth with eloquence our basic philosophy of liberty and representative democracy.

IN CONGRESS, JULY 4, 1776 (The unanimous Declaration of the Thirteen United States of America)

Preamble

When in the Course of human events, it becomes necessary for one people to dissolve the political bands which have connected them with another, and to assume, among the Powers of the earth, the separate and equal station to which the laws of nature and of nature's God entitle them, a decent respect to the opinions of mankind requires that they should declare the causes which impel them to the separation.

New Principles of Government

We hold these truths to be self-evident; that all men are created equal, that they are endowed by their Creator with certain unalienable Rights, that among these are life, liberty and the pursuit of happiness.

That, to secure these rights, governments are instituted among Men, deriving their just powers from the consent of the governed.

That whenever any form of government becomes destructive of these ends, it is the right of the people to alter or to abolish it, and to institute new government, laying its foundation on such principles, and organizing its powers in such form, as to them shall seem most likely to effect their safety and happiness. Prudence, indeed will dictate that governments long established should not be changed for light and transient causes; and accordingly all experience hath shown, that mankind are more disposed to suffer while evils are sufferable, than to right themselves by abolishing the forms to which they are accustomed. But when a long train of abuses and usurpations, pursuing invariably the same object evinces a design to reduce them under absolute despotism, it is their right, it is their duty, to throw off such government, and to provide new guards for their future security.

Reasons for Separation

Such has been the patient sufferance of these colonies; and such is now the necessity which constrains them to alter their former systems of government. The history of the present king of Great Britain is a history of repeated injuries and usurpations, all having in direct object the establishment of an absolute tyranny over these states. To prove this, let facts be submitted to a candid world.

He has refused his assent to laws, the most wholesome and necessary for the public good.

He has forbidden his governors to pass laws of immediate and pressing importance unless suspended in their operation till his assent should be obtained; and when so suspended, he has utterly neglected to attend to them.

He has refused to pass other laws for the accommodation of large districts of people, unless those people would relinquish the right of representation in the legislature, a right inestimable to them and formidable to tyrants only.

He has called together legislative bodies at places unusual, uncomfortable, and distant from the depository of their public records, for the sole purpose of fatiguing them into compliance with his measures.

He has dissolved representative houses repeatedly, for opposing, with manly firmness, his invasions on the rights of the people.

He has refused, for a long time, after such dissolutions, to cause others to be elected; whereby the legislative powers, incapable of annihilation, have returned to the people at large for their exercise; the state remaining in the mean-time, exposed to all the dangers of invasion from without and convulsions within.

He has endeavoured to prevent the population of these states; for that purpose obstructing the laws of naturalization of foreigners; refusing to pass others to encourage their migration hither, and raising the conditions of new appropriations of lands.

He has obstructed the administration of justice, by refusing his assent to laws for establishing judiciary powers.

He has made judges dependent on his will alone, for the tenure of their offices, and the amount and payment of their salaries.

He has erected a multitude of new offices, and sent hither swarms of officers to harass our People, and eat out their substance.

He has kept among us, in times of peace, standing armies without the consent of our legislature.

He has affected to render the Military independent of and superior to the Civil Power.

He has combined with others to subject us to a jurisdiction foreign to our constitution and unacknowledged by our laws, giving his assent to their acts of pretended legislation:

For quartering large bodies of armed troops among us;

For protecting them, by a mock trial, from punishment for any murders which they should commit on the Inhabitants of these States;

For cutting off our trade with all parts of the world;

For imposing taxes on us without our consent; For depriving us, in many cases, of the benefits of trial by jury;

For transporting us beyond seas to be tried for pretended offenses;

For abolishing the free system of English laws in a neighbouring province, establishing therein an arbitrary government, and enlarging its boundaries so as to render it at once an example and fit instrument for introducing the same absolute rule into these colonies;

For taking away our charters, abolishing our most valuable laws, and altering fundamentally the Forms of our Governments;

For suspending our own legislature, and declaring themselves invented with power to legislate for us in all cases whatsoever.

He has abdicated government here, by declaring us out of his protection and waging war against us.

He has plundered our seas, ravaged our coasts, burned our towns, and destroyed the lives of our people.

He is at this time transporting large armies of foreign mercenaries to complete the works of death, desolation and tyranny already begun with circumstances of cruelty & perfidy scarcely paralleled in the most barbarous ages and totally unworthy the head of a civilized nation.

He has constrained our fellow-citizens, taken captive on the high seas to bear arms against their country, to become the executioners of their friends and brethren, or to fall themselves by their hands.

He has excited domestic insurrections among us, and has endeavored to bring on the inhabitants of our frontiers the merciless Indian savages, whose known rule of warfare, is an undistinguished destruction of all ages, sexes and conditions.

In every stage of these oppressions we have petitioned for redress in the most humble terms; our repeated petitions have been answered only by repeated injury. A prince, whose character is thus marked by every act which may define a tyrant, is unfit to be the ruler of a free people.

Nor have we been wanting in attention to our British brethren. We have warned them from time to time, of attempts by their legislature to extend an unwarrantable jurisdiction over us. We have reminded them of the circumstances of our emigration and settlement here. We have appealed to their native justice and magnanimity; and we have conjured them by the ties of our common kindred to disavow these usurpations, which would inevitably interrupt our connections and correspondence. They, too, have been deaf to the voice of justice and of consanguinity. We must, therefore, acquiesce in the necessity which denounces our separation, and hold them, as we hold the rest of mankind, enemies in war, in peace, Friends.

We, therefore, the representatives of the United States of America, in General Congress, assembled, appealing to the Supreme Judge of the world for the rectitude of our intentions, do, in the name and by authority of the good people of these colonies, solemnly publish and declare, that these united colonies are, and of right ought to be, free and independent states; that they are absolved from all allegiance to the British crown, and that all political connection between them and the state of Great Britain, is and ought to be, totally dissolved; and that as free and independent states, they have full power to levy war, conclude peace, contract Alliances, establish commerce, and to do all other acts and things which independent states may of right do. And, for the support of this declaration, with a firm reliance of the protection of Divine Providence, we mutually pledge to each other our lives, our fortunes, and our sacred honor.

The Federalist No. 10

James Madison

Among the numerous advantages promised by a well-constructed Union, none deserves to be more accurately developed than its tendency to break and control the violence of faction. The friend of popular governments never finds himself so much alarmed for their character and fate, as when he contemplates their propensity to this dangerous vice. He will not fail, therefore, to set a due value on any plan which, without violating the principles to which he is attached, provides a proper cure for it. The instability, injustice, and confusion introduced into the public councils, have, in truth, been the mortal diseases under which popular governments have everywhere perished; as they continue to be the favorite and fruitful topics from which the adversaries to liberty derive their most specious declamations. The valuable improvements made by the American constitutions on the popular models, both ancient and modern, cannot certainly be too much admired; but it would be an unwarrantable partiality, to contend that they have as effectually obviated the danger on this side, as was wished and expected. Complaints are everywhere heard from our most considerate and virtuous citizens, equally the friends of public and private faith, and of public and personal liberty, that our governments are too unstable, that the public good is disregarded in the conflicts of rival parties, and that measures are too often decided, not according to the rules of justice and the rights of the minor party, but by the superior force of an interested and overbearing majority. However anxiously we may wish that these complaints had no foundation, the evidence, of known facts will not permit us to deny that they are in some degree true. It will be found, indeed, on a candid review of our situation, that some of the distresses under which we labor have been erroneously charged on the operation of our governments; but it will be found, at the same time, that other causes will not alone account for many of our heaviest misfortunes; and, particularly, for that prevailing and increasing distrust of public engagements, and alarm for private rights, which are echoed from one end of the continent to the other. These must be chiefly, if not wholly, effects of the unsteadiness and injustice with which a factious spirit has tainted our public administrations.

By a faction, I understand a number of citizens, whether amounting to a majority or a minority of the whole, who are united and actuated by some common impulse of passion, or of interest, adversed to the rights of other citizens, or to the permanent and aggregate interests of the community.

There are two methods of curing the mischiefs of faction: the one, by removing its causes; the other, by controlling its effects.

There are again two methods of removing the causes of faction: the one, by destroying the liberty which is essential to its existence; the other, by giving to every citizen the same opinions, the same passions, and the same interests.

It could never be more truly said than of the first remedy, that it was worse than the disease. Liberty is to faction what air is to fire, an aliment without which it instantly expires. But it could not be less folly to abolish liberty, which is essential to political life, because it nourishes faction, than it would be to wish the annihilation of air, which is essential to animal life, because it imparts to fire its destructive agency.

The second expedient is as impracticable as the first would be unwise. As long as the reason of man continues fallible, and he is at liberty to exercise it, different opinions will be formed. As long as the connection subsists between his reason and his self-love, his opinions and his passions will have a reciprocal influence on each other; and the former will be objects to which the latter will attach themselves. The diversity in the faculties of men, from which the rights of property originate, is not less an insuperable obstacle to a uniformity of interests. The protection of these faculties is the first object of government. From the protection of different and unequal faculties of acquiring property, the possession of different degrees and kinds of property immediately results; and from the influence of these on the sentiments and views of the respective proprietors, ensues a division of the society into different interests and parties.

The latent causes of faction are thus sown in the nature of man; and we see them everywhere brought into different degrees of activity, according to the different circumstances of civil society. A zeal for different opinions concerning religion, concerning government, and many other points, as well of speculation as of practice; an attachment to different leaders ambitiously contending for pre-eminence and power; or to persons of other descriptions whose fortunes have been interesting to the human passions, have, in turn, divided mankind into parties, inflamed them with mutual animosity, and rendered them much more disposed to vex and oppress each other than to co-operate for their common good. So strong is this propensity of mankind to fall into mutual animosities, that where no substantial occasion presents itself, the most frivolous and fanciful distinctions have been sufficient to kindle their unfriendly passions and excite their most violent conflicts. But the most common and durable source of factions has been the various and unequal distribution of property. Those who hold and those who are without property have ever formed distinct interests in society. Those who are creditors, and those who are debtors, fall under a like discrimination. A landed interest, a manufacturing interest, a mercantile interest, a moneyed interest, with many lesser interests, grow up of necessity in civilized nations, and divide them into different classes, actuated by different sentiments and views. The regulation of these various and interfering interests forms the principal task of modern legislation, and involves the spirit of party and faction in the necessary and ordinary operations of the government.

No man is allowed to be a judge in his own cause, because his interest would certainly bias his judgment, and, not improbably, corrupt his integrity. With equal, nay with greater reason, a body of men are unfit to be both judges and parties at the same time; yet what are many of the most important acts of legislation, but so many judicial determinations, not indeed concerning the rights of single persons, but concerning the rights of large bodies of citizens? And what are the different classes of legislators but advocates and parties to the causes which they determine? Is a law proposed concerning private debts? It is a question to which the creditors are parties on one side and the debtors on the other. Justice ought to hold the balance between them. Yet the parties are, and must be, themselves the judges; and the most numerous party, or, in other words, the most powerful faction must be expected to prevail. Shall domestic manufactures be encouraged, and in what degree, by restrictions on foreign manufactures? are questions which would be differently decided by the landed and the manufacturing classes, and probably by neither with a sole regard to justice and the public good. The apportionment of taxes on the various descriptions of property is an act which seems to require the most exact impartiality; yet there is, perhaps, no legislative act in which greater opportunity and temptation are given to a predominant party to trample on the rules of justice. Every shilling with which they overburden the inferior number, is a shilling saved to their own pockets.

It is in vain to say that enlightened statesmen will be able to adjust these clashing interests, and render them all subservient to the public good. Enlightened statesmen will not always be at the helm. Nor, in many cases, can such an adjustment be made at all without taking into view indirect and remote considerations, which will rarely prevail over the immediate interest which one party may find in disregarding the rights of another or the good of the whole.

The inference to which we are brought is, that the CAUSES of faction cannot be removed, and that relief is only to be sought in the means of controlling its EFFECTS.

If a faction consists of less than a majority, relief is supplied by the republican principle, which enables the majority to defeat its sinister views by regular vote. It may clog the administration, it may convulse the society; but it will be unable to execute and mask its violence under the forms of the Constitution. When a majority is included in a faction, the form of popular government, on the other hand, enables it to sacrifice to its ruling passion or interest both the public good and the rights of other citizens. To secure the public good and private rights against the danger of such a faction, and at the same time to preserve the spirit and the form of popular government, is then the great object to which our inquiries are directed. Let me add that it is the great desideratum by which this form of government can be rescued from the opprobrium under which it has so long labored, and be recommended to the esteem and adoption of mankind.

By what means is this object attainable? Evidently by one of two only. Either the existence of the same passion or interest in a majority at the same time must be prevented, or the majority, having such coexistent passion or interest, must be rendered, by their number and local situation, unable to concert and carry into effect schemes of oppression. If the impulse and the opportunity be suffered to coincide, we well know that neither moral nor religious motives can be relied on as an adequate control. They are not found to be such on the injustice and violence of individuals, and lose their efficacy in proportion to the number combined together, that is, in proportion as their efficacy becomes needful.

From this view of the subject it may be concluded that a pure democracy, by which I mean a society consisting of a small number of citizens, who assemble and administer the government in person, can admit of no cure for the mischiefs of faction. A common passion or interest will, in almost every case, be felt by a majority of the whole; a communication and concert result from the form of government itself; and there is nothing to check the inducements to sacrifice the weaker party or an obnoxious individual. Hence it is that such democracies have ever been spectacles of turbulence and contention; have ever been found incompatible with personal security or the rights of property; and have in general been as short in their lives as they have been violent in their deaths. Theoretic politicians, who have patronized this species of government, have erroneously supposed that by reducing mankind to a perfect equality in their political rights, they would, at the same time, be perfectly equalized and assimilated in their possessions, their opinions, and their passions.

A republic, by which I mean a government in which the scheme of representation takes place, opens a different prospect, and promises the cure for which we are seeking. Let us examine the points in which it varies from pure democracy, and we shall comprehend both the nature of the cure and the efficacy which it must derive from the Union.

The two great points of difference between a democracy and a republic are: first, the delegation of the government, in the latter, to a small number of citizens elected by the rest; secondly, the greater number of citizens, and greater sphere of country, over which the latter may be extended.

The effect of the first difference is, on the one hand, to refine and enlarge the public views, by passing them through the medium of a chosen body of citizens, whose wisdom may best discern the true interest of their country, and whose patriotism and love of justice will be least likely to sacrifice it to temporary or partial considerations. Under such a regulation, it may well happen that the public voice, pronounced by the representatives of the people, will be more consonant to the public good than if pronounced by the people themselves, convened for the purpose. On the other hand, the effect may be inverted. Men of factious tempers, of local prejudices, or of sinister designs, may, by intrigue, by corruption, or by other means, first obtain the suffrages, and then betray the interests, of the people. The question resulting is, whether small or extensive republics are more favorable to the election of proper guardians of the public weal; and it is clearly decided in favor of the latter by two obvious considerations:

In the first place, it is to be remarked that, however small the republic may be, the representatives must be raised to a certain number, in order to guard against the cabals of a few; and that, however large it may be, they must be limited to a certain number, in order to guard against the confusion of a multitude. Hence, the number of representatives in the two cases not being in proportion to that of the two constituents, and being proportionally greater in the small republic, it follows that, if the proportion of fit characters be not less in the large than in the small republic, the former will present a greater option, and consequently a greater probability of a fit choice.

In the next place, as each representative will be chosen by a greater number of citizens in the large than in the small republic, it will be more difficult for unworthy candidates to practice with success the vicious arts by which elections are too often carried; and the suffrages of the people being more free, will be more likely to centre in men who possess the most attractive merit and the most diffusive and established characters.

It must be confessed that in this, as in most other cases, there is a mean, on both sides of which inconveniences will be found to lie. By enlarging too much the number of electors, you render the representatives too little acquainted with all their local circumstances and lesser interests; as by reducing it too much, you render him unduly attached to these, and too little fit to comprehend and pursue great and national objects. The federal Constitution forms a happy combination in this respect; the great and aggregate interests being referred to the national, the local and particular to the State legislatures.

The other point of difference is, the greater number of citizens and extent of territory which may be brought within the compass of republican than of democratic government; and it is this circumstance principally which renders factious combinations less to be dreaded in the former than in the latter.

The smaller the society, the fewer probably will be the distinct parties and interests composing it; the fewer the distinct parties and interests, the more frequently will a majority be found of the same party; and the smaller the number of individuals composing a majority, and the smaller the compass within which they are placed, the more easily will they concert and execute their plans of oppression. Extend the sphere, and you take in a greater variety of parties and interests; you make it less probable that a majority of the whole will have a common motive to invade the rights of other citizens; or if such a common motive exists, it will be more difficult for all who feel it to discover their own strength, and to act in unison with each other. . . .

Hence, it clearly appears, that the same advantage which a republic has over a democracy, in controlling the effects of faction, is enjoyed by a large over a small republic,—is enjoyed by the Union over the States composing it. Does the advantage consist in the substitution of representatives whose enlightened views and virtuous sentiments render them superior to local prejudices and schemes of injustice? It will not be denied that the representation of the Union will be most likely to possess these requisite endowments. Does it consist in the greater security afforded by a greater variety of parties, against the event of any one party being able to outnumber and oppress the rest? In an equal degree does the increased variety of parties comprised within the Union, increase this security. Does it, in fine, consist in the greater obstacles opposed to the concert and accomplishment of the secret wishes of an unjust and interested majority? Here, again, the extent of the Union gives it the most palpable advantage.

The influence of factious leaders may kindle a flame within their particular States, but will be unable to spread a general conflagration through the other States. A religious sect may degenerate into a political faction in a part of the Confederacy; but the variety of sects dispersed over the entire face of it must secure the national councils against any danger from that source. A rage for paper money, for an abolition of debts, for an equal division of property, or for any other improper or wicked project, will be less apt to pervade the whole body of the Union than a particular member of it; in the same proportion as such a malady is more likely to taint a particular county or district, than an entire State.

In the extent and proper structure of the Union, therefore, we behold a republican remedy for the diseases most incident to republican government. And according to the degree of pleasure and pride we feel in being republicans, ought to be our zeal in cherishing the spirit and supporting the character of Federalists.

The Federalist No. 51

James Madison

To what expedient, then, shall we finally resort, for maintaining in practice the necessary partition of power among the several departments, as laid down in the Constitution? The only answer that can be given is, that as all these exterior provisions are found to be inadequate, the defect must be supplied, by so contriving the interior structure of the government as that its several constituent parts may, by their mutual relations, be the means of keeping each other in their proper places. . . .

In order to lay a due foundation for that separate and distinct exercise of the different powers of government, which to a certain extent is admitted on all hands to be essential to the preservation of liberty, it is evident that each department should have a will of its own; and consequently should be so constituted that the members of each should have as little agency as possible in the appointment of the members of the others. . . .

It is equally evident, that the members of each department should be as little dependent as possible on those of the others, for the emoluments annexed to their offices. Were the executive magistrate, or the judges, not independent of the legislature in this particular, their independence in every other would be merely nominal.

But the great security against a gradual concentration of the several powers in the same department, consists in giving to those who administer each department the necessary constitutional means and personal motives to resist encroachments of the others. The provision for defense must in this, as in all other cases, be made commensurate to the danger of attack. Ambition must be made to counteract ambition. The interest of the man must be connected with the constitutional rights of the place. It may be a reflection on human nature, that such devices should be necessary to control the abuses of government. But what is government itself, but the greatest of all reflections on human nature? If men were angels, no government would be necessary. If angels were to govern men, neither external nor internal controls on government would be necessary. In framing a government which is to be administered by men over men, the great difficulty lies in this: you must first enable the government to control the governed; and in the next place oblige it to control itself. A dependence on the people is, no doubt, the primary control on the government; but experience has taught mankind the necessity of auxiliary precautions.

This policy of supplying, by opposite and rival interests, the defect of better motives, might be traced through the whole system of human affairs, private as well as public. We see it particularly displayed in all the subordinate distributions of power, where the constant aim is to divide and arrange the several offices in such a manner as that each may be a check on the other that the private interest of every individual may be a sentinel over the public rights. These inventions of prudence cannot be less requisite in the distribution of the supreme powers of the State.

But it is not possible to give to each department an equal power of self-defense. In republican government, the legislative authority necessarily predominates. The remedy for this inconveniency is to divide the legislature into different branches; and to render them, by different modes of election and different principles of action, as little connected with each other as the nature of their common functions and their common dependence on the society will admit. It may even be necessary to guard against dangerous encroachments by still further precautions. As the weight of the legislative authority requires that it should be thus divided, the weakness of the executive may require, on the other hand, that it should be fortified. An absolute negative on the legislature appears, at first view, to be the natural defense with which the executive magistrate should be armed. But perhaps it would be neither altogether safe nor alone sufficient. On ordinary occasions it might not be exerted with the requisite firmness, and on extraordinary occasions it might be perfidiously abused. May not this defect of an absolute negative be supplied by some qualified connection between this weaker department and the weaker branch of the stronger department, by which the latter may be led to support the constitutional rights of the former, without being too much detached from the rights of its own department? If the principles on which these observations are founded be just, as I persuade myself they are, and they be applied as a criterion to the several State constitutions, and to the federal Constitution it will be found that if the latter does not perfectly correspond with them, the former are infinitely less able to bear such a test.

There are, moreover, two considerations particularly applicable to the federal system of America, which place that system in a very interesting point of view.

First. In a single republic, all the power surrendered by the people is submitted to the administration of a single government; and the usurpations are guarded against by a division of the government into distinct and separate departments. In the compound republic of America, the power surrendered by the people is first divided between two distinct governments, and then the portion allotted to each subdivided among distinct and separate departments.

Hence a double security arises to the rights of the people. The different governments will control each other, at the same time that each will be controlled by itself.

Second. It is of great importance in a republic not only to guard the society against the oppression of its rulers, but to guard one part of the society against the injustice of the other part. Different interests necessarily exist in different classes of citizens. If a majority be united by a common interest, the rights of the minority will be insecure. There are but two methods of providing against this evil: the one by creating a will in the community independent of the majority that is, of the society itself; the other, by comprehending in the society so many separate descriptions of citizens as will render an unjust combination of a majority of the whole very improbable, if not impracticable. The first method prevails in all governments possessing an hereditary or self-appointed authority. This, at best, is but a precarious security; because a power independent of the society may as well espouse the unjust views of the major, as the rightful interests of the minor party, and may possibly be turned against both parties. The second method will be exemplified in the federal republic of the United States. Whilst all authority in it will be derived from and dependent on the society, the society itself will be broken into so many parts, interests, and classes of citizens, that the rights of individuals, or of the minority, will be in little danger from interested combinations of the majority. In a free government the security for civil rights must be the same as that for religious rights. It consists in the one case in the multiplicity of interests, and in the other in the multiplicity of sects. The degree of security in both cases will depend on the number of interests and sects; and this may be presumed to depend on the extent of country and number of people comprehended under the same government. This view of the subject must particularly recommend a proper federal system to all the sincere and considerate friends of republican government, since it shows that in exact proportion as the territory of the Union may be formed into more circumscribed Confederacies, or States oppressive combinations of a majority will be facilitated: the best security, under the republican forms, for the rights of every class of citizens, will be diminished: and consequently the stability and independence of some member of the government, the only other security, must be proportionately increased. Justice is the end of government. It is the end of civil society. It ever has been and ever will be pursued until it be obtained, or until liberty be lost in the pursuit. In a society under the forms of which the stronger faction can readily unite and oppress the weaker, anarchy may as truly be said to reign as in a state of nature, where the weaker individual is not secured against the violence of the stronger; and as, in the latter state, even the stronger individuals are prompted, by the uncertainty of their condition, to submit to a government which may protect the weak as well as themselves; so, in the former state, will the more powerful factions or parties be gradnally induced, by a like motive, to wish for a government which will protect all parties, the weaker as well as the more powerful. It can be little doubted that if the State of Rhode Island was separated from the Confederacy and left to itself, the insecurity of rights under the popular form of government within such narrow limits would be displayed by such reiterated oppressions of factious majorities that some power altogether independent of the people would soon be called for by the voice of the very factions whose misrule had proved the necessity of it. In the extended republic of the United States, and among the great variety of interests, parties, and sects which it embraces, a coalition of a majority of the whole society could seldom take place on any other principles than those of justice and the general good; whilst there being thus less danger to a minor from the will of a major party, there must be less pretext, also, to provide for the security of the former, by introducing into the government a will not dependent on the latter, or, in other words, a will independent of the society itself. It is no less certain than it is important, notwithstanding the contrary opinions which have been entertained, that the larger the society, provided it lie within a practical sphere, the more duly capable it will be of self-government. And happily for the REPUBLICAN CAUSE, the practicable sphere may be carried to a very great extent, by a judicious modification and mixture of the FEDERAL PRINCIPLE.

Presidents and Vice Presidents

1. George Washington (1789) John Adams (1789)
2. John Adams (1797)
   Thomas Jefferson (1797)
3. Thomas Jefferson (1801)
   Aaron Burr (1801)
   George Clinton (1805)
4. James Madison (1809)
   George Clinton (1809)
   Elbridge Gerry (1813)
5. James Monroe (1817)
   Daniel D. Tompkins (1817)
6. John Quincy Adams (1825)
   John C. Calhoun (1825)
7. Andrew Jackson (1829)
   John C. Calhoun (1829)
   Martin Van Buren (1833)
8. Martin Van Buren (1837)
   Richard M. Johnson (1837)
9. William H. Harrison (1841)
   John Tyler (1841)
10. John Tyler (1841)
11. James K. Polk (1845)
    George M. Dallas (1845)
12. Zachary Taylor (1849)
    Millard Fillmore (1849)
13. Millard Fillmore (1850)
14. Franklin Pierce (1853)
    William R. King (1853)
15. James Buchanan (1857)
    John C. Breckinridge (1857)
16. Abraham Lincoln (1861)
    Hannibal Hamlin (1861)
    Andrew Johnson (1865)
17. Andrew Johnson (1865)
18. Ulysses S. Grant (1869)
    Schuyler Colfax (1869)
    Henry Wilson (1873)
19. Rutherford B. Hayes (1877)
    William A. Wheeler (1877)
20. James A. Garfield (1881)
    Chester A. Arthur (1881)
21. Chester A. Arthur (1881)
22. Grover Cleveland (1885)
    T.A. Hendricks (1885)
23. Benjamin Harrison (1889)
    Levi P. Morton (1889)
24. Grover Cleveland (1893)
    Adlai E. Stevenson (1893)
25. William McKinley (1897)
    Garret A. Hobart (1897)
    Theodore Roosevelt (1901)
26. Theodore Roosevelt (1901)
    Charles Fairbanks (1905)
27. William H. Taft (1909)
    James S. Sherman (1909)
28. Woodrow Wilson (1913)
    Thomas R. Marshall (1913)
29. Warren G. Harding (1921)
    Calvin Coolidge (1921)
30. Calvin Coolidge (1923)
    Charles G. Dawes (1925)
31. Herbert C. Hoover (1929)
    Charles Curtis (1929)
32. Franklin D. Roosevelt (1933)
    John Nance Garner (1933)
    Henry A. Wallace (1941)
    Harry S. Truman (1945)
33. Harry S. Truman (1945)
    Alben W. Barkley (1949)
34. Dwight D. Eisenhower (1953)
    Richard M. Nixon (1953)
35. John F. Kennedy (1961)
    Lyndon B. Johnson (1961)
36. Lyndon B. Johnson (1963)
    Hubert H. Humphrey (1965)
37. Richard M. Nixon (1969)
    Spiro T. Agnew (1969)
    Gerald R. Ford (1973)
38. Gerald R. Ford (1974)
    Nelson A. Rockefeller (1974)
39. James E. Carter Jr. (1977)
    Walter F. Mondale (1977)
40. Ronald W. Reagan (1981)
    George H.W. Bush (1981)
41. George H.W. Bush (1989)
    James D. Quayle III (1989)
42. William J.B. Clinton (1993)
    Albert Gore (1993)
43. George W. Bush (2001)
    Richard Cheney (2001)
44. Barack H. Obama (2009)
    Joseph R. Biden (2009)

GLOSSARY

19th Amendment The 1920 constitutional amendment guaranteeing women the right to vote.

26th Amendment The 1971 constitutional amendment guaranteeing 18-year-olds the right to vote.

A

ABM Treaty A formal treaty in 1972 between the United States and the Soviet Union in which each side agreed not to build or deploy antiballistic missiles.

abolition movement Social movement before the Civil War whose goal was to abolish slavery throughout the United States.

access Meeting and talking with decision makers, a prerequisite to direct persuasion.

adjudication Decision making by the federal bureaucracy as to whether an individual or organization has complied with or violated government laws and/or regulations.

adversarial system Method of decision making in which an impartial judge or jury or decision maker hears arguments and reviews evidence presented by opposite sides.

advice and consent The constitutional power of the U.S. Senate to reject or ratify (by a two-thirds vote) treaties made by the president.

affirmative action Any program, whether enacted by a government or by a private organization, whose goal is to overcome the results of past unequal treatment of minorities and/or women by giving members of these groups preferential treatment in admissions, hiring, promotions, or other aspects of life.

affirmative racial gerrymandering Drawing district boundary lines to maximize minority representation.

agenda setting Deciding what will be decided, defining the problems and issues to be addressed by decision makers.

aliens Persons residing in a nation who are not citizens.

amateurs People who have not worked in politics or public service professions who run for public office.

amendments Formal changes in a bill, law, or constitution.

amicus curiae Literally, "friend of the court"; a person, private group or institution, or government agency that is not a party to a case but participates in the case (usually through submission of a brief) at the invitation of the court or on its own initiative.

amnesty Government forgiveness of a crime, usually granted to a group of people.

Annapolis Convention A 1786 meeting at Annapolis, Maryland, to discuss interstate commerce, which recommended a larger convention—the Constitutional Convention of 1787.

Anti-Federalists Opponents of the ratification of the Constitution, who later coalesced into a political party supporting Thomas Jefferson for president in 1800.

appeal In general, requests that a higher court review cases decided at a lower level. In the Supreme Court, certain cases are designated as appeals under federal law; formally, these must be heard by the Court.

appellate jurisdiction Particular court's power to review a decision or action of a lower court.

apportionment The allocation of legislative seats to jurisdictions based on population. Seats in the U.S. House of Representatives are apportioned to the states on the basis of their population after every 10-year census.

appropriations act Congressional bill that provides money for programs authorized by Congress.

Articles of Confederation The original framework for the government of the United States, adopted in 1781 and superseded by the U.S. Constitution in 1789. It established a "firm league of friendship" among the states, rather than a government "of the people."

authoritarianism Monopoly of political power by an individual or small group that otherwise allows people to go about their private lives as they wish.

authorization Act of Congress that establishes a government program and defines the amount of money it may spend.

B

bail Release of an accused person from custody in exchange for promise to appear at trial, guaranteed by money or property that is forfeited to court if defendant does not appear.

***Bakke* case** U.S. Supreme Court case challenging affirmative action.

ballistic missile defense (BMD) Weapons systems capable of detecting, intercepting, and destroying missiles in flight.

battlefield sectionalism The historic partisan division of the Democratic South and the Republican North arising from the Civil War.

beliefs Shared ideas about what is true.

bicameral Any legislative body that consists of two separate chambers or houses; in the United States, the Senate represents 50 statewide voter constituencies, and the House of Representatives represents voters in 435 separate districts.

big-state strategy Presidential political campaign strategy in which a candidate focuses on winning primaries in large states because of their high delegate counts.

bill of attainder Legislative act inflicting punishment without judicial trial; forbidden under Article I of the Constitution.

Bill of Rights Written guarantees of basic individual liberties; the first 10 amendments to the U.S. Constitution.

bipartisanship Agreement by members of both the Democratic and the Republican parties.

block grants Federal grants to state or local governments for general government functions allowing greater flexibility in the use of money.

Bradley effect Tendency of white voters to not express opposition to a black candidate to pollsters, in order to not appear racist.

bribery Giving or offering anything of value in an effort to influence government officials in the performance of their duties.

briefs Documents submitted by an attorney to a court, setting out the facts of the case and the legal arguments in support of the party represented by the attorney.

budget maximization Bureaucrats' tendencies to expand their agencies' budgets, staff, and authority.

budget resolution Congressional bill setting forth target budget figures for appropriations to various government departments and agencies.

bureaucracy Departments, agencies, bureaus, and offices that perform the functions of government.

C

cabinet The heads (secretaries) of the executive departments together with other top officials accorded cabinet rank by the president; only occasionally does it meet as a body to advise and support the president.

campaign strategy Plan for a political campaign, usually including a theme, an attempt to define the opponent or the issues, and an effort to coordinate images and messages in news broadcasts and paid advertising.

capitalism Economic system asserting the individual's right to own private property and to buy, sell, rent, and trade that property in a free market.

careerism In politics, a reference to people who started young working in politics, running for and holding public office, and who made politics their career.

casework Services performed by legislators and their staffs on behalf of individual constituents.

categorical grants Federal grants to a state or local government for specific purposes or projects; may be allocated by formulas or by projects.

caucus Nominating process in which party members or leaders meet to nominate candidates or select delegates to conventions.

censure Public reprimand for wrongdoing, given to a member standing in the chamber before Congress.

centralized federalism Model of federalism in which the national government assumes primary responsibility for determining national goals in all major policy areas and directs state and local government activity through conditions attached to money grants.

chain of command Hierarchical structure of authority in which command flows downward; typical of a bureaucracy.

challengers In politics, a reference to people running against incumbent officeholders.

checks and balances Constitutional provisions giving each branch of the national government certain checks over the actions of other branches.

circuit courts The 12 appellate courts that make up the middle level of the federal court system.

civil cases Noncriminal court proceedings in which a plaintiff sues a defendant for damages in payment for harm inflicted.

civil disobedience Form of public protest involving the breaking of laws believed to be unjust.

class action suits Cases initiated by parties acting on behalf of themselves and all others similarly situated.

class conflict Conflict between upper and lower social classes over wealth and power.

class consciousness Awareness of one's class position and a feeling of political solidarity with others within the same class in opposition to other classes.

classical liberalism Political philosophy asserting the worth and dignity of the individual and emphasizing the rational ability of human beings to determine their own destinies.

clear and present danger doctrine Standard used by the courts to determine whether speech may be restricted; only speech that creates a serious and immediate danger to society may be restricted.

closed primaries Primary elections in which voters must declare (or have previously declared) their party affiliation and can cast a ballot only in their own party's primary election.

closed rule Rule that forbids adding any amendments to a bill under consideration by the House.

cloture Vote to end debate—that is, to end a filibuster—which requires a three-fifths vote of the entire membership of the Senate.

coalitions A joining together of interest groups (or individuals) to achieve common goals.

coercive federalism A term referring to direct federal orders (mandates) to state and local governments to perform a service or conform to federal law in the performance of a function.

COLAs Annual cost-of-living adjustments mandated by law in Social Security and other welfare benefits.

Cold War Political, military, and ideological struggle between the United States and the Soviet Union following the end of World War II and ending with the collapse of the Soviet Union's communist government in 1991.

collective security Attempt to bring order to international relations by all nations joining together to guarantee each other's "territorial integrity" and "independence" against "external aggression."

colonial charters Documents granted by the English Monarch to individuals, companies, and groups of settlers in the new American colonies, authorizing a degree of self-government, setting the precedent of written contracts defining governmental power.

commercial speech Advertising communications given only partial protection under the 1st Amendment to the Constitution.

common market Unified trade area in which all goods and services can be sold or exchanged free from customs or tariffs.

communism System of government in which a single totalitarian party controls all means of production and distribution of goods and services.

comparable worth Argument that pay levels for traditionally male and traditionally female jobs should be equalized by paying equally for all jobs that are "worth about the same" to an employer.

competitive federalism A theory that state and local governments compete for residents and industry by offering 'market baskets' of incentives, services, zoning, and taxes.

concurrent powers Powers exercised by both the national government and state governments in the American federal system.

concurring opinion Opinion by a member of a court that agrees with the result reached by the court in the case but disagrees with or departs from the court's rationale for the decision.

confederation Constitutional arrangement whereby the national government is created by and relies on subnational governments for its authority.

conference committees Meetings between representatives of the House and Senate to reconcile differences over provisions of a bill passed by both houses.

confirmation The constitutionally required consent of the Senate to appointments of high-level executive officials by the president and appointments of federal judges.

congressional hearings Congressional committee sessions in which members listen to witnesses who provide information and opinions on matters of interest to the committee, including pending legislation.

congressional investigation Congressional committee hearings on alleged misdeeds or scandals.

Connecticut Compromise A constitutional plan that merged elements of a Virginia plan and a New Jersey plan into the present arrangement of the U.S. Congress: one house in which each state has an equal number of votes (the Senate) and one house in which states' votes are based on population (the House of Representatives).

conservatism Belief in the value of free markets, limited government, and individual self-reliance in economic affairs, combined with a belief in the value of tradition, law, and morality in social affairs.

constituency The votes in a legislator's home district.

constitution The legal structure of a political system, establishing governmental bodies, granting their powers, determining how their members are selected, and prescribing the rules by which they make their decisions. Considered basic or fundamental, a constitution cannot be changed by ordinary acts of governmental bodies.

constitutional government A government limited by rule of law in its power over the liberties of individuals.

constitutionalism A government of laws, not people, operating on the principle that governmental power must be limited and government officials should be restrained in their exercise of power over individuals.

containment Policy of preventing an enemy from expanding its boundaries and/or influence, specifically the U.S. foreign policy vis-à-vis the Soviet Union during the Cold War.

contempt Willful disobedience to, or open disrespect of, a court or congressional body.

contingency fee Fee paid to attorneys to represent the plaintiff in a civil suit and receive in compensation an agreed-upon percentage of damages awarded (if any).

continuing resolution Congressional bill that authorizes government agencies to keep spending money for a specified period at the same level as in the previous fiscal year; passed when Congress is unable to enact final appropriations measures by October 1.

convention Nominating process in which delegates from local party organizations select the party's nominees.

cooperative federalism Model of federalism in which national, state, and local governments work together exercising common policy responsibilities.

covert actions Secret intelligence activities outside U.S. borders undertaken with specific authorization by the president; acknowledgment of U.S. sponsorship would defeat or compromise their purpose.

cracking Redistricting in which a strong minority is divided up and diluted to prevent it from electing a representative.

Cuban Missile Crisis The 1962 confrontation between the Soviet Union and the United States over Soviet placement of nuclear missiles in Cuba.

cyberculture The emergent culture that results from computerization, networking, and use of new media.

cyberpolitics The application of new media to campaign politics.

D

damages Financial compensation one can receive for an injury.

de facto segregation Racial imbalances not directly caused by official actions but rather by residential patterns.

dealignment Declining attractiveness of the parties to the voters, a reluctance to identify strongly with a party, and a decrease in reliance on party affiliation in voter choice.

Declaration of Independence The resolution adopted by the Second Continental Congress on July 4, 1776, that the American colonies are to be "free and Independent states." Drafted by Thomas Jefferson, it asserts natural law, inalienable rights, government by contract, and the right of revolution. John Hancock is said to have signed first in large letters so King George III could read it without his glasses.

deductibles Initial charges in insurance plans, paid by beneficiaries.

defendant Party against whom a criminal or civil suit is brought.

deferrals Items on which a president wishes to postpone spending.

deficits Imbalances in the annual federal budget in which spending exceeds revenues.

delegated, or enumerated, powers Powers specifically mentioned in the Constitution as belonging to the national government.

delegates (political parties) Accredited voting members of a party's national presidential nominating convention.

delegates (Congress) Legislators who feel obligated to present the views of their home constituents.

democracy Governing system in which the people govern themselves; from the Greek term meaning "rule by the many."

Democratic Party One of the main parties in American politics; it traces its origins to Thomas Jefferson's Democratic-Republican Party and acquired its current name under Andrew Jackson in 1828.

democratic principles Individual dignity, equality before the law, widespread participation in public decisions, and public decisions by majority rule, with one person having one vote.

dependency ratio In the Social Security system, the number of recipients as a percentage of the number of contributing workers.

deterrence U.S. approach to deterring any nuclear attack from the Soviet Union by maintaining a second-strike capability.

devolution Passing down of responsibilities from the national government to the states.

diffuse support (for the political system) Goodwill toward governmental authority learned early in life.

Dillon's Rule Named for a legal decision by Judge John Forrest Dillon in 1868, this rule holds that local governments, as municipal corporations, exist and get their powers from the state legislature. Cities and counties have lesser standing than individuals or states, and only possess the powers delegated to them.

diplomatic recognition Power of the president to grant or withhold "legitimacy" to or from a government of another nation (to declare or refuse to declare it "rightful").

direct democracy Governing system in which every person participates actively in every public decision, rather than delegating decision making to representatives.

direct discrimination Now illegal practice of differential pay for men versus women even when those individuals have equal qualifications and perform the same job.

discharge petition Petition signed by at least 218 House members to force a vote on a bill within a committee that opposes it.

discretionary funds Budgeted funds not earmarked for specific purposes but available to be spent in accordance with the best judgment of a bureaucrat.

discretionary spending Spending for programs not previously mandated by law.

dissenting opinion Opinion by a member of a court that disagrees with the result reached by the court in the case.

district courts Original jurisdiction trial courts of the federal system.

diversity Term in higher education that refers to racial, gender, and ethnic representation among students and faculty.

divided party government One party controls the presidency while the other party controls one or both houses of Congress.

division of labor Division of work among many specialized workers in a bureaucracy.

drafting a bill Actual writing of a bill in legal language.

dual federalism Early concept of federalism in which national and state powers were clearly distinguished and functionally separate.

E

earmarks Provisions in appropriation bills specifying particular projects for which federal money is to be spent.

Earned Income Tax Credit (EITC) Tax refunds in excess of tax payments for low-income workers.

economic cycles Fluctuations in real GDP growth followed by contraction.

Electoral College The 538 presidential electors apportioned among the states according to their congressional representation (plus three for the District of Columbia) whose votes officially elect the president and vice president of the United States.

elitism Political system in which power is concentrated in the hands of a relatively small group of individuals or institutions.

Emancipation Proclamation Lincoln's 1862 Civil War declaration that all slaves residing in rebel states were free. It did not abolish all slavery; that would be done by the 13th Amendment in 1865.

eminent domain The action of a government to take property for public use with just compensation even if the owner does not wish to sell.

end of history The collapse of communism and the worldwide movement toward free markets and political democracy.

Enlightenment Also known as the Age of Reason, a philosophical movement in eighteenth-century Western thought based on a belief in reason and the capacities of individuals, a faith in a scientific approach to knowledge, and a confidence in human progress.

entitlement programs Social welfare programs that provide classes of people with legally enforceable rights to benefits.

entitlements Benefits of social welfare programs for which individuals are eligible by law.

enumerated powers Powers specifically mentioned in the Constitution as belonging to the national government.

environmental federalism National laws that regulate environmental threats that cross state lines, and how the national government interacts with states on environmental policy.

environmental groups Groups primarily concerned with issues of conservation or preservation of natural resources.

Equal Rights Amendment (ERA) Proposed amendment to the Constitution guaranteeing that equal rights under the law shall not be denied or abridged on account of sex. Passed by Congress in 1972, the amendment failed to win ratification by three of the necessary three-fourths of the states.

equality of opportunity Elimination of artificial barriers to success in life and the opportunity for everyone to strive for success.

equality of results Equal sharing of income and material goods.

equal-time rule Federal Communications Commission (FCC) requirement that broadcasters who sell time to any political candidate must make equal time available to opposing candidates at the same price.

Establishment Clause Clause in the 1st Amendment to the Constitution that is interpreted to require the separation of church and state.

ex post facto law Retroactive criminal law that works against the accused; forbidden under Article I of the Constitution.

exclusionary rule Rule of law that evidence found in an illegal search or resulting from an illegally obtained confession may not be admitted at trial.

executive agreements Agreements with other nations signed by the president of the United States but less formal (and hence potentially less binding) than a treaty because it does not require Senate confirmation.

executive orders Formal regulations governing executive branch operations issued by the president.

executive privilege Right of a president to withhold from other branches of government confidential communications within the executive branch; although posited by presidents, it has been upheld by the Supreme Court only in limited situations.

externalities Costs imposed on people who are not direct participants in an activity.

F

Fair Deal Policies of President Harry Truman that extended Roosevelt's New Deal and maintained the Democratic Party's voter coalition.

Family Assistance (TANF) Public assistance program that provides monies to the states for their use in helping needy families with children.

fascism Political ideology in which the state and/or race is assumed to be supreme over individuals.

Federal Election Commission (FEC) Agency charged with enforcing federal election laws and disbursing public presidential campaign funds.

Federal Reserve Board (the Fed) Independent agency of the executive branch of the federal government charged with overseeing the nation's monetary policy.

federalism A constitutional arrangement whereby power is divided between national and subnational governments, each of which enforces its own laws directly on its citizens and neither of which can alter the arrangement without the consent of the other.

Federalists Supporters of the ratification of the Constitution, who later coalesced into a political party supporting John Adams for president in 1800.

"feeding frenzy" Intense media coverage of a scandal or event that blocks out most other news.

filibuster Delaying tactic by a senator or group of senators, using the Senate's unlimited debate rule to prevent a vote on a bill.

fiscal federalism The practice of different levels of government taxing different sources of revenue, based on the mobility of wealth and income.

fiscal policy Economic policies involving taxing, spending, and deficit levels of the national government.

fiscal year Yearly government accounting period, not necessarily the same as the calendar year. The federal government's fiscal year begins October 1 and ends September 30.

focus group In a political context, a small number of people brought together in a comfortable setting to discuss and respond to themes and issues, allowing campaign managers to develop and analyze strategies.

Food Stamp program (SNAP) Public assistance program that provides low-income households with coupons redeemable for enough food to provide a minimal nutritious diet.

fourth estate The free news press and the people and institutions of the free press.

franking privilege Free use of the U.S. mails granted to members of Congress to promote communication with constituents.

Free Exercise Clause Clause in the 1st Amendment to the Constitution that prohibits government from restricting religious beliefs and practices that do not harm society.

free market Free competition for voluntary exchange among individuals, firms, and corporations.

freedom of expression Collectively, the 1st Amendment rights to free speech, press, and assembly.

free-riders People who do not belong to an organization or pay dues, yet nevertheless benefit from its activities.

front-end strategy Presidential political campaign strategy in which a candidate focuses on winning early primaries to build momentum.

front-loading The scheduling of presidential primary elections early in the year.

G

gender gap A difference of opinion on issues or vote preference between men and women detected by opinion polling.

general election Election to choose among candidates nominated by parties and/or Independent candidates who gained access to the ballot by petition.

generation gap Differences in politics and public opinion among age groups.

gerrymandering Drawing district boundary lines for political advantage.

glass ceiling "Invisible" barriers to women rising to the highest positions in corporations and the professions.

GOP "Grand Old Party"—a popular label for the Republican Party.

Government Accountability Office An arm of Congress that undertakes oversight of the operations and finances of executive agencies as well as performing policy research and evaluation.

government Organization extending to the whole society that can legitimately use force to carry out its decisions.

grand jury Jury charged only with determining whether sufficient evidence exists to support indictment of an individual on a felony charge; the grand jury's decision to indict does not represent a conviction.

grant of immunity from prosecution Grant by the government to an individual of freedom from prosecution on a particular charge in return for testimony by that individual that might otherwise be self-incriminating.

grant-in-aid Payment of funds from the national government to state or local governments or from a state government to local governments for a specified purpose.

grassroots lobbying Attempts to influence government decision making by inspiring constituents to contact their representatives.

Great Society Policies of President Lyndon Johnson that promised to solve the nation's social and economic problems through government intervention.

gridlock Political stalemate between the executive and legislative branches arising when one branch is controlled by one major political party and the other branch by the other party.

gross domestic product (GDP) Measure of economic performance in terms of the nation's total production of goods and services for a single year, valued in terms of market prices.

H

halo effect Tendency of survey respondents to provide socially acceptable answers to questions.

health maintenance organizations (HMOs) Health care provider groups that provide a stipulated list of services to patients for a fixed fee that is usually substantially lower than such care would otherwise cost.

hold An informal request by a senator to his party's leader that a piece of legislation not be brought to the floor for consideration.

home rule Power of local government to pass laws affecting local affairs, so long as those laws do not conflict with state or federal laws.

home style Activities of Congress members specifically directed at their home constituencies.

honeymoon period Early months of a president's term in which his popularity with the public and influence with the Congress are generally high.

horse-race coverage Media coverage of electoral campaigns that concentrates on who is ahead and who is behind, and neglects the issues at stake.

I

ideological organizations Interest groups that pursue ideologically based (liberal or conservative) agendas.

ideological parties Third parties that exist to promote an ideology rather than to win elections.

ideology Consistent and integrated system of ideas, values, and beliefs.

illegal immigration The unlawful entry of a person into a nation.

immigration policy Regulating the entry of noncitizens into the country.

impeachment Formal charges of wrongdoing brought against a government official, resulting in a trial and upon conviction removal from office.

impersonality Treatment of all persons within a bureaucracy on the basis of "merit" and of all "clients" served by the bureaucracy equally according to rules.

implementation Development by the federal bureaucracy of procedures and activities to carry out policies legislated by Congress, it includes regulation as well as adjudication.

implied powers Powers not mentioned specifically in the Constitution as belonging to Congress but inferred as necessary and proper for carrying out the enumerated powers.

impoundment Refusal by a president to spend monies appropriated by Congress; outlawed except with congressional consent by the Budget and Impoundment Control Act of 1974.

inalienable rights The rights of all people derived from natural law and not bestowed by governments, including the rights to life, liberty, and property.

incidence Actual bearer of a tax burden.

income transfers Government transfers of income from taxpayers to persons regarded as deserving.

incorporation In constitutional law, the application of almost all of the Bill of Rights to the states and all of their subdivisions through the 14th Amendment.

incremental budgeting Method of budgeting that focuses on requested increases in funding for existing programs, accepting as legitimate their previous year's expenditures.

incumbent gerrymandering Drawing legislative district boundaries to advantage incumbent legislators.

incumbents Candidates currently in office seeking reelection.

independent counsel, or ("special prosecutor") A prosecutor appointed by a federal court to pursue charges against a president or other high official. This position was allowed to lapse by Congress in 1999 after many controversial investigations by these prosecutors.

indexing Tying of benefit levels in social welfare programs to the general price level.

indictment Determination by a grand jury that sufficient evidence exists to warrant trial of an individual on a felony charge; necessary before an individual can be brought to trial.

individual income tax Taxes on individuals' wages and other earned income, the primary source of revenue for the U.S. federal government.

individual mandate A requirement that every American purchase health insurance or face a tax penalty.

inflation Rise in the general level of prices; not just the prices of some products.

information overload Situation in which individuals are subjected to so many communications that they cannot make sense of them.

initiative Allows a specified number or percentage of voters by use of a petition to place a state constitutional amendment or a state law on the ballot for adoption or rejection by the state electorate.

in-kind (noncash) benefits Benefits of a social welfare program that are not cash payments, including free medical care, subsidized housing, and food stamps.

interest groups Organizations seeking to directly influence government policy.

interest-group entrepreneurs Leaders who create organizations and market memberships.

intergovernmental relations Network of political, financial, and administrative relationships between units of the federal government and those of state and local governments.

iron triangles Mutually supportive relationships among interest groups, government agencies, and legislative committees with jurisdiction over a specific policy area.

issue ads Ads that advocate policy positions rather than explicitly supporting or opposing particular candidates.

issue networks Coalitions of interest groups and governmental players who promote policy on a particular issue.

J

Jim Crow Second-class-citizen status conferred on blacks by Southern segregation laws; derived from a nineteenth-century song-and-dance act (usually performed by a white man in blackface) that stereotyped blacks.

judicial activism Making of new law through judicial interpretations of the Constitution.

judicial review Power of the U.S. Supreme Court and federal judiciary to declare laws of Congress and the states and actions of the president unconstitutional and therefore legally invalid.

judicial self-restraint Self-imposed limitation on judicial power by judges deferring to the policy judgments of elected branches of government.

jurisdiction Power of a court to hear a case in question.

K

K Street The primary location, in Washington, D.C., of many powerful lobbying organizations and interest groups.

"killer" amendments An amendment to a piece of legislation that is designed to ensure the defeat of the bill on final vote.

Korean War Communist North Korea invaded noncommunist South Korea in June 1950, causing President Harry S. Truman to intervene militarily, with UN support. General Douglas MacArthur defeated the North Koreans, but with China's entry into the war, a stalemate resulted. An armistice was signed in 1953, with Korea divided along nearly original lines.

laboratories of democracy A reference to the ability of states to experiment and innovate in public policy.

left A reference to the liberal, progressive, and/or socialist side of the political spectrum.

legal equality Belief that the laws should apply equally to all persons.

legitimacy Widespread acceptance of something as necessary, rightful, and legally binding.

Lemon test To be constitutional, a law must have a secular purpose; its primary effect must neither advance nor inhibit religion; and it must not foster excessive government entanglement with religion.

Leninism The theories of Vladimir Lenin, among them being that advanced capitalist countries turned toward war and colonialism to make their own workers relatively prosperous.

libel Writings that are false and malicious and intended to damage an individual.

liberalism Belief in the value of strong government to provide economic security and protection for civil rights, combined with a belief in personal freedom from government intervention in social conduct.

libertarian Opposing government intervention in both economic and social affairs, and favoring minimal government in all sectors of society.

limited government Principle that government power over the individual is limited, that there are some personal liberties that even a majority cannot regulate, and that government itself is restrained by law.

line-item veto Power of the chief executive to reject some portions of a bill without rejecting all of it.

literacy test Examination of a person's ability to read and write as a prerequisite to voter registration, outlawed by Voting Rights Act (1965) as discriminatory.

litigation Legal dispute brought before a court.

litmus test In political terms, a person's stand on a key issue that determines whether he or she will be appointed to public office or supported in electoral campaigns.

lobbying Activities directed at government officials with the hope of influencing their decisions.

lobbyist Person working to influence government policies and actions.

logrolling Bargaining for agreement among legislators to support each other's favorite bills, especially projects that primarily benefit individual members and their constituents.

M

machines Tightly disciplined party organizations, headed by a boss, that rely on material rewards—including patronage jobs—to control politics.

majoritarianism Tendency of democratic governments to allow the faint preferences of the majority to prevail over the intense feelings of minorities.

majority Election by more than 50 percent of all votes cast in the contest.

majority leader In the House, the majority-party leader and second in command to the Speaker, in the Senate, the leader of the majority party.

majority opinion Opinion in a case that is subscribed to by a majority of the judges who participated in the decision.

malapportionment Unequal numbers of people in legislative districts resulting in inequality of voter representation.

managed care Programs designed to keep health care costs down by the establishment of strict guidelines regarding when and what diagnostic and therapeutic procedures should be administered to patients under various circumstances.

mandates Perceptions of popular support for a program or policy based on the margin of electoral victory won by a candidate who proposed it during a campaign; direct federal orders to state and local governments requiring them to perform a service or to obey federal laws in the performance of their functions.

mandatory spending Spending for program commitments made by past congresses.

markup Line-by-line revision of a bill in committee by editing each phrase and word.

Marshall Plan U.S. program to rebuild the nations of Western Europe in the aftermath of World War II in order to render them less susceptible to communist influence and takeover.

Marxism The theories of Karl Marx, among them that capitalists oppress workers and that worldwide revolution and the emergence of a classless society are inevitable.

mass media All means of communication with the general public, including television, newspapers, magazines, radio, books, recordings, motion pictures, and the Internet.

Mayflower Compact Agreement among Pilgrim colonists to establish a government, setting the precedent of government by contract among the governed.

means-tested spending Spending for benefits that is distributed on the basis of the recipient's income.

media events Staged activities designed to attract media attention.

median voter theorem Two-party political systems tend to create centrist political parties who battle for decisive votes of moderate voters.

Medicaid Federal aid to the states to provide health insurance for low-income persons.

Medicare Social insurance program that provides health care insurance to elderly and disabled people.

merit system Selection of employees for government agencies on the basis of competence, with no consideration of an individual's political stance and/or power.

minority leader In both the House and Senate, the leader of the opposition party.

mobilize In politics, to activate supporters to work for candidates and turnout on Election Day.

monetary policy Economic policies involving the money supply, interest rates, and banking activity.

money bombs Large amounts of money raised in a brief period of time using only online resources.

"Motor Voter Act" Federal mandate that states offer voter registration at driver's licensing and welfare offices.

muckraking Journalistic exposés of corruption, wrongdoing, or mismanagement in government, business, and other institutions of society.

N

name recognition Public awareness of a candidate—whether people even know his or her name.

narrowcasting The emergence of news outlets on cable television and the Internet that offer specialty content for small, niche audiences.

national debt Total debt accumulated by the national government over the years.

National Security Council (NSC) "Inner cabinet" that advises the president and coordinates foreign, defense, and intelligence activities.

National Supremacy Clause Clause in Article VI of the U.S. Constitution declaring the constitution and laws of the national government "the supreme law of the land" superior to the constitutions and laws of the states.

nationalism Belief that shared cultural, historical, linguistic, and social characteristics of a people justify the creation of a government encompassing all of them and that the resulting nation-state should be independent and legally equal to all other nation-states.

natural law Rules governing human behavior that are morally superior to laws made by governments.

Necessary and Proper Clause Clause in Article I, Section 8, of the U.S. Constitution granting Congress the power to enact all laws that are "necessary and proper" for carrying out those responsibilities specifically delegated to it. Also referred to as the Implied Powers Clause.

negative campaigning Speeches, commercials, or advertising attacking a political opponent during a campaign.

New Deal Policies of President Franklin D. Roosevelt during the Depression of the 1930s that helped form a Democratic Party coalition of urban working-class, ethnic, Catholic, Jewish, poor, and southern voters.

new federalism Attempts to return power and responsibility to the states and reduce the role of the national government in domestic affairs.

new media Content and technology that result in the ability of individuals to actively and immediately share content generated in traditional media forms (text, image, sound, and video).

newsmaking Deciding what events, topics, presentations, and issues will be given coverage in the news.

nominations Political party's selections of its candidates for public office.

nominee Political party's entry in a general election race.

nonpartisan elections Elections in which candidates do not officially indicate their party affiliation; often used for city, county, school board, and judicial elections.

nonviolent direct action Strategy used by civil rights leaders such as Martin Luther King, Jr., in which protesters break "unjust" laws openly but in a "loving" fashion in order to bring the injustices of such laws to public attention.

North Atlantic Treaty Organization (NATO) Mutual-security agreement and joint military command uniting the nations of Western Europe, initially formed to resist Soviet expansionism.

O

obligational authority Feature of some appropriations acts by which an agency is empowered to enter into contracts that will require the government to make payments beyond the fiscal year in question.

one person, one vote The principle that legislative districts should have equal populations to ensure equal voting power of all individuals.

open primaries Primary elections in which a voter may cast a ballot in either party's primary election.

open rule Rule that permits unlimited amendments to a bill under consideration by the House.

open seat Seat in a legislature for which no incumbent is running for reelection.

organizational sclerosis Society encrusted with so many special benefits to interest groups that everyone's standard of living is lowered.

original intent Judicial philosophy under which judges attempt to apply the values of the Founders to current issues.

original jurisdiction Refers to a particular court's power to serve as the place where a given case is initially argued and decided.

outlays Actual dollar amounts to be spent by the federal government in a fiscal year.

outsourcing Government contracting with private firms to perform public services.

override Voting in Congress to enact legislation vetoed by the president; requires a two-thirds vote in both the House and Senate.

oversight Congressional monitoring of the activities of executive branch agencies to determine if the laws are being faithfully executed.

P

packing Redistricting in which partisan voters are concentrated in a single district, "wasting" their majority vote and allowing the opposition to win by modest majorities in other districts.

paradox of democracy Potential for conflict between individual freedom and majority rule.

parliamentary government A government in which power is concentrated in the legislature, which chooses from among its members a prime minister and cabinet.

partial preemption Federal government's assumption of some regulatory powers in a particular field, with the stipulation that a state law on the same subject as a federal law is valid if it does not conflict with the federal law in the same area.

party identification Self-described identification with a political party, usually in response to the question, "Generally speaking, how would you identify yourself: as a Republican, Democrat, Independent, or something else?"

party organization National and state party officials and workers, committee members, convention delegates, and others active in the party.

party polarization The tendency of the Democratic Party to take more liberal positions and the Republican Party to take more conservative positions on key issues.

party unity Percentage of Democrats and Republicans who stick with their party on party votes.

party votes Majority of Democrats voting in opposition to a majority of Republicans.

party-in-the-electorate Voters who identify themselves with a party.

party-in-the-government Public officials who were nominated by their party and who identify themselves in office with their party.

passport Evidence of U.S. citizenship, allowing people to travel abroad and reenter the United States.

patronage Appointment to public office based on party loyalty.

perjury Lying while under oath after swearing to tell the truth.

petit (regular) juries Juries called to determine guilt or innocence.

photo ops Staged opportunities for the media to photograph the candidate in a favorable setting.

plaintiff Individual or party who initiates a lawsuit or complaint.

platform Statement of principles adopted by a political party at its national convention (specific portions of the platform are known as planks); a platform is not binding on the party's candidates.

plea bargaining Practice of allowing defendants to plead guilty to lesser crimes than those with which they were originally charged in return for reduced sentences.

pluralism Theory that democracy can be achieved through competition among multiple organized groups and that individuals can participate in politics through group memberships and elections.

plurality Election by at least one vote more than any other candidate in the race.

pocket veto Effective veto of a bill when Congress adjourns within 10 days of passing it and the president fails to sign it.

political action committees (PACs) Organizations that solicit and receive campaign contributions from corporations, unions, trade associations, and ideological and issue-oriented groups, and their members, and then distribute these funds to political candidates.

political alienation Belief that politics is irrelevant to one's life and that one cannot personally affect public affairs.

political culture Widely shared views about who should govern, for what ends, and by what means.

political equality Belief that every person's vote counts equally.

political organizations Parties and interest groups that function as intermediaries between individuals and government.

political parties Organizations that seek to achieve power by winning public office.

political science The study of politics: who governs, for what ends, and by what means.

politically correct (PC) Repression of attitudes, speech, and writings that are deemed racist, sexist, homophobic (antihomosexual), or otherwise "insensitive."

politics Deciding who gets what, when, and how.

poll taxes Taxes imposed as a prerequisite to voting; prohibited by the 24th Amendment.

pork barreling Legislation designed to make government benefits, including jobs and projects used as political patronage, flow to a particular district or state.

poverty line Official standard regarding what level of annual cash income is sufficient to maintain a "decent standard of living"; those with incomes below this level are eligible for most public assistance programs.

power of the purse Congress's exclusive constitutional power to authorize expenditures by all agencies of the federal government.

precedent Legal principle that previous decisions should determine the outcome of current cases; the basis for stability in law.

precincts Subdivisions of a city, county, or ward for election purposes.

preemption Total or partial federal assumption of power in a particular field, restricting the authority of the states.

preemptive attacks The initiation of military action by the United States to prevent terrorists or rogue nations from inflicting heavy damage on the United States.

preferred position Refers to the tendency of the courts to give preference to the 1st Amendment rights to speech, press, and assembly when faced with conflicts.

preferred provider organizations (PPOs) Groups of hospitals and physicians who have joined together to offer their services to private insurers at a discount.

presidential primaries Primary elections in the states in which voters in each party can choose a presidential candidate for their party's nomination. Outcomes help determine the distribution of pledged delegates to each party's national nominating convention.

primary elections Elections to choose party nominees for public office; may be open or closed.

prior restraint Government actions to restrict publication of a magazine, newspaper, or books on grounds of libel, obscenity, or other legal violations prior to actual publication of the work.

professionalism In politics, a reference to the increasing number of officeholders for whom politics is a full-time occupation.

program budgeting Identifying items in a budget according to the functions and programs they are to be spent on.

progressive taxation System of taxation in which higher-income groups pay a larger percentage of their incomes in taxes than do lower-income groups.

property qualifications Early American state requirement of property ownership in order to vote.

proportional (flat) taxation System of taxation in which all income groups pay the same percentage of their income in taxes.

proportional representation Electoral system that allocates seats in a legislature based on the proportion of votes each party receives in a national election.

prospective voting Voting for or against a candidate or party on the expectations of their actions if they win.

protest parties Third parties that arise in response to issues of popular concern that have not been addressed by the major parties.

protests Public marches or demonstrations designed to call attention to an issue and motivate others to apply pressure on public officials.

public assistance Those social welfare programs for which no contributions are required and only those defined as low-income are eligible; includes food stamps, Medicaid, and Family Assistance.

public goods Goods and services that cannot readily be provided by markets, either because they are too expensive for a single individual to buy or because if one person bought them, everyone else would use them without paying.

public opinion Aggregate of preferences and opinions of individuals on significant issues.

"public option" A government-run nonprofit health insurance agency that would compete with private insurers; rejected by Congress.

public relations Building and maintaining goodwill with the general public.

public-interest groups Interest groups that claim to represent broad classes of people or the public as a whole.

pundits An individual who offers expert opinion to the mass media.

Q

quota Provision of some affirmative action programs in which specific numbers or percentages of positions are open only to minorities and/or women.

R

raiding Organized efforts by one party to get its members to cross over in a primary and defeat an attractive candidate in the opposition party's primary.

ranking minority member The minority-party committee member with the most seniority.

ratification Power of a legislature to approve or reject decisions made by other bodies. State legislators or state conventions must have the power to ratify constitutional amendments submitted by Congress. The U.S. Senate has the power to ratify treaties made by the president.

Reagan Coalition Combination of economic and social conservatives, religious fundamentalists, and defense-minded anticommunists who rallied behind Republican President Ronald Reagan.

realignment Long-term shift in social-group support for various political parties that creates new coalitions in each party.

recall An election to allow voters to decide whether or not to remove an elected official before his or her term expires.

recession Decline in the general level of economic activity.

Reconstruction The post–Civil War period when the Southern states were occupied by federal troops and newly freed African Americans occupied many political offices and exercised civil rights.

redistricting Drawing of legislative district boundary lines following each 10-year census.

reelection rates Percentages of incumbents running for reelection who are successful.

referenda Proposed laws or constitutional amendments submitted to the voters for their direct approval or rejection, found in state constitutions, but not in the U.S. Constitution.

regional security Attempt to bring order to international relations during the Cold War by creating regional alliances between a superpower and nations of a particular region.

registration Requirement that prospective voters establish their identity and place of residence prior to an election in order to be eligible to vote.

regressive taxation System of taxation in which lower-income groups pay a larger percentage of their incomes in taxes than do higher-income groups.

regulation Development by the federal bureaucracy of formal rules for implementing legislation.

remedies and relief Orders of a court to correct a wrong, including a violation of the Constitution.

rent A payment for a good beyond the marginal cost of the factors that enter its production and supply.

representational federalism Assertion that no constitutional division of powers exists between the nation and the states but the states retain their constitutional role merely by selecting the president and members of Congress.

representative democracy Governing system in which public decision making is delegated to representatives of the people chosen by popular vote in free, open, and periodic elections.

Republican Party One of the two main parties in American politics, it traces its origins to the antislavery and nationalist forces that united in the 1850s and nominated Abraham Lincoln for president in 1860.

republicanism Government by representatives of the people rather than directly by the people themselves.

rescissions Items on which a president wishes to cancel spending.

reserved powers Powers not granted to the national government or specifically denied to the states in the Constitution that are recognized by the 10th Amendment as belonging to the state governments. This guarantee, known as the Reserved Powers Clause, embodies the principle of American federalism.

responsible party model System in which competitive parties adopt a platform of principles, recruiting candidates and directing campaigns based on that platform and holding their elected officials responsible for enacting it.

restricted rule Rule that allows only specified amendments to be added to a bill under consideration by the House.

retail politics Direct candidate contact with individual voters.

retrospective voting Voting for or against a candidate or party on the basis of past performance in office.

revolving doors The movement of individuals from government positions to jobs in the private sector, using the experience, knowledge, and contacts they acquired in government employment.

rider Amendment to a bill that is not germane to the bill's purposes.

right A reference to the conservative, traditional, anticommunist side of the political spectrum.

roll-call vote Vote of the full House or Senate at which all members' individual votes are recorded and made public.

rule of four At least four justices must agree to hear an appeal (writ of certiorari) from a lower court in order to get a case before the Supreme Court.

rule Stipulation attached to a bill in the House of Representatives that governs its consideration on the floor, including when and for how long it can be debated and how many (if any) amendments may be appended to it.

runoff primary Additional primary held between the top two vote-getters in a primary where no candidate has received a majority of the vote.

S

safe seats Legislative districts in which the incumbent regularly wins by a large margin of the vote.

salient issues Issues about which most people have an opinion.

SALT I First arms limitation treaty between the United States and the Soviet Union, signed in 1972, limiting the total number of offensive nuclear missiles; it included the ABM Treaty that reflected the theory that the population centers of both nations should be left undefended.

SALT II Lengthy and complicated treaty between the United States and the Soviet Union, agreed to in 1979 but never ratified by the U.S. Senate, that set limits on all types of strategic nuclear launch vehicles.

SCHIP Federal grants to the states to extend health insurance to children of low-income families.

search warrant Court order permitting law-enforcement officials to search a location in order to seize evidence of a crime; issued only for a specified location, in connection with a specific investigation, and on submission of proof that "probable cause" exists to warrant such a search.

second-strike capability Ability of a nation's forces to survive a surprise nuclear attack by the enemy and then to retaliate effectively.

secular In politics, a reference to opposition to religious practices and symbols in public life.

selective perception Mentally screening out information or opinions with which one disagrees.

senatorial courtesy Custom of the U.S. Senate with regard to presidential nominations to the judiciary to defer to the judgment of senators from the president's party from the same state as the nominee.

seniority system Custom whereby the member of Congress who has served the longest on the majority side of a committee becomes its chair and the member who has served the longest on the minority side becomes its ranking member.

separate but equal Ruling of the Supreme Court in the case of Plessy v. Ferguson (1896) to the effect that segregated facilities were legal as long as the facilities were equal.

separation of powers Constitutional division of powers among the three branches of the national government—legislative, executive, and judicial.

set-aside program Program in which a specified number or percentage of contracts must go to designated minorities.

Shays's Rebellion An armed revolt in 1786, led by a Revolutionary War Officer Daniel Shays, protesting the discontent of small farmers over debts and taxes, and raising concerns about the ability of the U.S. government under the Articles of Confederation to maintain internal order.

shield laws Laws in some states that give reporters the right to refuse to name their sources or to release their notes in court cases; may be overturned by the courts when such refusals jeopardize a fair trial for a defendant.

single-issue groups Organizations formed to support or oppose government action on a specific issue.

single-issue parties Third parties formed around one particular cause.

slander Oral statements that are false and malicious and intended to damage an individual.

social contract The idea the government originates from an implied contract among people who agree to obey laws in exchange for the protection of their natural rights.

social insurance Social welfare programs to which beneficiaries have made contributions so that they are entitled to benefits regardless of their personal wealth.

social media applications Internet and new media applications that facilitate social coordination and interaction.

social mobility Extent to which people move upward or downward in income and status over a lifetime or over generations.

social movements Organized movements of persons who make "collective claims" on others.

Social Security Social insurance program composed of the Old Age and Survivors Insurance program, which pays benefits to retired workers who have paid into the program and their dependents and survivors, and the Disability Insurance program, which pays benefits to disabled workers and their families.

socialism System of government involving collective or government ownership of economic enterprise, with the goal being equality of results, not merely equality of opportunity.

socialization The learning of a culture and its values.

soft money Previously unregulated contributions to the parties, now prohibited; contributions to parties now limited.

soft news News featured in talk shows, late-night comedy, and TV news magazines—reaches more people than regular news broadcasts.

solicitor general Attorney in the Department of Justice who represents the U.S. government before the Supreme Court and any other courts.

Solid South An empirical theory of American politics stating that when the former Confederate states are unified and vote the same way, they determine who wins the presidency.

sound bites Concise and catchy phrases that attract media coverage.

sovereign immunity Legal doctrine that individuals can sue the government only with the government's consent.

Soviet Union The Union of Soviet Socialist Republics (USSR), consisting of Russia and its bordering lands and ruled by the communist regime in Moscow; officially dissolved in 1991.

Speaker of the House Presiding officer of the House of Representatives.

spin doctors Practitioners of the art of spin control, or manipulation of media reporting to favor their own candidate.

splinter parties Third parties formed by a dissatisfied faction of a major party.

spoils system Selection of employees for government agencies on the basis of party loyalty, electoral support, and political influence.

standard partial preemption Form of partial preemption in which the states are permitted to regulate activities already regulated by the federal government if the state regulatory standards are at least as stringent as the federal government's.

standing committee Permanent committee of the House or Senate that deals with matters within a specified subject area.

standing Requirement that the party who files a lawsuit have a legal stake in the outcome.

stare decisis Judicial precept that the issue has already been decided in earlier cases and the earlier decision need only be applied in the specific case before the bench; the rule in most cases, it comes from the Latin for "the decision stands."

START I First treaty between the United States and the Soviet Union that actually reduced the strategic nuclear arms of the superpowers, signed in 1991.

START II A treaty between the United States and Russia eliminating all multiwarhead land missiles and reducing nuclear weapons stockpiles; signed in 1993.

statutory laws Laws made by act of Congress or the state legislatures, as opposed to constitutional law.

strict scrutiny Supreme Court holding that race-based actions by governments can be done only to remedy past discrimination or to further a "compelling" interest and must be "narrowly tailored" to minimize effects on the rights of others.

subcommittees Specialized committees within standing committees; subcommittee recommendations must be approved by the full standing committee before submission to the floor.

subcultures Variations on the prevailing values and beliefs in a society.

subpoena A written command to appear before a court or a congressional committee.

suffrage Legal right to vote.

Sullivan rule Court guideline that false and malicious statements regarding public officials are protected by the 1st Amendment unless it can be proven they were known to be false at the time they were made or were made with "reckless disregard" for their truth or falsehood.

superdelegates Delegates to the Democratic Party national convention selected because of their position in the government or the party and not pledged to any candidate.

superpowers Refers to the United States and the Soviet Union after World War II, when these two nations dominated international politics.

Supplemental Security Income (SSI) Public assistance program that provides monthly cash payments to the needy elderly (65 or older), blind, and disabled.

survey research Gathering of information about public opinion by questioning a representative sample of the population.

swing states States that are not considered to be firmly in the Democratic or Republican column.

symbolic speech Actions other than speech itself but protected by the 1st Amendment because they constitute political expression.

System of Party Polarization The party alignment that emerged in the 1990s, characterized by intense, ideological identification of the parties in Congress and the electorate.

T

takings clause The 5th Amendment's prohibition against government taking of private property without just compensation.

tariff Tax imposed on imported products (also called a customs duty).

tax avoidance Taking advantage of exemptions, exclusions, deductions, and special treatments in tax laws (legal).

tax evasion Hiding income and/or falsely claiming exemptions, deductions, and special treatments (illegal).

tax expenditures Revenues lost to the federal government because of exemptions, exclusions, deductions, and special-treatment provisions in tax laws.

taxes Compulsory payments to the government.

television malaise Generalized feelings of distrust, cynicism, and powerlessness stemming from television's emphasis on the negative aspects of American life.

Temporary Assistance to Needy Families Welfare reform program replacing federal cash entitlement with grants to the states for welfare recipients.

term limits Limitations on the number of terms that an elected official can serve in office. The Constitution (Amendment XXII) limits the president to two terms. There are no limits on the terms of senators or representatives.

terrorism Title 22 of the U.S. Code, Section 2656 (d): "The term 'terrorism' means premeditated, politically motivated violence perpetrated against noncombatant targets by subnational groups or clandestine agents, usually intended to influence an audience."

third parties Political parties that challenge the two major parties in an election.

Three-Fifths Compromise A compromise in the Constitutional Convention of 1787 between pre- and slave states in which slaves would be counted as three-fifths of a person for both taxation and representation.

ticket splitters Persons who vote for candidates of different parties for different offices in a general election.

Title IX A provision in the Federal Education Act forbidding discrimination against women in college athletic programs.

tort claim When someone sues over a "civil duty" rather than over a contract.

total preemption Federal government's assumption of all regulatory powers in a particular field.

totalitarianism Rule by an elite that exercises unlimited power over individuals in all aspects of life.

trade associations Interest groups composed of businesses in specific industries.

transfer payments Direct payments (either in cash or in goods and/or services) by governments to individuals as part of a social welfare program, not as a result of any service or contribution rendered by the individual.

treaty A formal agreement with another nation (bilateral) or nations (multilateral) signed by the president and consented to by the Senate by a two-thirds vote.

Truman Doctrine U.S. foreign policy, first articulated by President Harry S. Truman, that pledged the United States to "support free peoples who are resisting attempted subjugation by armed minorities or by outside pressures."

trustees Legislators who feel obligated to use their own best judgment in decision making.

turnout Number of voters who actually cast ballots in an election, as a percentage of people eligible to register and vote.

turnover Replacement of members of Congress by retirement or resignation, by reapportionment, or (more rarely) by electoral defeat.

U

U.S. solicitor general The U.S. government's chief legal counsel, presenting the government's arguments in cases in which it is a party or in which it has an interest.

unanimous consent agreement Negotiated by the majority and minority leaders of the Senate, it specifies when a bill will be taken up on the floor, what amendments will be considered, and when a vote will be taken.

underclass People who have remained poor and dependent on welfare over a prolonged period of time.

unemployment compensation Social insurance program that temporarily replaces part of the wages of workers who have lost their jobs.

unemployment rate Percentage of the civilian labor force who are not working but who are looking for work or waiting to return to or to begin a job.

unfunded mandates Mandates that impose costs on state and local governments (and private industry) without reimbursement from the federal government.

unitary system Constitutional arrangement whereby authority rests with the national government; subnational governments have only those powers given to them by the national government.

V

values Shared ideas about what is good and desirable.

veto Rejection of a legislative act by the executive branch; in the U.S. federal government, overriding of a veto requires a two-thirds majority in both houses of Congress.

Vietnam War War between noncommunist South Vietnam and communist North Vietnam from 1956 to 1975, with increasing U.S. involvement, ending with U.S. withdrawal in 1973 and communist victory in 1975. The war became unpopular in the United States after 1968 and caused President Johnson not to run for a second term.

visa A document or stamp on a passport allowing a person to visit a foreign country.

voter targeting The use of voting record, polling, and market research data to identify and contact potential likely voters.

W

wall-of-separation doctrine The Supreme Court's interpretation of the No Establishment Clause that laws may not have as their purpose aid to one religion or aid to all religions.

War Powers Resolution Bill passed in 1973 to limit presidential war-making powers; it restricts when, why, and for how long a president can commit U.S. forces and requires notification of and, in many cases, approval by Congress.

wards Divisions of a city for electoral or administrative purposes or as units for organizing political parties.

Watergate The scandal that led to the forced resignation of President Richard M. Nixon. Adding "-gate" as a suffix to any alleged corruption in government suggests an analogy to the Watergate scandal.

wedge issue theorem Political parties run on polarizing issues to mobilize their ideological base and force moderate voters to make stark choices or not vote.

Whig Party Formed in 1836 to oppose Andrew Jackson's policies; it elected presidents Harrison in 1840 and Tyler in 1848 but soon disintegrated over the issue of slavery.

whips In both the House and Senate, the principal assistants to the party leaders and next in command to those leaders.

whistle-blowers Employees who expose waste, fraud or mismanagement in government or government contracting.

White House press corps Reporters from both print and broadcast media assigned to regularly cover the president.

white primary Democratic Party primary elections in many southern counties in the early part of the twentieth century that excluded black people from voting.

writ of certiorari Writ issued by the Supreme Court, at its discretion, to order a lower court to prepare the record of a case and send it to the Supreme Court for review. Most cases come to the Court as petitions for writs of certiorari.

writ of habeas corpus Court order directing public officials who are holding a person in custody to bring the prisoner into court and explain the reasons for confinement; the right to habeas corpus is protected by Article I of the Constitution.

Z

zero-based budgeting Method of budgeting that demands justification for the entire budget request of an agency, not just its requested increase in funding.

NOTES

1

1. Harold Lasswell, *Politics: Who Gets What, When, and How* (New York: McGraw-Hill, 1936).
2. For an update on the continuing discussion of whether political science is a "science," see Jon R. Bond, "The Scientification of the Study of Politics," *Journal of Politics* 69 (November 2007): 897–907.
3. For a discussion of various aspects of legitimacy and its measurement in public opinion polls, see M. Stephen Weatherford, "Measuring Political Legitimacy," *American Political Science Review* 86 (March 1992): 140–55.
4. Thomas Hobbes, *Leviathan* (1651).
5. John Locke, *Treatise on Government* (1688).
6. See Barbara S. Gamble, "Putting Civil Rights to a Popular Vote," *American Journal of Political Science* 41 (January 1997): 245–69. For an essay on the "paradox" of democracy, see Bonnie Honig, "Between Decision and Deliberation: Political Paradox in Democratic Theory," *American Political Science Review* 101 (February 2007): 1–25.
7. James Madison, Alexander Hamilton, and John Jay, *The Federalist Papers* (New York: Mentor Books, 1961), No. 10, p. 81. Madison's *Federalist Papers*, No. 10 and No. 51, are reprinted in the Appendix.
8. E. E. Schattschneider, *Two Hundred Million Americans in Search of a Government* (New York: Holt, Rinehart & Winston, 1969), p. 63.
9. Harold Lasswell and Daniel Lerner, *The Comparative Study of Elites* (Stanford, Calif.: Stanford University Press, 1952), p. 7.
10. C. Wright Mills's classic study, *The Power Elite* (New York: Oxford University Press, 1956), is widely cited by Marxist critics of American democracy, but it can be read profitably by anyone concerned with the effects of large bureaucracies—corporate, governmental, or military—on democratic government.
11. In *Who Rules America?* (New York: Prentice Hall, 1967) and its sequel, *Who Rules America Now?* (New York: Prentice Hall, 1983), sociologist G. William Domhoff argues that America is ruled by an "upper class" who attend the same prestigious private schools, intermarry among themselves, and join the same exclusive clubs. In *Who's Running America?* (New York: Prentice Hall, 1976) and *Who's Running America? The Bush Restoration* (New York: Prentice Hall, 2002), political scientist Thomas R. Dye documents the concentration of power and the control of assets in the hands of officers and directors of the nation's largest corporations, banks, law firms, networks, foundations, and so forth. Dye argues, however, that most of these "institutional elites" were not born into the upper class but instead climbed the ladder to success.
12. Yale political scientist Robert A. Dahl is an important contributor to the development of pluralist theory, beginning with his *Preface to Democratic Theory* (Chicago: University of Chicago Press, 1956). He often refers to a pluralist system as a *polyarchy*—literally, a system with many centers of power. See his *Polyarchy* (New Haven, Conn.: Yale University Press, 1971), and for a revised defense of pluralism, see his *Democracy and Its Critics* (New Haven, Conn.: Yale University Press, 1989).

2

1. Gunnar Myrdal, *An American Dilemma* (New York: Harper, 1944).
2. See Martin Luther King, Jr., "Letter from Birmingham City Jail," April 16, 1963.
3. For a discussion of the sources and consequences of intolerance in the general public, see James L. Gibson, "The Political Consequences of Intolerance: Cultural Conformity and Political Freedom," *American Political Science Review* 86 (June 1992): 338–52.
4. Alexis deTocqueville, *Democracy in America*, orig. 1835 (New York: Penguin Classic Books, 2003). See also Aurelian Craiutu and Jeremy Jennings, "The Third Democracy: Tocqueville's Views of America After 1840," *American Journal of Political Science* 98 (August 2004): 391–404.
5. Quoted in *The Ideas of Equality*, ed. George Abernathy (Richmond, Va.: John Knox Press, 1959), p. 185; also in Herbert McClosky and John Zaller, *The American Ethos: Public Attitudes toward Capitalism and Democracy* (Cambridge, Mass.: Harvard University Press, 1984), p. 72. For a more recent discussion of the American identity see Deborah J. Schildkraut, "Defining American Identity in the Twenty-First Century," *Journal of Politics* 69 (August 2007): 597–615.
6. Quoted in Richard Hofstadter, *The American Political Tradition* (New York: Knopf, 1948), p. 45. Historian Hofstadter describes the thinking of American political leaders from Jefferson and the Founders to Franklin D. Roosevelt.
7. See also Leslie McCall and Lane Kenworthy, "Americans' Social Policy Preferences in an Era of Rising Inequality," *Perspectives on Politics* 7 (September 2009): 459–84.
8. For a discussion of how people balance the values of individualism and opposition to big government with humanitarianism and the desire to help others, see Stanley Feldman and John Zaller, "The Political Culture of Ambivalence: Ideological Responses to the Welfare State," *American Journal of Political Science* 36 (February 1992): 268–307.
9. Lawrence R. Jacobs and Theda Skocpol, eds., *Inequality and American Democracy* (New York: Russell Sage Foundation, 2005).
10. *Sale v. Haitian Centers Council*, 125 L. Ed. 2d 128 (1993).
11. Poll figures in this section are derived from the Pew Research Center for the People & the Press, "Religion and American Life," August 24, 2004. www.people-press.org
12. *Congressional Quarterly*, March 7, 2005.
13. See Robert S. Erikson and Kent L. Tedin, *American Public Opinion*, 7th ed. (New York: Pearson, 2007), chap. 3.
14. Francis Fukuyama, *The End of History and the Last Man* (New York: Free Press, 1992).
15. Samuel P. Huntington, *The Clash of Civilizations and the Remaking of World Order* (New York: Simon & Schuster, 1996).
16. Herbert Marcuse, *One-Dimensional Man* (Boston: Beacon Press, 1964).

17. Allan Bloom, *The Closing of the American Mind* (New York: Simon & Schuster, 1987), p. 15.
18. Samuel P. Huntington *Who Are We? The Challenges to America's National Identity* (New York: Simon & Schuster, 2004).
19. Seymour Martin Lipset, *American Exceptionalism* (New York: Norton, 1999).
20. Huntington, op. cit.
21. For a contrary view, see Morris P. Fiorina et al., *Cultural Wars? The Myth of a Polarized America* (New York: Longman, 2006).

3

1. In *Federalist Papers*, No. 53, James Madison distinguishes a "constitution" from a law: a constitution is "established by the people and unalterable by the government, and a law established by the government and alterable by the government."
2. Another important decision on opening day of the Constitutional Convention was to keep the proceedings secret. James Madison made his own notes on the convention proceedings, and they were published many years later. See Max Ferrand, ed., *The Records of the Federal Convention of 1787* (New Haven, Conn.: Yale University Press, 1911).
3. See Edward Millican, *One United People: The Federalist Papers and the National Idea* (Lexington, Ky.: University Press of Kentucky, 1990).
4. See David Brian Robertson, "Madison's Opponents and Constitutional Design," *American Political Science Review* 99 (May 2005): 225–43.
5. Charles A. Beard, *An Economic Interpretation of the Constitution* (New York: Macmillan, 1913).
6. Robert E. Brown, *Charles Beard and the Constitution* (Princeton, N.J.: Princeton University Press, 1956).
7. James Madison, *Federalist Papers*, No. 51, reprinted in the Appendix.
8. Ibid.
9. Alexander Hamilton, *Federalist Papers*, No. 78.

4

1. The states are listed in the order in which their legislatures voted to secede. While occupied by Confederate troops, secessionist legislators in Missouri and Kentucky also voted to secede, but Unionist representatives from these states remained in Congress. The state of New Jersey debated secession but decided not to act.
2. *Texas v. White*, 7 Wallace 700 (1869).
3. James Madison, *Federalist Papers*, No. 51, reprinted in the Appendix.
4. Ibid.
5. The arguments for "competitive federalism" are developed at length in Thomas R. Dye, *American Federalism: Competition Among Governments* (Lexington, Mass.: Lexington Books, 1990).
6. David Osborne, *Laboratories of Democracy* (Cambridge, Mass.: Harvard Business School, 1988).
7. Morton Grodzins, *The American System* (Chicago, Ill.: Rand McNally, 1966), pp. 8–9.
8. Ibid., p. 265.
9. Charles Press, *State and Community Governments in the Federal System* (New York: Wiley, 1979), p. 78.
10. *Garcia v. San Antonio Metropolitan Transit Authority*, 469 U.S. 528 (1985).
11. See Michael S. Greve, *Real Federalism: Why It Matters, How It Could Happen* (Washington, D.C.: AEI Press, 1999).
12. *U.S. v. Lopez*, 514 U.S. 549 (1995).
13. *Seminole Tribe of Florida v. Florida*, 517 U.S. 44 (1996).
14. *Alden v. Maine*, 67 U.S.L.W. 1401 (1999).
15. *Printz v. U.S.,* 521 U.S. 890 (1997).
16. *U.S. v. Morrison,* 529 U.S. 598 (2000).
17. *Federal-State-Local Relations: Federal Grants in Aid*, House Committee on Government Operations, 85th Cong., 2d sess., p. 7.
18. Craig Volden, "Intergovernmental Political Competition in American Federalism," *American Journal of Political Science* 49 (April 2005): 327–42.

5

1. See James A. Stimson, Michael B. MacKuen, and Robert S. Erikson, "Dynamic Representation," *American Political Science Review* 89 (September 1995): 543–61.
2. Robert S. Erikson and Kent L. Tedin, *American Public Opinion*, 7th ed. (New York: Longman, 2007).
3. Carol Cassel, 2004. Voting Records and Validated Voting Studies, *Public Opinion Quarterly* 68 (1): 102–108.
4. Ibid., p. 35.
5. Sandra K. Schwartz, "Preschoolers and Politics," in *New Directions in Political Socialization*, eds. David C. Schwartz and Sandra K. Schwartz (New York: Free Press, 1975), p. 242.
6. See M. Kent Jennings, Laura Stoker, and Jake Bowers, "Politics Across Generations: Family Transmission Reexamined," *Journal of Politics* 71 (July 2009): 782–99.
7. John R. Alford, Carolyn L. Funk, and John R. Hibbing, "Are Political Orientations Genetically Transmitted?" *American Political Science Review* 99 (May 2005): 153–67; James H. Fowler and Christopher T. Dawes, "Two Genes Predict Voter Turnout," *Journal of Politics* 70 (July 2008): 579–94.
8. Robert D. Hess and Judith V. Torney, *The Development of Political Attitudes in Children* (Chicago, Ill.: Aldine, 1977), p. 42.
9. Cindy D. Kam and Carl L. Palmer, "Reconsidering the Effects of Education on Political Participation," *Journal of Politics* 70 (July 2008): 612–31.
10. Geoffrey C. Longman, "Religion and Political Behavior in the United States," *Public Opinion Quarterly* 61 (Summer 1997): 288–316.
11. See John C. Green, "The Christian Right in the 1994 Elections," *P.S.: Political Science & Politics* 28 (March 1995): 5–23.
12. See also Richard R. Lau and David P. Redlawsk, "Older but Wiser: Effects of Age on Political Cognition," *Journal of Politics* 70 (January 2008): 168–85.
13. Janet M. Box-Steffensmeier, Suzanna De Boef, and Tse-Min Lin, "The Dynamics of the Partisan Gender Gap," *American Political Science Review* 98 (August 2004): 515–28.
14. Jon Horwitz and Mark Peffley, "Explaining the Great Racial Divide: Perceptions of Fairness in the U.S. Criminal Justice System," *Journal of Politics* 67 (August 2005): 768–83.
15. See Marissa A. Abrajano, R. Michael Alvarez, and Jonathan Nagler, "The Hispanic Vote in the 2004 Presidential Election," *Journal of Politics* 70 (April, 2008): 368–82; Marco Battaglini, Rebecca Morton, and Thomas Palfrey, "*Si Se Puede!* Latino Candidates and the Mobilization of Latino Voters," *American Political Science Review* 101 (August 2007): 409–24. See also F. Chris Garcia and Gabriel Sanchez, *Hispanics and the U.S. Political System: Moving into the Mainstream* (New York: Longman, 2008).

16. V. O. Key, Jr., *Public Opinion and American Democracy* (New York: Knopf, 1967), p. 536.
17. *Smith v. Allwright*, 321 U.S. 649 (1944).
18. *Harper v. Virginia State Board of Elections*, 383 U.S. 663 (1966).
19. Staci L. Rhine, "Registration Reform and Turnout," *American Politics Quarterly* 23 (October 1995): 409–26; Stephen Knack, "Does 'Motor Voter' Work?" *Journal of Politics* 57 (August 1995): 796–811; Michael D. Martinez and David B. Hill, "Did Motor Voter Work?" *American Politics Quarterly* 27 (February 1997): 296–315.
20. Richard G. Niemi and Paul S. Herrnson, "Beyond the Butterfly: The Complexity of U.S. Ballots," *Perspectives on Politics* 1 (June, 2003): 317–26.
21. See R. Michael Alvarez, Thad E. Hall, Morgan H. Llewellyn, "Are Americans Confident Their Ballots Are Counted," *Journal of Politics* 70 (July 2008): 754–66.
22. *Crawford v. Marion County Election Board,* April 28, 2008.
23. *General Social Survey, 1998* (Chicago, Ill.: National Opinion Research Center, 1999).
24. Sidney Verba, Kay Scholzman, Henry Brady, and Norman Nie, "Citizen Activity: Who Participates? What Do They Say?" *American Political Science Review* 87 (June 1993): 303–18.
25. John Stuart Mill, *Considerations on Representative Government* (Chicago, Ill.: Regnery, Gateway, 1962; original publication 1859), p. 144.
26. Ibid., p. 130.
27. Quotation from Austin Ranney in "Non-Voting Is Not a Social Disease," *Public Opinion* 6 (November/December 1983): 18.
28. Martin Luther King, Jr., "Letter from Birmingham City Jail," April 16, 1963.

6

1. For an overview of the mass media in American politics, see Doris A. Graber, *Mass Media and American Politics*, 8th ed. (Washington, D.C.: CQ Press, 2009).
2. Pew Research Center for People & the Press, June 2000. http://people-press.org.
3. See Lance Bennett, *News: The Politics of Illusion*, 5th ed. (New York: Longman, 2007).
4. E. E. Schattschneider, *The Semisovereign People* (New York: Holt, Rinehart & Winston, 1961), p. 68.
5. William A. Henry, "News as Entertainment," in *What's News*, ed. Elie Abel (San Francisco, Calif.: Institute for Contemporary Studies, 1981), p. 133.
6. Shanto Iyengar, *Is Anyone Responsible? How Television Frames Political Issues* (Chicago: University of Chicago Press, 1991).
7. Graber, *Mass Media*, p. 35.
8. Matthew A. Baum, "Sex, Lies, and War: How Soft News Brings Foreign Policy to the Inattentive Public," *American Political Science Review* 96 (March 2002): 91–109.
9. Larry Sabato, Mark Stencel, and S. Robert Lichter, *Peep Show? Media Politics in an Age of Scandal* (Lanham, Md.: Rowman & Littlefield, 2001).
10. Ben J. Wattenberg, *The Good News Is the Bad News Is Wrong* (New York: Simon & Schuster, 1984).
11. Ted Smith, "The Watchdog's Bite," *American Enterprise* 2 (January/February 1990): 66.
12. Graber, *Mass Media*, p. 946.
13. S. Robert Lichter, Stanley Rothman, and Linda S. Lichter, *The Media Elite* (Bethesda, Md.: Adler and Adler, 1986).
14. David Prindle, "Hollywood Liberalism," *Social Science Quarterly* 71 (March 1993): 121.
15. David C. Barker, "Rushed Decisions: Political Talk Radio and Vote Choice," *Journal of Politics* 61 (May 1999): 527–39.
16. Phil Tetlock, *Expert Political Judgment: How Good Is It? How Can We Know?* (Princeton, N.J.: Princeton University Press, 2005); Richard Posner, *Public Intellectuals: A Study of Decline* (Cambridge, Mass.: Harvard University Press, 2003).
17. Diana C. Mutz and Byron Reeves, "The New Videomalaise: Effects of Televised Incivility on Political Trust," *American Political Science Review* 99 (February 2005): 1–15.
18. Marcus Prior, "News Versus Entertainment; How Increasing Media Choice Widens Gaps in Political Knowledge and Turnout," *American Journal of Political Science* 49 (July 2005): 577–92.
19. Shanto Iyengar et al "Selective Exposure to Campaign Communication," *Journal of Politics* 70 (January 2008): 186–200.
20. Julianne F. Flowers, Audrey A. Haynes, and Michael H. Crespin, "The Media, the Campaign, and the Message," *American Journal of Political Science* 47 (April 2003): 259–73.
21. See also Martin Gilens, Lynn Vavreck, and Martin Cohen, "The Mass Media and the Public's Assessment of Presidential Candidates, 1952–2000," *Journal of Politics* 69 (November 2007): 1160–75.
22. See David S. Castle, "Media Coverage of Presidential Primaries," *American Politics Quarterly* 19 (January 1991): 13–42; Christine F. Ridout, "The Role of Media Coverage of Iowa and New Hampshire," *American Politics Quarterly* 19 (January 1991): 43–58.
23. *New York Times v. U.S.*, 376 U.S. 713 (1971).
24. *New York Times v. Sullivan*, 376 U.S. 254 (1964).
25. Gary Wolf, "How the Internet Invented Howard Dean," *Wired* Magazine (January, 2004). http://www.wired.com/wired/archive/12.01/dean.html.
26. See Arthur Lupia and Tasha S. Philpot "Views from Inside the Net," *Journal of Politics* 67 (November 2005): 1122–42.
27. *Reno v. American Civil Liberties Union,* 117 S.Ct. 2329 (1997).
28. Bernard Cohen, *The Press and Foreign Policy* (Princeton, N.J.: Princeton University Press, 1963), p. 16.
29. Austin Ranney, *Channels of Power* (New York: Basic Books, 1983), p. 81.
30. Benjamin J. Page, Robert Y. Shapiro, and Glen R. Dempsey, "What Moves Public Opinion?" *American Political Science Review* 81 (March 1987): 23–43.
31. National Institute of Mental Health, *Television and Behavior* (Washington, D.C.: Government Printing Office, 1982).
32. Brandon Centerwall, "Exposure to Television as a Risk Factor for Violence," *American Journal of Epidemiology* 129 (April 1989): 643–52.

7

1. Gaetano Mosca, *The Ruling Class* (New York: McGraw-Hill, 1939), p. 51.
2. For a scholarly debate over realignment, see Byron E. Schafer, ed., *The End of Realignment: Interpreting American Election Eras* (Madison: University of Wisconsin Press, 1991); David Mayhew, *Electoral realignments: A critique of an American genre* (New Haven, Conn.: Yale University Press, 2002).
3. See John A. Clark, John M. Bruce, John H. Kessel, and William G. Jacoby, "I'd Rather Switch Than Fight: Lifelong Democrats and Converts to Republicanism among Campaign Activists," *American Journal of Political Science* 35 (August 1991): 577–97.
4. James Madison, *Federalist Papers*, No. 10, reprinted in the Appendix.

5. George Washington, "Farewell Address, September 17, 1796," in *Documents on American History*, 10th ed., eds. Henry Steele Commager and Milton Cantor (Upper Saddle River, N.J.: Prentice Hall, 1988): pp. 1–172.
6. Colleen A. Sheehan, "The Battle over Republicanism and the Role of Public Opinion," *American Political Science Review* 98 (August 2004): 405–24.
7. Samuel Merrill III, Bernard Grofman, and Thomas L. Brunell, "Cycles in American Electoral Politics, 1854–2006," *American Political Science Review* 102 (February 2008): 1–18.
8. E. E. Schattschneider, *Party Government* (New York: Holt, Rinehart & Winston, 1942), p. 1.
9. Geofrey C. Layman and Thomas M. Carsey, "Party Polarization and Conflict Extension in the American Electorate," *American Journal of Political Science* 46 (October 2002): 786–802.
10. See Thomas R. Dye and Susan MacManus, *Politics in States and Communities*, 13th ed. (Upper Saddle River, N.J.: Prentice Hall, 2008).
11. Parties may be increasing their influence in elections due to the growth of party committees in the financing of political campaigns. See Paul S. Herrnson, "The Roles of Party Organization, Party-Centered Committees, and Party Allies in Elections," *Journal of Politics* 71 (October, 2009): 1207–24.
12. Conventions continue to play a modest role in nominations in some states:
    - Colorado: Parties may hold a preprimary convention to designate a candidate tobe listed first on the primary ballot. All candidates receiving at least 30 percent of the delegate vote will be listed on the primary ballot.
    - Connecticut: Party conventions are held to endorse candidates. If no one challenges the endorsed candidate, no primary election is held. If a challenger receives 20 percent of the delegate vote, a primary election will be held to determine the party's nominee in the general election.
    - New York: Party conventions choose the party's "designated" candidate in primary elections. Anyone receiving 25 percent of the delegates also appears on the ballot.
    - Utah: Party conventions select party's nominees.
    - Illinois, Indiana, Michigan, and South Carolina: Party conventions nominate candidates for some minor state offices.
13. For an argument that primary elections force parties to be more responsive to voters, see John G. Geer and Mark E. Shere, "Party Competition and the Prisoner's Dilemma: An Argument for the Direct Primary," *Journal of Politics* 54 (August 1992): 365–74.
14. For an up-to-date listing of state primaries and relevant information about them, see *The Book of the States*, published biannually by the Council of State Governments, Lexington, Kentucky.
15. The U.S. Supreme Court declared that the "blanket primary" violated the 1st Amendment freedom of association right of political parties to choose their own candidates. California had adopted a primary system that gave all voters, regardless of party affiliation, ballots that included the names of *all* candidates in *both* parties. Candidates of each party who received the most votes were to become the nominees of those parties and move on to face each other in the general election. But the Supreme Court held that the blanket primary violated the 1st Amendment right of association *California Democratic Party v. Jones*, 530 U.S. 567 (2000).
16. Congressional Quarterly, *National Party Conventions 1811–1996* (Washington, D.C.: CQ Press, 1997).
17. For evidence that the national party conventions raise the poll standings of their presidential nominees, see James E. Campbell, Lynna L. Cherry, and Kenneth A. Wink, "The Convention Bump," *American Politics Quarterly* 20 (July 1992): 287–307.
18. Shigeo Hirano and James M. Snyder, Jr., "The Decline of Third-Party Voting in the United States," *Journal of Politics* 69 (February, 2007): 1–16.
19. Gary Miller and Norman Schofield, "Activists and Partisan Realignment in the United States," *American Political Science Review* 97 (May 2003): 245–60.

8

1. Gerald Pomper, *Elections in America* (New York: Dodd, Mead, 1968).
2. Morris P. Fiorina, *Retrospective Voting in American National Elections* (New Haven, Conn.: Yale University Press, 1981); V. O. Key, *The Responsible Electorate* (Cambridge , Mass.: Belknap Press, 1966).
3. Anthony Downs, *An Economic Theory of Democracy* (New York: Harper, 1957).
4. Quoted in *Congressional Quarterly Almanac, 1965* (Washington, D.C.: Congressional Quarterly, Inc., 1966), p. 267.
5. Ronald Keith Gaddie, *Born to Run: Origins of the Political Career* (Lanham, Md.: Rowman & Littlefield, 2004).
6. Alan Ehrenhalt, *The United States of Ambition: Politicians, Power and the Pursuit of Office* (New York: Random House, 1991), p. 22.
7. Heinz Eulau and John Sprague, *Lawyers in Politics* (Indianapolis, Ind.: Bobbs-Merrill, 1964).
8. David Canon, *Actors, Athletes, and Astronauts* (Chicago: University of Chicago Press, 1990).
9. See Jamie L. Carson, "Strategy, Selection and Candidate Competition in U.S. House and Senate Elections," *Journal of Politics* 67 (February 2005): 1–26.
10. Andrew Gelman and Gary King, "Estimating Incumbency Advantage Without Bias," *American Journal of Political Science* 34 (1990): 1142–64.
11. Alan I. Abramowitz, "Incumbency, Campaign Spending, and the Decline of Competition in U.S. House Elections," *Journal of Politics* 53 (February 1991): 55–70.
12. Michael Tomz and Robert P. Van Houweling, "The Electoral Implications of Candidate Ambiguity," *American Political Science Review* 103 (February 2009): 83–94.
13. Herbert Alexander, as quoted in Richard R. Lau et al., "The Effects of Negative Political Advertisements," *American Political Science Review* 93 (December 1999): 851–75.
14. Lee Sigelman and Emmett H. Buell, Jr., "You Take the High Road and I'll Take the Low Road? The Interplay of Attack Strategies and Tactics in Presidential Campaigns," *Journal of Politics* 46 (May 2003): 518–31; Richard R. Lau and Gerald M. Pomper, "Effectiveness of Negative Campaigning in U.S. Senate Elections," *American Journal of Political Science* 46 (January 2002): 47–66; Daniel Stevens et al., "What's Good for the Goose Is Bad for the Gander: Negative Political Advertising, Partisanship and Turnout," *Journal of Politics* 70 (April 2008): 527–41.
15. Ted Brader, "Striking a Responsive Chord: How Political Ads Motivate and Persuade Voters by Appealing to Emotions," *American Journal of Political Science* 49 (April 2005): 388–405.
16. Paul Friedman, Michael Franz, and Kenneth Goldstein, "Campaign Advertising and Democratic Citizenship," *American Journal of Political Science* 48 (October 2004): 723–41.

But see also Jonathan S. Krasno and Donald P. Green, "Do Televised Presidential Ads Increase Voter Turnout?" *Journal of Politics* 70 (January, 2008): 245–61.

17. Thomas M. Holbrook and Scott D. McClung, "The Mobilization of Core Supporters," *American Journal of Political Science*, 49 (October 2005): 689–703.
18. Center for Responsive Politics, *The Big Picture: The Money Behind the 2000 Elections* (Washington, D.C., 2001).
19. In the important U.S. Supreme Court decision in *Buckley v. Valeo* in 1976, James L. Buckley, former U.S. senator from New York, and his brother, William F. Buckley, the well-known conservative commentator, argued successfully that the laws limiting an individual's right to participate in political campaigns—financially or otherwise—violated 1st Amendment freedoms. Specifically, the U.S. Supreme Court held that no government could limit individuals' rights to spend money or publish or broadcast their own views on issues or elections. Candidates can spend as much of their own money as they wish on their own campaigns. Private individuals can spend as much as they wish to circulate their own views on an election, although their contributions to candidates and parties can still be limited. The Court, however, permitted governmental limitations on parties and campaign organizations and allowed the use of federal funds for financing campaigns. *Buckley v. Valeo*, 424 U.S. 1 (1976).
20. Sanford C. Gordon and Catherine Hafer, "Flexing Muscles: Corporate Political Expenditures As Signals to the Bureaucracy," *American Political Science Review* 99 (May 2005): 245–61.
21. *Buckley v. Valeo*, 424 U.S. 1 (1976).
22. *FEC v. Colorado Republican Committee*, 533 U.S. 431 (2001).
23. *McConnell v. FEC*, 540 U.S. 93 (2003).
24. Quotations from *Citizens United v. FEC*, January 21, 2010.
25. Lynn Vavreck, Constantine J. Spiliotes, and Linda L. Fowler, "The Effects of Retail Politics in the New Hampshire Primary," *American Journal of Political Science* 46 (July 2002): 595–610.
26. Matthew A. Baum, "Talking the Vote: Why Presidential Candidates Hit the Talk Show Circuit," *American Journal of Political Science* 49 (April 2005): 213–34.
27. University-based political scientists rely heavily on a series of National Election Studies, originated at the Survey Research Center at the University of Michigan, which have surveyed the voting-age population in every presidential election and most congressional elections since 1952.
28. For an updated summary of the extensive literature on voting behavior, see Michael S. Lewis-Beck, William G. Jakoby, Helmut Norpoth, and Herbert F. Weiberg, *The American Voter Revisited* (Ann Arbor: University of Michigan Press, 2008).
29. See Martin P. Wattenberg, *The Rise of Candidate-Centered Politics* (Cambridge, Mass.: Harvard University Press, 1991).
30. Responsibility for the economy, however, is also affected by the voters' partisanship, ideology and views about whether the president or Congress is chiefly responsible. See Joseph J. Rudolph, "Who's Responsible for the Economy?," *American Journal of Political Science* 47 (October 2003): 698–713.
31. For an argument that voters look ahead to the economic future and reward or punish the president based on rational expectations, see Michael B. MacKuen, Robert S. Erickson, and James A. Stimson, "Peasants or Bankers? The American Electorate and the U.S. Economy," *American Political Science Review* 86 (September 1992): 680–95.
32. Sunshine Hillygus and Todd G. Shields, *The Persuadable Voter* (Princeton, N.J.: Princeton University Press, 2008).

9

1. Political scientist David Truman's classic definition of an interest group: "any group that is based on one or more shared attitudes and makes certain demands upon other groups or organizations in society." See *The Governmental Process* (New York: Knopf, 1971), p. 33.
2. James Madison, *Federalist Papers*, No. 10, reprinted in the Appendix.
3. Gale Research Company, *Encyclopedia of Associations* (Detroit: Gale Research, 2004).
4. Frank R. Baumgartner and Beth L. Leech, "Interest Niches and Policy Bandwagons: Patterns of Interest Group Involvement in National Politics," *The Journal of Politics* 63 (November 2001): 1191–213.
5. Jeffrey M. Berry, *The New Liberalism: The Rising Power of Citizen Groups* (Washington, D.C.: Brookings Institution Press, 1999).
6. Kay Lehmann Scholzman, "What Accent the Heavenly Chorus? Political Equality and the American Pressure System," *Journal of Politics* 46 (November 1984): 1006–32; see also Jeffrey M. Berry, Kent E. Portney, and Ken Thomson, *The Case for Participatory Democracy* (Washington, D.C.: Brookings Institution Press, 1994).
7. Center for Responsive Politics, www.opensecrets.org (2009).
8. Leonard Silk and Mark Silk, *The American Establishment* (New York: Basic Books, 1980), p. 160.
9. Mark Green and Michelle Jolin, eds., *Change for America* (New York: Basic Books, 2009).
10. Jeffrey M. Berry, *The New Liberalism* (Washington, D.C.: Brookings Institution Press, 1999).
11. Quotation from Roger Kersh, "Corporate Lobbyists as Political Actors," in *Interest Group Politics*, 6th ed., ed. Allan J. Cigler and Burdett A. Loomis (Washington, D.C.: CQ Press, 2002).
12. For evidence that vote buying on congressional roll calls is rare, see Janet M. Grenzke, "Shopping in the Congressional Supermarket: The Currency Is Complex," *American Journal of Political Science* 33 (February 1989): 1–24. But for evidence that committee participation by members of Congress is influenced by political action committee money, see Richard L. Hall and Frank W. Wayman, "Buying Time: Moneyed Interests and the Mobilization of Bias in Congressional Committees," *American Political Science Review* 84 (September 1990): 797–819.
13. Robert H. Salisbury, "Who You Know versus What You Know: The Use of Government Experience by Washington Lobbyists," *American Journal of Political Science* 33 (February 1989): 175–95.
14. *Brown v. Board of Education of Topeka*, 349 U.S. 294 (1955).

10

1. James Madison, *Federalist Papers*, No. 10, reprinted in the Appendix.
2. Quoted in Jay M. Schafritz, *The Harper Collins Dictionary of American Government and Politics* (New York: HarperCollins, 1992), p. 56.
3. See David Auerswald and Forrest Maltzman, "Policymaking through Advice and Consent: Treaty Consideration by the United States Senate," *Journal of Politics* 65 (November 2003): 1097–110.
4. Jon R. Bond, Richard Fleisher, and Glen S. Krutz, "Malign Neglect: Evidence That Delay Has Become the Primary

Method of Defeating Presidential Appointments," *Congress and the Presidency* 36 (2009): pp. 226–243

5. *McGrain v. Doughtery*, 273 U.S. 13J (1927).
6. *Baker v. Carr*, 369 U.S. 186 (1962); *Wesberry v. Sanders*, 370 U.S. 1 (1964).
7. *Gray v. Sanders*, 322 U.S. 368 (1963).
8. *Department of Commerce v. U.S. House of Representatives*, 525 U.S. 316 (1999).
9. *Gaffney v. Cummings*, 412 U.S. 763 (1973).
10. *Davis v. Bandemer,* 478 U.S. 109 (1986).
11. *Vieth v. Jubelirer,* 241 F. Supp. 2d 478 (2004).
12. Scott W. Desposato and John R. Petrocik, "The Variable Incumbency Advantage: New Voters, Redistricting, and Personal Vote," *American Journal of Political Science* 47 (January 2003): 18–32; John N. Friedman and Richard T. Holden, "The Rising Incumbent Reelection Rate: What's Gerrymandering Got to Do With It?" *Journal of Politics* 71 (April 2009): 593–611.
13. *Thornburg v. Gingles*, 478 U.S. 30 (1986).
14. *Shaw v. Reno*, 125 I. Ed. 2d 511 (1993).
15. *Miller v. Johnson*, 115 S. Ct. 2475 (1995).
16. See Roger H. Davidson and Walter J. Oleszek, *Congress and Its Members*, 9th ed. (Washington, D.C.: CQ Press, 2004).
17. David Lublin, *The Paradox of Representation: Racial Gerrymandering and Minority Interests in Congress* (Princeton, N.J.: Princeton University Press, 1997). See also David Lublin and D. Stephen Voss, "The Missing Middle," *Journal of Politics* 65 (February 2003): 227–37.
18. For an in-depth analysis of who decides to run for Congress and who does not, see Linda L. Fowler and Robert D. McClure, *Political Ambition: Who Decides to Run for Congress* (New Haven, Conn.: Yale University Press, 1990).
19. See Michael K. Moore and John R. Hibbing, "Situational Dissatisfaction in Congress: Explaining Voluntary Departures," *Journal of Politics* 60 (November 1998): 1088–107.
20. *U.S. Term Limits v. Thornton*, 115 S.C. 1842, (1995).
21. See Gary Jacobson, *The Politics of Congressional Elections*, 5th ed. (New York: HarperCollins, 2000).
22. See David Epstein and Peter Zemsky, "Money Talks: Deterring Quality Challengers in Congressional Elections," *American Political Science Review* 89 (June 1995): 295–322.
23. See Richard Fenno, *Going Home: Black Representatives and Their Constituents* (Chicago: University of Chicago Press, 2003).
24. Paul S. Herrnson, J. Celeste Lay, and Atiya Kai Stokes, "Women Running 'As Women,'" *Journal of Politics* 65 (February 2003): 244–55; see also Jennifer Lawless and Kathryn Pearson, "The Primary Reason for Women's Underepresentation? Reevaluating the Conventional Wisdom," *Journal of Politics* 70 (January 2008): 67–82.
25. See Glen S. Krutz, "Issues and Institutions: 'Winnowing' in the U.S. Congress," *American Journal of Political Science* 49 (April 2005): 313–26.
26. U.S. House of Representatives, Commission on Administrative Review, *Administrative Reorganization and Legislative Management*, 95th Cong., 1st sess., H. Doc. 95–232, pp. 17–19.
27. Richard F. Fenno, *Home Style* (Boston: Little, Brown, 1978).
28. Roger H. Davidson and Walter J. Oleszek, *Congress and Its Members* (Washington, D.C.: CQ Press, 2000).
29. Glenn R. Parker, *Characteristics of Congress* (Upper Saddle River, N.J.: Prentice Hall, 1989), p. 30.
30. Richard F. Fenno, *The Making of a Senator: Dan Quayle* (Washington, D.C.: CQ Press, 1989), p. 119. Also cited in Davidson and Oleszek, *Congress and Its Members*, 9th ed., p. 120.
31. Davidson and Oleszek, *Congress and Its Members*, 9th ed., p. 129.
32. Gary W. Cox and Eric Magar, "How Much Is Majority Status in the U.S. Congress Worth?" *American Political Science Review* 93 (June 1999): 299–310.
33. See Roger H. Davidson, Walter J. Oleszek, and Frances E. Lee, *Congress and Its Members,* 11th ed. (Washington D.C.: CQ Press, 2008).
34. John R. Hibbing, *Congressional Careers* (Chapel Hill: University of North Carolina Press, 1991).
35. See Thomas E. Mann and Raymond Wolfinger, "Candidates and Parties in Congressional Elections," *American Political Science Review* 84 (September 1990): 545–64.
36. See Mary T. Hanna, "Political Science Caught Flat-Footed by Midterm Elections," *Chronicle of Higher Education*, November 30, 1994, pp. B1–2.
37. See Charles Stewart and Tim Groseclose, "The Value of Committee Seats in the United States Senate," *American Journal of Political Science* 43 (July 1999): 963–73; see also Kevin M. Esterling, "Buying Expertise: Campaign Contributions and Attention to Policy Analysis in Congressional Committees," *American Political Science Review* 101 (February 2007): 93–110.
38. See John W. Patty, "The House Discharge Procedure and Majoritarian Politics," *Journal of Politics* 69 (August 2007): 678–88.
39. Nathan W. Monroe and Gregory Robinson, "Do Restrictive Rules Produce Nonmedian Outcomes?" *Journal of Politics* 70 (January 2008): 217–31.
40. Charles J. Finocchiaro and Jeffery A. Jenkins, "In Search of Killer Amendments in the Modern U.S. House," *Legislative Studies Quarterly* 33 (2008): 263–94; Charles J. Finocchiaro and David W. Rohde, "War for the Floor: Partisan Theory and Agenda Control in the U.S. House of Representatives," *Legislative Studies Quarterly* 33 (2008): 35–61.
41. Larry Markinson, *The Cash Constituents of Congress* (Washington, D.C.: CQ Press, 1992).
42. Andrew Rehfield, "Representation Rethought: On Trustees, Delegates, and Gyroscopes in the Study of Representation and Democracy," *American Political Science Review* 101 (May 2009): 214–26.
43. Donald Matthews, *U.S. Senators and Their World* (New York: Vintage Books, 1960).
44. David Rohde, Norman J. Ornstein, and Robert L. Peabody, "Political Change and Legislative Norms," in *Studies of Congress*, ed. Glenn R. Parker (Washington, D.C.: CQ Press, 1985), p. 175.
45. See John R. Hibbing, "Contours of the Modern Congressional Career," *American Political Science Review* 85 (June 1991): 405–28.
46. Richard Fenno, *Power of the Purse* (Boston: Little, Brown, 1965), p. 620.
47. See David R. Mayhew, *Divided We Govern* (New Haven, Conn.: Yale University Press, 1991); Sarah A. Binder, "The Dynamics of Legislative Gridlock," *American Political Science Review* 93 (September 1999): 519–33.
48. *Congressional Quarterly Weekly Report*, November 23, 1991, p. 3437.
49. Alan J. Ziobrowski, Ping Cheng, James W. Boyd, and Brigitte J. Ziobrowski, 2004. "Abnormal Returns from the Common Stock Investments of the U.S. Senate," *Journal of Financial and Quantitative Analysis* 39 (4): 661–76.

11

1. See Michael Less Benedict, *The Impeachment and Trial of Andrew Johnson* (New York: Norton, 1973).
2. William Howard Taft, *Our Chief Magistrate and His Powers* (New York: Columbia University Press, 1938), p. 138,

reprinted in *The Presidency*, ed. John P. Roche (New York: Harcourt Brace Jovanovich, 1964), p. 23.

3. Quoted in Arthur B. Tourtellot, *Presidents on the Presidency* (New York: Doubleday, 1964), pp. 55–56.
4. *Youngstown Sheet & Tube Co. v. Sawyer*, 343 U.S. 579 (1952).
5. *United States v. Nixon*, 418 U.S. 683 (1974).
6. *Nixon v. Fitzgerald*, 457 U.S. 731 (1982).
7. *Clinton v. Jones*, 520 U.S. 681 (1997).
8. Quoted in Richard Neustadt, *Presidential Power* (New York: Wiley, 1960), p. 9.
9. See Paul Brace and Barbara Hinckley, "The Structure of Presidential Approval," *Journal of Politics* 53 (November 1991): 993–1017.
10. See Suzanne L. Parker, "Toward an Understanding of 'Rally' Effect," *Public Opinion Quarterly* 59 (September 1995): 526–46; Marc J. Hetherington and Michael Nelson, "Anatomy of a Rally Effect," *P.S. Political Science & Politics* 36 (January 2003): 37–42.
11. John Mueller, *War, Presidents, and Public Opinion* (New York: Wiley, 1973).
12. See George C. Edwards and B. Dan Wood, "Who Influences Whom," *American Political Science Review* 93 (June 1999): 327–44.
13. Garry Young and William B. Perkins, "Presidential Rhetoric, the Public Agenda, and the End of Presidential Television's 'Golden Age,'" *Journal of Politics* 67 (November 2005): 1190–205.
14. Michael Bailey, Lee Sigelman, and Clyde Wilcox, "Presidential Persuasion on Social Issues," *Political Research Quarterly* 56 (March 2003): 49–58.
15. William G. Howell. *Power without Persuasion: The Politics of Direct Presidential Action*. Princeton, N.J.: Princeton University Press, 2003.
16. George C. Edwards and Stephen J. Wayne, *Presidential Leadership,* 6th ed. (Belmont, Calif.: Wadsworth, 2003), p. 118.
17. Lawrence R. Jacobs and Robert Y. Schapiro, *Politicians Don't Pander* (Chicago: University of Chicago Press, 2000).
18. Brandice Canes-Wrone and Kenneth W. Shotts, "The Conditional Nature of Presidential Responsiveness to Public Opinion," *American Journal of Political Science* 48 (October 2004): 690–706.
19. Kenneth R. Mayer, "Executive Orders and Presidential Power," *Journal of Politics* 61 (May 1999): 445–66; Christopher J. Deering and Forrest Maltzman, "The Politics of Executive Orders," *Political Research Quarterly* 52 (December 1999): 767–83.
20. *Youngstown Sheet & Tube Co. v. Sawyer*, 343 U.S. 579 (1952).
21. See also Jeffrey E. Cohen, *The Politics of the U.S. Cabinet* (Pittsburgh: University of Pittsburgh Press, 1988).
22. John Kingdon, *Agenda, Alternatives, and Public Policies* (Boston: Little, Brown, 1984), p. 25.
23. Mathew N. Beckmann, "The President's Playbook: White House Strategies for Lobbying Congress," *Journal of Politics* 70 (April 2008): 407–19.
24. See Daniel E. Ingberman and Dennis A. Yao, "Presidential Commitment and the Veto," *American Journal of Political Science* 35 (May 1991): 357–89; Samuel B. Hoff, "Saying No," *American Politics Quarterly* 19 (July 1991): 310–23.
25. *Clinton v. City of New York*, 524 U.S. 417 (1998).
26. Brandice Canes-Wrone, William G. Howell, David E. Lewis, "Toward a Broader Understanding of Presidential Power," *Journal of Politics* 70 (January 2008): 1–16.
27. G. J. A. O'Toole, *Honorable Treachery: A History of U.S. Intelligence from the American Revolution to the CIA* (New York: Atlantic Monthly Press, 1991).
28. National Commission on Terrorist Attacks upon the United States, *The 9/11 Commission Report* (New York: W.W. Norton, 2004).
29. *Mora v. McNamara*, 389 U.S. 934 (1964); *Massachusetts v. Laird*, 400 U.S. 886 (1970). The Court specifically refused to intervene in the conduct of the Vietnam War by presidents Johnson and Nixon.
30. Jules Witcover, *Crap Shoot: Rolling the Dice on the Vice Presidency* (New York: Crow Publishing, 1992).

12

1. "Red tape" derives its meaning from the use of reddish tape by seventeenth-century English courts to bind legal documents. Unwrapping court orders entangled one in "red tape." See Herbert Kaufman, *Red Tape: Its Uses and Abuses* (Washington, D.C.: Brookings Institution, 1977).
2. H. H. Gerth and C. Wright Mills, *From Max Weber* (New York: Oxford Press, 1958).
3. Max Neiman, *Defending Government: Why Big Government Works* (Upper Saddle River, N.J.: Prentice Hall, 2000).
4. James Q. Wilson, *Bureaucracy: What Government Agencies Do and Why They Do It* (New York: Basic Books, 1989).
5. William Niskanen, *Bureaucracy and Representative Government* (Chicago, Ill.: Aldine, 1971).
6. The constitutional question of whether Congress can establish an executive branch commission and protect its members from dismissal by the president was settled in *Humphrey's Executor v. United States* (1935). Franklin Roosevelt fired Humphrey from the Federal Trade Commission despite a fixed term set by Congress. Humphrey died shortly afterward, and when the executors of his estate sued for his back pay, the Supreme Court ruled that his firing was illegal.
7. See Nicholas Henry, *Public Administration and Public Affairs*, 11th ed. (New York: Longman, 2010), Chapter 11.
8. Quoted in U.S. Civil Service Commission, *Biography of an Ideal: A History of the Civil Service System* (Washington, D.C.: Government Printing Office, 1973), p. 16.
9. See John D. Huber and Nalan McCarty, "Bureaucratic Capacity, Delegation, and Political Reform," *American Political Science Review* 98 (August 2004): 481–94.
10. Paul C. Light, *Thickening Government: Federal Hierarchy and the Diffusion of Accountability* (Washington, D.C.: Brookings Institution, 1995).
11. Michael M. Ting, "Whistleblowing," *American Political Science Review* 102 (May 2008): 249–60.
12. David Osborne and Ted Gaebler, *Reinventing Government* (New York: Addison-Wesley, 1992).
13. Al Gore, *Creating a Government That Works Better and Costs Less* (Washington, D.C.: Government Printing Office, 1993).
14. William G. Howell and David E. Lewis, "Agencies by Presidential Design," *Journal of Politics* 64 (November 2002): 1098–114.
15. OMB also forecasts economic activity, government spending and debt; see George A. Krause and J. Kevin Corder, "Explaining Bureaucratic Optimism," *American Political Science Review* 101 (February 2007): 129–42.
16. For research suggesting that the appointive power is a more important instrument of political control of the bureaucracy than budgets or legislation, see B. Dan Wood and Richard W. Waterman, "The Dynamics of Political Control of the Bureaucracy," *American Political Science Review* 83 (September 1991): 801–28.
17. Evidence of the effectiveness of interventions by members of Congress in local offices of federal agencies is provided by

John T. Scholz, Jim Twombly, and Barbara Headrick, "Street-Level Political Controls over Federal Bureaucracy," *American Political Science Review* 85 (September 1991): 829–50.

18. Bradley Canon and Michael Giles, "Recurring Litigants: Federal Agencies before the Supreme Court," *Western Political Quarterly* 15 (September 1972): 183–91; Reginald S. Sheehan, "Federal Agencies and the Supreme Court," *American Politics Quarterly* 20 (October 1992): 478–500.

13

1. Alexis de Tocqueville, *Democracy in America, 1835* (New York: Mentor Books, 1956), p. 75.
2. Felix Frankfurter, "The Supreme Court and the Public," *Forum* 83 (June 1930): 332.
3. Alexander Hamilton, *Federalist Papers*, No. 78 (New York: Modern Library, 1937), p. 505.
4. *Marbury v. Madison*, 1 Cranch 137 (1803).
5. *Brown v. Board of Education of Topeka*, 347 U.S. 483 (1954).
6. *Roe v. Wade*, 410 U.S. 113 (1973).
7. *Lawrence v. Texas,* 539 U.S. 558(2003).
8. *Buckley v. Valeo*, 424 U.S. 1 (1976).
9. *U.S. v. Morrison,* 529 U.S. 598 (2000).
10. *Ex parte Milligan*, 4 Wallace 2 (1866).
11. *Youngstown Sheet & Tube Co. v. Sawyer*, 343 U.S. 579 (1952).
12. *United States v. Nixon*, 418 U.S. 683 (1974).
13. *Clinton v. Jones*, 520 U.S. 681 (1997).
14. *West Virginia Board of Education v. Barnette*, 319 U.S. 624 (1943).
15. Quoted in Henry J. Abraham, *Justices and Presidents*, 3rd ed. (New York: Oxford University Press, 1992), p. 7.
16. Quoted in Charles P. Curtis, *Lions under the Throne* (Boston: Houghton Mifflin, 1947), p. 281.
17. See Michael A. Bailey and Forrest Maltzman. "Does Legal Doctrine Matter? Unpacking Law and Policy Preferences on the U.S. Supreme Court," *American Political Science Review* 102 (August 2008): 369–77.
18. William O. Douglas, "Stare Decisis," *Record*, April 1947, cited in Henry J. Abraham, *The Judicial Process* (New York: Oxford University Press, 1968), p. 58.
19. *Flast v. Cohen*, 392 U.S. 83 (1968).
20. *Gideon v. Wainwright*, 372 U.S. 335 (1963).
21. *Missouri v. Jenkins*, 110 S.C. 1651 (1990).
22. *Morrison v. Olson*, 487 U.S. 654 (1988).
23. Robert Scigliano, *The Supreme Court and the Presidency* (New York: Free Press, 1971), pp. 147–48.
24. See Bryon J. Moraski and Charles R. Shipan, "The Politics of Supreme Court Nominations," *American Journal of Political Science* 43 (October 1999): 1069–95.
25. See Charles R. Shipan and Megan L. Shannon, "Delaying Justices, *American Journal of Political Science* 47 (October 2003): 654–68; Sarah A. Binder and Forrest Maltzman, "Senatorial Delay in Confirming Federal Judges," *American Journal of Political Science* 46 (January 2002): 190–99; David W. Rohde and Kenneth A. Shepsle, "Advising and Consenting in the 60-Vote Senate: Strategic Appointments to the Supreme Court," *Journal of Politics* 69 (August 2007): 664–77.
26. At one time the U.S. Supreme Court was legally required to accept certain "writs of appeal," but today very few cases come to the Court in this fashion.
27. *University of California Regents v. Bakke*, 438 U.S. 265 (1978).
28. See Lee Epstein et al., *The Supreme Court Compendium*, 3rd ed. (Washington, D.C.: CQ Press, 2002).
29. Thomas Marshall, *Public Opinion and the Supreme Court* (New York: Unwin Hyman, 1989), p. 97; see also Michael W. Giles, Bethany Blackstone, and Richard L. Vining, Jr., "The Supreme Court in American Democracy: Unraveling the Linkages Between Public Opinion and Judicial Decision Making," *Journal of Politics* 70 (April 2008): 293–306.
30. Lee Epstein and C. K. Rowland, "Debunking the Myth of Interest Group Invincibility," *American Political Science Review* 85 (1991): 205–17.
31. James L. Gibson et al., "Measuring Attitudes toward the United States Supreme Court," *American Journal of Political Science* 47 (April 2003): 354–67; Stephen P. Nicholson and Robert H. Howard, "Framing Support for the Supreme Court in the Aftermath of *Bush v. Gore*," *Journal of Politics* 65 (August 2003): 676–95.
32. James R. Zink, James F. Spriggs II, and John T. Scott, "Courting the Public: The Influence of Decision Attributes on Individuals' Views of Court Opinions," *Journal of Politics,* 71 (July 2009): 909–25.
33. President Andrew Jackson's comments came in response to the Court's ruling in the case of *Cherokee Nation v. Georgia* (1831) and *Worcester v. Georgia* (1832), which forbade the federal or state governments from seizing Native American lands and forcing the people to move. Refusal by Jackson, an old "Indian fighter," to enforce the Court's decisions resulted in the infamous "Trail of Tears," the forced march of the Georgia Cherokees that left one-quarter of them dead along the path west.
34. *Grove City College v. Bell*, 465 U.S. 555 (1984).
35. *Pollock v. Farmer's Loan*, 158 U.S. 601 (1895).

14

1. James Madison, *Federalist Papers*, No. 10, reprinted in the Appendix.
2. *West Virginia Board of Education v. Barnette*, 319 U.S. 624 (1943).
3. *Slaughter-House Cases*, 16 Wallace 36 (1873).
4. *Hurtado v. California*, 110 U.S. 516 (1884).
5. *Gitlow v. New York*, 268 U.S. 652 (1925).
6. For an argument that Madison and some other Framers not only were concerned with lessening religious conflict but also were hostile to religion generally, see Thomas Lindsay, "James Madison on Religion and Politics," *American Political Science Review* 85 (December 1991): 1051–65.
7. *Reynolds v. United States*, 98 U.S. 145 (1879).
8. *Pierce v. Society of Sisters*, 268 U.S. 510 (1925).
9. *Cantwell v. Connecticut*, 310 U.S. 296 (1940).
10. *Employment Division v. Smith*, 494 U.S. 872 (1990).
11. *Wisconsin v. Yoder*, 406 U.S. 295 (1972).
12. *Church of Lukumi Babalu Aye v. City of Hialeah*, 508 U.S. 520 (1993).
13. *Bob Jones University v. United States*, 461 U.S. 574 (1983).
14. *Employment Division of Oregon v. Smith*, 494 U.S. 872 (1990).
15. *Goldman v. Weinberger*, 475 U.S. 503 (1986).
16. *City of Borne v. Flores*, 521 U.S. 507 (1997).
17. *Everson v. Board of Education*, 330 U.S. 1, 15, 16 (1947).
18. *Zorach v. Clausen*, 343 U.S. 306 (1952).
19. Opening public meetings with prayer was ruled constitutional as "a tolerable acknowledgment of beliefs widely held among the people of this country." *Marsh v. Chambers*, 463 U.S. 783 (1983).
20. *Lemon v. Kurtzman*, 403 U.S. 602 (1971).
21. *Muebler v. Adams*, 463 U.S. 388 (1983).
22. *Tilton v. Richardson*, 403 U.S. 672 (1971).
23. *Lambs Chapel v. Center Moriches Union Free School District*, 508 U.S. 384 (1993).

24. *Rosenberger v. University of Virginia*, 515 U.S. 819 (1995).
25. *Walz v. Tax Commission*, 397 U.S. 664 (1970).
26. *Board of Education v. Mergens*, 497 U.S. 111 (1990).
27. *McGowan v. Maryland*, 366 U.S. 429 (1961); *Braunfeld v. Brown*, 366 U.S. 599 (1961).
28. *County of Allegheny v. ACLU*, 492 U.S. 573 (1989).
29. *Edwards v. Aguillard*, 482 U.S. 578 (1987).
30. *VanOrden v. Perry*, 545 U.S. 677 (2005).
31. *Engel v. Vitale*, 370 U.S. 421 (1962).
32. *Abington School District v. Schempp*, 374 U.S. 203 (1963).
33. *Wallace v. Jaffree*, 472 U.S. 38 (1985).
34. *Lee v. Weisman*, 505 U.S. 577 (1992).
35. *Santa Fe Independent School District v. Doe*, 120 S.Ct. 2266 (2000).
36. *Zelman v. Simmons-Harris*, June 27, 2002.
37. *Schenck v. United States*, 249 U.S. 47 (1919).
38. *Gitlow v. New York*, 268 U.S. 652 (1925).
39. *Schenck v. United States*, 249 U.S. 47, 52 (1919).
40. *Whitney v. California*, 274 U.S. 357, 377 (1927), concurring opinion.
41. *Thomas v. Collins*, 323 U.S. 516 (1945).
42. *Dennis v. United States*, 341 U.S. 494 (1951).
43. *Yates v. United States*, 354 U.S. 298 (1957).
44. *Albertson v. Subversive Activities Control Board*, 382 U.S. 70 (1965).
45. *Whitehill v. Elkins*, 389 U.S. 54 (1967).
46. *United States v. Robel*, 389 U.S. 258 (1967).
47. *Aptheker v. Secretary of State*, 378 U.S. 500 (1964).
48. *Tinker v. Des Moines Independent Community School District*, 393 U.S. 503 (1969).
49. *Texas v. Johnson*, 491 U.S. 397 (1989).
50. *Texas v. Johnson*, 491 U.S. 397 (1989).
51. *Virginia v. Black*, 538 U.S. 343 (2003).
52. *Chaplinsky v. New Hampshire*, 315 U.S. 568 (1942).
53. *Terminiello v. Chicago*, 337 U.S. 1 (1949).
54. *Cohen v. California*, 403 U.S. 15 (1971).
55. *Hill v. Colorado*, 530 U.S. 703 (2000).
56. Justice Louis D. Brandeis opinion in *Whitney v. California*, 274 U.S. 357 (1927).
57. *R. A. V. v. City of St. Paul, Minnesota*, 505 U.S. 377 (1992).
58. *Wisconsin v. Mitchell*, 508 U.S. 476 (1993).
59. *Virginia State Board of Pharmacy v. Virginia Consumer Council, Inc.*, 425 U.S. 748 (1976).
60. *Bates v. Arizona State Bar*, 433 U.S. 350 (1977).
61. *Linmark Associates, Inc. v. Township of Willingboro*, 431 U.S. 85 (1977).
62. *New York Times v. Sullivan*, 376 U.S. 254 (1964).
63. *Gertz v. Robert Welch, Inc.*, 418 U.S. 323 (1974).
64. *Roth v. United States*, 354 U.S. 476 (1957).
65. *Jacobellis v. Ohio*, 378 U.S. 184 (1964).
66. *Jacobellis v. Ohio*, 378 U.S. 184 (1964).
67. Bob Woodward and Scott Armstrong, *The Brethren* (New York: Avon, 1979), p. 233.
68. *Miller v. California*, 5413 U.S. 15 (1973).
69. *Barnes v. Glenn Theatre*, 501 U.S. 560 (1991).
70. *Reno v. American Civil Liberties Union*, 117 S.Ct. 2329 (1997).
71. *New York v. Ferber*, 458 U.S. 747 (1982)
72. *Ashcroft v. Free Speech Coalition*, 535 U.S. 234 (2002)
73. *Near v. Minnesota*, 283 U.S. 697 (1931).
74. *New York Times v. United States*, 403 U.S. 713 (1971).
75. *Mutual Film Corp. v. Industrial Commission*, 236 U.S. 230 (1915).
76. *Times Film Corporation v. Chicago*, 365 U.S. 43 (1961).
77. *Freedman v. Maryland*, 380 U.S. 51 (1965).
78. *Young v. American Mini Theaters, Inc.*, 427 U.S. 50 (1976).
79. *Red Lion Broadcasting Co. v. Federal Communications Commission*, 395 U.S. 367 (1969).
80. *Miami Herald Publishing Co. v. Tornillo*, 418 U.S. 241 (1974).
81. *Branzburg v. Hayes*, 408 U.S. 665 (1972).
82. *Griswold v. Connecticut*, 381 U.S. 479 (1965).
83. *Roe v. Wade*, 410 U.S. 113 (1973).
84. *Harris v. McRae*, 448 U.S. 297 (1980).
85. *Planned Parenthood v. Casey*, 510 U.S. 110 (1992).
86. *Gonzales v. Carhart*, April 18, 2007.
87. *Bowers v. Hardwick*, 478 U.S. 186 (1986).
88. *Lawrence v. Texas*, 539 U.S. 558 (2003).
89. *Stanley v. Georgia*, 394 U.S. 557 (1969).
90. *Washington v. Glucksberg*, 117 S.Ct. 2258 (1997).
91. *Cruzan v. Missouri Department of Health*, 497 U.S. 261 (1990).
92. *NAACP v. Alabama ex rel. Patterson*, 357 U.S. 449 (1958).
93. *Aptheker v. Secretary of State*, 378 U.S. 500 (1964).
94. *Roberts v. United States Jaycees*, 468 U.S. 609 (1984).
95. *Hurley v. Irish-American Gay Lesbian and Bisexual Group of Boston*, 515 U.S. 557 (1995).
96. *Bay Scouts of America v. Dale*, 530 U.S. 640 (2000).
97. *California Democratic Party v. Jones*, 530 U.S. 567 (2000).
98. *Healy v. James*, 408 U.S. 169 (1972).
99. *National Socialist Party of America v. Skokie*, 432 U.S. 43 (1977).
100. *Frisby v. Schultz*, 487 U.S. 474 (1988).
101. *Schenck v. Pro Choice Network of Western New York*, 519 U.S. 357 (1997).
102. James Madison, *Federalist Papers*, No. 46.
103. *District of Columbia v. Heller*, 554 U.S. 126 (2008).
104. *Ex parte Milligan*, 4 Wallace 2 (1866).
105. *Duncan v. Kahanamosby*, 327 U.S. 304 (1946).
106. *Illinois v. Gates*, 462 U.S. 213 (1983).
107. *Arizona v. Hicks*, 480 U.S. 321 (1987).
108. *Knowles v. Iowa*, 525 U.S. 113 (1998).
109. *Youngstown Sheet & Tube Co. v. Sawyer*, 343 U.S. 579 (1952).
110. *Vernonia School District v. Acton*, 515 U.S. 646 (1995).
111. *Chandler v. Miller*, 520 U.S. 305 (1997).
112. *United States v. Watson*, 423 U.S. 411 (1976).
113. *Payton v. New York*, 445 U.S. 573 (1980).
114. *Spano v. New York*, 360 U.S. 315 (1959).
115. *Gideon v. Wainwright*, 372 U.S. 335 (1963).
116. *Escobedo v. Illinois*, 378 U.S. 478 (1964).
117. *Miranda v. Arizona*, 384 U.S. 436 (1966).
118. *Mapp v. Ohio*, 367 U.S. 643 (1961).
119. *United States v. Leon*, 468 U.S. 897 (1984).
120. *Illinois v. Perkins*, 497 U.S. 177 (1990).
121. *United States v. Salerno*, 481 U.S. 739 (1987).
122. *U.S. v. Marion*, 404 U.S. 307 (1971).
123. *Barker v. Wingo*, 407 U.S. 514 (1972).
124. *Illinois v. Allen*, 397 U.S. 337 (1970).
125. *Maryland v. Craig*, 497 U.S. 1 (1990).
126. *Brady v. Maryland*, 373 U.S. 83 (1963).
127. *Batson v. Kentucky*, 476 U.S. 79 (1986).
128. *Sheppard v. Maxwell*, 384 U.S. 333 (1966).
129. *Williams v. Florida*, 399 U.S. 78 (1970).
130. *Johnson v. Louisiana*, 406 U.S. 356 (1970); *Apodaca v. Oregon*, 406 U.S. 404 (1972).
131. *U.S. v. Perez*, 9 Wheat 579 (1824).
132. *Heath v. Alabama*, 474 U.S. 82 (1985).
133. *Furman v. Georgia*, 408 U.S. 238 (1972).
134. *Gregg v. Georgia*, 428 U.S. 153 (1976); *Proffitt v. Florida*, 428 U.S. 242 (1976); *Jurek v. Texas*, 428 U.S. 262 (1976).
135. *Ring v. Arizona*, 536 U.S. 550 (2002).
136. *Atkins v. Virginia*, 536 U.S. 304 (2002).
137. *Roper v. Simmons*, 543 U.S. 551 (2005).

15

1. *Dred Scott v. Sandford*, 60 U.S. 393 (1857).
2. See C. Vann Woodward, *Reunion and Reaction* (Boston: Little, Brown, 1951); Woodward, *The Strange Career of Jim Crow* (New York: Oxford University Press, 1957).
3. *Civil Rights Cases*, 100 U.S. 3 (1883).
4. *Plessy v. Ferguson*, 163 U.S. 537 (1896).
5. *Sweatt v. Painter*, 339 U.S. 629 (1950).
6. *Brown v. Board of Education of Topeka*, 347 U.S. 483 (1954).
7. Kenneth Clark, *Dark Ghetto* (New York: Harper & Row, 1965), p. 75.
8. The Supreme Court ruled that Congress was bound to respect the Equal Protection Clause of the 14th Amendment even though the amendment is directed at states, because equal protection is a liberty guaranteed by the 5th Amendment. *Bolling v. Sharpe*, 347 U.S. 497 (1954).
9. *Brown v. Board of Education of Topeka* (II), 349 U.S. 294 (1955).
10. *Alexander v. Holmes Board of Education*, 396 U.S. 19 (1969).
11. *Swann v. Charlotte-Mecklenburg County Board of Education*, 402 U.S. (1971).
12. *Milliken v. Bradley*, 418 U.S. 717 (1974).
13. *Board of Education v. Dowell*, 498 U.S. 550 (1991).
14. Martin Luther King, Jr., "I've Been to the Mountaintop" Speech, April 3, 1968. Memphis.
15. Ibid.
16. *University of California Regents v. Bakke*, 438 U.S. 265 (1978).
17. Bakke's overall grade point average was 3.46, and the average for special admissions students was 2.62. Bakke's MCAT scores were verbal, 96; quantitative, 94; science, 97; general information, 72. The average MCAT scores for special admissions students were verbal, 34; quantitative, 30; science, 37; general information, 18.
18. *United Steelworkers of America v. Weber*, 443 U.S. 193 (1979).
19. *United States v. Paradise*, 480 U.S. 149 (1987).
20. *Firefighters Local Union 1784 v. Stotts*, 467 U.S. 561 (1984).
21. *City of Richmond v. Crosen Co.*, 488 U.S. 469 (1989).
22. *Adarand Construction v. Pena*, 132 L. Ed., 2d 158 (1995).
23. *Parents Involved in Community Schools v. Seattle School District*, June 28, 2007.
24. *Hopwood v. Texas*, 513 U.S. 1033 (1996).
25. *Grutter v. Bollinger,* 539 U.S. 306 (2003).
26. *Gratz v. Bollinger,* 539 U.S. 244 (2003).
27. U.S. Department of Education, Office of Civil Rights, "Race-neutral Alternatives in Postsecondary Education," March 2003.
28. State of California, Proposition 209 "Prohibition Against Discrimination or Preferential Treatment by State and Other Public Entities," http://vote96.ss.ca.gov.
29. *Coalition for Economic Equity v. Pete Wilson*, Ninth Circuit Court of Appeals, April 1997.
30. Rodolfo O. de la Garza et al., *Latino Voices: Mexican, Puerto Rican, and Cuban Perspectives on American Politics* (Boulder, Colo.: Westview Press, 1992).
31. See F. Luis Garcia, *Latinos in the Political System* (Notre Dame, Ind.: Notre Dame University Press, 1988). John D. Griffin and Brian Newman, "The Unequal Representation of Latinos and Whites," *Journal of Politics* 69 (November, 2007), 1032–46; Matt A. Barreto, "Si Se Puede! Latino Candidates and the Mobilization of Latino Voters," *American Political Science Review*, 101 (August 2007): 425–38.
32. Linda Chavez, "Tequila Sunrise: The Slow but Steady Progress of Hispanic Immigrants," *Policy Review* (Spring 1989): 64–67.
33. Peter Mathiessen, *Sal Si Puedes: Cesar Chavez and the New American Revolution* (New York: Random House, 1969).
34. *Plyer v. Doe*, 457 U.S. 202 (1982).
35. See Marisa A. Abrajano, R. Michael Alvarez, and Jonathan Nagler, "The Hispanic Vote in the 2004 Presidential Election," *Journal of Politics* 70 (April 2008): 368–82.
36. *Morton v. Mancari*, 417 U.S. 535 (1974).
37. See Joseph P. Shapiro, *No Pity: People with Disabilities Forging a New Civil Rights Movement* (New York: Times Books/ Random House, 1993).
38. *The Chronicle of Higher Education*, December 8, 2000.
39. *Bradwell v. Illinois*, 16 Wall 130 (1873).
40. *Reed v. Reed*, 404 U.S. 71 (1971).
41. *Michael M. v. Superior Court of Sonoma County*, 450 U.S. 464 (1981).
42. *Statistical Abstract of the United States*, 2007, p. 379.
43. NCAA, *Participation Study*, www.ncaa.org.
44. http://www.wnba.com/sky/news/title_ix_history_2012_01_31.html last accessed 7/21/2012.
45. Susan Fraker, "Why Women Aren't Getting to the Top," *Fortune*, April 16, 1984, pp. 40–45.
46. *Mentor Savings Bank v. Vinson*, 477 U.S. 57 (1986).
47. *Harris v. Forklift Systems*, 510 U.S. 17 (1993).
48. *Bowers v. Hardwick,* 478 U.S. 186 (1986).
49. *Lawrence v. Texas*, 539 U.S. 558 (2003).
50. *Boy Scouts of America v. Dale*, 530 U.S. 640 (2000).
51. See Thomas B. Dye and Susan MacManus, *Politics in States and Communities,* 13th ed. (New York: Pearson, 2009), pp. 58, 545.
52. See Jeffery R. Lax and Justin H. Phillips, "Gay Rights in the States: Public Opinion and Policy Responsiveness," *American Political Science Review* 103 (August, 2009): 367–86.
53. See Margaret Ellis, "Gay Rights: Lifestyle or Immorality," in *Moral Controversies in American Politics*, 3rd ed., eds. Raymond Talalovich and Byron Daynes (Armonk. NY: M. E. Sharpe, 2005).

16

1. Paul Samuelson, *Economics*, 12th ed. (New York: McGraw-Hill, 1985), p. 5.
2. GDP differs very little from gross national product, GNP, which is often used to compare the performance of national economies.
3. For a revealing case study of interest-group efforts to maintain tax breaks during the struggle over the Tax Reform Act of 1986, see Jeffrey H. Birnbaum and Alan S. Murray, *Showdown at Gucci Gulch* (New York: Random House, 1986).
4. "The Underground Economy," National Center for Policy Analysis, 1998.
5. Joseph A. Pechman, *Federal Tax Policy*, 5th ed. (Washington, D.C.: Brookings Institution, 1987).
6. See Peter R. Orszag, *Taxing the Future* (Washington D.C.: Brookings Institute, 2006).

17

1. Christopher Jenks and Paul E. Peterson, eds., *The Urban Underclass* (Washington, D.C.: Brookings Institution, 1991). See also William A. Kelso, *Poverty and the Underclass* (New York: New York University Press, 1994).
2. See William Julius Wilson, *The Truly Disadvantaged* (Chicago: University of Chicago Press, 1987).
3. See Michael B. Katz, *In the Shadow of the Poorhouse* (New York: Basic Books, 1996).
4. See Charles Murray, *Losing Ground* (New York: Basic Books, 1984).
5. *Statistical Abstract of the United States, 2011*, p. 68.

6. Office of Management and Budget, *Budget of the United States Government, 2010*, p. 28.
7. *Federation of Independent Business v. Sebelius*, June 28, 2012.
8. *Federation of Independent Business v. Sebelius*, June 28, 2012.

18

1. Hans Morgenthau, *Politics Among Nations*, 5th ed. (New York: Knopf, 1973), p. 27.
2. George F. Kennan, writing under the pseudonym "X," "Sources of Soviet Conduct," *Foreign Affairs* 25 (July 1947): 25.
3. Frank Snepp, *Decent Interval* (New York: Random House, 1977).
4. George C. Herring, *America's Longest War* (New York: Random House, 1979), p. 262.
5. See Thomas E. Ricks, *Fiasco: The American Military Adventure in Iraq* (New York: Penguin Books, 2007). See also Michael R. Gordon and Bernard E. Trainor, *Cobra II: The Inside Story of the Invasion and Occupation of Iraq* (New York: Pantheon Books, 2006).
6. U.S. Department of Defense, *Afghanistan–Pakistan Review 2011*, as reported in International Institute for Strategic Studies, *The Military Balance 2011* (London: IISS, 2011), p 42.

CREDITS

Photo Credits

CHAPTER 1 Page 3: Sherry LaVars/KRT/Newscom; 6 tr: Pablo Martinez Monsivais, File/AP Images; 6 cr: Mary Altaffer/AP Images; 6 cl: Nicholas Kamm/Staff/AFP/Getty Images; 6 tl: Jeff Malet Photography/Newscom; 15: Mary Altaffer/AP Images; 16: Bettmann/Corbis; 17: China Daily China Daily Information Corp - CDIC/Reuters;19: Jeff Greenberg/ The Image Works; 22: Jason Reed/Reuters

CHAPTER 2 Page 29: David McNew/Staff/Getty Images; 37 br: Justin Sullivan/Getty Images News/Getty Images; 37 bl: onkey Business Images/Shutterstock; 41: Jack Kurtz/ZUMA Press/Newscom; 43 tr: Justin Sullivan/Getty Images; 43 b: Scott Olson/Getty Images; 48: Jim West/The Image Works; 54: Mark Wilson/Getty Images; 57: William West/AFP/Getty Images

CHAPTER 3 Page 63: Gerald Herbert/AP Images; 75: Pool/AP Images; 78: Ted S. Warren/AP Images; 81: Pearson Education; 81, 445, 465: Pearson Education; 84: Hisham Ibrahim pxcm/Getty Images; 88 c: Pearson Education; 88 tc: Pearson Education

CHAPTER 4 Page 97: Mike Stotts/ZUMAPRESS/Newscom; 99 bc: Oli Scarff/Getty Image; 99 c: Suzan Thierry/Maxppp/Landov; 99 t: Pearson Education; 103: AP Images; 104: Patrick Semansky/AP Images; 110: Rob Carr/Ap Images; 111: Franklin D. Roosevelt Library; 114: The Washington Post/Getty Images; 119: Cliff Owen/AP Images; 120: Wisconsin State Journal, John Hart/AP Images; 124: Chuck Kennedy/KRT/Newscom

CHAPTER 5 Page 135: Drew Perine/MCT/Newscom; 140: Shutterstock; 148: Andy Nelson/The Christian Science Monitor/Getty Images; 153: Bettmann/Corbis; 155: Bettmann/Corbis; 158: The Chronicle, Johnny Hanson/AP Images; 159: Journal Times, Gregory Shaver/AP Images; 169: AP Images; 170: Cincinnati Museum Center/Contributor/Archive Photos/Getty Images

CHAPTER 6 Page 175: Bloomberg/Getty Images; 176: Justin Sullivan/Getty Images; 182: Chad Buchanan/Contributor/Getty Images Entertainment/Getty Images; 184: Ron Sachs/UPI/Newscom; 185: Paul Fenton/ZUMA Press, Inc./Alamy; 191: Jim Sulley/Wirepix/The Image Works; 192: Rick Bowmer/Ap Images; 200: Craig Lassig/AFP/Getty Images; 207: Jason DeCrow/AP Images

CHAPTER 7 Page 213: Jae C. Hong/AP Images; 215 tl: Kean Collection/Staff/Archive Photos/Getty Images; 215 tr: Kean Collection/Staff/Archive Photos/Getty Images; 223: Bettmann/Corbis; 226: AP Images; 234 tr: Charlotte Observer/Contributor/McClatchy-Tribune/MCT via Getty Images; 234 br: Alex Wong/Getty Images; 242: John Bazemore/AP Images; 244: Jewel Sama/AFP/GettyImages; 246: The Yomiuri Shimbun/AP Images; 248: Ron Sachs/CNP/AdMedia/Newscom; 253: destina/Fotolia

CHAPTER 8 Page 259: ad; 262: Jay Paul/Getty Images; 266: Susan Walsh/AP Images; 268: AP Images; 269: Jae C. Hong/AP Images; 271: Shaun Best/Reuters; 272 tl, cl: Pearson Education; 275: The White House/Handout/Getty Images; 286: Jim Bourg/Getty Images News/Getty Images; 289: Rex Features/AP Images; 291: Rick Wilking/POOL/EPA/Newscom; 293: Reed Saxon/AP Images

CHAPTER 9 Page 307: Kris Tripplaar/Tripplaar Kristofer/SIPA/Newscom; 310: AP Images; 311: Buyenlarge/Contributor/Archive Photos/Getty Images; 315: Michal Czerwonka/Getty Images; 317: Smiley N. Pool/Houston Chronicle/AP Images; 322: Mike Segar/Reuters

CHAPTER 10 Page 345: Ron Sachs/CNP/AdMedia/Photoshot; 346: Mladen Antonov/AFP/Getty Images; 355: Dave Martin/AP Images; 358: Douglas Graham/Getty Images; 359: Win McNamee/Getty Images; 360: Tom Williams/CQ Roll Call/Newscom; 375: Alex Brandon/AP Images; 377: epa european pressphoto agency b.v./Alamy; 379: Jeff Malet Photography/Newscom; 380: Alex Wong/Getty Images; 385: Alex Wong/Getty Images

CHAPTER 11 Page 399: Tom Pennington/Getty Images; 400: Ralph Crane/Time Life Pictures/Getty Images; 406: Bettmann/Corbis; 408: Bob Daugherty/AP Images; 413: Chip Somodevilla/Getty Images; 414 bc: World History Archive/Alamy; 414 bc: GL Archive/Alamy; 414 br: GL Archive/Alamy; 414 bl: Library of Congress Prints and Photographs Division[LC-USZ62-117124]; 416: Getty Images; 421: Pool/Getty Images; 423: Mladen Antonov/AFP/Getty Images; 427: Larry Downing/Reuters; 430: AP Images; 432: Baz Ratner/Reuters; 434: Bettmann/Corbis; 436: Frederic J. Brown/AFP/Getty Images

CHAPTER 12 Page 443: Erik S. Lesser/EPA/Newscom; 445: Pearson Education; 453: Charlie Riedel/AP Images; 454: U.S. Coast Guard, Prentice Danner/AP Images; 455: J.M. Eddins, JR/Photoshot; 457: North Wind Picture Archives/AP Images; 462: Evan Vucci/AP Images; 465: Pearson Education; 472: Joe Burbank/Orlando Sentinel/MCT/Getty Images

CHAPTER 13 Page 479: Irene Springer/Pearson Education; 481: Carl Iwasaki//Time Life Pictures/Getty Images; 486: Irene Springer/Pearson Education; 493: Pablo Martinez Monsivais/AP Images; 493: Pablo Martinez Monsivais/AP Images; 499: Jose CABEZAS/AFP/Getty Images; 506: Lawrence Jackson/AP Images

CHAPTER 14 Page 515: CJ Gunther/EPA/Newscom; 520: Pearson Education; 521: Paul Hennessy/Polaris/Newscom; 522: MANDEL NGAN/AFP/Getty Images; 526: Jeffrey Z. Carney/AP Images; 528: AP images; 529: Getty Images; 530: Robyn Beck/AFP/Getty Images; 537: Bettmann/Corbis; 545: Joseph Kaczmarek/ZUMA Press/Newscom; 547: Stephen Chernin/AP Images; 554: John Spink/AP Images

CHAPTER 15 Page 561: Lisa F. Young/Fotolia; 570: PBR/AP Images; 572: Robert W. Kelley/Time & Life Pictures/Getty Images; 577: Timothy A. Clary/AFP/Getty Images; 579: Paul Sancya/AP Images; 584: Arthur Schatz/Time Life Pictures/Getty Images; 586: Jim Watson/AFP/Getty Images; 591: Greg Gilbert/KRT/Newscom; 593: Jeff Markowitz/AP Image; 594: U.S. Army/Getty Images; 595: Dave Weaver/AP Image

CHAPTER 16 Page 607: apops/Fotolia; 611: Zhang Jun/Xinhua/Photoshot; 613: Alex Wong/Staff/Getty Images; 623: Michael Shaw/The New Yorker Collection/Cartoon Bank; 627: Haraz N. Ghanbari/AP Images

CHAPTER 17 Page 635: Melanie Stetson Freeman/The Christian Science Monitor/Getty Images; 639: Nicholas Kamm/AFP/GettyImages; 641: Archive Photos/Getty Images; 648: Fabrizio Bensch/Reuters/Landov; 649: Kevin Lamarque/Reuters

CHAPTER 18 Page 659: Michele Sibiloni/AFP/Getty Images; 661: IS700/Image Source/Alamy; 665: JT/AP Images; 667: Haley/Sipa/AP Images; 667: Misha Japaridze, pool/AP Images; 670 tr: Anonymous/AP Images; 670 b: Anonymous/AP Images; 677: Maya Alleruzzo/AP Images; 680: Ahmed Deeb/AFP/Getty Images

Text Credits

CHAPTER 1 Page 7: Data for 2013 from the Pew Research Center (www.people-press.org/2013/10/18/trust-in-government-interactive); 10: "Gallup opinion poll, 2010, reported at www.gallup.com. Gallup opinion poll, July 13, 2011, reported at www.gallup.com. Gallup Opinion Poll, 2009, as reported in The Polling Report, www.pollingreport.com" 10: "Gallup opinion poll, 2010, reported at www.gallup.com.Gallup opinion poll, July 13, 2011, reported at www.gallup.com. Gallup Opinion Poll, 2009, as reported in The Polling Report, www.pollingreport.com"; 11: "Gallup opinion poll, 2010, reported at www.gallup.com.Gallup opinion poll, July 13, 2011, reported at www.gallup.com; Gallup Opinion Poll, 2009, as reported in The Polling Report, www.pollingreport.com"; 14: Based on data from Freedom House; 19: Copyright © 2011 The Gallup, Inc. All rights reserved. The content is used with permission; however, Gallup retains all rights of republication.

CHAPTER 2 Page 49: General Social Surveys, National Opinion Research Center, University of Chicago; updated from Gallup polls to 2012.

CHAPTER 5 Page 144: Data from the 2012 National Election Study (University of Michigan; 150: "British Broadcasting Corporation World Service Poll: "Negative views of Russia on the Rise: Global Poll," June 3 2014, accessed at http://downloads.bbc.co.uk/mediacentre/country-rating-poll.pdf. n = 24,542 in 24 countries, margin of error per country ranges from +/− 2.5 to 6.1 percent, with 95 percent confidence."; 161: Bureau of the Census, Data for 2012 presidential election., accessed at http://www.census.gov/hhes/www/socdemo/voting/publications/p20/2012/tables.html; 163: Based on Paul Taylor, et. al., "An Awaked Giant: The Hispanic Electorate is Likely to Double by 2030." Washington, DC: Pew Hispanic Trends Research Project, Nov. 14 2012.

CHAPTER 6 Page 177: Pew Research Center. Survey taken July 11–13 2013. www.people-press.org. Reprinted by permission; 178: Pew Research Center. Survey taken July 20–24 2011, July 17–21 2013. www.people-press.org. Reprinted by permission; 179: Adapted from the Pew Research Center for the People and the Press, 2013. www.people-press.org. Reprinted by permission; 188: Gallup News Service, September 5–8 2013. Copyright © 2013 The Gallup, Inc. All rights reserved. The content is used with permission; however, Gallup retains all rights of republication; 193: Adapted from Pew Research Center for the People & the Press, 2012. www.people-press.org. Reprinted by permission.

CHAPTER 7 Page 236: Center for Responsive Politics. Candidate committees, miscellaneous, and "retired" excluded from this table. Data from 2012 presidential election.

CHAPTER 8 Page 276: Data from Center for Responsive Politics, www.opensecrets.org.

CHAPTER 12 Page 447: Gallup Opinion Poll, May 20–21 2013. Copyright © 2013 The Gallup, Inc. All rights reserved. The content is used with permission; however, Gallup retains all rights of republication; 451: Sources: United States Census Bureau, Statistical Abstract of the United States, 2012, Table 1360; at page 863: Boris Gramc. "Factors in the Size of Government in Developed Countries." Prague Economic Papers 2 (2002): 130–142; 468: Sources: Gallup, Sept. 6–9 2012; Sept. 13–15 2004; 468: Sources: Washington Post/Kaiser Family Fund poll, July 25–Aug. 5, 2012.

CHAPTER 13 Page 490: Federal Court Management Statistics, March 2014. www.uscourts.gov.

CHAPTER 15 Page 575: U.S. Bureau of the Census, www.census.gov/2012. Bureau of Labor Statistics www.bls.gov/2012; 576: U.S. Census Bureau, Current Population Reports P60–245 Income, Poverty, and Health Insurance Coverage in the United States: 2012. 1968 to 2010 Annual Social and Economic Supplements; 579: Gallup, June 13–July 5 2013. Copyright © 2013 The Gallup, Inc. All rights reserved. The content is used with permission; however, Gallup retains all rights of republication; 584: Statistical Abstract of the United States 2012–13, p. 23. 587, Pew Research Center tabulations from the Current population Survey, November supplements. Reprinted by permission; 587: Based on www.hispanicvoters2012.com; 598: Statistical Abstract of the United States, 2012–2013 pp. 383–86.

CHAPTER 16 Page 612: Data from Bureau of Economic Analysis, 2013, www.bea.gov. 614: Data from Bureau of Economic Analysis, 2013, www.bea.gov. 615: Budget of the United States Government, 2015. 616: Budget of the United States Government, 2015. 619: Budget of the United States Government, 2014; 620: ??OECD (2013), Revenue Statistics 2013, OECD Publishing. http://dx.doi.org/10.1787/10.1787/rev_stats-2013-en-fr 629: Sources: Joint Economic Committee, U.S. Congress, April 2007, National Tax Foundation from US Internal Revenue Service, 2009.

CHAPTER 17 Page 636: www.census.gov/hhes/poverty00/2012; 637: Budget of the United States Government, 2015; 638: U.S. Bureau of the Census, 2012.

CHAPTER 18 Page 676: Author compilation of data from various editions of International Institute of Strategic Studies, The Military Balance. London: IISS; 675: US Department of Defense. Sustaining US Global Leadership: Priorities for 21st Century Defense, 2012; 678: Pew Research Center, www.pewglobal.org/2013. Reprinted by permission.

INDEX

Note: Page numbers in **bold** indicate definition of terms.

A

B

C

D

E

F

G

H

I

M

N

O

P

Q

R

S

T

U

W

TEST YOURSELF ANSWERS

	1	2	3	4	5	6	7	8	9
1.	b	d	c	d	d	e	c	e	c
2.	c	a	b	d	d	a	a	c	b
3.	d	c	c	a	a	b	b	d	c
4.	c	d	c	d	d	c	d	c	d
5.	a	a	d	a	e	e	d	a	c
6.	b	b	b	c	e	b	b	c	b
7.	a	b	c	c	c	c	e	e	e
8.	d	e	c	d	c	b	d		

	10	11	12	13	14	15	16	17	18
1.	d	a	d	e	e	c	c	b	a
2.	a	b	a	c	c	c	a	b	d
3.	c	e	b	c	c	c	d	c	d
4.	b	d	d	b	b	b	b	d	c
5.	a	b	c	b	d	b	b	d	b
6.	e	d	c	a	b	c	d	b	d
7.	b	e	e	c	a	c		b	
8.	a	c	e	d	e	d		c